Consumer price index manual

Theory and practice

Consumer price index manual

Theory and practice

International Labour Office

International Monetary Fund

Organisation for Economic Co-operation and Development

Statistical Office of the European Communities (Eurostat)

United Nations

The World Bank

First published 2004

ILO/IMF/OECD/UNECE/Eurostat/The World Bank
Consumer price index manual: Theory and practice
Geneva, International Labour Office, 2004

Guide, consumer price index, data collecting, statistical method, calculation, methodology, developed country, developing country. 09.02

ISBN 92-2-113699-X

ILO Cataloguing in Publication Data

ILO publications can be obtained through major booksellers or ILO local offices in many countries, or direct from ILO Publications, International Labour Office, CH-1211 Geneva 22, Switzerland. Catalogues or lists of new publications are available free of charge from the above address or by email: pubvente@ilo.org
Visit our website: www.ilo.org/publns

Pagesetted In India MAC
Printed in China

FOREWORD

This volume is an expanded revision of *Consumer price indices: An ILO manual*, published in 1989. Through the mechanism of the Intersecretariat Working Group on Price Statistics (IWGPS), the revision has been undertaken under the joint responsibility of six international organizations: the International Labour Office (ILO); the International Monetary Fund (IMF); the Organisation for Economic Co-operation and Development (OECD); the Statistical Office of the European Communities (Eurostat); the United Nations Economic Commission for Europe (UNECE); and the World Bank. It is also being published jointly by these organizations.

The manual contains detailed comprehensive information and explanations on compiling a consumer price index (CPI). It provides an overview of the conceptual and theoretical issues that statistical offices should consider when making decisions on how to deal with the various problems in the compilation of a CPI, and is intended for use by both developed and developing countries. The chapters cover many topics; they elaborate on the different practices currently in use, propose alternatives whenever possible, and discuss the advantages and disadvantages of each alternative. Given the comprehensive nature of the manual, we expect it to satisfy the needs of many users.

The main purpose of the manual is to assist producers of consumer price indices, particularly in countries that are revising or setting up their CPIs. It draws on a wide range of experience and expertise in an attempt to describe practical and suitable measurement methods. It should also help countries to produce their CPIs in a more comparable way so that statistical offices and international organizations can make meaningful international comparisons. Bringing together a large body of knowledge on the subject, the manual may be used for self-learning, or as a teaching tool for training courses on the CPI.

Other CPI users, such as employers, workers, policy-makers and researchers, are also targeted. The manual will inform them not only about the different methods that are employed in collecting data and compiling such indices, but also of the limitations, so that the results may be interpreted correctly.

The drafting and revision have entailed many meetings over a five-year period, in which CPI experts from national statistical offices, international and regional organizations, universities and research institutes have participated. The new manual owes much to their collective advice and wisdom.

The electronic version of the manual is available on the Internet at www.ilo.org/stat. The IWGPS views the manual as a "living document" that it will amend and update to address particular points in more detail. This is especially true for emerging discussions and recommendations made by international groups reviewing the CPI, such as the International Conference of Labour Statisticians (ICLS), meetings of the International Working Group on Price Indices (the "Ottawa Group"), and the Joint UNECE/ILO Meetings on Consumer Price Indices.

Comments on the manual are welcomed by the IWGPS, and should be sent to the ILO Bureau of Statistics (e-mail: stat@ilo.org). They will be taken into account in any future revisions.

International Labour Office (ILO): A. Sylvester Young, Director, Bureau of Statistics
International Monetary Fund (IMF): Horst Koehler, Managing Director
Organisation for Economic Co-operation and Development (OECD): Enrico Giovanini, Director, Statistical Directorate
Statistical Office of the European Communities (Eurostat): Bart Meganck, Director, Economic Statistics, and Economic and Monetary Convergence
United Nations Economic Commission for Europe (UNECE): Heinrich Brüngger, Director, Statistics Division
World Bank: Shaida Badiee, Director, Development Data Group

CONTENTS

List of tables

List of figures

List of boxes

PREFACE

The International Labour Office (ILO), the International Monetary Fund (IMF), the Organisation for Economic Co-operation and Development (OECD), the Statistical Office of the European Communities (Eurostat), the United Nations Economic Commission for Europe (UNECE) and the World Bank, together with experts from a number of national statistical offices and universities, have collaborated since 1998 on developing this manual. The sponsoring organizations endorse the principles and recommendations contained in it as good practice for statistical agencies in compiling their consumer price indices (CPIs). Because of practical and resource constraints, however, some of the current recommendations may not be immediately attainable by all statistical offices, and they should therefore serve as guidelines or targets for agencies as they revise their CPIs and improve their CPI programmes. There are not always clear-cut solutions to specific conceptual and practical problems such as sample design, choice of index formula, adjustment of prices for quality changes, and the treatment of new products. Statistical offices must therefore rely on the underlying economic and statistical principles laid out in this manual to arrive at practical solutions.

The consumer price index

The CPI is an index that measures the rate at which the prices of consumption goods and services are changing from month to month (or from quarter to quarter). The prices are collected from shops or other retail outlets. The usual method of calculation is to take an average of the period-to-period price changes for the different products, using as weights the average amounts that households spend on them. CPIs are official statistics that are usually produced by national statistical offices, ministries of labour or central banks. They are published as quickly as possible, typically about ten days after the end of the most recent month or quarter.

The manual is intended for the benefit of users of CPIs, as well as for the statistical agencies that compile the indices. It is designed to do two things. First, it explains in some detail the methods that are actually used to calculate a CPI. Second, it explains the underlying economic and statistical theory on which the methods are based.

A CPI measures the rate of price inflation as experienced and perceived by households in their role as consumers. It is also widely used as a proxy for a general index of inflation for the economy as a whole, partly because of the frequency and timeliness with which it is produced. It has become a key statistic for purposes of economic policy-making, especially monetary policy. It is often specified in legislation and in a wide variety of private contracts as the appropriate measure of inflation for the purposes of adjusting payments (such as wages, rents, interest and social security benefits) for the effects of inflation. It can therefore have substantial and wide-ranging financial implications for governments and businesses, as well as for households.

This manual provides guidelines for statistical offices or other agencies responsible for constructing a CPI, bearing in mind that the resources available for this purpose are limited. *Calculating a CPI cannot be reduced to a simple set of rules or standard set of procedures that can be mechanically followed in all circumstances.* While there are certain general principles that may be universally applicable, the procedures followed in practice, whether they concern the collection or processing of the prices or the methods of aggregation, have to take account of particular circumstances. These include the main use of the index, the nature of the markets and pricing practices within the country, and the resources available to the statistical office. Statistical offices have to make choices. The manual explains the underlying economic and statistical concepts and principles needed to enable statistical offices to make their choices in efficient and cost-effective ways and to be aware of the full implications of their choices.

The manual draws upon the experience of many statistical offices throughout the world. The procedures they use are not static, but continue to evolve and improve in response to several factors. First, research continually refines and strengthens the economic and statistical theory underpinning CPIs. For example, clearer insights have recently been obtained on the relative strengths and weaknesses of the various formulae and methods used to process the basic price data collected for CPI purposes. Second, recent advances in information and communications technology have affected CPI methods. Both of these theoretical and data developments can impinge on all the stages in compiling a CPI. New technology can affect the methods used to collect prices and transmit them to the central statistical office. It can also improve the processing and checking, including the methods used to adjust prices for changes in the quality of the goods and services covered. Finally, improved formulae help in calculating more accurate and reliable higher-level indices, including the overall CPI itself.

International standards for CPIs

Some international standards for economic statistics have evolved primarily in order to enable internationally comparable statistics to be compiled. However, individual countries also stand to benefit from international standards. The CPI standards described in this manual draw upon the collective experience and expertise accumulated in many countries. All countries can benefit by having easy access to this experience and expertise.

In many countries, CPIs were first compiled mainly in order to be able to adjust wages to compensate for the loss of purchasing power caused by inflation. Consequently, the responsibility for compiling CPIs was often entrusted to ministries, or departments, of labour. The International Conference of Labour Statisticians (ICLS), convened by the Governing Body of the ILO, therefore provided the natural forum in which to discuss CPI methodology and develop guidelines.

The first international standards for CPIs were promulgated in 1925 by the Second ICLS. The first set of standards referred to "cost of living" indices rather than CPIs. A distinction is now drawn between two different types of index. A consumer price index can be defined simply as measuring the change in the cost of purchasing a given "basket" of consumption goods and services, whereas a cost of living index is defined as measuring the change in the cost of maintaining a given standard of living, or level of utility. For this reason, the Tenth ICLS in 1962 decided to adopt the more general term "consumer price index", which should be understood to embrace both concepts. There need be no conflict between the two. As explained in the manual, the best-practice methods are likely to be very similar, whichever approach is adopted.

The international standards have been revised three times, in 1947, 1962 and 1987, in the form of resolutions adopted by the ICLS. The 1987 standards on CPI were followed by a manual on methods (Turvey, 1989), which provided guidance to countries on the practical application of the standards.

The background to the present revision

A few years after the publication of the 1989 ILO manual, it became clear that a number of outstanding and controversial methodological problems needed further investigation and analysis. An expert group was formed consisting of specialists in price indices from national statistical offices, international organizations and universities from around the world. It met for the first time in Ottawa in 1994, and became known as the "Ottawa Group", one of the city groups established by the United Nations Statistical Commission to address selected problems in statistical methods. During the course of seven meetings of the Ottawa Group between 1994 and 2003, over 100 research papers on the theory and practice of price indices were presented and discussed. One outcome was that it became apparent that existing CPI methods could be improved and strengthened in a number of ways.

At the same time, the control of inflation had become a high-priority policy objective in most countries. Not only is the CPI widely used to measure and monitor inflation, but inflation targets in many countries are set specifically in terms of a precise rate of change in the CPI. The slowing down of inflation in many parts of the world in the 1990s, as compared with the 1970s and 1980s, far from reducing interest in CPI methodology, actually stimulated a demand for more accurate, precise and reliable measures of inflation. When the rate of inflation slows to only 2 or 3 per cent per year, even a small error or bias in the CPI becomes relatively significant.

In order to be sure about the accuracy of CPIs, governments or research institutes in a few countries commissioned special groups of experts to investigate and evaluate the methods used. The methodology used to calculate CPIs was subjected to public interest and scrutiny unknown in the past. One conclusion reached was that existing methods might lead to some upward bias. Many academic and government economists and other users of CPIs became convinced of this, believing that insufficient allowance was being made for improvements in the quality of many goods and services. In fact, the extent and sometimes even the direction of such bias are uncertain. It will also, of course, vary between different types of consumption goods and services, and its total effect on the overall CPI will vary between countries. However, the bias is potentially large. For this reason, this manual addresses in some detail the issue of adjusting prices for changes in quality, drawing upon the most recent research in this area. There are other sources of possible bias, such as that resulting from working with an out-of-date and unrepresentative basket of goods and services. Bias may also result from the sampling and price collection methods used. Several chapters deal with these issues, with an overall summary of possible errors and biases given in Chapter 11.

CPIs are widely used for the index linking of social benefits such as pensions, unemployment benefits and other government payments, and also as escalators for adjusting prices in long-term contracts. The cumulative effects of even a small bias could be substantial over the long term and could have considerable financial consequences for government budgets. Government agencies, especially ministries of finance, have therefore taken a renewed interest in CPIs, examining their accuracy and reliability more closely and carefully than in the past.

In response to the various developments outlined above, the need to revise, update and expand the 1989 ILO manual was gradually recognized and accepted during the late 1990s. A formal recommendation to revise the manual was made at the joint UNECE/ILO Meeting on Consumer Price Indices, held in Geneva at the end of 1997. Responsibility for the revision was entrusted to the main international organizations interested in the measurement of inflation. This strategy was endorsed in 1998 by the United Nations Statistical Commission, which also agreed to the conversion of the Ottawa Group into a formal Intersecretariat Working Group on Price Statistics (IWGPS). The Sixteenth ICLS, meeting in 1998, also recommended that the Fourteenth ICLS resolution concerning consumer price indices, adopted in 1987, should be revised. The preparation of the draft revised resolution discussed at the Seventeenth ICLS (24 November–3 December 2003) was carried out by the ILO Bureau of Statistics in parallel with the preparation of this revised manual. Every effort has been made to ensure that the two documents are consistent and mutually supportive.[1]

Some concerns about current index methods

This new manual takes advantage of the wealth of new research on index number theory and methods in the last decade to address the kinds of concerns referred to above. It recommends some new practices and its purpose is not simply to codify existing statistical agency practices. It is useful to highlight a few of the main concerns that have led to many topics being dealt with in some depth in the manual.

The traditional standard methodology underlying a typical CPI is based on the concept of a Laspeyres price index. A Laspeyres index measures the change between two periods of time in the total cost of purchasing a basket of goods and services that is representative of the first, or base, period. The base period basket of consumer purchases is priced first at base period prices and then repeatedly priced at the prices of successive time periods. This methodology has at least three practical advantages. It is easily explained to the public; it can make repeated use of the same data on consumer purchases that date from some past household survey or administrative source (rather than requiring new data each month); and it need not be revised, assuming users are satisfied with the Laspeyres concept. Another notable advantage is that the Laspeyres is consistent in aggregation down to the lowest level of aggregation. The index can be broken down into sub-aggregates that are interrelated in a simple way.

Statistical agencies actually calculate their CPIs by implementing the Laspeyres index in its alternative form as a weighted average of the observed price changes, or price relatives, using the base period expenditure shares as weights. Unfortunately, although the Laspeyres is a simple concept, it is difficult to calculate a proper Laspeyres index in practice. Consequently, statistical agencies have to resort to approximations:

- It is generally impossible to obtain accurate expenditure shares for the base period at the level of individual commodities, so statistical agencies settle for getting base period expenditure weights at the level of 100–1,000 product groups.
- For each of the chosen product groups, agencies collect a sample of representative prices from outlets rather than attempting to collect every single transaction price. They use equally weighted (rather than expenditure-weighted) index formulae to aggregate these elementary product prices into an elementary aggregate index, which will in turn be used as the price relative for each of the 100–1,000 product groups when calculating the higher-level Laspeyres index. It is recognized that this two-stage procedure is not entirely consistent with the Laspeyres methodology (which requires weighting at each stage of aggregation). However, for a number of theoretical and practical reasons, statistical agencies judge the resulting elementary index price relatives to be sufficiently accurate to insert into the Laspeyres formula at the higher stage of aggregation.

This methodology dates back to the work of Mitchell (1927) and Knibbs (1924), and other pioneers who introduced it 80 or 90 years ago, and it is still used today.

Although most statistical agencies have traditionally used the Laspeyres index as their *target index*, both economic and index number theory suggest that some other types of indices may be more appropriate target indices to aim at: namely, the Fisher, Walsh or Törnqvist–Theil indices. As is well known, the Laspeyres index has an upward bias compared with these target indices. Of course, these target indices may not be achievable by a statistical agency, but it is necessary to have some sort of theoretical target to aim at. Having a target concept is also necessary so that the index that is actually produced by a statistical agency can be evaluated to see how close it comes to the theoretical ideal. In the theoretical chapters of the manual, four main approaches to index number theory are described:

[1]The 2003 resolution concerning consumer price indices is reproduced in Annex 3. It can also be found on the ILO Bureau of Statistics web site: http://www.ilo.org/public/english/bureau/stat.

(1) fixed basket approaches and symmetric averages of fixed baskets;
(2) the stochastic (statistical estimator) approach to index number theory;
(3) test (axiomatic) approaches; and
(4) the economic approach.

Approaches (3) and (4) will be familiar to many price statisticians and expert users, but perhaps a few words about approaches (1) and (2) are in order.

The Laspeyres index is an example of a basket index. The concern from a theoretical point of view is that there is an equally valid alternative for the two periods being compared: the Paasche index, which uses the basket of quantities from the current period. If there are two equally valid estimators for the same concept, then statistical theory suggests taking an average of the two. However, there is more than one kind of average and the question of which average to take is not trivial. The manual proposes that the "best" average is the geometric average of the Laspeyres and Paasche indices (the Fisher ideal). Alternatively, the "best" basket is one whose quantities are geometric averages of the quantities in both periods (the Walsh index). From the statistical estimation perspective, the "best" index number is a geometric average of the price relatives that uses the (arithmetic) average expenditure share in two periods as weights (the Törnqvist–Theil index).

One additional result from index number theory should be mentioned here: the problem of defining the price and quantity of a product that should be used for each period in the index number formula. The problem is that the same product may be sold at a number of different prices. So the question arises, what price would be most representative of the sales of this product for the period? The answer is the *unit value*, since this price multiplied by the total quantity sold during the period equals the value of sales. Of course, the manual does *not* endorse taking unit values over *heterogeneous* products; unit values should only be calculated for *identical* products.

Six *main areas of concern* with the standard methodology are listed below. They are not ranked in order of importance, and all are considered to be important:

1. At the final stage of aggregation, a conventional CPI is *not* a true Laspeyres index since the expenditure weights pertain to a reference base *year* that is different from the base *month* (or quarter) for prices. Thus, the expenditure weights are annual whereas the prices are collected monthly. To be a true Laspeyres index, the period that provides the expenditure weights must *coincide* with the reference period for the prices. In fact, the index actually calculated by many statistical agencies at the last stage of aggregation has a weight reference period that precedes the base price period. Indices of this type are likely to have some upward bias compared to a true Laspeyres index, especially if the expenditure weights are price-updated from the weight reference period to the Laspeyres base period. It follows that they must have definite upward biases compared to theoretical target indices such as the Fisher, Walsh or Törnqvist–Theil indices.
2. At the early stages of aggregation, unweighted averages of prices or price relatives are used. Until recently, when scanner data from electronic points of sale became more readily available, it was thought that the biases that might result from the use of unweighted indices were not particularly significant. However, recent evidence suggests that there is potential for significant upward bias at lower levels of aggregation compared to results that are generated by the preferred target indices mentioned above.
3. The third major concern with standard CPI methodology is that, although statistical agencies generally recognize that there is a problem with the treatment of quality change and new goods, it is difficult to work out a coherent methodology for these problems in the context of a Laspeyres index that uses a fixed set of quantities. The most widely received good practice in quality adjusting price indices is "hedonic regression", which characterizes the price of a product at any given time as a function of its physical and economic characteristics as compared with substitutes. In fact, there is a considerable amount of controversy on how to integrate hedonic regression methodology into the CPI's theoretical framework. Both the theoretical and the more practically oriented chapters in the manual devote a lot of attention to these methodological issues. The problems created by the disappearance of old, and the appearance of new, products are now much more severe than they were when the traditional CPI methodology was developed some 80 years ago (when the problem was mostly ignored). For many categories of products, such as models of consumer durables, those priced at the beginning of the year are simply no longer available by the end of the year. *Sample attrition* creates tremendous methodological problems. At lower levels of aggregation, it becomes necessary (at least in many product groups) to use chained indices rather than fixed base indices. Certain unweighted indices are liable to have substantial bias when chained.
4. A fourth major area of concern is related to the first: that is, the *treatment of seasonal commodities*. The use of annual quantities or annual expenditure shares is justified to a certain extent if one is interested in the longer-run trend of price changes. However, some users, such as central banks, focus on short-term, month-to-month changes, in which case the use of annual weights can lead to misleading signals. Monthly price changes for products that are out of season (i.e., the seasonal weights for the product class are small

for those months) can be greatly magnified by the use of annual weights. The problem is worse when the products are not available at all at certain months of the year. There are solutions to these seasonality problems, but they may not appeal to many CPI compilers and users since they involve the construction of *two* indices: one for the short-term measurement of price changes and another (more accurate) longer-term index that is adjusted for seasonal influences.

5. A fifth concern with standard CPI methodology is that, in common with most economic statistics, services have been comparatively neglected in CPIs, notwithstanding the fact that they have become extremely important. A typical CPI will collect many more goods prices than services prices and will have many more product groups for goods rather than services. Traditionally, there has not been much focus on the problems involved in measuring price and quantity changes for services, even though they raise serious conceptual and practical problems. Some examples of difficult-to-measure services are: insurance, gambling, financial services, advertising, telecommunications, entertainment and housing services. In many cases, statistical agencies simply do not have the resources or methodologies at their disposal to deal adequately with these difficult measurement problems.
6. A final concern with existing CPI methodology is that it tends not to recognize that more than one CPI may be required to meet the needs of different users. For example, some users may require information on the month-to-month movement of prices in a timely fashion. This requires a basket index with predetermined (even though possibly inappropriate and out-of-date) weights that are instantly available. However, other users may be more interested in a more accurate or representative measure of price change and may be willing to sacrifice timeliness for increased accuracy. For this reason, the United States Bureau of Labor Statistics provides, on a retrospective basis, a superlative index that uses both current and base period weight information in a symmetrical way. This is an entirely reasonable development, recognizing that different users have different needs. A second example where more than one index might be compiled relates to owner-occupied housing. Good cases have been made for three different treatments: the acquisitions approach, the rental equivalence approach and the user cost approach. However, these three approaches may give quite different numerical results in the short run. A statistical agency has to opt for one approach, but since all three command support, indices using the other two approaches could be made available as analytical series for interested users. A third example of where more than one index would be useful occurs when, because of seasonal commodities, the month-to-month index may not be based on the same set of products as one that compares the month with the same month a year earlier.

The above kinds of concern are addressed in this manual. Frank discussions of these matters should stimulate the interest of professional economists and statisticians in universities, government departments, central banks, and so on, to address these measurement problems and to provide new solutions that can be used by statistical agencies. Public awareness of these areas should also heighten awareness of the need for additional resources to be allocated to statistical agencies so that economic measurement will be improved.

The Harmonized Indices of Consumer Prices

Within the European Union (EU), the convergence of inflation in Member States was an important prerequisite for the formation of a monetary union in 1999. This required a precisely defined measure of inflation and an agreed methodology to ensure that the different countries' price indices are comparable. A detailed and systematic review of all aspects of the compilation of CPIs was therefore undertaken during the 1990s by all the national statistical offices of the EU Member States in collaboration with Eurostat, the Statistical Office of the EU. This work culminated in the elaboration of a new EU standard for the 29 Member and candidate States, and led to the development of the EU's Harmonized Indices of Consumer Prices (HICPs). A summary of HICP methodology is given in Annex 1 to this manual.

Work on the HICPs proceeded in parallel with that of the IWGPS, many of whose experts also participated both in work on the HICPs and in the present revision of this manual. Although the methodology elaborated here has much in common with that adopted for the HICPs, there are also differences. The HICPs were developed for a very specific purpose, whereas the methodology developed in this manual is intended to be flexible, multi-purpose and applicable to all countries, whatever their economic circumstances and level of development. The manual also provides considerably more detail, information, explanation and rationalization of CPI methodology and the associated economic and statistical theory than is to be found in the HICP standards.

The organization of the revision

The six international organizations listed at the beginning of this preface, concerned with both the measurement of inflation and policies designed to control it, have collaborated on the revision of this manual. They have provided, and continue to provide, technical assistance on CPIs to countries at all levels of development, including those in transition from planned to market economies. They joined forces for the revision of this manual, establishing the IWGPS for the purpose. The role of the IWGPS was to organize and manage the process rather than act as an expert group.

The responsibilities of the IWGPS were to:

- appoint the various experts on price indices who participated in the revision process, either as members of the Technical Expert Group (TEG/CPI), providing substantive advice on the content of the manual, or as authors;
- provide the financial and other resources needed;
- arrange meetings of the TEG/CPI, prepare the agendas and write the reports of the meetings; and
- arrange for the publication and dissemination of the manual.

Members of the IWGPS were also members of the TEG/CPI. It is important to note that the experts participating in the TEG/CPI were invited in their personal capacity as experts and not as representatives, or delegates, of the national statistical offices or other agencies in which they might be employed. Participants were able to give their expert opinions without in any way committing the offices from which they came.

The revision of the manual took five years, and involved multiple activities:

- the development of the manual outline and the recruitment of experts to draft the various chapters;
- the review of the draft chapters by the members of the TEG/CPI, the IWGPS and other experts;
- the posting of the draft chapters on a special web site for comment by interested individuals and organizations;
- discussions by a small group of experts from statistical agencies and universities on the finalization of all the chapters;
- final copy-editing of the whole manual.

Links with the *Producer price index manual*

One of the first decisions of the IWGPS was that a new international manual on producer price indices (PPIs) should be produced simultaneously with this manual. Whereas there have been international standards for CPIs for over 70 years, the first international manual on producer price indices was not produced until 1979 (United Nations, 1979). Despite the importance of PPIs for measuring and analysing inflation, the methods used to compile them have been comparatively neglected, at both national and international levels.

A new *Producer price index manual* (ILO, IMF, OECD, Eurostat, UNECE and the World Bank, forthcoming) has therefore been developed and written in parallel with this manual. The IWGPS established a second Technical Expert Group on PPIs whose membership overlapped with that of the Technical Expert Group on CPIs. The two groups worked in close liaison with each other. The methodologies of PPIs and CPIs have much in common. Both are based on essentially the same underlying economic and statistical theory, except that the CPI draws on the economic theory of consumer behaviour whereas the PPI draws on the economic theory of production. However, the two economic theories are isomorphic and lead to the same kinds of conclusions with regard to index number compilation. The two manuals have similar contents and are fully consistent with each other conceptually, sharing common text when appropriate.

Most members of the Technical Expert Groups on CPIs and PPIs also participated as active members of the Ottawa Group. The two manuals were able to draw upon the contents and conclusions of all the numerous papers presented at meetings of the Group.

ACKNOWLEDGEMENTS

The organizations of the IWGPS wish to thank all those involved in the drafting and production of the manual. Particular thanks go to Peter Hill, the editor, W. Erwin Diewert, who contributed extensively to the theoretical chapters of the manual, and Bert Balk, who acted as referee for all the theoretical chapters. Their efforts greatly enhanced the quality of the manual.

The authors of the chapters are as follows:

Preface Peter Hill, Paul Armknecht and W. Erwin Diewert
Reader's guide Peter Hill
1 *An introduction to consumer price index methodology* Peter Hill
2 *Uses of consumer price indices* Peter Hill
3 *Concepts and scope* Peter Hill and Fenella Maitland-Smith
4 *Expenditure weights and their sources* Valentina Stoevska and Carsten Boldsen
5 *Sampling* Jorgen Dalén, A. Sylvester Young and Bert Balk
6 *Price collection* David Fenwick
7 *Adjusting for quality change* Mick Silver
8 *Item substitution, sample space and new products* Mick Silver
9 *Calculating consumer price indices in practice* Carsten Boldsen and Peter Hill
10 *Some special cases* Keith Woolford, David Fenwick, contributors from several statistical offices
11 *Errors and bias* John Greenlees and Bert Balk
12 *Organization and management* David Fenwick
13 *Publication, dissemination and user relations* Tom Griffin
14 *The system of price statistics* Kimberly Zieschang
15 *Basic index number theory* W. Erwin Diewert
16 *The axiomatic and stochastic approaches to index number theory* W. Erwin Diewert
17 *The economic approach to index number theory: The single-household case* W. Erwin Diewert
18 *The economic approach to index number theory: The many-household case* W. Erwin Diewert
19 *Price indices using an artificial data set* W. Erwin Diewert
20 *Elementary indices* W. Erwin Diewert
21 *Quality change and hedonics* Mick Silver
22 *The treatment of seasonal products* W. Erwin Diewert
23 *Durables and user costs* W. Erwin Diewert
A glossary of main terms and annex to the glossary Peter Hill and Bert Balk

Annexes
1 *Harmonized Indices of Consumer Prices (European Union)* Alexandre Makaronidis, Keith Hayes
2 *Classification of Individual Consumption according to Purpose (COICOP)-Extract* United Nations
3 *Resolution concerning consumer price indices adopted by the Seventeenth International Conference of Labour Statisticians, 2003* ILO
4 *Spatial comparisons of consumer prices, purchasing power parities and the International Comparison Program* Prasada Rao

The affiliations of the authors are as follows:

Bert Balk	Statistics Netherlands
Carsten Boldsen	Statistics Denmark
Jorgen Dalén	Expert
W. Erwin Diewert	University of British Columbia, Canada
David Fenwick	United Kingdom Office of National Statistics (ONS)
John Greenlees	United States Bureau of Labor Statistics (BLS)
Tom Griffin	Expert
Keith Hayes	Eurostat
Peter Hill	Expert, manual editor
Fenella Maitland-Smith	OECD
Alexandre Makaronidis	Eurostat
Prasada Rao	University of Queensland, Australia
Mick Silver	Cardiff University, United Kingdom
Valentina Stoevska	ILO
Keith Woolford	Australian Bureau of Statistics (ABS)
A. Sylvester Young	ILO
Kimberly Zieschang	IMF

The manual has also benefited from valuable contributions by many other experts, including: Martin Boon (Statistics Netherlands); Heber Camelo and Ernestina Pérez (Economic Commission for Latin America and the Caribbean); Denis Fixler (United States Bureau of Economic Analysis); Leendert Hoven (Statistics Netherlands); Michel Mouyelo-Katoula (African Development Bank); Carl Obst (formerly OECD); Bouchaib Thich (Département de la prévision économique et du plan, Morocco); and Ralph Turvey (expert). The following also gave helpful advice and comments: Statistics Austria; Statistics Singapore; United States BLS; Michael Anderson (ABS); Rob Edwards (ABS); Eivind Hoffmann (ILO); participants at the International Workshop on Consumer Price Indices, Singapore, June 2001; and the members of the Ottawa Group.

The IWGPS established the Technical Expert Group on the CPI (TEG/CPI) for the revision of the manual. Members of the IWGPS were also members of the TEG/CPI, whose individual members were:

David Fenwick	Chair, United Kingdom ONS
Paul Armknecht	TEG/PPI chair, IMF
John Astin*	Eurostat
Bert Balk	Statistics Netherlands
W. Erwin Diewert	University of British Columbia, Canada
Yoel Finkel	Israel Central Bureau of Statistics
Carsten Boldsen	Statistics Denmark
John Greenlees	United States BLS
Paul Haschka	Statistics Austria
Peter Hill	Editor
Jean-Claude Roman*	Eurostat
Bohdan Schultz*	Statistics Canada
Mick Silver	Cardiff University, United Kingdom
Kimberly Zieschang	IMF

The UNECE (Jan Karlsson, Lidia Bratanova*, Miodrag Pesut*, Tihomira Dimova*) and the ILO (Valentina Stoevska) jointly acted as the Secretariat of the TEG/CPI.

The TEG/CPI met seven times: 11–12 February 1999 (Geneva), 2 November 1999 (Geneva), 5–6 February 2001 (Washington, DC), 25–26 June 2001 (Geneva), 31 October 2001 (Geneva), 19–21 March 2002 (London) and 14–15 October 2002 (London).

The IWGPS met formally five times: 24 September 1998 (Paris), 11 February 1999 (Geneva), 2 November 1999 (Geneva), 21–22 March 2002 (London) and 5 December 2003 (Geneva). A number of informal meetings were also held.

The ILO was the Secretariat of the Group and A. Sylvester Young the chairperson of the IWGPS. During the revision of the manual, the CPI manual editor (Peter Hill), the TEG-CPI chairperson (David Fenwick), the PPI manual editor and the TEG/PPI chairperson (Paul Armknecht) participated in the meetings of the IWGPS.

* These members served for only part of the period.

The final publication of the English version of this manual was coordinated, with the involvement of the IWGPS member organizations, by Valentina Stoevska of the ILO Bureau of Statistics. The ILO Bureau of Publications provided extensive editorial and support services for the production process. We should also like to thank Angela Haden and Barbara Campanini for their thorough copy-editing of the final draft.

READER'S GUIDE

International manuals in the field of economic statistics have traditionally been intended to provide guidance about concepts, definitions, classifications, coverage, valuation, the recording of data, aggregation procedures, formulae, and so on. They have been intended mainly to assist compilers of the relevant statistics in individual countries. This manual has the same principal objective.

The manual is also intended for the benefit of users of consumer price indices (CPIs), such as government and academic economists, financial experts and other informed users. The CPI is a key statistic for policy purposes. It attracts a great deal of attention from the media, governments and the public at large in most countries. Despite its apparent simplicity, the CPI is a sophisticated concept that draws upon a great deal of economic and statistical theory, and requires complex data manipulation. This manual is therefore also intended to promote greater understanding of the properties of CPIs.

In general, compilers and users of economic statistics must have a clear perception of what the statistics are supposed to measure, in principle. Measurement without theory is unacceptable in economics, as in other disciplines. The manual therefore contains a thorough, comprehensive and up-to-date survey of the relevant economic and statistical theory. This makes the manual completely self-contained on both the theory and practice of CPI measurement.

The resulting manual is large. As different readers may have different interests and priorities, it is not possible to devise a sequence of chapters that suits everyone. Indeed, because this manual is intended to serve as a reference source, it will not necessarily be read from cover to cover. Many readers may be interested in only a selection of chapters. The purpose of this reader's guide is to provide a map of the contents of the manual that will assist readers with different interests and priorities.

An overview of the sequence of chapters

Chapter 1 is a general introduction to CPI methodology, and is intended for all readers. It provides the basic information needed to understand the subsequent chapters. It summarizes index number theory, as explained in detail in Chapters 15 to 23, and outlines the main steps involved in the actual compilation of a CPI, drawing on material in Chapters 3 to 9. It does not provide a summary of the manual as whole, as it does not cover some specific topics and special cases that are not of general relevance.

Chapter 2 explains how CPIs have evolved in response to the demands made upon them and how the uses of CPIs affect the choice of methodology to be used. Chapter 3 is concerned with a number of basic concepts, principles and classifications, as well as with the scope or coverage of an index. The scope of a CPI can vary significantly from country to country.

Chapters 4 to 9 form an interrelated sequence describing the various steps involved in the compilation of a CPI from the collection and processing of the price data through to the calculation of the final index. Chapter 4 explains how the expenditure weights attached to the price changes for different goods and services are derived. These weights are typically based on household expenditure surveys supplemented by data from other sources.

Chapter 5 deals with sampling issues. A CPI is essentially an estimate based on a sample of prices. Chapter 5 considers sampling design, and the pros and cons of random versus purposive sampling. Chapter 6 is devoted to the procedures actually used to collect the prices from a selection of retail outlets or other suppliers. It deals with topics such as questionnaire design, the specification of the items selected, the use of scanner data and the use of hand-held computers.

Chapter 7 addresses the difficult question of how to adjust prices for changes over time in the quality of the goods or services selected. Changes in value resulting from changes in quality count as changes in quantity, not price. Disentangling the effects of quality change poses serious theoretical and practical problems for compilers. Chapter 8 covers the closely related question of how to deal with new goods or services not previously purchased and for which there are no prices in earlier periods.

Chapter 9 pulls together the material contained in the preceding five chapters and gives a step-by-step summary of the various stages of CPI calculation. It describes both the elementary price indices calculated from the raw prices collected for small groups of products and the subsequent averaging of the elementary indices to obtain indices at higher levels of aggregation up to the overall CPI itself.

Chapter 10 deals with a number of cases that require special treatment: for example, goods and services for which prices are not quoted separately, being embedded within composite transactions covering more than one item. It also examines the case of owner-occupied housing. Chapter 11 considers the errors and biases to which CPIs may be subject.

Chapter 12 deals with issues of organization and management. Conducting the price surveys and processing the results is a massive operation that requires careful planning and organization, and also efficient management. Chapter 13 is concerned with the publication or dissemination of the results.

Chapter 14 marks a break in the sequence of chapters, as it not concerned with the compilation of a CPI. Its purpose is different, namely to examine the place of the CPI in the general system of price statistics. The CPI should not be treated as an independent, isolated statistic. The flow of consumer goods and services to which it relates is itself only one of a set of interdependent flows within the economy as a whole. The analysis of inflation requires more than one index, and it is essential to know exactly how the CPI relates to the producer price index (PPI) and to other price indices, such as indices of export and import prices. The supply and use matrix of the System of National Acounts provides the appropriate conceptual framework within which to examine these interrelationships.

Chapters 15 to 18 provide a systematic and detailed exposition of the index number and economic theory underlying CPIs. Five different approaches to index number theory are examined that between them cover all aspects of index number theory. Collectively, they provide a comprehensive and up-to-date survey of index number theory, including recent methodological developments as reported in journals and conference proceedings.

Chapter 15 provides an introduction to index number theory focusing on the decomposition of value changes into their price and quantity components. Chapter 16 examines the axiomatic and stochastic approaches to CPIs. The axiomatic, or test, approach lists a number of properties that it is desirable for index numbers to possess and tests specific formulae to see whether or not they possess them.

Chapter 17 explains the economic approach based on the economic theory of consumer behaviour. On this approach, a CPI is defined as a cost of living index (COLI). Although COLIs cannot be calculated directly, a certain class of index numbers, known as superlative indices, can be expected to approximate COLIs in practice. An increasing number of economists and other users have concluded that, in principle, the preferred, ideal index for CPI purposes should be a superlative index, such as the Fisher index. This is reinforced by the fact that the Fisher also emerges as a very desirable index on axiomatic grounds.

Chapter 18 deals with aggregation issues. Chapter 19 uses a constructed data set to illustrate the numerical consequences of using different index number formulae. It demonstrates that, in general, the choice of index number formula can make a considerable difference, but that different superlative indices all tend to approximate each other.

Chapter 20 addresses the important question of what is the theoretically most appropriate form of elementary price index to calculate at the first stage of CPI compilation when no information is available on quantities or expenditures. This has been a comparatively neglected topic until recently, even though the choice of formula for an elementary index can have a significant impact on the overall CPI. The elementary indices are the basic building blocks from which CPIs are constructed.

Chapters 21 to 23 deal with difficult issues. Chapter 21 discusses adjusting for quality change, including the hedonic approach, from a theoretical viewpoint. Chapter 22 examines the treatment of seasonal products. Finally, Chapter 23 considers the treatment of durable goods. There is some tension in both national accounts and CPIs resulting from the fact that owner-occupied houses are treated as assets, whereas consumer durables are not. These treatments are not easy to reconcile conceptually and Chapter 23 discusses the theoretical issues involved.

The manual concludes with a glossary of terms, a bibliography, and four annexes on the following topics:

- the Harmonized Indices of Consumer Prices (HICPs) of the European Union;
- the Classification of Individual Consumption according to Purpose (COICOP), a household expenditure classification;
- the resolution concerning consumer prices indices adopted by the Seventeenth International Conference of Labour Statisticians, 2003;
- spatial comparisons of consumer prices, using purchasing power parities and the International Comparison Program.

Suggested reading plans

Different readers may have different needs and priorities. Readers interested mainly in the compilation of CPIs may not wish to pursue all the finer points of the underlying economic and statistical theory. Conversely, readers interested more in the use of CPIs for analytic or policy purposes may not be so interested in reading about the technicalities of conducting and managing price surveys.

Not all readers will want to read the entire manual but all readers, whatever their preferences, will find it useful to read the first three chapters. Chapter 1 provides a general introduction to the whole subject by giving an overview of the CPI theory and practice that is presented in the manual. It covers the basic knowledge required for understanding subsequent chapters. Chapter 2 explains why CPIs are calculated and what they are used for. Chapter 3 examines a number of fundamental concepts and the scope of a CPI.

A reading plan for compilers

Chapters 4 to 13 are primarily for compilers. They follow a logical sequence that roughly matches the various stages of the actual compilation of a CPI, starting with the derivation of the expenditure weights and the collection of the price data, and finishing with the publication of the final index.

Chapter 14 is intended equally for compilers and users of CPIs. It places CPIs in perspective within the overall system of price indices.

The remaining chapters from 15 to 23 are mainly theoretical. Compilers may find it necessary to pursue certain theoretical topics in greater depth, in which case they have immediate access to the relevant material. It would be desirable for compilers to be acquainted with at least the basic index number theory set out in Chapter 15 and the numerical example developed in Chapter 19. The material in Chapter 20 on elementary price indices is also particularly important for compilers.

A reading plan for users

Although all readers will find Chapters 1 to 3 useful, the subsequent ten chapters are designed primarily for compilers. Two topics that have, however, aroused considerable interest among many users are the treatment of quality change and new products. These are discussed at some length in Chapters 7 and 8. Users may also find Chapter 9 particularly helpful as it provides a concise description of the various stages of compiling a CPI.

Chapter 11 on errors and bias, and Chapter 14 on the system of price statistics are also of equal interest to users and compilers.

Chapters 15 to 23 covering the underlying economic and statistical theory are likely to be of interest to many users, especially professional economists and students of economics.

References

In the past, international manuals on economic statistics have not usually provided references to the associated literature. It was not considered helpful to cite references when the literature was mostly confined to printed volumes, including academic journals or proceedings of conferences, located only in university or major libraries. Compilers working in many statistical offices were unlikely to have ready access to such literature. This situation has been completely transformed by the Internet and the Web, which make all such literature readily accessible. Accordingly, this manual breaks with past tradition by including a comprehensive bibliography on the very large literature that exists on index number theory and practice.

AN INTRODUCTION TO CONSUMER PRICE INDEX METHODOLOGY

1

1.1 A price index is a measure of the proportionate, or percentage, changes in a set of prices over time. A consumer price index (CPI) measures changes in the prices of goods and services that households consume. Such changes affect the real purchasing power of consumers' incomes and their welfare. As the prices of different goods and services do not all change at the same rate, a price index can only reflect their average movement. A price index is typically assigned a value of unity, or 100, in some reference period and the values of the index for other periods of time are intended to indicate the average proportionate, or percentage, change in prices from this price reference period. Price indices can also be used to measure differences in price levels between different cities, regions or countries at the same point in time.

1.2 Much of this manual and the associated economic literature on price indices is concerned with two basic questions:

- Exactly what set of prices should be covered by the index?
- What is the most appropriate way in which to average their movements?

These two questions are addressed in the early sections of this introduction.

1.3 Consumer price indices (CPIs) are index numbers that measure changes in the prices of goods and services purchased or otherwise acquired by households, which households use directly, or indirectly, to satisfy their own needs and wants. Consumer price indices can be intended to measure either the rate of price inflation as perceived by households, or changes in their cost of living (that is, changes in the amounts that the households need to spend in order to maintain their standard of living). There need be no conflict between these two objectives. In practice, most CPIs are calculated as weighted averages of the percentage price changes for a specified set, or "basket", of consumer products, the weights reflecting their relative importance in household consumption in some period. Much depends on how appropriate and timely the weights are.

1.4 This chapter provides a general introduction to, and overview of, the methodology for compiling CPIs. It provides a summary of the relevant theory and practice of index number compilation that is intended to facilitate the reading and understanding of the detailed chapters that follow, some of which are inevitably quite technical. It describes all the various steps involved in CPI compilation starting with the basic concept, definition and purpose of a CPI, followed by the sampling procedures and survey methods used to collect and process the price data, and finishing with a summary of the actual calculation of the index and its dissemination.

1.5 An introductory presentation of CPI methodology has to start with the basic concept of a CPI and the underlying index number theory, including the properties and behaviour of the various kinds of index number that are, or might be, used for CPI purposes. In principle, it is necessary to settle what type of index to calculate before going on to consider the best way in which to estimate it in practice, taking account of the resources available.

1.6 The main topics covered in this chapter are as follows:

- the origins and uses of CPIs;
- basic index number theory, including the axiomatic and economic approaches to CPIs;
- elementary price indices and aggregate CPIs;
- the transactions, activities and households covered by CPIs;
- the collection and processing of the prices, including adjusting for quality change;
- the actual calculation of the CPI;
- potential errors and bias;
- organization, management and dissemination policy.

In contrast, in this manual, the chapters dealing with index theory come later on; thus the presentation in this chapter does not follow the same order as the corresponding chapters of the manual.

1.7 It is not the purpose of this introduction to provide a complete summary of the contents of the manual. The objective is rather to provide a short presentation of the core methodological issues with which readers need to be acquainted before tackling the detailed chapters that follow. Some special topics, such as the treatment of certain individual products whose prices cannot be directly observed, are not considered here as they are not central to CPI methodology.

The origins and uses of consumer price indices

1.8 CPIs must serve a purpose. The precise way in which they are defined and constructed depends very much on what they are meant to be used for, and by whom. As explained in Chapter 15, CPIs have a long history dating back to the eighteenth century. Laspeyres and Paasche indices, which are still widely used today, were first proposed in the 1870s. They are explained below. The concept of the cost of living index was introduced early in the twentieth century.

1.9 Traditionally, one of the main reasons for compiling a CPI was to compensate wage-earners for inflation by adjusting their wage rates in proportion to the percentage change in the CPI, a procedure known as indexation. For this reason, official CPIs tended to become the responsibility of ministries of labour, but most are now compiled by national statistical offices. A CPI that is specifically intended to be used to index wages is known as a compensation index.

1.10 CPIs have three important characteristics. They are published *frequently*, usually every month but sometimes every quarter. They are available *quickly*, usually about two weeks after the end of the month or quarter. They are also usually *not revised*. CPIs tend to be closely monitored and attract a lot of publicity.

1.11 As CPIs provide timely information about the rate of inflation, they have also come to be used for a wide variety of purposes in addition to indexing wages. For example:

- CPIs are widely used to index pensions and social security benefits.
- CPIs are also used to index other payments, such as interest payments or rents, or the prices of bonds.
- CPIs are also commonly used as a proxy for the general rate of inflation, even though they measure only consumer inflation. They are used by some governments or central banks to set inflation targets for purposes of monetary policy.
- The price data collected for CPI purposes can also be used to compile other indices, such as the price indices used to deflate household consumption expenditures in national accounts, or the purchasing power parities used to compare real levels of consumption in different countries.

1.12 These varied uses can create conflicts of interest. For example, using a CPI as an indicator of general inflation may create pressure to extend its coverage to include elements that are not goods and services consumed by households, thereby changing the nature and concept of the CPI. It should also be noted that because of the widespread use of CPIs to index a wide variety of payments – not just wages, but social security benefits, interest payments, private contracts, etc. – extremely large sums of money turn on their movements, enough to have a significant impact on the state of government finances. Thus, small differences in the movements of CPIs resulting from the use of slightly different formulae or methods can have considerable financial implications. CPI methodology is important in practice and not just in theory.

Choice of index number

1.13 The first question is to decide on the kind of index number to use. The extensive references dealing with index theory in the bibliography reflect the fact that there is a very large literature on this subject. Many different kinds of mathematical formulae have been proposed over the past two centuries. While there may be no single formula that would be preferred in all circumstances, most economists and compilers of CPIs seem to be agreed that, in principle, the index formula should belong to a small class of indices called *superlative* indices. A superlative index may be expected to provide an approximation to a cost of living index. A characteristic feature of a superlative index is that it treats the prices and quantities in both periods being compared symmetrically. Different superlative indices tend to have similar properties, yield similar results and behave in very similar ways. Because of their properties of symmetry, some kind of superlative index is also likely to be seen as desirable, even when the CPI is not meant to be a cost of living index.

1.14 When a monthly or quarterly CPI is first published, however, it is invariably the case that there is not sufficient information on the quantities and expenditures in the current period to make it possible to calculate a symmetric, or superlative, index. While it is necessary to resort to second-best alternatives in practice, being able to make a rational choice between the various possibilities means having a clear idea of the target index that would be preferred in principle. The target index can have a considerable influence on practical matters such as the frequency with which the weights used in the index should be updated.

1.15 A comprehensive, detailed, rigorous and up-to-date discussion of the relevant index number theory is provided in Chapters 15 to 23 of the manual. The following sections provide a summary of this material. Proofs of the various propositions or theorems stated in this chapter are to be found in the later chapters, to which the reader may refer for further explanation.

Price indices based on baskets of goods and services

1.16 The purpose of an index number may be explained as comparing the *values* of households' expenditures on consumer goods and services in two time periods. Knowing that expenditures have increased by 5 per cent is not very informative if we do not know how much of this change is attributable to changes in the *prices* of the goods and services, and how much to changes in the *quantities* purchased. The purpose of an index number is to decompose proportionate or percentage changes in value aggregates into their overall components of price and quantity change. A CPI is intended to measure the price component of the change in households' consumption expenditures. One way to do this is to measure the change in the value of an aggregate, holding the quantities constant.

Lowe indices

1.17 One very wide, and popular, class of price indices is obtained by defining the index as the percentage change, between the periods compared, in the total cost of purchasing a given set of quantities, generally described as a "basket". The meaning of such an index is easy to grasp and to explain to users. This class of index is called a Lowe index in this manual, after the index number pioneer who first proposed it in 1823 (see Chapter 15). Most statistical offices make use of some kind of Lowe index in practice.

1.18 Let there be n products in the basket with prices p_i and quantities q_i, and let the two periods compared be 0 and t. The Lowe index, P_{Lo}, is defined as follows:

$$P_{Lo} \equiv \frac{\sum_{i=1}^{n} p_i^t q_i}{\sum p_i^0 q_i}$$

1.19 In principle, any set of quantities could serve as the basket. The basket does not have to be restricted to the quantities purchased in one or other of the two periods compared, or indeed any actual period of time. The quantities could, for example, be arithmetic or geometric averages of the quantities in the two periods. For practical reasons, the basket of quantities used for CPI purposes usually has to be based on a survey of household consumption expenditures conducted in an earlier period than either of the two periods whose prices are compared. For example, a monthly CPI may run from January 2000 onwards, with January 2000 = 100, but the quantities may be derived from an annual expenditure survey made in 1997 or 1998, or even spanning both those years. As it takes a long time to collect and process expenditure data, there is usually a considerable time lag before such data can be introduced into the calculation of CPIs. The basket may also refer to a year, whereas the index may be compiled monthly or quarterly.

1.20 The period whose quantities are actually used in a CPI is described as the *weight reference period* and it will be denoted as period b. Period 0 is the *price reference period.* As just noted, b is likely to precede 0, at least when the index is first published, and this is assumed here, but b could be any period, including one between 0 and t, if the index is calculated some time after t. The Lowe index using the quantities of period b can be written as follows:

$$P_{Lo} \equiv \frac{\sum_{i=1}^{n} p_i^t q_i^b}{\sum_{i=1}^{n} p_i^0 q_i^b} \equiv \sum_{i=1}^{n} (p_i^t / p_i^0) s_i^{0b}$$

$$\text{where} \quad s_i^{0b} = \frac{p_i^0 q_i^b}{\sum_{i=1}^{n} p_i^0 q_i^b} \tag{1.1}$$

The index can be written, and calculated, in two ways: either as the ratio of two value aggregates, or as an arithmetic weighted average of the price ratios, or *price relatives*, p_i^t/p_i^0, for the individual products using the hybrid expenditure shares s_i^{0b} as weights. The expenditures are described as *hybrid* because the prices and quantities belong to two different time periods, 0 and b respectively. The hybrid weights may be obtained by updating the actual expenditure shares in period b, namely $p_i^b q_i^b / \sum p_i^b q_i^b$, for the price changes occurring between periods b and 0 by multiplying them by the price relatives b and 0, namely p_i^0/p_i^b. Lowe indices are widely used for CPI purposes.

Laspeyres and Paasche indices

1.21 Any set of quantities could be used in a Lowe index, but there are two special cases which figure very prominently in the literature and are of considerable importance from a theoretical point of view. When the quantities are those of the price reference period, that is when $b=0$, the *Laspeyres* index is obtained. When quantities are those of the other period, that is when $b=t$, the *Paasche* index is obtained. It is necessary to consider the properties of Laspeyres and Paasche indices, and also the relationships between them, in more detail.

1.22 The Laspeyres price index, P_L, is defined as:

$$P_L = \frac{\sum_{i=1}^{n} p_i^t q_i^0}{\sum_{i=1}^{n} p_i^0 q_i^0} \equiv \sum_{i=1}^{n} (p_i^t / p_i^0) s_i^0 \tag{1.2}$$

where s_i^0 denotes the share of the *actual* expenditure on commodity i in period 0: that is, $p_i^0 q_i^0 / \sum p_i^0 q_i^0$.

1.23 The Paasche index, P_P, is defined as:

$$P_P = \frac{\sum_{i=1}^{n} p_i^t q_i^t}{\sum_{i=1}^{n} p_i^0 q_i^t} \equiv \left\{ \sum_{i=1}^{n} (p_i^t / p_i^0)^{-1} s_i^t \right\}^{-1} \tag{1.3}$$

where s_i^t denotes the actual share of the expenditure on commodity i in period t; that is, $p_i^t q_i^t / \sum p_i^t q_i^t$. Notice that the Paasche index is a weighted *harmonic* average of the price relatives that uses the actual expenditure shares in the later period t as weights. It follows from equation (1.1) that the Paasche index can also be expressed as a weighted arithmetic average of the price relatives using hybrid expenditure weights, in which the quantities of t are valued at the prices of 0.

Decomposing current value changes using Laspeyres and Paasche indices

1.24 Laspeyres and Paasche quantity indices are defined in a similar way to the price indices, simply by interchanging the p and q values in formulae (1.2) and (1.3). They summarize changes over time in the flow of quantities of goods and services consumed. A Laspeyres quantity index values the quantities at the fixed prices of the earlier period, while the Paasche quantity index uses the prices of the later period. The ratio of the values of the expenditures in two periods (V) reflects the combined effects of both price and quantity changes. When Laspeyres and Paasche indices are used, the value change can be exactly decomposed into a price index times a quantity index only if the Laspeyres price (quantity) index is matched with the Paasche quantity (price) index. Let P_{La} and Q_{La} denote the Laspeyres price and quantity indices and let P_{Pa} and Q_{Pa} denote the Paasche price and quantity indices: then, $P_{La} Q_{Pa} \equiv V$ and $P_{Pa} Q_{La} \equiv V$.

1.25 Suppose, for example, a time series of household consumption expenditures at current prices in the national accounts is to be deflated by a price index to show changes in real consumption. To generate a series of consumption expenditures at constant base period prices (whose movements are identical with those of the Laspeyres volume index), the consumption expenditures at current prices must be deflated by a series of Paasche price indices.

Ratios of Lowe and Laspeyres indices

1.26 The Lowe index is transitive. The ratio of two Lowe indices using the same set of q^b values is also a Lowe index. For example, the ratio of the Lowe index for period $t+1$ with price reference period 0 divided by that for period t also with price reference period 0 is:

$$\frac{\sum_{i=1}^{n} p_i^{t+1} q_i^b \Big/ \sum_{i=1}^{n} p_i^0 q_i^b}{\sum_{i=1}^{n} p_i^t q_i^b \Big/ \sum_{i=1}^{n} p_i^0 q_i^b} = \frac{\sum_{i=1}^{n} p_i^{t+1} q_i^b}{\sum_{i=1}^{n} p_i^t q_i^b} = P_{Lo}^{t,t+1} \qquad (1.4)$$

This is a Lowe index for period $t+1$ with period t as the price reference period. This kind of index is, in fact, widely used to measure short-term price movements, such as between t and $t+1$, even though the quantities may date back to some much earlier period b.

1.27 A Lowe index can also be expressed as the ratio of two Laspeyres indices. For example, the Lowe index for period t with price reference period 0 is equal to the Laspeyres index for period t with price reference period b divided by the Laspeyres index for period 0 also with price reference period b. Thus,

$$P_{Lo} = \frac{\sum_{i=1}^{n} p_i^t q_i^b}{\sum_{i=1}^{n} p_i^0 q_i^b} = \frac{\sum_{i=1}^{n} p_i^t q_i^b \Big/ \sum_{i=1}^{n} p_i^b q_i^b}{\sum_{i=1}^{n} p_i^0 q_i^b \Big/ \sum_{i=1}^{n} p_i^b q_i^b} = \frac{P_{La}^t}{P_{La}^0} \qquad (1.5)$$

Updated Lowe indices

1.28 It is useful to have a formula that enables a Lowe index to be calculated directly as a chain index, in which the index for period $t+1$ is obtained by updating the index for period t. Because Lowe indices are transitive, the Lowe index for period $t+1$ with price reference period 0 can be written as the product of the Lowe index for period t with price reference period 0 multiplied by the Lowe index for period $t+1$ with price reference period t. Thus,

$$\frac{\sum_{i=1}^{n} p_i^{t+1} q_i^b}{\sum_{i-1}^{n} p_i^0 q_i^b} = \left[\frac{\sum_{i=1}^{n} p_i^t q_i^b}{\sum_{i=1}^{n} p_i^0 q_i^b}\right] \left[\frac{\sum_{i=1}^{n} p_i^{t+1} q_i^b}{\sum_{i=1}^{n} p_i^t q_i^b}\right]$$

$$= \left[\frac{\sum_{i=1}^{n} p_i^t q_i^b}{\sum_{i=1}^{n} p_i^0 q_i^b}\right] \left[\sum_{i=1}^{n} \left(\frac{p_i^{t+1}}{p_i^t}\right) s_i^{tb}\right] \qquad (1.6)$$

where the expenditure weights s_i^{tb} are hybrid weights defined as:

$$s_i^{tb} \equiv p_i^t q_i^b \Big/ \sum_{i=1}^{n} p_i^t q_i^b \qquad (1.7)$$

1.29 Hybrid weights of the kind defined in equation (1.7) are often described as *price-updated* weights. They can be obtained by adjusting the original expenditure weights $p_i^b q_i^b / \sum p_i^b q_i^b$ by the price relatives p_i^t / p_i^b. By price-updating the expenditure weights from b to t in this way, the index between t and $t+1$ can be calculated directly as a weighted average of the price relatives p_i^{t+1}/p_i^t without referring back to the price reference period 0. The index can then be linked on to the value of the index in the preceding period t.

Interrelationships between fixed basket indices

1.30 Consider first the interrelationship between the Laspeyres and the Paasche indices. A well-known result in index number theory is that if the price and quantity changes (weighted by values) are *negatively* correlated, then the Laspeyres index exceeds the Paasche index. Conversely, if the weighted price and quantity changes are *positively* correlated, then the Paasche index exceeds the Laspeyres index. The proof is given in Appendix 15.1 of Chapter 15.

1.31 As consumers are usually price-takers, they typically react to price changes by substituting goods or services that have become *relatively* cheaper for those that have become *relatively* dearer. This is known as the *substitution effect*, a phenomenon that figures prominently in this manual and the wider literature on index numbers. Substitution tends to generate a negative correlation between the price and quantity relatives, in which case the Laspeyres index is greater than the Paasche index, the gap between them tending to widen over time.

1.32 In practice, however, statistical offices do not calculate Laspeyres or Paasche indices but instead usually calculate Lowe indices as defined in equation (1.1). The question then arises of how the Lowe index relates to the Laspeyres and Paasche indices. It is shown in the text of Chapter 15, and also in Appendix 15.2, that if there are persistent long-term trends in relative prices and if the substitution effect is operative, the Lowe index will tend to exceed the Laspeyres, and therefore also the Fisher and the Paasche indices. Assuming that period b precedes period 0, the ranking under these conditions will be:

$$\text{Lowe} \geq \text{Laspeyres} \geq \text{Fisher} \geq \text{Paasche}$$

Moreover, the amount by which the Lowe exceeds the other three indices will tend to increase, the further back in time period b is in relation to period 0.

1.33 The positioning of period b is crucial. Given the assumptions about long-term price trends and substitution, a Lowe index will tend to increase as period b is moved backwards in time, or to decrease as period b is moved forwards in time. While b may have to precede 0 when the index is first published, there is no such restriction on the positioning of b as price and quantity data become available for later periods with passage of time. Period b can then be moved forwards. If b is positioned midway between 0 and t, the quantities are likely to be equi-representative of both periods, assuming that there is a fairly smooth transition from the relative quantities of 0 to those of t. In these circumstances, the Lowe index is likely to be close to the Fisher and other superlative indices, and cannot be presumed to have either an upward or a downward bias. These points are elaborated further below, and also in Chapter 15.

1.34 It is important that statistical offices take these relationships into consideration in deciding upon their policies. There are obviously practical advantages and financial savings from continuing to make repeated use over many years of the same fixed set of quantities to calculate a CPI. However, the amount by which such a CPI exceeds some conceptually preferred target index, such as a cost of living index (COLI), is likely to get steadily larger the further back in time the period b to which the quantities refer. Most users are likely to interpret the difference as upward bias. A large bias may undermine the credibility and acceptability of the index.

Young index

1.35 Instead of holding constant the quantities of period b, a statistical office may calculate a CPI as a weighted arithmetic average of the individual price relatives, holding constant the revenue shares of period b. The resulting index is called a *Young* index in this manual, again after another index number pioneer. The Young index is defined as follows:

$$P_{Yo} \equiv \sum_{i=1}^{n} s_i^b \left(\frac{p_i^t}{p_i^0} \right) \quad \text{where} \quad s_i^b \equiv \frac{p_i^b q_i^b}{\sum_{i=1}^{n} p_i^b q_i^b} \tag{1.8}$$

In the corresponding Lowe index, equation (1.1), the weights are hybrid revenue shares that value the quantities of b at the prices of 0. As already explained, the price reference period 0 is usually later than the weight reference period b because of the time needed to collect and process and revenue data. In that case, a statistical office has the choice of assuming that either the quantities of period b remain constant or the expenditure shares in period b remain constant. Both cannot remain constant if prices change between b and 0. If the expenditure shares actually remained constant between periods b and 0, the quantities must have changed inversely in response to the price changes, which implies an elasticity of substitution of unity.

1.36 Whereas there is a presumption that the Lowe index will tend to exceed the Laspeyres index, it is more difficult to generalize about the relationship between the Young index and the Laspeyres index. The Young could be greater or less than the Laspeyres depending on how sensitive the quantities are to changes in relative prices. It is shown in Chapter 15 that with high elasticities of substitution (greater than unity) the Young will tend to exceed the Laspeyres, whereas with low elasticities the Young will tend to be less than the Laspeyres.

1.37 As explained later in this chapter, the Lowe index may be preferred to the Young index because the Young index has some undesirable properties that cause it to fail some critical index number tests (see also Chapter 16).

Geometric Young, Laspeyres and Paasche indices

1.38 In the geometric version of the Young index, a weighted geometric average is taken of the price relatives using the expenditure shares of period b as weights. It is defined as follows:

$$P_{GYo} \equiv \prod_{i=1}^{n} \left(\frac{p_i^t}{p_i^0} \right)^{s_i^b} \tag{1.9}$$

where s_i^b is defined as above. The geometric Laspeyres is the special case in which $b=0$; that is, the expenditure shares are those of the price reference period 0. Similarly, the geometric Paasche uses the expenditure shares of period t. It should be noted that these geometric indices cannot be expressed as the ratios of value aggregates in which the quantities are fixed. They are not basket indices and there are no counterpart Lowe indices.

1.39 It is worth recalling that for any set of positive numbers the arithmetic average is greater than, or equal to, the geometric average, which in turn is greater than, or equal to, the harmonic average, the equalities holding only when the numbers are all equal. In the case of unitary cross-elasticities of demand and constant expenditure shares, the geometric Laspeyres and Paasche indices coincide. In this case, the ranking of the indices must be the ordinary Laspeyres $\geq$ the geometric Laspeyres and Paasche $\geq$ the ordinary Paasche, because the indices are, respectively, arithmetic, geometric and harmonic averages of the same price relatives which all use the same set of weights.

1.40 The geometric Young and Laspeyres indices have the same information requirements as their ordinary arithmetic counterparts. They can be produced on a timely basis. Thus, these geometric indices must be treated as serious practical possibilities for purposes of CPI calculations. As explained later, the geometric indices are likely to be less subject than their arithmetic counterparts to the kinds of index number biases discussed in later sections. Their main disadvantage may be that, because they are not fixed basket indices, they are not so easy to explain or justify to users.

Symmetric indices

1.41 A symmetric index is one that makes equal use of the prices and quantities in both the periods compared and treats them in a symmetric manner. There are three particular symmetric indices that are widely used in economic statistics. It is convenient to introduce them at this point. As already noted, these three indices are also superlative indices.

1.42 The first is the *Fisher price index*, P_F, defined as the *geometric* average of the Laspeyres and Paasche indices; that is,

$$P_F \equiv \sqrt{P_L P_P} \tag{1.10}$$

1.43 The second is the *Walsh price index, P_W*. This is a basket index whose quantities consist of *geometric* averages of the quantities in the two periods; that is,

$$P_W \equiv \frac{\sum_{i=1}^{n} p_i^t \sqrt{q_i^t q_i^0}}{\sum_{i=1}^{n} p_i^0 \sqrt{q_i^t q_i^0}} \tag{1.11}$$

By taking a *geometric* rather than an arithmetic average of the quantities, equal weight is given to the *relative* quantities in both periods. The quantities in the Walsh index can be regarded as being equi-representative of both periods.

1.44 The third index is the *Törnqvist price index, P_T*, defined as a *geometric* average of the price relatives weighted by the average expenditure shares in the two periods.

$$P_T = \prod_{i=1}^{n} (p_i^t / p_i^0)^{\sigma_i} \tag{1.12}$$

where σ_i is the arithmetic average of the share of expenditure on product i in the two periods.

$$\sigma_i = \frac{S_i^t + S_i^0}{2} \tag{1.13}$$

where the s_i values are defined as in equations (1.2) and (1.3) above.

1.45 The theoretical attractions of these indices become more apparent in the following sections on the axiomatic and economic approaches to index numbers.

Fixed base versus chain indices

1.46 This topic is examined in Chapter 15. When a time series of Lowe or Laspeyres indices is calculated using a fixed set of quantities, the quantities become progressively out of date and increasingly irrelevant to the later periods for which prices are being compared. The base period, in which quantities are set, has to be updated sooner or later and the new index series linked to the old. Linking is inevitable in the long run.

1.47 In a chain index, each link consists of an index in which each period is compared with the preceding one, the weight and price reference periods being moved forward each period. Any index number formula can be used for the individual links in a chain index. For example, it is possible to have a chain index in which the index for $t+1$ on t is a Lowe index defined as $\sum p^{t+1} q^{t-j} / \sum p^t q^{t-j}$. The quantities refer to some period that is j periods earlier than the price reference period t. The quantities move forward one period as the price reference period moves forward one period. If $j=0$, the chain Lowe becomes a chain Laspeyres, while if $j=-1$, it becomes a chain Paasche.

1.48 The CPIs in some countries are, in fact, annual chain Lowe indices of this general type, the quantities referring to some year or years that precede the price reference period 0 by a fixed period. For example, the 12 monthly indices from January 2000 to January 2001, with January 2000 as the price reference period, could be Lowe indices based on price-updated expenditures for 1998. The 12 indices from January 2001 to January 2002 are then based on price updated expenditures for 1999, and so on.

1.49 The expenditures lag behind the January price reference period by a fixed interval, moving forward a year each January as the price reference period moves forward one year. Although, for practical reasons, there has to be a time lag between the quantities and the prices when the index is first published, it is possible to recalculate the monthly indices for the current year later, using current expenditure data when they eventually become available. In this way, it is possible for the long-run index to be an annually chained monthly index, with contemporaneous annual weights. This method is explained in more detail in Chapter 9. It is used by one statistical office.

1.50 A chain index has to be "path dependent". It must depend on the prices and quantities in all the intervening periods between the first and last periods in the index series. Path dependency can be advantageous or disadvantageous. When there is a gradual economic transition from the first to the last period, with smooth trends in relative prices and quantities, chaining will tend to reduce the index number spread between the Lowe, Laspeyres and Paasche indices, thereby making the movements in the index less dependent on the choice of index number formula.

1.51 If there are fluctuations in the prices and quantities in the intervening periods, however, chaining may not only increase the index number spread but also distort the measure of the overall change between the first and last periods. For example, suppose all the prices in the last period return to their initial levels in period 0, which implies that they must have fluctuated in between; a chain Laspeyres index will not return to 100. It will tend to be greater than 100. If the cycle is repeated with all the prices periodically returning to their original levels, a chain Laspeyres index will tend to drift further and further above 100 even though there may be no long-term upward trend in the prices. Chaining is therefore not advised when prices fluctuate. When monthly prices are subject to regular and substantial seasonal fluctuations, for example, monthly chaining cannot be recommended. Seasonal fluctuations cause serious problems, which are analysed in Chapter 22. While a number of countries update their expenditure weights annually, the 12-monthly indices within each year are not chain indices but Lowe indices using fixed annual quantities.

1.52 *The Divisia index.* If the prices and quantities are continuous functions of time, it is possible to partition the change in their total value over time into price and quantity components following the method of Divisia. As shown in Chapter 15, the Divisia index may be derived mathematically by differentiating value (i.e. price multiplied by quantity) with respect to time to obtain two components: a relative-value-weighted price change and a relative-value-weighted quantity change.

These two components are defined to be price and quantity indices, respectively. The Divisia is essentially a theoretical index. In practice, prices can be recorded only at discrete intervals, even if they vary continuously with time. A chain index may, however, be regarded as a discrete approximation to a Divisia. The Divisia index itself offers limited practical guidance about the kind of index number formula to choose for the individual links in a chain index.

Axiomatic and stochastic approaches to index numbers

1.53 Various *axiomatic approaches* to index numbers are explained in Chapter 16. These approaches seek to determine the most appropriate functional form for an index by specifying a number of axioms, or tests, that the index ought to satisfy. They throw light on the properties possessed by different kinds of indices, some of which are not intuitively obvious. Indices that fail to satisfy certain basic or fundamental axioms, or tests, may be rejected completely because they are liable to behave in unacceptable ways. An axiomatic approach may also be used to rank indices on the basis of their desirable, and undesirable, properties.

First axiomatic approach

1.54 The first approach is the traditional test approach pioneered by Irving Fisher. The price and quantity indices are defined as functions of the two vectors of prices and two vectors of quantities relating to the two periods compared. The prices and quantities are treated as independent variables, whereas in the economic approach to index numbers considered later in this chapter the quantities are assumed to be functions of the prices.

1.55 Chapter 16 starts by considering a set of 20 axioms, but only a selection of them is given here by way of illustration.

T1: *positivity* – the price index and its constituent vectors of prices and quantities should be positive.

T3: *identity test* – if the price of every product is identical in both periods, then the price index should equal unity, no matter what the quantity vectors are.

T5: *proportionality in current prices* – if all prices in period t are multiplied by the positive number λ, then the new price index should be λ times the old price index; i.e., the price index function is (positively) homogeneous of degree one in the components of the period t price vector.

T10: *invariance to changes in the units of measurement* (commensurability test) – the price index does not change if the units in which the products are measured are changed.

T11: *time reversal test* – if all the data for the two periods are interchanged, then the resulting price index should equal the reciprocal of the original price index.

T14: *mean value test for prices* – the price index lies between the highest and the lowest price relatives.

T16: *Paasche and Laspeyres bounding test* – the price index lies between the Laspeyres and Paasche indices.

T17: *monotonicity in current prices* – if any period t price is increased, then the price index must increase.

1.56 Some of the axioms or tests can be regarded as more important than others. Indeed, some of the axioms seem so inherently reasonable that it might be assumed that any index number actually in use would satisfy them. For example, test T10, the commensurability test, says that if the unit of quantity in which a product is measured is changed, say, from a gallon to a litre, the index must be unchanged. One index that does not satisfy this test is the *Dutot* index, which is defined as the ratio of the arithmetic means of the prices in the two periods. As explained later, this is a type of elementary index that is in fact widely used in the early stages of CPI calculation.

1.57 Consider, for example, the average price of salt and pepper. Suppose it is decided to change the unit of measurement for pepper from grams to ounces while leaving the units in which salt is measured (for example, kilos) unchanged. As an ounce is equal to 28.35 grams, the absolute value of the price of pepper increases by over 28 times, which effectively increases the weight of pepper in the Dutot index by over 28 times.

1.58 When the products covered by an index are heterogeneous and measured in different physical units, the value of any index that does not satisfy the commensurability test depends on the purely arbitrary choice of units. Such an index must be unacceptable conceptually. If the prices refer to a strictly homogeneous set of products that all use the same unit of measurement, the test becomes irrelevant.

1.59 Another important test is T11, the time reversal test. In principle, it seems reasonable to require that the same result should be obtained whichever of the two periods is chosen as the price reference period: in other words, whether the change is measured forwards in time, i.e., from 0 to t, or backwards in time from t to 0. The Young index fails this test because an arithmetic average of a set of price relatives is not equal to the reciprocal of the arithmetic average of the reciprocals of the price relatives. The fact that the *conceptually* arbitrary decision to measure the change in prices forwards from 0 and t gives a different result from measuring backwards from t to 0 is seen by many users as a serious disadvantage. The failure of the Young index to satisfy the time reversal test needs to be taken into account by statistical offices.

1.60 Both the Laspeyres and Paasche fail the time reversal test for the same reasons as the Young index. For example, the formula for a Laspeyres calculated backwards from t to 0, P_{BL}, is:

$$P_{BL} = \frac{\sum_{i=1}^{n} p_i^0 q_i^t}{\sum_{i=1}^{n} p_i^t q_i^t} \equiv \frac{1}{P_P} \qquad (1.14)$$

This index is identical to the reciprocal of the (forwards) Paasche, not to the reciprocal of the (forwards) Laspeyres. As already noted, the (forwards) Paasche tends to register a smaller increase than the (forwards) Laspeyres so that the Laspeyres index cannot satisfy the time reversal test. The Paasche index also fails the time reversal test.

1.61 In contrast, the Lowe index satisfies the time reversal test *provided* that the quantities q_i^b remain fixed when the price reference period is changed from 0 to t. The quantities of a Laspeyres index are, however, those of the price reference period *by definition*, and must change whenever the price reference period is changed. The basket for a forwards Laspeyres is different from that for a backwards Laspeyres, and the Laspeyres fails the time reversal test in consequence.

1.62 Similarly, the Lowe index is transitive whereas the Laspeyres and Paasche indices are not. Assuming that a Lowe index uses a fixed set of quantities, q_i^b, whatever the price reference period, it follows that

$$Lo^{0,t} = Lo^{0,t-k} Lo^{t-k,t}$$

where $Lo^{0,t}$ is the Lowe index for period t with period 0 as the price reference period. The Lowe index that compares t directly with 0 is the same as that calculated indirectly as a chain index through period $t-k$.

1.63 If, on the other hand, the Lowe index is defined in such a way that quantities vary with the price reference period, as in the index $\sum p^{t+1}q^{t-j}/\sum p^t q^{t-j}$ considered earlier, the resulting chain index is not transitive. The chain Laspeyres and chain Paasche indices are special cases of this index.

1.64 In the real world, the quantities do change and the whole point of chaining is to enable the *quantities* to be continually updated to take account of the changing universe of products. Achieving transitivity by arbitrarily holding the quantities constant, especially over a very long period of time, does not compensate for the potential biases introduced by using out-of-date quantities.

Ranking of indices using the first axiomatic approach

1.65 In Chapter 16 it is shown not only that the Fisher price index satisfies all the 20 axioms listed but also, more remarkably, that it is the only possible index that can satisfy all 20 axioms. Thus, on the basis of this particular set of axioms, the Fisher clearly dominates other indices.

1.66 In contrast to Fisher, the other two symmetric (and superlative) indices defined in equations (1.11) and (1.12) above do not emerge so well from the 20 tests. In Chapter 16, it is shown that the Walsh price index fails four tests while the Törnqvist index fails nine tests. Nevertheless, the Törnqvist and the Fisher may be expected to approximate each other quite closely numerically when the data follow relatively smooth trends, as shown in Chapter 19.

1.67 One limitation of the axiomatic approach is that the list of axioms is inevitably somewhat arbitrary. Some axioms, such as the Paasche and Laspeyres bounding test failed by both Törnqvist and Walsh, could be regarded as dispensable. Additional axioms or tests can be envisaged, and two further axioms are considered below. Another problem with a simple application of the axiomatic approach is that it is not sufficient to know which tests are failed. It is also necessary to know how badly an index fails. Failing badly one major test, such as the commensurability test, might be considered sufficient to rule out an index, whereas failing several minor tests marginally may not be very disadvantageous.

Some further tests

1.68 Consider a further symmetry test. Reversing the roles of prices and quantities in a price index yields a quantity index of the same functional form as the price index. The *factor reversal test* requires that the product of this quantity index and the original price index should be identical with the change in the value of the aggregate in question. The test is important if, as stated earlier, price and quantity indices are intended to enable changes in the values of aggregates over time to be factored into their price and quantity components in an economically meaningful way. Another interesting result given in Chapter 16 is that the Fisher index is the only price index to satisfy four minimal tests: T1 (positivity), T11 (time reversal test), T12 (quantity reversal test) and T21 (factor reversal test). As the factor reversal test implicitly assumes that the prices and quantities must refer either to period 0 or to period t, it is not relevant to a Lowe index in which three periods are involved, b, 0 and t.

1.69 As shown earlier, the product of the Laspeyres price (quantity) index and the Paasche quantity (price) index is identical with the change in the total value of the aggregate in question. Thus, Laspeyres and Paasche indices may be said to satisfy a weak version of the factor reversal test in that dividing the value change by a Laspeyres (Paasche) price index does lead to a meaningful quantity index, i.e., the Paasche (Laspeyres), even though the functional forms of the price and quantity indices are not identical.

1.70 Another test discussed in Chapter 16 is the *additivity test*. This is more important from the perspective of quantity than price indices. Price indices may be used to deflate value changes to obtain implicit quantity changes. The results may be presented for sub-aggregates such as broad categories of household consumption. Just as expenditure aggregates at current prices are, by definition, obtained simply by summing individual expenditures, it is reasonable to expect that the changes in the sub-aggregates of a quantity index should add up to the changes in the totals – the additivity test. Quantity indices such as Laspeyres and Paasche that use a common set of prices to value quantities in both periods must satisfy the additivity test. Similarly, the Lowe quantity index defined as $\sum p^j q^t/\sum p^j q^0$ is also additive. The Geary–Khamis quantity index (see Annex 4) used to make international comparisons of real consumption and gross domestic product (GDP) between countries is an example of such a Lowe quantity index. It uses an arithmetically weighted average of the prices in the different countries as the common price vector p^j to compare the quantities in different countries.

1.71 Similarly, an average of the prices in two periods can be used to value the quantities in intertemporal indices. If the quantity index is also to satisfy the time reversal test, the average must be symmetrical. The *invariance to proportional changes in current prices test* (which corresponds to test T7 listed in Chapter 16, except that the roles of prices and quantities are reversed) requires that a quantity index depend only on the *relative*, not the absolute, level of the prices in each period. The Walsh quantity index satisfies this test, is additive and satisfies the time reversal test as well. It emerges as a quantity index with some very desirable properties.

1.72 Although the Fisher index itself is not additive, it is possible to decompose the overall *percentage change* in a Fisher price, or quantity, index into additive components that reflect the percentage change in each price or quantity. A similar multiplicative decomposition is possible for a Törnqvist price or quantity index.

The stochastic approach and a second axiomatic approach

1.73 Before considering a second axiomatic approach, it is convenient to take the stochastic approach to price indices. The stochastic approach treats the observed price *changes* or *relatives* as if they were a random sample drawn from a defined universe whose mean can be interpreted as the general rate of inflation. There can, however, be no single unique rate of inflation. Many possible universes can be defined, depending on which particular sets of expenditures or transactions the user is interested in. Clearly, the sample mean depends on the choice of universe from which the sample is drawn. Specifying the universe is similar to specifying the scope of a CPI. The stochastic approach addresses issues such as the appropriate form of average to take and the most efficient way to estimate it from a sample of price relatives, once the universe has been defined.

1.74 The stochastic approach is particularly useful when the universe is reduced to a single type of product. Because of market imperfections, there may be considerable variation in the prices at which the same product is sold in different outlets and also in the price changes observed. In practice, statistical offices have to estimate the average price change for a single product from a sample of price observations. Important methodological issues are raised, which are discussed in some detail in Chapter 7 and Chapter 20.

The unweighted stochastic approach

1.75 In Chapter 16, the unweighted stochastic approach to index number theory is explained. If simple random sampling has been used, equal weight may be given to each sampled price relative. Suppose each price relative can be treated as the sum of two components: a common inflation rate and a random disturbance with a zero mean. Using least squares or maximum likelihood, the best estimate of the common inflation rate is the unweighted *arithmetic* mean of price relatives, an index formula known as the *Carli* index. This index is the unweighted version of the Young index and is discussed further below, in the context of elementary price indices.

1.76 If the random component is multiplicative, not additive, the best estimate of the common inflation rate is given by the unweighted *geometric* mean of price relatives, known as the *Jevons* index. The Jevons index may be preferred to the Carli on the grounds that it satisfies the time reversal test, whereas the Carli does not. As explained below, this fact may be decisive when determining the functional form to be used to estimate the elementary indices compiled in the early stages of CPI calculations.

The weighted stochastic approach

1.77 As explained in Chapter 16, a *weighted* stochastic approach can be applied at an aggregative level covering sets of different products. As the products may be of differing economic importance, equal weight should not be given to each type of product. The products may be weighted on the basis of their share in the total value of the expenditures, or other transactions, in some period or periods. In this case, the index (or its logarithm) is the expected value of a random sample of price relatives (or their logarithms) whose probability of selection is proportional to the expenditure on that type of product in some period, or periods. Different indices are obtained depending on which expenditure weights are used and on whether the price relatives or their logarithms are used.

1.78 Suppose a sample of price relatives is randomly selected with the probability of selection proportional to the expenditure on that type of product in the price reference period 0. The expected price change is then the Laspeyres price index for the universe. Other indices may, however, also be obtained using the weighted stochastic approach. Suppose both periods are treated symmetrically and the probabilities of selection are made proportional to the arithmetic mean expenditure shares in both periods 0 and t. When these weights are applied to the logarithms of the price relatives, the expected value of the logarithms is the Törnqvist index, also known as the Törnqvist–Theil index. From an axiomatic viewpoint, the choice of a symmetric average of the expenditure shares ensures that the time reversal test is satisfied, while the choice of the arithmetic mean, as distinct from some other symmetric average, may be justified on the grounds that the fundamental proportionality in current prices test, T5, is thereby satisfied.

1.79 By focusing on price changes, the Törnqvist index emerges as an index with some very desirable properties. This suggests a second axiomatic approach to indices, in which the focus is shifted from the individual prices and quantities used in the traditional axiomatic approach, to price changes and values shares.

A second axiomatic approach

1.80 A second axiomatic approach is examined in Chapter 16 in which a price index is defined as a function of the two sets of prices, or their ratios, and two sets of values. Provided the index is invariant to changes in units of measurement, i.e., satisfies the commensurability test, it makes no difference whether individual prices or their ratios are specified. A set of 17 axioms is postulated which are similar to the 20 axioms considered in the first axiomatic approach.

1.81 It is shown in Appendix 16.1 that the Törnqvist, or Törnqvist–Theil, is the only price index to satisfy all 17 axioms, just as the Fisher price index is the only index to satisfy all 20 tests in the first approach. However, the Törnqvist index does not satisfy the factor reversal test, so that the implicit quantity index obtained by deflating the change in value by the Törnqvist price index is not the Törnqvist quantity index. The implicit quantity index is therefore not "best" in the sense of satisfying the 17 axioms when these are applied to the quantity, rather than price, indices.

1.82 Zero prices may cause problems for indices based on price ratios, and especially for geometric averages of price ratios. In particular, if any price tends to zero, one test that may be applied is that the price index ought not to tend to zero or plus infinity. The Törnqvist does not meet this test. It is therefore proposed in Chapter 16 that when using the Törnqvist index, care should be taken to bound the prices away from zero in order to avoid a meaningless index number.

1.83 Finally, Chapter 16 examines the axiomatic properties of the Lowe and Young indices. The Lowe index emerges quite well from the axiomatic approach, satisfying both the time reversal and circularity tests. On the other hand, the Young index, like the Laspeyres and Paasche indices, fails both tests. As already explained, however, the attractiveness of the Lowe index depends more on how relevant the fixed quantity weights are to the two periods being compared, that is on the positioning of period *b*, than its axiomatic properties.

1.84 Although the "best" indices emerging from the two axiomatic approaches, namely Fisher and Törnqvist, are not the same, they have much in common. As already noted, they are both symmetric indices and they are both superlative indices. Although their formulae are different, they may be expected to behave in similar ways and register similar price movements. The same *type* of indices keep emerging as having desirable properties whichever approach to index theory is adopted, a conclusion that is reinforced by the economic approach to index numbers, which is explained in Chapter 17.

Cost of living index

1.85 Approaching the consumer price index from the standpoint of economic theory has led to the development of the concept of a cost of living index (COLI). The theory of the COLI was first developed by Konus (1924). It rests on the assumption of optimizing behaviour on the part of a rational consumer. The COLI for such a consumer has been defined succinctly as the ratio of the minimum expenditures needed to attain the given level of utility, or welfare, under two different price regimes. A more precise definition and explanation are given in Chapter 17.

1.86 Whereas a Lowe index measures the change in the cost of purchasing a fixed basket of goods and services resulting from changes in their prices, a COLI measures the change in the *minimum* cost of maintaining a given level of utility, or welfare, that results from changes in the prices of the goods and services consumed.

1.87 A COLI is liable to possible misinterpretation because households' welfare depends on a variety of physical and social factors that have no connection with prices. Events may occur that impinge directly on welfare, such as natural or man-made disasters. When such events occur, households may need to increase their consumption of goods and services in order to compensate for the loss of welfare caused by those events. Changes in the costs of consumption triggered by events *other than changes in prices* are irrelevant for a CPI that is not merely intended to measure changes in the prices of consumer goods and services but is generally interpreted by users as measuring price changes, and only price changes. In order to qualify as a CPI, a COLI must therefore hold constant not only the consumer's preferences but all the non-price factors that affect the consumer's welfare and standard of living. If a CPI is intended to be a COLI it must be *conditional* on:

- a particular level of utility or welfare;
- a particular set of consumer preferences;
- a particular state of the physical and social environment.

Of course, Lowe indices are also conditional as they depend on the particular basket of goods and services selected.

1.88 Lowe indices and COLIs have in common the fact that they may both be defined as the ratios of expenditures in two periods. However, whereas, by definition, the quantities are fixed in Lowe indices, they vary in response to changes in relative prices in COLIs. In contrast to the fixed basket approach to index theory, the economic approach explicitly recognizes that the quantities consumed are actually dependent on the prices. In practice, rational consumers may be expected to adjust the *relative* quantities they consume in response to changes in *relative* prices. A COLI assumes that a consumer seeking to minimize the cost of maintaining a given level of utility will make the necessary adjustments. The baskets of goods and services in the numerator and denominator of a COLI are not therefore exactly the same.

1.89 The observed expenditure of a rational consumer in the selected base period may be assumed to be the minimum expenditure needed to achieve the level of utility enjoyed in that period. In order to calculate a COLI based on that period, it is necessary to know what would be the minimum expenditure needed to attain precisely the same level of utility if the prices prevailing were those of the second period, other things remaining equal. The quantities purchased under these assumed conditions are likely to be *hypothetical*. They will not be the quantities actually consumed in the second period if other factors, including the resources available to the consumer, have changed.

1.90 The quantities required for the calculation of the COLI in at least one of the periods are not likely to be observable in practice. The COLI is not an operational index that can be calculated directly. The challenge is therefore to see whether it is possible to find methods of estimating a COLI indirectly or at least to find upper and lower bounds for the index. There is also considerable interest in establishing the relationship between a COLI and Lowe indices, including Laspeyres and Paasche, that can be calculated.

Upper and lower bounds on a cost of living index

1.91 It follows from the definition of a Laspeyres index that, if the consumer's income were to change by the same proportion as the change in the Laspeyres index, the consumer must have the possibility of purchasing the same basket of products as in the base period. The consumer cannot be worse off. However, if *relative* prices have changed, a utility-maximizing consumer would not continue to purchase the same quantities as before. The consumer would be able to achieve a *higher level* of utility by substituting, at least marginally, products that have become relatively cheaper for those that have become dearer. As a COLI measures the change in the minimum expenditures needed to maintain a constant level of utility, the COLI based on the first period will increase by less than the Laspeyres index.

1.92 By a similar line of reasoning, it follows that when relative prices change, the COLI based on the second period must increase by more than the Paasche index. As explained in more detail in Chapter 17, the Laspeyres index provides an upper bound to the COLI based on the first period and the Paasche a lower bound to the COLI based on the second period. It should be noted that there are two different COLIs involved here: one based on the first period and the other based on the second period. In general, however, the two COLIs are unlikely to differ much.

1.93 Suppose that the theoretical target index is a COLI, but that, for practical reasons, the CPI is actually calculated as a Lowe index in which the quantities refer to some period b that precedes the price reference period 0. One important conclusion to be drawn from this preliminary analysis is that as the Lowe may be expected to exceed the Laspeyres, assuming long-term price trends and substitution, while the Laspeyres may in turn be expected to exceed the COLI, the widely used Lowe index may be expected to have an upward bias. This point has had a profound influence on attitudes towards CPIs in some countries. The bias results from the fact that, by definition, fixed basket indices, including Laspeyres, do not permit any substitution between products in response to changes in relative prices. It is therefore usually described as "substitution bias". A Paasche index would be expected to have a downward substitution bias.

Some special cases

1.94 The next step is to establish whether there are special conditions under which it may be possible to measure a COLI exactly. In Chapter 17 it is shown that if the consumer's preferences are homothetic – that is, each indifference curve has the same shape, each being a uniform enlargement, or contraction, of each other – then the COLI is independent of the utility level on which it is based. The Laspeyres and Paasche indices provide upper and lower bounds to the *same* COLI.

1.95 One interesting special case occurs when the preferences can be represented by the so-called "Cobb–Douglas" function in which the cross-elasticities of demand between the various products are all unity. Consumers adjust the relative quantities they consume inversely in proportion to the changes in relative prices so that expenditure shares remain constant. With Cobb–Douglas preferences, the geometric Laspeyres provides an exact measure of the COLI. As the expenditure shares remain constant over time, all three *geometric* indices – Young, Laspeyres and Paasche – coincide with each other and with the COLI. Of course, the arithmetic versions of these indices do not coincide in these circumstances, because the baskets in periods b, 0 and t are all different as substitutions take place in response to changes in relative prices.

1.96 One of the more famous results in index number theory is that if the preferences can be represented by a homogeneous quadratic utility function, the Fisher index provides an exact measure of the COLI (see Chapter 17). Even though consumers' preferences are unlikely to conform exactly with this particular functional form, this result does suggest that, in general, the Fisher index is likely to provide a close approximation to the underlying unknown COLI and certainly a much closer approximation than either the arithmetic Laspeyres or Paasche indices.

Estimating COLIs by superlative indices

1.97 The intuition – that the Fisher index approximates the COLI – is corroborated by the following line of reasoning. Diewert (1976) noted that a homogeneous quadratic is a flexible functional form that can provide a second-order approximation to other twice-differentiable functions around the same point. He then described an index number formula as *superlative* when it is exactly equal to the COLI based on a certain functional form *and* when that functional form is flexible, e.g., a homogeneous quadratic. The derivation of these results, and further explanation, is given in detail in Chapter 17. In contrast to the COLI based on the true but unknown utility function, a superlative index is an actual index number that can be calculated. The practical significance of these results is that they provide a theoretical justification for expecting a superlative index to provide a fairly close approximation to the underlying COLI in a wide range of circumstances.

1.98 *Superlative indices as symmetric indices.* The Fisher is by no means the only example of a superlative index. In fact, there is a whole family of superlative indices. It is shown in Chapter 17 that any quadratic mean of order r is a superlative index for each value of $r \neq 0$. A quadratic mean of order r price index P^r is defined as follows:

$$P^r \equiv \frac{\sqrt[r]{\sum_{i=1}^{n} s_i^0 \left(\frac{p_i^t}{p_i^0}\right)^{r/2}}}{\sqrt[r]{\sum_{i=1}^{n} s_i^t \left(\frac{p_i^0}{p_i^t}\right)^{r/2}}} \tag{1.15}$$

where s_i^0 and s_i^t are defined as in equations (1.2) and (1.3) above.

1.99 The symmetry of the numerator and denominator of equation (1.15) should be noted. A distinctive feature of equation (1.15) is that it treats the price changes and expenditure shares in both periods symmetrically, whatever value is assigned to the parameter r. Three special cases are of interest:

- when $r = 2$, equation (1.1) reduces to the Fisher price index;
- when $r = 1$ it is equivalent to the Walsh price index;
- in the limit as $r \rightarrow 0$, it equals the Törnqvist index.

These indices were introduced earlier as examples of indices that treat the information available in both periods *symmetrically*. Each was originally proposed long before the concept of a superlative index was developed.

1.100 *Choice of superlative index.* Chapter 17 addresses the question of which superlative formula to choose in practice. As each may be expected to approximate to the same underlying COLI, it may be inferred that they ought also to approximate to each other. The fact that they are all symmetric indices reinforces this conclusion. These conjectures tend to be borne out in practice by numerical calculations. So long as the parameter r does not lie far outside the range 0 to 2, superlative indices tend to be very close to each other. In principle, however, there is no limit on r and it has recently been shown that as r becomes larger, the formula tends to assign increasing weight to the extreme price relatives and the resulting superlative indices may diverge significantly from each other. Only when the absolute value of r is small, as in the case of the three commonly used superlative indices (Fisher, Walsh and Törnqvist), is the choice of superlative index unimportant.

1.101 Both the Fisher and the Walsh indices date back nearly a century. The Fisher index owes its popularity to the axiomatic, or test, approach, which Fisher himself was instrumental in developing. As already noted, it dominates other indices using the first axiomatic approach, while the Törnqvist dominates using the second axiomatic approach outlined above. The fact that the Fisher and the Törnqvist are both superlative indices whose use can be justified on economic grounds suggests that, from a theoretical point of view, it may not be possible to improve on them for CPI purposes.

Representativity bias

1.102 The fact that the Walsh index is a Lowe index that is also superlative suggests that the bias in other Lowe indices depends on the extent to which their quantities deviate from those in the Walsh basket. This can be viewed from another angle.

1.103 As the quantities in the Walsh basket are *geometric* averages of the quantities in the two periods, equal importance is assigned to the *relative*, as distinct from the *absolute*, quantities in both periods. The Walsh basket may therefore be regarded as being the basket that is most representative of *both* periods. If equal importance is attached to the consumption patterns in the two periods, the optimal basket for a Lowe index ought to be the most representative basket. The Walsh index then becomes the conceptually preferred target index for a Lowe index.

1.104 Suppose that period b, for which the quantities are actually used in the Lowe index, lies midway between 0 and t. In this case, assuming fairly smooth trends in the relative quantities, the actual basket in period b is likely to approximate to the most representative basket. Conversely, the further away that period b is from the midpoint between 0 and t, the more the relative quantities of b are likely to diverge from those in the most representative basket. In this case, the Lowe index between periods 0 and t that uses period b quantities is likely to exceed the Lowe index that uses the most representative quantities by an amount that becomes progressively larger the further back in time period b is positioned. The excess constitutes "bias" if the latter index is the target index. The bias can be attributed to the fact that the period b quantities tend to become increasingly unrepresentative of a comparison between 0 and t the further back period b is positioned. The underlying economic factors responsible are, of course, exactly the same as those that give rise to bias when the target index is the COLI. Thus, certain kinds of indices can be regarded as biased without invoking the concept of a COLI. Conversely, the same kinds of indices tend to emerge as being preferred, whether or not the objective is to estimate a cost of living bias.

1.105 If interest is focused on short-term price movements, the target index is an index between consecutive time periods t and $t+1$. In this case, the most representative basket has to move forward one period as the index moves forward. Choosing the most representative basket implies chaining. Similarly, chaining is also implied if the target index is a COLI between t and $t+1$. In practice, the universe of products is continually changing as well. As the most representative basket moves forward, it is possible to update the set of products covered, as well as take account of changes in the relative quantities of products that were covered previously.

Data requirements and calculation issues

1.106 As superlative indices require price and expenditure data for both periods, and as expenditure data are usually not available for the current period, it is not feasible to calculate a superlative CPI, at least at the time that a CPI is first published. In practice, CPIs tend to be Lowe indices with fixed quantities or annually updated chain Lowe indices. In the course of time, however, the requisite expenditure data may become available, enabling a superlative CPI to be calculated subsequently. Users will find it helpful for superlative CPIs to be published retrospectively as they make it possible to evaluate the properties and behaviour of the official index. Superlative CPIs can be treated as supplementary indices that complement, rather than replace, the original indices, if the policy is not to revise the official index.

1.107 Chapter 17 notes that, in practice, CPIs are usually calculated in stages (see also Chapters 9 and 20) and addresses the question of whether indices calculated this way are consistent in aggregation: that is, have the same values whether calculated in a single operation or in two stages. The Laspeyres index is shown to be exactly consistent, but the superlative indices are not. The widely used Fisher and Törnqvist indices are nevertheless shown to be approximately consistent.

Allowing for substitution

1.108 Chapter 17 examines one further index proposed recently, the Lloyd–Moulton index, P_{LM}, defined as follows:

$$P_{LM} \equiv \left\{ \sum_{i=1}^{n} s_i^0 \left(\frac{p_i^t}{p_i^0} \right)^{1-\sigma} \right\}^{\frac{1}{1-\sigma}} \qquad \sigma \neq 1 \qquad (1.16)$$

The parameter σ, which must be non-negative, is the elasticity of substitution between the products covered. It reflects the extent to which, on average, the various products are believed to be substitutes for each other. The advantage of this index is that it may be expected to be free of substitution bias to a reasonable degree of approximation, while requiring no more data than a Lowe or Laspeyres index. It is therefore a practical possibility for CPI calculation, even for the most recent periods, although it is likely to be difficult to obtain a satisfactory, acceptable estimate of the numerical value of the elasticity of substitution, the parameter used in the formula.

Aggregation issues

1.109 It has been assumed up to this point that the COLI is based on the preferences of a single representative consumer. Chapter 18 examines the extent to which the various conclusions reached above remain valid for CPIs that are actually compiled for groups of households. The general conclusion is that essentially the same relationships hold at an aggregate level, although some additional issues arise which may require additional assumptions.

1.110 One issue is how to weight individual households. Aggregate indices that weight households by their expenditures are called "plutocratic", while those that assign the same weight to each household are called "democratic". Another question is whether, at any one point of time, there is a single set of prices or whether different households face different prices. In general, when defining the aggregate indices it is not necessary to assume that all households are confronted by the same set of prices, although the analysis is naturally simplified if there is only a single set.

1.111 A plutocratic aggregate COLI assumes that each individual household minimizes the cost of attaining a given level of utility when confronted by two different sets of prices, the aggregate COLI being defined as the ratio of the aggregate minimum costs over all households. As in the case of a single household, it is recognized that the aggregate COLI that is appropriate for CPI purposes must be *conditional* on the state of a particular set of environmental variables, typically those in one or other of the periods compared. The environment must be understood in a broad sense to refer not only to the physical environment but also to the social and political environment.

1.112 Like the index for a single representative consumer, an aggregate COLI cannot be calculated directly, but it may be possible to calculate aggregate Laspeyres and Paasche indices that bound their respective COLIs from above or below. If there is only one single set of national prices, the aggregate plutocratic Laspeyres index reduces to an ordinary aggregate Laspeyres index. As the aggregate plutocratic Laspeyres and Paasche can, in principle, be calculated, so can the aggregate plutocratic Fisher index. It is argued in Chapter 18 that this should normally provide a good approximation to the aggregate plutocratic COLI.

1.113 Chapter 18 finally concludes that, in principle, both democratic and plutocratic Laspeyres, Paasche and Fisher indices could be constructed by a statistical agency, provided that information on household-specific price relatives and expenditures is available for both periods. If expenditure information is available only for the first period, then only the Laspeyres democratic and plutocratic indices can be constructed. The data requirements are rather formidable, however. The required data are unlikely to be available for *individual* households in practice and, even if they were to be, they could be subject to large errors.

Illustrative numerical data

1.114 Chapter 19 presents some numerical examples using an artificial data set. The purpose is not to illustrate the methods of calculation as such, but rather to demonstrate how different index number formulae can yield very different numerical results. Hypothetical but economically plausible prices, quantities and expenditures are given for six commodities over five periods of time. In general, differences between the different formulae tend to increase with the variance of the price relatives. They also depend on the extent to which the prices follow smooth trends or fluctuate.

1.115 The numerical results are striking. For example, the Laspeyres index over the five periods registers an increase of 44 per cent while the Paasche falls by 20 per cent. The two commonly used superlative indices, Törnqvist and Fisher, register increases of 25 per cent and 19 per cent respectively, an index number spread of only 6 points compared with the 64-point gap between the Laspeyres and Paasche. When the indices are chained, the chain Laspeyres and Paasche indices register increases of 33 per cent and 12 per cent respectively, reducing the gap between the two indices from 64 to 21 points. The chained Törnqvist and Fisher indices register increases of 22.26 per cent and 22.24 per cent respectively, being virtually identical numerically. These results show that the choice of index formula and method does matter.

Seasonal products

1.116 As explained in Chapter 22, the existence of seasonal products poses some intractable problems and serious challenges for CPI compilers and users. Seasonal products are products that are either:

- not available during certain seasons of the year; or
- are available throughout, but their prices or quantities are subject to regular fluctuations that are synchronized with the season or time of the year.

There are two main sources of seasonal fluctuations: the climate and custom. Month-to-month movements in a CPI may sometimes be so dominated by seasonal influences that it is difficult to discern the underlying trends in prices. Conventional seasonal adjustment programmes may be applied, but these may not always be satisfactory. The problem is not confined to interpreting movements in the CPI, as seasonality creates serious problems for the compilation of a CPI when some of the products in the basket regularly disappear and reappear, thereby breaking the continuity of the price series from which the CPI is built up. There is no panacea for seasonality. A consensus on what is best practice in this area has not yet been formed. Chapter 22 examines a number of different ways in which the problems may be tackled using an artificial data set to illustrate the consequences of using different methods.

1.117 One possibility is to exclude seasonal products from the index, but this may be an unacceptable reduction in the scope of the index, as seasonal products can account for a significant proportion of total household consumption. Assuming seasonal products are retained, one solution is to switch the focus from month-to-month movements in the index to changes between the same month in successive years. In some countries, it is common for the media and other users, such as central banks, to focus on the annual rate of inflation between the most recent month and the same month in the previous year. This year-on-year figure is much easier to interpret than month-to-month changes, which can be somewhat volatile, even in the absence of seasonal fluctuations.

1.118 This approach is extended in Chapter 22 to the concept of a rolling year-on-year index that compares the prices for the most recent 12 months with the corresponding months in the price reference year. The resulting *rolling year indices* can be regarded as seasonally adjusted price indices. They are shown to work well using the artificial data set. Such an index can be regarded as a measure of inflation for a year that is centred around a month that is six months earlier than the last month in the rolling index. For some purposes, this time lag may be disadvantageous, but in Chapter 22 it is shown that under certain conditions the current month year-on-year monthly index, together with the previous month's year-on-year monthly index, can successfully predict the rolling year index that is centred on the current month. Of course, rolling year indices and similar analytic constructs are not intended to replace the monthly or quarterly CPI but to provide supplementary information that can be extremely useful to users. They can be published alongside the official CPI.

1.119 Various methods of dealing with the breaks in price series caused by the disappearance and reappearance of seasonal products are examined in Chapter 22. However, this remains an area in which more research needs to be done.

Elementary price indices

1.120 As explained in Chapters 9 and 20, the calculation of a CPI proceeds in stages. In the first stage, *elementary price indices* are estimated for the *elementary expenditure aggregates* of a CPI. In the second stage, these elementary indices are aggregated, or averaged, to obtain higher-level indices using the elementary expenditure aggregates as weights. An elementary aggregate consists of the expenditures on a small and relatively homogeneous set of products defined within the consumption classification used in the CPI. As explained in Chapter 6, statistical offices usually select a set of representative products within each aggregate and then collect samples of their prices from a number of different outlets. The elementary aggregates serve as strata for sampling purposes.

1.121 The prices collected at the first stage are typically not prices observed in actual transactions between different economic units, but the prices at which the products are offered for sale in retail outlets of one kind or another. In principle, however, a CPI measures changes in the prices paid by households. These prices may actually vary during the course of a month, which is typically the time period to which the CPI relates. In principle, therefore, the first step should be to average the prices at which some product is sold during the period, bearing in mind that the price may vary even for the same product sold in the same outlet. In general, this is not a practical possibility. However, when the outlet is an electronic point of sale at which all the individual products are "scanned" as they are sold, the values of the transactions are actually recorded, thereby making it possible to calculate an average price instead of simply recording the offer price at a single point of time. Some use of scanner data is already made for CPI purposes and it may be expected to increase over the course of time.

1.122 Once the prices are collected for the representative products in a sample of outlets, the question arises of what is the most appropriate formula to use to estimate an elementary price index. This topic is considered in Chapter 20. It was comparatively neglected until a number of papers in the 1990s provided much clearer insights into the properties of elementary indices and their relative strengths and weaknesses. The quality of a CPI depends heavily on the quality of the elementary indices which are the building blocks from which CPIs are constructed.

1.123 Prices are collected for the same product in the same outlet over a succession of time periods. An elementary price index is therefore typically calculated from two sets of matched price observations. Here it is assumed that there are no missing observations and no changes in the quality of the products sampled so that the two sets of prices are perfectly matched. The treatment of new and disappearing products, and of quality change, is a separate and complex issue in its own right. It is outlined below, and discussed in detail in Chapters 7, 8 and 21.

Weights within elementary aggregates

1.124 In most cases, the price indices for elementary aggregates are calculated without the use of explicit expenditure weights. Whenever possible, however, weights should be used that reflect the relative importance of the sampled items, even if the weights are only approximate. In many cases, the elementary aggregate is simply the lowest level at which any reliable weighting information is available. In this case, the elementary index has to be calculated without the use of weights. Even in this case, however, it should be noted that when the items are selected with probabilities proportional to the size of some relevant variable such as sales, for example, weights are implicitly introduced by the sampling selection procedure.

1.125 For certain elementary aggregates, information about sales of particular items, market shares and regional weights may be used as explicit weights within an elementary aggregate. Weights within elementary aggregates may be updated independently, and possibly more often than the elementary aggregates themselves (which serve as weights for the higher-level indices).

1.126 For example, assume that the number of suppliers of a certain product, such as petrol, is limited. The market shares of the suppliers may be known from business survey statistics and can be used as weights in the calculation of an elementary aggregate price index for petrol. As another example, prices for water may be collected from a number of local water supply services where the population in each local region is known. The relative size of the population in each region may then be used as a proxy for the relative consumption expenditures to weight the price in each region to obtain the elementary aggregate price index for water.

Interrelationships between different elementary index formulae

1.127 Useful insights into the properties of various formulae that have been used, or considered, for elementary price indices may be gained by examining the mathematical interrelationships between them. Chapter 20 provides a detailed analysis of such relationships. As it is assumed that there are no explicit weights available, the various formulae considered all make use of unweighted averages: that is, *simple* averages in which the various items are *equally* weighted. There are two basic options for an elementary index:

- some kind of simple average of the price ratios or relatives;
- the ratio of some kind of simple average of the prices in the two periods.

In the case of a geometric average, the two methods coincide, as the geometric average of the price ratios or relatives is identical to the ratio of the geometric average prices.

1.128 Using the first of the above options, three possible elementary price indices are:

- a simple arithmetic average of the price relatives, known as the *Carli* index, or P_C; the Carli is the unweighted version of the Young index;
- a simple geometric average of the price relatives, known as the *Jevons* index, or P_J; the Jevons is the unweighted version of the geometric Young index;
- a simple harmonic average of the price relatives, or P_H.

As noted earlier, for any set of positive numbers the arithmetic average is greater than, or equal to, the geometric average, which in turn is greater than, or equal to, the harmonic average, the equalities holding only when the numbers are all equal. It follows that $P_C \geq P_J \geq P_H$.

1.129 It is shown in Chapter 20 that the gaps between the three indices widen as the variance of the price relatives increases. The choice of formula becomes more important the greater the diversity of the price movements. P_J can be expected to lie approximately halfway between P_C and P_H.

1.130 Using the second of the options, three possible indices are:

- the ratio of the simple arithmetic average prices, known as the *Dutot* index, or P_D;
- the ratio of the simple geometric averages, again the Jevons index, or P_J;
- the ratio of the simple harmonic averages, or P_H.

The ranking of *ratios* of different kinds of average are not predictable. For example, the Dutot, P_D, could be greater or less than the Jevons, P_J.

1.131 The Dutot can also be expressed as a weighted average of the price relatives in which the prices of period 0 serve as the weights:

$$P_D \equiv \frac{\sum_{i=1}^{n} p_i^t / n}{\sum_{i=1}^{n} p_i^0 / n} = \frac{\sum_{i=1}^{n} p_i^0 \left(\frac{p_i^t}{p_i^0} \right)}{\sum_{i=1}^{n} p_i^0} \qquad (1.17)$$

As compared with the Carli, which is a simple average of the price relatives, the Dutot gives more weight to the price relatives for the products with high prices in period 0. It is nevertheless difficult to provide an economic rationale for this kind of weighting. Prices are not expenditures. If the products are homogeneous, very few quantities are likely to be purchased at high prices if the same products can be purchased at low prices. If the products are heterogeneous, the Dutot should not be used anyway, as the quantities are not commensurate and not additive.

1.132 While it is useful to establish the interrelationships between the various indices, they do not actually help decide which index to choose. However, as the differences between the various formulae tend to increase with the dispersion of the price relatives, it is clearly desirable to define the elementary aggregates in such a way as to try to minimize the variation in the price movements within each aggregate. The less variation there is, the less difference the choice of index formula makes. As the elementary aggregates also serve as strata for sampling purposes, minimizing the variance in the price relatives within the strata will also reduce the sampling error.

Axiomatic approach to elementary indices

1.133 One way to decide between the various elementary indices is to exploit the axiomatic approach outlined earlier. A number of tests are applied to the elementary indices in Chapter 20.

1.134 The Jevons index, P_J, satisfies all the selected tests. It dominates the other indices in the way that the Fisher tends to dominate other indices at an aggregative level. The Dutot index, P_D, fails only one, the commensurability test. This failure is critical, however. It reflects the fundamental point made earlier that when the quantities are not additive from an economic viewpoint, the prices are also not additive and hence cannot be meaningfully averaged. However, P_D performs well when the sampled products are homogeneous. The key issue for the Dutot is therefore how heterogeneous are the products within the elementary aggregate. If the products are not sufficiently homogeneous for their quantities to be additive, the Dutot should not be used.

1.135 Although the Carli index, P_C, has been widely used in practice, the axiomatic approach shows it to have some undesirable properties. In particular, as the unweighted version of the Young index, it fails the time reversal and transitivity tests. This is a serious disadvantage, especially as elementary indices are often monthly chain indices. A consensus has emerged that the Carli may be unsuitable because it is liable to have a significant upward bias. This is illustrated by numerical example in Chapter 9. Its use is not sanctioned for the Harmonized Indices of Consumer Prices used within the European Union. Conversely, the harmonic average of the price relatives, P_H, is liable to have an equally significant downward bias; anyway, it does not seem to be used in practice.

1.136 Based on the axiomatic approach, the Jevons emerges as the preferred index, but its use may not be appropriate in all circumstances. If one observation is zero, the geometric mean is zero. The Jevons is sensitive to extreme falls in prices; it may be necessary to impose upper and lower bounds on the individual price relatives when using the Jevons.

Economic approach to elementary indices

1.137 The economic approach to elementary indices is explained in Chapter 20. The sampled products for which prices are collected are treated as if they constituted a basket of goods and services purchased by rational utility-maximizing consumers. The objective is then to estimate a conditional cost of living index covering the set of products in question.

1.138 It should be noted, however, that the differences between the prices of the sampled products do not necessarily mean that the products are qualitatively different. If markets were perfect, relative prices should reflect relative costs of production and relative utilities. In fact, price differences may occur simply because of market imperfections. For example, exactly the same products may be bought and sold at different prices in different outlets simply because consumers lack information about the prices charged in other outlets. Producers may also practise price discrimination, charging different customers different prices for exactly the same products. Price discrimination is widespread in many service industries. When the price differences are a result of market imperfections, consumers cannot be expected to react to changes in the relative prices of products in the same way as they would if they were well informed and had free choice.

1.139 In any case, assuming there is no information about quantities or expenditures within an elementary aggregate, it is not possible to calculate any kind of superlative index. So the conditional cost of living index at the level of an elementary aggregate can be estimated only on the assumption that certain special conditions apply.

1.140 There are two special cases of some interest. The first case is where the underlying preferences are so-called Leontief preferences. With these preferences *relative* quantities remain fixed whatever the relative prices. No substitutions are made in response to changes in relative prices. The cross-elasticities of demand are zero. With Leontief preferences, a Laspeyres index provides an exact measure of the cost of living index. In this case, the Carli calculated for a random sample would provide an estimate of the cost of living index provided that the items were selected with probabilities proportional to the population expenditure shares. It might appear that if the items were selected with probabilities proportional to the population quantity shares, the sample Dutot would provide an estimate of the population Laspeyres. However, assuming that the basket for the Laspeyres index contains a number of heterogeneous products whose quantities are not additive, the quantity shares, and hence the probabilities, are undefined.

1.141 The second case is one already considered above, namely when the preferences can be represented by a Cobb–Douglas function. As already explained, with these preferences, the geometric Laspeyres would provide an exact measure of the cost of living index. In this case, the Carli calculated for a random sample would provide an unbiased estimate of the cost of living index, provided that the items were selected with probabilities proportional to the population expenditure shares.

1.142 On the economic approach, the choice between the sample Jevons and the sample Carli rests on which is likely to approximate the more closely to the underlying COLI: in other words, on whether the demand cross-elasticities are likely to be closer to unity or zero, on average. In practice, the cross-elasticities could take on any value ranging up to plus infinity for an elementary aggregate in which the sampled products were strictly homogeneous, i.e., perfect substitutes. It should be noted that in the limiting case in which the sampled products are homogeneous, there is only a single kind of product and therefore no index number problem: the price index is given by the ratio of the unit values in the two periods. It may be conjectured that, on average, the cross-elasticities are likely to be closer to unity than zero for most elementary aggregates so that, in general, the Jevons index is likely to provide a closer approximation to the cost of living index than the Carli. In this case, the Carli must be viewed as having an upward bias.

1.143 It is worth noting that the use of the Jevons index does not imply, or assume, that expenditure shares remain constant. Obviously, a geometric average of the price relatives can be calculated whatever changes do or do not occur in the expenditure shares, in practice. What the economic approach shows is that *if* the expenditure shares remain constant (or roughly constant), *then* the Jevons can be expected to provide a good estimate of the underlying cost of living index. The insight provided by the economic approach is that the Jevons is likely to provide a closer approximation to the cost of living index than the Carli because a significant amount of substitution is more likely than no substitution, especially as elementary aggregates should be deliberately constructed in such a way as to group together similar items that are close substitutes for each other.

1.144 An alternative to the Jevons, P_J, would be a geometric average of P_C and P_H, an index labelled P_{CSWD} in Chapter 20. This could be justified on grounds of treating the data in both periods symmetrically without invoking any particular assumption about the form of the underlying preferences. It is also shown in Chapter 20 that the geometric average of P_C and P_H is likely to be very close to P_J, so that the latter may be preferred on the grounds that it is a simpler concept and easier to compile.

1.145 It may be concluded that, based on the economic approach, as well as the axiomatic approach, the Jevons emerges as the preferred index in general, although there may be cases in which little or no substitution takes place within the elementary aggregate and the Carli might be preferred. The index compiler must make a judgement on the basis of the nature of the products actually included in the elementary aggregate.

1.146 The above discussion has also thrown light on some of the sampling properties of the elementary indices. If the products in the sample are selected with probabilities proportional to expenditures in the price reference period:

- the sample (unweighted) Carli index provides an unbiased estimate of the population Laspeyres;
- the sample (unweighted) Jevons index provides an unbiased estimate of the population geometric Laspeyres.

These results hold irrespective of what the underlying cost of living index may be.

Concepts, scope and classifications

1.147 The purpose of Chapter 3 of the manual is to define and clarify a number of basic concepts underlying a CPI and to explain the scope of the index: that is, the set of goods and services and the set of households that the index is intended to cover, in principle. Chapter 3 also examines the structure of the classification of consumer goods and services used.

1.148 While the general purpose of a CPI is to measure changes in the prices of *consumption* goods and services, there are a number of concepts that need to be defined precisely before an operational definition of a CPI can be arrived at. The concept of consumption is an imprecise one that can be interpreted in several different ways, each of which may lead to a different CPI. It is also necessary to decide whether the index is meant to cover all consumers, i.e., all households, or just a particular group of households. The scope of a CPI is inevitably influenced by what is intended, or believed, to be the main use of the index. Compilers also need to remember that the index may be used as proxy for a general price index and used for purposes other than those for which it is intended.

1.149 The word "consumer" can be used to refer both to a type of economic unit and to a type of product. To avoid confusion here, the term *consumption* good or service will be used where necessary, rather than *consumer* good or service. A consumption good or service provides utility to its user. It may be defined as *a good or service that members of households use, directly or indirectly, to satisfy their own personal needs and wants*. "Utility" should be interpreted in a broad sense. It is simply the generic, technical term preferred by economists for the benefit or welfare that individuals or households derive from the use of a consumer good or service.

1.150 A CPI is generally understood to be a price index that measures changes in the prices of consumption goods and services acquired and used by households. In principle, more broadly based price indices can be defined whose scope extends beyond consumption goods and services to include the prices of physical assets such as land or dwellings. Such indices may be useful as broad measures of inflation as perceived by households, but most CPIs are confined to consumption goods and services. These may include the prices of the flows of services provided by assets such as dwellings, even though the assets themselves may be excluded. In any case, the prices of financial assets such as bonds, shares or other marketable securities purchased by households are generally regarded as being outside the scope of a CPI.

Acquisitions and uses

1.151 The times at which households acquire and use consumption goods or services are generally not the same. Goods are typically acquired at one point in time and used at some other point in time, or even used repeatedly over an extended period of time. The time of acquisition of a *good* is the moment at which the legal or effective economic ownership of the good passes to the consumer. In a market situation, this is the point at which the purchaser incurs a liability to pay. A *service* is acquired at the time that the producer provides it, no change of ownership being involved. The time at which acquisitions are recorded, and their prices, should also be consistent with the way in which the same transactions are recorded in the expenditure data used for weighting purposes.

1.152 The time at which payment is made may be determined mainly by institutional arrangements and administrative convenience. When payments are not made in cash, there may be a significant lapse of time before the consumer's bank account is debited for a purchase paid for by cheque, by credit card or similar arrangements. The time at which these debits are eventually made is irrelevant for the recording of the acquisitions and the prices. On the other hand, when the acquisition of a good or service is financed by the creation of a new financial asset at the time of acquisition, such as a loan to the purchaser, two economically separate transactions are involved, the purchase/sale of the good or service and the creation of the asset. The price to be recorded is the price payable at the time of acquisition, however the purchase is financed. Of course, the provision of finance may affect the price payable. The subsequent repayments of any debt incurred by the purchaser and the associated interest payments are financial transactions that are quite distinct from the purchase of the good or service whose price has to be recorded. The explicit or implicit interest payments payable on the amount depend on the capital market, the nature of the loan, its duration, the creditworthiness of the purchaser, and so on. These points are explained in more detail in Chapter 3.

1.153 The distinction between the *acquisition* and the *use* of a consumer good or service outlined above has led to two different concepts of a CPI being proposed:

- A CPI may be intended to measure the average change between two time periods in the prices of the consumer goods and services acquired by households.
- Alternatively, a CPI may be intended to measure the average change between two time periods in the prices of the consumer goods and services used by households to satisfy their needs and wants.

The distinction between time of acquisition and time of use is particularly important for durable goods and certain kinds of services.

1.154 *Durable and non-durable goods.* A "non-durable" good might be better described as a *single use* good. For example, food or drink are used once only to satisfy hunger or thirst. Many so-called non-durable consumer goods are in fact extremely durable physically. Households may hold substantial stocks of non-durables, such as many foodstuffs and fuel, for long periods of time before they are used.

1.155 The distinguishing feature of a durable consumption good is that it is durable under use. Consumer durables can be used repeatedly or continuously to satisfy the needs or wants of consumers over a long period of time, possibly many years: for example, furniture or vehicles. For this reason, a durable is often described as providing a flow of services to the consumer over the period it is used (see also Box 14.3 of Chapter 14). There is a close parallel between the definitions of consumer durables and fixed assets. Fixed assets are defined in national accounts as goods that are used repeatedly or continuously over long periods of time in processes of production: for example, buildings or other structures, machinery and equipment.

1.156 A list of the different kinds of consumer durables distinguished in the Classification of Individual Consumption according to Purpose (COICOP) is given in Chapter 3. Of course, some durables last much longer than others, the less durable ones being described as "semi-durables" in COICOP: for example, clothing. It should be noted that dwellings are classified as fixed assets, not durable consumption goods, and are therefore not included in COICOP. Dwellings are used to *produce* housing services. These services are consumed by tenants or owner-occupiers, as the case may be, and are therefore included in COICOP.

1.157 Many services are durable and are also not fully consumed, or used up, at the time they are acquired. Some services bring about long-lasting improvements from which the consumers derive enduring benefits. The condition and quality of life of persons receiving medical treatments such as hip replacements or cataract surgery, for example, are substantially and permanently improved. Similarly, consumers of educational services can derive lifetime benefits from them. Expenditures on education and health also share with durable goods the characteristic that they are also often so costly that they have to be financed by borrowing or by running down other assets.

1.158 Expenditures on durable goods and durable services are liable to fluctuate, whereas using up such goods and services is likely to be a fairly steady process. However, the using up cannot be directly observed and valued. It can only be estimated by making assumptions about the timing and duration of the flows of benefits. Partly because of the conceptual and practical difficulties involved in measuring uses, statistical offices tend to adopt the acquisitions approach to consumer durables in both their national accounts and CPIs.

1.159 *A consumer price index based on the acquisitions approach.* Households may acquire goods and services for purposes of consumption in four main ways. They may:

- purchase them in monetary transactions;
- produce them themselves for their own consumption;
- receive them as payments in kind in barter transactions, particularly as remuneration in kind for work done;
- receive them as free gifts, or transfers, from other economic units.

1.160 The broadest possible scope for goods and services based on the acquisitions approach would be one covering all four categories, irrespective of who bears the costs. It would therefore include all *social transfers in kind* in the form of education, health, housing and other goods and services provided free of charge, or at nominal prices, to individual households by governments or non-profit institutions (NPIs). Total acquisitions are equivalent to the total actual individual consumption of (non-institutional) households, as defined in the SNA (see Chapter 14). *Collective* services provided by governments to the community as whole, such as public administration and defence, are not included and are outside the scope of a CPI.

1.161 From the point of view of the government or NPI that provides and pays for them, social transfers are valued either by the market prices paid for them or by the costs of producing them. From the point of view of the receiving households they have zero or nominal prices. For CPI purposes, the appropriate price is that paid by the household. The price paid by the government belongs in a price index for government expenditures. When households incur zero expenditures, the services provided free carry zero weight in a CPI. However, when governments and NPIs introduce charges for goods or services that were previously provided free, the increase from a zero to a positive price could be captured by a CPI, as explained in Chapter 3.

1.162 *Expenditures versus acquisitions.* Expenditures need to be distinguished from acquisitions. Expenditures are incurred by the economic units that bear the costs. Households do not incur expenditures on social transfers in kind, so the scope of households' expenditures is generally narrower than the scope of their acquisitions. Moreover, not all expenditures are monetary. A *monetary expenditure* occurs when a household pays in cash, by cheque or credit card, or otherwise incurs a financial liability to pay. Only monetary expenditures generate monetary prices that can be observed and recorded for CPI purposes.

1.163 *Non-monetary expenditures* occur when households pay, but in other ways than cash. There are three important categories of non-monetary expenditures:

- In barter transactions, households exchange consumption goods and services among themselves. As the values of the goods and services surrendered as payments constitute negative expenditures, the expenditures should cancel out so that barter transactions between households carry zero weight on aggregate. They can be ignored in practice for CPI purposes.
- When employees are remunerated in kind, they purchase the goods or services, but pay with their labour, not cash. Monetary values can be imputed for the expenditures implicitly incurred by the households.
- Similarly, when households produce goods and services for themselves, they incur the costs, some of which may be monetary in the form of purchased inputs. The monetary values of the implicit expenditures on the outputs produced can be imputed on the basis of the corresponding market prices. If such imputed prices were to be included in the CPI, the prices of the inputs would have to be excluded to avoid double counting.

1.164 *A hierarchy of consumption aggregates.* A hierarchy of possible consumption aggregates may be envisaged, as explained in Chapter 14:

- total acquisitions of goods and services by households;
- *less* social transfers in kind = households' total expenditures;
- *less* non-monetary expenditures = households' monetary expenditures.

The choice of consumption aggregate is a policy matter. For example, if the main reason for compiling a CPI is to measure inflation, the scope of the index might be restricted to household monetary expenditures on consumption, inflation being essentially a monetary phenomenon. Prices cannot be collected for the consumer goods and services involved in non-monetary expenditures, although they can be estimated on the basis of the prices observed in corresponding monetary transactions. The European Union's Harmonized Indices of Consumer Prices, which are specifically intended to measure inflation within the EU, are confined to monetary expenditures.

Unconditional and conditional cost of living indices

1.165 Cost of living indices, or COLIs, are explained in Chapters 15 and 17. As also noted in Chapter 3, the scope of a COLI depends on whether it is conditional or unconditional. The welfare of a household depends not only on the utility derived from the goods and services it consumes, but on the social, political and physical environment in which the household lives. An *unconditional* cost of living index measures the change in the minimum cost of maintaining a given level of welfare in response to changes in any of the factors that affect welfare, whereas a *conditional* cost of living index measures the change in the minimum cost of maintaining a given level of utility or welfare resulting from changes in consumer prices, holding the environmental factors constant.

1.166 An unconditional COLI may be a more comprehensive *cost of living* index than a conditional COLI, but it is not a more comprehensive *price* index. An unconditional index does not include any more price information than a conditional index and it does not give more insight into the impact of price changes on welfare. On the contrary, the impact of the price changes is diluted and obscured the more environmental variables are included within the scope of an unconditional index. In order to qualify as a price index, a COLI must be conditional.

Specific types of transactions

1.167 Given that conceptually, a CPI is an index that measures changes in the prices of consumption goods and services, expenditures on items that are not consumption goods and services fall outside the scope of the CPI; for example, expenditures on assets such as land or bonds, shares and other financial assets. Similarly, payments that do not involve any flows of goods or services in return for the payments are outside the scope; for example, payments of income taxes or social security contributions.

1.168 *Transfers.* A transfer occurs when one economic unit provides a good, service or asset, including money, to another without receiving any counterpart good, service or asset in return. As no good or service is acquired when a household makes a transfer, the transfer must be outside the scope. For this reason, compulsory cash transfers, such as payments of direct taxes on income or wealth, must be outside the scope of a CPI. It is not always clear, however, whether certain payments to government are transfers or purchases of services. For example, payments to obtain certain kinds of licences are sometimes taxes under another name, whereas in other cases the government may provide a service by exercising some kind of supervisory, regulatory or control function. Gifts or donations must be transfers and therefore outside the scope. On the other hand, subscriptions to clubs and societies which provide their members with some kind of service in return are included. Tips and gratuities can be borderline cases. When they are effectively an expected, even obligatory, part of the payment for a service they are not transfers and should be treated as part of the price paid.

1.169 *Undesirable or illegal goods or services.* All goods and services that households *willingly* buy on the market to satisfy their own needs and wants should be included, even if most people might regard them as undesirable or even if they are prohibited by law. Of course, illegal goods and services may have to be excluded in practice because the requisite data cannot be collected.

1.170 *Financial transactions.* Financial transactions occur when one kind of financial asset is exchanged for another, bearing in mind that money is itself a financial asset. For example, the purchase of a bond or share is a financial transaction. Borrowing is a financial transaction in which cash is exchanged, the counterpart being the creation of a financial asset or liability.

1.171 No consumption occurs when a financial transaction takes place, even though financial transactions may be undertaken in order to facilitate future consumption. Financial transactions as such are not covered by CPIs because, by definition, no goods are exchanged, nor services provided, in financial transactions. However, some "financial" transactions may not be entirely financial because they may include an explicit or implicit service charge in addition to the provision of an asset, such as a loan. As a service charge constitutes the purchase of a service by the household, it should be included in a CPI, although it may be difficult to separate out the service charge in some cases. For example, foreign exchange transactions are financial transactions in which one financial asset is exchanged for another. Changes in the price of a foreign currency in terms of the domestic currency resulting from changes in the exchange rate are outside the scope of a CPI. On the other hand, the commission charges associated with the exchange of currencies are included as payments for the services rendered by the foreign exchange dealers.

1.172 Households may borrow in order to make large expenditures on durables or houses, but also to finance large educational or health expenses, or even expensive holidays. Whatever the purpose of the borrowing, the financial transaction in which the loan is contracted is outside the scope of a CPI. The treatment of the interest payable on loans is a separate issue considered below.

1.173 *Composite transactions.* As just noted, some transactions are composite transactions containing two or more components whose treatment may be quite different for CPI purposes. For example, part of a life insurance premium is a financial transaction leading to the creation of a financial claim and is therefore outside the scope, whereas the remainder consists of a service charge which should be covered by a CPI. The two components are not separately itemized, however.

1.174 As explained in Chapter 3, the treatment of payments of nominal interest is difficult because it may have four conceptually quite different components:

- a pure interest payment;
- a risk premium that depends on the creditworthiness of the borrower;
- a service charge payable to the bank, moneylender or other financial institution engaged in the business of making loans;
- a payment to compensate the creditor for the real holding loss incurred on the principal of the loan during inflation.

The fourth component is clearly outside the scope of a CPI as it is a capital flow. Conversely, the third component, the service charge, should clearly be included. The treatment of the first two components is controversial. When there is significant inflation or a very imperfect capital market, payments of nominal interest may be completely dominated by the last two components, both of which are conceptually quite different from the concept of pure interest. For example, the "interest" charged by a village moneylender may be mostly a high service charge. It may be impossible to decompose the various components of nominal interest in practice. The treatment of nominal interest as a whole remains difficult and somewhat controversial.

Household production

1.175 When households engage in production for the market, the associated business transactions are all outside the scope of a CPI. Expenditures incurred for business purposes are excluded, even though they involve purchases of goods and services that might be used to satisfy the personal needs and wants of members of the household instead.

1.176 Households also produce goods and services for their own consumption, mainly service production such as the preparation of meals, the care of children, the sick or the elderly, the cleaning and maintenance of durables and dwellings, the transportation of household members, and so on. Owner-occupiers produce housing services for their own consumption. Households also grow vegetables, fruit, flowers or other crops for their own use.

1.177 Many of the goods or services purchased by households do not provide utility directly but are used as inputs into the production of other goods and services that do provide utility: for example, raw foodstuffs, fertilizers, cleaning materials, paints, electricity, coal, oil, petrol, and so on.

1.178 In principle, a CPI should record changes in the prices of the outputs from these production activities, as it is the outputs rather than the inputs that are actually consumed and provide utility. However, as the outputs are not themselves purchased, no prices can be observed for them. Prices could be imputed for them equal to the prices they would fetch on the market, but this would make a CPI heavily dependent on assumed rather than collected prices. The pragmatic solution recommended in Chapter 3 is to treat all goods and services purchased on the market to be used exclusively as inputs into the production of other goods and services that are directly consumed by households as if they were themselves consumption goods and services. On this principle, goods such as insecticides and electricity are treated as providing utility indirectly and included in CPIs. This is, of course, the solution usually adopted in practice not only for CPIs but also in national accounts, where most expenditures on inputs into household production are classified as final consumption expenditures.

1.179 In some countries, there is an increasing tendency for households to purchase prepared, take-away meals rather than the ingredients. As the prices of such meals cost more than the sum of the ingredients that the households previously purchased, the weight attached to food consumption increases. This partly reflects the fact that the costs of the households' own labour inputs into the preparation of meals were previously ignored. Various kinds of household service activities that were previously outside the scope of a CPI may be brought within the scope if households choose to pay others to perform the services.

1.180 *Subsistence agriculture and owner-occupied housing*. In the case of two important types of production for own consumption within households, namely agricultural production for own consumption and housing services produced by owner-occupiers, the national accounts do actually try to record the values of the outputs produced and consumed rather than the inputs. Similarly, CPIs may also try to price the outputs rather than the inputs in these two cases.

1.181 In principle, the prices of the outputs from own-account agricultural production may be included in CPIs, even though they are imputed. On the other hand, for households relying on subsistence agriculture, the prices of inputs of agricultural materials purchased on the market may be their main exposure to inflation. Two points may be noted. First, the imputed market value of the output should usually be greater than the costs of the purchased inputs, if only because it should cover the costs of the labour inputs provided by the household. Thus, pricing the purchased inputs rather than the outputs may mean that the consumption of own agricultural production in CPIs does not receive sufficient weight. Second, double counting should be avoided. If the imputed prices of the outputs are included, the actual prices of the inputs consumed should not be included as well.

1.182 In the case of owner-occupied housing, the situation is complicated by the fact that the production requires the use of the capital services provided by a large fixed asset in the form of the dwelling itself. Even if the inputs into the production of housing services are priced for CPI purposes, it is still necessary to impute prices for the inputs of capital services (mainly depreciation plus interest) provided by the dwelling. Some countries therefore prefer to impute the prices of the outputs of housing services actually consumed on the basis of the rents payable for the same kind of dwellings rented on the market. The treatment of owner-occupied housing is complex, and somewhat controversial, and is considered in Chapters 3, 9, 10 and 23, among others.

Coverage of households and outlets

1.183 As explained in Chapter 3, households may be either individual persons or groups of persons living together who make common provision for food or other essentials for living. A CPI may be required to cover:

- *either* the consumption expenditures made by households resident in a particular area, usually a country or region, whether the expenditures are made inside or outside the area – this is called the "national" concept of expenditure;
- *or* the consumption expenditures that take place within a particular area, whether made by households resident in that area or residents of other areas – this is called the "domestic" concept.

Adopting the domestic concept may make it more difficult to collect the relevant disaggregated expenditure data in household surveys. A CPI may also be defined to cover a group of countries, such as the European Union.

1.184 Not all kinds of households have to be included. As explained in Chapter 3, some countries choose to exclude particular categories of households such as very wealthy households or households engaged in agriculture. Some countries also compile different indices designed to cover different groups of households, such as households resident in different regions. Another possibility is to compile a general CPI designed to cover all or most households and, in addition, one or more special indices aimed at particular sections of the community, such as households headed by pensioners. The precise coverage of households is a matter of choice. It is inevitably influenced by what are believed to be the main uses of the index. The set of households actually covered by the CPI is described as the "reference population".

Price variation

1.185 Prices for exactly the same good or service may vary between different outlets, while different prices may sometimes be charged to different types of customers. Prices may also vary during the course of the month to which the index relates. Conceptually, it is necessary to distinguish such pure price variation from price differences that are attributable to differences in the quality of the goods or services offered, although it is not always easy to distinguish between the two in practice. The existence of pure price differences reflects some form of market imperfections, such as consumers' lack of information or price discrimination.

1.186 When pure price differences exist, a change in market conditions may make it possible for some households to switch from purchasing at higher prices to purchasing at lower prices, for example if new outlets open that offer lower prices. The resulting fall in the average price paid by households counts as a price fall for CPI purposes, even though the price charged by each individual outlet may not change. If the prices are collected from the outlets and switches in households' purchasing habits remain unobserved, the CPIs are said to be subject to outlet substitution bias, as explained in more detail in Chapter 11. On the other hand, when the price differences reflect differences in the quality of the goods and services sold in the different outlets, switching from outlets selling at higher prices to outlets selling at lower prices simply means that households are choosing to purchase lower-quality goods or services. In itself, this does not imply any change in price.

Classifications

1.187 As explained in Chapter 3, the classification of household expenditures used in a CPI provides the necessary framework for the various stages of CPI compilation. It provides a structure for purposes of weighting and aggregation, and also a basis for stratifying the samples of products whose prices are collected. The goods and services covered by a CPI may be classified in several ways: not simply on the basis of their physical characteristics but also by the purposes they serve and the degree of similarity of their price behaviour. Product-based and purpose-based classifications differ but can usually be successfully mapped onto each other. In practice, most countries use a hybrid classification system in which the breakdown at the highest level is by purpose while the lower-level breakdowns are by product type. This is the case for the recently revised internationally agreed Classification of Individual Consumption according to Purpose (COICOP), which provides a suitable classification for CPI purposes.

1.188 The first level of classification in COICOP consists of 12 divisions covering total consumption expenditures of households. As just noted, the breakdown into divisions is essentially by purpose. At the second level of disaggregation, the 12 *divisions* are divided into 47 *groups* of products, which are in turn divided into 117 *classes* of products at the third level. Chapter 3 provides a listing of ten classes of goods defined as durables in COICOP. It also gives a list of seven classes described as semi-durables, such as clothing, footwear and household textiles.

1.189 The 117 classes at the lowest level of aggregation of COICOP are not sufficiently detailed for CPI purposes. They can be divided into sub-classes using the sub-classes of the internationally agreed Central Product Classification (CPC). Even some of these may require further breakdown in order to arrive at some of the elementary aggregates used for CPI purposes. In order to be useful for CPI purposes, expenditure weights must be available for the various sub-classes or elementary aggregates. From a sampling perspective, it is desirable for the price movements of the individual products within the elementary aggregates to be as homogeneous as possible. The elementary aggregates may also be divided into strata for sampling purposes, on the basis of location or the type of outlet in which the products are sold.

Consumer price indices and national accounts price deflators

1.190 Appendix 3.1 of Chapter 3 explains the differences between the overall CPI and the deflator for total household consumption expenditures in national accounts. In practice, CPIs may be designed to cover only a subset of the households and a subset of the expenditures covered by the national accounts. Moreover, the index number formulae needed for CPIs and national accounts deflators may be different. These differences mean that the overall CPI is generally not the same as the deflator for total household consumption expenditures in the national accounts. On the other hand, the basic price and expenditure data collected and used for CPI purposes are also widely used to build up the price indices needed to deflate the individual components of household consumption in the national accounts.

Expenditure weights

1.191 As already noted, there are two main stages in the calculation of a CPI. The first is the collection of the price data and the calculation of the elementary price indices. The second is the averaging of the elementary price indices to arrive at price indices at higher levels of aggregation up to the overall CPI itself. Expenditure data are needed for the elementary aggregates that can be used as weights in the second stage. These weights are needed whatever index number formula is used for aggregation purposes. Chapter 4 is concerned with the derivation, and sources, of the expenditure weights.

Household expenditure surveys and national accounts

1.192 The principal data source for household consumption expenditures in most countries is a household expenditure survey (HES). An HES is a sample survey of thousands of households that are asked to keep records of their expenditures on different kinds of consumer goods and services over a specified period of time, such as a week or longer. The size of the sample obviously depends on the resources available, but also on the extent to which it is desired to break down the survey results by region or type of household. HESs are costly operations. This manual is not concerned with the conduct of HESs or with general sampling survey techniques or procedures. There are several standard texts on survey methods to which reference may be made. Household expenditure surveys may be taken at specified intervals of time, such as every five years, or they may be taken each year on a continuing basis.

1.193 HESs can impose heavy burdens on the respondents, who have to keep detailed expenditure records of a kind that they would not normally keep, although this may become easier when supermarkets or other retail outlets provide detailed printouts of purchases. HESs tend to have some systematic biases. For example, many households either deliberately, or unconsciously, understate the amounts of their expenditures on certain "undesirable" products, such as gambling, alcoholic drink, tobacco or drugs. Corrections can be made for such biases. Moreover, the data collected in HESs may also need to be adjusted to bring them into line with the concept of expenditure required by the CPI. For example, the imputed expenditures on the housing services produced and consumed by owner-occupiers are not collected in HESs.

1.194 As explained in Chapter 14, the use of the commodity flow method within the supply and use tables of the SNA enables data drawn from different primary sources to be reconciled and balanced against each other. The commodity flow method may be used to improve estimates of household consumption expenditures derived from expenditure surveys by adjusting them to take account of the additional information provided by statistics on the sales, production, imports and exports of consumer goods and services. By drawing on various sources, the household expenditure data in the national accounts may provide the best estimates of aggregate household expenditures, although the classifications used may not be fine enough for CPI purposes. Moreover, because HESs may be conducted only at intervals of several years, the expenditure data in the national accounts may be more up to date, as national accounts are able to draw upon other kinds of more recent data, such as retail sales and the production and import of consumer goods and services. It is important to note, however, that national accounts should not be viewed as if they were an alternative, independent data source to HESs. On the contrary, HESs provide one of the main sources for the expenditure data on household consumption used to compile national accounts.

1.195 Household expenditure surveys in many countries may not be conducted as frequently as might be desired for CPI, or national accounts, purposes. National HESs can be very costly and onerous for the households, as already noted. They may be conducted only once every five or ten years, or even at longer intervals. In any case, conducting and processing HESs is time-consuming, so the results may not be available for CPI purposes until one or two years after the surveys have been conducted. It is for these practical reasons that CPIs in many countries are Lowe indices that use the quantities of some base period b that may precede the time reference period 0 by a few years and period t by many years.

1.196 Some countries conduct continuous HESs not only in order to update their CPI weights but also to improve their national accounts. Of course, the same panel of households does not have to be retained indefinitely; the panel can be gradually rotated by dropping some households and replacing them by others. Countries that conduct continuous expenditure surveys are able to revise and update their expenditure weights each year so that the CPI becomes a chain index with annual linking. Even with continuous expenditure surveys, however, there is a lag between the time at which the data are collected and the time at which the results are processed and ready for use, so that it is never possible to have survey results that are contemporaneous with the price changes. Thus, even when the weights are updated annually, they still refer to some period that precedes the time reference period. For example, when the price reference period is January 2000, the expenditure weights may refer to 1997 or 1998, or both years. When the price reference period moves forward to January 2001, the weights move forward to 1998 or 1999, and so on. Such an index is a chain Lowe index.

1.197 Some countries prefer to use expenditure weights that are the average rates of expenditure over periods of two or three years in order to reduce "noise" caused by errors of estimation (the expenditure surveys are only samples) or erratic consumer behaviour over short periods of time resulting from events such as booms or recessions, stock market fluctuations, oil shocks, or natural or other disasters.

Other sources for estimating expenditure weights

1.198 If expenditures need to be disaggregated by region for sampling or analytical purposes, it is possible to supplement whatever information may be available by region in HESs by using data from population censuses. Another data source may be food surveys. These are special surveys, conducted in some countries, that focus on households' expenditures on food products. They can provide more detailed information on food expenditures than that available from HESs.

1.199 Another possible source of information consists of points of purchase (POP) surveys, which are conducted in some countries. A POP survey is designed to provide information about the retail outlets at which households purchase specified groups of goods and services. Households are asked, for each item, about the amounts spent in each outlet and the names and addresses of the outlets. The main use for a POP survey is for selecting the sample of outlets to be used for price collection purposes.

Collection of price data

1.200 As explained in Chapter 9, there are two levels of calculation involved in a CPI. At the lower level, samples of prices are collected and processed to obtain lower-level price indices. These lower-level indices are the elementary indices, whose properties and behaviour are studied in Chapter 20. At the higher level, the elementary indices are averaged to obtain higher-level indices using expenditures as weights. At the higher level, all the index number theory elaborated in Chapters 15 to 18 comes into play.

1.201 Lower-level indices are calculated for elementary aggregates. Depending on the resources available and procedures adopted by individual countries, these elementary aggregates could be sub-classes or micro-classes of the expenditure classification described above. If it is desired to calculate CPIs for different regions, the sub-classes or micro-classes have to be divided into strata referring to the different regions. In addition, in order to improve the efficiency of the sampling procedures used to collect prices, it will usually be desirable, if feasible, to introduce other criteria into the definitions of the strata, such as the type of outlet. When the sub-classes or micro-classes are divided into strata for data collection purposes, the strata themselves become the elementary aggregates. As a weight needs to be attached to each elementary aggregate in order to calculate the higher-level indices, an estimate of the expenditure within each elementary aggregate must be available. Expenditure or quantity data are typically not available within an elementary aggregate, so the elementary indices have to be estimated from price data alone. This may change if scanner data from electronic points of sale become more available.

1.202 Chapter 5 is concerned with sampling strategies for price collection. Chapter 6 is concerned with the methods and operational procedures actually used to collect prices. In principle, the relevant prices for a CPI should be the purchasers' prices actually paid by households, but it is generally neither practical nor cost-effective to try to collect prices each month or quarter directly from households, even though expenditure data are collected directly from households in household expenditure surveys. In practice, the prices that are collected are not actual transaction prices, but rather the prices at which goods and services are offered for sale in outlets such as retail shops, supermarkets or service providers. However, it may become increasingly feasible to collect actual transactions prices as more goods and services are sold through electronic points of sale that record both prices and expenditures.

Random sampling and purposive sampling

1.203 Given that the prices are collected from the sellers, there are two different sampling problems that arise. The first is how to select the individual products within an elementary aggregate whose prices are to be collected. The second is how to select a sample of outlets selling those products. For some products, it may not be necessary to visit retail outlets to collect prices because there may be only a single price applying throughout the country. Such prices may be collected from the central organization responsible for fixing the prices. The following paragraphs refer to the more common situation in which prices are collected from a large number of outlets.

1.204 As explained in Chapter 5, the universe of products from which the sample is taken has several dimensions. The products may be classified not only on the basis of the characteristics and functions that determine their place in COICOP, but also according to the locations and outlets at which they are sold and the times at which they are sold. The fact that the universe is continually changing over time is a major problem, not only for CPIs but also for most other economic statistics. Products disappear to be replaced by other kinds of products, while outlets close and new ones open. The fact that the universe is changing over time creates both conceptual and practical problems, given that the measurement of price changes over time requires some continuity in the products priced. In principle, the price changes recorded should refer to matched products that are identical in both time periods. The problems created when products are not identical are considered in some detail later.

1.205 In designing the sample for price collection purposes, due attention should be paid to standard statistical criteria to ensure that the resulting sample estimates are not only unbiased and efficient in a statistical sense, but also cost-effective. There are two types of bias encountered in the literature on index numbers, namely *sampling bias* as understood here and the *non-sampling biases* in the form of substitution bias or representativity bias, as discussed in Chapter 10. It is usually clear from the context which type of bias is meant.

1.206 There is a large literature on sampling survey techniques to which reference may be made and which need not be summarized here. In principle, it would be desirable to select both outlets and products using random sampling with known probabilities of selection. This ensures that the sample of products selected is not distorted by subjective factors and enables sampling errors to be calculated. Many countries nevertheless continue to rely heavily on the purposive selection of outlets and products, because random sampling may be too difficult and too costly. Purposive selection is believed to be more cost-effective, especially when the sampling frames available are not comprehensive and not well suited to CPI purposes. It may also be cost-effective to collect a "cluster" of prices on different products from the same outlet, instead of distributing the price collection more thinly over a larger number of outlets.

1.207 Efficient sampling, whether random or purposive, requires comprehensive and up-to-date sampling frames. Two types of frames are needed for CPI purposes: one listing the universe of outlets, and the other listing the universe of products. Examples of possible sampling frames for outlets are business registers, central or local government administrative records or telephone directories. When the sampling frames contain the requisite information, it may be possible to increase efficiency by selecting samples of outlets using probabilities that are proportional to the size of some relevant economic characteristic, such as the total value of sales. Sampling frames for products are not always readily available in practice. Possible frames are catalogues or other product lists drawn up by major manufacturers, wholesalers or trade associations, or lists of products that are specific to individual outlets such as large supermarkets.

1.208 Depending on the information available in the sampling frame, it may be possible to group the outlets into strata on the basis of their location and size, as indicated by sales or employees. When there is information about size, it may be possible to increase efficiency by taking a random sample of outlets with probabilities proportional to size. In practice, however, there is also widespread use of purposive sampling.

1.209 In most countries, the selection of most of the individual items to be priced within the selected outlets tends to be purposive, being specified by the central office responsible for the CPI. The central office draws up lists of products that are deemed to be representative of the products within an elementary aggregate. The lists can be drawn up in collaboration with managers of wholesale or large retail establishments, or other experts with practical experience and knowledge. The actual procedures are described in more detail in Chapter 6.

1.210 It has been argued that the purposive selection of products is liable to introduce only a negligible amount of sampling bias, although there is not much conclusive evidence on this matter. In principle, random sampling is preferable and it is also quite feasible. For example, the United States Bureau of Labor Statistics makes extensive use of random selection procedures to select both outlets and products within outlets. When the selection of products is delegated to the individual price collectors, it is essential to ensure that they are well trained and briefed, and closely supervised and monitored.

Methods of price collection

1.211 The previous section focused on the sampling issues that arise when prices have to be collected for a large number of products from a large number of outlets. This section is concerned with some of the more operational aspects of price collection.

1.212 *Central price collection.* Many important prices can be collected directly by the central office responsible for the CPI from the head office of the organization responsible for fixing the prices. When prices are the same throughout the country, collection from individual outlets is superfluous:

- Some tariffs or service charges are fixed nationally and apply throughout the country. This may be the case for public utilities such as water, gas and electricity, postal services and telephone charges, or public transport. The prices or charges can be obtained from the relevant head offices.
- Some national chains of stores or supermarkets may charge the same prices everywhere, in which case the prices can be obtained from their head offices. Even when national chains do not charge uniform prices, there may be only a few minor regional differences in the prices and all the relevant information may be obtainable centrally.
- Many of these prices determined centrally may change very infrequently, perhaps only once or twice or year, so they do not have to be collected monthly. Moreover, many of these prices can be collected by telephone, fax or email and may not require visits to the head offices concerned.

1.213 *Scanner data.* One important new development is the increasing availability in many countries of large amounts of very detailed "scanner" data obtained from electronic points of sale. Such data are collated by commercial databases. Scanner data are up to date and comprehensive. An increasingly large proportion of all goods sold are being scanned as they pass through electronic points of scale.

1.214 The potential benefits of using scanner data are obviously considerable and could ultimately have a significant impact on the way in which price data are collected for CPI purposes. Not enough experience is yet available to provide general guidelines about the use of scanner data. Clearly, statistical offices should monitor developments in this field closely and explore the possibility of exploiting this major new source of data. Scanner data also increase the scope for using improved methods of quality adjustment, including hedonic methods, as explained in Chapter 7.

1.215 *Local price collection.* When prices are collected from local outlets, the individual products selected for pricing can be determined in two ways. One way is for a specific list of individual products to be determined in advance by the central office responsible for the CPI. Alternatively, the price collector can be given the discretion to choose from a specified range of products. The collector may use some kind of random selection procedure, or select the products that sell the most or are recommended by the shop owner or manager. An individual product selected for pricing in an individual outlet may be described as a sampled product. It may be a good or a service.

1.216 When the list of products is determined in advance by the central office, the objective is usually to select products that are considered to be representative of the larger group of products within an elementary aggregate. The central office also has to decide how loosely or tightly to describe, or specify, the representative products selected for pricing. In theory, the number of different products that might be identified is to some extent arbitrary, depending on the number of economic characteristics that are deemed to be relevant or important. For example, "beef" is a generic term for a group of similar but nevertheless distinct products. There are many different cuts of beef, such as minced beef, stewing steak or rump steak, each of which can be considered a different product and which can sell at very different prices. Furthermore, beef can also be classified according to whether it is fresh, chilled or frozen, and cross-classified again according to whether it comes from domestic or imported animals, or from animals of different ages or breeds.

1.217 Tightening the specifications ensures that the central office has more control over the items actually priced in the outlets, but it also increases the chance that some products may not actually be available in some outlets. Loosening the specifications means that more items may be priced but leaves the individual price collectors with more discretion with regard to the items actually priced. This could make the sample as a whole less representative.

Continuity of price collection

1.218 A CPI is intended to measure pure price changes. The products whose prices are collected and compared in successive time periods should ideally be perfectly *matched*; that is, they should be identical in respect of their physical and economic characteristics. When the products are perfectly matched, the observed price changes are *pure* price changes. When selecting representative products, it is therefore necessary to ensure that enough of them can be expected to remain on the market over a reasonably long period of time in exactly the same form or condition as when first selected. Without continuity, there would not be enough price changes to measure.

1.219 Having identified the items whose prices are to be collected, the normal strategy is to continue pricing exactly those same items for as long as possible. Price collectors can do this if they are provided with very precise, or tight, specifications of the items to be priced.

Alternatively, they must keep detailed records themselves of the items that they have selected to price.

1.220 The ideal situation for a price index would be one in which all the products whose prices are being recorded remain on the market indefinitely without any change in their physical and economic characteristics, except of course for the timing of their sale. It is worth noting that many theorems in index number theory are derived on the assumption that exactly the same set of goods and services is available in both the time periods being compared. Most products, however, have only a limited economic life. Eventually, they disappear from the market to be replaced by other products. As the universe of products is continually evolving, the representative products selected initially may gradually account for a progressively smaller share of total purchases and sales. As a whole, they may become less and less representative. As a CPI is intended to cover all products, some way has to be found to accommodate the changing universe of products. In the case of consumer durables whose features and designs are continually being modified, some models may have very short lives indeed, being on the market for only a year or less before being replaced by newer models.

1.221 At some point the continuity of the series of price observations may have to be broken. It may become necessary to compare the prices of some products with the prices of other new ones that are very similar but not identical. Statistical offices must then try to eliminate from the observed price changes the estimated effects of the changes in the characteristics of the products whose prices are compared. In other words, they must try to adjust the prices collected for any changes in the quality of the products priced, as explained in more detail below. At the limit, a completely new product may appear that is so different from those existing previously that quality adjustment is not feasible and its price cannot be directly compared with that of any previous product. Similarly, a product may become so unrepresentative or obsolete that it has to be dropped from the index because it is no longer worth trying to compare its price with those of any of the products that have displaced it.

Resampling

1.222 One strategy to deal with the changing universe of products would be to resample, or reselect, at regular intervals the complete set of items to be priced. For example, with a monthly index, a new set of items could be selected each January. Each set of items would be priced until the following January. Two sets have to be priced each January in order to establish a link between each set of 12 monthly changes. Resampling each year would be consistent with a strategy of updating the expenditure weights each year.

1.223 Although resampling may be preferable to maintaining an unchanged sample or selection, it is not used much in practice. Systematically resampling the entire set of products each year would be difficult to manage and costly to implement. Moreover, it does not provide a complete solution to the problem of the changing universe of products, as it does not capture price changes that occur at the moment of time when new products or new qualities are first introduced. Many producers deliberately use the time when products are first marketed to make significant price changes.

1.224 A more practical way in which to keep the sample up to date is to rotate it gradually by dropping certain items and introducing new ones. Items may be dropped for two reasons:

- The product is believed by the price collector or central office to be no longer representative. It appears to account for a steadily diminishing share of the total expenditures within the basic categories in question.
- The product may simply disappear from the market altogether. For example, it may have become obsolete as a result of changing technology or unfashionable because of changing tastes, although it could disappear for other reasons.

1.225 At the same time, new products or new qualities of existing products appear on the market. At some point, it becomes necessary to include them in the list of items priced. This raises the general question of the treatment of quality change and the treatment of new products.

Adjusting prices for quality changes

1.226 The treatment of quality change is perhaps the greatest challenge facing CPI compilers. It is a recurring theme throughout this manual. It presents both conceptual and practical problems for compilers of CPIs. The whole of Chapter 7 is devoted to the treatment of quality change, while Chapter 8 addresses the closely related topic of new goods and item substitution.

1.227 When a sampled product is dropped from the list of products priced in some outlet, the normal practice is to find a new product to replace it in order to ensure that the sample, or selection, of sampled products remains sufficiently comprehensive and representative. If the new product is introduced specifically to replace the old one, it is necessary to establish a link between the series of past price observations on the old item and the subsequent series for the new item. The two series of observations may, or may not, overlap in one or more periods. In many cases, there can be no overlap because the new quality, or model, is only introduced after the one which it is meant to replace is discontinued. Whether or not there is an overlap, the linking of the two price series requires some estimate of the change in quality between the old product and the product selected to replace it.

1.228 However difficult it is to estimate the contribution of the change in quality to the change in the observed price, it must be clearly understood that some estimate has to be made either explicitly or, by default, implicitly. The issue cannot be avoided or bypassed. All statistical offices have limited resources and many may not have the capacity to undertake the more elaborate explicit adjustments for quality change described in

Chapter 7. Even though it may not be feasible to undertake an explicit adjustment through lack of data or resources, it is not possible to avoid making some kind of implicit adjustment. Even apparently "doing nothing" necessarily implies some kind of implicit adjustment, as explained below. Whatever the resources available to them, statistical offices must be conscious of the implications of the procedures they adopt.

1.229 Three points are stressed in the introductory section of Chapter 7:

- The pace of innovation is high, and possibly increasing, leading to continual changes in the characteristics of products.
- There is not much consistency between countries in the methods they use to deal with quality change.
- A number of empirical studies have demonstrated that the choice of method does matter, as different methods can lead to very different results.

Evaluation of the effect of quality change on price

1.230 It is useful to try to clarify why one would wish to adjust the observed price change between two items that are similar, but not identical, for differences in their quality. A change in the quality of a good or service occurs when there is a change in some, but not most, of its characteristics. For purposes of a CPI, a quality change must be evaluated from the consumer's perspective. As explained in Chapter 7, the evaluation of the quality change is essentially an estimate of the additional amount that a consumer is willing to pay for the new characteristics possessed by the new quality. This additional amount is not a price increase because it represents the monetary value of the additional satisfaction or utility that is derived from the new quality. Of course, if the old quality is preferred to the new one, consumers would only be willing to buy the new quality if its price were lower.

1.231 Consider the following hypothetical experiment in which a new quality appears alongside an old one. Assume that the two products are substitutes and that the consumer is familiar with the characteristics of the old and the new qualities. Use lower case p to refer to prices of the old quality and upper case P for the prices of the new quality. Suppose that both qualities are offered to the consumer at the same price, namely the price P_t at which the new quality is actually being sold in period t. The consumer is then asked to choose between them and prefers the new quality.

1.232 Suppose next that the price of the old quality is progressively reduced until it reaches p_t^*, at which point the consumer becomes indifferent between purchasing the old quality at p_t^* and the new quality at P_t. Any further decrease below p_t^* causes the consumer to switch back to the old quality. The difference between P_t and p_t^* is a measure of the additional value that the consumer places on the new quality as compared with the old quality. It measures the maximum amount that the consumer is willing to pay for the new quality over and above the price of the old quality.

1.233 Let p_{t-1} denote the actual price at which the old quality was sold in period $t-1$. For CPI purposes, the price increase between the two qualities is not the observed difference $P_t - p_{t-1}$ but $p_t^* - p_{t-1}$. It is important to note that p_t^*, the hypothetical price for the old quality in period t, is directly comparable with the actual price of the old quality in period $t-1$ because both refer to the same identical product. The difference between them is a *pure* price change. The difference between P_t and p_t^* is not a price change but an evaluation of the difference in the quality of the two items in period t. The actual price of the new quality in period t needs to be multiplied by the ratio p_t^*/P_t in order to make the comparison between the prices in periods $t-1$ and t a comparison between products of equal quality in the eyes of the consumer. The ratio p_t^*/P_t is the required quality adjustment.

1.234 Of course, it is difficult to estimate the quality adjustment in practice, but the first step has to be to clarify conceptually the nature of the adjustment that is required in principle. In practice, producers often treat the introduction of a new quality, or new model, as a convenient opportunity at which to make a significant price change. They may deliberately make it difficult for consumers to disentangle how much of the observed difference in price between the old and the new qualities represents a price change.

1.235 Chapter 7 explains the two possibilities open to statistical offices. One possibility is to make an explicit adjustment to the observed price change on the basis of the different characteristics of the old and new qualities. The other alternative is to make an implicit adjustment by making an assumption about the pure price change; for example, on the basis of price movements observed for other products. It is convenient to take the implicit methods first.

Implicit methods for adjusting for quality changes

1.236 *Overlapping qualities*. Suppose that the two qualities overlap, both being available on the market at time t. If consumers are well informed, have a free choice and are collectively willing to buy some of both at the same time, economic theory suggests that the ratio of the prices of the new to the old quality should reflect their relative utilities to consumers. This implies that the difference in price between the old and the new qualities does not indicate any change in price. The price changes up to period t can be measured by the prices for the old quality, while the price changes from period t onwards can be measured by the prices for the new quality. The two series of price changes are linked in period t, the difference in price between the two qualities not having any impact on the linked series.

1.237 When there is an overlap, simple linking of this kind may provide an acceptable solution to the problem of dealing with quality change. In practice, however, this method is not used very extensively because the requisite data are seldom available. Moreover, the conditions may not be consistent with those assumed in the theory. Even when there is an overlap, consumers may not have had time to acquire sufficient knowledge of the characteristics to be able to evaluate the relative qualities properly, especially when there is a substantial change in quality. Not all consumers may have access to both qualities. When the new quality first appears, the market is liable to remain in disequilibrium for some time, as it takes time for consumers to adjust their consumption patterns.

1.238 There may be a succession of periods in which the two qualities overlap before the old quality finally disappears from the market. If the market is temporarily out of equilibrium, the relative prices of the two qualities may change significantly over time so that the market offers alternative evaluations of the relative qualities depending on which period is chosen. When new qualities that embody major new improvements appear on the market for the first time, there is often a tendency for their prices to fall relatively to older qualities before the latter eventually disappear. In this situation, if the price series for the old and new qualities are linked in a single period, the choice of period can have a substantial effect on the overall change in the linked series.

1.239 The statistician has then to make a deliberate judgement about the period in which the relative prices appear to give the best representation of the relative qualities. In this situation, it may be preferable to use a more complex linking procedure which uses the prices for both the new and the old qualities in several periods in which they overlap. However, the information needed for this more complex procedure will never be available if price collectors are instructed only to introduce a new quality when an old one is dropped. In this case, the timing of the switch from the old to the new can have a significant effect on the long-term change in the linked series. This factor must be explicitly recognized and taken into consideration.

1.240 If there is no overlap between the new and the old qualities, the problems just discussed do not arise as no choice has to be made about when to make the link. Other and more difficult problems nevertheless take their place.

1.241 *Non-overlapping qualities.* In the following sections, it is assumed that the overlap method cannot be used because there is a discontinuity between the series of price observations for the old and new qualities. Again, using lower case p for the old quality and upper case P for the new, it is assumed that the price data available to the index compiler take the following form:

$$\ldots, p_{t-3}, p_{t-2}, p_{t-1}, P_t, P_{t+1}, P_{t+2}, \ldots$$

The problem is to estimate the pure price change between $t-1$ and t in order to have a continuous series of price observations for inclusion in the index. Using the same notation as above:

- price changes up to period $t-1$ are measured by the series for the old quality;
- the change between $t-1$ and t is measured by the ratio p_t^*/p_{t-1} where p_t^* is equal to P_t *after* adjustment for the change in quality;
- price changes from period t onwards are measured by the series for the new quality.

1.242 The problem is to estimate p_t^*. This may be done explicitly by one of the methods described later. Otherwise, one of the implicit methods has to be used. These may be grouped into three categories:

- The first solution is to assume that $p_t^*/p_{t-1} = P_t/p_{t-1}$ or $p_t^* = P_t$. No change in quality is assumed to have occurred, so the whole of the observed price increase is treated as a pure price increase. In effect, this contradicts the assumption that there has been a change in quality.
- The second is to assume that $p_t^*/p_{t-1} = 1$, or $p_t^* = p_{t-1}$. No price change is assumed to have occurred, the whole of the observed difference between p_{t-1} and P_t being attributed to the difference in their quality.
- The third is to assume that $p_t^*/p_{t-1} = I$, where I is an index of the price change for a group of similar products, or possibly a more general price index.

1.243 The first two possibilities cannot be recommended as default options to be used automatically in the absence of any adequate information. The use of the first option can only be justified if the evidence suggests that the extent of the quality change is negligible, even though it cannot be quantified more precisely. "Doing nothing", in other words ignoring the quality change completely, is equivalent to adopting the first solution. Conversely, the second can only be justified if the evidence suggests that the extent of any price change between the two periods is negligible. The third option is likely to be much more acceptable than the other two. It is the kind of solution that is often used in economic statistics when data are missing.

1.244 Elementary indices are typically based on a number of series relating to different sampled products. The particular linked price series relating to the two qualities is therefore usually just one out of a number of parallel price series. What may happen in practice is that the price observations for the old quality are used up to period $t-1$ and the prices for the new quality from t onwards, the price change between $t-1$ and t being omitted from the calculations. In effect, this amounts to using the third option: that is, estimating the missing price change on the assumption that it is equal to the average change for the other sampled products within the elementary aggregate.

1.245 It may be possible to improve on this estimate by making a careful selection of the other sampled products whose average price change is believed to be more similar to the item in question than the average for the group of sampled products as a whole. This procedure is described in some detail in Chapter 7, where it is illustrated with a numerical example and described as "targeting" the imputation or estimation.

1.246 The general method of estimating the price on the basis of the average change for the remaining group of products is widely used. It is sometimes described as the "overall" class mean method. The more refined targeted version is the "targeted" mean method. In general, one or other method seems likely to be preferable to either of the first two options listed above, although each case must be considered on its individual merits.

1.247 While the class mean method seems a sensible practical solution, it may nevertheless give biased results, as explained in Chapter 7. The introduction of a new quality is precisely the occasion on which a producer may choose to make a significant price change. Many of the most important price changes may be missed if, in effect, they are assumed to be equal to the average price changes for products not subject to quality change.

1.248 It is necessary, therefore, to try to make an explicit adjustment for the change in quality, at least when a significant quality change is believed to have occurred. Again there are several methods that may be used.

Explicit quality adjustments

1.249 *Quantity adjustments.* The quality change may take the form of a change in the physical characteristics of the product that can easily be quantified, such as change in weight, dimensions, purity, or chemical composition of a product. It is generally a considerable oversimplification to assume that the quality of a product changes in proportion to the size of some single physical characteristic. For example, most consumers are very unlikely to rate a refrigerator that has three times the capacity of a smaller one as being worth three times the price of the latter. Nevertheless it is clearly possible to make some adjustment to the price of a new quality of different size to make it more comparable with the price of an old quality. There is considerable scope for the judicious, or common sense, application of relatively straightforward quality adjustments of this kind. A thorough discussion of quality adjustments based on "size" is given in Chapter 7.

1.250 *Differences in production or option costs.* An alternative procedure may be to try to measure the change in quality by the estimated change in the costs of producing the two qualities. The estimates can be made in consultation with the producers of the goods or services, if appropriate. This method, like the first, is only likely to be satisfactory when the changes take the form of relatively simple changes in the physical characteristics of the good, such as the addition of some new feature, or option, to an automobile. It is not satisfactory when a more fundamental change in the nature of the product occurs as a result of a new discovery or technological innovation. It is clearly inapplicable, for example, when a drug is replaced by another more effective variant of the same drug that also happens to cost less to produce.

1.251 Another possibility for dealing with a quality change that is more complex or subtle is to seek the advice of technical experts. This method is especially relevant when the general consumer may not have the knowledge or expertise to be able to assess or evaluate the significance of all of the changes that may have occurred, at least when they are first made.

1.252 *The hedonic approach.* Finally, it may be possible to systematize the approach based on production or option costs by using econometric methods to estimate the impact of observed changes in the characteristics of a product on its price. In this approach, the market prices of a set of different qualities or models are regressed on what are considered to be the most important physical or economic characteristics of the different models. This approach to the evaluation of quality change is known as *hedonic analysis.* When the characteristics are attributes that cannot be quantified, they are represented by dummy variables. The regression coefficients measure the estimated marginal effects of the various characteristics on the prices of the models and can therefore be used to evaluate the effects of changes in those characteristics, i.e., changes in quality, over time.

1.253 The hedonic approach to quality adjustment can provide a powerful, objective and scientific method of evaluating changes in quality for certain kinds of products. It has been particularly successful in dealing with computers. The economic theory underlying the hedonic approach is examined in more detail in Chapter 21. The application of the method is explained in some detail in Chapter 7. Products can be viewed as bundles of characteristics that are not individually priced, as the consumer buys the bundle as a single package. The objective is to try to "unbundle" the characteristics to estimate how much they contribute to the total price. In the case of computers, for example, three basic characteristics are the processor speed, the size of the RAM and the hard drive capacity. An example of a hedonic regression using these characteristics is given in Chapter 7.

1.254 The results obtained by applying hedonics to computer prices have had a considerable impact on attitudes towards the treatment of quality change in CPIs. They have demonstrated that for goods where there are rapid technological changes and improvements in quality, the size of the adjustments made to the market prices of the products to offset the changes in the quality can largely determine the movements of the elementary price index. For this reason, the manual contains a thorough treatment of the use of hedonics. Chapter 7 provides further analysis, including a comparison showing that the results obtained by using hedonics and matched models can differ significantly when there is a high turnover of models.

1.255 It may be concluded that statistical offices must pay close attention to the treatment of quality change and try to make explicit adjustments whenever possible. The importance of this topic can scarcely be over-emphasized. The need to recognize and adjust for changes in quality has to be impressed on price collectors. Failure to pay proper attention to quality changes can introduce serious biases into a CPI.

Item substitution and new goods

1.256 As noted above, ideally price indices would seek to measure pure price changes between matched products that are identical in the two periods compared. However, as explained in Chapter 8, the universe of products that a CPI has to cover is a dynamic universe that is gradually changing over time. Pricing matched products constrains the selection of products to a static universe of products given by the intersection of the two sets of products existing in the two periods compared.

This static universe, by definition, excludes both new products and disappearing products, whose price behaviour is likely to diverge from that of the matched products. Price indices have to try to take account of the price behaviour of new and disappearing products as far as possible.

1.257 A formal consideration and analysis of these problems are given in Appendix 8.1 to Chapter 8. A replacement universe is defined as one that starts with the base period universe but allows new products to enter as replacements as some products disappear. Of course, quality adjustments of the kind discussed above are needed when comparing the prices of the replacement products with those of the products that they replace.

1.258 One way in which to address the underlying problem of the changing universe is by sample rotation. This requires a completely new sample of products to be drawn to replace the existing one. The two samples must overlap in one period that acts as the link period. This procedure can be viewed as a systematic exploitation of the overlap method of adjusting for quality change. It may not therefore deal satisfactorily with all changes in quality that occur, because the relative prices of different goods and services at a single point of time may not provide satisfactory measures of the relative qualities of all the goods and services concerned. Nevertheless, frequent sample rotation helps by keeping the sample up to date and may reduce the extent to which explicit quality adjustments are required. Sample rotation is expensive, however.

New goods and services

1.259 The difference in quality between the original product and the one that it replaces may become so great that the new quality is better treated as a new good, although the distinction between a new quality and a new good is inevitably somewhat arbitrary. As noted in Chapter 8, a distinction is also drawn in the economics literature between evolutionary and revolutionary new goods. An evolutionary new good or service is one that meets existing needs in much more efficient or new ways, whereas a revolutionary new good or service provides completely new kinds of services or benefits. In practice, an evolutionary new good can be fitted into some sub-class of the product or expenditure classification, whereas a revolutionary new good will require some modification to the classification in order to accommodate it.

1.260 There are two main concerns with new goods or services. The first relates to the timing of the introduction of the new product into the index. The second relates to the fact that the mere availability of the new product on the market may bring a welfare gain to consumers, whatever the price at which it is sold initially. Consider, for example, the introduction of the first antibiotic drug, penicillin. The drug provided cures for conditions that previously might have been fatal. The benefit might be virtually priceless to some individuals. One way of gauging how much benefit is gained by the introduction of a new good is to ask how high its price would have to be to reduce the demand for the product to zero. Such a price is called the "demand reservation price". It could be very high indeed in the case of a new life-saving drug. If the demand reservation price could be estimated, it could be treated as the price in the period just before the new product appeared. The fall between the demand reservation price and the price at which the product actually makes its first appearance could be included in the CPI.

1.261 In practice, of course, statistical offices cannot be expected to estimate demand reservation prices with sufficient reliability for them to be included in a CPI. The concept is nevertheless useful because it highlights the fact that the mere introduction of a new good may bring a significant welfare gain that could be reflected in the CPI, especially if it is intended to be a COLI. In general, any enlargement of the set of consumption possibilities open to consumers has the potential to make them better off, other things being equal.

1.262 It is often the case that new goods enter the market at a higher price than can be sustained in the longer term, so their prices typically tend to fall relatively over the course of time. Conversely, the quantities purchased may be very small initially but increase significantly. These complications make the treatment of new products particularly difficult, especially if they are revolutionary new goods. Because of both the welfare gain from the introduction of a new product and the tendency for the price of a new good to fall after it has been introduced, it is possible that important price reductions may fail to be captured by CPIs because of the technical difficulties created by new products. Chapter 8 concludes by expressing concern about the capacity of CPIs to deal satisfactorily with the dynamics of modern markets. In any case, it is essential that statistical offices are alert to these issues and adopt procedures that take account of them to the maximum extent possible, given the data and resources available to them.

Calculation of consumer price indices in practice

1.263 Chapter 9 provides a general overview of the ways in which CPIs are calculated in practice. The methods used in different countries are by no means all the same, but they have much in common. There is clearly interest from users as well as compilers in knowing how most statistical offices set about calculating their CPIs. The various stages in the calculation process are illustrated by numerical examples. The chapter is descriptive and not prescriptive, although it does try to evaluate the strengths and weaknesses of existing methods. It makes the point that because of the greater insights into the properties and behaviour of indices gained in recent years, it is now recognized that not all existing practices are necessarily optimal.

1.264 As the various stages involved in the calculation process have, in effect, already been summarized in the preceding sections of this chapter, it is not proposed to repeat them all again in this section. It may be useful, however, to give an indication of the nature of the contents of Chapter 9.

Elementary price indices

1.265 Chapter 9 starts by describing how the elementary aggregates are constructed by working down from groups, classes and sub-classes of COICOP, or some equivalent expenditure classification. It reviews the principles underlying the delineation of the elementary aggregates themselves. Elementary aggregates are intended to be as homogeneous as possible, not merely in terms of the physical and economic characteristics of the products covered but also in terms of their price movements.

1.266 Chapter 9 then considers the consequences of using alternative elementary index formulae to calculate the elementary indices. It proceeds by means of a series of numerical examples that use simulated price data for four different products within an elementary aggregate. The elementary indices themselves, and their properties, have already been explained above. An elementary price index may be calculated either as a chain index or as a direct index; that is, either by comparing the price each month, or quarter, with that in the immediately preceding period or with the price in the fixed price reference period. Table 9.1 of Chapter 9 uses both approaches to illustrate the calculation of three basic types of elementary index, Carli, Dutot and Jevons. It is designed to highlight a number of their properties. For example, it shows the effects of "price bouncing" in which the same four prices are recorded for two consecutive months, but the prices are switched between the four products. The Dutot and Jevons indices record no increase but the Carli index registers an increase. Table 9.1 also illustrates the differences between the direct and the chain indices. After six months, each of the four prices is 10 per cent higher than at the start. Each of the three direct indices records a 10 per cent increase, as also do the chained Dutot and Jevons indices because they are transitive. The chained Carli, however, records an increase of 29 per cent, which is interpreted as illustrating the systematic upward bias in the Carli formula resulting from its failure to satisfy the time reversal test.

1.267 It is noted in Chapter 9 that the chaining and direct approaches have different implications when there are missing price observations, quality changes and replacements. The conclusion is that the use of a chain index can make the estimation of missing prices and the introduction of replacement items easier from a computational point of view.

1.268 Chapter 9 also examines the effects of missing price observations, distinguishing between those that are temporarily missing and those that have become permanently unavailable. Table 9.2 contains a numerical example of the treatment of the temporarily missing prices. One possibility is simply to omit the product whose price is missing for one month from the calculation of indices that compare that month with the preceding and following months, and also with the base period. Another possibility is to impute a price change on the basis of the average price for the remaining products, using one or other of the three types of average. The example is a simplified version of the kind of examples that are used in Chapter 7 to deal with the same problem.

1.269 Tables 9.3 and 9.4 illustrate the case in which one product disappears permanently to be replaced by another product. In Table 9.3 there is no overlap between the two products and the options considered are again to omit the products or to impute price changes for them based on averages for the other products. Table 9.4 illustrates the situation in which the products overlap in one month.

1.270 Chapter 9 also considers the possibility that there may be some expenditure weights available within an elementary aggregate, in which case it may be possible to calculate a Laspeyres or a geometric Laspeyres index, these being the weighted versions of the Carli and the Jevons.

Higher-level indices

1.271 Later sections of Chapter 9 illustrate the calculation of the higher-level indices using the elementary price indices and the weights provided by the elementary expenditure aggregates. It is at this stage that the traditional index number theory that was summarized earlier in this chapter and is explained in detail in Chapters 15 to 19 comes into play.

1.272 At the time the monthly CPI is first calculated, the only expenditure weights available must inevitably refer to some earlier period or periods of time. As explained earlier in this chapter, this predisposes the CPI to some form of Lowe or Young index in which the quantities, or expenditures, refer to some weight reference period b which precedes the price reference period 0. Such indices are often loosely described as Laspeyres type indices, but this description is inappropriate. At some later date, however, estimates may become available of the expenditures in both the price reference period 0 and the current period t, so that retrospectively the number of options open is greatly increased. It then becomes possible to calculate both Laspeyres and Paasche type indices, and also superlative indices such as Fisher or Törnqvist. There is some interest in calculating such indices later, if only to see how the original indices compare with the superlative indices. Some countries may wish to calculate retrospective superlative indices for that reason. Although most of the discussion in Chapter 9 focuses on some type of Lowe index because the official index first published will inevitably be of that type, this should not be interpreted as implying that such an index is the only possibility in the longer term.

1.273 *Production and maintenance of higher-level indices.* In practice, the higher-level indices up to and including the overall CPI are usually calculated as Young indices; that is, as weighted averages of the elementary price indices using weights derived from expenditures in some earlier weight reference period. This is a relatively straightforward operation, and a numerical example is given in Table 9.5 of Chapter 9 in which, for simplicity, the weight and price reference periods are assumed to be the same. Table 9.6 illustrates the case in which weight and price reference periods are not the same, and the weights are price updated between weight reference period b and the price reference period 0. It illustrates the point that statistical offices have two options when a new price reference period is introduced: they can either preserve the relative quantities of the weight reference period or they can preserve the relative expenditures, but they cannot do both. Price updating preserves the quantities.

1.274 The introduction of new weights is a necessary and integral part of the compilation of a CPI over the long run. Weights have to be updated sooner or later, some countries preferring to update their weights each year. Whenever the weights are changed, the index based on the new weights has to be linked to the index based on the old weights. Thus, the CPI inevitably becomes a chain index over the long term. An example of the linking is given in Table 9.7. Apart from the technicalities of the linking process, the introduction of new weights, especially if carried out at intervals of five years or so, provides an opportunity to undertake a major review of the whole methodology. New products may be introduced into the index, classifications may be revised and updated, while even the index number formula might be changed. Annual chaining facilitates the introduction of new products and other changes on a more regular basis, but in any case some ongoing maintenance of the index is needed whether it is annually chained or not.

1.275 Chapter 9 concludes with a section on data editing, a process that is very closely linked to the actual calculation of the elementary prices indices. Data editing comprises two steps: the detection of possible errors and outliers, and the verifying and correction of the data. Effective monitoring and quality control are needed to ensure the reliability of the basic price data fed into the calculation of the elementary prices indices, on which the quality of the overall index depends.

Organization and management

1.276 The collection of price data is a complex operation involving extensive fieldwork by a large number of individual collectors. The whole process requires careful planning and management to ensure that data collected conform to the requirements laid down by the central office with overall responsibility for the CPI. Appropriate management procedures are described in Chapter 12 of this manual.

1.277 Price collectors should be well trained to ensure that they understand the importance of selecting the right products for pricing. Inevitably, price collectors are bound to use their own discretion to a considerable extent. As already explained, one issue of crucial importance to the quality and reliability of a CPI is how to deal with the slowly evolving set of products with which a price collector is confronted. Products may disappear and have to be replaced by others, but it may also be appropriate to drop some products before they disappear altogether, if they have become unrepresentative. Price collectors need to be provided with appropriate training and very clear instructions and documentation about how to proceed. Clear instructions are also needed to ensure that price collectors collect the right prices when there are sales, special offers or other exceptional circumstances.

1.278 As just noted, the price data collected have also to be subjected to careful checking and editing. Many checks can be carried out by computer, using standard statistical control methods. It may also be useful to send out auditors to accompany price collectors and monitor their work. The various possible checks and controls are explained in detail in Chapter 12.

1.279 Improvements in information technology should obviously be exploited to the fullest extent possible. For example, collectors may use hand-held computers and transmit their results electronically to the central office.

Publication and dissemination

1.280 As noted above and in Chapter 2, the CPI is an extremely important statistic whose movements can influence the central bank's monetary policy, affect stock markets, influence wage rates and social security payments, and so on. There must be public confidence in its reliability, and in the competence and integrity of those responsible for its compilation. The methods used to compile it must therefore be fully documented, transparent and open to public scrutiny. Many countries have an official CPI advisory group consisting of both experts and users. The role of such a group is not just to advise the statistical office on technical matters but also to promote public confidence in the index.

1.281 Users of the index also attach great importance to having the index published as soon as possible after the end of each month or quarter, preferably within two or three weeks. There are also many users who do not wish the index to be revised once it has been published. Thus there is likely to be some trade-off between the timeliness and the quality of the index.

1.282 Publication should be understood to mean the dissemination of the results in any form. In addition to publication in print, or hard copy, the results should be released electronically and be available through the Internet on the web site of the statistical office.

1.283 As explained in Chapter 13, good publication policy goes beyond timeliness, confidence and transparency. The results should be made available to all users, in both the public and the private sectors, at the same time and according to a publication schedule announced in advance. There should be no discrimination among users in the timing of the release of the results. The results should not be subject to governmental scrutiny as a condition for their release, and should be seen to be free from political or other pressures.

1.284 There are many decisions to be taken about the degree of detail in the published data and the different ways in which the results may be presented. Users need to be consulted about these questions. These issues are discussed in Chapter 13. As they do not affect the actual calculation of the index, they need not be pursued further at this point.

USES OF CONSUMER PRICE INDICES 2

2.1 The consumer price index (CPI) is treated as a key indicator of economic performance in most countries. The purpose of this chapter is to explain why CPIs are compiled and what they are used for.

A range of possible consumer price indices

2.2 As noted in Chapter 1, compilers have to take into account the needs of users in deciding on the group of households and range of consumption goods and services covered by a CPI. As the prices of different goods and services do not all change at the same rate, or even all move in the same direction, changing the coverage of the index will change the value of the index. Thus, there can be no unique CPI and a range of possible CPIs could be defined.

2.3 While there may be interest in a CPI which is as broadly defined as possible, covering all the goods and services consumed by all households, there are many other options for defining CPIs covering particular sets of goods and services, which may be more useful for particular analytic or policy purposes. There is no necessity to have only a single CPI. When only a single CPI is compiled and published, there is a risk that it may be used for purposes for which it is not appropriate. More than one CPI could be published in order to meet different analytic or policy needs. It is important to recognize, however, that the publication of more than one CPI can be confusing to users who view consumer inflation as a pervasive phenomenon affecting all households equally. The coexistence of alternative measures could undermine their credibility for many users.

2.4 This chapter is intended not only to describe the most important uses for CPIs, but also to indicate how the coverage of a CPI can be affected by the use for which it is intended. The question of what is the most appropriate coverage of a CPI must be addressed before considering what is the most appropriate methodology to be used. Whether or not the CPI is intended to be a cost of living index (COLI), it is still necessary to determine exactly what kinds of good and services and what types of households are meant to be covered. This can only be decided on the basis of the main uses of the index.

Indexation

2.5 Indexation is a procedure whereby the monetary values of certain payments, or stocks, are increased or decreased in proportion to the change in the value of some price index. Indexation is most commonly applied to monetary flows such as wages, rents, interest or taxes, but it may also be applied to the capital values of certain monetary assets and liabilities. Under conditions of high inflation, the use of indexation may become widespread throughout the economy.

2.6 The objective of indexation of money incomes may be either to maintain the purchasing power of those incomes in respect of certain kinds of goods and services, or to preserve the standard of living or welfare of the recipients of the incomes. These two objectives are not quite the same, especially over the longer term. Maintaining purchasing power may be interpreted as changing money income in proportion to the change in the monetary value of a fixed basket of goods and services purchased out of that income. As explained further below and in detail in Chapter 3, maintaining the purchasing power of income over a fixed set of goods and services does not imply that the standard of living of the recipients of the income is necessarily unchanged.

2.7 When the indexation applies to monetary assets or liabilities, it may be designed to preserve the real value of the asset or liability relative to other assets or relative to the values of specified flows of goods and services.

Indexation of wages

2.8 As noted in Chapters 1 and 15, the indexation of wages seems to have been the main objective behind the original compilation of CPIs as the practice goes back over two centuries, although there has always been general interest in measuring inflation. If the indexation of wages is the main justification for a CPI, it has direct implications for the coverage of the index. First, it suggests that the index should be confined to expenditures made by households whose principal source of income is wages. Second, it may suggest excluding expenditures on certain types of goods and services which are considered to be luxurious or frivolous. If so, value judgements or political judgements may enter into the selection of goods and services covered. This point is elaborated further below.

Indexation of social security benefits

2.9 It has become common practice in many countries to index-link the rates at which social security benefits are payable. There are many kinds of benefits, such as retirement pensions, unemployment benefits, sickness benefits, child allowances, and so on. As in the case of wages, when index-linking to benefits of this kind is the main reason for compiling the CPI, it may suggest restricting the coverage of the index to certain types of households and goods and services. Many kinds of goods and services may then be excluded by political decision on the grounds that they are unnecessary or inappropriate. This type of thinking may lead to pressure to exclude expenditures on items such as holidays, gambling, tobacco or alcoholic drink.

2.10 An alternative procedure is to compile separate CPIs for different categories of households. For example, an index may be compiled covering the basket of goods and services purchased by households whose principal source of income is a social security pension. When this is done, it may be superfluous to decide to exclude certain types of luxury or inappropriate expenditures, as the actual expenditures on such items may be negligible anyway.

2.11 As already noted, publishing more than one CPI may be confusing if inflation is viewed as affecting everyone in the same way. Such confusion can be avoided by suitable publicity; it is not difficult to explain the fact that price changes are not the same for different categories of expenditures. In practice, some countries do publish more than one index.

2.12 The main reason why it may not be justifiable to publish more than one index is that the movements in the different indices may be virtually the same, especially in the short term. In such cases, the costs of compiling and publishing separate indices may not be worthwhile. In practice, it may need much bigger differences in patterns of expenditure than actually exist between different groups of households to yield significantly different CPIs.

2.13 Finally, it should be noted that the deliberate exclusion of certain types of goods and services by political decision on the grounds that the households towards whom the index is targeted ought not to be purchasing such goods, or ought not to be compensated for increases in the prices of such goods, cannot be recommended because it exposes the index to political manipulation. For example, suppose it is decided that certain products such as tobacco or alcoholic drink should be excluded from a CPI. There is then a possibility that when taxes on products have to be increased, these products may be deliberately selected in the knowledge that the resulting price increases do not increase the CPI. Such practices are not unknown.

The type of index used for indexation

2.14 When income flows such as wages or social security benefits are index-linked, it is necessary to consider the implications of choosing between a cost of living index and a price index that measures the changes in the cost of purchasing a fixed basket of goods and services, a type of index described here as a Lowe index. The widely used Laspeyres and Paasche indices are examples of Lowe indices. The Laspeyres index uses a typical basket purchased in the earlier of the two periods compared, while the Paasche uses a basket typical of the later period. This "fixed basket" method has a long history, as explained in Chapter 15. In contrast, a cost of living index (COLI) compares the cost of two baskets that may not be exactly the same but which bring the same satisfaction or utility to the consumer.

2.15 Indexation using a Laspeyres price index will tend to over-compensate the income recipients for changes in their cost of living. Increasing incomes in proportion to the change in the cost of purchasing a basket purchased in the past ensures that the income recipients have the opportunity to continue purchasing that same basket if they wish to do so. They would then be at least as well off as before. However, by adjusting their pattern of expenditures to take account of changes in the *relative* prices of the goods and services they buy, they will be able to improve their standard of living or welfare because they can substitute goods that have become relatively cheaper for ones that have become relatively dearer. In addition, they may be able to start to purchase completely new kinds of goods which provide new kinds of benefits that were not available in the earlier period. Such new goods tend to lower a cost of living index when they first appear even though no price can actually be observed to fall, as there was no previous price.

Indexation of interest, rents and other contractual payments

2.16 It is common for payments of both rents and interest to be index-linked. Governments may issue bonds with an interest rate specifically linked to the CPI. The interest payable in any given period may be equal to a fixed real rate of interest plus the percentage increase in the CPI. Payments of housing rents may also be linked to the CPI or possibly to some other index, such as an index of house prices.

2.17 Creditors receiving interest payments do not consist only of households, of course. In any case, the purpose of index-linking interest is not to maintain the standard of living of the creditors but rather to maintain their real wealth by compensating them for the real holding, or capital, losses on their loans incurred as a result of general inflation. A CPI may not be the ideal index for this purpose but may be used by default in the absence of any other convenient index, a point discussed further below.

2.18 Many other forms of contractual payments may be linked to the CPI. For example, legal obligations to pay alimony or for the support of children may be linked to the CPI. Payments of insurance premiums may be linked either to the index as a whole or to a sub-index relating to some specific types of expenditures, such the costs of repairs.

Taxation

2.19 Movements in a CPI may be used to affect the amounts payable in taxation in several ways. For example, liability for income tax may be affected by linking personal allowances that are deductible from taxable income to changes in the CPI. Under a system of progressive taxation, the various thresholds at which higher rates of personal income tax become operative may be changed in proportion to changes in the CPI. Liability for capital gains tax may be reduced by basing it on real rather than nominal capital gains through reducing the percentage increase in the value of the asset by the percentage change in the CPI over the same period, for taxation purposes. In general, there are various ways in which some form of indexation may be introduced into tax legislation.

Real consumption and real income

2.20 Price indices can be used to deflate expenditures at current prices or money incomes in order to derive measures of real consumption and real income. Real measures involve volume comparisons over time (or space). There are two different approaches to such comparisons which are analogous to the distinction between a Lowe, or basket, index and a cost of living index.

2.21 The first defines the change in real consumption as the change in the total value of the goods and services actually consumed measured at the fixed prices of some chosen period. This is equivalent to deflating the change in the current value of the goods and services consumed by an appropriately weighted Lowe price index. The change in real income can be measured by deflating the change in total money income by the same price index.

2.22 The alternative approach defines the change in real consumption as the change in welfare derived from the goods and services actually consumed. This may be estimated by deflating the change in the current value of consumption by using a COLI. Real income may be similarly obtained by deflating money income by the same COLI.

2.23 The two approaches cannot lead to the same results if the pure price index and the COLI diverge. The choice between the two approaches to the measurement of real consumption and real income will not pursued further here, as the issues involved are essentially the same as those already considered above in the parallel discussion of the choice between a Lowe, or basket, price index and a cost of living index.

Consistency between price indices and expenditure series

2.24 The data collected on prices and the data collected on household expenditures must be mutually consistent when measuring real consumption. This requires that both sets of data should cover the same set of goods and services and use the same concepts and classifications. Problems may arise in practice because the price indices and the expenditure series are often compiled independently of each other by different departments of a statistical agency or even by different agencies.

2.25 The coverage of a CPI need not be the same as that of total household consumption expenditures in the national accounts. The CPI may be targeted at selected households and expenditures for reasons given above. However, the difference in coverage between the CPI and the national accounts expenditures must be precisely identified so that it is possible to account for the differences between them. The price index used to deflate the expenditures ought to cover the additional goods and services not covered by the CPI. This may not be easy to achieve in practice because the relevant price data may not be easily available if the price collection procedures are geared to the CPI. Moreover, even if all the basic price data are available, the price index needed for deflation purposes is likely to be of a different type or formula from the CPI itself.

2.26 In principle, the deflation of national accounts estimates will normally require the compilation of appropriately defined price indices that differ from the CPI but may draw on the same price database. They may differ from the CPI not only in the range of the price and expenditure data they cover and the weighting and index number formula employed, but also in the frequency with which they are compiled and the length of the time periods they cover. The movements of the resulting indices will tend to differ somewhat from the CPI precisely because they measure different things. Although designed to be used to deflate expenditure data, they also provide useful additional information about movements in consumer prices. This information complements and supplements that provided by the CPI. The CPI itself is not designed to serve as a deflator. Its coverage and methodology should be designed to meet the needs of the CPI as described in other sections of this chapter.

2.27 When other types of consumer price indices are needed in addition to the CPI, this should be recognized at the data collection stage as it may be more efficient and cost effective to use a single collection process to meet the needs of more than one kind of price index. This may imply collecting rather more price data than are needed for the CPI itself if the coverage of the CPI has been deliberately restricted in some way.

Purchasing power parities

2.28 Many countries throughout the world, including all the member countries of the European Union (EU), participate in regular international programmes enabling purchasing power parities (PPPs) to be calculated for household consumption expenditures. The calculation of PPPs requires the prices of individual consumer goods and services to be compared directly between different countries. In effect, PPP programmes involve the compilation of international consumer price indices. Real expenditures and real incomes can then be compared between countries in much the same way as between different time periods in the same country.

2.29 It is not proposed to examine PPP methodology here but simply to note that PPPs create yet another demand for basic price data. When such data are being collected, therefore, it is important to recognize that they can be used for PPPs as well as CPIs. PPPs are essentially international deflators which are analogous to the inter-temporal deflators needed for the national accounts of a single country. Thus, while the processing and aggregation of the basic data for CPI purposes should be determined by the needs of the CPI itself, it is appropriate to take account of the requirements of these other kinds of price indices at the data collection stage. There may be important economies of scale to be realized by using a single collection process to meet the needs of several different types of indices.

2.30 Thus, operationally as well as conceptually, the CPI needs to be placed in the context of a wider set of interrelated price indices. The compilation of CPIs predates the compilation of national accounts by many years in some countries, so the CPI may have originated as a free-standing index. The CPI can, however, no longer be treated as an isolated index whose compilation and methodology can proceed quite independently of other interrelated statistics.

Use of the consumer price index for accounting under inflation

2.31 When there is inflation, both business and national accounts have to introduce adjustments which are not needed when the price level is stable. This is a complex subject which cannot be pursued in any depth here. Two methods of accounting are commonly used, and they are summarized below. Both require price indices for their implementation.

Current purchasing power accounts

2.32 Current purchasing power accounts are accounts in which the monetary values of the flows in earlier time periods are scaled up in proportion to the increase in some general index of inflation between the earlier period and the current period. In principle, the index used should be a general price index covering other flows in addition to household consumption expenditures, but in practice the CPI is often used by default in the absence of a suitable general index.

Current cost accounting

2.33 Current cost accounting is a method of accounting for the use of assets in which the cost of using the assets in production is calculated at the current prices of those assets as distinct from the prices at which the assets were purchased or otherwise acquired in the past (historic costs). The current cost of using an asset takes account not only of changes in the general price level but also of changes in the relative price of that type of asset since it was acquired. In principle, the price indices that are used to adjust the original prices paid for the assets should be specific price indices relating to that particular type of asset, and such indices are calculated and used in this way in some countries. However, when there are no such indices available there remains the possibility of using the CPI, or some sub-index of the CPI, by default, and CPIs have been used for this purpose.

Consumer price indices and general inflation

2.34 As already noted, measures of the general rate of inflation in the economy as a whole are needed for various purposes:

- Controlling inflation is usually one of the main objectives of government economic policy, although responsibility for controlling inflation may be delegated to the central bank. A measure of general inflation is needed in order to set targets and also to judge the degree of success achieved by the government or central bank in meeting anti-inflationary targets.
- As noted above, a measure of general inflation is also needed for both business and national accounting purposes, particularly for current purchasing power accounting.
- The concept of a relative price change is important in economics. It is convenient therefore to be able to measure the actual changes in the prices of individual goods or services relative to some measure of general inflation. There is also a need to be able to measure real holding (or capital) gains and losses on assets, including monetary assets and liabilities.

2.35 Suitable measures of general inflation are considered in Chapter 14, in which it shown that a hierarchy of price indices exists that includes the CPI. Clearly, a CPI is not a measure of general inflation, as it only measures changes in the prices of consumer goods and services purchased by households. A CPI does not cover capital goods, such as houses, or the goods and services consumed by enterprises or the government. Any attempt to analyse inflationary pressures in the economy must also take account of other price movements, such as changes in the prices of imports and exports, the prices of industrial inputs and outputs, and also asset prices.

Consumer price indices and inflation targets

2.36 Despite the obvious limitations of a CPI as a measure of general inflation, it is commonly used by governments and central banks to set inflation targets. Similarly, it is interpreted by the press and the public as the ultimate measure of inflation. Although governments and central banks are obviously well aware of the fact that the CPI is not a measure of general inflation, a number of factors help to explain the popularity of the CPI, and these are discussed below.

2.37 It may be noted, however, that even though the CPI does not measure general inflation its movements may be expected to be highly correlated with those of a more general measure, if only because consumption expenditures account for a large proportion of total final expenditures. In particular, the CPI should provide a reliable indicator of whether inflation is accelerating or decelerating and also of any turning points in the rate of inflation. This information is highly valuable even if the CPI may be systematically understating or overstating the general rate of inflation.

Consumer price indices and international comparisons of inflation

2.38 CPIs are also commonly used to make international comparisons of inflation rates. An important example of their use for this purpose is provided by the EU. In order to judge the extent to which rates of inflation in the different member countries were converging in the mid-1990s prior to the formation of the European Monetary Union, the member countries decided in the Maastricht Treaty that CPIs should be used. Although CPIs measure consumer inflation rather than general inflation, their use to evaluate the extent of convergence of inflation may be justified on similar grounds to those just mentioned. Presumably, the convergence in CPIs will be highly correlated with that in general inflation, so the use of a specific rather than a general measure of inflation may lead to the same conclusions about the extent of convergence and which countries diverge the most from the average.

Popularity of consumer price indices as economic statistics

2.39 CPIs seem to have acquired a unique status among economic statistics in most countries. There are several factors which help to explain this:

- First, all households have their own personal experience of the phenomenon the CPI is supposed to be measuring. The general public are very conscious of changes in the prices of consumer goods and services, and the direct impact those changes have on their living standards. Interest in CPIs is not confined to the press and politicians.
- Changes in the CPI tend to receive a lot of publicity. Their publication can make headline news. The CPI is a high-profile statistic.
- The CPI is published frequently, usually each month, so that the rate of consumer inflation can be closely monitored. The CPI is also a timely statistic that is released very soon after the end of the period to which it refers.
- The CPI is a statistic with a long history, as noted in Chapters 1 and 15. People have been familiar with it for a long time.
- Although price changes for certain kinds of consumer goods are difficult to measure because of quality changes, price changes for other kinds of goods and services such as capital goods and government services, especially public services, tend to be even more difficult to measure. The CPI may be a relatively reliable price index compared with the price indices for some other flows.
- The CPI is widely respected. Its accuracy and reliability are seldom seriously questioned.
- Most countries have deliberately adopted a policy of not revising the index once it has been published. This makes it more attractive for many purposes, especially those with financial consequences such as indexation. The lack of revisions may perhaps create a somewhat spurious impression of certainty, but it also seems to enhance the credibility and acceptability of the index.

2.40 The widespread use of the CPI for more purposes than it is designed for can be explained by the various factors listed above, together with the fact that no satisfactory alternative or more comprehensive measures of inflation are available monthly in most countries. For example, the CPI may be used as a proxy for a more general measure of inflation in business accounting, even though it may be clear that, conceptually, the CPI is not the ideal index for the purpose. Similarly, the fact that the CPI is not subject to revision, together with its frequency and timeliness, may explain its popularity for indexation purposes in business or legal contracts in contexts where it also may not be very appropriate conceptually. These practices may be defended on the grounds that the alternative to using the CPI may be to make no adjustment for inflation. Although the CPI may not be the ideal measure, it is much better to use it than to make no adjustment whatsoever.

2.41 Although the CPI is often used as a proxy for a general measure of inflation, this does not justify extending its coverage to include elements that go beyond household consumption. If broader indices of inflation are needed, they should be developed in addition to the CPI, leaving the CPI itself intact. Some countries are in fact developing additional and more comprehensive measures of inflation within the kind of conceptual framework outlined in Chapter 14 below.

The need for independence and integrity of consumer price indices

2.42 Because of the widespread use of CPIs for all kinds of indexation, movements in the CPI can have major financial ramifications throughout the economy. The implications for the government alone can be considerable, given that the CPI can affect interest payments and taxation receipts as well as the government's wage and social security outlays.

2.43 When financial interests are involved, there is always a risk that both political and non-political pressure groups may try to exert an influence on the methodology used to compile the CPI. The CPI, in common with other official statistics, must be protected from such pressures and be seen to be protected. Partly for this reason, many countries establish an advisory committee to ensure that the CPI is not subject to outside influence. The advisory committee may include representatives of a cross-section of interested parties as well as independent experts able to offer professional advice. Information about the methodology used to calculate CPIs should be publicly available.

CONCEPTS AND SCOPE

3

Introduction

3.1 The purpose of this chapter is to define and clarify the basic concepts of price and consumption used in a consumer price index (CPI) and to explain the scope of the index. While the general purpose of a *consumer* price index is to measure changes in the prices of consumption goods and services, the concept of "consumption" is an imprecise one that can be interpreted in several different ways, each of which may lead to a different CPI. The governmental agency or statistical office responsible for compiling a CPI also has to decide whether the index is meant to cover all consumers, i.e., all households, or to be restricted to a particular group of households. The precise scope of a CPI is inevitably influenced by what is intended, or believed, to be the main use of the index. Statistical offices should, however, bear in mind that CPIs are widely used as measures of general inflation, even though they may not have been designed for this purpose.

3.2 Consumption is an activity in which persons, acting either individually or collectively, use goods or services to satisfy their needs and wants. In economics, no attempt is made to observe and record such activities directly. Instead, consumption is measured either by the value of the goods and services wholly or partly used up in some period, or by the value of the goods and services that are purchased, or otherwise acquired, for purposes of consumption.

3.3 A consumer price index can have two different meanings, as "consumer" may refer either to a type of economic unit, typically a person or a household, or to a certain type of good or service. To avoid confusion, the term "consumer" will, so far as possible, be reserved here for persons or households, while so-called "consumer" goods will be described as "consumption" goods. *A consumption good or service is defined as one that members of households use, directly or indirectly, to satisfy their own personal needs and wants.* By definition, consumption goods or services provide *utility*. Utility is simply the generic, technical term preferred by economists for the satisfaction, benefit or welfare that people derive from consumption goods or services.

3.4 A CPI is generally understood to be a price index that measures changes in the prices of consumption goods and services acquired, or used, by households. As explained in Chapter 14, more broadly based price indices can be defined whose scope extends well beyond consumption goods and services, but a CPI is deliberately focused on household consumption. It is, however, possible to define a CPI that includes the prices of physical assets such as land or dwellings purchased by households. In the case of owner-occupied dwellings, a key issue is whether to include in the CPI the imputed rents for the flows of housing services provided by the dwellings, or alternatively whether to include the prices of the dwellings themselves in the index (notwithstanding the fact that they are treated as fixed assets and not consumption goods in the system of national accounts (SNA)). Views differ on this issue. In any case, purchases of financial assets, such as bonds or shares, are excluded because financial assets are not goods or services of any kind and are not used to satisfy the personal needs or wants of household members. Financial transactions do not change wealth as one type of financial asset is simply exchanged for another type of financial asset. For example, when securities are purchased, money is exchanged for a bond or share; or alternatively, when a debt is incurred, money is received in exchange for the creation of a liability.

3.5 Although, by definition, a CPI is confined to the prices of goods and services consumed by households, it does not necessarily follow that CPIs have to cover all households or all the goods and services they consume. For example, it might be decided to exclude publicly provided goods which households do not pay for. Many decisions have to be taken about the precise scope of a CPI even though the general purpose of the index may be determined. These issues are explored in this and the following chapter.

Alternative consumption aggregates

3.6 As already noted, the concept of consumption is not a precise one and may be interpreted in different ways. In this section, a hierarchy of different consumption concepts and aggregates is examined.

3.7 Households may acquire goods and services for purposes of consumption in four main ways:

- they may purchase them in monetary transactions;
- they may produce them themselves for their own consumption;
- they may receive them as payments in kind through barter transactions, particularly as remuneration in kind for work done;
- they may receive them as free gifts, or transfers, from other economic units.

3.8 The broadest concept of consumption for CPI purposes would be a price index embracing all four categories of consumption goods and services listed above. This set of consumption goods and services may be described as *total acquisitions*. Total acquisitions are equivalent to the total actual individual consumption of households as defined in the SNA (see Chapter 14). It should be noted that total acquisitions constitute a broader concept of consumption than total consumption expenditures.

Acquisitions and expenditures

3.9 Expenditures are made by the economic units who pay for the goods and services: in other words, who bear the costs. However, many of the goods and services consumed by households are financed and paid for by government units or non-profit institutions. They are mostly services such as education, health, housing and transport. Individual goods and services provided free of charge, or at nominal prices, to *individual* households by governments or non-profit institutions are described as *social transfers in kind*. They may make a substantial contribution to the welfare or standard of living of the individual households that receive them. (Social transfers in kind do not include *collective* services provided by governments to the community as whole, such as public administration and defence.)

3.10 The expenditures on social transfers in kind are incurred by the governments or non-profit institutions that pay for them and not by the households that consume them. It could be decided that the CPI should be confined to consumption expenditures incurred by households, in which case free social transfers in kind would be excluded from the scope of the index. Even if they were to be included, they can be ignored in practice when they are provided free, on the grounds that households incur zero expenditures on them. Of course, their prices are not zero from the perspective of the units that finance the social transfers, but the relevant prices for a CPI are those payable by the households.

3.11 Social transfers cannot be ignored, however, when governments and non-profit institutions decide to introduce charges for them, a practice that has become increasingly common in many countries. For example, if the CPI is intended to measure the change in the total value of a basket of consumption goods and services that includes social transfers, increases in their prices from zero to some positive amount increase the cost of the basket and ought to be captured by a CPI.

Monetary versus non-monetary expenditures

3.12 A distinction may also be drawn between monetary and non-monetary expenditures depending on the nature of the resources used to pay for the goods and services. A monetary expenditure occurs when a household pays in cash, by cheque or credit card, or otherwise incurs a financial liability to pay, in exchange for the acquisition of a good or service. Non-monetary expenditures occur when households do not incur a financial liability but bear the costs of acquiring the goods or services in some other way.

3.13 *Non-monetary expenditures*. Payments may be made in kind rather than cash, as in barter transactions. The goods and services offered as payment in barter transactions are equivalent to negative expenditures and their price changes should, in principle, carry negative weights in a CPI. If the price of goods sold increases, the household is better off. However, as the two sides of a barter transaction should in principle be equal in value, the net expenditure incurred by two households engaged in barter should be zero. Barter transactions between households may therefore be ignored in practice for CPI purposes.

3.14 Households also incur non-monetary expenditures when household members receive goods and services from their employers as remuneration in kind. The employees pay for the goods and services with their own labour rather than cash. Consumption goods and services received as remuneration in kind can, in principle, be included in a CPI using the estimated prices that would be payable for them on the market.

3.15 A third important category of non-monetary expenditure occurs when households consume goods and services that they have produced themselves. The households incur the costs, while the expenditures are deemed to occur when the goods and services are consumed. Own account expenditures of this kind include expenditures on housing services produced for their own consumption by owner-occupiers. The treatment of goods and services produced for own consumption raises important conceptual issues that are discussed in more detail below.

3.16 *Monetary expenditures*. The narrowest concept of consumption that could be used for CPI purposes is one based on monetary expenditures only. Such an aggregate would exclude many of the goods and services actually acquired and used by households for purposes of consumption. Only monetary expenditures generate the monetary prices needed for CPI purposes. The prices of the goods and services acquired through non-monetary expenditures can only be imputed on the basis of the prices observed in monetary transactions. Imputed prices do not generate more price information. Instead, they affect the weighting attached to monetary prices by increasing the weight of those monetary prices which are used to value non-monetary expenditures.

3.17 If the main reason for compiling a CPI is the measurement of inflation, it may be decided to restrict the scope of the index to monetary expenditures only, especially since non-monetary expenditures do not generate any demand for money. Harmonized Indices of Consumer Prices (HICPs), used to measure inflation within the European Union, are confined to monetary expenditures (see Annex 1).

Acquisitions and uses

3.18 It has been customary in the literature on CPIs to draw a distinction between acquisitions of consumption goods and services by households and their subsequent use to satisfy their households' needs or wants. Consumption goods are typically acquired at one point of time and used at some other point of time, often much later, or they may be used repeatedly, or even continuously, over an extended period of time. The times of acquisition and use nevertheless coincide for many services, although there are other kinds of services that provide lasting benefits and are not used up at the time they are provided.

3.19 The time at which a good is acquired is the moment at which ownership of the good is transferred to the consumer. In a market situation, it is the moment at which the consumer incurs a liability to pay, either in cash or in kind. The time at which a service is acquired is not so easy to determine precisely as the provision of a service does not involve any exchange of ownership. Instead, it typically leads to some improvement in the condition of the consumer. A service is acquired by the consumer at the same time that the producer provides it and the consumer accepts a liability to pay.

3.20 In a market situation, therefore, the time of acquisition for both goods and services is the time at which the liability to pay is incurred. When payments are not made immediately in cash, there may be a significant lapse of time before the consumer's bank account is debited for a purchase settled by cheque, by credit card or similar arrangement. The times at which these debits are eventually made depend on administrative convenience and on the particular financial and institutional arrangements in place. They have no relevance to the time of recording the transactions or the prices.

3.21 The distinction between time of acquisition and time of use is particularly important for durable goods and certain kinds of services.

Durables and non-durables

3.22 *Goods.* A "non-durable" good would be better described as a *single use* good. For example, food and drink are used once only to satisfy hunger or thirst. Heating oil, coal or firewood can be burnt once only, but they are nevertheless extremely durable physically and can be stored indefinitely. Households may hold substantial stocks of so-called non-durables, such as many foodstuffs and fuel, especially in periods of political or economic uncertainty.

3.23 Conversely, the distinguishing feature of consumer durables, such as furniture, household equipment or vehicles, is that they are durable under use. They can be used repeatedly or continuously to satisfy consumers' needs over a long period of time, possibly many years. For this reason, a durable is often described as providing a flow of "services"' to the consumer over the period it is used (see also Box 14.3 of Chapter 14). There is a close parallel between the definitions of consumer durables and fixed assets. Fixed assets are goods that are used repeatedly or continuously over long periods of time in processes of production: for example, buildings or other structures, machinery and equipment. A list of the different kinds of consumer durables distinguished in the Classification of Individual Consumption according to Purpose (COICOP) is given below. Some durables last much longer than others, the less durable ones being described as "semi-durables" in COICOP, for example clothing. Dwellings are not classified as consumer durables in COICOP. They are treated as fixed assets and not consumption goods and therefore fall outside the scope of COICOP. However, the housing services produced and consumed by owner-occupiers are included in COICOP and classified in the same way as the housing services consumed by tenants.

3.24 *Services.* Consumers may continue to benefit, and derive utility, from some services long after they were provided because they bring about substantial, long-lasting or even permanent improvements in the condition of the consumers. The quality of life of persons receiving medical treatments such as hip replacements or cataract surgery, for example, is substantially and permanently improved. Similarly, consumers of educational services can benefit from them over their entire lifetimes.

3.25 For some analytical purposes, it may be appropriate to treat certain kinds of services, such as education and health, as the service equivalents of durable goods. Expenditures on such services can be viewed as investments that augment the stock of human capital. Another characteristic that education and health services share with durable goods is that they are often so expensive that their purchase has to be financed by borrowing or by running down other assets.

Consumer price indices based on acquisitions and uses

3.26 The distinction between the *acquisition* and the *use* of a consumption good or service has led to two different concepts of a CPI being proposed.

- A CPI may be intended to measure the average change between two time periods in the prices of the consumption goods and services acquired by households.
- Alternatively, a CPI may be intended to measure the average change between two time periods in the prices of the consumption goods and services used by households to satisfy their needs and wants.

3.27 Flows of acquisitions and uses may be very different for durables. Acquisitions of durables, like producer capital goods, are liable to fluctuate, depending on the general state of the economy, whereas the using up of the stock of durables owned by households tends be a gradual and smooth process. A CPI based on the uses approach requires that the index should measure period-to-period changes in the *prices of the flows of services* provided by the durables. As explained in Chapter 23, the value of the flow of services from a durable may be estimated by its "user cost", which consists essentially of the depreciation on the asset (at current prices) *plus* the interest cost. The inclusion of the interest cost as well as the depreciation means that, over the long term, the weight given to durables is greater than when they are measured simply by acquisitions. In principle, the flows of services, or benefits, derived from major educational and medical expenditures might also be estimated on the basis of user costs.

3.28 When durables are rented on the market, the rentals have to cover not only the values of the service flows but additional costs such as administration and management, repairs and maintenance, and overheads. For example, the amount payable to use a washing machine in a launderette has to cover the costs of the room space in which the machine is housed, electricity, repairs and maintenance, the wages of supervisory staff, and so on, as well as the services provided by the machine itself. Similarly, the rentals payable for car hire may significantly exceed the cost of the service flow provided by the car on its own. In both cases, the customer is buying a bundle of services that includes more than just the use of the durable good.

3.29 Estimating the values and the prices of the flows of services provided by the stock of durables owned by households is difficult, whereas expenditures on durables are easily recorded, as are also the prices at which they are purchased. Partly because of these practical measurement difficulties, CPIs have, up to now, been based largely or entirely on the acquisitions approach. Similarly, national accounts tend to record expenditures on, or acquisitions of, durables rather than the flows of services they provide. As already noted, dwellings are treated as fixed assets and not consumer durables in the SNA. The treatment of owner-occupied housing is considered separately below.

Basket indices and cost of living indices

3.30 A fundamental conceptual distinction may be drawn between a *basket index* and a *cost of living index*. In a CPI context, a basket index is an index that measures the change between two time periods in the total expenditure needed to purchase a given set, or basket, of consumption goods and services. It is called a "Lowe index" in this manual. A cost of living index (COLI) is an index that measures the change in the minimum cost of maintaining a given standard of living. Both indices therefore have very similar objectives in that they aim to measure the change in the total expenditure needed to purchase *either* the same basket *or* two baskets whose composition may differ somewhat but between which the consumer is indifferent.

Lowe indices

3.31 CPIs are almost invariably calculated as Lowe indices in practice. Their properties and behaviour are described in detail in various chapters of this manual. The operational target for most CPIs is to measure the change over time in the total value of some specified basket of consumption goods and services purchased, or acquired, by some specified group of households in some specified period of time. The meaning of such an index is clear. It is, of course, necessary to ensure that the selected basket is relevant to the needs of users and also kept up to date. The basket may be changed at regular intervals and does not have to remain fixed over long periods of time. The determination of the basket is considered in more detail later in this chapter and in the following one.

Cost of living indices

3.32 The economic approach to index number theory treats the quantities consumed as being dependent on the prices. Households are treated as price takers who are assumed to react to changes in *relative* prices by adjusting the *relative* quantities they consume. A basket index that works with a fixed set of quantities fails to allow for the fact that there is a systematic tendency for consumers to substitute items that have become relatively cheaper for those that have become relatively dearer. A cost of living index based on the economic approach does take this substitution effect into account. It measures the change in the minimum expenditure needed to maintain a given standard when utility-maximizing consumers adjust their patterns of purchases in response to changes in relative prices. In contrast to a basket index, the baskets in the two periods in a cost of living index will generally not be quite the same in the two periods because of these substitutions.

3.33 The properties and behaviour of cost of living indices, or COLIs, are explained in some detail in Chapter 17. A summary explanation has already been given in Chapter 1. The maximum scope of a COLI would be the entire set of consumption goods and services consumed by the designated households from which they derive utility. It includes the goods and services received free as social transfers in kind from governments or non-profit institutions. Because COLIs measure the change in the cost of maintaining a given standard of living or level of utility, they lend themselves to a uses rather than an acquisitions approach, as utility is derived not by acquiring a consumer good or service but by using it to satisfy personal needs and wants.

3.34 Welfare may be interpreted to mean not only economic welfare, that is the utility that is linked to economic activities such as production, consumption and working, but also general well-being associated with other factors such as security from attack by others. It may not be possible to draw a clear distinction between economic and non-economic factors, but it is clear that total welfare is only partly dependent on the amount of goods and services consumed.

3.35 *Conditional and unconditional cost of living indices*. In principle, the scope of a COLI is influenced by whether or not it is intended to be a conditional and unconditional cost of living index. The *total welfare* of a household depends on a string of non-economic factors such as the climate, the state of the physical, social and political environment, the risk of being attacked either by criminals or from abroad, the incidence of diseases, and so on, as well as by the quantities of goods and services consumed. An *unconditional cost of living index* measures the change in the cost to a household of maintaining a given level of total welfare allowing the non-economic factors to vary as well as the prices of consumption goods and services. If changes in the non-economic factors lower welfare, then some compensating increase in the level of consumption will be needed in order to maintain the same level of total welfare. An adverse change in the weather, for example, requires more fuel to be consumed to maintain the same level of comfort as before. The cost of the *increased quantities* of fuel consumed drives up the unconditional cost of living index, irrespective of what has happened to prices. There are countless other events that can impact on an unconditional cost of living index, from natural disasters such as earthquakes to man-made disasters such as Chernobyl or acts of terrorism.

3.36 While there may be interest in an unconditional cost of living index for certain analytical and policy purposes, it is defined in such a way that it is deliberately intended to measure the effects of many other factors besides prices. If the objective is to measure the effects of price changes only, the non-price factors must be held constant. Given that a cost of living index is meant to serve as a consumer *price index*, its scope must be restricted to exclude the effects of events other than price changes. A *conditional* cost of living index is defined as the ratio of the minimum expenditures needed to maintain a given level of utility, or welfare, in response to price changes, assuming that all the other factors affecting welfare remain constant. It is conditional not only on a particular standard of living and set of preferences, but also on a particular state of the non-price factors affecting welfare. COLIs in this manual are to be understood as *conditional* cost of living indices.

3.37 A conditional COLI should not be viewed as second best. An unconditional COLI is a more comprehensive *cost of living* index than a conditional COLI, but it is not a more comprehensive *price* index than a conditional index. An unconditional index does not include more price information than a conditional index and it does not give more insight into the impact of price changes on households' welfare. On the contrary, the impact of the price changes is diluted and obscured as more variables impacting on welfare are included within the scope of the index.

3.38 Lowe indices, including Laspeyres and Paasche, are also conditional, being dependent on the choice of basket. The fact that the value of a basket index varies in predictable ways according to the choice of basket has generated much of the large literature on index number theory. Conceptually, Lowe indices and conditional COLIs have much in common. A Lowe index measures the change in the cost of a specified basket of goods and services, whereas a conditional COLI measures the change in the cost of maintaining the level of utility associated with some specified basket of goods and services, other things being equal.

Expenditures and other payments outside the scope of consumer price indices

3.39 Given that, conceptually, most CPIs are designed to measure changes in the prices of consumption goods and services, it follows that purchases of items that are not goods and services fall outside the intended scope of a CPI: for example, purchases of bonds, shares or other financial assets. Similarly, payments that are not even purchases because nothing is received in exchange fall outside the index: for example, payments of income taxes or social security contributions.

3.40 The implementation of these principles is not always straightforward, as the distinction between an expenditure on a good or service and other payments may not always be clear cut in practice. A number of conceptually difficult cases, including some borderline cases of a possibly controversial nature, are examined below.

Transfers

3.41 The definition of a transfer is a transaction in which one unit provides a good, service or asset to another without receiving any good, service or asset in return: i.e., transactions in which there is no counterpart. Transfers are unrequited. As no good or service of any kind is acquired by the household when it makes a transfer, the transfer must be outside the scope of a CPI. The problem is to determine whether or not certain kinds of transactions are in fact transfers, a problem common to both CPIs and national accounts.

3.42 *Social security contributions and taxes on income and wealth.* As households do not receive any specific, individual good or service in return for the payment of social security contributions, they are treated as transfers that are outside the scope of CPIs. Similarly, all payments of taxes based on income or wealth (the ownership of assets) are outside the scope of a CPI since they are unrequited compulsory transfers to government. Property taxes on dwellings (commonly levied as local authority taxes or rates) are outside the scope. It may be noted, however, that unrequited compulsory transfers could be incorporated within an unconditional COLI or within a more broadly defined conditional COLI that allows for changes in some other factors besides changes in the prices of consumption goods and services.

3.43 *Licences.* Households have to pay to obtain various kinds of licences and it is often not clear whether they are simply taxes under another name or whether the government agency providing the licence provides some kind of service in exchange, for example by exercising some supervisory, regulatory or control function. In the latter case, they could be regarded as purchases of services. Some cases are so borderline that they have been debated for years by taxation experts under the aegis of the International Monetary Fund (IMF) and other international agencies without reaching consensus. The experts therefore agreed to settle on a number of conventions based on practices followed in the majority of countries. It is appropriate to make use of these conventions for CPI, and also national accounts, purposes. These conventions are listed in the IMF's *Government Finance Statistics* (IMF, 2001) and have also been adopted in *SNA 1993*.

3.44 Payments by households for licences to own or use certain goods or facilities are, by convention, classified as consumption expenditures, not transfers, and are thus included within the scope of a CPI. For example, licence fees for radios, televisions, driving, firearms, and so on, as well as fees for passports, are included. On the other hand, licences for owning or using vehicles, boats and aircraft, and for hunting, shooting and fishing are conventionally classified as direct taxes and are therefore outside the scope of CPIs. Many countries, however, do include taxes for private vehicle use as they regard them as taxes on consumption for CPI purposes. As the actual circumstances under which licences are issued, and the conditions attaching to them, can vary significantly from country to country, statistical offices may wish to deviate from the proposed conventions in some instances. In general, however, it seems appropriate to make use of conventions internationally agreed by the relevant experts.

3.45 *Gifts and subscriptions.* Gifts are transfers, by definition, and thus outside the scope of a CPI. Payments of subscriptions or donations to charitable organizations for which no easily identifiable services are received in return are also transfers. On the other hand, payments of subscriptions to clubs and societies, including charities, which provide their members with some kind of service (e.g., regular meetings, magazines, etc.) can be regarded as final consumption expenditures and included in a CPI.

3.46 *Tips and gratuities.* Non-compulsory tips or gratuities are gifts that are outside the scope of a CPI. There may be cases, however, where, although tips are not compulsory, it can be very difficult to obtain a good or service without some form of additional payment, in which case this payment should be included in the expenditure on, and the price of, the good or service in question.

Insurance

3.47 There are two main types of insurance, life and non-life. In both cases the premiums have two components. One is a payment for the insurance itself, often described as the net premium, while the other is an implicit service charge payable to the insurance enterprise for arranging the insurance: i.e., a fee charged for calculating the risks, determining the premiums, administering the collection and investment of premiums, and the payment of claims.

3.48 The implicit service charge is not directly observable. It is an integral part of the gross premium that is not separately identified in practice. As a payment for a service it falls within the scope of a CPI, but it is difficult to estimate.

3.49 In the case of non-life insurance, the net premium is essentially a transfer that goes into a pool covering the collective risks of policy holders as a whole. As a transfer, it falls outside the scope of a CPI. In the case of life insurance, the net premium is essentially a form of financial investment. It constitutes the purchase of a financial asset, which is also outside the scope of a CPI.

3.50 Finally, it may be noted that when insurance is arranged through a broker or agent separate from the insurance enterprise, the fees charged by the brokers or agents for their services are included within the scope of the CPI, over and above the implicit service charges made by the insurers.

Gambling

3.51 The amounts paid for lottery tickets or placed in bets also consist of two elements that arc usually not separately identified – the payment of an implicit service charge (part of consumption expenditures) and a current transfer that enters the pool out of which the winnings are paid. Only the implicit or explicit service charges payable to the organizers of the gambling fall within the scope of a CPI. The service charges are usually calculated at an aggregate level as the difference between payables (stakes) and receivables (winnings).

Transactions in financial assets

3.52 Financial assets are not consumption goods or services. The creation of financial assets/liabilities, or their extinction, e.g., by lending, borrowing and repayments, are financial transactions that are quite different from expenditures on goods and services and take place independently of them. The purchase of a financial asset is obviously not expenditure on consumption, being a form of financial investment.

3.53 Some financial assets, notably securities in the form of bills, bond and shares, are tradable and have market prices. They have their own separate price indices, such as stock market price indices.

3.54 Many of the financial assets owned by households are acquired indirectly through the medium of pension schemes and life insurance. Excluding the service charges, pension contributions by households are similar to payments for life insurance premiums. They are essentially forms of investment made out of saving, and are thus excluded from CPIs. In contrast, the explicit or implicit fees paid by households for the services rendered by financial auxiliaries such as brokers, banks, insurers (life and non-life), pension fund managers, financial advisers, accountants, and so on, are within the scope of a CPI. Payments of such fees are simply purchases of services.

Purchases and sales of foreign currency

3.55 Foreign currency is a financial asset. Purchases and sales of foreign currency are therefore outside the scope of CPIs. Changes in the prices payable, or receivable, for foreign currencies resulting from changes in exchange rates are not included in CPIs. In contrast, the service charges made by foreign-exchange dealers are included within the scope of CPIs when households acquire foreign currency for personal use. These charges include not only explicit commission charges but also the margins between the buying or selling rates offered by the dealers and the average of the two rates.

Payments, financing and credit

3.56 Conceptually, the time at which an expenditure is incurred is the time at which the purchaser incurs a liability to pay: that is, when the ownership of the good changes hands or the service is provided. The time of payment is the time at which the liability is extinguished. The two may be simultaneous when payment is made immediately in cash, i.e., notes or coin, but the use of chcques, credit cards and other forms of credit facilities means that it is increasingly common for the payment to take place some time after the expenditure occurs. A further complication is that payments may be made in stages, with a deposit payable in advance. Given the time lags and complexity of financial instruments and institutional arrangements, it may be difficult to determine exactly when payment takes place. The time may even be different from the standpoint of the purchaser and the seller.

3.57 For consistency with the expenditure data used as weights in CPIs, the prices should be recorded at the times at which the expenditures actually take place. This is consistent with an acquisitions approach.

Financial transactions and borrowing

3.58 Some individual expenditures may be very large: for example, the purchase of expensive medical treatment, a large durable good, or an expensive holiday. If the household does not have sufficient cash, or does not wish to pay the full amount immediately in cash, various options are open.

- The purchaser may borrow from a bank, moneylender or other financial institution.
- The purchaser may use a credit card.
- The seller may extend credit to the purchaser, or the seller may arrange for a third party, some kind of financial institution, to extend credit to the purchaser.

The creation of a financial asset/liability

3.59 When a consumer borrows to purchase a good or service, two distinct transactions are involved: the purchase of the good or service, and the borrowing of the requisite funds. The latter is a purely financial transaction between a creditor and a debtor in which a new financial asset/liability is created. This financial transaction is outside the scope of a CPI. As already noted, a financial transaction does not change wealth and there is no consumption involved. A financial transaction merely rearranges the individual's asset portfolio by exchanging one type of asset for another. For example, when a loan is made, the lender exchanges cash for a financial claim over the debtor. Similarly, the borrower acquires cash counterbalanced by the creation of an equal financial liability. Such transactions are irrelevant for CPI purposes.

3.60 In general, when a household borrows from financial institutions, including moneylenders, the borrowed funds may be used for a variety of purposes including the purchase of assets such as dwellings or financial assets (for example, bonds or shares), as well as the purchase of expensive goods and services. Similarly, the credit extended to the holder of a credit card can be used for a variety of purposes. In itself, the creation of a financial asset and liability by new borrowing has no impact on a CPI. There is no good or service acquired, no expenditure and no price.

3.61 It should be noted that interest payments are not themselves financial transactions. The payment of interest is quite different from the borrowing, lending or other financial transactions that give rise to it. Interest is considered separately below.

3.62 Hire purchase and mortgage loans must be treated consistently with other loans. The fact that certain loans are conditional on the borrower using the funds for a particular purpose does not affect the treatment of the loan itself. Moreover, conditional loans are by no means confined to the purchase of durable goods on "hire purchase". Conditional personal loans may be made for other purposes, such as large expenditures on education or health. In each case, the contracting of the loan is a separate transaction from the expenditure on the good or service and must be distinguished from the latter. The two transactions may involve different parties and may take place at quite different times.

3.63 Although the provision of finance is a separate transaction from the purchase of a good or service for which it is used, it may affect the price paid. Each case needs to be carefully considered. For example, suppose the seller agrees to defer payment for one year. The seller appears to make an interest free loan for a year, but this is not the economic reality. The seller makes a loan but it is not interest free. Nor is the amount lent equal to the "full" price. Implicitly, the purchaser issues a short-term bill to the seller to be redeemed one year later and uses the cash received from the seller to pay for the good. However, the present value of a bill at the time it is issued is its redemption value discounted by one year's interest. The amount payable by the purchaser at the time the purchase of the good actually takes place is the present discounted price of the bill and not the full redemption price to be paid one year later. It is this discounted price that should be recorded for CPI purposes. The difference between the discounted price and the redemption price is, of course, the interest that the purchaser implicitly pays on the bill over the course of the year. This way of recording corresponds to the way in which bills and bonds are actually valued on financial markets and also to the way in which they are recorded in both business and economic accounts. Deferring payments in the manner just described is equivalent to a price reduction and should be recognized as such in CPIs. The implicit interest payment is not part of the price. Instead, it reduces the price. This example shows that in certain circumstances the market rate of interest can affect the price payable, but it depends on the exact circumstances of the credit arrangement agreed between the seller and the purchaser. Each individual case needs to be carefully considered on its merits.

3.64 This case needs to be clearly distinguished from hire purchase, considered in the next section, when the purchaser actually pays the full price and borrows an amount equal to the full price while contracting to make explicit interest payments in addition to repaying the amount borrowed.

Hire purchase

3.65 In the case of a durable good bought on hire purchase, it is necessary to distinguish the de facto, or economic, ownership of the good from the legal ownership. The time of acquisition is the time the hire purchase contract is signed and the purchaser takes possession of the durable. From then onwards, it is the purchaser who uses it and derives the benefit from its use. The purchasing household becomes the de facto owner at the time the good is acquired, even though legal ownership may not pass to the household until the loan is fully repaid.

3.66 By convention, therefore, the purchasing household is treated as buying the good at the time possession is taken and paying the full amount in cash at that point. At the same time, the purchaser borrows, either from the seller or some financial institution specified by the seller, a sum sufficient to cover the purchase price and the subsequent interest payments. The difference between the cash price and the sum total of all the payments to be made is equal to the total interest payable. The relevant price for CPI purposes is the cash price payable at the time the purchase takes place, whether or not the purchase is facilitated by some form of borrowing. The treatment of hire purchase is the same as that of "financial leasing" whereby fixed assets, such as aircraft, used for purposes of production are purchased by a financial institution and leased to the producer for most or all of the service life of the asset. This is essentially a method of financing the acquisition of an asset by means of a loan and needs to be distinguished from operational leasing such as hiring out cars for short periods of time. The treatment of hire purchase and financial leasing outlined here is followed in both business and economic accounting.

Interest payments

3.67 The treatment of interest payments on the various kinds of debt that households may have incurred raises both conceptual and practical difficulties. Nominal interest is a composite payment covering four main elements whose mix may vary considerably:

- The first component is the pure interest charge: i.e., the interest that would be charged if there were perfect capital markets and perfect information.
- The second component is a risk premium that depends on the creditworthiness of the individual borrower. It can be regarded as a built-in insurance charge under uncertainty against the risk of the debtor defaulting.
- The third component is a service charge incurred when households borrow from financial institutions that make a business of lending money.
- Finally, when there is inflation, the real value of a loan fixed in monetary terms (that is, its purchasing power over real goods and services) declines with the rate of inflation. However, creditors are able to offset the real holding, or capital, losses they expect to incur by charging appropriately high rates of nominal interest. For this reason, nominal interest rates vary directly with the rate of general inflation, a universally familiar phenomenon under inflationary conditions. In these circumstances, the main component of nominal interest may therefore be the built-in payment of compensation from the debtor to the creditor to offset the latter's real holding loss. When there is very high inflation it may account for almost all of the nominal interest charged.

3.68 The treatment of the first component, pure interest, is somewhat controversial but this component may account for only a small part of the nominal interest charged. The treatment of the second component, insurance against the risk of default, is also somewhat controversial.

3.69 The fourth component, the payment of compensation for the creditor's real holding loss, is clearly outside the scope of a CPI. It is essentially a capital transaction. It may account for most of nominal interest under inflationary conditions.

3.70 The third component constitutes the purchase of a service from financial institutions whose business it is to make funds available to borrowers. It is known as the *implicit service charge* and clearly falls within the scope of a CPI. It is included in COICOP. The service charge is not confined to loans made by "financial intermediaries", institutions that borrow funds in order to lend them to others. Financial institutions that lend out of their own resources provide the same kind of services to borrowers as financial intermediaries. When sellers lend out of their own funds, they are treated as implicitly setting up their own financial institution that operates separately from their principal activity. The rates of interest of financial institutions also include implicit service charges. Because some capital markets tend to be very imperfect and most households may not have access to proper capital markets, many lenders are effectively monopolists who charge very high prices for the services they provide, for example village moneylenders in many countries.

3.71 It is clear that interest payments should not be treated as if they were just pure interest or even pure interest plus a risk premium. It is very difficult to disentangle the various components of interest. It may be practically impossible to make realistic and reliable estimates of the implicit service charges embodied in most interest payments. Moreover, for CPI purposes it is necessary to estimate not only the values of the service charges but changes in the prices of the services over time. Given the complexity of interest flows and the fact that the different flows need to be treated differently, there seems to be little justification for including payments of nominal interest in a CPI, especially in inflationary conditions.

Household production

3.72 Households can engage in various kinds of productive activities that may be either aimed at the market or intended to produce goods or services for own consumption.

Business activities

3.73 Households may engage in business or commercial activities such as farming, retail trading, construction, the provision of professional or financial services, and so on. Goods and services that are used up in the process of producing other goods and services for sale on the market constitute *intermediate* consumption. They are not part of the *final* consumption of households. The prices of intermediate goods and services purchased by households are not to be included in CPIs. In practice, it is often difficult to draw a clear distinction between intermediate and final consumption, as the same goods may be used for either purpose.

Consumption of own produce

3.74 Households do not in fact consume directly all of the goods and services they acquire for purposes of consumption. Instead, they use them as inputs into the production of other goods or services which are then used to satisfy their needs and wants. There are numerous examples. For example, basic foodstuffs such as flour, cooking oils, raw meat and vegetables may be processed into bread, cakes or meals with the assistance of other inputs including fuels, the services provided by consumer durables, such as fridges and cookers, and the labour services of members of the household. Inputs of materials, equipment and labour are used to clean, maintain and repair dwellings. Inputs of seeds, fertilizers, insecticides, equipment and labour are used to produce vegetables or flowers, and so on.

3.75 Some of the production activities taking place within households' activities, for example gardening or cooking, may perhaps provide satisfaction in themselves. Others, such as cleaning, may be regarded as chores that reduce utility. In any case, the goods or services used as inputs into these productive activities do not provide utility in themselves. Again, there are numerous examples of such inputs: raw foodstuffs that are unsuitable for eating without being cooked; cleaning materials; fuels such as coal, gas, electricity or petrol; fertilizers; the services of refrigerators and freezers; and so on.

3.76 Utility is derived from consuming the outputs from household production undertaken for own consumption. It is necessary, therefore, to decide whether a CPI should try to measure the changes in the prices of the outputs, rather than the inputs. In principle, it seems desirable to measure the output prices, but there are serious objections to this procedure.

3.77 On a conceptual level, it is difficult to decide what are the real final outputs from many of the more nebulous household production activities. It is particularly difficult to specify exactly what are the outputs from important service activities carried out within households, such as child care or care of the sick or elderly. Even if they could be satisfactorily identified, conceptually they would have to be measured and priced. There are no prices to be observed, as there are no sales transactions. Prices would have to be imputed for them and such prices would be not only hypothetical but inevitably very speculative. Their use in CPIs is not a realistic possibility in general and almost certainly would not be acceptable to most users who are primarily interested in the market prices paid by households.

3.78 The practical alternative is to treat the goods and services acquired by households on the market for use as inputs into the various kinds of household production activities as if they were themselves final consumer goods and services. They provide utility *indirectly*, assuming that they are used exclusively to produce goods and services that are directly consumed by households. This is the practical solution that is generally adopted not only in CPIs but also in national accounts, where household expenditures on such items are classified as final consumption. Although this seems a simple and conceptually acceptable solution to an otherwise intractable problem, exceptions may be made for one or two kinds of household production that are particularly important and whose outputs can readily be identified.

3.79 *Subsistence agriculture*. In the national accounts, an attempt is made to record the value of the agricultural output produced for own consumption. In some countries, subsistence agriculture may account for a large part of the production and consumption of agricultural produce. The national accounts require such outputs to be valued at their market prices. It is doubtful whether it is appropriate to try to follow this procedure for CPI purposes.

3.80 A CPI may record either the actual input prices or the imputed output prices, but not both. If the imputed output prices for subsistence agriculture are included in a CPI, the prices of the purchased inputs should be excluded. This could remove from the index most of the market transactions made by such households. Expenditures on inputs may constitute the principal contact that the households have with the market and through which they experience the effects of inflation. It therefore seems preferable to record the actual prices of the inputs and not the imputed prices of the outputs in CPIs.

3.81 *Housing services produced for own consumption*. The treatment of owner-occupied housing is difficult and somewhat controversial. There may no consensus on what is best practice. This is discussed in several chapters of this manual, especially in Chapters 10 and 23. Conceptually, the production of housing services for own consumption by owner-occupiers is no different from other types of own account production taking place within households. The distinctive feature of the production of housing services for own consumption, as compared with other kinds of household production, is that it requires the use of an extremely large fixed asset in the form of the dwelling itself. In economics, and also national accounting, a dwelling is usually regarded as a fixed asset so that the purchase of a dwelling is classified as gross fixed capital formation and not as the acquisition of a durable consumer good. Fixed assets are used for purposes of production, not consumption. The dwelling is not consumed directly. The dwelling provides a stream of capital services that are consumed as inputs into the production of housing services. This production requires other inputs, such as repairs, maintenance and insurance. Households consume the housing services produced as outputs from this production.

3.82 It is important to note that there are two quite distinct service flows involved:

- One consists of the flow of *capital services* provided by the dwelling which are consumed as *inputs* into the production of housing services.
- The other consists of the flow of *housing services* produced as *outputs* which are consumed by members of the household.

The two flows are not the same. The value of the output flow will be greater than that of the input flow. The capital services are defined and measured in exactly the same way as the capital services provided by other kinds of fixed assets, such as equipment or structures other than dwellings. As explained in detail in Chapter 23, the value of the capital services is equal to the user cost and consists primarily of two elements, depreciation and the interest, or capital, costs. Capital costs are incurred whether or not the dwelling is purchased by borrowing on a mortgage. When the dwelling is purchased out of own funds, the interest costs represent the opportunity cost of the capital tied up in the dwelling; that is, the foregone interest that could have been earned by investing elsewhere.

3.83 There are two main options for the own-account production and consumption of housing services in CPIs. One is to price the output of housing services consumed. The other is to price the inputs, including the inputs of capital services. If housing services are to be treated consistently with other forms of production for own consumption within households, the input approach must be adopted. The production and consumption of housing services by owner-occupiers may, however, be considered to be so important as to merit special treatment.

3.84 If it is decided to price the outputs, the prices may be estimated using the market rents payable on rented accommodation of the same type. This is described as the rental equivalence approach. One practical problem is that there may be no accommodation of the same type that is rented on the market. For example, there may be no rental market for rural dwellings in developing countries where most of the housing may actually be constructed by the households themselves. Another problem is to ensure that the market rents do not include other services, such as heating, that are additional to the housing services proper. A further problem is that market rents, like the rentals charged when durables are leased, have to cover the operating expenses of the renting agencies as well as the costs of the housing services themselves, and also provide some profit to the owners. Finally, rented accommodation is inherently different from owner-occupied housing in that it may provide the tenants with more flexibility and mobility. The transaction costs involved in moving house may be much less for tenants.

3.85 In principle, if the output, or rental equivalence, approach is adopted then the prices of the inputs into the production of housing services for own consumption, such as expenditures on repairs, maintenance and insurance, should not be included as well. Otherwise, there would be double counting.

3.86 The alternative is to price the inputs into the production of housing services for own consumption in the same way that other forms of production for own consumption within households are treated. In addition to intermediate expenditures such as repairs, maintenance and insurance, the costs of the capital services must be estimated and their prices included in the CPI. The technicalities of estimating the values of the flow of capital services are dealt with in Chapter 23. As in the case of other types of production for own consumption within households, it is not appropriate to include the estimated costs of the labour services provided by the owners themselves.

3.87 Whether the input or the output approach is adopted, it is difficult to estimate the relevant prices. The practical difficulties experienced may sometimes be so great as to lead compilers and users to query the reliability of the results. There is also some reluctance to use imputed prices in CPIs, whether the prices refer to the inputs or the outputs. It has therefore been suggested that the attempt to measure the prices of housing service flows should be abandoned. Instead, it may be preferred to include the prices of the dwellings themselves in the CPI. In most cases these are observable market prices, although many dwellings, especially in rural areas in developing countries, are also built by their owners, in which case their prices still have to be estimated on the basis of their costs of production.

3.88 Including the prices of dwellings in CPIs involves a significant change in the scope of the index. A dwelling is clearly an asset and its acquisition is capital formation and not consumption. While the same argument applies to durables, there is a substantial difference of degree between a household durable and a dwelling, as reflected by the considerable differences in their prices and their service lives. In principle, therefore, extending the scope of a CPI to include dwellings implies extending the scope of the index to include household gross fixed capital formation.

3.89 The advantage of this solution is that it does not require estimates of either the input or output service flows, but conceptually it deviates significantly from the concept of a CPI as traditionally understood. In the case of both consumer durables and dwellings, the options are either to record the acquisitions of the assets in the CPIs at their market prices or to record the estimated prices of the service flows, but not both. Just as no service flows from durables are included in CPIs at present because their acquisitions are included, similarly if the prices of dwellings are included in CPIs the service flows would have to be excluded. As explained in Chapter 23, the acquisitions approach may give insufficient weight to durables and dwellings over the long run because it does not take account of the capital costs incurred by the owners of the assets.

Coverage of households and outlets

3.90 The group of households included in the scope of a CPI is often referred to as the "reference households", or the "reference population".

Definition of household

3.91 For CPI purposes, households may be defined in the same way as in population censuses. The following definition is recommended for use in population censuses (United Nations, 1998a):

> A household is classified as either (a) a one person household defined as an arrangement in which one person makes provision for his or her food or other essentials for living without combining with any other person to form part of a multi-person household; or (b) a multi-person

household, defined as a group of two or more persons living together who make common provision for food or other essentials for living. The persons in the group may pool their incomes and have a common budget to a greater or lesser extent; they may be related or unrelated persons or a combination of persons both related and unrelated.

3.92 This definition is essentially the same as that used in household budget surveys and in the SNA. The scope of a CPI is usually confined to private households, and excludes institutional households such as groups of persons living together indefinitely in religious institutions, residential hospitals, prisons or retirement homes. Nevertheless, convalescent homes, schools and colleges, the military, and so on are not treated as institutional households; their members are treated as belonging to their private households. The HICP coverage of households, however, is consistent with the *SNA 1993* definition and thus includes institutional households.

Types of household

3.93 In almost all countries, the CPI scope is designed to include as many private households as possible, and is not confined to those belonging to a specific socio-economic group. The HICP regulations require that coverage should be of households independent of their income level.

3.94 In some countries, however, extremely wealthy households are excluded for various reasons. Their expenditures may be considered to be very atypical, while their expenditure data, as collected in household budget surveys, may be unreliable. The response rates for wealthy households in household budget surveys are usually quite low. In addition, it may be too costly to collect prices for some of the consumer goods and services purchased exclusively by the wealthy. Some countries may decide to exclude other kinds of households. For example, the United Kingdom CPI excludes not only the top 4 per cent of households by income but also households mainly dependent on state pensions, with the net result that roughly 15 per cent of households, and 15 per cent of expenditure, is excluded. Japan and the Republic of Korea exclude households mainly engaged in agriculture, forestry and fishing, and all one-person households. Such exclusions affect the expenditure weights to the extent that the patterns of expenditures of the excluded groups differ from those of the rest of the population.

3.95 In addition to a single wide-ranging official (headline) CPI relevant to the country as a whole, many countries publish a range of subsidiary indices relating to sub-sectors of the population. For example, the Czech Republic compiles separate indices for:

- all households;
- all employees;
- employees with children;
- low-income employees;
- employees, incomplete families;
- pensioners;
- low-income pensioners;
- households in Prague;
- households in communities with populations of over 5,000.

3.96 In India, CPI compilation originated from a need to maintain the purchasing power of workers' incomes, and so four different CPIs are compiled at the national level for reference households headed by the following kinds of workers:

- agricultural labourers;
- industrial workers;
- rural labourers;
- urban non-manual employees.

Geographical coverage

3.97 *Urban and rural.* Geographical coverage may refer either to the geographical coverage of expenditures or the coverage of price collection. Ideally these two should coincide, whether the CPI is intended to be a national or a regional index. In most countries, prices are collected in urban areas only since their movements are considered to be representative of the price movements in rural areas. In these cases national weights are applied and the resulting index can be considered a national CPI. If price movements in urban and rural areas are felt to be sufficiently different – although price collection is restricted to urban areas because of resource constraints – then urban weights should be applied and the resulting index must be considered as purely an urban and not a national CPI. For example, the following countries cover urban households only (expenditure weights and prices): Australia, Mexico, Republic of Korea, Turkey, United States. Most other developed countries tend to use weights covering urban and rural households, although in nearly every case price collection takes place in urban areas only. Of course, the borderline between urban and rural is inevitably arbitrary and may vary from country to country. For example, in France urban price collection is interpreted to include villages with as few as 2,000 residents.

3.98 Decisions about geographical coverage in terms of urban versus rural coverage will depend on population distribution and the extent to which expenditure patterns and the movements of prices tend to differ between urban and rural areas.

3.99 *Foreign purchases of residents and domestic purchases of non-residents.* Problems arise when households make expenditures outside the boundaries of the area or country in which they are resident. Decisions about the treatment of such expenditures depend on the main use of a CPI. For inflation analysis, it is the price change within a country which is of interest. An index of inflation is needed that covers all so-called "domestic" consumption expenditures that take place within the geographical boundaries of the country, whether made by residents or non-residents. HICPs (see Annex 1) are defined in this way as indices of domestic inflation. Thus they exclude consumption expenditures made by residents when they are outside the country (which belong to the inflation indices of the countries where the purchases are made), and they include expenditures within the country made by residents of other countries. In practice, expenditures by visitors from abroad may be difficult to estimate, since household budget surveys do not cover non-resident households, although estimates might be possible for some commodities using retail sales data or special surveys of visitors. These issues become more important when there is significant cross-border shopping as well as tourism.

3.100 When CPIs are used for escalating the incomes of residents, it may be appropriate to adopt the so-called "national" concept of expenditure which covers all the expenditures of residents, whether inside or outside the country, including remote purchase from non-resident outlets, for example by the Internet, telephone or mail. Household budget surveys can cover all these types of expenditure, although it may be difficult to identify the country from which remote (Internet, mail, etc.) purchases are being made. The prices paid for airline tickets and package holidays bought within the domestic territory should also be covered. It can be difficult, however, to obtain price data for the goods and services purchased by residents when abroad, although in some cases sub-indices of the partner countries' CPIs might be used.

3.101 *Regional indices.* When compiling regional indices, the concept of residence applies to the region in which a household is resident. It is then possible to draw a distinction between the expenditures within a region and the expenditures of the residents of that region, analogous to the distinction between the "domestic" and "national" concepts of expenditure at the national level. The same issues arise for regional indices as were discussed in paragraph 3.97. The principles applying to cross-border shopping between regions are the same as for international cross-border shopping, but data availability is generally different. If the scope of the regional index is defined to include the purchases by regional residents when in other regions (abroad), then, although price data for the other regions should be readily available, it is unlikely that expenditure data will be available with the necessary split between expenditure within and expenditure outside the region of residence.

3.102 Care must be taken to treat cross-border shopping in the same way in all regions. Otherwise double counting, or omission, of expenditures may occur when regional data are aggregated. Where regional indices are aggregated to give a national index, the weights should be based on regional expenditure data rather than on population data alone.

3.103 Many countries try to satisfy the differing needs of their many CPI users by deriving a family of indices with differing coverage, headed by a single wide-ranging official (headline) CPI which is relevant to the country as a whole. In some large countries, regional indices are more widely used than the national CPI, particularly where the indices are used for escalating incomes. Thus, in addition to the headline CPI, which has the widest coverage possible, subsidiary indices are published which may relate to:

- sub-sectors of the population;
- geographical regions;
- specific commodity groups; sub-indices of the overall (official all-items) CPI should be published at as detailed a level as possible, since many users are interested in the price change of specific commodity groups.

3.104 In effect, many statistical offices are moving towards a situation in which a database of prices and weights is maintained from which a variety of subsidiary indices is derived.

Outlet coverage

3.105 The coverage of outlets is dictated by the purchasing behaviour of the reference households. As already stated, in principle, the prices relevant to CPIs are the prices paid by households. In practice, however, it is usually not feasible to collect price information directly from households, although as more sales are made through electronic points of sale which record and print out both the items purchased and their prices, it may become increasingly practical to collect information on the actual transaction prices paid by households. In the meantime, it is necessary to rely mainly on the prices at which products are offered for sale in retail shops or other outlets. All the outlets from which the reference population makes purchases are within the scope of the CPI, and should be included in the sampling frame from which the outlets are selected.

3.106 Examples of outlets are:

- retail shops – from very small permanent stalls to multinational chains of stores;
- market stalls and street vendors;
- establishments providing household services – electricians, plumbers, window cleaners, and so on;
- leisure and entertainment providers;
- health and education services providers;
- mail or telephone order agencies;
- the Internet;
- public utilities;
- government agencies and departments.

3.107 The principles governing the selection of a sample of outlets from which to collect prices are discussed in some detail in Chapters 5 and 6.

Price variation

3.108 Price variation occurs when exactly the same good or service is sold at different prices at the same moment of time. Different outlets may sell exactly the same product at different prices, or the same product may be sold from a single outlet to different categories of purchasers at different prices.

3.109 If markets were "perfect" in an economic sense, identical products would all sell at the same price. If more than one price were quoted, all purchases would be made at the lowest price. This suggests that products sold at different prices cannot be identical but must be qualitatively different in some way. When the price differences are, in fact, attributable to quality differences, the price differences are only apparent, not genuine. In such cases, a change in the average price resulting from a shift in the pattern of quantities sold at different prices would reflect a change in the average quality of the products sold. This would affect the volume and not the price index.

3.110 If statistical offices do not have enough information about the characteristics of goods and services selling at different prices, they have to decide whether to assume that the observed price differences are genuine or only apparent. The default procedure most commonly adopted in these circumstances is to assume that the price differences are apparent. This assumption is typically made for both CPI and national accounts purposes.

3.111 However, markets are seldom perfect. One reason for the co-existence of different prices for identical products may be that the sellers are able to practise price discrimination. Another reason may simply be that consumers lack information and may buy at higher prices out of ignorance. Also, markets may be temporarily out of equilibrium as a result of shocks or the appearance of new products. It must be recognized, therefore, that genuine price differences do occur.

Price discrimination

3.112 Economic theory shows that price discrimination tends to increase profits. It may not be feasible to practise price discrimination for goods because they can be retraded. Purchasers discriminated against would not buy directly but would try to persuade those who could purchase at the lowest prices to buy on their behalf. Services, however, cannot be retraded, as no exchange of ownership takes place.

3.113 Price discrimination appears to be extremely common, almost the norm, for many kinds of services including health, education and transport. For example, senior citizens may be charged less than others for exactly the same kinds of health or transportation services. Universities may charge foreign students higher fees than domestic students. As it is also easy to vary the qualities of the services provided to different consumers, it can be difficult to determine to what extent observed price differences are a result of quality differences or pure price discrimination. Sellers may even attach trivial or spurious differences in terms or conditions of sale to the services sold to different categories of purchasers in order to disguise the price discrimination.

3.114 Price discrimination can cause problems with regard to price indices. Suppose, for example, that a service supplier discriminates by age by charging senior citizens aged 60 years or over price p_2 and others price p_1, where $p_1 > p_2$. Suppose, further, that the supplier then decides to redefine senior citizens as those aged 70 years or over while otherwise keeping prices unchanged. In this case, although neither p_1 nor p_2 changes, the price paid by individuals aged 60 to 70 years changes and the average price paid by all households increases.

3.115 This example illustrates a point of principle. Although neither of the stated prices, p_1 and p_2, at which the services are on offer changes, the prices paid by certain households do change if they are obliged to switch from p_2 to p_1. From the perspective of the households, price changes have occurred and a CPI should, in principle, record a change. When prices are collected from sellers and not from households, such price changes are unlikely to be recorded.

Price variation between outlets

3.116 The existence of different prices in different outlets raises similar issues. Pure price differences are almost bound to occur when there are market imperfections, if only because households are not perfectly informed. When new outlets open selling at lower prices than existing ones, there may be a time lag during which exactly the same item sells at different prices in different outlets because of consumer ignorance or inertia.

3.117 Households may choose to switch their purchases from one outlet to another or even be obliged to switch because the universe of outlets is continually changing, some outlets closing down while new outlets open up. When households switch, the effect on the CPI depends on whether the price differences are pure or apparent. When the price differences are genuine, a switch between outlets changes the average prices paid by households. Such price changes ought to be captured by CPIs. On the other hand, if the price differences reflected quality differences, a switch would change the average quality of the products purchased, and hence affect volume, not price.

3.118 Most of the prices collected for CPI purposes are offer prices and not the actual transactions prices paid by households. In these circumstances, the effects of switches in the pattern of households' purchases between outlets may remain unobserved in practice. When the price differences reflect quality differences, the failure to detect such switches does not introduce any bias into the CPI. Buying at a lower price means buying a lower-quality product, which does not affect the price index. However, when the price differences are genuine, the failure to detect switches will tend to introduce an upward bias in the index, assuming households tend to switch towards outlets selling at lower prices. This potential bias is described as *outlet substitution bias.*

Outlet rotation

3.119 A further complication is that, in practice, prices are collected from only a sample of outlets and the samples may change, either because outlets open and close or because there is a deliberate rotation of the sample periodically. When the prices in the outlets newly included in the sample are different from those in the previous outlets, it is again necessary to decide whether the price differences are apparent or genuine. If they are assumed to be apparent, the difference between the price recorded previously in an old outlet and the new price in the new outlet is not treated as a price change for CPI purposes, the difference being treated as attributable to quality difference. As explained in more detail in Chapter 7, if this assumption is correct, the price changes recorded in the new outlets can simply be linked to those previously recorded in the old outlets without introducing any bias into the index. The switch from the old to the new outlets does not have any impact on the CPI.

3.120 If the price differences between the old and the new outlets are deemed to be genuine, however, the simple linking just described can lead to bias. When households change the price they pay for a product by changing outlets, the price changes should be captured by the CPI. As explained in more detail in Chapter 7, it seems that most statistical offices tend to assume that the price differences are not genuine and simply link the new price series on to the old. Given that it is unrealistic to assume that markets are always perfect and that pure price variation never occurs, this procedure, although widely used, is questionable and may lead to upward bias. Such bias is described as *outlet rotation bias*. One possible strategy that has been suggested is to assume that half of any observed price difference between old and new outlets is genuine and half is a result of quality difference, on the grounds that, although inevitably somewhat arbitrary, it is likely to be closer to the truth than assuming that the difference is either entirely genuine or entirely attributable to quality differences (see McCracken, Tobin et al., 1999).

Treatment of some specific household expenditures

3.121 Some of the expenditures made by households may not be on goods and services for household consumption and may therefore fall outside the scope of a CPI. One major category consists of the business expenditures made by households.

Fees of agents and brokers

3.122 When a house is purchased for own use by an owner-occupier, it can be argued that the transfer costs associated with purchase (and sale) should be treated as consumption expenditures in the same way as the brokers' fees incurred when financial assets are bought or sold. The fees paid to an agent to buy or sell houses are included in many national CPIs, provided that the house is to be occupied by the owner and not rented to a third party.

Undesirable or illegal goods and services

3.123 All the goods and services that households willingly purchase in order to satisfy their personal needs or wants constitute consumers' expenditures and therefore fall within the scope of a CPI, irrespective of whether their production, distribution or consumption is illegal or carried out in the underground economy or on the black market. Particular kinds of goods or services must not be excluded because they are considered to be undesirable, harmful or objectionable. Such exclusions could be quite arbitrary and undermine the objectivity and credibility of the CPI:

- First, it should be noted that some goods and services might be deemed to be undesirable at some times and desirable at others, or vice versa. People's attitudes change as they acquire more information, especially as a result of scientific advances. Similarly, some goods or services may be deemed to be undesirable in some countries but not in others at the same point of time. The concept of an undesirable good is inherently subjective and somewhat arbitrary and volatile.
- Second, if it is accepted that some goods and services may be excluded on the grounds that they are undesirable, the index is thereby exposed to actual or attempted manipulation by pressure groups.
- Third, attempts to exclude certain goods or services by pressure groups may be based on a misunderstanding of the implications of so doing. For example, if the CPI is used for escalating incomes, it may be felt that households ought not be compensated for increases in the prices of certain undesirable products. However, excluding them does not imply lowering the index. A priori, excluding some item is just as likely to increase the CPI as reduce it, depending on whether the price increase for the item in question is below or above the average for other goods and services. For example, if it is decided to exclude smoking from a CPI and the price increase for smoking products is below average, excluding smoking actually increases the income of smokers (just as it does for non-smokers).

3.124 While goods and services that households willingly choose to consume should not, in principle, be excluded from a CPI because they are acquired in the underground economy or even illegally, it may be impossible to obtain the requisite data on the expenditures or the prices, especially on illegal goods and services. They may well be excluded in practice.

Luxury goods and services

3.125 When a CPI is used as an index of general inflation, it ought to include all households regardless of their socio-economic group and also all consumer goods and services regardless of how expensive they are. Similarly, the scope of an index used for purposes of escalating incomes should include all the goods and services purchased by the reference households, irrespective of whether any of these goods and services are considered to be luxuries or otherwise unnecessary or undesirable.

3.126 Of course, if the reference households are confined to a select group of households, the index will effectively exclude all those items that are purchased exclusively by households that are not in the group. For example, excluding the wealthiest 5 per cent of households will, in practice, exclude many luxury items from the scope of the index. As already noted, such households may be excluded for various reasons, including the unreliability of their expenditure data and the fact that collecting prices for some items purchased exclusively by a tiny minority of households may not be cost-effective. Once the group of reference households has been decided and defined, however, judgements should not be made about whether to exclude certain of their expenditures that are considered to be non-essential or on luxuries.

Second-hand goods

3.127 Markets for used or second-hand goods exist for most durable goods. Household expenditures include expenditures on second-hand goods and are therefore within the scope of a CPI. Households' sales of durables constitute negative expenditures, however, so that the weights for second-hand goods are based on households' net expenditures: i.e., total purchases less sales. The total expenditure on a particular type of second-hand good is a function of the rate at which it is bought and sold, i.e., a higher turnover rate (number of transactions) gives a higher total expenditure. A higher turnover does not, however, increase the rate at which any individual good can be used for purposes of consumption or the flow of services that may be obtained from the good.

3.128 Households may buy second-hand goods through any of the following routes:

- *Directly from another household* – the selling household will record the proceeds of the sale as receipts. Net expenditures, i.e., expenditures *less* receipts, are zero so no weight is attached to purchases and sales from one household to another.
- *From another household via a dealer* – in principle, households' expenditures on the services of the dealers are given by the values of their margins (the difference between their buying and selling prices). These intermediation services should be included in CPIs. They should be treated in the same way as the fees charged by agents such as financial auxiliaries. The margins may be extremely difficult to estimate in practice. Care should be taken to include trade-ins either as purchases by the dealers or receipts of households.
- *Directly from another sector, i.e., from an enterprise or from abroad* – the weight would be household purchases of the second-hand goods from other sectors *less* sales to other sectors.
- *From an enterprise or from abroad via a dealer* – the appropriate weight is given by household purchases from dealers *less* any household sales to dealers *plus* the aggregate of dealers' margins on the products that they buy from and resell to households. Trade-ins should count as part of sales by households (in the case of cars, the weight given to new cars should not include any deduction for the value of trade-ins).

3.129 In some countries, many of the durables purchased by households, especially vehicles, may be imports of second-hand goods from other countries. The prices and expenditures on these goods enter the CPI in the same way as those for newly produced goods. Similarly, in some countries there may be significant net purchases of second-hand vehicles by households from the business sector, these vehicles possibly carrying more weight in the index than new vehicles purchased by households.

Imputed expenditures on goods and services

3.130 As explained in earlier sections, many of the goods and services acquired and used by households for purposes of their own final consumption are not purchased in monetary transactions but are acquired through barter or as remuneration in kind or are produced by households themselves. It is possible to estimate what households would have paid if they had purchased these goods and services in monetary transactions or, alternatively, what it cost to produce them. In other words, values may be imputed for these non-monetary expenditures.

3.131 The extent to which it is desirable to include imputed expenditures within the scope of a CPI depends partly on the main purpose of the index. If the CPI is intended to be a measure of consumer inflation, it can be argued that only monetary expenditures should be included. Inflation is a monetary phenomenon measured by changes in monetary prices recorded in monetary transactions. Even when the main use of a CPI is for indexation purposes, it can be argued that it should only reflect changes in the monetary prices actually paid by the reference population. Consistent with the objective of monitoring inflation in the European Union, the aim of the Harmonized Index of Consumer Prices (HICP) compiled by Eurostat is to measure inflation faced by consumers. The concept of "household final monetary consumption expenditure" (HFMCE) used in the HICP defines both the goods and services to be covered, and the price concept to be used, i.e., prices net of reimbursements, subsidies and discounts. HFMCE refers only to monetary transactions and includes neither consumption of own production (e.g., agricultural goods or owner-occupied housing services) nor consumption of goods and services received as income in kind.

3.132 When the CPI is intended to be a cost of living index, some imputed expenditures would normally be included within the scope of the CPI on the grounds that the goods and services acquired in non-monetary transactions affect households' living standards. As already noted, most countries include households' imputed expenditures on housing services produced by owner-occupiers but not imputed expenditures on goods such as agricultural goods produced for own consumption.

Price coverage

3.133 A CPI should reflect the experience of the consumers to whom it relates, and should therefore record what consumers actually pay for the goods and services which are included in the scope of the index. The expenditures and prices recorded should be those paid by consumers, including any taxes on the products, and taking account of all discounts, subsidies and most rebates, even if discriminatory or conditional. It may be virtually impossible, however, to take account of all discounts and rebates in practice. Sensible practical compromises are needed, for which recommendations and examples are given in Chapter 6.

3.134 When households pay the full market prices for products and are then subsequently reimbursed by governments or social security schemes for some of the amounts paid, CPIs should record the market prices *less* the amounts reimbursed. This kind of arrangement is common for educational and medical expenditures.

Taxes and subsidies

3.135 All taxes on products, such as sales taxes, excise taxes and value added tax (VAT), are part of the purchasers' prices paid by consumers that should be used for CPI purposes. Similarly, subsidies should be taken into account, being treated as negative taxes on products.

3.136 For some analytical and policy purposes, it may be useful to estimate a CPI that measures price movements excluding the effects of changes in taxes and subsidies. For monetary policy-makers, the price increases resulting from changes in indirect taxes or subsidies are not part of an underlying inflationary process but are attributable to their own manipulation of these economic levers. Similarly, when a CPI is used for escalation purposes, any increase in a CPI resulting from increases in indirect taxes leads to an increase in wages and benefits linked to the CPI, despite the fact that the aim of the tax increase might have been to reduce consumers' purchasing power. Alternatively, an increase in subsidies might be intended to stimulate consumption, but the resulting lower prices could be offset by a smaller increase in indexed wages and benefits.

3.137 *Net price indices.* Net price indices may be compiled in which taxes on consumer goods or services are deducted from the purchasers' prices, and subsidies are added back on. Such indices do not, however, necessarily show how prices would have moved if there were no taxes or changes in taxes. It is notoriously difficult to estimate the true incidence of taxes on products: that is, the extent to which taxes or subsidies, or changes therein, are passed on to consumers. It is also difficult to take account of the secondary effects of changes in taxes. In order to estimate the secondary effects, input–output analysis can be used to work out the cumulative impact of taxes and subsidies through all the various stages of production. For example, some of the taxes on vehicle fuel will enter the price of transport services which in turn will enter the prices of transported goods, some of which will enter the prices paid for consumer goods by retailers and hence the prices which they charge to consumers. To track all these impacts would demand a much more detailed and up-to-date input–output table than is available in most countries. A more practicable alternative is therefore simply to confine the taxes and subsidies for which correction is made to those levied at the final stage of sale at retail; that is, primarily to VAT, sales and excise taxes. Estimating prices less these taxes only, or corrected for changes in these taxes only, is more feasible. In the case of a percentage sales tax or VAT, the calculation is simple, but in the case of excise taxes, it is necessary to ascertain the percentage mark-up by the retailer, since the excise tax will also be marked up by this percentage.

Discounts, rebates, loyalty schemes and "free" products

3.138 CPIs should take into account the effects of rebates, loyalty schemes, and money-off vouchers. Given that a CPI is meant to cover all the reference households, whether in the country as a whole or in a particular region, discounts should be included even if they are available only to certain households or to consumers satisfying certain payment criteria.

3.139 It may be difficult to record discriminatory or conditional discounts for practical reasons. When only one selected group of households can enjoy a certain discount on a specific product, the original stratum for that product is split into two new strata, each experiencing different price changes and each requiring a weight. So, unless base period expenditures for all possible strata are known, it is not possible to record discriminatory discounts correctly. Similarly, with conditional discounts, e.g. discounts on utility bills for prompt payment, it can be difficult to record the effect of the introduction of such offers unless data are available on the proportion of customers taking advantage of the offer. These kinds of practical problems also arise when there is price discrimination and the sellers change the criteria that define the groups to whom different prices are charged, thereby obliging some households to pay more or less than before without changing the prices themselves. These cases are discussed further in Chapter 7.

3.140 Although it is desirable to record all price changes, it is also important to ensure that the qualities of the goods or services for which prices are collected do not change in the process. While discounted prices may be collected during general sales seasons, care should be taken to ensure that the quality of the products being priced has not deteriorated.

3.141 The borderline between discounts and rebates can be hazy and is perhaps best drawn according to timing. In other words, a discount takes effect at the time of purchase, whereas a rebate takes effect some time later. Under this classification, money-off vouchers are discounts, and as with the conditional discounts mentioned above, can only be taken into account in a CPI if they relate to a single product and if the take-up rate is known at the time of CPI compilation. Since this is highly unlikely, the effect of money-off vouchers is usually excluded from a CPI. It should be noted that the discount is recorded only when the voucher is used, not when the voucher is first made available to the consumer.

3.142 Rebates may be made in respect of a single product, e.g. air miles, or may be more general, e.g. supermarket loyalty schemes where a $10 voucher is awarded for every $200 spent. As with discounts discussed above, such rebates can only be recorded as price falls if they relate to single products and can be weighted according to take-up. Bonus products provided "free" to the consumer, either by larger pack sizes or offers such as "two packs for the price of one", should be treated as price reductions, although they may be ignored in practice when the offers are only temporary and quickly reversed. When permanent changes to pack sizes occur, quality adjustments should be made (see Chapter 7).

3.143 Given the practical difficulties in correctly recording all these types of price falls, it is usual to reflect discounts and rebates only if unconditional, whereas loyalty schemes, money-off coupons, and other incentives are ignored. Discounts during seasonal sales may be recorded provided that the quality of the goods does not change.

Classification

3.144 The classification system upon which any CPI is built provides the structure essential for many stages of CPI compilation. Most obviously, it provides the weighting and aggregation structure, but it also provides the scheme for stratification of products in the sampling frame, at least down to a certain level of detail, and it dictates the range of sub-indices available for publication. Several factors must be taken into account when a CPI classification system is being developed.

- First, the classification must reflect economic reality. For example, it must be possible to accommodate new goods and services in a manner that minimizes the need for later restructuring of the higher-level categories. Restructuring is undesirable because many users require long time series, and restructuring of the classification will produce breaks in the series.
- Second, the needs of users for sub-indices should be given a high priority when constructing aggregate groups, so that if, for example, some users are particularly interested in price change in food products, then the classification should provide sufficient detail in that area.
- Third, it is a requirement of any classification that its categories are unambiguously mutually exclusive, and at the same time provide complete coverage of all products considered to be within its scope. In practice this means that it should be a straightforward task to assign any particular expenditure, or price, to a single category of the classification system.

3.145 The availability and nature of the data themselves will also affect the design of a classification system. The availability of expenditure and price data will dictate the lowest level of detail that might be possible. Obviously it is not possible to produce a separate index for a product for which either weights or prices are not available. At the most detailed level, a high variance of the price changes, or relatives, will suggest where additional categories are needed. In line with standard sampling procedures, the stratification scheme should minimize the within-stratum variance while at the same time maximizing the between-stratum variance. The classification should reflect this requirement.

Criteria for classifying consumption expenditure

3.146 Although a classification may be conceived according to economic theory or user requirements using a top-down approach, in practice the statistical compiler collects data about individual products and then aggregates them according to the classification scheme (a bottom-up application). For example, the units of classification for the Classification of Individual Consumption according to Purpose (COICOP) are expenditures for the acquisition of consumer goods and services, not expenditures on purposes as such. Divisions 01 to 12 of COICOP convert these basic statistics into a purpose classification by grouping together the various goods and services which are deemed to fulfil particular purposes, such as nourishing the body, protecting it against inclement weather, preventing and curing illness, acquiring knowledge, travelling from one place to another, and so on.

3.147 Classifications of expenditure data are schemes for aggregating expenditures on products according to certain theoretical or user-defined criteria, such as:

- *Product type* – products may be aggregated by:
  - physical characteristics of goods and the nature of services; for example, biscuits are divided into those with and without a chocolate coat. This criterion can be meaningfully implemented down to the most detailed level, and is the basis of the Central Product Classification 1.0 (United Nations, 1998b);
  - economic activity from which the product originated. The International Standard Industrial Classification of All Economic Activities (ISIC), Revision 3.1 (United Nations, 2002) is the international standard classification;
  - production process from which the product originated;
  - retail outlet type from which the product was purchased;
  - geographical origin of the product.
- *Purpose* to which the products are put, e.g. to provide food, shelter, transport, etc. COICOP is the international standard.
- The *economic environment*, where products could be aggregated according to criteria such as:
  - substitutability of products;
  - complementarity of products;
  - application of sales taxes, consumer subsidies, excise taxes, customs duties, etc.;
  - imports from different countries (and in some cases, a classification of exportable products may be of interest).

Classification by product type

3.148 Where indices of price change for specific products groups are required, a product-based classification would be appropriate. Product classifications may combine several of the criteria listed above; for example, the Classification of Products by Activity (CPA) in the European Economic Community (Eurostat, 1993), which is linked to the CPC at the detailed level and the ISIC at the aggregate level.

3.149 Inevitably, price collectors and index compilers will encounter products for which no detailed class or sub-class exists, for example, entirely new products, or mixed products which are bundles of existing products. This is a problem frequently encountered with high technology goods, telecommunications goods and services, and food items in the form of "ready meals". Initially, the expenditure on these products may be recorded in an "other" or n.e.c. (not elsewhere classified) class, but once expenditure on these products becomes significant, a separate class should be created.

Classification by purpose

3.150 For a CPI compiler aiming to produce a measure of the change in the cost of satisfying particular needs, a purpose-based classification is appropriate. The COICOP breakdown at the highest level is by purpose such that the 12 divisions of COICOP are categories of purpose, and below this level the groups and classes are product types. In other words, products are allocated to purpose headings. The allocation of products is complicated by the existence of multi-purpose products (single products that can be used for a variety of purposes), such as electricity, and mixed purpose (bundled) products, such as package holidays comprising transport, accommodation, meals, and so on.

3.151 *Multi-purpose goods and services*. The majority of goods and services can be unambiguously assigned to a single purpose, but some goods and services could plausibly be assigned to more than one purpose. Examples include motor fuel, which may be used to power vehicles classified as transport as well as vehicles classified as recreational, and snowmobiles and bicycles which may be bought for transport or for recreation.

3.152 In drawing up COICOP, the general rule followed has been to assign multi-purpose goods and services to the division that represents the predominant purpose. Hence, motor fuel is shown under "Transport". Where the predominant purpose varies between countries, multi-purpose items have been assigned to the division that represents the main purpose in the countries where the item concerned is particularly important. As a result, snowmobiles and bicycles are both assigned to "Transport" because this is their usual function in the regions where most of these devices are purchased – that is, North America and the Nordic countries in the case of snowmobiles, and Africa, South-East Asia, China and the low countries of Northern Europe in the case of bicycles.

3.153 Examples of other multi-purpose items in COICOP include: food consumed outside the home, which is shown under "Hotels and restaurants", not "Food and non-alcoholic beverages"; camper vans, which are shown under "Recreation and culture", not "Transport"; and basket-ball shoes and other sports footwear suitable for everyday or leisure wear, which are shown under "Clothing and footwear", not "Recreation and culture".

3.154 National statisticians may wish to reclassify multi-purpose items if they consider that an alternative purpose is more appropriate in their country. Such reclassifications should be footnoted.

3.155 *Mixed purpose goods and services*. Single outlays may sometimes comprise a bundle of goods and services which serve two or more different purposes. For example, the purchase of an all-inclusive package tour will include payments for transport, accommodation and catering services, while the purchase of educational services may include payments for health care, transport, accommodation, board, educational materials, and so on.

3.156 Outlays covering two or more purposes are dealt with case by case with the aim of obtaining a breakdown by purpose that is as precise as possible and consistent with practical considerations of data availability. Hence, purchases for package holidays are shown under "Package holidays" with no attempt to isolate separate purposes such as transport, accommodation and catering. Payments for educational services, in contrast, should as far as possible be allocated to "Education", "Health", "Transport", "Hotels and restaurants" and "Recreation and culture".

3.157 Two other examples of mixed purpose items are: the purchase of in-patient hospital services which include payments for medical treatment, accommodation and catering; and the purchase of transport services which include meals and accommodation in the ticket price. In both cases, there is no attempt to isolate separate purposes. Purchases of in-patient hospital services are shown under "Hospital services" and purchases of transport services with accommodation and catering are shown under "Transport services".

Classifications for consumer price indices

3.158 In practice, most countries use a hybrid classification system for their CPI in the sense that the breakdown of expenditure at the highest level is by purpose, with breakdowns by product at the lower levels. In some countries the higher-level purpose classifications were developed many years ago for CPIs that were originally devised as measures of the changing cost of a basket of goods and services that were, at the time, considered necessary for survival or maintaining some "basic" standard of living. Thus, the classifications were based on consumer needs, where "need" may have had a somewhat subjective interpretation depending on political requirements.

3.159 The recommended practice today is still to use a purpose classification at the highest level, with product breakdowns below, but to use the recently developed international standard classifications as far as possible, with adaptations to national requirements where necessary. In other words, divisions 01 to 12 of COICOP, with Central Product Classification (CPC) product classes and sub-classes mapped onto them to provide the next two levels of detail.

Publication level

3.160 As mentioned above, any restructuring of the classification of published indices will inconvenience users and should be avoided so far as possible by careful planning and development of the classification scheme in the first place. There is a trade-off between providing users with as much detail as they would like in terms of product indices and weights, and preserving some freedom to restructure the lower levels (unpublished) without apparently affecting the published series.

3.161 Item samples below the level at which weights are published can be revised between major weight revisions. As explained in Chapter 9, new and replacement items and varieties can also be introduced provided they can be included within an existing published weight. A major new product, such as a personal computer, could only be introduced at the time of a major weight revision, whereas it might be possible to introduce mobile phones at any time if the lowest-level weight published in the telecommunications category is for telephone services.

Classification of Individual Consumption according to Purpose (COICOP)

3.162 *COICOP structure.* The international standard classification of individual consumption expenditures is the Classification of Individual Consumption according to Purpose (COICOP). COICOP is a functional classification that is also used in *SNA 1993* and covers the individual consumption expenditures incurred by three institutional sectors, i.e. households, non-profit institutions serving households (NPISHs), and general government. Individual consumption expenditures are those which benefit individual persons or households.

3.163 COICOP has 14 divisions:

- division 01 to 12 covering the final consumption expenditure of households;
- division 13 covering the final consumption expenditure of NPISHs;
- division 14 covering the individual consumption expenditure of general government.

The classification has three levels of detail:

- division or two-digit level, e.g. 01. Food and non-alcoholic beverages;
- group or three-digit level, e.g. 01.1 Food;
- class or four-digit level, e.g. 01.1.1 Bread and cereals.

3.164 The 12 divisions covering households consist of 47 groups and 117 classes and are listed in Annex 2. Below the level of class, CPI compilers have to create additional detail by further subdividing the classes according to their national needs. Of course, there are clear advantages, in terms of comparability between countries, and between the different uses of COICOP (CPIs, household expenditure statistics, national accounts aggregates), if the basic, higher-level structure of COICOP is maintained.

3.165 There are some COICOP classes which may, or may not, be included in most CPIs, or for which expenditure data cannot be collected directly from households. For example, COICOP has a class for the imputed rentals of owner-occupiers, which may be outside the scope of some CPIs. COICOP also has a class for financial intermediation services indirectly measured, which may be outside the scope of some CPIs because of practical measurement difficulties. In any case, the expenditures on these services cannot be collected in household budget surveys. Similarly, COICOP has a group for expenditure on insurance service charges, which may be within the scope of CPIs but cannot be measured using household surveys.

3.166 *Type of product.* COICOP classes are divided into: services (S), non-durables (ND), semi-durables (SD) and durables (D). This supplementary classification provides for other analytical applications. For example, an estimate may be required of the stock of consumer durables held by households, in which case the goods in COICOP classes that are identified as "durables" provide the basic elements for such estimates.

3.167 As explained above, the distinction between non-durable goods and durable goods is based on whether the goods can be used only once or whether they can be used repeatedly or continuously over a period of considerably more than one year. Moreover, durables, such as motor cars, refrigerators, washing machines and televisions, have a relatively high purchasers' value. Semi-durable goods differ from durable goods in that their expected lifetime of use, though more than one year, is often significantly shorter and their purchasers' value is substantially less. Because of the importance attached to durables, the categories of goods defined as durables in COICOP are listed below:

- furniture, furnishings, carpets and other floor coverings;
- major household appliances;
- tools and equipment for house and garden;
- therapeutic appliances and equipment;
- vehicles;
- telephone and fax equipment;
- audiovisual, photographic and information processing equipment (except recording media);
- major durables for recreation;
- electrical appliances for personal care;
- jewellery, clocks and watches.

The following goods are listed as semi-durables:

- clothing and footwear;
- household textiles;
- small electrical household appliances;
- glassware, tableware and household utensils;
- spare parts for vehicles;
- recording media;
- games, toys, hobbies, equipment for sport, camping, etc.

3.168 Some COICOP classes contain both goods and services because it is difficult for practical reasons to break them down into goods and services. Such classes are usually assigned an (S) when the service component is considered to be predominant. Similarly, there are classes which contain either both non-durable and semi-durable goods or both semi-durable and durable goods. Again, such classes are assigned a (ND), (SD) or (D) according to which type of good is considered to be the most important.

Appendix 3.1 Consumer price indices and national accounts price deflators

1. The purpose of this appendix is to explain why and how consumer price indices (CPIs) differ from the price indices used to deflate household consumption expenditures in national accounts. The differences between the two kinds of price index are often not well understood.

Coverage of households

2. The sets of households covered by CPIs and the national accounts are not intended to be the same, CPIs typically covering a smaller set of households. Household consumption expenditures in national accounts cover the expenditures made by all households, including institutional households resident in the country or region, whether those expenditures are made inside or outside the country or region of residence. CPIs tend to cover the expenditures and prices paid by households within the geographical boundaries of a country or region, whether the households are residents or visitors. More importantly, most CPIs are purposely defined to cover only selected groups of non-residential households. For example, CPIs may exclude very wealthy households or be confined to households in urban areas or headed by wage-earners.

Coverage of consumption expenditures

3. The sets of expenditures covered by CPIs and national accounts are not intended to be the same, CPIs typically covering a smaller set of expenditures. Most CPIs do not cover most of the imputed non-monetary consumption expenditures included in national accounts, either on principle or in practice because of lack of data. Many CPIs include the imputed rents on owner-occupied housing, but CPIs are not intended to cover the imputed expenditures and prices of agricultural products or other goods produced for own consumption that are included in national accounts.

Timing

4. Most CPIs measure price changes between two points of time or very short intervals of time such as a week. The price indices in national accounts are intended to deflate expenditures aggregated over long periods of time, generally a year. The ways in which monthly or quarterly CPIs are averaged to obtain annual CPI indices are unlikely to be conceptually consistent with the annual price indices in national accounts.

Index number formulae

5. The index number formulae used by CPIs and national accounts are not intended to be the same. In practice, most CPIs tend to use some kind of Lowe price index that uses the quantities of an earlier period, whereas the price indices, or price deflators, in national accounts are usually meant to be Paasche indices. Paasche indices are used in order to obtain Laspeyres volume indices. These differences, arising from the use of different index formulae, would tend to be reduced if both CPIs and national accounts adopted annual chaining.

Conclusions

6. It is clear that, in general, CPIs and the price deflators for national accounts can differ for a variety of reasons, such as major differences in the coverage of households and expenditures, differences in timing and differences in the underlying index number formulae. These differences are intentional and justified. Of course, the price data collected for CPI purposes may also be used to build up the detailed price deflators used for national accounts purposes, but at an aggregate level CPIs and national accounts deflators may be quite different for the reasons just given.

EXPENDITURE WEIGHTS AND THEIR SOURCES 4

Introduction

4.1 A consumer price index (CPI) is usually calculated as a weighted average of the price changes for the consumption goods and services covered by the index. The weights are meant to reflect the relative importance of the goods and services as measured by their shares in the total consumption of households. The weight attached to each good or service determines the impact that its price change will have on the overall index. The weights should be made publicly available in the interests of transparency, and for the information of the users of the index.

4.2 The weights depend on the scope of the index which, in turn, depends on the main use, or uses, for the index. The uses and scope of a CPI have already been explained in some detail in the two previous chapters. This chapter therefore focuses on the derivation and compilation of the weights and the data sources that may be used to estimate them. In practice, the weights usually refer to expenditures on consumption goods and services by households, as distinct from the actual use of those goods and services to satisfy the needs and wants of households. Expenditure-based weights are appropriate for a CPI based on the *acquisitions approach*. The difference between the acquisitions and uses approach to CPIs was explained in the previous chapter.

4.3 In the special case of owner-occupied housing, however, many countries adopt the uses rather than the acquisitions approach. They measure changes in the prices of the flows of housing services consumed by households as distinct from changes in the prices of dwellings. It is shown in Chapter 23 of this manual that one important consequence of adopting the uses approach to owner-occupied housing is that its weight in the overall CPI is considerably greater than when the acquisitions approach is used. The reason is that the values of the housing services consumed by owner-occupiers have to cover not only the depreciation on the houses purchased but also the interest costs on the capital invested in the dwellings. Over a period of years, the uses approach may well give twice as much weight to owner-occupied housing as the acquisitions approach. Reference may be made to Chapter 23 for further details and explanation.

The weighting structure of the consumer price index

4.4 As explained in more detail in Chapters 7 and 9, the calculation of a CPI usually proceeds in two stages. In the first stage, elementary indices are estimated for each of the elementary aggregates. Elementary indices are constructed by (a) collecting a sample of representative prices for each elementary aggregate, and then (b) calculating an average price change for the sample. In the second stage, a weighted average is taken of the elementary indices using the expenditures within the elementary aggregates as weights.

4.5 Elementary aggregates are usually the smallest groups of goods and services for which expenditure data are available to be used as weights. They may cover the whole country or separate regions within the country. Likewise, elementary aggregates may be distinguished for different types of outlets. The nature of the elementary aggregates depends on circumstances and the availability of expenditure data. Elementary aggregates may therefore be defined differently in different countries. In general:

- Elementary aggregates should consist of groups of goods or services that are as similar as possible.
- They should also consist of goods or services that may be expected to have similar price movements. The objective is to minimize the dispersion of price movements within the aggregate.
- The elementary aggregates should be appropriate to serve as strata for sampling purposes in the light of the sampling regime planned for the data collection.

4.6 The aggregation structure for a CPI is illustrated in Figure 4.1 using the Classification of Individual Consumption according to Purpose (COICOP) described in Chapter 3, although similar national classifications may be used instead:

- First, the entire set of consumption goods and services covered by the overall CPI is divided into *divisions*, such as "food and non-alcoholic beverages".
- Each *division* is then divided into *groups*, such as "food".
- Each *group* is further divided into *classes*, such as "bread and cereals".
- Each class may be divided into more homogeneous *sub-classes*, such as "rice".
- Finally, a *sub-class* may be further subdivided to obtain the *elementary aggregates*, by dividing according to region or type of outlet, as illustrated in Figure 4.1. In some cases, a particular sub-class cannot be, or does not need to be, further subdivided, in which case the sub-class becomes the elementary aggregate.

The sub-classes and elementary aggregates are not part of COICOP itself but more detailed breakdowns of COICOP classes that are needed for CPI purposes.

Figure 4.1 Typical aggregation structure of a consumer price index (CPI)

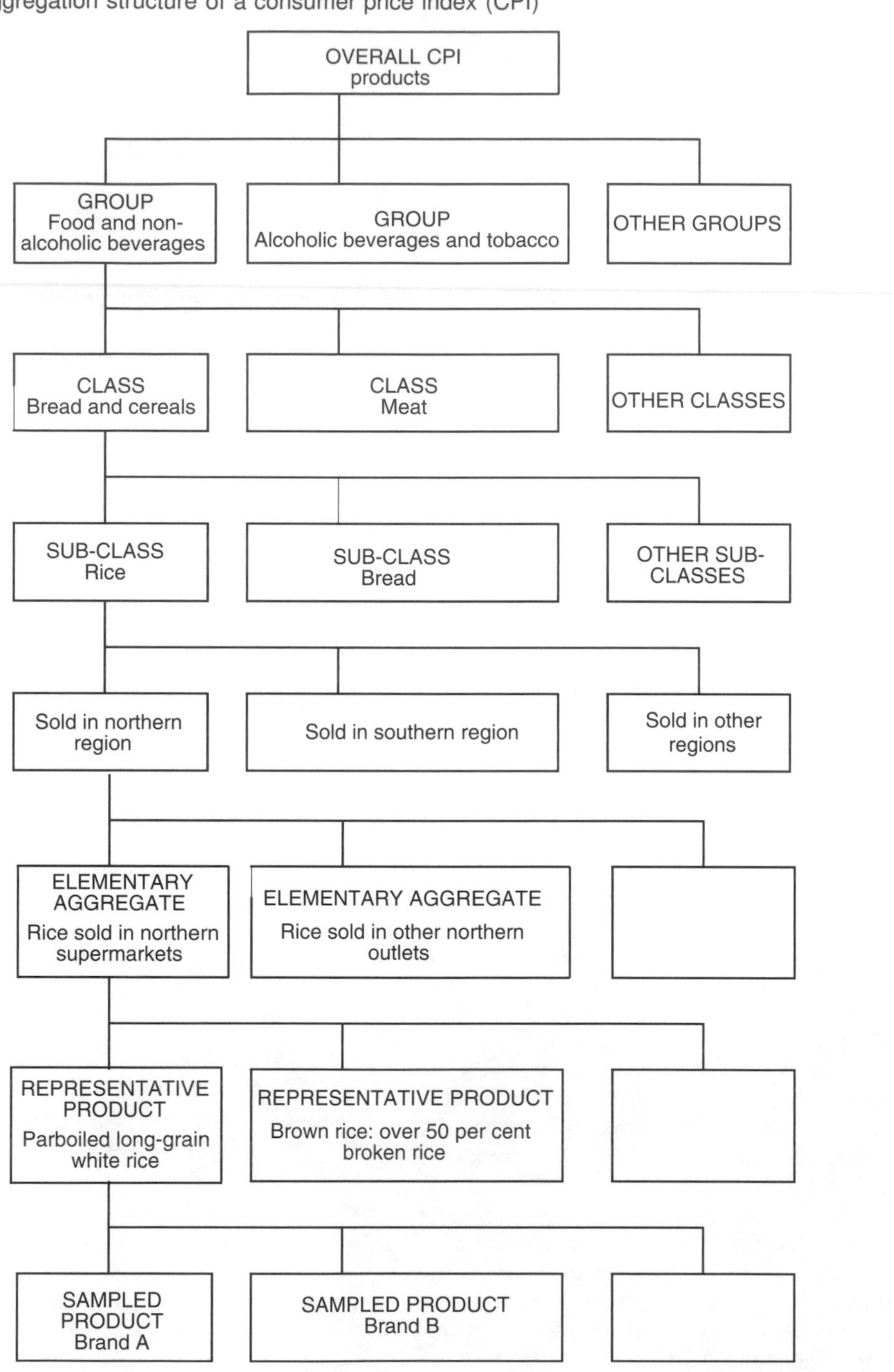

4.7 Within each elementary aggregate, one or more products are selected to represent the price movements of all the goods and services in the elementary aggregate. For example, the elementary aggregate consisting of rice sold in supermarkets in the northern region covers all types of rice, from which parboiled white rice and brown rice with over 50 per cent broken grains are selected as *representative products*. Of course, more representative products might be selected in practice. Finally, for each kind of representative product, a number of individual products can be selected for price collection, such as particular brands of parboiled rice. Again, the number of *sampled products* selected may vary depending on the nature of the representative product.

4.8 The methods used to calculate the *elementary price indices* from the individual price observations collected within each elementary aggregate are explained in Chapter 9, and are not of immediate concern here. Working upwards from the *elementary price indices*, all indices above the elementary aggregate level are described as *higher-level indices* that can be calculated from the elementary price indices using the elementary expenditure aggregates as weights. The aggregation structure is consistent, so that the weight at each level above the elementary aggregate is always equal to the sum of its components. The price index at each higher level of aggregation can be calculated on the basis of the weights and price indices for its components, that is, the lower-level or elementary price indices. The individual elementary price indices are not necessarily sufficiently reliable to be published separately, but they remain the basic building blocks of all higher-level indices. Above the level of the elementary aggregate, therefore, no new information is introduced into the calculation of the CPI.

Group, class and sub-class weights

4.9 The weights for the groups, classes and sub-classes are their shares in the total consumption expenditures of the reference population. They are most often derived from household expenditure surveys (HESs). These surveys are also described as household budget surveys (HBSs). As these surveys are sample surveys subject to reporting and non-response errors as well as sampling errors, the estimated shares for certain sub-classes are often modified or revised on the basis of supplementary or additional information from other sources.

Regional weights

4.10 Within a given sub-class, the regional weight shows the consumption expenditure in the region in proportion to the expenditure in the whole country for that sub-class. For example, if 60 per cent of the total expenditure on fresh fruit occurs in the North region and 40 per cent in the South region, then the regional weight for fresh fruit is 60 per cent for the North region and 40 per cent for the South region.

4.11 A region may also be a geographical area, a city or a group of cities, with a particular location or of a certain size. The rationale for introducing regional weights is to create more homogeneous entities which are likely to experience similar price movements and have similar consumption patterns. For example, there may be quite large differences in consumption patterns and price developments between urban and rural areas. It may be necessary to distinguish different regions in federal countries because CPIs for the provinces or local states may be required for administrative or political purposes. In addition, in federal countries indirect taxes and hence price development may differ between the provinces.

4.12 Regional weights may typically be obtained from the HES or they may be estimated from retail sales data or population data. Regional weights may or may not be introduced into the CPI, depending on the size and structure of the country, data availability, resources and the purpose of the index.

Outlet or outlet-type weights

4.13 Prices are collected from a variety of outlets and outlet types. Information about the sale or market share of the outlets may be used to form elementary aggregate weights specific to a given region and outlet type. One advantage from applying outlet weights is that it may allow prices to be collected centrally from supermarkets or other types of chain outlets.

Elementary aggregate weights

4.14 The elementary aggregate weights are the stratum weights according to expenditure class or sub-class, region and type of outlet. For example, expenditures within the sub-class "fresh fruit" may be divided into four regions, each having its own regional weight, as in Table 4.1. Assume further that it is known or estimated that 60 per cent is sold in supermarkets and 40 per cent in independent outlets, and that this same breakdown holds for all regions. Let the weight of fresh fruit in the CPI for the whole country be, say, 5 per cent. If no breakdown by region or outlet is carried out, then the sub-class as a whole becomes the elementary aggregate carrying a weight of 5 per cent in the overall index.

4.15 If weights are available by region but not by type of outlet, the 5 per cent is distributed over the four regions to obtain four separate elementary aggregates, one for each region. For example, the elementary aggregate for the North region will have a weight of $0.20 \times 0.05 = 1.0$ per cent in the overall CPI for the whole country. If a further division can be made according to type of outlet as well as region, then each region comprises two elementary aggregates: one for supermarkets and one for independent outlets. The weight for, say, the elementary aggregate for fresh fruit in the North region sold in supermarkets is then $0.12 \times 0.05 = 0.6$ per cent in the overall CPI for the whole country.

Data sources

4.16 The decision about what source or sources to use and how they should be used depends on an analysis of their respective advantages and disadvantages, and on the main purpose of the index. In most countries, the two main sources for calculation of the weights are the HES and the national accounts estimates for households' final consumption expenditures. Additional information may, however, be obtained from production and trade statistics, or from government departments, producers, marketing bodies and individual enterprises. Such additional information is particularly useful for estimating weights at the most detailed level. Although several of the sources may have been used to prepare the national

Table 4.1 Example of weights by region and outlet type for the sub-class "fresh fruit"

	Regional weights	Type of outlet	
		Supermarkets (60 per cent)	Independent (40 per cent)
North	20	12	8
South	40	24	16
West	30	18	12
East	10	6	4
Total	100	60	40

accounts estimates, they may be able to provide further details that were not used by the compilers of the national accounts.

Household expenditure surveys

4.17 As the HES may have been designed to serve more than one purpose, it is desirable to ensure that the survey design also meets the requirements for the CPI. The main requirements are that the survey should be representative of all private households in the country, and not exclude any particular group, and should include all types of consumption expenditures by households.

4.18 The HES may include payments that are outside the scope of the CPI: for example, payments of income taxes, life insurance premiums, remittances, gifts and other transfers, investments, savings and debt repayments. These should be excluded from the total used to calculate the expenditure shares that serve as the basis for estimating the CPI weights. There may also be a difference in the population coverage between the intended scope for the CPI and the actual scope of the HES, but the effects on the CPI of any consequent bias in the resulting weight estimates are likely to be very minor if the HES is designed to provide results for the whole population and not just a particular population group.

4.19 National food surveys are special surveys in which the primary emphasis is on collecting information on family expenditures for food products. These surveys provide a very detailed breakdown of food expenditures that can be used to derive the weights for elementary aggregates for food below the level of a COICOP class.

4.20 The HES may provide the basis for estimating specific weights for regions with different consumption patterns. These weights should be applied to the respective elementary price indices to calculate indices for the regions concerned.

4.21 In general, HES data for certain types of expenditures may not be sufficiently reliable and need to be checked against data from other sources. Certain types of expenditures may not even be covered by an HES so that they have to be estimated using other sources. The reliability of the CPI weights will obviously depend to a large extent on the reliability of the household expenditure data. As the HES is a sample survey, the estimates are bound to be subject to sampling errors, which may be relatively large for small or infrequent expenditures. The quality of the estimates will also suffer from non-response and from the under-reporting of some types of consumption. Under-reporting is probably the most serious and common problem affecting HESs. Some expenditures are not reported because the purchases are small or exceptional, and therefore easy to forget. Although large, estimates of expenditures on durable goods may also be problematic, since they are only purchased very infrequently. Some expenditures are not reported because the products have a social stigma or are illegal (e.g., drugs, alcohol and tobacco). When no adjustments are made for such under-reporting, the consequence is an under-estimation of the weights for these items and an over-estimation of the weights for the correctly reported items. For these reasons, to the extent possible, results from the HES should be compared and/or combined with the statistics from other sources when constructing CPI weights, especially when the HES sample is small.

4.22 For the purposes of the CPI, it is desirable for the HES to be conducted annually. This will allow countries to revise and update their expenditure weights each year. One advantage of annual updating of weights is that the differences between the results obtained from the use of different index number formulae tend to be reduced. Any bias which may follow from using a Lowe index that uses a fixed basket of goods and services will not have time to accumulate to a significant magnitude, as explained in Chapters 1, 9 and 15.

4.23 Some countries conduct continuous HESs with gradually rotating samples. A programme of annual surveys with samples large enough to provide the type of estimates required for CPI weights can, however, be very costly. For this reason, some countries conduct large-scale surveys at ten-year or five-year intervals, perhaps supplemented with a smaller annual sample. Other countries distribute a large sample over several years. The average of the results over several successive years of smaller-scale surveys may provide a set of satisfactory annual estimates. The weights derived in this way as the average rates of expenditure over periods of two or three years will also smooth any erratic consumer behaviour over a short period, for example as a result of events such as droughts or floods, civil strife, oil shocks, or exceptionally mild or cold winters.

4.24 It should be noted that in some countries it may be possible to experiment with new methods of recording expenditures in an HES by using scanner data generated by electronic points of sale. For example, by collecting the printed bar code receipts for cash which customers receive, the Icelandic HES could obtain, at virtually no cost to the surveyed households, precise information about types and brands of goods purchased in different outlets.

National accounts

4.25 There may be differences in the scope and definition of consumption between the national accounts and the CPI, and also a difference in the reference population of households between the national accounts and the HES.

4.26 First, in national accounts, the household sector consists of all resident households, including people living in institutional households. HESs, however, do not usually cover persons living permanently in institutional households, such as retirement homes or religious institutions. If the CPI is meant to cover all resident households, therefore, national accounts estimates may be used to adjust the HES data.

4.27 Second, as already explained in Chapter 3, it is possible to have two alternative concepts of total final consumption, *domestic* and *national*. The domestic concept refers to consumption on the economic territory, including the consumption of visiting foreign households but excluding the consumption of resident households when abroad. The national concept used in national accounts refers to the consumption of all the residents of the country, whether at home or abroad, the consumption of non-residents being excluded. The HES usually covers only resident households, and may or may not cover their expenditures abroad, depending on the instructions given to the respondents.

4.28 National accounts data may be used to improve HES weights for products that are under-reported in the HES. Note that national accounts figures for households' final consumption are usually based on statistics from the HES *and* from several other sources. This means that national accounts estimates are likely to be useful for estimating weights for consumption categories that tend to be wrongly reported in the HES, and where results from the HES suffer from a significant and distorting partial or total non-response rate.

Retail sales data

4.29 Statistics on retail sales by region and type of outlet may be available for broad groups of items. One disadvantage is that some of the sales may be to groups outside the reference population, perhaps to the business sector or to the government. The corresponding purchases do not form part of household private consumption. Some sales may also be to non-residents, who may or may not be part of the reference population. Furthermore, for regional sales data, it needs to be kept in mind that sales may include sales to people living in other regions.

Point-of-purchase surveys

4.30 Point-of-purchase surveys may provide statistics that can be used to estimate weights for price data, as they permit the analysis of shopping patterns for various segments of the population. Households are asked, for each item purchased, about the amounts spent in each outlet where purchases have been made, and the name and addresses of these outlets. On this basis, a list of outlets can be established, with the total sales for all the different items to the sample of households. A sample of outlets is then drawn from this list, with probability proportional to the sales. Given that household surveys are expensive and that there is an overlap between the HES and point-of-purchase survey, it is possible to combine the two data-collecting activities in an integrated survey that elicits expenditure and outlet data at detailed levels, along with the demographic information about the households needed for sub-group indices.

4.31 A simpler version of this survey may be conducted to obtain weights for groups of products by outlet type. In this case, a purposive sample of each outlet type should be selected. As an alternative, in the absence of this type of survey, national retail sales statistics by outlet type from a survey of outlets could be used to estimate a breakdown of sales by outlet type.

Scanner data

4.32 In the last few years some countries have started to use statistics obtained from cash register data to derive CPI weights. These statistics are based on electronic data records that are stored as scanner data in the databases of sellers. Such scanner data sets include the quantities sold and the corresponding value aggregates. (The cash register receipts usually give the following information: name of the outlet, date and time of purchase, description of items bought, quantity, price and value, form of payment, and VAT amount where relevant.) A comparison of the results from the HES with the corresponding scanner data from the biggest supermarket chains indicates that the use of scanner data can add to the reliability of the weights (Guðnason, 1999). This strengthens the case for using such data to revise CPI weights more often than otherwise would be possible, and probably at lower cost. The limitations of this source of information should, however, be borne in mind. The first one is that scanned data cannot be connected to a specific type of household, whereas the data from the HES can. Another important difference between HES data and scanner data from sellers is that the HES data cover goods bought from outlets that are not using this technology, as well as goods and services that do not carry scanner codes, regardless of where they are sold. Although the use of electronic data records is increasing every year, significant components of the retail trade market are not using scanner data even in countries that are electronically most advanced.

Population censuses

4.33 Population censuses provide statistics on the geographical distribution of the population and households, as well as on the regional differences in household size and composition. Combined with estimates of regional levels of household expenditure, these statistics can be used to estimate regional expenditure weights, especially when such estimates are not available from an HES with a satisfactory degree of precision. In the absence of any expenditure statistics, population statistics might be used as the basis for regional weights. Such estimates for the weights usually have to assume that expenditures per capita or per household are the same in all regions, and have to ignore the fact that there are usually large differences between the urban and rural populations in the level and pattern of items that they consume.

Deriving the weights in practice

4.34 Once the reference population and the coverage of goods and services have been decided, the weights need to be derived. In principle, this is a relatively simple matter, as the weights are calculated as the proportions of the total consumption expenditure of all goods and services included in the index basket for the reference population during the reference period. In practice, however, the calculation of weights is not so straightforward and involves a series of steps.

Payments that are not consumption expenditures

4.35 Only *consumption expenditures* are relevant for the construction of CPI weights. As explained in

Chapter 3, outlays such as payments of social security contributions or income taxes, or repayments of debts, are irrelevant and should be ignored because they are not consumption expenditures.

Unimportant expenditures

4.36 Each elementary aggregate consists of a fairly homogeneous group of products from which one or more representative products are selected for pricing. Some products may have a weight which for all practical purposes is negligible and for which prices are unlikely to be collected in practice. The HES, which in most cases is the main source for deriving the detailed weights, usually includes observations on a much larger variety of goods and services than it is practical to collect prices for. The prices of very minor products may not be worth collecting if they contribute almost nothing to the CPI.

4.37 Even though it may be decided not to collect prices for a certain product, it remains within the scope of the CPI. Some price change has to be explicitly or implicitly assumed, or imputed, and weighted by expenditures. There are two options:

- The product and the expenditures on it remain within the elementary aggregate, even though no prices are collected for it. The elementary price index for the aggregate as a whole is estimated entirely by the prices of the representative products for which prices are collected. This is equivalent to assuming that the price of the product changes at the same rate as the average for the prices of the representative products.
- The alternative is to reduce the weight for the elementary expenditure aggregate by excluding the expenditures on the product. This is equivalent to assuming that the price of the excluded product would have moved in the same way as the overall CPI for all the products actually included in the index.

4.38 In principle, the CPI should cover all types of products and expenditures within its scope, even if prices are not collected for some products. It might be decided, for example, to exclude from the index calculations groups with weights lower than, say, 0.1 per cent for food groups and 0.2 per cent for non-food groups. A lower minimum threshold for the food items might be set because the prices for these products tend to display greater variability and because prices for food products are normally less expensive to collect. If an expenditure group is excluded, its weight may be redistributed to another expenditure group that is similar in terms of content and price development. Alternatively, the expenditures may be completely excluded from the calculation of the weights.

Products that are difficult to price

4.39 Among the consumption expenditures, there are likely to be a few products for which the prices, or price changes, cannot be directly or satisfactorily measured, for example, illicit drugs or payments for catering and other service charges for private receptions and parties. Even if reliable prices cannot be obtained, these products should be included in the calculation of the weights if they are within the scope of the index. For difficult-to-price products, the options available are the same as those used for unimportant expenditures.

Use and combination of different sources

4.40 In most countries, the main source for deriving the weights is the HES. As noted above, however, the results from the HES need to be carefully examined and adjusted to take account of under- or over-reporting of certain types of products. The usual strategy is to use supplementary information from other relevant sources to adjust the HES results in order to derive the weights.

4.41 In countries where national accounts data provide reliable estimates of household expenditures, these data can be used to derive the weights at an aggregate level. Detailed HES data can then be used to break down or adjust these weights. In this way, it is possible to reconcile the detailed data from the HES with the aggregate national accounts data to calculate the weights. Weights for the main consumption groups can be obtained from the national accounts down to a certain level of disaggregation, say, 70 consumption groups or classes. Each of these weights can then be further distributed by applying the detailed HES expenditure groups to the national accounts consumption groups or classes. The combination of national accounts and HES data ensures consistency between the CPI and the national accounts data on consumption expenditure of households at the level of the main consumption groups.

Adjusting the weights derived from household expenditure surveys

4.42 As, in most cases, the information from a household expenditure survey is only available with a lag – often around 18 months or more – the new weights will lag behind the new price reference period for the index, which is the period when the new weights are introduced.

4.43 Adjustments might need to be made to the estimates based on the HES results to take into account any significant changes in expenditure patterns in the period between the time that the survey was carried out and the time that the new weights were introduced. Adjustments will typically be made for products which are significantly losing or gaining in importance during this period. It is also possible that expenditure on some products may not be available from the HES because the products appeared on the market after the survey had been completed. One example is mobile telephones and the corresponding charges, which emerged as significant new forms of expenditure in the late 1990s in many countries. Necessary adjustments then need to be made to the survey data to take into account the changes that have occurred. The expenditures on these new products should be estimated on the basis of information available from other sources (e.g., import and retail trade statistics), taking into account the need to exclude expenditures by enterprises and for business purposes.

Weight reference period

4.44 The weight reference period is the time period to which the estimated weights relate. The choice of the period covered by the expenditure statistics used to derive the weights is crucial. Generally speaking, the period chosen as the base should be long enough to cover a seasonal cycle. Further, if the index is not annually chained, the year chosen should have economic conditions that can be considered to be reasonably normal or stable. To achieve this, it may be necessary to adjust some of the values to normalize them and overcome any irregularities in the data for the particular period that constitutes the source of the information. The weight reference period should not be too distant from the price reference period. The weight reference period is typically a single calendar year. A month or quarter is too short a period to use as a weight base period, since any one month or quarter is likely to be affected by accidental or seasonal influences. In some instances, data for a single year may not be adequate either because of unusual economic conditions or because the sample is not large enough. An average of several years of expenditure data may then be used to calculate the weights. Countries in which this method is applied include the United States and the United Kingdom. In the United States, the expenditure information from the Consumer Expenditure Survey over a three-year period is used. In the United Kingdom, an average of three years of Expenditure and Food Survey data is used for regional weights, for stratification and for a limited number of groups of products where prices tend to be particularly volatile.

4.45 During periods of high inflation, multiple year weights may be calculated by averaging value shares rather than averaging actual value levels. Averaging the value levels will give too much weight to the data for the most recent year. Another option is to update the values for each year to a common period and then to compute a simple arithmetic average of adjusted yearly data.

4.46 As the weight reference period usually precedes the price reference period, the expenditure weights may be price updated to take account of the relative price changes from the weight reference period to the price reference period. Price updating of weights is discussed in more detail in Chapter 9, paragraphs 9.95 to 9.104.

Need for revising the weights

4.47 Most countries calculate their CPI as the change in the value of a specified basket of goods and services. An index of this general kind is described in this manual as a Lowe index. Its properties and behaviour are explained in Chapters 1, 9 and 15. Although CPIs are often described as Laspeyres indices, they are usually not Laspeyres indices in practice. A Laspeyres index is defined as an index in which the basket of goods and services is that of the price reference period, but a typical CPI basket uses the basket of some weight reference period that precedes the price reference period, as just explained. As many countries continue to use the same fixed basket of goods and services over a period of years, the question arises of how often the basket should be revised in order to ensure that it does not become out of date and irrelevant.

4.48 In the short run, consumers will change consumption patterns in response to shifts in relative prices, mostly between products included in the same class or sub-class. Over longer time periods, consumption patterns are also influenced by factors other than price changes. Most importantly, changes in the level and distribution of household income will cause a shift in demand for goods and services towards goods and services with higher income elasticities. Demographic factors such as ageing of the population, and technological changes, such as the increase in the use of computers, are examples of other factors that affect spending behaviour in the longer run. Furthermore, new products will be introduced and existing ones may be modified or become obsolete. A fixed basket will be unresponsive to all these changes.

4.49 As a result of both relative price changes and long-term effects, the weights may become out of date and less representative of current consumption patterns. As shown in Chapter 15, the bias in a Lowe index is likely to increase with the age of the weights. At some point, it therefore becomes desirable to use the weights of a more recent period to ensure that the index is weighting appropriately the price changes currently faced by consumers.

Frequency of updating the weights

4.50 The 1987 ICLS resolution concerning consumer price indices recommended that the weights should be updated periodically, and at least once every ten years, to guarantee the representativity of the index. However, the 2003 ICLS resolution proposes more frequent updates of the weights, such as once every five years, to ensure their relevance. Countries which are experiencing significant economic changes and thus more rapid changes in consumption patterns should update their weights even more frequently, say annually.

4.51 The need to revise the weights generally increases as the length of time from the weight reference period increases. The decision when to update the weights depends, for the most part, on the differences observed between the current weighting structure and that for the weight reference year. Changes in the relative importance of each item can be observed through expenditure survey results. If these statistics are available only at irregular intervals, the frequency of weight revision may necessarily be linked to the availability of results from the HES.

4.52 The introduction of new weights each year might possibly cause an upward drift in the index if there are big fluctuations in consumption caused by factors such as an economic blockade, or extremely favourable or unfavourable weather conditions. In general, the profile of the index time series can be sensitive to the selection of the weight reference period. It might be best to use a "normal" consumption period, if possible, as the basis for weighting information and to avoid periods in which there are special factors at work of a temporary nature. All available information concerning the nature of consumption in a weight reference period should be taken into consideration.

4.53 When the weights are to be fixed for several years, the objective should be to adopt weights that are not likely to change much in the future rather than precisely reflect the activity of a particular period that may be abnormal in some way.

4.54 Each year it is desirable to carry out a review of the weights in order to ensure that they are sufficiently reliable and representative. The review, which may be confined to weights at the level of sub-indices and their major components, should examine whether or not there are indications that important changes may have taken place in the consumption pattern since the weighting reference period.

4.55 Whenever the weighting pattern has been updated, the new index using updated weights should be calculated for an overlapping period with the old one so that the two can be linked.

Classification

4.56 In deriving the weights, the detailed expenditure items identified in the HES must be mapped to the CPI expenditure classes. If HES classes do not match CPI expenditure classes, the HES results must be transformed to match the CPI categories. This can be done by aggregating or disaggregating the relevant HES headings over the relevant CPI expenditure classes. Such transformation is achieved much more easily and more reliably if the coding list for expenditure items in the HES is coordinated with the corresponding list of items used for collecting price observations for the CPI.

4.57 For the purposes of international comparison, the classification scheme of goods and services should, to the extent practical, be in line with the United Nations Classification of Individual Consumption according to Purpose (COICOP) (see Annex 2). To facilitate estimation and application of weights, it is also desirable that the classification used be consistent with the classifications used for HESs and other statistics (for example, retail sales statistics). In the interests of maintaining both coordination of the statistical system and international comparability, the HES should also use a classification for types of expenditure that will be consistent with COICOP, and it should also be possible to establish a mapping between products in the retail sales price collections and COICOP. Another important objective is that the aggregation structure employed by the classification system should meet the major needs of users.

4.58 Using COICOP as an example, the classifications have the following hierarchical structure:

- *groups*: there are 47 of these in COICOP;
- *classes*: sub-divisions of the groups;
- *sub-classes*: the lowest-level categories that are weighted and usually the most detailed level of the structure for which index series are published – these are the expenditure components and weights that remain fixed when using a fixed weight index;
- *individual products*: the lowest level of the CPI basket, that is, the individual goods and services for which prices are actually collected – this is the level at which the composition of the CPI basket can be adjusted between two major revisions of the weighting structure to reflect changes in product supply and consumer behaviour.

4.59 Upper-level indices are formed by weighting together lower-level indices through progressive levels of aggregation, as defined by the classification structure. Weights are fixed for a period (say one, three or five years) between index reweighting.

4.60 The selection of the level in the index hierarchy at which the structure and weights are fixed for a period is particularly important. The main advantage of setting the level relatively high is that the actual samples of products and their prices below this level can be adjusted and updated as needed. New products can be introduced into the samples, and the weights at the lower level re-established on the basis of more recent information. There is thus a greater opportunity to keep the index representative, through an ongoing review of the sample of representative products.

4.61 If the level is set relatively low in the index structure, there is less freedom to maintain the representativeness of the index on an ongoing basis, and there will be a greater dependence on the periodic index review and reweighting process. In such circumstances, the arguments for frequent reweighting become stronger.

Items requiring special treatment

4.62 Some products, such as seasonal products, insurance, second-hand goods, expenditures abroad, etc., may need special treatment when constructing their weights. Reference may be made to Chapters 3, 10 and 22 for further details.

4.63 *Seasonal products*. Various approaches may be used to deal with seasonal products, for example:

- a fixed weights approach, which assigns the same weight for the seasonal product in all months, using an imputed price in the out-of-season months. Seasonal products are treated in the same way as other consumption products;
- a variable weights approach, in which a changing (or moving) weight is attached to the product in various months. In this method, the weights of the seasonal products change monthly according to changes in the quantities consumed during the different months of the weight reference period. The principle of a fixed basket – i.e. fixed weights – should, however, be maintained at least at some level of aggregation.

4.64 The advantage of applying the fixed weights method is mainly that it is consistent with the methods used for other consumption goods and services, and with the fixed basket index formula. In contrast to the moving weights method, the fixed weights method reflects monthly changes in prices only, and not in quantities. Another disadvantage of the moving weights method is that the weights are based on the monthly seasonal fluctuations in the weight reference period, whereas the monthly fluctuations in consumption may differ every year.

4.65 The fixed weights method may also have disadvantages, a major one being that during the months that fresh fruits or vegetables disappear, prices and indices have to be estimated or imputed for these items (or, as is done in some countries, prices and indices have to be frozen throughout the period of disappearance). These imputations need not be made when applying the moving weights method. In addition, the average fixed weight determined for all months of the year does not actually reflect the monthly consumption. Therefore, if there is a negative correlation between prices and quantities, there may be an upward bias in the index.

4.66 The choice of measuring seasonal goods according to the fixed weights method or the moving weights method should be based on whether the focus is on month-to-month changes or on the long-term index changes. The use of an annual basket and the use of annual expenditure shares are appropriate where the main interest is in the longer-run trend of price changes. On the other hand, if the focus is on month-to-month changes, then the annual weights attached to each month-to-month price relative can be unrepresentative of actual transactions that are taking place in the two consecutive months under consideration. In the latter case, monthly price changes for items that are out of season can be greatly magnified by the use of annual weights.[1] To satisfy the needs of different users, it may be appropriate to construct *two* indexes: one for the short-term measurement of price changes (with variable monthly weights) and another longer-term index (with fixed annual weights). The issue of seasonal items is dealt with in detail in Chapter 22.

4.67 *Insurance.* As explained in the section on insurance in Chapter 3, the weights for non-life insurance could be based on either the gross premiums paid or on the implicit service charges. The implicit service charges for administering the insurance and providing the insurance services are estimated by the gross premiums *plus* the income from investment of the insurance reserves *less* the amounts payable to policy holders in settlement of claims.[2] The net premiums are defined as the gross premiums less the service charges: in other words, the net premiums equal the claims. The net premiums and claims can be regarded as transfers, or redistributions, between policy-holding households. In general, it seems preferable to base the weights for non-life insurance on the service charges. These are the estimated amounts paid by households for the services provided by insurance firms. However, a case can also be made for basing the weights on the gross premiums. This is a difficult area in which there is not yet a consensus.

4.68 *Second-hand goods, including used cars.* As already explained in paragraphs 3.127 to 3.129 of Chapter 3, the prices of used or second-hand durable goods purchased by households are included in the CPI in the same way as the prices of new goods. However, households also sell used durables, such as cars. If the price of a second-hand good rises, a purchasing household is worse off, but a selling household is better off. From a weighting perspective, sales constitute negative expenditures, which implies that price changes for used goods *sold* by households implicitly carry a *negative* weight in the CPI. In effect, purchases and sales of second-hand goods *between households*, whether directly or indirectly through a dealer, cancel out (except for the dealers' margins, see Chapter 3) and carry no weight in the CPI. However, households also buy from, and sell to, other sectors. For the reference population as a whole, namely the entire set of households covered by the CPI, the weight to be attached to a particular kind of second-hand good is given by households' total expenditures on it *less* the value of the households' receipts from sales to/from *outside the household sector*. There is no reason why these should cancel out on aggregate. For example, many of the second-hand cars purchased by households may be imported from abroad. The difference between total expenditures and total sales is usually described as households' net expenditures. This is the weight to be attached the second-hand good in question.

4.69 Except in the case of used cars, however, it is practically impossible to estimate the net expenditure because most HESs do not collect the data that would allow for a comparison between expenditures and receipts from sales of individual kinds of second-hand goods. Usually, only the total amount received from the sale of second-hand goods is collected. This information does, however, give an idea of the volume and significance of these transactions in the national economy. In countries where this volume is small, second-hand goods (except used cars) may be ignored when calculating the weights of the index.

4.70 Because the amounts spent on purchasing second-hand cars are usually large, they should be included in the CPI basket if the data are available. In the absence of reliable data, however, their weight can be added to the weight of new cars.

4.71 Most countries include expenditure on second-hand goods in the estimation of CPI weights, but second-hand goods are not covered in the price collection (because of the difficulty of pricing the same good each month or, where the goods are different, making an appropriate quality adjustment). It is therefore assumed that the prices of new and second-hand goods move in the same way.

4.72 In countries where second-hand purchases are important and their prices are believed to change at different rates from those of new goods, separate weights are needed for them. The information could be obtained, at least for some major durables, from HESs, if the surveys ask about expenditure on second-hand and new goods.

4.73 *Expenditure abroad and expenditures by non-residents.* If the objective is to construct an index which

[1] For example, the impact of change in tomato prices at the beginning of the season would be overstated in the general index. Similarly, its impact in the peak months would be understated.

[2] In the national accounts, the gross premiums *plus* the investment income *less* the estimated service charges are described as "net premiums". By definition, "net premiums" equal claims payable, both flows being treated as transfers, or redistributions, between policy-holding households. The "net premiums" are not regarded as expenditures.

is representative of price movements within a given country or area, the weighting system must reflect purchases by both resident and non-resident households. In practice, the proportion of total purchases that are made by visitors from abroad or other areas may be difficult to estimate, except for certain types of purchases in geographical areas where foreign tourism is the dominant economic activity. Sources other than HESs must be used in order to ensure that the weights include the expenditures made by foreign tourists and reflect all purchases of consumer goods and services made by resident or non-resident households within the country. These sources may be national accounts or commercial sales statistics.

4.74 Where the main purpose of the index is to measure price changes experienced by the resident population, the weights should include their expenditures abroad. This would require collection, through the HES, of data on expenditures made outside the country (for example, expenditures on hotels and meals during holidays, durables, health and education). Possible ways of constructing the index to cover expenditure abroad would be:

- price collection outside the country of residence;
- the use of appropriate sub-indices provided by the statisticians in other countries for the kinds of products purchased there by residents;
- establishing a panel of residents who would report prices paid for their purchases abroad.

4.75 Given the limitations of HESs to provide reliable data on expenditures abroad, and the practical difficulties of constructing an index for expenditure abroad, the weights may have to be based on expenditure surveys without adjusting for the place of acquisition, and prices may be collected only for the goods and services acquired in the economic territory of the country. Such an approach assumes that the price changes of the goods and services acquired abroad are the same as those for the same goods and services acquired at home.

Errors in weighting

4.76 If all prices moved in the same way, weights would not matter. On the other hand, the greater the variation in price behaviour between products, the greater the role of weights in measuring aggregate price change.

4.77 Small changes in the weights usually have very little effect upon the overall CPI. An error in the weight for a given sub-index only matters to the extent that the change in the sub-index differs from the average change in the overall CPI. In general, the higher a sub-index's weight, the lower is the tolerable percentage error in that weight. It follows that the tolerable error in the weights declines as the rate of *relative* price change for the relevant items increases. Finally, it is also clear that while errors in weighting may not have a large influence on the overall index, the sub group-level errors could be significant. Australian experience shows that even items with relatively large weights can tolerate errors of 20–30 per cent in the weights (Australian Bureau of Statistics, 2000). According to Eurostat's studies, CPIs are fairly insensitive to changes in weights. Eurostat has, however, suggested developing quality control procedures for monitoring the weights of items for which changes in prices have diverged from the movement of the overall index (Eurostat, 2001). The question of the effects of weighting errors on the sub-index and the overall index is discussed in Rameshwar (1998).

SAMPLING

5

Introduction

5.1 The procedure used for price collection by a national statistical office in the production of a consumer price index (CPI) is a sample survey. In fact, in many countries, it might be better viewed as composed of many different surveys, each covering different subsets of the products covered by the index. We will therefore begin by outlining some of the general concepts of survey sampling which need to be kept in mind when looking at a particular survey such as price collection for a CPI.

5.2 There is a *target quantity*, for example a CPI, which is defined with respect to:

- a *universe* consisting of a finite population of units (e.g. products);
- one or more *variables* that are defined for each unit in the universe (e.g. price and quantity);
- a formula which combines the values of one or more of these variables for all units in the universe into a single value called a *parameter* (e.g. the Laspeyres index).

The interest is in the value of this parameter.

5.3 The universe usually has three dimensions. There is a *product dimension*, consisting of all purchased products and varieties of products. There is a *geographical and outlet dimension* consisting of all places and channels where a product is sold. Finally, there is a *time dimension* consisting of all sub-periods within an index period. The time dimension will be given less attention since price variation is usually smaller over a short time span and since temporal aspects may be dealt with in product and outlet specifications.

5.4 In this chapter, the first two dimensions will be regarded as being static over the time periods considered in the index. In other words, it will be assumed that the same products and outlets are in the universe in both periods, or that replacements between old and new products or outlets are one to one and without problems. For the complications arising from dynamic changes in the universe, please refer to Chapter 8, where replacement, resampling and quality adjustment are discussed.

5.5 Why take only a sample of units? Apart from the near physical impossibility and prohibitive cost of trying to cover all products in all outlets, the data are likely to be of better quality if there are fewer units to deal with because of the use of more specialized and better trained data collectors. Also, the time required to complete the exercise is shorter.

5.6 In *probability sampling*, the units are selected in such a way that each unit (an outlet or a product) has a known non-zero probability of selection. For example, outlets are selected at random from a business register in which each outlet has an equal chance of being selected. Traditionally, however, *non-probability sampling* methods have mainly been used in the compilation of a CPI for choosing outlets or products. The representative item method is particularly popular for selecting items. Other methods used are cut-off sampling and quota sampling (see below). There are also instances of a mixture of the two methods of sampling; for example, outlets are selected using probability sampling techniques, whilst products are selected using the representative item method.

5.7 Having decided to sample, there are two issues to be considered: how to select the sample; and how to use the sample values to estimate the parameter. The former reflects the choice of sampling design, and the latter constitutes the estimation procedure. We first take a look at sampling design.

Probability sampling techniques

5.8 This section presents some general concepts and techniques of survey sampling that have important applications for price indices. This brief presentation covers those concepts of survey sampling that are of immediate interest in price index applications. For a full treatment of the subject, please refer to one of the many textbooks available, for example Särndal, Swensson and Wretman (1992) or Cochran (1977).

5.9 Survey sampling theory views the universe as composed of a finite number (N) of observational units denoted $j = 1, \ldots, N$. Sampling then amounts to selecting n units out of N by attaching an inclusion probability, π_j, to each unit. For price indices there are two sampling designs that are of particular interest.

5.10 In *simple random sampling* and *systematic sampling* each unit is sampled with equal probability and we have $\pi_j = n/N$. In simple random sampling, all units are selected using a random mechanism. In systematic sampling, the sampling units are selected at equal distances from each other in the frame, with random selection of only the first unit. These techniques are usually recommended in situations where the units are relatively homogeneous.

5.11 In *probability proportional to size (pps) sampling* the inclusion probability is proportional to some auxiliary variable x_j and we have $\pi_j = nx_j / \sum_{j=1}^{N} x_j$. Units for which initially this quantity is larger than one are selected with certainty, whereafter the inclusion probabilities are calculated for the remainder of the universe.

5.12 The universe may be divided into strata, denoted $h = 1, \ldots, H$. In each stratum, there are then N_h

units and we have $\sum_{h=1}^{H} N_h = N$. The purpose of stratification is usually to group units together that are either homogeneous in some sense or satisfy some administrative convenience such as being physically close together. Each stratum is a mini-universe with sampling taking place independently in each one. In a CPI, the practice is to use elementary aggregates as strata. In the remainder of this chapter, we look at sampling in a single stratum, corresponding to an elementary aggregate, and drop the subscript h.

Implementing probability sampling in consumer price indices

5.13 A *sampling frame* is a list of all (or most) of the N units in the universe. A frame may have overcoverage to the extent that it includes units that are not in the universe or includes duplicates of units. It may have undercoverage to the extent that some units in the universe are missing from the frame.

5.14 Sampling frames for the outlet dimension could be:

- Business registers. These should include locations of retail trade businesses with addresses and be updated regularly. If a size measure (turnover or number of employees) is included in the register, it is a useful device for performing probability proportional to size (pps) sampling and this size measure would then be included in the universe parameter also.
- Telephone directories ("yellow pages"). These usually do not include size measures so simple random sampling or systematic sampling would then be necessary. Sometimes informal knowledge of the importance of different outlets could be used to stratify the universe into two or more categories and then draw a relatively larger sample from the more important strata.
- Records of local administrations, organizations of enterprises, and so on, could be used for local markets and suchlike, which are especially important in developing countries.

5.15 Sampling frames for the product dimension could be:

- product lists provided by major wholesalers showing sales values for varieties in an earlier period. Sales values provide an obvious size measure for weights and pps sampling;
- outlet-specific lists of products. These lists could also be drawn up by the price collectors themselves by noting the products displayed on the shelf. Shelf space could then be used as a size measure for pps sampling.

Sampling techniques based on probability proportional to size

5.16 Several techniques exist for drawing pps samples. They fall into two main categories according to whether the size of the sample is fixed or random. A fixed, predetermined sample size is clearly desirable for CPIs since the sample size in each stratum is often small and a random size would entail the risk of an empty sample. We therefore present two techniques here that provide fixed size pps samples.

Table 5.1 Systematic sample of 3 out of 10 outlets, based on probability proportional to size

Outlet	Number of employees = x	Cumulative x	Inclusion interval	Included when starting point is 25
1	13	13	1–13	
2	2	15	14–15	
3	5	20	16–20	
4	9	29	21–29	X
5	1	30	30	
6	25	55	31–55	X
7	10	65	56–65	
8	6	71	66–71	
9	11	82	72–82	
10	8	90	83–90	X

5.17 *Systematic pps sampling*. The procedure is best explained by an example. In Table 5.1 we show how a sample of 3 outlets can be drawn from 10. In this case we have the number of employees as our size measure. We look at the list, where we have included the cumulative sizes and the inclusion intervals. We take the total number of our size measure, which is 90 in this case, and divide it by the sample size, 3. This gives us a sampling interval of 30. We next choose a random number between 1 and 30 (random number functions are given in, for example, the Excel spreadsheet software). Say that we get 25. The sample will then consist of the outlets whose inclusion intervals cover the numbers 25, 25 + 30 and 25 + 2 × 30.

5.18 Systematic sampling is easy to execute. If, however, the frame has some overcoverage, the sample size will not be the predetermined one. Let us say that, at the first visit to the outlets, we discover that outlet 6 does not sell the products in the product sample. We would then be left with a sample of only two outlets. We would either be content with that, or somehow seek a replacement for the invalid outlet, which is not determined by the basic sampling procedure. Moreover, the selected sample depends on the order in which the outlets or products are listed. This might be important, especially if the listing order is correlated to the size measure.

5.19 *Order pps sampling*. This is a relatively new method for drawing pps samples. Rosén (1997a, 1997b) gives its theory. In this case, a uniform random number U_i between 0 and 1 and a variable $z_i = nx_i/\sum_i x_i$, where x_i is a size variable, are associated with each sampling unit and a *ranking variable* is constructed as a function of these two variables. The units in the universe are then sorted in ascending order and the n units with the smallest values of the ranking variable are included in the sample. Two important examples of such ranking variables Q_i are:

- for sequential pps sampling: $Q_i = U_i/z_i$;
- for Pareto pps sampling: $Q_i = U_i(1-z_i)/z_i(1-U_i)$.

5.20 For the same universe as above and with Pareto pps as our example, we show in Table 5.2 how this works. We have now ordered the universe in ascending order with respect to the ranking variable. Our first

Table 5.2 Pareto sample of 3 out of 10 outlets, based on probability proportional to size

Outlet	x_i	U_i	Q_i	Sample
6	25	0.755509	0.036943	X
1	13	0.198082	0.207721	(X)
8	6	0.915131	0.310666	X
9	11	0.277131	0.346024	X
10	8	0.834138	0.380468	
7	10	0.709046	0.412599	
4	9	0.46373	0.580264	
3	5	0.500162	1.25	
5	1	0.067941	1.836435	
2	2	0.297524	2.926051	

sample turns out to consist of outlets 6, 1 and 8. Say that we now discover, however, that it is inappropriate to include outlet 1. We then turn to the fourth unit in order – outlet 9 – and include that one instead. Thus, order pps sampling is easy to combine with a fixed sample size and more flexible than systematic sampling.

5.21 Neither of the two order sampling procedures is, however, exactly pps, because the obtained inclusion probabilities vary somewhat from the desired ones. Rosén (1997b) shows, however, that for the purpose of estimating means and variances, they are approximately pps. In the case of the price index, this still holds when there is sample substitution resulting from overcoverage. Pareto pps is marginally better than sequential pps and should therefore be preferred.

5.22 Order pps sampling is at present used in many areas of the Swedish CPI, for example for sampling:

- outlets from the business register (the size measure is number of employees +1);
- products from databases provided by major retail chains (the size measure is historic sales);
- car models from the central car register (the size measure is number of cars registered in the reference period).

5.23 Further details on the application of these procedures are given in Statistics Sweden (2001). Rosén (1997b) shows that Pareto pps and systematic pps are the two optimal pps sampling methods. Pareto pps permits an objective assessment of estimation precision. With regard to final precision, however, Pareto pps is best in some situations whereas systematic pss is best in other situations. The choice between them is therefore a matter of judgement and practicality in a particular sampling situation. The great flexibility of order pps sampling with regard to imperfections in the frame, an aspect of importance in CPI applications, leads us to make this procedure our first recommendation among pps procedures.

Sampling methods used by the US Bureau of Labor Statistics

5.24 The US Bureau of Labor Statistics (BLS) uses probability methods in all stages of sample selection. In the last stage, individual items in outlets are selected in a process designed to approximate pps sampling with respect to the sales of each such item. To this end, the BLS field representatives are allowed to use any of four procedures for determining the sales proportions (U.S. BLS, 1997):

- obtaining the proportions directly from a respondent;
- ranking the subgroups/items by importance of sales as indicated by the respondent and then obtaining the proportions directly or using pre-assigned proportions;
- using shelf space to estimate the proportions where applicable;
- using equal probability.

5.25 The advantages of this procedure, according to the BLS, are that it ensures an objective and efficient probability sampling procedure, where no other such procedure would be available. It allows broad definitions of the item strata so that the same tight specification need not be priced everywhere. The wide variety of specific items greatly reduces the within-item component of variance, reduces the correlation of price movement between areas, and allows a reduction of the sample size needed for a given variance.

5.26 A potential pitfall in this approach is that, if the sales value measure is taken during a very short period, it may coincide with a special campaign with temporarily reduced prices. It could then happen that an item with a temporarily reduced price is given a large inclusion probability. Since this price will tend to increase more than average, an overestimating bias may result. It is thus essential that the sampling of the item takes place at an earlier point in time than the first price collection or that sales values from an earlier period are used. Okamoto (1999) emphasizes this point for Japan, where price bouncing seems to be a very common phenomenon.

Non-probability sampling techniques

5.27 Modern statistical sampling theory focuses on probability sampling. Use of probability sampling is also strongly recommended and standard practice for all kinds of statistical surveys, including economic surveys. But price index practice in most countries is still dominated by non-probability techniques. It may then be fruitful to speculate somewhat about the rational and irrational reasons for this situation. In the following section we discuss a number of such possible reasons, one by one. We then go on to consider some non-probability techniques.

Reasons for using non-probability sampling

5.28 *No sampling frame is available.* This is often true for the product dimension but less frequently so for the outlet dimension, for which business registers or telephone directories do provide frames, at least in some countries, notably in Western Europe, North America and Oceania. There is also the possibility of constructing tailor-made frames in a limited number of cities or locations, which are sampled as clusters in a first stage. For products, it may be noted that the product assortment exhibited in an outlet provides a natural sampling frame, once the outlet is sampled as a kind of cluster, as in the BLS sampling procedure presented above. So the absence of sampling frames is not a good enough excuse for not applying probability sampling.

5.29 *Bias resulting from non-probability sampling is negligible.* There is some empirical evidence to support this assertion for highly aggregated indexes. Dalén (1998b) and De Haan, Opperdoes and Schut (1999) both simulated cut-off sampling of products within item groups. Dalén looked at about 100 groups of items sold in supermarkets and noted large biases for the sub-indices of many item groups, which however almost cancelled out after aggregation. De Haan, Opperdoes and Schut used scanner data and looked at three categories (coffee, babies' napkins and toilet paper) and, although the bias for any one of these was large, the mean square error (defined as the variance plus the squared bias) was often smaller than that for pps sampling. Biases were in both directions and so could be interpreted to support Dalén's findings. The large biases for item groups could, however, still be disturbing. Both Dalén and De Haan, Opperdoes and Schut report biases for single-item groups of many index points.

5.30 *We need to ensure that samples can be monitored for some time.* If we are unlucky with our probability sample, we may end up with a product that disappears immediately after its inclusion in the sample. We are then faced with a replacement problem, with its own bias risks. Against this, it may happen that short-lived products have a different price movement from the price movement of long-lived ones and constitute a significant part of the market, so leaving them out will create bias.

5.31 *A probability sample with respect to the base period is not a proper probability sample with respect to the current period.* This argument anticipates some of the discussion in Chapter 8 below. It is certainly true that the bias protection offered by probability sampling is to a large extent destroyed by the need for non-probabilistic replacements later on.

5.32 *Price collection must take place where there are price collectors.* This argument applies to geographical sampling only. It is, of course, cheaper to collect prices near the homes of the price collectors, and it would be difficult and expensive to recruit and dismiss price collectors each time a new sample is drawn. This problem can be reduced by having good coverage of the country in terms of price collectors. One way to achieve this is to have a professional and geographically distributed interviewer organization within the national statistical agency, which works on many surveys at the same time. Another way of reducing the problem is to have a first-stage sample of regions or cities or locations which changes only very slowly.

5.33 *The sample size is too small.* Stratification is sometimes made so fine that there is room for only a very small sample in the final stratum. A random selection of 1–5 units may sometimes result in a final sample that is felt to be skewed or otherwise to have poor representativity properties. Unless the index for this small stratum is to be publicly presented, however, the problem is also small. The skewness of small low-level samples will even out at higher levels. The argument that sample size is too small has a greater validity when it relates to first-stage clusters (geographical areas) that apply to most subsequent sampling levels simultaneously.

5.34 *Sampling decisions have to be taken at a low level in the organization.* Unless price collectors are well versed in statistics, it may be difficult for them to perform probability sampling on site. Such sampling would be necessary if the product specification that has been provided centrally covers more than one product (price) in an outlet. Nevertheless, in the United States (U.S. BLS, 1997) field representatives do exactly this. In Sweden, where central product sampling (for daily necessities) is carried to the point of specifying well-defined varieties and package sizes, no sampling in the outlets is needed. In countries where neither of these possibilities is at hand, full probability sampling for products would be more difficult.

5.35 In some situations, there are thus valid reasons for using non-probability techniques. We discuss two such techniques below.

Cut-off sampling

5.36 Cut-off sampling refers to the practice of choosing the n largest sampling units with certainty and giving the rest a zero chance of inclusion. In this context, the term "largeness" relates to some measure of size that is highly correlated with the target variable. The word "cut-off" refers to the borderline value between the included and the excluded units.

5.37 In general, sampling theory tells us that cut-off sampling does not produce unbiased estimators (see paragraphs 5.51 to 5.60 below for a discussion of bias and variance), since the small units may display price movements which systematically differ from those of the larger units. Stratification by size or pps sampling also has the advantage of including the largest units with certainty while still giving all units a non-zero probability of inclusion.

5.38 If the error criterion is not minimal bias but minimal *mean square error* (= variance + squared bias) then, since any estimator from cut-off sampling has zero variance, cut-off sampling might be a good choice where the variance reduction more than offsets the introduction of a small bias. De Haan, Opperdoes and Schut (1999) demonstrate that this may indeed be the case for some item groups.

5.39 Often, in a multi-stage sampling design there is room for only a very small number of units at a certain stage. Measurement difficulties that are sometimes associated with small units may then be a reason, in addition to large variances, for limiting price collection to the largest units.

5.40 Note that a hybrid design can also be applied in which there is a certainty stratum part, some probability sampling strata and a low cut-off point below which no sample at all is drawn. In practice, this design is very often used where the "below cut-off section" of the universe is considered insignificant and perhaps difficult to measure.

5.41 A particular CPI practice that is akin to cut-off sampling is for the price collector to select the most sold product in an outlet, within a centrally defined specification. In this case, the sample size is one (in each outlet) and the cut-off rule is judgemental rather than exact, since exact size measures are only rarely available. In all cases of size-dependent sampling in an outlet, it is crucial to take a long-term view of size, so that temporarily large sales during a short period of reduced prices are not taken as a size measure. Such products will tend to increase in price in the immediate future much more than the product group which they represent and thus create a serious overestimating bias.

Quota sampling

5.42 Many product groups, even rather small ones, are quite heterogeneous in nature, and the price varies according to a large number of subgroups or characteristics. There may well be different price movements going on within such a product group, and a procedure to represent the group by just one or a few tightly specified product types may then carry an unnecessarily great risk of bias.

5.43 The definition of quota sampling is that the selected sample shall have the same proportions of units as the universe with respect to a number of known characteristics, such as product subgroup, type of outlet, and location. The actual selection of sampling units is then done by judgemental procedures in such a manner that the composition of the final sample meets the quota criteria.

5.44 The following example illustrates the concept of quota sampling. A sample of 20 package holidays is desired. It is known that, in the universe, 60 per cent of the holidays are to Spain, 30 per cent to Greece, and 10 per cent to Portugal. Of the travel groups, 70 per cent comprise 2 adults, 20 per cent comprise 2 adults + 1 child, and 10 per cent comprise 2 adults + 2 children. Of the sample, 20 per cent stay in 2-star hotels, 40 per cent in 3-star hotels, 30 per cent in 4-star hotels, and 10 per cent in 5-star hotels. With this information, it is possible to design the sample purposively so that all these proportions are retained in the sample, which then becomes self-weighted. Note that these proportions reflect volumes, not values, and may need to be adjusted depending on the elementary aggregate formula used.

5.45 Quota sampling requires central management of the whole sampling process, which may limit its usefulness in some situations. It is more difficult, but not impossible, to manage a quota sampling system where local price collection is used. One would then need to divide the price collectors into subgroups with somewhat different instructions for selecting products. A limitation of quota sampling, as in other non-probability sampling, is that the standard error of the estimate cannot be determined.

The representative item method

5.46 This is the traditional CPI method. The central office draws up a list of product types, with product-type specifications. These specifications may be tight, in that they narrowly prescribe for the price collectors what products they are permitted to select, or they may be loose, giving the price collector freedom to choose locally popular varieties.

5.47 The method with tight specifications is in a sense diametrically opposite to the quota sampling method discussed above. Unless the product groups are defined so as to include a very large number of product types, representativity will suffer in this procedure, since no products falling outside the specification will enter the index. Another disadvantage with the method is that it may lead to more missing products in the outlets and thus reduce the effective sample. Its main advantage is simplicity. It is easy to maintain a central control over the sample. If quality adjustments are needed, they can be decided in the central office, which may or may not be an advantage.

5.48 The method with loose specifications gives price collectors the chance to adjust the sample to local conditions and will normally lead to greater representativity of the sample as a whole. Where it is combined with the "most sold" criterion it will, however, systematically underrepresent the smaller brands and products that may be bought by important minorities.

Sampling in time

5.49 A CPI usually refers to a month, during which prices are not constant. The issue of sampling in time then arises. Often, this problem is ignored, for example by using the 15th day of the month, or the days surrounding the 15th, as the target date for price measurement. In some areas, there is a day-of-the-week effect on prices, for example in cinemas, theatres and restaurants, but this may be taken into account in the product specification rather than in sampling, for example by specifying a weekday evening price.

5.50 As far as is known, random sampling in time is not used anywhere. The method used in some countries is to spread price collection over several weeks according to some pattern, for example different weeks in different regions or for different product groups. In some cases, more frequent pricing than monthly is also used, for example for fresh produce. There is not yet any systematic knowledge about the pros and cons of such practices. Chapter 6 discusses the more practical aspects of distributing price collection over time.

Choice of sampling method

5.51 In this section, we discuss how choices in sampling method could depend on specific factors in a country. But first we consider the matter of sample size.

5.52 *Sample size.* The final precision of a sample estimate depends only on the size and allocation of the sample and not on the size of the country, so in this sense there is no need for a larger sample in a larger country. Larger samples are called for if regional differences in price change are of interest and if the amount of product disaggregation that is desired in presenting the indices is very high. Of course, the budget allocated to CPI work may be larger in large countries, allowing for larger samples.

5.53 Studies of bias (not the sampling bias described in paragraphs 5.61 to 5.64) and of sampling error show that bias in CPIs is generally a much greater problem than sampling error. This leads to the conclusion that, in many cases, smaller samples that are better monitored with respect to replacements, resampling and quality adjustment could give a higher quality index for the same budget. In some countries, local price collection is a fixed resource and it is therefore difficult to move resources from local price collection to central analytical work. Still, it is advisable to try to use local resources for higher quality price collection rather than just for many observations. The quality of price collection is further discussed in Chapter 6.

5.54 Monthly sample sizes in different countries seem to vary from several thousand to several hundred thousand. Often, the reasons for these differences lie more in tradition than in a rational analysis of the needs of precision. Countries with very large sample sizes would probably do well to look at ways of reallocating their total resources.

5.55 *Geographical distribution of price collectors.* Sampling is more expensive further away from the homes of the price collectors. If the organization for price collection is centralized in a few main cities, it will be difficult to sample outlets elsewhere. It should be borne in mind, however, that rural and urban inflation may well be different, so failure to collect prices in both rural and urban areas would be detrimental to efforts to achieve the best measure of average national inflation. It would be better to have at least a small sample in the rural areas so that this factor can be taken into account. The major part of the saving arising from allocating outlets close to price collectors can then still be realized.

5.56 *Sophistication of price collectors.* If price collectors are well educated, they may be instructed to carry out more complex sampling schemes such as pps sampling in the outlets. Otherwise, simpler methods are called for.

5.57 *Access to sampling expertise in the central office.* Probability sampling requires access to methodological expertise in the central statistical office.

5.58 *Homogeneous versus heterogeneous product groups.* The representative item method is more suitable for homogeneous product groups. In heterogenous groups, it is more likely that important segments of the product universe, with different price movement, will be left out.

5.59 *Access to sampling frames and their quality.* Probability sampling requires sampling frames. But they do not necessarily have to be available at the national level. By applying geographical cluster sampling in the first stage (where the sampling frame is just a map), a list of relevant outlets can be constructed in each sampled cluster using telephone directories or local enumeration, as is done in the United Kingdom. This method is also used to select urban areas for the United States CPI (Dippo and Jacobs, 1983).

5.60 *Scanner data.* The discussion in this chapter is based on the traditional situation, where prices have to be collected locally and centrally, and entered individually into a central database. Where prices and possibly quantities are collected electronically, as is the case with sale point scanner data, sampling could be different. There is then no need for sampling products or varieties or points in time, since they are completely enumerated automatically. Nevertheless, not all outlets selling a product will be covered by scanner data in the foreseeable future. Since all kinds of outlets should be represented in the index, there will be continue to be a need to combine scanner data samples with traditional samples for non-scanner outlets.

Estimation procedures

5.61 There is a crucial distinction to be made between what is to be estimated, the *parameter*, which is defined for the whole universe, and the *estimator*, which is a formula to be calculated using the sample values as an estimate of the parameter. Now, in survey sampling in general we want to estimate a population total or a function of several such totals, for example a ratio of totals. So, if we have two variables y and z defined for each sampling unit (for example, prices at two different periods), we may want to estimate the following parameters:

$$Y=\sum_{j=1}^{N} y_j \quad \text{and} \quad Z=\sum_{j=1}^{N} z_j \quad \text{or} \quad R=Y/Z$$

5.62 Several different estimators may be proposed for the same population parameter, in which case we need to decide which of these estimators to use. In assessing the quality of a sample estimator, i.e. how well it estimates the parameter, two measures are often considered in the probability sampling paradigm. The first measure is the bias of an estimator, which is the difference between the universe parameter and the average of the estimator over all possible samples that could be drawn under the specified sample design (referred to as the mean of the sampling distribution of the estimator). Note that this bias refers to something different from the index number bias discussed elsewhere in this manual. An estimator is unbiased if it has zero bias. The second measure is the variance of the estimator with respect to this sampling distribution. An estimator is considered good if both its bias and variance are small; that is, the estimator is on average very close to the parameter and does not vary much from its mean.

5.63 The good fortune of finding an estimator that minimizes both bias and variance at the same time does not often happen. An estimator with a small bias may have a large variance, and one with a small variance may have a large bias. So use is frequently made of a criterion called the mean square error, which is the sum of the bias squared and the variance. A "good" estimator is then one which minimizes this criterion.

5.64 Sampling theory tells us that the following estimators are unbiased, respectively, for the parameters Y and Z above: $\hat{Y}=\sum_{j\in S} y_j/\pi_j$, $\hat{Z}=\sum_{j\in S} z_j/\pi_j$, where S is the sample, and that $\hat{R}=\hat{Y}/\hat{Z}$ is approximately unbiased for R, subject to a (usually negligible) technical ratio estimator bias.

Implementing estimation procedures for consumer price indices

5.65 As stated earlier, sampling for CPIs is usually stratified, with elementary aggregates as strata. Let us assume that the universe parameter is I and that the parameter in stratum h is labelled I_h. Then we have:

$$I = \sum_h w_h I_h$$

where w_h is the weight of stratum h. The issue then is to estimate I_h for each stratum. In the following discussion, we therefore concentrate on estimating for a single stratum and drop the subscript h.

5.66 Depending on the content, degree of homogeneity, price elasticity and access to weighting information within the stratum, different parameters may be appropriate in different strata. The choice of parameter is an index number problem, to be solved by reference to the underlying economic concepts. As discussed in Chapter 20, it could be the unit value index, the Laspeyres index, the Lowe index, or the geometric Laspeyres index.

5.67 Suppose we have a sample of size n and that the units in the sample are labelled 1,2, . . . , n. Very often, one of the three formulae below is used as an estimator of the stratum index:

The arithmetic mean of price relatives (Carli index):

$$r = \frac{1}{n} \sum_{j \in S} \frac{p_j^1}{p_j^0} \tag{5.1}$$

The ratio of mean prices (Dutot index):

$$a = \frac{\frac{1}{n} \sum_{j \in S} p_j^1}{\frac{1}{n} \sum_{j \in S} p_j^0} \tag{5.2}$$

The geometric mean (Jevons index):

$$g = \prod_{j \in S} \left(\frac{p_j^1}{p_j^0} \right)^{\frac{1}{n}} \tag{5.3}$$

For discussion below, we also need to introduce the ratio of harmonic mean prices:

$$h = \frac{\frac{1}{n} \sum_{j \in S} 1/p_j^0}{\frac{1}{n} \sum_{j \in S} 1/p_j^1} \tag{5.4}$$

5.68 When comparing the above estimators with the functional form of the parameters in Chapter 20, we realize that very special conditions are needed to make them unbiased estimators of those parameters. For one thing, unlike the parameters in Chapter 20, there are no quantities involved in the sample estimators.

5.69 We state, without proof, some results concerning the statistical properties of the above estimators (see Balk (2002) for details). Suppose we have N products in the universe labelled 1,2, . . . , N. Let p_j^t, q_j^t be respectively the price and quantity for product j in period t ($t=0$ for base period and 1 for current period), and let

$$w_j^0 = \frac{q_j^0 p_j^0}{\sum_{j=1}^{N} q_j^0 p_j^0} \quad (j=1, \ldots, N)$$

be the base period expenditure share of product j. Then:

- Under simple random sampling, none of r, a or g estimates any of the population parameters without bias. Instead, weights need to be used in the estimators also.
- Under pps, if $\pi_j \propto w_j^0$ for all j, then r, the average of relatives, is unbiased for the Laspeyres index (the symbol "$\propto$" means "proportional to").
- Under pps, if $\pi_j \propto q_j^0$ for all j, then a, the ratio of averages, is approximately unbiased for the Laspeyres index.
- Under pps, if $\pi_j \propto w_j^0$ for all j, then g is approximately unbiased for the geometric Laspeyres index. In this case log g is unbiased for the logarithm of the geometric Laspeyres index. The remaining bias tends to be of a similar order to that of a.

5.70 All these results are somewhat theoretical in nature since neither w_j^0 nor q_j^0 are known at the time when the sample could be drawn. This is a reason for introducing the Lowe index:

- Under pps, if $\pi_j \propto q_j^b$ (where b is some period before 0) for all j, then a is approximately unbiased for the Lowe index.

5.71 There is no simple way to relate any of the estimators to the unit value index. In fact, estimating that index requires separate samples in the two time periods, since its numerator and denominator refer to different universes.

- Under two separate sample designs, one for period 0 and one for period 1, which are both pps and where $\pi_j^0 \propto q_j^0$ and $\pi_j^1 \propto q_j^1$, then a is approximately unbiased for the unit value index. In this case, however, the interpretation of the a formula will be different, since the samples in the numerator and the denominator are different.
- Under two separate sample designs, one for period 0 and one for period 1, which are both pps and where $\pi_j^0 \propto v_j^0 = p_j^0 q_j^0$ and $\pi_j^1 \propto v_j^1 = p_j^1 q_j^1$, then h, the ratio of harmonic mean prices, is approximately unbiased for the unit value index. The following algebraic reformulation of the unit value index helps to clarify that fact:

$$UV = \frac{\sum_{j \in S} v_j^1 \Big/ \sum_{j \in S} v_j^1 / p_j^1}{\sum_{j \in S} v_j^0 \Big/ \sum_{j \in S} v_j^0 / p_j^0}.$$

As for a, however, the interpretation of the h formula will be different, since the samples in the numerator and the denominator are different.

5.72 The phrase "approximately unbiased" needs some explanation. It refers to the fact that the estimator is not exactly unbiased but that the bias is small and decreases towards zero as the sample size and the size of the universe simultaneously go to infinity in a certain, mathematically well-defined manner. In the ratio estimator case applicable to a, the sign of this bias is indeterminate and its size after aggregation is probably negligible. In the case of the geometric mean, however, the bias is always positive, i.e. the sample geometric mean tends to overestimate the universe geometric mean on average over many sample drawings. In the case of simple random sampling and an unweighted geometric mean in both the universe and the sample, the bias expression is: $b \approx \sigma^2/2n$, where σ^2 is the variance of the price ratios. For small universes, a finite population correction needs to be multiplied to this expression. This result is easily derived from expression (4.1.4) in Dalén (1999b). The bias may be significant for small sample sizes, so that a caution against very small samples in a stratum may be warranted when the geometric mean is applied.

Variance estimation

5.73 A CPI is a complex statistic, usually with a complex design. It is thus not a routine task to estimate the variance of a CPI. To the extent that samples are not probability based, variance estimates need to make use of some kind of model in which random sampling is assumed. In the absence of systematic and generally accepted knowledge, the approaches to variance estimation used in four countries will be briefly described.

Variances of elementary index formulae

5.74 As a preliminary, some variance estimators for elementary aggregate formulae will be provided. In order not to overburden the text with formulae, the variance estimators, not the exact variance, will be given. The variance estimators are approximately unbiased under simple random sampling, where the corresponding universe parameter is unweighted. They are also applicable to the case of pps sampling for a weighted universe parameter, where the size measure is the same as the parameter weight. For definitions of the formulae, see equations (5.1)–(5.3).

$$V(r) = \frac{\sigma_r^2}{n}, \text{ where } \sigma_r^2 = \frac{1}{n-1}\sum_{j \in S}(r_j - r)^2$$

$$\text{and } r_j = \frac{p_j^1}{p_j^0}; \qquad (5.5)$$

$$V(a) = \frac{1}{n(\bar{p}^0)^2}(\sigma_1^2 + r^2\sigma_0^2 - 2r\sigma_{01}), \qquad (5.6)$$

where $\sigma_1^2 = \frac{1}{n-1}\sum_{j \in S}(p_j^1 - \bar{p}^1)^2$, $\sigma_0^2 = \frac{1}{n-1}\sum_{j \in S}(p_j^0 - \bar{p}^0)^2$, $\sigma_{01} = \frac{1}{n-1}\sum_{j \in S}(p_j^1 - \bar{p}^1)(p_j^0 - \bar{p}^0)$, $\bar{p}^1 = \frac{1}{n}\sum_{j \in S} p_j^1$ and $\bar{p}^0 = \frac{1}{n}\sum_{j \in S} p_j^0$.
This estimate follows from the fact that a, unlike r, is a ratio of stochastic variables. See, for example, Cochran (1977) for a derivation of this formula.

5.75 The geometric mean is more complex, since it is not a linear estimator. However, Dalén (1999b) derived the following easily applied variance expression, which holds with good approximation if price ratios do not have too extreme variation ($\sigma_r/r < 0.2$, say):

$$V(g) = \frac{\sigma_r^2}{n}\left(1 - \frac{\sigma_r^2}{r^2}\right) \qquad (5.7)$$

The United States approach

5.76 The United States CPI uses sampling and estimation procedures which are in many ways unique in comparison to those of other countries. The exact design obviously varies somewhat over time. The following description is based on U.S. BLS (1997) and Leaver and Valliant (1995).

5.77 The United States CPI is composed of building blocks consisting of geographical areas crossed with product strata to a total of 8,487 "basic CPI strata" corresponding to elementary aggregates. The 88 geographical areas were selected by pps in a controlled selection procedure and 29 of them were included with certainty (self-representing). Within each basic CPI stratum an estimation procedure is applied in which indices for a particular time period are based on the overlapping sample units (outlets and items) between this time period and the immediately preceding period. The period-to-period indices are then multiplied to obtain an index from the base period to the current period. Sampling within the basic CPI strata is approximately pps according to the description above.

5.78 Variance estimation for this design proves to be too complex for the use of a direct design-based variance estimator. Instead a random group replication method, using the so-called VPLX software, is applied. Other methods have also been tried.

5.79 Leaver and Swanson (1992) provide a detailed account of the variance estimation methods used up to then. They also present the following numerical estimates of (median) standard errors for CPI changes for various intervals over the 1987–91 period: 1 month – standard error 0.074; 2 months – standard error 0.103; 6 months – standard error 0.130; and 12 months – standard error 0.143.

The Swedish approach

5.80 The following outline summarizes the description given by Dalén and Ohlsson (1995). The Swedish CPI uses a primary stratification into product groups, which are measured in separate and independent price surveys. The first step in the Swedish approach is therefore to note that the variance of the all items price index is a weighted sum of the variances of the separate surveys:

$$V(I) = \sum_h w_h^2 V(I_h) \qquad (5.8)$$

5.81 The reason that all these surveys can reasonably be assumed to be independent is that there is no common regional sampling scheme used in them. Altogether, there are about 60 different surveys. Some of them cover many product groups and have a complex design and there is stochastic dependence between them. Other surveys cover only one group and have simple designs. Some cover their universes, without any sampling, so they have zero variance.

5.82 In many simple product groups it is fairly reasonable to assume that the price ratios obtained are effectively random samples. In some cases this may lead to some overestimation of variance since there is in fact some substratification or quota sampling within the group. In those product groups, stratum variances could then be estimated according to formulae (5.5) (5.7). When a price survey is stratified, formula (5.8) can be applied at lower levels above the elementary aggregate.

5.83 Some price surveys are more complex, however. This is especially the case for that large part of the index where outlets and products are simultaneously sampled. In the Swedish case these surveys are called the local price survey and the daily necessities survey. In both these cases, outlets are sampled by probability (pps) from the central business register. Products are sampled by pps in the daily necessities survey but by the representative item method in the local price survey. In the Swedish variance estimation model, the final sample is in these cases considered as drawn from a two-dimensional universe of products and outlets. The final sampling units are thus sampled products sold in sampled outlets – a cross-classified sample.

5.84 In a cross-classified sample, the total variance can be decomposed into three parts:

- variance between products (in the same outlet);
- variance between outlets (for the same product);
- outlet and product interaction variance.

Dalén and Ohlsson (1995) provide the exact formulae used.

5.85 In the daily necessities survey, the cross-classified model comes fairly close to the actual sampling design. In the local price survey, it is more of a model, since the products are in fact purposively drawn. It has nevertheless been considered a useful model for the purpose of getting a first idea of the sampling error and for analysing allocation problems.

5.86 The total variance of the Swedish CPI, according to this model, was estimated to be 0.04, corresponding to a 95 per cent confidence interval of ±0.4. This estimate appeared to be fairly stable over the period 1991–95 for which the model was tried.

The French approach

5.87 In France, variance calculation at present only takes into consideration items accounting for 65 per cent of the total weight of the index.

5.88 The smallest element of the calculation is a product type in an urban area. For these elements one of two formulae are applied, depending on whether the product is homogeneous (ratio of arithmetic means) or heterogeneous (geometric means). A two-stage random sample is assumed, first of urban areas and then of a particular item (variety) in an outlet. The variance obtained is thus the sum of a "between urban areas" and a "within urban areas" component. Linearization based on second-degree expansions is done, because of the non-linear nature of the estimators. Higher-level variances are obtained by weighting the elementary level variances.

5.89 After an optimization exercise which took place in 1997, the standard deviation of the all-products index (for 65 per cent of the total weight of the index) was computed as 0.03. This value is close to that estimated in 1993, although the number of observations was reduced. The precision of a number of sub-indices was also improved.

5.90 Covariance terms are ignored. In fact, this makes a very small difference in the "between urban areas" component. In the "within urban areas" component it has undoubtedly a greater influence. The effect is, however, seen as limited because of a rule which limits the number of products observed in the same outlet.

5.91 For the 35 per cent of the weight that is at present excluded from the variance calculation (called the "tariffs"), such calculations will be introduced for insurance. The necessary elements for variance calculation are also present for physicians' and dentists' services. Variances will soon be calculated for these products, as well as for new cars. For a certain number of sub-indices (tobacco and pharmaceuticals) the sample is in effect a total count. Their variances are thus zero.

5.92 A 95 per cent confidence interval for a 12-month comparison can be expressed as the estimated index ±0.06 for the ordinary, non-tariff items. If zero variance is assumed for the remaining 35 per cent of the index, the confidence interval for the all-products index would become ±0.04. This assumption is clearly too optimistic, but from the work on variance estimation done so far, it can be concluded that the confidence interval is certainly smaller than 0.1.

5.93 More details on the French computations can be found in Ardilly and Guglielmetti (1993).

The Luxembourg approach

5.94 The Luxembourg CPI can be described as a stratified purposive sample with 258 product strata. There are slightly fewer than 7,000 observations each month, giving an average of 27 observations per stratum. In each stratum, observations are taken from several different outlets; but the same outlet is represented in many product strata. The outlet is here used as the identifier for the price-setting organization (for rents it is a landlord, for insurance it is the companies, and so on). In each stratum, there are observations from several outlets. Since there is good reason to believe that each outlet has its own price-setting behaviour, prices and price changes in the same outlet tend to be correlated, resulting in positive covariances in the general variance expression:

$$V(I) = \sum_k w_k^2 V(I_k) + \sum_k \sum_l w_k w_l Cov(I_k, I_l) \qquad (5.9)$$

5.95 In the sampling model, each separate outlet sample within a product stratum is regarded as a simple random sample. Further, a two-stage model was assumed such that, in the first stage, a simple random sample of outlets was assumed to have been drawn from a (fictitious) sampling frame of all outlets in Luxembourg. Then, in each sampled outlet, a second-stage sample of observations was assumed to be drawn in product stratum h so that the combined product–outlet stratum became the lowest computational level in the index. All second-stage samples were assumed to be mutually independent and sampling fractions to be small. This model resulted in three components of total variance:

- variance within outlets;
- variance between outlets;
- covariance between outlets.

Covariances are difficult to calculate, even with a computer. Luckily, however, it was possible algebraically to combine the last two components into one, with the number of summation levels reduced.

5.96 Numerical estimates were made with this model for 22 consecutive 12-month changes starting from the period January 1996 to January 1997 and ending with the period October 1997 to October 1998. The average variance estimate was 0.02 (corresponding to a standard error of 0.14), which is surprisingly small given the small sample size. The reason for this small value was not explored in detail but may lie in a combination of the special circumstances in the markets in Luxembourg and in procedures used in the index estimation system.

5.97 The full variance estimation model for the Luxembourg CPI and the results from it are presented in Dalén and Muelteel (1998).

Other approaches

5.98 A number of experimental models have been tried out and calculations done for the United Kingdom. None of them has so far been acknowledged as an official method or estimate. Kenny (1995 and earlier reports) experimented with the Swedish approach on United Kingdom data. He found a standard error of the United Kingdom Retail Price Index as a whole of around 0.1, which was reasonably constant over several years, although the detailed composition of the variance varied quite a lot. Sitter and Balshaw (1998) used a pseudo-population approach but did not present any overall variance estimates.

5.99 For Finland, Jacobsen (1997) provided partial calculations according to a similar design as in the Swedish approach. His analysis was used to suggest changes in the allocation of the sample.

Optimal allocation

5.100 Producing a consumer price index is a major operation in any country and a great deal of resources are spent on price collection. It is therefore worthwhile to devote some effort to allocating these resources in the most efficient way.

5.101 The general approach to sample allocation was established by Neyman and is described in any sampling textbook. It uses a mathematical expression for the variance of the estimate and another expression for the cost. Both variance and cost are functions of sample size. Optimal allocation then amounts to minimizing variance for a given cost or minimizing cost for a given variance.

5.102 Variance estimation was discussed above. As for cost, it is important to note that not all price observations are equally costly. It is less expensive to collect an extra price in an outlet that is already in the sample than to add a price in an outlet that is new to the sample. For example, in the Swedish CPI, the following cost function was used:

$$C = C_0 + \sum_h n_h \left\{ a_h + b_h \sum_g m_g r_{gh} \right\} \qquad (5.10)$$

where C refers to total cost and C_0 to the fixed part of the cost that is independent of sample size,

n_h is the number of outlets in outlet stratum h,

m_g is the number of product varieties in product stratum g,

a_h is the unit cost per outlet and reflects travelling time to the outlet,

b_h is the unit cost per product, which reflects the additional cost for observing a product, when the price collector is already in the outlet,

r_{gh} is the average relative frequency of products in stratum g sold in outlets of stratum h.

5.103 In formula (5.10), a_h is usually much larger than b_h. This fact calls for an allocation with relatively more products than outlets, i.e. of several products per outlet. This allocation is further reinforced to the extent that variances between products in the same outlet and product stratum are usually larger than variances between outlets for the same product. This is the case, at least according to experience in Sweden.

5.104 With a specified variance function and a specified cost function, it is possible, using the mathematical technique of Lagrange multipliers, to derive optimal sample sizes in each stratum. It is usually not possible to obtain explicit expressions, however, since we run into a non-linear optimization problem for which it is not possible to find an explicit solution.

5.105 In a CPI, the all-products index is usually the most important statistic. Therefore, the allocation of the sample should be directed towards the minimization of its error. It is also important that other published sub-indices are of high quality, but the sub-index quality can often be taken as the criterion for publication, rather than the other way round.

Summary

5.106 The above discussion can be summarized in the form of a small number of specific recommendations.

5.107 *Clarity* – sampling rules should be well defined. In many CPIs, there is a wide range of sampling and other solutions for different product groups. A fairly well-defined method is often used for the field collection of prices, but the exact methods used for the central price collection of many products are commonly in the hands of one or a few responsible persons and are sometimes poorly documented. It is essential for the basic credibility of the CPI that rules for sampling and estimation (e.g. the treatment of outliers) are well defined and described.

5.108 *Probability sampling should be seriously considered.* The use of probability sampling designs should be increased. In many areas, useful sampling frames do exist or could be constructed without excessive difficulties. Stratified, order pps sampling is an important type of design that ought to be considered in many situations. Size measures used for sampling must have a long-term interpretation, so that they are uncorrelated with price movements.

5.109 *Representativity – no large part of the universe should be left out.* When sampling designs are planned, the full universe of items and outlets belonging to the item group in question should be taken into account. All significant parts of that universe should be appropriately represented, unless there are excessive costs or estimation problems involved in doing so.

5.110 *Variance or mean square error should be as low as possible.* Samples should be reasonably optimized, based on at least a rudimentary analysis of sampling variance. As a first-order approximation, sample sizes could be set approximately proportional to the weights of the commodity groups. A better approximation is obtained by multiplying each weight by a measure of price change dispersion in the group. Variance and cost considerations together call for allocations where relatively many products are measured per outlet and relatively few outlets are contained in the sample. Since biases are generally a greater problem than sampling errors, smaller but better samples, allowing for more frequent renewal and careful monitoring of replacements and quality adjustments, generally make good sense.

PRICE COLLECTION

6

Introduction

6.1 The most appropriate sampling and survey methods for a price survey will vary depending on the use of the price index and local circumstances. For instance, the diversity of available goods and services, their turnover and the range of prices charged, the frequency and size of price changes, consumers' purchasing habits (including the use of telephone, catalogue and Internet shopping) and the structure of retailing in terms of the local economy, types of outlets and geographical spread will all have a bearing.

6.2 This chapter gives an overview of some of the issues, but bearing the above in mind it is clear that the treatment of these will require different solutions in different countries according to local circumstances. Solutions cannot be too prescriptive, and the compiler should always be guided by the fundamental principles and objectives of a price index as addressed in earlier chapters. The structure of Western economies together with the retailing patterns and associated consumer purchasing habits lend themselves to more structured price collections. In contrast, subsistence economies and developing economies will require more flexible price collection techniques.

6.3 Consideration has to be given as to how best to collect prices in terms of efficiency, accuracy and representation of consumers' purchasing patterns. In some cases, price collection directly from individual shops around the region or country (local price collection) may be considered appropriate. In other circumstances, prices collected centrally by staff located in the headquarters or regional offices of the national statistical institute (central price collection) may be more appropriate. Many of the issues covered in this chapter are relevant to both local and central price collection.

6.4 The advantages and disadvantages of local versus central price collection for different types of prices are covered later in this chapter. Briefly, local price collection has the advantage of covering a wide range of locations and item selections, particularly for food, alcohol, tobacco and durable goods (for example, clothing, furniture and electrical goods). Central collection is useful for prices that are difficult to observe directly (for example, costs of housing or utilities), where there are national pricing policies, for goods sold through mail order and catalogues, or for items where there are limited collection opportunities or difficulties in making an adjustment for technical and quality charges (particularly transport and services).

Frequency and timing of collection

6.5 The type of economy can initially govern the frequency and timing of price collection. Where transient markets are important to a wide spectrum of the population, the timing of these markets will affect the timing of price collecting because of the need to consider the availability of goods and services to consumers.

6.6 A fundamental decision about the frequency and timing of price collection is whether the index should relate to monthly average prices or prices for a specific point in time (for example, a single day or week in a month). This decision is related to a number of factors, including the uses of the index, the practicalities of carrying out price collections, the pattern of price movements and the timing of index publication. These factors are discussed in turn below.

6.7 It has been argued that the question of whether the index should relate to a period or to a point in time generally becomes less of an issue the more frequently the prices are collected. But it is far from certain whether this is true in all circumstances. For instance, prices over certain holiday periods or at particular times of year might be especially volatile. In such cases, the smoothness resulting from a period rather than a point estimate may be considered an advantage over a potentially misleading short-term trend shown by a more highly volatile point estimate. In answering this question, there is also a need to take into account the primary use of the index.

6.8 In principle, if used for deflating income, expenditure or sales, the index should relate to the period of time of these money flows. For economic analysis, where the index will be used in conjunction with other economic statistics, most of which relate to a period rather than to a point in time, it seems logical, again in principle, that the consumer price index should do the same.

6.9 In reality, when making this choice, considerations of principle have to be weighed against various practical considerations. The first point to note is that when inflation is low and stable there will be little difference between, for example, the annual rate of change in the index from Monday 3 January 2000 to Wednesday 1 January 2001 and the corresponding annual rate of change between the complete months of January 2000 and January 2001. This will not be the case if inflation is rapid or the rate changes significantly during the year. The difference between 1 January and 1 February and average January to average February inflation rates may be different – particularly if so-called "sale" periods are limited by laws or local ordinance, as they are in some countries. For certain products with high index weights, where price changes are sudden and tend to affect the whole market on about the same day, the choice between time period and point is important. Examples are petrol, electricity and telecommunication prices. Here the case for an average price for the period is strong. Obviously, the weights should relate to the periodicity of the collection taking into account the appropriate expenditure and pricing periods (for example, if prices are increased one-third of the way through the period then two-thirds of the weight should reflect the higher pricing).

6.10 Not all price observations can be made within a single day, let alone at one point in time during that day. This is particularly true of local price collections, but may also be true of central price collections, depending on the resources available at head office. In practice, the real issue is whether the observations are spread over a few days to provide an approximation to a point-in-time estimate (for example, Monday to Wednesday to represent prices on a specific Tuesday) or spread over the whole month to provide an estimate for the average for that month.

6.11 It should also be borne in mind that the sampling variance will differ according to whether a period or point-in-time index is compiled and, in the case of the latter, the frequency of collection. In considering the timing and frequency of price collection, consideration also needs to be given more generally to the trade-off between statistical accuracy and cost. It should be noted that collecting prices locally from shops is normally a relatively expensive activity. In practice, the budget for price collection usually limits the available options.

6.12 The desired frequency of price collection may vary by commodity, depending on how frequently the prices to be observed change. For example, it is possible that prices charged by public utilities, central or local government fees or charges, or mail order catalogue prices will change annually or quarterly according to a known timetable, and therefore these price collections can be carried out according to the timetable of changes rather than every month. In contrast, food prices – where shopkeepers may review the prices they charge on a continuous basis to reflect market conditions and the prices charged by their suppliers – need to be collected more frequently. Clearly, statisticians will need to be absolutely sure about the frequency of price changes for any specific good or service before coming to a decision to collect prices on a less frequent basis. They will also need to keep in touch with current pricing policies to monitor whether the position changes, so that they can immediately reflect these changes in their price collection procedures. In addition, statisticians need to be aware of any unusual price changes that could be missed by less frequent price collections, for example, changes to indirect taxation rates or one-off timing changes of increases (for example, service providers moving annual increases from April to March or prices of school dinners changing each term, with terms starting in different months from one year to the next).

6.13 Another point to note is the timing of publication of the resulting price indices. There may be legal constraints on the timing of the publication of indices. In such cases, prices must be collected in time to allow quality assurance, processing and aggregation procedures to be completed before the deadline.

6.14 As mentioned above, in cases where inflation is stable and where collection costs are not an issue, collection can be spread over a whole month. In these cases, different neighbourhoods should be scheduled for price collection at different times of the month according to a regular pattern to be repeated every month. This not only makes the use of the collectors' time more efficient, but also has the advantage of providing a spread of collection dates for many representative items. It is also important that individual price observations are carried out at the same time each month so that the index does not move as a result of a change in the length of interval between collection dates. A further important consideration, particularly of consequence in Middle Eastern countries, is in cases where prices can vary by day of the week (for example, depending when market day is) or time of the day according to various marketing special offers to attract more customers at less busy times or to reflect the freshness of the goods.

6.15 When the aim is to compute a point-in-time index, price observations need to be spread over a very small number of days each month. The interval between price observations should be uniform for each outlet. Since the length of the month varies, this uniformity has to be defined carefully.

6.16 Preferably, days of the week and times of the month should be chosen taking into account when purchases are concentrated and where prices and goods in stock are known to be representative of the month as a whole. In Middle Eastern countries, results of the household expenditure surveys suggest that most households do the shopping on the day of the souk (market). It should also be borne in mind, however, that retailers may be less prepared to cooperate when they are busy, so a balance needs to be struck between the ideal timing for collection and the impact on response rates. It should be noted that a fixed interval is impossible because of the varying length of a month and the timing of public and religious holidays. One solution is to take sequences of four and five weeks, so maintaining a relatively stable monthly or quarterly period; another is to follow a rule such as collecting on the regular market day or on Wednesday through to Friday of the first full week in the month.

6.17 Price collection days (and sometimes times) need to be set in advance. In some countries or economies, decisions need to be taken in advance about whether and how these days should be kept confidential to avoid key sources, such as major stores or governments, adjusting prices for collection days and thus distorting the price indices. It is nevertheless important for public perception about the integrity of the index that a statistical office is able to explain the procedures used for setting collection dates and the underlying objectivity of its method. Any price collection agencies carrying out the collection for national statistical institutes need to know collection dates a long way in advance for resource planning purposes. In addition, any data suppliers who supply prices direct to head office staff need to know the collection date a short time in advance to be able to prepare and supply the necessary price returns.

6.18 Regular timing is particularly important when inflation is rapid. Where there is a specific collection day, it is most important that the most volatile prices are collected on that specific day rather than the days around it. Particular items may include fresh fruit and vegetables, fresh meat, and items subject to varying indirect taxation and duties (such as tobacco and petrol). In the case of foodstuffs sold in marketplaces, the time of day as well as the day of the week is important. In Middle Eastern countries, at least, these prices are usually higher in the mornings and lower in the evenings.

6.19 Price collection days need to be set after considering a variety of factors that affect prices and shopping patterns. Holidays and weekends should be avoided except for items with large sales during these times, such as petrol, leisure services and entertainment (for example, restaurant meals and tourist attractions). Some countries have limited shop openings on some days or half-day closing on other days, which can limit the number of prices that can be collected or bias the location sample to certain types of outlets or service providers. On the days approaching long holiday periods when many shops are shut, there can be limited supplies of fresh food and many abnormal price reductions to clear stocks before the shops shut for the holiday period. The implications of any sale periods controlled by law should also be considered.

6.20 Whether collection is continuous or point-in-time, the interval between successive price observations at each outlet must be held constant by visiting that outlet during a fixed time period each month (or quarter).

6.21 Another issue is raised by the pricing of tariffs (telephone charges, for example, depend on the time of day and the destination of the call), variable pricing policies dependent on demand (sporting and leisure fees, for example, depend on the time of day – peak demand times attracting higher prices) and prices where there is potentially limited availability (such as air, rail and taxi fares). For each of these, price collections should be made consistently over time and in a way that represents consumer purchasing patterns. The selection of the representative items should represent consumer behaviour (for example, air fares may be priced 6, 3, 2 and 1 month in advance and include last-minute booking options too) and be weighted by consumer spending patterns (for example, weighting together prices for peak and off-peak entry to a swimming pool).

6.22 A final point to note is that with the point-in-time approach, major price setters, notably the government, can influence the index according to whether their price changes take effect on a day just before or after the day for which their price information is obtained, or on the day of collection. Since prices are often collected centrally from such price setters, it should be possible to obtain information from them about both the amount and timing of price changes at the end of each month, so that in applying the period-of-time approach, an average price for the whole month can be calculated. For example, if electricity charges are made quarterly and prices increase part way through the 3-month period, individual customers' payments could include 0, 1, 2 or 3 months at the higher rate.

Taking account of hyperinflation

6.23 Special arrangements may need to be put into place where there is hyperinflation. In these circumstances it becomes even more important that the prices of individual items in individual shops are collected at precisely the same time each month, otherwise misleading figures may result. Consideration should be given to the more frequent collection of prices and correspondingly a more frequent compilation of the index. Where prices are normally collected on a quarterly basis, it may be sensible to collect them more frequently. If this is not feasible, it may be appropriate to up-rate prices proportionately by some relevant indicator to provide an approximation to a monthly index. If this is done, however, great care needs to be taken in choosing the appropriate comparator, particularly as relativities between prices can change dramatically in periods of hyperinflation.

6.24 In some circumstances, rapid or frequent price changes may be associated with certain items only and action should be taken accordingly. By way of example, food prices may rise disproportionately because of a bad harvest and it may be sensible to increase the frequency of the index for food items only. Alternatively, a simpler way of dealing with this situation may be to monitor a small number of relevant prices on a regular basis without producing a full price index. Such sub-indices could be published separately or used to up-rate the later prices collected in the period, as mentioned above. These items may be chosen according to their importance for the family budget and whether they are particularly susceptible to big price increases.

Item specification

6.25 Specific representative items should be chosen to be typical of price movements in the consumer price index basket. An item consumed by households or individuals that has a price is a definable good or service. In some cases, however, such as à la carte restaurant meals, cars (where the purchaser may be able to buy optional extras on top of the basic model) and car rentals (where insurance may be extra), a decision needs to be taken about whether to treat the package as a single item or whether to price components separately. As a general rule, the package should be considered a single item when it can be expected that the offer is not temporary and where the purchaser typically buys the whole bundle of goods and services on offer. Otherwise, the components should be treated as separate items and individual cost quotes obtained. Where the purchase is not normally of the whole bundle, it is usual to be able to pick up individual quotes for the different parts of the package. This provides some indication of whether packages or individual items are being purchased.

6.26 Ideally, the selection of items should be based upon a complete census of relevant transactions relating to different items purchased by individuals. In practice, this is not normally universally available, although in some countries useful data may be generated by point-of-sale and scanner data.

6.27 How tightly defined (narrow) or general (broad) the item specification should be is an issue of great theoretical and practical importance. Whether specifications are broad or narrow can vary according to individual circumstances and may differ throughout the basket of goods and services being priced. Narrow item descriptions are generally more effective for controlling sample representativeness (assuming that a reliable sampling frame or set of reference data is available) and for controlling for quality differences, and can also reduce the variance of prices and price relatives, thus optimizing the performance of some aggregation formulae. But they can result in a smaller achieved sample, as there is less flexibility for price collectors to choose an appropriate item in a particular shop. In contrast, broad item descriptions can increase the size of the achieved sample but can be more difficult to control for sample representativity and will normally result in higher variances.

6.28 In some countries, prices for clothing are specified very tightly to ensure that quality differences are minimized. A description might be as detailed as "knitted top; mid-season; with sleeves; no collar; no buttons; made in Morocco; acrylic; mid to light thickness". In comparison, a general description used in another consumer price index for an equivalent item might be "men's formal shirt; long sleeved".

6.29 Whichever of the two approaches is used, rules should be established for selecting representative items that fit the item descriptions (for example, best-selling lines as reported by the individual retailer, or items selected by probability proportional to size sampling). It is important that the representative items chosen, whether with tight or general product descriptions, are actually representative of the consumer spending patterns. There is no point, for instance, in pricing an item that is rarely sold but looks good in the shop window, or is just in a convenient location for the collector to find it each month. The rules for selection should also take account of the sampling methodology underlying the selection of shops. There is a stronger argument for using some form of probability sampling for the selection of items using tight descriptions when the selection of shops is more loosely specified, and vice versa. This is because the broader the item descriptions and the more loosely controlled the item selection in the field, the more the representativity of the sample is reliant on the quality of the initial selection of shops.

6.30 It is also important under either specification regime that instructions to price collectors give an adequate description of the item to be priced. For instance, in the case of a washing machine the information required for a tight specification may include make, model number, capacity, whether automatic, whether top or front loaded, and spin speed. As well as providing effective sampling control, this will also be useful information if a price collector has to choose the nearest equivalent should the particular model cease to be available. It is important that the number of prices obtained for tightly specified goods or services are regularly reviewed so that specifications can be updated if these items are being phased out or if consumer purchasing patterns are changing.

6.31 A loose specification may simply specify a washing machine with a particular range either for the capacity or the spin speed. In this case it is still important that the collector records a detailed description of the washing machine being priced to enable the selection of a comparable model if that model is discontinued or so that a future collector can carry out the price collection when the original collector is not available.

Collection procedures

6.32 An important consideration in the collection of prices is the scope of the price index being constructed. For example, should black market or contraband goods be priced as part of the price collection? In general, if such purchases constitute a significant part of expenditure then there is an argument in principle that they should be considered for inclusion. This, however, leads to price collection difficulties such as finding the necessary outlets, which may be transient and not advertise themselves, as well as the actual pricing of goods and services. Another difficulty regarding scope concerns activities that are considered illegal in some countries but not in others (for example, prostitution, gambling or sales of alcohol).

6.33 The greatest difficulty in collecting prices arises for goods and services in economies where bartering plays an important part. Examples range from prices for cars, which can be individually negotiated (including the possibility of trading in an old car), to market stalls in some communities. Ultimately the price obtained depends on the likelihood of a real purchase, and the negotiating skills of the price collector, as well as factors such as how desperate the retailer is for a sale. Ideally the price collector should obtain the price that a consumer would actually pay. In some cases it may be appropriate to look at alternative price collection methods or indicators instead (such as the advertised price, which could be assumed to move in the same way as the bartered price depending on circumstances).

6.34 In some Middle Eastern countries where prices vary according to the time of day and where prices are not usually advertised (for example, in the souk), it is necessary to employ a variety of collection procedures. Prices for fresh meat and vegetables may be collected three to six times in a day, including a morning, lunchtime and evening visit. In addition, collectors can be trained to recognize "deceptive" prices and can be encouraged to linger and listen to transaction prices for genuine sales.

6.35 Different collection procedures may be applicable for different outlets. Permanent outlets can sometimes be selected on the basis of a sampling frame either held centrally or through local enumeration (see Chapter 5). In the souk or marketplace it may be appropriate to use other collection procedures, particularly where the opening times and the variety of stalls and goods for sale vary at different times. In these cases, the item list may be restricted to items known to be available in the souk and price collectors may be asked to obtain a fixed number of price quotes for each item, the number being determined by local knowledge of the varieties on sale and the variation in price. Some items, such as fruit and vegetables, may warrant more quotes than others and prices may need to be collected at intervals throughout the day (for example, three times in the morning, three times during lunchtime and three times in the afternoon or evening) to ensure that any variability in price according to time of day is taken into account. Consideration may also need to be given to collecting from farmers (who travel to the souk to sell their wares) and middlemen (who buy the food from the farmers and then sell it on).

6.36 Another difference between countries may be where a significant proportion of expenditure occurs abroad and then the purchased items are imported by individuals (for example, car sale markets in Lithuania are frequented by the population of other Baltic States). Under such circumstances, price collections need to be considered in terms of the scope of the index (for example, should prices in other countries be considered?) as well as the more complicated matter of pricing the same or similar quality car each month.

6.37 An overview of local price collection for straightforward outlets is given in Figure 6.1. This diagram assumes that outlets have already been enumerated and selected, that the shopkeeper or head office of a chain has agreed that price collectors may visit on a regular basis, and that usual identification formalities on arrival and departure will have been carried out. In addition, it assumes that item selections have already been made in previous months. This is usually best done on a separate pre-collection visit where the price collectors introduce themselves, familiarize themselves with the shop, and explain the price collection procedure to the shopkeeper.

6.38 The diagram details different decisions and actions that a price collector must make to price any individual item. The diagram starts with arrival of the price collector at the outlet, at a mutually agreed time, which may or may not coincide with the usual shop opening times. Having gained entry to the outlet (or a replacement outlet), the collector attempts to price the necessary item or items. In a straightforward situation the item is immediately available for purchase and priced. More complicated situations arise when the item is different from the previous collection in some way (such as in size, description, weight, or quantity), in which case the usual procedure is to price the item and report the facts to head office. Finally, if the item is unavailable, another item has to be selected as a replacement comparable item or a replacement new item. Having priced all the items required in that outlet, the collector can move on to the next outlet.

6.39 The choice of a comparable item is made using the same bundle of key characteristics as that potentially affecting the price. For example, the brand name, wash cycles, capacity, energy consumption and spin speed may affect the price of a washing machine.

6.40 The most complicated situation arises when a different item that is not of a comparable quality has to be priced. How this is treated depends on the procedures in place for adjusting prices for changes in quality. For example, quality changes may be treated implicitly by considering the item as a new item with an imputed base price. The latter may be calculated by head office staff who may require supplementary information from the price collection or by the price collector in the outlet with the assistance of sales staff.

6.41 Seasonal items require special attention. In some situations, seasonal items such as fruit, vegetables or clothing may not be available for pricing all year round. One way of reflecting this in the index is to use seasonal weights, which differ for each month of the year and reflect expenditure information from household budget surveys or other sources. Alternatively, other seasonal items may be priced at different times of the year to directly replace the unavailable items (for example, bathing costumes and shorts may be priced for six months, and gloves and scarves for six months).

6.42 One possibility for data collection is to collect some items less often than monthly, thereby making possible a larger total sample. Many items in the United States Consumer Price Index (CPI) are collected only bimonthly in any given area; similarly, the rent samples are divided into six panels, each priced twice each year. It makes the calculation more complex but may be more efficient from both a statistical standpoint and also for collectors.

Price collection techniques

6.43 For many items, prices will be collected locally by price collection agencies employed by the national statistical institute, or their own employees, visiting retail outlets and recording current prices for an agreed selection of items. But some prices may be collected centrally from catalogues, by retailers providing list prices covering a range of outlets, by telephone, fax, letter, emails or from Internet sites. All these methods may be cost-effective or necessary to represent different aspects of consumer purchasing behaviour and so it is not surprising that many statistical offices use a variety of data collection techniques. In addition, such price collections can allow for the implementation of specific methodological procedures by head office staff (for example, quality changes). Either local collection agents or head office staff can use these varying collection methods. Examples of price collection techniques include the following:

- Prices may be obtained from mail catalogues to represent a certain type of retail outlet, or where high street catalogue stores have nationwide coverage with uniform pricing policies. Increasingly in some countries mail order suppliers are offering their own Internet services. In the case of both mail order and Internet shopping, care has to be taken to treat delivery prices and sales taxes consistently and correctly.
- Prices may be obtained over the Internet either for convenience (where major stores offer the same prices

Figure 6.1 Price collection procedures

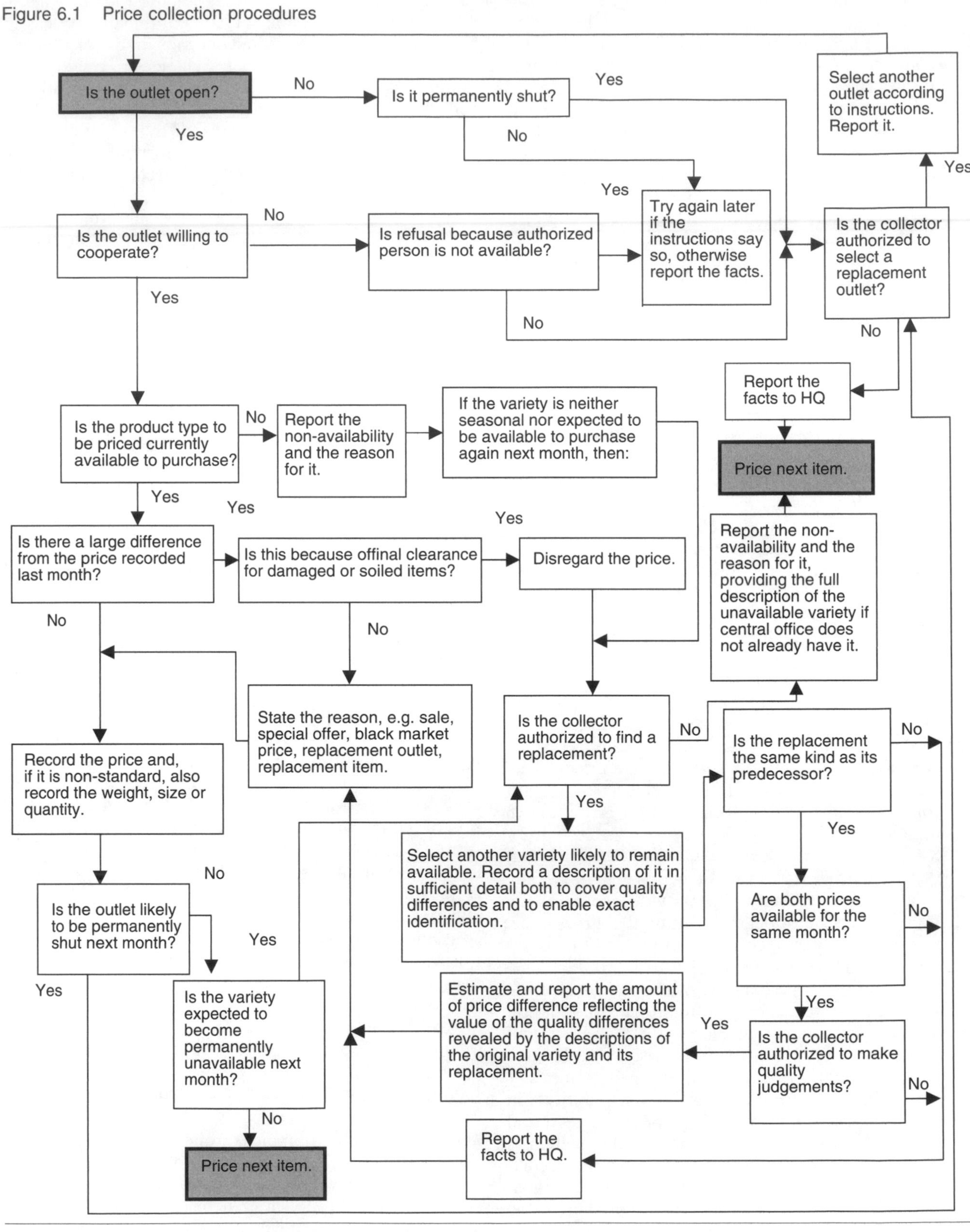

on the Internet as in the shops) or through necessity in order to maintain a representative sample where this type of retail outlet is increasingly used (for example, for books).

- Some retailers have national pricing policies with no individual pricing discretion, even for sales and special offers. In these cases, a single store can be visited or the retailer's head office may agree to supply a single price list (covering all items or prices for the specific selected items).
- Prices may be obtained over the telephone or by fax where there will be no ambiguity in price because the item being priced is standard and the contractor will quote a standard charge (for example, electricians may be telephoned for charges for providing a new single electricity socket). In addition, obtaining a price over the telephone will reflect what the consumer will often do in practice. A further factor is that many service providers (such as plumbers or window cleaners) tend not to work from retail outlets and it would be difficult to visit due to their variable working hours off-site at the customer's own premises.
- Prices may be obtained by letter, fax or email, accompanied by relevant head office forms for completion and return in cases where central office collection is deemed more efficient or where local price collection is not possible (for example, tariff prices). Examples include prices collected from a sample of local authorities, insurance companies, public utilities, and telephone companies.
- Prices may be obtained from other government agencies or regulatory authorities, which can act as intermediaries in the price collection process. In some countries, for example, this would be the case for electricity prices.
- In some cases, secondary sources can provide data on specific goods. Two examples, taken from the United States CPI but by no means unique to that country, are airline fares and used vehicles. A sample of scheduled airline flights is selected using detailed ticket data from the United States Department of Transportation. Monthly pricing is then carried out by online reference to a private-sector computerized fare database widely used by travel agents and others. In the case of used cars and trucks, both sampling and pricing employ published data from a dealer trade association. The benefits of using secondary data may include larger sample sizes, faster or less expensive access to data, or the avoidance of particularly difficult collection problems.

6.44 When using other sources such as catalogues or the Internet for prices, special care must be taken to ensure that they are correctly recorded with or without sales taxes, or with or without delivery charges. In these cases, procedures should include a check that the prices are relevant for the index period.

6.45 It is important to remember that all the usual price collection principles and quality assurance concerns remain relevant for prices collected from the Internet (including the need for detailed descriptions, immediate availability of the item for purchase, treatment of special offers, and possibility of substituting comparable or new items).

6.46 Where prices are taken over the telephone it is recommended that the retailer be visited occasionally, where practicable, to maintain personal contact and response rates and to ensure that no misunderstandings of items or pricing are occurring. As far as possible, prices collected by telephone should also be confirmed in writing to provide confirmation for quality assurance procedures (see Chapter 12).

6.47 Many households may be unable to access the Internet, and Internet shopping provides additional services, such as home delivery. This means that collecting prices from the Internet can be considered either as the introduction of a new outlet or a new item. In both instances action should be taken as part of the procedure for maintaining a representative sample at the time of the regular updating of the item and location selections, usually at the time of chain linking. It should be noted that consideration will also need to be given to whether a move to Internet shopping involves a quality change. For example, in the case of food shopping, free delivery may be included for payment over a certain level, or the average "use by" date may differ from that found in traditional outlets.

6.48 The scope for improving the efficiency of data collection can increase with the arrival of technological advances in the marketplace. New collection methods are continually becoming available, particularly in the technologically advanced countries. Methods for future collection include touch-tone dialling facilities and scanner data, both of which have the advantage of offering new ways for businesses to reduce the burden or inconvenience of supplying data.

6.49 It should be remembered that to keep the index representative, it might be appropriate to collect prices for an item in more than one way. For example, people may buy books from catalogues, from a variety of shops (bookshops, newsagents, supermarkets, department stores, and so on) and through the Internet. In these circumstances, it is appropriate to collect prices through all types of outlet where transactions are significant.

Questionnaire design

6.50 Good design of the questionnaire form (or its electronic equivalent) is essential for the successful collection of prices. Not only is it important that the price collectors find it easy to use, but the format and layout should facilitate the extraction of data (price, item description, comments, and so on) by head office for effective quality assurance.

6.51 The first step in designing a questionnaire is to define the information that needs to be gathered and how it will be collected. Different forms will be appropriate for each of the collection methods that are deployed, for instance visiting retailers compared with collecting by post. There will, however, be a number of common principles. The questionnaire should be practical for the price collector to use in the field and should also facilitate basic quality assurance. It is for the latter reason that it has been argued that the price recorded last time the item was surveyed should be shown on the questionnaire, as this will prompt the collector to ask questions if the previous price is very different from the current price. The converse to this argument is that the recording of the last price may mistakenly lead price collectors to identify the item to be priced by reference to price rather than item description, or at the extreme to estimate the price or repeat the previous price without actually visiting the shop.

6.52 It should be remembered that, at the time an index is chained, the questionnaire will need to list all items included in the old as well as the new basket. For example, an index chained annually on January prices requires both the old sample of locations and items and the new sample of locations and items for the base month.

6.53 An example of a price collection form is given in Appendix 6.1. This example is of a form used by the collector for recording prices when visiting an outlet and could be either a paper or electronic version. It is also possible to ask the shopkeepers concerned to complete the form themselves and to send it to the national statistical institute. Such a form may therefore serve for reporting as well as for collecting. If the form has space for recording prices over a whole sequence of months, the collector may keep the form and transcribe the prices from it each month onto a separate report form, which is sent to the national statistical institute. Where the form used for collection is also used for reporting, there are two main possibilities: either the form has space for recording prices over a whole sequence of months, and the form is shuttled backwards and forwards monthly between the collector and the office; or new forms for collection and reporting are printed out by the computer each month. In the latter case, if considered desirable, the form may contain the prices recorded in the previous month alongside the spaces for recording the current month's prices. It should be noted that the transfer of the prices to another form or system, whether done by computer or manually, may lead to transcription errors.

6.54 Increasingly, the use of an electronic version of the questionnaire on a hand-held computer or "personal assistant", with built-in validation checks, is seen as advantageous for local price collection by price collectors. The data can then be transferred electronically from collector to head office via a variety of intermediate steps for further validation checks by the price collection agency.

6.55 It is recommended that price collectors be required to provide full descriptions of the items being priced. This enables checks to be put in place to ensure that collectors are properly following instructions, particularly on the selection of items to be priced. It also ensures that any changes, including changes in the quality of the items, are being properly identified, with enough detailed information to enable decisions to be taken on quality adjustment. Price collectors should be given a checklist or set of codes to record relevant information on changes relating to outlets, items or prices. The information needs to be systematically collected. For instance, codes to help with quality adjustment need to reflect those characteristics that most influence price. Prior research, for example, based on the hedonic method, can help to predetermine these (see Chapters 7 and 21).

6.56 Codes for managing the sample of outlets may include:

- *closed down*: outlet permanently shut or closed down;
- *temporarily unavailable*: outlet temporarily closed, but likely to be open next month;
- *refusal*: owner or staff refuses to cooperate;
- *change of details*: change of ownership or name, or change of purpose.

6.57 Continuity is one of the most important principles of price collection. As the index measures price *changes*, it is vital that the same item is priced every month in order to establish a true picture of price changes. So if, for example, a jar of a supermarket's own brand strawberry jam has been selected, that particular brand and flavour should continue to be collected; if it is out of stock, another brand and flavour should not be used without further investigation to establish whether this is a temporary situation or likely to be permanent. In the latter case, and if another flavour of the same brand, size and quality is available, then this item should in normal circumstances be chosen as a "comparable" item and the item description suitably amended. If a different brand, size or quality product is available then this should be selected as a "new" item, but only where no comparable items are available. The same principles apply to other items, such as clothes, and fresh fruit and vegetables. With clothes, it may be important that colour, fabric, country of origin, logos and size are specified to ensure that the same item is priced each month. For fresh fruit and vegetables, useful attributes to record may be "country of origin", "class" and variety. For electrical equipment, it may be the specifications and features given in the manufacturer's catalogue that are important.

6.58 It is not possible to be prescriptive because the concept of equivalence will vary between different countries; but for practical purposes it is important that a detailed description of the items being priced is recorded. Item descriptions will assist the price collector and head office in choosing or confirming the suitability of a replacement for an item that has been withdrawn and will also help identify changes in quality. The focus should be on recording price-determining characteristics.

6.59 Should the regular price collector, for whatever reason, be unable to carry out the normal collection, full and accurate descriptions will enable a relief collector to carry out the collection without any doubt as to the correct items.

6.60 Most of the time, the item will be exactly as collected the previous month and all that will be recorded is a new price. However, should there be a change or uncertainty in the item, then it will be necessary for price collectors to use their own judgement and to inform head office, bearing in mind that head office staff are responsible for making the final decision. A pre-coded specification will be less time-consuming and will provide better guidance to the price collector on what information should be reported. The codes might include:

Comparable (C): The original item is no longer stocked but a similar alternative has been collected that does not differ in terms of major attributes. The price is likely to be in a similar range although this may not always be the case.

New (N): The item has been replaced by something new that is not really comparable but is equally representative of that commodity group. If possible the collector should try to find out the price of the "new" item in the chain link or base period.

Sale or special offer (S): A price decrease because of a genuine sale or special offer, with a sale or discount sticker present. This does not include damaged or out of date stock or clearance goods. The latter should never be included. A price reduction where there is no notice of a sale or special offer is not a "sale"; the item should still be priced, but without the S indicator code.

Recovery (R): A return to the normal selling price, for example after a sale or special offer. This need not be a return to the same price as before the sale or special offer.

Temporarily out of stock (T): Guidance will need to be given to the price collector concerning the meaning of "temporarily" (in terms of expected duration, which may vary for different items). It may be advisable to replace items immediately (for example, fashion clothing, if it is unlikely that the identical item will come back into stock). Typically, T indicators should not be used for more than two consecutive months – in the third month, a replacement should be chosen. In food outlets, it is very unusual for items to go permanently out of stock. The collector should always try to check future availability with the retailer.

Missing (M): Used where the outlet has never stocked or no longer intends to stock an item and there is no appropriate alternative item. In these circumstances it is recommended that the item is checked at subsequent collections to ensure that a suitable replacement item has not come into stock.

Weight (W): A permanent weight or quantity change to the product.

Query (Q): Such a code may be used to supply extra retail information to head office (for example, "10 per cent extra free", "3 for the price of 2", or a strange price difference that is not covered by one of the other indicators, such as a bumper issue of a magazine at an increased price). Arrangements need to be in place for head office to respond to these comments and to treat the price quotes accordingly.

6.61 The use of these codes is illustrated in Appendix 6.1. Even if the retailer says there have been no price changes since the previous month, the price collector should confirm prices anyway. This will require some diplomacy, but it is important because it is easy for the shopkeeper to overlook a small number of price increases, forget when the last increase occurred or even deliberately mislead the price collectors. The use of codes is important for operational reasons. For example, if an item is unlikely to remain available the next month, then a substitute can be selected in advance and an overlap price collected.

6.62 As a general rule, a price should be recorded only if the exact product being priced is on display and immediately available for sale. No price should be recorded if a product is temporarily out of stock. For certain large items such as furniture, however, where the item must normally be ordered, the price should be recorded as long as the retailer confirms that it is available for delivery within an "acceptable" time period.

6.63 Some food items, such as meat, fish and cheese, can be sold in variable weights, so it is sensible to collect prices per unit of weight. This should be taken from the package labelling or calculated directly by the collector. Roughly the same package size and type should be used each month, as the unit price might be lower for larger pack sizes or differ between package types. Other items, such as eggs, are often sold in specified quantities. For these, it is essential that collectors record prices for the specified quantity, as total and unit prices usually depend on the number bought. If X eggs are to be priced and the price for the number is not quoted directly, then the price of one egg can be obtained and multiplied by X to get the required price. Care does need to be taken, however, to ensure that unit price does not decrease with quantity. Another example is mint. This herb is often sold in bunches of variable size, so a number of bunches should be weighed and priced to obtain a price per kilogram.

6.64 Certain food items, such as fruit or vegetables, are more difficult to price as some outlets might price items per number purchased while others might price by weight. For example, peppers may be priced by weight or by unit no matter what the size. Garlic may be priced per bulb, clove or by weight. Various types of berries may be priced by weight or by punnet, which may differ in size or how full they are. In these instances, care has to be taken with the product descriptions. Collectors need to be aware of the importance of collecting the same thing from one month to another, so that genuine price changes are recorded and not quantity or quality price changes.

6.65 The use of hand-held computers for local price collection provides more scope for quality assurance both in the field and at head office, without some of the disadvantages associated with paper forms. Price collection using hand-held computers is discussed in more detail below. Use of electronic forms on floppy disks or by email, for example for central price collection from the head offices of large retail chains, may be more cost-effective than sending price collectors into individual outlets. But in these circumstances, care needs to be taken to check that there are no price variations between different outlets in a chain and that any special offers given locally are covered. Where there are such local factors, adequate account will need to be taken of them, otherwise the price recorded for the index may be misleading.

6.66 A decision needs to be taken over whether large retail chains should be placed in separate strata (treating the chain rather than an individual outlet as the sampling unit) or whether a sample of outlets from each chain is taken (thus taking as the sampling unit an outlet from a particular chain). As a general rule, a retail chain with no national pricing policy cannot be treated as a single sampling unit, but it may be possible to visit only a few of their outlets if it can be established that each outlet visited reflects the chain's prices over a wide area. In these situations, it is usual to approach the management of the chain's head office to confirm their pricing policies and obtain permission for the collection. Each year, when approached again for permission to continue the price collection, the management should be asked to confirm that their regional pricing policy remains unchanged. The prices collected are then given a weight to reflect the market share they represent, in the same fashion as the weights applied to prices collected centrally for a chain where there are no price variations between outlets. Issues relating to central collection of prices from local businesses and outlets (for instance, over the telephone by staff located in the national statistical institute) and the collection of prices for retail chains from their corresponding head office are discussed further below.

Field procedures

6.67 Adequate field procedures are required to ensure that the quality of the price index is not compromised through errors in price collection. Price collection needs to be carefully planned and managed, and effective instructions and training given to price collectors. Most prices are likely to be collected through price collectors visiting individual outlets. Guidance on the organization and management of field procedures relating to local price collection is given in Chapter 12.

6.68 In some circumstances it may be more efficient for prices to be obtained from one source rather than through surveys in the field. These are covered in the section that follows.

Central and head office collection

6.69 One form of central and head office price collection is where price data representing a number of shops are collected from one single source. This can take place when chains of shops have proven national pricing policies, with no local variations between stores in terms of either price normally paid or special offers and discounts. In these cases, the chains' outlets should be excluded from local price collection and the prices collected should be weighted according to the market share of sales.

6.70 The selection of this type of central collection and calculation is usually dependent on one or more of the following considerations: national or local pricing policies; available sources of data (including willingness of chains to assist in this way and forward commitment by them to provide data centrally); data presentation and format (advertised prices or average transaction prices provided by email, on floppy disk or paper); reference point of available data (price lists match the collection day or period); and frequency of price changes.

6.71 Central price collection may also be appropriate for some service prices. These could include:

- fees set by a professional or trade association or union;
- charges for public utilities or services provided by deregulated (and regulated) bodies or government (such as: water, gas and electricity tariffs; bus and train fares; birth, marriage and death registration fees);
- prices centrally determined by government (for example, fees to be paid for services, such as health care and education, that may be partially or fully funded by government);
- taxes and licence fees paid to government (for example, television licences and vehicle excise duties).

In some instances, data may need to be requested from regional authorities, for example where there are regional utility providers.

6.72 Data may be requested in writing, or by telephone or electronically. Where letters are sent, consideration should be given to using office automation for the generation of data requests (for example, mail merge facilities), logging responses, monitoring progress and sending reminders to non-respondents. Useful categories for informing progress might include: return received; return being checked; query sent and awaiting resolution of query; figures finalized.

6.73 The greatest gains from electronic reporting of centrally collected prices are likely to be efficiency gains from automation, better work monitoring and fewer problems arising from transcription errors. The risk – one that is associated with all central price collection – is that the impact of an undetected error can be compounded because of the relatively large weight that may be placed on one price or set of prices. Clearly, this factor should be reflected in the quality assurance procedures as well as in the sampling procedures. It has been observed that national statistical institutes can be slow in reviewing their quality assurance procedures following a move to greater central price collecting. This can lead to a disproportionate amount of effort at head office being focused on the checking of local prices. This is particularly so if local prices have been rigorously scrutinized in the field; any individual error will not have a noticeable impact on the index unless it is part of a systematic bias, for example arising from inadequate instructions to collectors.

6.74 Providers of goods and services may send either a full price list or a tariff from which an appropriate sample of prices and weights can be extracted or just those prices required for compilation of the index. In some instances, for example a regional transport authority, it may be acceptable for data to be provided in the form of a price index. In these cases it is clearly important to ensure that the index has been calculated accurately and in accordance with the requirements of the consumer price index, using agreed methodology, and that the central office exercises strict quality control. The latter may be done by, for example, checking the computation once a year or more frequently against the basic data or by setting up automated systems to detect abnormal changes. Agreements on the methodology of the computation should include such things as item selection, weighting of components and timing of collection, as well as the mathematical construction of the index. The index should also be made available to the central office with supplementary briefing and explanations for price movements. Any potential problems, such as the need to resample where previously quoted items are no longer available, should be discussed with the national statistical institute in advance. A continuous quality control may take the form of a reconciliation analysis against other related data (including announced price changes) and identifying outliers when compared to previous values of the index. Data and prices published by another organization or government body may provide a useful comparator. Where prices are taken over the telephone, it is highly recommended that all price quotations are subsequently confirmed in writing to ensure that any queries may be resolved and that an audit trail is maintained for future months in case of subsequent discrepancies that cannot be resolved.

6.75 In all instances it is important to check on a regular basis that the item or service being provided has not changed in any respect, because if this is the case a quality adjustment may need to be applied. In the case of supermarkets and other large suppliers of data, confirmation should be sought from head office that code numbers have not changed to ensure that the items being priced do not change unexpectedly between one price collection period and the next.

6.76 As stated previously, the frequency of collection depends on both the range of prices being monitored and when the prices are known or expected to change. For instance, bus and rail fares may change once a year on a prespecified date. In other instances, prices may change throughout the year as different providers review their pricing structures, but the expectation may be that prices will show little volatility. For example, it may be necessary only to contact health insurance companies on a quarterly basis or local authorities for prices of school dinners only at the start of each term. Decisions on these issues will need to be based on knowledge of local circumstances, with satisfactory procedures in place to detect any change in procedures.

6.77 The number of price quotes required at each collection will depend on individual circumstances and will need to take account of the weights and homogeneity of the index as well as the underlying volatility of prices (see Chapter 5). It is also best to avoid situations where a handful of price quotes from, say, an individual retail chain represents a large weight in the index. The number of prices collected centrally should where possible reflect the importance of that item in the shopping basket and the range and volatility of the prices.

6.78 All the data collection principles above are to be followed for all central and head office price collection, regardless of whether these forms of collection have been introduced for reasons of practicality, cost-effectiveness, or special methodological concerns.

6.79 Further examples of items that may be collected centrally include: some aspects of transport, such as tolls for bridges; situations where there may be a variety of different outlets but where there is uniform pricing for all consumers; and instances where the data requirements for quality adjustment are better met by exploiting a single data source. By way of elaboration, if none of the towns or cities selected for local price collections have tolls on roads, bridges or tunnels, then these could be unintentionally excluded from the index; but by selecting a sample of these across the country – with prices collected centrally – the index remains representative of these types of expenditure. Similarly, if the prices of goods and services are the same all over the country, regardless from whom they are bought (for example, newspapers and magazines), then these prices are most cost-effectively collected centrally. The more complex methodological calculations of prices, including quality adjustments, may also be best collected centrally. Examples of these include some housing costs, and computers and cars (where information on technical specifications at the level of detail required for quality adjustment may not be available from shopkeepers).

Price reductions

6.80 One of the principles relating to consumer price indices, which is applied with few exceptions (such as owner-occupier housing costs), is that only transaction prices, that is prices actually paid by individuals or households, should be included in the index. This may differ from the advertised price if, for example, a discount is offered. In practice, however, discriminatory discounts, which are available only to a restricted group of households (as opposed to non-discriminatory discounts that are available to all), are generally excluded on principle. For example, money-off coupons and loyalty rewards for previous expenditure are normally ignored and the non-discounted price is recorded. Also, it may be difficult to obtain the price paid if this is subject to individual bargaining. It may therefore not come as a surprise that, while the general rule above may appear simple, there are a number of instances requiring special treatment either because of conceptual issues or because of practical difficulties. The following guidelines reflect practices followed by a number of countries. They do not represent a set of rules because the appropriate practice to be followed will be determined by individual circumstances, which might vary between different countries.

6.81 *Discounted prices* should only be taken if generally available to anyone with no conditions attached; otherwise the non-discounted or unsubsidized price is recorded. In particular, the general practice is to ignore money-off coupons and loyalty rewards. A judgement needs to be made, however, relating to the interpretation of "generally available". For instance, reduced prices for payment by direct debit may be taken into account depending on the extent to which consumers as a whole have access to and use such a service. A judgement is required in the latter case on the threshold to be set for access, above which action is taken for inclusion in the index. Alternatively, different payment methods may all be priced individually (for example, separate data collection for electricity payments by cash, direct debit and pre-payment) and weighted together to form a single price index for that item.

6.82 *Price discrimination.* Discounts available only to a restricted group of households should be disregarded because they are discriminatory, unless they are significant and are available either to the vast majority of the population or to identifiable subgroups who qualify for such discounts on the basis of demographic or other characteristics not requiring action by the individuals concerned at the time of purchase. In the latter case, they should be treated as stratification or coverage issues in item sampling. Some judgement is required. Examples of allowable price discrimination may include lower prices offered to pensioners (for example, discounted travel or haircuts) and discounts for people who receive state benefits. Another example of a case where prices are not universally available to all, and where judgement is required, is where a nominal or token membership fee is required by the retail outlet. In these cases, the take-up of such membership – which is widely available to all – needs to be considered in terms of thresholds and general spending patterns of the consumers and the conditions placed on membership which may make the latter restrictive (for example, minimum levels of purchase). Ease of access to the outlets in question may be a relevant factor as well, say, if in practice the customers need to have the use of a private car.

6.83 *Sale or special offer prices* should be recorded if these are either temporary reductions on goods that are likely to be available again at normal prices, or are stock-clearing sales (such as January sales or summer sales). Before designating a price as a "sale" price, however, special care should be taken to ascertain that there is a genuine sale with price reductions on normal stock. On occasion, stock is continually sold below the recommended retail price or advertised as a special offer even though these prices are available all year. In such cases, prices should not be considered as sale prices, but can still be collected. Special purchases of end-of-range, damaged, shop-soiled or defective goods should not normally be priced, as they are likely not to be the same quality as, or comparable with, goods previously priced and are unlikely to be available in future. If the special offer is limited to the first customers, the item should not be priced, as the offer is not available to everyone. Introductory special offers may be included if they are available to all. In reality, however, given the need to price the same "basket" each month, such offers will not be chosen as representative items unless they are introduced at the time of an update of the "basket" or when a replacement item needs to be chosen. Discounts on goods close to expiry dates should be disregarded or treated as specification or quality changes.

6.84 *Bonus offers, extras and free gifts.* Prices for items temporarily bearing extra quantities (for example, 30 per cent extra free) should not be adjusted to take account of the increased quantity if it is thought that the extra quantities involved may not be wanted by most consumers, will not have influenced the decision to purchase or will not be consumed. Similarly, free items with other purchases (such as buy 2 get 1 free or free gift with every product purchased) should be disregarded. Money-off coupons for future purchases should be disregarded, as these may not be used or wanted. Free gifts such as plastic toys in cereal boxes should be ignored because they are not included in the list for price observations; it is the price to be paid to get the cereal in the box that is relevant. Collectors should be aware that temporary "special offer" weight changes (X per cent extra free) could become a permanent weight change (for example, cans of alcoholic drinks changing size from 440 ml to 500 ml) and should feed the information back to head office as they become aware of it. In this way, head offices can issue new or amended guidance to price collectors about item specifications.

6.85 *Stamps.* Sometimes purchasers are given special stamps, which can be accumulated and subsequently exchanged for goods and services. If a discount is available as an alternative to such stamps, then the discounted price should be recorded. Otherwise, the stamps should be disregarded.

6.86 *Trade-ins.* In general the price reduction obtained by trading in an old item (for example, a car) compared with the nominal full price should be ignored. This treatment follows convention, as the transaction essentially relates to a second-hand good and only the service charge levied by the outlet in buying and selling the good comes under the scope of the index. In reality, however, the situation is not so clear-cut. For instance, a garage may well give a discount which is greater than the retail value of the traded-in car and, therefore, in effect gives a genuine discount on the new car. In many cases, discounts from trade-ins are very difficult to evaluate. The trade-in value may be negotiable in each case, and the full nominal price – which is used as the benchmark against which the discount is measured – may not be known. It may therefore be best to report the list price or asking price.

6.87 *Sales taxes.* When an indirect tax is not included in the price of individual items in a shop, but is instead added on when the customer pays for the item, great care must be taken to record the price including tax. To make sure of this, with items for which the price is normally quoted pre-tax, and in areas where a general sales tax is added to the bill, the price collection forms should require the collector to indicate whether or not the price recorded does include the tax – as a price check – so that it can be added where necessary.

6.88 *Tips for services.* If a compulsory service charge is included, for example on a restaurant bill, only the compulsory amount should be included in the price, but not any additional discretionary tips. For services which are free in principle, but which in practice can rarely be obtained without what amounts to a tip, or where tipping at a standard rate is the common practice, such tips should be added to the specified price.

6.89 *Regular rebates or refunds* should only be taken into account when attributable to the purchase of an individual identifiable product and granted within a time period from the actual purchase such that they are expected to have a significant influence on the quantities buyers wish to buy. For example, money-back deposits on bottles should be deducted from the price if they are a sufficient incentive for returning the bottle, while money-back offers on lawn mowers after a five-year period should be disregarded. In all cases, a consistent decision for each item must be applied over time. Decisions about the treatment of rebates are not easy to recommend, as many decisions are made on an individual basis. They may reflect income rather than expenditure changes and may require different treatment for, say, national accounts uses.

6.90 *Irregular rebates or refunds* should only be taken into account when they apply to the purchase of an individual product and are granted within a time period such that they are expected to have a significant influence on the quantities purchasers are willing to buy. Loyalty rebates or coupons associated with previous expenditure at the outlet, to be used for similar or other purchases, should generally be disregarded, as they are discriminatory. If they are significant factors, they should be treated as stratification or coverage aspects of sampling (see Chapter 5). One off rebates (for example, associated with privatization) should be disregarded as they do not relate to the specific time period of the consumption and are unlikely to affect levels of consumption. They can be viewed more as a source of additional income.

6.91 *Credit card and other payment arrangements involving interest, service charges or extra charges* incurred as a consequence of failing to pay within a specified period of time from the purchase should be disregarded. For example, zero interest as well as positive interest loans granted to finance a purchase should be disregarded when determining the price. Reductions for cash payments may be included but care should be taken to ensure consistent treatment from one period to the next.

Price bargaining

6.92 Bargaining relates to a situation where prices are individually negotiated between sellers and purchasers, and are not predetermined. The process of negotiation is a characteristic of, for example, marketplaces in many African countries where almost everything to be purchased must be negotiated to arrive at an agreed price, including a wide range of life's daily necessities that can account for a large part of household consumption. The system of bargaining is characterized by its great flexibility in the setting of prices. Final transaction prices and quantities will vary from one transaction to another and cannot be determined until the purchase has been made. Similarly, there will be variations between transactions in the quality of the goods being purchased. Clearly, these special conditions require special methods to determine purchasers' prices for inclusion in the consumer price index.

6.93 It can be argued from the viewpoint of the system of national accounts that bargaining is a form of price discrimination. A purchaser is not free to choose the purchase price because the seller can charge different categories of purchasers different prices for identical goods and services sold under exactly the same circumstances. It follows that "identical" products sold at different prices should be recognized as having the same quality, and their prices must be averaged to obtain a single price relative to calculating price indices. In reality, the variation in transaction price can rarely be associated with identifiable price-related categories of customers. Rather, purchasers may inadvertently buy at a higher price than may be found elsewhere or could have been finally negotiated. Notwithstanding this, collectors of prices should guard against the presumption that price differences do not relate to quality (or quantity) differences.

6.94 Where prices are determined by bargaining, standard price survey methods – which consist of collecting prices directly from sellers – can generate erratic price indices that do not reflect actual price movements in a market. For example, prices collected by enumerators depend on their ability, willingness and power to bargain, in the same way as actual prices paid by genuine purchasers. In addition, prices can vary during the course of a day as well as from one day to the next, adding an extra dimension to the concept of representativeness. A number of survey methods and price collection techniques have been developed to overcome the difficulties inherent in measuring prices that have been bargained.

6.95 *Survey by purchase of products*. The principle is that price collection should be carried out in conditions that simulate as closely as possible situations in which real transactions actually take place. Price collectors behave like regular purchasers by actually purchasing items to be priced and spreading their purchases over the day to ensure representativeness. In each case, the field manager will need to carry out regular checks on quantities and prices obtained by collectors. The following approaches may be taken:

- Price collectors buy items to determine the relevant price through bargaining. They should be trained to behave as normal purchasers and strive to get the lowest possible price from selected outlets and sellers. Given the high turnover of sellers, the sample of sellers should be partially renewed on a regular basis to ensure that it remains representative and chained in as appropriate.
- Price collectors buy items and, in addition, are given an incentive to get the best price. For example, a price ceiling may be set and the collector may receive a proportion of the difference between the ceiling and the bargained price. This incentive system guards against potential difficulties caused by the collector not getting the lowest price because, unlike an ordinary customer, he or she is not concerned with maximizing value for money and is not constrained by income.

6.96 *Survey of purchasers*. The prices purchasers have paid are collected throughout the day immediately after the purchaser leaves the outlet or market stall, together with a record of the quantity and quality of the product purchased. The extent of the haggling should be determined (for example, opening and closing prices) together with an indication of the relevant parameters determining the price. A form of incentive payment for survey participation may be needed where there is reluctance among purchasers to submit to such time-consuming questions.

6.97 For the survey by purchase of products and the survey of purchasers, all items in the basket of items used to calculate the consumer price index that are subject to bargaining should be covered. The number of prices collected needs to be sufficient both to cover all relevant items and to provide a reliable guide to average price. This may be difficult to determine beforehand, although previous price collections should provide some guidance. It is suggested that price collectors engaging in a survey of purchasers are given a form on which to record the number of quotations per stall or shop, as indicated by the various respondents. This can be used to check the number of quotes obtained against the target number set by head office. An example of such a form is given in Table 6.1.

6.98 *Survey of trends in wholesale prices.* A limited parallel collection of wholesale prices can be a useful supplement for problematic items where the information obtained from the above survey techniques is only partially successful, for example where there is a deficit in the number of observations obtained. Ideally, prices should be obtained from the particular wholesalers where the relevant retailers get their goods. All factors should be observed which might result in increases in the corresponding retail prices, such as changes in taxes on retail activities, licence fees and the rental for the market stall. Assuming that those factors remain constant over time, the evolution of wholesale prices may be used as a proxy for the retail price index of relevant items. The price of an item for the current period would be estimated by multiplying the price of the previous period by the corresponding evolution in wholesale price.

6.99 Determination of the prices paid by a purchaser can be problematic where the final price is for a bundle of items, for example where a stall holder gives the purchaser extra quantities as a bonus for buying a number of goods. If the bonus comprises several categories of items, including the item on which a transaction price was being directly negotiated, then the purchase has to be split into as many sub-transactions as item categories. In these cases, a commonsense approach is needed. There is a fine dividing line between this type of circumstance and the "two-for-one" offers sometimes found, for example, in Western-style supermarkets. The latter form of discount is often excluded from price calculations on the basis that the purchaser does not want or use the additional amount supplied. Additional perishable goods, for example, will become out of date and be thrown away. This argument is less relevant in market purchases in a developing country, where many consumers will be living on a subsistence income and therefore will consume all purchases. In such cases, purchasers will have actively bartered an overall price for the total basket of purchases, including any "free" goods thrown in.

Table 6.1 Example of a survey form showing the number of price quotations by shop or stall

Items	Targeted number of quotations (set by head office)	Actual number of quotations			
		Shop/Stall 1	Shop/Stall 2	....	Shop/Stall n
Item 1	5	0	3		5
Item 2	4	4	5		4
Item 3	8	5	8		8
...					
Item k	5	7	2		6

6.100 The method for determining the price paid by the purchaser is illustrated in the following example: a purchaser wants to buy 5 kg of carrots and is offered a bonus consisting of 500 grams of carrots, 100 grams of lettuce and 200 grams of baby marrow.

6.101 Three transactions can be identified, involving: 5.5 kg of carrots; 100 grams of lettuce; and 200 grams of marrow. The bonus has to be valued at prices at which the seller would have sold and the purchaser would have bought the items. The assumption made is that prices, in local currency units (LCU), would have been determined through bargaining on the same conditions as the price of the item needed (carrots). If the opening value of 5 kg of carrots is LCU 15,000 and the closing value LCU 12,000, whereas the opening values of other foodstuffs included in the bonus are LCU 990 for a bunch of 264 grams of lettuce and LCU 4,620 for a heap of baby marrow of 4.4 kg, the actual closing price of carrots will be determined as shown in Table 6.2. The actual purchaser's price of carrots is found to be LCU 2.0967 per gram or LCU 2,096.7 per kilo.

6.102 If the price collector does not know the closing price at which lettuce and baby marrow would have been sold by the seller of the carrots, then it can be estimated. This is done by collecting opening values and standard quantities from a sample of sellers in the same market or at different outlets in the same area. The average opening price of an item is equal to the sum of opening values of the item divided by the sum of relevant standard quantities. For each bonus item (lettuce and baby marrow), the resulting average opening price will be divided by the bargaining ratio calculated on the item needed (carrots) to estimate a closing price for that bonus item. The value of each bonus item is obtained by multiplying the closing price by the quantity offered. If the packet of bonus items contains an item of the same quality as the requested item, that bonus item will be valued on the basis of the closing value of the requested item.

Forced replacements, product substitution and quality adjustment

6.103 A difficulty which confronts both local and central price collections occurs when an item that was being priced is no longer available and a substitute needs to be found. This is briefly discussed here because it relates to real decisions facing price collectors in the field, but the issues are covered in more depth in Chapters 7 and 8. In cases where a replacement has to be found, the price collector should normally take the nearest equivalent product available in the outlet, taking into account those characteristics which will be most influential in determining price and purchasing habits (for example, one out-of-date or obsolete item should

Table 6.2 Example illustrating the method for determining the actual price paid by the purchaser when bargaining takes place

	Requested item	Bonus items		
	Carrots	Carrots	Lettuce	Baby marrow
Opening value of standard/requested quantity (local currency units)	15 000	15 000	990	4 620
Standard/requested quantity (grams)	5 000	5 000	264	4 400
Opening unit price of standard/requested quantity (local currency units per gram)	3	3	3.75	1.05
Opening unit price of bonus quantity (local currency units per gram)		3	3.75	1.05
Bonus quantity (grams)		500	100	200
Opening value of bonus quantity (local currency units)		1 500	375	210
Closing value of items received (local currency units)	12 000	1 200	300	168
New price (local currency units per gram)	2.4	2.4	3	0.8
Bargaining ratio	1.25	1.25	1.25	1.25
Payment (local currency units)	12 000			
Estimated closing value of bonus (local currency units)	1 668			
Actual value of requested item (all carrots) (local currency units)	10 332			
Quantity received of requested item (grams)	5 500			
Actual purchaser's unit price of requested item (local currency units per gram)	2.0967[1]			
Improved bargaining ratio	1.52[2]			

[1](12000−300−168) ÷ 5500 = 2.0967. [2]3 ÷ 2.0967 = 1.52.

not be replaced with a close item which may also shortly suffer the same fate). Nevertheless, where it is considered desirable to take the opportunity provided by product substitution to update the sample, a "most representative" replacement may be chosen. In the latter case, care must be taken to ensure that sufficient controls are in place to achieve the desirable end.

6.104 When a replacement is made, it is important for the price collector to provide a detailed specification of the new item so that head office can identify any associated quality change. This is to ensure that the consumer price index continues to reflect the cost of buying a fixed, constant quality basket of goods. Head office should then use the information collected to decide on any relevant quality adjustment to be applied.

6.105 When such a situation occurs, a nominal price in the base month (which for some indices will be the previous month) is needed for the new or replacement item. The latter may be obtained from the shopkeeper or one of three methods can be applied to take account of quality differences, which can then be used to estimate a new base price. These are direct comparison (that is, when there is no change in quality), direct (explicit) quality adjustment, or indirect (implicit) quality adjustment. When a new rather than a comparable replacement item is priced, it may be necessary for the new item to be kept out of the index for a short period until there is sufficient evidence of its longer-term availability and price stability.

6.106 In some countries, a table of quality coefficients is used to adjust prices. In one North African country, for example, the item "green tea" should be represented by Minara tea; however, if this is unavailable an alternative tea may be collected and that price scaled by the relevant coefficient (for example, Oudaya tea × 1.20). More detailed guidance on direct and indirect quality adjustment is given in Chapter 7.

6.107 If an outlet closes or refuses to allow further price collection, then another similar outlet should be selected from the same location and the indirect quality adjustment approach used to calculate new base prices. See Chapter 5 on sampling for replacing outlets within locations.

Related issues

Electronic reporting

6.108 Electronic reporting for centrally collected prices and use of hand-held computers for local price collection can introduce greater efficiency into price collection and processing, as well as providing more scope for effective auditing, but both are dependent on the introduction of effective quality control procedures. Electronic reporting through the use of electronic point of sale (EPOS) or scanner data is also likely to increase over time.

6.109 *Electronic reporting for centrally collected prices.* Centrally collected data can be collected electronically in a number of ways. Once initial contact has been made with data suppliers, a mutually convenient electronic data collecting procedure can be initiated. Options include:

- emailing data collection spreadsheets between the national statistics institute and the retailer;
- emailing of price lists at agreed times by retailers;
- touch-tone dialling facilities for data to be supplied in an agreed format;
- use of the Internet (supplemented if necessary by telephone calls to clarify definitions and availability).

6.110 *Hand-held computers*. The greatest gains from the use of hand-held computers for local price collection are likely to be drawn from efficiency in data transmission, better quality data as a result of the additional editing facilities available in the field, and the elimination of transcription errors. In addition, hand-held computers can generally speed up timetables.

6.111 The validation checks made during local price collection using hand-held computers will generally differ very little from those that should be carried out at central office when paper forms are received under the more traditional methods of collecting price data. The advantage of hand-held computers is that they provide the opportunity to validate prices in the field and in consequence correct errors at the time of price collection, rather than attempting to do so afterwards. In practice, it may be expensive and very difficult to check prices after collection. For example, prices may have changed in the intervening period and the price collector may have to rely on the shopkeeper's memory.

6.112 The choice of hand-held computer will depend on a number of factors, including price, reliability, maintenance and ease of use. The computing functions of data transfer, including back-up and downloading of data, as well as compatibility with office systems, are also important. Other considerations of particular concern to the price collector include ergonomic aspects, size and weight, editing facilities, and expected battery life. The risk of theft and other security matters will also play a part.

6.113 The introduction of hand-held computers can involve a significant initial outlay associated with purchasing the computers, developing the software and training price collectors. In addition there will be ongoing maintenance costs. These costs can sometimes be reduced or spread either by using the machines for other data collection in the national statistical institute, for example a household budget survey, or by contracting out to another organization that may already deploy these machines for other statistical surveys. These costs can be offset, at least in part, by more efficient working by price collectors and savings generated by less transcribing and inputting of data by hand, and a reduction in data editing by head office staff.

6.114 Careful planning is required in moving from a paper-based collection system to one using computers in order to avoid the risks inherent in such a change. National statistical institutes planning a move to price collection using hand-held computers should embark on extensive pilot testing and should also consider some limited double-running in parallel with the old paper collection system to ensure the robustness of the new method and that it is producing the same numerical results.

6.115 The additional facilities offered by hand-held computers, including local editing of prices, plus the elimination of the need for data transcription, may necessitate a general reorganization of the process for producing the consumer price index, and a redefining of roles and interaction between different members of the production team and between head office and price collectors.

6.116 It is important that clear rules and procedures are set out controlling the changes that can be made in the field by the price collector and the changes that should be made centrally. For example, replacement outlets could be pre-programmed in the event that outlets close down or refuse entry. Flexibility should allow price collectors to select and key in the new attributes for replacement items subject to procedures controlled centrally.

6.117 *EPOS or scanner data*. Electronic point of sale (EPOS) data usually refers to data obtained directly from a retailer's electronic point of sale, while scanner data usually refers to a commercial database that collates individual EPOS data. National statistical institutes are increasingly looking towards EPOS or scanner data as a convenient method of obtaining up-to-date and accurate information, not only on the quantity and prices of goods sold but also on their specification. The latter can be used to control the representativity of the sample and also to measure changes in quality. The advantage of this is that data are collated electronically without the necessity of sending price collectors into the field.

6.118 When considering the use of scanner data, account needs to be taken of such matters as the representativity of outlet and product coverage, and also whether the average prices given in scanner data accurately reflect actual transaction prices in the outlets themselves. In addition, it cannot be assumed that the geographical and population coverage or the treatment of goods and transactions matches the scope of the index. Scanner data are also likely to be of little use in collecting prices of services, which in many countries comprise an increasing share of transactions and thus of weights in consumer price indices. On a practical front, the unique identification of products can sometimes be problematical, as one item might be covered by more than one code number, and code numbers may not be uniquely assigned to one product and may be recycled as items disappear.

Purchasing power parities

6.119 Purchasing power parities are used to deflate major economic aggregates, such as gross domestic product, to enable intercountry comparisons of real income levels to be made in terms of real volume, that is, adjusted to account for local prices and different consumption patterns. Purchasing power parities consist of intercountry comparisons of prices for a basket of goods and services that is both representative of and comparable between the countries involved. The underlying price data therefore differ from those used in consumer price indices in so far as the latter basket is designed to be representative solely of private household consumption in the economic territory of an individual country.

6.120 It would be attractive in principle to construct consumer price indices and purchasing power parities from the same basic set of price data. In practice, the scope for this may be limited because of the differing objectives of the two exercises. In particular, the additional need for prices collected in the context of purchasing power parities to be comparable between countries will generally result in a more tightly defined basket compared with that likely to be available and used for a consumer price index.

6.121 An investigation of the potential overlap between the two baskets may, however, identify potential areas where one price collection may suit both purposes. This may be the case particularly for unbranded goods and locally produced fresh fruit and vegetables, for example, where a locally produced dessert apple of a standard quality may be compared across countries without recourse to a reference to the variety concerned. In contrast, branded items – whether food or non-food – may be more problematical because of differences in availability and specification between countries.

6.122 In some cases, scanner data might provide a useful common source of price data for at least some elements of the purchasing power parities calculation, notwithstanding the drawbacks mentioned above. Annex 4 goes into more detail on issues relating to purchasing power parities and the International Comparison Program (ICP).

Data quality and quality assurance

6.123 Checks should be carried out to ensure the accuracy of the data on prices and that the index itself has been compiled according to the proper methodology. Checks to ensure that data are complete and correct should be carried out as early as possible in the collection and compilation processes. A return to the shop to re-input prices becomes increasingly less feasible as time goes on, and there is a greater risk that the prices in the shops will have changed since the initial collection. It is not possible to prescribe the type and range of checks that should be carried out. The checks will depend on individual circumstances, including sample design and the medium used for the collection of prices. For example, the use of hand-held computers by price collectors facilitates much more detailed checking at the time of the initial collection of prices in the shop than the equivalent paper system. Further guidance on quality assurance is given in Chapter 12.

Documentation

6.124 The importance of good documentation cannot be overemphasized. Documents are needed to explain what is to be done, when it should be done, how it should be done and why it should be done. Preparing such documents provides a useful opportunity to ensure the quality of current procedures used to collect prices and compile the index. It also provides an opportunity to review and improve these procedures. Once in place, documentation serves two purposes in the context of producing the index. First, it enables somebody to take over the work if the person responsible falls ill or leaves. Second, it provides a quality check to ensure that the procedures that should be carried out are indeed being carried out in practice. More generally, documentation can provide a useful reference for users of consumer price indices. Documentation is discussed in more detail in Chapter 12.

Appendix 6.1 Extract from a simple price collection form

Notes: The collector fills in the last four columns, leaving "brand or make" blank when inapplicable. There will usually be a separate questionnaire for each type of item or for each outlet.

Collection date: Collector's name: Outlet name:

Item	Retail outlet	Description: brand or make	Price	Indicator code[1]	Further explanation (complete as necessary for outlet/item using agreed electronic pre-coded messages as appropriate)
Potatoes – new, loose per kg	Green Fingers Green Grocers	Jersey Royals	59p	C	Comparable item. Last month Egyptian Queens. Seasonal variation.
Home killed beef, best mince per kg	SuperBuys Supermarket	Own brand. Premium cut, low fat. Red and blue packaging.	£3.45	S	Special Offer. Half price.
Frozen pizza, medium size 300–450 g	SuperBuys Supermarket	Own Brand. Meat Feast. Red box with pizza pictured.	400 g	W	Previous size 450 g.
Milk, pasteurized, 4 pt or 2 l	SuperBuys Supermarket	Full cream pasteurized. Plastic bottle with blue label.	89p		
Men's formal shirt, long sleeved	Formal For Men	"Dickie Dirts" brand. White. 75 per cent cotton, 25 per cent polyester. Made in England. Blue flash on packet.	£34.99	Q	Includes free tie.
Women's shoes, fashion	Steps	Black court shoes. Shoe name "Sleekie". Leather uppers and leather soles. Made in China. Near till.	£30.00	R	Recovery from 25 per cent off.
Restaurant meal, main course, evening meal, specify	Fill Up	Cod, chips and salad. Main menu.	£7.50	C	Previously served as "Plaice, chips and salad".
Theatre admission, evening, front stalls, adult	Civic Theatre	Jack and the Beanstalk. Weekday (Mon–Thurs) evening performance.	£12.00	N	Previously, "Talking heads".

[1] C = comparable; S = sale or special offer; W = weight; Q = query; R = recovery; N = new.

ADJUSTING FOR QUALITY CHANGE

7

Introduction

7.1 The measurement of changes in the level of consumer prices is complicated by the appearance and disappearance of new and old goods and services, as well as changes in the quality of existing ones. If there were no such complications, then a representative sample could be taken of the items households consume in period 0, their prices recorded and compared with the prices of the same matched items in subsequent periods, say t. In this way the prices of like would be compared with like. However, such complications do exist. For example, an item may no longer be produced in period $t+1$, so its price comparison cannot be undertaken between periods 0 and $t+1$.

7.2 A number of methods are available to remedy this. A replacement item may exist in period $t+1$. If it is of the same quality, its price can be compared with the "old" item's price in period t. But the replacement item may well be of a different quality. One option is to ignore the quality difference and continue comparing the price of the "new" replacement item in $t+1$ with that of the old one in period t to continue the series. An adjustment for the difference in quality is still being made; it is just that it is a very poor adjustment, because the change in quality has no effect on the price. A second option is to exclude from the index those items for which quality changes, and to compile the index link between t and $t+1$ only for matched items having characteristics that are the same. This exclusion amounts to an implicit quality adjustment, one that assumes the overall price change of existing matched items will be the same as the quality-adjusted price change between the missing old and replacement new items. In reality, however, price changes generally vary over the stages of a product's life cycle. Price changes at the time of, say, a model's upgrade – when an item is missing and replaced – may be quite different from those at other stages. The implicit assumption may therefore be inappropriate. Third, the price change of a new replacement item may be spliced onto the index if the prices of the disappearing and replacement items are available in a common overlap period, say period t. The old item's price change between periods 0 and t is multiplied by the replacement item's price change between periods t and $t+1$. Yet again, there is an implicit quality adjustment, one that requires the price difference between the old item and its replacement in period t to reflect the effect of the quality difference on price. Such differences may also be in part the result of strategic price-setting behaviour related to the period in the item's life cycle.

7.3 There are other methods of adjusting the prices of non-comparable replacements for quality differences, including ones that use explicit estimates of the effect of the quality change on price. There are a number of methods of deriving such explicit estimates, and the suitability of explicit quality adjustments depends as much on the method used as on the availability of appropriate data to implement the method. In each case, whatever procedure a statistical office follows, a quality adjustment to prices *is* made in every period when an item is not available. The purpose of this chapter is to help ensure that these quality adjustments are the appropriate ones.

7.4 There are three main reasons for considering how to adjust for quality change. First, the scale and pace of methodological innovations are substantial. Second, there is a lack of consistency in the methods chosen by statistical offices for dealing with quality changes; thus comparisons of consumer price indices between product areas, across countries, and over time may be misleading. Finally, a number of empirical studies on the effects of using different methods found that choice of method does indeed matter (Dulberger, 1989; Armknecht and Weyback, 1989; Moulton and Moses, 1997; Lowe, 1996).

7.5 Against these concerns, it must be recognized that statistical agencies do guard against quality changes by using the matched models method. Price collectors record the features of selected items and collect prices for the very same models in subsequent periods in order to compare like with like. If a product group exists in which there are no items whose quality changes and no new or disappearing goods and services, then the matched models method based on representative items works. More generally, three potential sources of error arise from the matched models approach: missing items, sample space change, and new products.

Why the matched models method may fail

7.6 The long-run price change for an item is measured by comparing the price of the item in the current period with that in the price reference period, the period in which it, along with most other items, entered the sample.

Missing items

7.7 The first source of error, and the focus of this chapter, is when an item is no longer available in the outlet. It may be discontinued or it may not be available to the same specification – its quality has changed – and it is effectively missing in the current period. The item's price may be missing for other reasons. It may be a seasonal item or one whose price does not need to be recorded so frequently, or it may be that the item is a custom-made product or service, supplied each time to the customer's specification.

7.8 It is necessary to distinguish between items that are permanently and temporarily missing. Items that are *temporarily* missing are items not available and not priced in the month in question, but that are priced in subsequent months. The items may be missing because, for example, demand is seasonal, as is the case with some fruits and vegetables, or there are shortages. Some commodities are priced on a less frequent basis, maybe quarterly or biannually, because their price changes are irregular. They are therefore missing when they are "off cycle".

7.9 The concern with seasonal items is to impute their missing prices until the item reappears. The imputation methods used are similar in some cases to those used for quality adjustment. The temporary nature of the imputation, however, requires that they be separately identified by the respondent as "temporarily missing" or "seasonal". Principles and methods for such imputations are outlined by Armknecht and Maitland-Smith (1999) and Feenstra and Diewert (2001), and in Chapter 22. The concern in this chapter is with permanently missing items and with making imputations on a continuing basis or using a replacement item.

7.10 A number of approaches are available for dealing with missing items:

- The item may be dropped on the assumption that the aggregate price change of a group of other items reflects change in the missing item – an implicit quality adjustment to price.
- A replacement item may be selected and the replacement item's price may be used for the comparison because the replacement is deemed to be comparable in quality to the missing item.
- The replacement may be deemed to be non-comparable with the missing item, but prices on both the missing and replacement items may be available in an overlap period before the former item was missing. The price difference in this overlap period may be used as an estimate of the quality difference to quality-adjust the replacement item's price.
- The replacement price of a non-comparable replacement may be used, with an explicit estimate of the adjustment for the quality difference to extricate the "pure" price and quality change.

7.11 In many cases, therefore, there is a need to make a quality adjustment to the replacement item's price. A quality adjustment in this instance is an adjustment to the price (price change) of the replacement item (compared with the missing item) to remove that part of the price change that results from quality differences. A quality adjustment can be taken to be a coefficient that multiplies the price of, say, the replacement item to make it commensurate, from the consumer's point of view, with the price of the original.

7.12 To take a simple example, suppose that the size (or quantity) an item is sold in is a quality feature. Suppose that the size of the missing item and its replacement differ. Assume that a quantity k of the replacement is sold for the same price as a quantity j of the original. Whether the consumer buys one unit of the original or j/k units of the replacement makes no difference – they are worth the same. In order to make the price of one unit of the replacement commensurate with the price of one unit of the original, the replacement must be multiplied by k/j. This is the required quality adjustment. For example, if 2 units of the replacement item were equivalent to 3 of the original, the required quality adjustment to be applied to the price of the replacement item is 2/3. Suppose one unit of the replacement actually sells at the same price as one unit of the original, then the price of the replacement, after adjusting for the change in quality, is only 2/3 that of the price of the original. If one unit of the replacement sells for twice the price of the original, then the quality-adjusted price is 4/3 that of the original: the price increase is 33 per cent, not 100 per cent. The consumer price index seeks to record the change between the price of the original and the quality-adjusted price of the replacement.

7.13 The approaches listed in paragraph 7.10 will be discussed later in some detail, along with the assumptions implied by them. By definition, the prices of the unavailable items cannot be determined. The veracity of some of the assumptions about their price changes, had they been available, is therefore difficult to establish. What is stressed here is that the matching of prices of items allows for the measurement of price changes untainted by quality changes. When items are replaced with new ones of a different quality, then a quality-adjusted price is required. If the adjustment is inappropriate, there is an error, and if it is inappropriate in a systematic direction, there is a bias. Careful quality adjustment practices are required to avoid error and bias. Such adjustments are the subject of this chapter.

Sampling concerns

7.14 There are four main concerns with regard to sampling. First, the matching of prices of identical items over time, by its nature, is likely to lead to the monitoring of a sample of items increasingly unrepresentative of the population of transactions. It may be that the prices of old items being dropped are relatively low and the prices of new ones relatively high, and such differences in price remain even after quality differences have been taken into account (Silver and Heravi, 2002). For strategic reasons, firms may wish to dump old models, perhaps to make way for the introduction of new models priced relatively high. Ignoring such "unmatched" models in measuring a consumer price index will bias the index downwards (see paragraphs 7.150 to 7.152 below). Therefore, in a curious way, the very method of matching, used to ensure constant quality, may itself lead to bias by omitting items whose price changes are unusual (see also Koskimäki and Vartia (2001) for an example). Chapter 8 suggests that the strategy for quality adjustment of prices should be linked to one of item selection and chaining. The strategy is particularly pertinent to sectors with dynamic technological innovations (see also the discussion of hedonic price indices, below).

7.15 Second, because of the additional resources required for quality adjustments to prices, it may be in the interests of the price collectors and desk statisticians, and indeed fall within their guidelines, to avoid making non-comparable replacements and quality adjustments. Thus items continue to be monitored until they are no longer produced. This means that old items with limited sales are monitored. Such items may exhibit unusual price changes as they near the end of their life cycle, because of the marketing strategies of firms. Firms typically identify gains to be made from different pricing strategies at different times in the life cycle of products, particularly at the introduction and end of the cycle (Parker, 1992). The (implicit or otherwise) weight of end-of-cycle items in the index would thus remain relatively high, being based on their sales share when they were sampled. Furthermore, new unmatched items with possibly relatively large sales would be ignored. As a consequence, undue weight would be given to the unusual price changes of matched items at the end of their life cycle.

7.16 A third sampling concern relates to the timing of item substitution: when a replacement item is chosen to substitute for an old one. Instructions to pick a comparable replacement to avoid messy quality adjustments to prices compound the problem. Obsolete items are by their nature at the end of their cycles and comparable replacements, to be comparable, must also be near or at the end of their cycles. Obsolete items with unusual price changes at the end of their cycles are thus replaced by obsolete items with, again, unusual price changes. This compounds the problem of unrepresentative samples and continues to bias the index against technically superior items delivering cheaper service flows.

7.17 The final sampling problem with the matching procedure is when the price collector continues to report prices of items until replacements are forced, that is, until the items are no longer available, and has instructions to replace those items with typically consumed or popular items. This improves the coverage and representativity of the sample. But it also makes reliable quality adjustments of prices between the old obsolete and new popular items more difficult. The differences in quality are likely to be beyond those that can be attributed to price differences in some overlap period, as one item is in the last stages of its life cycle and the other in its first. Furthermore, the technical differences between the items are likely to be of an order that makes it more difficult to provide reliable, explicit estimates of the effect of quality differences on prices. Finally, the (quality-adjusted) price changes of very old and very new items are unlikely to meet assumptions of "similar price changes to existing items or classes of items", as required by the imputation methods. Many of the methods of dealing with quality adjustment for unavailable items may be better served if the switch to a replacement item is made earlier rather than later. Sampling concerns can be seen to be inextricably linked to quality adjustment methods. This will be taken up in Chapter 8 on item selection and the need for an integrated approach to dealing with both representativity and quality-adjusted prices.

New products

7.18 A third potential source of error arises when something new is introduced into the marketplace. It is difficult to distinguish between new items and quality changes in old ones; this difficulty will be discussed in Chapter 8. When a really new item is introduced, there is an immediate gain in welfare or utility as demand switches from the previous technology and other goods. For example, the introduction of the zip fastener for clothing, instead of buttons, was a completely new good that led to an initial gain in utility or welfare to consumers as they switched from the old to the new technology. This gain from its introduction would not be properly brought into the index by waiting until the index was rebased, or by waiting for at least two successive periods of prices for zip fasteners and linking the new price comparison to the old index. Subsequent prices might be constant or even fall. The initial welfare gain would be calculated from a comparison between the price in the period of introduction and the hypothetical price in the *preceding* period, during which supply would be zero. The practical tools for estimating such a hypothetical price are not well developed, though this subject is discussed in more detail in Chapter 21. For a consumer price index built on the concept of a base period and a fixed basket, there is, strictly speaking, no problem. The new good was not in the old basket and should be excluded. Although an index properly measuring an old fixed basket would be appropriate in a definitional sense, it would not be representative of what we buy. Such an index would thus be inappropriate. For a cost of living index concerned with measuring the change in expenditure necessary to maintain a constant level of utility (see Chapter 17), there is no doubt that it would be conceptually appropriate to include the new good.

The nature of quality change

7.19 This section considers what is meant by quality change and then outlines the methods available for dealing with unavailable price quotes. To understand the "meaning" of quality change requires a conceptual and theoretical platform, so that adjustments to prices for quality differences are made against a well-considered framework.

7.20 A starting point is to appreciate that over time the quality of what is produced changes. The example of new cars is used here. Bode and van Dalén (2001) undertook an extensive study of the price measurement of new cars in the Netherlands between 1990 and 1999. The average nominal price increase over this period was found to be around 20 per cent, but the mix of average quality characteristics changed over this period. For example, the horsepower (HP) increased on average from 79 to 92 HP; the average efficiency of fuel consumption improved from 9.3 to 8.4 litres/100 km; the share of cars with fuel injection rose from 51 per cent to 91 per cent; the proportion of cars with power steering increased from 27 per cent to 94 per cent; airbags from 6 per cent to 91 per cent, and similarly for central locking, tinted glass and much more. This churning in the quality mix of what is purchased is one aspect of quality change. In matching the prices of a sample of models in, for example, January with the self-same models in subsequent months, the quality mix is kept constant in an attempt to avoid contaminating the price measurement through quality differences. As will be seen later, however, the resulting sample of models is one that gives less emphasis to models subsequently introduced which may have benefited from more recent technological change and have different price changes given the quality of services they provide. One approach, which corrects for such quality changes but uses the whole sample, is that of the dummy variable hedonic regressions (see below). Bode and van Dalén (2001), using a variety of formulations of hedonic regressions, found quality-corrected prices of these new automobiles to be about constant over this period, while their average nominal price increase was around 20 per cent.

7.21 It will be argued in Chapter 21 that observed changes in prices arise in theory from a number of sources, including quality changes, changes in tastes and preferences, and changes in the technology of producers. More formally, the observed data on prices are the locus of intersection of the demand curves of different consumers with varying tastes and the supply curves of different producers with possibly varying technologies of production. The separation of the effects of changes in tastes and preferences from quality changes is only possible in highly restrictive circumstances. Chapter 8 suggests chaining or regular rebasing, so that weights – which reflect tastes and preferences – are not unduly out of date.

7.22 The changing mix of the observed characteristics of items is not the only concern. There is also the practical problem of not always being able to observe or quantify characteristics such as the style, reliability, ease of use and safety of what is produced. Chapter 16 of the *System of National Accounts, 1993* (*SNA 1993*) on price and volume measurement notes factors other than changes in physical characteristics that give rise to improved quality. These include "transporting a good to a location in which it is in greater demand is a process of production in its own right in which the good is transformed into a higher quality good". The same good provided at a different and more convenient location may command a higher price and be of a higher quality. Furthermore, different times of the day or periods of the year may also give rise to quality differences: "For example, electricity or transport provided at peak times must be treated as being of higher quality than the same amount of electricity or transport provided at off-peak times. The fact that peaks exist shows that purchasers or users attach greater utility to the services at these times, while the marginal costs of production are usually higher at peak times. . . ." Other differences, including the conditions of sale and circumstances or environment in which the goods or services are supplied or delivered, can make an important contribution to differences in quality. A retailer, for example, may attract customers by providing free delivery, credit opportunity or better variety, by being more accessible, by offering shorter order times, smaller tailor-made orders, clearer labelling, better support and advice, more convenient car parking or a wider range of brands, or simply by operating in a more pleasant or fashionable environment. These sorts of benefits are not always specified in the item description because, first, the services are provided without specific charge – they are incorporated in the prices of the goods sold. Second, by matching the prices of models in specific outlets the level of such services is assumed to remain constant. This does not mean, however, that conceptually such quality improvements should be outside the scope of the index. If any such benefits change, a price adjustment for the estimated value of the benefits should be made.

7.23 To ask how to adjust prices for quality changes, it is first necessary to ask what is meant by quality. While there may be an intuition as to whether an item consumed in one period is better than its counterpart in the next, a theoretical framework will help in establishing the basis for such comparisons. For example, an item of clothing is sampled and, after a few months, it is missing. One option is to replace it with a similar item. The nearest comparable option may have more cloth in it, or have a lining, be a different colour, have different buttons, have better stitching or be considered to be better styled in some fashionable sense. There is a need to put a price estimate on the difference in quality between the old and new items so that like can be compared with like. To propose or criticize a quality adjustment procedure requires some concept of what is ideally required and how the procedure stands up to this. Although such a discussion takes us away from the practicalities of the procedures for a while, its use will become apparent in subsequent sections.

A utility-based approach

7.24 In Chapter 17 a cost of living index (COLI) is defined as the ratio of the minimum expenditures in the base and current period required to achieve a given standard of living or "utility". Quality adjustments to prices involve trying to measure the price change for a product which has exhibited some change in its characteristics from an earlier period that provides a different level of utility to the consumer. The equating of the value of a quality change with the change in utility derived by the consumer, while falling naturally under a COLI framework, is not exclusive to it. A cost of a fixed basket of goods index (COGI) can also benefit from regarding quality in this way. While a COGI requires the pricing of a fixed basket of products, some items will become unavailable and the replacement items selected to maintain the sample may not be of the same quality. The aim is to determine what proportion of the total price change results from a change in quality and what results from pure price change. The concept of utility will be used to help with the former.

7.25 Note that the definition of a quality change is based on equating some change in characteristics to a different level of utility provided. Consider an example in which a new, improved quality item is substituted for an old one in period t, the consumer having to choose between the two. Suppose that after the new quality item appeared, both qualities were offered to a consumer at the same price, say $p^t = 100$. The consumer was then asked to choose between them and naturally preferred the new quality. Say the price of the old quality was then progressively reduced until it reached a point, say $p^{t*} = 75$, at which the consumer was indifferent as regards the choice between purchasing the old quality at $p^{t*} = 75$ and the new quality at $p^t = 100$. The consumer might then select the old quality at 75 or the new one at 100. Either way, the consumer would obtain the same utility, because of being indifferent as to which to choose. Any further decrease below $p^{t*} = 75$ would cause the consumer to switch back to the old quality.

7.26 The difference between p^t and p^{t*} would be a measure of the additional utility that the consumer placed on the new quality as compared with the old quality. It would measure the maximum amount that the consumer was prepared to pay for the new quality over and above the price of the old quality. In economic theory, as will be outlined in Chapter 21, if consumers (or households) are indifferent between two purchases, the utility derived from them is the same. The difference between 75 and 100 must therefore arise from the consumers' valuation of the utility they derive from the two items: their quality difference. The definition is sensible as a conceptual framework. It naturally has problems relating to implementation, but this is not our concern here. Our initial concern is with the provision of an analytical framework on which to ground our thinking and analysis.

7.27 The utility-based framework is concerned with the question of how consumers choose between items of different qualities. The answer, in part, is because more utility is derived from an item of higher quality than from an item of lower quality, and thus consumers prefer it. But this does not explain why one item is bought rather than the other. For this it is also necessary to know the relative price of one item with respect to the other, since if the lower-quality item is cheaper, it may still be purchased. The above thought experiment to determine the price below which the old quality would be purchased, $p^{t*} \leq 75$, serves this purpose.

7.28 Defining quality change in terms of its effect on utility is of obvious benefit to the economic approach to index numbers (Chapter 21). Fixler and Zieschang (1992), Feenstra (1995), Triplett (1987) and Diewert (2003a) have developed theoretical frameworks for COLIs akin to those defined in Chapter 21, but which also incorporate goods and services whose quality changes. Silver and Heravi (2001a and 2003) and Kokoski et al. (1999) have undertaken empirical studies based on these frameworks for comparisons over time and between geographical areas, respectively. The use of utility as a guide towards understanding quality adjustments to prices is not, however, confined to the economic theory of cost of living indices (Chapter 21). Consumer price indices based on a fixed basket concept have the pragmatic need to adjust for quality differences when an item is unavailable, and there is nothing in the definition of a fixed basket index that precludes differences in utility being used as a guideline. If item A is better than its old version, item B, it is because it delivers something more to the consumer who is willing to pay more. That "thing" is called utility.

7.29 It is as well to distinguish between two concepts of value used in the analysis of quality adjustment: *resource cost* and *user value*. The value users derive from their consumption is their utility. Triplett (1990, pp. 222–223) considers how a consumer price index differs from a producer price index:

> Fisher and Shell (1972) were the first to show that different index number measurements (they considered output price indexes and consumer price indexes) imply alternative treatments of quality change, and that the theoretically appropriate treatments of quality change for these two indexes correspond respectively, to "resource-cost" and "user-value" measures. Triplett (1983) derives this same result for cases where "quality change" is identified with characteristics of goods – and therefore with empirical hedonic methods; the conclusions are that the resource cost of a characteristic is the appropriate quality adjustment for the output price index, and its user value is the quality adjustment for the COLI index or input index.

7.30 This position is not without difficulties. Diewert (2002d) has advocated a user cost approach for the producer price output index. This in part arises from the need to consolidate the inputs and outputs at constant prices in national accounts. If different quality adjustments are used for the same items in the producer price *input* index and the producer price *output* index, then the deflated constant price value added series, as their difference, will not balance. The issue arises generally in the field of producer price indices, since it concerns the question of whether the producer price output index should use a user value concept. It does not dispute the use of this concept in consumer price indices.

Conditional indices

7.31 The domain of a COGI is its fixed basket of goods and services. The use of a COLI framework requires consideration of wider issues concerning our quality of life. There are changes in the social, physical and economic environment that require more or less expenditure to maintain a given level of utility. Many factors affect our welfare, and in practice not all can be included in a consumer price index. It is thus appropriate to consider indices that are *conditional* on excluded factors remaining constant. These generally include health status, the environment and the quantity and quality of government-provided goods and services. The minimum expenditure necessary for achieving a given level of utility will increase as, for example, the police become less effective. Expenditure would then be necessary for better household security. It would cost more to maintain a given level of utility than in the previous period. Similarly, an outbreak of illness would lead to increased expenditure on medicines to maintain a given level of utility. Bad winter weather increases heating bills to maintain the same utility as before. In each case there is a very real sense in which the cost of living will have changed. Yet it is not generally accepted that the consumer price index should directly reflect such changes. What should be reflected are changes in the prices of locks, medicines and fuel that arise because the demand for such items changes. In addition, as more or less is spent on such items, the index should eventually incorporate such changes in the weighting as and when the weights are updated – and the more frequent the update, the better are such effects incorporated. But the index should not normally reflect short-run changes in the *quantities* used of security, medicine, heat and the like as a result of such external factors. Gordon and Griliches (1997, p. 87) comment in a similar vein:

> It is not clear, moreover, whether events such as a colder winter, the appearance of AIDS, or a rise in the crime rate should be included in the definition of a *price* index. A change in expenditures due to an unanticipated change in the weather should raise the price index only to the extent that energy prices go up, not quantities consumed. If the event persists, ultimately it will affect the commodity weights in the index, but that is a different matter. (Authors' emphasis)

7.32 It may be inappropriate to disregard environmental factors if they seriously affect a given group of people. In such cases, indexing for special factors sometimes takes place outside the index. For example, a government may provide cold-weather payments to pensioners if the temperature falls below a threshold condition. If a specific factor has a substantial effect for a significant group of households, an additional index might be compiled which includes the effect.

An overview of methods of quality adjustment when matched items are unavailable

7.33 It is apparent from the above that quality adjustments to prices are not a simple matter of applying routine methods to prices in specified product areas. A number of alternative approaches are suggested below. Some will be more appropriate than others for specific product areas. An understanding of the consumer market, technological features of the producing industry, and alternative data sources will all be required for the successful implementation of quality adjustments. Specific attention will need to be devoted to product areas with relatively high weights, where large proportions of items are turned over. Some of the methods are not straightforward and require a level of expertise. Quality adjustment needs to be implemented by developing a gradual approach on a product-by-product basis. Such concerns should not be used as excuses for failing to attempt to estimate quality-adjusted prices. The practice of statistical agencies in dealing with missing items, even if it is to ignore them, implicitly involves a quality adjustment. Such an implicit approach may not be the most appropriate method, and may even be misleading. The extent of quality changes and the pace of technological change require that appropriate methods be used.

7.34 To measure aggregate price changes, a representative sample of items is selected from a sample of outlets, along with a host of details that define each price. The items are repriced each month. The detailed specifications are included on the repricing form each month as a prompt to help ensure that the same items are being priced. Merkel (2000) has proposed that detailed checklists of item descriptions should be used, as any lack of clarity in the specifications may lead to errors. It should be borne in mind that price collectors may have no incentive to report changes in specifications, since this will invariably involve additional work. Attention should also be devoted to ensuring that the specifications used contain all pertinent, price-determining elements, otherwise there may be cases in which the quality change would become invisible in the price measurement process.

7.35 When an item is missing in a month for reasons other than being off season or off cycle, the replacement may be of a different quality – like may no longer be compared with like. A number of approaches exist for dealing with such situations and are well documented for the consumer price index (CPI), as outlined in Turvey et al. (1989), Moulton and Moses (1997), Armknecht et al. (1997), Moulton et al. (1999) and Triplett (2002). Though the terminology differs between authors and statistical agencies, they include:

- imputation – where no information is available to allow reasonable estimates to be made of the effect on price of a quality change. The price changes of all items, or of more or less similar items, are assumed to be the same as that for the missing item;
- overlap – used where no information is available to allow reasonable estimates to be made of the effect on price of a quality change, but where a replacement item exists in the same period as the old item. The price difference between the old item and its replacement in the overlap period is then used as a measure of the quality difference;
- direct comparison – if another item is directly comparable, that is, it is so similar that it can be assumed to have had more or less the same quality characteristics as the missing one, its price replaces the unavailable price. Any difference in price level between the new and old is assumed to arise from price changes and not quality differences;
- explicit quality adjustment – where there is a substantial difference between the quality of the old and replacement items, estimates of the effect of quality differences on prices are made to enable quality-adjusted price comparisons to be made.

7.36 Before outlining and evaluating these methods it is as well to say something about the extent of the problem. This arises when the item is unavailable. It is not just a problem when *comparable* items are unavailable, for the judgement as to what is and what is not comparable itself requires an estimate of quality differences. Part of a statistical meta-information system for statistical offices (outlined in Chapter 8) is to identify and monitor sectors that are prone to such replacements and whether the replacements used really are comparable. Seminal studies in Canada and the United States throw some light on the extent of such replacements. Moulton et al. (1999) examined the extent to which items became unavailable for televisions in the compilation of the United States CPI. Between 1993 and 1997, a total of 10,553 prices on televisions were used, of which 1,614 (15 per cent) were replacements, of which, in turn, 934 (57 per cent) were judged to be directly comparable. Thus a typical television remained in the sample less than a year. The Canadian experience for televisions over an almost identical period (1993 to November 1997) found 750 of the 10,050 prices (7.5 per cent) to be replacements. Of these, 178 (24 per cent) were directly comparable, 162 (22 per cent) required a judgement and 410 (55 per cent) were "spliced" – the price difference between the replacement and the unavailable model in the two periods being attributed to quality differences (Lowe, 1999). Thus, there was wide variation in the frequency of total replacements, although the frequency of non-comparable replacements was roughly similar (6.4 per cent in the United States sample and 5.7 per cent in Canada). Liegey (2000) found that of the 215 average (August 1999 to April 2000) monthly prices collected for major appliances for the United States CPI, 22 item replacements were required because of missing prices, of which comparable replacements were found for 16 and non-comparable replacements for the remaining six.

7.37 Information across a wider range of items is available for the United States. Armknecht (1996) found that, over the three years 1993 to 1995, the annual average number of price observations collected for the United States CPI was 835,443, of which 59,385 (7.1 per cent) were substitutions (as opposed to imputations for missing values). Of these substitutes, about half were carried out using comparable replacements, under a quarter using overall mean imputation, about 12 per cent using direct quality adjustment, and 10 per cent using class mean imputation. It should be borne in mind that these figures ignore the implicit quality adjustments that take place when the Bureau of Labor Statistics rotates its sample between rebasing. The *overlap* method is effectively applied on sample rotation, the outlet and item samples being reselected for about one-fifth of the geographical areas, with prices of old and new items sampled in the same month. All price-level differences between the old and new items are treated as quality differences as the new sample is spliced onto the old.

7.38 Methods of quality adjustment for prices are generally classified into implicit/imputed (or indirect) quality adjustment methods – the differences in terminology are notorious in this area – and explicit (or direct) methods. Implicit and explicit methods are discussed below. Both decompose the price change between the old item and its replacement into quality and pure price changes. For explicit adjustments, however, an explicit estimate is made of the quality difference, usually on the basis of external information, and the pure price effect is identified as a remainder. For implicit adjustments, a measurement technique is used to compare the old item to the replacement item, in which the extent of the quality and pure price change is implicitly determined by the assumptions of the method. The accuracy of the method relies on the veracity of the assumptions as opposed to the quality of the explicit estimate. Explicit adjustments make use of separate estimates of the portion of prices ascribed to quality differences, so that the price of the original item can be compared with that of a replacement of the same quality. The suitability of the explicit methods thus depends to a large extent on how good such estimates are, on average. Implicit adjustments involve assumptions about price movements, and for these informed intuition or theory is relied upon – though in some cases national statistical offices may make use of more specific empirical market knowledge.

Additive versus multiplicative adjustment

7.39 The quality adjustments to prices may be undertaken either by adding a fixed amount or multiplication by a ratio. For example, where m is the old item and n its replacement for a comparison over periods t, $t+1$, $t+2$, the use of the overlap method in period $t+1$ requires the ratio p_n^{t+1}/p_m^{t+1} to be used as a measure of the relative quality difference between the old item and its replacement. This ratio could then be *multiplied* by the price of the old item in period t, p_m^t, to obtain the quality-adjusted prices p_m^{*t} as follows:

	t	t+1	t+2
old item m		p_m^{t+1}	
replacement n	p_m^{*t}	p_n^{t+1}	p_n^{t+2}

7.40 Such multiplicative formulations are generally advised, as the adjustment is invariant to the absolute value of the price. It would otherwise be possible for the absolute value of the change in specifications to exceed the value of the item in some earlier or (with technological advances) later period. Yet there may be some items for which the worth of the constituent parts is not considered to be in proportion to the price. In other words, the constituent parts have their own, intrinsic, absolute, additive worth, which remains constant over time. Producers selling over the World Wide Web may, for example, include postage, which in some instances may remain the same irrespective of what is happening to price. If postage is subsequently excluded from the price, this fall in quality should be valued as a fixed sum.

Base versus current period adjustment

7.41 Two variants of the approaches to quality adjustment are to make the adjustment either to the price in the base period or to the price in the current period. For example, in the overlap method, described above, the implicit quality adjustment coefficient was used to adjust p_m^t. An alternative procedure would have been to multiply the ratio p_m^{t+1}/p_n^{t+1} by the price of the replacement item p_n^{t+2} to obtain the quality-adjusted price p_n^{*t+2}, etc. The first approach is easier since, once the base period price has been adjusted, no subsequent adjustments are required. Each new replacement price can be compared with the adjusted base period price. For multiplicative adjustments, the end result is the same whichever approach is used. For additive adjustments, the results differ and it is more appropriate to make the adjustment to prices near to the overlap period.

Long-run versus short-run comparisons

7.42 Much of the analysis of quality adjustments in this manual has been undertaken by comparing prices between two periods, say, period 0 prices with those in a subsequent period 1. For long-run comparisons the base period is taken as, say, period t and the index is compiled by comparing prices in period t first with $t+1$; then t with $t+2$; then t with $t+3$, etc. The short-run framework allows long-run comparisons, say, between periods t and $t+3$, to be built up as a sequence of links joined together by successive multiplication, say period t with $t+2$ and period $t+2$ with $t+3$; or with chaining, period t with $t+1$, $t+1$ with $t+2$ and $t+2$ with $t+3$. The advantages of the short-run framework for imputations are discussed in paragraphs 7.165 to 7.173.

7.43 Following a discussion of implicit and explicit methods of quality adjustment, issues relating to choice of method are considered. The implicit and explicit adjustment methods are outlined under a standard long-run Laspeyres framework, in which prices in a base (or reference) period are compared with those in each subsequent period. Where products are experiencing rapid technological change, however, these methods may be unsuitable. The matching and repricing of like items, and "patching in" of quality-adjusted replacement prices when the matching fails, are appropriate when failures are the exception. But in high-technology product markets likely to experience rapid turnover of models, they are the rule. Alternative methods using chained or hedonic frameworks are therefore also considered. These are quite radical approaches to meet the needs of rapidly changing production portfolios. Finally, the use of short-run comparisons as an alternative to long-run ones is considered as an intermediary – and for imputation a more appropriate – approach. Chapter 22 discusses issues relating to seasonal items in more detail.

Implicit methods of quality adjustment

7.44 This section discusses the following implicit methods of quality adjustment: overlap; overall mean or targeted mean imputation; class mean imputation; comparable replacement; linked to show no price change; and carry-forward.

Overlap

7.45 Consider for illustration the case where the items are sampled in, say, January and prices are compared over the remaining months of the year. Matched comparisons are undertaken between the January prices and their counterparts in successive months. Five items are assumed to exist in January sold by two outlet types with prices $p^{11}, p^{21}, p^{51}, p^{61}$ and p^{81} (Table 7.1(a)). At this level of aggregation, the weights can be ignored assuming only one quote is taken on each item. A price index for February compared with January = 100.0 is straightforward, in that prices of items 1, 2, 5, 6 and 8 only are used and compared by way of the geometric mean of price ratios, the Jevons index (which is equivalent to the ratio of the geometric mean in February over the geometric mean in January – see Chapter 20). In March the prices for items 2 and 6 are missing, one from specialized chain stores and one from department stores.

Table 7.1 Example of the implicit methods of quality adjustment

(a) General illustration

Outlet	Item	January	February	March	April
Specialized chain stores	1	p^{11}	p^{12}	p^{13}	p^{14}
	2	p^{21}	p^{22}		
	3			p^{33}	p^{34}
	4		p^{42}	p^{43}	p^{44}
Department stores	5	p^{51}	p^{52}	p^{53}	p^{54}
	6	p^{61}	p^{62}		
	7			p^{73}	p^{74}
	8	p^{81}	p^{82}	p^{83}	p^{84}

(b) Numerical illustration

Outlet	Item	January	February	March
Specialized chain stores	1	4	5	6
	2	5	6	
	2. overlap			**6.9**
	– imputation			**6.56**
	– targeted imputation			**7.2**
	– comparable replacement			**6.5**
	3			6.5
	4		7.5	8
Department stores	5	10	11	12
	6	12	12	
	– imputation			**13.13**
	– targeted imputation			**12.533**
	7			14
	8	10	10	10

7.46 Table 7.1(b) is a numerical counterpart to Table 7.1(a) to further illustrate the calculations. The overlap method requires prices of the old and replacement items to be available in the same period. In Table 7.1(a), in March item 2 has no price quote. Its new replacement is, say, item 4. The overlap method simply measures the ratio, in a common overlap period (February), of the prices of the old and replacement items (items 2 and 4, respectively). This is taken to be an indicator of their quality differences. The two approaches outlined above are apparent: either to insert a quality-adjusted price in January for item 4 and continue to use the replacement item 4 series, or to continue the item 2 series by patching in quality-adjusted item 4 prices. Both yield the same answer. Consider the former. For a Jevons geometric mean for January to March *for specialized chain stores only*, assuming equal weights of unity:

$$P_J(p^1, p^3) = [p^{13}/p^{11} \times p^{43}/((p^{42}/p^{22}) \times p^{21})]^{1/2}$$
$$= [6/4 \times 8/((7.5/6) \times 5)]^{1/2} = 1.386. \qquad (7.1)$$

Note that the comparisons are long-run ones. That is, they are between January and the month in question. The short-run modified Laspeyres framework provides a basis for short-run changes based on data in each current month and the immediately preceding one. In Tables 7.1(a) and (b) the comparison for specialized chain stores only would first be undertaken between January and February using items 1 and 2, and this would be multiplied by the comparison between February and March using items 1 and 4. This still implicitly uses the differences in prices in the overlap in February between items 2 and 4 as a measure of this quality difference. It yields the same result as before:

$$\left[\frac{5}{4}\times\frac{6}{5}\right]^{\frac{1}{2}}\times\left[\frac{6}{5}\times\frac{8}{7.5}\right]^{\frac{1}{2}}=1.386$$

The advantage of recording price changes for, say, January to October in terms of January to September, and September to October, is that it allows the compiler to compare immediate month-on-month price changes for data editing purposes. Moreover, it has quite specific advantages for the use of imputations (as discussed in paragraphs 7.53 to 7.68 below) for which different results arise for the long- and short-run methods. The long-run and short-run frameworks are discussed more fully in paragraphs 7.159 to 7.173.

7.47 The method is only as good as the validity of its underlying assumptions. Consider $i=1\ldots m$ items where p_m^t is the price of item m in period t, p_n^{t+1} is the price of a replacement item n in period $t+1$, and there are overlap prices for both items in period t. Now item n replaces m, but is of a different quality. So let $A(z)$ be the quality adjustment to p_n^{t+1} which equates its quality to p_m^{t+1} such that the quality-adjusted price $p_m^{*t+1}=A(z^{t+1})p_n^{t+1}$. Very simply, the index for the item in question over the period $t-1$ to $t+1$ is:

$$(p_m^t/p_m^{t-1})\times(p_n^{t+1}/p_n^t)=I^{t-1,t+1}$$
$$=\frac{p_n^{t+1}}{p_m^{t-1}}\times\frac{p_m^t}{p_n^t} \qquad (7.2)$$

7.48 Now the quality adjustment to prices in period $t+1$ is defined as previously, $p_m^{*t+1}=A(z^{t+1})p_n^{t+1}$, which is the adjustment to p_n in period $t+1$ which equates its utility to p_m in period $t+1$ (had it existed then). A desired measure of price changes between periods $t-1$ and $t+1$ is thus:

$$(p_m^{*t+1}/p_m^{t-1}) \qquad (7.3)$$

The overlap formulation equals this when:

$$\frac{p^{*t+1}}{p_m^{t-1}}=A(z^{t+1})\frac{p_n^{t+1}}{p_m^{t-1}}=\frac{p_n^{t+1}}{p_n^t}\times\frac{p_m^t}{p_m^{t-1}}$$

$A(z^{t+1})=\frac{p_m^t}{p_n^t}$ and similarly for future periods of the series

$$A(z^{t+1})=\frac{p_m^t}{p_n^t}\quad\text{for}\quad\frac{p_m^{*t+i}}{p_m^{t-1}}\quad\text{for}\quad i=2,\ldots T \qquad (7.4)$$

The assumption is that the quality difference in any period equates to the price difference at the *time of the splice*. The *timing* of the switch from m to n is thus crucial. Unfortunately, price collectors usually hang onto an item so that the switch may take place at an unusual period of pricing, near the end of item m's life cycle and the start of item n's life cycle.

7.49 But what if the assumption does not hold? What if the relative prices in period t, $R^t=p_m^t/p_n^t$, do not equal $A(z)$ in some future period, say $A(z^{t+i})=\alpha_i R^t$? If $\alpha_i=\alpha$, the comparisons of prices between future successive periods, say between $t+3$ and $t+4$, are unaffected, as would be expected, since item n is effectively being compared with itself,

$$\frac{p_m^{*t+4}}{p_m^{t-1}}\Big/\frac{p_m^{*t+3}}{p_m^{t-1}}=\frac{\alpha R^t p_n^{t+4}}{\alpha R^t p_n^{t+3}}=\frac{p_n^{t+4}}{p_n^{t+3}} \qquad (7.5)$$

However, if differences in the relative prices of the old and replacement items vary over time, then:

$$\frac{p_m^{*t+4}}{p_m^{t-1}}\Big/\frac{p_m^{*t+3}}{p_m^{t-1}}=\frac{\alpha_4 p_n^{t+4}}{\alpha_3 p_n^{t+3}} \qquad (7.6)$$

Note that the quality difference here is not related to the technical specifications or resource costs, but to the relative prices consumers pay.

7.50 Relative prices may also reflect unusual pricing policies aimed at minority segments of the market. In the example of pharmaceutical drugs (Berndt et al., 2003), the overlap in prices of a generic with a branded product was argued to reflect the needs of two different market segments. The overlap method can be used with a judicious choice of the overlap period. It should if possible be a period before the use of the replacement since in such periods the pricing may reflect a strategy to dump the old model to make way for the new one.

7.51 The overlap method is implicitly employed when samples of items are rotated. That is, the old sample of items is used to compute the category index price change between periods $t-1$ and t, and the new sample is used between t and $t+1$. The "splicing" together of these index movements is justified by the assumption that – on a group-to-group rather than item-to-item level – differences in price levels at a common point in time accurately reflect differences in qualities.

7.52 The overlap method has at its roots a basis in the law of one price: that when a price difference is observed it must arise from some difference in physical quality or some such factors for which consumers are willing to pay a premium, such as the timing of the sale, location, convenience or conditions. Economic theory would dictate that such price differences would not persist, given markets made up of rational producers and consumers. However, Chapter 16 of *SNA 1993* notes three reasons why this might fail:

> First, purchasers may not be properly informed about existing price differences and may therefore inadvertently buy at higher prices. While they may be expected to search out for the lowest prices, costs are incurred in the process.

Secondly, purchasers may not be free to choose the price at which they purchase because the seller may be in a position to charge different prices to different categories of purchasers for identical goods and services sold under exactly the same circumstances – in other words, to practise price discrimination.

Thirdly, buyers may be unable to buy as much as they would like at a lower price because there is insufficient supply available at that price. This situation typically occurs when there are two parallel markets. There may be a primary, or official, market in which the quantities sold, and the prices at which they are sold, are subject to government or official control, while there may be a secondary market – a free market or unofficial market – whose existence may or may not be recognized officially.

Overall mean or targeted mean imputation

7.53 This method uses the price changes of other items as estimates of the price changes of the missing items. Consider a Jevons elementary price index, i.e., a geometric mean of price relatives (Chapter 20). The prices of the missing items in the current period, say $t+1$, are imputed by multiplying their prices in the immediately preceding period t by the geometric mean of the price relatives of the remaining matched items between these two periods. The comparison is then linked by multiplication to the price changes for previous periods. It is the computationally most straightforward of methods since the estimate can be undertaken by simply dropping the items that are missing from both periods from the calculation. In practice, the series is continued by including in the database the imputed prices. It is based on the assumption of similar price movements. A targeted form of the method would use similar price movements of a cell or elementary aggregate of similar items, or be based on price changes at a higher level of aggregation if either the lower level had an insufficient sample size or price changes at the higher level were judged to be more representative of the price changes of the missing item.

7.54 In the example in Table 7.1, the January to February comparison for both outlet types is based on items 1, 2, 5, 6 and 8. For March compared with January – weights all equal to unity – the item 2 and item 6 prices are imputed using the short-run price change for February (p^2) compared with March (p^3) based on items 1, 5 and 8. Since different formulae are used for elementary aggregation, the calculations for the main three formulae are illustrated here (but see Chapter 20 on choice of formulae). The geometric mean of the price ratios – the Jevons index – is:

$$P_J(p^2,p^3)=\prod_{i=1}^{N}[p_i^3/p_i^2]^{1/N} \tag{7.7}$$

$$=[(p^{13}/p^{12})\times(p^{53}/p^{52})\times(p^{83}/p^{82})]^{1/3}$$

$$=[(6/5)\times(12/11)\times(10/10)]^{1/3}=1.0939,$$

or a 9.39 per cent increase.

The ratio of the average (mean) prices – the Dutot index – is:

$$P_D(p^2,p^3)=\left(\sum_{i=1}^{N}p_i^3/N\right)\Big/\left(\sum_{i=1}^{N}p_i^2/N\right) \tag{7.8}$$

$$=[(p^{13}+p^{53}+p^{83})/3\div(p^{12}+p^{52}+p^{82})/3]$$

$$=(6+12+10)/(5+11+10)=1.0769,$$

or a 7.69 per cent increase.

The average (mean) of the price ratios – the Carli index – is:

$$P_C(p^3,p^2)=\sum_{i=1}^{N}(p_i^3/p_i^2)/N \tag{7.9}$$

$$=[(p^{13}/p^{12})+(p^{53}/p^{52})+(p^{83}/p^{82})]/3$$

$$=[6/5+12/11+10/10]/3=1.09697,$$

or a 9.697 per cent increase.

In practice, the imputed figure would be entered on the data sheet. In Table 7.1(b) the overall mean imputations in March for items 2 and 6, using the Jevons index, are $1.0939\times6=6.563$ and $1.0939\times12=13.127$, respectively: these are shown in bold. It should be noted that the Dutot index is in this instance lower that the Jevons index, a result not expected from the relationship established in Chapter 20. The relationship in Chapter 20 assumed that the variance of prices would increase over time, while in Table 7.1(b) it decreases for the three items. The arithmetic mean of relatives, the Carli index, equally weights each price change while the ratio of arithmetic means, the Dutot index, weights price changes according to the prices of the item in the base period relative to the sum of the base period prices. Item 1 has a relatively low price (4), and thus weight, in the base period, but this item has the highest price increase (6/5). The Dutot index is thus lower than the Carli index.

7.55 As noted above, it is also possible to refine the imputation method by "targeting" the imputation: by including the weight for the unavailable items in groupings likely to experience similar price changes, say by outlet type, specific product area or geographical region. Any stratification system used in the selection of outlets would facilitate this. For example, in Table 7.1 assume that the price change of the missing item 2 in March is more likely to follow price changes of item 1 in specialized chain stores, and item 6 is more likely to experience similar price changes to those of items 5 and 8 in department stores. For March compared with February, and weights all equal to unity, the geometric mean of the price ratios – the Jevons index – is:

$$P_J(p^2,p^3)=\prod_{i=1}^{N}(p_i^3/p_i^2)^{1/N} \tag{7.10}$$

$$=[(p^{13}/p^{12})^2\times(p^{53}/p^{52}\times p^{83}/p^{82})^{3/2}]^{1/5}$$

$$=[(6/5)^2\times(12/11\times10/10)^{3/2}]^{1/5}-1.1041.$$

Note the weights used: for specialized chain stores the one price represents two prices, while for department stores the two prices represent three prices, or $3/2=1.5$ each.

The ratio of the average (mean) prices – the Dutot index – is:

$$P_D(p^2,p^3)=\left(\sum_{i=1}^{N}p_i^3\Big/N\right)\Big/\left(\sum_{i=1}^{N}p_i^2\Big/N\right) \quad (7.11)$$
$$=[(2p^{13}+1.5p^{53}+1.5p^{83})/5 \div(2p^{12}+1.5p^{52}+1.5p^{82})/5]$$
$$=[(2\times 6+1.5\times 12+1.5\times 10) \div(2\times 5+1.5\times 11+1.5\times 10)]=1.0843$$

The average (mean) of the price ratios – the Carli index – is:

$$P_C(p^2,p^3)=\sum_{i=1}^{N}(p_i^3/p_i^2)\Big/N \quad (7.12)$$
$$=\frac{2}{5}(p^{13}/p^{12})+\frac{3}{5}[(p^{53}/p^{52}+p^{83}/p^{82})/2]$$
$$=\frac{2}{5}(6/5)+\frac{3}{5}[(12/11+10/10)/2]=1.1073$$

7.56 Alternatively, and more simply, imputed figures could be entered in Table 7.1(b) for items 2 and 6 in March, just using specialized chain stores and department store price movements for items 2 and 6 respectively, and indices calculated accordingly. Using a Jevons index, for item 2 the imputed value in March would be $6/5\times 6=7.2$ and for item 6 it would be $[(12/11)\times(10/10)]^{1/2}=12.533$. It is thus apparent that not only does the choice of formula matter, as discussed in Chapter 20, but so too may the targeting of the imputation. In practice, the sample of items in a targeted subgroup may be too small. An appropriate stratum is required with a sufficiently large sample size, but there may be a trade-off between the efficiency gains from the larger sample and the representativity of price changes achieved by that sample. Stratification by product area and region may be preferred to stratification just by product area, if regional differences in price changes are expected, but the resulting sample size may be too small. In general, the stratum used for the target should be based on the analyst's knowledge of the market, as well as an understanding of similarities of price changes between and within strata, and the reliability of the sample available to be representative of price changes.

7.57 The underlying assumptions of these methods require some analysis since, as discussed by Triplett (1999 and 2002), they are often misunderstood. Consider $i=1\ldots m$ items where, as before, p_m^t is the price of item m in period t, p_n^{t+1} is the price of a replacement item n in period $t+1$. Now n replaces m, but is of a different quality. So, as before, let $A(z)$ be the quality adjustment to p_n^{t+1} which equates its quality services or utility to p_m^{t+1} such that the quality-adjusted price $p_m^{*t+1}=A(z)p_n^{t+1}$. For the imputation method to work, the average price changes of the $i=1\ldots m$ items, including the quality-adjusted price p_m^{*t+1}, given on the left-hand side of equation (7.13), must equal the average price change from just using the overall mean of the rest of the $i=1\ldots m-1$ items, on the right-hand side of equation (7.13). The discrepancy or bias from the method is the balancing term Q. It is the implicit adjustment that allows the method to work. The arithmetic formulation is given here, though a similar geometric one can be readily formulated. The equation for one unavailable item is given by:

$$\frac{1}{m}\left[\frac{p_m^{*t+1}}{p_m^t}+\sum_{i=1}^{m-1}\frac{p_i^{t+1}}{p_i^t}\right]=\left[\frac{1}{(m-1)}\sum_{i=1}^{m-1}\frac{p_i^{t+1}}{p_i^t}\right]+Q \quad (7.13)$$

$$Q=\frac{1}{m}\frac{p_m^{*t+1}}{p_m^t}-\frac{1}{m(m-1)}\sum_{i=1}^{m-1}\frac{p_i^{t+1}}{p_i^t} \quad (7.14)$$

and for x unavailable items by:

$$Q=\frac{1}{m}\sum_{i=1}^{x}\frac{p_m^{*t+1}}{p_m^t}-\frac{x}{m(m-x)}\sum_{i=1}^{m-x}\frac{p_i^{t+1}}{p_i^t} \quad (7.15)$$

7.58 The relationships are readily visualized if r_1 is defined as the arithmetic mean of price changes of items that continue to be recorded and r_2 of quality-adjusted unavailable items. For the arithmetic case,

$$\text{where } r_1=\left[\sum_{i=1}^{m-x}p_i^{t+1}/p_i^t\right]\div(m-x) \text{ and } r_2=\left[\sum_{i=1}^{x}p_i^{*t+1}/p_i^t\right]\div x \quad (7.16)$$

then the ratio of arithmetic mean biases from substituting equation (7.16) in (7.15) is:

$$Q=\frac{x}{m}(r_2-r_1) \quad (7.17)$$

which equals zero when $r_1=r_2$. The bias depends on the ratio of unavailable values and the difference between the mean of price changes for existing items and the mean of quality-adjusted replacement price changes. The bias decreases as either (x/m) or the difference between r_1 and r_2 decreases. Furthermore, the method is reliant on a comparison between price changes for existing items and quality-adjusted price changes for the replacement or unavailable comparison. This is more likely to be justified than a comparison without the quality adjustment to prices. For example, suppose there were $m=3$ items, each with a price of 100 in period t. Let the $t+1$ prices be 120 for two items, but assume the third is unavailable, i.e., $x=1$ and is replaced by an item with a price of 140, of which 20 is attributable to quality differences. Then the arithmetic bias as given in equations (7.16) and (7.17), where $x=1$ and $m=3$, is

$$\frac{1}{3}\left[(-20+140)/100-\left(\frac{120}{100}+\frac{120}{100}\right)/2\right]=0$$

Had the bias depended on the unadjusted price of 140 compared with 100, the imputation would be prone to serious error. In this calculation, the direction of the bias is given by (r_2-r_1) and does not depend on whether quality is improving or deteriorating, in other words whether $A(z)>p_n^{t+1}$ or $A(z)<p_n^{t+1}$. If $A(z)>p_n^{t+1}$, a quality improvement, it is still possible that $r_2<r_1$ and for the bias to be negative, a point stressed by Triplett (2002).

7.59 The analysis here is framed in terms of a short-run price change framework. That is, the short-run price changes between the prices in a period and those in the preceding period are used for the imputation. This is different from the long-run imputation where a base period price is compared with prices in subsequent months, and where the implicit assumptions are more restrictive.

7.60 Table 7.2 provides an illustration in which the (mean) price change of items that continue to exist, r_1, is allowed to vary for values between 1.00 and 1.5 – corresponding to a variation between no price change and a 50 per cent increase. The (mean) price change of the quality-adjusted new items compared with the items they are replacing is assumed not to change, i.e., $r_2 = 1.00$. The bias is given for ratios of missing values of 0.01, 0.05, 0.1, 0.25 and 0.5, both for arithmetic means and geometric means. For example, if 50 per cent of price quotes are missing and the missing quality-adjusted prices do not change, but the prices of existing items increase by 5 per cent ($r_1 = 1.05$), then the bias for the geometric mean is represented by the proportional factor 0.9759; i.e., instead of 1.05, the index should be $0.9759 \times 1.05 = 1.0247$. For an arithmetic mean, the bias is -0.025; instead of 1.05 it should be 1.025.

7.61 Equation (7.17) shows that the ratio x/m and the difference between r_1 and r_2 determine the bias. Table 7.2 shows that the bias can be quite substantial when x/m is relatively large. For example, for $x/m = 0.25$, an inflation rate of 5 per cent for existing items translates to an index change of 3.73 per cent and 3.75 per cent for the geometric and arithmetic formulations, respectively, when $r_2 = 1.00$, i.e., when quality-adjusted prices of unavailable items are constant. Instead of being 1.0373 or 1.0375, ignoring the unavailable items would give a result of 1.05. Even with 10 per cent missing ($x/m = 0.1$), an inflation rate of 5 per cent for existing items translates to 4.45 per cent and 4.5 per cent for the geometric and arithmetic formulations, respectively, when $r_2 = 1.00$. Considering a fairly low ratio of x/m, say 0.05, then even when $r_2 = 1.00$ and $r_1 = 1.20$, Table 7.2 shows that the corrected rates of inflation should be 18.9 per cent and 19 per cent for the geometric and arithmetic formulations, respectively. In competitive markets, r_1 and r_2 are unlikely to differ by substantial amounts since r_2 is a price comparison between the new item and the old item after adjusting for quality differences. If r_1 and r_2 are the same, then there would be no bias from the method even if $x/m = 0.9$. There may, however, be more sampling error. It should be borne in mind that it is not appropriate to compare bias between the arithmetic and geometric means, at least in the form they take in Table 7.2. The latter would have a lower mean, rendering comparisons of bias meaningless.

7.62 An awareness of the market conditions relating to the commodities concerned is instructive in understanding likely differences between r_1 and r_2. The concern here is when prices vary over the life cycle of the items. Thus, for example, at the introduction of a new model, the price change may be quite different from price changes of other existing items. Thus assumptions of similar price changes, even with quality adjustment, might be inappropriate. Greenlees (2000) gives the example of personal computers: new computers enter the market at prices equal to, or lower than, prices of previous models, but with greater speed and capability. An assumption that $r_1 = r_2$ could not be justified. He continues with the example of apparel, in which new clothing enters the market at relatively high quality-adjusted prices, while old, end-of-season or out-of-style clothes are being discounted. Again there will be bias, as r_1 differs from r_2.

7.63 Some of these differences arise because markets are composed of different segments of consumers. Indeed, the very training of consumer marketers involves consideration of developing different market segments and ascribing to each appropriate pricing, product quality, promotion and place (method of distribution) – the 4Ps of the marketing mix (Kotler, 1991). In addition, consumer marketers are taught to plan the marketing mix for the life cycle of items. Such planning allows for different inputs of each of these marketing mix variables at different points in the life cycle. This includes "price skimming" during the period of introduction, when

Table 7.2 Example of the bias from implicit quality adjustment when the (mean) price change of quality-adjusted new items compared with the items they are replacing is assumed not to change (r_2=1.00)

	Geometric mean					Arithmetic mean				
	Ratio of missing items, x/m					Ratio of missing items, x/m				
	0.01	0.05	0.1	0.25	0.5	0.01	0.05	0.1	0.25	0.5
r_1										
1	1	1	1	1	1	0	0	0	0	0
1.01	0.999901	0.999503	0.999005	0.997516	0.995037	−0.0001	−0.0005	−0.001	−0.0025	−0.005
1.02	0.999802	0.99901	0.998022	0.995062	0.990148	−0.0002	−0.001	−0.002	−0.005	−0.01
1.03	0.999704	0.998523	0.997048	0.992638	0.985329	−0.0003	−0.0015	−0.003	−0.0075	−0.015
1.04	0.999608	0.998041	0.996086	0.990243	0.980581	−0.0004	−0.002	−0.004	−0.01	−0.02
1.05	0.999512	0.997563	0.995133	0.987877	0.9759	−0.0005	−0.0025	−0.005	−0.0125	−0.025
1.1	0.999047	0.995246	0.990514	0.976454	0.953463	−0.001	−0.005	−0.01	−0.025	−0.05
1.15	0.998603	0.993036	0.986121	0.965663	0.932505	−0.0015	−0.0075	−0.015	−0.0375	−0.075
1.2	0.998178	0.990925	0.981933	0.955443	0.912871	−0.002	−0.01	−0.02	−0.05	−0.1
1.3	0.99738	0.986967	0.974105	0.936514	0.877058	−0.003	−0.015	−0.03	−0.075	−0.15
1.5	0.995954	0.979931	0.960265	0.903602	0.816497	−0.005	−0.025	−0.05	−0.125	−0.25

r_1=(mean) price change for items that continue to exist.

higher prices are charged to skim off the surplus from segments of consumers willing to pay more. The economic theory of price discrimination would also predict such behaviour. Thus the quality-adjusted price change of an old item compared with a new replacement item may be higher than price changes of other items in the product group. After the introduction of the new item its prices may fall relative to others in the group. There may be no law of one price change for differentiated items within a market. Berndt et al. (2003) clearly show how, after patents expire, the price of branded prescription pharmaceuticals can increase with the entry of new generic pharmaceuticals at a lower price, as particularly loyal, less price-sensitive customers maintain their allegiance to the branded pharmaceuticals.

7.64 There is thus little in economic or marketing theory to support any expectation of similar (quality-adjusted) price changes for new and replacement items, as compared to other items in the product group. Some knowledge of the realities of the particular market under study would be helpful when considering the suitability of this approach. Two aspects need to be considered in any decision to use the imputation approach. The first is the proportion of replacements; Table 7.2 provides guidance here. The second is the expected difference between r_1 and r_2. It is clear from the above discussion that there are markets in which they are unlikely to be similar. This is not to say the method should not be used. It is a simple and expedient approach. What arguably should not happen is that it is used by default, without any prior evaluation of expected price changes and the timing of the switch. Furthermore, its use should be targeted, by selecting items expected to have similar price changes. The selection of such items, however, should take account of the need to include a sufficiently large sample so that the estimate is not subject to undue sampling error.

7.65 The manner in which these calculations are undertaken is also worth considering. In its simplest form, the pro forma setting for the calculations, say on a spreadsheet, would usually have each item description and its prices recorded on a monthly basis. The imputed prices of the missing items are inserted into the spreadsheet, and are highlighted to show that they are imputed. The need to highlight such prices is, first, because they should not be used in subsequent imputations as if they were actual prices. Second, the inclusion of imputed values may give a false impression of a larger sample size than actually exists. Care should be taken in any audit of the number of prices used in the compilation of the index to code such observations as "imputed".

7.66 The method described above is an illustration of a short-run imputation. As is discussed in paragraphs 7.165 to 7.173 below, there is a strong case for using short-run imputations as against long-run ones.

Class mean imputation

7.67 The class mean (or substitution relative) method of implicit quality adjustment to prices as used in the United States CPI is discussed by Schultz (1996), Reinsdorf, Liegey and Stewart (1996), Armknecht, Lane and Stewart (1997), and Armknecht and Maitland-Smith (1999). It arose from concerns similar to those considered in the previous section, that unusual price changes were found in the early introductory period, when new models were being introduced, particularly for consumer durables. Moulton and Moses (1997), using United States CPI data for 1995 in their study of selected products, found the average pure price change to be only 0.12 per cent for identical items being repriced (on a monthly or bimonthly basis), compared to an average 2.51 per cent for comparable substitutes – items judged equivalent to the items they replaced. The corresponding average price change for directly substituted quality-adjusted price changes was 2.66 per cent. Thus, the price movement of continuing items appears to be a flawed proxy for the pure price component of the difference between old and replacement items.

7.68 The class mean method was adopted in the United States CPI for cars in 1989 and was phased in for most other non-food commodities, beginning in 1992. It differed from the overall mean imputation method only in the source for the imputed rate of price change for the old item in period $t+1$. Rather than using the category index change, obtained using all the non-missing items in the category, the imputed rate of price change was based on constant quality replacement items – those items that were judged comparable or that were quality-adjusted directly. The class mean approach was seen as an improvement on the overall mean imputation approach because the imputed price changes were based on items that had not just been replaced, but whose replacement price had benefited from a quality adjustment or the new replacement item had been judged to be directly comparable. It may be the case, however, that sufficiently large samples of comparable substitutes or directly quality-adjusted items are unavailable. Or it may be that the quality adjustments and selection of comparable items are not deemed sufficiently reliable. In that case, a targeted imputation might be considered. The targeted mean is less ambitious in that it seeks only to capture price changes of similar items, irrespective of their point in the life cycle. Yet it is an improvement on the overall mean imputation, as long as sufficiently large sample sizes are used.

Comparable replacement

7.69 The comparable replacement method requires the respondent to make a judgement that the replacement is of a similar quality to the old item and any price changes are untainted by quality changes. For specialized chain stores in Table 7.1(b), item 3 might be judged to be comparable to item 2 and its prices in subsequent months might be used to continue the series. The price of item 3 (6.5) in March would be used as the price in March of item 2, whose January to March price change would be $6.5/6 \times 100 = 1.0833$ or 8.33 per cent. Lowe (1999) notes the common practice of manufacturers of television sets to change model numbers with a new production run, though nothing physically has changed, or when small changes take place in specifications, such as the type of remote controls, or the number or placement of jacks. The method of comparable replacement relies on the efficacy of the price collectors and, in turn, on the adequacy of the specifications used as a description of the items. Statistical agencies may rightly be wary of sample sizes being reduced by dropping items for which prices need to be imputed, and also wary of the intensive use of resources to make explicit estimates as outlined below. The use of repriced items of a comparable specification has much to commend it. If the quality of items is improving, however, the preceding item will be inferior to the current one. Continually ignoring small changes in the quality of replacements can lead to an upward bias in the index. The extent of the problem will depend on the proportion of such occurrences, the extent to which comparable items are accepted as being so despite quality differences, and the weight attached to those items. Proposals in Chapter 8 to monitor types of quality adjustment methods by product area provide a basis for a strategy for applying explicit adjustments where they are most needed.

Linked to show no price change

7.70 Linking attributes any price change between the replacement item in the current period and the old item in the preceding period to the change in quality. For example, in Table 7.1(b), a replacement item 7 is selected from a department store for the missing March item 6. Items 6 and 7 may be of different quality, the price difference being quite large. The change in price is assumed to be attributable to a change in quality. An estimate is made for p^{72} by equating it to p^{73}, to show no change, i.e., the assumed price of item 7 in February is 14 in Table 7.1(b). There is thus assumed to be no price change over the period February to March for item 7. The January to March result for item 6 is $(12/12)\times(14/14)=1.00$, indicating no change. For the period March to April, however, the price of item 7 in March can be compared with the imputed p^{72} for February and linked to the preceding results. So the January to April comparison is composed of the January to February comparison for item 6, linked to (multiplied by) the February to April comparison for item 7. This linking is analogous to the procedures used for the chained and short-run framework discussed in paragraphs 7.153 to 7.158 and 7.171 to 7.173 below. The method is born out of circumstances where comparable replacement items are not available and there are relatively large price differences between the old and replacement items, these being from different price bases and of different qualities. It is not possible to separate out how much of this difference is attributable to price changes and how much to quality changes, so the method attributes it all to quality and holds price constant. The method introduces a degree of undue price stability into the index. It may well be the case that the period of replacement is when substantial price changes are taking place and that these are wrongly attributed to quality changes by this method. Article 5 of the European Commission (EC) Regulation No. 1749/96 requires Member States to avoid "automatic linking". Such linking is equivalent to the assumption that the difference in price between two successive models is wholly attributable to a difference in quality (Eurostat, 2001a, p. 125).

Carry-forward

7.71 With the carry-forward method, when an item becomes unavailable, say in period t, the price change calculation uses the old $t-1$ price, simply carried forward as if there were no change. Thus from Table 7.1(a) for specialized chain stores for the period January to March, the Jevons and Dutot indices (Chapter 20) are:

$$P_J(p^1,p^3)=[(p^{13}/p^{11}\times p^{22}/p^{21})]^{1/2} \quad \text{and}$$
$$P_D(p^1,p^3)=[(p^{13}+p^{22})/(p^{11}+p^{21})] \qquad (7.18)$$

with p^{22} filling in for the missing p^{23}. This introduces undue stability into the index, which is aggravated if the old price, p^{22}, continues to be used to fill in the unobserved prices in subsequent periods. It induces an inappropriate amount of stability into the index and may give a misleading impression of the active sample size. The practice of the carry-forward method is banned under Article (6) of the EC Regulation No. 1749/96 for Harmonized Indices of Consumer Prices (Eurostat, 2001a, p. 126). To use this method an assumption is made that the price from this outlet would not change. This method should only be used if it is fairly certain that there would be no price change.

Explicit methods of quality adjustment

7.72 The aforementioned methods do not rely on explicit information on the value of the change in quality, $A(z)$. This section discusses the following methods that rely on obtaining an explicit valuation of the quality difference: expert judgement; quantity adjustment; differences in production or option costs; and the hedonic approach.

Expert judgement

7.73 Hoven (1999) describes comparable replacement as a special case of subjective quality adjustment, because the determination of product equivalence is based on the judgement of the commodity specialist. One objection to subjective methods is the inability to provide results that can be independently replicated. Yet in comparable replacement, and for the selection of representative items, a subjective element is part of normal procedure. This is not, of course, an argument for expanding the use of subjective methods.

7.74 Hoffman (1999) describes a possibly unique alternative for quality adjustment of replacement items in the German CPI. When a new product is more expensive than the item it replaces, a flexible adjustment factor can be employed, attributing none, some, or all of the price difference to improved quality. In particular, when no precise information is available on which to make a quality determination, it is permissible for an adjustment to be made of 50 per cent of the price difference. The guidelines used in Germany since 1997 replaced flawed procedures in which the particular methods chosen for individual quality adjustments depended on the difference in price alone. As Hoffmann notes, however, even in the current approach no quality adjustment is made if the new item is less expensive than the old. Consequently, problems could arise if an increase in quality were accompanied by a decrease in price (or *vice versa*). The methods used in the German CPI are needed because quality adjustments for most goods are made not in the central CPI office but by price collectors in the field. Wide use of the hedonic and production cost approaches is precluded under these conditions. Thus, the organizational structure of the statistical agency, as well as its funding level, will necessarily influence its choice of quality adjustment methods.

7.75 Reports by consumer associations and product evaluations in consumer magazines are not advised by Turvey (1998), who cites a study which correlated quality ratings and prices for 135 products categories using *Consumer Reports*. The average correlation was 0.26, with over half having a positive association, just over a third no association and the rest a negative one. He also argues against "best buy" estimates, which are expert views as to what a sensible consumer should pay, as opposed to what the market price will be (see also Combris, Lecocqs and Visser, 1997).

7.76 The use of expert views as to consumer calculations may be appropriate for highly complex items where alternative methods are not feasible. Experts should be guided with regard to the nature of the estimate required. More than one expert should be chosen and, where possible, the experts should be from different backgrounds. It is also advisable to give the experts some indication of the interval in which their estimate should lie. The well-known Delphi method (for example, see Czinkota and Ronkainen, 1997) may be applicable. In this approach a panel of experts never meet, to avoid any "bandwagon" effect regarding their estimates. They are asked to provide an estimate of the average response and the range of likely responses. The median is taken of these estimates and any estimate that is considered extreme is sent back to the expert concerned, who is asked to account for possible reasons behind the difference. It may be that the particular expert has a useful perspective on the problem, which the other experts had not considered. If the expert argues the case convincingly, the response is fed back to the panel who are asked if they wish to change their views. A new median is taken, and further iterations are possible. The Delphi method is time-consuming and expensive, but it reflects the care needed in such matters. If an adjustment is required for a product area with a large weighting in the CPI, and no other techniques are available, it is a possible alternative.

Quantity adjustment

7.77 Quantity adjustment is one of the most straightforward explicit adjustments to undertake. It is applicable when the site of the replacement item differs from that of the available item. In some situations there is a readily available quantity metric that can be used to compare the items. Examples are the number of units in a package (e.g., paper plates or vitamin pills), the size or weight of a container (e.g., kilogram of flour, litre of cooking oil), or the size of sheets or towels. Quality adjustment to prices can be accomplished by scaling the price of the old or new item by the ratio of quantities. The index production system may do this scaling adjustment automatically, by converting all prices in the category to a price per unit of size, weight or number. Scaling is important. For example, if cooking oil is now sold in 5 litre containers instead of 2.5 litre ones, it should not be the case that prices have doubled.

7.78 There is, however, a second aspect. In the pharmaceutical context, for example, prices of bottles of pills of different sizes differ. A bottle of 100 pills, each having 50 milligrams of a drug, is not the same as a bottle of 50 pills of 100 milligrams, even though both bottles contain 5,000 milligrams of the same drug. If there is a change, say, to a larger size container, and a *unit* price decrease of 2 per cent accompanies this change, then it should not be regarded as a price fall of 2 per cent if consumers gain less utility from the larger and more inconvenient containers. In practice it will be difficult to determine what proportion of the price fall is attributable to quality and what proportion to price. A general policy is not to automatically interpret unit price changes arising from packaging size changes as pure price changes, if contrary information is available.

7.79 Consider a further example: a branded bag of flour previously available in a 0.5 kilogram bag priced at 1.5 is replaced by a 0.75 kilogram bag priced at 2.25. The main concern here is with rescaling the quantities. The method would use the relative quantities of flour in each bag for the adjustment. The prices may have increased by $[(2.25/1.5) \times 100 = 150]$ 50 per cent but the quality-adjusted prices (i.e. prices adjusted by size) have remained constant $[(2.25/1.5) \times (0.5/0.75) \times 100 = 100]$. The approach can be outlined in a more elaborate manner by recourse to Figure 7.1. The concern here is with the part of the unbroken line between the (price, quantity) coordinates (1.5, 0.5) and (2.25, 0.75), both of which have *unit* prices of 3 (price = 1.5/0.5 and 2.25/0.75). There should be no change in quality-adjusted prices. The symbol Δ denotes a change. The slope of the line is β

Figure 7.1 Quality adjustment for different-sized items

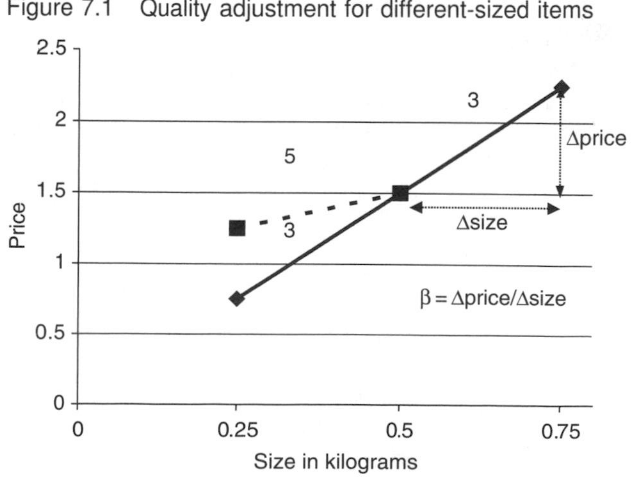

which is $\Delta price/\Delta size = (2.25 - 1.5)/(0.75 - 0.50) = 3$, i.e., the change in price arising from a unit (kilogram) change in size. The quality- (size-) adjusted price in period $t-1$ of the old m bag is:

$$\hat{p}_m^{t-1} = p_m^{t-1} + \beta \Delta size = 1.5 + 3(0.75 - 0.5) = 2.25 \quad (7.19)$$

The quality-adjusted price change shows no change, as before:

$$p_n^t / \hat{p}_m^{t-1} = 2.25/2.25 = 1.00$$

The approach is outlined in this form so that it can be seen as a special case of the hedonic approach (discussed below), where price is related to a number of quality characteristics of which size may be only one.

7.80 The method can be seen to be successful on intuitive grounds as long as the unit price of different-sized bags remains constant. If the switch was from the replacement of the 0.5 kilogram bag to a 0.25 kilogram one priced at 0.75, as shown by the continuation to coordinate (0.75, 0.25) of the unbroken line in Figure 7.1, the quality-adjusted prices would again not change, assuming, however, that the unit (kilogram) prices were 5, 3 and 3 for the 0.25, 0.5 and 0.75 kilogram bags, respectively, as shown in Table 7.3 and in Figure 7.1 (including the broken line). Then the measure of quality-adjusted price change would depend on whether the 0.5 kilogram bag was replaced by the 0.25 kilogram one (a 67 per cent increase) or the 0.75 kilogram one (no change). This is not satisfactory because the choice of replacement size is arbitrary. The rationale behind the quality adjustment process is to ask: does the difference in unit price in each case reflect different levels of utility? If so, adjustments should be made to the unit prices to bring them into line. If not, adjustments should be made to the unit prices for that proportion attributable to differences in utility gained from, say, more convenient packaging or the availability of smaller lots. It may be obvious from the nature of the product that an item packaged in a very small size with a disproportionately high unit price carries an unusually high profit margin, and that an appropriate replacement for a large-sized item would not be this very small one.

Table 7.3 Example of size, price and unit price of bags of flour

Size (kilograms)	First price	First unit price	Second price	Second unit price
0.25	0.75	3	1.25	5
0.5	1.50	3	1.50	3
0.75	2.25	3	2.25	3

Differences in production or option costs

7.81 A natural approach to quality adjustment is to adjust the price of an old item by an amount equal to the resource costs of the additional features of the new item; i.e., to compare relative prices using:

$$p_n^t / \hat{p}_m^{t-1} \quad \text{where} \quad \hat{p}_m^{t-1} = p_m^{t-1} + x \qquad (7.20)$$

and x is the value of the additional features in period $t-1$ prices. This value should be a consumer's valuation, reflecting the additional flow of services or utility. One source of data is the manufacturers. They would be asked to provide data on production costs, to which retail mark-ups and associated indirect taxes would be added. This approach is most practicable in markets where there is a relatively small number of manufacturers, and where updates of models are infrequent and predictable. It only works if there is good communication between manufacturers and the statistical agency staff. It is particularly suitable when the quality adjustments are also being undertaken to calculate the producer price index (PPI) or other price programmes. Greenlees (2000) provides an example for new trucks and motor vehicles in the United States in 1999. Just prior to the introduction of the annual models, BLS staff visit selected manufacturers to collect cost information. The data are used in the PPI and International Comparison Programmes as well as in the CPI, and the information-gathering activity is a joint operation of the three programmes. Allowable product changes for the purpose of quality adjustments include occupant safety enhancements, mechanical and electrical improvements to overall vehicle operation or efficiency, changes that affect length of service or need for repair, and changes affecting comfort or convenience.

7.82 Bearing in mind the caveat in paragraph 7.30, the producer orientation of the PPI implies that resource cost is the appropriate criterion for quality adjustment to prices (Triplett, 1983). One distinction, then, between the use of producer cost estimates in the CPI and PPI is that only the former programme will add retail mark-ups and indirect taxes. Another important difference may occur in situations where product improvements are mandated by government. Some of these mandated improvements provide no direct benefit to the purchaser. In these cases it is appropriate to make a quality adjustment to prices for the associated resource cost in the PPI, but not in the CPI, where the appropriate criterion is user value. If only production cost data are available, then estimates of the retail mark-up must take into account the (average) age of the models under consideration. Mark-ups will decrease as models come to the end of their life cycles. Therefore, mark-ups based on models at the end of their life cycle should not be applied to the production costs of models at the start of their life cycle.

7.83 Because of these difficulties in using the production cost approach, the option cost method is generally preferred. Often it is the retail price of an option that is available and this of course includes the mark-up for profit. Consider an example of the *price* of an option being used to adjust for quality. Let the prices for an item in periods $t-1$ and t be 10,000 and 10,500, respectively, but assume the price in period t is for the item with a new feature or "option", and let the price of the additional feature in period t be known to be 300. Then the price change would be $10,200/10,000 = 1.02$ or 2.0 per cent. The adjustment may take a multiplicative form (see paragraphs 7.39–7.40 above): the additional option is worth $300/10,500 = 0.028571$ of the period t price. The adjusted price in period $t-1$ is therefore $10{,}000 \times 1.028571 = 10{,}285.71$ and the price change 10,500/10,285.71 = 1.020833 or about 2.08 per cent. If in subsequent periods either of these elements changes, then so too must $\hat{p}_{n,t-1}$ for those comparisons. The option cost method is thus a method for use in stable markets with stable technologies. Alternatively, it may be preferable to estimate a one-off adjustment to the preceding base period price and then compare all subsequent prices with the new option to this estimate; i.e. 10,500/10,300 = 1.019417 or approximately 2 per cent.

7.84 Option costs are thus useful in situations in which the old and new items differ by quantifiable characteristics that can be valued in monetary terms by reference to market prices. For example, nuts may be available roasted or unroasted, and food items may be available cooked or uncooked. Consider the addition of a feature to a car model. The feature may have been available as an option either in the prior period or currently for other models, providing an absolute or proportional consumer valuation. Armknecht and Maitland-Smith (1999) note that when radial tyres became a standard feature on new cars, the price of adding optional radial tyres was used to determine the quality adjustments in the United States CPI. The valuation of a quantifiable product feature may be readily available from the comparison of different product prices. Turvey et al. (1989) give the example of whiskies of different proofs (percentage alcohol content). The quality adjustment for a change in the alcohol content of one product may be inferred from the market relationship between proof and price.

7.85 Consider the addition of a feature to a product – say an installed automatic ice-maker in a refrigerator (Shepler, 2000). Refrigerators can be sold as standard or with an installed automatic ice-maker. The price collector may always have collected prices on the standard model, but this may no longer be in production, being replaced by a model with an installed automatic ice-maker. The cost of the option is thus known from before and a continuing series can be developed by using equation (7.20) and simply adjusting the old price in the base period for the option cost. Even this process may have its problems. First, the cost of producing something as standard may be lower than when it was an option, all new refrigerators now having the installed automatic ice-maker. This saving may be passed on, at least in part, to the consumer. The option cost method would thus understate a price increase. Triplett (2002) cites a study by Levy et al. (1999) in which a car theft system was installed as standard but disabled when the option was not required. It was seemingly cheaper to produce this way. Second, by including something as standard the consumer's valuation of the option may fall since buyers cannot refuse it. Some consumers may attribute little value to the option. The overall effect would be that the estimate of the option cost, priced for those who choose it, is likely to be higher than the implicit average price consumers would pay for it as standard. Estimates of the effect on price of this discrepancy should in principle be made, though in practice are quite difficult.

7.86 Option cost adjustments can be seen to be similar to quantity adjustments, except that instead of size being the additional quality feature of the replacement, the added quality can be any other individual feature. The comparison is: $p_n^t/\hat{p}_m^{t-1}$ where $\hat{p}_m^{t-1} = p_m^{t-1} + \beta\Delta z$ for an individual z characteristic where $\Delta z = (z_n^t - z_m^{t-1})$. The characteristics may be the size of the random access memory (RAM) of a personal computer (PC) when a specific model of PC is replaced by a model that is identical except for the amount of RAM it possesses. If the relationship between price and RAM is linear, the above formulation is appropriate. Many web pages give the price of additional RAM as being independent of other features of PCs, and a linear adjustment is appropriate. Bear in mind that a linear formulation values the worth of a fixed additional amount of RAM to be the same, irrespective of the amount of RAM the machine possesses.

7.87 The relationship may, of course, be non-linear. Say, for example, for every additional 1 per cent of x, y increases by 1.5 per cent ($\beta = 1.015$). In this case,

$$\hat{p}_m^{t-1} = p_m^{t-1}\beta^z \tag{7.21}$$

for $p_n^t/\hat{p}_m^{t-1}$ as a measure of quality-adjusted price changes. Again the z change may reflect the service flow, but the non-linearity in the price–z relationship may reflect the increasing or decreasing utility to the scale of the provision. Possession of the characteristic in up-market models of the item may be priced at a higher rate than in a lower-priced one, i.e. $\beta \geq 1$ in equation (7.21).

7.88 Consider Figure 7.1 with the z characteristic being the option on the horizontal axis. The similarity between the quantity adjustment and the option cost approaches is apparent since both relate price to some dimension of quality: the size or the option. The option cost approach can be extended to more than one quality dimension. Both approaches rely on the acquisition of estimates of the change in price resulting from a change in the option or size: the β slope estimates. In the case of the quantity adjustment, this was taken from an item identical to the one being replaced, aside from the fact that it was of a different size. The β slope estimate in this case was perfectly identified from the two pieces of information. It is as if the nature of the experiment controlled for changes in the other quality factors by comparing prices of what is essentially the same thing except for the quantity (size) change.

7.89 The same reasoning applies to option costs. There may be, for example, two items, identical but for the possession of a feature. This allows the value of the feature to be determined. Yet sometimes the value of a feature or option has to be extracted from a much larger data set. This may be because the quality dimension takes a relatively large range of possible numerical values without an immediately obvious consistent valuation. Consider the simple example of only one feature varying for a product, the speed of processing of a PC. It is not a straightforward matter to determine the value of an additional unit of speed. To complicate matters, there may be several quality dimensions to the items and not all combinations of these may exist as items in the market in any one period. Furthermore, the combinations existing in the second period being compared may be quite different to those in the first. Considering these aspects leads to a more general framework, known as the hedonic approach.

Hedonic approach

7.90 The hedonic approach is an extension of the two preceding approaches in that, first, the change in price arising from a unit change in quality – the slope of the line in Figure 7.1 – is now estimated from a data set comprising prices and quality characteristic values of a larger number of varieties. Second, the quality characteristic set is extended to cover, in principle, all major characteristics that might influence price, rather than just the quantity or option adjustment. The theoretical basis for hedonic regressions will be covered in Chapter 21 and is briefly reviewed below, following an example based on personal computers.

7.91 It should be noted that the method requires an extension of the data set to include values of the price-determining quality characteristics for each item. Under the matched models method each price collector needed only to collect sufficient data on each model to allow the model to be identified for subsequent repricing. The extension required in the hedonic approach is that all price-determining characteristics should be collected for each model. Checklists for the characteristics of a product have been found by Merkel (2000) to improve the quality of data collected, as well as serving the needs of hedonic adjustments (see also Chapter 6 on price collection and Liegey, 1994). If an item goes missing, any difference in the characteristics of its replacement can be identified and, as will be shown, a valuation can be ascribed to such differences using the hedonic approach.

7.92 Appendix 7.1 to this chapter provides data taken from the United Kingdom Compaq and Dell web sites in July 2000 on the prices and characteristics of 64 desktop personal computers (PCs). Figure 7.2 is a scatter diagram constructed from this information, relating the price (£ sterling) to the processing speed (MHz). It is apparent that PCs with higher speeds command higher prices – a positive relationship. Under the option cost framework above, a switch from a 733 MHz to a 933 MHz PC would involve a measure of the slope of the line between two unique points. The approach requires that there are 733 MHz and 933 MHz PCs that are identical except for their processing speed. From Figure 7.2 and Appendix 7.1 it is apparent that there are several PCs with the same speed but different prices, resulting from the fact that other things differ. To estimate the value given to additional units of speed, an estimate of the slope of the line that best fits the data is required. In Figure 7.1 the actual slope was used; for the data in Figure 7.2 an estimate of the slope needs to be derived from an estimate of the equation of the line that best fits the data, using ordinary least squares regression. Facilities for regression are available on standard statistical and econometric software, as well as spreadsheets. The estimated (linear) equation in this instance is:

$$\hat{\text{P}}\text{rice} = -658.436 + 3.261\ \text{Speed} \quad \bar{R}^2 = 0.820 \qquad (7.22)$$

The coefficient of speed is the estimated slope of the line: the change in price (£3,261) resulting from a 1 MHz change in speed. This can be used to estimate quality-adjusted price changes for PCs of different speeds. The value of $\bar{R}^2$ indicates that 82 per cent of price variation is explained by variation in processing speed. A t-statistic to test the null hypothesis of the coefficient being zero was found to be 18.83: recourse to standard tables on t-statistics found the null hypothesis was rejected at a 1 per cent level. The fact that the estimated coefficient differs from zero cannot be attributed to sampling errors at this level of significance. There is a probability of 1 per cent that the test has wrongly rejected the null hypothesis.

7.93 The range of prices for a given speed – for example for 933 MHz – can, however, be seen from Appendix 7.1 to be substantial. There is a price range of about £1,000, which suggests that other quality characteristics may be involved. Table 7.4 provides the results of a regression equation that relates price to a number of quality characteristics using the data in Appendix 7.1. Such estimates can be provided by standard statistical and econometric software, as well as spreadsheets.

7.94 The second column provides the results from a linear regression model, the dependent variable being price. The first variable is (processor) speed, with a coefficient of 2.731 – a unit MHz increase in processing speed leads to an estimated £2.731 increase (positive sign) in price. A change from 733 MHz to 933 MHz would be valued at an estimated 200×2.731=£546.20. The coefficient is statistically significant – its difference from zero (no effect) not being attributable to sampling errors at a 0.1 per cent level of significance. This estimated coefficient is based on a multivariate model: it is the effect of a unit change in processing speed on price, having controlled for the effect of other variables in the equation. The preceding result of 3.261 in equation (7.22) was based on only one variable, and is different from this improved result.

7.95 The brand variables are dummy intercepts taking values of 1 for, say, a Dell computer, and zero otherwise. While brands are not in themselves quality characteristics, they may be proxy variables for other factors such as reliability or after-sales service. The

Figure 7.2 Scatter diagram showing prices and processing speeds of personal computers

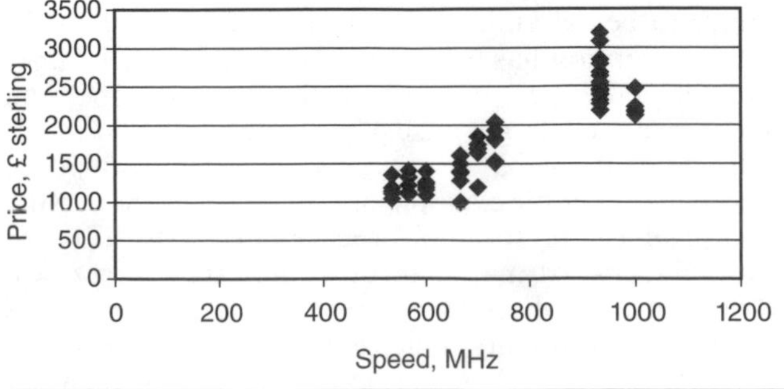

Table 7.4 Hedonic regression results for Dell and Compaq personal computers

Dependent variable	Price	ln price
Constant	– 725.996 (2.71)**	6.213 (41.95)***
Speed (processor, MHz)	2.731 (9.98)***	0.001364 (9.02)***
RAM (random access memory, MB)	1.213 (5.61) ***	0.000598 (5.00) ***
HD (hard drive capacity, MB)	4.517 (1.96)*	0.003524 (2.76)**
Brand (benchmark: Compaq Deskpro)		
Compaq Presario	– 199.506 (1.89)*	– 0.152 (2.60)**
Compaq Prosignia	– 180.512 (1.38)*	– 0.167 (2.32)*
Dell	– 1330.784 (3.74)***	– 0.691 (3.52)***
Processor (benchmark: AMD Athlon)		
Intel Celeron	393.325 (4.38)***	0.121 (2.43)**
Intel Pentium III	282.783 (4.28)***	0.134 (3.66)***
ROM-drive (benchmark: CD-ROM)†		
CD-RW (compact disk, re-writable)	122.478 (56.07)***	0.08916 (2.88)**
DVD (digital video drive)	85.539 (1.54)	0.06092 (1.99)*
Dell* Speed (MHz)	1.714 (4.038)***	0.000820 (3.49)***
N	63	63
$\bar{R}^2$	0.934	0.934

† Read only memory.
Figures in parentheses are *t*-statistics testing a null hypothesis of the coefficient being zero.
***,** and * denote statistically significant at 0.1 per cent, 1 per cent and 5 per cent levels, respectively, tests being one-tailed.

inclusion of such brand dummies also goes some way towards reflecting segmented markets as communities of buyers, as discussed in Chapter 21. Similar dummy variables were used for the other makes or brands (Compaq Presario and Compaq Presignia), except for one brand (Compaq Deskpro) which, in this case, was taken to form the benchmark against which other models are compared. The coefficient of the Dell brand is an estimate of the difference between a Dell brand's worth and that of a Compaq Deskpro, other variables being constant, i.e. £1,330.78 cheaper. Similarly, an Intel Pentium III commands an estimated £282.78 premium on an AMD Athlon.

7.96 The estimate for processor speed was based on data for Dell and Compaq PCs. If the adjustment for quality is between two Dell PCs, it might be argued that data on Compaq PCs should be ignored. Separate regressions could be estimated for each make, but this would severely restrict the sample size. Alternatively, an interaction term or slope dummy can be used for variables which are believed to have a distinctive brand-interaction effect. An example of such a dummy would be, say, Dell * Speed, which takes the value of "speed" when the PC is a Dell and zero otherwise. The coefficient of this variable (see Table 7.4) is 1.714; it is an estimate of the additional (positive sign) price arising for a Dell PC over and above that already arising from the standard valuation of a 1 MHz increase in speed. For Dell PCs it is £2.731 + £1.714 = £4.445. Thus if the replacement Dell PC is 200 MHz faster than the unavailable PC, the price adjustment to the unavailable PC is to add 200 × £4.465 = £893. Interactive terms for other variables can similarly be defined and used. The estimation of regression equations is easily undertaken using econometric or statistical software, or data analysis facilities in spreadsheets. An explanation of the techniques is given in many texts, including Kennedy (1998) and Maddala (1988). In Chapter 21, econometric concerns particular to the estimation of hedonic regressions are discussed.

7.97 The value $\bar{R}^2$ is the proportion of variation in price explained by the estimated equation. More formally, it is 1 minus the ratio of the variance of the residuals, $\sum_{i=1}^{N}(p_i^t - \hat{p}_i^t)^2/N$, of the equation to the variance of prices, $\sum_{i=1}^{N}(p_i^t - \bar{p}_i^t)^2/N$. The bar on the term R^2 denotes that an appropriate adjustment for degrees of freedom is made to this expression, which is necessary when comparing equations with different numbers of explanatory variables. At 0.934 (see Table 7.4), the value $\bar{R}^2$ is very high. A high value of $\bar{R}^2$ can, however, be misleading for the purpose of quality adjustment. First, such values indicate that the explanatory variables account for much of the price variation. This may be over a relatively large number of varieties of goods in the period concerned. This, of course, is not the same as implying a high degree of prediction for an adjustment to a replacement item of a single brand in a subsequent time period. Predicted values depend for their accuracy not just on the fit of the equation, but also on how far the characteristics of the item whose price is to be predicted are from the means of the sample. The more unusual the item, the higher the prediction probability interval. Second, the value $\bar{R}^2$ indicates the proportion of variation in prices explained by the estimated equation. It may be that 0.90 is explained while 0.10 is not explained. If the dispersion in prices is very large, this still leaves a large absolute margin of prices unexplained. Nonetheless, a high $\bar{R}^2$ is a necessary condition for the use of hedonic adjustments.

7.98 Hedonic regressions should generally be conducted using a semi-logarithmic formulation (Chapter 21). The dependent variable is the (natural) logarithm of the price, but the variables on the right-hand side of the equation are kept in their normal units, hence the semi-logarithmic formulation. A double-logarithmic formulation would also take logarithms of the right-hand side z variables. However, if any of these z variables are dummy variables which take the value of zero in some instances, the double-logarithmic formulation would break down because logarithms of zero cannot be taken. The focus is thus on the semi-logarithmic form. This concern with linear and semi-logarithmic formulations is equivalent to the consideration of additive and multiplicative formulations discussed in paragraphs 7.39 to 7.40 above. A linear model would, for example, ascribe an extra £282.78 to a PC with an Intel Pentium III as opposed to an AMD Athlon, irrespective of the price of the PC. This is common in pricing strategies using the World Wide Web. More often than not, however, the same options are valued at a higher price for up-market goods and services. In this case, equation (7.22) for a multivariate model becomes:

$$\text{Price} = \beta_0 \beta_1^{z_1} \beta_2^{z_2} \beta_3^{z_3} \ldots \beta_n^{z_n} \varepsilon$$

$$\text{or } \ln \text{Price} = \ln \beta_0 + z_1 \ln \beta_1 + z_2 \ln \beta_2 + z_3 \ln \beta_3 + \ldots\ldots z_n \ln \beta_n + \ln \varepsilon. \quad (7.23)$$

Note that this is a semi-logarithmic form; logarithms are taken of only the left-hand-side variable, i.e., price. Each of the z characteristics enters the regression without having logarithms taken. This has the advantage of allowing dummy variables for the possession or otherwise of a feature to be included on the right-hand side. Such dummy variables take the value of one if the item possesses the feature and zero otherwise. Matters relating to the choice of functional form are discussed in more detail in Chapter 21.

7.99 The taking of logarithms of the first equation (7.23) allows it to be transformed in the second equation to a linear form. This allows the use of a conventional ordinary least squares (OLS) estimator to yield estimates of the logarithms of the coefficients. These are given in the third column of Table 7.4 and have a useful direct interpretation: if these coefficients are multiplied by 100, they are the percentage change in price arising from a 1 unit change in the explanatory variable. For (processor) speed there is an estimated 0.1364 per cent change in price for each additional MHz the replacement item has over and above the unavailable item. When dummy variables are used, the coefficients, when multiplied by 100, are estimates of the percentage change in price, given by $(e^{\beta}-1)100$. For example, for a rewritable CD-RW compared to a read-only CD-ROM the change in price is 8.916 per cent. There is some bias in these coefficients; and in the (semi-) logarithmic equation, half the variance of each coefficient should be added to the coefficient before using it (Teekens and Koerts, 1972). For a read-only CD-ROM, the t-statistic is 2.88; this is equal to the coefficient divided by its standard error, the standard error being $0.08916/2.88 = 0.03096$ and the variance: $0.03096^2 = 0.000958$. The adjustment is to add 0.000958/2 to 0.08916, giving 0.089639 or 8.9639 per cent.

7.100 The approach is particularly useful when the market does not reveal the price of the quality characteristics required for the adjustment. Markets reveal prices of items, not quality characteristics, so it is useful to consider items as tied bundles of characteristics. A sufficiently large data set of items with their characteristics and sufficient variability in the mix of characteristics between the items allows the hedonic regression to provide estimates of the implicit prices of the characteristics. The theory behind such estimates is discussed in Chapter 21. A number of ways of implementing the method are outlined below.

7.101 Some mention should first be made of the interpretation of the coefficients from hedonic regressions. The matter is discussed in detail in Chapter 21; only the conclusions are summarized here. There used to be an erroneous perception that the coefficients from hedonic methods represented estimates of user value as opposed to resource cost. The former is the relevant concept in constructing a consumer price index, while for PPI construction it is the latter. Rosen (1974) found that hedonic coefficients may reflect both user value and resource cost – both supply and demand influences. There is what is referred to in econometrics as an identification problem; in other words, the observed data do not permit the estimation of the underlying demand and supply parameters. Suppose that the production technology of sellers is the same, but that buyers differ. Then the hedonic function describes the prices of characteristics that the firm will supply with the given ruling technology to the current mixture of tastes. There are different tastes on the consumer side, so what appears in the market is the result of firms trying to satisfy consumer preferences for a constant technology and profit level. The structure of supply is revealed by the hedonic price function. Now suppose that sellers differ, but that buyers' tastes are the same. Here the hedonic function $p(z)$ identifies the structure of demand. Of these two possible assumptions, uniformity of tastes is unlikely, while uniformity of technologies is more likely, especially when access to technology is unrestricted in the long run. Griliches (1988, p. 120) has argued in the context of a consumer price index:

> My own view is that what the hedonic approach tries to do is to estimate aspects of the budget constraint facing consumers, allowing thereby the estimation of "missing" prices when quality changes. It is not in the business of estimating utility functions *per se*, though it can also be useful for these purposes ... what is being estimated is the actual locus of intersection of the demand curves of different consumers with varying tastes and the supply curves of different producers with possible varying technologies of production. One is unlikely, therefore, to be able to recover the underlying utility and cost functions from such data alone, except in very special circumstances.

It is thus necessary to take a pragmatic stance. In many cases the implicit quality adjustment to prices outlined in paragraphs 7.44 to 7.71 may be inappropriate because the implicit assumptions are unlikely to be valid. In such instances, the practical needs of economic statistics require explicit quality adjustments. Not to do anything on the grounds that the measures are not conceptually appropriate would be to ignore quality change and provide wrong results. Hedonic techniques provide an important tool, making effective use of data on the price quality relationship derived from other items in the market to adjust for changes in one or more characteristics.

7.102 The proper use of hedonic regression requires an examination of the coefficients of the estimated equations to see if they make sense. It might be argued that the very multitude of distributions of tastes and technologies, along with the interplay of supply and demand, that determine the estimated coefficients (Chapter 21) make it unlikely that "reasonable" estimates will arise from such regressions. A firm may, for example, cut a profit margin relating to a characteristic for reasons related to long-run strategic plans; this may yield a coefficient on a desirable characteristic that may even be negative (Pakes, 2001). This does not negate the usefulness of examining hedonic coefficients as part of a strategy for evaluating estimated hedonic equations. First, there has been extensive empirical work in this field and the results for individual coefficients are, for the most part, quite reasonable. Even over time individual coefficients can show quite sensible patterns of decline (van Mulligen, 2003). Unreasonable coefficients on estimated equations are the exception and should be treated with some caution. Second, one can have more faith in an estimated equation whose coefficients make sense and which predicts well, than one which may also predict well but whose coefficients do not make sense. Third, if a coefficient for a characteristic does not make sense, it may be due to multicollinearity, a data problem, and should be examined to see if this is the case (see Appendix 21.1 to Chapter 21).

7.103 The implementation of hedonic methods to estimate quality adjustments for matched items which are no longer available is considered below. Consider items l, m and n where item l is available in periods t and $t+2$, the "old" item m is only available in period t and the replacement item n only in period $t+2$. The items are defined by their z quality characteristics, item m for example being z^t_m and the price of item m in period t is p^t_m, as depicted below. There is no problem with comparing the prices p^t_l and p^{t+2}_l of matched items with characteristics z^t_l with z^{t+2}_l, for they have the same l quality characteristics. But there is a problem with item m. A hedonic *imputation* approach would predict the price of item m's characteristics in period $t+2$ at the characteristic prices taken from a hedonic regression estimated in period $t+2$, i.e. $\hat{p}^{t+2}_m$.

Item/period	t	$t+2$
l	p^t_l	p^{t+2}_l
m	p^t_m	$\hat{p}^{t+2}_m$
n	$\hat{p}^t_n$	p^{t+2}_n

In this case, item m's characteristics are held constant in the comparison $\hat{p}^{t+2}_m/p^t_m$. A similar exercise can be conducted for the replacement item n using $p^{t+2}_n/\hat{p}^t_n$. In this comparison, item n's characteristics are held constant and compared at period $t+2$ and period t prices. These imputation approaches are outlined below. Yet there is a second approach, an *adjustment* one. Here the characteristics of the replacement item n are identified and compared with those of the old item m, $(z^{t+2}_n - z^t_m)$, and estimated coefficients from hedonic equations used to estimate the value of the changes. These two approaches, hedonic imputations and hedonic adjustments, are considered below in further detail. This "patching" of missing prices is quite different from the use of hedonic price indices discussed in paragraphs 7.132 to 7.149 and Chapter 21. These use hedonic regressions to provide hedonic price indices of overall quality-adjusted prices using a sample of all of the data in each period with no patching. The "patching" of missing prices is a partial application of the hedonic approach, used in imputations for missing items or on non-comparable replacements for missing items when the matched models approach is being used and an item's price is missing.

7.104 *Hedonic imputation: Predicted vs. actual.* In this approach a hedonic regression of the natural logarithm of the price of model i in period t on its characteristics set z^t_{ki} is estimated for each month, using the equation:

$$\ln p^t_i = \beta^t_0 + \sum_{k=1}^{K} \beta^t_k \, z^t_{ki} + \varepsilon^t_i \qquad (7.24)$$

Say the price of an item m available in January (period t) is unavailable in March (period $t+2$). The price of item m can be predicted for March by inserting the characteristics of the old unavailable item m into the estimated regression equation for March, and similarly for successive months. The predicted price for this old item in March and price comparison with January (period t) are given, respectively, by:

$$\hat{p}^{t+2}_m = \exp\left[\beta^{t+2}_0 + \textstyle\sum_k \beta^{t+2}_k \, z^t_{k,m}\right] \quad \text{and} \quad \hat{p}^{t+2}_m / p^t_m \qquad (7.25a)$$

That is, the old model's price is predicted for period $t+2$ and patched in. In the example in Table 7.1(a), $\hat{p}^{23}$, $\hat{p}^{24}$, etc. and $\hat{p}^{63}$, $\hat{p}^{64}$, etc. would be estimated and compared with p^{21} and p^{61} respectively. The blanks for items 2 and 6 in Table 7.1(a) would be effectively filled in by the estimated price from the regression equation.

7.105 An alternative procedure is to select for each unavailable m item a replacement item n. In this case the price of n in period $t+2$ is known, and a predicted price for n in period t is required. The predicted price for the new item and the required price comparison are:

$$\hat{p}^t_n = \exp\left[\beta^t_0 + \textstyle\sum_k \beta^t_k \, z^{t+2}_{k,m}\right] \quad \text{and} \quad p^{t+2}_n / \hat{p}^t_n \qquad (7.25b)$$

That is, the new model's price is adjusted. In this case the characteristics of item n are inserted into the right-hand side of an estimated regression for period t. The price comparisons of equation (7.25a) may be weighted by w^t_m, as would those of its replaced price comparison in equation (7.25b).

7.106 Another option is to take the geometric mean of the formulations in equations (7.25a) and (7.25b) on grounds analogous to those discussed in Chapter 15 and by Diewert (1997) with regard to similar index numbers.

7.107 *Hedonic imputation: Predicted vs. predicted.* This approach uses predicted values for, say, item n in both periods, e.g., $\hat{p}^{t+2}_n/\hat{p}^t_n$. Consider a misspecification problem in the hedonic equation. For example, there may be an interaction effect between a brand dummy and a characteristic – say for Dell and speed in the example in Table 7.4. Possession of both characteristics may be worth more in terms of price (in a semi-logarithmic form) than their separate individual components (for evidence of interactive effects see Curry et al., 2001). The use of $p_n^{t+2}/\hat{p}_n^t$ would be misleading since the actual price in the numerator would incorporate the 5 per cent premium, while the one predicted from a straightforward semi-logarithmic form would not. It is stressed that, in adopting this approach, a recorded actual price is being replaced by an imputation. This is not desirable, but neither is the form of bias discussed above. Diewert (2002e) considers a similar problem and suggests an adjustment to bring the actual price back in line with the hedonic one. The comparisons using predicted values in both periods are given as:

$\hat{p}_n^{t+2}/\hat{p}_n^t$ for the new item

$\hat{p}_m^{t+2}/\hat{p}_m^t$ for the disappearing or old item, or

$$[(\hat{p}_n^{t+2}/\hat{p}_n^t)(\hat{p}_m^{t+2}/\hat{p}_m^t)]^{1/2} \tag{7.26}$$

as a geometric mean of the two.

7.108 *Hedonic adjustments.* In this approach a replacement item is used and any differences between the k characteristics of the replacement n in, for example, period $t+2$ and m in period t are ascertained. A predicted price for m adjusted to be compatible with n is estimated for period t, i.e., $\hat{p}_m^{t+2}$ and is compared with the actual price, p_m^t, where

$$\hat{p}_m^{t+2} \equiv p_n^{t+2} \exp[-\textstyle\sum_k \beta_k^{t+2}(z_{nk}^{t+2} - z_{mk}^t)] \tag{7.27a}$$

or alternatively, a predicted price for n adjusted to be compatible with m is estimated for period t, i.e. $\hat{p}_n^t$ is compared with the actual price, p_n^{t+2}, where

$$\hat{p}_n^t \equiv p_m^t \exp[\textstyle\sum_k \beta_k^t(z_{nk}^{t+2} - z_{mk}^t)] \tag{7.27b}$$

The adjustments here are undertaken using predicted values. However, unlike the formulations in equation (7.27b), for example, $\hat{p}_n^t$ may be estimated by applying the subset of the k characteristics that distinguished m from n to their respective implicit prices in period t estimated from the hedonic regression, and adjusting the price of p_m^t. For example, if the nearest replacement for item 2 is item 3, then the characteristics that differentiated item 3 from item 2 are identified and the price in the base period, p^{31}, is estimated by adjusting p^{21} using the appropriate coefficients from the hedonic regression in that month. For example, for washing machines, if item 2 had a spin speed of 800 rpm and item 3 a spin speed of 1,100 rpm, other things being equal, the shadow price of the 300 rpm differential would be estimated from the hedonic regression and p^{21} would be adjusted for comparison with p^{33}. Note that if the z variables in the characteristic set are perfectly independent of each other, the results from this approach will be similar to those from equation (7.25). This is because interdependence between the variables on the right-hand side of the hedonic equation – multicollinearity – leads to imprecise estimates of the coefficients (see Chapter 21). Hedonic imputations and adjustments of the form (7.25b) and (7.27b) have an advantage over their counterparts (7.25a) and (7.27a) since the regression equation does not have to be updated in each period. However, (7.25b) and (7.27b) effectively compare a constant fixed basket of current period characteristics while (7.25a) and (7.27a) compare a fixed basket of price reference period characteristics. There is no reason to prefer one to the other and if the difference or spread between the two indices is large, this is reason for caution over the use of one against a geometric mean of the two. Regular updating of hedonic regressions would be likely to minimize spread.

7.109 *Hedonic: Indirect adjustment.* An indirect adjustment may be made for the current period, which only requires the hedonic regression to be estimated in the base period t, using:

$$\frac{p_n^{t+2}}{p_m^t} \Big/ \frac{\hat{p}_n^t}{\hat{p}_m^t} \tag{7.28}$$

The first term is the change in price between the old and replacement items in periods t and $t+2$ respectively. But the quality of the item has also changed, so this price change needs to be divided by a measure of the change in quality. The second term uses the hedonic regression in period t in both the numerator and denominator. The coefficients – the shadow prices of each characteristic – are held constant. The predicted prices nevertheless differ because different quantities of the characteristics are being inserted into the numerator and denominator: the characteristics of the replacement item n in the former and the old item m in the latter. The measure is the change in price after removing (by division) the change in quantity of characteristics for each item at a constant period t price. Of course, conceptually, the constant valuation by a period $t+2$ regression would be equally valid and a geometric mean of the two ideal. However, if hedonic regressions cannot be run in real time this is a compromise. As the spread between the current and base period results increases, its validity decreases. As such, the regression estimates should be updated regularly using old and current period estimates and results compared retrospectively as a check on the validity of the results.

Limitations of the hedonic approach

7.110 The limitations of the hedonic approach should be borne in mind. Some points are summarized below (see also Chapter 21). First, the approach requires statistical expertise for the estimation of the equations. The availability of user-friendly software with regression facilities makes this less problematic. Statistical and econometric software carries a range of diagnostic tests to help judge if the final formulation of the model is satisfactory. These include $\bar{R}^2$ as a measure of the overall explanatory power of the equation, and F-test and t-test statistics to enable tests to be conducted as to whether the differences between the coefficients of the explanatory variables are jointly and individually different from zero at specified levels of statistical significance. Most of these statistics make use of the errors from the estimated equation. The regression equation can be used to predict prices for each item by inserting the values of the characteristics of the items into the explanatory variables. The differences between the actual prices and these predicted results are the residual errors. Bias or imprecise, and thus misleading, results may arise from a range of factors including heteroscedasticity (non-constant variances in the residuals suggesting non-linearities or omission of relevant explanatory variables), a non-normal distribution for the errors, and multicollinearity, where two or more explanatory variables are related. The latter in particular has been described as the "bane of hedonic regressions" (Triplett, 1990). Such econometric issues have been discussed in the context of hedonic regressions (Berndt, 1991; Berndt et al., 1995; Triplett, 1990; Gordon, 1990; Silver, 1999; and in Chapter 21) and more generally by Kennedy (1998) and Maddala (1988). For the reasons discussed above, when multicollinearity is suspected, the use of predicted values rather than individual coefficients is advised.

7.111 Second, the estimated coefficients should be updated regularly. If the adjustment is to the old model, then the price comparison is between the price of the old model in some reference period adjusted for the quality difference between the old and new models, using coefficients from an estimated hedonic equation in the price reference period as estimates of the value of such differences, as in (7.27b). There is, at first sight, no need to update the estimated coefficients each month. Yet the valuation of a characteristic in the price reference period may be quite out of line with its valuation in the new period. For example, a feature may be worth an additional 5 per cent in the reference period instead of 10 per cent in the current period, because it might have been introduced at a discount at that point in its life cycle to encourage usage. Continuing to use the coefficients from some far-off period to make adjustments to prices in the current period is akin to using out-of-date base period weights. The comparison may be well defined, but have little meaning. If price adjustments for quality differences are being made to the old item in the price reference period using hedonic estimates from that period, then there is a need to update the estimates if they are considered to be out of date, say because of changing tastes or technology, and splice the new estimated comparisons onto the old. The regular updating of hedonic estimates when using imputations or adjustments is thus recommended, especially when there is evidence of parameter instability over time. Ideally a geometric mean of either (7.25a) and (7.25b) or of (7.27a) and (7.27b) should be used, but this requires an updating of hedonic regressions in real time.

7.112 Third, the sample of prices and characteristics used for the hedonic adjustments should be suitable for the purpose. If they are taken from a particular outlet or outlet type, trade source or web page and then used to adjust non-comparable prices for items sold in quite different outlets, then there must at least be an intuition that the marginal utilities for characteristics are similar between the outlets. A similar principle applies for the brands of items used in the sample for the hedonic regression. It should be borne in mind that high $\bar{R}^2$ statistics do not alone ensure reliable results. Such high values arise from regressions in periods prior to their application and indicate the proportion of variation in prices across many items and brands. They are not in themselves a measure of the prediction error for a particular item, sold in a specific outlet, of a given brand in a subsequent period, though they can be an important constituent of this.

7.113 Fourth, there is the issue of functional form and the choice of variables to include in the model. Simple functional forms generally work well. These include linear, semi-logarithmic (logarithm of the left-hand side) and double-logarithmic (logarithms of both sides) forms. Such issues are discussed in Chapter 21. The specification of a model should include all price-determining characteristics. Some authors advise quite simple forms with only the minimum number of variables, as long as the predictive capacity is high (Koskimäki and Vartia, 2001). Shepler (2000) included 33 variables in her hedonic regressions of refrigerators – a fairly homogeneous product. These included nine dummy variables for brand and four for colour, five types of outlets, three regions as control variables, and 11 characteristics including capacity, types of ice-maker, energy-saving control, extra drawers, sound insulation, humidifier and filtration device. Typically, a study would start with a large number of explanatory variables and a general econometric model of the relationship, while the final model would be more specific, having dropped a number of variables. The dropping of variables would depend on the result of experimenting with different formulations, and seeing their effects on diagnostic test statistics, including the overall fit of the model and the accordance of signs and magnitudes of coefficients with prior expectations. Reese (2000), for example, started with a hedonic regression for United States college textbooks which included about 50 explanatory variables, subsequently reduced to 14 such variables with little loss of explanatory power.

7.114 Finally, Bascher and Lacroix (1999) list several requirements for successful design and use of hedonic quality adjustment in the consumer price index, noting that these require heavy investments over a long period involving:

- intellectual competencies and sufficient time to develop and re-estimate the model, and to employ it when products are replaced;
- access to detailed, reliable information on product characteristics;
- a suitable organization of the infrastructure for collecting, checking and processing information.

7.115 Hedonic methods may also improve quality adjustment in the consumer price index by indicating which product attributes do *not* appear to have material impacts on price. That is, if a replacement item differs from the old item only in characteristics that have been rejected as price-determining variables in a hedonic study, this would support a decision to treat the items as comparable or equivalent to and include the entire price difference, if any, as pure price change. Care has to be exercised in such analysis because a feature of multicollinearity in regression estimates is that the imprecision of the parameter estimates may give rise to statistical tests that do not reject null hypotheses that are false, i.e., they do not find significant parameter estimates that are significant. The results from such regressions can nonetheless provide valuable information on the extent to which different characteristics influence price variation, and this in turn can help in the selection of replacement items. Enhanced confidence in item substitution and the quality adjustment of prices that arises from using the hedonic approach, and the parallel reduction in reliance on "linking", has been cited as a significant benefit in terms of the reliability of the measurement of price changes for apparel in the United States consumer price index (Reinsdorf, Liegey and Stewart, 1996). The results from hedonic regressions have a role to play in identifying price-determining characteristics and may be useful in the design of quality checklists in price collection (Chapter 6).

Choice between quality adjustment methods

7.116 Choice of method for quality adjustments to prices is not straightforward. The analyst must consider the technology and market for each commodity and devise appropriate methods. This is not to say the methods selected for one product area will be independent of those selected for other areas. Expertise built up using one method may encourage its use elsewhere, and intensive use of resources for one commodity may lead to less resource-intensive methods for others. The methods adopted for individual product areas may vary between countries as access to data, relationships with the outlet managers, resources, expertise and features of the production, and market for the product vary. Guidelines on choice of method arise directly from the features of the methods outlined above. A good understanding of the methods, and their implicit and explicit assumptions, is essential to the choice of an appropriate method.

7.117 Figure 7.3 provides a guide to the decision-making process. Assume that the matched models method is being used. If the item is matched for re-pricing, there being no change in the specification, no quality adjustment is required. This is the simplest of procedures. However, a caveat applies. If the item belongs to a high-technology industry where model replacement is rapid, the matched sample may become unrepresentative of the universe of transactions. Alternatively, matching may be under a chained framework, where prices of items in a period are matched to those in the preceding period to form a link. A series of successive links of matched comparisons combined by successive multiplication makes up the chained matched index. Or hedonic indices may be used which require no matching. The use of such methods is discussed in paragraphs 7.132 to 7.149. At the very least, attention should be directed to more regular item re-sampling. Continued long-run matching would deplete the sample and an alternative framework to long-run matching would be required.

7.118 Consider a change in the quality of an item and assume that a replacement item is available. The selection of a comparable item to the same specification and the use of its price as a *comparable replacement* require that none of the price difference is attributable to quality. It also requires confidence that all price-determining factors are included in the specification. The replacement item should also be representative and account for a reasonable proportion of sales. Caution is required when replacing near obsolete items with unusual pricing at the end of their life cycles with similar ones that account for relatively low sales, or with ones that have quite substantial sales but are at different points in their cycle. Strategies for ameliorating such effects are discussed below and in Chapter 8, including early substitutions before pricing strategies become dissimilar.

7.119 Figure 7.3 illustrates the case where quality differences can be quantified. *Explicit estimates* are generally considered to be more reliable, although they are also more resource intensive, at least initially. Once an appropriate methodology has been developed, they can often be easily replicated. General guidelines are more difficult here as the choice depends on the host of factors discussed above, which are likely to make the estimates more reliable in each situation. Central to all of this is the quality of the data upon which the estimates are based. If reliable data are unavailable, subjective judgements may be used. Product differences are often quite technical and very difficult to specify and quantify. The reliability of the method depends on the expertise of the experts and the variance in opinions. Estimates based on objective data are thus preferred. Good *production cost* estimates in industries with stable technologies and identifiable constant retail mark-ups and where differences between the old and replacement items are well specified and exhaustive are, by definition, reliable. Estimates of the retail mark-up are, however, prone to error and the *option cost* approach is generally preferable. This requires that the old and new items differ by easily identifiable characteristics which are or have been separately priced as options.

7.120 The use of *hedonic regressions* for partial patching is most appropriate where data on price and characteristics are available for a range of models and where the characteristics are found to predict and explain price variability well in terms of a priori reasoning and econometric terms. Their use is appropriate where the cost of an option or change in characteristics cannot be separately identified and has to be gleaned from the prices of items sold with different specifications in the market. The estimated regression coefficients are the estimate of the contribution to price of a unit change in a characteristic, having controlled for the effects of variations in the quantities of other characteristics. The estimates are particularly suited to valuing changes in the quality of an item when only a given set of characteristics changes and the valuation is required for changes in these characteristics only. The results from hedonic regressions may be used to target the salient characteristics for item selection. The synergy between the selection of prices according to characteristics defined as price determining by the hedonic regression, and their subsequent use for quality adjustment, should reap rewards. The method should be applied where there are high ratios of non-comparable replacements and where the differences between the old and new items can be well defined by a large number of characteristics.

Figure 7.3 Flowchart for making decisions on quality change

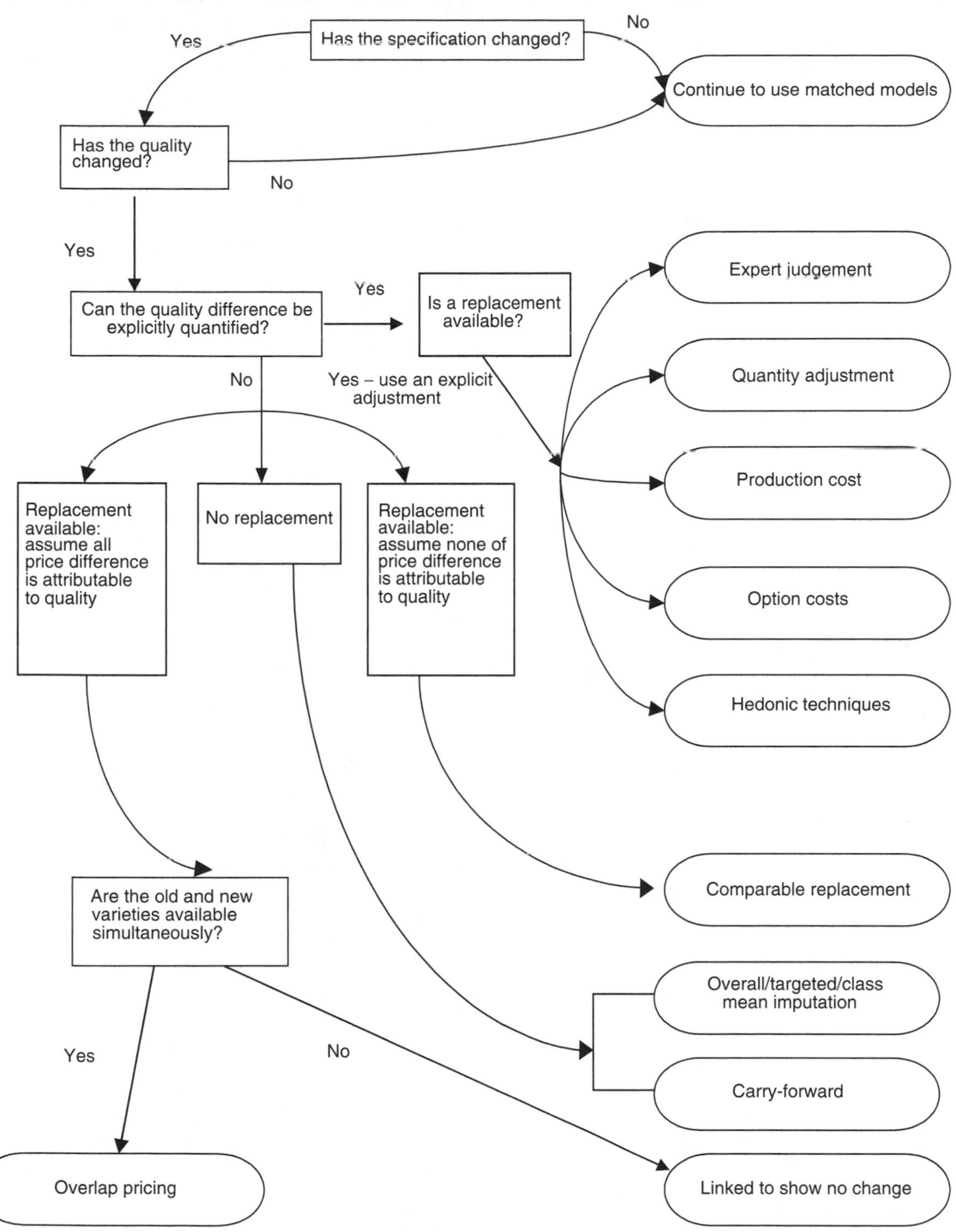

Source: Chart developed from a version by Fenella Maitland-Smith and Rachel Bevan, OECD; see also a version in Triplett (2002).

7.121 If explicit estimates of quality are unavailable, and no replacement items are deemed appropriate, then imputations may be used. The use of *imputations* has much to commend it resource-wise. It is relatively easy to employ – though some verification of the validity of the implicit assumptions might be appropriate. It requires no judgement (unless targeted) and is therefore objective. Targeted mean imputation is preferred to overall mean imputation as long as the sample size upon which the target is based is adequate. Class mean imputation is preferred when models at the start of their life cycles are replacing those around the end of their life cycle, although the approach requires faith in the adequacy of the explicit and comparable replacements being made.

7.122 Bias from using imputation is directly related to the proportion of missing items and the difference between quality-adjusted prices of available matched items and the quality-adjusted prices of unavailable ones (see Table 7.2 on page 110). The nature and extent of the bias depends on whether short-run or long-run imputations are being used (the former being preferred) and on market conditions (see paragraphs 7.159 to 7.173). Imputation, in practical terms, produces the same result as deletion of the item. The inclusion of imputed prices may give the illusion of larger sample sizes. Imputation is less likely to introduce bias where the proportion of missing prices is low. Table 7.2 can be used to estimate likely error margins arising from its use and a judgement can be made as to whether they are acceptable. The use of imputation across many products need not necessarily compound the errors since, as noted in the above discussion of this method, the direction of bias need not be systematic. It is cost-effective for product areas with a large number of missing items because of its ease of use. But the underlying assumptions required by imputation must be very carefully considered if it is widely used. Imputation should by no means be the overall catch-all strategy, and statistical agencies are advised against its use as a default device without due consideration of the nature of the markets, the possibility of targeting the imputation and the viability of estimates from the sample sizes involved if such targeting is employed.

7.123 If the old and replacement items are available simultaneously, and if the quality difference cannot be quantified, an implicit approach can be used whereby the price difference between the old and replacement items in a period in which they both exist is assumed to be attributable to quality. This *overlap* method, in replacing the old item by a new one, takes the ratio of prices in a period to be a measure of their quality difference. It is implicitly used when new samples of items are taken. The assumption of relative prices equating to quality differences at the time of the splice is unlikely to hold if the old and replacement items are at different stages in their life cycles and different pricing strategies are used at these stages. For example, there may be deep discounting of the old item to clear inventories, and price skimming of market segments that will purchase new models at relatively high prices. As with comparable replacements, early substitutions are advised so that the overlap is at a time when items are at similar stages in their life cycles.

7.124 For the reasons discussed, the use of the *linked to show no change* method and the *carry-forward* method is not generally advised for making quality adjustment imputations, unless the implicit assumptions are deemed to be valid.

High-technology and other sectors with a rapid turnover of models

7.125 The measurement of price changes of items unaffected by quality changes is primarily achieved by matching models, the above techniques being applicable when the matching breaks down. But what of industries where the matching breaks down on a regular basis because of the high turnover in new models of different qualities to the old ones? The matching of prices of identical models over time, by its nature, is likely to lead to a seriously depleted sample. There is both a dynamic universe of all items consumed and a static universe of the items selected for repricing (Dalén, 1998a). If, for example, the sample is initiated in December, by the subsequent May the static universe will be matching prices of those items available in the static universe in both December and May, but will omit the unmatched new items introduced in January, February, March, April and May, and the unmatched old ones available in December but unavailable in May. Two empirical questions show whether there will be any significant bias. First, is sample depletion substantial? Substantial depletion of the sample is a necessary condition for such bias. Second, are the unmatched new and unmatched old items likely to have quality-adjusted prices that substantially differ from those of the matched items in the current and the base periods?

7.126 The matching of prices of identical models over time may lead to the monitoring of a sample of models that is increasingly unrepresentative of the population of transactions. Some of the old models that existed when the sample was drawn are not available in the current period; and new models that enter the sample are not available in the base period. It may be that the models that are going out have relatively low prices, while the entrants have relatively high ones. By ignoring these prices, a bias is being introduced. Using old low-priced items and ignoring new high-priced ones has the effect of biasing the index downwards. In some industries, the new item may be introduced at a relatively low price and the old one may become obsolete at a relatively high price, serving a minority segment of the market (Berndt et al., 2003). In this case, the bias would take the opposite direction. The nature of the bias will depend on the pricing strategies of firms for new and old items.

7.127 This sampling bias exists for most products. Our concern here, however, is with product markets where the statistical agencies are finding the frequency of new item introductions and old item obsolescence sufficiently high that they may have little confidence in their results. First, some examples of such product markets will be given and then two procedures will be considered: the use of hedonic price indices (as opposed to the partial, hedonic patching discussed above) and chaining.

Some examples

7.128 Koskimäki and Vartia (2001) attempted to match prices of models of personal computers (PCs) over three two-month periods (spring, summer and autumn) using a sample of prices collected as part of standard price collection for the Finnish consumer price index. Of the 83 spring prices, only 55 matched comparisons could be made with the summer prices, and then only 16 continued through to the autumn. The sample of matched pairs became increasingly rapidly biased: of the 79 models in the autumn, the 16 matched ones had a mean processor speed of 518 MHz compared with 628 MHz for the remaining 63 unmatched ones; the hard disk sizes were, respectively, 10.2 and 15.0 Gigabytes, and the percentages of high-end processors (Pentium III and AMD Atl.) were 25 per cent and 49.2 per cent, respectively. Hardly any change in *matched* prices was found over this six-month period, while a hedonic regression analysis using all of the data found quality-adjusted price falls of around 10 per cent. Instructions to price collectors to hold onto models until forced replacements are required may thus lead to a sample that is increasingly unrepresentative of the population and is biased towards technically inferior variants. In this instance, the hedonic price changes fell faster since the newer models became cheaper for the services supplied.

7.129 Kokoski et al. (1999) used hedonic regressions in an empirical study of inter-area price comparisons of food products across urban areas in the United States using the United States consumer price index data. They found a negative sign on the coefficients of dummy variables for whether or not the sample items were from newly rotated samples (dummy variable = 1) or samples prior to rotation (dummy variable = 0). This indicated that quality-adjusted prices were lower for the newly included items compared with the quality-adjusted prices of the old items.

7.130 Silver and Heravi (2002) found evidence of sample degradation when matching prices of United Kingdom washing machines over a year. By December, only 53 per cent of the January basket of model varieties was used for the December/January index, although this accounted for 81.6 per cent of January expenditure. Models of washing machines with lower sales values dropped out faster. However, the remaining models in December accounted for only 48.2 per cent of the value of transactions in December. The active sample relating to the universe of transactions in December had substantially deteriorated. The prices of unmatched and matched models were found to differ, as were their vintage and quality. Even when prices were adjusted for quality using hedonic regressions, prices of unmatched old models were found to be lower than matched ones, there also being evidence of higher prices for unmatched new models. Quality-adjusted prices fell faster for the matched sample than for the full sample: about 10 per cent compared with about 7 per cent. Residuals from a common hedonic surface and their leverage were also examined. The residuals from unmatched new models were higher than matched ones, while residuals from unmatched old models were much lower. Unmatched observations had nearly twice the (unweighted) leverage as matched ones – their influence in the estimation of the parameters of the regression equation was much greater, and their exclusion more serious.

7.131 The above studies demonstrate how serious sample degradation can occur and how unmatched excluded items may be quite different from included ones. Two procedures for dealing with such situations will be considered: the use of hedonic price indices (as opposed to the partial, hedonic patching discussed above) and chaining. Both rely on a data set of a representative sample of items and their characteristics in each period. Price collectors might use a checklist of characteristics in gathering the data (Merkel, 2000). They will be asked to collect prices and characteristics of more than one item in each store, the items being the major or typical ones sold. If a new item is introduced which has or is likely to have substantial sales, then it is included as a replacement or even addition, and its characteristics are marked off against a checklist of salient characteristics. The list will be developed at the time of initiating the sample, and updated as required. Alternatively, market research agencies, web pages and trade associations may also be able to provide lists of models and their prices. Nevertheless, there is a need to collect transaction prices, as opposed to list prices.

Hedonic price indices

7.132 It is important to distinguish between the use of hedonic regressions to make adjustments for quality differences when a non-comparable substitute is used, as in paragraphs 7.90 to 7.115, and their use in their own right as *hedonic price indices*, which are measures of quality-adjusted price changes. Hedonic price indices are suitable when the pace and scale of replacements of items are substantial because, first, an extensive use of quality adjustments may lead to errors and, second, the sampling will be from a matched/replacement universe likely to be biased. With new models being continually introduced and old ones disappearing, the coverage of a matched sample may deteriorate and bias may be introduced as the price changes of new/old models differ from those of the matched ones. What is required is a sample to be drawn in each month and price indices constructed; but instead of controlling for quality differences by matching, they will be controlled for, or "partialled out", in the hedonic regression. Note that all the indices described below use a fresh sample of the data available in each period. If there is a new item in a period, it is included in the data set and its quality differences controlled for by the regression. Similarly, if old items drop out, they are still included in the data for the indices in the periods in which they exist. Paragraphs 7.110 to 7.115 stress the need for caution in the use of hedonic regressions for quality adjustments; some of the theoretical and econometric aspects are considered in Chapter 21. This need for caution extends to the use of the results from hedonic indices, and the discussion is not repeated here for the sake of brevity.

7.133 In Chapter 17, theoretical price indices are defined and practical index number formulae are considered as bounds or estimates of these indices. Theoretical index numbers are also defined in Chapter 21 to include goods made up of tied characteristics, so something can be said about how such theoretical indices relate to different forms of hedonic indices. A number of forms are considered in Chapter 21; they are summarized below.

7.134 *Hedonic functions with dummy variables for time.* The sample covers the two time periods being compared, say t and $t+2$, and does not have to be matched. The hedonic formulation regresses the price of item i, p_i, on the $k=2, \ldots K$ characteristics of the items z_{ki}. A single regression is estimated on the data in the two time periods compared, the equation also including a dummy variable D^{t+2} being 1 in period $t+2$, zero otherwise:

$$\ln p_i = \beta_0 + \beta_1 D^{t+2} + \sum_{k=2}^{K} \beta_k z_{ki} + \varepsilon_i \qquad (7.29)$$

The coefficient β_1 is an estimate of the quality-adjusted price change between period t and period $t+2$. It is an estimate of the change in the logarithm of price, having controlled for the effects of variation in quality via $\sum_{k=2}^{K} \beta_k z_{ki}$. Note that an adjustment is required for β_1: the addition of ½ (standard error)^2 of the estimate, as discussed in Goldberger (1968) and Teekens and Koerts (1972). Two variants of equation (7.28) are considered. The first is the direct *fixed base version*, that compares period t with $t+2$ as outlined: January–February, January–March, etc. The second is a rolling *chained version* evaluated for period t with $t+1$; then again for $t+1$ with $t+2$, the links in the chain being combined by successive multiplication. A January–March comparison, for example, would be the January–February index multiplied by the February–March one. There is, of course, a *fully constrained version*: a single constrained regression for, say, January to December with dummy variables for each month, but this is impractical in real time since it requires data on future observations.

7.135 The above approach uses the dummy variables on time to compare prices in period 1 with prices in each subsequent period. In doing so, the β parameters are constrained to be constant over the period being compared. A fixed base, bilateral comparison using equation (7.29) makes use of the constrained parameter estimates over the two periods and, given an equal number of observations in each period, is a form of a symmetric average. A *chained* formulation would estimate $I_{1,4}$, for example, as: $I_{1,4} = I_{1,2} \times I_{2,3} \times I_{3,4}$. In each binary comparison for matched data, equal weight is also given to the data in each period.

7.136 There is no explicit weighting in these formulations and this is a serious disadvantage. In practice, "cut-off" sampling might be employed to include only the most important items. If sales data are available, a weighted least squares (WLS) estimator should be used, as opposed to an ordinary least squares (OLS) estimator. It is axiomatic in normal index number construction that the same weight should not be given to each price comparison, since some items may account for much larger sales revenues than others. The same consideration applies to these hedonic indices. Diewert (2002e) has argued for a preference for sales *value* weights over quantity weights. Two items may have sales equal to the same quantity, but if one is priced higher than another, its price changes should be accordingly weighted higher for the result to be meaningful in an economic sense. Additionally, Diewert (2002e) has shown that value *shares* should form the weights, since values will increase, in say period $t+2$, with prices, the residuals and their variance thus being higher in period $t+2$ than in t. This heteroscedasticity is an undesirable feature of a regression model, resulting in increased standard errors. Silver (2002) has further shown that a WLS estimator does not purely weight the observations by their designated weights, the actual influence given being also the result of a combination of the residuals and the leverage effect. The latter is higher as the characteristics of the observations diverge from the average characteristics of the data. Silver suggests that observations with relatively high leverage and low weights be deleted and the regression re-run.

7.137 *Period-to-period hedonic indices.* An alternative approach for a comparison between periods t and $t+2$ is to estimate a hedonic regression for period $t+2$, and insert the values of the characteristics of each model existing in period t into the period $t+2$ regression to predict, for each item, its price. This would generate predictions of the prices of items existing in period t based on their z_i^t characteristics, at period $t+2$ shadow prices, $\hat{p}_i^{t+2}(z_i^t)$. These prices (or an average) can be compared with the actual prices (or the average of prices) of models in period t, $p_i^t(z_i^t)$ as, for example, a Jevons hedonic base period index:

$$P_{JHB} = \frac{\left[\prod_{i=1}^{N^t} \hat{p}_i^{t+2}(z_i^t)\right]^{1/N^t}}{\left[\prod_{i=1}^{N^t} p_i^t(z_i^t)\right]^{1/N^t}} = \frac{\left[\prod_{i=1}^{N^t} \hat{p}_i^{t+2}(z_i^t)\right]^{1/N^t}}{\left[\prod_{i=1}^{N^t} \hat{p}_i^t\right]^{1/N^t}} = \frac{\left[\prod_{i=1}^{N^t} \hat{p}_i^{t+2}(z_i^t)\right]^{1/N^t}}{\left[\prod_{i=1}^{N^t} p_i^t\right]^{1/N^t}} \qquad (7.30a)$$

7.138 Alternatively, the characteristics of models existing in period $t+2$ can be inserted into a regression for period t. Predicted prices of period $t+2$ items generated at period t shadow prices, $p_i^t(z_i^{t+2})$, are the prices of items existing in period $t+2$ estimated at period t prices and these prices (or an average) can be compared with the actual prices (or the average of prices) in period $t+2$, $p_i^{t+2}(z_i^{t+2})$; a Jevons hedonic current period index is:

$$P_{JHC} = \frac{\left[\prod_{i=1}^{N^{t+2}} p_i^{t+2}(z_i^{t+2})\right]^{1/N^{t+2}}}{\left[\prod_{i=1}^{N^{t+2}} p_i^t(z_i^{t+2})\right]^{1/N^{t+2}}} = \frac{\left[\prod_{i=1}^{N^{t+2}} \hat{p}_i^{t+2}\right]^{1/N^{t+2}}}{\left[\prod_{i=1}^{N^{t+2}} p_i^t\,(z_i^{t+2})\right]^{1/N^{t+2}}} = \frac{\left[\prod_{i=1}^{N^{+2t}} p_i^{t+2}\right]^{1/N^{t+2}}}{\left[\prod_{i=1}^{N^{t+2}} p_i^t(z_i^{t+2})\right]^{1/N^{t+2}}} \qquad (7.30b)$$

7.139 For a fixed base bilateral comparison using either equation (7.30a) or equation (7.30b), the hedonic equation is only estimated for one period, the current period $t+2$ in equation (7.30a) and the base period t in equation (7.30b). For reasons analogous to those explained in Chapters 15, 16 and 17, a symmetric average of these indices would have some theoretical support.

7.140 Note that a geometric mean of (7.30) uses all the data available in each period, as does the hedonic index using a time dummy variable in (7.29). If in (7.29) there is a new item in, say, period $t+2$, it is included in the data set and its quality differences controlled for by the regression. Similarly, if old items drop out, they are still included in the indices in the periods in which they exist. This is part of the natural estimation procedure, unlike using matched data and hedonic adjustments on non-comparable replacements when items are no longer available.

7.141 With the dummy variable approach, there is no explicit weighting in its formulation in (7.29), and this is a serious disadvantage. In practice, cut-off sampling might be employed to include only the most important items; or if expenditure data are available, a WLS as opposed to an OLS estimator might be used, with expenditure value shares as weights, as discussed in Appendix 21.1 to Chapter 21.

7.142 *Superlative and exact hedonic indices (SEHI).* In Chapter 17, Laspeyres and Paasche bounds are defined on a theoretical basis, as are superlative indices, which treat both periods' data symmetrically. These superlative formulae, in particular the Fisher index, are also seen in Chapter 16 to have desirable axiomatic properties. Furthermore, the Fisher index is supported by economic theory as a symmetric average of the Laspeyres and Paasche bounds, being found to be the most suitable such average on axiomatic grounds. The Törnqvist index is seen to be best from the stochastic viewpoint, and also does not require strong assumptions for its derivation from the economic approach as a superlative index. The Laspeyres and Paasche indices are found to correspond to (be exact for) underlying Leontief aggregator functions with no substitution possibilities, while superlative indices are exact for flexible functional forms, including the quadratic and translogarithmetic forms for the Fisher and Törnqvist indices, respectively. If data on prices, characteristics and quantities are available, analogous approaches and findings arise for hedonic indices (Fixler and Zieschang, 1992 and Feenstra, 1995). Exact theoretical bounds on a hedonic index have been defined by Feenstra (1995). Consider the theoretical index in Chapter 17, equation (17.3), but now defined only over items in terms of their characteristics z_i. The prices (and quantities) are still of items, but they are wholly defined through their characteristics $p_i\,(z_i)$. An arithmetic aggregation for a linear hedonic equation finds a Laspeyres upper bound (as quantities demanded *decrease* with increasing relative prices) given by:

$$\frac{\sum_{i=1}^{N} q_i^t \hat{p}_i^{t+2}}{\sum_{i=1}^{N} q_i^t p_i^t} = \sum_{i=1}^{N} s_i^t \left(\frac{\hat{p}_i^{t+2}}{p_i^t}\right) \geq \frac{C(u^t, p(z)^{t+2})}{C(u^t, p(z)^t)} \qquad (7.31a)$$

where the right-hand-side expression is the ratio of the cost of achieving a period t level of utility (u^t), where utility is a function of the vector of quantities, i.e., $u^t = f(q^t)$. The price comparison is evaluated at a fixed level of period t quantities, and s_i^t are the shares in total value of expenditure on product i in period t, $s_i^t = q_i^t p_i^t / \sum_{i=1}^{N} q_i^t p_i^t$ and

$$\hat{p}_i^{t+2} \equiv p_i^{t+2} - \sum_{i=1}^{N} \beta_k^{t+2}(z_{ik}^{t+2} - z_{ik}^t) \qquad (7.31b)$$

are prices in period $t+2$ adjusted for the sum of the changes in each quality characteristic weighted by their coefficients derived from a linear hedonic regression. Note that the summation is over the same i in both periods, since replacements are included when an item is missing and equation (7.31b) adjusts their prices for quality differences.

7.143 A Paasche lower bound is estimated as:

$$\frac{\sum_{i=1}^{N} q_i^{t+2} p_i^{t+2}}{\sum_{i=1}^{N} q_i^{t+2} \hat{p}_i^t} = \left[\sum_{i=1}^{N} s_i^{t+2} \left(\frac{p_i^{t+2}}{\hat{p}_i^t}\right)\right]^{-1} \leq \frac{C(u^{t+2}, p(z)^{t+2})}{C(u^{t+2}, p(z)^t)} \qquad (7.32a)$$

where $s_i^{t+2} = q_i^{t+2} p_i^{t+2} / \sum_{i=1}^{N} q_i^{t+2} p_i^{t+2}$ and

$$\hat{p}_i^t \equiv p_i^t + \sum_{i=1}^{N} \beta_k^t (z_{ik}^{t+2} - z_{ik}^t) \qquad (7.32b)$$

which are prices in periods t adjusted for the sum of the changes in each quality characteristic weighted by its respective coefficients derived from a linear hedonic regression.

7.144 In Chapter 17 it is shown that Laspeyres P_L and Paasche P_P price indices form bounds on their respective "true" economic theoretic indexes. Using similar reasoning to that in Chapter 17 applied to equations (7.31a) and (7.32a), it can be shown that under homothetic preferences these true economic indices collapse into a single theoretical index $c(p^{t+2})/c(p^t)$, and:

$$P_L \geq c(p^{t+2})/c(p^t) \geq P_P \qquad (7.33)$$

7.145 The approach is akin to that used for adjustments to non-comparable replacement items in equations (7.27a) and (7.27b), above. However, the SEHI approach first uses all the data in each period, not just the matched sample and selected replacements. Second, it uses the coefficients from hedonic regressions on changes in the characteristics to adjust observed prices for quality changes. Third, it incorporates a weighting system using data on the expenditure shares of each model and their characteristics, rather than treating each model as equally important. Finally, it has a direct correspondence to formulations defined from economic theory.

7.146 Semi-logarithmic hedonic regressions would supply a set of β coefficients suitable for use with these base and current period geometric bounds:

$$\prod_{i=1}^{N} \left(\frac{p_i^{t+2}}{\hat{p}_i^t}\right)^{s_i^{t+2}} \leq \frac{C(u, p(z)^{t+2})}{C(u, p(z)^t)} \leq \prod_{i=1}^{N} \left(\frac{\hat{p}_i^{t+2}}{p_i^t}\right)^{s_i^t} \qquad (7.34a)$$

$$\hat{p}_i^t \equiv p_i^t \exp\left[\sum_{i=1}^{N} \beta_k^t (z_{ik}^{t+2} - z_{ik}^t)\right]$$

$$\hat{p}_i^{t+2} \equiv p_i^{t+2} \exp\left[-\sum_{i=1}^{N} \beta_k^{t+2} (z_{ik}^{t+2} - z_{ik}^t)\right] \qquad (7.34b)$$

7.147 In equation (7.34a) the two bounds on the respective theoretical indices have been shown to be brought together under an assumption of homothetic preference (see Chapter 17). The calculation of such indices is no small task. For examples of their application, see Silver and Heravi (2001a and 2003) for comparisons over time and Kokoski et al. (1999) for price comparisons across areas of a country. Kokoski et al. (1999) used a sample from a replacement universe of otherwise matched data from the United States Bureau of Labor Statistics consumer price index, though the sample benefited from rotation. Silver and Heravi (2001a and 2003) used scanner data for the universe of transactions via a two-stage procedure in which cells were defined according to major price-determining features such as all combinations of brand, outlet type and (for television sets) screen size – much like strata. There may be a gain in the efficiency of the final estimate since the adjustment is for within-strata variation, much in the way that stratified random sampling improves on simple random sampling. The average price in each matched cell could then be used for the price comparisons using equations (7.32a) and (7.34a), except that – to ensure that the quality differences in each cell from characteristics other than these major ones did not influence the price comparison – adjustments were made for quality changes using equations (7.32b) and (7.34b). This allowed all matched, old unmatched and new unmatched data to be included since, if the average price in, say, a cell of equation (7.32a) was increased because of the inclusion of a new improved item, equation (7.32b) would be used to remove such improvements, on average. Consider, for example, a brand X, 14-inch television set with stereo sound sold to multiple outlets. There might be matched cells for brand X television sets sold in multiples, but not matched cells also including stereo. The new model may have to be grouped in a cell with the brand X, 14-inch television sets sold in multiples, and the average price of the cells compared in equation (7.32a) or (7.34a), and making a quality adjustment for the stereo in the form of equation (7.32b) or (7.34b). The estimated coefficient for stereo would be derived from a hedonic equation estimated from data of other television sets, some of which possess stereo.

7.148 The above description illustrates how weighted index number formulae such as Laspeyres, Paasche, Fisher and Törnqvist might be constructed using data on prices, quantities and characteristics of an item. Silver and Heravi (2003) show that as the number of characteristics over which the summation takes place in equations (7.32a) and (7.34a) increases, the more redundant the adjustment in equations (7.32b) and (7.34b) becomes, until, when all combinations of characteristics are used in equations (7.32a) and (7.34a) as strata, the calculation extends to a matched models problem in which each cell uniquely identifies an item. For matched data, equations (7.32b) and (7.34b) serve no purpose; the aggregation in equations (7.32a) and (7.34a) would be over all items, and would reduce to the usual index number problem. Diewert (2003a), commenting on the method, explains why, when matching is relatively large, the results given are similar to those from superlative hedonic index numbers.

7.149 Weighted index number formulae might thus be constructed using data on prices, quantities and characteristics of an item when the data are not matched. This is because continuing with matched data may lead to errors from two sources: multiple quality adjustments from items no longer available and their non-comparable replacements; and sample selectivity bias from sampling from a replacement universe as opposed to a double universe.

The difference between hedonic indices and matched indices

7.150 In previous sections, the advantages of hedonic indices over matched comparisons are referred to in terms of the inclusion by the former of unmatched data. This relationship is discussed more formally here. Triplett (2002) argued and Diewert (2002e) showed that an unweighted geometric mean (Jevons) index for matched data gives the same result as a logarithmic hedonic index run on the same data. Consider the matched sample m and Z^{t+2} and Z^t as overall quality adjustments to the dummy variables for time in equation (7.29), that is, $\sum_{k=2}^{K}\beta_k z_{ki}$. The very first line in equation (7.35) below is shown by Aizcorbe et al. (2001) to equal the difference between two geometric means of quality-adjusted prices. The sample space $m=M^t=M^{t+2}$ is the same model in each period. Consider the introduction of a new model n introduced in period $t+2$ with no counterpart in t and the demise of an old model o so it has no counterpart in $t+2$. So M^{t+2} is composed of m and n, and M^t is composed of m and o, while M consists only of the matched models m. Silver and Heravi (2002) have shown the dummy variable hedonic comparison to now be:

$$\begin{aligned}\ln p^{t+2}/p^t = &\left[m/(m+n)\sum_m \ln(p_m^{t+2}-Z_m)/m\right.\\&\left.+n/(m+n)\sum_n \ln(p_n^{t+2}-Z_n)/n\right]\\&\times\left[m/(m+o)\sum_m \ln(p_m^{t}-Z_m)/m\right.\\&\left.+o/(m+o)\sum_o \ln(p_o^{t}-Z_o)/o\right]\\&=\left[m/(m+n)\sum_m \ln(p_m^{t+2}-Z_m)/m\right.\\&\left.-m/(m+o)\sum_m \ln(p_m^{t}-Z_m)/m\right]\\&\times\left[n/(m+n)\sum_n \ln(p_n^{t+2}-Z_n)/n\right.\\&\left.-o/(m+o)\sum_o \ln(p_o^{t}-Z_o)/o\right]\end{aligned} \tag{7.35}$$

7.151 Consider the second expression in equation (7.35). First, there is the change for the m matched observations. This is the change in mean prices of matched models m in period $t+2$ and t, adjusted for quality. Note that the weight in period $t+2$ for this matched component is the proportion of matched to all observations in period $t+2$. Similarly, for period t, the matched weight depends on how many unmatched old observations are in the sample. In the last line of equation (7.35), the change is between the unmatched new and the unmatched old mean (quality-adjusted) prices in periods

$t+2$ and t. Thus matched methods can be seen to ignore the last line in equation (7.35) and will thus differ from the hedonic dummy variable approach in at least this respect. The hedonic dummy variable approach, in its inclusion of unmatched old and new observations, can be seen from equation (7.35) possibly to differ from a geometric mean of matched prices changes, the extent of any difference depending, in this unweighted formulation, on the proportions of old and new items leaving and entering the sample and on the price changes of old and new items relative to those of matched ones. If the market for products is one in which old quality-adjusted prices are unusually low while new quality-adjusted prices are unusually high, then the matched index will understate price changes (see Silver and Heravi, 2002 and Berndt et al., 2003 for examples). Different market behaviour will lead to different forms of bias.

7.152 If sales weights replace the number of observations in equation (7.35), then different forms of weighted hedonic indices can be derived, as explained in Chapter 21. Silver (2002) has also shown that the hedonic approach will differ from a corresponding weighted or unweighted hedonic regression in respect of the leverage and influence that the hedonic regression gives to observations.

Chaining

7.153 An alternative approach to dealing with products with a high turnover of items is to use a chained, say monthly, index instead of the long-term fixed base comparison. A chained index compares prices of items in period t with period $t+1$ ($\text{Index}_{t,t+1}$) and then, as a new exercise, studies the universe of items in period $t+1$ and matches them with items in period $t+2$. These links ($\text{Index}_{t,t+1}$ and $\text{Index}_{t,t+2}$) are combined by successive multiplication, continuing to, say, $\text{Index}_{t+5,t+6}$ to form $\text{Index}_{t+1,t+6}$. Only items available in both period t and period $t+6$ would be used in a fixed base consumer price index. Consider the five items 1, 2, 5, 6 and 8 over the four months January–April, as shown in Table 7.1. The price index for January compared with February (J:F) involves price comparisons for all five items. For February–March (F:M) it involves items 1, 4, 5 and 8 and for March–April (M:A) six items: 1, 3, 4, 5, 7 and 8. The sample composition changes for each comparison as old items disappear and new items come in. Price indices can be calculated for each of these successive price comparisons using any of the unweighted formulae described in Chapter 21. The sample will grow in size when new products appear and shrink when old products disappear, changing in composition through time (Turvey, 1999).

7.154 Sample depletion may be reduced in long-run comparisons by the judicious use of replacement items. As discussed in Chapter 8, however, the replacement sample would only include a new item as and when a replacement was needed, irrespective of the number of new items entering the market. Furthermore, the replacement item is likely to be either of a similar quality, to facilitate quality adjustment, and thus have relatively low sales, or of a different quality with relatively high sales, but requiring an extensive quality adjustment. In either case this is unsatisfactory.

7.155 Chaining, unlike hedonic indices, does not use all the price information in the comparison for each link. Items 2 and 6, for example, may be missing in March. The index makes use of the price information on items 2 and 6 when they exist, for the January–February comparison, but does not allow their absence to disrupt the index for the February–March comparison. It may be that item 4 is a replacement for item 2. Note how easily it is included as soon as two price quotes become available. There is no need to wait for rebasing or sample rotation. It may be that item 7 is a replacement for item 6. A quality adjustment to prices may be required for the February–March comparison between items 6 and 7, but this is a short-run one-off adjustment, the compilation of the index continuing in March–April using item 7 instead of item 6. *SNA 1993* (Chapter 16, para. 54) on price and volume measurement picks up on the point:

> In a time series context, the overlap between the products available in the two periods is almost bound to be greatest for consecutive time periods (except for sub-annual data subject to seasonal fluctuations). The amount of price and quantity information that can be utilized directly for the construction of the price or volume indices is, therefore, likely to be maximized by compiling chain indices linking adjacent time periods. Conversely, the further apart the two time periods are, the smaller the overlap between the ranges of products available in the two periods is likely to be, and the more necessary it becomes to resort to implicit methods of price comparisons based on assumptions. Thus, the difficulties created by the large spread between the direct Laspeyres and Paasche indices for time periods that are far apart are compounded by the practical difficulties created by the poor overlap between the sets of products available in the two periods.

7.156 The chained approach has been justified as the natural discrete approximation to a theoretical Divisia index (Forsyth and Fowler, 1981 and Chapter 16). Reinsdorf (1998) has formally determined the theoretical underpinnings of the index, concluding that in general chained indices will be good approximations to the theoretical ideal – though they are prone to bias when price changes "swerve and loop", as Szulc (1983) has demonstrated (see also Forsyth and Fowler, 1981 and de Haan and Opperdoes, 1997).

7.157 The dummy variable hedonic index uses all the data in January and March for a price comparison between the two months. Yet the chained index ignores unmatched successive pairs, as outlined above; but this is preferable to its fixed base equivalent. The hedonic approach, in predicting from a regression equation, naturally has a confidence interval attached to such predictions. The width of the interval is dictated by the fit of the equation, the distance of the characteristics from their mean and the number of observations. Matching, chained or otherwise, does not suffer from any prediction error. Aizcorbe et al. (2001) undertook an extensive and meticulous study of high-technology goods (personal computers and semiconductors) using quarterly data for the period 1993 to 1999. The results from comparable hedonic and chained indices were remarkably similar over the seven years of the study. For, example, for desktop central processing units (CPUs) the index fell between the seven years from 1993:Q1 to 1999:Q4 by 60.0 per cent (dummy variable hedonic), 59.9 per cent (chained Fisher) and 57.8 per cent (chained geometric mean). The results differed only for quarters when there was a high turnover of items, and in these cases such differences could be substantial. For example, for desktop CPUs in 1996:Q4 the 38.2 per cent annual fall measured by the dummy variable hedonic method differed from the chained geometric mean index by 17 percentage points. Thus with little model turnover there is little discrepancy between hedonic and chained matched models methods and, for that matter, fixed base matched indices. It is only when binary comparisons or links have a high model turnover that differences arise (see also Silver and Heravi, 2001a and 2003).

7.158 Of course it is possible to make up for missing prices by using partial, patched hedonic estimates, as discussed above. Dulberger (1989) computed hedonic indices for computer processors and compared the results to those from a matched models approach. The hedonic dummy variable index fell by about 90 per cent over the period 1972 to 1984, about the same as for the matched models approach where missing prices for new or discontinued items were derived from a hedonic regression. However, when using a chained matched models approach with no estimates or imputations for missing prices, the index fell by 67 per cent. It is also possible to combine methods; de Haan (2003) used matched data when available and the time dummy only for unmatched data – his double imputation method.

Long-run and short-run comparisons

7.159 This section describes a useful formulation to aid quality adjustment. Its innovation arises from a possible concern with the long-run nature of the quality-adjusted price comparisons being undertaken. In the example in Table 7.1, prices in March were compared with those in January. Assumptions of similar price changes are required by the imputation method to hold over this period for long-run imputations – something that gives rise to increasing concern when price comparisons continue over longer periods, between January and October, January and November, January and December, and even subsequently. To help alleviate such concerns, this section considers a short-run formulation, mentioned in paragraph 7.42. Consider Table 7.5, which, for simplicity, has a single item A that exists throughout the period, an item B which is permanently missing in April, and a possible replacement item C in April.

Quality adjustment methods in short-run comparisons

7.160 A *comparable replacement* C may be found. In the previous example the focus was on the use of the Jevons index at the elementary level, since it is shown in Chapter 20 that this has much to commend it. The example here uses the Dutot index, the ratio of arithmetic means. This is not to advocate it, but only to provide an example using a different formulation. The Dutot index also has much to commend it on axiomatic grounds, but fails the commensurability (units of measurement) test and should only be used for relatively homogeneous items. The long-run Dutot index for April compared with January is:

$$P_D \equiv \frac{\sum_{i=1}^{N} p_i^{Apr}/N}{\sum_{i=1}^{N} p_i^{Jan}/N}$$

which is 8/5 = 1.30, a 30 per cent increase.

Table 7.5 Example of long-run and short-run comparisons

Item	January	February	March	April	May	June
Comparable replacement						
A	2	2	2	2	2	2
B	3	3	4			
C				6	7	8
Total	*5*	*5*	*6*	*8*	*9*	*10*
Explicit adjustment						
A	2	2	2	2	2	2
B	3	3	4	**(5/6) × 6=5**	**(5/6) × 7=5.8**	**(5/6) × 8=6.67**
C	**(6/5) × 3=3.60**			6	7	8
Total	*5*	*5*	*6*	*8*	*9*	*10*
Overlap						
A	2	2	2	2	2	2
B	3	3	4	**6 × (4/5)=4.8**		
C			5	6	7	8
Total	*5*	*5*	*6*	*6.8*		
Imputation						
A	2	2	2.5	3.5	4	5
B	3	3	4	**(3.5/2.5) × 4=5.6**	**(4/3.5) × 5.6=6.4**	**(5/4) × 6.4=8**
Total	*5*	*5*	*6.5*	*9.1*	*8.4*	*13*

Figures in bold are estimated quality-adjusted prices described in the text.

The short-run equivalent is the product of a long run index up to the immediately preceding period, and an index for the preceding to the current period, i.e., for period $t+4$ compared with period t:

$$P_D \equiv \left[\frac{\sum_{i=1}^{N} p_i^{t+3}/N}{\sum_{i=1}^{N} p_i^{t}/N}\right] \times \left[\frac{\sum_{i=1}^{N} p_i^{t+4}/N}{\sum_{i=1}^{N} p_i^{t+3}/N}\right]$$

or for January with April:

$$P_D \equiv \left[\frac{\sum_{i=1}^{N} p_i^{Mar}/N}{\sum_{i=1}^{N} p_i^{jan}/N}\right] \times \left[\frac{\sum_{i=1}^{N} p_i^{Apr}/N}{\sum_{i=1}^{N} p_i^{Mar}/N}\right] \qquad (7.36)$$

which is, of course, $\frac{6}{5} \times \frac{8}{6} - 1.30$ as before.

7.161 Consider a *non-comparable replacement with an explicit quality adjustment*. Say, for example, that C's value of 6 in April is quality-adjusted to be considered to be worth only 5 when compared to the quality of B. The quality adjustment to prices may have arisen from an option cost estimate, a quantity adjustment, a subjective estimate or a hedonic coefficient, as outlined above. Say that the long-run comparison uses an adjusted January price for C, which is B's price of 3 multiplied by 6/5 to upgrade it to the quality of C, i.e., $(6/5) \times 3 = 3.6$. From April onwards, the prices of the replacement item C can be readily compared to its January reference period price. Alternatively, the prices of C in April onwards might have been adjusted by multiplying them by 5/6 to downgrade them to the quality of B and enable comparisons to take place with item B's price in January: for April the adjusted price is $(5/6) \times 6 = 5$; for May the adjusted price is 5.8 and for June it is 6.67 (see Table 7.5). Both procedures yield the same results for long-run price comparisons. The results from both methods (rounding errors aside) are the same for item B.

7.162 For the overall Dutot index, however, the results will differ, since the Dutot index weights price changes by their price in the initial period as a proportion of total price (see Chapter 20, footnote 27). The two quality adjustment methods will have the same price changes, but different implicit weights. The Dutot index in May is $9/5.6 = 1.607$ if an adjustment is made to the initial (January) price or $7.8/5 = 1.56$ if an adjustment is made to the current period (May) price. The short-run indices give the same results for each adjustment:

$\frac{8}{5.6} \times \frac{9}{8} = 1.607$ using an adjustment to the initial (January) price, and

$\frac{7}{5} \times \frac{7.8}{7} = 1.56$ using an adjustment to the current period (May) price.

7.163 The *overlap method* may also take the short-run form. In Table 7.5 there is a price for C in March of 5 that overlaps with B in March. The ratio of these prices is an estimate of their quality difference. A long-run comparison between January and April would be $\left(6 \times \frac{4}{5} + 2\right)/5 = 1.36$. The short-run comparison would be based on the product of the January to March and March to April link: $\frac{6.8}{6} \times \frac{6}{5} = 1.36$.

7.164 At this unweighted level of aggregation it can be seen that there is no difference between the long-run and short-run results when items do not go missing, when comparable replacements are available, when explicit adjustments are made for quality or when the overlap method is used. The separation of short-run (most recent month-on-month) and long-run changes may have advantages for quality assurance to help spot unusual short-run price changes. But this is not the concern of this chapter. The short-run approach does, however, have advantages when imputations are made.

Implicit short-run comparisons using imputations

7.165 The use of the short-run framework has been mainly considered for temporarily missing values, as outlined by Armknecht and Maitland-Smith (1999) and Feenstra and Diewert (2001). Similar issues nevertheless arise in the context of quality adjustment. Consider again Table 7.5, but this time there is no replacement item C and item A's prices have been changed to show an upward trend. Item B is again missing in April. A long-run imputation for item B in April is given by $(3.5/2) \times 3 = 5.25$. The price change is thus $(5.25 + 3.5)/5 = 1.75$ or 75 per cent. This is, of course, the same result as that obtained by simply using item A $(3.5/2 = 1.75)$, since the implicit assumption is that price movements of item B, had it continued to exist, would have followed those of A. The assumption of similar long-run price movements may, in some instances, be difficult to support over very long periods. An alternative approach would be to use a short-run framework in which the imputed price for April is based on the (say, overall) mean price change between the preceding and current period, i.e. $(3.5/2.5) \times 4 = 5.6$ in the above example. In this case, the price change between March and April is $(5.6 + 3.5)/(2.5 + 4) = 1.40$. This is combined with the price change between January and March $6.5/5 = 1.30$, to give the January to April change of $1.30 \times 1.40 = 1.82$, an 82 per cent increase.

7.166 Consider why the short-run result of 82 per cent is larger than the long-run result of 75 per cent. The price change for A between March and April of 40 per cent, upon which the short-run imputation is based, is larger than the average *annual* change of A, which is just over 20 per cent. The extent of any bias from this approach was found, above, to depend on the ratio of missing values, and the difference between the average price change of the matched sample and the quality-adjusted price change of the item that went missing, had it continued to exist. The short-run comparison is to be favoured if the assumption of similar price changes is considered more likely to hold than the long-run assumption.

7.167 There are data on price changes of the item that are no longer available, item B in Table 7.5, up to the period preceding the period in which it is missing. In Table 7.5, item B has price data for January, February and March. The long-run imputation makes no use of such data, simply assuming that price changes over the period of January to April, for example, are the same for B as for A. Let the data for B's prices in Table 7.5 (penultimate row) now be 3, 4 and 6 in January, February and March, respectively, instead of 3, 3 and 4. The long-run estimate for B in April is 5.25, as before. The estimated price change between March and April for B is now a fall from 6 to 5.25. A short-run imputation based on the price movements of A between March and April would more correctly show an increase from 6 to $(3.5/2.5) \times 6 = 8.4$.

7.168 There may, however, be a problem with the continued use of short-run imputations. Returning to the data for A and B in Table 7.5, consider what happens in May. Adopting the same short-run procedure, the imputed price change is given in Table 7.5 as $(4/3.5) \times 5.6 = 6.4$ and for June as $(5/4) \times 6.4 = 8$. In the former case, the January to May price change is:

$$\left[\frac{(6.4+4)}{(5.6+3.5)}\right] \times \left[\frac{(5.6+3.5)}{(3+2)}\right] = 2.08$$

and in the latter, for June:

$$\left[\frac{(8+5)}{(6.4+4)}\right] \times \left[\frac{(6.4+4)}{(3+2)}\right] = 2.60$$

compared with long-run comparisons for May and June, respectively, of:

$$\left[\frac{((4/2) \times 3+4)}{(3+2)}\right] = 2.00$$

$$\left[\frac{((5/2) \times 3+5)}{(3+2)}\right] = 2.50$$

7.169 A note of caution is required. The comparisons here use an imputed value for item B in April and also an imputed value for May. The price comparison for the second term in equation (7.36) above, for the current versus immediately preceding period, uses imputed values for item B. Similarly, for the January to June results, the May to June comparison uses imputed values for item B for both May and June. The pragmatic needs of quality adjustment may of course demand this. If comparable replacements, overlap links and resources for explicit quality adjustment are unavailable, an imputation must be considered. However, using imputed values as lagged values in short-run comparisons introduces a level of error into the index which will be compounded with their continued use. Long-run imputations are likely to be preferable to short-run changes based on lagged imputed values, unless there is something in the nature of the industry that cautions against such long-run imputations. There are circumstances in which the price collector may believe the missing item to be temporarily missing, and the imputation is conducted in the expectation that production will subsequently continue; a wait-and-see policy is adopted under some rule, say that the item is missing for a maximum of three months, after which the item is deemed to be permanently missing. Such pragmatic situations require imputations to extend values over consecutive periods and call for the use of lagged imputed values to be compared with current imputed values, despite the fact that this is cautioned against, especially over several months. There is an intuitive feeling that the period over which this is undertaken should not be extensive. First, the effective sample size decreases as the use of imputation increases. Second, the implicit assumptions of similar price movements inherent in imputations are less likely to hold over the longer run. Finally, there is some empirical evidence, albeit from a different context, against the use of imputed values as if they were lagged actual values (see Feenstra and Diewert's study (2001) using data from the United States Bureau of Labor Statistics for their International Price Program).

7.170 The above short-run approach will be developed in the next section, where weighted indices are considered. The practice of estimating quality-adjusted prices is usually carried out at the elementary item level. At this lower level, the prices of items may subsequently be missing, and replacements with or without adjustments and imputations are used to allow the series to continue. New items are also being introduced, as are newer varieties and switching of sales between sections of the index. The turmoil of changing quality is not just about maintaining similar price comparisons, but also about the accurate reweighting of the mix of what is consumed. Under a Laspeyres framework, the bundle is held constant in the base period, so any change in the relative importance of items consumed is held to be of no concern until the next re-basing of the index. Yet procedures for updating the weights are required to capture something of the very real changes in the mix of what is consumed. This is considered in Chapter 9. The concern here is with an equivalent higher-level procedure to the short-run adjustments discussed above. It is one particularly suited to countries where resource constraints prohibit the regular updating of weights through regular household surveys.

Single-stage and two-stage indices

7.171 Consider aggregation at the elementary level. This is the level at which prices are collected from a representative selection of outlets across regions in a period and compared with the matched prices of the same items in a subsequent period to form an index for, say, lamb. Each price comparison is equally weighted unless the sample design gives proportionately more chance of selection to items with more sales. The elementary price index for lamb is then weighted, and combined with the weighted elementary indices for other products to form the consumer price index. A Jevons elementary aggregate index for period $t+6$ compared with period t, for example, is given as:

$$P_J \equiv \prod_{i \in N(t+6) \cap N(t)}^{N} (p_i^{t+6}/p_i^T). \tag{7.37}$$

Compare this with a two-stage procedure:

$$P_J \equiv \prod_{i \in N(t+5) \cap N(t)}^{N} (p_i^{t+5}/p_i^T) \quad \prod_{i \in N(t+6) \cap N(t+5)}^{N} (p_i^{t+6}/p_i^{T+5}) \tag{7.38}$$

7.172 If an item is missing in period $t+6$, an imputation may be undertaken. If equation (7.37) is used, the requisite assumption is that the price change of the missing item, had it continued, is equal to that of the average of the remaining items over the period t to $t+6$. In equation (7.38), the missing item in period $t+6$ may be included in the first stage of the calculation, between periods t and $t+5$, but excluded in the second stage, between periods $t+5$ and $t+6$. The requisite assumption is that price changes between $t+5$ and $t+6$ are equal. Assumptions of short-run price changes are generally considered to be more valid than their long-run counterparts. The two-stage framework also has the advantage of including in the worksheet prices for the current period and the immediately preceding one which, as is shown in Chapter 9, promotes good data validity checks.

7.173 Feenstra and Diewert (2001) applied a number of mainly short-run imputation procedures to price comparisons for the United States Bureau of Labor Statistics International Price Program. Although such price indices are not the direct interest of this manual, the fact that about one-quarter of the individual items tracked did not have price quotations in any given month makes it an interesting area in which to explore the results from different imputation procedures. When using the two-stage procedure, Feenstra and Diewert (2001) advise against carrying forward imputed period prices as if they were actual values, for the subsequent price comparison. The resulting price relatives for the subsequent period based on prior imputations had a standard deviation about twice that of price relatives where no imputation was required, leading the authors to conclude that such a practice introduced a significant amount of error into the calculation. Feenstra and Diewert (2001) found that higher variances of price changes arose from long-run imputation compared with the short-run imputation method. They also found, from both theory and empirical work, that when actual prices become available in a future data set and were used to interpolate back on a linear basis the missing prices, then such estimates lead to much lower variances than the short-run imputation approach. Such linear interpolations, however, require the statistical agency to store past information until a price quote becomes available, interpolate back the missing price, and then publish a revised consumer price index.

Appendix 7.1 Data on personal computers, obtained from United Kingdom Compaq and Dell web sites, July 2000, to illustrate hedonic regression

PRICE (£)	SPEED (MHz)	RAM, MB.	HD, MB.	DELL	PRESARIO	PROSIGNIA	CELERON	PENTIUM III	CD-RW	DVD	DELL*SPEED (MHz)
2123	1000	128	40	0	1	0	0	0	0	0	0
1642	700	128	40	0	1	0	0	0	0	0	0
2473	1000	384	40	0	1	0	0	0	0	0	0
2170	1000	128	60	0	1	0	0	0	0	0	0
2182	1000	128	40	0	1	0	0	0	0	1	0
2232	1000	128	40	0	1	0	0	0	1	0	0
2232	1000	128	40	0	1	0	0	0	0	0	0
1192	700	384	40	0	1	0	0	0	0	0	0
1689	700	384	60	0	1	0	0	0	0	0	0
1701	700	384	40	0	1	0	0	0	0	1	0
1751	700	384	40	0	1	0	0	0	1	0	0
1851	700	384	40	0	1	0	0	0	0	0	0
2319	933	128	15	0	0	0	0	1	0	0	0
2512	933	256	15	0	0	0	0	1	0	0	0
2451	933	128	30	0	0	0	0	1	0	0	0
2270	933	128	10	0	0	0	0	1	0	0	0
2463	933	256	10	0	0	0	0	1	0	0	0
2183	933	64	10	0	0	0	0	1	0	0	0
1039	533	64	8	0	0	1	1	0	0	0	0
1139	533	128	8	0	0	1	1	0	0	0	0
1109	533	64	17	0	0	1	1	0	0	0	0
1180	533	64	8	0	0	1	1	0	1	0	0
1350	533	128	17	0	0	1	1	0	1	0	0
1089	600	64	8	0	0	1	0	1	0	0	0
1189	600	128	8	0	0	1	0	1	0	0	0
1159	600	64	17	0	0	1	0	1	0	0	0
1230	600	64	8	0	0	1	0	1	1	0	0
1259	600	128	17	0	0	1	0	1	0	0	0
1400	600	128	17	0	0	1	0	1	1	0	0
2389	933	256	40	0	1	0	0	1	0	0	0
1833	733	256	40	0	1	0	0	1	0	0	0
2189	933	128	40	0	1	0	0	1	0	0	0
2436	933	256	60	0	1	0	0	1	0	0	0
2397	933	256	40	0	1	0	0	1	0	1	0
2447	933	256	40	0	1	0	0	1	1	0	0
2547	933	256	40	0	1	0	0	1	0	0	0
2845	933	384	60	0	1	0	0	1	0	0	0
2636	933	384	60	0	1	0	0	1	0	0	0
1507	733	64	30	0	1	0	0	1	0	0	0
1279	667	64	10	1	0	0	0	1	0	0	667
1379	667	128	10	1	0	0	0	1	0	0	667
1399	667	64	30	1	0	0	0	1	0	0	667
1499	667	128	30	1	0	0	0	1	0	0	667
1598	667	128	30	1	0	0	0	1	1	0	667

1609	667	128	30	1	0	0	0	1	0	1	667
1389	667	64	10	1	0	0	0	1	0	1	667
999	667	64	10	1	0	0	1	0	0	0	667
1119	566	64	30	1	0	0	1	0	0	0	566
1099	566	128	10	1	0	0	1	0	0	0	566
1097	566	64	10	1	0	0	1	0	1	0	566
1108	566	64	10	1	0	0	1	0	0	1	566
1219	566	128	30	1	0	0	1	0	0	0	566
1318	566	128	30	1	0	0	1	0	1	0	566
1328	566	128	30	1	0	0	1	0	0	1	566
1409	566	128	10	1	0	0	0	1	0	0	733
1809	733	384	10	1	0	0	0	1	0	0	733
1529	733	128	30	1	0	0	0	1	0	0	733
1519	733	128	10	1	0	0	0	1	0	1	733
1929	733	384	30	1	0	0	0	1	0	0	733
2039	733	384	30	1	0	0	0	1	0	1	933
2679	933	128	30	1	0	0	0	1	0	0	933
3079	933	384	10	1	0	0	0	1	0	0	933
2789	933	128	10	1	0	0	0	1	0	1	933
3189	933	384	10	1	0	0	0	1	0	1	933

ITEM SUBSTITUTION, SAMPLE SPACE AND NEW PRODUCTS

8

Introduction

8.1 As new items are introduced and old items no longer sold, the universe of items from which prices are sampled changes. Yet index number methodology may constrain the sampling to subsets of the universe. The samples selected from such subsets are referred to here as the "sample space" of the index. A focus of this chapter is the limitations of such sample spaces. In Chapter 7 the use of the matched models method was recognized as the accepted approach to ensuring that the measurement of price changes was untainted by changes in quality. It was noted, however, that the approach might fail in three respects: missing items, the limited sample space, and new goods and services (in the remainder of this chapter "goods" is taken to include services). In Chapter 7, several implicit and explicit methods of quality adjustment to prices, and the choice between them, are discussed as ways of dealing with missing items. In this chapter, attention is turned to the two other reasons why the matched models method may fail: sampling concerns (the limited sample space) and new products. The three sources of potential error are first briefly outlined below.

8.2 *Missing items.* A problem arises when an item is no longer produced. An implicit quality adjustment may be made using the overlap or imputation method, or the respondent may choose a replacement item of a comparable quality and its price may be directly compared with the missing item's price. If the replacement is of a non-comparable quality, an explicit price adjustment is required. This was the subject of Chapter 7, paragraphs 7.72 to 7.115. In paragraphs 7.125 to 7.158 a caveat was added. It was recognized that for items in industries where model replacements are rapid, continued long-run matching depletes the sample and quality adjustment becomes unfeasible on the scale required. Chained matching or hedonic indices are deemed preferable.

8.3 *Sampling concerns.* The matching of prices of identical items over time, by its very nature, is likely to lead to the monitoring of a sample of items that is increasingly unrepresentative of the population of transactions. Price collectors may keep following those selected items until they are no longer available. Thus, price collectors may continue to monitor old items, with unusual price changes and limited sales. With regard to item replacement, price collectors may select unpopular comparable items in order to avoid explicit quality adjustments. Thus obsolete items with unusual price changes may be replaced by near obsolete items, again with unusual price changes. That the replacement items are near obsolete will mean that their expenditure shares will be relatively small. This will compound the problem of unrepresentative samples. The substitution of an item with relatively high sales for an obsolete one has its own problems, since the difference in quality is likely to be substantial and substantive, beyond that which can be attributed to, say, the price difference in some overlap period. One item might be in the last stage of its life cycle and the other in the first stage of its life cycle. The problem has implications for sample rotation and item substitution.

8.4 *New products.* A third potential difficulty arises when something "new" is produced. There is a difficulty in distinguishing between new items and quality changes in old ones, and this is discussed below. When a quite new good is produced, there is a need for it to be included in the index as soon as possible, especially if the product is expected to be responsible for relatively high sales. New goods might have quite different price changes from those of existing ones, especially at the start of the life cycle. Furthermore, in the initial period of introduction there is often a welfare gain to the consumer. The new good is not a perfect substitute for the old good and this uniqueness gives economic value to the consumer which would have otherwise not been obtained, had the new good not been available (Trajtenberg, 1989). But by definition, there is no price for the new product in the period preceding its introduction. So even if prices of new products are obtained and included in the index from the initial introduction date, there is still something missing – the initial gain in welfare that consumers experience in the period of introduction. The difficulties in capturing such effects are discussed in paragraphs 8.59–8.60 and Appendix 8.2.

8.5 The problem of missing items was the subject of Chapter 7. This chapter considers sampling concerns arising out of the matched models approach and the problem of introducing new products into the index.

Matched samples

8.6 The matching procedure has at its roots a conundrum. Matching is designed to avoid price changes being contaminated by quality changes. Yet its adoption constrains the sampling to a static universe of items that exist in both the reference and base periods. Outside this matched sample, there are of course the items that exist in the reference period but not in the current period, and are therefore not matched, and similarly those new items existing in the current period but not in the reference period – the dynamic universe (Dalén, 1998a; Sellwood, 2001). The conundrum is that the items not in the matched universe – the new items appearing after the reference period and the old items that disappeared from the current period – may experience price changes that differ substantially from the price changes of existing matched items. This is because these products will embody different technologies and be subject to different (quality-adjusted) strategic price changes. The very device used to maintain a sample of constant quality, i.e., matching, may itself give rise to a sample that is biased away from technological developments. Furthermore, when this matched sample is used to impute the price changes of missing items (see Chapter 7, paragraphs 7.53 to 7.68), it will reflect the technology of a sample that is not representative of current technological changes.

8.7 A formal consideration of matching and the dynamic universe is provided in Appendix 8.1 to this chapter. Three universes are considered:

- an *intersection universe*, which includes only matched items;
- a dynamic *double universe*, which includes all items in the base comparison period and all in the current period, although they may be of different qualities;
- a *replacement universe*, which starts with the base period universe, but also includes one-to-one replacements when an item from the sample in the base period is missing in the current period.

8.8 It is, of course, difficult to ascertain the extent to which matching from the intersection universe constrains the penetration of the sample into the dynamic, double universe, since statistical agencies generally do not collect data for the latter. Its extent will in any event vary between products. Sellwood (2001) advocated simulations using the universe of scanner data. Silver and Heravi (2002) undertook such an experiment using scanner data on the consumer prices of washing machines in the United Kingdom in 1998. A matched Laspeyres index, based on price comparisons with matched models existing in both January and December, covered only 48 per cent of December expenditure on washing machines, as a result of new models introduced after January not being included in the matched index. Furthermore, the January to December matched comparison covered slightly more than 80 per cent of January expenditure, resulting from the exclusion of models available in January but not in December. A biannual sample rotation (rebasing) increased the December expenditure coverage to just over 70 per cent, while a monthly (chained) rotation increased that coverage to 98 per cent (see also Chapter 7, paragraphs 7.128 to 7.131 for further examples). Two implications arise from this. First, the selection of item substitutes (replacements) puts the coverage of the sample to some extent under the control of the price collectors. Guidelines on directed replacements in particular product areas have some merit. Second, chaining, hedonic indices (as considered in Chapter 7, paragraphs 7.125 to 7.158) and regular sample rotation have merit in some product areas as devices to refresh the sample. These are considered in turn.

Sample space and item replacement or substitution

8.9 When an item goes missing, one possibility is for the price collector to select a replacement item. The sample space of the index is thus the matched items initially selected and replacement items selected when matched items are missing. Price collectors are often best placed to select replacement items. The price collectors are often physically present in the same store as the missing item and thus any replacement price selected is likely to be unaffected by price differences which may be attributed to differences in the services (ease of location, parking, warranties, service) provided by different stores. It may also be the case that an obvious replacement is provided by a store which wishes to cater to the same market segment, and this will be conspicuous to the price collector. Sometimes the replacement may have a different code or model number which a desk officer may take to indicate a different item, but which the price collector can identify as simply being a difference of, say, a colour or packaging. Price collectors can also identify whether a new (replacement) model of an item has styling and other qualitative factors so different from the old model that in themselves they would account for substantial price differences. In such instances, a desk officer may only focus on the technical specifications and be unaware of these other differences. Against this, desk officers have additional information. This might include information from a similar store in a different location on the price of the missing item, which might be temporarily out of stock.

8.10 The price collector takes on the task of identifying whether an item is of comparable quality or not. If the price collector judges the item to be comparable when in fact it is not, the quality difference will be taken to be a price difference, resulting in bias where the unrecognized quality changes are in a consistent direction. Informed comparable substitution requires general guidelines on what makes a good substitute, as well as product-specific information on characteristics likely to determine price. It also requires timely substitution, to maximize the probability of an appropriate substitute being available.

8.11 Guidelines for selection of comparable items and monitoring of the nature of the selections are good practice. Liegey (1994) notes how useful the results from hedonic regressions are in the selection of items. The results provide an indication of the major quality factors that explain price variation in the product or service. Price collectors can thus be given guidelines as to which characteristics are important – in the sense that they are price determining – in the selection of the sample and replacement items.

8.12 The matter of sample space requires consideration regarding the selection of replacement items/substitutes for missing items. The initial selection of items whose prices are matched may best be made at random, though such items are more often selected as those "typically" purchased. Similarly items "typically" purchased should be included as replacements. Not all price collectors should aim to sample the same "most typical" item. It is desirable to sample a distribution of items which broadly represents the distribution of purchases. For example, a particular brand – one that accounts for, say, 40 per cent of sales revenue – may be known to be the market leader. This common knowledge should not lead all price collectors to select that brand on rebasing. A representative sample is required.

8.13 Replacement items should intrude into the universe of transactions so that the sample is broadly representative of the dynamic universe. The inclusion of a popular replacement item to refresh the sample – one at the same point in its life cycle as the original popular one selected in the base period – allows for a useful and accurate price comparison, assuming that an appropriate quality adjustment is made. Substitute or replacement items should, where possible, not merely be comparable in quality, but should also be likely to account for a relatively substantial amount of sales value. It is of little merit to substitute a new item with limited sales for a missing item, again with limited sales, just because they have similar features, both being "old"; the index would become more unrepresentative. The replacement of an item only when the item is no longer available may be ineffectual with regard to the representativity of the index. In that case, items with relatively low sales would continue to be monitored until they died. And even replacement might not remedy the situation. If the replacement guidelines indicate that the price collector should select a similar item sold in the outlet, then the replacement selected will be almost as obsolete (Lane, 2001, p. 21).

8.14 Guidelines to select "similar" items are given to ease quality adjustment between the old and new items; at best the items are "comparable" and require no quality adjustment. The institutional mechanism devised to help in making quality adjustments to prices can lead to bias because of its adherence to a sample of items which do not enjoy the benefits of recent technological innovations and are unrepresentative of what is produced. Bear in mind that an index number methodology based on an initially selected matched sample and a sample of substitute replacement items, when items go missing, may not be representative of the universe of all items being consumed. In particular, if the index number methodology is biased to the selection of replacement items with relatively low sales, so that they are comparable with obsolete items, then the sampling from new items and the sample space of the index are biased. Quality adjustment and representativity are interrelated, since the former affects the sample space of the index.

8.15 The importance of, and care required in, the use of replacements to militate against sample depletion is worth reiterating. Consider the case where there is only one model of a product available in the market at the start of the price comparison in period t. A price collector includes it in the sample in period t and then monitors its price in subsequent periods. A new (replacement) model enters the market in, say, period $t+2$, but it is ignored since the original model continues to exist for several months. However, in, say, period $t+9$ the old item is no longer on the market and is replaced, with a quality adjustment, by the new item. The long-run price comparison between the new model's price in period $t+9$ and the old model's price in period t has no sampling bias. Both account for 100 per cent of the market in their respective periods, being the only items available. Both are near the start of their life cycles, so the price comparison is a fair one. If the new and old items have different price changes, sampling bias will occur between periods $t+2$ and $t+8$, when only one of the two items is being sampled, but sampling will be unbiased once the model is replaced in period $t+9$.

8.16 There is thus a case for managing the replacement strategy to minimize sample depletion. In that respect, the following points should be borne in mind:

- Replacements offer an opportunity to cut back on, and possibly remove, sample bias in the period of replacement, though not prior to it.
- The more frequent is the replacement, the less the sample bias.
- If there is more than one new (replacement) item in the market, there may still be bias as only the most popular one will be selected and it may well be at a different stage in its life cycle and thus be experiencing different price changes in comparison with other new (replacement) models.
- The analysis assumes that perfect quality adjustments are made on replacement. The less frequent the replacement, the more difficult this might be to achieve, as the very latest replacement item on the market may have more substantial differences in quality than earlier ones.
- If the best-selling replacement item is of comparable quality and at the same stage in its life cycle as the missing item, then its selection will minimize sample bias.
- If there is more than one replacement item and the most comparable one – having the old technology – is selected, it will have low market share and unusual price changes.
- Given advance information on market conditions, replacements that are included in the sample well before the old item becomes obsolescent are likely to increase the sample's share of the market, include items that are more representative of the market, and facilitate quality adjustment.

8.17 The problem of item substitution is analogous to the problems that arise when an outlet closes. It may be possible to find a comparable outlet not already in the sample, or a non-comparable one for which, in principle, an adjustment can be made for the better quality of service provided. It is not unusual for an outlet to close following the introduction of a new, more competitive outlet. Where the matching of prices between these outlets broadly follows the consumption patterns of the clients of the original outlet, there is an obvious replacement outlet. If, however, the new outlet has comparable prices but, say, a better range of items, parking and service, there is a gain to consumers from substituting one outlet for the other. Yet since such facilities have no direct price, it is difficult to provide estimates of their value in order to make an adjustment for the better quality of service of the new outlet. The index would thus have an upward bias, which would be lost on rebasing. In such cases, replacing the old outlet by a new one that provides a similar standard of service may be preferable to replacing it by one that has a different standard but serves the same catchment area. In their regression analyses for consumer durables, Liegey (2000), Shepler (2000) and Silver and Heravi (2001b) found "outlet type" to be a substantial and statistically significant explanatory variable for price variation, while for a particular outlet type – grocery outlets, for food and petrol prices in the United States – Reinsdorf (1993) found much smaller differences.

Sample rotation, chaining and hedonic indices

8.18 It is important to recognize the interrelationships among the methods for handling item rotation, item replacement and quality adjustment. When consumer price index (CPI) item samples are rotated, this is a form of item substitution, except that it is not "forced" by a missing item, but is undertaken for a general group of items to update the sample of items. It has the effect of making future forced replacements less likely. Yet the assumption implicit in its use is equivalent to that for the overlap adjustment technique: that price differences are an adequate proxy for the change in price per unit of quality between items disappearing from the sample and replacement items.

8.19 Consider the initiation of a new sample of items. This may be by probability or judgemental methods, or a combination of the two. Prices for the old and new samples are returned in the same month, and the new index is compiled on the basis of the new sample, the results being linked to the old. This is an implicit use of the overlap method, in which all price differences between the new and old items in that month are taken to be quality changes. Assume that the new sample is initiated, say, in January. Assume also that the prices of an old item in December and January are $10 and $11 respectively, a 10 per cent increase, while those for the new replacement item in January and February are $16 and $18 respectively, an increase of 12.5 per cent. The new item in January is of a better quality than the old, and this difference in quality may be worth $16−11=5 to the consumer. That is, the price difference is assumed to be equal to the quality difference, which is the assumption implicit in the overlap method. Had the price of the old item in December been compared with the quality-adjusted price of the new item in January under this assumption, the price change would in this case be the same, 10 per cent (i.e. (16−5)/10=1.10). In practice, the need to simultaneously replace and update a large number of items requires the assumptions of the overlap method, the point being that this process should not be regarded as error free. In cases where the assumptions are considered likely to be particularly untenable (discussed in Chapter 7, paragraphs 7.44 to 7.52), explicit adjustments of the form discussed in paragraphs 7.72 to 7.115 should be used.

8.20 It was noted above that when samples are updated, any difference in the average quality of items between the samples is dealt with in a way that is equivalent to the overlap adjustment technique. Sample rotation to refresh the sample between rebasing is an expensive exercise. If rebasing is infrequent, however, and if there is a substantial loss of items in particular product areas, then sample rotation might be appropriate for those areas. A *metadata* system (described below) will aid such decision-making. More frequent sample rotation aids the process of quality adjustment in two ways. First, the new sample will include newer varieties. Comparable replacements with substantial sales will be more likely to be available and non-comparable ones will be of a similar quality, which facilitates good explicit adjustments. Second, because the sample has been rotated, there will be fewer missing items than otherwise and thus less need for quality adjustments.

8.21 A natural extension of more frequent sample rotation is to use a chained formulation in which the sample is reselected each period. In Chapter 7, paragraphs 7.153 to 7.158, the principles and methods were outlined in the context of sectors in which there was a rapid turnover of items. These principles are echoed here. Similarly, the use of hedonic indices (as outlined in paragraphs 7.132 to 7.152) or the use of short-run comparisons (discussed in paragraphs 7.159 to 7.173) might be useful in this context.

Information requirements for a quality adjustment strategy

8.22 It should be apparent from the above that a strategy for quality adjustment must not only be linked to one relating to sample representativity, but must also require the building of a statistical metadata system. This is not an area where the approach for the index as a whole can be simply described, but one that requires the continual development of market information and the recording and evaluation of methods on a product-by-product basis.

Statistical metadata system

8.23 The methods used for estimating quality-adjusted prices should be well documented as part of a statistical metadata system. Metadata are systematic descriptive information about data content and organization that help those who operate the systems that produce statistics to remember what tasks they should perform and how they should perform them. A related purpose is to train new staff and introduce them to the production routines (Sundgren, 1993). Metadata systems also help to identify where current methods of quality adjustment require reconsideration, and prompt the use of alternative methods. They may also serve user needs, the oldest and most extensive form being footnotes.

8.24 The dramatic increase in volume of statistical data in machine-readable form, with a concomitant increase in metadata, argues for keeping the metadata in such a form. This is to enhance transparency in the methods used and help ensure that the methods are understood and continued, as staff leave the CPI team and new staff join it. Changes in quality adjustment methodology can in themselves lead to changes in the index. Indices produced using new procedures should be spliced onto existing indices. The metadata system should also be used as a tool to help with quality adjustment. Because so much of the rationale for the employment of different methods is specific to the features of the products concerned, data should be held on such features.

8.25 Statistical agencies should monitor the incidence of missing items against each Classification of Individual Consumption according to Purpose (COICOP) group. If that incidence is high, then the monitoring should be carried out by class within each group. Again, if that incidence is high, the monitoring should be done by elementary aggregate or selected representative items within each group, or at the most detailed level of the system. Where the incidence is high, the ratios of temporary missing prices, comparable replacements and non-comparable replacements to the overall number of prices, and the methods for dealing with each of these three circumstances, should also be monitored to provide the basis of a statistical metadata system. The advantage of a top-down approach is that resources are saved by monitoring only at the detailed level product areas which are problematic.

8.26 Product-specific information, such as the timing of the introduction of new models, pricing policies (especially with regard to months in which no changes were made) and the popularity of models and brands according to different data sources, should be included in the metadata as the system develops. An estimate, if available, of the weight of the product concerned should be given, so that a disproportionate effort is not given to relatively low-weighted items. All this will lead to increased transparency in the procedures used and allow effort to be directed where it is most needed.

8.27 For items for which replacement levels are high, the metadata system would benefit from contacts between statistical agencies and market research organizations, retailers, manufacturers and trade associations. Such links will allow staff to better judge the validity of the assumptions underlying implicit quality adjustments. Where possible, staff should be encouraged to be responsible for learning more about specific industries whose weights are relatively high and where item replacement is common.

8.28 Statistical staff should identify price-determining characteristics for product areas using hedonic regressions, information from market research, store managers, trade associations and other such bodies, and the experience of price collectors. This information should contribute to the statistical metadata system and be particularly useful in providing subsequent guidelines on item selection.

8.29 When hedonic regressions are used either for partial patching of missing prices or as indices in their own right, information on the specification, estimated parameters and diagnostic tests of the regression equations should be kept, along with the data and with notes as to why the final formulation was chosen and used. This will allow the methodology for subsequent updated equations to be benchmarked and tested against the previous versions.

8.30 The metadata system should help statistical staff to:

- identify product areas likely to be undergoing regular technological change;
- ascertain the pace at which models change and, possibly, the timing of changes;
- undertake an analysis of what have in the past been judged to be "comparable" replacements in terms of the factors that distinguish the replacement and old items;
- identify whether different price collectors are making similar judgements regarding comparable replacements, and whether such judgements are reasonable.

8.31 Price statisticians may have more faith in the use of some quality adjustment procedures than others. When such procedures are used extensively it might be useful to note, as part of the metadata system, the degree of faith the statistician has in the procedures. Following Shapiro and Wilcox (1997b), this may be envisaged as a traditional confidence interval: the statistician may believe at, say, a 90 per cent level of confidence that the quality-adjusted price change is 2 per cent (0.02) with an interval of plus or minus 0.5 per cent (0.005). There may be an indication as to whether the interval is symmetric, or positively or negatively one-sided. Alternatively, statisticians may use a simple subjective coding on a scale of, say, 1 to 5.

New products and how they differ from products with quality changes

8.32 The question arises of how to define new products (goods and services) and to distinguish them from existing products whose quality has changed. A new model of a good may provide more of a currently available set of service flows. For example, a new car model may differ from existing ones in that it may have a bigger engine. There is a continuation of a service and production flow, and this may be linked to the service flow and production technology of the existing models. A practical definition of a new good, as against quality changes in an updated existing model, is that, first, the new good cannot easily be linked to an existing item as a continuation of an existing resource base and service flow, because of the very nature of its "newness". For example, frozen foods, microwave ovens and mobile phones, while extensions of existing flows of services to the consumer, have a dimension of service that is quite new. Second, as discussed below, new goods can generate a welfare gain to consumers by their very introduction. The simple introduction of the new good into the index, once two successive price quotes are available, misses this gain.

8.33 Oi (1997) directs the problem of defining "new" goods to that of defining a monopoly. If there is no close substitute, the good is new. He argues that individual new books, new videos and new television serials may have quite small cross-price elasticities in some cases; their shared service is to provide entertainment and they are similar in this respect. Hausman (1997), however, found cross-elasticities for substitution to be quite substantial for new television serials (though see Bresnahan (1977)). There are many new forms of existing products, such as fashionable toys and clothes, which are not easily substitutable for similar items and for which consumers would be willing to pay a premium.

8.34 Bresnahan (1997, p. 237) notes that *Brandweek* counted over 22,000 new-product introductions for the United States for 1994 – the purpose of their introduction being, as differentiated products, not to be exact substitutes for existing ones, but to be distinct. Their distinctiveness is in many cases the rationale behind their launch. The extent of differentiated markets nevertheless makes the definition and treatment of such things as "new" impractical. Oi (1997, p. 110) sets out the pragmatic case: "Our theory and statistics would be unduly cluttered if separate product codes had to be set aside for Clear Coke and Special K." Furthermore, the techniques for including such products are not, as indicated below, readily applicable. The sound practical advice given by Oi (1997) to keep matters "uncluttered" is therefore not unreasonable.

8.35 The terminology adopted here is that used by Merkel (2000) for producer price index (PPI) measurement, but considered in a CPI context. It distinguishes between *evolutionary* goods and *revolutionary* goods. Evolutionary goods are replacement or supplementary models that continue to provide a similar service flow, but maybe in new ways or to different degrees. These are distinguished from revolutionary goods, which are entirely new goods not closely tied to a previously available product. Although revolutionary goods may satisfy a long-standing consumer need in a novel way, they do not fit into any established CPI item category (Armknecht et al., 1997). Problems are associated with incorporating distinctly new revolutionary goods. This is because a good, which by its nature is unique, is unlikely to be incorporated into the sample as a replacement for an existing item. It would neither be comparable nor be amenable to explicit adjustments to its price for quality differences with existing goods. Since a distinctly new item is not replacing an item, it does not have an existing weight; its introduction therefore implies a need to re-weight the index.

Incorporation of new products

8.36 There are three major concerns regarding the incorporation of new goods into the CPI. The first concern is the detection and identification of the new good; these are facilitated by close links with market research, and producer and trade associations. The second concern, which is related to the first, is the decision on the need and timing for their inclusion. This refers to both the weight and price changes of the new good. The third concern relates to the incorporation of the initial welfare to the consumer arising from the switch from the old technology.

8.37 Consider some examples on the timing of the introduction of new goods. The sales of mobile phones were at such a significant level in some countries that their early inclusion in the CPI became a matter of priority. They simply rose from nothing to relatively quickly account for quite a large proportion of sales in their product classification. Furthermore, their price changes were atypical of other goods in their product classification. Being new, they might be produced using inputs and technologies quite different from those used for existing telephones. Because of substantial marketing campaigns, many new goods command substantial sales and are the subject of distinct pricing strategies at launch. For radical innovations, however, there may be a delay in their incorporation into the index since they cannot be defined within existing classification systems.

8.38 Armknecht et al. (1997) cite the example of the incorporation of video cassette recorders (VCRs) into the United States CPI. VCRs were launched in 1978 with a sales value of US$299 million and estimated average retail price of US$1,240. Because the CPI was rebased every ten years, VCRs were introduced into the CPI only in 1987 when their sales value was US$3,442 million and average price had fallen to US$486. All the extraordinary price movements between 1978 and 1987 were thus missed by the index.

8.39 Dulberger (1993) provides some estimates for United States PPIs for dynamic random access memory (DRAM) computer memory chips. She calculated price indices for the period 1982 to 1988 with varying amounts of delay in introducing new chips into the index. The indices were chained so that new chips could be introduced, or not, as soon as they had been available for two successive years. Using a Laspeyres chained index, there was a fall of 27 per cent if there was no delay in introducing the new goods, as compared with falls of 26.2 per cent, 24.7 per cent, 19.9 per cent, 7.1 per cent and 1.8 per cent if the introductions were delayed by, respectively, 1, 2, 3, 4 or 5 years. In all cases the index was biased downwards because of the delay. Berndt et al. (1997) provide a detailed study of a new anti-ulcer drug, Tagamet. They found that the effects of pre-introduction marketing of the drug on its price and market share at introduction were substantial. Not unexpectedly, there were price falls for the generic form of a pharmaceutical on the expiry of the patent, but there were increases for the branded form; loyal customers were found to be willing to pay a premium over the price prior to the patent expiry (Berndt et al., 2003).

8.40 Waiting for a new good to be established or waiting for the rebasing of an index before incorporating new products may lead to errors in the measurement of price changes if the unusual price movements at critical stages in the product life cycles arc ignored. Strategies are required for the early identification of new products, and mechanisms are needed for their incorporation either at launch (if preceded by major marketing strategies) or soon after (if there is evidence of market acceptance).

These strategies and mechanisms should form part of the metadata system. Waiting for new products to achieve market maturity may result in an implicit policy of ignoring the quite disparate price movements that accompany their introduction (Tellis, 1988, and Parker, 1992). This is not to say that new goods will always have different price changes. Merkel (2000) gives the example of "light" varieties of foods and beverages, which are similar to the original varieties but with fewer calories. The prices of "light" products are very close to the prices of the original products. The introduction of "light" varieties simply serves to expand the market. While there is a need to capture such expansion when the weights are revised, the price changes for the existing items can be used to capture those of the "light" items.

8.41 The second measurement concern with respect to new products is the incorporation of the effect of those products at launch. The preceding discussion is concerned with the incorporation of price changes into the index once two successive quotations are available. Yet there is a gain to the consumer when comparing the price in the first of these periods with the price in the period that preceded the introduction of the product. This latter price is a hypothetical price. It is the price which would make the demand from the community for the product equal to zero; that is, it is the reservation price which, when inserted into the demand function, sets demand to zero. If a demand system can be estimated, so too can the reservation price. The virtual reservation price is compared with the actual price in the period of introduction, and this is used to estimate the surplus from the introduction of the good. If the reservation price is relatively high, then the introduction of the new good is clearly of some benefit to the consumer. To ignore this benefit, and the change from the shadow price to the actual price in its period of launch, is to ignore something of the price movements that give rise to improvements in the standard of living. Of course, if a "new" good is a close substitute – at the price it is brought into the index – for goods already in existence, then no additional consumer surplus is generated.

8.42 It should be noted that a consumer may be in a geographical area in which a new good or service, say, cable television, a video rental outlet or health facility, is not present. The benefits of the new good on its introduction to different geographical areas will therefore develop over time as the new good becomes more generally available. The benefits will emerge again and again for each sector of the population that benefits from access to the new product. In practice, such items gain increasing weight as the index is rebased or the sample rotated.

8.43 The methods outlined below for the inclusion of substitute and new goods include both normal CPI procedures and exceptional treatments. In regard to the former, consideration is given in paragraphs 8.44 to 8.58 to the rebasing of the index, rotating of items, introduction of new goods as replacements for discontinued ones on rotating, and a strategy for dealing with new item bias. In regard to the latter, techniques that require different sets of data are outlined. The use of chained matched models and hedonic indices was discussed in Chapter 7 in the context of products experiencing rapid turnover in models. Analytic frameworks that consider new goods bias by way of reservation prices and substitution effects are considered in paragraphs 8.59 and 8.60 and Appendix 8.2. The data requirements and econometric expertise are much more demanding for these approaches.

Sample rebasing and rotation

8.44 A new good may be readily incorporated in the index at the time of rebasing the index, or when the whole or the pertinent part of the sample is rotated. If the new good has, or is likely to have, substantial sales, and is not a replacement for a pre-existing one, or is likely to command a much higher or lower market share than the pre-existing one it is replacing, then new weights are necessary to reflect this. New weights are only fully available on rebasing, not on sample rotation. There will thus be a delay in the new item's inclusion in the index. The extent of the delay will depend on how close the introduction of the item is to the next rebasing and, more generally, the frequency with which the index is rebased. This discussion of rebasing is effectively concerned with the use of new weights for the index. Even if the index is rebased annually and chained, there will be a delay until the annual rebasing before weights can be assigned, and there may even be a further six-month delay for the sampling and collating of the survey results for the weights. Such frequent rebasing allows for the early introduction of a new good and is to be advised when the weights are not keeping pace with product innovations.

8.45 At the elementary level of aggregation, an implicit weight equal to the expenditure share is given by the Jevons index, for example, to each price relative. The Dutot index gives each price change the weight of its price relative to the sum of the prices in the initial base period of the comparison (see Chapter 7). If a product area is expected to be subject to dynamic innovations, then the sample may be increased on rotation, without any changes to the weight for the group. There would simply be more items selected to form the arithmetic or geometric average price change. As new varieties become available, they could be substituted for some of the existing ones, there being a wider range from which to draw a comparable item, or less effort involved in the quality adjustment procedure for a non-comparable one.

8.46 Some statistical agencies rotate (resample) items within product groups. Opportunities exist to introduce new items within a weighted group under such circumstances. The resource practicalities of such schemes require items to be rotated on a staggered basis for different product groups. Product groups experiencing rapid change should be rotated more frequently. The incorporation of new goods using sample rotation allows some of the existing weight of the product group to be re-allocated to the new good. Yet it implicitly uses the overlap method for the introduction of the new good of a different quality. The difference in prices in the overlap period of the new and obsolete items is assumed to be equal to their quality difference. The assumptions implicit in such procedures have been outlined above and their likely veracity needs to be considered. Since evolutionary items are defined as continuations of the service flow of existing (and possibly exiting) ones, the hedonic framework may be more suitable in some cases to the use of the overlap method. These and other methods and the choice between methods are discussed in Chapter 7.

8.47 In many countries, rebasing is infrequent and sample rotation is not undertaken, despite their advantages. The rotating of samples on a frequent basis should not, however, be considered a panacea. Sample rotation is an arduous task, especially when performed over a range of product groups experiencing rapid change. Even frequent rotation, say, every four years, may miss many new goods. Yet it is not necessary for statistical agencies to wait until an item is obsolete before a new one is introduced. It is quite feasible for statistical agencies to pre-empt the obsolescence of an old item and decide on its early substitution by a new one. In some product areas, the arrival of a new good is well advertised in advance of the launch. In other areas, it is feasible for a statistical agency to have general procedures for substitutions, as outlined below. Without such a strategy, and where rotation or rebasing is infrequent, a country would be open to serious new product bias.

8.48 In summary:

- The treatment of a new good as a replacement for an existing one can be undertaken if the old item's weight suitably reflects the new good's sales and if a suitable quality adjustment can be made to its price to link it to the existing, old, price series.
- If the new good does not fit into the pre-existing weighting structure, it can be included on rebasing, though this may be infrequent in some countries.
- Regular sample rotation provides a means by which the inclusion of such items can be formally reconsidered, though since this is undertaken on a staggered basis, only the weights within the product group are reallocated, not those between the groups.
- Directed sample substitution, as opposed to waiting for sample rotation, may be used to pre-empt the arrival of new goods.
- Revolutionary items will not fit into existing weighting structures and alternative means are required.
- The modified short-run or chained framework outlined in Chapter 7, paragraphs 7.153 to 7.173, may be more appropriate for product areas with high turnover of items.

Directed replacements for evolutionary items and directed augmentation of the sample for revolutionary goods are considered below.

Directed replacements and sample augmentation

8.49 For evolutionary goods in product areas where there is a rapid replacement and introduction of such goods, a policy of directed replacements might be adopted. Judgement, experience, discussions with store managers, market research companies and a statistical metadata system should help identify such products. The selection of replacements is directed to evolutionary items in order to ensure that the index maintains its representativity. If the new version of a product is designed as a replacement for an existing one, then substitution might be automatic. Once a substitute has been made, the prices require an adjustment for the quality difference using, perhaps, the overlap method, imputation, or an explicit estimate based on production or option costs, or a hedonic regression as discussed in Chapter 7.

8.50 The management of the directed substitution can take a number of forms. It can comprise instructions to price collectors who are informed of defined configurations of a product, such as "high end", "mainstream", "economy", "entry level" and "other" (Lane, 2001). Directions might also be given as to the proportions expected of items at these levels, say, 20 per cent of the market should be "high end". Such information should be based on actual data or judgement of specialists. The configurations are revised, say, every six months. What was "high end" at the start of the period may now be "entry level" and the price collectors will have new configurations indicating what the desired replacements should look like. They are directed to particular replacements. Alternatively, the price collector might be responsible for the selection of replacements, either after discussion with store managers or, if an indication of the market share of the popular makes is given, with probability proportionate to size. There are, of course, other variants. In such markets, the desired end effect is that replacement items likely to be representative of substantial sales are selected and that this selection is made earlier rather than later. The point is not to miss the birth of such items and to facilitate quality adjustment.

8.51 It is important to emphasize that, on the introduction of new versions of these evolutionary goods, a particularly high price may be charged to take advantage of segments of the market willing to pay a premium for the "newness" of the item. Alternatively, a particularly low price may be charged to introduce the good to the market in order to help gain acceptance. After a while, prices may be changed as the novelty of the item wears off or as it gains acceptance, or as competitors bring out improved products. Directed substitution is important in ensuring that the CPI captures the unusual price increases at the launch. It is also necessary in ensuring that the coverage of items becomes more representative. Although directed substitution allows for both, a caveat applies. If the overlap method is used, the item is introduced on the assumption that the price difference between the old and new items equates to their quality difference. For example, if a new type of detergent is introduced with a new, biological cleaning action, it may be that the typical consumer is willing to pay a price of 10 against the existing standard detergent's price of 8. With no explicit estimate of the additional usefulness or utility to be gained from the biological action, the overlap method implicitly assumes it is worth 2. Yet there may be an introductory launch price of 8 and the price may later increase to 10. At the time of the overlap, the two prices would be the same, there being no adjudged quality difference. In fact, the quality-adjusted price would be falling; there is a quality difference of 2, but this cannot be deduced by the statistical office. In general, therefore, when there is evidence of items being launched at unusual prices and the overlap method is used, it is better to make the replacement later when the market has settled.

8.52 For revolutionary goods, substitution may not be appropriate. First, they may not be able to be defined within the existing classification systems. Second, a major part of their uniqueness may be the manner in which they are sold, which will require extending the sample to such new sales channels. Third, there will be no previous items to match such goods against in order to make a quality adjustment to prices since, by definition, they are substantially different from pre-existing goods. Finally, there is no weight to attach to the new outlets or items.

8.53 The first need is to identify new goods. The suggested contacts with market research companies, outlet managers and manufacturers, mentioned above in relation to producing a supportive metadata system, are also pertinent here. Once the new goods are identified, sample augmentation is appropriate for the introduction of revolutionary goods. It is necessary to bring the new revolutionary goods into the sample, in addition to what already exists in the sample. This may involve extending the classification, the sample of outlets, and the item list within new or existing outlets. The choice of means by which the new goods are introduced is more problematic.

8.54 Once two price quotes are available, it should be possible to splice the new good onto an existing or obsolete one. This of course misses the impact of the new item in its initial period. As discussed below, however, including such effects is not a trivial exercise. Consider the linking of a good that is likely to be replaced in the market by the new good. For example, a relatively new electrical kitchen appliance might follow the price index for existing kitchen appliances up to the period of the link, and then the price changes for the new good in subsequent periods. This would create a separate and additional price series for a new good that augments the sample, as illustrated in Table 8.1. Item C is new in period 2 and has no base period weight. Its price change between periods 1 and 2, had it existed, is assumed to follow the overall index for products A and B. For period 3 onwards, a new linked price series is formed for C, which for period 3 is $101.40 \times 0.985 = 99.88$ and for period 4 is $101.40 \times 0.98 = 99.37$. New revised weights in period 2 show C's weight to be 20 per cent of all the items. The new index for period 3 is:

$$101.40 \times [0.8 \times (101.9/101.4) + 0.2 \times (99.88/101.4)]$$
$$= 0.8 \times 101.9 + 0.2 \times 99.88 = 101.50$$

and for period 4:

$$101.40 \times [0.8 \times (102.7/101.4) + 0.2 \times (99.37/101.4)]$$
$$= 0.8 \times 102.7 + 0.2 \times 99.37 = 102.05$$

8.55 If C were an evolutionary good replacing B, then there would be no need to introduce new weights and no need to augment the sample. The revolutionary good C has no weight in the base period; the splicing thus

Table 8.1 Example of sample augmentation

Products	Base weight	Revised weight	Period 1	Period 2	Period 3	Period 4
A	0.6	0.5	100.00	101.00	101.50	102.50
B	0.4	0.3	100.00	102.00	102.50	103.00
All items		*0.8*	*100.00*	*101.40*	*101.90*	*102.70*
C				100.00	98.50	98.00
Spliced C		0.2	100.00	101.40	99.88	99.37
All items (revised)			*100.00*	*101.40*	*101.50*	*102.05*

requires a revision of the weights at the same time. Both the selection of the series onto which the new item is spliced, and the product groups selected for the weight revision, require some judgement. Items whose market share is likely to be affected by the introduction of the new good should be selected. If the new good is likely to be responsible for a significant share of expenditure, such that it will affect the weights of a broad class of product groups, then there may be a case for a realignment of the overall weighting procedure. Such seismic shifts can of course occur, especially in the communications industries, and for a wider range of markets when trade barriers are relaxed in less-developed economies or when regulations are removed. The change in weights may also be required for disappearing goods no longer sold in an economy. In that case, the weights of these goods need to be reassigned. As noted in Chapter 7, paragraphs 7.132 to 7.158, chaining and hedonic indices may well be appropriate when there is a rapid turnover in such new and obsolete goods. Chaining is an extension of the above procedure and can be used to introduce a new good as soon as it is available for two successive periods.

8.56 Item augmentation may also be used for evolutionary goods that are likely to be responsible for a substantial share of the market, while not displacing the existing goods. Say, for example, that a country has a local brewery and that a licensing agreement with a foreign brewery has led to the joint production of two beers, under different brand names. Say the market share for beer from the brewery remains the same, but one segment of the market now drinks foreign as opposed to domestic beer. Price collectors may be directed to a forced substitution of some of the sample of domestic beers for foreign ones, the weight remaining the same. This would be similar to a quality adjustment using a non-comparable replacement, as discussed in Chapter 7, paragraphs 7.72 to 7.115. Alternatively, the sample may be augmented since there is concern that a smaller sample of domestic beers may now not be sufficiently representative. The augmentation process may be similar to that outlined in Table 8.1, with the new foreign beer C accounting for 20 per cent of the market. If the advent of foreign beers displaced some of the alcoholic spirits market, say, then the revision of weights would extend into that product group. As noted in Chapter 7, paragraphs 7.125 to 7.158, chaining and hedonic indices may well be appropriate when there is a rapid turnover in such new and obsolete goods. With chaining, the good needs to be available for only two successive periods to allow for its introduction.

8.57 In some instances a directed replacement is required for evolutionary and revolutionary outlets. Forced augmentation of the sample of outlets may be implemented so that new goods available only in specific outlets are included. This is especially likely in the service sector, where a new service is particular to specific outlets, for example cyber cafés or online retailers. The procedures are similar to those described for items. For example, in the above example, instead of products A, B and C, consider C as a new outlet in addition to outlets A and B. Some estimate would be required of its expected sales share to form the revised weights.

8.58 The effect of a new outlet on the index depends on how it is included, as well as the nature of the market and its reaction to the new outlet. First, if a new outlet offers some innovation which induces some consumers to shop there, there is an increase in usefulness or utility. Because of imperfect knowledge about the new outlet or different preferences of different segments of the market, the old outlet may not close down. There is no natural prompt for the new outlet to be introduced into the CPI, as there is with the closure of an old outlet. The start-up of the new outlet may have been apparent to the statistical office. If the new outlet is expected to have substantial sales, it may augment the sample. It may be spliced onto the index in the manner of item C above. Such a methodology would not include the welfare gain to consumers arising from the uniqueness of the outlet (Trajtenberg, 1989), since price comparisons are only being undertaken once it has been introduced. The initial welfare effect is between the period prior to its existence and the period of its introduction. Second, all other outlets might lower their quality-adjusted prices to match those from the new outlet. The fall in price and gain in usefulness or utility arising from the new outlet's technology would then be captured by the CPI. Finally, outlets may appear that offer a wider range of options in terms of goods and service, which is valued by consumers and is therefore an improvement in the standard of living via the gain in utility. There is nothing in current CPI methodology that allows for the valuation of such gains (Shapiro and Wilcox, 1997a).

Reservation prices

8.59 Shapiro and Wilcox (1997a, p. 144) expressed concerns over:

> ...the rare new item that delivers services radically different from anything previously available. For example, even the earliest generation of personal computers allowed consumers to undertake tasks that previously would have been prohibitively expensive. This problem can be solved only by estimating the consumer surplus created by the introduction of each new item. Hausman (1994) [republished as Hausman (1997)] argues that this must involve explicit modeling of the demand for each new item. Although explicit modeling of demand may be of dubious practicality for widespread implementation in the CPI, strategic application in a few selected cases might be worthwhile.

8.60 The technical means for such estimates is recognized as being beyond the practical capabilities of a statistical agency. More disturbing is that the argument for the inclusion of such effects extends from revolutionary new goods to the clutter of evolutionary items such as new breakfast cereals. Appendix 8.2 provides some details of a generalized Laspeyres approach which takes account of substitution between new and old models. Given the complexity of the estimation systems involved, however, this manual envisages a pragmatic approach which would initially exclude such effects.

Summary

8.61 The need to consider the sample space of the items selected by the index number methodology and new goods arises out of a very real concern with the dynamic nature of modern markets. New goods and quality changes are far from being a new phenomenon. As Triplett (1999) has argued, it has not been demonstrated that the rate of new product development and introduction is much higher now than in the past. It is certainly accepted, however, that the number of new products and varieties is substantially greater than before. Computer technology provides cost-effective means for collecting and analysing very large sets of data. Chapter 6 considers the use of hand-held computers for data capture, and the availability of bar-code scanner data. The proper handling of such data requires consideration of aspects beyond those normally taken into account in regard to the static intersection universe which underscores matched samples. Appendix 8.1 to this chapter provides an outline of these sampling issues.

8.62 The following important points should be borne in mind:

- Where nothing much in the quality and range of goods available changes, use of the matched models method presents many advantages. The matched models method compares like with like, from like outlets.
- Statistical metadata systems are needed to help identify the product areas in which matching provides few problems, and to focus attention on those areas that are problematic. They show how to collect and provide the information that will facilitate quality adjustment. They also allow for transparency in methods and they facilitate retraining.
- Where there is a very rapid turnover in items such that serious sample depletion takes place quickly, replacements cannot be relied upon to make up the sample. Alternative mechanisms, which sample from or use the double universe of items in each period, are required. These include chained formulations and hedonic indices, as discussed in Chapter 7, paragraphs 7.125 to 7.158.
- Some new goods can be treated as evolutionary and incorporated using non-comparable replacements with associated quality adjustments. The timing of the replacement is critical for both the efficacy of the quality adjustment and the representativity of the index.
- Instructions to price collectors on the selection of replacements are important, for they too have a bearing

on the representativity of the index. The replacement of obsolete items with newly introduced items, in turn, leads to difficulties in undertaking quality adjustments, while their replacement with similar items leads to problems with representativity.

- Sample rotation is an extreme form of the use of replacements, and is one mechanism for refreshing the sample and thus increasing its representativity. Against this, however, is the possibility of bias arising from the implicit assumptions underlying the overlap procedure for quality adjustment not being met.
- Revolutionary goods may require the augmentation of the sample to make room for new price series and new weighting procedures. The classification of new goods into evolutionary goods and revolutionary goods has a bearing on the strategy for their introduction, directed replacement (substitution) and sample augmentation.
- The initial gain in consumer welfare arising from new items and loss in welfare because items disappear are not captured by either of these procedures. Econometric estimates of reservation prices provide an approach that is theoretically appropriate, although problematic in practice.

Appendix 8.1 Appearance or disappearance of products or outlets

1. In previous chapters, it was generally assumed that the target quantity for estimation could be defined in terms of a fixed set of products. Here we consider the complications arising from the fact that the products and outlets are continually changing. The rate of change is rapid in many industries. Sampling to estimate price changes is thus a dynamic rather than a static problem. Somehow, the prices of new products and the prices in new outlets have to be compared to old ones. Whatever methods and procedures are used in a price index to handle these dynamic changes, the effects of these procedures will always amount to an explicit or implicit estimation approach for this dynamic universe.

The representation of change in a price index

2. From a sample selection perspective, there are three ways of handling dynamic changes in an elementary aggregate universe (Dalén, 1998a), where varieties and outlets move in and out:

- by resampling the whole elementary aggregate at certain points in time;
- by a one-to-one replacement of one variety or outlet for another;
- by adding and deleting single observation points (items in outlets) within an index link.

Sample rotation

3. By resampling it is meant that the old sample is reconsidered as a whole so as to make it representative of the universe in a later period. This does not necessarily mean that all or even most sampling units have to be changed, only that a fresh look is taken at the representativity of the whole sample and changes are undertaken, as appropriate. The methods used for resampling could be any of those used for the initial sampling. In the case of probability sampling, every unit belonging to the universe in the later period needs to have a non-zero probability, equal to its relative market share, of being included in the sample.

4. Resampling (or sample rotation) is traditionally combined with the overlap method outlined in Chapter 7, paragraphs 7.45 to 7.52. It is a similar procedure to that used when combining two links in chain indices. The first period for which the new sample is used is also the last period for which the old sample is used. Thereby, price change estimation is always based on one sample only – the old sample up to the overlap period and the new sample from the overlap period onwards (see below). Resampling is the only method that is fully able to maintain the representativity of the sample. Resources permitting, resampling should be undertaken frequently. The appropriate frequency, of course, depends on the rate of change in a particular product group. It also relies on the assumption that the price differences between the old and new items are appropriate estimates of quality differences. At its extreme, resampling amounts to drawing a new sample in each period and comparing the average price between the samples, instead of the usual procedure of averaging price changes for matched samples. Although logical from the point of view of representativity, resampling in each period would aggravate the problem of quality adjustment by its implicit procedure of quality adjustment, and is thus not recommended.

Replacements

5. A replacement can be defined as an individual successor to a sampled product that has either disappeared completely from the market or lost market share in either the market as a whole or a specific outlet. Criteria for selecting replacements may differ considerably. First, there is the question of when to make the replacement. The usual practice is to do it either when an item disappears completely or when its share of the sales is reduced significantly. Another possible, but less-used rule, would be to replace an item when another variety within the same group, or representative item definition, has become larger with regard to sales, even if the old variety is still sold in significant quantities.

6. The second question is how to select the replacement item. If the rule for initial selection was "most sold" or with probability proportionate to (sales) size, then the replacement rule could follow the same selection rule. Alternatively, the replacement could be that item which is "most like" the old one. The advantage of the former rule is that it produces better representativity. The advantage of the "most like" rule is that, at least superficially, it might reduce the quality adjustment problem.

7. It is important to realize that, under current conditions, replacements cannot adequately represent new items that are coming onto the market. This is because what triggers a replacement is not the appearance of something new, but the disappearance or reduced importance of something old. For example, if the range of varieties in a certain group is increasing, sampling can only represent this increase directly from the set of new varieties, say by sample rotation.

Adding and deleting

8. It is possible to add a new observation point into an elementary aggregate within an index link. For example, if a new brand or model of a durable is introduced without replacing any particular old model, it is desirable to add it to the sample, starting from the time of its introduction. In order to accommodate this new observation in the index system, a reference price needs to be imputed. A practical way to do this is to use the ratio of the price of the new item in the month of its introduction to the average of all other items in the elementary aggregate from the reference period to the month of introduction. In this way, the effect of the new item on the index for months up to the introduction month will be neutral.

9. Similarly, an item that disappears could just be deleted from the sample without replacement. Price change can then be computed over the remaining items. If no further action is taken, this means that the price change for the deleted item, which was measured up to the month prior to deletion, will be disregarded from the month of deletion. This may or may not be desirable, depending on the circumstances in the particular product group.

Formulating an operational target in a dynamic universe

10. A rigorous approach to statistical estimation requires an index estimation strategy, including both the operational target of measurement and the sampling strategy (design and estimator) needed for estimating this target. This strategy would have to consist of the following components:

- a definition of the universe of transactions or observation points (usually a product variety in an outlet) in each of the two time periods between which we want to estimate price change;
- a list of all variables defined for these units. These variables should include prices and quantities (number of units sold at each price), but also all relevant price-determining characteristics of the products (and possibly also of the outlets). This forms the price basis;

- the target algorithm (index formula) that combines the values of the defined variables for the observation points in the defined universe into a single value;
- procedures used for initial sampling of items and outlets from the defined universe;
- procedures within the time span for replacing, sample rotation, adding or deleting observations;
- the estimation algorithm (index formula) applied to the sample with the purpose of minimizing the expected error of the sample estimate compared with the target algorithm. In principle, the estimation needs to consider all the procedures undertaken in replacement and sample rotation situations, including procedures for quality adjustment.

11. Because of its complexity, the rigorous strategy out lined above is generally not used in practical index construction, although the associated information (statistical metadata) system is discussed in paragraphs 8.23 to 8.31 above. A few comments on such possible strategies are made below.

A two-level aggregation system

12. A starting point for discussing an objective of estimating a price index from a sample drawn from a dynamic universe is a two-level structuring of the universe of items and outlets that are considered in the scope of a price index. These levels are:

- the *aggregate* level: at this level there is a fixed structure of item groups $h = 1, \ldots, H$ (or perhaps a fixed cross-structure of item groups by regions and outlet types) within an index link. In terms of updating the universe of items, new goods and services would be defined as new groups at the aggregate level and moved into the index only in connection with a new index link;
- the *elementary* level: at this level the aim is to capture the properties of a changing universe in the index by comparing new and old items. The micro-comparison from period s to period t must be defined so that new products or outlets enter the market and old products or outlets disappear from the market.

13. The common starting point for the three alternative approaches at the elementary level presented here is a basket index from period s to period t at the aggregate level:

$$I_{st} = \frac{\sum_h Q_h P_h^t}{\sum_h Q_h P_h^s} = \sum_h W_h^s I_h^{st},$$

$$\text{where} \quad W_h^s = \frac{Q_h P_h^s}{\sum_h Q_h P_h^s} \quad \text{and} \quad I_h^{st} = \frac{P_h^t}{P_h^s}. \qquad \text{(A8.1)}$$

The quantities, Q_h, are for $h = 1 \ldots H$ item groups from any period, or functions of quantities from several periods, for example, a symmetric average of the base and current periods s and t. Special cases of such a basket index are the Laspeyres ($Q_h = Q_h^s$), Paasche ($Q_h = Q_h^t$), Edgeworth ($Q_h = Q_h^s + Q_h^t$) and Walsh ($Q_h = [Q_h^s Q_h^t]^{1/2}$) price indices outlined in Chapters 15 to 17. Alternative formulations for an elementary-level estimation strategy now enter in the definition of I_h^{st}. As a further common starting point, the set of items or outlets belonging to h in period u ($= s$ or t) is defined as Ω_h^u. The concept of an *observation point* is introduced, usually a tightly specified item in a specific outlet. For each observation point $j \in \Omega_h^u$, there is a price p_j^u and a quantity sold q_j^u. There are now three possibilities for defining the operational target.

The intersection universe

14. The elementary index is defined over the intersection universe, that is, only over observation points existing in both s and t. This index may also be called the *identical units index*. It is equivalent to starting out with the observation points existing in s and then dropping (deleting) missing or disappearing points. An example of such an index is:

$$I_h^{st} = \frac{\sum_{j \in \Omega_h^s \cap \Omega_h^t} q_j p_j^t}{\sum_{j \in \Omega_h^s \cap \Omega_h^t} q_j p_j^s} \qquad \text{(A8.2)}$$

The intersection universe decreases successively over time, as fewer matches are found for each long-run comparison between s and t, s and $t+1$, s and $t+2$ etc., until it eventually becomes empty. An attraction of the intersection universe is that there are, by definition, no replacements involved, and thus, normally, no quality adjustments. If the identical units index is combined with a short index link, followed by *resampling* from the universe in a later period, sampling from the intersection universe is a perfectly reasonable strategy, as long as the assumption implicit in the overlap procedure, that the price differences at that point in time reflect the quality differences, is valid.

The double universe

15. The polar opposite approach to the intersection universe is to consider P_h^s and P_h^t as average prices defined over two separately defined universes in the two periods. A double universe could then be considered as the operational target of measurement: one universe in period s and another in period t. This seems to be a natural way of defining the target, since both time periods should be of equal status and all products existing in either of them should be taken into account. The difficulty with this approach is that the two universes are rarely comparable in terms of quality. Some kind of adjustment for average quality change would need to be brought into the index. The natural definition of the average prices involved in this approach is based on unit values. This would lead to the following definition of a *quality-adjusted unit value index*:

$$I_h^{st} = \frac{\bar{P}_h^t}{\bar{P}_h^s g_h^{st}},$$

$$\text{where} \quad \bar{P}_h^t = \frac{\sum_{j \in \Omega_h^t} q_j^t p_j^t}{\sum_{j \in \Omega_h^t} q_j^t} \quad \text{and} \quad \bar{P}_h^s = \frac{\sum_{j \in \Omega_h^s} q_j^s p_j^s}{\sum_{j \in \Omega_h^s} q_j^s} \qquad \text{(A8.3)}$$

where g_h^{st} is the average quality change in h (also interpretable as a *quality index*), which of course needs further definition. For example, g_h^{st} could be thought of as a hedonic adjustment procedure, where characteristics are held constant. Equation (A8.3) was discussed in Chapter 7, paragraphs 7.142–7.149, as part of Laspeyres, Paasche, Fisher and Törnqvist indices (as opposed to unit value ones), in a form which includes explicit hedonic quality adjustments, g_h^{st}. This operational target is attractive for products where the rate of turnover of varieties is very fast, but where average quality changes only slowly or where reliable estimates of quality changes can be made. The commonly used representative-item method is not really compatible with a double universe target. It implicitly focuses on pre-selected primary sampling units that are used for both period s and t.

The replacement universe

16. Neither sampling from the intersection universe nor from the double universe bears a close resemblance to usual practices for constructing price indices. The most common sampling method used in practice – the representative-item method combined with one-to-one replacements – needs a rationalization in terms of operational targets which differs from these alternatives. Such a rationalization of sampling from a *replacement universe* is considered below.

17. For each $j \in \Omega_h^s$ and $j \notin \Omega_h^t$ we define replacement items $a_j \in \Omega_h^t$ whose price replaces that of j in the formula. Obviously, for $j \in \Omega_h^s$ and $j \in \Omega_h^t$, $a_j = j$. In addition to a replacement, a quality change from j to a_j is included. This gives rise to a quality adjustment factor g_j, interpreted as the factor with which p_j^s must be multiplied for the consumer to be indifferent between consuming items j and a_j at prices p_j^s and p_{aj}^t.

$$I_h^{st} = \frac{\sum_{j \in \Omega_h^s} q_j p_{aj}^t}{\sum_{j \in \Omega_h^s} q_j p_j^s g_j}. \tag{A8.4}$$

18. This step towards an operational use of the formula requires, first, a definition of g_j, which is possible using a hedonic regression as described in Chapter 7, paragraphs 7.132 to 7.152. Second, there is a need to define a_j. A natural procedure is to use a *dissimilarity function* from j to a_j. The notation $d(j, a_j)$ is introduced for this function. The common procedure of choosing the most similar item in cases of replacement now corresponds to minimizing the dissimilarity function. Some further specifications nevertheless need to be made. When is the replacement defined to take place? In practice, this ought to be done when the first chosen variety is no longer representative. Mathematically, this could be defined as follows: observation point j should be replaced in the first period in which $q_j^t < cq_j^s$, where c is a suitably chosen constant between 0 and 1 (a modification being required for seasonal items). The choice of replacement point would then be governed by a rule such as: a_j should be chosen so that $d(j, a_j)$ is minimized for j. Since some priority should be given to observation points that are important in terms of quantities or values, that definition can be modified to become, for example: a_j should be chosen so that $d(j, a_j)/q_{aj}^t$ is minimized for j. Other rules for the choice of replacement point or function to be minimized can of course be chosen.

19. The dissimilarity function needs to be specified; it may depend on the item group h. In general, it must be some kind of metric defined on the set of characteristics of the product and outlet in question. For example, priority could be given to dissimilarity either to "same outlet" or "same product", concepts which could easily be worked into such a metric. A more troublesome concern is the inclusion of as many new points in Ω_h^t as possible in the index definition, in order to ensure that the sample is representative. As the above definitions now stand, the same new point could replace many predecessors, whereas there might be many new points which will not be sampled unless there is a need for a replacement. This shortcoming of the replacement universe is an inherent trait in the replacement method as such. The replacement method is designed to maintain only the representativity of the old sample, not that of the new sample.

Appendix 8.2 New goods and substitution

1. An alternative approach to estimating the effect of introducing new goods is to see new goods as a special case of substitution. In each period a consumer, faced with a set of prices, decides what to consume. The relative sales of the different items sold may change over time. Consumers may decide to consume less of one existing item and more of another existing one, or substitute consumption of an existing old item by a new one not previously available, or discontinue consumption of an existing item and substitute it by consumption of an existing or new one. Such changes are generally prompted by changes in relative prices. In many cases the "decision" of the consumer is tied to that of the producer or retailer, as items are no longer produced or sold so as to make way for new ones. Such substitutions between items apply as much to radically new goods as to new models of existing goods. In economic theory, the *elasticity of substitution*, denoted as σ, is a measure of the change in the quantity of, say, item i relative to item j, that would arise from a unit change in the price of item i relative to item j. A value of zero would imply that a change in price would lead to no substitution between the consumption of items and $\sigma > 1$ implies that the change in expenditure arising as a result of substituting items is positive: it is worth switching.

2. There is an intuition here that, if σ is known, and the extent to which substitutions occur in terms of their expenditure shares is also known, then estimates of the underlying price change that prompted the substitution can be derived. This applies as much to substitution between existing items as to substitution between existing, discontinued and new ones. The framework for operationalizing this institution for CPI use is proposed by Shapiro and Wilcox (1997b) – see also Lloyd (1975) and Moulton (1996a) – whereby the usual Laspeyres formulation is generalized to include the (demand) elasticity of substitution:

$$\left[\sum_{n \in 0,t} w_0 \left(\frac{p_{it}}{p_{i0}}\right)^{1-\sigma}\right]^{1/(1-\sigma)} \quad \text{(A8.5)}$$

where w_0 are expenditure shares in the base period and the summation is over matched items available in both periods. The correction, using σ, incorporates a substitution effect into the basic Laspeyres formula. If $\sigma = 0$, the formula is the traditional Laspeyres one. As $\sigma \rightarrow 1$, the formula tends towards a base-period weighted geometric mean. To use this formulation to generalize across the items in the summation, the restriction must apply that for any pair of items, the elasticity of substitution must be the same. The elasticity of substitution must also be the same over time. Such forms are referred to as constant elasticity of substitution (CES) functional relationships.

3. Feenstra (1994), Feenstra and Shiells (1997) and Balk (2000b) have extended the substitution to discontinued and new items. The advantage of equation (A8.5) is that, given an estimate of σ, a cost of living index which includes an estimate of substitution effects can be measured in real time. The incorporation of the effects of new and discontinued items follows directly from this. Alternative frameworks for including substitution effects (discussed in Chapter 17) require expenditure data for the base and current periods.

4. To extend the framework to new items, it is necessary to know how expenditures shift between new, existing and discontinued items. Let λ^t be the expenditure share of matched existing items out of the total in period t. The total includes existing and new items, so $1-\lambda^t$ is the share of new items in period t. Similarly, $1-\lambda^0$ is the expenditure share of old, discontinued items in period 0. The generalized Laspeyres index, which includes substitution between existing and old and new items, is given by:

$$\left[\frac{\lambda^t}{\lambda^0}\right]^{1/(\sigma-1)} \left[\sum_{n \in 0,t} w_0 \left(\frac{p_{it}}{p_{i0}}\right)^{1-\sigma}\right]^{1/(1-\sigma)} \quad \text{(A8.6)}$$

Like the usual Laspeyres index, it requires only the price relatives, the base period weights, the ratio of expenditure shares and an estimate of the elasticity of substitution. It can be derived in a number of alternative forms, including generalized, Paasche, Fisher or Sato–Vartia indices.

5. While there is an intuition behind the above formula, its formal correspondence to an index of consumer prices defined in economic theory is given by Balk (2000b). De Haan (2001) shows how the Fisher equivalent could be derived from a decomposition of a Fisher index when there are new and disappearing goods. The derivations show how the framework requires that $\sigma > 1$, a factor prompting Balk (2000b) to argue for its use for lower-level index aggregation, where this is more likely. The remaining problems are the estimation of σ, the availability of data on current expenditure shares, and the validity of the implied constant σ. There are also some conceptual issues. Increases in utility are regarded as having resulted from increases in the desirability of the items included in the above aggregation. If such items improve, then utility increases. Yet there are other goods outside the aggregation or system of demand equations. Deterioration in such goods will lead to increases in the desirability of the included items and decreases in utility. For example, if a consumer switches to private transport as a result of a deterioration in public transport, this should not be measured as a welfare gain resulting from better private transport, even though the expenditure flows in equation (A8.6) shift that way (Nevo, 2001).

6. The direct estimation of σ requires considerable econometric expertise. This puts it outside the routine construction of index numbers (see Hausman, 1997). Balk (2000b) shows how an alternative numerical routine might work. De Haan (2001) used scanner data to apply the methodology to a generalized Fisher index. He applied Balk's routine to nine product groups, using data from the Netherlands CPI, and found values of σ that exceeded unity. He advised the use of chained indices to maximize the matching of ongoing items, a principle discussed in Chapter 7, paragraphs 7.153 to 7.158. De Haan (2001) found major discrepancies between a generalized and ordinary Fisher index for at least six of the products, arguing for the need to incorporate the effects of new goods (see also Opperdoes, 2001). He also demonstrates how sensitive the procedure is to the selection of σ: for a share in current expenditure for new items of 4.8 per cent, and $\sigma = 1.2$, a Paasche-type index which includes new goods would be 93 per cent below the Paasche price change for ongoing goods only. For $\sigma = 5.0$ and the same expenditure share, the discrepancy falls to 34.1 per cent. For very large values, say $\sigma > 100$, the two indices would be relatively close. In such cases, the goods are almost identical, being near-perfectly substitutable; a switch to a new good would have little effect, the new and existing goods having similar prices.

CALCULATING CONSUMER PRICE INDICES IN PRACTICE

9

Introduction

9.1 The purpose of this chapter is to provide a general description of the ways in which consumer price indices (CPIs) are calculated in practice. The methods used in different countries are not exactly the same, but they have much in common. There is clearly interest from both compilers and users of CPIs in knowing how most statistical offices actually set about calculating their CPIs.

9.2 As a result of the greater insights into the properties and behaviour of price indices that have been achieved in recent years, it is now recognized that some traditional methods may not necessarily be optimal from a conceptual and theoretical viewpoint. Concerns have also been voiced in a number of countries about possible biases that may be affecting CPIs. These issues and concerns need to be considered in this manual. Of course, the methods used to compile CPIs are inevitably constrained by the resources available, not merely for collecting and processing prices, but also for gathering the expenditure data needed for weighting purposes. In some countries, the methods used may be severely constrained by lack of resources.

9.3 The calculation of CPIs usually proceeds in two stages. First, price indices are estimated for the elementary expenditure aggregates, or simply elementary aggregates. Then these elementary price indices are averaged to obtain higher-level indices using the relative values of the elementary expenditure aggregates as weights. This chapter starts by explaining how the elementary aggregates are constructed, and what economic and statistical criteria need to be taken into consideration in defining the aggregates. The index number formulae most commonly used to calculate the elementary indices are then presented, and their properties and behaviour illustrated using numerical examples. The pros and cons of the various formulae are considered, together with some alternative formulae that might be used instead. The problems created by disappearing and new items are also explained, as well as the different ways of imputing values for missing prices.

9.4 The second part of the chapter is concerned with the calculation of higher-level indices. The focus is on the ongoing production of a monthly price index in which the elementary price indices are averaged, or aggregated, to obtain higher-level indices. Price-updating of weights, chain linking and reweighting are discussed, with examples being provided. The problems associated with introduction of new elementary price indices and new higher-level indices into the CPI are also dealt with. It is explained how it is possible to decompose the change in the overall index into its component parts. Finally, the possibility of using some alternative and rather more complex index formulae is considered.

9.5 The chapter concludes with a section on data editing procedures, as these are an integral part of the process of compiling CPIs. It is essential to ensure that the right data are entered into the various formulae. There may be errors resulting from the inclusion of incorrect data or from entering correct data inappropriately, and errors resulting from the exclusion of correct data that are mistakenly believed to be wrong. The section examines data editing procedures which try to minimize both types of errors.

The calculation of price indices for elementary aggregates

9.6 CPIs are typically calculated in two steps. In the first step, the elementary price indices for the elementary aggregates are calculated. In the second step, higher-level indices are calculated by averaging the elementary price indices. The elementary aggregates and their price indices are the basic building blocks of the CPI.

Construction of elementary aggregates

9.7 Elementary aggregates are groups of relatively homogeneous goods and services. They may cover the whole country or separate regions within the country. Likewise, elementary aggregates may be distinguished for different types of outlets. The nature of the elementary aggregates depends on circumstances and the availability of information. Elementary aggregates may therefore be defined differently in different countries. Some key points, however, should be noted:

- Elementary aggregates should consist of groups of goods or services that are as similar as possible, and preferably fairly homogeneous.
- They should also consist of items that may be expected to have similar price movements. The objective should be to try to minimize the dispersion of price movements within the aggregate.
- The elementary aggregates should be appropriate to serve as strata for sampling purposes in the light of the sampling regime planned for the data collection.

9.8 Each elementary aggregate, whether relating to the whole country or an individual region or group of outlets, will typically contain a very large number of individual goods or services, or items. In practice, only a small number can be selected for pricing. When selecting the items, the following considerations need to be taken into account:

- The items selected should be ones for which price movements are believed to be representative of all the products within the elementary aggregate.
- The number of items within each elementary aggregate for which prices are collected should be large enough for the estimated price index to be statistically reliable. The minimum number required will vary between elementary aggregates depending on the nature of the products and their price behaviour.
- The object is to try to track the price of the same item over time for as long as possible, or as long as the item continues to be representative. The items selected should therefore be ones that are expected to remain on the market for some time, so that like can be compared with like.

9.9 *The aggregation structure*. The aggregation structure for a CPI is illustrated in Figure 9.1. Using a classification of consumers' expenditures such as the Classification of Individual Consumption according to Purpose (COICOP), the entire set of consumption goods and services covered by the overall CPI can be divided into groups, such as "food and non-alcoholic beverages". Each group is further divided into classes, such as "food". For CPI purposes, each class can then be further divided into more homogeneous sub-classes, such as "rice". The sub-classes are the equivalent of the basic headings used in the International Comparison Program (ICP), which calculates purchasing power parities (PPPs) between countries. Finally, the sub-class may be further subdivided to obtain the elementary aggregates, by dividing according to region or type of outlet, as in Figure 9.1. In some cases, a particular sub-class cannot be, or does not need to be, further subdivided, in which case the sub-class becomes the elementary aggregate. Within each elementary aggregate, one or more items are selected to represent all the items in the elementary aggregate. For example, the elementary aggregate consisting of rice sold in supermarkets in the northern region covers all types of rice, from which parboiled white rice and brown rice with over 50 per cent broken grains are selected as representative items. Of course, more representative items might be selected in practice. Finally, for each representative item, a number of specific products can be selected for price collection, such as particular brands of parboiled rice. Again, the number of sampled products selected may vary depending on the nature of the representative product.

9.10 Methods used to calculate the elementary indices from the individual price observations are discussed below. Working upwards from the elementary price indices, all indices above the elementary aggregate level are higher-level indices that can be calculated from the elementary price indices using the elementary expenditure aggregates as weights. The aggregation structure is consistent, so that the weight at each level above the elementary aggregate is always equal to the sum of its components. The price index at each higher level of aggregation can be calculated on the basis of the weights and price indices for its components, that is, the lower-level or elementary indices. The individual elementary price indices are not necessarily sufficiently reliable to be published separately, but they remain the basic building blocks of all higher-level indices.

9.11 *Weights within elementary aggregates*. In most cases, the price indices for elementary aggregates are calculated without the use of explicit expenditure weights. Whenever possible, however, weights should be used that reflect the relative importance of the sampled items, even if the weights are only approximate. Often, the elementary aggregate is simply the lowest level at which reliable weighting information is available. In this case, the elementary index has to be calculated as an unweighted average of the prices of which it consists. Even in this case, however, it should be noted that when the items are selected with probabilities proportional to the size of some relevant variable such as sales, weights are implicitly introduced by the sampling selection procedure.

9.12 For certain elementary aggregates, information about sales of particular items, market shares and regional weights may be used as explicit weights within an elementary aggregate. Weights within elementary aggregates may be updated independently and possibly more often than the elementary aggregates themselves (which serve as weights for the higher-level indices).

9.13 For example, assume that the number of suppliers of a certain product such as fuel for cars is limited. The market shares of the suppliers may be known from business survey statistics and can be used as weights in the calculation of an elementary aggregate price index for car fuel. Alternatively, prices for water may be collected from a number of local water supply services where the population in each local region is known. The relative size of the population in each region may then be used as a proxy for the relative consumption expenditures to weight the price in each region to obtain the elementary aggregate price index for water.

9.14 A special situation occurs in the case of tariff prices. A tariff is a list of prices for the purchase of a particular kind of good or service under different terms and conditions. One example is electricity, where one price is charged during daytime while a lower price is charged at night. Similarly, a telephone company may charge a lower price for a call at the weekend than in the rest of the week. Another example may be bus tickets sold at one price to ordinary passengers and at lower prices to children or old age pensioners. In such cases, it is appropriate to assign weights to the different tariffs or prices in order to calculate the price index for the elementary aggregate.

9.15 The increasing use of electronic points of sale in many countries, in which both prices and quantities are scanned as the purchases are made, means that valuable new sources of information may become increasingly available to statistical offices. This could lead to significant changes in the ways in which price data are collected and processed for CPI purposes. The treatment of scanner data is examined in Chapters 7, 8 and 21.

Construction of elementary price indices

9.16 An elementary price index is the price index for an elementary aggregate. Various different methods and formulae may be used to calculate elementary price indices. The methods that have been most commonly

Figure 9.1 Typical aggregation structure of a consumer price index (CPI)

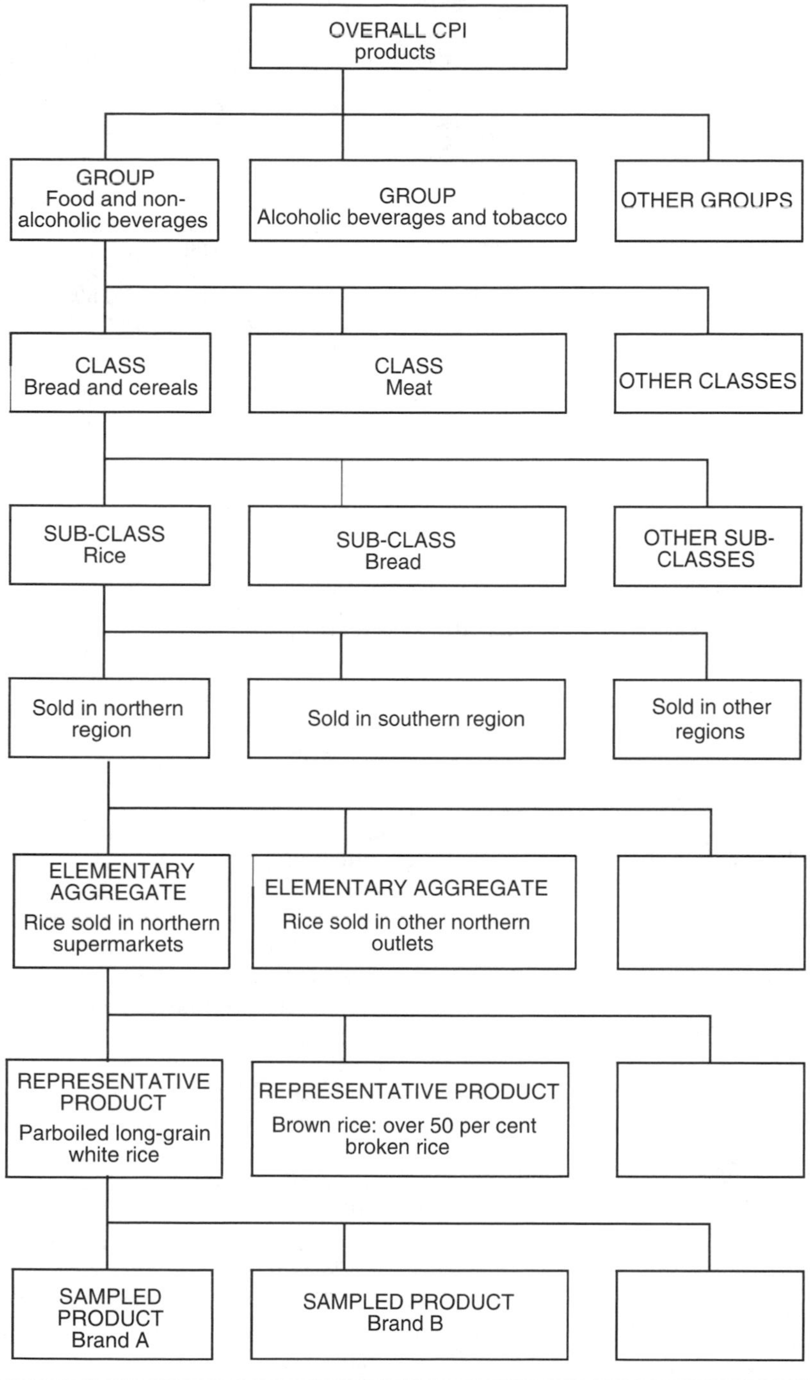

used are illustrated by means of a numerical example in Table 9.1. In the example, it is assumed that prices are collected for four items within an elementary aggregate. The quality of each item remains unchanged over time, so the month-to-month changes compare like with like. It is assumed initially that prices are collected for all four items in every month covered, so that there is a complete set of prices. There are no disappearing items, no missing prices and no replacement items. This is quite a strong assumption because many of the problems encountered in practice are attributable to breaks in the continuity of the price series for the individual items for one reason or another. The treatment of disappearing and replacement items is taken up later. It is also assumed that there are no explicit weights available.

9.17 Three widely used formulae that have been, or still are, in use by statistical offices to calculate elementary price indices are illustrated in Table 9.1. It should be noted, however, that these are not the only possibilities and some alternative formulae are considered later.

- The first is the Carli index for $i = 1, \ldots, n$ items. It is defined as the simple, or unweighted, arithmetic mean

Table 9.1 Calculation of price indices for an elementary aggregate[1]

	January	February	March	April	May	June	July
				Prices			
Item A	6.00	6.00	7.00	6.00	6.00	6.00	6.60
Item B	7.00	7.00	6.00	7.00	7.00	7.20	7.70
Item C	2.00	3.00	4.00	5.00	2.00	3.00	2.20
Item D	5.00	5.00	5.00	4.00	5.00	5.00	5.50
Arithmetic mean prices	5.00	5.25	5.50	5.50	5.00	5.30	5.50
Geometric mean prices	4.53	5.01	5.38	5.38	4.53	5.05	4.98
				Month-to-month price ratios			
Item A	1.00	1.00	1.17	0.86	1.00	1.00	1.10
Item B	1.00	1.00	0.86	1.17	1.00	1.03	1.07
Item C	1.00	1.50	1.33	1.25	0.40	1.50	0.73
Item D	1.00	1.00	1.00	0.80	1.25	1.00	1.10
				Current-to-reference-month (January) price ratios			
Item A	1.00	1.00	1.17	1.00	1.00	1.00	1.10
Item B	1.00	1.00	0.86	1.00	1.00	1.03	1.10
Item C	1.00	1.50	2.00	2.50	1.00	1.50	1.10
Item D	1.00	1.00	1.00	0.80	1.00	1.00	1.10
Carli index – the arithmetic mean of price ratios							
Month-to-month index	100.00	112.50	108.93	101.85	91.25	113.21	100.07
Chained month-to-month index	100.00	112.50	122.54	124.81	113.89	128.93	129.02
Direct index on January	100.00	112.50	125.60	132.50	100.00	113.21	110.00
Dutot index – the ratio of arithmetic mean prices							
Month-to-month index	100.00	105.00	104.76	100.00	90.91	106.00	103.77
Chained month-to-month index	100.00	105.00	110.00	110.00	100.00	106.00	110.00
Direct index on January	100.00	105.00	110.00	110.00	100.00	106.00	110.00
Jevons index – the ratio of geometric mean prices = geometric mean of price ratios							
Month-to-month index	100.00	110.67	107.46	100.00	84.09	111.45	98.70
Chained month-to-month index	100.00	110.67	118.92	118.92	100.00	111.45	110.00
Direct index on January	100.00	110.67	118.92	118.92	100.00	111.45	110.00

[1] All price indices have been calculated using unrounded figures.

of the price relatives, or price ratios, for the two periods, 0 and t, to be compared:

$$I_C^{0:t} = \frac{1}{n}\sum\left(\frac{p_i^t}{p_i^0}\right) \tag{9.1}$$

- The second is the Dutot index, defined as the ratio of the unweighted arithmetic mean prices:

$$I_D^{0:t} = \frac{\frac{1}{n}\sum p_i^t}{\frac{1}{n}\sum p_i^0} \tag{9.2}$$

- The third is the Jevons index, defined as the unweighted geometric mean of the price relative or ratio which is identical to the ratio of the unweighted geometric mean prices:

$$I_J^{0:t} = \prod\left(\frac{p_i^t}{p_i^0}\right)^{1/n} = \frac{\prod (p_i^t)^{1/n}}{\prod (p_i^0)^{1/n}} \tag{9.3}$$

9.18 The properties of the three indices are examined and explained in some detail in Chapter 20. Here, the purpose is to illustrate how they perform in practice, to compare the results obtained by using the different formulae and to summarize their strengths and weaknesses.

9.19 Each *month-to-month* index shows the change in the index from one month to the next. The *chained monthly* indices link together these month-to-month changes by successive multiplication. The *direct* indices compare the prices in each successive month directly with those of the reference month, January. By simple inspection of the various indices, it is clear that the choice of formula and method can make a substantial difference to the results obtained. Some results are striking, in particular the large difference between the chained Carli index for July and each of the direct indices for July, including the direct Carli.

9.20 The properties and behaviour of the different indices are summarized in the following paragraphs (see also Chapter 20). First, the differences between the results obtained by using the different formulae tend to increase as the variance of the price relatives, or ratios, increases. The greater the dispersion of the price movements, the more critical the choice of index formula, and method, becomes. If the elementary aggregates are defined in such a way that the price movements within the aggregate are minimized, the results obtained become less sensitive to the choice of formula and method.

9.21 Certain features displayed by the data in Table 9.1 are systematic and predictable; they follow from the mathematical properties of the indices. For example, it is well known that an arithmetic mean is always greater than, or equal to, the corresponding geometric mean, the equality holding only in the trivial case in which the numbers being averaged are all the same. The direct Carli indices are therefore all greater than the Jevons indices, except in May and July when the four price relatives based on January are all equal. In general, the Dutot may be greater or less than the Jevons, but tends to be less than the Carli.

9.22 One general property of geometric means should be noted when using the Jevons index. If any one observation out of a set of observations is zero, their geometric mean is zero, whatever the values of the other observations. The Jevons index is sensitive to extreme falls in prices and it may be necessary to impose upper and lower bounds on the individual price ratios of say 10 and 0.1, respectively, when using the Jevons. Of course, extreme observations often result from errors of one kind or another, so extreme price movements should be carefully checked anyway.

9.23 Another important property of the indices illustrated in Table 9.1 is that the Dutot and the Jevons indices are transitive, whereas the Carli is not. Transitivity means that the chained monthly indices are identical to the corresponding direct indices. This property is important in practice, because many elementary price indices are in fact calculated as chain indices which link together the month-on-month indices. The intransitivity of the Carli index is illustrated dramatically in Table 9.1 when each of the four individual prices in May returns to the same level as it was in January, but the chain Carli registers an increase of almost 14 per cent over January. Similarly, in July, although each individual price is exactly 10 per cent higher than in January, the chain Carli registers an increase of 29 per cent. These results would be regarded as perverse and unacceptable in the case of a direct index, but even in the case of a chain index the results seems so intuitively unreasonable as to undermine the credibility of the chain Carli. The price changes between March and April illustrate the effects of "price bouncing" in which the same four prices are observed in both periods but they are switched between the different items. The monthly Carli index from March to April increases whereas both the Dutot and the Jevons indices are unchanged.

9.24 The message emerging from this brief illustration of the behaviour of just three possible formulae is that different index numbers and methods can deliver very different results. Index compilers have to familiarize themselves with the interrelationships between the various formulae at their disposal for the calculation of the elementary price indices so that they are aware of the implications of choosing one formula rather than another. Knowledge of these interrelationships is nevertheless not sufficient to determine which formula should be used, even though it makes it possible to make a more informed and reasoned choice. It is necessary to appeal to other criteria in order to settle the choice of formula. There are two main approaches that may be used, the axiomatic and the economic approaches.

Axiomatic approach to elementary price indices

9.25 As explained in Chapters 16 and 20, one way in which to decide upon an appropriate index formula is to require it to satisfy certain specified axioms or tests. The tests throw light on the properties possessed by different kinds of indices, some of which may not be intuitively obvious. Four basic tests will be cited here to illustrate the axiomatic approach:

- *Proportionality test* – if all prices are λ times the prices in the price reference period (January in the example), the index should equal λ. The data for July, when every price is 10 per cent higher than in January, show that all three direct indices satisfy this test. A special case of this test is the *identity test*, which requires that if the price of every item is the same as in the reference period, the index should be equal to unity (as in May in the example).
- *Changes in the units of measurement test (commensurability test)* – the price index should not change if the quantity units in which the products are measured are changed (for example, if the prices are expressed per litre rather than per pint). The Dutot index fails this test, as explained below, but the Carli and Jevons indices satisfy the test.
- *Time reversal test* – if all the data for the two periods are interchanged, then the resulting price index should equal the reciprocal of the original price index. The Carli index fails this test, but the Dutot and the Jevons indices both satisfy the test. The failure of the Carli to satisfy the test is not immediately obvious from the example, but can easily be verified by interchanging the prices in January and April, for example, in which case the backwards Carli for January based on April is equal to 91.3 whereas the reciprocal of the forwards Carli is 1/132.5 or 75.5.
- *Transitivity test* – the chain index between two periods should equal the direct index between the same two periods. It can be seen from the example that the Jevons and the Dutot indices both satisfy this test, whereas the Carli index does not. For example, although the prices in May have returned to the same levels as in January, the chain Carli registers 113.9. This illustrates the fact that the Carli may have a significant built-in upward bias.

9.26 Many other axioms or tests can be devised, but the above are sufficient to illustrate the approach and also to throw light on some important features of the elementary indices under consideration here.

9.27 The sets of products covered by elementary aggregates are meant to be as homogeneous as possible. If they are not fairly homogeneous, the failure of the Dutot index to satisfy the units of measurement or commensurablity test can be a serious disadvantage. Although defined as the ratio of the unweighted arithmetic average prices, the Dutot index may also be interpreted as a weighted arithmetic average of the price ratios in which each ratio is weighted by its price in the base period. This can be seen by rewriting formula (9.2) above as

$$I_D^{0:t} = \frac{\frac{1}{n}\sum p_i^0(p_i^t/p_i^0)}{\frac{1}{n}\sum p_i^0}$$

However, if the products are not homogeneous, the relative prices of the different items may depend quite arbitrarily on the quantity units in which they are measured.

9.28 Consider, for example, salt and pepper, which are found within the same sub-class of COICOP. Suppose the unit of measurement for pepper is changed from grams to ounces, while leaving the units in which salt is measured (say kilos) unchanged. As an ounce of pepper is equal to 28.35 grams, the "price" of pepper increases by over 28 times, which effectively increases the weight given to pepper in the Dutot index by over 28 times. The price of pepper relative to salt is inherently arbitrary, depending entirely on the choice of units in which to measure the two goods. In general, when there are different kinds of products within the elementary aggregate, the Dutot index is unacceptable conceptually.

9.29 The Dutot index is acceptable only when the set of items covered is homogeneous, or at least nearly homogeneous. For example, it may be acceptable for a set of apple prices even though the apples may be of different varieties, but not for the prices of a number of different kinds of fruits, such as apples, pineapples and bananas, some of which may be much more expensive per item or per kilo than others. Even when the items are fairly homogeneous and measured in the same units, the Dutot's implicit weights may still not be satisfactory. More weight is given to the price changes for the more expensive items, but in practice they may well account for only small shares of the total expenditure within the aggregate. Consumers are unlikely to buy items at high prices if the same items are available at lower prices.

9.30 It may be concluded that from an axiomaic viewpoint, both the Carli and the Dutot indices, although they have been, and still are, widely used by statistical offices, have serious disadvantages. The Carli index fails the time reversal and transitivity tests. In principle, it should not matter whether we choose to measure price changes forwards or backwards in time. We would expect the same answer, but this is not the case for the Carli. Chained Carli indices may be subject to a significant upward bias. The Dutot index is meaningful for a set of homogeneous items but becomes increasingly arbitrary as the set of products becomes more diverse. On the other hand, the Jevons index satisfies all the tests listed above and also emerges as the preferred index when the set of tests is enlarged, as shown in Chapter 20. From an axiomatic point of view, the Jevons index is clearly the index with the best properties, even though it may not have been used much until recently. There seems to be an increasing tendency for statistical offices to switch from using Carli or Dutot indices to the Jevons index.

Economic approach to elementary price indices

9.31 In the economic approach, the objective is to estimate an economic index – that is, a *cost of living index* for the elementary aggregate (see Chapter 20). The items for which prices are collected are treated as if they constituted a basket of goods and services purchased by consumers, from which the consumers derive utility. A cost of living index measures the minimum amount by which consumers would have to change their expenditures in order to keep their utility level unchanged, allowing consumers to make substitutions between the items in response to changes in the relative prices of items. In the absence of information about quantities or expenditures within an elementary aggregate, the index can only be estimated when certain special conditions are assumed to prevail.

9.32 There are two special cases of some interest. The first case is when consumers continue to consume the same *relative* quantities whatever the relative prices. Consumers prefer not to make any substitutions in reponse to changes in relative prices. The cross-elasticities of demand are zero. The underlying preferences are described in the economics literature as "Leontief". With these preferences, a Laspeyres index would provide an exact measure of the cost of living index. In this first case, the Carli index calculated for a random sample would provide an estimate of the cost of living index provided that the items are selected with probabilities proportional to the population expenditure shares. It might appear that if the items were selected with probabilities proportional to the population quantity shares, the sample Dutot would provide an estimate of the population Laspeyres. If the basket for the Laspeyres index contains different kinds of products whose quantities are not additive, however, the quantity shares, and hence the probabilities, are undefined.

9.33 The second case occurs when consumers are assumed to vary the quantities they consume in inverse proportion to the changes in relative prices. The cross-elasticities of demand between the different items are all unity, the expenditure shares being the same in both periods. The underlying preferences are described as "Cobb–Douglas". With these preferences, the *geometric Laspeyres* would provide an exact measure of the cost of living index. The geometric Laspeyres is a weighted geometric average of the price relatives, using the expenditure shares in the earlier period as weights (the expenditure shares in the second period would be the same in the particular case under consideration). In this second case, the Jevons index calculated for a random sample would provide an unbiased estimate of the cost of living index, provided that the items are selected with probabilities proportional to the population expenditure shares.

9.34 On the basis of the economic approach, the choice between the sample Jevons and the sample Carli rests on which is likely to approximate the more closely to the underlying cost of living index: in other words, on whether the (unknown) cross-elasticities are likely to be closer to unity or zero, on average. In practice, the cross-elasticities could take on any value ranging up to plus infinity for an elementary aggregate consisting of a set of strictly homogeneous items, i.e., perfect substitutes. It should be noted that in the limit when the products really are homogeneous, there is no index number problem, and the price "index" is given by the ratio of the unit values in the two periods, as explained later. It may be conjectured that the average cross-elasticity is likely to be closer to unity than zero for most elementary aggregates so that, in general, the Jevons index is likely to provide a closer approximation to the cost of living index than the Carli. In this case, the Carli index must be viewed as having an upward bias.

9.35 The insight provided by the economic approach is that the Jevons index is likely to provide a closer approximation to the cost of living index for the elementary aggregate than the Carli because, in most cases, a significant amount of substitution is more likely than no substitution, especially as elementary aggregates should be deliberately constructed in such a way as to group together similar items that are close substitutes for each other.

9.36 The Jevons index does not imply, or assume, that expenditure shares remain constant. Obviously, the Jevons can be calculated whatever changes do, or do not occur in the expenditure shares in practice. What the economic approach shows is that if the expenditure shares remain constant (or roughly constant), then the Jevons index can be expected to provide a good estimate of the underlying cost of living index. Similarly, if the relative quantities remain constant, then the Carli index can be expected to provide a good estimate, but the Carli does not actually imply that quantities remain fixed.

9.37 It may be concluded that, on the basis of the economic approach as well as the axiomatic approach, the Jevons emerges as the preferred index in general, although there may be cases in which little or no substitution takes place within the elementary aggregate and the Carli might be preferred. The index compiler must make a judgement on the basis of the nature of the products actually included in the elementary aggregate.

9.38 Before leaving this topic, it should be noted that it has thrown light on some of the sampling properties of the elementary indices. If the products in the sample are selected with probabilities proportional to expenditures in the price reference period:

- the sample (unweighted) Carli index provides an unbiased estimate of the population Laspeyres;
- the sample (unweighted) Jevons index provides an unbiased estimate of the population geometric Laspeyres.

These results hold irrespective of the underlying cost of living index.

Chain versus direct indices for elementary aggregates

9.39 In a direct elementary index, the prices of the current period are compared directly with those of the price reference period. In a chain index, prices in each period are compared with those in the previous period, the resulting short-term indices being chained together to obtain the long-term index, as illustrated in Table 9.1.

9.40 Provided that prices are recorded for the same set of items in every period, as in Table 9.1, any index formula defined as the ratio of the average prices will be transitive: that is, the same result is obtained whether the index is calculated as a direct index or as a chain index. In a chain index, successive numerators and denominators will cancel out, leaving only the average price in the last period divided by the average price in the reference period, which is the same as the direct index. Both the Dutot and the Jevons indices are therefore transitive. As already noted, however, a chain Carli index is not transitive and should not be used because of its upward bias. Nevertheless, the direct Carli remains an option.

9.41 Although the chain and direct versions of the Dutot and Jevons indices are identical when there are no breaks in the series for the individual items, they offer different ways of dealing with new and disappearing items, missing prices and quality adjustments. In practice, products continually have to be dropped from the index and new ones included, in which case the direct and the chain indices may differ if the imputations for missing prices are made differently.

9.42 When a replacement item has to be included in a direct index, it will often be necessary to estimate the price of the new item in the price reference period, which may be some time in the past. The same happens if, as a result of an update of the sample, new items have to be linked into the index. Assuming that no information exists on the price of the replacement item in the price reference period, it will be necessary to estimate it using price ratios calculated for the items that remain in the elementary aggregate, a subset of these items or some other indicator. However, the direct approach should only be used for a limited period of time. Otherwise, most of the reference prices would end up being imputed, which would be an undesirable outcome. This effectively rules out the use of the Carli index over a long period of time, as the Carli can only be used in its direct form anyway, being unacceptable when chained. This implies that, in practice, the direct Carli may be used only if the overall index is chain linked annually, or at intervals of two or three years.

9.43 In a chain index, if an item becomes permanently missing, a replacement item can be linked into the index as part of the ongoing index calculation by including the item in the monthly index as soon as prices for two successive months are obtained. Similarly, if the sample is updated and new products have to be linked into the index, this will require successive old and new prices for the present and the preceding months. For a chain index, however, the missing observation will have an impact on the index for two months, since the missing observation is part of two links in the chain. This is not the case for a direct index, where a single, non-estimated missing observation will only have an impact on the index in the current period. For example, for a comparison between periods 0 and 3, a missing price of an item in period 2 means that the chain index excludes the item for the last link of the index in periods 2 and 3, while the direct index includes it in period 3 since a direct index will be based on items whose prices are available in periods 0 and 3. In general, however, the use of a chain index can make the estimation of missing prices and the introduction of replacements easier from a computational point of view, whereas it may be inferred that a direct index will limit the usefulness of overlap methods for dealing with missing observations.

9.44 The direct and the chain approaches also produce different by-products that may be used for monitoring price data. For each elementary aggregate, a chain index approach gives the latest monthly price change, which can be useful for both data editing and imputation of missing prices. By the same token, however, a direct index derives average price levels for each elementary aggregate in each period, and this information may be a useful by-product. Nevertheless, because the availability of cheap computing power and of spreadsheets allows such by-products to be calculated whether a direct or a chained approach is applied, the choice of formula should not be dictated by considerations regarding by-products.

Consistency in aggregation

9.45 Consistency in aggregation means that if an index is calculated stepwise by aggregating lower-level indices to obtain indices at progressively higher levels of aggregation, the same overall result should be obtained as if the calculation had been made in one step. For presentational purposes this is an advantage. If the elementary aggregates are calculated using one formula and the elementary aggregates are averaged to obtain the higher-level indices using another formula, the resulting CPI is not consistent in aggregation. It may be argued, however, that consistency in aggregation is not necessarily an important or even appropriate criterion, or that it is unachievable when the amount of information available on quantities and expenditures is not the same at the different levels of aggregation. In addition, there may be different degrees of substitution within elementary aggregates as compared to the degree of substitution between products in different elementary aggregates.

9.46 As noted earlier, the Carli index would be consistent in aggregation with the Laspeyres index if the items were to be selected with probabilities proportional to expenditures in the reference period. This is typically not the case. The Dutot and the Jevons indices are also not consistent in aggregation with a higher-level Laspeyres. As explained below, however, the CPIs actually calculated by statistical offices are usually not true Laspeyres indices anyway, even though they may be based on fixed baskets of goods and services. As also noted earlier, if the higher-level index were to be defined as a geometric Laspeyres, consistency in aggregation could be achieved by using the Jevons index for the elementary indices at the lower level, provided that the individual items are sampled with probabilities proportional to expenditures. Although unfamiliar, a geometric Laspeyres has desirable properties from an economic point of view and is considered again later.

Missing price observations

9.47 The price of an item may fail to be collected in some period either because the item is missing temporarily or because it has permanently disappeared. The two classes of missing prices require different treatment. Temporary unavailability may occur for seasonal items (particularly for fruit, vegetables and clothing), because of supply shortages or possibly because of some collection difficulty (say, an outlet was closed or a price collector was ill). The treatment of seasonal items raises a number of particular problems. These are dealt with in Chapter 22 and will not be discussed here.

9.48 *The treatment of temporarily missing prices.* In the case of temporarily missing observations for non-seasonal items, one of four actions may be taken:

- omit the item for which the price is missing so that a matched sample is maintained (like is compared with like) even though the sample is depleted;
- carry forward the last observed price;
- impute the missing price by the average price change for the prices that are available in the elementary aggregate;
- impute the missing price by the price change for a particular comparable item from another similar outlet.

9.49 Omitting an observation from the calculation of an elementary index is equivalent to assuming that the price would have moved in the same way as the average of the prices of the items that remain included in the index. Omitting an observation changes the implicit weights attached to the other prices in the elementary aggregate.

9.50 Carrying forward the last observed price should be avoided wherever possible and is acceptable only for a very limited number of periods. Special care needs to be taken in periods of high inflation or when markets are changing rapidly as a result of a high rate of innovation and product turnover. While simple to apply, carrying forward the last observed price biases the resulting index towards zero change. In addition, there is likely to be a compensating step-change in the index when the price of the missing item is recorded again, which will be wrongly missed by a chain index, but will be included in a direct index to return the index to its proper value. The adverse effect on the index will be increasingly severe if the item remains unpriced for some length of time. In general, to carry forward is not an acceptable procedure or solution to the problem.

9.51 Imputation of the missing price by the average change of the available prices may be applied for elementary aggregates where the prices can be expected to move in the same direction. The imputation can be made using all of the remaining prices in the elementary aggregate. As already noted, this is numerically equivalent to omitting the item for the immediate period, but it is useful to make the imputation so that if the price becomes available again in a later period the sample size is not reduced in that period. In some cases, depending on the homogeneity of the elementary aggregate, it may be preferable to use only a subset of items from the elementary aggregate to estimate the missing price. In some instances, this may even be a single comparable item from a similar type of outlet whose price change can be expected to be similar to the missing one.

9.52 Table 9.2 illustrates the calculation of the price index for an elementary aggregate consisting of three items where one of the prices is missing in March. Section (a) of Table 9.2 shows the indices where the missing price has been omitted from the calculation. The direct indices are therefore calculated on the basis of items A, B and C for all months except March, where they are calculated on the basis of items B and C only. The chained indices are calculated on the basis of all three prices from January to February and from April to May. From February to March and from March to April the monthly indices are calculated on the basis of items B and C only.

9.53 For both the Dutot and the Jevons indices, the direct and chain indices now differ from March onwards. The first link in the chain index (January to February) is the same as the direct index, so the two indices are

Table 9.2 Imputation of temporarily missing prices

	January	February	March	April	May
			Prices		
Item A	6.00	5.00		7.00	6.60
Item B	7.00	8.00	9.00	8.00	7.70
Item C	2.00	3.00	4.00	3.00	2.20
(a) Omit missing prices from the index calculation					
Carli index – the arithmetic mean of price ratios					
Direct index	100.00	115.87	164.29	126.98	110.00
Dutot index – the ratio of arithmetic mean prices					
Month-to-month index	100.00	106.67	118.18	84.62	91.67
Chained month-to-month index	100.00	106.67	126.06	106.67	97.78
Direct index	100.00	106.67	144.44	120.00	110.00
Jevons index – the ratio of geometric mean prices = geometric mean of price ratios					
Month-to-month index	100.00	112.62	122.47	81.65	87.31
Chained month-to-month index	100.00	112.62	137.94	112.62	98.33
Direct index	100.00	112.62	160.36	125.99	110.00
(b) Imputation					
Carli index – the arithmetic mean of price ratios					
Impute price for item A in March as $5 \times (9/8+4/3)/2 = 6.15$					
Direct index	100.00	115.87	143.67	126.98	110.00
Dutot index – the ratio of arithmetic mean prices					
Impute price for item A in March as $5 \times ((9+4)/(8+3)) = 5.91$					
Month-to-month index	100.00	106.67	118.18	95.19	91.67
Chained month-to-month index	100.00	106.67	126.06	120.00	110.00
Direct index	100.00	106.67	126.06	120.00	110.00
Jevons index – the ratio of geometric mean prices = geometric mean of price ratios					
Impute price for item A in March as $5 \times (9/8) \times (4/3)^{0.5} = 6.12$					
Month-to-month index	100.00	112.62	122.47	91.34	87.31
Chained month-to-month index	100.00	112.62	137.94	125.99	110.00
Direct index	100.00	112.62	137.94	125.99	110.00

identical numerically. The direct index for March completely ignores the price decrease of item A between January and February, while this is taken into account in the chain index. As a result, the direct index is higher than the chain index for March. On the other hand, in April and May, when all prices are again available, the direct index captures the price development, whereas the chain index fails to track the development in the prices.

9.54 In section (b) of Table 9.2 the missing price for item A in March is imputed by the average price change of the remaining items from February to March. While the index may be calculated as a direct index, comparing the prices of the present period with the reference period prices, the imputation of missing prices should be made on the basis of the average price change from the preceding to the present period, as shown in the table. Imputation on the basis of the average price change from the base period to the present period should not be used as it ignores the information about the price change of the missing item that has already been included in the index. The treatment of imputations is discussed in more detail in Chapter 7.

9.55 *Treatment of items that have permanently disappeared and their replacements.* Items may disappear permanently for a variety of reasons. The item may disappear from the market because new items have been introduced or the outlets from which the price has been collected have stopped selling the product. Where products disappear permanently, a replacement product has to be sampled and included in the index. The replacement product should ideally be one that accounts for a significant proportion of sales, is likely to continue to be sold for some time, and is likely to be representative of the sampled price changes of the market that the old product covered.

9.56 The timing of the introduction of replacement items is important. Many new products are initially sold at high prices which then gradually drop over time, especially as the volume of sales increases. Alternatively, some products may be introduced at artificially low prices to stimulate demand. In such cases, delaying the introduction of a new or replacement item until a large volume of sales is achieved may miss some systematic price changes that ought to be captured by CPIs. It may be desirable to try to avoid forced replacements caused when products disappear completely from the market, and to try to introduce replacements when sales of the items they replace are falling away, but before they cease altogether.

9.57 Table 9.3 shows an example where item A disappears after March and item D is included as a replacement from April onwards. Items A and D are not available on the market at the same time and their price series do not overlap.

9.58 To include the new item in the index from April onwards, an imputed price needs to be calculated either for the base period (January) if a direct index is being calculated, or for the preceding period (March) if a chain index is calculated. In both cases, the imputation method ensures that the inclusion of the new item does not, in itself, affect the index. In the case of a chain index, imputing the missing price by the average change of the available prices gives the same result as if the item is simply omitted from the index calculation until it has

Table 9.3 Disappearing items and their replacements with no overlapping prices

	January	February	March	April	May
			Prices		
Item A	6.00	7.00	5.00		
Item B	3.00	2.00	4.00	5.00	6.00
Item C	7.00	8.00	9.00	10.00	9.00
Item D				9.00	8.00
(a) Imputation					
Carli index – the arithmetic mean of price ratios					
Impute price for item D in January as 9/((5/3+10/7) × 0.5) = 5.82					
Direct index	100.00	99.21	115.08	154.76	155.38
Dutot index – the ratio of arithmetic mean prices					
Impute price for item D in March as 9/((5+10)/(4+9)) = 7.80					
Month-to-month index	100.00	106.25	105.88	115.38	95.83
Chained month-to-month index	100.00	106.25	112.50	129.81	124.40
Impute price for item D in January as 9/((5+10)/(3+7)) = 6.00					
Direct index	100.00	106.25	112.50	150.00	143.75
Jevons index – the ratio of geometric mean prices = geometric mean of price ratios					
Impute price for item D in March as 9/((5/4 × 10/9)$^{0.5}$) = 7.64					
Month-to-month index	100.00	96.15	117.13	117.85	98.65
Chained month-to-month index	100.00	96.15	112.62	132.73	130.94
Impute price for item D in January as 9/((5/3 × 10/7)$^{0.5}$) = 5.83					
Direct index	100.00	96.15	112.62	154.30	152.22
(b) Omit missing prices					
Dutot index – the ratio of arithmetic mean prices					
Month-to-month index	100.00	106.25	105.88	115.38	95.83
Chained month-to-month index	100.00	106.25	112.50	129.81	124.40
Jevons index – the ratio of geometric mean prices = geometric mean of price ratios					
Monthly index	100.00	96.15	117.13	117.85	98.65
Chained month-to-month index	100.00	96.15	112.62	132.73	130.94

been priced in two successive periods. This allows the chain index to be compiled by simply chaining the month-to-month index between periods $t-1$ and t, based on the matched set of prices in those two periods, onto the value of the chain index for period $t-1$. In the example, no further imputation is required after April, and the subsequent movement of the index is unaffected by the imputed price change between March and April.

9.59 In the case of a direct index, however, an imputed price is always required for the reference period in order to include a new item. In the example, the price of the new item in each month after April still has to be compared with the imputed price for January. As already noted, to prevent a situation in which most of the reference period prices end up being imputed, the direct approach should only be used for a limited period of time.

9.60 The situation is somewhat simpler when there is an overlap month in which prices are collected for both the disappearing and the replacement item. In this case, it is possible to link the price series for the new item to the price series for the old item that it replaces. Linking with overlapping prices involves making an implicit adjustment for the difference in quality between the two items, as it assumes that the relative prices of the new and old item reflect their relative qualities. For perfect or nearly perfect markets this may be a valid assumption, but for certain markets and products it may not be so reasonable. The question of when to use overlapping prices is dealt with in detail in Chapter 7. The overlap method is illustrated in Table 9.4.

9.61 In the example in Table 9.4, overlapping prices are obtained for items A and D in March. Their relative prices suggest that one unit of item D is worth two units of item A. If the index is calculated as a direct Carli, the January base period price for item D can be imputed by dividing the price of item A in January by the price ratio of items A and D in March.

9.62 A monthly chain index of arithmetic mean prices will be based on the prices of items A, B and C until March, and from April onwards on the prices of items B, C and D. The replacement item is not included until prices for two successive periods are obtained. Thus, the monthly chain index has the advantage that it is not necessary to carry out any explicit imputation of a reference price for the new item.

9.63 If a direct index is calculated defined as the ratio of the arithmetic mean prices, the price of the new item needs to be adjusted by the price ratio of A and D in March in every subsequent month, which complicates computation. Alternatively, a reference period price of item D for January may be imputed. This, however, results in a different index because the price ratios are implicitly weighted by the relative base period prices in the Dutot index, which is not the case for the Carli or the Jevons indices. For the Jevons index, all three methods give the same result, which is an additional advantage of this approach.

Other formulae for elementary price indices

9.64 A number of other formulae have been suggested for the price indices for elementary aggregates.

Table 9.4 Disappearing and replacement items with overlapping prices

	January	February	March	April	May
			Prices		
Item A	6.00	7.00	5.00		
Item B	3.00	2.00	4.00	5.00	6.00
Item C	7.00	8.00	9.00	10.00	9.00
Item D			10.00	9.00	8.00
Carli index – the arithmetic mean of price ratios					
Impute price for item D in January as 6/(5/10)=12.00					
Direct index	100.00	99.21	115.08	128.17	131.75
Dutot index – the ratio of arithmetic mean prices					
Chain the monthly indices based on matched prices					
Month-to-month index	100.00	106.25	105.88	104.35	95.83
Chained month-to-month index	100.00	106.25	112.50	117.39	112.50
Divide item D's price in April and May by 10/5–2 and use item A's price in January as base price					
Direct index	100.00	106.25	112.50	121.88	118.75
Impute price for item D in January as 6/(5/10)=12.00					
Direct index	100.00	106.25	112.50	109.09	104.55
Jevons index – the ratio of geometric mean prices = geometric mean of price ratios					
Chain the monthly indices based on matched prices					
Month-to-month index	100.00	96.15	117.13	107.72	98.65
Chained month-to-month index	100.00	96.15	112.62	121.32	119.68
Divide item D's price in April and May with 10/5=2 and use item A's price in January as base price					
Direct index	100.00	96.15	112.62	121.32	119.68
Impute price for item D in January as 6/(5/10)=12.00					
Direct index	100.00	96.15	112.62	121.32	119.68

The most important are presented below and discussed further in Chapter 20.

9.65 *Laspeyres and geometric Laspeyres indices*. The Carli, Dutot and Jevons indices are all calculated without the use of explicit weights. However, as already mentioned, in certain cases there may be weighting information that could be exploited in the calculation of the elementary price indices. If the reference period expenditures for all the individual items within an elementary aggregate, or estimates thereof, were to be available, the elementary price index could itself be calculated as a Laspeyres price index, or as a geometric Laspeyres. The Laspeyres price index is defined as:

$$I_{La}^{0:t} = \sum w_i^0 \left(\frac{p_i^t}{p_i^0}\right), \ \sum w_i^0 = 1 \qquad (9.4)$$

where the weights, w_i^0, are the expenditure shares for the individual items in the reference period. If all the weights were equal, the formula (9.4) would reduce to the Carli index. If the weights were proportional to the prices in the reference period, the formula (9.4) would reduce to the Dutot index.

9.66 The geometric version of the Laspeyres index is defined as:

$$\mathrm{I}_{JW}^{0:t} = \prod \left(\frac{p_i^t}{p_i^0}\right)^{w_0^i} = \frac{\prod (p_i^t)^{w_i^0}}{\prod (p_i^0)^{w_i^0}}, \ \sum w_i^0 = 1 \qquad (9.5)$$

where the weights, w_i^0, are again the expenditure shares in the reference period. When the weights are all equal, the formula (9.5) reduces to the Jevons index.

9.67 *Some alternative index formulae*. Another widely used type of average is the harmonic mean. In the present context, there are two possible versions: either the harmonic mean of price ratios or the ratio of harmonic mean prices. The harmonic mean of price relatives, or ratios, is defined as:

$$I_{HR}^{0:t} = \frac{1}{\frac{1}{n}\sum \frac{p_i^0}{p_i^t}} \qquad (9.6)$$

The ratio of harmonic mean prices is defined as:

$$I_{RH}^{0:t} = \frac{\sum \frac{n}{p_i^0}}{\sum \frac{n}{p_i^t}} \qquad (9.7)$$

Formula (9.7), like the Dutot index, fails the commensurability test and would only be an acceptable possibility when the items are all fairly homogeneous. Neither formula appears to be used much in practice, perhaps because the harmonic mean is not a familiar concept and would not be easy to explain to users. Nevertheless, at an aggregate level, the widely used Paasche index is a weighted harmonic average.

9.68 The ranking of the three common types of mean is always arithmetic $\geq$ geometric $\geq$ harmonic. It is shown in Chapter 20 that, in practice, the Carli index (the arithmetic mean of the relatives) is likely to exceed the Jevons index (the geometric mean) by roughly the same amount that the Jevons exceeds the harmonic mean given by the formula (9.6). The harmonic mean of the price relatives has the same kinds of axiomatic properties as the Carli index, but with opposite tendencies and biases. It fails the transitivity, time reversal and price bouncing tests. As it can be viewed conceptually as the complement, or rough mirror image, of the Carli index, it has been argued that a suitable elementary index would be provided by a geometric mean of the two, in the same way that, at an aggregate level, a geometric mean is taken of the Laspeyres and Paasche indices to obtain the Fisher index. Such an index has been proposed by Carruthers, Sellwood and Ward (1980) and Dalén (1992), namely:

$$I_{CSWD}^{0:t} = (I_C^{0:t} I_{HR}^{0:t})^{1/2} \tag{9.8}$$

I_{CSWD} is shown in Chapter 20 to have very good axiomatic properties, although not quite as good as the Jevons index, which is transitive, whereas the I_{CSWD} is not. It can, however, be shown to be approximately transitive, and it has been observed empirically to be very close to the Jevons index.

9.69 In recent years, attention has focused on formulae that can take account of the substitution that may take place within an elementary aggregate. As already explained, the Carli and the Jevons indices may be expected to approximate to the cost of living index if the cross-elasticities of substitution are close to 0 and 1, respectively, on average. A more flexible formula that allows for different elasticities of substitution is the unweighted Lloyd–Moulton (LM) index:

$$I_{LM}^{0:t} = \left[\sum \frac{1}{n} \left(\frac{P_i^t}{P_i^0} \right)^{1-\sigma} \right]^{\frac{1}{1-\sigma}} \tag{9.9}$$

where σ is the elasticity of substitution. The Carli and the Jevons indices can be viewed as special cases of the LM in which $\sigma = 0$ and $\sigma = 1$. The advantage of the LM formula is that σ is unrestricted. Provided a satisfactory estimate can be made of σ, the resulting elementary price index is likely to approximate to the underlying cost of living index. The LM index reduces "substitution bias" when the objective is to estimate the cost of living index. The difficulty is the need to estimate elasticities of substitution, a task that will require substantial development and maintenance work. The formula is described in more detail in Chapter 17.

Unit value indices

9.70 The unit value index is simple in form. The unit value in each period is calculated by dividing total expenditure on some product by the related total quantity. It is clear that the quantities must be strictly additive in an economic sense, which implies that they should relate to a single homogeneous product. The unit value index is then defined as the ratio of unit values in the current period to that in the reference period. It is not a price index as normally understood, as it is essentially a measure of the change in the average price of a *single* product when that product is sold at different prices to different consumers, perhaps at different times within the same period. Unit values, and unit value indices, should not be calculated for sets of heterogeneous products.

9.71 Unit values do play an important part in the process of calculating an elementary price index, as they are the appropriate average prices that need to be entered into an elementary price index. Usually, prices are sampled at a particular time or period each month, and each price is assumed to be representative of the average price of that item in that period. In practice, this assumption may not hold. In this case, it is necessary to estimate the unit value for each item, even though this will inevitably be more costly. Thus, having specified the item to be priced in a particular store, data should be collected on both the value of the total sales in a particular month and the total quantities sold in order to derive a unit value to be used as the price input into an elementary aggregate formula. It is particularly important to do this if the item is sold at a sale price for part of the period and at the regular price in the rest of the period. Under these conditions, neither the sale price nor the regular price is likely to be representative of the average price at which the item has been sold or the price change between periods. The unit value over the whole month should be used. With the possibility of collecting more and more data from electronic points of sale, such procedures may be increasingly used. It should be stressed, however, that the item specifications must remain constant through time. Changes in the item specifications could lead to unit value changes that reflect quantity or quality changes, and should not be part of price changes.

Formulae applicable to scanner data

9.72 Scanner data obtained from electronic points of sale are becoming an increasingly important source of data for CPI compilation. Their main advantage is that the number of price observations can be enormously increased and that both price and quantity information is available in real time. There are, however, many practical considerations to be taken into consideration which are discussed in other chapters of this manual.

9.73 Access to detailed and comprehensive quantity and expenditure information within an elementary aggregate means that there are no constraints on the type of index number that may be employed. Not only Laspeyres and Paasche but superlative indices such as Fisher and Törnqvist may be envisaged. As noted at the beginning of this chapter, it is preferable to introduce weighting information as it becomes available rather than continuing to rely on simple unweighted indices such as Carli and Jevons. Advances in technology, both in the retail outlets themselves and in the computing power available to statistical offices, suggest that traditional elementary price indices may eventually be replaced by superlative indices, at least for some elementary aggregates in some countries. The methodology must be kept under review in the light of the resources available.

The calculation of higher-level indices

9.74 A statistical office must have some target index at which to aim. Statistical offices have to consider what kind of index they would choose to calculate in the ideal hypothetical situation in which they had complete information about prices and quantities in both time periods compared. If the CPI is meant to be a *cost of living index*, then a superlative index such as a Fisher, Walsh or Tornqvist–Theil would have to serve as the theoretical target, as a superlative index may be expected to approximate to the underlying cost of living index.

9.75 Many countries do not aim to calculate a cost of living index and prefer the concept of a *basket index*. A basket index is one that measures the change in the total value of a given basket of goods and services between two time periods. This general category of index is described here as a *Lowe index* (see Chapters 1 and 15). The meaning of a Lowe index is clear and can be easily explained to users, these being important considerations for many statistical offices. It should be noted that, in general, there is no necessity for the basket to be the actual basket in one or other of the two periods compared. If the theoretical target index is to be a basket or Lowe index, the preferred basket might be one that attaches equal importance to the baskets in both periods; for example, the Walsh index. The quantities that make up the basket in the Walsh index are the geometric means of the quantities in the two periods. Thus, the same kind of index may emerge as the theoretical target in both the basket and the cost of living approaches. In practice, a statistical office may prefer to designate a basket index that uses the actual basket in the earlier of the two periods as its target index on grounds of simplicity and practicality. In other words, the Laspeyres index may be the target index.

9.76 The theoretical target index is a matter of choice. In practice, it is likely to be either a Laspeyres or some superlative index. Even when the target index is the Laspeyres, there may a considerable gap between what is actually calculated and what the statistical office considers to be its target. It is now necessary to consider what statistical offices tend to do in practice.

Consumer price indices as weighted averages of elementary indices

9.77 A higher-level index is an index for some expenditure aggregate above the level of an elementary aggregate, including the overall CPI itself. The inputs into the calculation of the higher-level indices are:

- the elementary price indices;
- weights derived from the values of elementary aggregates in some earlier year or years.

9.78 The higher-level indices are calculated simply as weighted arithmetic averages of the elementary price indices. This general category of index is described here as a *Young index* after another nineteenth-century index number pioneer who advocated this type of index.

9.79 The weights typically remain fixed for a sequence of at least 12 months. Some countries revise their weights at the beginning of each year in order to try to approximate as closely as possible to current consumption patterns, but many countries continue to use the same weights for several years. The weights may be changed only every five years or so. The use of fixed weights has the considerable practical advantage that the index can make repeated use of the same weights. This saves both time and money. Revising the weights can be both time-consuming and costly, especially if it requires new household expenditure surveys to be carried out.

9.80 The second stage of calculating a CPI does not involve individual prices or quantities. Instead, a higher-level index is a Young index in which the elementary price indices are averaged using a set of pre-determined weights. The formula can be written as follows:

$$I^{0:t} = \sum w_i^b I_i^{0:t}, \quad \sum w_i^b = 1 \tag{9.10}$$

where $I^{0:t}$ denotes the overall CPI, or any higher-level index, from period 0 to t; w_i^b is the weight attached to each of the elementary price indices; and $I_i^{0:t}$ is the corresponding elementary price index. The elementary indices are identified by the subscript i, whereas the higher-level index carries no subscript. As already noted, a higher-level index is any index, including the overall CPI, above the elementary aggregate level. The weights are derived from expenditures in period b, which in practice has to precede period 0, the price reference period.

9.81 It is useful to recall that three kinds of reference period may be distinguished for CPI purposes:

- *Weight reference period.* The period covered by the expenditure statistics used to calculate the weights. Usually, the weight reference period is a year.
- *Price reference period.* The period for which prices are used as denominators in the index calculation.
- *Index reference period.* The period for which the index is set to 100.

9.82 The three periods are generally different. For example, a CPI might have 1998 as the weight reference year, December 2002 as the price reference month and the year 2000 as the index reference period. The weights typically refer to a whole year, or even two or three years, whereas the periods for which prices are compared are typically months or quarters. The weights are usually estimated on the basis of an expenditure survey that was conducted some time before the price reference period. For these reasons, the weight reference period and the price reference period are invariably separate periods in practice.

9.83 The index reference period is often a year; but it could be a month or some other period. An index series may also be re-referenced to another period by simply dividing the series by the value of the index in that period, without changing the rate of change of the index. The expression "base period" can mean any of the three reference periods and is ambiguous. The expression "base period" should only be used when it is absolutely clear in context exactly which period is referred to.

9.84 Provided the elementary aggregate indices are calculated using a transitive formula such as the Jevons or Dutot, but not the Carli, and provided that there are no new or disappearing items from period 0 to t, equation (9.10) is equivalent to:

$$I^{0:t} = \sum w_i^b I_i^{0:t-1} I_i^{t-1:t}, \quad \sum w_i^b = 1, \tag{9.11}$$

The advantage of this version of the index is that it allows the sampled products within the elementary price index from $t-1$ to t to differ from the sampled products in the periods from 0 to $t-1$. Hence, it allows replacement items and new items to be linked into the index from period $t-1$ without the need to estimate a price for period 0. For example, if one of the sampled items in periods 0 and $t-1$ is no longer available in period t, and the price of a replacement product is available for $t-1$ at t, the new replacement product can be included in the index using the overlap method.

A numerical example

9.85 Equation (9.10) applies at each level of aggregation. The index is additive; that is, the overall index is the same whether calculated on the basis of the original elementary price indices or on the basis of the intermediate higher-level indices. This facilitates the presentation of the index.

9.86 Table 9.5 illustrates the calculation of higher-level indices in the special case where the weight and the price reference period are identical, i.e. $b=0$. The index consists of five elementary aggregate indices and two intermediate higher-level indices, G and H. The overall index and the higher-level indices are all calculated using equation (9.10). Thus, for example, the overall index for April can be calculated from the two intermediate higher-level indices for April as:

$$I^{Jan:Apr} = 0.6 \times 103.92 + 0.4 \times 101.79 = 103.06$$

or directly from the five elementary indices as:

$$I^{Jan:Apr} = 0.2 \times 108.75 + 0.25 \times 100 + 0.15 \times 104 + 0.1 \times 107.14 + 0.3 \times 100 = 103.06$$

Note from equation (9.11) that:

$$I^{0:t} = \sum w_i^b I_i^{0:t-1} I_i^{t-1:t} \neq I^{0:t-1} \sum w_i^b I_i^{t-1:t} \Rightarrow \frac{I^{0:t}}{I^{0:t-1}} \neq \sum w_i^b I_i^{t-1:t} \qquad (9.12)$$

This shows that if the month-to-month indices are averaged using the fixed weights w_i^b, the resulting index is *not* equal to the month-to-month higher-level index. As explained later, in order to be able to obtain the month-to-month higher-level index, the weights applied to the month-to-month indices need to be updated to reflect the effects of the price changes that have taken place since January.

Young and Lowe indices

9.87 It is useful to clarify the relationship between Lowe and Young indices. As already noted, when statistical offices explain their CPIs to users they often describe them as Lowe indices, which measure the change over time in the value of a fixed basket of goods and services. But when they calculate their CPIs, the formula they actually use is that of a Young index. The relationship between the two indices is given in equation (9.13), where I_{Lo} is the Lowe index and I_{Yo} is the Young index:

$$I_{Lo} = \frac{\sum p_j^t q_j^b}{\sum p_j^0 q_j^b} = \frac{\sum p_j^t q_j^b}{\sum p_j^b q_j^b} \Big/ \frac{\sum p_j^0 q_j^b}{\sum p_j^b q_j^b} = \sum w_j \left(\frac{p_j^t}{p_j^0}\right) = I_{Yo}$$

$$\text{where} \quad w_j = \frac{p_j^o q_j^b}{\sum p_j^0 q_j^b} \qquad (9.13)$$

The values q_j^b, the individual quantities in the weight reference period b, make up the basket. Assume initially that the weight reference period b has the same duration as that of the two periods 0 and t that are being compared. It can be seen from the relationship (9.13) that:

- the Lowe index is equal to a Young index in which the weights are *hybrid* value shares obtained by revaluing the values q^b, the quantities in the weight reference period b, at the prices of the price reference month 0;
- the Lowe index can be expressed as the ratio of the two Laspeyres indices for periods t and 0, respectively, based on month b;
- the Lowe index reduces to the Laspeyres index when $b = 0$, and to the Paasche index when $b=t$.

9.88 In practice, the situation is more complicated for actual CPIs because the duration of the reference period b is typically much longer than periods 0 and t. The weights w_j usually refer to the expenditures over a period of a year, or longer, while the price reference period is usually a month in some later year. For example, a monthly index may be compiled from January 2003 onwards with December 2002 as the price reference

Table 9.5 The aggregation of elementary price indices

	Weight	January	February	March	April	May	June
Month-to-month elementary price indices							
A	0.20	100.00	102.50	104.88	101.16	101.15	100.00
B	0.25	100.00	100.00	91.67	109.09	101.67	108.20
C	0.15	100.00	104.00	96.15	104.00	101.92	103.77
D	0.10	100.00	92.86	107.69	107.14	100.00	102.67
E	0.30	100.00	101.67	100.00	98.36	103.33	106.45
Direct or chained monthly elementary price indices with January=100							
A	0.20	100.00	102.50	107.50	108.75	110.00	110.00
B	0.25	100.00	100.00	91.67	100.00	101.67	110.00
C	0.15	100.00	104.00	100.00	104.00	106.00	110.00
D	0.10	100.00	92.86	100.00	107.14	107.14	110.00
E	0.30	100.00	101.67	101.67	100.00	103.33	110.00
Total		100.00	100.89	99.92	103.06	105.03	110.00
Higher-level indices							
G=A+B+C	0.60	100.00	101.83	99.03	103.92	105.53	110.00
H=D+E	0.40	100.00	99.46	101.25	101.79	104.29	110.00
Total		100.00	100.89	99.92	103.06	105.03	110.00

month, but the latest available weights during the year 2003 may refer to the year 2000 or even some earlier year.

9.89 Conceptually, a typical CPI may be viewed as a Lowe index that measures the change from month to month in the total cost of an annual basket of goods and services that may date back several years before the price reference period. Because it uses the fixed basket of an earlier period, it is sometimes loosely described as a "Laspeyres-type index", but this description is unwarranted. A true Laspeyres index would require the basket to be that consumed in the price reference month, whereas in most CPIs the basket not only refers to a different period from the price reference month but to a period of a year or more. When the weights are annual and the prices are monthly, it is not possible, even retrospectively, to calculate a monthly Laspeyres price index.

9.90 As shown in Chapter 15, a Lowe index that uses quantities derived from an earlier period than the price reference period is likely to exceed the Laspeyres, and by a progressively larger amount, the further back in time the weight reference period is. The Lowe index is likely to have an even greater upward bias than the Laspeyres as compared with some target superlative index or underlying cost of living index. Inevitably, the quantities in any basket index become increasingly out of date and irrelevant the further back in time the period to which they relate. To minimize the resulting bias, the weights should be updated as often as possible.

9.91 A statistical office may not wish to estimate a cost of living index and may prefer to choose some basket index as its target index. In that case, if the theoretically attractive Walsh index were to be selected as the target index, a Lowe index would have the same bias as just described, given that the Walsh index is also a superlative index.

Factoring the Young index

9.92 It is possible to calculate the change in a higher-level Young index between two consecutive periods, such as $t-1$ and t, as a weighted average of the individual price indices between $t-1$ and t provided that the weights are updated to take account of the price changes between the price reference period 0 and the previous period, $t-1$. This makes it possible to factor the formula (9.10) into the product of two component indices in the following way:

$$I^{0:t} = I^{0:t-1}\sum w_i^{b(t-1)} I_i^{t-1:1}$$

$$\text{where} \quad w_i^{b(t-1)} = w_i^b I_i^{0:t-1} \Big/ \sum w_i^b I_i^{0:t-1}. \qquad (9.14)$$

$I^{0:t-1}$ is the Young index for period $t-1$. The weight $w_i^{b(t-1)}$ is the original weight for elementary aggregate i price-updated by multiplying it by the elementary price index for i between 0 and $t-1$, the adjusted weights being rescaled to sum to unity. The price-updated weights are hybrid weights because they implicitly revalue the quantities of b at the prices of $t-1$ instead of at the average prices of b. Such hybrid weights do not measure the actual expenditure shares of any period.

9.93 The index for period t can thus be calculated by multiplying the already calculated index for $t-1$ by a separate Young index between $t-1$ and t with hybrid price-updated weights. In effect, the higher-level index is calculated as a chain index in which the index is moved forward period by period. This method gives more flexibility to introduce replacement items and makes it easier to monitor the movements of the recorded prices for errors, as month-to-month movements are smaller and less variable than the total changes since the base period.

9.94 Price-updating may also occur between the weight reference period and the price reference period, as explained in the next section.

Price-updating from the weight reference period to the price reference period

9.95 When the weight reference period b and the price reference period 0 are different, as is normally the case, the statistical office has to decide whether or not to price-update the weights from b to 0. In practice, the price-updated weights can be calculated by multiplying the original weights for period b by elementary indices measuring the price changes between periods b and 0 and rescaling to sum to unity.

9.96 The issues involved are best explained with the help of a numerical example. In Table 9.6, the base period b is assumed to be the year 2000, so the weights are the expenditure shares in 2000. In section (a) of Table 9.6, 2000 is also used as the price reference period. In practice, however, weights based on 2000 cannot be introduced until some time after 2000 because of the time needed to collect and process the expenditure data. In section (b) of Table 9.6, it is assumed that the 2000 weights are introduced in December 2002 and that this is also chosen as the new price reference base.

9.97 Note that it would be possible in December 2002 to calculate the indices based on 2000 shown in section (a) of the table, but it is decided to make December 2002 the price reference base. This does not prevent the index with the December 2002 price reference period from being calculated backwards a few months into 2002, if desired.

9.98 The statistical office compiling the index has two options at the time the new index is introduced. It has to decide whether the weights in the new index should preserve the quantities in 2000 or the expenditures in 2000. It cannot do both.

9.99 If it is decided to preserve the quantities, the resulting index is a basket index, or Lowe index, in which the quantities are those of the year 2000. This implies that the *movements* of the index must be identical with those of the index based on 2000 shown in section (a) of the table. In this case, if the index is to be presented as a weighted average of the elementary price indices with December 2002 as the price reference period, the expenditure weights for 2000 have to be price-updated to December 2002. This is illustrated in section (b) of Table 9.6, where the updated weights are obtained by multiplying the original weights for 2000 in section (a) of the

Table 9.6 Price-updating of weights between the weight and price reference periods

	Weight	2000	Nov. 02	Dec. 02	Jan. 03	Feb. 03	Mar. 03
(a) Index with 2000 as weight and price reference period							
				Elementary price indices			
	w_{00}						
A	0.20	100.00	98.00	99.00	102.00	101.00	104.00
B	0.25	100.00	106.00	108.00	107.00	109.00	110.00
C	0.15	100.00	104.00	106.00	98.00	100.00	97.00
D	0.10	100.00	101.00	104.00	108.00	112.00	114.00
E	0.30	100.00	102.00	103.00	106.00	105.00	106.00
				Higher-level indices			
G = A + B + C	0.60	100.00	102.83	104.50	103.08	104.08	104.75
H = D + E	0.40	100.00	101.75	103.25	106.50	106.75	108.00
Total		100.00	102.40	104.00	104.45	105.15	106.05
(b) Index re-referenced to December 2002 and weights price-updated to December 2002							
				Elementary price indices			
	$w_{00(Dec02)}$						
A	0.190	101.01	98.99	100.00	103.03	102.02	105.05
B	0.260	92.59	98.15	100.00	99.07	100.93	101.85
C	0.153	94.34	98.11	100.00	92.45	94.34	91.51
D	0.100	96.15	97.12	100.00	103.85	107.69	109.62
E	0.297	97.09	99.03	100.00	102.91	101.94	102.91
				Higher-level indices			
G = A + B + C	0.603	95.69	98.41	100.00	98.64	99.60	100.24
H = D + E	0.397	96.85	98.55	100.00	103.15	103.39	104.60
Total		96.15	98.46	100.00	100.43	101.11	101.97
Rescaled to 2000 = 100		100.00	102.40	104.00	104.45	105.15	106.05

table by the price indices for the elementary aggregates between 2000 and December 2002, and then rescaling the results to sum to unity. These are the weights labelled $w_{00(Dec02)}$ in the table.

9.100 The indices with price-updated weights in section (b) of Table 9.6 are Lowe indices in which b = 2000 and 0 = December 2002. These indices can be expressed as ratios of the indices in the upper part of the table. For example, the overall Lowe index for March 2003 with December 2002 as its price reference base, namely 101.97, is the ratio of the index for March 2003 based on 2000 shown in section (a) of the table, namely 106.05, divided by the index for December 2002 based on 2000, namely 104.00. Thus, the price-updating preserves the movements of the indices in section (a) of the table while shifting the price reference period to December 2002.

9.101 Alternatively, it could be decided to calculate a series of Young indices using the expenditure weights from 2000 as they stand without updating. If the expenditure shares were actually to remain constant, the quantities would have had to move inversely with the prices between 2000 and December 2002. The quantities that make up the basket for the new Young index could not be the same as those of 2000. The movements of this index would have to be slightly different from those of the price-updated index.

9.102 The issue is whether to stick with the known quantities of the weight reference period 2000, which are the latest for which firm data have been collected, or to stick with the known expenditure shares of the weight reference period. If the official objective is to measure a Lowe index that uses a fixed basket, the issue is decided and the statistical office is obliged to price-update. On the other hand, some statistical offices may have to decide for themselves which option to adopt.

9.103 Updating the prices without updating the quantities does not imply that the resulting expenditure weights are necessarily more up to date. When there is a strong inverse relation between movements of price and quantities, price-updating on its own could produce perverse results. For example, the prices of computers have been declining rapidly in recent years. If the quantities are held fixed while the prices are updated, the resulting expenditures on computers would also decline rapidly. In practice, however, the share of expenditures on computers might be actually be rising because of a very rapid increase in quantities of computers purchased.

9.104 When there are rapid changes taking place in relative quantities as well as relative prices, statistical offices are effectively obliged to change their expenditure weights more frequently, even if this means conducting more frequent expenditure surveys. Price-updating on its own cannot cope with this situation. The expenditure weights have to be updated with respect to their quantities as well as their prices, which, in effect, implies collecting new expenditure data.

The introduction of new weights and chain linking

9.105 From time to time, the weights for the elementary aggregates have to be revised to ensure that they reflect current expenditure patterns and consumer behaviour. When new weights are introduced, the price reference period for the new index can be the last period of the old index, the old and the new indices being linked together at this point. The old and the new indices make a chain index.

9.106 The introduction of new weights is often a complex operation because it provides the opportunity to introduce new items, new samples, new data sources, new compilation practices, new elementary aggregates, new higher-level indices or new classifications. These tasks are often undertaken simultaneously at the time of reweighting to minimize overall disruption to the time series and any resulting inconvenience to users of the indices.

9.107 In many countries, reweighting and chaining are carried out about every five years, but some countries introduce new weights each year. Chain indices do not have to be linked annually; the linking may be done less frequently. The real issue is not whether to chain or not but how frequently to chain. Reweighting is inevitable sooner or later, as the same weights cannot continue to be used for ever. Whatever the time frame, statistical offices have to address the issue of chain linking sooner or later. It is inevitable and a major task for index compilers.

9.108 *Frequency of reweighting.* It is reasonable to continue to use the same set of elementary aggregate weights so long as consumption patterns at the elementary aggregate level remain fairly stable. Over time, consumers will tend to substitute away from products of which the prices have increased relatively. Thus, in general, movements in prices and quantities tend to be inversely related. This kind of substitution behaviour on the part of consumers implies that a Lowe index based on the fixed basket of an earlier period will tend to have an upward bias compared with a basket index using up-to-date weights.

9.109 Another reason why consumption patterns change is that new products are continually being introduced on the market while others drop out. Over the longer term, consumption patterns are also influenced by several other factors. These include rising incomes and standards of living, demographic changes in the structure of the population, changes in technology, and changes in tastes and preferences.

9.110 There is wide consensus that regular updating of weights – at least every five years, and more often if there is evidence of rapid changes in consumption patterns – is a sensible and necessary practice. The question of how often to change the weights and chain link the index is nevertheless not straightforward, as frequent linking can also have some disadvantages. It can be costly to obtain new weights, especially if they require more frequent expenditure surveys. Annual chaining has the advantage that changes (such as the inclusion of new goods) can be introduced on a regular basis, although every index needs some ongoing maintenance, whether annually chained or not.

9.111 Expenditures on certain types of products are strongly influenced by short-term fluctuations in the economy. For example, expenditures on cars, major durables, expensive luxuries, and so on, may change drastically from year to year. In such cases, it may be preferable to base the weight on an average of two or more years of expenditure.

9.112 *The calculation of a chain index.* Assume that a series of fixed weight Young indices has been calculated with period 0 as the price reference period and that in a subsequent period, k, a new set of weights has to be introduced in the index. The new set of weights may, or may not, have been price-updated from the new weight reference period to period k. A chain index is then calculated as:

$$\begin{aligned} I^{0:t} &= I^{0:k}\sum w_i^k I_i^{k:t-1} I_i^{t-1:t} \\ &= I^{0:k}\sum w_i^k I_i^{k:t} \\ &= I^{0.k} I^{k.t} \end{aligned} \qquad (9.15)$$

9.113 There are several important features of a chain index:

- The chain index formula allows weights to be updated, and facilitates the introduction of new items and sub-indices and the removal of obsolete ones.
- In order to be able to link the old and the new series, an overlapping period (k) is needed in which the index has to be calculated using both the old and the new set of weights.
- A chain index may have two or more links. Between each link period, the index may be calculated as a fixed weight index using the formula (9.10), or indeed using any other index formula. The link period may be a month or a year, provided the weights and indices refer to the same period.
- Chaining is intended to ensure that the individual indices on all levels show the correct development through time.
- Chaining leads to non-additivity. When the new series is chained onto the old, as in equation (9.15), the higher-level indices after the link cannot be obtained as weighted arithmetic averages of individual indices using the new weights. If, on the other hand, the index reference period is changed and the index series prior to the link period is rescaled to the new index reference period, this series cannot be aggregated to higher-level indices by use of the new weights. Such results need to be carefully explained and presented.

9.114 An example of the calculation of a chain index is presented in Table 9.7. From 1998 to December 2002 the index is calculated with the year 1998 as weight and price reference period. From December 2002 onwards, a new set of weights is introduced. The weights may refer to the year 2000, for example, and may or may not have been price-updated to December 2002. A new fixed weight index series is then calculated with December 2002 as the price reference month. Finally, the new index series is linked onto the old index with 1998 = 100 by multiplication to get a continuous index from 1998 to March 2003. The chained higher-level indices in Table 9.7 are calculated as:

$$I^{00:t} = I^{98:Dec02}\sum w_i^{00(Dec\,02)} I_i^{Dec\,02:t} \qquad (9.16)$$

Because of the lack of additivity, the overall chain index for March 2003 (129.07), for example, cannot be calculated as the weighted arithmetic mean of the chained higher-level indices G and H using the weights from December 2002.

Table 9.7 Calculation of a chain index

	Weight 1998	1998	Nov. 2002	Dec. 2002	Weight 2000	Dec. 2002	Jan. 2003	Feb. 2003	Mar. 2003
		1998 = 100				*December 2002 = 100*			
Elementary price indices									
A	0.20	100.00	120.00	121.00	0.25	100.00	100.00	100.00	102.00
B	0.25	100.00	115.00	117.00	0.20	100.00	102.00	103.00	104.00
C	0.15	100.00	132.00	133.00	0.10	100.00	98.00	98.00	97.00
D	0.10	100.00	142.00	143.00	0.18	100.00	101.00	104.00	104.00
E	0.30	100.00	110.00	124.00	0.27	100.00	103.00	105.00	106.00
Total		100.00	119.75	124.90		100.00	101.19	102.47	103.34
Higher-level indices									
G = A + B + C	0.60	100.00	120.92	122.33	0.55	100.00	100.36	100.73	101.82
H = D + E	0.40	100.00	118.00	128.75	0.45	100.00	102.20	104.60	105.20
Total		100.00	119.75	124.90		100.00	101.19	102.47	103.34
Chaining of higher-level indices to 1998 = 100									
G = A + B + C	0.60	100.00	120.92	122.33	0.55	122.33	122.78	123.22	124.56
H = D + E	0.40	100.00	118.00	128.75	0.45	128.75	131.58	134.67	135.45
Total		100.00	119.75	124.90		124.90	126.39	127.99	129.07

9.115 *The introduction of new elementary aggregates.* First, consider the situation in which new weights are introduced and the index is chain linked in December 2002. The overall coverage of the CPI is assumed to remain the same, but certain items have increased sufficiently in importance to merit recognition as new elementary aggregates. Possible examples are the introduction of new elementary aggregates for mobile telephones or Internet access.

9.116 Consider the calculation of the new index from December 2002 onwards, the new price reference period. The calculation of the new index presents no special problems and can be carried out using formula (9.10). However, if the weights are price-updated from, say, 2000 to December 2002, difficulties may arise because the elementary aggregate for mobile telephones did not exist prior to December 2002, so there is no price index with which to price-update the weight for mobile telephones. Prices for mobile telephones may have been recorded prior to December 2002, possibly within another elementary aggregate (communications equipment), so it may be possible to construct a price series which can be used for price-updating. Otherwise, price information from other sources, such as purchasing power parity (PPP) surveys, business statistics, or industry sources, may have to be used. If no information is available, then movements in the price indices for similar elementary aggregates may be used as proxies for price-updating.

9.117 The inclusion of a new elementary aggregate means that the next higher-level index contains a different number of elementary aggregates before and after the linking. Therefore, the rate of change of the higher-level index whose composition has changed may be difficult to interpret. However, failing to introduce new goods or services for this reason would result in an index that does not reflect the actual dynamic changes taking place in the economy. If it is customary to revise the CPI backwards, then the prices of the new product and their weights might be introduced retrospectively. If the CPI is not revised backwards, which is usually the case, there is little that can be done to improve the quality of the chain index. In many cases, the addition of a single elementary aggregate is unlikely to have a significant effect on the next higher-level index into which it enters. If the addition of an elementary aggregate is believed to have a significant impact on the time series of the higher-level index, it may be necessary to discontinue the old series and commence a new higher-level index. These decisions can only be made on a case-by-case basis.

9.118 *The introduction of new higher-level indices.* It may be necessary to introduce a new higher-level index in the overall CPI. This situation may occur if the coverage of the CPI is enlarged or the grouping of elementary aggregates is changed. It then needs to be decided what the initial value of the new higher-level index should be when it is included in the calculation of the overall CPI. Take as an example the situation in Table 9.7 and assume that a new higher-level index from January 2003 has to be included in the index. The question is then what should be the December 2002 value to which the new higher-level index is to be linked. There are two options:

- Estimate the value in December 2002 that the new higher-level index would have had with 1998 as the price reference period, and link the new series from January 2003 onwards on to this value. This procedure will prevent any break in the index series.
- Use 100 in December 2002 as the starting point for the new higher-level index. This simplifies the problem from a calculation perspective, although there remains the difficulty of explaining the index break to users.

In any case, major changes such as those just described should, so far as possible, be made in connection with the regular reweighting and chaining in order to minimize disruptions to the index series.

9.119 A final case to consider concerns classification change. For example, a country may decide to change from a national classification to an international one, such as the Classification of Individual Consumption according to Purpose (COICOP). The changes in the composition of the aggregates within the CPI may then be so large that it is not meaningful to link them. In such cases, it is recommended that the CPI with the new classification should be calculated backwards for at least one year so that consistent annual rates of change can be calculated.

9.120 *Partial reweighting*. The weights for the elementary aggregates may be obtained from a variety of sources over a number of different periods. Consequently, it may not be possible to introduce all the new weighting information at the same time. In some cases, it may be preferable to introduce new weights for some elementary aggregates as soon as possible after the information is received. The introduction of new weights for a subset of the overall index is known as partial reweighting.

9.121 Partial reweighting has particular implications for the practice of price-updating the weights. Weighting information may not be available for some elementary aggregates at the time of rebasing. Thus, it may be necessary to consider price-updating not only the new weights, but also the old weights for those elementary aggregates for which no new weights are available. The weights for the latter may have to be price-updated over a long period, which, for reasons given earlier, may give rise to serious problems if relative quantities have changed inversely to the relative price changes. Data on both quantity and price changes should be sought before undertaking such updates. The disadvantage of partial reweighting is that the implicit quantities belong to different periods, so that the composition of the basket is obscure and not well defined.

9.122 It may be concluded that the introduction of new weights and the linking of a new series to an old series is not difficult in principle. The difficulties arise in practice when trying to align weight and price reference periods and when deciding whether higher-level indices comprising different elementary aggregates should be chained over time. It is not possible for this manual to provide specific guidance on decisions such as these, but compilers should consider carefully the economic logic and statistical reliability of the resulting chained series and also the needs of users. In order to facilitate the decision-making process, careful thought should be given to these issues in advance during the planning of a reweighting exercise, paying particular attention to which of the indices are to be published.

9.123 *Long-term and short-term links*. Consider a long-term chain index in which the weights are changed annually. In any given year, the current monthly indices are first calculated using the latest set of available weights, which cannot be those of the current year. However, when the weights for the year in question become available subsequently, the monthly indices can then be recalculated on the basis of the weights for that same year. The resulting series can then be used in the long-term chain index, rather than the original indices first published. Thus, the movements of the long-term chain index from, say, any one December to the following December are based on weights of that same year, the weights being changed each December. This method has been developed by the Central Statistical Office of Sweden, where it is applied in the calculation of the CPI. It is described in *Swedish Consumer Price Index: A Handbook of Methods* (Statistics Sweden, 2001).

9.124 Assume that each link runs from December to December. The long-term index for month m of year Y with December of year 0 as index reference period is then calculated using the formula:

$$I^{Dec0:mY} = \left(\prod_{y=1}^{Y-1} I^{Decy-1:Decy} \right) I^{DecY-1:mY} = I^{Dec0:Dec1} I^{Dec1:Dec2} \ldots I^{DecY-2:DecY-1} I^{DecY-1:mY} \quad (9.17)$$

In the actual Swedish practice, a factor scaling the index from December year 0 to the average of year 0 is multiplied onto the right-hand side of the formula (9.19) to have a full year as the reference period. The long-term movement of the index depends on the long-term links only, as the short-term links are successively replaced by their long-term counterparts. For example, let the short-term indices for January to December 2001 be calculated as:

$$I^{Dec00:m01} = \sum w_i^{00(Dec00)} I_i^{Dec00:m01} \quad (9.18)$$

where $W_i^{00(Dec00)}$ are the weights from 2000 price-updated to December 2000. When weights for 2001 become available, this is replaced by the long-term link:

$$I^{Dec00:Dec01} = \sum w_i^{01(Dec00)} I_i^{Dec00:Dec01} \quad (9.19)$$

where $W_i^{01(Dec00)}$ are the weights from 2001 price-backdated to December 2000. The same set of weights from 2001 price-updated to December 2001 is used in the new short-term link for 2002:

$$I^{Dec01:m02} = \sum w_i^{01(Dec01)} I_i^{Dec01:m02}. \quad (9.20)$$

9.125 Using this method, the movement of the long-term index is determined by contemporaneous weights. The method is conceptually attractive because the weights that are most relevant for most users are those based on consumption patterns at the time the price changes actually take place. The method takes the process of chaining to its logical conclusion, at least assuming the indices are not chained more frequently than once a year. As the method uses weights that are continually revised to ensure that they are representative of current consumer behaviour, the resulting index also largely avoids the substitution bias that occurs when the weights are based on the consumption patterns of some period in the past. The method may therefore appeal to statistical offices whose objective is to estimate a cost of living index.

9.126 Finally, it may be noted that the method involves some revision of the index first published. In some countries, there is opposition to revising a CPI once it has been first published, although it is standard practice for other economic statistics, including the national accounts, to be revised as more information and more up-to-date information become available. This point is considered further below.

Decomposition of index changes

9.127 Users of the index are often interested in how much of the change in the overall index is attributable to the change in the price of some particular good or group of products, such as oil or food. Alternatively, there may be interest in what the index would be if housing or energy were left out. Questions of this kind can be answered by decomposing the change in the overall index into its constituent parts.

9.128 Assume that the index is calculated as in equation (9.10) or (9.11). The relative change of the index from $t-m$ to t can then be written as:

$$\frac{I^{0:t}}{I^{0:t-m}} - 1 = \frac{\sum w_i^b I_i^{0:t-m} I_i^{t-m:t}}{\sum w_i^b I_i^{0:t-m}} - 1 \qquad (9.21)$$

Hence, a sub-index from $t-m$ to 0 enters the higher-level index with a weight of:

$$\frac{w_i^b I_i^{0:t-m}}{\sum w_i^b I_i^{0:t-m}} = \frac{w_i^b I_i^{0:t-m}}{I^{0:t-m}} \qquad (9.22)$$

The effect on the higher-level index of a change in a sub-index can then be calculated as:

$$Effect = \frac{w_i^b I_i^{0:t-m}}{I^{0:t-m}} \left(\frac{I_i^{0:t}}{I_i^{0:t-m}} - 1 \right)$$
$$= \frac{w_i^b}{I^{0:t-m}} (I_i^{0:t} - I_i^{0:t-m}) \qquad (9.23)$$

With $m=1$, the formula (9.23) gives the effect of a monthly change; with $m=12$, it gives the effect of the change over the past 12 months.

9.129 If the index is calculated as a chain index, as in equation (9.15), then a sub-index from $t-m$ enters the higher-level index with a weight of:

$$\frac{w_i^0 I_i^{k:t-m}}{I^{k:t-m}} = \frac{w_i^0 (I_i^{0:t-m} / I_i^{0:k})}{(I^{0:t-m} / I^{0:k})} \qquad (9.24)$$

The effect on the higher-level index of a change in a sub-index can then be calculated as:

$$Effect = \frac{w_i^0}{I^{k:t-m}} (I_i^{k:t} - I_i^{k:t-m})$$
$$= \frac{w_i^0}{(I^{0:t-m} / I^{0:k})} \left(\frac{I_i^{0:t} - I_i^{0:t-m}}{I_i^{0:k}} \right) \qquad (9.25)$$

It is assumed that $t-m$ lies in the same link (i.e. $t-m$ refers to a period later than k). If the effect of a sub-index on a higher-level index is to be calculated across a chain, the calculation needs to be carried out in two steps: one with the old series up to the link period, and one from the link period to period t.

9.130 The calculation of the effect of a change in a sub-index on a higher-level index is illustrated in Table 9.8. The index is calculated in one link so that equation (9.25) may be applied for the decomposition. For instance, the effect in percentage points of the increase for housing from January 2002 to January 2003 can be calculated as $0.25/118.6 \times (120.0 - 110.0) = 2.11$ percentage points. This means that, of the increase of 10.03 per cent in the all-items index, 2.11 percentage points can be attributed to the increase in the index for housing.

Some alternatives to fixed weight indices

9.131 Monthly CPIs are, typically, arithmetic weighted averages of the price indices for the elementary aggregates, in which the weights are kept fixed over a number of periods – which may range from 12 months to many years. The repeated use of the same weights relating to some past period b simplifies calculation procedures and reduces data collection requirements. It is also cheaper to keep using the results from an old expenditure survey than to conduct an expensive new one. Moreover, when the weights are known in advance of the price collection, the index can be calculated immediately after the prices have been collected and processed.

9.132 The longer the same weights are used, however, the less representative they become of current consumption patterns, especially in periods of rapid technical change when new kinds of goods and services are continually appearing on the market and old ones disappearing. This may undermine the credibility of an index that purports to measure the rate of change in the total cost of a basket of goods and services typically consumed by households. Such a basket needs to be representative not only of the households covered by the index, but also of expenditure patterns at the time the price changes occur.

9.133 Similarly, if the objective is to compile a cost of living index, the continuing use of the same fixed basket is likely to become increasingly unsatisfactory the longer the same basket is used. The longer the same basket is used, the greater the upward bias in the index is likely to become. It is well known that the Laspeyres index has an upward bias compared with a cost of living index. However, a Lowe index between periods 0 and t with weights from an earlier period b will tend to exceed the Laspeyres between 0 and t by an amount that increases the further back in time period b is (see Chapter 15).

Table 9.8 Decomposition of index changes

	Weight	Index			Change in % from Jan. 02 to Jan. 03	Effect (contribution)	
		2000	Jan. 02	Jan. 03		% points of total change	% of total change
1 Food	0.30	100.0	120.0	130.0	8.33	2.53	25.21
2 Clothing	0.10	100.0	130.0	145.0	11.54	1.26	12.61
3 Housing	0.25	100.0	110.0	120.0	9.09	2.11	21.01
4 Transport	0.20	100.0	125.0	130.0	4.00	0.84	8.40
5 Miscellaneous	0.15	100.0	114.0	140.0	22.81	3.29	32.77
All items	1.00	100.0	118.6	130.5	10.03	10.03	100.00

9.134 There are several possible ways of minimizing or avoiding the potential biases from the use of fixed weight indices. These are outlined below.

9.135 *Annual chaining*. One way in which to minimize the potential biases from the use of fixed-weight indices is obviously to keep the weights and the base period as up to date as possible by frequent rebasing and chaining. Quite a number of countries have adopted this strategy and revise their weights annually. In any case, as noted earlier, it would be impossible to deal with the changing universe of products without some chaining of the price series within the elementary aggregates, even if the weights attached to the elementary aggregates remain fixed. Annual chaining eliminates the need to choose a base period, as the weight reference period is always the previous year, or possibly the preceding year.

9.136 *Annual chaining with current weights*. When the weights are changed annually, it is possible to replace the original weights based on the previous year, or years, by those of the current year, if the index is revised retrospectively as soon as information on the current year's expenditures becomes available. The long-term movements in the CPI are then based on the revised series. This is the method adopted by the Swedish Statistical Office, as explained above. This method could provide unbiased results.

9.137 *Other index formulae*. When the weights are revised less frequently, say every five years, another possibility would be to use a different index formula for the higher-level indices instead of an arithmetic average of the elementary price indices. One possibility would be a weighted geometric average. This is not subject to the same potential upward bias as the arithmetic average. More generally, a weighted version of the Lloyd–Moulton formula might be considered. This formula takes account of the substitutions that consumers make in response to changes in relative prices, and should be less subject to bias for this reason. It reduces to the geometric average when the elasticity of substitution is unity, on average. It is unlikely that such a formula could replace the arithmetic average in the foreseeable future and gain general acceptance, if only because it cannot be interpreted as measuring changes in the value of a fixed basket. It could, however, be compiled on an experimental basis and might well provide a useful supplement to the main index. It could at least flag the extent to which the main index is liable to be biased and throw light on its properties.

9.138 *Retrospective superlative indices*. Finally, it is possible to calculate a superlative index retrospectively. Superlative indices, such as Fisher and Törnqvist indices, treat both periods compared symmetrically and require expenditure data for both periods. Although the CPI may have to be some kind of Lowe index when it is first published, it may be possible to estimate a superlative index later when much more information becomes available about consumers' expenditures period by period. At least one office, the United States Bureau of Labor Statistics, publishes such an index. The publication of revised or supplementary CPIs raises matters of statistical policy, although users readily accept revisions in other fields of economic statistics. Moreover, users are already confronted with more than one CPI in the European Union (EU) where the harmonized index for EU purposes may differ from the national CPI. Thus the publication of supplementary indices which throw light on the properties of the main index and which may be of considerable interest to some users seems justified and acceptable.

Data editing

9.139 This chapter has been concerned with the methods used by statistical offices to calculate their CPIs. This concluding section considers the data editing carried out by statistical offices, a process that is very closely linked to the calculation of the price indices for the elementary aggregates. Data collection, recording and coding – the data capture processes – are dealt with in Chapters 5 to 7. The next step in the production of price indices is data editing. Data editing is here meant to comprise two steps:

– detection of possible errors and outliers;
– verifying and correction of data.

9.140 Logically, the purpose of detecting errors and outliers is to exclude errors or outliers from the index calculation. Errors may be falsely reported prices, or they may be caused by recording or coding mistakes. Also, missing prices because of non-response may be dealt with as errors. Possible errors and outliers are usually identified as observations that fall outside some pre-specified acceptance interval or are judged to be unrealistic by the analyst on some other ground. It may also be the case, however, that even if an observation is not identified as a potential error, it may actually show up to be false. Such observations are sometimes referred to as inliers. Sometimes, by chance, the sampling may have captured an exceptional price change, which falls outside the acceptance interval but has been verified as correct. In some discussions of survey data, any extreme value is described as an outlier. The term is reserved here for extreme values that have been verified as being correct.

9.141 When a possible error has been identified, it needs to be verified whether it is in fact an error or not. This clarification can usually be made by asking the respondent to verify the price, or by comparison with the price change of comparable items. If the value is in fact an error, it needs to be corrected. This can be done easily if the respondent can provide the correct price or, where this is not possible, by imputation or omitting the price from the index calculation. If the value proves to be correct, it should be included in the index. If it proves to be an outlier, it can be accepted or corrected according to a pre-defined practice, e.g. omitting or imputation.

9.142 Although the power of computers provides obvious benefits, not all of these activities have to be computerized. There should be a complete set of procedures and records that controls the processing of data, even though some or all of it may be undertaken without the use of computers. It is not always necessary for all of one step to be completed before the next is started. If the process uses spreadsheets, for example, with default imputations predefined for any missing data, the index can be estimated and re-estimated whenever a new observation is added or modified. The ability to examine the impact of individual price observations on elementary aggregate indices and the impact of elementary indices on various higher-level aggregates is a useful aid in all aspects of the computation and analytical processes.

9.143 It is neither necessary nor desirable to apply the same degree of scrutiny to all reported prices. The price changes recorded by some respondents carry more weight than others, and statistical analysts should be aware of this. For example, one elementary aggregate with a weight of 2 per cent, say, may contain 10 prices, while another elementary aggregate of equal weight may contain 100 prices. Obviously, an error in a reported price will have a much smaller effect in the latter, where it may be negligible, while in the former it may cause a significant error in the elementary aggregate index and even influence higher-level indices.

9.144 There may be an interest in the individual elementary indices, as well as in the aggregates built from them. Since the sample sizes used at the elementary level may often be small, any price collected, and error in it, may have a significant impact on the results for individual products or industries. The verification of reported data usually has to be done on an index-by-index basis, using the statistical analysts' experience. Analysts will also need the cooperation and support of the respondents to the survey to help explain unusual price movements.

9.145 Obviously, the design of the survey and questionnaires also influences the occurrence of errors. Hence, price reports and questionnaires should be as clear and unambiguous as possible to prevent misunderstandings and errors. Whatever the design of the survey, it is important to verify that the data collected are those that were requested initially. The survey questionnaire should prompt the respondent to indicate if the requested data could not be provided. If, for example, a product is not produced any more and thus is not priced in the current month, a possible replacement would be requested along with details as to the extent of its comparability with the old one. In the event that a respondent cannot supply a replacement, there are a number of procedures for dealing with missing data (also discussed in Chapter 7).

Identifying possible errors and outliers

9.146 One of the ways in which price surveys are different from other economic surveys is that, although prices are recorded, the measurement concern is with price *changes*. As the index calculations consist of comparing the prices of matching observations from one period to another, editing checks should focus on the price changes calculated from pairs of observations, rather than on the reported prices themselves.

9.147 Identification of unusual price changes can be accomplished by:

- non-statistical checking of input data;
- statistical checking of input data;
- output checking.

These will be described in turn.

9.148 *Non-statistical checking of input data.* Non-statistical checking can be undertaken by manually checking the input data, by inspection of the data presented in comparable tables, or by setting filters.

9.149 When the price reports or questionnaires are received in the statistical office, the reported prices can be checked manually by comparing these to the previously reported prices of the same items or by comparing them to prices of similar items from other outlets. While this procedure may detect obvious unusual price changes, it is far from certain that all possible errors will be detected. It is also extremely time-consuming and, of course, it does not identify coding errors.

9.150 After the price data have been coded, the statistical system can be programmed to present the data in a comparable tabular form. For example, a table showing the percentage change for all reported prices from the previous to the current month may be produced and used for detection of possible errors. Such tables may also include, for comparison, the percentage changes of previous periods and 12-month changes. Most computer programs and spreadsheets can easily sort the observations according to, say, the size of the latest monthly rate of change, so that extreme values can easily be identified. It is also possible to group the observations by elementary aggregates.

9.151 The advantage of grouping observations is that it highlights potential errors so that the analyst does not have to look through all observations. A hierarchical strategy whereby all extreme price changes are first identified and then examined in context may save time, though the price changes underlying elementary aggregate indices, which have relatively high weights, should also be examined in context.

9.152 Filtering is a method by which possible errors or outliers are identified according to whether the price changes fall outside some predefined limits, such as plus or minus 20 per cent or even 50 per cent. This test should capture any serious errors of data coding, as well as some of the cases where a respondent has erroneously reported on a different product. It is usually possible to identify these errors without reference to any other observations in the survey, so this check can be carried out at the data capture stage. The advantage of filtering is that it avoids the analyst having to look through a lot of individual observations. The upper and lower limits may be set for the latest monthly change, or change over some other period. Again, they should take account of the context of the price change, in that they may be specified by item or elementary aggregates or higher-level indices. Larger changes for items with prices that are known to be volatile might be accepted without question. For example, for monthly changes, limits of plus or minus 10 per cent might be set for oil prices, while for professional services the limits might be zero per cent to plus 5 per cent (as any price that falls is suspect), and for computers it might be −5 per cent to zero per cent (as any price that rises is suspect). The limits can also be changed over time. If it is known that oil prices are rising, the limits could be 10 per cent to 20 per cent, while if they are falling, the limits might be −10 per cent to −20 per cent. The count of failures should be monitored regularly to examine the limits. If too many observations are being identified for review, the limits will need to be adjusted, or the scope refined.

9.153 The use of automatic deletion systems is not advised, however. It is a well-recorded phenomenon in pricing that price changes for many products, especially durables, are not undertaken smoothly over time, but saved up to avoid what are termed "menu costs" associated with making a price change. These relatively substantial increases may take place at different times for different models of products and have the appearance of extreme, incorrect values. To delete a price change for each model of the product as being "extreme" at the time it occurs is to ignore all price changes for the industry.

9.154 *Statistical checking of input data.* Statistical checking of input data compares, for some time period, each price change with the change in prices in the same or a similar sample. Two examples of such filtering are given here, the first based on non-parametric summary measures and the second on the log normal distribution of price changes.

9.155 The first method involves tests based on the median and quartiles of price changes, so they are unaffected by the impact of any single "extreme" observation. Define the median, first quartile and third quartile price ratios as R_M, R_{Q1}, and R_{Q3}, respectively. Then any observation with a price ratio that is more than a certain multiple C of the distance between the median and the quartile is identified as a potential error. The basic approach assumes that price changes are normally distributed. Under this assumption, it is possible to estimate the proportion of price changes that are likely to fall outside given bounds expressed as multiples of C. Under a normal distribution, R_{Q1} and R_{Q3} are equidistant from R_M. Thus, if C is measured as $R_M - (R_{Q1} + R_{Q3})/2$, then 50 per cent of observations would be expected to lie within plus or minus C from the median. From the tables of the standardized normal distribution this is equivalent to about 0.7 times the standard deviation (σ). If, for example, C was set to 6, the distance implied is about 4σ of the sample, so about 0.17 per cent of observations would be identified this way. With $C = 4$, the corresponding figures are 2.7σ, or about 0.7 per cent of observations. If $C = 3$, the distance is 2.02σ, so about 4 per cent of observations would be identified.

9.156 In practice, most prices may not change each month and the share of observations identified as possible errors as a percentage of all changes would be unduly high. Some experimentation with alternative values of C for different industries or sectors may be appropriate. If this test is to be used to identify possible errors for further investigation, a relatively low value of C should be used.

9.157 To use this approach in practice, three modifications should be made:

- First, to make the calculation of the distance from the centre the same for extreme changes on the low side as well as on the high side, a transformation of the ratios should be made. The transformed distance for the ratio of one price observation i, S_i, should be:

$$S_i = 1 - R_M/R_i \text{ if } 0 < R_i < R_M \text{ and}$$
$$S_i = R_i/R_M - 1 \text{ if } R_i \geq R_M.$$

- Second, if the price changes are grouped closely together, the distances between the median and quartiles may be very small, so that many observations would be identified that had quite small price changes. To avoid this, some minimum distance, say 5 per cent for monthly changes, should also be set.
- Third, with small samples the impact of one observation on the distances between the median and quartiles may be too great. Because sample sizes for some elementary indices are small, samples for similar elementary indices may need to be grouped together.

9.158 For a detailed presentation of this method, see Hidiroglou and Berthelot (1986). The method can be expanded to also take into account the level of the prices. Thus, for example, a price increase from 100 to 110 will be attributed a different weight from the weight attributed to a price increase from 10 to 11.

9.159 An alternative method can be used if it is thought that the price changes may be distributed log normally. To apply this method, the standard deviation of the log of all price changes in the sample (excluding unchanged observations) is calculated and a goodness of fit test (χ^2) is undertaken to identify whether the distribution is log normal. If the distribution satisfies the test, all price changes outside two times the exponential of the standard deviation are highlighted for further checking. If the test rejects the log normal hypothesis, all the price changes outside three times the exponential of the standard deviation are highlighted. The same caveats mentioned before about clustered changes and small samples apply.

9.160 The second example is based on the Tukey algorithm. The set of price ratios is sorted and the highest and lowest 5 per cent flagged for further attention. In addition, having excluded the top and bottom 5 per cent, exclude the price ratios that are equal to 1 (no change). The arithmetic (trimmed) mean (AM) of the remaining price ratios is calculated. This mean is used to separate the price ratios into two sets, an upper and a lower one. The upper and lower "mid-means", that is, the means of each of these sets (AM_L, AM_U), are then calculated. Upper and lower Tukey limits (T_L, T_U) are then established as the mean plus (minus) 2.5 times the difference between the mean and the mid-means:

$$T_U = AM + 2.5\,(AM_U - AM)$$
$$T_L = AM - 2.5\,(AM - AM_L)$$

Then all those observations that fall above T_U and below T_L are flagged for attention.

9.161 This is a simpler method similar to that based on the normal distribution. Since it excludes all cases of no change from the calculation of the mean, it is unlikely to produce limits that are very close to the mean, so there is no need to set a minimum difference. Its success will also depend on there being a large number of observations on the set of changes being analysed. Again, it will often be necessary to group observations from similar elementary indices. For any of these algorithms, the comparisons can be made for any time periods, including the latest month's changes or longer periods, in particular, 12-month changes.

9.162 The advantage of these two models of filtering compared to the simple method of filtering is that for each period the upper and lower limits are determined by the data and hence are allowed to vary over the year, given that the analyst has decided on the value of the parameters entering the models. A disadvantage is that, unless the analyst is prepared to use approximations from earlier experience, all the data have to be collected before the filtering can be undertaken. Filters should be set tightly enough so that the percentage of potential errors that turn out to be real errors is high. As with all automatic methods, the flagging of an unusual observation is for further investigation, as opposed to automatic deletion.

9.163 *Checking by impact, or data output checking.* Filtering by impact, or output editing, is based on calculating the impact that an individual price change has on an index to which it contributes. This index can be an elementary aggregate index, the total index, or some other aggregate index. The impact that a price change has on an index is its percentage change times its effective weight. In the absence of sample changes, the calculation is straightforward: it is the nominal (reference period) weight, multiplied by the price relative, and divided by the level of the index to which it is contributing. So the impact on the index I of the change of the price of product i from time t to $t+1$ is $\pm w_i\,(p_{t+1}/p_t)/I_t$ where w_i is the nominal weight in the base period. A minimum value for this impact can be set, so that all price changes that cause an impact greater than this change can be flagged for review. If index I is an elementary index, then all elementary indices may be reviewed, but if I is an aggregative index, prices that change by a given percentage will be flagged or not depending on how important the elementary index to which they contribute is in the aggregate.

9.164 At the lowest level, the appearance and disappearance of products in the sample cause the effective weight of an individual price to change substantially. The effective weight is also affected if a price observation is used as an imputation for other missing observations. The evaluation of effective weights in each period is possible, though complicated. As an aid to highlighting potential errors, the nominal weights, as a percentage of their sum, will usually provide a reasonable approximation. If the impact of 12-month changes is required to highlight potential errors, approximations are the only feasible filters to use, as the effective weights will vary over the period.

9.165 One advantage of identifying potential errors in this way is that it focuses on the results. Another advantage is that this form of filtering also helps the analyst to describe the contributions to change in the price indices. In fact, much of this kind of analysis is done after the indices have been calculated, as the analyst often wishes to highlight those indices that have contributed the most to overall index changes. Sometimes the analysis results in a finding that particular industries have a relatively high contribution to the overall price change, and that is considered unrealistic. The change is traced back to an error, but it may be late in the production cycle and jeopardize the schedule release date. There is thus a case for identifying such unusual contributions as part of the data editing procedures. The disadvantage of this method is that an elementary index's change may be rejected at that stage. It may be necessary to over-ride the calculated index, though this should be only a stopgap measure until the index sample is redesigned.

Verifying and correcting data

9.166 Some errors, such as data coding errors, can be identified and corrected easily. Ideally, these errors are caught at the first stage of checking, before they need to be viewed in the context of other price changes. Dealing with other potential errors is more difficult. Many results that fail a data check may be judged by the analyst to be quite plausible, especially if the data checking limits are broad. Some potential failures may only be resolved by checking the data with the respondent.

9.167 If a satisfactory explanation can be obtained from the respondent, the data can be verified or corrected. If not, procedures may differ. Rules may be established that if a satisfactory explanation is not obtained, then the reported price is omitted from the index calculation. Alternatively, it may be left to the analyst to make the best judgement as to the price change. If an analyst makes a correction to some reported data without verifying it with the respondent, the change may subsequently cause problems with the respondent. If the respondent is not told of the correction, the same error may persist in the future. The correct action depends on a combination of confidence in the analysts, the revision policy of the survey, and the degree of communication with respondents. Most statistical organizations do not want to burden respondents unduly.

9.168 In many organizations, a disproportionate share of activity is devoted to identifying and following up potential errors. If this practice leads to little change in the results, as a result of most reports finally being accepted, then the "bounds" on what are considered to be extreme values should be relaxed. More errors are likely to be introduced by respondents failing to report changes that occur than from wrongly reporting changes, and the good will of respondents should not be unduly undermined.

9.169 Generally, the effort spent on identifying potential errors should not be excessive. Obvious mistakes should be caught at the data capture stage. The time spent in identifying observations to query, unless they are highly weighted and excessive, is often better spent treating those cases in the production cycle where things have changed – quality changes or unavailable prices – and reorganizing activities towards maintaining the relevance of the sample, and checking for errors of omission.

9.170 If the price observations are collected in a way that prompts the respondent with the previously reported price, the respondent may report the same price as a matter of convenience. This can happen even though the price may have changed, or even when the particular product being surveyed is no longer available. As prices for many items do not change frequently, this kind of error is unlikely to be spotted by normal checks. Often the situation comes to light when the contact at the responding outlet changes and the new contact has difficulty in finding something that corresponds to the price previously reported. It is advisable, therefore, to keep a record of the last time a particular respondent reported a price change. When that time has become suspiciously long, the analyst should verify with the respondent that the price observation is still valid. What constitutes too long will vary from product to product and the level of overall price inflation, but, in general, any price that has remained constant for more than a year is suspect.

9.171 *Treatment of outliers.* Detection and treatment of outliers (extreme values that have been verified as being correct) is an insurance policy. It is based on the fear that a particular data point collected is exceptional by chance, and that if there were a larger survey, or even a different one, the results would be less extreme. The treatment, therefore, is to reduce the impact of the exceptional observation, though not to ignore it as, after all, it did occur. The methods to test for outliers are the same as those used to identify potential errors by statistical filtering, described above. For example, upper and lower bounds of distances from the median price change are determined. In this case, however, when observations are found outside those bounds, they may be changed to be at the bounds or imputed by the rate of change of a comparable set of prices. This outlier adjustment is sometimes made automatically, on the grounds that the analyst by definition has no additional information on which to base a better estimate. While such automatic adjustment methods are employed, this manual proposes caution in their use. If an elementary aggregate is relatively highly weighted and has a relatively small sample, an adjustment may be made. The general prescription should be to include verified prices; the exception should be to dampen them.

9.172 *Treatment of missing price observations.* It is likely that not all the requested data will have been received by the time the index needs to be calculated. It is generally the case that missing data turn out to be delayed. Sometimes, the respondent may report that a price cannot be reported because neither the product, nor any similar substitute is being made any more. Sometimes, of course, what started apparently as a late report becomes a permanent loss to the sample. Different actions need to be taken depending on whether the situation is temporary or permanent.

9.173 For temporarily missing prices, the most appropriate strategy is to minimize the occurrence of missing observations. Survey reports are likely to come in over a period of time before the indices need to be calculated. In many cases, they follow a steady routine; some respondents will tend to file quickly, others typically will be later in the processing cycle. An analyst should become familiar with these patterns. A computerized data capture system can flag those reports that appear to be later than usual, well before the processing deadline. Also, some data are more important than others. Depending on the weighting system, some respondents may be particularly important, and important products should be flagged as requiring particular scrutiny.

9.174 For those reports for which no estimate can be made, two basic alternatives are considered here (see Chapter 7 for a full range of approaches): imputation, preferably targeted, in which the missing price change is assumed to be the same as some other set of price changes; or an assumption of no change, as the preceding period's price is used. This latter procedure ignores the fact that some prices will prove to have changed, and if prices are generally moving in one direction, this will mean that the change in the index will be understated. It is not advised. However, if the index is periodically revised, this approach will lead to fewer subsequent revisions than imputations, since for most products, prices do not generally change in any given period. Standard imputation is to base the estimate of the missing price observation on the change of some similar group of observations.

9.175 There will be situations where the price is permanently missing because the product no longer exists. As there is no replacement for the missing price, an imputation will have to be made for each period until either the sample is redesigned or until a replacement can be found. It is, therefore, more important than in the case of temporarily missing reports, and requires closer attention.

9.176 The missing price can be imputed by using the change in the remaining price observations in the elementary aggregate, which has the same effect as removing the missing observation from the sample, or by the change in a subset of other price observations for comparable items. The series should be flagged as being based on imputed values.

9.177 Samples are designed on the basis that the products chosen for observation are representative of a wider range of products. Imputations for permanently missing prices are indications of weakness in the sample, and their accumulation is a signal that the sample should be redesigned. For indices where there are known to be a large number of disappearances in the sample, the need for replacements should be anticipated.

SOME SPECIAL CASES

10

Introduction

10.1 This chapter focuses on a number of expenditure areas that pose particular problems for price index compilers, both in terms of identifying an agreed conceptual approach and also overcoming practical measurement difficulties. Six areas have been selected for discussion, mainly from the service sector. They are:

- owner-occupied housing;
- clothing;
- telecommunication services;
- financial services;
- real estate agency services;
- property insurance services.

10.2 This chapter is therefore structured into six sections, in turn dealing with the problem areas listed above. Under each section, any necessary theoretical considerations are discussed and relevant measurement issues explored. Where appropriate, illustrative examples of alternative approaches to the measurement of weights or price changes are provided, and the advantages and disadvantages are outlined.

10.3 It is important to note that the examples shown are neither definitive nor prescriptive, but rather provide broad guidance as to how the problem areas can be approached. User requirements, data availability and the statistical resources available are important factors that need to be taken into consideration in choosing an appropriate methodology. Market conditions and product market regulations, which can differ widely between countries, also have a critical impact on the choice of method.

Owner-occupied housing

10.4 The treatment of owner-occupied housing in consumer price indices (CPIs) is arguably the most difficult issue faced by CPI compilers. Depending on the proportion of the reference population that are owner-occupiers, the alternative conceptual treatments can have a significant impact on the CPI, affecting both weights and, at least, short-term measures of price change.

10.5 Ideally, the approach chosen should align with the conceptual basis that best satisfies the principal purpose of the CPI. However, the data requirements for some (or even all) of these options may be such that it is not feasible to adopt the preferred treatment. Equally important, it may be difficult to identify a single principal purpose for the CPI. In particular, the dual use of CPIs as both macroeconomic indicators and also for indexation purposes can lead to clear tensions in designing an appropriate treatment for owner-occupied housing costs. In these circumstances, it may be necessary to adopt a treatment that is not entirely consistent with the approach adopted for other items in the CPI. In some countries, the difficulties in resolving such tensions have led to the omission of owner-occupied housing from the CPI altogether or the publication of more than one index.

10.6 The remainder of this section discusses the conceptual basis and data requirements for the *use*, *payments* and *acquisitions* approaches in turn.

Use

10.7 The general objective of this approach is to measure the change over time in the value of the flow of shelter services consumed by owner-occupiers. Detailed approaches fall under one of two broader headings: user cost or rental equivalence.

10.8 The *user cost* approach attempts to measure the changes in the cost to owner-occupiers of using the dwelling. In the weighting base period, these costs comprise two elements: recurring actual costs, such as those for repairs and maintenance, and property taxes; and the opportunity cost of having money tied up in the dwelling rather than being used for some other purpose. At its simplest, and where houses are purchased outright, this latter element is represented by the rate of return available on alternative assets. More usually, house purchase will be at least part financed through mortgage borrowing. In this case, opportunity cost can be viewed as an average of interest rates on mortgages and alternative assets, weighted by the proportion of the purchase price borrowed and paid outright, respectively.

10.9 Estimation of the base period weight for recurring actual costs such as expenditures on repairs and maintenance is relatively straightforward and generally obtainable from household expenditure surveys. Similarly, the construction of price measures for these items presents few difficulties.

10.10 Estimation of the base period weight for opportunity costs is more complicated and will require modelling. One approach is to assume that all owner-occupiers purchased their dwellings outright at the beginning of the period and sold them at the end. During the period their opportunity costs comprise the amount of interest forgone (i.e. the amount of interest they might have earned by investing this money elsewhere) and depreciation. Offsetting these costs would be any capital gains earned on the sale of the dwellings. Construction of the required measures of price change is likewise quite complicated (see Chapter 23 for a more complete discussion) and, particularly for the depreciation element, a good deal of imputation is required. Allowing for house purchases part financed by mortgage borrowing, a typical formula for user cost (UC) is:

$$UC = rM + iE + D + RC - K$$

where M and E represent mortgage debt and equity in the home, and r and i represent mortgage interest rates and the rate of return available on alternative assets, respectively. D is depreciation, RC other recurring costs and K capital gains.

10.11 No national statistical office is currently using the full user cost approach. This partly reflects the conceptual and methodological complexity of the measure, which may also make it difficult to obtain widespread public support for the approach. For this reason, the methodology is not discussed in detail here. It is, however, worth noting that both the weights and the ongoing measures of price change are significantly influenced by the relative rate of change in house prices. Since the user cost formula is typically dominated by capital gains and interest rates, where house price inflation exceeds nominal interest rates the user cost weight is likely to be negative (implying a negative price for user cost).

10.12 In practice, it is possible to avoid some of these difficulties by adopting a variant or a narrower definition of user cost. For example, some countries have adopted a variant of the user cost approach focusing on gross mortgage interest payments and depreciation, in part because these items are readily recognizable as key costs by home owners. The former may be viewed as the cost of retaining housing shelter today, while the depreciation element represents current expenditure that would be required to offset the deterioration and obsolescence in dwellings that would otherwise occur over time. Methodologies for calculating actual average mortgage interest payments for index households are described in the section on the payments approach to owner-occupied housing costs, below.

10.13 Depreciation is a gradual process and so is best represented by the amount that needs to be put aside year by year as opposed to actual expenditures (which will typically be large but infrequent). The base period weight for depreciation may be estimated from the current market value of the owner-occupied housing stock excluding land values, multiplied by an average rate of depreciation. The latter may be derived from national accounts estimates of housing capital consumption. Imputed this way, the appropriate price indicator should ideally be an index of house prices excluding land rather than an index of the costs of renovation work.

10.14 The *rental equivalence* approach attempts to measure the change in the price of the housing service consumed by owner-occupiers by estimating the market value of those services. In other words, it is based on estimating how much owner-occupiers would have to pay to rent their dwelling. Under this approach, it would be inappropriate also to include those input costs normally borne by landlords such as dwelling insurance, major repair and maintenance, and property taxes as this would involve an element of double counting. The rental equivalence approach is recommended in *SNA 1993* for measuring household consumption and is also used in constructing international comparisons of living standards.

10.15 Deriving the weight for rental equivalence requires estimating how much owner-occupiers would have paid in the weighting base period to rent their dwellings. This is not something that owner-occupiers can normally be expected to estimate reliably in a household expenditure survey. In principle, however, it can be estimated by matching the dwellings of owner-occupiers with comparable dwellings that are being rented and applying those rents to the owner-occupied dwellings.

10.16 In practice, this raises a number of problems, particularly in countries where the overall size of the private rental market is small or if rented housing is of a different type from owner-occupied housing in terms of general quality, age, size and location. Direct imputation from actual rents may also be inappropriate if the rental market is subject to price control. In addition, owner-occupiers may be considered to derive significant additional utility from features such as security of tenure and the ability to modify the dwelling, implying a need to make additional adjustments to the initial imputations.

10.17 In those countries where the reference population for the CPI corresponds to all resident households, the estimation problem is identical to that faced by the national accountants and a collaborative approach would be beneficial.

10.18 The corresponding price series for owner-occupiers' rent can be derived from an actual rent index, except where such rents are subject to price control. Depending on both the relative significance of owner-occupiers to renters and the composition of the two markets in terms of dwelling characteristics, any existing rent surveys may need to be modified to meet the particular requirements of an owners' equivalent rent series. If the total value of owners' equivalent rent is significantly larger than actual rents, the absolute size of the existing price sample may be deemed insufficient. If the characteristics of owner-occupied dwellings differ significantly from the overall rental market, the existing rent survey may also require stratifying more finely (e.g. by type and size of dwelling, and by location). The price measures for the different strata can then be given different weights when calculating the actual rents and the owners' equivalent rent series, respectively.

10.19 While it may be acceptable to include subsidized and controlled prices in the actual rent series, these should not be used in calculating the owners' equivalent rent series. Given the increased significance of rent prices in the overall index, it may also be necessary to pay greater attention to the measurement of price change for individual properties when tenancies change. As this often presents landlords with an opportunity to refurbish properties and increase rents, the practice of regarding the whole of all such price changes as arising from quality change should be avoided. Furthermore, the rent series may need to be quality-adjusted to take account of ongoing depreciation to housing structures.

This question is discussed in Chapter 23, paragraphs 23.69 to 23.78.

Payments

10.20 The item domain for a payments index is defined by reference to actual outlays made by households to gain access to consumer goods and services. The set of outlays peculiar to owner-occupiers in the weighting base period includes:

- down payments or deposits on newly purchased dwellings;
- legal and real estate agency fees payable on property transfers;
- repayments of mortgage principal;
- mortgage interest payments;
- alterations and additions to the dwelling;
- insurance of the dwelling;
- repair and maintenance of the dwelling;
- property rates and taxes.

10.21 While it is conceivable to include all of these items in the index, it is generally agreed that at least some represent capital transactions that ought to be excluded from a CPI. For example, while down payments and repayments of mortgage principal result in a running down of household cash reserves, they also result in the creation of a real asset (at least part of a dwelling) or in the reduction of a liability (the amount of mortgage debt outstanding). Similarly, any cash expenditures on alterations and additions result in a running down of cash reserves offset by increases in dwelling values. In other words, those transactions which result in no net change to household balance sheets should be excluded.

10.22 The remaining items can be regarded as current expenditures which do not result in any offsetting adjustments to household balance sheets. It is therefore considered appropriate that these items be included in a payments-based CPI. By defining a payments index in this way, it is clear that the aggregate payments equal a household's source of funds which comprise income after tax (wages, transfers, property income, insurance claims, etc.) and net savings (as a balancing item). It is for this reason that a payments-based CPI is commonly considered to be the best construct for assessing changes in net money incomes over time.

10.23 Estimation of gross expenditures on these items in the weighting base period is readily achievable via a household expenditure survey, as the items are generally reportable by households. The construction of price indices for real estate agency fees and insurance is discussed later in this chapter. Indices for repair and maintenance, and property rates and taxes are not considered particularly problematic so are not discussed here. The remainder of this section is therefore devoted to the construction of price measures for mortgage interest charges.

10.24 The construction of price indices for mortgage interest charges is not altogether straightforward. The degree of complexity will vary from country to country depending on the operation of domestic financial markets and the existence (or otherwise) of any income tax provisions applying to mortgage interest payments. What follows therefore is a description of an overall objective and an illustrative methodology for producing the required index in the most straightforward of cases. The methodology will require modifying to account for additional complexities that may be encountered in some countries.

10.25 The general approach may be summarized briefly as follows. Under a fixed basket approach, the objective of the index is to measure the change over time in the interest that would be payable on a set of mortgages equivalent to those existing in the weighting base period. This base stock of mortgages will, of course, vary widely in age, from those taken up in the base period itself to those taken up many years previously. In compiling a fixed base index, the distribution of mortgages by age is required to be held constant.

10.26 The amount of interest payable on a mortgage is determined by applying some rate of interest, expressed as a percentage, to the monetary value of debt. Changes in mortgage interest charges over time therefore can, in principle, be measured by periodically collecting information on a representative selection of mortgage interest rates, using these to derive an average interest rate, and then applying this to an appropriate debt figure. At least for standard variable rate mortgages, interest due on the revalued stock of base period mortgages may be derived simply with reference to current mortgage interest rates.

10.27 The main problem then is in determining the appropriate debt figure in each of the comparison periods. Since the real value of any monetary amount of debt varies over time according to changes in the purchasing power of money, it is not appropriate to use the actual base period monetary value of debt in calculations for subsequent periods. Rather, it is necessary first to update that monetary value in each comparison period so that it remains constant in real terms (i.e. so that the quantities underpinning the base period amount are held constant).

10.28 In order to do this, it is necessary to form at least a theoretical view of the quantities underpinning the amount of debt in the base period. The amount of mortgage debt outstanding for a single household in the base period depends on the original house purchase price and loan-to-value ratio, and also the rate of repayment of principal since the house was purchased. An equivalent value of debt can be calculated in subsequent comparison periods by holding constant the age of the debt, the original value of the debt (as some fixed proportion of the total value of the dwelling when the mortgage was initially entered into) and the rate of repayment of the principal (as some proportion of the original debt), and applying these factors to house prices for periods corresponding to the age of the debt.

10.29 To illustrate, suppose a base period household purchased a dwelling five years earlier for $100,000 and financed 50 per cent by mortgage. If, between the time of purchase and the base period, the household repaid 20 per cent of this debt, then the outstanding debt on which base period interest charges were calculated would have been $40,000. Now move to some subsequent comparison period and suppose that it is known that house prices doubled between the period when the household originally purchased and the period five years prior to the comparison period. The equivalent amount of outstanding debt in the comparison period would be calculated by first taking 50 per cent of the revalued house price (of $200,000) to give $100,000, and then reducing this by the principal repayment rate (of 20 per cent) to give $80,000.

10.30 Under these assumptions, it is clear that the comparison period value of outstanding debt may be estimated directly from the base period value of outstanding debt solely on the basis of house price movements between five years prior to the base period and five years prior to the comparison period. In other words, while preservation of original debt/equity ratios and rates of repayment of principal help in understanding the approach, estimates of these variables are not strictly required to calculate the required comparison period debt. All that is required is the value of the outstanding debt in the base period, the age of that debt and a suitable measure of changes in dwelling prices.

10.31 Now suppose that all mortgages are of the variable rate type, and that average nominal interest rates rose from 5 per cent in the base period to 7.5 per cent in the comparison period. Interest payments in the two periods can be calculated as $2,000 and $6,000 respectively, and so the mortgage interest payments index for the comparison period is 300.0. An identical result may of course be found directly from index number series for debt and nominal interest rates. The mortgage interest charges index equals the debt index multiplied by the nominal interest rate index divided by 100. In this example, the debt index equals 200.0 and the nominal interest rate index equals 150.0. Therefore the mortgage interest rate index equals (200.0×150.0)/100 or 300.0. This simple example also serves to illustrate the very important point that percentages (interest rates, taxes, etc.) are not prices and cannot be used as if they were. Percentages must be applied to some monetary value in order to determine a monetary price.

10.32 While the single-household example shown above is useful in explaining the basic concepts, it is necessary to devise a methodology that can be employed to calculate a mortgage interest charges index for the reference population as a whole. The main complication when moving from the single-household to the many-household case is the fact that the age of the debt will vary across households. Given the importance of revaluing base period debt to maintain a constant age, this is no trivial matter. While it is conceivable that information on the age of mortgage debt could be collected in household expenditure surveys, the additional respondent burden and the generally small number of households reporting mortgages often serve to make estimates from this source unreliable. Another option is to approach a sample of providers of mortgages (banks, building societies, etc.) for an age profile of their current mortgage portfolio. This type of data is normally available and is generally reliable.

10.33 Table 10.1 illustrates how an aggregate debt price index can be constructed. For the purpose of illustrating the methodology, some simplifying assumptions have been made:

- The index is assumed to be quarterly rather than monthly.
- The oldest age of mortgage debt is assumed to be between three and four years (in practice, it is normally the case that debt older than eight years is insignificant).
- Each annual cohort of debt is assumed to be distributed evenly across the year.
- A quarterly index of dwelling prices (new and second-hand dwellings, including land) is available.

10.34 Column (1) of Table 10.1(a) contains index numbers for dwelling prices extending back four years prior to the base period for the debt series (quarter 1 of year 0). Column (2) contains a four-quarter moving average of the first series – this is required to reflect "yearly" prices to correspond with the debt cohorts, which are only available in yearly age groups in this example (if quarterly cohorts were available it would not be necessary to calculate the moving average series).

10.35 Columns (1) to (4) of Table 10.1(b) contain the calculated debt indices for each cohort re-referenced to Y0 Q1 = 100. These series are simple transformations of the series in column (2) of Table 10.1(a), each with a different starting point. For example, the debt series for that cohort contracted for between three and four years ago has as a starting point the index number from Y−4 Q4 (i.e. 113.9) in column (2), and the series for debt aged between two and three years starts from Y−3 Q4 (i.e. 118.7) and so on. Column (5) of Table 10.1(b) contains the aggregate debt index which is derived by weighting together the indices for the four age cohorts. The weights are derived from data from financial institutions on debt outstanding by age, revalued to period Y0 Q1 prices.

10.36 A nominal mortgage interest rate index number series is obtained by calculating average quarterly interest rates on variable rate mortgages from a sample of lending institutions (starting in period Y0 Q1) and presenting them in index number form. The nominal interest rate series can then be combined with the debt series to calculate the final mortgage interest rate charges series, as illustrated in Table 10.2.

10.37 The construction of equivalent indices for fixed interest mortgages is more complicated in so far as an interest charges index has to be calculated separately for each age cohort of debt to reflect the fact that interest payable today, on a loan four years old, depends on the interest rate prevailing four years ago. This requires the compilation of a nominal fixed interest rate index extending back as far as the dwelling price series. To the extent that the interest rates charged on fixed interest loans also depend on the duration of the loan, calculation of the nominal fixed interest rate series is also more complex. The additional complexity of these indices may make the construction of a mortgage interest charges index impractical for countries where fixed interest rate mortgages predominate.

10.38 The construction of the index for mortgage interest payments is predicated on the assumption that

Table 10.1 Calculation of a mortgage debt series
(a) Dwelling price index

Year	Quarter	Original house price index (1)	Four quarter moving average of (1) (2)
Y–4	Q1	111.9	
	Q2	112.8	
	Q3	114.7	
	Q4	116.2	113.9
Y–3	Q1	117.6	115.3
	Q2	118.5	116.8
	Q3	119.0	117.8
	Q4	119.8	118.7
Y–2	Q1	120.1	119.4
	Q2	120.3	119.8
	Q3	120.5	120.2
	Q4	122.0	120.7
Y–1	Q1	122.3	121.3
	Q2	123.8	122.2
	Q3	124.5	123.2
	Q4	125.2	124.0
Y0	Q1	125.9	124.9
	Q2	126.1	125.4
	Q3	127.3	126.1
	Q4	129.2	127.1

(b) Debt index

Year	Quarter	Age of debt				
		3–4 years Wt = 10% (1)	2–3 years Wt = 20% (2)	1–2 years Wt = 30% (3)	0–1 year Wt = 40% (4)	Weighted average (5)
Y0	Q1	100.0	100.0	100.0	100.0	100.0
	Q2	101.2	100.6	100.7	100.7	100.7
	Q3	102.5	100.9	101.6	101.1	101.4
	Q4	103.4	101.3	102.2	101.7	101.9

the purpose of the mortgage is to finance the purchase of the dwelling (hence revaluation of debt by changes in dwelling prices). However, it is increasingly common, particularly in developed countries, for households to draw down on the equity they have in their home. That is, households may take new or additional mortgages, or redraw part of the principal already paid to finance other activities, for example to purchase a large consumer durable such as a car or a boat, to go on holiday or even to purchase stocks and bonds. If these alternative uses of the funds made available by way of mortgages are significant, it may be appropriate to regard at least some proportion of mortgage interest charges as the cost of a general financial service rather than a housing cost. For that proportion of the debt deemed to be used for other purposes, it would be more appropriate to use a general index of price inflation for debt revaluation purposes.

Table 10.2 Calculation of a mortgage interest charges series

Year	Quarter	Debt index (1)	Nominal interest rates index (2)	Mortgage interest charges index (1) × (2)/100 (3)
Y0	Q1	100.0	100.0	100.0
	Q2	100.7	98.5	99.2
	Q3	101.4	100.8	102.2
	Q4	101.9	101.5	103.4

Acquisitions

10.39 The item domain for an acquisitions index is defined as all those consumer goods and services acquired by households. Those countries which compile their CPIs on an acquisitions basis have generally concluded that the principal purpose of their CPI is to provide a measure of price inflation for the household sector as a whole. Based on the view that price inflation is a phenomenon peculiar to the operation of markets, the domain is also normally restricted to those consumer goods and services acquired in monetary transactions. That is, consumer goods and services provided at no cost to households by governments and non-profit institutions serving households are excluded.

10.40 The expenditures of owner-occupiers that could be included in an acquisitions index are:

- net purchases of dwellings (i.e. purchases less sales by the reference population);
- direct construction of new dwellings;
- alterations and additions to existing dwellings;

- legal and real estate agency fees payable on property transfers;
- repair and maintenance of dwellings;
- insurance of dwellings;
- property rates and taxes.

10.41 The construction of price indices for real estate agency fees and insurance is discussed later in this chapter. Indices for repair and maintenance, and property rates and taxes are not considered particularly problematic so are not discussed here. The remainder of this section is therefore devoted to a discussion of the issues involved in constructing measures for dwelling purchase, construction, and alterations and additions. An advantage of the acquisitions approach is that, consistent with the treatment of most other goods and services in the CPI, the owner-occupied housing index will reflect the full price paid for housing. Moreover, it is not affected by methods of financing for house purchase.

10.42 As CPIs are constructed to measure price change for a group of households in aggregate (the reference or target population), the index should not include any transactions that take place between those households. In the case of an index covering all private households, the weight should only reflect net additions to the household sector owner-occupied housing stock. In practice, net additions will mainly comprise those dwellings purchased from businesses (newly constructed dwellings, company houses, or rental dwellings) and those purchased from or transferred from the government sector plus any purchases, for owner-occupation, of rental dwellings from reference population households. If the CPI is constructed for some subgroup of the population (e.g. wage and salary earners), the weight should also include purchases from other household types.

10.43 Economists regard all housing as fixed capital and hence would exclude purchases of dwellings from household consumption. While this is unambiguously the case for housing purchased for rental, the case is less clear-cut when it comes to housing for owner-occupation. Although households recognize the likelihood of making capital gains when they purchase housing and invariably regard their dwelling as an asset, they also commonly cite the primary motivation for the purchase of a dwelling as being to gain access to a service (i.e. shelter and security of tenure). From the households' perspective, therefore, the costs borne by owner-occupiers in respect of their principal dwelling represent a mix of investment and consumption expenditure, and the total exclusion of these costs from an acquisitions-based CPI can lead to a loss of confidence in the CPI by the population at large. Particularly in those countries where rental sectors are relatively small, with limited opportunities for substitution between owner-occupation and renting, it might be argued that the consumption element dominates.

10.44 The problem confronting compilers of CPIs is how to separate the two elements so as to include only the consumption element in the CPI. Although there is no single agreed technique, one approach is to regard the cost of the land as representing the investment element and the cost of the structure as representing the consumption element. The rationale for this is that while the structure may deteriorate over time and hence be "consumed", the land remains at constant quality for all time (except under extremely unusual circumstances). As the land (or location element) accounts for most of the variation in observable prices for otherwise identical dwellings sold at the same point in time, the exclusion of land values may also be seen as an attempt to exclude asset price inflation from the CPI. (Measures of asset price inflation are, of course, useful in their own right.)

10.45 Derivation of weighting base period expenditures on the net acquisition of dwellings (excluding land), the construction of new dwellings, and alterations and additions to existing dwellings poses some problems. Although household expenditure surveys may yield reliable estimates of the amounts households spend on alterations and additions, and construction of dwellings, it is unlikely that they will provide reliable estimates of net expenditures on existing dwellings exclusive of the value of the land.

10.46 An alternative approach is to combine data from censuses of population and housing and building activity surveys. Population censuses normally collect information on housing tenure, from which average annual growth in the number of owner-occupier households represents a good proxy for net additions to the housing stock. Building activity surveys are also conducted in most countries, providing data on the total value of dwellings constructed. These data can be used to estimate the average value of new dwellings, which can then be applied to the estimated volumes derived from the population census. Of course, the suitability of this approach would need to be assessed by each country and may be complicated if the CPI relates only to some subset of the total population.

10.47 The price index is required to measure the change over time in existing dwelling structures, newly constructed dwellings, and alterations and additions. As the appropriate price for existing dwelling structures is current replacement cost, an index measuring changes in prices of newly constructed dwellings is also appropriate for this purpose. Given that the prices for both newly constructed dwellings and alterations and additions are, in principle, determined by costs of building materials, labour costs and producers' profits, it may also be satisfactory to construct a single price sample for all elements. The requirement for a separate price sample for alterations and additions will depend on the relative significance of this activity and whether the material and labour components differ significantly from those for a complete dwelling (e.g. if alterations and additions are predominantly to kitchens and bathrooms). In all cases, it is important that the price indices are mix-adjusted to eliminate price variations that reflect changes in the characteristics of newly constructed dwellings.

10.48 The type of dwelling constructed in individual countries will significantly influence the complexity and cost of constructing appropriate price measures. If each newly constructed dwelling is essentially unique (i.e. designed to meet site or other requirements) it will be necessary to adopt "model pricing". This requires selection of a sample of building firms, identifying samples of recently constructed dwellings and collecting prices for constructing identical dwellings in subsequent periods (exclusive of site preparation costs, which will vary from site to site). This approach is likely to entail significant costs for the respondents. Moreover, care needs to be taken to ensure that the supplied prices truly reflect all prevailing market conditions. That is, prices need to reflect the amount builders could realistically expect to be able to charge in the current market rather than the prices they would like to be able to charge based on conditions prevailing in some prior period.

10.49 In a number of countries, a significant proportion of newly constructed dwellings are of the type referred to as "project homes". These are homes that builders construct on a regular basis from a suite of standard designs maintained for this purpose. This practice is most feasible in countries where a significant proportion of new dwelling construction takes place in new developments (i.e. land recently developed or redeveloped specifically for residential housing). Where project home construction is significant in scale, then it is possible to select a sample of these project homes for pricing over time, safe in the knowledge that the prices provided will be actual transaction prices (again, priced net of any site preparation costs). Even if project homes do not account for the majority of new dwellings constructed, they may still provide a representative measure of overall price change.

10.50 In pricing project homes, it is necessary to monitor the selected sample to ensure that the selected plans remain representative and to detect changes in quality arising from modifications in design and changes to basic inclusions. Whenever a change is made to the plans, the change in overall quality has to be estimated. For physically measurable characteristics, such as a small increase in the overall size of the dwelling, it may be assumed that the change in quality is proportional to the change in the relevant quantity. Other changes, such as the addition of insulation, inclusion of a free driveway and so on, will need to be valued, preferably in terms of current value to the consumer. These could be estimated by obtaining information on the amounts that consumers would have to pay if they were to have the items provided separately (the option cost method). An alternative is to ask the builder if a cash rebate is available in lieu of the additional features. Where plans are modified to meet changed legal requirements, the consumer has no choice in purchase and so it is acceptable to classify the full change in price as pure price movement (even though there may be some discernible change in quality).

Clothing

10.51 Clothing is a semi-durable good and its treatment is not affected by the conceptual basis chosen for the CPI (acquisitions, use or payments). Particular features of the clothing market do, however, create problems for price index compilers. Although clothing is purchased throughout the year, many types of clothing are only available in particular seasons and, unlike seasonal fruit and vegetables, the specific items on sale in one season (say summer) may not return the following year. In addition to seasonal availability, the physical characteristics of some items of clothing can also change as a result of changing fashions.

10.52 The remainder of this section seeks to provide a general description of the clothing market applicable to most countries, discusses the most significant problems faced by index compilers and looks at some options for overcoming or at least minimizing these.

The clothing market

10.53 Most countries experience at least some climatic variation throughout the year. The number of discrete "seasons" may range from two ("wet" and "dry", summer and winter) up to the four experienced in most regions (winter, spring, summer and autumn). Items of clothing tend to fall into two categories: those that are available in one season only, and those that are available all year round.

10.54 Clothing (whether seasonal or not) is also subject to changes in fashion. The fashion for trousers can change from straight legged to flared; jackets from single-breasted to double-breasted; shirts from button-down collar to not; skirts from long length to short length, and so on.

10.55 Even within categories of garments which are not unduly affected by seasonal influences or general changes in fashions, the garments that are available for pricing from one period to the next can vary greatly. Retailers change suppliers in order to seek the best prices or to maintain an image of a constantly changing range in order to attract shoppers. Many producers will also frequently change product lines in order to maintain buyer appeal. The practice of single producers using different and changing brands as a marketing tool is also common. Isolated countries that rely predominantly on imported clothing also face the additional problem of discontinuities in supply because of shipping failures or even the whim of importers.

10.56 The often short life cycles of specific items, and whole categories of items in the case of seasonal items, mean that retailers have to pay particular attention to inventory control, since they cannot afford to be left with large volumes of stock that they cannot sell. This is most commonly handled by progressively discounting or marking down prices throughout the estimated life cycle of an item.

10.57 The fragmented and changing nature of the clothing market invariably means that price index compilers have to strike a balance between the ideal requirements for index purposes and the cost of data collection (of both prices and characteristics that may be required to make quality adjustments).

Approaches to constructing indices for non-seasonal clothing

10.58 Even where seasonality is not a problem, the construction of a price index for clothing is not a simple task. The range of available items can differ significantly across outlets, making central determination and detailed specification of items to be priced ineffective. The brands and styles of particular garment types can also vary significantly over time in individual outlets, requiring close attention to procedures for replacing items and making quality adjustments.

10.59 Although it is virtually impossible to set out specific procedures that will be applicable in all countries, it is possible to develop a set of guidelines to help avoid the most significant pitfalls. In developing these guidelines, the key objective is to maximize the number of usable price quotations (for a given collection cost) in any month, and to minimize the incidence of measures of price change being affected by changes in quality.

10.60 In some circumstances, it may be possible to identify "national" specifications to be priced at each outlet (e.g. brand X, model Y jeans). The use of these types of specifications can help minimize the effort that needs to be put into quality adjustment, and movements in prices of these items can provide a useful benchmark against which to assess the movements of other items. Reliable identification of such items necessitates ongoing relationships with the buyers for large chains, or large domestic producers or importers. These sources need to be contacted on a regular basis to identify the current range of items, the extent of their availability across the country and any planned changes (including changes in style and quality as well as deletions from and additions to the range). This information may be used proactively to update specifications or descriptions of items to be priced in the field, so minimizing the incidence of price collectors attempting to price items that are no longer available. It can also be used to assist in the quantification of any quality changes.

10.61 For some items where availability by brand varies, it may be possible to identify a number of brands which are assessed as being of equal quality (e.g. different brands of T-shirts). In these cases, price collectors could be provided with the list of equivalent brands and instructed to price the cheapest one of these available at each outlet without having to ensure that the same brand is priced this time as on the last visit. The argument for this practice is that, if the brands are truly equivalent, discerning shoppers will purchase the cheapest at the time of purchase, and to reflect this in the CPI will result in an index that more closely follows the experience of households. Clearly, the success or otherwise of this technique depends vitally on the assessment of the "equality" of brands which, while largely a matter of judgement, may be assisted by an analysis of past price behaviour. In general, brand equality might be indicated by narrow longer-term price dispersion and a tendency for brands to swap prices over time or outlets.

10.62 In other cases it might be appropriate to restrict sampled items to a subset of brands without regarding the brands as equivalent. For example, a number of brands of jeans might together dominate the market but with the availability of the individual brands varying by outlet. In these cases, price collectors could be provided with a list of acceptable brands and instructed to price the most representative of these brands at each outlet. Once the initial selection has been made, price collectors should be instructed to record the specific brand and model priced at each outlet, and should continue to price that specification on subsequent visits until such time as it ceases to be stocked (or it becomes clear that it is no longer representative of the sales of that particular outlet).

10.63 The clothing market has become so diverse that it is not always possible to specify centrally either the item to be priced or even the brand (or brands). In these cases, it is necessary to give price collectors much greater discretion when it comes to selecting the individual items for pricing. To avoid the selection of inappropriate items, it is important for price collectors to be provided with guidelines to assist in this process. At the very least, they should be instructed to select the brand and model that the retailer advises is both representative and is expected to be stocked for some time (little advantage is to be gained from selecting an item which, while popular, has been purchased by the retailer on a one-off basis and is thus unlikely to be available for pricing in subsequent periods).

10.64 More sophisticated guidelines can incorporate a checklist of features that the selected item should match as closely as possible. These features should be ranked from most to least important, and it should be clear which features the selected item possesses and which it does not (either from the detailed description recorded by the price collector or through the completion of a separate feature pro-forma). In addition to brand (or acceptable brands), where possible, the list might include features such as:

- fabric type (e.g. cotton, wool, linen);
- weight of the fabric (e.g. heavy, medium, light);
- existence of a lining;
- number of buttons;
- type of stitching (e.g. single, double).

10.65 It is recognized that high fashion items pose particular difficulties in terms of quality adjustment. There is certainly clear potential for such items to bias the CPI towards the end of their life cycle when prices may be heavily discounted and sales volumes are low. For example, compilers need to guard against the danger that items leave the index at a heavily discounted price to be replaced by items that are on sale at the full price (which for a highly fashionable item may be at a premium). More generally, any decision on the inclusion of high fashion items ought certainly to reflect the intended reference population of the index, for example where this excludes households at the upper end of the income distribution.

Replacement of items and quality change

10.66 Even for garment types that are available all year round, there remains a strong need to replace items or to otherwise recognize changes in item characteristics. It is therefore important to ensure that procedures are established to minimize any bias resulting from changes in the quality of items priced.

10.67 The appropriate conceptual basis for assessing changes in the quality of garments is from the perspective of value to the consumer. In other words, a garment can be said to be of different quality to another garment if it is valued differently by the consumer. The difficulty confronted by index compilers is that quality differences are only observable in terms of changes in the physical characteristics of garments (including brand), some of which will have an impact on customer value and some of which will not. The problem is how to distinguish between them.

10.68 To assist in this task it is important to develop guidelines for selecting replacement items, with the general objective of minimizing the quality difference between the old and new items. For most items, research has shown that brand is an important price- and quality-determining characteristic (particularly for items that have a significant fashion element) and so, in the first instance, an effort should be made to select a replacement from the same brand (but noting the danger that as brands go out of fashion they become less representative). As this will not always be possible, it is useful to enlist experts in the trade to assist in drawing up a list that classifies brands into quality groups along the following lines:

- exclusive brands, usually international brands, mostly sold in exclusive stores;
- higher-quality brands, well-known brands at the national level (which may also include international brands);
- average quality brands;
- other or unknown brands.

10.69 If it is not possible to select a replacement from the same brand, the fallback should be to select a replacement from a brand in the same quality group. Similarity of price should never be the guiding objective when a substitute variety has to be chosen.

10.70 Once a replacement item has been selected, a detailed description of the new item needs to be recorded. The physical differences between the old and new items should be described in as much detail as possible to enable the index compiler to assess whether the replacement item is comparable (i.e. of equal quality) to the old item or not. As a general guide, changes such as single rows of stitching replacing double rows, of lighter-weight fabrics replacing heavier-weight ones, reductions in the number of buttons on shirts, reductions in the length of shirt tails, disappearance of linings and so on should be regarded as changes in quality. Changes in physical characteristics attributable solely to changes in fashion (e.g. straight leg to flared leg trousers) should not be regarded as quality changes.

10.71 Where an item is assessed as not being comparable, action will need to be taken to remove the impact of the quality change from the index. There are a number of approaches that may be taken to value the quality difference:

- Industry experts may be asked to place a cash value on the differences.
- The statistical office may arrange for some index compilers to receive additional training to become commodity experts able to estimate the value of such changes themselves.
- Hedonic methods may be employed if resources permit. Descriptions of hedonic techniques for clothing can be found in Liegey (1992) and Norberg (1999).

10.72 Each of these methods requires that the changes in the quality-determining characteristics (such as quality of material and standard of manufacture) are quantifiable. If such information is not available, implicit quality adjustment methods may have to be used. In this case, it is important that the price for the outgoing specification is returned to a normal price before it is removed from index calculation.

Approaches to including seasonal clothing in the consumer price index

10.73 The practices adopted by statistical agencies for handling seasonal clothing in CPIs vary widely, ranging from complete exclusion of such items to various methods of imputation of prices of items that are unavailable at a particular time of year, or to systems of weights that vary throughout the year. In some respects, the treatment of seasonal clothing raises similar issues to those found in dealing with fashion items, in particular reflecting the short life cycles of products and the likelihood of price-discounting during those cycles.

10.74 This section describes some practical alternatives for indices constructed using the traditional annual basket approach to produce a monthly CPI (i.e. systems of explicitly changing weights are not explored, nor is the use of year-on-year changes as proposed in Chapter 22). Further, the examples will be restricted to the so-called multiple basket approach because of the inherent difficulty of making quality adjustments between seasons in the so-called single basket approach. (The single basket approach takes the view that, say, summer and winter seasonal items are different varieties of the same article, whereas the multiple basket approach takes the view that they are completely different articles.)

10.75 CPI compilers may choose to exclude seasonal clothing from the CPI altogether. While this might simplify the job of compiling the index, it clearly reduces the representativeness of the basket. This might be considered as the option of last resort and will cause presentational difficulties from the point of view of external users, particularly where relative expenditure on seasonal clothing is high. Including seasonal items makes the basket more representative of consumption patterns but complicates the process of compiling the index. In reaching a decision, it will be necessary to strike a balance between representativeness and complexity (cost). Where seasonal items are excluded, their expenditure weight should be distributed among non-seasonal counterparts.

10.76 Six possible approaches to constructing aggregate clothing price indices in the presence of seasonal items are described below. A synthetic set of prices is used (see Table 10.3) to illustrate the various options. For simplicity, it is assumed that there are only three categories of clothing: those available all year (non-seasonal); and two seasonal categories (labelled summer and winter here). The two seasons are assumed to be

Table 10.3 Synthetic price data to illustrate approaches to constructing clothing price indices

Month	Year Y − 1			Year Y			Year Y + 1		
	Non-seasonal	Summer seasonal	Winter seasonal	Non-seasonal	Summer seasonal	Winter seasonal	Non-seasonal	Summer seasonal	Winter seasonal
1	100	100		113	110		127	125	
2	101	80		114	90		128	100	
3	102	60		115	70		130	80	
4	103			116			131		
5	104			117			132		
6	105			118			133		
7	106		100	120		110	135		125
8	107		80	121		90	136		100
9	108		60	122		70	137		80
10	109			123			139		
11	110			124			140		
12	112			126			142		

non-overlapping and the prices of the seasonal varieties are contrived to show progressive discounting over the course of each season. The prices of the non-seasonal items show a steady rate of growth. Within each category, prices are assumed to be for items of identical physical characteristics (or alternatively, to have been adjusted to remove the effects of changes in physical characteristics).

10.77 The price indices have been compiled with a base period of month 1 in year 0 and extend for 24 months (prices are provided for year Y−1 in order to impute base period prices for the winter seasonal item). For the purpose of weighting, it is assumed that each of the seasonal categories accounts for 25 per cent of expenditure, while non-seasonal items account for the remaining 50 per cent. For ease of computation, imputation is based on the simple arithmetic average of the price movements of the available series (including movements from imputed to real prices), though in practice these imputations would be based on weighted averages. Tables 10.4 to 10.6 present the calculated indices and monthly percentage changes for summer seasonal, winter seasonal and total clothing, respectively, based on the alternative methodologies described below.

10.78 *Exclude seasonal items*. This is the simplest option from an index construction point of view, but suffers from a lack of representativeness, which may be a cause of concern to some users. In this example, only 50 per cent of expenditures would be directly represented in the index. Clearly, the greater the relative expenditure on seasonal items, the more users are likely to be concerned about the lack of representativeness of the index. The results for this index are shown in column (1) of Table 10.6 and may be used as a benchmark against which the following options can be assessed.

10.79 *Impute only on items available all year*. This approach is one of the targeted imputation approaches. In this case, the out of season prices for both summer and winter items are imputed based only on the movement in the prices of those items available all year round. The results for the summer and winter items are shown in column (1) of Tables 10.4 and 10.5, respectively, while the total clothing index is shown in column (2) of Table 10.6.

10.80 *Impute on all available items*. This approach imputes all missing prices based on the movements in all available prices of related or similar items. This approach is similar in principle to the approach that would be taken in the case of a missing price observation. Prices for seasonal items are collected while they are observable, and when out of season are imputed based on items available all year round together with other seasonal items if available. The results are shown in column (2) in Tables 10.4 and 10.5, and in column (3) of Table 10.6.

10.81 *Carry forward of last observed price*. This simpler variant of the methods described above involves the carry forward of the last observed prices for seasonal items during the months when such prices are unavailable. This approach would not normally be recommended in the general case where prices are not available for non-seasonal items, on the grounds that the likely downward bias imparted could easily be avoided by observing the price of some similar item that is available. But where a whole class of goods is unavailable and hence unobservable, and particularly where price movements are not strongly correlated with other items, carry forward of prices may be seen as an acceptable approach. The results are shown in column (3) in Tables 10.4 and 10.5, and in column (4) of Table 10.6.

10.82 Under this approach, it is preferable to determine in advance during which months seasonal prices will be collected. This helps prevent distortion of the index through collection of possibly atypical prices for seasonal items unexpectedly available outside those periods when they would normally be available. Such decisions should be subject to regular review on the basis of market developments.

10.83 *Return to normal, then impute*. This approach requires the index compiler to estimate the "normal" price for the item during the first month when it is unavailable (out of season). This estimated normal price is then imputed forward until such time as the item becomes available again. Compared to the methods discussed so far, this approach is designed to avoid artificial depression of the aggregate index beyond the end of season, following progressive discounts over the item's short life cycle.

Table 10.4 Alternative price indices for summer seasonal clothing

Month	Impute only on items available all year (1)	Impute on all available items (2)	Carry forward of last observed price (3)	Return to normal, then impute (4)	Include first seasonal observation, then impute (5)
			Index numbers		
1	100.0	100.0	100.0	100.0	100.0
2	81.8	81.8	81.8	81.8	100.9
3	63.6	63.6	63.6	63.6	101.8
4	64.2	64.2	63.6	100.0	102.7
5	64.7	64.7	63.6	100.9	103.5
6	65.3	65.3	63.6	101.7	104.4
7	66.4	77.0	63.6	102.9	105.4
8	67.0	70.3	63.6	94.0	106.3
9	67.5	62.8	63.6	83.9	107.1
10	68.1	63.3	63.6	108.3	108.0
11	68.6	63.8	63.6	109.2	108.9
12	69.7	64.9	63.6	110.9	110.7
13	113.6	113.6	113.6	113.6	113.6
14	90.9	90.9	90.9	90.9	114.5
15	72.7	72.7	72.7	72.7	116.3
16	73.3	73.3	72.7	113.6	117.2
17	73.8	73.8	72.7	114.5	118.1
18	74.4	74.4	72.7	115.4	119.0
19	75.5	93.3	72.7	117.4	120.8
20	76.1	84.3	72.7	106.1	121.7
21	76.6	76.2	72.7	95.8	122.6
22	77.8	77.3	72.7	123.5	124.4
23	78.3	77.9	72.7	124.4	125.3
24	79.4	79.0	72.7	126.2	127.1
			Monthly percentage changes		
2	−18.2	−18.2	−18.2	−18.2	0.9
3	−22.2	−22.2	−22.2	−22.2	0.9
4	0.9	0.9	0.0	57.2	0.9
5	0.8	0.8	0.0	0.9	0.8
6	0.9	0.9	0.0	0.8	0.9
7	1.7	17.9	0.0	1.2	1.0
8	0.9	−8.7	0.0	−8.6	0.9
9	0.7	−10.7	0.0	−10.7	0.8
10	0.9	0.8	0.0	29.1	0.8
11	0.7	0.8	0.0	0.8	0.8
12	1.6	1.7	0.0	1.6	1.7
13	63.0	75.0	78.6	2.4	2.6
14	−20.0	−20.0	−20.0	−20.0	0.8
15	−20.0	−20.0	−20.0	−20.0	1.6
16	0.8	0.8	0.0	56.3	0.8
17	0.7	0.7	0.0	0.8	0.8
18	0.8	0.8	0.0	0.8	0.8
19	1.5	25.4	0.0	1.7	1.5
20	0.8	−9.6	0.0	−9.6	0.7
21	0.7	−9.6	0.0	−9.7	0.7
22	1.6	1.4	0.0	28.9	1.5
23	0.6	0.8	0.0	0.7	0.7
24	1.4	1.4	0.0	1.4	1.4

Table 10.5 Alternative price indices for winter seasonal clothing

Month	Impute only on items available all year (1)	Impute on all available items (2)	Carry forward of last observed price (3)	Return to normal, then impute (4)	Include first seasonal observation, then impute (5)
			Index numbers		
1	100.0	100.0	100.0	100.0	100.0
2	100.9	91.4	100.0	91.4	100.9
3	101.8	81.6	100.0	81.6	101.8
4	102.7	82.3	100.0	105.3	102.7
5	103.5	83.0	100.0	106.2	103.5
6	104.4	83.7	100.0	107.1	104.4
7	175.2	112.4	183.3	107.8	104.6
8	143.4	91.9	150.0	88.2	105.4
9	111.5	71.5	116.7	68.6	106.3
10	112.4	72.1	116.7	107.8	107.2
11	113.3	72.7	116.7	108.7	108.1
12	115.2	73.9	116.7	110.4	109.8
13	116.1	101.9	116.7	112.2	111.7
14	117.0	92.1	116.7	101.5	112.6
15	118.8	83.6	116.7	92.1	114.4
16	119.7	84.3	116.7	118.4	115.2
17	120.6	84.9	116.7	119.3	116.1
18	121.6	85.6	116.7	120.2	117.0
19	199.1	127.7	208.3	122.5	118.8
20	159.3	102.2	166.7	98.0	119.7
21	127.4	81.7	133.3	78.4	120.6
22	129.3	82.9	133.3	122.5	122.4
23	130.2	83.5	133.3	123.4	123.2
24	132.1	84.7	133.3	125.2	125.0
			Monthly percentage changes		
2	0.9	−8.6	0.0	−8.6	0.9
3	0.9	−10.7	0.0	−10.7	0.9
4	0.9	0.9	0.0	29.0	0.9
5	0.8	0.9	0.0	0.9	0.8
6	0.9	0.8	0.0	0.8	0.9
7	67.8	34.3	83.3	0.7	0.2
8	−18.2	−18.2	−18.2	−18.2	0.8
9	−22.2	−22.2	−22.2	−22.2	0.9
10	0.8	0.8	0.0	57.1	0.8
11	0.8	0.8	0.0	0.8	0.8
12	1.7	1.7	0.0	1.6	1.6
13	0.8	37.9	0.0	1.6	1.7
14	0.8	−9.6	0.0	−9.5	0.8
15	1.5	−9.2	0.0	−9.3	1.6
16	0.8	0.8	0.0	28.6	0.7
17	0.8	0.7	0.0	0.8	0.8
18	0.8	0.8	0.0	0.8	0.8
19	63.7	49.2	78.6	1.9	1.5
20	−20.0	−20.0	−20.0	−20.0	0.8
21	−20.0	−20.1	−20.0	−20.0	0.8
22	1.5	1.5	0.0	56.3	1.5
23	0.7	0.7	0.0	0.7	0.7
24	1.5	1.4	0.0	1.5	1.5

10.84 There are some problems with this procedure. Particularly during periods of high inflation, it will be difficult to determine what the normal price is. More generally, it can be argued that the procedure reduces the objectivity of the index. In the illustrative examples presented here, the normal price to which the item is returned is the price observed at the start of the season. Compared with the previous three approaches, it can be seen that this has the effect of shifting the price increase from the commencement of the next season to immediately after the current season, i.e. the index records a sharp price change when none is observable. The results are shown in column (4) in Tables 10.4 and 10.5, and in column (5) of Table 10.6.

10.85 *Include only the first seasonal observation, then impute*. This approach requires that seasonal items be priced only once per season, when they first appear in the marketplace. This first observed price is then imputed forward until the item is priced again at the commencement of the next season. The rationale for this technique

Table 10.6 Alternative price indices for total clothing

Month	Only items available all year round (1)	Impute only on items available all year (2)	Impute on all available items (3)	Carry forward of last observed price (4)	Return to normal, then impute (5)	Include first seasonal observation, then imput (6)
			Index numbers			
1	100.0	100.0	100.0	100.0	100.0	100.0
2	100.9	96.1	93.8	95.9	93.8	100.9
3	101.8	92.3	87.2	91.8	87.2	101.8
4	102.7	93.1	88.0	92.2	102.7	102.7
5	103.5	93.8	88.7	92.7	103.5	103.5
6	104.4	94.6	89.5	93.1	104.4	104.4
7	106.2	113.5	100.5	114.8	105.8	105.6
8	107.1	106.2	94.1	106.9	99.1	106.5
9	108.0	98.8	87.6	99.1	92.1	107.4
10	108.8	99.5	88.3	99.5	108.4	108.2
11	109.7	100.3	89.0	99.9	109.3	109.1
12	111.5	102.0	90.5	100.8	111.1	110.9
13	112.4	113.6	110.1	113.8	112.7	112.5
14	113.3	108.6	102.4	108.5	104.8	113.4
15	115.0	105.4	96.6	104.9	98.7	115.2
16	115.9	106.2	97.4	105.3	116.0	116.1
17	116.8	107.0	98.1	105.8	116.9	117.0
18	117.7	107.9	98.9	106.2	117.8	117.9
19	119.5	128.4	115.0	130.0	119.7	119.7
20	120.4	119.1	106.8	120.0	111.2	120.6
21	121.2	111.6	100.1	112.1	104.2	121.4
22	123.0	113.3	101.6	113.0	123.0	123.2
23	123.9	114.1	102.3	113.5	123.9	124.1
24	125.7	115.7	103.8	114.3	125.7	125.9
			Monthly percentage changes			
2	0.9	−3.9	−6.2	−4.1	−6.2	0.9
3	0.9	−4.0	−7.0	−4.3	−7.0	0.9
4	0.9	0.9	0.9	0.5	17.8	0.9
5	0.8	0.8	0.8	0.5	0.8	0.8
6	0.9	0.9	0.9	0.5	0.9	0.9
7	1.7	20.0	12.3	23.3	1.3	1.1
8	0.8	−6.4	−6.4	−6.9	−6.3	0.9
9	0.8	−7.0	−6.9	−7.4	−7.1	0.8
10	0.7	0.7	0.8	0.4	17.7	0.7
11	0.8	0.8	0.8	0.4	0.8	0.8
12	1.6	1.7	1.7	0.9	1.6	1.6
13	0.8	11.4	21.7	12.8	1.4	1.4
14	0.8	−4.4	−7.0	−4.6	−7.0	0.8
15	1.5	−2.9	−5.7	−3.4	−5.8	1.6
16	0.8	0.8	0.8	0.4	17.5	0.8
17	0.8	0.8	0.7	0.4	0.8	0.8
18	0.8	0.8	0.8	0.4	0.8	0.8
19	1.5	19.0	16.3	22.4	1.6	1.5
20	0.8	−7.2	−7.1	−7.7	−7.1	0.8
21	0.7	−6.3	−6.3	−6.6	−6.3	0.7
22	1.5	1.5	1.5	0.8	18.0	1.5
23	0.7	0.7	0.7	0.4	0.7	0.7
24	1.5	1.4	1.5	0.8	1.5	1.5

is that it is a means of adjusting for the quality degradation of seasonal items associated with the commonly observed feature of falling prices throughout the season. Further, if it is desirable that the index behave as if it were constructed as a moving year index (see Chapter 22), then this approach provides a cost-effective alternative that also accommodates changing seasons (e.g. when the items that were in season last March do not appear until April this year).

10.86 On the downside, in fully discounting observable price movements through a seasonal item's life cycle, an implicit assumption is made that all such movements reflect quality changes with no change in underlying price. This is not likely to fully accord with user perceptions of price evolution and, unless similar techniques are employed for fashion items, it can be argued that the approach is inconsistent. The results are shown in column (5) in Tables 10.4 and 10.5, and column (6) in Table 10.6.

Summary comments

10.87 First, it is worth noting that the consequences of imputing price changes for baskets of seasonal items based on the price movements for other items of clothing is equivalent to allocating the weight for seasonal items to other items when they are out of season, so avoiding the complexity involved in systems of explicitly changing weights. In these circumstances, some care needs to be taken in the presentation of estimates of the contribution of both seasonal and non-seasonal items to the change in the aggregate CPI. The standard practice of determining an item's contribution to the total change in the CPI is to multiply the item's previous period (price-updated) weight by its percentage change. Only those seasonal items for which prices are actually measured in the current period will contribute to the change in the aggregate index. Similarly, though only non-seasonal items will contribute to the change in the aggregate index when seasonal items are out of season, the standard measure of their contribution will be understated. This is mainly an issue of presentation, although some compilers might prefer to present assessments of contributions only down to the level that includes both the seasonal and non-seasonal baskets.

10.88 There is likely to be a range of views across countries, and indeed users, concerning the appropriate treatment of seasonal items within a CPI. There is likely to be a particular diversity of views about whether the quality of seasonal items should be regarded as diminishing over the life of the season or not and, if so, whether a similar approach should (or can) be taken in respect of fashion items. The example data set was contrived so that each category displayed broadly constant growth in prices on a year-on-year basis. Those users primarily interested in measures that best capture persistent or underlying price pressures in the economy are likely to prefer those approaches which do not yield significant variations in the rate of price change that are solely attributable to how the statistical agency treats seasonal items. Such users may prefer that seasonal items be excluded altogether or that only the first seasonal observation be included with prices for other months being imputed.

10.89 What is clear is that national statistical offices need to carefully weigh up user requirements, theoretical issues, costs and the implications of alternative approaches before settling on the methodology to be adopted.

Telecommunication services

10.90 The global telecommunications sector has undergone rapid change in recent years. Technological innovation has resulted in a proliferation of new services while deregulation has led to sharp growth in the number of providers in many countries. Taken together, these factors have resulted in suppliers adopting a range of new strategies to differentiate their services in order to attract and retain customers.

10.91 Characteristics of particular significance to compilers of price indices are:

- fewer linear pricing schedules and the adoption of different pricing structures across providers;
- the increasing tendency to offer contracts that bundle services together in different ways to appeal to different types of consumers;
- rapid changes in the contracts offered to consumers as an effective means of encouraging the take-up of the ever-increasing range of services.

10.92 Increasingly, telecommunication companies offer services via plans that require customers to enter into longer-term contractual arrangements with the providers. This also poses problems for index compilation. Two broad types of plan are typically offered. The first has no fixed duration and makes allowance for the provider to change pricing structures with advance notice to the consumer. The second and increasingly more popular type provides a fixed term contract (generally of one to two years) with prices fixed for the duration of the contract. These plans are differentiated by charging different prices for different services. For example, a simple plan may be differentiated by charging more for monthly line rental but less for local calls, so appealing to users who make a higher volume of local calls. The emergence of new tailored plans designed to maximize customer demand overall is continuous.

10.93 If statistical agencies follow traditional sampling approaches and select price schedules according to some base period set of plans, and follow them until they expire, no price changes will be observed (likewise if plans expire and replacements are linked to show no change). The marketplace reality, by contrast, is that unit values for telecommunication services have been declining significantly in many countries.

10.94 All statistical agencies are struggling to develop methodologies capable of coping with the complexities of this sector. In particular, it is recognized that current best practice approaches have difficulty in accounting for substitutions across providers and in adequately accounting for changes in the quality of the services provided.

10.95 With the telecommunications sector under continual change, statistical practices need to be kept under constant review. Statistical agencies that are considering the construction of telecommunications indices for the first time, or considering reviewing their current practices, are advised to seek out the most recent research in this field. Nevertheless, this section seeks to provide a general description of four approaches that are currently used by national statistical agencies to measure changes in the prices of telecommunication services. The approaches, in increasing order of cost, are:

- representative items – matched samples;
- representative items – unit values;
- customer profiles;
- sample of bills.

10.96 Each approach is briefly described and potential deficiencies noted. There is no firm recommendation on the best approach as the choice will depend largely on the market conditions prevailing in individual countries, the sophistication of the index compilation system in use, and the extent of access to accurate and timely telecommunication services data. Depending on these factors, it may be appropriate to use different approaches for different telecommunication services, or even for the different services of specific providers.

Representative items – matched samples

10.97 This approach mirrors traditional techniques adopted elsewhere in the CPI. Total expenditure of reference group households on telecommunication services in the weighting base period is derived from sources such as household expenditure surveys. A sample of service providers is approached to obtain information on revenue by types of services (such as line rental, local calls, international calls, handset sales or rentals, connection fees, voicemail services, Internet charges and so on) and a number of these are selected as *representative items* with weights derived from the revenue data.

10.98 For each representative item, a sample of detailed specifications (such as a telephone call from location A to location B, at time X, of duration Y minutes) is drawn up sufficient to represent the range of specific services purchased by consumers within each representative item. This sample of specifications is held constant from period to period, and movements in the indices for representative items are computed, based on the movements in the prices of this *matched sample* of specifications. Table 10.7 illustrates the approach.

10.99 The list of representative items (the lowest level in the structure) generally does not need to cover all telecommunication services, but those selected should be sufficient to be representative of price behaviour as a whole, in particular taking account of published tariffs. Expenditures on those services not selected for pricing should be distributed over the other services within that general class for the purpose of deriving weights. For example, the expenditures on any fixed line services not selected for pricing should be distributed over those fixed line services selected.

10.100 Compared to suppliers of goods, service providers have an almost infinite capacity to tailor both the services and the prices they charge, for example based on the time at which the service is provided. A telephone call of five minutes' duration at 8 a.m. can be regarded as a different product to an equivalent call made at 8 p.m., and service providers are able to charge different prices for these calls. Representative items therefore need to be described in sufficient detail to capture all the price-determining characteristics.

10.101 Furthermore, given the ease with which providers can adjust the differential aspects of their pricing schedules (such as the time span designated as peak and the duration of a call before a different rate applies), it is necessary to use a sufficient number of varied specifications to capture these aspects reliably. It is not sufficient to simply describe a call as peak or off-peak, or from zone 1 to zone 2. Illustrative examples of the types of specifications that may be applicable for two representative items – international calls (fixed line) and usage fees (Internet services) – are provided in Table 10.8.

10.102 It is assumed that the origin of both the telephone calls and Internet access is also identified. All times are domestic. It should also be noted that the nature of Internet access generally precludes pricing on the basis of access, and hence the timing of access cannot be as tightly defined as for international telephone calls; instead, all specifications are for total monthly use.

10.103 The most costly aspect of this approach therefore is obtaining the data required to establish the representative items and to identify suitable specifications, as this will require detailed information from service providers. Once implemented, most price information should be readily available from published fee schedules, so minimizing the burden on respondents between reviews of the specifications.

10.104 The dynamic nature of the telecommunication sector and the common use of the pricing mechanism to change consumer behaviour are likely to require that the specifications be updated relatively frequently. When a specification disappears (i.e. a particular plan is no longer offered), all efforts must be made to find a suitable comparison specification. Where specifications are replaced, it is possible to argue that because different plans involve different conditions of sale they are fundamentally different products. It is equally reasonable

Table 10.7 An illustrative index structure for telecommunication services (representative item approach)

Fixed line services
Telephone connection costs
Telephone line rental
Local calls
Long-distance national calls
International calls
Mobile telephones
Connection costs
Handset purchase or rental
National calls
International calls
Payphones
Local calls
Internet services
Connection fees
Usage fees

Table 10.8 Examples of specifications of telecommunication services

Representative item	Examples of specifications
International calls (fixed line)	Plan A: Call to Athens at 8 a.m. on a Friday, duration 10 minutes Plan B: Call to London at 9 p.m. on a Saturday, duration 5 minutes Plan A: Call to New York at 11 a.m. on a Wednesday, duration 20 minutes Plan B: Call to Paris at 7 p.m. on a Sunday, duration 15 minutes Plan A: Call to Durban at 8 p.m. on a Monday, duration 30 minutes
Usage fees (Internet)	Plan A: 10 hours dial-up connect time between 4 p.m. and 7 p.m. weekends, total download 20 Mb Plan B: 20 hours dial-up connect time between 6 p.m. and midnight weekdays, total download 50 Mb Plan C: Permanent broadband connection, total download 100 Mb

to question whether all of the price difference between plans is due to quality differences, particularly in light of the evidence of ever-increasing volumes and reductions in unit values. The difficulty lies in quantifying the quality differences. Although hedonic techniques offer some prospects for resolving this dilemma, they are costly to implement.

Representative items – unit values

10.105 The unit value approach is similar to the previous approach, with the exception that specifications are not priced. The price for each representative item is calculated from revenue and quantity data collected from the service provider. For example, the price for national long-distance calls can be derived as the total revenue received from such calls divided by the number of call-minutes. Similarly, in the case of monthly line rental fees, the price can be calculated as the total revenue from line rental divided by the total number of subscribers.

10.106 Compared to the matched sample approach, the unit value approach attributes all of the difference between plans, and time and duration of calls to price (i.e. the quality difference is assumed to be zero). The unit value approach is also seen as providing a method for accounting for price change when the items are subject to a proliferation of discount schemes or promotions (e.g. $2 to call anywhere for as long as you like for the next week). While the approach avoids some of the customer sampling choices inherent in other methodologies, compilation does rest on analysis of aggregate company data and so is likely to be less timely than methodologies based on pre-published prices. Moreover, care needs to be exercised with this approach to ensure that the measure is not affected by undesirable compositional changes (see Chapter 9, where unit value indices are discussed in more detail). A unit value index should only be constructed for truly homogeneous items. This points to a requirement for defining the representative items at a relatively fine level of disaggregation. For example, international calls may need to be further subdivided by destination to avoid changes in unit values arising purely from shifts in the numbers of calls made to different destinations.

10.107 Although this approach appears to address at least some of the known deficiencies of the matched sample approach, it is likely to have a medium- to long-term downward bias and, unless implemented carefully, it is likely to exhibit period-to-period volatility because of compositional shifts, if only as a result of seasonal variations in usage patterns. There are also a number of respondent and data quality aspects that need to be considered. The unit value approach imposes a greater data burden on service providers, who often regard revenue and quantity data as highly commercially sensitive. To be effective, the service providers also need to be able to furnish data relating only to households (i.e. they have to be able to separate out revenue and quantities relating to businesses) and the revenue information needs to conform to the requirements of the index. For example, some service providers may record certain discounts as a marketing expense, rather than a reduction in revenue as is required for the unit value index.

Customer profiles

10.108 For marketing purposes, telecommunication companies often classify their customers according to their volume of service use. Although the number of categories can vary, a common approach is to use a three-way classification: low-volume, medium-volume and high-volume customers. Service providers analyse customer usage patterns by category when developing new plans targeted specifically at each group. National regulatory authorities may also be in a position to provide detailed customer use profiles on a confidential basis.

10.109 Statistical agencies can take a similar approach for the construction of price indices by devising profiles which reflect the average usage patterns for each category of consumer. Costs faced by these average consumers in each period can then be estimated by reference to the rates set out in that plan that is currently most commonly applicable to each customer category. Variations on this general theme include estimation of costs based on the plan that would deliver the cheapest overall cost to the consumer (based on the simplifying assumption of cost-minimizing consumer behaviour with perfect knowledge). This has the advantage of providing a clear basis for choosing a comparable replacement should an existing package cease to be available. Alternatively, costs to each customer group may be estimated with reference to several plans, where sales information indicates that this is a closer approximation to reality. The overall index is derived by weighting together the results from these user profiles according to information about the relative importance of each category of consumer.

10.110 In constructing the aggregate index, these calculations are likely to be made for a representative sample of service providers, exploiting information on their overall market share for sampling or weighting purposes if available. This opens up the possibility of fully exploiting all the possible relevant permutations of profiles and companies. Information on the distribution of customer profiles by service provider may, however, not be available or at least very costly to obtain. Table 10.9 gives an example of a profile for mobile telephone services, taken from Beuerlein (2001), which describes the current approach used in the German CPI.

10.111 Consistent with the fixed basket approach, the activity of consumers (in terms of numbers and types of calls) is held constant between comparison periods. Prices may, of course, change when not fixed by contract or when plans are replaced. Index compilers may also allow rates to change in response to a changing mix of plans within customer categories. This approach assumes that plan changes, as such, fundamentally represent price change rather than quality change, but it eliminates the cruder compositional effects associated with the unit value approach, which does not take account of customer profiles.

10.112 The success of this approach is determined by the degree to which the profiles truly reflect consumer

Table 10.9 Example of a user profile for mobile phone services

Specification	Unit	Rare callers	Low-volume callers	Average callers
Total length of calls	Minutes	16	42	96
Length of individual call				
Type A	Seconds	35	45	45
Type B	Seconds	65	95	115
Calls[1]	Number	20	36	72
Within the same network	Number	8	12	24
Beyond the network	Number	12	24	48

[1]The calls are distributed over times of the day and days of the week so that it is possible to take account of changes in the delimitation of between peak and off-peak, weekday and weekend tariffs.
Source: Beuerlein (2001).

behaviour and therefore a great deal of thought needs to be put into their development. The construction of the customer profiles will require a high degree of co-operation from service providers and, given the known volume changes, they will require updating at reasonably regular intervals, possibly more frequently than other items in the CPI basket. Data on plan usage by customer category for each index compilation period (month or quarter) may also be required if compilers decide to allow for such effects.

Sample of bills

10.113 This method can be seen as a more refined application of the customer profile approach. A fixed level of service activity from an actual sample of customers is priced each month rather than defining profiles representative of the average monthly activities of customers. A sample of customers should be selected from each category of customer (low-, medium- and high-volume customers) and, ideally, the bills (or activity statements) should cover a full year's activity.

10.114 The advantages of this approach compared to the customer profile approach are:

- It is able to take account of any within-year variations in customer behaviour (e.g. a higher incidence of international calls associated with religious or cultural events of significance).
- It better reflects the diversity of consumer behaviour by identifying actual activities (i.e. calls actually made by a sample of consumers).
- It accommodates within each bill any instances of annual charges.
- It allows for the detection and recording of other sources of price change associated with customers' overall relationship with the service provider (e.g. where overall discounts are provided when aggregate monthly spending exceeds certain values, or where an aggregate discount is provided if customers acquire bundles of services from a single provider, such as fixed line phone plus Internet).

10.115 Calculation of the index still requires monthly information on the relative significance of various plans by customer category (which can then be randomly allocated across the sampled bills). With the bill sample repriced each period, the resulting index measures the cost of a full year's consumption at the prices prevailing in each index period compared to the same cost at base prices. This assumes that the quality difference between old and new plans is zero for households' changing plans. Because of the generally larger number of bills (compared with the number of available profiles), price changes can be reflected more gradually, as the proportion of bills priced using each plan can better mirror the changing population distribution.

10.116 As with the profile approach, it is important that the sample of bills is updated regularly to reflect changes in consumption patterns and the take-up of new services such as call-waiting, voicemail and text messaging. Although, with adequate sampling, the bill approach is likely to provide a better measure of the aggregate rate of price change for telecommunication services as a whole, it may not be best suited to the calculation of separate indices for the components of those services (depending on whether overall or bottom-line discounts are offered). The approach is also data intensive, requiring a large number of calculations each period and thus a sophisticated data processing system.

Financial services

10.117 The construction of reliable, comprehensive price indices for financial services in CPIs is in its infancy. Given the increasing use of financial services by households, however, national statistical agencies are coming under pressure to account for at least some financial services in their CPIs. There is a particularly strong demand for CPIs to include those fees and charges faced by households in respect of deposit and loan accounts held with financial institutions.

10.118 The construction of price indices for financial services is inherently difficult, as there is no unanimous view about which financial services ought to be included in the CPI, or indeed about precisely how they should be measured. The discussion in this section attempts to present what might be regarded as the majority view based on what is practically feasible. Much of the material is based on Fixler and Zieshang (2001), Frost (2001) and Woolford (2001).

10.119 Common examples of financial services acquired by households include financial advice, currency exchange, services associated with deposit and loan facilities, services provided by fund managers, life insurance offices and superannuation funds, stockbroking services, and real estate agency services. The range of items explicitly regarded as financial services for inclusion in a CPI, and also the way in which they are measured, will depend on the principal purpose of the CPI and hence on whether an acquisitions, use or payments approach is employed.

10.120 Where a *payments* approach is used, the gross interest payable on mortgages is often included as a cost of owner-occupied housing (see paragraphs 10.4 to 10.50 above). In the interests of strict consistency, this might imply that the CPI should also include consumer credit charges (measured in a similar way to mortgage interest charges), as well as gross outlays on direct fees and charges paid in respect of other financial services. In practice, and as noted in the earlier section on housing costs, the treatment of housing sometimes differs in concept from other interest charges in national CPIs, partly reflecting mixed objectives for the overall index combined with public perceptions of the importance of this item within overall budgets. The specific requirements for a payments approach will not be discussed further here as the principles are either described elsewhere (e.g. under owner-occupied housing) or are relatively straightforward.

10.121 Assuming that households acquire all of their financial services from the private sector (i.e. they are not generally subsidized by governments or provided by nonprofit institutions serving households), the *acquisitions* and *use* approaches take an identical view of the measurement of financial services. In terms of coverage, however, some proponents of the use approach take a more restrictive view of which services should be included by limiting the scope to only those financial services which are acquired to directly facilitate current household consumption.

10.122 Under the more restrictive view of coverage, it is argued that the use of some financial services is inextricably linked with capital (or investment) activity. This suggests that such activities should be considered outside the scope of CPIs intended to provide measures of changes in consumption prices. Proponents of this view often draw upon national accounts practices as the starting point. For example, *SNA 1993* classifies expenses associated with the transfer of real estate (real estate agents' commissions, legal fees, and government taxes and charges) as part of gross fixed capital formation. It is important to note, however, that the CPI is not constrained to follow the practices adopted for national accounting. Rather, individual countries will need to make decisions on the item coverage of the CPI which best meets the domestic requirements of the price index itself.

10.123 One broad definition that could be adopted for the coverage of financial services within the CPI is: *all those services acquired by households in relation to the acquisition, holding and disposal of financial and real assets, including advisory services, except those acquired for business purposes*. This definition serves two purposes. First, it distinguishes between the services facilitating the transfer and holding of assets and the assets themselves. Second, it makes no distinction between whether the underlying asset is a real asset or a financial asset.

10.124 The degree of complexity involved in placing a value on financial services acquired by households and constructing the companion price indices varies markedly by service. Three specific examples reflecting current Australian research are used to illustrate the issues: currency exchange, stockbroking, and deposit and loan facilities. Real estate agency services are discussed separately in this chapter (see paragraphs 10.149 to 10.155) because they may be classified as either a housing expense or a financial service.

Currency exchange

10.125 For weighting purposes, the estimation of the base period expenditures incurred by households in exchanging domestic currency for currencies of other countries is, in principle, relatively straightforward and should be reportable in household expenditure surveys.

10.126 Construction of the companion price index is more complex. The service for which a price is required is that of facilitating the exchange of domestic currency for that of another country (the acquisition of an asset – foreign currency). The price for the service is usually specified in terms of some percentage of the domestic currency value of the transaction. These percentage margins may change only rarely, with service providers relying on the nominal value of the transactions increasing over time to deliver increases in fee receipts. The price required for index construction purposes is the monetary value of the margin (i.e. the amount determined by applying the percentage rate to the value of the currency transaction). To measure price change over time, the index compiler has to form a view about the quantity underpinning the original transaction.

10.127 The purchase of foreign currency can be seen as facilitating the purchase of some desired quantity of foreign goods and services (e.g. expenditure on foreign travel, or direct import of a commodity). The service price in comparison periods would be expressed as the amount payable on the conversion of a sum of domestic currency corresponding to that sum of foreign currency required to purchase the same quantum of foreign goods and services purchased in the base period.

10.128 A practical translation implies that the original foreign currency amount is indexed forward using changes in foreign prices, and then converted to domestic currency at the prevailing exchange rate, with the prevailing percentage margin applied to this new amount to deliver the current price. This current price would be compared to the base price to derive the measure of price change. Although the ideal measure for indexing forward the foreign currency amount would be an index specifically targeting those foreign goods and services purchased by resident households, this is unlikely to be feasible. A practical alternative is to use the published aggregate CPI for the foreign countries.

10.129 If a single margin (percentage rate) does not apply to all transactions (e.g. different rates apply to different size transactions), then the price measure should be constructed by reference to a representative sample of base period transactions. The value margin for each transaction in the current period in the domestic currency would be determined by the current domestic currency value of each transaction and the current period percentage margin applying to each. This captures any price change resulting from the value of an underlying transaction moving from one price band to another.

Stockbroking services

10.130 Consider the case of the purchase of a parcel of shares in a publicly listed company. In most countries, the purchase has to be arranged through a licensed broker (stockbroker). The total amount paid by the purchaser generally comprises three elements: an amount for the shares (the asset); a fee for the brokerage service; and some form of transaction tax (stamp duty).

10.131 The tax should be considered part of the cost of acquiring the shares, as opposed to being part of the price of the security. The tax should be included along with the brokerage cost in the CPI. This is consistent with both the intention of the tax and the more commonly accepted basis for the valuation of the shares. (It also proves convenient to adopt this principle here, as it allows for the – perhaps less contentious – comparable treatment of taxes on banking services.) Allowing for current tax schedules poses no difficulty in that they will be widely available in all countries.

10.132 Working from the premise that stockbrokers' fees are more likely to follow a step function than a linear function, a price measure would be constructed as follows. First, select a representative sample of transactions (domestic currency values) and calculate the tax payable and the fees payable by reference to the respective schedules. The taxes and fees payable in subsequent periods are calculated by first indexing forward the values of the sample transactions and then applying current fee and tax schedules to the revalued transactions. This methodology raises two main issues. First, what is the most appropriate index for revaluing the transactions and, second, how should the current schedule of fees be determined?

10.133 The quantum underlying share transactions can be regarded as forgone consumption, i.e. the quantity of goods and services that could have been purchased instead. The value of a constant quantum of consumption forgone in successive comparison periods therefore will vary with consumer prices. In this case, the obvious choice for an escalator would be the CPI itself, based on current period preliminary estimates, or the previous period's result. However, the use of a single period's movement in the CPI (either previous or current) has the potential to result in the prices of stockbroking services moving in a way that is unlikely to reflect reality. This would be particularly evident where, for example, the current or previous period's CPI was influenced significantly by some one-off, temporary or unusual price change (e.g. an oil price shock, or change to health care arrangements). Any "echoing" of abnormal shorter-term price changes through the precise treatment of stockbrokers' or similar fees is likely to stretch public credibility in the CPI. As an alternative, a 12-month moving average CPI might be employed, itself consistent with a base period comprising a full year's activity.

10.134 Alternatively, it might be argued that the quantum of shares could be revalued in subsequent periods in line with movements in equity prices themselves. According to this view, the price of equities may be seen as an important influence on the actual costs of storing forgone consumption in much the same way as tax and fee schedules specific to equity purchases are allowed to enter the calculations described above. The strong argument against this treatment is that it assumes that households have a desire to own equities per se, rather than using them simply as an appropriate vehicle to store forgone consumption. Moreover, the introduction of equity prices within the price indicator is likely to impart additional short-term volatility to the CPI.

10.135 Competition in the stockbroking industry means that there is unlikely to be a common fee schedule. If individual brokers adhere reasonably closely to an in-house fee schedule, obtaining copies of these schedules should be a relatively simple matter. On the other hand, if no such fee schedules exist, then a survey of stockbrokers may be required to collect information on a sample of trades (value of trade and fee charged), and this information used to derive a current period fee schedule.

10.136 In the case of sales of shares, the underlying transaction represents the exchange of one asset for another (shares for cash). Quantities underlying sales can be viewed similarly to share purchases (i.e. some current period basket of consumption goods and services). In reality, households review their investment strategies regularly in order to "store" their deferred consumption in whatever asset class they believe offers the greatest security or prospect for growth. A symmetrical treatment of the purchase and sale of shares is particularly appealing. Unless different fees or taxes apply to sales, there is no need to distinguish between the two in constructing the index.

Deposit and loan facilities

10.137 Accounting for the costs of services provided by financial intermediaries represents a significant step up in complexity. Even where a prior decision has been made to include such facilities within the scope of the CPI, the service being provided is difficult to visualize comprehensively, and the prices comprise significant elements that are not directly observable.

10.138 *SNA 1993* recommends (6.125 and Annex III) that the value of financial intermediation services output produced by an enterprise should be valued as the following sum:

- for financial assets involved in financial intermediation, such as loans, the value of services provided by the enterprise to the borrower per monetary unit on account is the margin between the rate payable by the borrower and a reference rate; plus
- for financial liabilities involved in financial intermediation, such as deposits, the value of services provided by the enterprise to the lender or depositor per monetary unit on account is the margin between the reference rate and the rate payable by the enterprise to the lender; plus
- the value of actual or explicit financial intermediation service charges levied.

10.139 For a summary of the developments in national accounts treatment in this area, and a discussion of the notion of a reference rate, see OECD (1998). In concept, *SNA 1993* describes the reference rate as the risk-free or pure interest rate. The value of the service provided to a borrower is the difference between the actual amount of interest paid by the borrower and the lower amount that would have been paid had the reference rate applied. The converse applies for depositors. In practice, it is very difficult to identify the reference rate, and in particular to avoid either volatility in or even negative measures of the value of such services (as would occur if the reference rate lay above the lending rate or below the deposit rate). As a matter of practical expediency, an average of borrowing and lending rates may be used (with the mid-point being favoured).[1] Given the complexities involved, expenditures on financial intermediation required for index weighting purposes cannot be collected from households in expenditure surveys and so must be estimated by collecting data from financial institutions.

10.140 In thinking about the construction of the index number, it is useful to start by considering the case of a traditional bank providing a single loan product and a single deposit product; the example will then be extended to a typical bank. In some countries, the traditional bank does not charge direct fees, but all income is derived through an interest margin on lending rates over deposit rates.

10.141 The base period weighting value of the financial service (and so household consumption of such services) therefore is estimated by applying a margin (the absolute difference between the reference rate and the rate of interest charged to borrowers or paid to depositors) to an aggregate balance (loan or deposit). In line with the suggested treatment of other financial transactions, the construction of accompanying price measures should allow for the indexation forward of base period balances, applying comparison period margins to calculate a money value. The price index is then calculated as the ratio of comparison period and base period money values.

10.142 Again, the issue of an appropriate escalator needs to be addressed. While the base period flows of deposits and withdrawals can readily be conceptualized as forgone consumption at base period prices, how should the balances (stocks) reflecting an accumulation of flows over a number of years be viewed? If an age profile for balances were available, accumulated consumption forgone could be computed as a moving average of the CPI. The more practical alternative is to view base period balances as representing some quantum of consumption goods and services at base period prices, in which case the 12-month moving average CPI can be used. This is consistent with the idea that households review temporal consumption or investment decisions (and so accumulated financial balances) on a regular basis, in this case annually.

10.143 The traditional bank has all but disappeared in some countries and most financial institutions now derive income from a combination of indirect fees (margins) and direct fees and charges, with the trend being for a move from margins towards direct fees. In this case, the challenge is to construct measures of price change that reflect the total price of the service and therefore capture any offsets between margins and direct fees. As with stockbroking services, there may also be taxes levied on financial transactions or balances and these should also be included in the "price". Frost (2001), for example, provides a description of the more practical aspects of constructing price indices for deposit and loan facilities based on recent Australian experience.

10.144 Given the clear scope for financial intermediaries to shift charges between the direct (fee) and indirect (margin) elements, there are clear dangers in constructing broad measures of margins – known by national accountants as financial intermediation services indirectly measured (FISIM) – independent of direct fees and taxes. Rather, the approach should be to construct price measures for specific (relatively homogeneous) products that can then be weighted together to provide a measure for deposit and loan facilities in aggregate, and taking account of both the direct and indirect elements in total price. This represents a similar strategy to that adopted throughout the CPI. For example, the index for motor vehicles is constructed by pricing a sample of individual vehicles and weighting these price measures to derive an aggregate, instead of, for example, attempting to directly construct an index for the supplier or producer of a range of vehicles.

10.145 The basic process is: first, to select a sample of representative products from each sampled institution; second, to select a sample of customers for each product, and third, to estimate the total base period value of the service associated with each product by element (margin, direct fees and taxes). These value aggregates can be viewed as being equivalent to prices for some quantum. Comparison period prices are derived by moving forward the base period value aggregates as follows:

- Margin – index forward the base period balance and apply the comparison period margin (the difference between the comparison period reference rate and the product yield). In practice, the "price" movement is given as the product of the indexation factor and the ratio of margins.
- Fees – index forward the transaction values for each sampled account (or profile) and apply the comparison period fee structure. The ratio of new aggregate fees to base fees is used to move the fee value aggregate. The aggregate fees in the base and comparison periods can be constructed as either arithmetic or geometric averages of the fees calculated for the individual customers.
- Taxes – as for fees, but use tax schedules instead of fee schedules.

10.146 Appendix 10.1 contains a worked example of the calculation of a price index for a single deposit product.

10.147 Since step function pricing and taxing schedules (for example, fees that are only payable after some number of transactions or if balances fall below some level) are prevalent in financial services, samples of detailed customer accounts with all the necessary charging variables identified will be required. These samples

[1]OECD (1998) expresses some concerns about the use of a mid-point reference rate as a measure of the risk-free rate of interest. There are, however, some doubts about whether the conceptual ideal is for some "risk-free" interest rate, or whether a more appropriate concept might be the interest rate that would have been struck in the absence of financial intermediaries (i.e. the rate that would have been struck by depositors dealing directly with borrowers). Such a rate would have incorporated the lenders' knowledge of risk. Taking the mid-point of the borrowing and lending rates would appear to be a good means of estimating this market-clearing rate.

should cover a full year's activity. If it is not possible to sample actual accounts, customer profiles may be developed as a fallback option.

10.148 To minimize problems associated with non-response and changing industry structures, a separate reference rate should be constructed for each sampled service provider. The reference rate should be calculated in respect of all loans and deposits (including those to businesses). Further, to avoid problems that may arise in the timing of accounting entries (e.g. revisions, or interest income on credit cards), monthly yields, reference rates and margins should be constructed by reference to three-month moving averages of the reported underlying balances and interest flows.

Real estate agency services

10.149 The services provided by real estate agencies in the acquisition and disposal of properties can be treated in a number of ways. If the CPI is constructed as an economic cost of *use* index, these services are out of scope as they form part of the input costs of the notional landlords (*SNA 1993* also assigns all transfer costs on dwellings to gross fixed capital formation). The transfer costs associated with the acquisition of a dwelling (legal fees, real estate agency fees and taxes) can be included in both a *payments* and an *acquisitions* CPI. They can be classified as either a cost of home ownership or as a distinctly separate financial service. Although all transfer costs should be included in such measures, the discussion below focuses on real estate agents' fees for simplicity. Price measures for the other elements are calculated using similar procedures. In all cases, the general approach is to estimate the current cost of the various services relative to, and as they would apply to, some fixed basket of activity in the base period. Consistent with some of the areas already discussed, this involves indexing forward the base period expenditures on which the fees are charged (to preserve the underlying quantum) via some appropriate price index, and then estimating the fees payable in the comparison period.

10.150 Real estate agents typically quote their fees as some percentage of the price received for the dwelling. In common with other items where charges are determined as a margin, this needs to be converted to a domestic currency price. If the percentage margin is known, the agents' price for any given transaction (sale/purchase of a dwelling for a known price) can be computed by multiplying the value of the dwelling by the percentage margin, and the index can be constructed on the basis of estimates of both components.

10.151 The methodology chosen for estimating the percentage margin will depend upon an assessment of the variation in margins across and within individual agencies. In the most straightforward case, firms may operate with a single percentage margin applicable to all transactions regardless of value. In other words, at any point in time the percentage margins charged may vary by agency, but not by value of transaction within agency. In this case, what is required is an estimate, in each comparison period, of the average percentage margin charged by agencies. This can be achieved by collecting the percentage margins, exclusive of any taxes levied on agents' fees such as value added tax (VAT) or goods and services tax (GST), from a sample of agencies and deriving an average.

10.152 Percentage margins charged by individual agencies sometimes vary with transaction price (typically declining with increasing prices of dwellings). Where tariffs do vary within agencies, a more sophisticated estimation procedure may be required. Using data from a sample of transactions from a sample of agents, the relationship between the value of transaction and the percentage margin can be derived through econometric analysis. Empirical analysis will be required to determine the precise functional form for this relationship. For example, in the Australian case research has shown that ordinary least squares regression can be used to estimate this relationship and that the following functional form is adequate:

$$R = a + b_1(1/p) + b_2(1/p)^2$$

where: R = the commission rate, p = the house price, a = a constant, and b_1 and b_2 are parameters to be estimated.

10.153 Estimation of the current period value of transactions to which the percentage margin applies depends on whether real estate agency fees are classified as a cost of housing or as a separate financial service. If the former, the value of the current period transaction, relative to the value of the base period transaction, would reflect changes in house prices. If the latter, where the purchase of a dwelling is regarded as forgone consumption, the current period value would reflect changes in the CPI itself.

10.154 If a single percentage margin is assumed to operate, then only a single current period transaction is required, i.e. an estimate of the average value of base period transactions at comparison period prices. For example, if real estate agency fees are classified as a housing cost, then the base period price is calculated by applying the average base period percentage margin to the average house price in the base period, with any VAT or GST then added. The comparison period price is calculated by indexing forward the average base period house price, applying the average comparison period percentage margin and adding GST or VAT.

10.155 If a single percentage margin is not assumed to operate, then a sample of representative base period transactions is required. The monetary value of the margin on each representative transaction is then calculated from published tariffs or from an estimated functional relationship, such as that described above. Comparison period prices are likewise estimated by first indexing forward each of the base period representative transactions and then applying the same model. Note that, in this case, there is no need to exclude any GST or VAT from the initial margins data.

Property insurance services

10.156 The construction of reliable price indices for insurance can be difficult to achieve in practice. This section is restricted to a discussion of property insurance, as this type of insurance can be assumed to operate in similar ways across countries. It nevertheless provides only an illustration of the issues that index compilers face, with each sector raising specific conceptual and measurement difficulties. For example, in the case of life insurance, insurance policies are often bundled with a long-term investment service yielding a financial payout when insured persons survive the policy term. Separation of the service charges relating to the insurance and investment elements within a single premium poses significant problems for index compilers.

10.157 For the purposes of the discussion below, property insurance is defined to include:

- dwelling insurance;
- household contents insurance;
- motor vehicle insurance.

10.158 The common feature of these policies is that for a fee (premium), households receive financial compensation if a nominated event results in the loss of, or damage to, designated property. The alternative to purchasing insurance is for the household to self-insure. For households as a group, the service received is represented by the elimination of the risk of a financial loss. The appropriate treatment of property insurance in the CPI depends on whether the CPI is constructed using the acquisitions, use or payments approach.

Payments

10.159 Under the *payments* approach, each of the above policy types is in scope. In thinking about how this property insurance should be included in the CPI, it is necessary to consider both the gross premiums payable and the claims receivable by households. The definitions of gross premiums payable and claims receivable are straightforward. It is possible, however, to treat claims receivable in a number of ways, which will have an impact on either the weight assigned to insurance or the weight assigned to the items insured. Spending on insurance can be weighted on either a gross basis (i.e. valued using gross premiums payable) or on a net basis (i.e. valued using gross premiums payable *less* claims receivable). Likewise, items which are insured against loss may also be weighted gross or net (in the latter case, excluding purchases explicitly financed by insurance claims receivable). Taken together, this suggests three plausible alternative treatments:

- gross premiums, net expenditures;
- net premiums, gross expenditures;
- gross premiums, gross expenditures.

10.160 *Gross premiums, net expenditures.* It may be argued that calculating expenditures net of purchases financed by insurance claims avoids double counting of that portion of gross premiums which funds the claims. There are some problems with this approach. First, it is necessary to assume that all proceeds from insurance claims are used to purchase replacement items or to repair damaged items. In some cases, claims receivable may be to compensate for damage or destruction to the property of agents beyond the scope of the index (e.g. businesses, government or even other households where the CPI reference group covers only some subset of households). Households may also choose to use the proceeds for entirely different purposes. Thus the estimation of the net expenditure weights is likely to involve some arbitrary choices. More generally, because money is fungible, attempts to restrict coverage only to those expenditures made from selected sources of funds are questionable. Finally, the potential distortion of weights for these items may reduce the usefulness of sub-indices for other purposes.

10.161 *Net premiums, gross expenditures.* Within a payments index, the "net premiums, gross expenditures" approach is based on the view that claims receivable should be regarded as negative expenditure on insurance. This may be seen as an attempt to avoid the double counting of expenditures on items financed by claims receivable and already included in gross expenditures on other items elsewhere in the index. The net premiums approach is much less problematic than the net expenditures approach (as at least the impact is restricted to the weights for insurance). It may, however, be argued that the net premiums approach is inconsistent with approaches adopted for other items in a payments index, in particular mortgage interest and consumer credit charges, where weights are based on gross payments. Any allowance for interest receipts would be likely to yield negative weights since households are generally net savers overall.

10.162 The fact that the net premiums approach effectively measures the value of the insurance service as required for indices constructed according to both the acquisitions and use approaches is incidental. The task here is to determine the appropriate treatment for a payments-based index.

10.163 *Gross premiums, gross expenditures.* The "gross premiums, gross expenditures" approach is based on the view that the claims receivable by households simply represent one of the sources of funds from which expenditures are made. This is the most appealing approach for a payments index, as it recognizes the fungible nature of money and provides a consistent means of identifying both the item coverage of the index and the relative weights by reference only to the actual outlays of households.

Use

10.164 Under the *use* approach, dwelling insurance is out of scope as an input cost of the notional landlord. The weights should relate to the value of the insurance service consumed by households. This is defined as being equal to: gross insurance premiums payable by households, *plus* premium supplements, *less* provisions for claims, *less* changes in actuarial reserves.

10.165 It is not possible to estimate the nominal value of the net insurance service from household expenditure surveys alone. For weighting purposes, the most appealing approach is to obtain data from a sample of insurance providers, permitting estimation of the ratio of net insurance services to gross premiums, and to apply this ratio to the estimated value of gross premiums obtained from household expenditure surveys. However, it has not been possible to devise a corresponding price measure that is conceptually sound. For this reason, those countries that have adopted the net concept for weighting purposes are using movements in gross insurance premiums as a proxy price measure.

Acquisitions

10.166 Under the *acquisitions* approach, all three items are in scope. Because the objective is to measure price inflation for the household sector, the expenditures required for weighting purposes should reflect the insurance companies' contribution to the inflationary process, which equates to the value of the insurance service as per the use approach.

Pricing gross insurance premiums

10.167 The gross insurance premium payable by households in any one period is determined by the conditions of the policy, the administration costs and profit objectives of the insurance provider, the risk of a claim being made and any relevant taxes. For any single policy, the principal quality-determining characteristics (generally specified in the conditions of the policy) can be summarized as being:

- the type of property being covered (dwellings, motor vehicles, etc.);
- the type of cover provided (physical damage, liability, etc.);
- the nature of the compensation (replacement cost, current market value, etc.);
- any limits on the amount claimable;
- the location of the property;
- amount of any excess payable by the insured;
- risks (or events) covered.

10.168 While it is clear that pricing to constant quality requires these conditions to be held fixed, there is also a question about whether the risk of a claim being made should be held constant. In other words, if the incidence of, say, vehicle theft increases, should this be regarded as a quality improvement or simply a price change? If, on the one hand, it is argued that as the consumers' decision to insure is based on their assessment of the likelihood of suffering a loss compared to the premium charged, the risk factors should be held constant. On the other hand, it may be argued that, once insured, the consumer simply expects to be compensated for any loss. From the perspective of the consumer, any increase in risk simply represents an increase in the insurer's cost base (which may or may not be passed on to the consumer by way of a price change). Obtaining data of sufficient reliability to make quality adjustments in response to changes in risk is problematic, so in practice most indices reflect changes in risk as a price change.

10.169 In pricing insurance policies, the approach should be to select a sample of policies representative of those policies held in the base period and to reprice these in subsequent periods. Taking dwelling insurance as an example, base period insurance policies would be taken out to insure dwellings of various values and types (e.g. timber or brick) in different locations. The price samples should therefore consist of specifications that aim to cover, in aggregate, as many combinations of these variables as is reasonable. While the conditions of the policy, the dwelling type and location should be held constant over time, the value of the dwelling should be updated each period to reflect changes in house prices (i.e. the underlying real quantity needs to be preserved). It is important to note that, as the premiums will be related in some way to the value of the insured property, the price index for insurance can change without there being any change in premium schedules.

10.170 Every effort should be made to identify any changes in the conditions applying to selected policies in order to facilitate appropriate quality adjustments. Examples would include cessation of coverage for specific conditions and changing the excess (or deductible) paid by the consumer when a claim is made. Estimates of the value of such changes may be based on the insurance company's own assessments of their likely impact on the value of total claims payable. If it is assumed that the change in the aggregate value of claims can be equated to the change in service to the consumer (compared to the service that would have been provided prior to policy renewal), then an appropriate adjustment can be made to the premium to provide a (quality-adjusted) movement in price. For example, consider the case where the excess on a policy is doubled and advice from the company is that this will result in a 3 per cent drop in the aggregate value of claims payable. This could be considered as equivalent to a 3 per cent increase in price.

Using gross premiums as a proxy for the net insurance service

10.171 The net insurance service charge captures the administration costs and profits of the insurance provider along with any taxes. The problem is that taxes on insurance are normally levied on the gross premiums. Therefore, if the gross insurance premiums are subject to a high rate of tax, then the taxes will account for an even higher proportion of the net insurance service charge. Simply using the gross insurance premium inclusive of taxes as the price measure understates the real effect of any increase in the tax rates. This is best illustrated by way of an example.

10.172 For the sake of simplicity, assume that there are no premium supplements and no actuarial reserves. Then the insurance service charge is given by gross premiums less provisions for claims. Suppose the only change between two periods is a change in the tax rate – from 5 per cent of gross premiums to 20 per cent. Then the values in Table 10.10 are likely to be observed. Under this scenario it is clear that the insurance service charge has increased from $45 to $60 (an increase of 33.3 per cent), yet gross premiums have only increased by 14.3 per cent.

Table 10.10 Illustration of the impact of taxes on measures of insurance services ($)

Period	Premiums before tax	Tax	Gross premiums	Claims	Insurance service
1	100	5	105	60	45
2	100	20	120	60	60

10.173 Given that changes in the tax rates on gross insurance premiums are often subject to significant variation, this is a non trivial problem. A practical solution is to decompose insurance service into two components – insurance service before tax (or net of tax) and tax on insurance services. The price measure for the first is constructed by reference to movements in gross premiums net of tax, and the price measure for the second is given by changes in taxes on gross premiums. Further research is required to develop a workable methodology for directly measuring changes in prices of insurance services before tax.

Appendix 10.1 Calculation of a price index for a deposit product

(a) Base period sample account. Only a single month's data is used in this example. In practice, many accounts would be sampled with each account containing data for a full year.

Taxes

Date	Debit (D) or Credit (C)	Transaction	Transaction value ($)	Tax ($)	Balance ($)
					456.23
2 Jan	D	Over the counter withdrawal	107.05	0.70	348.48
12 Jan	C	Deposit	4 000.00	2.40	4 346.08
13 Jan	D	EFTPOS[1] transaction	50.62	0.30	4 295.16
13 Jan	D	Over the counter withdrawal	371.00	0.70	3 923.46
14 Jan	D	Own ATM[2] cash	300.00	0.70	3 622.76
14 Jan	D	Own ATM cash	100.00	0.70	3 522.06
16 Jan	D	Own ATM cash	100.00	0.70	3 421.36
16 Jan	D	Over the counter withdrawal	371.00	0.70	3 049.66
16 Jan	D	Cheque	90.00	0.30	2 959.36
19 Jan	D	Own ATM cash	100.00	0.70	2 858.66
19 Jan	D	Own ATM cash	100.00	0.70	2 757.96
19 Jan	C	Deposit	4 000.00	2.40	6 755.56
19 Jan	D	Cheque	740.00	1.50	6 014.06
20 Jan	D	EFTPOS transaction	76.42	0.30	5 937.34
21 Jan	D	Other ATM cash	20.00	0.30	5 917.04
21 Jan	D	Cheque	100.00	0.70	5 816.34
22 Jan	D	Cheque	43.40	0.30	5 772.64
22 Jan	D	Cheque	302.00	0.70	5 469.94
22 Jan	D	Cheque	37.00	0.30	5 432.64
23 Jan	D	Over the counter withdrawal	371.00	0.70	5 060.94
23 Jan	D	Cheque	72.00	0.30	4 988.64
27 Jan	D	Own ATM cash	150.00	0.70	4 837.94
27 Jan	D	Cheque	73.50	0.30	4 764.14
27 Jan	D	Cheque	260.00	0.70	4 503.44
27 Jan	D	EFTPOS transaction	51.45	0.30	4 451.69
28 Jan	D	Over the counter withdrawal	19.95	0.30	4 431.44
28 Jan	D	Cheque	150.00	0.70	4 280.74
29 Jan	D	Cheque	140.00	0.70	4 140.04
30 Jan	D	Over the counter withdrawal	371.00	0.70	3 768.34
30 Jan	D	Cheque	8.00	0.30	3 760.04
30 Jan	D	Cheque	60.00	0.30	3 699.74
Total taxes				**21.10**	

[1]EFTPOS (Electronic Funds Transfer Point Of Sale).
[2]ATM (Automatic Teller Machine).

Fees

Activity	Total no.	No. charged	Amount($)
Over the counter withdrawal	6	2	6.00
EFTPOS transaction	3	0	0.00
Own ATM cash	6	0	0.00
Own ATM cash	1	1	1.20
Cheque	13	3	3.00
Deposit	2	2	0.00
Total fees			**10.20**

Fees and taxes are calculated using data in tables (b) and (c), respectively.
Source: Woolford (2001)

(b) Fee schedule. This is a summary of the information typically available from financial institutions. For each period, the table includes the number of free transactions and the per transaction charge for additional transactions. A zero number free indicates that no transactions are free and a zero charge indicates that all transactions are free.

Description	Base period		Current period	
	No. free	Charge ($)	No. free	Charge ($)
Over the counter withdrawal	4	3.00	4	3.00
EFTPOS transaction	10	0.50	9	0.50
Own ATM cash	10	0.50	9	0.50
Other ATM cash	0	1.20	0	1.20
Cheque	10	1.00	9	1.00
Deposit	0	0.00	0	0.00

Source: Woolford (2001).

(c) Tax schedule. This is a table of tax rates of the type that used to be employed in Australia. The debits tax is levied on all debit transactions to eligible accounts, with the amount charged being set for ranges of transaction values (i.e. using a step function). Financial institutions duty is levied on all deposits, the amount being determined as a percentage of the value of the deposit.

Bank accounts debit tax

Transaction value ($)		Tax ($)	
Min.	Max.	Base period	Current period
0	1	0.00	0.00
1	100	0.30	0.30
100	500	0.70	0.70
500	5 000	1.50	1.50
5 000	10 000	3.00	3.00
10 000+		4.00	4.00

Financial institutions duty (%)

Base period	Current period
0.06	0.06

Source: Woolford (2001).

(d) Interest data. The table presents, in summary form, the balances and annualized interest flows derived by taking moving averages of data reported by financial institutions. Interest rates and margins are calculated from the balances and flows.

	Base period				Current period			
	Balance ($ million)	Interest ($ million)	Interest rate (%)	Margin (%)	Balance ($ million)	Interest ($ million)	Interest rate (%)	Margin (%)
Deposit products								
Personal accounts	22 000	740	3.3636	2.4937	23 600	775	3.2839	2.3971
Current accounts	6 000	68	1.1333	4.7241	6 600	75	1.1364	4.5446
Other accounts	16 000	672	4.2000	1.6574	17 000	700	4.1176	1.5634
Business accounts	25 000	920	3.6800	2.1774	28 000	1 000	3.5714	2.1096
Total deposit accounts	47 000	1 660	3.5319	2.3255	51 600	1 775	3.4399	2.2411
Loan products								
Personal accounts	42 000	3 188	7.5905	1.7331	46 000	3 400	7.3913	1.7103
Business accounts	28 000	2 540	9.0714	3.2140	31 000	2 700	8.7097	3.0287
Total loan accounts	70 000	5 728	8.1829	2.3255	77 000	6 100	7.9221	2.2411
Reference rate			**5.8574**				**5.6810**	

Source: Woolford (2001).

(e) CPI data. The table presents data required to derive the indexation factor. This example follows the Australian practice of a quarterly CPI. If a monthly CPI is produced, 12-term moving averages would be required.

	t–5	t–4	t–3	t–2	t–1
All groups	117.5	121.2	123.4	127.6	129.1
4-term moving average				122.4	125.3
Indexation factor (movement)					1.0237

Source: Woolford (2001).

(f) Projected current period sample account. The opening balance and transaction values are derived by applying the indexation factor to the base period amounts. The tax payable is determined by reference to the data in table (c). Fees payable are determined by reference to the data in table (b).

Taxes

Date	Debit (D) or Credit (C)	Transaction	Transaction value ($)	Tax ($)	Balance ($)
					467.04
2 Jan	D	Over the counter withdrawal	109.59	0.70	356.75
12 Jan	C	Deposit	4 094.75	2.46	4 449.05
13 Jan	D	EFTPOS transaction	51.82	0.30	4 396.93
13 Jan	D	Over the counter withdrawal	379.79	0.70	4 016.44
14 Jan	D	Own ATM cash	307.11	0.70	3 708.63
14 Jan	D	Own ATM cash	102.37	0.70	3 605.56
16 Jan	D	Own ATM cash	102.37	0.70	3 502.50
16 Jan	D	Over the counter withdrawal	379.79	0.70	3 122.01
16 Jan	D	Cheque	92.13	0.30	3 029.57
19 Jan	D	Own ATM cash	102.37	0.70	2 926.51
19 Jan	D	Own ATM cash	102.37	0.70	2 823.44
19 Jan	C	Deposit	4 094.75	2.46	6 915.73
19 Jan	D	Cheque	757.53	1.50	6 156.70
20 Jan	D	EFTPOS transaction	78.23	0.30	6 078.17
21 Jan	D	Other ATM cash	20.47	0.30	6 057.40
21 Jan	D	Cheque	102.37	0.70	5 954.33
22 Jan	D	Cheque	44.43	0.30	5 909.60
22 Jan	D	Cheque	309.15	0.70	5 599.75
22 Jan	D	Cheque	37.88	0.30	5 561.57
23 Jan	D	Over the counter withdrawal	379.79	0.70	5 181.08
23 Jan	D	Cheque	73.71	0.30	5 107.08
27 Jan	D	Own ATM cash	153.55	0.70	4 952.83
27 Jan	D	Cheque	75.24	0.30	4 877.28
27 Jan	D	Cheque	266.16	0.70	4 610.43
27 Jan	D	EFTPOS transaction	52.67	0.30	4 557.46
28 Jan	D	Over the counter withdrawal	20.42	0.30	4 536.73
28 Jan	D	Cheque	153.55	0.70	4 382.48
29 Jan	D	Cheque	143.32	0.70	4 238.46
30 Jan	D	Over the counter withdrawal	379.79	0.70	3 857.98
30 Jan	D	Cheque	8.19	0.30	3 849.49
30 Jan	D	Cheque	61.42	0.30	3 787.77
Total taxes				**21.21**	

Fees

Activity	Total No.	No. charged	Amount ($)
Over the counter withdrawal	6	2	6.00
EFTPOS transaction	3	0	0.00
Own ATM cash	6	0	0.00
Own ATM cash	1	1	1.20
Cheque	13	4	4.00
Deposit	2	2	0.00
Total fees			**11.20**

Source: Woolford (2001).

(g) Indices for current accounts. This table brings the results together. The current period value aggregates are derived as follows. For margins – the base period aggregate is multiplied by the product of the indexation factor (e) and the ratio of the current and base period margins for current accounts (d). For fees – the base period aggregate is multiplied by the ratio of total fees payable on the sample account in the current period (f) and the base period (a). For taxes – the same procedure is followed as for fees.

Component	Base period		Current period	
	Value aggregate ($)	Index	Value aggregate ($)	Index
Margins	28 344	100.0	27 913	98.5
Fees	11 904	100.0	13 071	109.8
Taxes	14 739	100.0	14 818	100.5
Total	54 987	100.0	55 803	101.5

Source: Woolford (2001).

ERRORS AND BIAS

11

Introduction

11.1 This chapter discusses the general types of potential error to which all price indices are subject. The literature on consumer price indices (CPIs) discusses these errors from two perspectives, and this chapter presents the two perspectives in turn. First, the chapter describes the sources of sampling and non-sampling error that arise in estimating a population CPI from a sample of observed prices. Second, the chapter reviews the arguments made in numerous recent studies that attribute bias to CPIs as a result of insufficiently accurate treatment of quality change, consumer substitution and other factors. It should be emphasized that many of the underlying issues discussed here are dealt with in much greater detail elsewhere in the manual.

Types of error

11.2 One of the main objectives of a sample survey is to compute estimates of population characteristics. Such estimates will never be exactly equal to the population characteristics. There will always be some error. Table 11.1 gives a taxonomy of the different types of error. See also Balk and Kersten (1986) and Dalén (1995) for overviews of the various sources of stochastic and non-stochastic errors experienced in calculating a CPI. Two broad categories can be distinguished: sampling errors and non-sampling errors.

Sampling error

11.3 *Sampling errors* are due to the fact that an estimated CPI is based on samples and not on a complete enumeration of the populations involved. Sampling errors vanish if observations cover the complete population. As mentioned in previous chapters, statistical offices usually adopt a fixed weight price index as the object of estimation. A fixed weight index can be seen as a weighted average of partial indices of commodity groups, with weights being expenditure shares. The estimation procedures that most statistical offices apply to a CPI involve different kinds of samples. The most important kinds are:

- for each commodity group, a sample of commodities to calculate the partial price index of the commodity group;
- for each commodity, a sample of outlets to calculate the elementary price index of the commodity from individual price observations;
- a sample of households needed for the estimation of the average expenditure shares of the commodity groups. (Some countries use data from national accounts instead of a household expenditure survey to obtain the expenditure shares.)

11.4 The sampling error can be split into a selection error and an estimation error. A *selection error* occurs when the actual selection probabilities deviate from the selection probabilities as specified in the sample design. The *estimation error* denotes the effect caused by using a sample based on a random selection procedure. Every new selection of a sample will result in different elements, and thus in a possibly different value of the estimator.

Table 11.1. A taxonomy of errors in a consumer price index

Total error:
- Sampling error
  - Selection error
  - Estimation error
- Non-sampling error
  - Observation error
    - Overcoverage
    - Response error
    - Processing error
  - Non-observation error
    - Undercoverage
    - Non-response

Non-sampling error

11.5 *Non-sampling errors* may occur even when the whole population is observed. They can be subdivided into observation errors and non-observation errors. *Observation errors* are the errors made during the process of obtaining and recording the basic observations or responses.

11.6 *Overcoverage* means that some elements are included in the survey which do not belong to the target population. For outlets, statistical offices usually have inadequate sampling frames. In some countries, for instance, a business register is used as the sampling frame for outlets. In such a register, outlets are classified according to major activity. The register thus usually exhibits extensive overcoverage, because it contains numerous outlets which are out of scope from the CPI perspective (e.g. firms that sell to businesses rather than to households). In addition, there is usually no detailed information on all the commodities sold by an outlet, so it is possible that a sampled outlet may turn out not to sell a particular commodity at all.

11.7 *Response errors* in a household expenditure survey or price survey occur when the respondent does not understand the question, or does not want to give the right answer, or when the interviewer or price collector makes an error in recording the answer. In household expenditure surveys, for example, households appear to systematically underreport expenditures on commodity groups such as tobacco and alcoholic beverages. In most countries, the main price collection method is by persons who regularly visit outlets. They may return with prices of unwanted commodities.

11.8 The price data are processed in different stages, such as coding, entry, transfer and editing (control and correction). At each step mistakes, so-called *processing errors*, may occur. For example, at the outlets the price collectors write down the prices on paper forms. After the collectors have returned home, a computer is used as the input and transmission medium for the price information. It is clear that this way of processing prices is susceptible to errors.

11.9 *Non-observation errors* are made when the intended measurements cannot be carried out. *Undercoverage* occurs when elements in the target population do not appear in the sampling frame. The sampling frame of outlets can have undercoverage, which means that some outlets where relevant commodities are purchased cannot be contacted. Some statistical offices appear to exclude mail order firms and non-food market stalls from their outlet sampling frame.

11.10 Another non-observation error is *non-response*. Non-response errors may arise from the failure to obtain the required information in a timely manner from all the units selected in the sample. A distinction can be drawn between total and partial (or item) non-response. Total non-response occurs when selected outlets cannot be contacted or refuse to participate in the price survey. Another instance of total non-response occurs when mail questionnaires and collection forms are returned by the respondent and the price collector, respectively, after the deadline for processing has passed. Mail questionnaires and collection forms that are only partially filled in are examples of partial non-response. If the price changes of the non-responding outlets differ from those of the responding outlets, the results of the price survey will be biased.

11.11 Total and partial non-response may also be encountered in a household expenditure survey. Total non-response occurs when households drawn in the sample refuse to cooperate. Partial non-response occurs, for instance, when certain households refuse to give information about their expenditure on certain commodity groups.

Measuring error and bias

Estimation of variance

11.12 The variance estimator depends on both the chosen estimator of a CPI and the sampling design. Boon (1998) gives an overview of the sampling methods that are applied in the compilation of CPIs by various European statistical institutes. It appeared that only four of them use some sort of probability techniques for outlet selection, and only one uses probability sampling for item selection. In the absence of probability techniques, so-called judgemental and cut-off selection methods are applied.

11.13 In view of the complexity of the (partially connected) sample designs in compiling a CPI, an integrated approach to variance estimation appears to be problematic. That is, it appears to be difficult to present a single formula for measuring the variance of a CPI, which captures all sources of sampling error. It is, however, feasible to develop partial (or conditional) measures, in which only the effect of a single source of variability is quantified. For instance, Balk and Kersten (1986) calculated the variance of a CPI resulting from the sampling variability of the household expenditure survey, conditional on the assumption that the partial price indices are known with certainty. Ideally, all the conditional sampling errors should be put together in a unifying framework in order to assess the relative importance of the various sources of error. Under rather restrictive assumptions, Balk (1989a) derived an integrated framework for the overall sampling error of a CPI.

11.14 There are various procedures for trying to estimate the sampling variance of a CPI. Design-based variance estimators (that is, variances of Horvitz–Thompson estimators) can be used, in combination with Taylor linearization procedures, for sampling errors arising from a probability sampling design. For instance, assuming a cross-classified sampling design, in which samples of commodities and outlets are drawn independently from a two-dimensional population, with probabilities proportional to size (PPS) in both dimensions, a design-based variance formula can be derived. In this way Dalén and Ohlsson (1995) found that the sampling error for a 12-month change of the all-commodity Swedish CPI was of the order of 0.1–0.2 per cent.

11.15 The main problem with non-probability sampling is that there is no theoretically acceptable way of knowing whether the dispersion in the sample data accurately reflects the dispersion in the population. It is then necessary to fall back on approximation techniques for variance estimation. One such technique is quasi-randomization (see Särndal, Swensson and Wretman (1992, p. 574)), in which assumptions are made about the probabilities of sampling commodities and outlets. The problem with this method is that it is difficult to find a probability model that adequately approximates the method actually used for outlet and item selection. Another possibility is to use a replication method, such as the method of random groups, balanced half-samples, jackknife, or bootstrap. This is a completely non-parametric class of methods to estimate sampling distributions and standard errors. Each replication method works by drawing a large number of sub-samples from the given sample. From each sub-sample the parameter of interest can be estimated. Under rather weak conditions, it can be shown that the distribution of the resulting estimates approximates the sampling distribution of the original estimator. For more details on the replication methods see Särndal, Swensson and Wretman (1992, pp. 418–445).

Qualitative descriptions of non-sampling errors

11.16 It is still more difficult to obtain quantitative measures of the non-sampling errors. Thus the use of qualitative indications is the only possibility. For instance, the coverage of the sampling frames as a proxy of the target populations can be addressed (including gaps, duplications and definitional problems). The percentage of the target outlet samples from which responses or usable price data were obtained (i.e. the response rates) can be provided. Any known difference in the prices of responding outlets and non-responding outlets can be described, as can an indication of the method of imputation or estimation used to compensate for non-response. Several categories of non-sampling errors provide the bulk of the bias issues discussed below.

Procedures to minimize errors

11.17 The *estimation error* can be controlled by means of the sampling design. For example, by increasing the sample size, or by taking selection probabilities proportional to some well-chosen auxiliary variable, the error in the estimated CPI can be reduced. The choice of an adequate sampling design for the CPI is an extremely complex matter. The target population is the set of all goods and services that are acquired, used or paid for by households from outlets in a particular time period. A proper probability sampling procedure selects a sample by a random mechanism in which each good or service in the population has a known probability of selection. In combination with a Horvitz–Thompson estimator, such a probability sampling design will produce an index that is (approximately) unbiased and precise.

11.18 The following three probability sampling designs are used extensively in survey practice: simple random (SI) sampling, probability proportional to size (PPS) sampling, and stratified sampling with SI or PPS sampling per stratum. The advantage of SI sampling is its simplicity; it gives each population element the same probability of being included in the sample. PPS sampling has the advantage that the more important elements have a larger chance of being sampled than the less important ones. For instance, at Statistics Sweden the outlets are selected with probabilities proportional to some proxy for size, namely their number of employees. Unequal probability designs can lead to a substantial variance reduction in comparison with equal probability designs. In stratified sampling, the population is divided into non-overlapping sub-populations called strata. For instance, at the United Kingdom Office for National Statistics the population of outlets is split by outlet type (multiple, independent or specialist) to form different strata. In each stratum a sample is selected according to a certain design. One of the reasons why stratified sampling is so popular is that most of the potential gain in precision of PPS sampling can be captured through stratified selection with SI sampling within well-constructed strata. Stratified sampling is in several aspects simpler than PPS sampling.

11.19 Because appropriate sampling frames are lacking, samples are frequently obtained by non-probability methods. Judgemental (or expert choice) sampling is one form of non-random selection. In this case an expert selects certain "typical" elements where data are to be collected. With skill on the part of the expert a fairly good sample might result, but there is no way to be sure. A more sophisticated non-probability method is quota sampling. In quota sampling the population is firstly divided into certain strata. For each stratum, the number (quota) of elements to be included in the sample is fixed. Next the interviewer in the field simply fills the quotas, which means in the case of outlet sampling that the selection of the outlets is ultimately based on the judgement of the price collectors. Another non-probability method is cut-off sampling, which means that a part of the target population is deliberately excluded from the sample selection process. In particular, this procedure is used when the distribution of the value of some auxiliary variable is highly skewed. For instance, a large part of the population may consist of small outlets whose contribution to total sales is modest. A decision may then be taken to exclude from the sampling frame the outlets with the lowest sales. Because the selection is non-random, non-probability methods usually lead to more or less biased estimates. Empirical results of research undertaken by Statistics Netherlands nevertheless show that non-probability selection methods do not necessarily perform worse, in terms of the mean square error, than probability sampling techniques (De Haan, Opperdoes and Schut, 1997).

11.20 Provided that the sampling design is given, the sampling variance of an estimated (all-commodities) CPI can in general be lowered by:

- enlarging the samples of households, commodities and outlets;
- the application of suitable stratifications to the various populations (e.g. grouping commodities with respect to similarity of price changes).

11.21 It is important to allocate optimally the available resources both between and within the different CPI samples, since badly allocated samples may lead to unnecessarily high sampling errors. The Swedish variance estimation results, presented in Dalén and Ohlsson (1995), show that the error resulting from commodity sampling is relatively high compared with the error resulting from outlet sampling. In this case, it is worthwhile increasing the sample size of commodities and reducing the sample size of outlets.

11.22 A systematic analysis of sampling errors offers possibilities for improving or reducing cost. The problem of optimum sample allocation is usually formulated as the determination of the sizes of the samples of commodities and outlets, and their distribution over the strata that minimizes the sampling error of an all-commodities CPI, subject to the available budget.

11.23 As already mentioned, a business register is usually not an adequate sampling frame for outlets, because it provides extensive *overcoverage*. It is recommended to set up an appropriate sampling frame by enumeration of the main outlets within each sampled municipality. Such enumeration yields a list of all outlets in a municipality together with the commodity groups that belong to their assortments. A less expensive way to organize an outlet sampling frame is to ask the price collectors – who may be assumed to know the local situation well – to make a list of outlets where purchases are made by households.

11.24 The populations of commodities (and varieties) and outlets are continually changing through time. The composition of most commodity groups is not constant over time, because commodities disappear from the market and new ones appear. The passage of time also plays a disturbing role with respect to the outlet population: outlets close, temporarily or permanently; new outlets emerge; the importance of some outlets diminishes or increases. The samples of commodities (and varieties) and outlets should be reviewed and updated periodically to maintain their representativity with respect to the current buying habits of the households.

11.25 *Response errors* caused by the underreporting of certain categories of household expenditure can be adjusted by using producer-based estimates from the national accounts (see Linder (1996) for an example). Measurement errors by price collectors can be reduced by providing them with hand-held computers for data entry. In this way the validation of observed prices can be executed at the point of price collection (i.e. in the outlet), by means of an automatic comparison of the currently observed price quote with the previously observed one (by setting a limit on the percentage price change) and with the price quotes obtained from other outlets (by setting suitable upper and lower limits). Details are provided by Haworth, Fenwick and Beaven (1997).

11.26 It is useful to appoint data collection supervisors to conduct quality assurance checks on the data collectors. It is also a good idea to organize regularly meetings where price collectors and statisticians from the head office can share their experiences. In this way, the statisticians will keep in touch with the conditions in the field, and may take the opportunity to provide more information about frequently made price collection errors and new representative goods.

11.27 It is important to check the collected price data for *processing errors* and, where possible, to correct these errors. This activity is called data editing. When editing is carried out on individual observations, it is called micro-editing. When the resources to spend on data editing must be minimized, while at the same time maintaining a high level of data quality, selective editing and macro-editing are possibilities. Selective editing is a form of traditional micro-editing, in which the number of edits is kept to a minimum. Only those edits which have an impact on the survey results are carried out. Macro-editing offers a top-down approach. The edits are carried out on aggregated data (for instance, the price index numbers of a commodity group) instead of individual records (for example, price observations). Micro-editing of individual records is then carried out only if macro-edits raise suspicion. In particular, attention should be paid to outliers among the observations.

11.28 *Non-response* usually introduces selection bias. There are three methods for the treatment of missing price observations. First, the corresponding price can be excluded from the data set of previous prices, so that the set of previous prices is "matched" with the set of current prices. Second, this matching can be achieved by using an imputed (or artificial) price for the missing one. The imputed price can be calculated by either carrying forward the previous price observation or by extrapolating the previous price observation using the change of other price observations for the same commodity. Third, there is the possibility to reweight the sample. The objective of reweighting is to inflate the weight given to the prices of the responding outlets. This compensates for those prices that are lost by non-response.

11.29 In a household expenditure survey, missing data are usually imputed with the help of information on the same household from a previous observation period or other households from the same observation period. To reduce bias in the average expenditure pattern arising from selective non-response, a household expenditure survey sample of households is generally post-stratified by a number of household characteristics, such as income, composition and size.

Types of bias

11.30 This section reviews several categories of error, either in pricing or in index construction, that potentially can lead to bias in the overall CPI. The emphasis here is on the categorization of errors, along with some consideration of their likely size, rather than on methods to reduce or eliminate the errors. The question might arise of why such a discussion is necessary, since such issues as quality change, and the appropriate methods for handling them in the CPI, are dealt with at both a conceptual and operational level in other chapters.

11.31 The reason this chapter addresses the topic of CPI bias per se is the great surge in interest in price measurement problems during the mid-1990s. Especially in the United States, the view became widespread that the CPI was subject to systematic upward biases because of the failure to deal adequately with consumer substitution, product quality improvements, and the introduction of new items and services. Moreover, it was recognized, first, that the existence of such upward bias would have fundamental implications for the measurement of recent trends in output and productivity, and second, that the elimination of upward bias could substantially improve the government budget situation through reduced government expenditures and increased tax revenues (see, for example, Eldridge (1999) and Duggan and Gillingham (1999)). These discoveries led to a series of papers and reports on CPI measurement problems, often accompanied by point estimates of aggregate bias.

11.32 Prominent examples of these quantitative studies of bias are those by the Advisory Commission to Study the CPI (United States Senate, 1996), Congressional Budget Office (1994), Crawford (1998), Cunningham (1996), Dalén (1999a), Diewert (1996c), Lebow, Roberts and Stockton (1994), Lebow and Rudd (2003), Shapiro and Wilcox (1997b), Shiratsuka (1999),

White (1999), and Wynne and Sigalla (1994). Responses and estimates by statistical agencies include those provided by Abraham et al. (1998), US Bureau of Labor Statistics (1998), Ducharme (1997), Edwards (1997), Fenwick (1997), Lequiller (1997), Moulton (1996b), and Moulton and Moses (1997). Among the many other discussions of the CPI bias issue are those reported by Baker (1998), Boskin et al. (1998), Deaton (1998), Diewert (1998a), Krueger and Siskind (1998), Nordhaus (1998), Obst (2000), OECD (1997), Pollak (1998), Popkin (1997), and Triplett (1997).

11.33 Two points are worth making at the outset with respect to measuring bias in CPIs. First, the issue has usually been addressed in the context of the cost of living index (COLI). That is, the CPI bias has been defined as the difference between the rate of increase in the CPI and the rate of increase in a true COLI. Many authors on bias have taken as given that the COLI should be the CPI's measurement objective. Somewhat different conclusions might be reached if the index objective were taken to be a pure price index. Notably, the gains in consumer welfare from a widening array of new goods, or the ability of consumers to substitute away from items with increasing relative prices, might be deemed irrelevant and an index that ignored those factors might not be judged biased on that account.

11.34 The second point is that CPI bias is not amenable to estimation with the same level of rigour as that used in CPI variance estimation. Since the COLI or other ideal target index is unobserved, analysts have been forced to rely in part on conjectures and on generalizations from fragmentary empirical evidence in order to quantify the extent of bias. The notable exceptions are with respect to substitution bias, when traditional Laspeyres indices and indices using superlative formulae can be computed using the same underlying price and expenditure data, and the differences construed as a measure of the upward bias from use of the Laspeyres formula.

11.35 Several different taxonomies of bias have appeared in the literature mentioned above. It is sufficient, however, to employ four categories roughly corresponding to those set forth in the best-known study, namely the *Final report of the Advisory Commission to Study the CPI* (the Boskin Commission), established by the United States Senate Finance Committee in 1995. These categories are: upper-level substitution bias; elementary aggregate bias; quality change and new goods bias; and new outlet bias.

11.36 These categories can be further broken down into two subgroups according to whether they refer to errors in individual price measurements or errors in computing index series. Quality change bias and new goods bias arise because of failures to measure adequately the value to consumers of individual goods and services that appear in (or disappear from) the marketplace. It should be recognized that discussions of "new goods" problems apply equally to all products, whether goods or services. At a conceptual level, it can be difficult to distinguish these two biases from each other. Operationally, however, quality change bias pertains to the procedures for comparing new products or models with the older products they replace in the CPI samples. In general, new goods bias can be thought of as applying to wholly new types of products, or products that would not enter samples routinely through forced replacement. New outlet bias, sometimes referred to as outlet substitution bias, is similar to new goods bias but is focused on the appearance of new types of stores or marketing methods that offer goods at lower prices or higher quality.

11.37 The other categories of bias refer to the procedures for constructing index values from component series. As noted throughout this manual, CPI construction can be thought of as taking place in two steps, or at two levels. At the lower level, individual price quotations are combined; at the upper level, these basic indices are aggregated together. Corresponding to these two levels are two forms of potential bias. Elementary aggregate bias involves the averaging formulae used to combine price quotations into basic indices. Upper-level substitution bias applies to the formulae used to combine those elementary aggregates into higher-level indices. These components of potential bias, and the means used to measure them, are discussed in more detail below.

Components of bias

Upper-level substitution bias

11.38 Upper-level substitution bias is perhaps the most widely accepted source of CPI bias, and the kind with which economists are most familiar from textbook expositions of price index theory and practice. Simply stated, it arises when CPIs employ the Laspeyres formula (see Chapter 17), which is well known to provide an upper bound on a cost of living index under certain assumptions about consumer behaviour. As noted in paragraph 11.34 above, quantitative measures of upper-level substitution bias can be generated by comparing Laspeyres price indices to Fisher ideal, Törnqvist or other superlative indices. Under certain assumptions about, for example, constant preferences, these will stand as relatively precise bias estimates.

11.39 Genereux (1983) and Aizcorbe and Jackman (1993) provide such index comparisons and estimates of upper-level substitution bias using actual CPI index series for Canada and the United States, respectively. Other early studies by Braithwait (1980) and Manser and McDonald (1988) estimate the substitution bias in United States national account indices. In lieu of superlative indices, the Braithwait study uses estimated exact cost of living indices based on demand system estimation. A similar estimate for the Netherlands is provided by Balk (1990). In these studies, the existence of an upward bias from the Laspeyres formula is demonstrated consistently. The biases in the annual index changes in individual years are relatively small, averaging 0.1 to 0.3 percentage points, and depend empirically on such factors as the distance from the Laspeyres base period, the level of index detail at which the alternative formulae are applied, and whether the superlative index is of the fixed base or chained variety.

11.40 The major differences between Laspeyres and superlative indices derive from the variation in relative prices over the period being compared, and from the shift in quantities consumed towards those index categories that have fallen in relative price. This leads to several conclusions:

- If index movements are characterized by continuing, uniform drift in relative prices over time, with accompanying drifts in consumption, the size of the annual Laspeyres bias will tend to increase with the distance from the base period. (Greenlees (1997) notes, however, that there is little evidence for this phenomenon in the United States; see also Szulc (1983).)
- Under the same circumstances, reducing the expenditure weight chaining interval will work to reduce the upper-level substitution bias in the Laspeyres CPI. The more frequent chaining will increase the weight given to indices that are falling in relative price, thereby reducing the rate of CPI growth. Conversely, if there is "bouncing" in relative index movements, frequent chaining can lead to an upward "chain drift" in a Laspeyres index.
- Upper-level substitution bias will tend to be larger during periods of higher inflation, if these periods also have greater relative price variation. Little empirical evidence exists on this point, however.

11.41 The concept of upper-level substitution bias has been derived and discussed in the context of cost of living index theory, but an equivalent bias may be defined from the perspective of the pure price index. If the Fisher ideal or other superlative index is judged preferable on the basis of its symmetric treatment of base period and current period expenditure patterns, then the difference between that index and a Laspeyres could be interpreted as a measure of representativity bias. A similar argument could be applied with respect to lower-level substitution bias within elementary index cells.

11.42 Recently, Lebow and Rudd (2003) have defined and estimated another category of bias related to upper-level aggregation. They concluded that the consumer expenditure survey weights used in the United States CPI were subject to error because of, for example, under-reporting of alcohol and tobacco expenditures. This will lead to a weighting bias if the errors in relative weight are correlated with component index changes. (Sources for, and problems in, expenditure weight estimation are discussed in detail in Chapter 4.)

Elementary aggregate bias

11.43 Elementary aggregate bias can be divided into two components: formula bias and lower-level substitution bias. An elementary index in the CPI is biased if its expectation differs from its measurement objective. The term formula bias (or functional form bias) is used here to denote a situation in which the elementary index formula has an upward bias relative to the pure price index. When the measurement objective is a cost of living index, the elementary index formula suffers from lower-level substitution bias (or within-stratum substitution bias) if it does not reflect consumer substitution among the items contained in that index cell. Thus, given any elementary index formula, the two forms of bias can be distinguished according to the objective of the elementary index.

11.44 Chapters 9 and 20 of this manual discuss the characteristics of alternative elementary index formulae. A key result is that the Carli formula for the arithmetic average of ratios has an upward bias relative to the trend in average item prices. Consequently, Eurostat has prohibited use of this formula in computations for the Harmonized Indices of Consumer Prices (HICPs). The weighted formulae used in basic indices of the United States CPI had some characteristics of the Carli formula prior to procedural and computational changes made in 1995 and 1996. The problems and the methods chosen to address them are discussed, for example, by Reinsdorf and Moulton (1997) and Moulton (1996b).

11.45 The ratio of arithmetic averages (Dutot) and geometric mean (Jevons) formulae eliminate formula bias as defined here, and both are permitted by Eurostat. Their expectations differ, however, when item prices do not change at a uniform rate. The differences provide one way of evaluating the potential importance of lower-level substitution bias. The geometric mean formula is exact for a cost of living index if consumers follow the Cobb–Douglas behavioural model, whereas the formula based on the ratio of arithmetic averages corresponds to zero-substitution behaviour. Thus, if the goal is to approximate a cost of living index, the geometric mean formula is likely to be judged preferable.

11.46 In the future, scanner data may make it possible to record item-level consumption data at a daily, weekly or monthly frequency and to use those data in superlative index calculations. Currently, however, it is impossible to employ superlative formulae to compute elementary CPI indices. Some assumption, such as the Cobb–Douglas, must be made in order to approximate a cost of living index. Note that the substitution that the index ideally should reflect involves consumer choice among all the items in the cell: different products, products in different outlets, different package sizes of the same product, or the same product offered for sale at different times of the period to which the index applies (see Dalton, Greenlees and Stewart (1998)). Thus, the appropriate degree of assumed substitution behaviour should depend, in principle, on the dimensions of variety within the item category.

11.47 The method used by the statistical agency for sampling items within a category will determine the effectiveness of formula choice in dealing with lower-level substitution bias. For example, if only a single representative item is chosen to represent the category, the index formula will fail to reflect the consumer response to any relative price change in the universe of items. More generally, the geometric mean formula index suffers from an upward bias in small samples, so lower-level substitution bias may be underestimated in empirical comparisons of the geometric mean to other index formulae. White (1999) discusses the relationship between sampling error and bias estimates. See also McClelland and Reinsdorf (1999) on the small sample bias in the geometric mean.

11.48 The impact of formula choice can be estimated with some degree of precision over a given historical period. Any corresponding bias, however, can be estimated only by assuming that the geometric mean or other functional form successfully approximates the index's measurement objective.

11.49 As implied by the above discussion, the importance of elementary aggregate bias will vary by country, depending on the particular index formulae used, the degree of heterogeneity within index strata, and the sampling methods employed. Also, as with upper-level substitution bias, elementary aggregate bias will vary with the overall level of inflation in the economy if absolute and relative price changes are correlated.

11.50 The performance of any formula for elementary aggregate calculation will also be affected by the methods used by the statistical agency to handle special situations, such as seasonal goods and other products that are temporarily unavailable. Armknecht and Maitland-Smith (1999) discuss how the failure to impute missing prices can lead to bias in the modified Laspeyres and other index formulae.

Quality change and new products bias

11.51 Discussion of potential CPI biases arising from inadequate quality adjustment has a long history. For example, the Stigler Committee report on United States price statistics (Price Statistics Review Committee, 1961) indicated that "if a poll were taken of professional economists and statisticians, in all probability they would designate (and by a wide majority) the failure of the price indices to take full account of quality changes as the most important defect of these indices". In most studies of bias, unmeasured or mismeasured quality change is also the largest contributor to the total estimated bias. Just as quality adjustment is widely recognized as an extremely difficult process, however, it is correspondingly difficult to measure any quality change bias.

11.52 Unlike substitution bias, which can be estimated by comparison of alternative formulae, quality change bias must be analysed on a product-by-product basis. Products and their associated index components will experience widely varying rates of quality change over time. Moreover, the methods used for quality adjustment will also vary. Whereas the linking method may dominate in terms of frequency of use, important index components may employ production cost, hedonic adjustment, or the other methods described in Chapters 7 and 21.

11.53 A crucial point to recognize is that the direction of overall quality change does not imply the direction of any quality change bias. Non-experts sometimes assume that the CPI does little or no quality adjustment, and that it therefore must overestimate price change in view of the many demonstrable improvements over time in the quality of goods and services. Rather, for any component index, the issue is whether the direct or indirect method chosen for quality adjustment overestimates or underestimates the relative quality of replacement items in the CPI sample. The resulting bias can be either positive or negative.

11.54 Empirical evidence on quality change bias has been based largely on extrapolation from individual studies of particular products. These individual studies may involve, for example, comparisons of hedonic regression indices to the corresponding CPI series or estimates of the value of some product improvement that is ignored in CPI calculations. Although the majority of such studies have suggested upward rather than downward bias, the reliance on fragmentary evidence has led to criticism by observers who point to evidence of quality declines that have not been subjected to systematic analysis.

11.55 Especially for services, overall quality trends can also be a matter of subjective valuation. New technology has led to unambiguous improvements in the quality of many consumer durables and other goods. By contrast, in service sectors such as mail delivery, public transport and medical care, it can be difficult to evaluate changes in quality. Airline travel, for example, has become safer and faster but perhaps less comfortable and reliable in recent decades, and the lack of cross-sectional variation in these characteristics makes the use of hedonic quality adjustment problematic.

11.56 New product bias, like elementary aggregate bias, can be divided conceptually into two components. The first concerns the failure to bring new products into the CPI sample with sufficient speed. This can lead to upward bias if those new products later experience large price reductions that are not reflected in the index. The second component is the welfare gain that consumers experience when a new product appears. This may not be viewed as a bias, however, when the cost of living index is not accepted as the CPI's measurement objective.

11.57 As discussed in Chapter 8, "new goods" can be: products that replace predecessor items, for example CDs replacing vinyl records and tapes; product varieties that widen the range of consumer choice, such as imported beers and ethnic restaurants; or products that represent wholly new categories of consumption, such as microwave ovens or mobile telephones.

11.58 Like quality change bias, new product bias has sometimes been estimated primarily by generalization from individual product evidence. A frequent approach has been to measure the price change for a product or category during a period prior to its entry into the CPI sample. Studies by Hausman (1997, 1999) of breakfast cereals and cellular telephones provided quantitative measures of the consumer surplus gain from the new products, but this complex econometric approach has not been applied widely. Some of the Boskin Commission's estimates of new product bias, notably those for food, were necessarily based on conjecture.

11.59 Also, like quality change bias, new product bias could be negative if the range of products decreases, if valuable consumer goods disappear from the market, or if the index fails to capture phases of rapid price increase for items. Most observers, however, seem to agree on the direction of bias as upward, and that the uncertainty concerns the magnitude.

New outlet bias

11.60 Conceptually, new outlet bias is identical to new product bias. It arises because of the failure to reflect either price changes in new outlets not yet sampled, or the welfare gain to consumers when the new outlets appear. The explanation for its existence as a separate bias category is twofold. The first reason is historical: new outlet bias was identified by Reinsdorf (1993) as a potentially major explanation for anomalous movements in the United States CPI. Second, the methods used to sample and compare outlets differ from those used with products, and the problems in controlling new outlet bias are somewhat different.

11.61 A failure to maintain a current outlet sample can introduce bias because the new outlets are distinctive in their pricing or service policy. Reinsdorf (1993), for example, focused on the growth of discount stores. It should be noted, however, that the problem could also be geographical in nature; it is important to employ outlet sampling frames that reflect new as well as traditional shopping locations.

11.62 One way that new products enter the CPI sample is through forced replacement, when exiting or less successful products disappear from shelves. Outlet disappearance is less frequent, and agency procedures may not provide for automatic replacement. Moreover, when a new outlet enters the sample there are no standard procedures for comparing data at the new and old outlets. Thus, the index will not incorporate any effects of, for example, lower price or inferior service quality at the new outlet.

11.63 Reinsdorf (1993) estimated the degree of new outlet bias by comparing average prices at outlets entering and disappearing from United States CPI samples. There has been little or no empirical work, however, on the measurement or consumer valuation of outlet quality. As a consequence, there is little evidence on which to evaluate the accuracy of new outlet bias estimates.

Summary of bias estimates

11.64 The 1996 Boskin Commission report gave a range of estimates for the total upward United States CPI bias of 0.8 to 1.6 percentage points, with the point estimate being 1.1 percentage point. This total reflects the straightforward summation of the component bias estimates. As reported by the United States in United States General Accounting Office (2000), however, changes in CPI methods subsequent to 1996 led the Boskin Commission members to reduce their estimates of total bias. Lacking evidence to the contrary, additivity of biases has been assumed in most such studies. Shapiro and Wilcox (1997b) provide probability distributions and correlations of their component bias estimates, yielding an overall confidence interval for the total bias. Most detailed studies of bias also conclude that the CPI bias is in an upward direction, although there have been numerous criticisms of that conclusion.

11.65 It is apparent that statistical agencies cannot compute or publish CPI bias estimates on a regular basis. Many of the same obstacles that prevent the elimination of bias also stand in the way of estimating bias. These include the lack of complete data on product-level consumer preferences and spending behaviour, and the inability to observe and value all differences in quality among items in the marketplace. Without such information it is impossible to calculate a true cost of living index, and similarly impossible to measure the divergence between its rate of growth and the growth rate of the CPI.

11.66 Statistical agencies have been reluctant to provide their own estimates of CPI bias. In some cases, they have accepted the existence of substitution bias, recognizing that the use of a Laspeyres formula implies that the CPI usually will overstate price change relative to a cost of living index. Statistical agencies have, however, been reluctant to draw even qualitative conclusions from the fragmentary and speculative evidence on quality change, new products and new outlet bias.

Conclusion

11.67 In order to ensure public confidence in a CPI, a detailed and up-to-date description of the methods and data sources should be published. The document should include, among other things, the objectives and scope of the index, details of the weights, and last but not least, a discussion of the accuracy of the index. A description of the sources and magnitude of the sampling and non-sampling errors (coverage, non-response rates, etc.) in a CPI provides users with valuable information on the limitations that might apply to their uses of the index. One example of a handbook of CPI methods is that published by the United States Bureau of Labor Statistics (1997), which devotes a section to the varieties and sources of possible error in the index.

ORGANIZATION AND MANAGEMENT 12

Introduction

12.1 Consumer price indices (CPI) are one of the most important and widely used of macroeconomic indicators. As well as informing economic policy, they are used for indexation of welfare benefits, pensions, gilts and securities, and also for escalation clauses in private contracts. Accuracy and reliability are paramount for a statistic as important as a CPI.

12.2 The process of producing a consumer price index needs to be carefully planned. Individual circumstances vary to such an extent that this manual cannot be too prescriptive about timetables or critical path analysis of all the steps involved. Figure 12.1 nevertheless provides an outline of the kind of schedule of activities that should result from a detailed examination of the logistics of the whole periodic operation of data collection and the computation of the index.

12.3 The guidance given in this chapter, which is based on the experiences of a number of national statistical institutes, presents a range of organizational options. As individual circumstances can vary, the examples given of good practice may be for some offices aspirational.

12.4 In reviewing these options, this chapter covers the relationships between the field and central office (which kind of work is carried out in central office, the flow of information between each part of the organization, etc.). The size, frequency, cost or complexity of the collection of prices as the basis of the index may mean that in some countries not all these operations and relationships will be appropriate. The use of both a central and a local collection, or outsourcing of certain elements of the collection, may not always be effective. If the index is compiled infrequently, from a relatively small number of outlets, or concentrates on only specific location types, different circumstances will demand different solutions.

Local collection

12.5 A local price collection involves collectors visiting individual outlets to collect prices for a variety of goods and services. This is the predominant method of price collection in most countries. The range and number of outlets visited and the types of goods and services priced will vary between countries.

12.6 Although the precise method of local price collection will vary, each price collector will usually be responsible for collection from a certain location or from certain types of outlet. Collectors will visit the same outlets in each collection period to attempt to price the same items. Through this type of arrangement, price collectors are able to build up effective relationships with retailers and specialist knowledge.

12.7 There are a number of important criteria relating to the conduct of the collection, whether the national statistical institute uses its own staff or contracts out the collection (as discussed below). These criteria include:

- Collectors should always be smartly dressed and polite – whoever employs them, they are representing the national statistical institute.
- They should carry identification to confirm their role and status.
- They should make themselves known to the retailer or store manager when they arrive, and before they begin collecting prices.
- They should comply with any request from the shopkeeper whenever possible, for instance, if the store is very busy and the shopkeeper asks the collector to return later in the day.
- The collection should be carried out as quickly as possible, causing minimal disruption to store business.

12.8 Collectors should also follow rules of common sense in preparing for a collection. These may include making sure that they have: spare pens; the appropriate forms; a clipboard; a local map; spare batteries (if the collection is computerized); money for shopping centre car-parks; and wet weather clothing, if appropriate. In some circumstances a mobile telephone will also be useful.

Contracting out

12.9 One of the decisions facing any statistical agency carrying out a price collection is whether to use in-house staff or to tender the collection to an external organization, such as a private market research company, another part of the agency, or another governmental department that specializes in surveys.

12.10 The nature of the price collection and the distribution and profile of statistical staff may help to determine whether the collection is suitable for contracting out. Where price collection is continuous, or involves complicated decision-making (such as quality adjustment), or where prices are collected from a small number of locations, it may be advantageous to keep the collection in-house. However, if the collection takes place over a small number of days per month, from a large number of locations, is relatively straightforward and involves routine or simple decision-making (perhaps selecting from a prespecified list of codes), then contracting out may be considered if there are enough

Figure 12.1 Price collection procedures

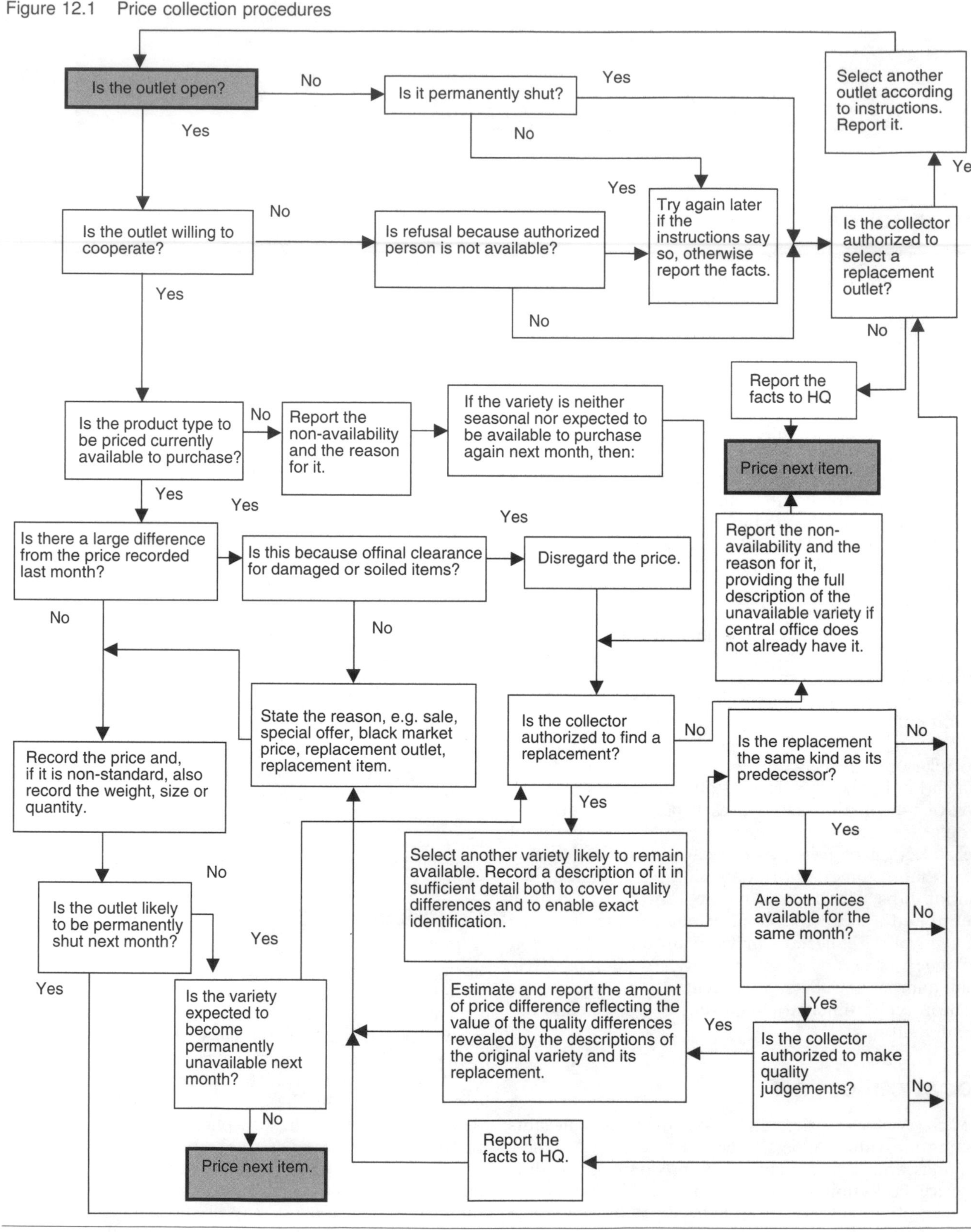

market research companies with suitable skills existing in the country.

12.11 Contracting out local collection can lead to reduced costs. Where price collection is carried out electronically, the responsibility for purchase and maintenance of data capture devices may be transferred to the contractor.

12.12 Contracting out may also allow statistical staff to spend more time analysing data rather than collecting them. By divorcing the role of data collector and data checker, statistical staff may feel more comfortable questioning the validity of price data. Accuracy of data collected can be directly linked to the performance of the contractor through performance measures which drive incentive payments (and penalties if targets are not achieved).

Central collection

12.13 Central shop-collected prices are prices obtained from the central offices of major retailing chains with national pricing policies. Branches of these chains may be excluded from the local collection if data can be collected more effectively centrally. Data suppliers may provide information on paper forms, or by entering price data on spreadsheets and forwarding them to the national statistical institute by email, CD-ROM or on floppy disks. Mail order catalogues can also be treated as central shops: prices are recorded as and when the catalogues are issued. These prices are then combined with those for the same items from the local collection.

12.14 Price data for services or fees may be collected centrally from organizations such as trade associations, national or local governmental departments and so on. Whenever possible, these prices are obtained from one central source, although there will have to be contact with regional or competing companies if there are local variations. Data may be requested in writing or by telephone, or may come automatically because the national statistical institute is on a provider's mailing list. Providers may send either a full price list or tariff sheet, from which the relevant prices will be extracted by the CPI staff, or just the prices of those items specified in the data request. All price quotations should be confirmed by some form of written documentation. Frequency of enquiry varies across the range of items and depends on when prices are known or expected to change. The most common frequencies are monthly or quarterly, but there are also instances of collecting as and when necessary, although in these cases checks must be in place to ensure that all price data are reported. For instance, this may be the case where tariffs for gas, electricity and water change once a year on a predetermined date.

Quality in the field

12.15 Quality is an important aspect of price collection. A high-quality price collection enables a statistical agency to have confidence in the index it produces, and ensure that observed price changes are genuine and not the result of collector error. It is important that procedures are developed to ensure that the standard of collection is maintained at a high level for every collection period. These procedures will form the basis of collector training and should be included in any training material developed for price collectors. Guidance to collectors should cover price index principles, organizational issues and validation procedures.

Descriptions

12.16 Accurate item descriptions are vitally important in ensuring item continuity. Collectors' descriptions should be comprehensive enough to ensure that collectors are able to price the same item in each collection period. It is therefore important that contributors record the attributes which uniquely define the item they are pricing. For example, for clothes it will be important that colour, size and fabric composition are specified to ensure that the same item is priced each month. For fresh fruit and vegetables, useful attributes to record may be country of origin, class and variety.

12.17 Accurate item descriptions will assist the price collector and head office in choosing a replacement for an item that has been withdrawn and will also help to identify changes in quality. Head office staff should be encouraged to spend some time, each collection period, going through collectors' descriptions to ensure that the correct items are being priced. Collectors should also be encouraged to review their descriptions to ensure that they contain all of the relevant information. It may be useful to ask collectors occasionally to switch collections with another collector so that they understand the importance of good descriptions.

Continuity

12.18 Continuity is one of the most important principles of price collection. Because a price index measures price *changes*, it is vital that the same item is priced every month in order to establish a true picture of price changes. So if, for example, a jar of a supermarket's own brand of strawberry jam has been selected, that particular brand and flavour should continue to be collected. If it is out of stock in the collection period, another brand and flavour should not be used. If, however, in subsequent collection periods, the selected jam continues to be out of stock, but another flavour of the same brand and price is available, then this item should be chosen as a comparable item and the item description suitably amended. If no comparable item exists, then a new item must be chosen, and the description amended. Thus a new price chain will begin. It is not possible to be prescriptive because the concept of equivalence will vary between different countries; but for practical purposes it is important that a detailed description of the items being priced is kept.

12.19 As continuity is so important in the compilation of an accurate price index, collectors should be encouraged to check with the retailer that an item is out of stock before replacing it. Some guidelines may be drawn up by the head office of the national statistical institute to cover different items. Food items, for example, will usually come back into stock in the following collection period, and so should not be replaced immediately, whereas fashion clothing will rarely come back into stock once a "season" has ended or the stock has been exhausted, and so should be replaced immediately in the collection.

12.20 Collectors should also be encouraged to plan their route for price collection to take account of outlet opening and closing times and any special retailer requests. Collectors may find it useful to compile a route map, listing the order in which outlets should be visited. This is particularly useful when the collection in a location has to be undertaken by a different collector, for example to cover for sick leave. Collectors should be encouraged to try to collect prices at similar times within each collection period. This is particularly important when pricing volatile items, such as petrol and oil, where there can be sharp fluctuations.

Data entry queries

12.21 Once the price data are correct and complete, a series of validation checks may be run. In deciding on what checks should be carried out, account should be taken of the validation checks carried out in the field. For example, the use of hand-held computers will increase the potential for validation at time of price collection and reduce the need for detailed scrutiny at head office. In addition, it would clearly not be productive or cost-effective to repeat tests already carried out.

12.22 The range of tests carried out may include:

- *Price change*: The price entered is compared with the price for the same product in the same shop in the previous month, and triggers a query where the price difference is outside preset percentage limits. These limits vary, depending on the item or group of items, and may be determined by looking at historical evidence of price variation. If there is no valid price for the previous month, for example because the item was out of stock, the check can be made against the price two months or three months ago.
- *Maximum/minimum prices*: A query is raised if the price entered exceeds a maximum or is below a minimum price for the item of which the particular product is representative. The range may be derived from the validated maximum and minimum values observed for that item in the previous month expanded by a standard scaling factor. This factor may vary between items, again based on previous experience.

12.23 If a hand-held computer is used, both of these tests can be implemented easily to take place at the time of collection, otherwise they will need to be conducted in the head office as soon as possible after collection and before prices are processed on the main system. A failure in either test should not result in the collector being unable to price the item, but should prompt the collector to check and confirm the entry, and prompt for an explanatory comment.

12.24 Queries raised may be either dealt with at head office or sent to the price collector for resolution. For example, scrutiny of a form might show that a big price difference has arisen because the item priced was a new product replacing another that has been discontinued. In this case there may be no need to raise a query with the price collector unless there is evidence to suggest that to label the item "new product" is incorrect.

12.25 Where an error is discovered too late in the process to resolve, head office will need to reject it and exclude that item from that month's index. Care should be taken that the item is also excluded from the base month so that the basket is kept constant.

Feedback

12.26 Collectors should be encouraged to give feedback to head office on their experiences of price collecting. Collectors are a valuable source of information and often give good early feedback on changes in the marketplace. Collectors can often warn of size or product changes before the head office is able to derive this information from other sources such as trade magazines. Collectors' feedback can be used to support observed price movements and to provide supplementary briefing material. It can also form the basis of a newsletter for collectors.

Quality checks in local collection: The role of auditors

12.27 The whole periodic routine of collecting prices in the field needs to be carefully planned and monitored, with arrangements in place to reflect local conditions. Circumstances vary, so it is not appropriate to be too prescriptive. It is, however, important to ensure that price collectors send in information when it is due. If they do not do so, it is necessary to find out the reason and to take appropriate action. It is also important to check that the information sent in is accurate and complete.

12.28 One way of monitoring the work being carried out by price collectors is to employ auditors to occasionally accompany collectors during the field collection, or to carry out a retrospective check on the data that have been collected.

Monitoring

12.29 If an auditor intends to accompany a price collector, he or she will need to inform the collector in advance in order to arrange meeting details. In general, the auditor will not accompany the whole price collection but will spend a few hours observing the price collection in a specific location. For example, it may be desirable to observe the collection of certain items or in particular outlets where collection might be problematical, and the price collector may need to rearrange his or her route accordingly.

12.30 Prior to monitoring, the auditor will need to carry out preparation work – a pre-monitoring check. Such a check might involve looking at descriptions, prices, price history and indicator codes of the items collected in the chosen location. This type of check will enable the auditor to have a good idea of the standard of collection prior to going into the field and may suggest on which areas of the collection the auditor should concentrate his or her efforts.

12.31 An auditor's main duty is to ensure that the price collector is following the procedures and instructions laid down for price collection and that the collection is being performed competently. While the auditor may not have the role of a trainer, the opportunity may be taken to give some coaching when errors are noted. There should also be the opportunity for the collector to ask the auditor relevant questions during the monitoring exercise.

12.32 Auditors may undertake other duties at a location besides accompanying the collector. For instance, they may enumerate outlets or carry out an item review. Following a monitoring visit, the auditor should compile a report detailing the observations made while accompanying the collector. This report should include a summary of findings, a list of points for action, and a recommended course of action. Auditors may advise that a collector receive extra training on certain aspects of the price collection; head office (or the contractor, if the collection has been outsourced) should act on this. This report will then be used as a starting point on the auditor's next visit. In other instances, general problems may arise where solutions need to be disseminated to all price collectors, perhaps by issuing revised instructions or through a newsletter.

Backchecking

12.33 Another approach to monitoring the standard of price collection is to carry out a backcheck, a retrospective check of a proportion of the prices recorded during the collection.

12.34 Backchecks can be used to:

- assess the standard of competence of individual price collectors;
- audit the overall standard of price collection;
- identify general training needs or the specific needs of an individual;
- highlight any key issues including, for example, problems with documentation or instructions issued by head office;
- identify areas where collection is problematical; for example all collectors may have problems in certain types of outlets, prompting the need for more detailed head office instructions.

12.35 Backchecking should be done by an expert independent of the process (preferably employed by the national statistical institute). Backchecking is carried out by visiting the selected outlet and re-collecting the prices and other relevant information, such as attribute or description codes. This activity should be carried out close to the original collection period to avoid problems of price changes occurring in the interim. It is important that backcheckers seek permission from the shopkeeper beforehand and follow the general criteria of conduct for local collection, as described in paragraphs 12.5 to 12.12.

12.36 For a backcheck to be a useful exercise it is important that performance criteria are determined to which all backcheck results can be compared. These criteria should set, for example, the acceptable number of price errors per number of items checked. Well-defined criteria will enable easy identification of a poorly performing collector or location following a backcheck.

12.37 A backcheck may include a range of tests to identify the following:

- price difference – if the price is different, the auditor should check with shopkeepers to see if there has been a price change since the original collection took place;
- insufficient item description – each item should be uniquely defined so that another collector can step in to cover the absence of the usual collector, for example in the event of illness;
- wrong item priced – such as incorrect size being chosen;
- items wrongly recorded as missing or temporarily out of stock.

12.38 A report should be sent to head office for scrutiny once the backcheck has been completed. Head office will then need to take appropriate action, which may include, for example, retraining or sending out supplementary instructions.

Other auditor functions

12.39 The range of tasks that an auditor carries out will vary from one statistical agency to another. Monitoring the standard of price collection will always be the main focus of the auditor. There are a number of other areas, however, in which auditors can be called upon to contribute.

12.40 Auditors may be required to help with the sampling of locations and items. Auditors can check that proposed collection locations contain an adequate range of shops. They can also advise on economic conditions in these locations and on any dangerous areas. Auditors can carry out commodity work. For example, if a particular item seems to be causing difficulty for price collectors, auditors can speak to collectors and retailers with a view to determining reasons for these difficulties. Auditors can also advise on changes to basket composition. They can ensure that products suggested by head office are available across the country, and can suggest item descriptions and weight bands. Furthermore, auditors can provide reports on collection in existing locations. For example, head office may raise a query about a particular outlet in a particular location; auditors can visit this outlet to find the answer to the question or to persuade a retailer to continue with the survey.

Quality checks in head office

12.41 Four kinds of regular checking are necessary in head office:

- to ensure that the price collectors' reports are sent in when they are due. If this is not done, it is necessary to find out the reason and to take appropriate action to obtain the reports;
- to confirm that the reports contain what they are supposed to contain, i.e. that fields which must be filled in have not been left blank, that numeric fields contain numbers and that non-numeric fields do not;

- to review and edit each return. Substitutions may have to be made centrally or those made by the collectors may have to be approved. Unusual (or simply large) price changes may need to be queried. Items priced in multiple units or varying weights may have to be converted to price per standard unit. Missing prices must be dealt with according to standard rules relating to the cause;
- errors introduced when keying the numbers into the computer or transcribing them onto worksheets must be found and corrected, and preferably avoided in the first place by eliminating the need to transcribe.

12.42 It should be noted that the way the data are organized in worksheets or in the computer may differ from the way they are organized on receipt, since they will arrive at the central office organized by collector, outlet and item. Their origin should, however, be recorded so that reference to it can be made should processing disclose any problems with the data. Furthermore, even if codes provided to the collectors to list items and to describe or qualify the prices are used unchanged in the processing, other codes may have to be used for information which comes in from the collectors in non-coded form.

12.43 How the checking is organized will vary from country to country. In some cases, local or regional supervisors will do some of it; in other cases, it will be more appropriate for it all to be done centrally. Some of these tasks can be done by computer, others manually. Therefore, no general suggestion can be made about the sequence of the work or about its division into different parts.

12.44 Procedures should be in place to check that all documents, messages or files are returned from the field so that price collectors can be contacted about missing returns. Initial checks should then be carried out to ensure that data are complete and correct. For instance, checks should be run to ensure that unexpected duplicate prices (i.e. for the same item, in the same shops, in the same location) are not taken on, and that the location, outlet and item identifier codes which accompany each price exist and are valid. If any prices fail these checks, a query should be raised with the price collector for clarification. Since some of the checking may require reference back to the price collectors (or to their supervisors or respondents when direct mail questionnaires are used), the timetable for producing the index must allow for this communication to take place.

12.45 Following the checks that the price data are correct and complete, a series of validation checks may be run. In deciding on what checks should be done, account should be taken of the validation checks carried out in the field. The use of hand-held computers will increase the potential for validation at the time of price collection and reduce the need for detailed scrutiny at head office. It would clearly not be productive or cost-effective to repeat all the tests already carried out locally, except as a secondary audit or random check that those checks have been completed.

12.46 The range of checks that might be carried out is covered in paragraphs 12.21 to 12.25. In addition, it is possible for the head office to use the price data received that month to identify outliers.

Reports

12.47 Reports should routinely be generated for most representative items, to help the analyst pick out particular prices for which the level or change stands out as different from that reported for similar varieties elsewhere, or simply where the change lies outside certain specified limits. Thus, a computer printout can list all prices which either fall well outside the range of prices obtained last time for that representative item, or for which the percentage change from last time for the same item in the same outlet falls outside a specified range. The limits used will vary from item to item and can be amended in the light of experience. The analyst can then work through the printout, first ascertaining whether there has been a keying-in error, and then examining whether any explanation furnished by the collector adequately explains the divergent price behaviour or whether a query should be sent back to the supervisor or collector. The timetable should allow for this, and anomalous observations should be discarded where an acceptable explanation or correction cannot be obtained in time.

12.48 Other reports may be produced regularly on the basis of reports for several periods (e.g. several months) to detect accumulated patterns, thus enabling broader problems to be detected. For example:

- One collector's reports might show many more "outlet closed" remarks than those of other collectors, perhaps indicating either a motivational or training need on the part of that collector, or a change in retail trade patterns in a particular area.
- Variety substitution for a particular representative item might become more numerous than hitherto, suggesting a possible need for revision of the specification or the choice of another representative item.
- Where tight specifications list a number of brands and models of which one is to be chosen, but a large number of prices are for items not specified in the original list, this will suggest that the specified brands and models are no longer appropriate and a review of the list is required.
- The dispersion of price changes for a particular representative item might be much larger than it used to be, raising the question of whether it has been appropriately specified.

12.49 Routine computer-generated reports should enable those in charge of the index to detect the existence of all such problems. Two types of reports are particularly useful: index dispersion reports, and price quote reports.

12.50 *Index dispersion report.* This is a list of items indicating the current index for each item, the number of valid quotes for each item, and the number of price relatives (the ratio of current price to previous valid price) in each of a series of pre-selected ranges (for example, less than 40, 40–49, ... 190–199, greater than 199). The index dispersion reports can be used to identify quotes with price relatives that fall outside the range of the main bulk of quotes. These quotes can be identified from quote reports for the item, then investigated and appropriate action taken if necessary.

12.51 *Price quote report*. This consists of a range of information on an item that the index dispersion report has highlighted as warranting further investigation. Information listed may include current price, recent previous prices and base price, together with locations and types of shop. The report can be used to identify the quotes that require further investigation and also to investigate rejected prices.

Algorithms

12.52 Algorithms can be created which may be used to identify and invalidate price movements that differ significantly from the norm for an item. For some seasonal items for which price movements are erratic, it may be more appropriate to construct an algorithm to look at price level rather than price change.

12.53 An example is the Tukey algorithm. This operates as follows:

- The ratio of current price to previous valid price (the price relative) is calculated for each price. (In the case of items tested by price level rather than price change, this stage is omitted.)
- For each item, the set of all such ratios is sorted into ascending order, and ratios of 1 (unchanged prices) are excluded. (In the case of items tested by price level rather than price change, the prices themselves are sorted.)
- The top and bottom 5 per cent of the list are removed (this 5 per cent is parameter 1).
- The "midmean" is the mean of what is left.
- The upper and lower "semi-midmeans" are the midmeans of all observations above or below the median.
- The upper (lower) Tukey limit is the midmean plus (minus) 2.5 times the difference between the midmean and the upper (lower) semi-midmean. This figure of 2.5 represents parameters 2 and 3. The upper and lower values can be set independently if desired but are currently set to be equal.
- If the upper limit is negative, it is set to zero. (If price levels are used, the lower limit is set to zero.)
- Price relatives, or price levels, outside the Tukey limits are flagged as unacceptable and requiring amendment or further investigation.

12.54 The Tukey algorithm has a number of advantageous characteristics. In particular, it produces intuitively reasonable results; is consistent from month to month; is robust in the presence of outliers (in other words, adding in one or two rogue observations does not affect very much the limits set by the algorithm); and is robust as data volume changes (i.e. limits calculated from a subset of the data do not vary much from those calculated on the full data set).

12.55 Whilst algorithms can be an efficient way of highlighting problematical data, a word of caution should be expressed about using them. Analysts will want to assure themselves that their use does not result in systematic bias in the index. This is a matter that may also need to be taken into account in any editing routines, although it is less likely to be problematical in the context of manual editing.

Producing and publishing the index

12.56 In regard to producing and publishing the index, there are a number of organizational models that could be adopted for effective working. Considerations to be taken into account in deciding on the appropriate organizational structure include:

- the need for clarity of reporting lines;
- the need for a clear division of responsibilities;
- centralized or decentralized management of fieldwork (see above discussion on local collection, and the outsourcing of fieldwork, paragraphs 12.6 to 12.14);
- production management versus technical development;
- compatibility with corporate structures in the national statistical institute, for example, in relation to quality management, methodological research, and dissemination.

12.57 In some cases, for instance where little in-house expertise in fieldwork practice exists, it may be advantageous for fieldwork to be conducted by a different organization in either the public or private sector. In these circumstances it is important that an effective contractual relationship exists with regard to the data. There should also be agreed delivery targets and performance measures to cover such things as data delivery timetables, response rates and levels of accuracy. Consideration should also be given to the independent auditing of the contractor's work on a sample basis.

Monthly compilation

12.58 The system used for the regular computation of the index must be sufficiently flexible to allow for changes in the kind of data obtained. For example, local price collection for purposively sampled products from the branches of a large supermarket chain may be superseded by centrally collected prices for a statistical sample drawn from complete sales data made available by the head office of the chain. In these circumstances, a modular approach may be seen as an advantage.

12.59 Analytical computations provide comparisons between the published index, or one or more sub-indices, and what they would have been using different methods or data. They help to explain why the index has moved as it has and they allow methodological experimentation. The following examples of such investigations serve to make clear some of the computational capabilities and data that are required:

- alternative aggregations of sub-indices;
- the effects of different weights; the effects of introducing newly significant product categories; and price-updating of weights;

- number and duration of missing observations; how a different method of estimating them would affect the index;
- comparison of indices computed with various sub-samples of the data as a means of estimating variance; variances of price ratios;
- computation of a standard reference index (one with no explicit quality adjustments) so that an implicit quality index is obtained;
- numbers of sampled products; rates of forced replacements; and lengths of time products remain in the sample;
- frequency distributions of quality adjustments.

12.60 To examine such matters, the database must contain not only prices but detailed descriptions of product replacements, explanatory remarks attached to observed prices, and so on. Generally, it will be found that historical databases will be too large to be stored live on the system and therefore will need to be archived. Detailed documentation relating to the archived material will need to be kept to guard against loss of vital information caused by changes in computing staff or computers. Consideration should also be given to appointing a data custodian with responsibility for all archived records.

Spreadsheets

12.61 Spreadsheets may be used for compiling sub-indices that require special procedures, or where data are collected centrally, or on an uncertain timetable or to a different timetable from that of other data collection, but effective control procedures need to be put in place. Examples of types of prices for which the use of separate spreadsheets may be useful include: air fares, hotel accommodation, newspapers and car rental. Such use of a spreadsheet has the advantage of additional flexibility and scope for combining responsibility for data collection, data input and computation. The compiler's specialized knowledge about the markets or outlets where these prices may be observed, combined with analytical tools applied to the spreadsheet, will help the compiler to detect any irregularities in the data, facilitate investigation of whether these reflect reporting or input errors, and allow for rapid rectification. The ability to jump between numerical data entry and a chart displaying, for example, current-month and previous-month entries, helps the rapid and simple detection of anomalies. The same person can then follow this up with the data supplier.

12.62 As time passes, the resolution of problems that have arisen and adaptation to new circumstances will result in changes in the spreadsheet. Unless quality management controls are put in place, there is a danger that the spreadsheet will be understandable only by the person responsible and that it will not be properly documented. If so, two unfortunate consequences can arise:

- If that person is absent, retires or moves to another job, his or her successor will find it very difficult to maintain the continuity and quality of the sub-index.
- New procedures introduced to deal with new circumstances may be inconsistent with procedures used for other sub-indices for which other people are responsible.

12.63 Good documentation and good communication with colleagues will diminish these risks. At a minimum, there should be an insistence that the spreadsheets and changes in them are made understandable by the provision of adequately explicative row and column headings or of notes attached to headings. Furthermore, changes in procedures or formulae, rebasing and the application of new weights should always be introduced by moving computation over to a new sheet within the workbook, not by modifying the old sheet. The new sheet and the old sheet will then exist side by side so that they can be compared.

12.64 Inadvertent changes may be prevented by using passwords to cells containing formulae and by locking cells containing input data once editing is completed. Passwords should be known only to a limited number of people with authority to edit the spreadsheets. Regular back-up by copying the whole workbook to another disk is also essential.

Introducing changes

12.65 Various checks should be carried out when introducing changes. These may include a comparison of the old and new basis using data from parallel running of collections (e.g. when handing over to a new collection contractor) or re-estimating backwards – for example, when new base prices are being imputed for a complete range of goods or services. Any anomalies can then be investigated further.

Disaster recovery

12.66 A consumer price index will arguably be the most important and highest-profile statistic that a national statistical institute produces and can affect the widest range of users. There is often a legal obligation for the CPI to be published within a short time period after the end of the month to which the data refer. For example, in the European Union, there is a legal requirement to publish within 30 days of the reference period the Harmonized Index of Consumer Prices (HICP), which uses the CPI data sets from member States (although the Eurostat timetable is for publication two weeks earlier than this). Any delay in publication can have a significant impact on subsequent months, threatening future publications. Significant delays could take months to catch up, in order to return to the existing tight publication timetables. It is critical, therefore, that national statistical institutes develop a robust and tested disaster recovery plan, however unlikely the need to implement it.

12.67 There are a number of possible causes of disaster:

- failure of an external contractor to fulfil obligations to supply information;
- failure of the computer system;

- major natural disaster or other event (e.g. terrorist activity) affecting the operations centres or head office of the national statistical institute.

12.68 Where the collection is contracted out, one of the most important requirements of a disaster recovery plan is to recruit an alternative permanent service supplier as soon as possible. It is probable that, on termination of a contract with an external provider, the national statistical institute could arrange to have the services supplied by a third party, but only on a temporary basis prior to re-letting the contract through a competitive tendering process.

12.69 Additional money may need to be obtained for implementing a computing disaster recovery plan. Consideration needs to be given as to whether outsourcing the disaster recovery plan to a company specializing in the provision of back-up support or maintaining an in-house capability is the best option. This will, in part, depend on the number of sites and locations at which the national statistical institute operates. If the organization has a number of sites, some distance apart but linked by modern communications infrastructure, then there is less likelihood that they will all be affected by a natural disaster.

12.70 The managers of disaster recovery plans will also need to consider:

- full specification of accommodation and associated requirements (e.g. personal computers, telephones) associated with each site;
- allocation of specific officers to specific duties for the disaster recovery period and identification of each individual's training needs;
- investigation of practicalities and associated expenses for matters such as access to shared drives and systems, including communication and the quality management systems, from other sites;
- confirmation of costs, arrangement of site visits and liaison with procurement units in negotiating contracts.

Quality management and quality management systems

12.71 Statistical offices are faced with the continuous challenge of providing a wide range of outputs and services to meet user, i.e. customer, needs. Thus a key element of quality is customer focus and the effective dissemination of relevant, accurate and timely statistics. In addition, it can be argued that quality management should include effective customer education on the use of such statistics. In these terms, success can be measured by the achievement of a high level of satisfaction amongst well-informed users.

12.72 For the quality management of a CPI, it can be argued that the priority area is quality control of the production process itself. For most national statistical institutes, quality control of production will be an area which represents a high risk, given the complexity of the process and the financial implications of an error in the index.

12.73 If the principles of organizing and managing the collection of data, and subsequent processing of information to produce a consumer price index, are to be adopted, then it is vital that a system is in place to ensure that the data obtained, the processes involved in achieving the specified outputs, and the formulation of the policies and strategies that drive them are managed in an effective, consistent manner. The processes should, wherever possible, be open to verification; and mechanisms should be put in place to ensure that outputs meet requirements – in other words, customer satisfaction. Taken together, these elements form the basis of a quality management system.

12.74 There are varying perceptions about the meaning of quality but an important common thread is the requirement to react to and serve users of the CPI and to ensure continuous improvement in that service. Thus the implementation of an effective quality management system requires a high level of understanding of customer needs and the translation of this into a coherent statistical and quality framework. Such a framework is also necessary for putting together criteria for judging success. User needs can be canvassed either formally through negotiation of contractual obligations which may or may not be legally binding, or less formally through talking to customers on a one-to-one basis or through customer surveys.

12.75 In many countries, issues relating to the governance of the national statistical institute are set down in a "framework" or similar document. This defines the functions and responsibilities of the national statistical institute, and generally guides and directs the work of the office. For instance, an objective stated in the framework document "to improve the quality and relevance of service to customers – both in government and the wider user community" provides a powerful statement for determining workplans.

12.76 This recognition of the importance of quality can be further endorsed by a published vision of the national statistical institute as a key supplier of authoritative, timely and high-quality information. Such a vision can be encapsulated by publishing objectives in an annual business plan. These objectives can include improving quality and relevance, thereby increasing public confidence in the integrity and validity of outputs.

12.77 Performance can be measured against a combination of a number of factors, including accuracy, timeliness, efficiency and relevance. There are a number of practical examples and case studies of quality systems, illustrating how different models may be applied.

Quality management systems

12.78 Various standards of best-practice standards can be exploited to help organizations to improve quality management. Some of these standards have the added advantage of being internationally recognized.

12.79 *Total quality management*. Total quality management (TQM) is more closely identified with a management philosophy rather than a highly specified and structured system. The characteristics associated with

TQM and an effective culture of quality in an organization include:

- clearly defined organizational goals;
- strong customer focus;
- strategic quality planning;
- process orientation;
- employee empowerment;
- information sharing;
- continuous quality improvement.

12.80 *Benchmarking.* Benchmarking is a process of comparing with others, and learning from them about what you do and how well you do it, with the aim of bringing about improvements.

12.81 There are already a number of benchmarking partnerships operating within national statistical institutes, some specifically considering the CPI. The Australian Bureau of Statistics has been particularly active in this area, and undertook an exercise in 1998–2000 in partnership with the United Kingdom. Benchmarking projects have also been undertaken in New Zealand, the Scandinavian countries and the United States.

12.82 Areas that can be considered when benchmarking a CPI collection may include:

- timelines, accuracy and coverage of collection;
- benefits of index methodologies for various items, e.g. geometric mean as against average of relatives;
- frequency of collection and publication;
- cost of collection per unit of commodity, etc.

12.83 *European Foundation for Quality Management Excellence Model.* The Excellence Model (1994) constructed by the European Foundation for Quality Management (EFQM) is a diagnostic tool for self-assessment. The model is widely used by governmental organizations across Europe to improve quality and performance. It may be described as a tool that drives the philosophy of TQM.

12.84 The EFQM Excellence Model focuses on general business areas and assesses performance against two sets of criteria – the first consists of five criteria covering what the business area does (the enablers: leadership; people; policy and strategy; partnership and resources; and process), and the second consists of four criteria on what the business area achieves (the results: people results; customer results; society results; and key performance results). Evidence based on feedback from focus groups, questionnaires and personal interviews is used to score performance, and a resulting action plan for improvement is introduced which is then included in the business plan.

12.85 Underlying the EFQM Excellence Model is the realization that business excellence – measured through customer satisfaction – is achieved through effective leadership which drives policy and strategy, allocates resources compatible with that policy, and manages employees in such a way as to enable them to manage the processes.

12.86 In the case of national statistical institutes, where some procedures are governed by statute or regulation, the use of the EFQM Excellence Model enables continuous improvement to be taken forward across a range of processes and functions. To work effectively, it needs the commitment of senior managers, who must be responsible for leading any self-assessment. However, unlike ISO 9000, where assessment is carried out by qualified auditors often from outside the work area (see below), the EFQM Excellence Model relies on the input from all staff.

12.87 *ISO 9000.* The International Standard ISO 9000 is an international quality standard for management systems (ISO, 1994). A quality system is a common-sense, well-documented business management system that is applicable to all business sectors. It helps to ensure consistency and improvement of working practices, including the products and services produced.

12.88 The ISO standards were fully revised as ISO 9001 in November 2000 to match current philosophies of quality management and views regarding the structures that need to be in place to ensure that continuous improvement is maintained (ISO, 2000).

12.89 The revised standards give users the opportunity to add value to their activities and to improve their performance continually by focusing on the major processes within the organization. They will result in a closer alignment of the quality management system with the needs of the organization and reflect the way the organization runs its business activities. By meeting the ISO 9000 standard, an organization will come more into line with TQM and the EFQM Excellence Model.

Scope for greater use of quality management techniques

12.90 Both ISO 9000 and the EFQM Excellence Model have received a great deal of international recognition over recent years. At the same time, the use of benchmarking networks has also grown in prominence. It is therefore pertinent to ask whether more coordinated use should be made of these and other quality management techniques at a strategic level in fields of statistics where the focus is on international comparability. This is particularly so with statistics that are compiled for treaty purposes, for example by member States of the European Union following detailed methodological guidelines laid down in law.

12.91 The arguments are fivefold:

- It is paramount that such important non-optional statistics whose production and uses are enshrined in legislation have the full trust of users.
- The quality of international comparisons is dependent on the weakest link, thus good-quality statistics from one country may be of little value if not matched by statistics of equally good quality from other countries.
- There is a potential for misleading analysis and conclusions arising from differences in the application of standard methodology.
- Empowerment in ensuring the establishment of adequate control processes is reduced when production is delegated to member States.

- There is limited scope for centralized validation and quality management when production is decentralized.

Performance management, development and training

12.92 An effective performance management system for individuals is just as important as applying such a system to management structure. Performance management can be seen as a continuous process designed to improve work outputs by focusing on what people actually achieve rather than the amount of effort they put into the work. It should provide the link between the objectives of the individuals, those of their team and those of the wider organization, so that workplans are coherent across the organization, and everybody knows what they are doing and why they are doing it. The performance management system should provide clear objectives for monitoring and evaluation, to enable feedback on performance and also to assist with the identification of the development needs of individuals. Performance management should be continuous.

Training requirements

12.93 Effective training will help motivate staff and equip them to deliver a good-quality CPI. At its simplest, training will give a background understanding of the nature and uses of the index and how it is compiled. Training and development takes many different forms and may include:

- tutoring by the line manager or supervisor;
- attending an induction course or reading a manual;
- accompanying an experienced price collector.

12.94 A written training plan is useful in identifying training and development needs in relation to the organization's goals and targets. It can also be used to identify the resources required to deliver the training to meet these needs, and to evaluate whether the training has been delivered effectively and objectives have been met.

Specific training for compilers and collectors

12.95 Further training will be required for specific skills, depending on the roles of the individuals and their jobs. Training should continue beyond the induction stage to cover changed procedures, and retraining where performance is unsatisfactory.

12.96 Price collectors will need to be trained specifically in field procedures, including relations with shopkeepers, the selection and definition of a valid price, special rules for certain individual items (including seasonal items), how to complete forms and, where appropriate, how to use hand-held computers. Compilers of the index will need to be trained specifically on validation procedures and consistency checking, the calculation of centrally collected indices, weighting procedures and how to aggregate prices, as well as on the treatment of seasonal items and special procedures relating to some sections (e.g. housing). It may also be beneficial to provide training in local or national trading or statistical regulations, economics, and commodity information.

12.97 Significant benefits may result from the interaction between price collectors and index compilers. Benefits will also be gained from liaison between the national statistical institute and commodity experts from industry. Such experts can advise on issues such as how to identify quality features on particular items, for example electrical goods, personal computers, or clothing and footwear.

12.98 It may be beneficial if statisticians from headquarters are personally responsible for supervising price collection in the area where the head office is situated, so that they can have first-hand experience of the problems involved. This will put them in a position to provide assistance where difficulties arise. Equally, it is a good idea to arrange for regular visits to headquarters by groups of collectors and their supervisors. It is good for morale. Price collectors will, arguably, do a better job if they feel that they belong to a team, if they can see that their work is appreciated and if they feel that their problems are understood. Visits to headquarters will help convey that the accuracy and conscientiousness of their contribution is recognized as being crucial to the quality of the index. Visits to head office by price collectors also will help the statisticians to keep in touch with conditions in the field and, for example, to obtain more information about new goods and aspects of quality change.

12.99 Similarly, compilers of the index may wish to visit the field occasionally and participate in or simply observe the price collection. This will provide them with a better appreciation of the practical problems associated with price collection and a better feel for data (and in consequence for the quality of the index), together with the skills required to help with price collection in the event of an emergency.

Documentation

12.100 A manual and other documents such as desk instructions may serve for initial training. Later on such documents should enable the collectors and compilers to remind themselves of all the relevant rules and procedures. The documentation should be well organized and well indexed so that answers to problems can quickly be found.

12.101 Documentation should be checked by all concerned and updated regularly. The pile of pieces of paper containing amendments should never grow large, but should be replaced by a new consolidated version. One way of achieving this is to have a loose-leaf manual so that individual pages can be replaced whenever necessary. Another option is to keep an electronic version that can be updated by nominated individuals. It is important that the updating of documentation is done in a systematic and controlled way. A variety of software is available to help the statistician to do this.

12.102 The benefits of using standard electronic software for documentation are threefold:

- more efficient production of documentation, because the software helps with the initial compilation of information and reduces the need to print and circulate paper copies;
- better-informed staff, because they have immediate electronic access to the latest documentation, including desk instructions, with a search facility by subject and author;
- better quality control, because authors can readily amend and date-stamp updates and because access to non-authors is restricted to "read only".

Reviews

12.103 Training may be seen as an essential part of continuous quality improvement. Staff may be invited to operational reviews where all team members have the opportunity to raise concerns and, where appropriate, tackle specific issues through individual or group training.

PUBLICATION, DISSEMINATION AND USER RELATIONS

13

Introduction

13.1 The consumer price index (CPI) is one of the most important statistical series. Where statistics are categorized according to their potential impact, the CPI and its variants are always in the first rank. It follows therefore that it must be published, and otherwise disseminated, according to the policies, codes of practice and standards set for such data.

13.2 The CPI should therefore be:

- released as soon as possible;
- made available to all users at the same time;
- released according to pre-announced timetables;
- released separately from ministerial comment;
- made available in convenient form for users;
- accompanied by methodological explanation;
- backed up by professional statisticians and economists who can answer questions and provide further information.

13.3 Above all, the CPI should meet the *Fundamental Principles of Official Statistics* (United Nations, 1994). These principles are published in several languages on the websites of the United Nations and the United Nations Economic Commission for Europe (UNECE). They refer to dissemination and to all aspects of statistical work. These and other standards are discussed in this chapter.

Time series presentation of level and change

13.4 It is common, though not universal, to give greatest prominence to indices that show changes in aggregate prices between the month for which the most up-to-date data are available and the same month one year earlier. It is also usual to compare this annual change with the annual change shown one month previously. The model presentation in Box 13.1 on page 230 provides an example of this. It is also possible to focus on the latest one-month change or to give some emphasis to quarter-on-quarter changes.

13.5 The arguments for the choices shown in the example are as follows. The 12-month comparison provides an indication of price changes in a reasonably long time frame, by reference to periods which may otherwise be expected to be similar year to year. Thus, seasonal factors are unlikely to be influential. Also, price changes that are often decided centrally, such as those relating to the tariffs of utilities, and changes in indirect taxes (which have a direct impact on prices), are usually on an annual timetable and occur in the same month or months each year. There may nevertheless be one-off changes that can have an influence on the index.

13.6 Some press releases may give prominence to the month-on-previous-month change, especially for some components of the CPI. Such data have to be presented with care to avoid suggesting, for example, that a 2 per cent change in one month is similar to a 24 per cent change over a year.

13.7 It is also virtually universal to set a reference month (or longer period) in the past for which the price index is set at 100. All subsequent months then have index numbers which are percentages of the reference month or period. Indeed, it is that index which is used as the basic figure from which the other changes are calculated.

13.8 Indices are usually shown only to one decimal place, as are the other changes mentioned here, so figures have to be rounded. Rounding in these circumstances can, however, give a false impression of comparative change and must thus be explained, especially where prices are changing relatively little.

13.9 Care has also to be taken to differentiate between percentage points in the basic monthly index (which usually has 100 per cent set several years earlier) and, for example, percentage changes between one month and the next. If in one month the index is, for example, 200 and the following month it is 201, then the change can be described as one percentage point (above the period when the index was set at 100) or as half a percentage point (where the previous month is taken as 100 per cent). Both are valid, but they are percentages of different points in the past. It is therefore important to specify which is the base point of reference.

13.10 The reference period which is set at 100 is often referred to as "the base period". But it is often a relatively arbitrarily chosen date, changed every few years, and not necessarily related to any point in time when methodologies may have changed or when a new basket of goods and services was introduced. The status of the reference period should be made clear in the methodological explanation.

13.11 The CPI is, by definition, an index and therefore not a level or a series of absolute changes in prices. Nevertheless, in the process of presenting the CPI, average prices are calculated for categories of goods and services. It is thus possible to publish some average prices for groups of goods or services, and also to show the upper and lower bands of the prices from which the averages have been calculated. Some users of the index find average price levels useful; these averages should therefore be made available to researchers who may want them. It has to be noted, however, that data on price levels may be less reliable than the price change indices for any given group of goods or services.

13.12 So far this chapter has referred only to the broadest aggregates, without reference to subgroups of prices or to variants of the CPI which may include or exclude certain items. All of the foregoing refers to the most common form of CPI, which is usually intended to refer to the "average consumer" in a specific country and to include virtually all consumer prices in that country. But it can equally refer to regions of a country or to subgroups (such as pensioners), or to related or alternative measures of price change. Related or alternative measures, and sub-aggregate indices, are discussed in paragraphs 13.24 to 13.37 below.

Seasonal adjustment and smoothing of the index

13.13 The treatment of seasonal products and the estimation of seasonal effects are discussed in Chapter 22. In the present chapter we discuss the dissemination of such adjusted or smoothed series.

13.14 Most series of economic statistics are shown seasonally adjusted, as well as unadjusted. Consumer price indices are, however, not usually seasonally adjusted, although they sometimes are. Seasonal factors, for any series, are usually frequently recalculated using the latest data, so seasonally adjusted series can be changed in retrospect, but unadjusted CPIs are not usually revised.

13.15 In comparing one month with the same month a year earlier, it is assumed that seasonal patterns are much the same from one year to the next. There may be, however, exceptional months when the usual seasonal change is advanced or delayed. Such exceptional circumstances should be noted as one of the likely causes of a change in the CPI or in one of its components.

13.16 Changes over periods of less than a year are of course subject to seasonal factors and, in order to differentiate seasonal factors from other factors, it is necessary to make estimates of seasonal effects and to note them as factors that have contributed to changes in the index.

13.17 Although the CPI itself is not usually seasonally adjusted, some variants of the CPI may be seasonally adjusted, perhaps because they are more subject to seasonality and because they can be revised in retrospect if necessary. If such variants are seasonally adjusted, it is important to explain why. Seasonal adjustment usually leads to a smoother series than the original unadjusted one. There are also other ways of smoothing a monthly series, for example using three-month moving averages.

13.18 Statistical offices do not usually smooth the CPI series in their published presentations. Consumer price changes are not usually so erratic from month to month as to disguise price trends. If there is an erratic change, the producers of the index can usually explain the reasons for it. In any case, where any seasonally adjusted or smoothed series is published, it is important to publish the unadjusted as well as the adjusted series, so that the effect of the adjustment process is clear to users who may wish to know what has happened to prices, whether or not the changes can be put down to seasonal factors. Similarly, a full explanation should be given for the reasons why a particular seasonal adjustment procedure has been followed.

Analysis of contributions to change

13.19 The CPI is an aggregate of many different goods and services whose prices are changing at different rates, some of which may be going up while others are going down. Many users of the index want to know which goods or services have contributed most to changes in the index, and which prices may be out of step with general price trends.

13.20 The statisticians who calculate the index are well placed to provide analyses of the contributions to the price change, and to do so at the same time as the index is published. Sufficient detail should be made available so that users can see for themselves what has happened to various groups of prices. In addition, to assist journalists and others working under time constraints, the statistician should indicate the goods or group of products whose changes in price are the main contributors to the aggregate CPI, and also goods whose changes in price are the most different from the aggregate. The statistics can be presented in the form of tables and charts so that the trends may be compared. Similarly, statisticians should indicate any reasons for price changes which may not be immediately obvious but are nevertheless discernible from the published figures. For example, if there has been a sharp price rise or fall one year earlier, then it will affect the current year-on-year change, whatever happens to prices currently.

13.21 Analysis of contributions to change should also refer to any pre-announced price changes, or major changes since the last price-reporting date, which will affect the outlook for the index over the following months.

Economic commentary and interpretation of the index

13.22 In undertaking an analysis such as that described above, statisticians must be objective so that users of the data may differentiate clearly between the figures themselves and the interpretation of them. It is therefore essential to take care to avoid expressing any judgement of the impact of current policy on price changes or the possible implications of price changes for future policies. Whether the figures should be seen as good news or bad news is for the users to decide for themselves. The statistician's role here is to make it as easy as possible for users to form their own judgements from the perspective of their own economic or political views.

13.23 There are several ways of avoiding any apparent or real lapses in objectivity in the analysis. The first, and perhaps the most important, is to publish the figures independently of any ministerial or other political comment. Another is to be consistent in the way the analysis is presented. That is to say, the data should be presented in much the same format every month (see paragraphs 13.38 to 13.41 below). For example, tables and charts should cover the same periods every month, and use the same baselines.

Presentation of related or alternative measures

Core inflation

13.24 For the purposes of economic analysis, it is desirable to construct measures of "core" or "underlying" inflation which exclude movements in the inflation rate that are attributable to transient factors. In other words, measures of core or underlying inflation seek to measure the persistent or generalized trend of inflation. Central banks, for example, need to have measures of the general trend of inflation when setting monetary policy. For this reason, economists and statisticians are increasingly interested in developing measures of "underlying inflation".

13.25 Several methods can be used to derive a measure of underlying inflation. Most measures focus on reducing or eliminating the influence of exceptionally volatile prices, or of exceptionally large individual price changes. The most traditional approach is to exclude particular components of the CPI on a discretionary basis. The items to be excluded would be based on the statistician's knowledge of the volatility of particular items, depending on the economic conditions of the country. Items commonly excluded under this approach are fresh meat, fruit and vegetables, and petroleum. Many countries also exclude imported goods, government charges, and government-controlled prices. In some countries, a calculation is made to exclude the effect of indirect taxes such as VAT. Of course, care must be taken so as not to exclude so many items that the remainder becomes only a small and unrepresentative component of the total.

13.26 Other methods include smoothing techniques, for example annualizing three-month average inflation. A more difficult method is to exclude outliers, that is those items with the highest or lowest increases.

Alternative indices

13.27 An example of an alternative index is a "tax and prices index" in which income tax and sometimes social security payments are taken into account. Such an index estimates how much a taxpayer's gross income needs to change in order to maintain his or her spending power. It combines changes in direct (income) tax with changes in consumer prices.

13.28 Another example is an index which reflects changes in prices excluding indirect taxes (such as sales taxes) and duties. When compared to the CPI itself, such an index indicates the effects on prices of changes in indirect (e.g. sales) taxation.

13.29 Both of these examples involve allowing for taxes in one form or another. They are more complex than the CPI itself, and do not have the intuitive attraction of an index which aims at tracking the change in prices of a typical basket of consumer goods and services. As such, they should be presented as interesting and enlightening constructs based on the core index. It must be made clear that they are not replacements for, or superior to, the CPI itself.

13.30 A further example is the European Union's Harmonized Indices of Consumer Prices (HICPs), which are used to compare and aggregate price movements across European Union economies. The HICPs do not use a common basket of goods for all the countries in which they are calculated, because buying habits are different from one country to another, but the concepts and methods are nevertheless harmonized in other ways. No European Union member uses the HICPs as its national CPI, and therefore member countries also produce and publish their own indices. Although the HICPs are already used as an important indicator in the zone within Europe which uses the Euro as its underlying unit of currency, the HICPs are nevertheless relatively new, and are still under development. This is a case where the presentation of an alternative index may raise serious questions about whether it may be superior to the national CPI. It is therefore important to explain clearly the underlying concepts (which generally differentiate the HICPs from national CPIs) and to explain in some detail the reasons why the results are different. The HICPs were not calculated before 1996, and therefore do not enable price comparisons before that date. The starting date should be indicated if it is not obvious in any presentation.

13.31 Another concept is the cost of living index (COLI), which is usually defined as an index that indicates the changes in the costs associated not just with buying the same basket of goods, but with providing the same utility or usefulness to the consumer. Countries do not usually attempt to calculate a COLI on a regular basis, but users frequently refer to the CPI as a cost of living index. It should be made clear, in any background notes, whether this is indeed the concept underlying the CPI.

Sub-aggregate indices

13.32 Countries commonly calculate price indices for hundreds of products (for example bread or footwear), based on thousands of individual price records. The number of possible sub-aggregates is therefore very large indeed.

13.33 One kind of sub-aggregation is the grouping of sets of items or products which, when the sets are taken together, comprise the whole of the CPI. An important consideration here is the relationship of products within the subgroups. For example, an index may be presented for food and, under the heading of food, indices may be presented for subgroups such as cereals and vegetables.

13.34 One of the first considerations in presenting such sub-aggregate data for related products is consistency. That is to say, there should be a set of sub-aggregates for which indices are calculated and presented each month. Users commonly attach great importance to being able to continue their analysis from month to month.

13.35 Another consideration is international standardization of the division of the index into groups of goods and services, which enables comparison between countries. Some countries also have their own sub-aggregate groupings which may predate the current international standard. The generally accepted international standard for the presentation of sub-aggregates is the Classification of Individual Consumption according to Purpose (COICOP). It is used, for example, in the HICPs. Because COICOP defines groups of items by the general purpose for which they are used (e.g. "transport" or "housing and household services"), it combines goods and services within the same subgroups. Many national classifications are, however, composed of subgroups in which goods and services are never in the same subgroup. Where the national CPI is sub-aggregated by divisions other than the international standard, it is advisable either to present a breakdown also by COICOP or at least to show how the national classification compares to the international standard. COICOP and the related Central Product Classification (CPC) are discussed in more detail in Chapter 3 of this manual.

13.36 A further type of sub-aggregate index is an index which is essentially the same as the CPI except that it excludes certain items from it. The core index discussed earlier is an example. It could also be argued that the HICPs are such an index because they exclude certain non-monetary expenditures. Some countries publish, in addition to their all-items CPI, an index or indices which exclude certain expenditures. An example is an index which excludes mortgage interest payments from housing costs.

13.37 In the presentation of all related or alternative measures, their definitions should be made clear. It is also advisable to give the reasons for their publication. Most importantly, it should not be suggested that the sub-aggregate index is more meaningful than or superior to the CPI itself.

Press release, bulletin and methodological statement

13.38 The model presentation of a CPI in Box 13.1 is an example of the first page of a press release for a fictitious country. Other formats are possible. For example, the presentation might include a seasonally adjusted index. As indicated in the model, the presentation should contain the following information:

- details of issuing office;
- date and time of release;
- percentage change in new month over the same month one year earlier;
- comparison with change in previous month;

Box 13.1 Model presentation of consumer price index

Office of [name of country] Statistics
Friday 18 February 2000, for release at 11.00 a.m.

CONSUMER PRICE INDEX (CPI)
JANUARY 2000: PRESS RELEASE

In January 2000, consumers were paying 1.0 per cent more than they did in January 1999 for the goods and services in the CPI basket. This 12-month change was lower than the 12-month change recorded in December (1.5 per cent) but higher than in November (0.9 per cent).

Percentage change in the consumer price index over the same month of the previous year, for the last five years

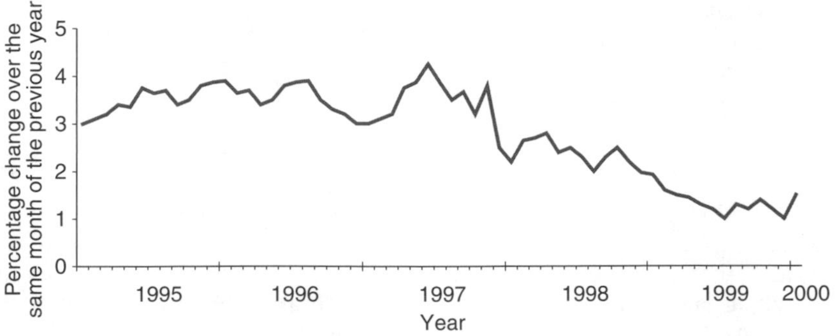

Main contributions to the overall 1.0 per cent increase

The largest increase was in the prices of clothing and footwear, with smaller increases in recreation and culture. Within the energy group of prices, there was a significant increase in gas tariffs. There were falls in the prices of furnishings and household goods. The changes in product groups are shown in the table on page x of this release.

Issued by the Office of Xxxxx Statistics, address xxxxxx
Press enquiries 1 111 1111; Public enquiries 2 222 2222 (name of a contact is helpful)
Background notes on the CPI are given in the annex to this note.
More notes and more details are given in our Internet site at XXX

– information on the product groups which contributed to the change and on any significant component price;
– reference to where more information can be found.

Note that no judgements are offered on policy or economic reasons for the price change, and no judgement is given on whether the change is good or bad.

13.39 What is not obvious from just one example is that the format of the press release should be the same from month to month. Using a consistent format is important in order to avoid appearing to choose a different format to indicate a preferred trend, for example from a selected starting date.

13.40 Other pages of the press release should give the monthly indices (base period equals 100) from which the percentage changes are calculated. Similar indices should also be given for major groups of goods and services. Charts may also be used to illustrate, for example, which prices have contributed most or least to the overall CPI.

13.41 If any other consumer price variant is also being published, then the differences between the indices should be briefly explained, including any methodological differences. Such variants that require explanation include, for example, a national index based on the European Union's HICPs methodology, any regional indices, or versions of the CPI that exclude particular components of consumer expenditure such as house purchase. The press release should include a short note on methodology, similar to that given in Box 13.2. More detailed explanation could be given in a handbook.

Box 13.2 Model note on methodology – to be included in press releases on consumer price indices

What is the consumer price index (CPI) measuring and how is it done?

The all-items consumer price index (CPI) is the main measure of what is commonly called inflation. It measures the change in prices, on average, from month to month, of the goods and services bought by most households.

Prices are collected each month from shops and other suppliers of goods and services. The pattern of household expenditure on these goods and services is derived from a regular household budget (or expenditure) survey. The prices and spending patterns are then combined to calculate the price indices for groups of goods and services and for the all-items index.

The overall index, with all of its component indices, is published each month in our *CPI Bulletin*. The *Bulletin* also contains more information on the methodology used in calculating the CPI. A small booklet is also available. For a detailed account of the methodology used in calculating the CPI, please see the *CPI technical manual*. For more information on these publications, and how they may be obtained, please refer to our web site at www.ous.gov or telephone the numbers given on the front of this press release.

International standards concerning the dissemination of consumer price indices

13.42 There are many international standards which apply, in general terms or specifically, to the CPI. The introduction to this chapter lists some of the broad principles which are reflected in many of the international standards in some form. One very general standard, but by its nature a fundamental one, is the United Nations *Fundamental Principles of Official Statistics*. It is available on the web sites of the UNECE and the United Nations in several languages. It refers not just to dissemination but to all aspects of statistical work.

13.43 The International Monetary Fund (IMF) standards are particularly pertinent in regard to dissemination. There are two which refer to statistics including consumer price indices. One is the General Data Dissemination System (GDDS), and the other is the Special Data Dissemination Standard (SDDS). The GDDS provides a general framework, with some specific indicators defined as "core" and others defined as "encouraged". The SDDS is based on the GDDS framework, but is more demanding and applies only to those countries that choose to subscribe to it in writing to the IMF Board. Both standards are available on the IMF web site.

13.44 Under the heading of quality, the GDDS refers to the necessity to provide information on sources and methods, as well as on component details and checking procedures. Under the heading "integrity", it refers to declared standards of confidentiality, internal government access before data release, identification of ministerial commentary, and information on revision and advance notice of changes in methodology. Under the heading "access by the public", it refers to the need for pre-announced release dates and simultaneous access for all users. In the tables of data categories, it refers to the CPI as a core indicator which should be issued monthly, within one to two months of the data collection date. All of these standards are reflected in the present manual. The ILO has also published guidelines concerning dissemination practices for labour statistics (ILO, 1998), which are available on the ILO web site.

Timing of dissemination of the consumer price index

13.45 The CPI should be released as soon as possible, but it is equally important to release the index according to a strict timetable. It is also important to publish the timetable of release dates as far in advance as possible. Having a fixed release date, published well in advance, is important for two main reasons. First, it reduces the scope for the manipulation of the release date for political expediency. Second, it gives confidence to users that the release date is as soon as possible and has not been delayed (or brought forward) for purely political reasons. A third advantage is that users know when to expect the figures and can be prepared to use them.

Timeliness of release versus data accuracy

13.46 The IMF's GDDS, discussed in paragraphs 13.43 and 13.44 above, recommends that the CPI be released within one to two months of data collection each month. It is usual, in practice, for most countries to release the CPI in the middle of the month after the month to which the index refers. This is possible because, in many cases, the data are collected mainly over a limited period in the middle of the month to which the latest data refer. Thus the statisticians have some time to check and analyse the data, and to prepare the many tables and charts in which the data will be disseminated.

13.47 The accuracy of the index is particularly important because so much depends on the CPI. In addition to the economic policy implications of the index, the CPI is used in most countries in a variety of contracts. Perhaps the best-known contractual use is the indexing of wages and salaries. Also, partly because it is rare for more data to emerge after the CPI is published, and partly because of the way in which the index is used in contracts, it is very rarely revised. This represents a major difference between the CPI and other economic or socioeconomic aggregates.

13.48 It follows that, although timeliness is important, the timetable must allow time for the data to be properly prepared and thoroughly checked. After the release date, in most cases, a revision to the non-seasonally adjusted CPI would not be permissible. The HICPs of the European Union are an exception and are revised from time to time. If any series is revised, then of course the changes must be fully described and explained when the new data are released. If there is any methodological change, this is usually known in advance. Users should be warned before any such change occurs.

Access to data

13.49 With the CPI as with other statistics, users should be allowed access to as much data as possible for two main reasons. First, some users find the detailed data very useful in their analysis. Second, access to the data inspires confidence in the data.

13.50 There are, however, limits on the quantity of data that can be made available to users. One reason is confidentiality, which is addressed in the next section of this chapter. Another is the quantity of data that most users can absorb. A further reason is the cost of publishing large quantities of data which few users may need.

13.51 In general, the CPI and its major components are deemed to be of such wide importance that they are made available free through press releases. More detailed data are, however, often published only in books and other media, and are charged for in order to recover some of the dissemination costs. Similarly, special analyses made at the request of particular users are usually charged for at a rate commensurate with the work involved.

13.52 The quantity of data to which users should be given access through the various possible media is also discussed in paragraphs 13.53 to 13.58 below.

Confidentiality

13.53 Although, in general, as much data as possible should be made available to users, there are reasons why confidentiality is important in some instances. First, some data are supplied by retailers and others on the understanding that the data will be used only for the purpose of aggregation with other data and will not be released in any other form. This can be especially important where the data are given voluntarily, as they often are. Second, only a sample of particular brands is priced as representative of a much larger group of products. If it is known which brands are included in the index and which are not, then it might be possible to bias components of the index by manipulating a small number of prices.

13.54 Even the knowledge that price data are, or might be, collected on one particular day in the month could enable some component price indices to be biased by retailers or others choosing to change prices on a particular day. This is, however, only a short-run danger and cannot be sustained.

Electronic dissemination

13.55 The World Wide Web has several advantages as a dissemination medium. For the data producer, distribution costs are relatively small. No printing or mailing costs are involved. As soon as the data are on the Web, they are available to all Web users at the same time. Putting a large amount of data on the Web costs little more than putting on a smaller amount. Web users can download the data without re-keying, thus increasing speed and reducing transmission or transposition errors.

13.56 Among the disadvantages of dissemination via the World Wide Web is that not all data users have equal access to the Web. Another important disadvantage is that users may go straight to the data, without reading the metadata which may be crucial to the proper understanding of the data. Also, it may be as easy for a user to disseminate the CPI widely by electronic means as it is for the statistical office, thus enabling users to preempt the producers by circulating the index in advance of the release time, perhaps without the metadata which may be essential to a proper understanding of the figures.

13.57 Ideally the CPI, complete with any essential metadata, should be released simultaneously to the press and other users. One way in which some statistical offices are ensuring this is to bring the journalists together perhaps half an hour before the official release time, provide them with the printed press release, explain the data and answer any questions. Then, at release time, the journalists are permitted to transmit the figures to their offices for wider distribution.

13.58 In essence, care must be taken to ensure that the CPI is available at the same time to all users, regardless of the dissemination medium used.

User consultation

Different uses of consumer price indices

13.59 The different uses of CPIs are discussed in some detail in Chapter 2. It is important to explain to potential users of the CPI which are suitable uses and which are not. To this end, it is important to explain how the CPI is constructed, and to provide details of its sources and methods. It is also important to make readily available explanations of alternative indices or sub-indices, indicating how their uses differ from the uses of the CPI itself.

Presentation of methodology

13.60 When the CPI is published each month, users are anxious to see the main figures and to use them. Users do not generally want to be burdened with explanations of the methodology underlying the data. Nevertheless, methodological explanations must be accessible to those who may want them, and in forms which are comprehensible to users with different levels of expertise and interest. Any significant changes in methodology must be fully explained, and notified as far in advance as possible of the change being made.

13.61 In addition to a brief statement in press releases (see paragraphs 13.38 to 13.41 above), methodological explanations should be available on at least two levels. Non-experts should be able to refer to a booklet which explains the history, principles and practice underlying the CPI and any alternative measures which may also be available. A more thorough explanation of sources and methods should also be readily available for those users who are sufficiently interested and, for example, for statisticians who may be working on the production of the CPI for the first time. The information must also be kept up to date despite the pressures to devote time to the output at the expense of documentation. As noted elsewhere, the ready availability of a full explanation of sources and methods is essential to confidence and trust in the CPI.

Role of advisory committees

13.62 For a statistical series as important as the CPI, it is essential for there to be an advisory committee, or set of committees, representing users and producers. There are many contentious issues in the construction of the CPI. In many countries there have been fierce arguments about, for example, which components should be included and excluded. The role of an advisory committee is to consider and to advise on contentious and other issues. Perhaps an equally important role of an advisory committee is that its very existence provides reassurance that the CPI can be trusted and is not a tool of government propaganda.

13.63 In those countries where advisory committees have not been the norm, there may be a fear on the part of statisticians that including non-governmental participants may raise expectations beyond what the statisticians can deliver, thereby increasing dissatisfaction among the general public. In fact, the inclusion of non-governmental users can lead to a greater understanding of the realities and the practical constraints to meeting theoretical needs. This is the usual experience of offices that already have advisory bodies which include representatives of all the major constituencies, both inside and outside government. It is therefore important that the advisory committee should comprise people such as academics, employers, trade union representatives and others who have an interest in the index from differing points of view. It is also important that the reports of the advisory committee are made available to the public fully and without undue delay.

Explaining index quality

13.64 The CPI is regarded with suspicion at many different levels. It usually refers to the average consumer, but each consumer has a different spending pattern from the spending patterns of others and may notice changes in one set of prices but not in others. More importantly, perhaps, there is criticism of the index because of suspicion that it does not keep track of newer types of goods and services, changes in the quality of products, or newer types of retailing.

13.65 In the light of such suspicion, it is important for the producers of the index to be willing to discuss these issues and to explain how they are being dealt with. As with other issues discussed here, the producers of the index must be open about their methods and the extent to which they can, or cannot, overcome the potential or real problems which have been identified. It follows that the statisticians who produce the index should publish explanations of quality aspects, whether or not the quality of the index is currently being questioned.

THE SYSTEM OF PRICE STATISTICS 14

Introduction

14.1 This chapter focuses on the value aggregates for goods and services that relate the major price indices, including the consumer price index (CPI), to one another. The chapter provides a deeper context for the domain of the CPI covered in Chapter 3 and the index weights dealt with in Chapter 4. It also deepens the context for defining the sample unit and the set of products, discussed in Chapter 5.

14.2 We begin by defining a value aggregate for a domain of goods and services as the sum of the products of the prices and quantities of those goods and services. A price index may be characterized as the factor giving the relative change in this value aggregate arising from changes in prices. As such, all the major price index formulae can be expressed as weighted averages of price relatives whose weights are the shares of items in the value aggregate. For the best-known price index formulae expressed as value aggregates of share-weighted averages of price relatives, see Chapter 1, equation (1.2) and Chapter 15, equation (15.8) for the Laspeyres index. See Chapter 1, equation (1.3) and Chapter 15, equation (15.9) for the Paasche index, and Chapter 1, equations (1.11)–(1.12) and Chapter 15, equations (15.21) and (15.81) for the Walsh and Törnqvist indices. As the geometric mean of the Laspeyres and Paasche indices, the Fisher ideal index of Chapter 1, equation (1.10) and Chapter 15, equation (15.12) is also a function of expenditure shares derived directly from the value aggregate.

14.3 To define a price index, we first need to know several things about the value aggregate. The value aggregate defines the following aspects of a price index:

- which commodities or items to include in the index;
- how to determine the item prices;
- which transactions that involve these items to include in the index;
- how to determine the weights, and from which sources these weights should be drawn.

Besides the content of the value aggregates for the major price indices, we also discuss in this chapter their valuation and timing properties. These properties bear importantly on how compilers define the prices and weights of price indices.

14.4 The four principal price indices in the system of economic statistics are the consumer price index (CPI), the producer price index (PPI), and the export and import price indices (XPI and MPI). They are well-known and closely watched indicators of macroeconomic performance. They are direct indicators of the purchasing power of money in various types of transactions and other flows involving goods and services. Consequently, these indices are important tools in the design and conduct of the monetary and fiscal policy of the government. They also are used as deflators to provide summary measures of the volume of goods and services produced and consumed. They thus are also used to inform economic decisions throughout the private sector. They do not, or should not, comprise merely a collection of unrelated price indicators, but provide instead an integrated and consistent view of price developments pertaining to production, consumption, and international transactions in goods and services. By implication, the meaningfulness of all of these indices derives in no small measure from the meaningfulness of the value aggregates to which each refers. Although there are other important price indices, most of which also are discussed in this chapter, these four constitute the backbone of the system of price statistics in most countries, and they will be given special attention.

14.5 Paragraphs 14.8 onwards establish the relationships among the four major price series by associating them with certain of the interlocking aggregates defined in the *System of National Accounts 1993* (*SNA 1993*). The system of national accounts (SNA) has gone through various versions over the years, the 1993 edition of this manual being the latest. We will use SNA to refer to the system of national accounts generically, and *SNA 1993* to refer specifically to the most recent version, as appropriate. The CPI draws its coverage from a variety of accounts in the SNA. At various points along the way, we note whether and how the composition of each value aggregate in the national accounts relates to the aggregate on which the CPI may be defined. Besides the four main price indices and an array of additional useful price indices, we briefly consider labour compensation indices and purchasing power parities in the system of economic statistics.

14.6 As noted in Chapter 2, the CPI is constructed for a range of uses in various countries, but we can identify two broad themes: the *consumption* (sometimes called the cost of living) CPI, and the *transactions* (often called the inflation) CPI. Advocates for the transactions CPI often refer to it as an acquisitions CPI, following the language of the earlier *Consumer price indices: An ILO manual* (Turvey et al., 1989) which used this terminology to distinguish alternative treatments of, for example, owner-occupied housing (p. 15). The term "acquisitions CPI" has a different meaning in the SNA, referring to households' consumption of goods and services secured not only by themselves, but also by non-profit institutions and government on their behalf. We thus use the term "transactions" instead. In the ILO manual's terminology, what we call a consumption CPI would have been called a "uses" CPI. Either is consistent with current SNA terminology.

14.7 Both types of CPI are oriented towards the price experience of households, but, as its name implies, the consumption CPI focuses on the prices of items on which households make final consumption expenditures, while the transactions CPI focuses on the prices of items on which households make monetary final expenditures on consumption *and* capital formation. Consumption CPIs thus *exclude* capital formation expenditures by households (for example, on their own dwellings), but *may include* both monetary and imputed consumption expenditures (for example, the imputed rent paid by homeowners on their own dwellings). Transactions CPIs focus only on the prices of items on which households make monetary final expenditures, and thus *may include* household capital formation expenditures (for example, net acquisitions of dwellings), but categorically *exclude* expenditures that must be imputed in order to cover households' effective consumption of goods and services. In this chapter, we will further explain the concepts of institutional sector and type of transaction from the SNA that define the distinction and the relationship between the consumption and transactions CPI. In each of the following sections, as relevant, we will discuss the kinds of expenditures defining the items and weights appropriate for each of these two main types, referring to the sum of expenditures corresponding to the consumption CPI as *expenditure aggregate #1* and that for the transactions CPI as *expenditure aggregate #2*.

National accounts as a framework for the system of price statistics

14.8 The system of national accounts is the core system of value aggregates for transactions and other flows in goods and services. It is clearly of broad economic interest. Granted, the value aggregates of the major price indices need not be coincident with the major value aggregates in the national accounts. The national accounts aggregates, however, represent the major flows of goods and services and levels of tangible and intangible stocks in the economy. The major price indices therefore should have a clear relationship to these aggregates. This chapter explains the value aggregates now in common use by national authorities for the major price indices, or planned for future use, by assembling them from components identified in the SNA.

14.9 The *SNA 1993* describes the system of national accounts as follows:

> 1.1 The System of National Accounts (SNA) consists of a coherent, consistent and integrated set of macroeconomic accounts, balance sheets and tables based on a set of internationally agreed concepts, definitions, classifications and accounting rules. It provides a comprehensive framework within which economic data can be compiled and presented for purposes of economic analysis, decision taking and policy making. The accounts cover the major economic activities taking place within an economy, such as production, consumption, financing and the accumulation of capital goods. Some of the flows involved, such as income, saving, lending and borrowing, do not relate to goods and services and do not factor into price and quantity components. However, the SNA also contains a comprehensive framework, the supply and use table, discussed in more detail below, which establishes and displays the interrelationships between all the main flows of goods and services in the economy. The coverage and contents of these flows are defined, classified and measured in a conceptually consistent manner. Within this table, the linkages between major flows of goods and services associated with activities such as production, consumption, distribution, importing and exporting can be seen in a simple and direct way. The table provides an ideal framework for designing and organizing a system of internally consistent price statistics that relate to a set of economically interdependent flows of goods and services. The table not only establishes the interrelationships between consumer, producer, import and export prices themselves, but also their linkages with price indices for major macroeconomic aggregates such as gross domestic product (GDP).

14.10 In this overview of price indices, we first take a top-level view of the major national accounts aggregates. We then begin a review of the underlying construction of these aggregates by considering first the types of economic agents in the economy that are recognized in the national accounting system, and second, the economic accounts kept on them involving goods and services flows that build up to the main aggregates. As these accounts are built up from their foundations, precise relationships emerge between the well-known headline price indicators – the PPI, CPI, XPI and MPI – and the closely watched national accounts aggregates.

Aggregate supply and use of goods and services

14.11 At the most aggregate level, the supply and use of goods and services in the national accounts is the simple textbook macroeconomic identity equating total supply with total uses. Total supply is the sum of output Y, imports M, and taxes less subsidies on products T. Total use is the sum of intermediate consumption Z, the final consumption of households C and government G, capital formation I, and exports X:

$$Y + M + T = Z + C + G + I + X \tag{14.1}$$

14.12 Rearranging this identity by subtracting intermediate consumption and imports from both sides, we arrive at the familiar alternative expressions for GDP from the production (value added) and expenditure approaches:

$$(Y - Z) + T = \text{Value added} + T \equiv C + C + I + X - M = \text{Gross domestic product} \tag{14.2}$$

GDP is, of course, internationally recognized as the central national accounts aggregate for measuring economic performance. It is essentially a measure of production, as distinct from final demand. More precisely, it measures the value added of the productive activities carried out by all the economic agents resident in an economy. As imports are not included in GDP, a price index for GDP tracks internally generated inflation. Compiling indices for tracking the parts of relative change in GDP and its components that can be attributed to price and volume change is among the most important objectives for the development of price statistics in modern statistical systems.

14.13 As explained in more detail later, the supply and use table in the SNA is a comprehensive matrix covering the economy as a whole that exploits the identities (14.1) and (14.2) at a disaggregated level. Each row of the matrix shows the total uses of a commodity, or group of commodities, while each column shows the total supplies from domestic industries and imports. The table provides an accounting framework that imposes the discipline of both conceptual and numerical consistency on data on flows of goods and services drawn from different sources. The flows have to be defined, classified and valued in the same way, while any errors have to be reconciled. The table provides a good basis for compiling a set of interdependent price and quantity indices. In the following sections, we consider the various elements or building blocks that make up the table before examining the table as a whole.

Institutional units and establishments

14.14 In building the accounting system and the major aggregates Y, M, T, Z, C, G, I and X of equations (14.1) and (14.2), the *SNA 1993* first organizes the economy of a country into the kinds of entities or agents that undertake economic activity. These agents are called *institutional units* and comprise five types resident in the economy, as well as a single non-resident category, the rest of the world. An institutional unit is said to be resident in an economy if its primary centre of economic interest is located there. A centre of economic interest is operationally defined in part by the duration of physical presence. For example, a household is resident in an economic territory if it lives within the territory's boundaries for a year or more. The five types of resident institutional units are: non-financial corporations; financial corporations; general government; households; and non-profit institutions serving households (NPISHs). The *SNA 1993* associates with institutional units the ability to hold title to productive assets, and thus they represent the smallest units on which complete balance sheets can be compiled.

14.15 As noted earlier, institutional units can engage in producing and consuming goods and services and in capital formation, accumulating goods and services as productive tangible and intangible assets. To analyse production, the *SNA 1993* identifies a smaller unit or agent than an institutional unit, called an *establishment* or *local kind of activity unit* (LKAU). Within an institutional unit, the establishment is the smallest unit organized for production whose costs and output can be separately identified. Generally, establishments specialize in the production of only a few types of output at a single geographical location. To compile productivity statistics, analysts also need detail on produced and non-produced *non-financial* assets (capital) by establishment from multi-establishment institutional units. This is because, as we will see, these statistics use an industry or activity classification of establishments rather than institutional units. Some institutional units may own establishments in more than one industry. On the other hand, an account of financial assets and liabilities by establishment is not needed and not generally available from the accounts of institutional units owning multiple establishments. The latter would be necessary to make establishment balance sheets.

14.16 The *SNA 1993* classification of institutional units into sectors is shown in Box 14.1. The *SNA 1993* classification of institutional units does not strictly follow the legal status of institutional units, but rather their function. Hence, a government-owned non-financial enterprise producing output sold at prices substantially covering its costs and for which a balance sheet can be compiled would be classified as a non-financial corporation, along with non-financial corporations that are corporate legal entities. For further details, see *SNA 1993*, Chapter IV. Notice that the *SNA 1993* institutional sectors represent the units typically covered in economic and household censuses and surveys. The SNA focuses on the activities of institutional units that are resident in a nation or economic territory. It makes provision for the rest of the world (S.2 in Box 14.1) only to capture the transactions of resident institutional units with non-residents. Transactions of non-residents with other non-residents are out of scope for the national or regional accounts of a given country or region.

14.17 The classification of household institutional units into sectors is highly relevant for analysing the incidence of price change. As shown in Box 14.1, the *SNA 1993* defines household subsectors according to the major source of income: mixed income (mostly profits of household enterprises), compensation (wages, salaries and compensation in kind), or property income (rents, dividends and interest). There are not the only sectors of households that may be of interest to users of the CPI, however. In addition to the *source* of income, analysts often (perhaps more often) are interested in the *level* of income. The shares of particular goods and services in household expenditures are likely to show more variation across income level than across major source of income. For example, to shed light on the price experience of poor (low-income) households we would want to know whether there is a significant difference in the shares of expenditure on specific goods and services for poor as compared with non-poor households. A good example would be the relative importance of expenditures for used durable goods. As we will see, consumer durables are measured in the SNA on an acquisitions-less-disposals basis. While poor households normally would be net purchasers of such goods, richer households would tend to be net sellers. A change in the prices of used goods thus would have a very different impact on the CPIs for the two groups of households.

Box 14.1 Institutional sectors in the *System of National Accounts 1993*

S.1 Total economy
- **S.11 Non-financial corporations**
  - *Ultimate subdivisions: public, national private and foreign controlled*
- **S.12 Financial corporations**
  - *Ultimate subdivisions: public, national private and foreign controlled*
  - S.121 Central bank
  - S.122 Other depository corporations
    - S.1221 Deposit money corporations
    - S.1222 Other depository corporations, except deposit money corporations
  - S.123 Other financial intermediaries, except insurance corporations and pension funds
  - S.124 Financial auxiliaries
  - S.125 Insurance corporations and pension funds
- **S.13 General government**
  - *Alternate scheme n = 1, social security funds shown as a separate branch of government S.1314*
  - *Alternate scheme n = 2, social security funds included as components of central, state, and local branches, and S.1314 deleted*
  - S.13*n*1 Central government
  - S.13*n*2 State government
  - S.13*n*3 Local government
  - S.1314 Social security funds
- **S.14 Households**
  - *Classified according to the largest source of income received*
  - S.141 Employers *(mixed income, owning an unincorporated enterprise with paid employees)*
  - S.142 Own account workers *(mixed income,[1] owning an unincorporated enterprise without paid employees)*
  - S.143 Employees *(compensation of employees)*[2]
  - S.144 Recipients of property and transfer income[3]
    - S.1441 Recipients of property income
    - S.1442 Recipients of pensions
    - S.1443 Recipients of other transfers
- **S.15 Non-profit institutions serving households (NPISHs)**

S.2 Rest of the world

[1]To understand how subsectors S.141 and S.142 of households are formed, an explanation of the term "mixed income" is in order. This, in turn, requires consideration of the national accounts income concept of operating surplus. The operating surplus of an enterprise is the residual of the value of output less purchases of goods and services, inputs, wages and salaries, employers' social contributions (social security and pension payments), and taxes net of subsidies payable on production that are unrelated to products. The mixed income of household unincorporated enterprises is algebraically defined identically with the operating surplus of other enterprises. However, for unincorporated household enterprises, the compensation of the owners or proprietors of the enterprise may not be included in the recorded compensation of employees item, and thus the difference between output and operating cost will include compensation for the owners' labour. The distinct terminology merely recognizes that the owners' wages are often inextricably mixed with the operating surplus for these units. [2]Compensation of employees comprises wages and salaries, and employer-provided benefits comprising employers' social contributions. [3]Property income comprises interest, dividends and rent.

Accounts of institutional units

14.18 In equations (14.1) and (14.2), we identified the basic aggregates comprising the total supply and use of goods and services in the economy, and derived GDP in terms of these aggregates. To see how to separate the price and volume components of supply and use, it is necessary to build these basic aggregates up from the institutional sector accounts of the economy's economic agents. In this process it is important to detail the production and consumption activities of these agents, as well as the types of goods and services they produce and consume. The framework organizing this information is the supply and use table. As this table is built up, we effectively also begin to accumulate data on the product share weights s needed for computing price index formulae (Chapters 1, 3, and 15–17). The basic accounts of the SNA in which all of these aggregates are recorded at the level of institutional units are the production, use of income, capital, and external goods and services accounts. These accounts organize the information for the following top-level aggregates:

- *Production account*: output Y, intermediate consumption Z, and value added $Y-Z$;
- *Use of income account*: household consumption C and government consumption G;
- *Capital account*: capital formation I;
- *External goods and services account*: exports X and imports M.

Recording transactions in goods and services

14.19 Before turning to further elaboration on these four goods and services accounts, it is important to specify how each entry in the value aggregates comprising them is to be recorded. The items i in the value aggregate equation (15.1) of Chapter 15 represent detailed goods and services flows classified into categories of transactions. There are two defining aspects of recording transactions: timing and valuation.

14.20 Regarding the *timing* of transactions, to associate each transaction with a date, the national accounts consider a transaction to have been consummated when a liability to pay is created between the units involved. For flows of goods and services, this occurs when the ownership of the good is exchanged or when the service is delivered. When change of ownership occurs or the service is delivered, a transaction is said to have accrued. In general, this time need not be the same as the moment at which the payment actually takes place.

14.21 There are two *valuation* principles in the national accounts, one for suppliers and one for users. For suppliers, transactions in goods and services are to be valued at basic prices. The basic price is the price per unit of good or service receivable by the producer. We use the term receivable to indicate that the price refers to an accrued transaction for the seller, and the term payable to indicate a transaction that has accrued to the purchaser. As the producer does not receive taxes (if any) on products, but does receive subsidies (if any) on products, taxes on products are excluded from the basic price, while subsidies on products are included. The producer also does not receive separately invoiced transport and insurance charges provided by other suppliers, or any distribution margins added by other, retail or wholesale service producers, and these are also excluded from the basic price. In contrast, the user, as purchaser, pays all of these charges, and users' purchases are therefore valued at purchasers' prices, which add taxes net of subsidies on products and margins for included transport, insurance and distribution services to the basic price.

14.22 The *SNA 1993* distinguishes between taxes on products and other taxes on production. Taxes net of subsidies on products *T* include all taxes payable per unit or as a fraction of the value of goods or services transacted. Included in *T* are excise, sales, and the non-refundable portion of value added taxes, duties on imports and taxes on exports. Subsidies on products include all subsidies receivable per unit or as a fraction of the value of goods or services produced, including in particular subsidies paid on imports and exports. Other taxes on production comprise, for example, taxes on real property and taxes on profits. Other subsidies on production include, for example, regular payments by the government to cover the difference between the costs and revenues of loss-making enterprises. Of total taxes and subsidies on production, only taxes and subsidies on products are considered in defining basic and purchasers' prices. By implication, there are no taxes payable on products included in either of the aggregates *Y* or *M*, while subsidies receivable on products are included in these aggregates.

14.23 Accordingly, output *Y* and imports *M* in equations (14.1) and (14.2) are valued at basic prices, to which are added taxes less subsidies on products *T* to arrive at total supply. The reader may have noted that transport, insurance and distribution margins have somehow disappeared after having been introduced. Whether these services are included with the good or invoiced separately does not affect the total expenditure on goods and services by the purchaser. For the economy as a whole, these transactions cancel out, but when we consider industry or activity and product detail, they will have redistributive effects among goods and services products. This point is revisited in the discussion of the supply and use table below.

14.24 The components of total uses are valued at purchasers' prices. This is straightforwardly interpreted for the final consumption of households and government. For capital formation expenditures, the notion of purchasers' prices also includes the costs of "setting up" fixed capital equipment. For exports, purchasers' prices also include export taxes net of subsidies, according to the "free on board" (fob) value at the national frontier. We now discuss each of the four major goods and services accounts in turn.

Production

14.25 An institutional unit engaged in production is said to be an *enterprise*. By implication, any of the five types of resident institutional units can be an enterprise. The production account for enterprises in the *SNA 1993* appears, with minor reordering of elements, essentially as shown in Table 14.1. An identical presentation also applies to the establishments or local kind of activity units (LKAUs) owned by enterprises. In fact, an establishment can be defined operationally as the smallest unit for which a production account can be constructed. There are cases in which an establishment or LKAU is synonymous with or at least inseparable from the institutional unit that owns it. This is true of single-establishment corporations and of household unincorporated enterprises, for example. In other cases, an enterprise may own multiple establishments. The

Table 14.1 Production account for an establishment, institutional unit or institutional sector

SNA 1993 items in bold refer to flows in goods and services

Uses	Resources
P.2 Intermediate consumption (purchasers' prices)	**P.1 Output (basic prices)**
B.1 *Gross value-added* (balances the account; that is, it is the difference between output P.1 and intermediate consumption P.2)	
	Of which, memorandum items breaking down total output for classifying the market/non-market status of the producer unit: **P.11 Market output** **P.12 Output for own final use** **P.13 Other non-market output**

production account can also be produced for various establishment and enterprise groupings, including, of course, institutional sectors, but also for establishment industry or activity groups. In the production account and throughout the *SNA 1993*, the transaction codes beginning with P refer to entries for transactions in goods and services. The codes beginning with B refer to so-called "balancing items", which are defined residually as the difference between a resources total and the sum of itemized uses of those resources.

14.26 For classifying an establishment or LKAU, output is broken down into market output (P.11), which is sold at "economically significant prices" substantially covering the cost of production, and two types of non-market output that are provided without charge or at prices so low they bear no relationship to production cost. The two types of non-market output are output for own final use (P.12) and other non-market output (P.13). Output for own final use includes the production of, for example, machine tools and structures (fixed capital formation items) by an establishment for the use of the establishment itself or other establishments in the same enterprise, the imputed rental value of certain productive assets owned by households, such as (and currently limited to) owner-occupied dwellings, and the production of certain other unincorporated household enterprises, such as agricultural products produced by farmers for consumption by their own families or employees. Other non-market output comprises the output of general government and non-profit institutions serving households distributed free of charge or sold at prices that are not economically significant. In constructing a price index, we will necessarily be focusing on those transactions of establishment units that involve economically significant prices, and thus on market output (P.11). The prices collected for market output items may also, however, be used to value the own final use portion of non-market output (P.12). Our scope of coverage for price indices thus extends to cover this component of non-market output as well.

14.27 A production unit's resources derive from the value of its output, and its uses of resources are the costs it incurs in carrying out production. The production account therefore uses both the basic price and purchasers' price methods of valuation, as appropriate to a production unit in its roles as a supplier and a user of products. For the supply (resources) of goods and services, products are valued at basic prices, the national currency value receivable by the producer for each unit of a product. The prices include subsidies, and exclude the taxes on products and additional charges or margins on products to pay for included retail and wholesale trade services, and for included transport and insurance. For uses of goods and services, products are valued at purchasers' prices, the national currency value payable by the user for each unit of a product, including taxes on products as well as trade and transport margins, and excluding subsidies on products.

14.28 *Product detail in the production account.* In addition to breaking output down into its market and non-market components, output and intermediate consumption also can be broken down by type of product. Classifying product types using, for example, the international standard Central Product Classification (CPC), the production account for each establishment could be arranged to appear as in Table 14.2. Table 14.2 effectively gives the core structure of the report form of the typical establishment survey providing source data on production for the national accounts.

14.29 *Industry detail in the production account.* With the values of total output by product, and total market and non-market outputs in Table 14.2 for each establishment, we then classify the establishment by its principal activity or industry, and market/non-market status. To reflect the information required for this classification, positions for the activity and market/non-market classification codes of the establishment are shown at the top of Table 14.2. The activity classification involves principally, if not exclusively, sorting establishments according to the types of product produced (CPC or other product code, such as the Classification of Products by Activity) for which the total output is greatest. The major categories of the International Standard Industrial Classification of All Economic Activities (ISIC), Revision 3, are shown in Box 14.2 below.

14.30 As indicated in Table 14.2, The *SNA 1993* recommends use of the International Standard Industrial Classification (ISIC) for all economic activities, the CPC for domestic products, and the closely related Harmonized Commodity Description and Classification System (HS) for exported and imported products. Each country may adapt the international standard to its specific circumstances. If the adaptation amounts to adding further detail, the classification is said to be derived from the international standard. The *Nomenclature générale des Activités économiques dans les Communautés européennes* (NACE, the General Industrial Classification of Economic Activities within the European Communities) is an industrial classification derived from the ISIC. If the adaptation reorganizes the way in which detailed categories are grouped compared with the international standard, but provides for a cross-classification at some level of detail, it is said to be related. The North American Industrial Classification System (NAICS) of Canada, Mexico and the United States is an industrial classification related to the ISIC. The European Commission's PRODCOM classification of industrial products is derived from its Classification of Products by Activity (CPA) which, in turn, is related to the international standard CPC through a cross-classification defined at a high level of product detail.

14.31 *The output aggregate of the producer price index and the production account.* The producer price index (PPI) is an index of the prices of the outputs of establishments. The position of the PPI in the *SNA 1993* is defined by the relationship of its output value aggregate to those defined in the national accounts. In Box 14.2, we consider the composition of the PPI value aggregate according to its industry coverage, arguing that the PPI's industry coverage should be complete. Considering further market and non-market production within an industry group of establishments that are classified according to market status, the PPI's coverage could extend both to the market output (P.11) and output for own final use

Table 14.2 Production account with product detail for an establishment or local kind of activity unit

SNA 1993 items in bold refer to flows in goods and services

Establishment ID: eeeeeeee | *Institutional unit ID: uuuuuuuu*
Activity/Industry code (ISIC): aaaa | *Institutional sector code:* S.nnnnn
Market status: P.1*n*

Uses		Resources	
P.2	**Intermediate consumption (purchasers' prices), *of which:***	**P.1**	**Output (basic prices), *of which:***
CPC 0	Agriculture, forestry and fishery products	CPC 0	Agriculture, forestry and fishery products
CPC 1	Ores and mineral; electricity, gas, and water	CPC 1	Ores and mineral; electricity, gas, and water
CPC 2	Food products, beverages and tobacco; textiles, apparel and leather products	CPC 2	Food products, beverages and tobacco; textiles, apparel and leather products
CPC 3	Other transportable goods, except metal products, machinery and equipment	CPC 3	Other transportable goods, except metal products, machinery and equipment
CPC 4	Metal products, machinery and equipment	CPC 4	Metal products, machinery and equipment
CPC 5	Intangible assets; land; constructions; construction services	CPC 5	Intangible assets; land; constructions; construction services
CPC 6	Distributive trade services; lodging; food and beverage serving services; transport services; and utilities distribution services	CPC 6	Distributive trade services; lodging; food and beverage serving services; transport services; and utilities distribution services
CPC 7	Financial and related services; real estate services; and rental and leasing services	CPC 7	Financial and related services; real estate services; and rental and leasing services
CPC 8	Business and production services	CPC 8	Business and production services
CPC 9	Community, social and personal services	CPC 9	Community, social and personal services
B.1	*Gross value-added*		
			Memorandum items breaking down total output for classifying the market/non-market status of the producer:
		P.11	**Market output**
		P.12	**Output for own final use**
		P.13	**Other non-market output**

(P.12) identified in Table 14.2 when this account is considered for all establishments in the economy. Although the latter is technically non-market output, it would be valued at the basic prices the establishment would receive were that own-use production to be sold.

14.32 *The expenditure aggregate of the consumer price index and the production account.* Consumption from own production is a significant fraction of total consumption, comprising both goods and services. For goods produced by households, as noted in the *SNA 1993*:

> 6.24 The System includes the production of all goods within the production boundary. At the time the production takes place it may not even be known whether, or in what proportions, the goods produced are destined for the market or for own use. The following types of production by households are, therefore, included whether intended for own final consumption or not:
>
> (a) The production of agricultural products and their subsequent storage; the gathering of berries or other uncultivated crops; forestry; wood-cutting and the collection of firewood; hunting and fishing;
>
> (b) The production of other primary products such as mining salt, cutting peat, the supply of water, etc.;
>
> (c) The processing of agricultural products; the production of grain by threshing; the production of flour by milling; the curing of skins and the production of leather; the production and preservation of meat and fish products; the preservation of fruit by drying, bottling, etc.; the production of dairy products such as butter or cheese; the production of beer, wine, or spirits; the production of baskets or mats; etc.;
>
> (d) Other kinds of processing such as weaving cloth; dress making and tailoring; the production of footwear; the production of pottery, utensils or durables; making furniture or furnishings; etc.
>
> The storage of agricultural goods produced by households is included within the production boundary as an extension of the goods-producing process. The supply of water is also considered a goods-producing activity in this context. In principle, supplying water is a similar kind of activity to extracting and piping crude oil.
>
> 6.25 It is not feasible to draw up a complete, exhaustive list of all possible productive activities but the above list covers the most common types. When the amount of a good produced within households is believed to be quantitatively important in relation to the total supply of that good in a country, its production should be recorded. Otherwise, it is not worthwhile trying to estimate it in practice.

For services, the *SNA 1993* notes housing services as the sole – but for most countries extremely important – item of production for own consumption:

> 6.29 The production of housing services for their own final consumption by owner-occupiers has always been included within the production boundary in national accounts, although it constitutes an exception to the general exclusion of own-account service production. The ratio of owner-occupied to rented dwellings can vary significantly between countries and even over short periods of time within a single country, so that both international and intertemporal comparisons of the production and consumption of housing services could be distorted if no imputation were made for the value of

Box 14.2 Coverage of industries or activities by the producer price index in terms of aggregate output value

The principal economic activities of the International Standard Industrial Classification of All Economic Activities (ISIC), Revision 3, are:

A Agriculture, hunting and forestry
B Fishing
C Mining and quarrying
D Manufacturing
E Electricity, gas and water supply
F Construction
G Wholesale and retail trade; repair of motor vehicles, motorcycles, and personal and household goods
H Hotels and restaurants
I Transport, storage and communications
J Financial intermediation
K Real estate, renting and business activities
L Public administration and defence; compulsory social security
M Education
N Health and social work
O Other community, social and personal service activities
P Private households with employed persons
Q Extra-territorial organizations and bodies

These are characteristic of the activities identified in most national industrial classifications. In assembling data on the supply and use flows in the economy, a detailed industry production account such as given in Table 14.2 is effectively constructed for each type of activity in the economy, whose major categories are shown in the ISIC list above. With the product output and expenditure detail in Table 14.2, we can show more explicitly the typical goods and services coverage of the PPI within the output aggregate (P.1) of the production account for each industry. In most countries, PPIs cover industries that produce goods, such as the mining and manufacturing activities (C–D) and sometimes also agriculture (A) and fishing (B), and construction (F), as well as the two industrial service activities – electricity, gas and water supply (E) and transport, storage and communications (I). In principle, the PPI should cover the market output of all activities, and a number of countries are currently working on extending PPI coverage to the remaining service-producing activities besides transport and utilities.

own-account housing services. The imputed value of the income generated by such production is taxed in some countries.

The SNA imputes the value of such consumption at the equivalent market value of the output households produce for their own purposes.

14.33 In some cases, however, the market equivalent method of valuing production for own consumption is not viable because sufficiently similar market equivalents to the items supplied from own production are not available, or they are sufficiently rare that it is too expensive to obtain information on them or too unreliable to base estimates on such information. In these cases, production cost approaches are taken. The source of data for the production cost approaches is, in part, the household production account as regards goods and services purchased for intermediate consumption. The ultimate source of primary information for the household production account is principally the household expenditure survey, though specialized surveys of household business activity may also be undertaken for this purpose. For the shelter services provided by houses occupied by their owners, for example, the production account would be the source of expenditures on utilities, maintenance, and do-it-yourself repair items of intermediate consumption that would be used, in part, to determine the cost to an owner-occupant of the services he or she derives from his or her own dwelling. For the own production of agricultural produce, purchases of seed, fertilizer, and small garden tools might be recorded as intermediate consumption. Particularly for the latter, however, it is often difficult to distinguish between the intermediate production expense of production for own consumption and final consumption expenditure for maintaining decorative landscaping.

Final consumption

14.34 Consumption of goods and services in the *SNA 1993* is shown in the use of income account, which appears essentially as in Table 14.3 for each institutional unit. It is recalled that the accounts pertaining to goods and services in the *SNA 1993* that can be decomposed into price and volume components, and that would thus draw our interest as price index compilers, are designated by the codes P.n. Items of final consumption are designated by P.3 with extensions: P.3 comprises individual consumption expenditure (P.31) and collective consumption expenditure (P.32).

14.35 *Individual consumption, actual consumption, and household consumption expenditures*. The SNA distinguishes individual from collective goods and services, a distinction that is equivalent to that between private and public goods in economic theory. The distinction is mainly relevant to services. Individual services are provided to individual households and benefit those particular households, whereas collective services are provided to the community, for example services such as public order, administration, security and defence. Many individual services, however, such as education, health, housing and transport, may be financed and paid for by government or non-profit institutions and provided free or at a nominal price to individual households. A large part of government consumption expenditure is not on public goods but on goods or services supplied to individual households. These individual consumption expenditures by governments and NPISHs are described as *social transfers in kind* in the *SNA 1993*.

14.36 The concept of "household consumption" can have three distinct meanings. First, it can mean the total set of individual consumption goods and services actually acquired by households, including those received as

Table 14.3 Use of income account for institutional units and sectors

SNA 1993 items in bold refer to flows in goods and services

Institutional unit ID: uuuuuuuu Institutional sector code: S.*nnnnn*

Uses	Resources
P.3 Final consumption expenditure (purchasers' prices)[1]	B.6 *Disposable income[2]*
P.31 Individual consumption expenditure, *of which:* P.311 Individual consumption expenditure, except from production on own account, and imputed consumption expenditure, household sector S.14 only P.312 Imputed expenditure on owner-occupied housing services, household sector S.14 only P.313 Financial intermediation services implicitly measured (FISIM) P.314 Other imputed individual consumption expenditure **P.32 Collective consumption expenditure (general government sector S.13 only)** D.8 Adjustment for the change in the net equity of households in pension funds[3]	
B.8 *Saving* (balances the account; that is, it is the difference between disposable income B.6 and the sum of expenditures P.3 and adjustment D.8)	

[1]By definition, corporations have no final consumption in the *SNA 1993*. Thus, item P.3 and its subdivisions appear with non-zero entries only for household, government, and non-profit institutions serving households (NPISH) units. [2] The *SNA 1993* derives disposable income in a sequence of accounts producing the balancing items: value added B.1 (production account), operating surplus B.2 and mixed income B.3 (generation of income account), balance of primary incomes B.5 (allocation of primary income account), and disposable income B.6 (secondary distribution of income account). Collapsing all of these steps, disposable income B.6 is value added B.1 less (net) taxes on production and imports (payable) D.2 plus (net) subsidies D.3 (receivable), plus compensation of employees receivable, plus (net) property income (receivable) D.4, less (net) taxes on income and wealth (payable) D.5, less (net) social contributions (payable) D.61, plus (net) social benefits (receivable) D.62, less (net) other transfers (payable) D.7. [3] This adjustment reflects the treatment by the *SNA 1993* of privately funded pensions as owned by the household beneficiaries of such plans. It maintains consistency between the income and accumulation accounts in the system. It is not relevant to price and volume measurement (see *System of National Accounts 1993*, Chapter IX, Section A.4 for further details).

social transfers in kind. Second, it can mean the subset which households actually pay for themselves. To distinguish between these two sets, the SNA describes the first as the *actual final consumption* of households and the second as *household final consumption expenditures*. A third possible interpretation of household consumption is that it means the actual physical process of consuming the goods and services. It is this process from which utility is derived and that determines the household's standard of living. The process of consuming or using the goods or services can take place some time after the goods or services are acquired, as most consumer goods can be stored. The distinction between acquisition and use is most pronounced in the case of consumer durables that may be used over very long periods of time. The treatment of durables is discussed further in Box 14.3.

14.37 The existence of social transfers in kind is not generally recognized in CPIs, although it is desirable to take account of them, especially when considering changes in the cost of living. Moreover, governments may start to charge for services that were previously provided free, a practice that has become increasingly common in many countries in recent years. The goods and services provided free as social transfers could, in principle, be regarded as also being part of household consumption expenditures but as having a zero price. The shift from a zero to positive price is then a price increase that could be captured by a consumer price index.

14.38 *Monetary and imputed expenditures*. Not all household expenditures are monetary. A monetary expenditure is one in which the counterpart to the good or service acquired is the creation of some kind of financial liability. This may be immediately extinguished by a cash payment, but many monetary expenditures are made on credit. Household consumption expenditures also include certain imputed expenditures on goods or services that households produce for themselves. These are treated as expenditures because households incur the costs of producing them (in contrast to social transfers in kind, which are paid for by government or non-profit institutions).

14.39 The imputed household expenditures recognized in the SNA include all those on goods that households produce for themselves (mainly agricultural goods in practice), but exclude all household services produced for own consumption *except* for housing services produced by owner-occupants. The imputed prices at which the included goods and services are valued are their estimated prices on the market. In the case of housing services, these are imputed market rentals. In practice, most countries follow the SNA by including owner-occupied housing in the CPI. Other imputed prices, such as the prices of vegetables, fruit, or dairy or meat products produced for own consumption, may be included if they comprise a sufficiently large component of household consumption expenditure.

14.40 *Product detail in the use of income account*. As with the production accounts of the establishments owned by institutional units, we can consider extending the product detail of goods and services consumption in the use of income account according to the type of product consumed. In order to maintain the integration of the system of price and volume statistics on consumption with those we have just covered on production, products

Box 14.3 Treatment of housing and consumer durables in the system of national accounts and in consumer price indices

Dwellings are fixed assets. Purchases of dwellings by households therefore constitute household gross fixed capital formation and are not part of household consumption. They cannot enter into a price index for household consumption. Fixed assets are used for purposes of production, not consumption. Dwellings have therefore to be treated as fixed assets that are used by their owners to produce housing services. The system of national accounts (SNA) actually sets up a production account in which this production is recorded. The services are consumed by the owners. The expenditures on the services are imputed, the services being valued by the estimated rentals payable on the market for equivalent accommodation. The rentals have to cover both the depreciation of the dwellings and the associated interest charges or capital costs.

The existence of these imputed expenditures on owner-occupied housing services has always been recognized in national accounts and most countries have also included them in their consumer price indices (CPIs), even though other imputed expenditures are not included.

Consumer durables, such as automobiles, cookers and freezers, are also assets that are used by their owners over long periods of time. In principle, they could be treated in the same way as dwellings and be reclassified as fixed assets that produce flows of services that are consumed by their owners. For certain analytic purposes, it may be desirable to treat them this way. To do so in the SNA, however, would not simply be a matter of estimating the market rentals that would be payable for hiring the assets. It would also be necessary to set up production accounts in which the durables are used as fixed assets. This has traditionally been regarded as too difficult and artificial. There are also objections to extending further the range of imputed flows included in the SNA and gross domestic product. In practice, therefore, expenditures on durables are classified in the SNA as consumption expenditures and not as gross fixed capital formation, a practice that is carried over into CPIs.

would be classified according to the same system as in the production account. We show the major categories of the CPC 1.0 within the components of final consumption expenditure in Table 14.4.

14.41 Although the discussion in this chapter maintains a consistent classification of expenditure by product across all goods and services accounts, other functional classifications of expenditure have been developed for each institutional sector for specific purposes. The international standard versions of these classifications included in the *SNA 1993* comprise the Classification of Individual Consumption according to Purpose (COICOP), the Classification of the Purposes of Non-profit Institutions Serving Households (COPNI), the Classification of the Functions of Government (COFOG), and the Classification of the Purposes of Producers (COPP). The first column of Tables 14.4 and 14.5 is often compiled using data from household expenditure surveys. These data are collected using functional classifications such as COICOP, rather than product classifications. To facilitate constructing the cross-economy framework of the *SNA 1993* considered in this chapter, there is a concordance between the CPC and the COICOP.

14.42 *A hierarchy of household consumption aggregates.* It is worth noting that all household consumption expenditures (that is, of the households institutional sector S.14) are individual expenditures, by definition. The following hierarchy of household consumption aggregates that are relevant to CPIs may be distinguished in the SNA:

- P.41 Actual individual consumption, of which:
  - D.63 Social transfers in kind (the individual consumption expenditure P.31 of general government S.13 and NPISHs S.15)
  - P.31 Individual consumption expenditure, of which:
    - P.311 Monetary consumption expenditure
    - P.312 Financial intermediation services implicitly measured (FISIM)
    - P.313 Imputed expenditure on owner-occupied housing services
    - P.314 Other imputed individual consumption expenditure

The codes P.311, P.312, P.313 and P.314 do not exist in the *SNA 1993* but are introduced for convenience here. These four sub-categories of household consumption expenditures are separately identified in Tables 14.4 and 14.5. As already noted, D.63 is usually excluded from the expenditure coverage of CPIs.

14.43 It is worth noting the special treatment of financial services in the *SNA 1993*. FISIM comprises expenditures on those market services provided by financial institutions that are not separately distinguished from interest charges. Expenditures on financial services on which there is an explicit charge are already covered in P.311. Although FISIM P.312 requires an implicit measurement as the difference between a market interest rate and a reference rate, it is part of an observed interest payment and thus is not considered an imputed expenditure in the same sense as imputed rent P.313 and other imputed expenditure P.314.

14.44 Our item P.314, other imputed individual consumption, includes, besides households' production of goods for their own consumption, expenditures on goods and services that employers make on behalf of their employees as non-cash compensation. The SNA calls this item D.12, employers' social contributions, and considers it in the generation of income account. It is recognized as a component of the labour services price index, but is not customarily included in the CPI despite its dual role as an item of consumption (see paragraph 14.75 below).

14.45 *The expenditure aggregate of the consumer price index and the use of income account.* The detailed use of income accounts for institutional sectors can be assembled into a consolidated framework by choosing columns from Table 14.4 for each sector and displaying them together as in Table 14.5, which gives an economy-wide presentation of final consumption and saving. Table 14.5, for the total economy, shows individual consumption as comprising the individual consumption entries P.31 of the use of income accounts for households, NPISHs and the general government sector. It also aggregates the disposable income B.6 of all three. It shows separately the final collective consumption of government P.32. The account in Table 14.5 has been arranged specifically to show the *consumption* coverage

Table 14.4 Use of income account with product detail for institutional units and sectors

Left columns (Uses) show detail of far right column (Resources); SNA 1993 items in bold refer to flows in goods and services, sector titles in italics indicate whether the column appears in the use of income account for that sector

Institutional unit ID: uuuuuuu *Institutional sector code:* S.nnnnn

Uses					Resources
P.31 Individual consumption expenditure			**P.32 Collective consumption expenditure**	**P.3 Final consumption expenditure (total, purchasers' prices)**	B.6 *Disposable income*
P.311 Monetary consumption expenditure *P.313 Financial intermediation services implicitly measured (FISIM)*	*P.312 Imputed expenditure on owner-occupied housing services*	*P.314 Other individual consumption expenditure[1] of households*	*P.32 Collective consumption expenditure: general government S.13 only*		
CPC 0 Agriculture, forestry and fishery products		CPC 0 Agriculture, forestry and fishery products	CPC 0 Agriculture, forestry and fishery products	CPC 0 Agriculture, forestry and fishery products	
CPC 1 Ores and mineral; electricity, gas, and water		CPC 1 Ores and mineral; electricity, gas, and water	CPC 1 Ores and mineral; electricity, gas, and water	CPC 1 Ores and mineral; electricity, gas, and water	
CPC 2 Food products, beverages and tobacco; textiles, apparel and leather products		CPC 2 Food products, beverages and tobacco; textiles, apparel and leather products	CPC 2 Food products, beverages and tobacco; textiles, apparel and leather products	CPC 2 Food products, beverages and tobacco; textiles, apparel and leather products	
CPC 3 Other transportable goods, except metal products, machinery and equipment		CPC 3 Other transportable goods, except metal products, machinery and equipment	CPC 3 Other transportable goods, except metal products machinery and equipment	CPC 3 Other transportable goods, except metal products, machinery and equipment	
CPC 4 Metal products, machinery and equipment		CPC 4 Metal products, machinery and equipment	CPC 4 Metal products, machinery and equipment	CPC 4 Metal products, machinery and equipment	
CPC 6 Distributive trade services; lodging; food and beverage serving services; transport services; and utilities distribution services		CPC 6 Distributive trade services; lodging; food and beverage serving services; transport services; and utilities distribution services	CPC 6 Distributive trade services; lodging; food and beverage serving services; transport services; and utilities distribution services	CPC 6 Distributive trade services; lodging; food and beverage serving services; transport services; and utilities distribution services	
CPC 7 Financial and related services; real estate services; and rental and leasing services	CPC 7 Financial and related services; real estate services; and rental and leasing services	CPC 7 Financial and related services; real estate services; and rental and leasing services[2]	CPC 7 Financial and related services; real estate services; and rental and leasing services	CPC 7 Financial and related services; real estate services; and rental and leasing services	
CPC 8 Business and production services		CPC 8 Business and production services	CPC 8 Business and production services	CPC 8 Business and production services	
CPC 9 Community, social and personal services		CPC 9 Community, social and personal services	CPC 9 Community, social and personal services	CPC 9 Community, social and personal services	
				D.8 Adjustment for the change in the net equity of households in pension funds	
				B.8 *Saving*	

[1]The "Other individual consumption of households" comprises D.12 "Employers' social contributions, consumption in-kind of goods and services supplied to households by their employers in lieu of cash wages, and consumption from the households' own production of goods". D.12 appears in the Generation of Income Account and is a factor in the discussion of the price index of labour services to employers. Among "Employers' social contributions" are provision of housing, transport, child care, medical insurance and services, and life insurance services. "Employers' social contributions" also include contributions to pension plans, which are not consumption except for a small part attributable to pension administration services. The residual part of pension contributions is an important component of household saving. [2]In addition to the real estate, rental and leasing services of homeowners, the *SNA 1993* treats financial services consumption expenditure as the sum of measured and imputed components. Measured expenditures comprise explicit service charges levied by financial institutions for deposit, loan, advisory services and the like, while imputed expenditures reflect the income forgone because the household does not lend (keep deposits with a financial institution) or borrow at a reference rate. In principle, these imputed expenditures, as well as those for other imputed consumption, are of the same market-equivalent valued type as for owner-occupied housing services and could be covered in the CPI.

Table 14.5 Use of income account with product detail for the total economy

Institutional unit ID: uuuuuuuu	*Institutional sector code: S.nnnnn*	*Left columns show detail of far right column; SNA 1993 items in bold refer to flows in goods and services*			B.6 *Disposable income*, Total economy S.1, *with uses comprising:*
P.31 Individual consumption expenditure, Total economy S.1 (purchasers' prices), *comprising:*				**P.32 Collective consumption expenditure, Total economy S.1 (purchasers' prices),** ***comprising:***	**P.3 Final consumption expenditure, total economy S.1,** ***of which***
P.31 Individual consumption expenditure, Household sector S.14			**P.31 Individual consumption expenditure, general government S.13 and NPISH[1] S.15 sectors**	**P.32 Collective consumption expenditure, general government sector S.13**	
Consumer Price Index reference aggregate #1[2]					
P.311 Monetary consumption expenditure *P.312 Financial intermediation services implicitly measured (FISIM)*	*P.313 Imputed expenditure on owner-occupied housing services*	*P.314 Other imputed individual consumption expenditure: households S.14*	*D.63 Social transfers in kind*		
CPC 0 Agriculture, forestry and fishery products		CPC 0 Agriculture, forestry and fishery products	CPC 0 Agriculture, forestry and fishery products	CPC 0 Agriculture, forestry and fishery products	CPC 0 Agriculture, forestry and fishery products
CPC 1 Ores and mineral; electricity, gas, and water		CPC 1 Ores and mineral; electricity, gas, and water	CPC 1 Ores and mineral; electricity, gas, and water	CPC 1 Ores and mineral; electricity, gas, and water	CPC 1 Ores and mineral; electricity, gas, and water
CPC 2 Food products, beverages and tobacco; textiles, apparel and leather products		CPC 2 Food products, beverages and tobacco; textiles, apparel and leather products	CPC 2 Food products, beverages and tobacco; textiles, apparel and leather products	CPC 2 Food products, beverages, tobacco; textiles, apparel, leather products	CPC 2 Food products, beverages, tobacco; textiles, apparel, leather products
CPC 3 Other transportable goods, except metal products, machinery and equipment		CPC 3 Other transportable goods, except metal products, machinery and equipment	CPC 3 Other transportable goods, except metal products, machinery and equipment	CPC 3 Other transportable goods, except metal products, machinery and equipment	CPC 3 Other transportable goods, except metal products, machinery and equipment
CPC 4 Metal products, machinery and equipment		CPC 4 Metal products, machinery and equipment	CPC 4 Metal products, machinery and equipment	CPC 4 Metal products, machinery and equipment	CPC 4 Metal products, machinery and equipment
CPC 6 Distributive trade services; lodging; food and beverage serving services; transport services; and utilities distribution services		CPC 6 Distributive trade services; lodging; food and beverage serving services; transport services; and utilities distribution services	CPC 6 Distributive trade services; lodging; food and beverage serving services; transport services; and utilities distribution services	CPC 6 Distributive trade services; lodging; food and beverage serving services; transport services; and utilities distribution services	CPC 6 Distributive trade services; lodging; food and beverage serving services; transport services; and utilities distribution services
CPC 7 Financial and related services; real estate services; and rental and leasing services	CPC 7 Financial and related services; real estate services; and rental and leasing services	CPC 7 Financial and related services; real estate services; and rental and leasing services	CPC 7 Financial and related services; real estate services; and rental and leasing services	CPC 7 Financial and related services; real estate services; and rental and leasing services	CPC 7 Financial and related services; real estate services; and rental and leasing services
CPC 8 Business and production services		CPC 8 Business and production services	CPC 8 Business and production services	CPC 8 Business and production services	CPC 8 Business and production services
CPC 9 Community, social and personal services		CPC 9 Community, social and personal services	CPC 9 Community, social and personal services	CPC 9 Community, social and personal services	CPC 9 Community, social and personal services
					D.8 Adjustment for the change in the net equity of households *S.14* in pension funds
					B.8 *Saving, Total economy S.1*

[1]Non-profit institutions serving households. [2]P.313 Financial intermediation services implicitly measured (FISIM) are market services supplied to households by financial institutions and thus are included along with the monetary consumption expenditure of households. FISIM are in scope for inflation or transaction CPIs, for example. They are separately distinguished from non-FISIM monetary expenditures here because they require implicit measurement comparing a market interest rate with a reference rate. Other monetary expenditures are measured at least in principle by direct observation.

of the typical CPI, which comprises the first and second columns and is labelled *CPI reference aggregate #1*. This aggregate corresponds with the practice of most, but not all, countries and comprises, as shown in Table 14.5, the monetary (non-imputed) individual consumption expenditure of the household sector (P.311) plus the implicit rent paid by homeowners on their own residences (P.313). Box 14.3 contains further discussion on housing and durables in the CPI consumption expenditure aggregate.

Capital formation

14.46 Capital formation comprises: the accumulation of fixed tangible and intangible assets, such as equipment, structures and software; changes in inventories and work in progress; and acquisitions less disposals of valuables, such as works of art. These items are accounted for in the SNA capital account, which appears, with minor resorting, essentially as in Table 14.6 for each institutional unit. *Net lending (+)/net borrowing (−)* is the balancing item of the capital account, making the uses on the left, comprising net acquisitions of stocks of various tangible and intangible items, add up to the resources on the right, comprising the sources of income financing them. From our earlier discussion on institutional units and establishments, it would be easy to conclude that the smallest economic unit to which the capital account can apply is the institutional unit. It was asserted earlier that only institutional units maintain balance sheets and can monitor the stock variables that are the focus of this account. Nevertheless, the physical capital assets for which changes are tracked in the capital account can and should be compiled, if possible, at the establishment/LKAU. Such data are particularly useful for productivity analysis, even though complete capital accounts cannot be compiled at the establishment level.

14.47 *Product detail in the capital account*. As with the other goods and services-related accounts in the *SNA 1993*, the capital account's goods and services items, designated by the codes P.5 with extensions, can be expanded by product type. The account therefore can be rearranged to show details of goods and services as in Table 14.7, which, as Table 14.6, may pertain to an institutional unit, an institutional sector aggregate, or the total economy. For an institutional unit, Table 14.6 contains the core set of items in the report form of the typical capital formation survey for the national accounts. Our focus is on the CPI here, and thus on the version of the form that typically would be part of the package a respondent would fill out in a household expenditure survey. In addition to the Central Product Classification (CPC), version 1.0 shown here, the *SNA 1993*, Annex V contains a Non-financial assets

Table 14.6 Capital account

Items in bold refer to flows of goods and services

Institutional unit ID: uuuuuuuu — *Institutional sector:* S.*nnnnn*

Uses	Resources
P.5 Gross capital formation, *of which:*	B.10.1 *Changes in net worth due to saving and capital transfers, of which:*
P.51 Gross fixed capital formation	
P.511 Acquisitions less disposals of tangible fixed assets	
P.5111 Acquisitions of new tangible fixed assets	
P.5112 Acquisitions of existing tangible fixed assets	
P.5113 Disposals of existing tangible fixed assets	
P.512 Acquisitions less disposals of intangible fixed assets	
P.5121 Acquisitions of new intangible fixed assets	
P.5122 Acquisitions of existing intangible fixed assets	
P.5123 Disposals of existing intangible fixed assets	
P.513 Additions to the value of non-produced non-financial assets	
P.5131 Major improvements to non-produced non-financial assets	
P.5132 Costs of ownership transfer on non-produced non-financial assets	
P.52 Change in inventories	
P.53 Acquisitions less disposals of valuables	
	B.8n *Saving, net*
	B.8 *Saving (gross, from use of income account)*
K.1 Consumption of fixed capital (−)	K.1 Consumption of fixed capital (−)
K.2 Acquisitions less disposals of non-produced non-financial assets	
K.21 Acquisitions less disposals of land and other tangible non-produced assets	
K.22 Acquisitions less disposals of intangible non-produced assets	
	D.9 Capital transfers receivable (+)
	D.91 Investment grants
	D.92 Other capital transfers receivable
	D.9 Capital transfers payable (−)
	D.91 Capital taxes payable
	D.91 Other capital transfers payable
B.9 *Net lending (+)/net borrowing (−)*	

Table 14.7 Capital account with product detail

Institutional unit ID: uuuuuuuu | *Institutional sector code: S.nnnnn* | *SNA 1993 items in bold refer to flows in goods and services* | B.10.1 *Change in net worth resulting from saving and capital transfers, with uses comprising*

P.51 Gross fixed capital formation			**P.52 Change in inventories**[1]	**P.53 Acquisitions less disposals of valuables**[2]	**P.5 Gross capital formation**
P.511 Acquisitions less disposals of tangible fixed assets, *of which:*[3]	**P.512 Acquisitions less disposals of intangible fixed assets, *of which:***[4]	**P.513 Additions to the value of non-produced non-financial assets, *of which:***[5]			
CPC 0 Agriculture, forestry and fishery products			CPC 0 Agriculture, forestry and fishery products	CPC 0 Agriculture, forestry and fishery products	CPC 0 Agriculture, forestry and fishery products
			CPC 1 Ores and mineral; electricity, gas, and water	CPC 1 Ores and mineral; electricity, gas, and water	CPC 1 Ores and mineral; electricity, gas, and water
			CPC 2 Food products, beverages and tobacco; textiles, apparel and leather products	CPC 2 Food products, beverages and tobacco; textiles, apparel and leather products	CPC 2 Food products, beverages and tobacco; textiles, apparel and leather products
			CPC 3 Other transportable goods, except metal products, machinery and equipment	CPC 3 Other transportable goods, except metal products, machinery and equipment	CPC 3 Other transportable goods, except metal products, machinery and equipment
CPC 4 Metal products, machinery and equipment			CPC 4 Metal products, machinery and equipment	CPC 4 Metal products, machinery and equipment	CPC 4 Metal products, machinery and equipment
CPC 5 Intangible assets; land; constructions; construction services *Of which:*	CPC 5 Intangible assets; land; constructions; construction services	CPC 5 Intangible assets; land; constructions; construction services	CPC 5 Intangible assets; land; constructions; construction services		CPC 5 Intangible assets; land; constructions; construction services
P.511a Residential structures, Household sector S.14					
P.511b Other capital formation in CPC 5					
					K.1 Consumption of fixed capital K.2 Acquisitions less disposals of non-produced non-financial assets
					B.9 *Net borrowing(–)/ net lending(+)*

[1]*SNA 1993* asset code AN.12 Inventories. Excludes intangible assets, land, and constructions. [2]*SNA 1993* asset code AN.13 Valuables. Excludes intangible assets, land, constructions, and construction services. [3]*SNA 1993* asset code AN.111 Tangible fixed assets. Excludes intangible assets, land, and construction services. [4]*SNA 1993* asset code AN.112 Intangible fixed assets. Excludes land, constructions, and construction services. [5]*SNA 1993* asset code AN.2 Non-produced assets. Excludes intangible assets, constructions, and construction services

classification identifying the specific tangible, intangible, produced, and non-produced fixed assets, as well as inventory and valuables items, recognized by the *SNA 1993*.

14.48 *The expenditure aggregate of the CPI and the capital account*. The CPI may be defined to include the household sector's final expenditure not only for consumption but also for capital formation. This brings into the CPI expenditure aggregate the purchase of new residential structures or expenditure on major improvements to existing residential structures. *Consumer price index expenditure aggregate #2* is defined as the monetary individual consumption expenditure of households P.311 in Table 14.5, which excludes all imputed expenditure, plus household expenditure on residential fixed capital formation shown as item *P.511a Residential structures, Household sector S.14* (shown in a box in Table 14.7).

External trade

14.49 The external account of goods and services is shown in Table 14.8. It contains the transactions of the non-resident institutional units sector – S.2 Rest of the world – with the five types of resident units taken together and determines the trade deficit (B.11) as imports (resources to rest of the world S.2) less exports (use or resources by the rest of the world). The external goods and services account generally is taken from the balance of payments, which uses adjusted merchandise trade information from the customs services for goods P.61 and P.71, and assembles services data on P.62 and P.72 from various sources. For further details, see International Monetary Fund: *Balance of payments manual* (fifth edition, 1993). Although the account of external goods and services is shown as an aggregate of the external transactions of all resident institutional units by the *SNA 1993*, it may be possible to disaggregate it to distinguish the external goods and services expenditures of institutional sectors, hence the institutional sector designation *S.1.nnnn* at the top of Table 14.8 to include this possibility. Our principal interest would be in the household sector S.14 and its subsectors S.14*nn*, as these would relate to the CPI.

14.50 *Product detail in the external account of goods and services*. As with the other accounts, the external goods and services account can be expanded to show product detail, as in Table 14.9. Regarding Table 14.9, the *SNA 1993* states (*SNA 1993*, paragraph 15.68) that imported goods should be valued at cost-insurance-freight (cif) at the level of detailed products. On the other hand, the *SNA 1993* requires that, in total, imports of goods be valued free-on-board (fob) at the border of the exporting country, thus excluding insurance and transport in a single adjustment to total imports of goods cif (*SNA 1993* paragraphs 14.36–14.41). That part of freight services on imports provided by non-residents is included in imports of transport services, and that part of insurance services provided on imports by non-residents is added to imports of insurance services. Transport and insurance services provided by residents on imports are included in exports of transport and insurance services. This rather roundabout approach is taken to imports by product because, as a practical matter, it may be difficult to obtain insurance and freight charges on imports from customs administrative data systems at the product level of detail (see *SNA 1993*, paragraphs 14.40–14.41). Recent developments in computerized customs documentation have made the itemization of insurance and freight more straightforward, and the *SNA 1993* does also allow for the possibility of determining imports by product at their fob values, consistent with the aggregate valuation of imports. If trade data are collected by a survey of resident institutional units, the core elements of the report form for such a survey would be as given in Table 14.9.

14.51 *The export and import price indices and the external account of goods and services*. From the point of view of the residents of an economic territory, exports are a supply of goods and services to non-residents. The SNA, however, records exports from the non-resident's point of view, as a non-resident use of goods and services supplied by residents. Accordingly, the relevant valuation principle for exports determining the behaviour of the non-resident user is the purchasers' price. The SNA takes the purchasers' price to the non-resident user to be the fob price at the frontier of the resident supplier's economic territory or country.

14.52 From the resident's point of view, imports are a use of goods and services supplied by non-residents. The SNA, however, records international trade from the non-resident's point of view, as the supply of goods and services to residents by non-residents. Accordingly, the relevant valuation principle for imports determining the behaviour of the non-resident supplier is the basic price. The SNA takes the basic price to the non-resident supplier to be the fob price at the frontier of the non-resident supplier's country in the rest of the world.

The supply and use table

14.53 Arraying elements of resources and uses from the production account, use of income account, capital account, and external accounts of goods and services in a particular configuration, we can derive a format for the production portion of an analytical presentation of the data called a supply and use table (SUT). An SUT is shown in Table 14.10. It arrays various accounts relevant to monitoring developments in production and consumption within a country according to the supply and uses of goods and services.

14.54 In terms of the *SNA 1993* codes, the supply of goods and services comes from:

- resident establishments (arranged in industries) in the form of domestic output (P.1), given by Y in equations (14.1) and (14.2);
- the rest of the world as imports (P.7), given by M in equations (14.1) and (14.2), adjusted for trade and transport margins and taxes less subsidies on products (D.21–D.31), given by T in equations (14.1) and (14.2);

and the uses of goods and services are for:

- current inputs into production by resident producers (arranged in industries) in the form of intermediate consumption (P.2), given by Z in equations (14.1) and (14.2);

Table 14.8 External account of goods and services

Resident institutional units classified into sectors S.1.nnnn with non-resident institutional units S.2; SNA 1993 goods and services items shown in bold

Uses	Resources
P.6 Exports of goods and services **P.61 Exports of goods** **P.62 Exports of services**	**P.7 Imports of goods and services** **P.71 Imports of goods** **P.72 Imports of services**
B.11 *External balance of goods and services*	

Table 14.9 External account of goods and services with product detail

Resident institutional units classified into sectors S.1.nnnn with non-resident institutional units S.2; SNA 1993 goods and services items shown in bold

Uses	Resources
P.6 Exports of goods and services ***Export price index uses aggregate*** **P.61 Exports of goods** *At fob values*	**P.7 Imports of goods and services** ***Import price index supply aggregate*** **P.71 Imports of goods** *At fob values, of which:* *At cif values:*[1]
CPC 0 Agriculture, forestry and fishery products CPC 1 Ores and mineral; electricity, gas, and water CPC 2 Food products, beverages and tobacco; textiles, apparel and leather products CPC 3 Other transportable goods, except metal products, machinery and equipment CPC 4 Metal products, machinery and equipment	CPC 0 Agriculture, forestry and fishery products CPC 1 Ores and mineral; electricity, gas, and water CPC 2 Food products, beverages and tobacco; textiles, apparel and leather products CPC 3 Other transportable goods, except metal products, machinery and equipment CPC 4 Metal products, machinery and equipment
	Less: Adjustment to total imports of goods cif for insurance and freight provided by both residents and non-residents for delivery to the first resident recipient.
P.62 Exports of services CPC 5 Intangible assets; land; constructions; construction services[2] CPC 6 Distributive trade services; lodging; food and beverage serving services; transport services; and utilities distribution services, *of which:* • Distributive trade services; lodging; food and beverage serving services; transport services; and utilities distribution services; *except* transport services on imports and exports rendered by residents • Transport services on imports and exports rendered by residents CPC 7 Financial and related services; real estate services; and rental and leasing services, *of which:* • Financial and related services; real estate services; and rental and leasing services; *except* insurance services on imports rendered by residents • Insurance services on imports rendered by residents CPC 8 Business and production services CPC 9 Community, social and personal services	**P.72 Imports of services** CPC 5 Intangible assets; land; constructions; construction services[2] CPC 6 Distributive trade services; lodging; food and beverage serving services; transport services; and utilities distribution services, *of which:* • Distributive trade services; lodging; food and beverage serving services; transport services; and utilities distribution services; *except* transport services on imports rendered by non-residents • Transport services on imports and exports rendered by non-residents CPC 7 Financial and related services; real estate services; and rental and leasing services, *of which:* • Financial and related services; real estate services; and rental and leasing services; *except* insurance services on imports rendered by non-residents • Insurance services on imports rendered by non-residents CPC 8 Business and production services CPC 9 Community, social and personal services
B.11 *External balance of goods and services*	

[1]The *SNA 1993* values imports fob, but it allows for the fact that while fob valuation by product would be consistent and preferred, compiling such data may be problematic at the product level of detail. Imports of goods cif by product may be all that are available because the insurance and freight data are often not separately compiled by product in customs systems (see *SNA 1993*, paragraph 15.68). Totals for these data may be obtained instead from resident and non-resident shippers in the process of compiling the balance of payments. Insurance and freight services provided by residents on imports are a services export. Regarding goods and services valuations in the import price and volume indices, see *MPI* in Tables 14.12 and 14.15, where it is explained that both fob and purchasers' price valuations are important in constructing the *MPI* as a deflator for imports fob. Imports at purchasers' prices would be imports cif plus import tariffs, as well as domestic insurance and freight for delivery to the first domestic owner. [2]Construction services only.

Table 14.10 The supply and use table (SUT)

Production account: double outlines and no shading; **Use of income account:** single outlines and no shading; **Capital account:** diagonal shading; **External account of goods and services:** vertical shading

Supply							*Use*						
P.1 Output at basic prices *of establishments producing for:*			Transport and distribution margin adjustment[1]	D.21-D.31 Taxes less subsidies products[2]	Imports cif[3]		P.2 Intermediate consumption at purchasers' prices *of establishments producing for:*			P.31 Individual consumption	P.32 Collective consumption	P.5 Gross capital formation	P.6 Exports fob
P.11 Market	P.12 Own use	P.13 Other non-market			P.7 Imports fob	cif/fob adjustment[4]	P.11 Market	P.12 Own use	P.13 Other non-market				
Product × *Industry*	*Product* × *Industry*	*Product* × *Industry*	+ **Goods (+)** / ***Services (–)***	+ ***Product* × 1**	+ **Goods fob** / ***Services***[6]	+ **Goods (+)**[5] / ***Services (–)***	= *Product* × *Industry*	*Product* × *Industry*	*Product* × *Industry*	+ *Product* × 1	*Product* × 1	***Product* × 1**	+ ***Product* × 1**
							+	+	+				
							B.1 Value added 1 × *Industry*	B.1 Value added 1 × *Industry*	B.1 Value added 1 × *Industry*				
=	=	=					=	=	=				
P.11 Output at basic prices 1 × *Industry*	P.12 Output at basic prices 1 × *Industry*	P.13 Output at basic prices 1 × *Industry*				=	P.11 Output at basic prices 1 × *Industry*	P.12 Output at basic prices 1 × *Industry*	P.13 Output at basic prices 1 × *Industry*				

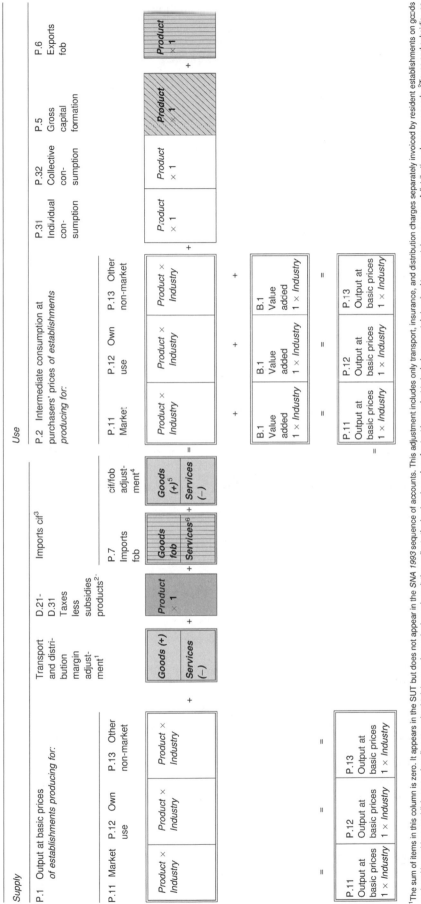

[1]The sum of items in this column is zero. It appears in the SUT but does not appear in the *SNA 1993* sequence of accounts. This adjustment includes only transport, insurance, and distribution charges separately invoiced by resident establishments on goods produced by resident establishments. As a first stage in obtaining purchasers' price values, it thus adjusts the basic price value of output by product to include separately invoiced transport, insurance and distribution charges on goods. [2]Taxes and subsidies on products are shown in the *SNA 1993* allocation of primary income account for the general government institutional sector S.13, which derives the balancing item B.5 *Balance of primary incomes* (*SNA 1993*, Annex V, Table A.V.5). B.5 is B.2 Operating surplus plus D.2 Taxes on production and imports less D.3 Subsidies plus D.4 Property income (net). This account is the source of data for construction of this column in the SUT, when expanded to show product detail for the items D.21 Taxes on products and D.31 Subsidies on products. It includes taxes and subsidies on both domestic output and imports. [3]As noted elsewhere, the *SNA 1993* values goods imports cif at the product level of detail but fob in total. Thus, the *SNA 1993* presentation of goods imports in the supply matrix is the sum of P.7 Imports fob and the cif/fob adjustment on goods imports shown in Table 14.10. To simplify this presentation of the SUT and clarify the nature of the negative adjustment to services, we assume that insurance and freight provided on imports can be compiled by product and thus imports fob can be compiled by product. Insurance and freight provided on imports by residents are already included in the insurance and transport rows of the P.1 matrix. [4]The sum of items in this column is zero. It appears in the SUT but does not appear in any *SNA 1993* account. [5]Insurance and freight on imports of goods by product provided by both residents and non-residents. [6]Including insurance and freight on imports provided by non-residents. Insurance and freight provided on imports by residents are included in the insurance and transport rows of the P.1 matrix.

- final domestic consumption, including individual consumption by resident households, resident non-profit institutions serving households (NPISHs), and the government (P.31), and collective consumption by the government (P.32), given by, respectively, *C* and *G* in equations (14.1) and (14.2);
- capital formation by resident enterprises (P.5) (comprising fixed capital formation (P.51), inventory change (P.52), and acquisitions less disposals of valuables (P.53)), given by *I* in equations (14.1) and (14.2);
- export (P.6) and use by the rest of the world, given by *X* in equations (14.1) and (14.2).

14.55 Trade and transport margins do not appear in the standard sequence of accounts in the *SNA 1993* because these accounts are not shown with product detail. Although these margins are non-zero for individual products, they add up to zero in total because the amount added to the domestic supply of *goods* comes from the domestic supply of distribution, insurance and transport *services*. Margins are thus shown in Table 14.10 separately for margins on domestic production and imports (cif/fob adjustment), because the SUT displays product detail down the columns. In the aggregate, of course, these adjustments for trade and transport margins on domestic production and the cif/fob adjustment for imports cancel each other out.

14.56 The SUT is primarily a matrix of flows of goods and services designed to highlight the relationship between production and consumption, not between institutional units per se. For example, households may undertake production in unincorporated enterprises for which activity appears in the production for own final use part of the SUT, but also consume goods and services, as represented in individual consumption. The current production transactions of the establishments of all institutional units are grouped together and summarized in one part of the SUT, and the remaining transactions are summarized and organized in another part. Each institutional sector, including households (S.14), has its own SUT in principle. The SUT for the total economy (S.1) is the cell-by-cell sum of the institutional sector SUTs.

The consumer price index among major price indices

14.57 It is instructive at this point to associate the SUT with the component aggregates and matrices of the four major, headline price indices that are compiled by most countries. In so doing, we form a more precise impression of the central purpose of the major price indices in the overall economic statistical system represented by the *SNA 1993*. The four main price indices and their associated national accounts aggregates and matrices in the SUT are:

- producer price index (PPI): output of resident producers (P.1);
- consumer price index (CPI): final consumption of households (P.31) for CPI reference aggregate #1, *plus* gross fixed capital formation of households (P.51) for CPI reference aggregate #2;
- export price index (XPI): exports (P.6);
- import price index (MPI): imports (P.7).

14.58 The location and coverage of these major price indicators as they directly apply to goods and services value aggregates in the national accounts are shown diagrammatically in Table 14.11. Chapter 15 characterizes a price index as a function of price relatives and weights, noting that, other than the formula for the index itself, the requisite features of the relatives and weights would be determined by the value aggregate. These factors are:

- what items to include in the index;
- how to determine the item prices;
- what transactions that involve these items to include in the index;
- from what source to draw the weights used in the selected index formula.

Based on our survey of the goods and services accounts of the *SNA 1993* culminating in the SUT, these particulars for each of the four major indices can summarized as in Table 14.12.

Scope of the expenditure aggregates of the consumer price index

14.59 As noted in paragraphs 14.6 and 14.7, there are two principal expenditure sub-aggregates of the total final expenditure of the households (S.14) institutional sector employed in most national CPIs that we can now see are transparently linked to the SNA:

- *CPI reference aggregate #1*, comprising the *consumption* items:

  P.311 Monetary consumption expenditure (Table 14.5)

  P.313 Financial intermediation services implicitly measured (FISIM) (Table 14.5)

  P.312 Imputed expenditure on owner-occupied housing services (Table 14.5)
- *CPI reference aggregate #2*, comprising the *consumption* and *capital formation* items:

  P.311 Monetary consumption expenditure (Table 14.5)

  P.313 Financial intermediation services implicitly measured (FISIM) (Table 14.5)

  P.511a Gross fixed capital formation in residential structures (Table 14.9)

14.60 Proponents of CPI reference aggregate #1 generally take a consumption or cost of living view of the CPI, seeing household welfare as determined by the flow of goods and services, including the services of residential structures that are owned wholly or in part by the occupants, that households consume. On this view, households' fixed capital formation, which is effectively limited to the purchase of residences for own use, is a business-related activity of unincorporated enterprises that households own and thus not in the scope of the CPI. The customary version of aggregate #1 excludes non-housing consumption from own production P.314. Although compensation in kind in the form of benefits

Table 14.11 Location and coverage of major price indices: Columns in the supply and use table

The effective coverage of the major indices is shown by shaded areas

Total supply

SNA 1993 transaction	P.1 Output, *of which, establishments producing principally*			Transport and distribution margin adjustment	Taxes *less* subsidies on domestic products	P.7 Imports, fob	Cif/fob adjustment	Taxes *less* subsidies on imports
	P.11 Market output	P.12 Output for own final use	P.13 Other non-market output			Imports at purchasers' prices		
PPI reference aggregate								
MPI reference aggregate								
Resources by product: Goods	*Product × Industry*	*Product × Industry*	*Product × Industry*	*Product × 1* +	*Product × 1*	*Product × 1*	*Product × 1*	*Product × 1*
Resources by product: Services				–				
Total resources				0				

Final uses

SNA 1993 transaction	P.31 Individual consumption				P.32 Collective consumption	P.5 Gross capital formation				P.6 Exports, fob	
SNA 1993 institutional sector	Households S.14			Government S.13 NPISHs[1] S.15	Government S.13	Households S.14			All institutional sectors, except households	All institutional sectors	
Detailed expenditure categories	P.311 Monetary consumption P.313 FISIM[2]	P.312 Imputed rent of owner-occupants	P.314 Other imputed individual consumption expenditure	D.36 Social transfers in kind		P.51 Gross fixed capital formation		P.52 Inventories P.53 valuables		Output (at basic prices) sold to non-residents	Taxes less subsidies on export products, transport to international shipment point
						P.511a Residential structures for own use	Other fixed capital formation				
CPI reference aggregate #1											
CPI reference aggregate #2											
XPI reference aggregate											
Expenditures by product: Goods	*Product × 1*	*Product × 1*	*Product × 1*	*Product × 1*	*Product × 1*	*Product × 1*	*Product × 1*	*Product × 1*	*Product × 1*	*Product × 1*	*Product × 1*
Expenditures by product: Services											
Total expenditure											

[1]Non-profit institutions serving households. [2]Financial intermediation services implicitly measured.

Table 14.12 Definition of scope, price relatives, coverage and weights for major price indices

Index	Items to include	Price determination	Transactions coverage	Sources of weights
PPI	All types of domestically produced or processed goods and services that are valued at market prices	Basic prices, determined for goods as the date when available for sale (available for change of ownership) or service price when service rendered	Output of resident enterprises, comprising sales plus change in finished goods inventories for goods, and sales for services	The product by industry matrices of Market output P.11 and Output for own final use P.12 in the expanded Industry production account and the supply and use table (SUT)
CPI	*Reference expenditure aggregate #1:* All types of goods and services purchased explicitly or implicitly by households for individual consumption	Purchasers' prices, determined for goods on the change of ownership date and for services when used, including taxes on products, excluding subsidies on products, and including transport and distribution margins	*Reference expenditure aggregate #1:* Consumption expenditures of the Households sector S.13 of institutional units, excluding consumption from own production except for imputed expenditures for rental of owner-occupied dwellings	*Reference expenditure aggregate #1:* The product column of the CPI consumption sub-aggregate of Individual consumption P.31 of the Household sector S.13 in the expanded Use of Income account and in the SUT
	Reference expenditure aggregate #2: All types of goods and services purchased explicitly by households for individual consumption, plus all types of goods and services purchased explicitly by households for residential capital formation		*Reference expenditure aggregate #2*: Reference expenditure aggregate #1, less imputed expenditures for rental of owner-occupied dwellings, plus net acquisition of or major improvements in residential housing	*Reference expenditure aggregate #2*: The product column of the monetary consumption sub-aggregate of individual consumption P.31 of the Household sector S.13 in the expanded Use of income account plus the product column of acquisitions less disposals of fixed assets P.511 for residential housing
XPI	All types of transportable goods and services purchased by non-residents from residents. Goods exported without change of ownership for significant processing by non-residents and subsequent re-import are included	Purchasers' prices at the national frontier of the exporting country (fob), including export taxes and excluding export subsidies, and including transport and distribution margins from the production location to the national frontier	All transportable goods and services produced or processed by residents and purchased by non-residents except goods in transit or goods exported and minimally processed by non-residents for re-import	The product column of Exports P.6 in the expanded External account of goods and services and the SUT
MPI	All types of transportable goods and services purchased by residents from non-residents. Goods imported without change of ownership for significant processing by residents and subsequent re-export are included	Basic prices at the national frontier of the exporting country (fob), excluding import taxes and including import subsidies, and excluding transport and distribution margins from the production location to the national frontier[1]	All transportable goods and services produced or processed by non-residents and purchased by residents except goods in transit or goods imported and minimally processed by residents for re-export	The product column of Imports P.7 in the expanded External account of goods and services and the SUT

PPI = producer price index; CPI = consumer price index; XPI = export price index; MPI = import price index.

[1]In defining the import price index, however, the price index maker would, in fact, first consider an economic input price index valuing imported goods and services at the purchasers' price payable by their first resident owner. The import price index would be obtained by adjusting (multiplying) the import purchasers' price index by a "markdown" index tracking the movement in the ratio of imports fob to imports at purchasers' prices. This is required for it to be properly matched in valuation with imports fob and yield the conceptually correct import volume index when used as an imports fob deflator.

provided by the employer is an important part of this item, households often are only vaguely aware of its value, since the employer actually makes the payments to the providers of the benefits. An argument nevertheless could be made for including this item, as households sometimes are able to exercise control over how this part of their compensation income is spent.

14.61 Proponents of CPI reference aggregate #2 generally take a transactions or inflation view of the CPI, tailoring the index to measuring the rate of change in the prices of an expenditure aggregate broadly covering the monetary final expenditures that households make on goods and services, including their capital formation in residential structures via purchase of their own dwellings and the major improvements they make to them.

14.62 Both CPI concepts are useful. The cost of living view provides a price index whose dual is the volume of household consumption. The inflation view provides a price index whose dual is the volume of households' final monetary purchases, which represent the demand pressure they put on the markets in which they participate. Table 14.11 illustrates the coverage of both indices.

The consumer price index as a measure of inflation in market transactions

14.63 Central banks take an interest in the major price indices, particularly if they are implementing a monetary policy that targets inflation. Indeed, reference aggregate #2 has been seen as a better measure of change in the prices of actual transactions in goods and services than CPIs based on reference aggregate #1, which gives substantial weight to the imputed rent of owner-occupied housing.

14.64 Both reference aggregates for the CPI are an important component of total final expenditure and GDP in virtually all countries, but the total value of transactions in goods and services also includes intermediate consumption, so as an inflation index for total goods and services transactions, the CPI's coverage is rather limited under either definition #1 or #2 compared with, for example, the PPI, which covers, in principle, total output. Progress in extending the industry coverage of the PPI to cover all output-producing activities, services in particular, has, however, proceeded slowly owing to the technical difficulty of specifying service products and measuring the associated prices. The combination of the PPI, covering output, and the import price index provides a price index for total market supply, and is seen by at least one monetary authority as a useful inflation measure. Another central bank targets the total domestic supply price index, which is based on total supply less exports (that is, covering the aggregate comprising output plus imports minus exports).

14.65 The CPI's purchasers' price valuation principle also includes taxes less subsidies on products, which may not be desired in an inflation indicator for underlying price change. Nevertheless, the CPI is the most widely available macroeconomic price statistic, and may in many countries be the only available option for inflation measurement. Monetary authorities also may find the CPI the most socially acceptable inflation target precisely because of its focus on households.

Treatment of cross-border shopping in the consumer price index

14.66 Exports P.6 are not an expenditure of any resident institutional unit and thus would not be the focus of a price index covering its expenditure. By implication, they would not appear in any CPI expenditure aggregate. Imports are, however, an expenditure of resident units and it is often relevant to consider the importance of imports in the expenditure aggregates of such units. In many countries, imports acquired by households directly through cross-border shopping are a significant fraction of household consumption expenditure.

14.67 Of particular note here is that imported goods P.71 and services P.72 in Table 14.8 for the household sector would contain only the direct expenditures of households on goods and services secured from non-residents, that is, in cross-border shopping. This should include purchases of transportable goods and services by households from non-resident suppliers through all means, including in person, by mail order and through the Internet. These expenditures in transactions with non-residents are already covered in households' individual consumption P.31 and capital formation P.5, so the purpose of identifying imports P.7 in the context of the CPI is to identify the importance of transactions with non-residents in the final expenditure aggregates of households and that part of those aggregates covered by the CPI expenditure aggregate.

14.68 Note that under both CPI reference aggregates #1 and #2 we would include expenditures on consumption goods and services provided by non-residents to resident households as the imported component of Individual consumption P.31. To assess the importance of imports when considering CPI reference expenditure aggregate #2, we also would include households' Fixed capital formation P.51 expenditures on imported transportable goods such as building materials for residences, as well as residential construction services provided by non-residents.

Other price indicators in the national accounts

Price indices for total supply

14.69 Consistent with our earlier discussion of the coverage of the PPI, we define total market-valued output as the sum of market output P.11 and output for own final use P.12. Total output P.1 is the sum of market-valued output and other non-market output P.13. Total supply at basic prices is the sum of output and imports P.7. Mark-up adjustments at the product level for trade and transport margins on domestic production, insurance and freight on imports, and taxes D.21 less subsidies D.31 on products would be added to total supply at basic prices to produce total supply at purchasers' prices.

14.70 In decomposing total supply into price and volume components, the total supply price index (SPI) at basic prices can be seen to be a weighted mean of the total output price index YPI and the import price index MPI. The YPI comprises in turn the PPI and an implicit deflator index (IDI) for other non-market output. To obtain the price index for total supply at purchasers' prices, the SPI would be multiplied by an index of the total mark-up for trade, insurance, and transport margins, and taxes net of subsidies on products. The margins only matter when developing supply price indices at purchasers' prices for individual products and product sub-aggregates. For all products, they cancel out, leaving only taxes less subsides on products contributing to the total mark-up on total supply at basic prices. Total supply price indices at product levels of detail are useful in compiling and reconciling discrepancies in supply and use tables expressed in volume terms. In addition, they are employed in producing industry price indices for intermediate consumption P.2, which are useful for compiling gross domestic product (GDP) volume measures from the production approach. Although principally used as a compilation aid and in deflation of value added at basic prices via the double deflation approach (see paragraphs 14.71 and 14.73), supply price indices could also serve as analytical indicators in their own right because of their coverage of all goods and services transactions in the economy relating to production and external trade. As such, they may be useful as indicators for the analysis and evaluation of economic policy, where broad coverage of transactions is required, for example in formulating monetary policy.

Price indices for intermediate consumption

14.71 In considering intermediate consumption price indices (IPIs) for the total economy and for industry, the weights correspond to a column-wise reading of the intermediate consumption part of the SUT's use matrix, which is derived from Table 14.2 and shown in Table 14.10 as the region labelled P.2. Because the various margins on basic prices inherent in prevailing purchasers' prices may vary from user industry to user industry, the ideal sources for purchasers' prices for intermediate consumption price indices would be enterprise surveys. Unfortunately, such surveys are generally burdensome and expensive. Instead, as noted in the discussion above on price indices for total supply, the price index of intermediate consumption by industry can be derived from detailed product components of the SPI, which will result in indices of acceptable accuracy if the variation in the total tax, subsidy, transport and distribution margin is not too great from industry to industry within product class. For the total economy, the price index of intermediate consumption is obtained as a weighted average of industries' intermediate input price indices, where the weights are the share of each industry's intermediate consumption in the total intermediate consumption in the economy.

Price indices for final uses

14.72 The price indices for final use comprise deflators for individual consumption P.31, collective consumption P.32, gross fixed capital formation P.51, change in inventories P.52, acquisitions less disposals of valuables P.53 and exports P.6. Of the major price indices discussed above, the CPI is the principal source of detailed (product level) information for P.31, while the PPI is a significant source of detailed information for P.51 and the principal source for the finished goods component of P.52. When the CPI is defined on the basis of CPI reference expenditure aggregate #2, the CPI could also be the source of data on capital formation in residential structures. The SPI may be the principal source for the input inventories component of P.52 in the absence of a detailed survey of the purchase price of intermediate inputs, and the XPI is the deflator for P.6. The SPI can serve, as well, as a source of detailed product information for P.32, P.51 and P.53. We will designate the deflator for total final uses as the final uses price index (FPI), which would be computed as a weighted mean (formula to be determined) of the component indices just discussed.

Price indices for gross domestic product

14.73 As noted above in the discussion of the SPI and the intermediate consumption price index, the

Table 14.13 Generation of income account for establishment, institutional unit or institutional sector

SNA 1993 goods and services items shown in bold

Uses	Resources
D.1 Compensation of employees	B.1 *Value added*[1]
D.11 Wages and salaries	
D.12 Employers' social contributions	
D.121 Employers' actual social contributions	
D.122 Employers' imputed social contributions	
D.2 Taxes on production and imports	
D.29 Other taxes on production[2]	
D.3 Subsidies	
D.39 Other subsidies on production (−)[3]	
B.2 *Operating surplus*[4]	

[1]From the production account. [2]Taxes on production unrelated to products. [3]Subsidies on production unrelated to products. [4]Balancing item of the generation of income account.

GDP price index can be compiled in two ways, corresponding to the two goods and services methods of compiling GDP: the production approach and the expenditure approach. Recall that the production approach derives from the definition of value added implicit in equation (14.2), as the difference between output P.1 (at basic prices) and intermediate consumption P.2 (at purchasers' prices). The *SNA 1993* recommends the use of double deflation for value added, by which output at basic prices Y is deflated by all the items YPI to obtain output volume, and intermediate purchases are deflated by an intermediate purchases price index to obtain intermediate input volume. Real value added is then computed as the difference between output volume and intermediate input volume (see *SNA 1993*, Chapter XVI). This operation is equivalent to deflating value added in current prices with a double deflation-type price index having a positive weight on the YPI and a negative weight on the IPI. In the usual case just described, we have the value added deflator as a Paasche index of the output price index $YPI^{s,t}$ and the intermediate input price index $IPI^{s,t}$, where the weight on the $IPI^{s,t}$ is

$$w_I^t = \frac{-\text{P.}2^t}{\text{P.}1^t - \text{P.}2^t}$$

and the weight on the $YPI^{s,t}$ is $1 - w_I^t$. The corresponding volume index has the Laspeyres or "constant price" form, which is equivalent to the double deflation measure of the volume of real value added divided by current price value added in period s. The total value added at current basic prices divided by real value added, obtained via double deflation, yields the implicit deflator for value added at basic prices. Finally, the GDP deflator at purchasers' prices is the value added price index (at basic prices for output and purchasers' prices for intermediate input) multiplied by the index of the mark-up on value added of output taxes less output subsidies on products.

14.74 Alternatively, the final expenditure deflator FPI may be combined with the MPI using a double deflation-type approach. GDP volume is calculated from expenditure data by deflating imports P.7 by the MPI, and subtracting the result from the volume of final uses, calculated by deflating final uses by the FPI. The implicit GDP deflator would be the ratio of GDP at current prices to GDP volume so calculated. The aggregate index of GDP volume and the aggregate index of real value added should agree with one another, as should, by implication, the implicit GDP deflator calculated from the two approaches.

Price indices for labour services

14.75 Value added appears first in the production account, calculated as the balancing item between output and intermediate consumption. This margin is used to pay for, among other things, labour services. The *SNA 1993* provides for the income components comprising value added in the generation of income account, shown in Table 14.13. The largest of the income components itemized in this account is compensation of employees D.1, comprising wages and salaries D.11 and employers' social contributions D.12. D.1 represents a value aggregate for a flow of labour services and is thus susceptible to decomposition into price and volume components. Table 14.14 shows the same account expanded by type of labour service (occupation) for an establishment or industry. The price index for labour services (LPI) measures developments in total compensation, by occupation, within industry. The price of labour services in total compensation terms is of particular interest when compared with the GDP deflator, which indicates the relative purchasing power of labour compensation in terms of production for final consumption. This comparison is useful in assessing cost-push pressures on output prices and as an input into compiling measures of the productivity of labour. A second useful comparison is between the wages and salaries sub-index of the LPI and the CPI. The ratio of the LPI to the CPI indicates the purchasing power of wages in terms of consumption goods and services, and tracks the material welfare, particularly of the employees subsector S.143 of the household institutional sector S.14 (see Box 14.1 on page 238). In the LPI, the price of labour services comprises all the components of compensation of employees, including employers' social contributions (benefits), as well as wages and salaries. The wages and salaries sub-index of the LPI would be another example of a price index adjusted by a mark-up index. Analogously with the price index for total supply at purchasers' prices or for GDP by production in Table 14.10, the LPI would be adjusted in this case by a "markdown index", deducting employers' social contributions.

Framework for a system of price statistics for goods and services

14.76 To summarize this overview of the main price indicators and the national accounts, Table 14.15 shows in tabular form the price indices needed for the value aggregates in the national accounts and their relation to the four main price indicators. Indices that are functions of two other indices are shown with the notation

$$f(I_1, I_2; w)$$

where f is an index formula, I_1 and I_2 are price indices, w is the weight of the second index, with the weight of the first index understood to be $1-w$. For example, if f is the Laspeyres formula, then the output price index (YPI) would be calculated by making the following substitutions: $P_L^{s,t} = YPI^{s,t}$ $r_1^{s,t} = PPI^{s,t}$, $w_1^s = 1 - w_D^s$, $r_2^{s,t} = IDI^{s,t}$, $w_2^s = w_D^s$. f could also be chosen as a Paasche formula (with the same substitutions except for change in the time superscript on the weights $w_1^t = 1 - w_D^t$ and $w_2^t = w_D^t$), Fisher ideal formula, or other index formula.

Table 14.14 Generation of income account for establishment and industry with labour services (occupational[1]) detail

SNA 1993 goods and services items shown in bold

Establishment ID: eeeeeeee	*Activity/Industry code (ISIC): aaaa* *Market status:* P.1*n*	*Institutional unit ID: uuuuuuuu* *Institutional sector code:* S.*nnnnn*	
Uses			Resources
D.11 Wages and salaries	**D.12 Employers' social contributions**	**D.1 Compensation of employees**	B.1 *Value added*[2]
1: Legislators, senior officials and managers	1: Legislators, senior officials and managers	1: Legislators, senior officials and managers	
2: Professionals	2: Professionals	2: Professionals	
3: Technicians and associate professionals	3: Technicians and associate professionals	3: Technicians and associate professionals	
4: Clerks	4: Clerks	4: Clerks	
5: Service workers and shop and market sales workers	5: Service workers and shop and market sales workers	5: Service workers and shop and market sales workers	
6: Skilled agricultural and fishery workers	6: Skilled agricultural and fishery workers	6: Skilled agricultural and fishery workers	
7: Craft and related trades workers	7: Craft and related trades workers	7: Craft and related trades workers	
8: Plant and machine operators and assemblers	8: Plant and machine operators and assemblers	8: Plant and machine operators and assemblers	
9: Elementary occupations	9: Elementary occupations	9: Elementary occupations	
0: Armed forces	0: Armed forces	0: Armed forces	
		D.2 Taxes on production and imports	
		D.29 Other taxes on production	
		D.3 Subsidies (–)	
		D.39 Other subsidies on production	
		B.2 *Operating surplus*[3]	

[1]Showing major groups of ILO: *International Standard Classification of Occupations 1988* (ISCO-88) (Geneva, 1990). [2]From the production account. [3]Balancing item of the generation of income account.

International comparisons of expenditure on goods and services

14.77 The main price statistics discussed thus far trace price developments of goods and services through time. Purchasing power parities (PPPs) compare price levels between different countries or geographical areas for a given accounting period and are generally used to eliminate the effect of prices in different currency units when comparing the levels of GDP between two countries or areas. The price relatives in bilateral PPPs comprise the ratios of the local currency prices of identical goods and services between the two countries or areas. The weights are proportional to the shares of these items in expenditure on GDP within the two countries or areas. The sources of price relatives are the same as those for the final uses GDP deflator, and the weights are simply the total final uses, net of imports fob, by product. In order to ensure that the PPP between area A and area B is the reciprocal of the PPP between B and A, bilateral PPPs need to be computed using symmetric index numbers such as the Fisher.

14.78 A matrix of bilateral PPPs provides a means of making not only direct bilateral comparisons, but also bilateral comparisons between any two areas as the product of a sequence of bilateral PPPs through any set of intervening areas, beginning with the first area and ending with the second. In order to ensure the consistency of such multilateral comparisons – for example, that a chain beginning with a given area and ending with the same area produces a PPP of unity – bilateral PPPs are adjusted to produce a transitive set of comparisons.

14.79 The four main index series dealt with in this chapter are related to PPPs because the prices collected for the CPI, PPI, XPI and MPI, in addition to their use in these temporal indices and in the temporal GDP price index, can also be used in international comparisons of expenditures on consumption, capital formation and trade. See Annex 4 on the International Comparison Program for further details on PPPs.

Table 14.15 A framework for price statistics

SNA 1993 aggregate	*SNA 1993* transaction codes[1]	Valuation and needed detail	*SNA 1993* source account	Price index[2]	Derivation from other price indices
			Supply		
Market-valued output	**P.11 + P.12**	**Basic prices, product by industry**	**Production account with industry and product detail, total economy S.1**	***Producer price index (PPI)***	
Other non-market output[3]	P.13	Basic prices (cost of production), product by industry	Production account with industry and product detail, total economy S.1	*Implicit deflator for other non-market output (IDI)*	Derived from volume indicator
Total output	P.1 = P.11 + P.12 + P.13	Basic prices, by product	Production account with industry and product detail, total economy S.1	*Output price index (YPI)*	$YPI = f(PPI, IDI; w_m),\ w_m = \frac{P.13}{P.1}$
Imports	**P.7**	**Basic prices (goods fob frontier of exporting country, including the freight and insurance on imports provided by non-residents), by product**	**External transactions in goods and services account with product detail, total economy S.1**	***Import price index (MPI), comprising an import purchasers' price index multiplied by an fob/purchasers' price markdown index***	
Total supply, basic prices	P.1 + P.7	Basic prices, by product	Supply and use table, total economy S.1	*Supply price index (SPI)*	$SPI = f(MPI, YPI; w_y),\ w_y = \frac{P.1}{P.1+P.7}$
Total domestic supply	P.1 + P.7 – P.6	Basic prices, by product (P.1 and P.7); purchasers' prices (P.6 exports fob, see "Uses" entry below)	Supply and use table, total economy S.1	*Domestic supply price index (DSPI)*	$SPI = f(MPI, YPI, XPI; w_y, -w_x)$, $w_y = \frac{P.1}{P.1+P.7-P.6},\ w_x = \frac{P.6}{P.1+P.7-P.6}$
Domestic trade, insurance, and transport margin adjustment		Basic prices, for services provided for transport and distribution within national frontiers, by product	Supply and use table, total economy S.1	*Supply mark-up index (SMI)*	$SMI = \frac{\frac{P.1^t+P.7^t+D.21^t-D.31^t}{P.1^t+P.7^t}}{\frac{P.1^s+P.7^s+D.21^s-D.31^s}{P.1^s+P.7^s}}$ *(in the aggregate)*. Product-level total output mark-up indices would also include trade and transport margins in the numerator of the above expression
Freight and insurance on imports adjustment		Basic prices (for services provided from exporter frontier to domestic frontier, regardless of residency of provider), by product	Supply and use table, total economy S.1		
Taxes less subsidies on products	D.21 – D.31	Payable, by product	Allocation of primary income account, general government sector S.13		
Total supply, purchasers' prices	P.11 + P.12 + P.7 + D.21 – D.31	Purchasers' prices			$SPI \times SMI$

			Uses		
Intermediate consumption	P.2	Purchasers' prices, products by industries	Production account with product and industry detail, total economy S.1	*Intermediate consumption price index (IPI)*	Usually incorporates product-level information from the total supply price index at purchasers' prices
Individual consumption	P.31	Purchasers' prices, by product	Use of income account with product detail, total economy S.1	*Household consumption price index (HPI)*	Incorporates the CPI, and may incorporate product-level information from the CPI and PPI regarding goods and services produced from own consumption and provided to individuals by NPISHs and general government
Household sector S.14	**P.31, except imputed consumption and consumption from production for own final use, but including imputed rent of home-owners**	**Purchasers' prices, by product**	**Use of income account with product detail, household sector S.14, with special sub-classification of P.31**	***Consumer price index (CPI) and other sub-indices as needed***	
Collective consumption	P.32	Purchasers' prices, by product	Use of income account with product detail, general government sector S.13	*Government price index (GPI)*	*May incorporate product indices from the **CPI** and **PPI***
Gross fixed capital formation	P.51	Purchasers' prices, by product	Capital account with product detail, total economy S.1	*Fixed capital formation price index (KPI)*	*May incorporate product indices from the **PPI***
Change in inventories	P.52	Purchasers' prices, by product	Capital account with product detail, total economy S.1	*Inventory price index (NPI)*	*Price index of inventory stocks*
Acquisitions less disposals of valuables	P.53	Purchasers' prices, by product	Capital account with product detail, total economy S.1	*Valuables price index (VPI)*	*Price index of valuables stocks*
Exports	**P.6**	**Purchasers' prices (fob domestic frontier), by product**	**External transactions in goods and services account with product detail, total economy S.1**	***Export price index (XPI)***	
Total final uses	P.3 + P.5 + P.6	Purchasers' prices, by product	Supply and use table, total economy S.1	*Total uses price index (FPI)*	$FPI = f(HPI, GPI, KPI, NPI, VPI, XPI, \vec{w})$ *where*[4] $\vec{w} = [w_G, w_K, w_N, w_V, w_X]^3$ *and* $w_G = \frac{P.32}{P.3+P.4+P.5+P.6}$, $w_K = \frac{P.51}{P.3+P.4+P.5+P.6}$, $w_N = \frac{P.52}{P.3+P.4+P.5+P.6}$, $w_V = \frac{P.53}{P.3+P.4+P.5+P.6}$, $w_X = \frac{P.6}{P.3+P.4+P.5+P.6}$

Table 14.15 A framework for price statistics (*contd.*)

SNA 1993 aggregate	*SNA 1993* transaction codes[1]	Valuation and needed detail	*SNA 1993* source account	Price index[2]	Derivation from other price indices
			Gross domestic product		
Gross domestic product	GDP = P.3 + P.5 + P.6 – P.7, or GDP = P.1 – P.2 + D.21 – D.31	By product when assembled from final consumption net of imports By industry when assembled from value added at basic prices, with industry and total value added price indices adjusted by a mark-up factor for taxes net of subsidies on products	Supply and use table, total economy S.1	*GDP deflator*	$GDP\ deflator = f(FPI, MPI; w_M), = SMI^* \times f(SPI, IPI; w_I)$ *where*[5] $w_M = \frac{-P.7}{GDP}$ $w_I = \frac{-P.2^4}{GDP}$ $SMI^* = \frac{\frac{P.1^t - P.2^t + D.21^t - D.31^t}{P.1^t - P.2^t}}{\frac{P.1^s - P.2^s + D.21^s - D.31^s}{P.1^s - P.2^s}}$ *(in the aggregate)* Industry-level value added mark-up indices *SMI** would include the total trade and transport margins on output in the numerator
Compensation of employees	D.1	By industry and occupation	Generation of income account, total economy S.1	*Employment cost index*	

[1]P.11 = market output, P.12 = output for own final use, D.21 = taxes on products, and D.31 = subsidies on products. [2]The four major price indices are shown in bold. [3]This category comprises public services output provided free of charge or at economically insignificant prices by general government and non-profit institutions serving households (NPISHs). This output is valued at cost because it has no market comparator. A price index cannot be directly constructed for this aggregate because there are no economically significant prices for other non-market output. The implicit deflator for other non-market output P.13 is derived by dividing a directly compiled volume indicator into the value of other non-market output. [4]Unlike our other aggregations of indices that involve the combination of two component indices, we show the FPI as a simultaneous aggregation of six price indices for the components of final uses. Again, *f* can be any of the indices introduced in Chapters 1 and 15, with the weight of the first item, here of individual consumption P.31, determined as one minus the rest of the weights, and the price relatives given by the list of index arguments. [5]The negative weight of the second index argument of both of these formulae for GDP is an indication that they represent a "double deflation-type" price index (see *SNA 1993*, Chapter XVI, Section E).

15

BASIC INDEX NUMBER THEORY

Introduction

The answer to the question what is the Mean of a given set of magnitudes cannot in general be found, unless there is given also the object for the sake of which a mean value is required. There are as many kinds of average as there are purposes; and we may almost say in the matter of prices as many purposes as writers. Hence much vain controversy between persons who are literally at cross purposes. (Edgeworth (1888, p. 347)).

15.1 The number of physically distinct goods and unique types of services that consumers can purchase is in the millions. On the business or production side of the economy, there are even more commodities that are actively traded. This is because firms not only produce commodities for final consumption, but they also produce exports and intermediate commodities that are demanded by other producers. Firms collectively also use millions of imported goods and services, thousands of different types of labour services and hundreds of thousands of specific types of capital. If we further distinguish physical commodities by their geographical location or by the season or time of day that they are produced or consumed, then there are billions of commodities that are traded within each year in any advanced economy. For many purposes, it is necessary to summarize this vast amount of price and quantity information into a much smaller set of numbers. The question that this chapter addresses is: how exactly should the microeconomic information involving possibly millions of prices and quantities be aggregated into a smaller number of price and quantity variables? This is the basic problem of index numbers.

15.2 It is possible to pose the index number problem in the context of microeconomic theory; i.e., given that we wish to implement some economic model based on producer or consumer theory, what is the "best" method for constructing a set of aggregates for the model? When constructing aggregate prices or quantities, however, other points of view (that do not rely on economics) are possible. Some of these alternative points of view are considered in this chapter and the next. Economic approaches are pursued in Chapters 17 and 18.

15.3 The index number problem can be framed as the problem of decomposing the value of a well-defined set of transactions in a period of time into an aggregate price term times an aggregate quantity term. It turns out that this approach to the index number problem does not lead to any useful solutions. So, in paragraphs 15.7 to 15.17, the problem of decomposing a value ratio pertaining to two periods of time into a component that measures the overall change in prices between the two periods (this is the price index) times a term that measures the overall change in quantities between the two periods (this is the quantity index) is considered. The simplest price index is a fixed basket type index; i.e., fixed amounts of the n quantities in the value aggregate are chosen and then the values of this fixed basket of quantities at the prices of period 0 and at the prices of period 1 are calculated. The fixed basket price index is simply the ratio of these two values where the prices vary but the quantities are held fixed. Two natural choices for the fixed basket are the quantities transacted in the base period, period 0, or the quantities transacted in the current period, period 1. These two choices lead to the Laspeyres (1871) and Paasche (1874) price indices, respectively.

15.4 Unfortunately, the Paasche and Laspeyres measures of aggregate price change can differ, sometimes substantially. Thus in paragraphs 15.18 to 15.32, taking an average of these two indices to come up with a single measure of price change is considered. In paragraphs 15.18 to 15.23, it is argued that the "best" average to take is the geometric mean, which is Irving Fisher's (1922) ideal price index. In paragraphs 15.24 to 15.32, instead of averaging the Paasche and Laspeyres measures of price change, taking an average of the two baskets is considered. This fixed basket approach to index number theory leads to a price index advocated by Correa Moylan Walsh (1901; 1921a). Other fixed basket approaches are, however, also possible. Instead of choosing the basket of period 0 or 1 (or an average of these two baskets), it is possible to choose a basket that pertains to an entirely different period, say period b. In fact, it is typical statistical agency practice to pick a basket that pertains to an entire year (or even two years) of transactions in a year prior to period 0, which is usually a month. Indices of this type, where the weight reference period differs from the price reference period, were originally proposed by Joseph Lowe (1823), and indices of this type are studied in paragraphs 15.64 to 15.84. Such indices are also evaluated from the axiomatic perspective in Chapter 16 and from the economic perspective in Chapter 17.[1]

15.5 In paragraphs 15.65 to 15.75, another approach to the determination of the *functional form* or the *formula* for the price index is considered. This approach is attributable to the French economist Divisia (1926) and is based on the assumption that price and quantity data are available as continuous functions of time. The theory of differentiation is used in order to decompose the rate of change of a continuous time value aggregate into two

[1] Although indices of this type do not appear in Chapter 19, where most of the index number formulae exhibited in Chapters 15–18 are illustrated using an artificial data set, indices where the weight reference period differs from the price reference period are illustrated numerically in Chapter 22, in which the problem of seasonal commodities is discussed.

components that reflect aggregate price and quantity change. Although the approach of Divisia offers some insights,[2] it does not offer much guidance to statistical agencies in terms of leading to a definite choice of index number formula.

15.6 In paragraphs 15.76 to 15.97, the advantages and disadvantages of using a *fixed base* period in the bilateral index number comparison are considered versus always comparing the current period with the previous period, which is called the *chain system*. In the chain system, a *link* is an index number comparison of one period with the previous period. These links are multiplied together in order to make comparisons over many periods.

The decomposition of value aggregates into price and quantity components

The decomposition of value aggregates and the product test

15.7 A *price index* is a measure or function which summarizes the *change* in the prices of many commodities from one situation 0 (a time period or place) to another situation 1. More specifically, for most practical purposes, a price index can be regarded as a weighted mean of the change in the relative prices of the commodities under consideration in the two situations. To determine a price index, it is necessary to know:

- which commodities or items to include in the index;
- how to determine the item prices;
- which transactions that involve these items to include in the index;
- how to determine the weights and from which sources these weights should be drawn;
- what formula or type of mean should be used to average the selected item relative prices.

All the above questions regarding the definition of a price index, except the last, can be answered by appealing to the definition of the *value aggregate* to which the price index refers. A value aggregate V for a given collection of items and transactions is computed as:

$$V = \sum_{i=1}^{n} p_i q_i \qquad (15.1)$$

where p_i represents the price of the ith item in national currency units, q_i represents the corresponding quantity transacted in the time period under consideration and the subscript i identifies the ith elementary item in the group of n items that make up the chosen value aggregate V. Included in this definition of a value aggregate is the specification of the group of included commodities (which items to include) and of the economic agents engaging in transactions involving those commodities (which transactions to include), as well as principles of the valuation and time of recording that motivate the behaviour of the economic agents undertaking the transactions (determination of prices). The included elementary items, their valuation (the p_i), the eligibility of the transactions and the item weights (the q_i) are all within the domain of definition of the value aggregate. The precise determination of the p_i and q_i is discussed in more detail elsewhere in this manual, in particular in Chapter 5.[3]

15.8 The value aggregate V defined by equation (15.1) refers to a certain set of transactions pertaining to a single (unspecified) time period. Now the same value aggregate for two places or time periods, periods 0 and 1, is considered. For the sake of convenience, period 0 is called the *base period* and period 1 is called the *current period* and it is assumed that observations on the base period price and quantity vectors, $p^0 \equiv [p_1^0, \ldots, p_n^0]$ and $q^0 \equiv [q_1^0, \ldots, q_n^0]$ respectively, have been collected.[4] The value aggregates in the base and current periods are defined in the obvious way as:

$$V^0 \equiv \sum_{i=1}^{n} p_i^0 q_i^0; \; V^1 \equiv \sum_{i=1}^{n} p_i^1 q_i^1 \qquad (15.2)$$

In the previous paragraph, a price index was defined as a function or measure which summarizes the change in the prices of the n commodities in the value aggregate from situation 0 to situation 1. In this paragraph, a *price index* $P(p^0, p^1, q^0, q^1)$ along with the corresponding *quantity index* (or *volume index*) $Q(p^0, p^1, q^0, q^1)$ is defined to be two functions of the $4n$ variables p^0, p^1, q^0, q^1 (these variables describe the prices and quantities pertaining to the value aggregate for periods 0 and 1) where these two functions satisfy the following equation:[5]

$$V^1/V^0 = P(p^0, p^1, q^0, q^1)\, Q(p^0, p^1, q^0, q^1) \qquad (15.3)$$

If there is only one item in the value aggregate, then the price index P should collapse down to the single price ratio, p_1^1/p_1^0, and the quantity index Q should collapse down to the single quantity ratio, q_1^1/q_1^0. In the case of many items, the price index P is to be interpreted as some sort of weighted average of the individual price ratios, $p_1^1/p_1^0, \ldots, p_n^1/p_n^0$.

15.9 Thus the first approach to index number theory can be regarded as the problem of decomposing the change in a value aggregate, V^1/V^0, into the product of a part that is attributable to *price change*, $P(p^0, p^1, q^0, q^1)$, and a part that is attributable to *quantity change*, $Q(p^0, p^1, q^0, q^1)$. This approach to the determination of the price index is the approach that is taken in the national accounts, where a price index is used to deflate a value ratio in order to obtain an estimate of quantity change. Thus, in this approach to index number theory, the primary use for the price index is as a *deflator*. Note that once the functional form for the price index $P(p^0, p^1, q^0, q^1)$ is known, then the corresponding

[2] In particular, it can be used to justify the chain system of index numbers (discussed in paragraphs 15.86 to 15.97).

[3] Ralph Turvey has noted that some values may be difficult to decompose into unambiguous price and quantity components. Examples of difficult-to-decompose values are bank charges, gambling expenditures and life insurance payments.

[4] Note that it is assumed that there are no new or disappearing commodities in the value aggregates. Approaches to the "new goods problem" and the problem of accounting for quality change are discussed in Chapters 7, 8 and 21.

[5] The first person to suggest that the price and quantity indices should be jointly determined in order to satisfy equation (15.3) was Fisher (1911, p. 418). Frisch (1930, p. 399) called equation (15.3) the *product test*.

quantity or volume index $Q(p^0, p^1, q^0, q^1)$ is completely determined by P; i.e., rearranging equation (15.3):

$$Q(p^0, p^1, q^0, q^1) = (V^1/V^0)/P(p^0, p^1, q^0, q^1) \quad (15.4)$$

Conversely, if the functional form for the quantity index $Q(p^0, p^1, q^0, q^1)$ is known, then the corresponding price index $P(p^0, p^1, q^0, q^1)$ is completely determined by Q. Thus using this deflation approach to index number theory, separate theories for the determination of the price and quantity indices are not required: if either P or Q is determined, then the other function is implicitly determined by the product test equation (15.4).

15.10 In the next section, two concrete choices for the price index $P(p^0, p^1, q^0, q^1)$ are considered and the corresponding quantity indices $Q(p^0, p^1, q^0, q^1)$ that result from using equation (15.4) are also calculated. These are the two choices used most frequently by national income accountants.

The Laspeyres and Paasche indices

15.11 One of the simplest approaches to the determination of the price index formula was described in great detail by Lowe (1823). His approach to measuring the price change between periods 0 and 1 was to specify an approximate *representative commodity basket*,[6] which is a quantity vector $q \equiv [q_1, \ldots, q_n]$ that is representative of purchases made during the two periods under consideration, and then calculate the level of prices in period 1 relative to period 0 as the ratio of the period 1 cost of the basket, $\sum_{i=1}^{n} p_i^1 q_i$, to the period 0 cost of the basket, $\sum_{i=1}^{n} p_i^0 q_i$. This *fixed basket approach* to the determination of the price index leaves open the question as to how exactly is the fixed basket vector q to be chosen.

15.12 As time passed, economists and price statisticians demanded a little more precision with respect to the specification of the basket vector q. There are two natural choices for the reference basket: the base period commodity vector q^0 or the current period commodity vector q^1. These two choices lead to the Laspeyres (1871) price index[7] P_L defined by equation (15.5) and the Paasche (1874) price index[8] P_P defined by equation (15.6):[9]

$$P_L(p^0, p^1, q^0, q^1) \equiv \frac{\sum_{i=1}^{n} p_i^1 q_i^0}{\sum_{i=1}^{n} p_i^0 q_i^0} \quad (15.5)$$

$$P_P(p^0, p^1, q^0, q^1) \equiv \frac{\sum_{i=1}^{n} p_i^1 q_i^1}{\sum_{i=1}^{n} p_i^0 q_i^1} \quad (15.6)$$

15.13 The formulae (15.5) and (15.6) can be rewritten in an alternative manner that is more useful for statistical agencies. Define the period t expenditure share on commodity i as follows:

$$s_i^t \equiv p_i^t q_i^t \Big/ \sum_{j=1}^{n} p_j^t q_j^t \quad \text{for } i = 1, \ldots, n \text{ and } t = 0, 1 \quad (15.7)$$

Then the Laspeyres index (15.5) can be rewritten as follows:[10]

$$\begin{aligned} P_L(p^0, p^1, q^0, q^1) &= \sum_{i=1}^{n} p_i^1 q_i^0 \Big/ \sum_{j=1}^{n} p_j^0 q_j^0 \\ &= \sum_{i=1}^{n} (p_i^1/p_i^0) p_i^0 q_i^0 \Big/ \sum_{j=1}^{n} p_j^0 q_j^0 \\ &= \sum_{i=1}^{n} (p_i^1/p_i^0) s_i^0 \end{aligned} \quad (15.8)$$

using definitions (15.7). The Laspeyres price index P_L can thus be written as an arithmetic average of the n price ratios, p_i^1/p_i^0, weighted by base period expenditure shares. The Laspeyres formula (until very recently) has been widely used as the intellectual base for consumer price indices (CPIs) around the world. To implement it, a statistical agency needs only to collect information on expenditure shares s_n^0 for the index domain of definition for the base period 0, and then collect information on item *prices* alone on an ongoing basis. *Thus the Laspeyres CPI can be produced on a timely basis without having quantity information for the current period.*

15.14 The Paasche index can also be written in expenditure share and price ratio form as follows:[11]

$$\begin{aligned} P_P(p^0, p^1, q^0, q^1) &= \frac{1}{\left\{ \sum_{i=1}^{n} p_i^0 q_i^1 \Big/ \sum_{j=1}^{n} p_j^1 q_j^1 \right\}} \\ &= \frac{1}{\left\{ \sum_{i=1}^{n} (p_i^0/p_i^1) p_i^1 q_i^1 \Big/ \sum_{j=1}^{n} p_j^1 q_j^1 \right\}} \end{aligned}$$

[6] Lowe (1823, Appendix, p. 95) suggested that the commodity basket vector q should be updated every five years. Lowe indices are studied in more detail in paragraphs 15.45 to 15.85.

[7] This index was actually introduced and justified by Drobisch (1871a, p. 147) slightly earlier than Laspeyres. Laspeyres (1871, p. 305) in fact explicitly acknowledged that Drobisch showed him the way forward. However, the contributions of Drobisch have been forgotten for the most part by later writers because Drobisch aggressively pushed for the ratio of two unit values as being the "best" index number formula. While this formula has some excellent properties where all the n commodities being compared have the same unit of measurement, it is useless when, say, both goods and services are in the index basket.

[8] Drobisch (1871b, p. 424) also appears to have been the first to define explicitly and justify the Paasche price index formula, but he rejected this formula in favour of his preferred formula, the ratio of unit values, and so again he did not gain any credit for his early suggestion of the Paasche formula.

[9] Note that $P_L(p^0, p^1, q^0, q^1)$ does not actually depend on q^1 and $P_P(p^0, p^1, q^0, q^1)$ does not actually depend on q^0. It does no harm to include these vectors, however, and the notation indicates that the reader is in the realm of bilateral index number theory; i.e., the prices and quantities for a value aggregate pertaining to two periods are being compared.

[10] This method of rewriting the Laspeyres index (or any fixed basket index) as a share weighted arithmetic average of price ratios is attributable to Fisher (1897, p. 517) (1911, p. 397) (1922, p. 51) and Walsh (1901, p. 506; 1921a, p. 92).

[11] This method of rewriting the Paasche index (or any fixed basket index) as a share weighted harmonic average of the price ratios is attributable to Walsh (1901, p. 511; 1921a, p. 93) and Fisher (1911, p. 397–398).

$$= \frac{1}{\left\{\sum_{i=1}^{n} (p_i^1/p_i^0)^{-1} s_i^1\right\}}$$

$$= \left\{\sum_{i=1}^{n} (p_i^1/p_i^0)^{-1} s_i^1\right\}^{-1} \quad (15.9)$$

using definitions (15.7). The Paasche price index P_P can thus be written as a *harmonic* average of the n item price ratios, p_i^1/p_i^0, weighted by period 1 (current period) expenditure shares.[12] The lack of information on current period quantities prevents statistical agencies from producing Paasche indices on a timely basis.

15.15 The quantity index that corresponds to the Laspeyres price index using the product test in equation (15.3) is the Paasche quantity index; i.e., if P in equation (15.4) is replaced by P_L defined by equation (15.5), then the following quantity index is obtained:

$$Q_P(p^0, p^1, q^0, q^1) \equiv \frac{\sum_{i=1}^{n} p_i^1 q_i^1}{\sum_{i=1}^{n} p_i^1 q_i^0} \quad (15.10)$$

Note that Q_P is the value of the period 1 quantity vector valued at the period 1 prices, $\sum_{i=1}^{n} p_i^1 q_i^1$, divided by the (hypothetical) value of the period 0 quantity vector valued at the period 1 prices, $\sum_{i=1}^{n} p_i^1 q_i^0$. Thus the period 0 and 1 quantity vectors are valued at the same set of prices, the current period prices, p^1.

15.16 The quantity index that corresponds to the Paasche price index using the product test (15.3) is the Laspeyres quantity index; i.e., if P in equation (15.4) is replaced by P_P defined by equation (15.6), then the following quantity index is obtained:

$$Q_L(p^0, p^1, q^0, q^1) \equiv \frac{\sum_{i=1}^{n} p_i^0 q_i^1}{\sum_{i=1}^{n} p_i^0 q_i^0} \quad (15.11)$$

Note that Q_L is the (hypothetical) value of the period 1 quantity vector valued at the period 0 prices, $\sum_{i=1}^{n} p_i^0 q_i^1$, divided by the value of the period 0 quantity vector valued at the period 0 prices, $\sum_{i=1}^{n} p_i^0 q_i^0$. Thus the period 0 and 1 quantity vectors are valued at the same set of prices, the base period prices, p^0.

15.17 The problem with the Laspeyres and Paasche index number formulae is that, although they are equally plausible, in general they will give different answers. For most purposes, it is not satisfactory for the statistical agency to provide two answers to the question:[13] What is the "best" overall summary measure of price change for the value aggregate over the two periods in question? In the following section, we consider how "best" averages of these two estimates of price change can be constructed. Before doing so, we ask: What is the "normal" relationship between the Paasche and Laspeyres indices? Under "normal" economic conditions when the price ratios pertaining to the two situations under consideration are negatively correlated with the corresponding quantity ratios, it can be shown that the Laspeyres price index will be larger than the corresponding Paasche index.[14] A precise statement of this result is presented in Appendix 15.1.[15] The divergence between P_L and P_P suggests that if a *single estimate* for the price change between the two periods is required, then some sort of evenly weighted average of the Laspeyres and Paasche indices should be taken as the final estimate of price change between periods 0 and 1. As mentioned above, this strategy will be pursued in the following section. It should, however, be kept in mind that statistical agencies will not usually have information on current expenditure weights, hence averages of Paasche and Laspeyres indices can be produced only on a delayed basis (perhaps using national accounts information) or not at all.

Symmetric averages of fixed basket price indices

The Fisher index as an average of the Paasche and Laspeyres indices

15.18 As mentioned above, since the Paasche and Laspeyres price indices are equally plausible but often give different estimates of the amount of aggregate price change between periods 0 and 1, it is useful to consider taking an evenly weighted average of these fixed basket price indices as a single estimator of price change between the two periods. Examples of such *symmetric averages*[16] are the arithmetic mean, which leads to the

[12] Note that the derivation in the formula (15.9) shows how harmonic averages arise in index number theory in a very natural way.

[13] In principle, instead of averaging the Paasche and Laspeyres indices, the statistical agency could think of providing both (the Paasche index on a delayed basis). This suggestion would lead to a matrix of price comparisons between every pair of periods instead of a time series of comparisons. Walsh (1901, p. 425) noted this possibility: "In fact, if we use such direct comparisons at all, we ought to use all possible ones."

[14] Peter Hill (1993, p. 383) summarized this inequality as follows:

> It can be shown that relationship (13) [i.e., that P_L is greater than P_P] holds whenever the price and quantity relatives (weighted by values) are negatively correlated. Such negative correlation is to be expected for price takers who react to changes in relative prices by substituting goods and services that have become relatively less expensive for those that have become relatively more expensive. In the vast majority of situations covered by index numbers, the price and quantity relatives turn out to be negatively correlated so that Laspeyres indices tend systematically to record greater increases than Paasche with the gap between them tending to widen with time.

[15] There is another way to see why P_P will often be less than P_L. If the period 0 expenditure shares s_i^0 are exactly equal to the corresponding period 1 expenditure shares s_i^1, then by Schlömilch's (1858) inequality (see Hardy, Littlewood and Polyá (1934, p. 26)), it can be shown that a weighted harmonic mean of n numbers is equal to or less than the corresponding arithmetic mean of the n numbers and the inequality is strict if the n numbers are not all equal. If expenditure shares are approximately constant across periods, then it follows that P_P will usually be less than P_L under these conditions (see paragraphs 15.70 to 15.84).

[16] For a discussion of the properties of symmetric averages, see Diewert (1993c). Formally, an average $m(a, b)$ of two numbers a and b is symmetric if $m(a, b) = m(b, a)$. In other words, the numbers a and b are treated in the same manner in the average. An example of a nonsymmetric average of a and b is $(1/4)a + (3/4)b$. In general, Walsh (1901, p. 105) argued for a symmetric treatment if the two periods (or countries) under consideration were to be given equal importance.

Drobisch (1871b, p. 425), Sidgwick (1883, p. 68) and Bowley (1901, p. 227)[17] index, $P_D \equiv (1/2)P_L + (1/2)P_P$, and the geometric mean, which leads to the Fisher (1922)[18] ideal index, P_F, defined as

$$P_F(p^0, p^1, q^0, q^1) \equiv \{P_L(p^0, p^1, q^0, q^1) P_P(p^0, p^1, q^0, q^1)\}^{1/2} \tag{15.12}$$

At this point, the fixed basket approach to index number theory is transformed into the *test approach* to index number theory; i.e., in order to determine which of these fixed basket indices or which averages of them might be "best", desirable *criteria* or *tests* or *properties* are needed for the price index. This topic will be pursued in more detail in the next chapter, but an introduction to the test approach is provided in the present section because a test is used to determine which average of the Paasche and Laspeyres indices might be "best".

15.19 What is the "best" symmetric average of P_L and P_P to use as a point estimate for the theoretical cost of living index? It is very desirable for a price index formula that depends on the price and quantity vectors pertaining to the two periods under consideration to satisfy the *time reversal test*.[19] An index number formula $P(p^0, p^1, q^0, q^1)$ satisfies this test if

$$P(p^1, p^0, q^1, q^0) = 1/P(p^0, p^1, q^0, q^1) \tag{15.13}$$

i.e., if the period 0 and period 1 price and quantity data are interchanged, and then the index number formula is evaluated, then this new index $P(p^1, p^0, q^1, q^0)$ is equal to the reciprocal of the original index $P(p^0, p^1, q^0, q^1)$. This is a property that is satisfied by a single price ratio, and it seems desirable that the measure of aggregate price change should also satisfy this property so that it does not matter which period is chosen as the base period. Put another way, the index number comparison between any two points of time should not depend on the choice of which period we regard as the base period: if the other period is chosen as the base period, then the new index number should simply equal the reciprocal of the original index. It should be noted that the Laspeyres and Paasche price indices do not satisfy this time reversal property.

15.20 Having defined what it means for a price index P to satisfy the time reversal test, then it is possible to establish the following result.[20] The Fisher ideal price index defined by equation (15.12) is the *only* index that is a homogeneous[21] symmetric average of the Laspeyres and Paasche price indices, P_L and P_P, and satisfies the time reversal test (15.13). The Fisher ideal price index thus emerges as perhaps the "best" evenly weighted average of the Paasche and Laspeyres price indices.

15.21 It is interesting to note that this *symmetric basket approach* to index number theory dates back to one of the early pioneers of index number theory, Arthur L. Bowley, as the following quotations indicate:

> If [the Paasche index] and [the Laspeyres index] lie close together there is no further difficulty; if they differ by much they may be regarded as inferior and superior limits of the index number, which may be estimated as their arithmetic mean ... as a first approximation (Bowley (1901, p. 227)).
>
> When estimating the factor necessary for the correction of a change found in money wages to obtain the change in real wages, statisticians have not been content to follow Method II only [to calculate a Laspeyres price index], but have worked the problem backwards [to calculate a Paasche price index] as well as forwards. ... They have then taken the arithmetic, geometric or harmonic mean of the two numbers so found (Bowley (1919, p. 348)).[22]

15.22 The quantity index that corresponds to the Fisher price index using the product test (15.3) is the Fisher quantity index; i.e., if P in equation (15.4) is replaced by P_F defined by equation (15.12), the following quantity index is obtained:

$$Q_F(p^0, p^1, q^0, q^1) \equiv \{Q_L(p^0, p^1, q^0, q^1) Q_P(p^0, p^1, q^0, q^1)\}^{1/2} \tag{15.14}$$

Thus the Fisher quantity index is equal to the square root of the product of the Laspeyres and Paasche quantity indices. It should also be noted that $Q_F(p^0, p^1, q^0, q^1) = P_F(q^0, q^1, p^0, p^1)$; i.e., if the role of prices and quantities is interchanged in the Fisher price index formula, then the Fisher quantity index is obtained.[23]

15.23 Rather than take a symmetric average of the two basic fixed basket price indices pertaining to two situations, P_L and P_P, it is also possible to return to Lowe's basic formulation and choose the basket vector q to be a symmetric average of the base and current period basket vectors, q^0 and q^1. This approach

[17] Walsh (1901, p. 99) also suggested the arithmetic mean index P_D (see Diewert (1993a, p. 36) for additional references to the early history of index number theory).

[18] Bowley (1899, p. 641) appears to have been the first to suggest the use of the geometric mean index P_F. Walsh (1901, pp. 428–429) also suggested this index while commenting on the big differences between the Laspeyres and Paasche indices in one of his numerical examples: "The figures in columns (2) [Laspeyres] and (3) [Paasche] are, singly, extravagant and absurd. But there is order in their extravagance; for the nearness of their means to the more truthful results shows that they straddle the true course, the one varying on the one side about as the other does on the other."

[19] See Diewert (1992a, p. 218) for early references to this test. If we want the price index to have the same property as a single price ratio, then it is important to satisfy the time reversal test. However, other points of view are possible. For example, we may want to use our price index for compensation purposes, in which case satisfaction of the time reversal test may not be so important.

[20] See Diewert (1997, p. 138).

[21] An average or mean of two numbers a and b, $m(a, b)$, is *homogeneous* if when both numbers a and b are multiplied by a positive number λ, then the mean is also multiplied by λ; i.e., m satisfies the following property: $m(\lambda a, \lambda b) = \lambda m(a, b)$.

[22] Fisher (1911, pp. 417–418; 1922) also considered the arithmetic, geometric and harmonic averages of the Paasche and Laspeyres indices.

[23] Fisher (1922, p. 72) said that P and Q satisfied the *factor reversal test* if $Q(p^0, p^1, q^0, q^1) = P(q^0, q^1, p^0, p^1)$ and P and Q satisfied the product test (15.3) as well.

to index number theory is pursued in the following section.

The Walsh index and the theory of the "pure" price index

15.24 Price statisticians tend to be very comfortable with a concept of the price index that is based on pricing out a constant "representative" basket of commodities, $q \equiv (q_1, q_2, \ldots, q_n)$, at the prices of periods 0 and 1, $p^0 \equiv (p_1^0, p_2^0, \ldots, p_n^0)$ and $p^1 \equiv (p_1^1, p_2^1, \ldots, p_n^1)$ respectively. Price statisticians refer to this type of index as a *fixed basket index* or a *pure price index*[24] and it corresponds to Sir George H. Knibbs's (1924, p. 43) *unequivocal price index*.[25] Since Lowe (1823) was the first person to describe systematically this type of index, it is referred to as a Lowe index. Thus the general functional form for the *Lowe price index* is

$$P_{Lo}(p^0, p^1, q) \equiv \sum_{i=1}^{n} p_i^1 q_i \Big/ \sum_{i=1}^{n} p_i^0 q_i = \sum_{i=1}^{n} s_i (p_i^1 / p_i^0) \quad (15.15)$$

where the (hypothetical) *hybrid expenditure shares* s_i[26] corresponding to the quantity weights vector q are defined by:

$$s_i \equiv p_i^0 q_i \Big/ \sum_{j=1}^{n} p_j^0 q_j \quad \text{for } i = 1, 2, \ldots, n \quad (15.16)$$

15.25 The main reason why price statisticians might prefer a member of the family of Lowe or fixed basket price indices defined by equation (15.15) is that the fixed basket concept is easy to explain to the public. Note that the Laspeyres and Paasche indices are special cases of the pure price concept if we choose $q = q^0$ (which leads to the Laspeyres index) or if we choose $q = q^1$ (which leads to the Paasche index).[27] The practical problem of picking q remains to be resolved, and that is the problem that will be addressed in this section.

15.26 It should be noted that Walsh (1901, p. 105; 1921a) also saw the price index number problem in the above framework:

> Commodities are to be weighted according to their importance, or their full values. But the problem of axiometry always involves at least two periods. There is a first period, and there is a second period which is compared with it. Price variations have taken place between the two, and these are to be averaged to get the amount of their variation as a whole. But the weights of the commodities at the second period are apt to be different from their weights at the first period. Which weights, then, are the right ones – those of the first period? Or those of the second? Or should there be a combination of the two sets? There is no reason for preferring either the first or the second. Then the combination of both would seem to be the proper answer. And this combination itself involves an averaging of the weights of the two periods (Walsh (1921a, p. 90)).

Walsh's suggestion will be followed and thus the ith quantity weight, q_i, is restricted to be an average or *mean* of the base period quantity q_i^0 and the current period quantity for commodity iq_i^1, say $m(q_i^0, q_i^1)$, for $i = 1, 2, \ldots, n$.[28] Under this assumption, the Lowe price index (15.15) becomes:

$$P_{Lo}(p^0, p^1, q^0, q^1) \equiv \frac{\sum_{i=1}^{n} p_i^1 m(q_i^0, q_i^1)}{\sum_{j=1}^{n} p_j^0 m(q_j^0, q_j^1)} \quad (15.17)$$

15.27 In order to determine the functional form for the mean function m, it is necessary to impose some *tests* or *axioms* on the pure price index defined by equation (15.17). As above, we ask that P_{Lo} satisfy the *time reversal test* (15.13). Under this hypothesis, it is immediately obvious that the mean function m must be a *symmetric mean*;[29] i.e., m must satisfy the following property: $m(a,b) = m(b,a)$ for all $a > 0$ and $b > 0$. This assumption still does not pin down the functional form for the pure price index defined by equation (15.17). For example, the function $m(a,b)$ could be the *arithmetic mean*, $(1/2)a + (1/2)b$, in which case equation (15.17) reduces to the *Marshall* (1887) and *Edgeworth* (1925) *price index* P_{ME}, which was the pure price index preferred by Knibbs (1924, p. 56):

$$P_{ME}(p^0, p^1, q^0, q^1) \equiv \frac{\sum_{i=1}^{n} p_i^1 \{(q_i^0 + q_i^1)/2\}}{\sum_{j=1}^{n} p_j^0 \{(q_j^0 + q_j^1)/2\}} \quad (15.18)$$

15.28 On the other hand, the function $m(a,b)$ could be the *geometric mean*, $(ab)^{1/2}$, in which case equation

[24] See section 7 in Diewert (2001).

[25] Suppose however that, for each commodity, Q′ = Q, then the fraction, ∑(P′Q)/∑(PQ), viz., the ratio of aggregate value for the second unit-period to the aggregate value for the first unit-period is no longer merely a ratio of totals, it also shows unequivocally the effect of the change in price. Thus it is an unequivocal price index for the quantitatively unchanged complex of commodities, A, B, C, etc.

It is obvious that if the quantities were different on the two occasions, and if at the same time the prices had been unchanged, the preceding formula would become ∑(PQ′)/∑(PQ). It would still be the ratio of the aggregate value for the second unit-period to the aggregate value for the first unit period. But it would be also more than this. It would show in a generalized way the ratio of the quantities on the two occasions. Thus it is an unequivocal quantity index for the complex of commodities, unchanged as to price and differing only as to quantity.

Let it be noted that the mere algebraic form of these expressions shows at once the logic of the problem of finding these two indices is identical (Knibbs (1924, pp. 43–44)).

[26] Note that Fisher (1922, p. 53) used the terminology "weighted by a hybrid value", while Walsh (1932, p. 657) used the term "hybrid weights".

[27] Note that the ith share defined by equation (15.16) in this case is the hybrid share $s_i \equiv p_i^0 q_i^1 / \sum_{i=1}^{n} p_i^0 q_i^1$, which uses the prices of period 0 and the quantities of period 1.

[28] Note that we have chosen the mean function $m(q_i^0, q_i^1)$ to be the same for each item i. We assume that $m(a,b)$ has the following two properties: $m(a,b)$ is a positive and continuous function, defined for all positive numbers a and b and $m(a,a) = a$ for all $a > 0$.

[29] For more on symmetric means, see Diewert (1993c, p. 361).

(15.17) reduces to the *Walsh* (1901, p. 398; 1921a, p. 97) *price index*, P_W:[30]

$$P_W(p^0,p^1,q^0,q^1) \equiv \frac{\sum_{i=1}^{n} p_i^1 \sqrt{q_i^0 q_i^1}}{\sum_{j=1}^{n} p_j^0 \sqrt{q_j^0 q_j^1}} \tag{15.19}$$

15.29 There are many other possibilities for the mean function m, including the mean of order r, $[(1/2)a^r + (1/2)b^r]^{1/r}$ for $r \neq 0$. Obviously, in order to completely determine the functional form for the pure price index P_{Lo}, it is necessary to impose at least one additional test or axiom on $P_{Lo}(p^0,p^1,q^0,q^1)$.

15.30 There is a potential problem with the use of the Edgeworth–Marshall price index (15.18) that has been noticed in the context of using the formula to make international comparisons of prices. If the price levels of a very large country are compared to the price levels of a small country using formula (15.18), then the quantity vector of the large country may totally overwhelm the influence of the quantity vector corresponding to the small country.[31] In technical terms, the Edgeworth–Marshall formula is not homogeneous of degree 0 in the components of both q^0 and q^1. To prevent this problem from occurring in the use of the pure price index $P_K(p^0,p^1,q^0,q^1)$ defined by equation (15.17), it is asked that P_{Lo} satisfy the following *invariance to proportional changes in current quantities test*:[32]

$$P_{Lo}(p^0,p^1,q^0,\lambda q^1) = P_{Lo}(p^0,p^1,q^0,q^1) \quad \text{for all } p^0,p^1,q^0,q^1 \text{ and all } \lambda > 0 \tag{15.20}$$

The two tests, the time reversal test (15.13) and the invariance test (15.20), make it possible to determine the precise functional form for the pure price index P_{Lo} defined by formula (15.17): the pure price index P_K must be the Walsh index P_W defined by formula (15.19).[33]

15.31 In order to be of practical use by statistical agencies, an index number formula must be able to be expressed as a function of the base period expenditure shares, s_i^0, the current period expenditure shares, s_i^1, and the n price ratios, p_i^1/p_i^0. The Walsh price index defined by the formula (15.19) can be rewritten in the following format:

$$\begin{aligned} P_W(p^0,p^1,q^0,q^1) &\equiv \frac{\sum_{i=1}^{n} p_i^1 \sqrt{q_i^0 q_i^1}}{\sum_{j=1}^{n} p_j^0 \sqrt{q_j^0 q_j^1}} \\ &= \frac{\sum_{i=1}^{n} \left(p_i^1/\sqrt{p_i^0 p_i^1}\right) \sqrt{s_i^0 s_i^1}}{\sum_{j=1}^{n} \left(p_j^0/\sqrt{p_j^0 p_j^1}\right) \sqrt{s_j^0 s_j^1}} \\ &= \frac{\sum_{i=1}^{n} \sqrt{s_i^0 s_i^1} \sqrt{p_i^1/p_i^0}}{\sum_{j=1}^{n} \sqrt{s_j^0 s_j^1} \sqrt{p_j^0/p_j^1}} \end{aligned} \tag{15.21}$$

15.32 The approach taken to index number theory in this section was to consider averages of various fixed basket type price indices. The first approach was to take an even-handed average of the two primary fixed basket indices: the Laspeyres and Paasche price indices. These two primary indices are based on pricing out the baskets that pertain to the two periods (or locations) under consideration. Taking an average of them led to the Fisher ideal price index P_F defined by equation (15.12). The second approach was to average the basket quantity weights and then price out this average basket at the prices pertaining to the two situations under consideration. This approach led to the Walsh price index, P_W, defined by equation (15.19). Both of these indices can be written as a function of the base period expenditure shares, s_i^0, the current period expenditure shares, s_i^1, and the n price ratios, p_i^1/p_i^0. Assuming that the statistical agency has information on these three sets of variables, which index should be used? Experience with normal time series data has shown that these two indices will not differ substantially and thus it is a matter of indifference which of these indices is used in practice.[34] Both of these indices are examples of *superlative indices*, which are defined in Chapter 17. Note, however, that both of these indices treat the data pertaining to the two situations in a *symmetric* manner. Hill[35] commented on superlative price indices and the importance of a symmetric treatment of the data as follows:

> Thus economic theory suggests that, in general, a symmetric index that assigns equal weight to the two situations being compared is to be preferred to either the Laspeyres or Paasche indices on their own. The precise choice of superlative index – whether Fisher, Törnqvist or other superlative index – may be of only secondary importance as all the symmetric indices are likely to approximate each other, and the underlying theoretic index fairly closely, at least when the index number spread between the Laspeyres and Paasche is not very great (Hill (1993, p. 384)).

[30] Walsh (1921a, p. 103) endorsed P_W as being the best index number formula: "We have seen reason to believe formula 6 better than formula 7. Perhaps formula 9 is the best of the rest, but between it and Nos. 6 and 8 it would be difficult to decide with assurance." His formula 6 is P_W defined by equation (15.19) and his 9 is the Fisher ideal defined by equation (15.12). The *Walsh quantity index*, $Q_W(p^0,p^1,q^0,q^1)$, is defined as $P_W(q^0,q^1,p^0,p^1)$; i.e., the role of prices and quantities in definition (15.19) is interchanged. If the Walsh quantity index is used to deflate the value ratio, an implicit price index is obtained, which is Walsh's formula 8.

[31] This is not likely to be a severe problem in the time series context, however, where the change in quantity vectors going from one period to the next is small.

[32] This is the terminology used by Diewert (1992a, p. 216); Vogt (1980) was the first to propose this test.

[33] See section 7 in Diewert (2001).

[34] Diewert (1978, pp. 887–889) showed that these two indices will approximate each other to the second order around an equal price and quantity point. Thus for normal time series data where prices and quantities do not change much going from the base period to the current period, the indices will approximate each other quite closely.

[35] See also Hill (1988).

Annual weights and monthly price indices

The Lowe index with monthly prices and annual base year quantities

15.33 It is now necessary to discuss a major practical problem with the above theory of basket type indices. Up to now, it has been assumed that the quantity vector $q \equiv (q_1, q_2, \ldots, q_n)$ that appeared in the definition of the Lowe index, $P_{Lo}(p^0, p^1, q)$ defined by equation (15.15), is either the base period quantity vector q^0 or the current period quantity vector q^1 or an average of these two quantity vectors. In fact, in terms of actual statistical agency practice, the quantity vector q is usually taken to be an annual quantity vector that refers to a *base year*, say b, that is prior to the base period for the prices, period 0. Typically, a statistical agency will produce a consumer price index at a monthly or quarterly frequency, but for the sake of argument a monthly frequency will be assumed in what follows. Thus a typical price index will have the form $P_{Lo}(p^0, p^t, q^b)$, where p^0 is the price vector pertaining to the base period month for prices, month 0, p^t is the price vector pertaining to the current period month for prices, say month t, and q^b is a reference basket quantity vector that refers to the base year b, which is equal to or prior to month 0.[36] Note that this Lowe index $P_{Lo}(p^0, p^t, q^b)$ is *not* a true Laspeyres index (because the annual quantity vector q^b is not equal to the monthly quantity vector q^0 in general).[37]

15.34 The question is: why do statistical agencies *not* pick the reference quantity vector q in the Lowe formula to be the monthly quantity vector q^0 that pertains to transactions in month 0 (so that the index would reduce to an ordinary Laspeyres price index)? There are two main reasons why this is not done:

- Most economies are subject to seasonal fluctuations, and so picking the quantity vector of month 0 as the reference quantity vector for all months of the year would not be representative of transactions made throughout the year.
- Monthly household quantity or expenditure weights are usually collected by the statistical agency using a household expenditure survey with a relatively small sample. Hence the resulting weights are usually subject to very large sampling errors and so standard practice is to average these monthly expenditure or quantity weights over an entire year (or in some cases, over several years), in an attempt to reduce these sampling errors.

The index number problems that are caused by seasonal monthly weights are studied in more detail in Chapter 22. For now, it can be argued that the use of annual weights in a monthly index number formula is simply a method for dealing with the seasonality problem.[38]

15.35 One problem with using annual weights corresponding to a perhaps distant year in the context of a monthly consumer price index must be noted at this point: if there are systematic (but divergent) trends in commodity prices and households increase their purchases of commodities that decline (relatively) in price and reduce their purchases of commodities that increase (relatively) in price, then the use of distant quantity weights will tend to lead to an upward bias in this Lowe index compared to one that used more current weights, as will be shown below. This observation suggests that statistical agencies should strive to get up-to-date weights on an ongoing basis.

15.36 It is useful to explain how the annual quantity vector q^b could be obtained from monthly expenditures on each commodity during the chosen base year b. Let the month m expenditure of the reference population in the base year b for commodity i be $v_i^{b,m}$ and let the corresponding price and quantity be $p_i^{b,m}$ and $q_i^{b,m}$ respectively. Of course, value, price and quantity for each commodity are related by the following equations:

$$v_i^{b,m} = p_i^{b,m} q_i^{b,m} \quad \text{where } i = 1, \ldots, n \text{ and } m = 1, \ldots, 12 \tag{15.22}$$

For each commodity i, the annual total, q_i^b, can be obtained by price deflating monthly values and summing over months in the base year b as follows:

$$q_i^b = \sum_{m=1}^{12} \frac{v_i^{b,m}}{p_i^{b,m}} = \sum_{m=1}^{12} q_i^{b,m}; \quad i = 1, \ldots, n \tag{15.23}$$

where equation (15.22) was used to derive the second equation in (15.23). In practice, the above equations will be evaluated using aggregate expenditures over closely related commodities and the price $p_i^{b,m}$ will be the month m price index for this elementary commodity group i in year b relative to the first month of year b.

15.37 For some purposes, it is also useful to have annual prices by commodity to match up with the annual quantities defined by equation (15.23). Following national income accounting conventions, a reasonable[39]

[36] Month 0 is called the price reference period and year b is called the weight reference period.

[37] Triplett (1981, p. 12) defined the Lowe index, calling it a Laspeyres index, and calling the index that has the weight reference period equal to the price reference period a pure Laspeyres index. Balk (1980c, p. 69), however, asserted that although the Lowe index is of the fixed base type; it is not a Laspeyres price index. Triplett also noted the hybrid share representation for the Lowe index defined by equations (15.15) and (15.16). Triplett noted that the ratio of two Lowe indices using the same quantity weights was also a Lowe index. Baldwin (1990, p. 255) called the Lowe index an *annual basket index*.

[38] In fact, the use of the Lowe index $P_{Lo}(p^0, p^t, q^b)$ in the context of seasonal commodities corresponds to Bean and Stine's (1924, p. 31) Type A index number formula. Bean and Stine made three additional suggestions for price indices in the context of seasonal commodities. Their contributions are evaluated in Chapter 22.

[39] These annual commodity prices are essentially unit value prices. Under conditions of high inflation, the annual prices defined by equation (15.24) may no longer be "reasonable" or representative of prices during the entire base year because the expenditures in the final months of the high inflation year will be somewhat artificially blown up by general inflation. Under these conditions, the annual prices and annual commodity expenditure shares should be interpreted with caution. For more on dealing with situations where there is high inflation within a year, see Hill (1996).

price p_i^b to match up with the annual quantity q_i^b is the value of total consumption of commodity i in year b divided by q_i^b. Thus we have:

$$\begin{aligned} p_i^b &\equiv \sum_{m=1}^{12} v_i^{b,m}/q_i^b \qquad i=1,\ldots,n \\ &= \frac{\sum_{m=1}^{12} v_i^{b,m}}{\sum_{m=1}^{12} v_i^{b,m}/p_i^{b,m}} \quad \text{using (15.23)} \\ &= \left[\sum_{m=1}^{12} s_i^{b,m}(p_i^{b,m})^{-1}\right]^{-1} \qquad (15.24) \end{aligned}$$

where the share of annual expenditure on commodity i in month m of the base year is

$$s_i^{b,m} \equiv \frac{v_i^{b,m}}{\sum_{k=1}^{12} v_i^{b,k}}; \quad i=1,\ldots,n \qquad (15.25)$$

Thus the annual base year price for commodity i, p_i^b turns out to be a monthly expenditure weighted *harmonic mean* of the monthly prices for commodity i in the base year, $p_i^{b,1}, p_i^{b,2}, \ldots, p_i^{b,12}$.

15.38 Using the annual commodity prices for the base year defined by equation (15.24), a vector of these prices can be defined as $p^b \equiv [p_1^b, \ldots, p_n^b]$. Using this definition, the Lowe index $P_{Lo}(p^0, p^t, q^b)$ can be expressed as a ratio of two Laspeyres indices, where the price vector p^b plays the role of base period prices in each of the two Laspeyres indices:

$$\begin{aligned} P_{Lo}(p^0,p^t,q^b) &\equiv \frac{\sum_{i=1}^n p_i^t q_i^b}{\sum_{i=1}^n p_i^0 q_i^b} = \frac{\sum_{i=1}^n p_i^t q_i^b \Big/ \sum_{i=1}^n p_i^b q_i^b}{\sum_{i=1}^n p_i^0 q_i^b \Big/ \sum_{i=1}^n p_i^b q_i^b} \\ &= \frac{\sum_{i=1}^n s_i^b (p_i^t/p_i^b)}{\sum_{i=1}^n s_i^b (p_i^0/p_i^b)} \\ &= P_L(p^b,p^t,q^b)/P_L(p^b,p^0,q^b) \qquad (15.26) \end{aligned}$$

where the Laspeyres formula P_L was defined by equation (15.5). Thus the above equation shows that the Lowe monthly price index comparing the prices of month 0 to those of month t using the quantities of base year b as weights, $P_{Lo}(p^0, p^t, q^b)$, is equal to the Laspeyres index that compares the prices of month t to those of year b, $P_L(p^b, p^t, q^b)$, divided by the Laspeyres index that compares the prices of month 0 to those of year b, $P_L(p^b, p^0, q^b)$. Note that the Laspeyres index in the numerator can be calculated if the base year commodity expenditure shares, s_i^b, are known along with the price ratios that compare the prices of commodity i in month t, p_i^t, with the corresponding annual average prices in the base year b, p_i^b. The Laspeyres index in the denominator can be calculated if the base year commodity expenditure shares, s_i^b, are known along with the price ratios that compare the prices of commodity i in month 0, p_i^0, with the corresponding annual average prices in the base year b, p_i^b.

15.39 There is another convenient formula for evaluating the Lowe index, $P_{Lo}(p^0, p^t, q^b)$, and that is to use the hybrid weights formula (15.15). In the present context, the formula becomes:

$$P_{Lo}(p^0,p^t,q^b) \equiv \frac{\sum_{i=1}^n p_i^t q_i^b}{\sum_{i=1}^n p_i^0 q_i^b} = \frac{\sum_{i=1}^n (p_i^t/p_i^0) p_i^0 q_i^b}{\sum_{i=1}^n p_i^0 q_i^b} = \sum_{i=1}^n \left(\frac{p_i^t}{p_i^0}\right) s_i^{0b} \qquad (15.27)$$

where the hybrid weights s_i^{0b} using the prices of month 0 and the quantities of year b are defined by

$$\begin{aligned} s_i^{0b} &\equiv \frac{p_i^0 q_i^b}{\sum_{j=1}^n p_j^b q_j^b}; \quad i=1,\ldots,n \\ &= \frac{p_i^b q_i^b (p_i^0/p_i^b)}{\sum_{j=1}^n \left[p_j^b q_j^b (p_j^0/p_j^b)\right]} \qquad (15.28) \end{aligned}$$

The second equation in (15.28) shows how the base year expenditures, $p_i^b q_i^b$, can be multiplied by the commodity price indices, p_i^0/p_i^b, in order to calculate the hybrid shares.

15.40 There is one additional formula for the Lowe index, $P_{Lo}(p^0, p^t, q^b)$, that will be exhibited. Note that the Laspeyres decomposition of the Lowe index defined by the third term in equation (15.26) involves the long-term price relatives, p_i^t/p_i^b, which compare the prices in month t, p_i^t, with the possibly distant base year prices, p_i^b, and that the hybrid share decomposition of the Lowe index defined by the third term in equation (15.27) involves the long-term monthly price relatives, p_i^t/p_i^0, which compare the prices in month t, p_i^t, with the base month prices, p_i^0. Both of these formulae are unsatisfactory in practice because of sample attrition: each month, a substantial fraction of commodities disappears from the marketplace. Thus it is useful to have a formula for updating the previous month's price index using just month-over-month price relatives. In other words, long-term price relatives disappear at too fast a rate to make it viable, in practice, to base an index number formula on their use. The Lowe index for month $t+1$, $P_{Lo}(p^0, p^{t+1}, q^b)$, can be written in terms of the Lowe index for month t, $P_{Lo}(p^0, p^t, q^b)$, and an updating factor as follows:

$$\begin{aligned} P_{Lo}(p^0,p^{t+1},q^b) &\equiv \frac{\sum_{i=1}^n p_i^{t+1} q_i^b}{\sum_{i=1}^n p_i^0 q_i^b} = \left[\frac{\sum_{i=1}^n p_i^t q_i^b}{\sum_{i=1}^n p_i^0 q_i^b}\right]\left[\frac{\sum_{i=1}^n p_i^{t+1} q_i^b}{\sum_{i=1}^n p_i^t q_i^b}\right] \\ &= P_{Lo}(p^0,p^{t+1},q^b)\left[\frac{\sum_{i=1}^n p_i^{t+1} q_i^b}{\sum_{i=1}^n p_i^t q_i^b}\right] \end{aligned}$$

$$= P_{Lo}(p^0, p^{t+1}, q^b) \left[\frac{\sum_{i=1}^{n} \left(\frac{p_i^{t+1}}{p_i^t} \right) p_i^t q_i^b}{\sum_{i=1}^{n} p_i^t q_i^b} \right]$$

$$= P_{Lo}(p^0, p^{t+1}, q^b) \left[\sum_{i=1}^{n} \left(\frac{p_i^{t+1}}{p_i^t} \right) s_i^{tb} \right] \quad (15.29)$$

where the hybrid weights s_i^{tb} are defined by:

$$s_i^{tb} \equiv \frac{p_i^t q_i^b}{\sum_{j=1}^{n} p_j^t q_j^b}; \quad i = 1, \ldots, n \quad (15.30)$$

Thus the required updating factor, going from month t to month $t+1$, is the chain link index $\sum_{i=1}^{n} s_i^{tb}(p_i^{t+1}/p_i^t)$, which uses the hybrid share weights s_i^{tb} corresponding to month t and base year b.

15.41 The Lowe index $P_{Lo}(p^0, p^t, q^b)$ can be regarded as an approximation to the ordinary Laspeyres index, $P_L(p^0, p^t, q^0)$, that compares the prices of the base month 0, p^0, to those of month t, p^t, using the quantity vectors of month 0, q^0, as weights. It turns out that there is a relatively simple formula that relates these two indices. In order to explain this formula, it is first necessary to make a few definitions. Define the ith price relative between month 0 and month as

$$r_i \equiv p_i^t / p_i^0; \quad i = 1, \ldots, n \quad (15.31)$$

The ordinary Laspeyres price index, going from month 0 to t, can be defined in terms of these price relatives as follows:

$$P_L(p^0, p^t, q^0) \equiv \frac{\sum_{i=1}^{n} p_i^t q_i^0}{\sum_{i=1}^{n} p_i^0 q_i^0} = \frac{\sum_{i=1}^{n} \left(\frac{p_i^t}{p_i^0} \right) p_i^0 q_i^0}{\sum_{i=1}^{n} p_i^0 q_i^0}$$

$$= \sum_{i=1}^{n} \left(\frac{p_i^t}{p_i^0} \right) s_i^0 = \sum_{i=1}^{n} s_i^0 r_i \equiv r^* \quad (15.32)$$

where the month 0 expenditure shares s_i^0 are defined as follows:

$$s_i^0 \equiv \frac{p_i^0 q_i^0}{\sum_{j=1}^{n} p_j^0 q_j^0}; \quad i = 1, \ldots, n \quad (15.33)$$

15.42 Define the ith quantity relative t_i as the ratio of the quantity of commodity i used in the base year b, q_i^b, to the quantity used in month 0, q_i^0, as follows:

$$t_i \equiv q_i^b / q_i^0; \quad i = 1, \ldots, n \quad (15.34)$$

The Laspeyres quantity index, $Q_L(q^0, q^b, p^0)$, that compares quantities in year b, q^b, to the corresponding quantities in month 0, q^0, using the prices of month 0, p^0, as weights can be defined as a weighted average of the quantity ratios t_i as follows:

$$Q_L(q^0, q^b, p^0) \equiv \frac{\sum_{i=1}^{n} p_i^0 q_i^b}{\sum_{i=1}^{n} p_i^0 q_i^0} = \frac{\sum_{i=1}^{n} \left(\frac{q_i^b}{q_i^0} \right) p_i^0 q_i^0}{\sum_{i=1}^{n} p_i^0 q_i^0} = \sum_{i=1}^{n} \left(\frac{q_i^b}{q_i^0} \right) s_i^0$$

$$= \sum_{i=1}^{n} s_i^0 t_i \text{ using definition (15.34)}$$

$$\equiv t^* \quad (15.35)$$

15.43 Using formula (A15.2.4) in Appendix 15.2 to this chapter, the relationship between the Lowe index $P_{Lo}(p^0, p^t, q^b)$ that uses the quantities of year b as weights to compare the prices of month t to month 0, and the corresponding ordinary Laspeyres index $P_L(p^0, p^t, q^0)$ that uses the quantities of month 0 as weights is the following one:

$$P_{Lo}(p^0, p^t, q^b) \equiv \frac{\sum_{i=1}^{n} p_i^t q_i^b}{\sum_{i=1}^{n} p_i^0 q_i^b}$$

$$= P_L(p^0, p^t, q^0) + \frac{\sum_{i=1}^{n} (r_i - r^*)(t_i - t^*) s_i^0}{Q_L(q^0, q^b, p^0)} \quad (15.36)$$

Thus the Lowe price index using the quantities of year b as weights, $P_{Lo}(p^0, p^t, q^b)$, is equal to the usual Laspeyres index using the quantities of month 0 as weights, $P_L(p^0, p^t, q^0)$, plus a covariance term $\sum_{i=1}^{n}(r_i - r^*)(t_i - t^*)s_i^0$ between the price relatives $r_i \equiv p_i^t/p_i^0$ and the quantity relatives $t_i \equiv q_i^b/q_i^0$, divided by the Laspeyres quantity index $Q_L(q^0, q^b, p^0)$ between month 0 and base year b.

15.44 Formula (15.36) shows that the Lowe price index will coincide with the Laspeyres price index if the covariance or correlation between the month 0 to t price relatives $r_i \equiv p_i^t/p_i^0$ and the month 0 to year b quantity relatives $t_i \equiv q_i^b/q_i^0$ is zero. Note that this covariance will be zero under three different sets of conditions:

- if the month t prices are proportional to the month 0 prices so that all $r_i = r^*$;
- if the base year b quantities are proportional to the month 0 quantities so that all $t_i = t^*$;
- if the distribution of the relative prices r_i is independent of the distribution of the relative quantities t_i.

The first two conditions are unlikely to hold empirically, but the third is possible, at least approximately, if consumers do not systematically change their purchasing habits in response to changes in relative prices.

15.45 If this covariance in formula (15.36) is negative, then the Lowe index will be less than the Laspeyres index. Finally, if the covariance is positive, then the Lowe index will be greater than the Laspeyres index. Although the sign and magnitude of the covariance term, $\sum_{i=1}^{n}(r_i - r^*)(t_i - t^*)s_i^0$, is ultimately an empirical matter, it is possible to make some reasonable conjectures about its likely sign. If the base year b precedes the price reference month 0 and there are long-term trends in prices, then it is likely that this covariance is positive and hence that the Lowe index will exceed the corresponding Laspeyres price index;[40] i.e.,

$$P_{Lo}(p^0,p^t,q^b) > P_L(p^0,p^t,q^0) \tag{15.37}$$

To see why the covariance is likely to be positive, suppose that there is a long-term upward trend in the price of commodity i so that $r_i - r^* \equiv (p_i^t/p_i^0) - r^*$ is positive. With normal consumer substitution responses,[41] q_i^t/q_i^0 less an average quantity change of this type is likely to be negative, or, upon taking reciprocals, q_i^0/q_i^t less an average quantity change of this (reciprocal) type is likely to be positive. But if the long-term upward trend in prices has persisted back to the base year b, then $t_i - t^* \equiv (q_i^b/q_i^0) - t^*$ is also likely to be positive. Hence, the covariance will be positive under these circumstances. Moreover, the more distant is the base year b from the base month 0, the bigger the residuals $t_i - t^*$ are likely to be and the bigger will be the positive covariance. Similarly, the more distant is the current period month t from the base period month 0, the bigger the residuals $r_i - r^*$ are likely to be and the bigger will be the positive covariance. Thus, under the assumptions that there are long-term trends in prices and normal consumer substitution responses, the Lowe index will normally be greater than the corresponding Laspeyres index.

15.46 Define the Paasche index between months 0 and t as follows:

$$P_P(p^0,p^t,q^t) \equiv \frac{\sum_{i=1}^{n} p_i^t q_i^t}{\sum_{i=1}^{n} p_i^0 q_i^t} \tag{15.38}$$

As discussed in paragraphs 15.18 to 15.23, a reasonable target index to measure the price change going from month 0 to t is some sort of symmetric average of the Paasche index $P_P(p^0,p^t,q^t)$, defined by formula (15.38), and the corresponding Laspeyres index, $P_L(p^0,p^t,q^0)$, defined by formula (15.32). Adapting equation (A15.1.5) in Appendix 15.1, the relationship between the Paasche and Laspeyres indices can be written as follows:

$$P_P(p^0,p^t,q^t) = P_L(p^0,p^t,q^0) + \frac{\sum_{i=1}^{n} (r_i - r^*)(u_i - u^*)s_i^0}{Q_L(q^0,q^t,p^0)} \tag{15.39}$$

where the price relatives $r_i \equiv p_i^t/p_i^0$ are defined by equation (15.31) and their share-weighted average r^* by equation (15.32) and the u_i, u^* and Q_L are defined as follows:

$$u_i \equiv q_i^t/q_i^0; \quad i=1,\ldots,n \tag{15.40}$$

$$u^* \equiv \sum_{i=1}^{n} s_i^0 u_i = Q_L(q^0,q^t,p^0) \tag{15.41}$$

and the month 0 expenditure shares s_i^0 are defined by the identity (15.33). Thus u^* is equal to the Laspeyres quantity index between months 0 and t. This means that the Paasche price index that uses the quantities of month t as weights, $P_P(p^0,p^t,q^t)$, is equal to the usual Laspeyres index using the quantities of month 0 as weights, $P_L(p^0,p^t,q^0)$, plus a covariance term $\sum_{i=1}^{n}(r_i - r^*)(u_i - u^*)s_i^0$ between the price relatives $r_i \equiv p_i^t/p_i^0$ and the quantity relatives $u_i \equiv q_i^t/q_i^0$, divided by the Laspeyres quantity index $Q_L(q^0,q^t,p^0)$ between month 0 and month t.

15.47 Although the sign and magnitude of the covariance term, $\sum_{i=1}^{n}(r_i - r^*)(u_i - u^*)s_i^0$, is again an empirical matter, it is possible to make a reasonable conjecture about its likely sign. If there are long-term trends in prices and consumers respond normally to price changes in their purchases, then it is likely that this covariance is negative and hence the Paasche index will be less than the corresponding Laspeyres price index; i.e.,

$$P_P(p^0,p^t,q^t) < P_L(p^0,p^t,q^0) \tag{15.42}$$

To see why this covariance is likely to be negative, suppose that there is a long-term upward trend in the price of commodity i[42] so that $r_i - r^* \equiv (p_i^t/p_i^0) - r^*$ is positive. With normal consumer substitution responses, q_i^t/q_i^0 less an average quantity change of this type is likely to be negative. Hence $u_i - u^* \equiv (q_i^t/q_i^0) - u^*$ is likely to be negative. Thus, the covariance will be negative under these circumstances. Moreover, the more distant is the base month 0 from the current month t, the bigger in magnitude the residuals $u_i - u^*$ are likely to be and the bigger in magnitude will be the negative covariance.[43] Similarly, the more distant is the current period month t from the base period month 0, the bigger the residuals $r_i - r^*$ will probably be and the bigger in magnitude will be the covariance. Thus under the assumptions that there are long-term trends in prices and normal consumer substitution responses, the Laspeyres index will be greater than the corresponding Paasche index, with the divergence likely to grow as month t becomes more distant from month 0.

15.48 Putting the arguments in the three previous paragraphs together, it can be seen that under the

[40] For this relationship to hold, it is also necessary to assume that households have normal substitution effects in response to these long-term trends in prices; i.e., if a commodity increases (relatively) in price, its consumption will decline (relatively) and if a commodity decreases relatively in price, its consumption will increase relatively.

[41] Walsh (1901, pp. 281–282) was well aware of consumer substitution effects, as can be seen in the following comment which noted the basic problem with a fixed basket index that uses the quantity weights of a single period: "The argument made by the arithmetic averagist supposes that we buy the same quantities of every class at both periods in spite of the variation in their prices, which we rarely, if ever, do. As a rough proposition, we – a community – generally spend more on articles that have risen in price and get less of them, and spend less on articles that have fallen in price and get more of them."

[42] The reader can carry through the argument if there is a long-term relative decline in the price of the ith commodity. The argument required to obtain a negative covariance requires that there be some differences in the long-term trends in prices; i.e., if all prices grow (or fall) at the same rate, there will be price proportionality and the covariance will be zero.

[43] However, $Q_L = u^*$ may also be growing in magnitude, so the net effect on the divergence between P_L and P_P is ambiguous.

assumptions that there are long-term trends in prices and normal consumer substitution responses, the Lowe price index between months 0 and t will exceed the corresponding Laspeyres price index, which in turn will exceed the corresponding Paasche price index; i.e., under these hypotheses,

$$P_{Lo}(p^0,p^t,q^b) > P_L(p^0,p^t,q^0) > P_P(p^0,p^t,q^t) \quad (15.43)$$

Thus, if the long-run target price index is an average of the Laspeyres and Paasche indices, it can be seen that the Laspeyres index will have an upward bias relative to this target index and the Paasche index will have a downward bias. In addition, if the base year b is prior to the price reference month, month 0, then the Lowe index will also have an upward bias relative to the Laspeyres index and hence also to the target index.

The Lowe index and mid-year indices

15.49 The discussion in the previous paragraph assumed that the base year b for quantities preceded the base month for prices, month 0. If the current period month t is quite distant from the base month 0, however, then it is possible to think of the base year b as referring to a year that lies between months 0 and t. If the year b does fall between months 0 and t, then the Lowe index becomes a *mid-year index*.[44] It turns out that the Lowe mid-year index no longer has the upward biases indicated by the inequalities in the inequality (15.43) under the assumption of long-term trends in prices and normal substitution responses by quantities.

15.50 It is now assumed that the base year quantity vector q^b corresponds to a year that lies between months 0 and t. Under the assumption of long-term trends in prices and normal substitution effects so that there are also long-term trends in quantities (in the opposite direction to the trends in prices so that if the ith commodity price is trending up, then the corresponding ith quantity is trending down), it is likely that the intermediate year quantity vector will lie between the monthly quantity vectors q^0 and q^t. The mid-year Lowe index, $P_{Lo}(p^0,p^t,q^b)$, and the Laspeyres index going from month 0 to t, $P_L(p^0,p^t,q^0)$, will still satisfy the exact relationship given by equation (15.36). Thus $P_{Lo}(p^0,p^t,q^b)$ will equal $P_L(p^0,p^t,q^0)$ plus the covariance term $[\sum_{i=1}^n (r_i - r^*)\ (t_i - t^*)s_i^0]/Q_L(q^0,q^b,p^0)$, where $Q_L(q^0,q^b,p^0)$ is the Laspeyres quantity index going from month 0 to t. This covariance term is likely to be negative so that

$$P_L(p^0,p^t,q^0) > P_{Lo}(p^0,p^t,q^b). \quad (15.44)$$

To see why this covariance is likely to be negative, suppose that there is a long-term upward trend in the price of commodity i so that $r_i - r^* \equiv (pi^t/p_i^0) - r^*$ is positive. With normal consumer substitution responses, q_i will tend to decrease relatively over time and since q_i^b is assumed to be between q_i^0 and q_i^t, q_i^b/q_i^0 less an average quantity change of this type is likely to be negative. Hence $u_i - u^* \equiv (q_i^b/q_i^0) - t^*$ is likely to be negative. Thus, the covariance is likely to be negative under these circumstances. Therefore, under the assumptions that the quantity base year falls between months 0 and t and that there are long-term trends in prices and normal consumer substitution responses, the Laspeyres index will normally be larger than the corresponding Lowe mid-year index, with the divergence probably growing as month t becomes more distant from month 0.

15.51 It can also be seen that under the above assumptions, the mid-year Lowe index is likely to be greater than the Paasche index between months 0 and t; i.e.,

$$P_{Lo}(p^0,p^t,q^b) > P_P(p^0,p^t,q^t) \quad (15.45)$$

To see why the above inequality is likely to hold, think of q^b starting at the month 0 quantity vector q^0 and then trending smoothly to the month t quantity vector q^t. When $q^b = q^0$, the Lowe index $P_{Lo}(p^0,p^t,q^b)$ becomes the Laspeyres index $P_L(p^0,p^t,q^0)$. When $q^b = q^t$, the Lowe index $P_{Lo}(p^0,p^t,q^b)$ becomes the Paasche index $P_P(p^0,p^t,q^t)$. Under the assumption of trending prices and normal substitution responses to these trending prices, it was shown earlier that the Paasche index will be less than the corresponding Laspeyres price index; i.e., that $P_P(p^0,p^t,q^t)$ was less than $P_L(p^0,p^t,q^0)$, recalling the inequality (15.42). Thus, under the assumption of smoothly trending prices and quantities between months 0 and t, and assuming that q^b is between q^0 and q^t, we will have

$$P_P(p^0,p^t,q^t) < P_{Lo}(p^0,p^t,q^b) < P_L(p^0,p^t,q^0) \quad (15.46)$$

Thus if the base year for the Lowe index is chosen to be in between the base month for the prices, month 0, and the current month for prices, month t, and there are trends in prices with corresponding trends in quantities that correspond to normal consumer substitution effects, then the resulting Lowe index is likely to lie between the Paasche and Laspeyres indices going from months 0 to t. If the trends in prices and quantities are

[44] The concept of the mid-year index can be traced to Hill (1998, p. 46):

> When inflation has to be measured over a specified sequence of years, such as a decade, a pragmatic solution to the problems raised above would be to take the middle year as the base year. This can be justified on the grounds that the basket of goods and services purchased in the middle year is likely to be much more representative of the pattern of consumption over the decade as a whole than baskets purchased in either the first or the last years. Moreover, choosing a more representative basket will also tend to reduce, or even eliminate, any bias in the rate of inflation over the decade as a whole as compared with the increase in the CoL index.

Thus, in addition to introducing the concept of a mid-year index, Hill also introduced the terminology *representativity bias*. Baldwin (1990, pp. 255–256) also introduced the term *representativeness*: "Here representativeness [in an index number formula] requires that the weights used in any comparison of price levels are related to the volume of purchases in the periods of comparison."

However, this basic idea dates back to Walsh (1901, p. 104; 1921a, p. 90). Baldwin (1990, p. 255) also noted that his concept of representativeness was the same as Drechsler's (1973, p. 19) concept of *characteristicity*. For additional material on mid-year indices, see Schultz (1999) and Okamoto (2001). Note that the mid-year index concept could be viewed as a close competitor to Walsh's (1901, p. 431) multi-year fixed basket index where the quantity vector was chosen to be an arithmetic or geometric average of the quantity vectors in the span of periods under consideration.

smooth, then choosing the base year half-way between periods 0 and t should give a Lowe index that is approximately half-way between the Paasche and Laspeyres indices; hence it will be very close to an ideal target index between months 0 and t. This basic idea has been implemented by Okamoto (2001), using Japanese consumer data, and he found that the resulting mid-year indices approximated very closely to the corresponding Fisher ideal indices.

15.52 It should be noted that these mid-year indices can only be computed on a retrospective basis; i.e., they cannot be calculated in a timely fashion, as can Lowe indices that use a base year that is prior to month 0. Thus mid-year indices cannot be used to replace the more timely Lowe indices. The above material indicates, however, that these timely Lowe indices are likely to have an upward bias that is even bigger than the usual Laspeyres upward bias compared to an ideal target index, which was taken to be an average of the Paasche and Laspeyres indices.

15.53 All the inequalities derived in this section rest on the assumption of long-term trends in prices (and corresponding economic responses in quantities). If there are no systematic long-run trends in prices, but only random fluctuations around a common trend in all prices, then the above inequalities are not valid and the Lowe index using a prior base year will probably provide a perfectly adequate approximation to both the Paasche and Laspeyres indices. There are, however, reasons for believing that there are some long-run trends in prices. In particular:

- The computer chip revolution of the past 40 years has led to strong downward trends in the prices of products that use these chips intensively. As new uses for chips have been developed over the years, the share of products that are chip intensive has grown and this implies that what used to be a relatively minor problem has become a more major problem.
- Other major scientific advances have had similar effects. For example, the invention of fibre optic cable (and lasers) has led to a downward trend in telecommunications prices as obsolete technologies based on copper wire are gradually replaced.
- Since the end of the Second World War, a series of international trade agreements has dramatically reduced tariffs around the world. These reductions, combined with improvements in transport technologies, have led to a very rapid growth of international trade and remarkable improvements in international specialization. Manufacturing activities in the more developed economies have gradually been outsourced to lower-wage countries, leading to deflation in goods prices in most countries around the world. In contrast, many services cannot be readily outsourced[45] and so, on average, the price of services trends upwards while the price of goods trends downwards.
- At the microeconomic level, there are tremendous differences in growth rates of firms. Successful firms expand their scale, lower their costs, and cause less successful competitors to wither away with their higher prices and lower volumes. This leads to a systematic negative correlation between changes in item prices and the corresponding changes in item volumes that can be very large indeed.

Thus there is some a priori basis for assuming long-run divergent trends in prices. Hence there is some basis for concern that a Lowe index that uses a base year for quantity weights that is prior to the base month for prices may be upwardly biased, compared to a more ideal target index.

The Young index

15.54 Recall the definitions for the base year quantities, q_i^b, and the base year prices, p_i^b, given by equations (15.23) and (15.24) above. The base year expenditure shares can be defined in the usual way as follows:

$$s_i^b \equiv \frac{p_i^b q_i^b}{\sum_{k=1}^{n} p_k^b q_k^b}; \quad i=1,\ldots,n \qquad (15.47)$$

Define the vector of base year expenditure shares in the usual way as $s^b \equiv [s_1^b, \ldots, s_n^b]$. These base year expenditure shares were used to provide an alternative formula for the base year b Lowe price index going from month 0 to t, defined in equation (15.26) as $P_{Lo}(p^0, p^t, q^b) = \left[\sum_{i=1}^{n} s_i^b (p_i^t/p_i^b)\right] / \left[\sum_{i=1}^{n} s_i^b (p_i^0/p_i^b)\right]$. Rather than using this index as their short-run target index, many statistical agencies use the following closely related index:

$$P_Y(p^0, p^t, s^b) \equiv \sum_{i=1}^{n} s_i^b (p_i^t/p_i^0) \qquad (15.48)$$

This type of index was first defined by the English economist, Arthur Young (1812).[46] Note that there is a change in focus when the Young index is used compared to the other indices proposed earlier in this chapter. Up to this point, the indices proposed have been of the fixed basket type (or averages of such indices) where a *commodity basket* that is somehow representative for the two periods being compared is chosen and then "purchased" at the prices of the two periods and the index is taken to be the ratio of these two costs. In contrast, for the Young index, *representative expenditure shares* are chosen that pertain to the two periods under consideration, and then these shares are used to calculate the overall index as a share-weighted average of the individual price ratios, p_i^t/p_i^0. Note that this view of index number theory, based on the share-weighted average of price ratios, is a little different from the view taken at the beginning of this chapter, which saw the

[45] Some services, however, can be internationally outsourced; e.g., call centres, computer programming and airline maintenance.

[46] This formula is attributed to Young by Walsh (1901, p. 536; 1932, p. 657).

index number problem as that of decomposing a value ratio into the product of two terms, one of which expresses the amount of price change between the two periods and the other which expresses the amount of quantity change.[47]

15.55 Statistical agencies sometimes regard the Young index, defined above, as an approximation to the Laspeyres price index $P_L(p^0, p^t, q^0)$. Hence, it is of interest to see how the two indices compare. Defining the long-term monthly price relatives going from month 0 to t as $r_i \equiv p_i^t/p_i^0$ and using definitions (15.32) and (15.48):

$$\begin{aligned} P_Y(p^0,p^t,s^b) - P_L(p^0,p^t,q^0) &\equiv \sum_{i=1}^n s_i^b\left(\frac{p_i^t}{p_i^0}\right) - \sum_{i=1}^n s_i^0\left(\frac{p_i^t}{p_i^0}\right) \\ &= \sum_{i=1}^n \left[s_i^b - s_i^0\right]\left(\frac{p_i^t}{p_i^0}\right) \\ &= \sum_{i=1}^n \left[s_i^b - s_i^0\right] r_i \\ &= \sum_{i=1}^n \left[s_i^b - s_i^0\right]\left[r_i - r^*\right] \\ &\quad + r^* \sum_{i=1}^n \left[s_i^b - s_i^0\right] \\ &= \sum_{i=1}^n \left[s_i^b - s_i^0\right]\left[r_i - r^*\right] \qquad (15.49) \end{aligned}$$

since $\sum_{i=1}^n s_i^b = \sum_{i=1}^n s_i^0 = 1$ and defining $r^* \equiv \sum_{i=1}^n s_i^0 r_i = P_L(p^0, p^t, q^0)$. Thus the Young index $P_Y(p^0, p^t, s^b)$ is equal to the Laspeyres index $P_L(p^0, p^t, q^0)$, plus the *covariance* between the difference in the annual shares pertaining to year b and the month 0 shares, $s_i^b - s_i^0$, and the deviations of the relative prices from their mean, $r_i - r^*$.

15.56 It is no longer possible to guess at what the likely sign of the covariance term is. The question is no longer whether the *quantity* demanded goes down as the price of commodity i goes up (the answer to this question is usually "yes") but the new question is: does the *share* of expenditure go down as the price of commodity i goes up? The answer to this question depends on the elasticity of demand for the product. Let us provisionally assume, however, that there are long-run trends in commodity prices and if the trend in prices for commodity i is above the mean, then the expenditure share for the commodity trends *down* (and vice versa). Thus we are assuming high elasticities or very strong substitution effects. Assuming also that the base year b is prior to month 0, then under these conditions, suppose that there is a long-term upward trend in the price of commodity i so that $r_i - r^* \equiv (p_i^t/p_i^0) - r^*$ is positive. With the assumed very elastic consumer substitution responses, s_i will tend to decrease relatively over time and since s_i^b is assumed to be prior to s_i^0, s_i^0 is expected to be less than s_i^b or $s_i^b - s_i^0$ will probably be positive. Thus, the covariance is likely to be positive under these circumstances. *Hence with long-run trends in prices and very elastic responses of consumers to price changes, the Young index is likely to be greater than the corresponding Laspeyres index.*

15.57 Assume that there are long-run trends in commodity prices. If the trend in prices for commodity i is above the mean, then suppose that the expenditure share for the commodity trends *up* (and vice versa). Thus we are assuming low elasticities or very weak substitution effects. Assume also that the base year b is prior to month 0 and suppose that there is a long-term upward trend in the price of commodity i so that $r_i - r^* \equiv (p_i^t/p_i^0) - r^*$ is positive. With the assumed very inelastic consumer substitution responses, s_i will tend to increase relatively over time and since s_i^b is assumed to be prior to s_i^0, it will be the case that s_i^0 is greater than s_i^b or $s_i^b - s_i^0$ is negative. Thus, the covariance is likely to be negative under these circumstances. *Hence with long-run trends in prices and very inelastic responses of consumers to price changes, the Young index is likely to be less than the corresponding Laspeyres index.*

15.58 The previous two paragraphs indicate that, a priori, it is not known what the likely difference between the Young index and the corresponding Laspeyres index will be. If elasticities of substitution are close to one, then the two sets of expenditure shares, s_i^b and s_i^0, will be close to each other and the difference between the two indices will be close to zero. If monthly expenditure shares have strong seasonal components, however, then the annual shares s_i^b could differ substantially from the monthly shares s_i^0.

15.59 It is useful to have a formula for updating the previous month's Young price index using just month-over-month price relatives. The Young index for month $t+1$, $P_Y(p^0, p^{t+1}, s^b)$, can be written in terms of the Young index for month t, $P_Y(p^0, p^t, s^b)$, and an updating factor as follows:

$$\begin{aligned} P_Y(p^0,p^{t+1},s^b) &\equiv \sum_{i=1}^n s_i^b\left(\frac{p_i^{t+1}}{p_i^0}\right) \\ &= P_Y(p^0,p^t,s^b)\frac{\sum_{i=1}^n s_i^b(p_i^{t+1}/p_i^0)}{\sum_{i=1}^n s_i^b(p_i^t/p_i^0)} \end{aligned}$$

[47] Fisher's 1922 book is famous for developing the value ratio decomposition approach to index number theory, but his introductory chapters took the share-weighted average point of view: "An index number of prices, then shows the *average percentage change* of prices from one point of time to another" (Fisher (1922, p. 3)). Fisher went on to note the importance of economic weighting: "The preceding calculation treats all the commodities as equally important; consequently, the average was called 'simple'. If one commodity is more important than another, we may treat the more important as though it were two or three commodities, thus giving it two or three times as much 'weight' as the other commodity" (Fisher (1922, p. 6)). Walsh (1901, pp. 430–431) considered both approaches: "We can either (1) draw some average of the total money values of the classes during an epoch of years, and with weighting so determined employ the geometric average of the price variations [ratios]; or (2) draw some average of the mass quantities of the classes during the epoch, and apply to them Scrope's method." Scrope's method is the same as using the Lowe index. Walsh (1901, pp. 88–90) consistently stressed the importance of weighting price ratios by their economic importance (rather than using equally weighted averages of price relatives). Both the value ratio decomposition approach and the share-weighted average approach to index number theory are studied from the axiomatic perspective in Chapter 16.

$$= P_Y(p^0, p^t, s^b) \frac{\sum_{i=1}^{n} p_i^b q_i^b (p_i^{t+1}/p_i^0)}{\sum_{i=1}^{n} p_i^b q_i^b (p_i^t/p_i^0)}$$

using definition (15.47)

$$= P_Y(p^0, p^t, s^b) \frac{\sum_{i=1}^{n} p_i^b q_i^b \left(\frac{p_i^t}{p_i^0}\right)\left(\frac{p_i^{t+1}}{p_i^t}\right)}{\sum_{i=1}^{n} p_i^b q_i^b (p_i^t/p_i^0)}$$

$$= P_Y(p^0, p^t, s^b) \left[\sum_{i=1}^{n} s_i^{b0t} (p_i^{t+1}/p_i^t)\right] \qquad (15.50)$$

where the hybrid weights s_i^{b0t} are defined by

$$s_i^{b0t} \equiv \frac{p_i^b q_i^b (p_i^t/p_i^0)}{\sum_{k=1}^{n} p_k^b q_k^b (p_k^t/p_k^0)} = \frac{s_i^b (p_i^t/p_i^0)}{\sum_{k=1}^{n} s_k^b (p_k^t/p_k^0)} \quad i = 1, \ldots, n \qquad (15.51)$$

Thus the hybrid weights s_i^{b0t} can be obtained from the base year weights s_i^b by updating them; i.e., by multiplying them by the price relatives (or *indices* at higher levels of aggregation), p_i^t/p_i^0. Thus the required updating factor, going from month t to month $t+1$, is the chain link index, $\sum_{i=1}^{n} s_i^{b0t}(p_i^{t+1}/p_i^t)$, which uses the hybrid share weights s_i^{b0t} defined by equation (15.51).

15.60 Even if the Young index provides a close approximation to the corresponding Laspeyres index, it is difficult to recommend the use of the Young index as a final estimate of the change in prices going from period 0 to t, just as it was difficult to recommend the use of the Laspeyres index as the *final* estimate of inflation going from period 0 to t. Recall that the problem with the Laspeyres index was its lack of symmetry in the treatment of the two periods under consideration; i.e., using the justification for the Laspeyres index as a good fixed basket index, there was an identical justification for the use of the Paasche index as an equally good fixed basket index to compare periods 0 and t. The Young index suffers from a similar lack of symmetry with respect to the treatment of the base period. The problem can be explained as follows. The Young index, $P_Y(p^0, p^t, s^b)$, defined by equation (15.48) calculates the price change between months 0 and t treating month 0 as the base. But there is no particular reason to necessarily treat month 0 as the base month other than convention. Hence, if we treat month t as the base and use the same formula to measure the price change from month t back to month 0, the index $P_Y(p^t, p^0, s^b) = \sum_{i=1}^{n} s_i^b (p_i^0/p_i^b)$, would be appropriate. This estimate of price change can then be made comparable to the original Young index by taking its reciprocal, leading to the following *rebased Young index*,[48] $P_Y^*(p^t, p^0, s^b)$, defined as

$$P_Y^*(p^0, p^t, s^b) \equiv 1 \Big/ \sum_{i=1}^{n} s_i^b (p_i^0/p_i^t)$$

$$= \left[\sum_{i=1}^{n} s_i^b (p_i^t/p_i^0)^{-1}\right]^{-1} \qquad (15.52)$$

The rebased Young index, $P_Y^*(p^0, p^t, s^b)$, which uses the current month as the initial base period, is a *share-weighted harmonic mean* of the price relatives going from month 0 to month t, whereas the original Young index, $P_Y(p^0, p^t, s^b)$, is a *share-weighted arithmetic mean* of the same price relatives.

15.61 Fisher argued as follows that an index number formula should give the same answer no matter which period was chosen as the base:

> Either one of the two times may be taken as the "base". Will it make a difference which is chosen? Certainly, it *ought* not and our Test 1 demands that it shall not. More fully expressed, the test is that the formula for calculating an index number should be such that it will give the same ratio between one point of comparison and the other point, *no matter which of the two is taken as the base* (Fisher (1922, p. 64)).

15.62 The problem with the Young index is that not only does it not coincide with its rebased counterpart, but there is a definite inequality between the two indices, namely:

$$P_Y^*(p^0, p^t, s^b) \le P_Y(p^0, p^t, s^b) \qquad (15.53)$$

with a strict inequality provided that the period t price vector p^t is not proportional to the period 0 price vector p^0.[49] A statistical agency that uses the direct Young index $P_Y(p^0, p^t, s^b)$ will generally show a higher inflation rate than a statistical agency that uses the same raw data but uses the rebased Young index, $P_Y^*(p^0, p^{tl}, s^b)$.

15.63 The inequality (15.53) does not tell us by how much the Young index will exceed its rebased time antithesis. In Appendix 15.3, however, it is shown that to the accuracy of a certain second-order Taylor series approximation, the following relationship holds between the direct Young index and its time antithesis:

$$P_Y(p^0, p^t, s^b) \approx P_Y^*(p^0, p^t, s^b) + P_Y(p^0, p^t, s^b)\mathrm{Var}\ e \qquad (15.54)$$

[48] Using Fisher's (1922, p. 118) terminology, $P_Y^*(p^0, p^t, s^b) \equiv 1/[P_Y(p^t, p^0, s^b)]$ is the *time antithesis* of the original Young index, $P_Y(p^0, p^t, s^b)$.

[49] These inequalities follow from the fact that a harmonic mean of M positive numbers is always equal to or less than the corresponding arithmetic mean; see Walsh (1901, p. 517) or Fisher (1922, pp. 383–384). This inequality is a special case of Schlömilch's (1858) inequality; see Hardy, Littlewood and Pólya (1934, p. 26). Walsh (1901, pp. 330–332) explicitly noted the inequality (15.53) and also noted that the corresponding geometric average would fall between the harmonic and arithmetic averages. Walsh (1901, p. 432) computed some numerical examples of the Young index and found big differences between it and his "best" indices, even using weights that were representative for the periods being compared. Recall that the Lowe index becomes the Walsh index when geometric mean quantity weights are chosen and so the Lowe index can perform well when representative weights are used. This is not necessarily the case for the Young index, even using representative weights. Walsh (1901, p. 433) summed up his numerical experiments with the Young index as follows: "In fact, Young's method, in every form, has been found to be bad."

where Var e is defined as

$$\text{Var } e \equiv \sum_{i=1}^{n} s_i^b \left[e_i - e^*\right]^2 \tag{15.55}$$

The deviations e_i are defined by $1+e_i=r_i/r^*$ for $i=1, \ldots, n$ where the r_i and their weighted mean r^* are defined by

$$r_i \equiv p_i^t/p_i^0; \quad i=1, \ldots, n; \tag{15.56}$$

$$r^* \equiv \sum_{i=1}^{n} s_i^b r_i \tag{15.57}$$

which turns out to equal the direct Young index, $P_Y(p^0, p^t, s^b)$. The weighted mean of the e_i is defined as

$$e^* \equiv \sum_{i=1}^{n} s_i^b e_i \tag{15.58}$$

which turns out to equal 0. *Hence the more dispersion there is in the price relatives p_i^t/p_i^0, to the accuracy of a second-order approximation, the more the direct Young index will exceed its counterpart that uses month* t *as the initial base period rather than month 0.*

15.64 Given two a priori equally plausible index number formulae that give different answers, such as the Young index and its time antithesis, Fisher (1922, p. 136) generally suggested taking the geometric average of the two indices.[50] A benefit of this averaging is that the resulting formula will satisfy the time reversal test. Thus rather than using *either* the base period 0 Young index, $P_Y(p^0, p^t, s^b)$, *or* the current period t Young index, $P_Y^*(p^0, p^t, s^b)$, which is always below the base period 0 Young index if there is any dispersion in relative prices, it seems preferable to use the following index, which is the *geometric average* of the two alternatively based Young indices:[51]

$$P_Y^{**}(p^0, p^t, s^b) \equiv \left[P_Y(p^0, p^t, s^b) P_Y^*(p^0, p^t, s^b)\right]^{1/2} \tag{15.59}$$

If the base year shares s_i^b happen to coincide with both the month 0 and month t shares, s_i^0 and s_i^t respectively, it can be seen that the time-rectified Young index $P_Y^{**}(p^0, p^t, s^b)$ defined by equation (15.59) will coincide with the Fisher ideal price index between months 0 and t, $P_F(p^0, p^t, q^0, q^t)$ (which will also equal the Laspeyres and Paasche indices under these conditions). Note also that the index P_Y^{**} defined by equation (15.59) can be produced on a timely basis by a statistical agency.

The Divisia index and discrete approximations to it

The Divisia price and quantity indices

15.65 The second broad approach to index number theory relies on the assumption that price and quantity data change in a more or less continuous way.

15.66 Suppose that the price and quantity data on the n commodities in the chosen domain of definition can be regarded as continuous functions of (continuous) time, say $p_i(t)$ and $q_i(t)$ for $i=1, \ldots, n$. The value of consumer expenditure at time t is $V(t)$ defined in the obvious way as:

$$V(t) \equiv \sum_{i=1}^{n} p_i(t) q_i(t) \tag{15.60}$$

15.67 Now suppose that the functions $p_i(t)$ and $q_i(t)$ are differentiable. Then both sides of the definition (15.60) can be differentiated with respect to time to obtain:

$$V'(t) = \sum_{i=1}^{n} p_i'(t) q_i(t) + \sum_{i=1}^{n} p_i(t) q_i'(t) \tag{15.61}$$

Divide both sides of equation (15.61) through by $V(t)$ and using definition (15.60), the following equation is obtained:

$$\frac{V'(t)}{V(t)} = \frac{\sum_{i=1}^{n} p_i'(t) q_i(t) + \sum_{i=1}^{n} p_i(t) q_i'(t)}{\sum_{j=1}^{n} p_j(t) q_j(t)} = \sum_{i=1}^{n} \frac{p_i'(t)}{p_i(t)} s_i(t) + \sum_{i=1}^{n} \frac{q_i'(t)}{q_i(t)} s_i(t) \tag{15.62}$$

where the time t expenditure share on commodity i, $s_i(t)$, is defined as:

$$s_i(t) \equiv \frac{p_i(t) q_i(t)}{\sum_{m=1}^{n} p_m(t) q_m(t)} \quad \text{for } i=1, 2, \ldots, n \tag{15.63}$$

15.68 Divisia (1926, p. 39) argued as follows: *suppose* the aggregate value at time t, $V(t)$, can be written as the product of a time t price level function, $P(t)$ say, times a time t quantity level function, $Q(t)$ say; i.e., we have:

$$V(t) = P(t) Q(t) \tag{15.64}$$

Suppose further that the functions $P(t)$ and $Q(t)$ are differentiable. Then differentiating the equation (15.64) yields:

$$V'(t) = P'(t) Q(t) + P(t) Q'(t) \tag{15.65}$$

[50] We now come to a third use of these tests, namely, to "rectify" formulae, i.e., to derive from any given formula which does not satisfy a test another formula which does satisfy it; .... This is easily done by "crossing", that is, by averaging antitheses. If a given formula fails to satisfy Test 1 [the time reversal test], its time antithesis will also fail to satisfy it; but the two will fail, as it were, in opposite ways, so that a cross between them (obtained by *geometrical* averaging) will give the golden mean which does satisfy (Fisher (1922, p. 136)).
Actually the basic idea behind Fisher's rectification procedure was suggested by Walsh, who was a discussant for Fisher (1921), where Fisher gave a preview of his 1922 book: "We merely have to take any index number, find its antithesis in the way prescribed by Professor Fisher, and then draw the geometric mean between the two" (Walsh (1921b, p. 542)).

[51] This index is a base year weighted counterpart to an equally weighted index proposed by Carruthers, Sellwood and Ward (1980, p. 25) and Dalén (1992, p. 140) in the context of elementary index number formulae. See Chapter 20 for further discussion of this unweighted index.

Dividing both sides of equation (15.65) by $V(t)$ and using equation (15.64) leads to the following equation:

$$\frac{V'(t)}{V(t)} = \frac{P'(t)}{P(t)} + \frac{Q'(t)}{Q(t)} \qquad (15.66)$$

15.69 Divisia compared the two expressions for the logarithmic value derivative, $V'(t)/V(t)$, given by equations (15.62) and (15.66), and he simply defined the logarithmic rate of change of the *aggregate price level*, $P'(t)/P(t)$, as the first set of terms on the right-hand side of (15.62). He also simply defined the logarithmic rate of change of the *aggregate quantity level*, $Q'(t)/Q(t)$, as the second set of terms on the right-hand side of equation (15.62). That is, he made the following definitions:

$$\frac{P'(t)}{P(t)} \equiv \sum_{i=1}^{n} s_i(t)\frac{p_i'(t)}{p_i(t)} \qquad (15.67)$$

$$\frac{Q'(t)}{Q(t)} \equiv \sum_{i=1}^{n} s_i(t)\frac{q_i'(t)}{q_i(t)} \qquad (15.68)$$

15.70 Definitions (15.67) and (15.68) are reasonable definitions for the proportional changes in the aggregate price and quantity (or quantity) levels, $P(t)$ and $Q(t)$.[52] The problem with these definitions is that economic data are not collected in *continuous* time; they are collected in *discrete* time. In other words, even though transactions can be thought of as occurring in continuous time, no consumer records his or her purchases as they occur in continuous time; rather, purchases over a finite time period are cumulated and then recorded. A similar situation occurs for producers or sellers of commodities; firms cumulate their sales over discrete periods of time for accounting or analytical purposes. If it is attempted to approximate continuous time by shorter and shorter discrete time intervals, empirical price and quantity data can be expected to become increasingly erratic since consumers only make purchases at discrete points of time (and producers or sellers of commodities only make sales at discrete points of time). It is, however, still of some interest to approximate the continuous time price and quantity levels, $P(t)$ and $Q(t)$ defined implicitly by equations (15.67) and (15.68), by discrete time approximations. This can be done in two ways. Either methods of numerical approximation can be used or assumptions can be made about the path taken through time by the functions $p_i(t)$ and $q_i(t)$ $(i=1, \ldots, n)$. The first strategy is used in the following section. For discussions of the second strategy, see Vogt (1977; 1978), Van Ijzeren (1987, pp. 8–12), Vogt and Barta (1997) and Balk (2000a).

15.71 There is a connection between the Divisia price and quantity levels, $P(t)$ and $Q(t)$, and the economic approach to index number theory. This connection is, however, best made after studying the economic approach to index number theory. Since this material is rather technical, it has been relegated to Appendix 15.4.

Discrete approximations to the continuous time Divisia index

15.72 In order to make operational the continuous time Divisia price and quantity levels, $P(t)$ and $Q(t)$ defined by the differential equations (15.67) and (15.68), it is necessary to convert to discrete time. Divisia (1926, p. 40) suggested a straightforward method for doing this conversion, which we now outline.

15.73 Define the following price and quantity (forward) differences:

$$\Delta P \equiv P(1) - P(0) \qquad (15.69)$$

$$\Delta p_i \equiv p_i(1) - p_i(0); \quad i=1, \ldots, n \qquad (15.70)$$

Using the above definitions:

$$\frac{P(1)}{P(0)} = \frac{P(0)+\Delta P}{P(0)} = 1 + \frac{\Delta P}{P(0)} \approx 1 + \frac{\sum_{i=1}^{n} \Delta p_i q_i(0)}{\sum_{m=1}^{n} p_m(0) q_m(0)}$$

using (15.67) when $t=0$ and approximating $p_i'(0)$ by the difference Δp_i

$$= \frac{\sum_{i=1}^{n} \{p_i(0)+\Delta p_i\} q_i(0)}{\sum_{m=1}^{n} p_m(0) q_m(0)} = \frac{\sum_{i=1}^{n} p_i(1) q_i(0)}{\sum_{m=1}^{n} p_m(0) q_m(0)}$$

$$= P_L(p^0, p^1, q^0, q^1) \qquad (15.71)$$

where $p^t \equiv [p_1(t), \ldots, p_n(t)]$ and $q^t \equiv [q_1(t), \ldots, q_n(t)]$ for $t=0,1$. Thus, it can be seen that Divisia's discrete approximation to his continuous time price index is just the Laspeyres price index, P_L, defined above by equation (15.5).

15.74 But now a problem noted by Frisch (1936, p. 8) occurs: instead of approximating the derivatives by the discrete (forward) differences defined by equations (15.69) and (15.70), other approximations could be used and a wide variety of discrete time approximations could be obtained. For example, instead of using forward differences and evaluating the index at time $t=0$, it would be possible to use backward differences and evaluate the index at time $t=1$. These backward differences are defined as:

$$\Delta_b p_i \equiv p_i(0) - p_i(1); \quad i=1, \ldots, n \qquad (15.72)$$

This use of backward differences leads to the following approximation for $P(0)/P(1)$:

[52] If these definitions are applied (approximately) to the Young index studied in the previous section, then it can be seen that in order for the Young price index to be consistent with the Divisia price index, the base year shares should be chosen to be average shares that apply to the entire time period between months 0 and t.

$$\frac{P(0)}{P(1)}=\frac{P(1)+\Delta_b P}{P(1)}=1+\frac{\Delta_b P}{P(1)}\approx 1+\frac{\sum_{i=1}^{n}\Delta_b p_i q_i(1)}{\sum_{m=1}^{n} p_m(1)q_m(1)}$$

using (15.67) when $t=1$ and approximating $p_i'(1)$ by the difference $\Delta_b p_i$

$$=\frac{\sum_{i=1}^{n}\{p_i(1)+\Delta_b p_i\}q_i(1)}{\sum_{m=1}^{n} p_m(1)q_m(1)}$$

$$=\frac{\sum_{i=1}^{n} p_i(0)q_i(1)}{\sum_{m=1}^{n} p_m(1)q_m(1)}=\frac{1}{P_P(p^0,p^1,q^0,q^1)} \quad (15.73)$$

where P_P is the Paasche index defined above by equation (15.6). Taking reciprocals of both sides of equation (15.73) leads to the following discrete approximation to $P(1)/P(0)$:

$$\frac{P(1)}{P(0)}\approx P_P \quad (15.74)$$

15.75 Thus, as Frisch[53] noted, both the Paasche and Laspeyres indices can be regarded as (equally valid) approximations to the continuous time Divisia price index.[54] Since the Paasche and Laspeyres indices can differ considerably in some empirical applications, it can be seen that Divisia's idea is not all that helpful in determining a *unique* discrete time index number formula.[55] What is useful about the Divisia indices is the idea that as the discrete unit of time gets smaller, discrete approximations to the Divisia indices can approach meaningful economic indices under certain conditions. Moreover, if the Divisia concept is accepted as the "correct" one for index number theory, then the corresponding "correct" discrete time counterpart might be taken as a weighted average of the chain price relatives pertaining to the adjacent periods under consideration, where the weights are somehow representative of the two periods under consideration.

Fixed base versus chain indices

15.76 In this section,[56] we discuss the merits of using the chain system for constructing price indices in the time series context versus using the fixed base system.[57]

15.77 The chain system[58] measures the change in prices going from one period to a subsequent period using a bilateral index number formula involving the prices and quantities pertaining to the two adjacent periods. These one-period rates of change (the links in the chain) are then cumulated to yield the relative levels of prices over the entire period under consideration. Thus if the bilateral price index is P, the chain system generates the following pattern of price levels for the first three periods:

$$1, P(p^0,p^1,q^0,q^1), P(p^0,p^1,q^0,q^1)\,P(p^1,p^2,q^1,q^2) \quad (15.75)$$

15.78 In contrast, the fixed base system of price levels, using the same bilateral index number formula P, simply computes the level of prices in period t relative to the base period 0 as $P(p^0,p^t,q^0,q^t)$. Thus the fixed base pattern of price levels for periods 0,1 and 2 is:

$$1, P(p^0,p^1,q^0,q^1), P(p^0,p^2,q^0,q^2) \quad (15.76)$$

15.79 Note that in both the chain system and the fixed base system of price levels defined by the formulae (15.75) and (15.76), the base period price level is set equal to 1. The usual practice in statistical agencies is to set the base period price level equal to 100. If this is done, then it is necessary to multiply each of the numbers in the formulae (15.75) and (15.76) by 100.

15.80 Because of the difficulties involved in obtaining current period information on quantities (or equivalently, on expenditures), many statistical agencies loosely base their consumer price index on the use of the Laspeyres formula (15.5) and the fixed base system. Therefore, it is of interest to look at some of the possible problems associated with the use of fixed base Laspeyres indices.

[53] "As the elementary formula of the chaining, we may get Laspeyres' or Paasche's or Edgeworth's or nearly any other formula, according as we choose the approximation principle for the steps of the numerical integration" (Frisch (1936, p. 8)).

[54] Diewert (1980, p. 444) also obtained the Paasche and Laspeyres approximations to the Divisia index, using a somewhat different approximation argument. He also showed how several other popular discrete time index number formulae could be regarded as approximations to the continuous time Divisia index.

[55] Trivedi (1981) systematically examined the problems involved in finding a "best" discrete time approximation to the Divisia indices using the techniques of numerical analysis. These numerical analysis techniques depend on the assumption that the "true" continuous time micro-price functions, $p_i(t)$, can be adequately represented by a polynomial approximation. Thus we are led to the conclusion that the "best" discrete time approximation to the Divisia index depends on assumptions that are difficult to verify.

[56] This section is largely based on the work of Hill (1988; 1993, pp. 385–390).

[57] The results in Appendix 15.4 provide some theoretical support for the use of chain indices in that it is shown that under certain conditions, the Divisia index will equal an economic index. Hence any discrete approximation to the Divisia index will approach the economic index as the time period gets shorter. Thus under certain conditions, chain indices will approach an underlying economic index.

[58] The chain principle was introduced independently into the economics literature by Lehr (1885, pp. 45–46) and Marshall (1887, p. 373). Both authors observed that the chain system would mitigate the difficulties arising from the introduction of new commodities into the economy, a point also mentioned by Hill (1993, p. 388). Fisher (1911, p. 203) introduced the term "chain system".

15.81 The main problem with the use of fixed base Laspeyres indices is that the period 0 fixed basket of commodities that is being priced out in period t can often be quite different from the period t basket. Thus if there are systematic trends in at least some of the prices and quantities[59] in the index basket, the fixed base Laspeyres price index $P_L(p^0, p^t, q^0, q^t)$ can be quite different from the corresponding fixed base Paasche price index, $P_P(p^0, p^t, q^0, q^t)$.[60] This means that both indices are likely to be an inadequate representation of the movement in average prices over the time period under consideration.

15.82 The fixed base Laspeyres quantity index cannot be used for ever: eventually, the base period quantities q^0 are so far removed from the current period quantities q^t that the base must be changed. Chaining is merely the limiting case where the base is changed each period.[61]

15.83 The main advantage of the chain system is that under normal conditions, chaining will reduce the spread between the Paasche and Laspeyres indices.[62] These two indices each provide an asymmetric perspective on the amount of price change that has occurred between the two periods under consideration and it could be expected that a single point estimate of the aggregate price change should lie between these two estimates. Thus the use of either a chained Paasche or Laspeyres index will usually lead to a smaller difference between the two and hence to estimates that are closer to the "truth".[63]

15.84 Hill (1993, p. 388), drawing on the earlier research of Szulc (1983) and Hill (1988, pp. 136–137), noted that it is not appropriate to use the chain system when prices oscillate or bounce. This phenomenon can occur in the context of regular seasonal fluctuations or in the context of price wars. However, in the context of roughly monotonically changing prices and quantities, Hill (1993, p. 389) recommended the use of chained symmetrically weighted indices (see paragraphs 15.18 to 15.32). The Fisher and Walsh indices are examples of symmetrically weighted indices.

15.85 It is possible to be a little more precise about the conditions under which to chain or not to chain. Basically, chaining is advisable if the prices and quantities pertaining to adjacent periods are *more similar* than the prices and quantities of more distant periods, since this strategy will lead to a narrowing of the spread between the Paasche and Laspeyres indices at each link.[64] Of course, one needs a measure of how similar are the prices and quantities pertaining to two periods. The similarity measures could be *relative* ones or *absolute* ones. In the case of absolute comparisons, two vectors of the same dimension are similar if they are identical and dissimilar otherwise. In the case of relative comparisons, two vectors are similar if they are proportional and dissimilar if they are non-proportional.[65] Once a similarity measure has been defined, the prices and quantities of each period can be compared to each other using this measure, and a "tree" or path that links all of the observations can be constructed where the most similar observations are compared with each other using a bilateral index number formula.[66] Hill (1995) defined the price structures between two countries to be more dissimilar the bigger the spread between P_L and P_P; i.e., the bigger is $\{P_L/P_P, P_P/P_L\}$. The problem with this measure of dissimilarity in the price structures of the two countries is that it could be the case that $P_L = P_P$ (so that the Hill measure would register a maximal degree of similarity), but p^0 could be very different from p^t. Thus there is a need for a more systematic study of similarity (or dissimilarity) measures in order to pick the "best" one that could be used as an input into Hill's (1999a; 1999b; 2001) spanning tree algorithm for linking observations.

[59] Examples of rapidly downward trending prices and upward trending quantities are computers, electronic equipment of all types, Internet access and telecommunication charges.

[60] Note that $P_L(p^0, p^t, q^0, q^t)$ will equal $P_P(p^0, p^t, q^0, q^t)$ if *either* the two quantity vectors q^0 and q^t are proportional *or* the two price vectors p^0 and p^t are proportional. Thus in order to obtain a difference between the Paasche and Laspeyres indices, non-proportionality in *both* prices and quantities is required.

[61] Regular seasonal fluctuations can cause monthly or quarterly data to "bounce"—using the term coined by Szulc (1983, p. 548)—and chaining bouncing data can lead to a considerable amount of index "drift"; i.e., if after 12 months, prices and quantities return to their levels of a year earlier, then a chained monthly index will usually not return to unity. Hence, the use of chained indices for "noisy" monthly or quarterly data is not recommended without careful consideration.

[62] See Diewert (1978, p. 895) and Hill (1988; 1993, pp. 387–388).

[63] This observation will be illustrated with an artificial data set in Chapter 19.

[64] Walsh, in discussing whether fixed base or chained index numbers should be constructed, took for granted that the precision of all reasonable bilateral index number formulae would improve, provided that the two periods or situations being compared were more similar, and hence favoured the use of chained indices: "The question is really, in which of the two courses [fixed base or chained index numbers] are we likely to gain greater exactness in the comparisons actually made? Here the probability seems to incline in favor of the second course; for the conditions are likely to be less diverse between two contiguous periods than between two periods say fifty years apart" (Walsh (1901, p. 206)).

Walsh (1921a, pp. 84–85) later reiterated his preference for chained index numbers. Fisher also made use of the idea that the chain system would usually make bilateral comparisons between price and quantity data that were more similar, and hence the resulting comparisons would be more accurate:

> The index numbers for 1909 and 1910 (each calculated in terms of 1867–1877) are compared with each other. But direct comparison between 1909 and 1910 would give a different and more valuable result. To use a common base is like comparing the relative heights of two men by measuring the height of each above the floor, instead of putting them back to back and directly measuring the difference of level between the tops of their heads (Fisher (1911, p. 204)).
>
> It seems, therefore, advisable to compare each year with the next, or, in other words, to make each year the base year for the next. Such a procedure has been recommended by Marshall, Edgeworth and Flux. It largely meets the difficulty of non-uniform changes in the Q's, for any inequalities for successive years are relatively small (Fisher (1911, pp. 423–424)).

[65] (Diewert (2002b) takes an axiomatic approach to defining various *indices* of absolute and relative dissimilarity.)

[66] Fisher (1922, pp. 271–276) hinted at the possibility of using spatial linking; i.e., of linking countries that are similar in structure. The modern literature has, however, grown as a result of the pioneering efforts of Robert Hill (1995; 1999a; 1999b; 2001). Hill (1995) used the spread between the Paasche and Laspeyres price indices as an indicator of similarity, and showed that this criterion gives the same results as a criterion that looks at the spread between the Paasche and Laspeyres quantity indices.

15.86 The method of linking observations explained in the previous paragraph, based on the similarity of the price and quantity structures of any two observations, may not be practical in a statistical agency context since the addition of a new period may lead to a reordering of the previous links. The above "scientific" method for linking observations may be useful, however, in deciding whether chaining is preferable or whether fixed base indices should be used while making month-to-month comparisons within a year.

15.87 Some index number theorists have objected to the chain principle on the grounds that it has no counterpart in the spatial context:

> They [chain indices] only apply to intertemporal comparisons, and in contrast to direct indices they are not applicable to cases in which no natural order or sequence exists. Thus the idea of a chain index for example has no counterpart in interregional or international price comparisons, because countries cannot be sequenced in a "logical" or "natural" way (there is no $k+1$ nor $k-1$ country to be compared with country k) (von der Lippe (2001, p. 12)).[67]

This is of course correct, but the approach of Hill does lead to a "natural" set of spatial links. Applying the same approach to the time series context will lead to a set of links between periods which may not be month-to-month but it will in many cases justify year-over-year linking of the data pertaining to the same month. This problem is reconsidered in Chapter 22.

15.88 It is of some interest to determine if there are index number formulae that give the same answer when either the fixed base or chain system is used. Comparing the sequence of chain indices defined by the expression (15.75) to the corresponding fixed base indices, it can be seen that we will obtain the same answer in all three periods if the index number formula P satisfies the following functional equation for all price and quantity vectors:

$$P(p^0,p^2,q^0,q^2)=P(p^0,p^1,q^0,q^1)P(p^1,p^2,q^1,q^2) \qquad (15.77)$$

If an index number formula P satisfies the equation (15.77), then P satisfies the *circularity test*.[68]

15.89 If it is assumed that the index number formula P satisfies certain properties or tests in addition to the circularity test above,[69] then Funke, Hacker and Voeller (1979) showed that P must have the following functional form, originally established by Konüs and Byushgens[70] (1926, pp. 163–166):[71]

$$P_{KB}(p^0,p^1,q^0,q^1)\equiv\prod_{i=1}^{n}\left(\frac{p_i^1}{p_i^0}\right)^{\alpha_i} \qquad (15.78)$$

where the n constants α_i satisfy the following restrictions:

$$\sum_{i=1}^{n}\alpha_i=1 \text{ and } \alpha_i>0 \quad \text{for } i=1,\ldots,n \qquad (15.79)$$

Thus under very weak regularity conditions, the only price index satisfying the circularity test is a weighted geometric average of all the individual price ratios, the weights being constant through time.

15.90 An interesting special case of the family of indices defined by equation (15.78) occurs when the weights α_i are all equal. In this case, P_{KB} reduces to the Jevons (1865) index:

$$P_J(p^0,p^1,q^0,q^1)\equiv\prod_{i=1}^{n}\left(\frac{p_i^1}{p_i^0}\right)^{\frac{1}{n}} \qquad (15.80)$$

15.91 The problem with the indices defined by Konüs and Byushgens, and Jevons is that the individual price ratios, p_i^1/p_i^0, have weights (either α_i or $1/n$) that are *independent* of the economic importance of commodity i in the two periods under consideration. Put another way, these price weights are independent of the quantities of commodity i consumed or the expenditures on commodity i during the two periods. Hence, these indices are not really suitable for use by statistical agencies at higher levels of aggregation when expenditure share information is available.

15.92 The above results indicate that it is not useful to ask that the price index P satisfy the circularity test *exactly*. It is nevertheless of some interest to find index number formulae that satisfy the circularity test to some degree of approximation, since the use of such an index number formula will lead to measures of aggregate price change that are more or less the same no matter whether we use the chain or fixed base systems. Fisher (1922, p. 284) found that deviations from circularity using his data set and the Fisher ideal price index P_F defined by equation (15.12) above were quite small. This relatively high degree of correspondence between fixed base and

[67] It should be noted that von der Lippe (2001, pp. 56–58) is a vigorous critic of all index number tests based on symmetry in the time series context, although he is willing to accept symmetry in the context of making international comparisons. "But there are good reasons *not* to insist on such criteria in the *intertemporal* case. When no symmetry exists between 0 and t, there is no point in interchanging 0 and t" (von der Lippe (2001, p. 58)).

[68] The test name is attributable to Fisher (1922, p. 413) and the concept originated from Westergaard (1890, pp. 218–219).

[69] The additional tests referred to above are: (i) positivity and continuity of $P(p^0,p^1,q^0,q^1)$ for all strictly positive price and quantity vectors p^0,p^1,q^0,q^1; (ii) the identity test; (iii) the commensurability test; (iv) $P(p^0,p^1,q^0,q^1)$ is positively homogeneous of degree one in the components of p^1, and (v) $P(p^0,p^1,q^0,q^1)$ is positively homogeneous of degree zero in the components of q^1.

[70] Konüs and Byushgens show that the index defined by equation (15.78) is exact for Cobb–Douglas (1928) preferences; see also Pollak (1983, pp. 119–120). The concept of an exact index number formula is explained in Chapter 17.

[71] The result in equation (15.78) can be derived using results in Eichhorn (1978, pp. 167–168) and Vogt and Barta (1997, p. 47). A simple proof can be found in Balk (1995). This result vindicates Irving Fisher's (1922, p. 274) intuition that "the only formulae which conform perfectly to the circular test are index numbers which have *constant weights* . . . ". Fisher (1922, p. 275) went on to assert: "But, clearly, constant weighting is not theoretically correct. If we compare 1913 with 1914, we need one set of weights; if we compare 1913 with 1915, we need, theoretically at least, another set of weights. . . . Similarly, turning from time to space, an index number for comparing the United States and England requires one set of weights, and an index number for comparing the United States and France requires, theoretically at least, another."

chain indices has been found to hold for other symmetrically weighted formulae, such as the Walsh index P_W defined by equation (15.19).[72] In most time series applications of index number theory where the base year in fixed base indices is changed every five years or so, it will not matter very much whether the statistical agency uses a fixed base price index or a chain index, provided that a symmetrically weighted formula is used.[73] The choice between a fixed base price index or chain index will depend, of course, on the length of the time series considered and the degree of variation in the prices and quantities as we go from period to period. The more prices and quantities are subject to large fluctuations (rather than smooth trends), the less the correspondence.[74]

15.93 It is possible to give a theoretical explanation for the approximate satisfaction of the circularity test for symmetrically weighted index number formulae. Another symmetrically weighted formula is the Törnqvist index P_T.[75] The natural logarithm of this index is defined as follows:

$$\ln P_T(p^0, p^1, q^0, q^1) \equiv \sum_{i=1}^{n} \frac{1}{2}(s_i^0 + s_i^1) \ln\left(\frac{p_i^1}{p_i^0}\right) \quad (15.81)$$

where the period t expenditure shares s_i^t are defined by equation (15.7). Alterman, Diewert and Feenstra (1999, p. 61) show that if the logarithmic price ratios $\ln(p_i^t/p_i^{t-1})$ trend linearly with time t and the expenditure shares s_i^t also trend linearly with time, then the Törnqvist index P_T will satisfy the circularity test exactly.[76] Since many economic time series on prices and quantities satisfy these assumptions approximately, the Törnqvist index P_T will satisfy the circularity test approximately. As is seen in Chapter 19, the Törnqvist index generally closely approximates the symmetrically weighted Fisher and Walsh indices, so that for many economic time series (with smooth trends), all three of these symmetrically weighted indices will satisfy the circularity test to a high enough degree of approximation so that it will not matter whether we use the fixed base or chain principle.

15.94 Walsh (1901, p. 401; 1921a, p. 98; 1921b, p. 540) introduced the following useful variant of the circularity test:

$$1 = P(p^0, p^1, q^0, q^1)P(p^1, p^2, q^1, q^2)\ldots P(p^T, p^0, q^T, q^0) \quad (15.82)$$

The motivation for this test is the following. Use the bilateral index formula $P(p^0, p^1, q^0, q^1)$ to calculate the change in prices going from period 0 to 1, use the same formula evaluated at the data corresponding to periods 1 and 2, $P(p^1, p^2, q^1, q^2)$, to calculate the change in prices going from period 1 to 2, ... , use $P(P^{T-1}, p^T, q^{T-1}, q^T)$ to calculate the change in prices going from period $T-1$ to T, introduce an artificial period $T+1$ that has exactly the price and quantity of the initial period 0 and use $P(p^T, p^0, q^T, q^0)$ to calculate the change in prices going from period T to 0. Finally, multiply all of these indices together. Since we end up where we started, the product of all of these indices should ideally be one. Diewert (1993a, p. 40) called this test a *multiperiod identity test*.[77] Note that if $T=2$ (so that the number of periods is three in total), then Walsh's test reduces to Fisher's (1921, p. 534; 1922, p. 64) time reversal test.[78]

15.95 Walsh (1901, pp. 423–433) showed how his circularity test could be used in order to evaluate how "good" any bilateral index number formula was. What he did was invent artificial price and quantity data for five periods, and he added a sixth period that had the data of the first period. He then evaluated the right-hand side of equation (15.82) for various formulae, $P(p^0, p^1, q^0, q^1)$, and determined how far from unity the results were. His "best" formulae had products that were close to one.[79]

15.96 This same framework is often used to evaluate the efficacy of chained *indices* versus their direct counterparts. Thus if the right-hand side of equation (15.82) turns out to be different from unity, the chained indices are said to suffer from "chain drift". If a formula does suffer from chain drift, it is sometimes recommended that fixed base indices be used in place of chained ones. However, this advice, if accepted, would *always* lead to the adoption of fixed base indices, provided that the bilateral index formula satisfies the identity test, $P(p^0, p^0, q^0, q^0) = 1$. Thus it is not recommended that Walsh's circularity test be used to decide whether fixed base or chained indices should be calculated. It is fair to use Walsh's circularity test, as he originally used it as an

[72] See, for example, Diewert (1978, p. 894)). Walsh (1901, pp. 424 and 429) found that his three preferred formulae all approximated each other very well, as did the Fisher ideal for his artificial data set.

[73] More specifically, most superlative indices (which are symmetrically weighted) will satisfy the circularity test to a high degree of approximation in the time series context. See Chapter 17 for the definition of a superlative index. It is worth stressing that fixed base Paasche and Laspeyres indices are very likely to diverge considerably over a five-year period if computers (or any other commodity which has price and quantity trends that are quite different from the trends in the other commodities) are included in the value aggregate under consideration (see Chapter 19 for some "empirical" evidence on this topic).

[74] Again, see Szulc (1983) and Hill (1988).

[75] This formula was implicitly introduced in Törnqvist (1936) and explicitly defined in Törnqvist and Törnqvist (1937).

[76] This exactness result can be extended to cover the case when there are monthly proportional variations in prices, and the expenditure shares have constant seasonal effects in addition to linear trends; see Alterman, Diewert and Feenstra (1999, p. 65).

[77] Walsh (1921a, p. 98) called his test the *circular test*, but since Fisher also used this term to describe his transitivity test defined earlier by equation (15.77), it seems best to stick to Fisher's terminology since it is well established in the literature.

[78] Walsh (1921b, pp. 540–541) noted that the time reversal test was a special case of his circularity test.

[79] This is essentially a variant of the methodology that Fisher (1922, p. 284) used to check how well various formulae corresponded to his version of the circularity test.

approximate method for deciding how "good" a particular index number formula is. To decide whether to chain or use fixed base indices, look at how similar the observations being compared are and choose the method which will best link up the most similar observations.

15.97 Various properties, axioms or tests that an index number formula could satisfy have been introduced in this chapter. In the following chapter, the test approach to index number theory is studied in a more systematic manner.

Appendix 15.1 The relationship between the Paasche and Laspeyres indices

1. Recall the notation used in paragraphs 15.11 to 15.17, above. Define the ith relative price or price relative r_i and the ith quantity relative t_i as follows:

$$r_i \equiv \frac{p_i^1}{p_i^0};\ t_i \equiv \frac{q_i^1}{q_i^0};\quad i=1,\ldots,n \qquad \text{(A15.1.1)}$$

Using formula (15.8) for the Laspeyres price index P_L and definitions (A15.1.1), we have:

$$P_L = \sum_{i=1}^{n} r_i s_i^0 \equiv r^* \qquad \text{(A15.1.2)}$$

i.e., we define the "average" price relative r^* as the base period expenditure share-weighted average of the individual price relatives, r_i.

2. Using formula (15.6) for the Paasche price index P_P, we have:

$$P_P \equiv \frac{\sum_{i=1}^{n} p_i^1 q_i^1}{\sum_{m=1}^{n} p_m^0 q_m^1} = \frac{\sum_{i=1}^{n} r_i t_i p_i^0 q_i^0}{\sum_{m=1}^{n} t_m p_m^0 q_m^0} \quad \text{using definitions (A15.1.1)}$$

$$= \frac{\sum_{i=1}^{n} r_i t_i s_i^0}{\sum_{m=1}^{n} t_m s_m^0} = \left\{ \frac{1}{\sum_{m=1}^{n} t_m s_m^0} \sum_{i=1}^{n} (r_i - r^*)(t_i - t^*) s_i^0 \right\} + r^* \qquad \text{(A15.1.3)}$$

using (A15.1.2) and $\sum_{i=1}^{n} s_i^0 = 1$ and where the "average" quantity relative t^* is defined as

$$t^* \equiv \sum_{i=1}^{n} t_i s_i^0 = Q_L \qquad \text{(A15.1.4)}$$

where the last equality follows using equation (15.11), the definition of the Laspeyres quantity index Q_L.

3. Taking the difference between P_P and P_L and using equations (A15.1.2) (A15.1.4) yields:

$$P_P - P_L = \frac{1}{Q_L} \sum_{i=1}^{n} (r_i - r^*)(t_i - t^*) s_i^0 \qquad \text{(A15.1.5)}$$

Now let r and t be discrete random variables that take on the n values r_i and t_i respectively. Let s_i^0 be the joint probability that $r = r_i$ and $t = t_i$ for $i = 1, \ldots, n$ and let the joint probability be 0 if $r = r_i$ and $t = t_j$ where $i \neq j$. It can be verified that the summation $\sum_{i=1}^{n} (r_i - r^*)(t_i - t^*) s_i^0$ on the right-hand side of equation (A15.1.5) is the covariance between the price relatives r_i and the corresponding quantity relatives t_i. This covariance can be converted into a correlation coefficient.[80] If this covariance is negative, which is the usual case in the consumer context, then P_P will be less than P_L.

[80] See Bortkiewicz (1923, pp. 374–375) for the first application of this correlation coefficient decomposition technique.

Appendix 15.2 The relationship between the Lowe and Laspeyres indices

1. Recall the notation used in paragraphs 15.33 to 15.48, above. Define the ith relative price relating the price of commodity i of month t to month 0, r_i, and the ith quantity relative, t_i, relating quantity of commodity i in base year b to month 0 t_i as follows:

$$r_i \equiv \frac{p_i^t}{p_i^0}\ t_i \equiv \frac{q_i^b}{q_i^0};\quad i=1,\ldots,n \qquad \text{(A15.2.1)}$$

As in Appendix A15.1, the Laspeyres price index $P_L(p^0, p^t, q^0)$ can be defined as r^*, the month 0 expenditure share-weighted average of the individual price relatives r_i defined in (A15.2.1) except that the month t price, p_i^t, now replaces period 1 price, p_i^1, in the definition of the ith price relative r_i:

$$r^* \equiv \sum_{i=1}^{n} r_i s_i^0 = P_L \qquad \text{(A15.2.2)}$$

2. The "average" quantity relative t^* relating the quantities of base year b to those of month 0 is defined as the month 0 expenditure share-weighted average of the individual quantity relatives t_i, defined in (A15.2.1):

$$t^* \equiv \sum_{i=1}^{n} t_i s_i^0 = Q_L \qquad \text{(A15.2.3)}$$

where $Q_L = Q_L(q^0, q^b, p^0)$ is the Laspeyres quantity index relating the quantities of month 0, q^0, to those of the year b, q^b, using the prices of month 0, p^0, as weights.

3. Using definition (15.26), the Lowe index comparing the prices in month t to those of month 0, using the quantity weights of the base year b, is equal to:

$$P_{Lo}(p^0, p^t, q^b) \equiv \frac{\sum_{i=1}^{n} p_i^t q_i^b}{\sum_{i=1}^{n} p_i^0 q_i^b} = \frac{\sum_{i=1}^{n} p_i^t t_i q_i^0}{\sum_{i=1}^{n} p_i^0 t_i q_i^0} \quad \text{using (A15.2.1)}$$

$$= \left\{ \frac{\sum_{i=1}^{n} p_i^t t_i q_i^0}{\sum_{i=1}^{n} p_i^0 q_i^0} \right\} \left\{ \frac{\sum_{i=1}^{n} p_i^0 t_i q_i^0}{\sum_{i=1}^{n} p_i^0 q_i^0} \right\}^{-1}$$

$$= \left\{ \frac{\sum_{i=1}^{n} \left(\frac{p_i^t}{p_i^0}\right) t_i p_i^0 q_i^0}{\sum_{i=1}^{n} p_i^0 q_i^0} \right\} \Big/ t^* \quad \text{using (A15.2.3)}$$

$$= \left\{ \frac{\sum_{i=1}^{n} r_i t_i p_i^0 q_i^0}{\sum_{i=1}^{n} p_i^0 q_i^0} \right\} \Big/ t^* \quad \text{using (A15.2.1)}$$

$$= \frac{\sum_{i=1}^{n} r_i t_i s_i^0}{t^*} = \frac{\sum_{i=1}^{n} (r_i - r^*) t_i s_i^0}{t^*} + \frac{\sum_{i=1}^{n} r^* t_i s_i^0}{t^*}$$

$$= \frac{\sum_{i=1}^{n} (r_i - r^*) t_i s_i^0}{t^*} + \frac{r^* \left[\sum_{i=1}^{n} r_i t_i s_i^0 \right]}{t^*}$$

$$= \frac{\sum_{i=1}^{n}(r_i - r^*)t_i s_i^0}{t^*} + \frac{r^*[t^*]}{t^*} \quad \text{using (A15.2.3)}$$

$$= \frac{\sum_{i=1}^{n}(r_i - r^*)(t_i - t^*)s_i^0}{t^*} + \frac{\sum_{i=1}^{n}(r_i - r^*)t^* s_i^0}{t^*} + r^*$$

$$= \frac{\sum_{i=1}^{n}(r_i - r^*)(t_i - t^*)s_i^0}{t^*} + \frac{t^*\left[\sum_{i=1}^{n} r_i s_i^0 - r^*\right]}{t^*} + r^*$$

$$= \frac{\sum_{i=1}^{n}(r_i - r^*)(t_i - t^*)s_i^0}{t^*} + r^* \quad \text{since } \sum_{i=1}^{n} r_i s_i^0 = r^*$$

$$= P_L(p^0, p^t, q^0) + \frac{\sum_{i=1}^{n}(r_i - r^*)(t_i - t^*)s_i^0}{Q_L(q^0, q^b, p^0)} \qquad \text{(A15.2.4)}$$

since using (A15.2.2), r^* equals the Laspeyres price index, $P_L(p^0, p^t, q^0)$, and using (A15.2.3), t^* equals the Laspeyres quantity index, $Q_L(q^0, q^b, p^0)$. Thus equation (A15.2.4) tells us that the Lowe price index using the quantities of year b as weights, $P_{Lo}(p^0, p^t, q^b)$, is equal to the usual Laspeyres index using the quantities of month 0 as weights, $P_L(p^0, p^t, q^0)$, plus a covariance term $\sum_{i=1}^{n}(r_i - r^*)(t_i - t^*)s_i^0$ between the price relatives $r_i \equiv p_i^t/p_i^0$ and the quantity relatives $t_i \equiv q_i^b/q_i^0$, divided by the Laspeyres quantity index $Q_L(q^0, q^b, p^0)$ between month 0 and base year b.

Appendix 15.3 The relationship between the Young index and its time antithesis

1. Recall that the direct Young index, $P_Y(p^0, p^t, s^b)$, was defined by equation (15.48) and its time antithesis, $P_Y^*(p^0, p^t, s^b)$, was defined by equation (15.52). Define the ith relative price between months 0 and t as

$$r_i \equiv p_i^t/p_i^0; \quad i = 1, \ldots, n \qquad \text{(A15.3.1)}$$

and define the weighted average (using the base year weights s_i^b) of the r_i as

$$r^* \equiv \sum_{i=1}^{n} s_i^b r_i \qquad \text{(A15.3.2)}$$

which turns out to equal the direct Young index, $P_Y(p^0, p^t, s^b)$. Define the deviation e_i of r_i from their weighted average r^* using the following equations:

$$r_i = r^*(1 + e_i); \quad i = 1, \ldots, n \qquad \text{(A15.3.3)}$$

If equation (A15.3.3) is substituted into equation (A15.3.2), the following equation is obtained:

$$r^* \equiv \sum_{i=1}^{n} s_i^b r^*(1 + e_i)$$

$$= r^* + r^* \sum_{i=1}^{n} s_i^b e_i \quad \text{since} \sum_{i=1}^{n} s_i^b = 1 \qquad \text{(A15.3.4)}$$

$$e^* \equiv \sum_{i=1}^{n} s_i^b e_i = 0 \qquad \text{(A15.3.5)}$$

Thus the weighted mean e^* of the deviations e_i equals 0.

2. The direct Young index, $P_Y(p^0, p^t, s^b)$, and its time antithesis, $P_Y^*(p^0, p^t, s^b)$, can be written as functions of r^*, the weights s_i^b and the deviations of the price relatives e_i as follows:

$$P_Y(p^0, p^t, s^b) = r^* \qquad \text{(A15.3.6)}$$

$$P_Y^*(p^0, p^t, s^b) = \left[\sum_{i=1}^{n} s_i^b \{r^*(1 + e_i)\}^{-1}\right]^{-1}$$

$$= r^*\left[\sum_{i=1}^{n} s_i^b (1 + e_i)^{-1}\right]^{-1} \qquad \text{(A15.3.7)}$$

3. Now regard $P_Y^*(p^0, p^t, s^b)$ as a function of the vector of deviations, $e \equiv [e_1, \ldots, e_n]$, say $P_Y^*(e)$. The second-order Taylor series approximation to $P_Y^*(e)$ around the point $e = 0_n$ is given by the following expression:[81]

$$P_Y^*(e) \approx r^* + r^* \sum_{i=1}^{n} s_i^b e_i + r^* \sum_{i=1}^{n}\sum_{j=1}^{n} s_i^b s_j^b e_i e_j - r^* \sum_{i=1}^{n} s_i^b [e_i]^2$$

$$= r^* + r^* 0 + r^* \sum_{i=1}^{n} s_i^b \left[\sum_{j=1}^{n} s_j^b e_j\right] e_i - r^* \sum_{i=1}^{n} s_i^b [e_i - e^*]^2$$

using (A15.3.5)

[81] This type of second-order approximation is attributable to Dalén (1992; 143) for the case $r^* = 1$ and to Diewert (1995a, p. 29) for the case of a general r^*.

$$= r^* + r^* \sum_{i=1}^{n} s_i^b[0]e_i - r^* \sum_{i=1}^{n} s_i^b[e_i - e^*]^2 \quad \text{using (A15.3.5)}$$

$$= P_Y(p^0, p^t, s^b) - P_Y(p^0, p^t, s^b) \sum_{i=1}^{n} s_i^b[e_i - e^*]^2$$

using (A15.3.6)

$$= P_Y(p^0, p^t, s^b) - P_Y(p^0, p^t, s^b)\text{Var } e$$

where the weighted sample variance of the vector e of price deviations is defined as

$$\text{Var } e \equiv \sum_{i=1}^{n} s_i^b[e_i - e^*]^2 \qquad \text{(A15.3.9)}$$

4. Rearranging equation (A15.3.8) gives the following approximate relationship between the direct Young index $P_Y(p^0, p^t, s^b)$ and its time antithesis $P_Y^*(p^0, p^t, s^b)$, to the accuracy of a second-order Taylor series approximation about a price point where the month t price vector is proportional to the month 0 price vector:

$$P_Y(p^0, p^t, s^b) \approx P_Y^*(p^0, p^t, s^b) + P_Y(p^0, p^t, s^b)\text{Var } e \qquad \text{(A15.3.10)}$$

Thus, to the accuracy of a second-order approximation, the direct Young index will exceed its time antithesis by a term equal to the direct Young index times the weighted variance of the deviations of the price relatives from their weighted mean. Thus the bigger is the dispersion in relative prices, the more the direct Young index will exceed its time antithesis.

Appendix 15.4 The relationship between the Divisia and economic approaches

1. Divisia's approach to index number theory relied on the theory of differentiation. Thus it does not appear to have any connection with economic theory. However, starting with Ville (1946), a number of economists[82] have established that the Divisia price and quantity indices *do* have a connection with the economic approach to index number theory. This connection is outlined in this appendix.

2. The economic approach to the determination of the price level and the quantity level is first outlined. The particular economic approach that is used here is attributable to Shephard (1953; 1970), Samuelson (1953) and Samuelson and Swamy (1974).

3. It is assumed that "the" consumer has well-defined *preferences* over different combinations of the n consumer commodities or items. Each combination of items can be represented by a positive vector $q \equiv [q_1, \ldots, q_n]$. The consumer's preferences over alternative possible consumption vectors q are assumed to be representable by a continuous, non-decreasing and concave utility function f. It is further assumed that the consumer minimizes the cost of achieving the period t utility level $u^t \equiv f(q^t)$ for periods $t = 0, 1, \ldots, T$. Thus it is assumed that the observed period t consumption vector q^t solves the following period t cost minimization problem:

$$C(u^t, p^t) \equiv \min_q \left\{ \sum_{i=1}^{n} p_i^t q_i : f(q) = u^t = f(q^t) \right\}$$
$$= \sum_{i=1}^{n} p_i^t q_i^t; \; t = 0, 1, \ldots, T \qquad \text{(A15.4.1)}$$

The period t price vector for the n commodities under consideration that the consumer faces is p^t. Note that the solution to the period t cost or expenditure minimization problem defines the *consumer's cost function*, $C(u^t, p^t)$.

4. An additional regularity condition is placed on the consumer's utility function f. It is assumed that f is (positively) linearly homogeneous for strictly positive quantity vectors. Under this assumption, the consumer's expenditure or cost function, $C(u, p)$, decomposes into $uc(p)$ where $c(p)$ is the consumer's unit cost function.[83] The following equation is obtained:

$$\sum_{i=1}^{n} p_i^t q_i^t = c(p^t) f(q^t) \quad \text{for } t = 0, 1, \ldots, T \qquad \text{(A15.4.2)}$$

Thus the period t total expenditure on the n commodities in the aggregate, $\sum_{i=1}^{n} p_i^t q_i^t$, decomposes into the product of two terms, $c(p^t) f(q^t)$. The period t unit cost, $c(p^t)$, can be identified as the period t price level P^t and the period t level of utility, $f(q^t)$, can be identified as the period t quantity level Q^t.

5. The economic price level for period t, $P^t \equiv c(p^t)$, defined in the previous paragraph, is now related to the Divisia price level for time t, $P(t)$, that was implicitly defined by the differential equation (15.67). As in paragraphs 15.65 to 15.71, think of the prices as being continuous, differentiable functions of

[82] See for example Malmquist (1953, p. 227), Wold (1953, pp. 134–147), Solow (1957), Jorgenson and Griliches (1967) and Hulten (1973), and see Balk (2000a) for a recent survey of work on Divisia price and quantity indices.

[83] See Diewert (1993b, pp.120–121) for material on unit cost functions. This material will also be covered in Chapter 17.

time, $p_i(t)$ say, for $i \equiv 1, \ldots, n$. Thus the unit cost function can be regarded as a function of time t as well; i.e., define the unit cost function as a function of t as

$$c^*(t) \equiv c[p_1(t), p_2(t), \ldots, p_n(t)] \quad \text{(A15.4.3)}$$

6. Assuming that the first-order partial derivatives of the unit cost function $c(p)$ exist, calculate the logarithmic derivative of $c^*(t)$ as follows:

$$\frac{d \ln c^*(t)}{dt} \equiv \frac{1}{c^*(t)} \frac{dc^*(t)}{dt} = \frac{\sum_{i=1}^{n} c_i[p_1(t), p_2(t), \ldots, p_n(t)] p_i'(t)}{c[p_1(t), p_2(t), \ldots, p_n(t)]} \quad \text{(A15.4.4)}$$

where $c_i[p_1(t), p_2(t), \ldots, p_N(t)] \equiv \partial c[p_1(t), p_2(t), \ldots, p_n(t)]/\partial p_i$ is the partial derivative of the unit cost function with respect to the ith price, p_i, and $p_i'(t) \equiv dp_i(t)/dt$ is the time derivative of the ith price function, $p_i(t)$. Using Shephard's (1953, p. 11) Lemma, the consumer's cost minimizing demand for commodity i at time t is:

$$q_i(t) = u(t) c_i\{p_1(t), p_2(t), \ldots, p_n(t)\} \quad \text{for } i = 1, \ldots, n \quad \text{(A15.4.5)}$$

where the utility level at time t is $u(t) = f[q_1(t), q_2(t), \ldots, q_n(t)]$. The continuous time counterpart to equations (A15.4.2) above is that total expenditure at time t is equal to total cost at time t which in turn is equal to the utility level, $u(t)$, times the period t unit cost, $c^*(t)$:

$$\sum_{i=1}^{n} p_i(t) q_i(t) = u(t) c^*(t) = u(t) c\{p_1(t), p_2(t), \ldots, p_n(t)\} \quad \text{(A15.4.6)}$$

7. The logarithmic derivative of the Divisia price level $P(t)$ can be written as (recall equation (15.67) above):

$$\frac{P'(t)}{P(t)} = \frac{\sum_{i=1}^{n} p_i'(t) q_i(t)}{\sum_{i=1}^{n} p_i(t) q_i(t)} = \frac{\sum_{i=1}^{n} p_i'(t) q_i(t)}{u(t) c^*(t)} \quad \text{using (A15.4.6)}$$

$$= \frac{\sum_{i=1}^{n} p_i'(t)[u(t) c\{p_1(t), p_2(t), \ldots, p_n(t)\}]}{u(t) c^*(t)} \quad \text{using (A15.4.5)}$$

$$= \frac{\sum_{i=1}^{n} c_i\{p_1(t), p_2(t), \ldots, p_n(t)\} p_i'(t)}{c^*(t)} = \frac{1}{c^*(t)} \frac{dc^*(t)}{dt}$$

using (A15.4.4)

$$\equiv \frac{c^{*\prime}(t)}{c^*(t)} \quad \text{(A15.4.7)}$$

Thus under the above continuous time cost-minimizing assumptions, the Divisia price level, $P(t)$, is essentially equal to the unit cost function evaluated at the time t prices, $c^*(t) \equiv c[p_1(t), p_2(t), \ldots, p_N(t)]$.

8. If the Divisia price level $P(t)$ is set equal to the unit cost function $c^*(t) \equiv c[p_1(t), p_2(t), \ldots, p_N(t)]$, then from equation (A15.4.2), it follows that the Divisia quantity level $Q(t)$ defined by equation (15.68) will equal the consumer's utility function regarded as a function of time, $f^*(t) \equiv f[q_1(t), \ldots, q_n(t)]$. Thus, under the assumption that the consumer is continuously minimizing the cost of achieving a given utility level where the utility or preference function is linearly homogeneous, it has been shown that the Divisia price and quantity levels $P(t)$ and $Q(t)$, defined implicitly by the differential equations (15.67) and (15.68), are essentially equal to the consumer's unit cost function $c^*(t)$ and utility function $f^*(t)$ respectively.[84] These are rather remarkable equalities since in principle, given the functions of time, $p_i(t)$ and $q_i(t)$, the differential equations that define the Divisia price and quantity indices can be solved numerically and hence $P(t)$ and $Q(t)$ are in principle observable (up to some normalizing constants).

9. For more on the Divisia approach to index number theory, see Vogt (1977; 1978) and Balk (2000a). An alternative approach to Divisia indices using line integrals may be found in the forthcoming companion volume *Producer price index manual* (Eurostat et al., 2004).

[84] Obviously, the scale of the utility and cost functions are not uniquely determined by the differential equations (15.62) and (15.63).

THE AXIOMATIC AND STOCHASTIC APPROACHES TO INDEX NUMBER THEORY 16

Introduction

16.1 As was seen in Chapter 15, it is useful to be able to evaluate various index number formulae that have been proposed in terms of their properties. If a formula turns out to have rather undesirable properties, this casts doubts on its suitability as an index that could be used by a statistical agency as a target index. Looking at the mathematical properties of index number formulae leads to the *test* or *axiomatic approach to index number theory*. In this approach, desirable properties for an index number formula are proposed, and it is then attempted to determine whether any formula is consistent with these properties or tests. An ideal outcome is the situation where the proposed tests are both desirable and completely determine the functional form for the formula.

16.2 The axiomatic approach to index number theory is not completely straightforward, since choices have to be made in two dimensions:

- The index number framework must be determined.
- Once the framework has been decided upon, it must be decided what tests or properties should be imposed on the index number.

The second point is straightforward: different price statisticians may have different ideas about which tests are important, and alternative sets of axioms can lead to alternative "best" index number functional forms. This point must be kept in mind while reading this chapter, since there is no universal agreement on what the "best" set of "reasonable" axioms is. Hence the axiomatic approach can lead to more than one best index number formula.

16.3 The first point about choices listed above requires further discussion. In the previous chapter, for the most part, the focus was on *bilateral index number theory*; i.e., it was assumed that prices and quantities for the same n commodities were given for two periods and the object of the index number formula was to compare the overall level of prices in one period with the other period. In this framework, both sets of price and quantity vectors were regarded as variables which could be independently varied so that, for example, variations in the prices of one period did not affect the prices of the other period or the quantities in either period. The emphasis was on comparing the overall cost of a fixed basket of quantities in the two periods or taking averages of such fixed basket indices. This is an example of an index number framework.

16.4 However, other index number frameworks are possible. For example, instead of decomposing a value ratio into a term that represents price change between the two periods times another term that represents quantity change, an attempt could be made to decompose a value aggregate for one period into a single number that represents the price level in the period times another number that represents the quantity level in the period. In the first variant of this approach, the price index number is supposed to be a function of the n commodity prices pertaining to that aggregate in the period under consideration, while the quantity index number is supposed to be a function of the n commodity quantities pertaining to the aggregate in the period. The resulting price index function was called an *absolute index number* by Frisch (1930, p. 397), a *price level* by Eichhorn (1978, p. 141) and a *unilateral price index* by Anderson, Jones and Nesmith (1997, p. 75). In a second variant of this approach, the price and quantity functions are allowed to depend on both the price and quantity vectors pertaining to the period under consideration.[1] These two variants of unilateral index number theory will be considered in paragraphs 16.11 to 16.29.[2]

16.5 The remaining approaches in this chapter are largely bilateral approaches; i.e., the prices and quantities in an aggregate are compared for two periods. In paragraphs 16.30 to 16.73 and 16.94 to 16.129, the value ratio decomposition approach is taken.[3] In paragraphs 16.30 to 16.73, the bilateral price and quantity indices, $P(p^0,p^1,q^0,q^1)$ and $Q(p^0,p^1,q^0,q^1)$, are regarded as functions of the price vectors pertaining to the two periods, p^0 and p^1, and the two quantity vectors, q^0 and q^1. Not only do the axioms or tests that are placed on the price index $P(p^0,p^1,q^0,q^1)$ reflect "reasonable" price index properties, but some tests have their origin as "reasonable" tests on the quantity index $Q(p^0,p^1,q^0,q^1)$. The approach in paragraphs 16.30 to 16.73 simultaneously determines the "best" price and quantity indices.

16.6 In paragraphs 16.74 to 16.93, attention is shifted to the *price ratios* for the n commodities between

[1] Eichhorn (1978, p. 144) and Diewert (1993d, p. 9) considered this approach.

[2] In these unilateral index number approaches, the price and quantity vectors are allowed to vary independently. In yet another index number framework, prices are allowed to vary freely but quantities are regarded as functions of the prices. This leads to the *economic approach to index number theory*, which is considered briefly in Appendix 15.4 of Chapter 15, and in more depth in Chapters 17 and 18.

[3] Recall paragraphs 15.7 to 15.17 of Chapter 15 for an explanation of this approach.

periods 0 and 1, $r_i \equiv p_i^1/p_i^0$ for $i=1,\ldots,n$. In the *unweighted stochastic approach to index number theory*, the price index is regarded as an evenly weighted average of the n price relatives or ratios, r_i. Carli (1764) and Jevons (1863; 1865) were the earlier pioneers in this approach to index number theory, with Carli using the arithmetic average of the price relatives and Jevons endorsing the geometric average (but also considering the harmonic average). This approach to index number theory will be covered in paragraphs 16.74 to 16.79. This approach is consistent with a statistical approach that regards each price ratio r_i as a random variable with mean equal to the underlying price index.

16.7 A major problem with the unweighted average of price relatives approach to index number theory is that this approach does not take into account the economic importance of the individual commodities in the aggregate. Young (1812) did advocate some form of rough weighting of the price relatives according to their relative value over the period being considered, but the precise form of the required value weighting was not indicated.[4] It was Walsh (1901, pp. 83–121; 1921a, pp. 81–90), however, who stressed the importance of weighting the individual price ratios, where the weights are functions of the associated values for the commodities in each period and each period is to be treated symmetrically in the resulting formula:

> What we are seeking is to average the variations in the exchange value of one given total sum of money in relation to the several classes of goods, to which several variations [price ratios] must be assigned weights proportional to the relative sizes of the classes. Hence the relative sizes of the classes at both the periods must be considered (Walsh (1901, p. 104)).

> Commodities are to be weighted according to their importance, or their full values. But the problem of axiometry always involves at least two periods. There is a first period and there is a second period which is compared with it. Price variations[5] have taken place between the two, and these are to be averaged to get the amount of their variation as a whole. But the weights of the commodities at the second period are apt to be different from their weights at the first period. Which weights, then, are the right ones – those of the first period or those of the second? Or should there be a combination of the two sets? There is no reason for preferring either the first or the second. Then the combination of both would seem to be the proper answer. And this combination itself involves an averaging of the weights of the two periods (Walsh (1921a, p. 90)).

16.8 Thus Walsh was the first to examine in some detail the rather intricate problems[6] involved in deciding how to weight the price relatives pertaining to an aggregate, taking into account the economic importance of the commodities in the two periods being considered. Note that the type of index number formula that Walsh was considering was of the form $P(r, v^0, v^1)$, where r is the vector of price relatives which has ith component $r_i = p_i^1/p_i^0$ and v^t is the period t value vector which has ith component $v_i^t = p_i^t q_i^t$ for $t=0,1$. His suggested solution to this weighting problem was not completely satisfactory but he did at least suggest a very useful framework for a price index, as a value-weighted average of the n price relatives. The first satisfactory solution to the weighting problem was obtained by Theil (1967, pp. 136–137) and his solution is explained in paragraphs 16.79 to 16.93.

16.9 It can be seen that one of Walsh's approaches to index number theory[7] was an attempt to determine the "best" weighted average of the price relatives, r_i. This is equivalent to using an axiomatic approach to try to determine the "best" index of the form $P(r, v^0, v^1)$. This approach is considered in paragraphs 16.94 to 16.129.[8]

16.10 The Young and Lowe indices, discussed in Chapter 15, do not fit precisely into the bilateral framework since the value or quantity weights used in these indices do not necessarily correspond to the values or quantities that pertain to either of the periods that correspond to the price vectors p^0 and p^1. The axiomatic properties of these two indices with respect to their price variables are studied in paragraphs 16.130 to 16.134.

---

[4] Walsh (1901, p. 84) refers to Young's contributions as follows:

> Still, although few of the practical investigators have actually employed anything but even weighting, they have almost always recognized the theoretical need of allowing for the relative importance of the different classes ever since this need was first pointed out, near the commencement of the century just ended, by Arthur Young. ... Arthur Young advised simply that the classes should be weighted according to their importance.

[5] A price variation is a price ratio or price relative in Walsh's terminology.

[6] Walsh (1901, pp. 104–105) realized that it would not do simply to take the arithmetic average of the values in the two periods, $[v_i^0 + v_i^1]/2$, as the "correct" weight for the ith price relative r_i since, in a period of rapid inflation, this would give too much importance to the period that had the highest prices and he wanted to treat each period symmetrically:

> But such an operation is manifestly wrong. In the first place, the sizes of the classes at each period are reckoned in the money of the period, and if it happens that the exchange value of money has fallen, or prices in general have risen, greater influence upon the result would be given to the weighting of the second period; or if prices in general have fallen, greater influence would be given to the weighting of the second period. Or in a comparison between two countries greater influence would be given to the weighting of the country with the higher level of prices. But it is plain that *the one period, or the one country, is as important, in our comparison between them, as the other, and the weighting in the averaging of their weights should really be even.*

However, Walsh was unable to come up with Theil's (1967) solution to the weighting problem, which was to use the average expenditure share $[s_i^0 + s_i^1]/2$, as the "correct" weight for the ith price relative in the context of using a weighted geometric mean of the price relatives.

[7] Walsh also considered basket-type approaches to index number theory, as was seen in Chapter 15.

[8] In paragraphs 16.94 to 16.129, rather than starting with indices of the form $P(r, v^0, v^1)$, indices of the form $P(p^0, p^1, v^0, v^1)$ are considered. However, if the test of invariance to changes in the units of measurement is imposed on this index, it is equivalent to studying indices of the form $P(r, v^0, v^1)$. Vartia (1976) also used a variation of this approach to index number theory.

The levels approach to index number theory

An axiomatic approach to unilateral price indices

16.11 Denote the price and quantity of commodity n in period t by p_i^t and q_i^t respectively for $i=1,2,\ldots,n$ and $t=0,1,\ldots,T$. The variable q_i^t is interpreted as the total amount of commodity i transacted within period t. In order to conserve the value of transactions, it is necessary that p_i^t be defined as a unit value; i.e., p_i^t must be equal to the value of transactions in commodity i for period t divided by the total quantity transacted, q_i^t. In principle, the period of time should be chosen so that variations in commodity prices within a period are very small compared to their variations between periods.[9] For $t=0,1,\ldots,T$, and $i=1,\ldots,n$, define the value of transactions in commodity i as $v_i^t \equiv p_i^t q_i^t$ and define the *total value of transactions in period t* as:

$$V^t \equiv \sum_{i=1}^{n} v_i^t = \sum_{i=1}^{n} p_i^t q_i^t \quad t=0,1,\ldots,T \tag{16.1}$$

16.12 Using the above notation, the following *levels version of the index number problem* is defined as follows: for $t=0,1,\ldots,T$, find scalar numbers P^t and Q^t such that

$$V^t = P^t Q^t \quad t=0,1,\ldots,T \tag{16.2}$$

The number P^t is interpreted as an aggregate period t price level, while the number Q^t is interpreted as an aggregate period t quantity level. The aggregate price level P^t is allowed to be a function of the period t price vector, p^t, while the aggregate period t quantity level Q^t is allowed to be a function of the period t quantity vector, q^t; hence:

$$P^t = c(p^t) \text{ and } Q^t = f(q^t) \quad t=0,1,\ldots,T \tag{16.3}$$

16.13 The functions c and f are to be determined somehow. Note that equation (16.3) requires that the functional forms for the price aggregation function c and for the quantity aggregation function f be independent of time. This is a reasonable requirement since there is no reason to change the method of aggregation as time changes.

16.14 Substituting equations (16.3) and (16.2) into equation (16.1) and dropping the superscripts t means that c and f must satisfy the following functional equation for all strictly positive price and quantity vectors:

$$c(p)f(q) = \sum_{i=1}^{n} p_i q_i \quad \text{for all } p_i > 0 \text{ and for all } q_i > 0 \tag{16.4}$$

16.15 It is natural to assume that the functions $c(p)$ and $f(q)$ are positive if all prices and quantities are positive:

$$c(p_1,\ldots,p_n) > 0; \quad f(q_1,\ldots,q_n) > 0 \quad \text{if all } p_i > 0 \text{ and all } q_i > 0 \tag{16.5}$$

16.16 Let 1_n denote an n-dimensional vector of ones. Then (16.5) implies that when $p=1_n$, $c(1_n)$ is a positive number, a for example, and when $q=1_n$, then $f(1_n)$ is also a positive number, b for example; i.e., (16.5) implies that c and f satisfy:

$$c(1_n) = a > 0; \quad f(1_n) = b > 0 \tag{16.6}$$

16.17 Let $p=1_n$ and substitute the first equation in (16.6) into equation (16.4) in order to obtain the following equation:

$$f(q) = \sum_{i=1}^{n} \frac{q_i}{a} \quad \text{for all } q_i > 0 \tag{16.7}$$

16.18 Now let $q=1_n$ and substitute the second equation in (16.6) into equation (16.4) in order to obtain the following equation:

$$c(p) = \sum_{i=1}^{n} \frac{p_i}{b} \quad \text{for all } p_i > 0 \tag{16.8}$$

16.19 Finally substitute equations (16.7) and (16.8) into the left-hand side of equation (16.4) to obtain the following equation:

$$\left(\sum_{i=1}^{n} \frac{p_i}{b}\right)\left(\sum_{i=1}^{n} \frac{q_i}{a}\right) = \sum_{i=1}^{n} p_i q_i \quad \text{for all } p_i > 0 \text{ and for all } q_i > 0 \tag{16.9}$$

If n is greater than one, it is obvious that equation (16.9) cannot be satisfied for all strictly positive p and q vectors. Thus if the number of commodities n exceeds one, then there do not exist any functions c and f that satisfy equations (16.4) and (16.5).[10]

[9] This treatment of prices as unit values over time follows Walsh (1901, p. 96; 1921a, p. 88) and Fisher (1922, p. 318). Fisher and Hicks both had the idea that the length of the period should be short enough so that variations in price within the period could be ignored, as the following quotations indicate:

> Throughout this book "the price" of any commodity or "the quantity" of it for any one year was assumed given. But what is such a price or quantity? Sometimes it is a single quotation for January 1 or July 1, but usually it is an average of several quotations scattered throughout the year. The question arises: On what principle should this average be constructed? The *practical* answer is *any* kind of average since, ordinarily, the variations during a year, so far, at least, as prices are concerned, are too little to make any perceptible difference in the result, whatever kind of average is used. Otherwise, there would be ground for subdividing the year into quarters or months until we reach a small enough period to be considered practically a point. The quantities sold will, of course, vary widely. What is needed is their sum for the year (which, of course, is the same thing as the simple arithmetic average of the per annum rates for the separate months or other subdivisions). In short, the simple arithmetic average, both of prices and of quantities, may be used. Or, if it is worth while to put any finer point on it, we may take the weighted arithmetic average for the prices, the weights being the quantities sold (Fisher (1922, p. 318)).
>
> I shall define a week as that period of time during which variations in prices can be neglected. For theoretical purposes this means that prices will be supposed to change, not continuously, but at short intervals. The calendar length of the week is of course quite arbitrary; by taking it to be very short, our theoretical scheme can be fitted as closely as we like to that ceaseless oscillation which is a characteristic of prices in certain markets (Hicks (1946, p. 122)).

[10] Eichhorn (1978, p. 144) established this result.

16.20 Thus this levels test approach to index number theory comes to an abrupt halt; it is fruitless to look for price and quantity level functions, $P^t = c(p^t)$ and $Q^t = f(q^t)$, that satisfy equations (16.2) or (16.4) and also satisfy the very reasonable positivity requirements (16.5).

16.21 Note that the levels price index function, $c(p^t)$, did not depend on the corresponding quantity vector q^t and the levels quantity index function, $f(q^t)$, did not depend on the price vector p^t. Perhaps this is the reason for the rather negative result obtained above. Hence, in the next section, the price and quantity functions are allowed to be functions of both p^t and q^t.

A second axiomatic approach to unilateral price indices

16.22 In this section, the goal is to find functions of $2n$ variables, $c(p,q)$ and $f(p,q)$, such that the following counterpart to equation (16.4) holds:

$$c(p,q)f(p,q) = \sum_{i=1}^{n} p_i q_i \quad \text{for all } p_i > 0 \text{ and for all } q_i > 0 \qquad (16.10)$$

16.23 Again, it is natural to assume that the functions $c(p,q)$ and $f(p,q)$ are positive if all prices and quantities are positive:

$$c(p_1,\ldots,p_n;q_1,\ldots,q_n) > 0; f(p_1,\ldots,p_n;q_1,\ldots,q_n) > 0 \text{ if all } p_i > 0 \text{ and all } q_i > 0 \qquad (16.11)$$

16.24 The present framework does not distinguish between the functions c and f, so it is necessary to require that these functions satisfy some "reasonable" properties. The first property imposed on c is that this function be homogeneous of degree one in its price components:

$$c(\lambda p, q) = \lambda c(p,q) \quad \text{for all } \lambda > 0 \qquad (16.12)$$

Thus, if all prices are multiplied by the positive number λ, then the resulting price index is λ times the initial price index. A similar linear homogeneity property is imposed on the quantity index f; i.e., f is to be homogeneous of degree one in its quantity components:

$$f(p, \lambda q) = \lambda f(p,q) \quad \text{for all } \lambda > 0 \qquad (16.13)$$

16.25 Note that properties (16.10), (16.11) and (16.13) imply that the price index $c(p,q)$ has the following homogeneity property with respect to the components of q:

$$\begin{aligned} c(p,\lambda q) &= \sum_{i=1}^{n} \frac{p_i \lambda q_i}{f(p,\lambda q)} \quad \text{where } \lambda > 0 \\ &= \sum_{i=1}^{n} \frac{p_i \lambda q_i}{\lambda f(p,q)} \quad \text{using (16.3)} \\ &= \sum_{i=1}^{n} \frac{p_i q_i}{f(p,q)} \\ &= c(p,q) \quad \text{using (16.10) and (16.11)} \end{aligned} \qquad (16.14)$$

Thus $c(p,q)$ is homogeneous of degree zero in its q components.

16.26 A final property that is imposed on the levels price index $c(p,q)$ is the following one. Let the positive numbers d_i be given. Then it is asked that the price index be invariant to changes in the units of measurement for the n commodities so that the function $c(p,q)$ has the following property:

$$c(d_1p_1,\ldots,d_np_n;q_1/d_1,\ldots,q_n/d_n) = c(p_1,\ldots,p_n;q_1,\ldots,q_n) \qquad (16.15)$$

16.27 It is now possible to show that properties (16.10), (16.11), (16.12), (16.14) and (16.15) on the price levels function $c(p,q)$ are inconsistent; i.e., there does not exist a function of $2n$ variables $c(p,q)$ that satisfies these very reasonable properties.[11]

16.28 To see why this is so, apply the equation (16.15), setting $d_i = q_i$ for each i, to obtain the following equation:

$$c(p_1,\ldots,p_n;q_1,\ldots,q_n) = c(p_1q_1,\ldots,p_nq_n;1,\ldots,1) \qquad (16.16)$$

If $c(p,q)$ satisfies the linear homogeneity property (16.12) so that $c(\lambda p,q) = \lambda c(p,q)$, then equation (16.16) implies that $c(p,q)$ is also linearly homogeneous in q so that $c(p,\lambda q) = \lambda c(p,q)$. But this last equation contradicts equation (16.14), which establishes the impossibility result.

16.29 The rather negative results obtained in paragraphs 16.13 to 16.21 indicate that it is fruitless to pursue the axiomatic approach to the determination of price and quantity levels, where both the price and quantity vector are regarded as independent variables.[12] Hence, in the following sections of this chapter, the axiomatic approach to the determination of a *bilateral price index* of the form $P(p^0,p^1,q^0,q^1)$ will be pursued.

The first axiomatic approach to bilateral price indices

Bilateral indices and some early tests

16.30 In this section, the strategy will be to assume that the bilateral price index formula, $P(p^0,p^1,q^0,q^1)$, satisfies a sufficient number of "reasonable" tests or properties so that the functional form for P is determined.[13] The word "bilateral"[14] refers to the assumption that the function P depends only on the data pertaining to the two situations or periods being compared; i.e., P is regarded as a function of the two sets of price and quantity vectors, p^0,p^1,q^0,q^1, that

[11] This proposition is due to Diewert (1993d, p. 9), but his proof is an adaptation of a closely related result due to Eichhorn (1978, pp. 144–145).

[12] Recall that in the economic approach, the price vector p is allowed to vary independently, but the corresponding quantity vector q is regarded as being determined by p.

[13] Much of the material in this section is drawn from sections 2 and 3 of Diewert (1992a). For more recent surveys of the axiomatic approach see Balk (1995) and von Auer (2001).

[14] Multilateral index number theory refers to the case where there are more than two situations whose prices and quantities need to be aggregated.

are to be aggregated into a single number that summarizes the overall change in the n price ratios, $p_1^1/p_1^0, \ldots, p_n^1/p_n^0$.

16.31 In this section, the value ratio decomposition approach to index number theory will be taken; i.e., along with the price index $P(p^0, p^1, q^0, q^1)$, there is a companion quantity index $Q(p^0, p^1, q^0, q^1)$ such that the product of these two indices equals the value ratio between the two periods.[15] Thus, throughout this section, it is assumed that P and Q satisfy the following *product test*:

$$V^1/V^0 = P(p^0, p^1, q^0, q^1)\, Q(p^0, p^1, q^0, q^1). \qquad (16.17)$$

The period t values, V^t, for $t=0,1$ are defined by equation (16.1). As soon as the functional form for the price index P is determined, then equation (16.17) can be used to determine the functional form for the quantity index Q. A further advantage of assuming that the product test holds is that, if a reasonable test is imposed on the quantity index Q, then equation (16.17) can be used to translate this test on the quantity index into a corresponding test on the price index P.[16]

16.32 If $n=1$, so that there is only one price and quantity to be aggregated, then a natural candidate for P is p_1^1/p_1^0, the single price ratio, and a natural candidate for Q is q_1^1/q_1^0, the single quantity ratio. When the number of commodities or items to be aggregated is greater than 1, then what index number theorists have done over the years is propose properties or tests that the price index P should satisfy. These properties are generally multidimensional analogues to the one good price index formula, p_1^1/p_1^0. Below, some 20 tests are listed that turn out to characterize the Fisher ideal price index.

16.33 It will be assumed that every component of each price and quantity vector is positive; i.e., $p^t \gg 0_n$ and $q^t \gg 0_n$[17] for $t=0,1$. If it is desired to set $q^0 = q^1$, the common quantity vector is denoted by q; if it is desired to set $p^0 = p^1$, the common price vector is denoted by p.

16.34 The first two tests, denoted T1 and T2, are not very controversial, so they will not be discussed in detail.

T1: *Positivity*:[18] $P(p^0, p^1, q^0, q^1) > 0$

T2: *Continuity*:[19] $P(p^0, p^1, q^0, q^1)$ is a continuous function of its arguments

16.35 The next two tests, T3 and T4, are somewhat more controversial.

T3: *Identity or constant prices test*:[20]

$$P(p, p, q^0, q^1) = 1$$

That is, if the price of every good is identical during the two periods, then the price index should equal unity, no matter what the quantity vectors are. The controversial aspect of this test is that the two quantity vectors are allowed to be different in the test.[21]

T4: *Fixed basket or constant quantities test*:[22]

$$P(p^0, p^1, q, q) = \frac{\sum_{i=1}^{n} p_i^1 q_i}{\sum_{i=1}^{n} p_i^0 q_i}$$

That is, if quantities are constant during the two periods so that $q^0 = q^1 \equiv q$, then the price index should equal the expenditure on the constant basket in period 1, $\sum_{i=1}^{n} p_i^1 q_i$, divided by the expenditure on the basket in period 0, $\sum_{i=1}^{n} p_i^0 q_i$.

16.36 If the price index P satisfies Test T4 and P and Q jointly satisfy the product test (16.17) above, then it is easy to show[23] that Q must satisfy the identity test $Q(p^0, p^1, q, q) = 1$ for all strictly positive vectors p^0, p^1, q. This *constant quantities test* for Q is also somewhat controversial since p^0 and p^1 are allowed to be different.

Homogeneity tests

16.37 The following four tests, T5–T8, restrict the behaviour of the price index P as the scale of any one of the four vectors p^0, p^1, q^0, q^1 changes.

T5: *Proportionality in current prices*:[24]

$$P(p^0, \lambda p^1, q^0, q^1) = \lambda P(p^0, p^1, q^0, q^1) \quad \text{for } \lambda > 0$$

That is, if all period 1 prices are multiplied by the positive number λ, then the new price index is λ times

[15] See paragraphs 15.7 to 15.25 of Chapter 15 for more on this approach, which was initially due to Fisher (1911, p. 403; 1922).

[16] This observation was first made by Fisher (1911, pp. 400–406), and the idea was pursued by Vogt (1980) and Diewert (1992a).

[17] The notation $q \gg 0_n$ means that each component of the vector q is positive; $q \geq 0_n$ means each component of q is non-negative and $q > 0_n$ means $q \geq 0_n$ and $q \neq 0_n$.

[18] Eichhorn and Voeller (1976, p. 23) suggested this test.

[19] Fisher (1922, pp. 207–215) informally suggested the essence of this test.

[20] Laspeyres (1871, p. 308), Walsh (1901, p. 308) and Eichhorn and Voeller (1976, p. 24) have all suggested this test. Laspeyres came up with this test or property to discredit the ratio of unit values index of Drobisch (1871a), which does not satisfy this test. This test is also a special case of Fisher's (1911, pp. 409–410) price proportionality test.

[21] Usually, economists assume that, given a price vector p, the corresponding quantity vector q is uniquely determined. Here, the same price vector is used but the corresponding quantity vectors are allowed to be different.

[22] The origins of this test go back at least 200 years to the Massachusetts legislature, which used a constant basket of goods to index the pay of Massachusetts soldiers fighting in the American Revolution; see Willard Fisher (1913). Other researchers who have suggested the test over the years include: Lowe (1823, Appendix, p. 95), Scrope (1833, p. 406), Jevons (1865), Sidgwick (1883, pp. 67–68), Edgeworth (1925, p. 215) originally published in 1887, Marshall (1887, p. 363), Pierson (1895, p. 332), Walsh (1901, p. 540; 1921b, pp. 543–544), and Bowley (1901, p. 227). Vogt and Barta (1997, p. 49) correctly observe that this test is a special case of Fisher's (1911, p. 411) proportionality test for quantity indexes which Fisher (1911, p. 405) translated into a test for the price index using the product test (15.3).

[23] See Vogt (1980, p. 70).

[24] This test was proposed by Walsh (1901, p. 385), Eichhorn and Voeller (1976, p. 24) and Vogt (1980, p. 68).

the old price index. Put another way, the price index function $P(p^0, p^1, q^0, q^1)$ is (positively) homogeneous of degree one in the components of the period 1 price vector p^1. Most index number theorists regard this property as a very fundamental one that the index number formula should satisfy.

16.38 Walsh (1901) and Fisher (1911, p. 418; 1922, p. 420) proposed the related proportionality test $P(p, \lambda p, q^0, q^1) = \lambda$. This last test is a combination of T3 and T5; in fact Walsh (1901, p. 385) noted that this last test implies the identity test, T3.

16.39 In the next test, instead of multiplying all period 1 prices by the same number, all period 0 prices are multiplied by the number λ.

T6: *Inverse proportionality in base period prices*:[25]

$$P(\lambda p^0, p^1, q^0, q^1) = \lambda^{-1} P(p^0, p^1, q^0, q^1) \quad \text{for } \lambda > 0$$

That is, if all period 0 prices are multiplied by the positive number λ, then the new price index is $1/\lambda$ times the old price index. Put another way, the price index function $P(p^0, p^1, q^0, q^1)$ is (positively) homogeneous of degree minus one in the components of the period 0 price vector p^0.

16.40 The following two homogeneity tests can also be regarded as invariance tests.

T7: *Invariance to proportional changes in current quantities*:

$$P(p^0, p^1, q^0, \lambda q^1) = P(p^0, p^1, q^0, q^1) \text{ for all } \lambda > 0$$

That is, if current period quantities are all multiplied by the number λ, then the price index remains unchanged. Put another way, the price index function $P(p^0, p^1, q^0, q^1)$ is (positively) homogeneous of degree zero in the components of the period 1 quantity vector q^1. Vogt (1980, p. 70) was the first to propose this test[26] and his derivation of the test is of some interest. Suppose the quantity index Q satisfies the quantity analogue to the price test T5; i.e., suppose Q satisfies $Q(p^0, p^1, q^0, \lambda q^1) = \lambda Q(p^0, p^1, q^0, q^1)$ for $\lambda > 0$. Then, using the product test (16.17), it can be seen that P must satisfy T7.

T8: *Invariance to proportional changes in base quantities*:[27]

$$P(p^0, p^1, \lambda q^0, q^1) = P(p^0, p^1, q^0, q^1) \quad \text{for all } \lambda > 0$$

That is, if base period quantities are all multiplied by the number λ, then the price index remains unchanged. Put another way, the price index function $P(p^0, p^1, q^0, q^1)$ is (positively) homogeneous of degree zero in the components of the period 0 quantity vector q^0. If the quantity index Q satisfies the following counterpart to T8: $Q(p^0, p^1, \lambda q^0, q^1) = \lambda^{-1} Q(p^0, p^1, q^0, q^1)$ for all $\lambda > 0$, then using equation (16.17), the corresponding price index P must satisfy T8. This argument provides some additional justification for assuming the validity of T8 for the price index function P.

16.41 T7 and T8 together impose the property that the price index P does not depend on the *absolute* magnitudes of the quantity vectors q^0 and q^1.

Invariance and symmetry tests

16.42 The next five tests, T9–T13, are invariance or symmetry tests. Fisher (1922, pp. 62–63, 458–460) and Walsh (1901, p. 105; 1921b, p. 542) seem to have been the first researchers to appreciate the significance of these kinds of tests. Fisher (1922, pp. 62–63) spoke of fairness but it is clear that he had symmetry properties in mind. It is perhaps unfortunate that he did not realize that there were more symmetry and invariance properties than the ones he proposed; if he had, it is likely that he would have been able to provide an axiomatic characterization for his ideal price index, as is done in paragraphs 16.53 to 16.56. The first invariance test is that the price index should remain unchanged if the *ordering* of the commodities is changed:

T9: *Commodity reversal test* (or invariance to changes in the ordering of commodities):

$$P(p^{0*}, p^{1*}, q^{0*}, q^{1*}) = P(p^0, p^1, q^0, q^1)$$

where p^{t*} denotes a permutation of the components of the vector p^t and q^{t*} denotes the same permutation of the components of q^t for $t = 0,1$. This test is attributable to Fisher (1922, p. 63)[28] and it is one of his three famous reversal tests. The other two are the time reversal test and the factor reversal test, which are considered below.

16.43 The next test asks that the index be invariant to changes in the units of measurement.

T10: *Invariance to changes in the units of measurement* (commensurability test):

$$\begin{aligned} &P(\alpha_1 p_1^0, \ldots, \alpha_n p_n^0; \alpha_1 p_1^1, \ldots, \alpha_n p_n^1; \alpha_1^{-1} q_1^0, \ldots, \alpha_n^{-1} q_n^0; \\ &\alpha_1^{-1} q_1^1, \ldots, \alpha_n^{-1} q_n^1) = P(p_1^0, \ldots, p_n^0; p_1^1, \ldots, p_n^1; \\ &q_1^0, \ldots, q_n^0; q_1^1, \ldots, q_n^1) \quad \text{for all } \alpha_1 > 0, \ldots, \alpha_n > 0 \end{aligned}$$

That is, the price index does not change if the units of measurement for each commodity are changed. The concept of this test is attributable to Jevons (1863, p. 23) and the Dutch economist Pierson (1896, p. 131), who criticized several index number formulae for not satisfying this fundamental test. Fisher (1911, p. 411) first called this test the *change of units test*; later, Fisher (1922, p. 420) called it the *commensurability test*.

[25] Eichhorn and Voeller (1976, p. 28) suggested this test.

[26] Fisher (1911, p. 405) proposed the related test $P(p^0, p^1, q^0, \lambda q^0) = P(p^0, p^1, q^0, q^0) = \sum_{i=1}^n p_i^1 q_i^0 / \sum_{i=1}^n p_i^0 q_i^0$.

[27] This test was proposed by Diewert (1992a, p. 216).

[28] "This [test] is so simple as never to have been formulated. It is merely taken for granted and observed instinctively. Any rule for averaging the commodities must be so general as to apply interchangeably to all of the terms averaged" (Fisher (1922, p. 63)).

16.44 The next test asks that the formula be invariant to the period chosen as the base period.

T11: *Time reversal test*:

$$P(p^0,p^1,q^0,q^1)=1/P(p^1,p^0,q^1,q^0)$$

That is, if the data for periods 0 and 1 are interchanged, then the resulting price index should equal the reciprocal of the original price index. Obviously, in the one good case when the price index is simply the single price ratio, this test will be satisfied (as are all the other tests listed in this section). When the number of goods is greater than one, many commonly used price indices fail this test; e.g., the Laspeyres (1871) price index, P_L defined by equation (15.5) in Chapter 15, and the Paasche (1874) price index, P_P defined by equation (15.6) in Chapter 15, both fail this fundamental test. The concept of the test is attributable to Pierson (1896, p. 128), who was so upset by the fact that many of the commonly used index number formulae did not satisfy this test that he proposed that the entire concept of an index number should be abandoned. More formal statements of the test were made by Walsh (1901, p. 368; 1921b, p. 541) and Fisher (1911, p. 534; 1922, p. 64).

16.45 The next two tests are more controversial, since they are not necessarily consistent with the economic approach to index number theory. These tests are, however, quite consistent with the weighted stochastic approach to index number theory, discussed later in this chapter.

T12: *Quantity reversal test* (quantity weights symmetry test):

$$P(p^0,p^1,q^0,q^1)=P(p^0,p^1,q^1,q^0)$$

That is, if the quantity vectors for the two periods are interchanged, then the price index remains invariant. This property means that if quantities are used to weight the prices in the index number formula, then the period 0 quantities q^0 and the period 1 quantities q^1 must enter the formula in a symmetric or even-handed manner. Funke and Voeller (1978, p. 3) introduced this test; they called it the *weight property*.

16.46 The next test is the analogue to T12 applied to quantity indices:

T13: *Price reversal test* (price weights symmetry test):[29]

$$\left(\frac{\sum_{i=1}^{n} p_i^1 q_i^1}{\sum_{i=1}^{n} p_i^0 q_i^0}\right)\Bigg/ P(p^0,p^1,q^0,q^1)=\left(\frac{\sum_{i=1}^{n} p_i^0 q_i^1}{\sum_{i=1}^{n} p_i^1 q_i^0}\right)\Bigg/ P(p^1,p^0,q^0,q^1) \qquad (16.18)$$

Thus if we use equation (16.17) to define the quantity index Q in terms of the price index P, then it can be seen that T13 is equivalent to the following property for the associated quantity index Q:

$$Q(p^0,p^1,q^0,q^1)=Q(p^1,p^0,q^0,q^1) \qquad (16.19)$$

That is, if the price vectors for the two periods are interchanged, then the quantity index remains invariant. Thus if prices for the same good in the two periods are used to weight quantities in the construction of the quantity index, then property T13 implies that these prices enter the quantity index in a symmetric manner.

Mean value tests

16.47 The next three tests, T14–T16, are mean value tests.

T14: *Mean value test for prices*:[30]

$$\min_i(p_i^1/p_i^0 : i=1,\ldots,n) \le P(p^0,p^1,q^0,q^1) \le \max_i(p_i^1/p_i^0 : i=1,\ldots,n) \qquad (16.20)$$

That is, the price index lies between the minimum price ratio and the maximum price ratio. Since the price index is supposed to be interpreted as some sort of an average of the n price ratios, p_i^1/p_i^0, it seems essential that the price index P satisfy this test.

16.48 The next test is the analogue to T14 applied to quantity indices:

T15: *Mean value test for quantities*:[31]

$$\min_i(q_i^1/q_i^0 : i=1,\ldots,n) \le \frac{(V^1/V0)}{P(p^0,p^1,q^0,q^1)} \le \max_i(q_i^1/q_i^0 : i=1,\ldots,n) \qquad (16.21)$$

where V^t is the period t value for the aggregate defined by equation (16.1). Using the product test (16.17) to define the quantity index Q in terms of the price index P, it can be seen that T15 is equivalent to the following property for the associated quantity index Q:

$$\min_i(q_i^1/q_i^0 : i=1,\ldots,n) \le Q(p^0,p^1,q^0,q^1) \le \max_i(q_i^1/q_i^0 : i=1,\ldots,n) \qquad (16.22)$$

That is, the implicit quantity index Q defined by P lies between the minimum and maximum rates of growth q_i^1/q_i^0 of the individual quantities.

16.49 In paragraphs 15.18 to 15.32 of Chapter 15, it was argued that it is very reasonable to take an average of the Laspeyres and Paasche price indices as a single "best" measure of overall price change. This point of

[29] This test was proposed by Diewert (1992a, p. 218).

[30] This test seems to have been first proposed by Eichhorn and Voeller (1976, p. 10).

[31] This test was proposed by Diewert (1992a, p. 219).

view can be turned into a test:

T16: *Paasche and Laspeyres bounding test*:[32]

The price index P lies between the Laspeyres and Paasche indices, P_L and P_P, defined by equations (15.5) and (15.6) in Chapter 15.
A test could be proposed where the implicit quantity index Q that corresponds to P via equation (16.17) is to lie between the Laspeyres and Paasche quantity indices, Q_P and Q_L, defined by equations (15.10) and (15.11) in Chapter 15. However, the resulting test turns out to be equivalent to test T16.

Monotonicity tests

16.50 The final four tests, T17–T20, are monotonicity tests; i.e., how should the price index $P(p^0,p^1,q^0,q^1)$ change as any component of the two price vectors p^0 and p^1 increases or as any component of the two quantity vectors q^0 and q^1 increases?

T17: *Monotonicity in current prices*:

$$P(p^0,p^1,q^0,q^1) < P(p^0,p^2,q^0,q^1) \text{ if } p^1 < p^2$$

That is, if some period 1 price increases, then the price index must increase, so that $P(p^0,p^1,q^0,q^1)$ is increasing in the components of p^1. This property was proposed by Eichhorn and Voeller (1976, p. 23) and it is a very reasonable property for a price index to satisfy.

T18: *Monotonicity in base prices*: $P(p^0,p^1,q^0,q^1) >$

$$P(p^2,p^1,q^0,q^1) \text{ if } p^0 < p^2$$

That is, if any period 0 price increases, then the price index must decrease, so that $P(p^0,p^1,q^0,q^1)$ is decreasing in the components of p^0. This very reasonable property was also proposed by Eichhorn and Voeller (1976, p. 23).

T19: *Monotonicity in current quantities*:

if $q^1 < q^2$, then

$$\left(\frac{\sum_{i=1}^{n} p_i^1 q_i^1}{\sum_{i=1}^{n} p_i^0 q_i^0}\right) \Big/ P(p^0,p^1,q^0,q^1)$$

$$< \left(\frac{\sum_{i=1}^{n} p_i^1 q_i^2}{\sum_{i=1}^{n} p_i^0 q_i^0}\right) \Big/ P(p^0,p^1,q^0,q^2) \qquad (16.23)$$

T20: *Monotonicity in base quantities*: if $q^0 < q^2$, then

$$\left(\frac{\sum_{i=1}^{n} p_i^1 q_i^1}{\sum_{i=1}^{n} p_i^0 q_i^0}\right) \Big/ P(p^0,p^1,q^0,q^1)$$

$$> \left(\frac{\sum_{i=1}^{n} p_i^1 q_i^1}{\sum_{i=1}^{n} p_i^0 q_i^2}\right) \Big/ P(p^0,p^1,q^2,q^1) \qquad (16.24)$$

16.51 Let Q be the implicit quantity index that corresponds to P using equation (16.17). Then it is found that T19 translates into the following inequality involving Q:

$$Q(p^0,p^1,q^0,q^1) < Q(p^0,p^1,q^0,q^2) \quad \text{if } q^1 < q^2 \quad (16.25)$$

That is, if any period 1 quantity increases, then the implicit quantity index Q that corresponds to the price index P must increase. Similarly, we find that T20 translates into:

$$Q(p^0,p^1,q^0,q^1) > Q(p^0,p^1,q^2,q^1) \quad \text{if } q^0 < q^2 \quad (16.26)$$

That is, if any period 0 quantity increases, then the implicit quantity index Q must decrease. Tests T19 and T20 are attributable to Vogt (1980, p. 70).

16.52 This concludes the listing of tests. The next section offers an answer to the question of whether any index number formula $P(p^0,p^1,q^0,q^1)$ exists that can satisfy all 20 tests.

The Fisher ideal index and the test approach

16.53 It can be shown that the only index number formula $P(p^0,p^1,q^0,q^1)$ which satisfies tests T1–T20 is the Fisher ideal price index P_F defined as the geometric mean of the Laspeyres and Paasche indices:[33]

$$P_F(p^0,p^1,q^0,q^1) \equiv \{P_L(p^0,p^1,q^0,q^1)P_p(p^0,p^1,q^0,q^1)\}^{1/2} \qquad (16.27)$$

16.54 It is relatively straightforward to show that the Fisher index satisfies all 20 tests. The more difficult part of the proof is to show that the Fisher index is the *only* index number formula that satisfies these tests. This part of the proof follows from the fact that, if P satisfies the positivity test T1 and the three reversal tests, T11–T13, then P must equal P_F. To see this, rearrange the terms in the statement of test T13 into the

[32] Bowley (1901, p. 227) and Fisher (1922, p. 403) both endorsed this property for a price index.

[33] See Diewert (1992a, p. 221).

following equation:

$$\frac{\sum_{i=1}^{n} p_i^1 q_i^1 \Big/ \sum_{i=1}^{n} p_i^0 q_i^0}{\sum_{i=1}^{n} p_i^0 q_i^1 \Big/ \sum_{i=1}^{n} p_i^1 q_i^0} = \frac{P(p^0,p^1,q^0,q^1)}{P(p^1,p^0,q^0,q^1)}$$

$$= \frac{P(p^0,p^1,q^0,q^1)}{P(p^1,p^0,q^1,q^0)}$$

using T12, the quantity reversal test

$$= P(p^0,p^1,q^0,q^1)P(p^0,p^1,q^0,q^1)$$

using T11, the time reversal test (16.28)

Now take positive square roots of both sides of equation (16.28). It can be seen that the left-hand side of the equation is the Fisher index $P_F(p^0,p^1,q^0,q^1)$ defined by equation (16.27) and the right-hand side is $P(p^0,p^1,q^0,q^1)$. Thus if P satisfies T1, T11, T12 and T13, it must equal the Fisher ideal index P_F.

16.55 The quantity index that corresponds to the Fisher price index using the product test (16.17) is Q_F, the Fisher quantity index, defined by equation (15.14) in Chapter 15.

16.56 It turns out that P_F satisfies yet another test, T21, which was Fisher's (1921, p. 534; 1922, pp. 72–81) third reversal test (the other two being T9 and T11):

T21: *Factor reversal test* (functional form symmetry test):

$$P(p^0,p^1,q^0,q^1)P(q^0,q^1,p^0,p^1) = \frac{\sum_{i=1}^{n} p_i^1 q_i^1}{\sum_{i=1}^{n} p_i^0 q_i^0} \qquad (16.29)$$

A justification for this test is the following: if $P(p^0, p^1,q^0,q^1)$ is a good functional form for the price index, then, if the roles of prices and quantities are reversed, $P(q^0,q^1,p^0,p^1)$ ought to be a good functional form for a quantity index (which seems to be a correct argument) and thus the product of the price index $P(p^0,p^1,q^0,q^1)$ and the quantity index $Q(p^0,p^1,q^0,q^1) = P(q^0,q^1,p^0,p^1)$ ought to equal the value ratio, V^1/V^0. The second part of this argument does not seem to be valid, and thus many researchers over the years have objected to the factor reversal test. Nevertheless, if T21 is accepted as a basic test, Funke and Voeller (1978, p. 180) showed that the only index number function $P(p^0,p^1,q^0,q^1)$ which satisfies T1 (positivity), T11 (time reversal test), T12 (quantity reversal test) and T21 (factor reversal test) is the Fisher ideal index P_F defined by equation (16.27). Thus the price reversal test T13 can be replaced by the factor reversal test in order to obtain a minimal set of four tests that lead to the Fisher price index.[34]

The test performance of other indices

16.57 The Fisher price index P_F satisfies all 20 of the tests T1–T20 listed above. Which tests do other commonly used price indices satisfy? Recall the Laspeyres index P_L defined by equation (15.5), the Paasche index P_P defined by equation (15.6), the Walsh index P_W defined by equation (15.19) and the Törnqvist index P_T defined by equation (15.81) in Chapter 15.

16.58 Straightforward computations show that the Paasche and Laspeyres price indices, P_L and P_P, fail only the three reversal tests, T11, T12 and T13. Since the quantity and price reversal tests, T12 and T13, are somewhat controversial and hence can be discounted, the test performance of P_L and P_P seems at first sight to be quite good. The failure of the time reversal test, T11, is nevertheless a severe limitation associated with the use of these indices.

16.59 The Walsh price index, P_W, fails four tests: T13, the price reversal test; T16, the Paasche and Laspeyres bounding test; T19, the monotonicity in current quantities test; and T20, the monotonicity in base quantities test.

16.60 Finally, the Törnqvist price index P_T fails nine tests: T4 (the fixed basket test), the quantity and price reversal tests T12 and T13, T15 (the mean value test for quantities), T16 (the Paasche and Laspeyres bounding test) and the four monotonicity tests T17 to T20. Thus the Törnqvist index is subject to a rather high failure rate from the viewpoint of this axiomatic approach to index number theory.[35]

16.61 The tentative conclusion that can be drawn from the above results is that, from the viewpoint of this particular bilateral test approach to index numbers, the Fisher ideal price index P_F appears to be "best" since it satisfies all 20 tests. The Paasche and Laspeyres indices are next best if we treat each test as being equally important. Both of these indices, however, fail the very important time reversal test. The remaining two indices, the Walsh and Törnqvist price indices, both satisfy the time reversal test but the Walsh index emerges as being "better" since it passes 16 of the 20 tests whereas the Törnqvist only satisfies 11 tests.[36]

The additivity test

16.62 There is an additional test that many national income accountants regard as very important: the *additivity test*. This is a test or property that is placed on the implicit quantity index $Q(p^0,p^1,q^0,q^1)$ that corresponds to the price index $P(p^0,p^1,q^0,q^1)$ using the product test (16.17). This test states that the implicit quantity index has the

[34] Other characterizations of the Fisher price index can be found in Funke and Voeller (1978) and Balk (1985; 1995).

[35] It is shown in Chapter 19, however, that the Törnqvist index approximates the Fisher index quite closely using "normal" time series data that are subject to relatively smooth trends. Hence, under these circumstances, the Törnqvist index can be regarded as passing the 20 tests to a reasonably high degree of approximation.

[36] This assertion needs to be qualified: there are many other tests that we have not discussed, and price statisticians might hold different opinions regarding the importance of satisfying various sets of tests. Other tests are discussed by von Auer (2001; 2002), Eichhorn and Voeller (1976), Balk (1995) and Vogt and Barta (1997), among others. It is shown in paragraphs 16.101 to 16.135 that the Törnqvist index is ideal when considered under a different set of axioms.

following form:

$$Q(p^0,p^1,q^0,q^1)=\frac{\sum_{i=1}^{n} p_i^* q_i^1}{\sum_{m=1}^{n} p_m^* q_m^0} \quad (16.30)$$

where the common across-periods *price* for commodity i, p_i^* for $i=1,\ldots,n$, can be a function of all $4n$ prices and quantities pertaining to the two periods or situations under consideration, p^0,p^1,q^0,q^1. In the literature on making multilateral comparisons (i.e., comparisons between more than two situations), it is quite common to assume that the quantity comparison between any two regions can be made using the two regional quantity vectors, q^0 and q^1, and a common reference price vector, $P^* \equiv (p_1^*,\ldots,p_n^*)$.[37]

16.63 Obviously, different versions of the additivity test can be obtained if further restrictions are placed on precisely which variables each reference price p_i^* depends. The simplest such restriction is to assume that each p_i^* depends only on the commodity i prices pertaining to each of the two situations under consideration, p_i^0 and p_i^1. If it is further assumed that the functional form for the weighting function is the same for each commodity, so that $p_i^*=m(p_i^0,p_i^1)$ for $i=1,\ldots,n$, then we are led to the *unequivocal quantity index* postulated by Knibbs (1924, p. 44).

16.64 The theory of the *unequivocal quantity index* (or the *pure quantity index*)[38] parallels the theory of the pure price index outlined in paragraphs 15.24 to 15.32 of Chapter 15. An outline of this theory is given here. Let the pure quantity index Q_K have the following functional form:

$$Q_K(p^0,p^1,q^0,q^1)\equiv\frac{\sum_{i=1}^{n} q_i^1 m(p_i^0,p_i^1)}{\sum_{k=1}^{n} q_k^0 m(p_k^0,p_k^1)} \quad (16.31)$$

It is assumed that the price vectors p^0 and p^1 are strictly positive and the quantity vectors q^0 and q^1 are non-negative but have at least one positive component.[39] The problem is to determine the functional form for the averaging function m if possible. To do this, it is necessary to impose some tests or properties on the pure quantity index Q_K. As was the case with the pure price index, it is very reasonable to ask that the quantity index satisfy the *time reversal test*:

$$Q_K(p^1,p^0,q^1,q^0)=\frac{1}{Q_K(p^0,p^1,q^0,q^1)} \quad (16.32)$$

16.65 As was the case with the theory of the unequivocal price index, it can be seen that if the unequivocal quantity index Q_K is to satisfy the time reversal test (16.32), the mean function in equation (16.31) must be *symmetric*. It is also asked that Q_K satisfy the following *invariance to proportional changes in current prices test*.

$$Q_K(p^0,\lambda p^1,q^0,q^1)=Q_K(p^0,p^1,q^0,q^1)$$
$$\text{for all } p^0,p^1,q^0,q^1 \text{ and all } \lambda>0 \quad (16.33)$$

16.66 The idea behind this invariance test is this: the quantity index $Q_K(p^0,p^1,q^0,q^1)$ should depend only on the *relative* prices in each period and it should not depend on the amount of inflation between the two periods. Another way to interpret test (16.33) is to look at what the test implies for the corresponding implicit price index, P_{IK}, defined using the product test (16.17). It can be shown that if Q_K satisfies equation (16.33), then the corresponding implicit price index P_{IK} will satisfy test T5 above, the *proportionality in current prices test*. The two tests, (16.32) and (16.33), determine the precise functional form for the pure quantity index Q_K defined by equation (16.31): the *pure quantity index* or Knibbs' *unequivocal quantity index* Q_K must be the Walsh quantity index Q_W[40] defined by:

$$Q_W(p^0,p^1,q^0,q^1)\equiv\frac{\sum_{i=1}^{n} q_i^1\sqrt{p_i^0p_i^1}}{\sum_{k=1}^{n} q_k^0\sqrt{p_k^0p_k^1}} \quad (16.34)$$

16.67 Thus with the addition of two tests, the pure price index P_K must be the Walsh price index P_W defined by equation (15.19) in Chapter 15 and with the addition of the same two tests (but applied to quantity indices instead of price indices), the pure quantity index Q_K must be the Walsh quantity index Q_W defined by equation (16.34). Note, however, that the product of the Walsh price and quantity indices is *not* equal to the expenditure ratio, V^1/V^0. Thus believers in the pure or unequivocal price and quantity index concepts have to choose one of these two concepts; they cannot both apply simultaneously.[41]

16.68 If the quantity index $Q(p^0,p^1,q^0,q^1)$ satisfies the additivity test (16.30) for some price weights p_i^*, then the percentage change in the quantity aggregate, $Q(p^0,p^1,q^0,q^1)-1$, can be rewritten as follows:

$$Q(p^0,p^1,q^0,q^1)-1=\frac{\sum_{i=1}^{n} p_i^* q_i^1}{\sum_{m=1}^{n} p_m^* q_m^0}-1=\frac{\sum_{i=1}^{n} p_i^* q_i^1-\sum_{m=1}^{n} p_m^* q_m^0}{\sum_{m=1}^{n} p_m^* q_m^0}$$
$$=\sum_{i=1}^{n} w_i(q_i^1-q_i^0) \quad (16.35)$$

[37] Hill (1993, p. 395–397) termed such multilateral methods *the block approach* while Diewert (1996a, pp. 250–251) used the term *average price approaches.* Diewert (1999b, p. 19) used the term *additive multilateral system.* For axiomatic approaches to multilateral index number theory, see Balk (1996a; 2001) and Diewert (1999b).

[38] Diewert (2001) used this term.

[39] It is assumed that $m(a,b)$ has the following two properties: $m(a,b)$ is a positive and continuous function, defined for all positive numbers a and b, and $m(a,a)=a$ for all $a>0$.

[40] This is the quantity index that corresponds to the price index 8 defined by Walsh (1921a, p. 101).

[41] Knibbs (1924) did not notice this point.

where the *weight* for commodity i, w_i, is defined as

$$w_i \equiv \frac{p_i^*}{\sum_{m=1}^{n} p_m^* q_m^0}; \quad i=1,\ldots,n \tag{16.36}$$

Note that the change in commodity i going from situation 0 to situation 1 is $q_i^1 - q_i^0$. Thus the ith term on the right-hand side of equation (16.35) is the contribution of the change in commodity i to the overall percentage change in the aggregate going from period 0 to 1. Business analysts often want statistical agencies to provide decompositions such as equation (16.35) so that they can decompose the overall change in an aggregate into sector-specific components of change.[42] Thus there is a demand on the part of users for additive quantity indices.

16.69 For the Walsh quantity index defined by equation (16.34), the ith weight is

$$w_{W_i} \equiv \frac{\sqrt{p_i^0 p_i^1}}{\sum_{m=1}^{n} q_m^0 \sqrt{p_m^0 p_m^1}}; \quad i=1,\ldots,n \tag{16.37}$$

Thus the Walsh quantity index Q_W has a percentage decomposition into component changes of the form of equation (16.35), where the weights are defined by equation (16.37).

16.70 It turns out that the Fisher quantity index Q_F, defined by equation (15.14) in Chapter 15, also has an additive percentage change decomposition of the form given by equation (16.35).[43] The ith weight w_{F_i} for this Fisher decomposition is rather complicated and depends on the Fisher quantity index $Q_F(p^0,p^1,q^0,q^1)$ as follows:[44]

$$w_{F_i} \equiv \frac{w_i^0 + (Q_F)^2 w_i^1}{1+Q_F}; \quad i=1,\ldots,n \tag{16.38}$$

where Q_F is the value of the Fisher quantity index, $Q_F(p^0,p^1,q^0,q^1)$, and the period t normalized price for commodity i, w_i^t, is defined as the period i price p_i^t divided by the period t expenditure on the aggregate:

$$w_i^t \equiv \frac{p_i^t}{\sum_{m=1}^{n} p_m^t q_m^t}; \quad t=0,1; \quad i=1,\ldots,n \tag{16.39}$$

16.71 Using the weights w_{F_i} defined by equations (16.38) and (16.39), the following exact decomposition is obtained for the Fisher ideal quantity index:

$$Q_F(p^0,p^1,q^0,q^1)-1 = \sum_{i=1}^{n} w_{F_i}(q_i^1 - q_i^0) \tag{16.40}$$

Thus the Fisher quantity index has an additive percentage change decomposition.[45]

16.72 Because of the symmetric nature of the Fisher price and quantity indices, it can be seen that the Fisher price index P_F defined by equation (16.27) also has the following additive percentage change decomposition:

$$P_F(p^0,p^1,q^0,q^1)-1 = \sum_{i=1}^{n} v_{F_i}(p_i^1 - p_i^0) \tag{16.41}$$

where the commodity i weight v_{F_i} is defined as

$$v_{F_i} \equiv \frac{v_i^0 + (P_F)^2 v_i^1}{1+P_F}; \quad i=1,\ldots,n \tag{16.42}$$

where P_F is the value of the Fisher price index, $P_F(p^0,p^1,q^0,q^1)$, and the period t normalized quantity for commodity i, v_i^t, is defined as the period i quantity q_i^t divided by the period t expenditure on the aggregate:

$$v_i^t \equiv \frac{q_i^t}{\sum_{m=1}^{n} p_m^t q_m^t}; \quad t=0,1; \quad i=1,\ldots,n \tag{16.43}$$

16.73 The above results show that the Fisher price and quantity indices have exact additive decompositions into components that give the contribution to the overall change in the price (or quantity) index of the change in each price (or quantity).

The stochastic approach to price indices

The early unweighted stochastic approach

16.74 The stochastic approach to the determination of the price index can be traced back to the work of Jevons (1863; 1865) and Edgeworth (1888) over 100 years ago.[46] The basic idea behind the (unweighted) stochastic approach is that each price relative, p_i^1/p_i^0 for $i=1,2,\ldots,n$, can be regarded as an estimate of a common inflation rate α between periods 0 and 1.[47]

It is assumed that

$$\frac{p_i^1}{p_i^0} = \alpha + \varepsilon_i; \quad i=1,2,\ldots,n \tag{16.44}$$

where α is the common inflation rate and the ε_i are random variables with mean 0 and variance σ^2. The least

[42] Business and government analysts also often demand an analogous decomposition of the change in price aggregate into sector-specific components that add up.

[43] The Fisher quantity index also has an additive decomposition of the type defined by equation (16.30) attributable to Van Ijzeren (1987, p. 6). The ith reference price p_i^* is defined as $p_i^* \equiv (1/2)p_i^0 + (1/2)p_i^1 / P_F(p^0,p^1,q^0,q^1)$ for $i=1,\ldots,n$ and where P_F is the Fisher price index. This decomposition was also independently derived by Dikhanov (1997). The Van Ijzeren decomposition for the Fisher quantity index is currently being used by the US Bureau of Economic Analysis; see Moulton and Seskin (1999, p. 16) and Ehemann, Katz and Moulton (2002).

[44] This decomposition was obtained by Diewert (2002a) and Reinsdorf, Diewert and Ehemann (2002). For an economic interpretation of this decomposition, see Diewert (2002a).

[45] To verify the exactness of the decomposition, substitute equation (16.38) into equation (16.40) and solve the resulting equation for Q_F. It is found that the solution is equal to Q_F defined by equation (15.14) in Chapter 15.

[46] For references to the literature, see Diewert (1993a, pp. 37–38; 1995a; 1995b).

[47] "In drawing our averages the independent fluctuations will more or less destroy each other; the one required variation of gold will remain undiminished" (Jevons (1863, p. 26)).

squares or maximum likelihood estimator for α is the Carli (1764) price index P_C defined as

$$P_C(p^0,p^1) \equiv \sum_{i=1}^{n} \frac{1}{n}\frac{p_i^1}{p_i^0} \qquad (16.45)$$

A drawback of the Carli price index is that it does not satisfy the time reversal test, i.e., $P_C(p^1,p^0) \neq 1/P_C(p^0,p^1)$.[48]

16.75 Now change the stochastic specification and assume that the logarithm of each price relative, $\ln(p_i^1/p_i^0)$, is an unbiased estimate of the logarithm of the inflation rate between periods 0 and 1, β say. The counterpart to equation (16.44) is:

$$\ln\left(\frac{p_i^1}{p_i^0}\right) = \beta + \varepsilon_i; \quad i=1,2,\ldots,n \qquad (16.46)$$

where $\beta \equiv \ln \alpha$ and the ε_i are independently distributed random variables with mean 0 and variance σ^2. The least squares or maximum likelihood estimator for β is the logarithm of the geometric mean of the price relatives. Hence the corresponding estimate for the common inflation rate α[49] is the Jevons (1865) price index P_J defined as follows:

$$P_J(p^0,p^1) \equiv \prod_{i=1}^{n} \sqrt[n]{\frac{p_i^1}{p_i^0}}. \qquad (16.47)$$

16.76 The Jevons price index P_J does satisfy the time reversal test and hence is much more satisfactory than the Carli index P_C. Both the Jevons and Carli price indices nevertheless suffer from a fatal flaw: each price relative p_i^1/p_i^0 is regarded as being equally important and is given an equal weight in the index number formulae (16.45) and (16.47). John Maynard Keynes was particularly critical of this unweighted stochastic approach to index number theory.[50] He directed the following criticism towards this approach, which was vigorously advocated by Edgeworth (1923):

> Nevertheless I venture to maintain that such ideas, which I have endeavoured to expound above as fairly and as plausibly as I can, are root-and-branch erroneous. The "errors of observation", the "faulty shots aimed at a single bull's eye" conception of the index number of prices, Edgeworth's "objective mean variation of general prices", is the result of confusion of thought. There is no bull's eye. There is no moving but unique centre, to be called the general price level or the objective mean variation of general prices, round which are scattered the moving price levels of individual things. There are all the various, quite definite, conceptions of price levels of composite commodities appropriate for various purposes and inquiries which have been scheduled above, and many others too. There is nothing else. Jevons was pursuing a mirage.
>
> What is the flaw in the argument? In the first place it assumed that the fluctuations of individual prices round the "mean" are "random" in the sense required by the theory of the combination of independent observations. In this theory the divergence of one "observation" from the true position is assumed to have no influence on the divergences of other "observations". But in the case of prices, a movement in the price of one commodity necessarily influences the movement in the prices of other commodities, whilst the magnitudes of these compensatory movements depend on the magnitude of the change in expenditure on the first commodity as compared with the importance of the expenditure on the commodities secondarily affected. Thus, instead of "independence", there is between the "errors" in the successive "observations" what some writers on probability have called "connexity", or, as Lexis expressed it, there is "sub-normal dispersion".
>
> We cannot, therefore, proceed further until we have enunciated the appropriate law of connexity. But the law of connexity cannot be enunciated without reference to the relative importance of the commodities affected—which brings us back to the problem that we have been trying to avoid, of weighting the items of a composite commodity (Keynes (1930, pp. 76–77)).

The main point Keynes seemed to be making in the above quotation is that prices in the economy are not independently distributed from each other and from quantities. In current macroeconomic terminology, Keynes can be interpreted as saying that a macroeconomic shock will be distributed across all prices and quantities in the economy through the normal interaction between supply and demand; i.e., through the workings of the general equilibrium system. Thus Keynes seemed to be leaning towards the economic approach to index number theory (even before it was developed to any great extent), where quantity movements are functionally related to price movements. A second point that Keynes made in the above quotation is that there is no such thing as *the* inflation rate; there are only price changes that pertain to well-specified sets of commodities or transactions; i.e., the domain of definition of the price index must be carefully specified.[51] A final point that Keynes made is that price

[48] In fact, Fisher (1922, p. 66) noted that $P_C(p^0,p^1)P_C(p^1,p^0) \geq 1$ unless the period 1 price vector p^1 is proportional to the period 0 price vector p^0; i.e., Fisher showed that the Carli index has a definite upward bias. He urged statistical agencies not to use this formula. Walsh (1901, pp. 331, 530) also discovered this result for the case $n=2$.

[49] Greenlees (1999) pointed out that although $(1/n)\sum_{i=1}^{n} \ln(p_i^1/p_i^0)$ is an unbiased estimator for β, the corresponding exponential of this estimator, P_J defined by equation (16.47), will generally not be an unbiased estimator for α under our stochastic assumptions. To see this, let $x_i = \ln p_i^1/p_i^0$. Taking expectations, we have: $Ex_i = \beta = \ln \alpha$. Define the positive, convex function f of one variable x by $f(x) \equiv e^x$. By Jensen's (1906) inequality, $Ef(x) \geq f(Ex)$. Letting x equal the random variable x_i, this inequality becomes: $E(p_i^1/p_i^0) = Ef(x_i) \geq f(Ex_i) = f(\beta) = e^\beta = e^{\ln \alpha} = \alpha$. Thus for each n, $E(p_i^1/p_i^0) \geq \alpha$, and it can be seen that the Jevons price index will generally have an upward bias under the usual stochastic assumptions.

[50] Walsh (1901, p. 83) also stressed the importance of proper weighting according to the economic importance of the commodities in the periods being compared: "But to assign uneven weighting with approximation to the relative sizes, either over a long series of years or for every period separately, would not require much additional trouble; and even a rough procedure of this sort would yield results far superior to those yielded by even weighting. It is especially absurd to refrain from using roughly reckoned uneven weighting on the ground that it is not accurate, and instead to use even weighting, which is much more inaccurate."

[51] See paragraphs 15.7 to 15.17 in Chapter 15 for additional discussion on this point.

movements must be weighted by their economic importance, i.e., by quantities or expenditures.

16.77 In addition to the above theoretical criticisms, Keynes also made the following strong empirical attack on Edgeworth's unweighted stochastic approach:

> The Jevons–Edgeworth "objective mean variation of general prices", or "indefinite" standard, has generally been identified, by those who were not as alive as Edgeworth himself was to the subtleties of the case, with the purchasing power of money – if only for the excellent reason that it was difficult to visualise it as anything else. And since any respectable index number, however weighted, which covered a fairly large number of commodities could, in accordance with the argument, be regarded as a fair approximation to the indefinite standard, it seemed natural to regard any such index as a fair approximation to the purchasing power of money also.
>
> Finally, the conclusion that all the standards "come to much the same thing in the end" has been reinforced "inductively" by the fact that rival index numbers (all of them, however, of the wholesale type) have shown a considerable measure of agreement with one another in spite of their different compositions... On the contrary, the tables given above (pp. 53, 55) supply strong presumptive evidence that over long period as well as over short period the movements of the wholesale and of the consumption standards respectively are capable of being widely divergent (Keynes (1930, pp. 80–81)).

In the above quotation, Keynes noted that the proponents of the unweighted stochastic approach to price change measurement were comforted by the fact that all of the then existing (unweighted) indices of wholesale prices showed broadly similar movements. Keynes showed empirically, however, that his wholesale price indices moved quite differently from his consumer price indices.

16.78 In order to overcome the above criticisms of the unweighted stochastic approach to index numbers, it is necessary to:

- have a definite domain of definition for the index number;
- weight the price relatives by their economic importance.[52]

Alternative methods of weighting are discussed in the following sections.

The weighted stochastic approach

16.79 Walsh (1901, pp. 88–89) seems to have been the first index number theorist to point out that a sensible stochastic approach to measuring price change means that individual price relatives should be weighted according to their economic importance or their *transactions value* in the two periods under consideration:

> It might seem at first sight as if simply every price quotation were a single item, and since every commodity (any kind of commodity) has one price-quotation attached to it, it would seem as if price-variations of every kind of commodity were the single item in question. This is the way the question struck the first inquirers into price-variations, wherefore they used simple averaging with even weighting. But a price-quotation is the quotation of the price of a generic name for many articles; and one such generic name covers a few articles, and another covers many.... A single price-quotation, therefore, may be the quotation of the price of a hundred, a thousand, or a million dollar's worths, of the articles that make up the commodity named. Its weight in the averaging, therefore, ought to be according to these money-unit's worth (Walsh (1921a, pp. 82–83)).

But Walsh did not give a convincing argument on exactly how these economic weights should be determined.

16.80 Henri Theil (1967, pp. 136–137) proposed a solution to the lack of weighting in the Jevons index, P_J defined by equation (16.47). He argued as follows. Suppose we draw price relatives at random in such a way that each dollar of expenditure in the base period has an equal chance of being selected. Then the probability that we will draw the ith price relative is equal to $s_i^0 \equiv p_i^0 q_i^0 / \sum_{k=1}^n p_k^0 q_k^0$, the period 0 expenditure share for commodity i. Then the overall mean (period 0 weighted) logarithmic price change is $\sum_{i=1}^n s_i^0 \ln(p_i^1/p_i^0)$.[53] Now repeat the above mental experiment and draw price relatives at random in such a way that each dollar of expenditure in period 1 has an equal probability of being selected. This leads to the overall mean (period 1 weighted) logarithmic price change of $\sum_{i=1}^n s_i^1 \ln(p_i^1/p_i^0)$.[54]

16.81 Each of these measures of overall logarithmic price change seems equally valid, so we could argue for taking a symmetric average of the two measures in order to obtain a final single measure of overall logarithmic price change. Theil[55] argued that a "nice" symmetric index number formula can be obtained if the probability of selection for the nth price relative is made equal to the arithmetic average of the period 0 and 1 expenditure shares for commodity n. Using these probabilities of selection, Theil's final measure of overall logarithmic price change was

$$\ln P_T(p^0, p^1, q^0, q^1) \equiv \sum_{i=1}^n \frac{1}{2}(s_i^0 + s_i^1) \ln\left(\frac{p_i^1}{p_i^0}\right) \qquad (16.48)$$

Note that the index P_T defined by equation (16.48) is equal to the Törnqvist index defined by equation (15.81) in Chapter 15.

16.82 A statistical interpretation of the right-hand side of equation (16.48) can be given. Define the ith

[52] Walsh (1901, pp. 82–90; 1921a, pp. 82–83) also objected to the lack of weighting in the unweighted stochastic approach to index number theory.

[53] In Chapter 19, this index is called the *geometric Laspeyres index*, P_{GL}. Vartia (1978, p. 272) referred to this index as the *logarithmic Laspeyres index*. Yet another name for the index is the *base weighted geometric index*.

[54] In Chapter 19, this index is called the *geometric Paasche index*, P_{GP}. Vartia (1978, p. 272) referred to this index as the *logarithmic Paasche index*. Yet another name for the index is the *current period weighted geometric index*.

[55] "The price index number defined in (1.8) and (1.9) uses the n individual logarithmic price differences as the basic ingredients. They are combined linearly by means of a two-stage random selection procedure: First, we give each region the same chance ½ of being selected, and second, we give each dollar spent in the selected region the same chance ($1/m_a$ or $1/m_b$) of being drawn" (Theil (1967, p. 138)).

logarithmic price ratio r_i by:

$$r_i \equiv \ln\left(\frac{p_i^1}{p_i^0}\right) \quad \text{for } i=1, \ldots, n \tag{16.49}$$

Now define the discrete random variable, R say, as the random variable which can take on the values r_i with probabilities $\rho_i \equiv (1/2)[s_i^0 + s_i^1]$ for $i=1,\ldots,n$. Note that, since each set of expenditure shares, s_i^0 and s_i^1, sums to one over i, the probabilities ρ_i will also sum to one. It can be seen that the expected value of the discrete random variable R is

$$E[R] \equiv \sum_{i=1}^{n} \rho_i r_i = \sum_{i=1}^{n} \frac{1}{2}(s_i^0 + s_i^1)\ln\left(\frac{p_i^1}{p_i^0}\right) = \ln P_T(p^0, p^1, q^0, q^1). \tag{16.50}$$

Thus the logarithm of the index P_T can be interpreted as *the expected value of the distribution of the logarithmic price ratios* in the domain of definition under consideration, where the n discrete price ratios in this domain of definition are weighted according to Theil's probability weights, $\rho_i \equiv (1/2)[s_i^0 + s_i^1]$ for $i=1,\ldots,n$.

16.83 Taking antilogs of both sides of equation (16.48), the Törnqvist (1936; 1937) and Theil price index, P_T, is obtained.[56] This index number formula has a number of good properties. In particular, P_T satisfies the proportionality in current prices test T5 and the time reversal test T11, discussed above. These two tests can be used to justify Theil's (arithmetic) method of forming an average of the two sets of expenditure shares in order to obtain his probability weights, $\rho_i \equiv (1/2)[s_i^0 + s_i^1]$ for $i=1,\ldots,n$. Consider the following *symmetric mean class of logarithmic index number formulae*:

$$\ln P_S(p^0, p^1, q^0, q^1) \equiv \sum_{i=1}^{n} m(s_i^0, s_i^1)\ln\left(\frac{p_i^1}{p_i^0}\right) \tag{16.51}$$

where $m(s_i^0, s_i^1)$ is a positive function of the period 0 and 1 expenditure shares on commodity i, s_i^0 and s_i^1 respectively. In order for P_S to satisfy the time reversal test, it is necessary that the function m be symmetric. Then it can be shown[57] that for P_S to satisfy test T5, m must be the arithmetic mean. This provides a reasonably strong justification for Theil's choice of the mean function.

16.84 The stochastic approach of Theil has another "nice" symmetry property. Instead of considering the distribution of the price ratios $r_i = \ln p_i^1/p_i^0$, we could also consider the distribution of the *reciprocals* of these price ratios, say:

$$t_i \equiv \ln\frac{p_i^0}{p_i^1} = \ln\left(\frac{p_i^1}{p_i^0}\right)^{-1} = -\ln\frac{p_i^1}{p_i^0} = -r_i \quad \text{for } i=1, \ldots, n \tag{16.52}$$

The symmetric probability, $\rho_i \equiv (1/2)[s_i^0 + s_i^1]$, can still be associated with the ith reciprocal logarithmic price ratio t_i for $i=1,\ldots,n$. Now define the discrete random variable, T say, as the random variable which can take on the values t_i with probabilities $\rho_i \equiv (1/2)[s_i^0 + s_i^1]$ for $i=1,\ldots,n$. It can be seen that the expected value of the discrete random variable T is

$$\begin{aligned} E[T] &\equiv \sum_{i=1}^{n} \rho_i t_i \\ &= -\sum_{i=1}^{n} r_i t_i \text{ using (16.52)} \\ &= -E[R] \text{ using (16.50)} \\ &= -\ln P_T(p^0, p^1, q^0, q^1) \end{aligned} \tag{16.53}$$

Thus it can be seen that the distribution of the random variable T is equal to minus the distribution of the random variable R. Hence it does not matter whether the distribution of the original logarithmic price ratios, $r_i \equiv \ln p_i^1/p_i^0$, is considered or the distribution of their reciprocals, $t_i \equiv \ln p_i^0/p_i^1$, is considered: essentially the same stochastic theory is obtained.

16.85 It is possible to consider weighted stochastic approaches to index number theory where the distribution of the price ratios, p_i^1/p_i^0, is considered rather than the distribution of the logarithmic price ratios, ln p_i^1/p_i^0. Thus, again following in the footsteps of Theil, suppose that price relatives are drawn at random in such a way that each dollar of expenditure in the *base period* has an equal chance of being selected. Then the probability that the ith price relative will be drawn is equal to s_i^0, the period 0 expenditure share for commodity i. Thus the overall mean (period 0 weighted) price change is:

$$P_L(p^0, p^1, q^0, q^1) = \sum_{i=1}^{n} s_i^0 \frac{p_i^1}{p_i^0} \tag{16.54}$$

which turns out to be the Laspeyres price index, P_L. This stochastic approach is the natural one for studying *sampling problems* associated with implementing a Laspeyres price index.

16.86 Now repeat the above mental experiment and draw price relatives at random in such a way that each dollar of expenditure in period 1 has an equal probability of being selected. This leads to the overall mean (period 1 weighted) price change equal to:

$$P_{PAL}(p^0, p^1, q^0, q^1) = \sum_{i=1}^{n} s_i^1 \frac{p_i^1}{p_i^0} \tag{16.55}$$

This is known as the Palgrave (1886) index number formula.[58]

16.87 It can be verified that neither the Laspeyres nor Palgrave price indices satisfy the time reversal test, T11. Thus, again following in the footsteps of Theil, it might be attempted to obtain a formula that satisfies the time reversal test by taking a symmetric average of the

[56] The sampling bias problem studied by Greenlees (1999) does not occur in the present context because there is no sampling involved in definition (16.50): the sum of the $p_i^t q_i^t$ over i for each period t is assumed to equal the value aggregate V^t for period t.

[57] See Diewert (2000) and Balk and Diewert (2001).

[58] It is formula number 9 in Fisher's (1922, p. 466) listing of index number formulae.

two sets of shares. Thus consider the following class of *symmetric mean index number formulae*:

$$P_m(p^0,p^1,q^0,q^1) \equiv \sum_{i=1}^{n} m(s_i^0,s_i^1)\frac{p_i^1}{p_i^0} \tag{16.56}$$

where $m(s_i^0,s_i^1)$ is a symmetric function of the period 0 and 1 expenditure shares for commodity i, s_i^0 and s_i^1 respectively. In order to interpret the right hand-side of equation (16.56) as an expected value of the price ratios p_i^1/p_i^0, it is necessary that

$$\sum_{i=1}^{n} m(s_i^0,s_i^1) = 1 \tag{16.57}$$

In order to satisfy equation (16.57), however, m must be the arithmetic mean.[59] With this choice of m, equation (16.56) becomes the following (unnamed) index number formula, P_u:

$$P_u(p^0,p^1,q^0,q^1) \equiv \sum_{i=1}^{n} \frac{1}{2}(s_i^0+s_i^1)\frac{p_i^1}{p_i^0} \tag{16.58}$$

Unfortunately, the unnamed index P_u does not satisfy the time reversal test either.[60]

16.88 Instead of considering the distribution of the price ratios, p_i^1/p_i^0, the distribution of the *reciprocals* of these price ratios could be considered. The counterparts to the asymmetric indices defined earlier by equations (16.54) and (16.55) are now $\sum_{i=1}^{n} s_i^0(p_i^0/p_i^1)$ and $\sum_{i=1}^{n} s_i^1 (p_i^0/p_i^1)$, respectively. These are (stochastic) price indices going *backwards* from period 1 to 0. In order to make these indices comparable with other previous forward-looking indices, take the reciprocals of these indices (which leads to harmonic averages) and the following two indices are obtained:

$$P_{HL}(p^0,p^1,q^0,q^1) \equiv \frac{1}{\sum_{i=1}^{n} s_i^0 \frac{p_i^0}{p_i^1}} \tag{16.59}$$

$$P_{HP}(p^0,p^1,q^0,q^1) \equiv \frac{1}{\sum_{i=1}^{n} s_i^1 \frac{p_i^0}{p_i^1}} = \frac{1}{\sum_{i=1}^{n} s_i^1 \left(\frac{p_i^1}{p_i^0}\right)^{-1}} = P_P(p^0,p^1,q^0,q^1) \tag{16.60}$$

using equation (15.9) in Chapter 15. Thus the reciprocal stochastic price index defined by equation (16.60) turns out to equal the fixed basket Paasche price index, P_P. This stochastic approach is the natural one for studying sampling problems associated with implementing a Paasche price index. The other asymmetrically weighted reciprocal stochastic price index defined by the formula (16.59) has no author's name associated with it but it was noted by Fisher (1922, p. 467) as his index number formula 13. Vartia (1978, p. 272) called this index *the harmonic Laspeyres index* and his terminology will be used.

16.89 Now consider the class of *symmetrically weighted reciprocal price indices* defined as:

$$P_{mr}(p^0,p^1,q^0,q^1) \equiv \frac{1}{\sum_{i=1}^{n} m(s_i^0,s_i^1)\left(\frac{p_i^1}{p_i^0}\right)^{-1}} \tag{16.61}$$

where, as usual, $m(s_i^0,s_i^1)$ is a homogeneous symmetric mean of the period 0 and 1 expenditure shares on commodity i. However, none of the indices defined by equations (16.59) to (16.61) satisfies the time reversal test.

16.90 The fact that Theil's index number formula P_T satisfies the time reversal test leads to a preference for Theil's index as the "best" weighted stochastic approach.

16.91 The main features of the weighted stochastic approach to index number theory can be summarized as follows. It is first necessary to pick two periods and a transactions domain of definition. As usual, each value transaction for each of the n commodities in the domain of definition is split up into price and quantity components. Then, assuming there are no new commodities or no disappearing commodities, there are n price relatives p_i^1/p_i^0 pertaining to the two situations under consideration along with the corresponding $2n$ expenditure shares. The weighted stochastic approach just assumes that these n relative prices, or some transformation of these price relatives, $f(p_i^1/p_i^0)$, have a discrete statistical distribution, where the ith probability, $\rho_i = m(s_i^0,s_i^1)$, is a function of the expenditure shares pertaining to commodity i in the two situations under consideration, s_i^0 and s_i^1. Different price indices result, depending on how the functions f and m are chosen. In Theil's approach, the transformation function f is the natural logarithm and the mean function m is the simple unweighted arithmetic mean.

16.92 There is a third aspect to the weighted stochastic approach to index number theory: it has to be decided what *single number* best summarizes the distribution of the n (possibly transformed) price relatives. In the above analysis, the *mean* of the discrete distribution was chosen as the "best" summary measure for the distribution of the (possibly transformed) price relatives; but other measures are possible. In particular, the *weighted median* or various *trimmed means* are often suggested as the "best" measure of central tendency because these measures minimize the influence of outliers. Detailed discussion of these alternative measures of central tendency is, however, beyond the scope of this chapter. Additional material on stochastic approaches to index number theory and references to the literature can be found in Clements and Izan (1981; 1987), Selvanathan and Rao (1994),

[59] For a proof of this assertion, see Balk and Diewert (2001).

[60] In fact, this index suffers from the same upward bias as the Carli index in that $P_u(p^0,p^1,q^0,q^1)P_u(p^1,p^0,q^1,q^0) \geq 1$. To prove this, note that the previous inequality is equivalent to $[P_u(p^1,p^0,q^1,q^0)]^{-1} \leq P_u(p^0,p^1,q^0,q^1)$ and this inequality follows from the fact that a weighted harmonic mean of n positive numbers is equal or less than the corresponding weighted arithmetic mean; see Hardy, Littlewood and Pólya (1934, p. 26).

Diewert (1995b), Cecchetti (1997) and Wynne (1997; 1999).

16.93 Instead of taking the above stochastic approach to index number theory, it is possible to take the same raw data that are used in this approach but use an axiomatic approach. Thus, in the following section, the price index is regarded as a value-weighted function of the n price relatives and the test approach to index number theory is used in order to determine the functional form for the price index. Put another way, the axiomatic approach in the next section looks at the *properties* of alternative descriptive statistics that aggregate the individual price relatives (weighted by their economic importance) into summary measures of price change in an attempt to find the "best" summary measure of price change. Thus the axiomatic approach pursued below can be viewed as a branch of the theory of descriptive statistics.

The second axiomatic approach to bilateral price indices

The basic framework and some preliminary tests

16.94 As mentioned in paragraphs 16.1 to 16.10, one of Walsh's approaches to index number theory was an attempt to determine the "best" weighted average of the price relatives, r_i.[61] This is equivalent to using an axiomatic approach to try to determine the "best" index of the form $P(r, v^0, v^1)$, where v^0 and v^1 are the vectors of expenditures on the n commodities during periods 0 and 1.[62] Initially, rather than starting with indices of the form $P(r, v^0, v^1)$, indices of the form $P(p^0, p^1, v^0, v^1)$ will be considered, since this framework will be more comparable to the first bilateral axiomatic framework taken in paragraphs 16.30 to 16.73. As will be seen below, if the invariance to changes in the units of measurement test is imposed on an index of the form $P(p^0, p^1, v^0, v^1)$, then $P(p^0, p^1, v^0, v^1)$ can be written in the form $P(r, v^0, v^1)$.

16.95 Recall that the product test (16.17) was used to define the quantity index $Q(p^0, p^1, q^0, q^1) \equiv V^1/V^0P(p^0, p^1, q^0, q^1)$ that corresponded to the bilateral price index $P(p^0, p^1, q^0, q^1)$. A similar product test holds in the present framework; i.e., given that the functional form for the price index $P(p^0, p^1, v^0, v^1)$ has been determined, then the corresponding *implicit quantity index* can be defined in terms of P as follows:

$$Q(p^0, p^1, v^0, v^1) \equiv \frac{\sum_{i=1}^{n} v_i^1}{\left(\sum_{i=1}^{n} v_i^0\right) P(p^0, p^1, v^0, v^1)} \qquad (16.62)$$

16.96 In paragraphs 16.30 to 16.73, the price and quantity indices $P(p^0, p^1, q^0, q^1)$ and $Q(p^0, p^1, q^0, q^1)$ were determined *jointly*; i.e., not only were axioms imposed on $P(p^0, p^1, q^0, q^1)$ but they were also imposed on $Q(p^0, p^1, q^0, q^1)$ and the product test (16.17) was used to translate these tests on Q into tests on P. In this section, this approach will not be followed: only tests on $P(p^0, p^1, v^0, v^1)$ will be used in order to determine the "best" price index of this form. Thus there is a parallel theory for quantity indices of the form $Q(q^0, q^1, v^0, v^1)$, where it is attempted to find the "best" value-weighted average of the quantity relatives, q_i^1/q_i^0.[63]

16.97 For the most part, the tests which will be imposed on the price index $P(p^0, p^1, v^0, v^1)$ in this section are counterparts to the tests that were imposed on the price index $P(p^0, p^1, q^0, q^1)$ in paragraphs 16.30 to 16.73. It will be assumed that every component of each price and value vector is positive; i.e., $p^t \gg 0_n$ and $v^t \gg 0_n$ for $t = 0,1$. If it is desired to set $v^0 = v^1$, the common expenditure vector is denoted by v; if it is desired to set $p^0 = p^1$, the common price vector is denoted by p.

16.98 The first two tests are straightforward counterparts to the corresponding tests in paragraph 16.34.

T1: *Positivity*: $P(p^0, p^1, v^0, v^1) > 0$

T2: *Continuity*: $P(p^0, p^1, v^0, v^1)$ is a continuous function of its arguments

T3: *Identity or constant prices test*: $P(p, p, v^0, v^1) = 1$

That is, if the price of every good is identical during the two periods, then the price index should equal unity, no matter what the value vectors are. Note that the two value vectors are allowed to be different in the above test.

[61] Fisher also took this point of view when describing his approach to index number theory:

> An index number of the prices of a number of commodities is an average of their price relatives. This definition has, for concreteness, been expressed in terms of prices. But in like manner, an index number can be calculated for wages, for quantities of goods imported or exported, and, in fact, for any subject matter involving divergent changes of a group of magnitudes. Again, this definition has been expressed in terms of time. But an index number can be applied with equal propriety to comparisons between two places or, in fact, to comparisons between the magnitudes of a group of elements under any one set of circumstances and their magnitudes under another set of circumstances (Fisher (1922, p. 3)).

In setting up his axiomatic approach, Fisher imposed axioms on the price and quantity indices written as functions of the two price vectors, p^0 and p^1, and the two quantity vectors, q^0 and q^1; i.e., he did not write his price index in the form $P(r, v^0, v^1)$ and impose axioms on indices of this type. Of course, in the end, his ideal price index turned out to be the geometric mean of the Laspeyres and Paasche price indices and, as was seen in Chapter 15, each of these indices can be written as expenditure share-weighted averages of the n price relatives, $r_i \equiv p_i^1/ip_i^0$.

[62] Chapter 3 in Vartia (1976) considered a variant of this axiomatic approach.

[63] It turns out that the price index that corresponds to this "best" quantity index, defined as $P^*(q^0, q^1, v^0, v^1) \equiv \sum_{i=1}^{n} v_i^1 / [\sum_{i=1}^{n} v_i^0 Q(q^0, q^1, v^0, v^1)]$, will not equal the "best" price index, $P(p^0, p^1, v^0, v^1)$. Thus the axiomatic approach used here generates *separate* "best" price and quantity indices whose product does not equal the value ratio in general. This is a disadvantage of the second axiomatic approach to bilateral indices compared to the first approach studied above.

Homogeneity tests

16.99 The following four tests restrict the behaviour of the price index P as the scale of any one of the four vectors p^0, p^1, v^0, v^1 changes.

T4: *Proportionality in current prices*:

$$P(p^0, \lambda p^1, v^0, v^1) = \lambda P(p^0, p^1, v^0, v^1) \quad \text{for } \lambda > 0$$

That is, if all period 1 prices are multiplied by the positive number λ, then the new price index is λ times the old price index. Put another way, the price index function $P(p^0, p^1, v^0, v^1)$ is (positively) homogeneous of degree one in the components of the period 1 price vector p^1. This test is the counterpart to test T5 in paragraph 16.37.

16.100 In the next test, instead of multiplying all period 1 prices by the same number, all period 0 prices are multiplied by the number λ.

T5: *Inverse proportionality in base period prices*:

$$P(\lambda p^0, p^1, v^0, v^1) = \lambda^{-1} P(p^0, p^1, v^0, v^1) \quad \text{for } \lambda > 0$$

That is, if all period 0 prices are multiplied by the positive number λ, then the new price index is $1/\lambda$ times the old price index. Put another way, the price index function $P(p^0, p^1, v^0, v^1)$ is (positively) homogeneous of degree minus one in the components of the period 0 price vector p^0. This test is the counterpart to test T6 in paragraph 16.39.

16.101 The following two homogeneity tests can also be regarded as invariance tests.

T6: *Invariance to proportional changes in current period values*:

$$P(p^0, p^1, v^0, \lambda v^1) = P(p^0, p^1, v^0, v^1) \quad \text{for all } \lambda > 0$$

That is, if current period values are all multiplied by the number λ, then the price index remains unchanged. Put another way, the price index function $P(p^0, p^1, v^0, v^1)$ is (positively) homogeneous of degree zero in the components of the period 1 value vector v^1.

T7: *Invariance to proportional changes in base period values*:

$$P(p^0, p^1, \lambda v^0, v^1) = P(p^0, p^1, v^0, v^1) \quad \text{for all } \lambda > 0$$

That is, if base period values are all multiplied by the number λ, then the price index remains unchanged. Put another way, the price index function $P(p^0, p^1, v^0, v^1)$ is (positively) homogeneous of degree zero in the components of the period 0 value vector v^0.

16.102 T6 and T7 together impose the property that the price index P does not depend on the *absolute* magnitudes of the value vectors v^0 and v^1. Using test T6 with $\lambda = 1/\sum_{i=1}^{n} v_i^1$ and using test T7 with $\lambda = 1/\sum_{i=1}^{n} v_i^0$, it can be seen that P has the following property:

$$P(p^0, p^1, v^0, v^1) = P(p^0, p^1, s^0, s^1) \qquad (16.63)$$

where s^0 and s^1 are the vectors of expenditure shares for periods 0 and 1; i.e., the ith component of s^t is $s_i^t \equiv v_i^t / \sum_{k=1}^{n} v_k^t$ for $t = 0,1$. Thus the tests T6 and T7 imply that the price index function P is a function of the two price vectors p^0 and p^1 and the two vectors of expenditure shares, s^0 and s^1.

16.103 Walsh (1901, p. 104) suggested the spirit of tests T6 and T7 as the following quotation indicates: "What we are seeking is to average the variations in the exchange value of one given total sum of money in relation to the several classes of goods, to which several variations [i.e., the price relatives] must be assigned weights proportional to the relative sizes of the classes. Hence the relative sizes of the classes at both the periods must be considered."

16.104 Walsh also realized that weighting the ith price relative r_i by the arithmetic mean of the value weights in the two periods under consideration, $(1/2)[v_i^0 + v_i^1]$ would give too much weight to the expenditures of the period that had the highest level of prices:

> At first sight it might be thought sufficient to add up the weights of every class at the two periods and to divide by two. This would give the (arithmetic) mean size of every class over the two periods together. But such an operation is manifestly wrong. In the first place, the sizes of the classes at each period are reckoned in the money of the period, and if it happens that the exchange value of money has fallen, or prices in general have risen, greater influence upon the result would be given to the weighting of the second period; or if prices in general have fallen, greater influence would be given to the weighting of the first period. Or in a comparison between two countries, greater influence would be given to the weighting of the country with the higher level of prices. But it is plain that *the one period, or the one country, is as important, in our comparison between them, as the other, and the weighting in the averaging of their weights should really be even* (Walsh (1901, pp. 104–105)).

16.105 As a solution to the above weighting problem, Walsh (1901, p. 202; 1921a, p. 97) proposed the following *geometric price index*:

$$P_{GW}(p^0, p^1, v^0, v^1) \equiv \prod_{i=1}^{n} \left(\frac{p_i^1}{p_i^0} \right)^{w(i)} \qquad (16.64)$$

where the ith weight in the above formula was defined as

$$w(i) \equiv \frac{(v_i^0 v_i^1)^{1/2}}{\sum_{k=1}^{n} (v_k^0 v_k^1)^{1/2}} = \frac{(s_i^0 s_i^1)^{1/2}}{\sum_{k=1}^{n} (s_k^0 s_k^1)^{1/2}} \qquad i = 1, \ldots, n \quad (16.65)$$

The second equation in (16.65) shows that Walsh's geometric price index $P_{GW}(p^0, p^1, v^0, v^1)$ can also be written as a function of the expenditure share vectors, s^0 and s^1; i.e., $P_{GW}(p^0, p^1, v^0, v^1)$ is homogeneous of degree zero in the components of the value vectors v^0 and v^1 and so $P_{GW}(p^0, p^1, v^0, v^1) = P_{GW}(p^0, p^1, s^0, s^1)$. Thus Walsh came very close to deriving the Törnqvist–Theil index defined earlier by equation (16.48).[64]

[64] Walsh's index could be derived using the same arguments as Theil, except that the geometric average of the expenditure shares $(s_i^0 s_i^1)^{1/2}$ could be taken as a preliminary probability weight for the ith logarithmic price relative, ln r_i. These preliminary weights are then normalized to add up to unity by dividing by their sum. It is evident that Walsh's geometric price index will closely approximate Theil's index using normal time series data. More formally, regarding both indices as functions of p^0, p^1, v^0, v^1, it can be shown that $P_W(p^0, p^1, v^0, v^1)$ approximates $P_T(p^0, p^1, v^0, v^1)$ to the second order around an equal price (i.e., $p^0 = p^1$) and quantity (i.e., $q^0 = q^1$) point.

Invariance and symmetry tests

16.106 The next five tests are *invariance* or *symmetry tests* and four of them are direct counterparts to similar tests in paragraphs 16.42 to 16.46 above. The first invariance test is that the price index should remain unchanged if the *ordering* of the commodities is changed.

T8: *Commodity reversal test* (or invariance to changes in the ordering of commodities):

$$P(p^{0*}, p^{1*}, v^{0*}, v^{1*}) = P(p^0, p^1, v^0, v^1)$$

where p^{t*} denotes a permutation of the components of the vector p^t and v^{t*} denotes the same permutation of the components of v^t for $t=0,1$.

16.107 The next test asks that the index be invariant to changes in the units of measurement.

T9: *Invariance to changes in the units of measurement* (commensurability test):

$$P(\alpha_1 p_1^0, \ldots, \alpha_n p_n^0; \alpha_1 p_1^1, \ldots, \alpha_n p_n^1; v_1^0, \ldots, v_n^0; v_1^1, \ldots, v_n^1) = P(p_1^0, \ldots, p_n^0; p_1^1, \ldots, p_n^1; v_1^0, \ldots, v_n^0; v_1^1, \ldots, v_n^1)$$
$$\text{for all } \alpha_1 > 0, \ldots, \alpha_n > 0$$

That is, the price index does not change if the units of measurement for each commodity are changed. Note that the expenditure on commodity i during period t, v_i^t, does not change if the unit by which commodity i is measured changes.

16.108 The last test has a very important implication. Let $\alpha_1 = 1/p_1^0, \ldots, \alpha_n = 1/p_n^0$ and substitute these values for the α_i into the definition of the test. The following equation is obtained:

$$P(p^0, p^1, v^0, v^1) = P(1_n, r, v^0, v^1) \equiv P^*(r, v^0, v^1) \quad (16.66)$$

where 1_n is a vector of ones of dimension n and r is a vector of the price relatives; i.e., the ith component of r is $r_i \equiv p_i^1/p_i^0$. Thus, if the commensurability test T9 is satisfied, then the price index $P(p^0, p^1, v^0, v^1)$, which is a function of $4n$ variables, can be written as a function of $3n$ variables, $P^*(r, v^0, v^1)$, where r is the vector of price relatives and $P^*(r, v^0, v^1)$ is defined as $P(1_n, r, v^0, v^1)$.

16.109 The next test asks that the formula be invariant to the period chosen as the base period.

T10: *Time reversal test*: $P(p^0, p^1, v^0, v^1) = 1/P(p^1, p^0, v^1, v^0)$

That is, if the data for periods 0 and 1 are interchanged, then the resulting price index should equal the reciprocal of the original price index. Obviously, in the one good case when the price index is simply the single price ratio, this test will be satisfied (as are all the other tests listed in this section).

16.110 The next test is a variant of the circularity test, introduced in paragraphs 15.76 to 15.97 of Chapter 15.[65]

T11: *Transitivity in prices for fixed value weights*:

$$P(p^0, p^1, v^r, v^s) P(p^1, p^2, v^r, v^s) = P(p^0, p^2, v^r, v^s)$$

In this test, the expenditure weighting vectors, v^r and v^s, are held constant while making all price comparisons. Given that these weights are held constant, however, the test asks that the product of the index going from period 0 to 1, $P(p^0, p^1, v^r, v^s)$, times the index going from period 1 to 2, $P(p^1, p^2, v^r, v^s)$, should equal the direct index that compares the prices of period 2 with those of period 0, $P(p^0, p^2, v^r, v^s)$. Obviously, this test is a many-commodity counterpart to a property that holds for a single price relative.

16.111 The final test in this section captures the idea that the value weights should enter the index number formula in a symmetric manner.

T12: *Quantity weights symmetry test*:

$$P(p^0, p^1, v^0, v^1) = P(p^0, p^1, v^1, v^0)$$

That is, if the expenditure vectors for the two periods are interchanged, then the price index remains invariant. This property means that, if values are used to weight the prices in the index number formula, then the period 0 values v^0 and the period 1 values v^1 must enter the formula in a symmetric or even-handed manner.

A mean value test

16.112 The next test is a *mean value test*.

T13: *Mean value test for prices*:

$$\min_i (p_i^1/p_i^0 : i=1, \ldots, n) \le P(p^0, p^1, v^0, v^1) \le \max_i (p_i^1/p_i^0 : i=1, \ldots, n) \quad (16.67)$$

That is, the price index lies between the minimum price ratio and the maximum price ratio. Since the price index is to be interpreted as an average of the n price ratios, p_i^1/p_i^0, it seems essential that the price index P satisfy this test.

Monotonicity tests

16.113 The next two tests in this section are *monotonicity tests*; i.e., how should the price index $P(p^0, p^1, v^0, v^1)$ change as any component of the two price vectors p^0 and p^1 increases?

T14: *Monotonicity in current prices*:

$$P(p^0, p^1, v^0, v^1) < P(p^0, p^2, v^0, v^1) \quad \text{if } p^1 < p^2$$

That is, if some period 1 price increases, then the price index must increase (holding the value vectors fixed), so that $P(p^0, p^1, q^0, q^1)$ is increasing in the components of p^1 for fixed p^0, v^0 and v^1.

T15: *Monotonicity in base prices*:

$$P(p^0, p^1, v^0, v^1) > P(p^2, p^1, v^0, v^1) \text{ if } p^0 < p^2$$

That is, if any period 0 price increases, then the price index must decrease, so that $P(p^0, p^1, q^0, q^1)$ is decreasing in the components of p^0 for fixed p^1, v^0 and v^1.

[65] See equation (15.77) in Chapter 15.

Weighting tests

16.114 The above tests are not sufficient to determine the functional form of the price index; for example, it can be shown that both Walsh's geometric price index $P_{GW}(p^0, p^1, v^0, v^1)$ defined by equation (16.65) and the Törnqvist–Theil index $P_T(p^0, p^1, v^0, v^1)$ defined by equation (16.48) satisfy all of the above axioms. Thus, at least one more test will be required in order to determine the functional form for the price index $P(p^0, p^1, v^0, v^1)$.

16.115 The tests proposed thus far do not specify exactly how the expenditure share vectors s^0 and s^1 are to be used in order to weight, say, the first price relative, p_1^1/p_1^0. The next test says that only the expenditure shares s_1^0 and s_1^1 pertaining to the first commodity are to be used in order to weight the prices that correspond to commodity 1, p_1^1 and p_1^0.

T16: *Own share price weighting*:

$$P(p_1^0, 1, \ldots, 1; p_1^1, 1, \ldots, 1; v^0, v^1) = f\left(p_1^0, p_1^1, \left[v_1^0 \Big/ \sum_{k=1}^{n} v_k^0\right], \left[v_1^1 \Big/ \sum_{k=1}^{n} v_k^1\right]\right) \quad (16.68)$$

Note that $v_1^t / \sum_{k=1}^{n} v_k^t$ equals s_1^t, the expenditure share for commodity 1 in period t. The above test says that if all the prices are set equal to 1 except the prices for commodity 1 in the two periods, but the expenditures in the two periods are arbitrarily given, then the index depends only on the two prices for commodity 1 and the two expenditure shares for commodity 1. The axiom says that a function of $2+2n$ variables is actually only a function of four variables.[66]

16.116 Of course, if test T16 is combined with test T8, the commodity reversal test, then it can be seen that P has the following property:

$$P(1, \ldots, 1, p_i^0, 1, \ldots, 1; 1, \ldots, 1, p_i^1, 1, \ldots, 1; v^0; v^1) = f\left(p_i^0, p_i^1, \left[v_i^0 \Big/ \sum_{k=1}^{n} v_k^0\right], \left[v_i^1 \Big/ \sum_{k=1}^{n} v_k^1\right]\right) \quad i = 1, \ldots, n \quad (16.69)$$

Equation (16.69) says that, if all the prices are set equal to 1 except the prices for commodity i in the two periods, but the expenditures in the two periods are arbitrarily given, then the index depends only on the two prices for commodity i and the two expenditure shares for commodity i.

16.117 The final test that also involves the weighting of prices is the following one:

T17: *Irrelevance of price change with tiny value weights*:

$$P(p_1^0, 1, \ldots, 1; p_1^1, 1, \ldots, 1; 0, v_2^0, \ldots, v_n^0; 0, v_2^1, \ldots, v_n^1) = 1 \quad (16.70)$$

The test T17 says that, if all the prices are set equal to 1 except the prices for commodity 1 in the two periods, and the expenditures on commodity 1 are 0 in the two periods but the expenditures on the other commodities are arbitrarily given, then the index is equal to 1.[67] Thus, roughly speaking, if the value weights for commodity 1 are tiny, then it does not matter what the price of commodity 1 is during the two periods.

16.118 Of course, if test T17 is combined with test T8, the commodity reversal test, then it can be seen that P has the following property: for $i = 1, \ldots, n$:

$$P(1, \ldots, 1, p_i^0, 1, \ldots, 1; 1, \ldots, 1, p_i^1, 1, \ldots, 1; v_1^0, \ldots, 0, \ldots, v_n^0; v_1^1, \ldots, 0, \ldots, v_n^1) = 1 \quad (16.71)$$

Equation (16.71) says that, if all the prices are set equal to 1 except the prices for commodity i in the two periods, and the expenditures on commodity i are 0 during the two periods but the other expenditures in the two periods are arbitrarily given, then the index is equal to 1.

16.119 This completes the listing of tests for the approach to bilateral index number theory based on the weighted average of price relatives. It turns out that the above tests are sufficient to imply a specific functional form for the price index, as seen in the next section.

The Törnqvist–Theil price index and the second test approach to bilateral indices

16.120 In Appendix 16.1 to this chapter, it is shown that, if the number of commodities n exceeds two and the bilateral price index function $P(p^0, p^1, v^0, v^1)$ satisfies the 17 axioms listed above, then P must be the Törnqvist–Theil price index $P_T(p^0, p^1, v^0, v^1)$ defined by equation (16.48).[68] Thus the 17 properties or tests listed in paragraphs 16.94 to 16.129 provide an axiomatic characterization of the Törnqvist–Theil price index, just as the 20 tests listed in paragraphs 16.30 to 16.73 provided an axiomatic characterization of the Fisher ideal price index.

16.121 Obviously, there is a parallel axiomatic theory for quantity indices of the form $Q(q^0, q^1, v^0, v^1)$ that depend on the two quantity vectors for periods 0 and 1, q^0 and q^1, as well as on the corresponding two expenditure vectors, v^0 and v^1. Thus, if $Q(q^0, q^1, v^0, v^1)$ satisfies the quantity counterparts to tests T1 to T17, then Q must be equal to the Törnqvist–Theil quantity index

[66] In the economics literature, axioms of this type are known as separability axioms.

[67] Strictly speaking, since all prices and values are required to be positive, the left-hand side of equation (16.70) should be replaced by the limit as the commodity 1 values, v_1^0 and v_1^1, approach 0.

[68] The Törnqvist–Theil price index satisfies all 17 tests, but the proof in Appendix 16.1 does not use all these tests to establish the result in the opposite direction: tests 5, 13, 15 and one of 10 or 12 were not required in order to show that an index satisfying the remaining tests must be the Törnqvist–Theil price index. For alternative characterizations of the Törnqvist–Theil price index, see Balk and Diewert (2001) and Hillinger (2002).

$Q_T(q^0, q^1, v^0, v^1)$ defined, as follows:

$$\ln Q_T(q^0, q^1, v^0, v^1) \equiv \sum_{i=1}^{n} \frac{1}{2}(s_i^0 + s_i^1) \ln\left(\frac{q_i^1}{q_i^0}\right) \quad (16.72)$$

where as usual, the period t expenditure share on commodity i, s_i^t, is defined as $v_i^t / \sum_{k=1}^{n} v_k^t$ for $i = 1, \ldots, n$ and $t = 0, 1$.

16.122 Unfortunately, the implicit Törnqvist–Theil price index, $P_{IT}(q^0, q^1, v^0, v^1)$ that corresponds to the Törnqvist–Theil quantity index Q_T, defined by equation (16.72) using the product test, is not equal to the direct Törnqvist–Theil price index $P_T(p^0, p^1, v^0, v^1)$, defined by equation (16.48). The product test equation that defines P_{IT} in the present context is given by the following equation:

$$P_{IT}(q^0, q^1, v^0, v^1) \equiv \frac{\sum_{i=1}^{n} v_i^1}{\left(\sum_{i=1}^{n} v_i^0\right) Q_T(q^0, q^1, v^0, v^1)} \quad (16.73)$$

The fact that the direct Törnqvist–Theil price index P_T is not in general equal to the implicit Törnqvist–Theil price index P_{IT}, defined by equation (16.73), is something of a disadvantage compared to the axiomatic approach outlined in paragraphs 16.30 to 16.73, which led to the Fisher ideal price and quantity indices being considered "best". Using the Fisher approach meant that it was not necessary to decide whether the aim was to find a "best" price index or a "best" quantity index: the theory outlined in paragraphs 16.30 to 16.73 determined both indices simultaneously. In the Törnqvist–Theil approach outlined in this section, however, it is necessary to choose between a "best" price index or a "best" quantity index.[69]

16.123 Other tests are of course possible. A counterpart to Test T16 in paragraph 16.49, the Paasche and Laspeyres bounding test, is the following *geometric Paasche and Laspeyres bounding test*:

$$P_{GL}(p^0, p^1, v^0, v^1) \le P(p^0, p^1, v^0, v^1) \le P_{GP}(p^0, p^1, v^0, v^1) \text{ or}$$
$$P_{GP}(p^0, p^1, v^0, v^1) \le P(p^0, p^1, v^0, v^1) \le P_{GL}(p^0, p^1, v^0, v^1) \quad (16.74)$$

where the logarithms of the geometric Laspeyres and geometric Paasche price indices, P_{GL} and P_{GP}, are defined as follows:

$$\ln P_{GL}(p^0, p^1, v^0, v^1) \equiv \sum_{i=1}^{n} s_i^0 \ln\left(\frac{p_i^1}{p_i^0}\right) \quad (16.75)$$

$$\ln P_{GP}(p^0, p^1, v^0, v^1) \equiv \sum_{i=1}^{n} s_i^1 \ln\left(\frac{p_i^1}{p_i^0}\right) \quad (16.76)$$

As usual, the period t expenditure share on commodity i, s_i^t, is defined as $v_1^t / \sum_{k=1}^{n} v_k^t$ for $i = 1, \ldots, n$ and $t = 0, 1$. It can be shown that the Törnqvist–Theil price index $P_T(p^0, p^1, v^0, v^1)$ defined by equation (16.48) satisfies this test, but the geometric Walsh price index $P_{GW}(p^0, p^1, v^0, v^1)$ defined by equation (16.65) does not. The geometric Paasche and Laspeyres bounding test was not included as a primary test in this section because it was not known a priori what form of averaging of the price relatives (e.g., geometric or arithmetic or harmonic) would turn out to be appropriate in this test framework. The test (16.74) is an appropriate one if it has been decided that geometric averaging of the price relatives is the appropriate framework, since the geometric Paasche and Laspeyres indices correspond to "extreme" forms of value weighting in the context of geometric averaging and it is natural to require that the "best" price index lies between these extreme indices.

16.124 Walsh (1901, p. 408) pointed out a problem with his geometric price index defined by equation (16.65), which also applies to the Törnqvist–Theil price index, $P_T(p^0, p^1, v^0, v^1)$, defined by equation (16.48): these geometric type indices do not give the "right" answer when the quantity vectors are constant (or proportional) over the two periods. In this case, Walsh thought that the "right" answer must be the Lowe index, which is the ratio of the costs of purchasing the constant basket during the two periods. Put another way, the geometric indices P_{GW} and P_T do not satisfy the fixed basket test T4 in paragraph 16.35. What then was the argument that led Walsh to define his geometric average type index P_{GW}? It turns out that he was led to this type of index by considering another test, which will now be explained.

16.125 Walsh (1901, pp. 228–231) derived his test by considering the following very simple framework. Let there be only two commodities in the index and suppose that the expenditure share on each commodity is equal in each of the two periods under consideration. The price index under these conditions is equal to $P(p_1^0, p_2^0; p_1^1, p_2^1; v_1^0, v_2^0; v_1^1, v_2^1) = P^*(r_1, r_2; 1/2, 1/2; 1/2, 1/2) \equiv m(r_1, r_2)$, where $m(r_1, r_2)$ is a symmetric mean of the two price relatives, $r_1 \equiv p_1^1/p_1^0$ and $r_2 \equiv p_2^1/p_2^0$.[70] In this framework, Walsh then proposed the following *price relative reciprocal test*:

$$m(r_1, r_1^{-1}) = 1 \quad (16.77)$$

Thus, if the value weighting for the two commodities is equal over the two periods and the second price relative is the reciprocal of the first price relative r_1, then Walsh (1901, p. 230) argued that the overall price index under these circumstances ought to equal 1, since the relative fall in one price is exactly counterbalanced by a rise in the other and both commodities have the same expenditures in each period. He found that the geometric mean satisfied this test perfectly but the arithmetic mean led to index values greater than 1 (provided that r_1 was not equal to 1) and the harmonic mean led to index values that were less than 1, a situation which was not at all satisfactory.[71] Thus he was led to some form of geometric

[69] Hillinger (2002) suggested taking the geometric mean of the direct and implicit Törnqvist–Theil price indices in order to resolve this conflict. Unfortunately, the resulting index is not "best" for either set of axioms that were suggested in this section.

[70] Walsh considered only the cases where m was the arithmetic, geometric and harmonic means of r_1 and r_2.

[71] "This tendency of the arithmetic and harmonic solutions to run into the ground or to fly into the air by their excessive demands is clear indication of their falsity" (Walsh (1901, p. 231)).

averaging of the price relatives in one of his approaches to index number theory.

16.126 A generalization of Walsh's result is easy to obtain. Suppose that the mean function, $m(r_1, r_2)$, satisfies Walsh's reciprocal test (16.77) and, in addition, m is a homogeneous mean, so that it satisfies the following property for all $r_1>0$, $r_2>0$ and $\lambda>0$:

$$m(\lambda r_1, \lambda r_2)=\lambda m(r_1, r_2). \qquad (16.78)$$

Let $r_1>0, r_2>0$. Then

$$\begin{aligned} m(r_1, r_2) &= \left(\frac{r_1}{r_1}\right) m(r_1, r_2) \\ &= r_1 m\left(\frac{r_1}{r_1}, \frac{r_2}{r_1}\right) \quad \text{using (16.78) with } \lambda=\frac{1}{r_1} \\ &= r_1 m\left(1, \frac{r_2}{r_1}\right)=r_1 f\left(\frac{r_2}{r_1}\right) \qquad (16.79) \end{aligned}$$

where the function of one (positive) variable $f(z)$ is defined as

$$f(z) \equiv m(1, z) \qquad (16.80)$$

Using equation (16.77):

$$\begin{aligned} 1 &= m(r_1, r_1^{-1}) \\ &= \left(\frac{r_1}{r_1}\right) m(r_1, r_1^{-1}) \\ &= r_1 m(1, r_1^{-2}) \quad \text{using (16.78) with } \lambda=\frac{1}{r_1} \qquad (16.81) \end{aligned}$$

Using equation (16.80), equation (16.81) can be rearranged in the following form:

$$f(r_1^{-2})=r_1^{-1} \qquad (16.82)$$

Letting $z \equiv r_1^{-2}$ so that $z^{1/2}=r_1^{-1}$, equation (16.82) becomes:

$$f(z)=z^{1/2} \qquad (16.83)$$

Now substitute equation (16.83) into equation (16.79) and the functional form for the mean function $m(r_1, r_2)$ is determined:

$$m(r_1, r_2)=r_1 f\left(\frac{r_2}{r_1}\right)=r_1\left(\frac{r_2}{r_1}\right)^{1/2}=r_1^{1/2} r_2^{1/2} \qquad (16.84)$$

Thus, the geometric mean of the two price relatives is the only homogeneous mean that will satisfy Walsh's price relative reciprocal test.

16.127 There is one additional test that should be mentioned. Fisher (1911, p. 401) introduced this test in his first book that dealt with the test approach to index number theory. He called it the *test of determinateness as to prices* and described it as follows: "A price index should not be rendered zero, infinity, or indeterminate by an individual price becoming zero. Thus, if any commodity should in 1910 be a glut on the market, becoming a 'free good', that fact ought not to render the index number for 1910 zero." In the present context, this test could be interpreted as the following one: if any single price p_i^0 or p_i^1 tends to zero, then the price index $P(p^0, p, v^0, v^1)$ should not tend to zero or plus infinity. However, with this interpretation of the test, which regards the values v_i^t as remaining constant as the p_i^0 or p_i^1 tends to zero, none of the commonly used index number formulae would satisfy this test. Hence this test should be interpreted as a test that applies to price indices $P(p^0, p^1, q^0, q^1)$ of the type studied in paragraphs 16.30 to 16.73, which is how Fisher intended the test to apply. Thus, Fisher's price determinateness test should be interpreted as follows: if any single price p_i^0 or p_i^1 tends to zero, then the price index $P(p^0, p, q^0, q^1)$ should not tend to zero or plus infinity. With this interpretation of the test, it can be verified that Laspeyres, Paasche and Fisher indices satisfy this test but the Törnqvist–Theil price index does not. Thus, when using the Törnqvist–Theil price index, care must be taken to bound the prices away from zero in order to avoid a meaningless index number value.

16.128 Walsh was aware that geometric average type indices such as the Törnqvist–Theil price index P_T or Walsh's geometric price index P_{GW} defined by equation (16.64) become somewhat unstable[72] as individual price relatives become very large or small:

> Hence in practice the geometric average is not likely to depart much from the truth. Still, we have seen that when the classes [i.e., expenditures] are very unequal and the price variations are very great, this average may deflect considerably (Walsh (1901, p. 373)).
>
> In the cases of moderate inequality in the sizes of the classes and of excessive variation in one of the prices, there seems to be a tendency on the part of the geometric method to deviate by itself, becoming untrustworthy, while the other two methods keep fairly close together (Walsh (1901, p. 404)).

16.129 Weighing all the arguments and tests presented above, it seems that there may be a slight preference for the use of the Fisher ideal price index as a suitable target index for a statistical agency, but, of course, opinions may differ on which set of axioms is the most appropriate to use in practice.

The test properties of the Lowe and Young indices

16.130 The Young and Lowe indices were defined in Chapter 15. In the present section, the axiomatic properties of these indices with respect to their price arguments are developed.[73]

16.131 Let $q^b \equiv [q_1^b, \ldots, q_n^b]$ and $p^b \equiv [p_1^b, \ldots, p_n^b]$ denote the quantity and price vectors pertaining to some base year. The corresponding *base year expenditure*

[72] That is, the index may approach zero or plus infinity.

[73] Baldwin (1990, p. 255) worked out a few of the axiomatic properties of the Lowe index.

shares can be defined in the usual way as

$$s_i^b \equiv \frac{p_i^b q_i^b}{\sum_{k=1}^{n} p_k^b q_k^b} \quad i=1,\ldots,n \tag{16.85}$$

Let $s^b \equiv [s_1^b, \ldots, s_n^b]$ denote the vector of base year expenditure shares. The Young (1812) price index between periods 0 and t is defined as follows:

$$P_Y(p^0, p^t, s^b) \equiv \sum_{i=1}^{n} s_i^b \left(\frac{p_i^t}{p_i^0}\right) \tag{16.86}$$

The Lowe (1823, p. 316) price index[74] between periods 0 and t is defined as follows:

$$P_{Lo}(p^0, p^t, q^b) \equiv \frac{\sum_{i=1}^{n} p_i^t q_i^b}{\sum_{k=1}^{n} p_k^0 q_k^b} = \frac{\sum_{i=1}^{n} s_i^b \left(\frac{p_i^t}{p_i^b}\right)}{\sum_{k=1}^{n} s_k^b \left(\frac{p_k^0}{p_k^b}\right)} \tag{16.87}$$

16.132 Drawing on the axioms listed above in this chapter, 12 desirable axioms for price indices of the form $P(p^0, p^1)$ are listed below. The period 0 and t price vectors, p^0 and p^t, are presumed to have strictly positive components.

T1: *Positivity*: $P(p^0, p^t) > 0$ if all prices are positive

T2: *Continuity*: $P(p^0, p^t)$ is a continuous function of prices

T3: *Identity test*: $P(p^0, p^0) = 1$

T4: *Homogeneity test for period* t *prices*: $P(p^0, \lambda p^t) = \lambda P(p^0, p^t)$ for all $\lambda > 0$

T5: *Homogeneity test for period* 0 *prices*: $P(\lambda p^0, p^t) = \lambda^{-1} P(p^0, p^t)$ for all $\lambda > 0$

T6: *Commodity reversal test*: $P(p^t, p^0) = P(p^{0*}, p^{t*})$ where p^{0*} and p^{t*} denote the same permutation of the components of the price vectors p^0 and p^t[75]

T7: *Invariance to changes in the units of measurement* (*commensurability test*)

T8: *Time reversal test*: $P(p^t, p^0) = 1/P(p^0, p^t)$

T9: *Circularity or transitivity test*: $P(p^0, p^2) = P(p^0, p^1) P(p^1, p^2)$

T10: *Mean value test*: $\min\{p_i^t/p_i^0 : i=1, \ldots, n\} \leq P(p^t, p^0) \leq \max\{p_i^t/p_i^0 : i=1, \ldots, n\}$

T11: *Monotonicity test with respect to period* t *prices*: $P(p^0, p^t) < P(p^0, p^{t*})$ if $p^t < p^{t*}$

T12: *Monotonicity test with respect to period* 0 *prices*: $P(p^0, p^t) > P(p^{0*}, p^t)$ if $p^0 < p^{0*}$

16.133 It is straightforward to show that the Lowe index defined by equation (16.87) satisfies all 12 of the axioms or tests listed above. Hence the Lowe index has very good axiomatic properties with respect to its price variables.[76]

16.134 It is straightforward to show that the Young index defined by equation (16.86) satisfies 10 of the 12 axioms, failing the time reversal test T8 and the circularity test T9. Thus the axiomatic properties of the Young index are definitely inferior to those of the Lowe index.

[74] This index number formula is also precisely Bean and Stine's (1924, p. 31) Type A index number formula. Walsh (1901, p. 539) initially mistakenly attributed Lowe's formula to G. Poulett Scrope (1833), who wrote *Principles of Political Economy* in 1833 and suggested Lowe's formula without acknowledging Lowe's priority. But in his discussion of Fisher's (1921) paper, Walsh (1921b, p. 543–544) corrects his mistake on assigning Lowe's formula:

> What index number should you then use? It should be this: $\sum qp_1/\sum qp_0$. This is the method used by Lowe within a year or two of one hundred years ago. In my [1901] book, I called it Scrope's index number; but it should be called Lowe's. Note that in it are used quantities neither of a base year nor of a subsequent year. The quantities used should be rough estimates of what the quantities were throughout the period or epoch.

[75] In applying this test to the Lowe and Young indices, it is assumed that the base year quantity vector q^b and the base year share vector s^b are subject to the same permutation.

[76] From the discussion in Chapter 15, it will be recalled that the main problem with the Lowe index occurs if the quantity weight vector q^b is not representative of the quantities that were purchased during the time interval between periods 0 and 1.

Appendix 16.1 Proof of the optimality of the Törnqvist–Theil price index in the second bilateral test approach

The tests (T1, T2, etc.) mentioned in this appendix are those presented in paragraphs 16.98 to 16.119.

1. Define $r_i \equiv p_i^1/p_i^0$ for $i=1,\ldots,n$. Using T1, T9 and equation (16.66), $P(p^0,p^1,v^0,v^1)=P^*(r,v^0,v^1)$. Using T6, T7 and equation (16.63):

$$P(p^0,p^1,v^0,v^1)=P^*(r,s^0,s^1) \qquad \text{(A16.1.1)}$$

where s^t is the period t expenditure share vector for $t=0,1$.

2. Let $x\equiv(x1,\ldots,xn)$ and $y\equiv(y1,\ldots,yn)$ be strictly positive vectors. The transitivity test T11 and equation (A16.1.1) imply that the function P^* has the following property:

$$P^*(x;\,s^0,s^1)P^*(y;\,s^0,s^1)=P^*(x_1y_1,\,\ldots,x_ny_n;\,s^0,s^1). \qquad \text{(A16.1.2)}$$

3. Using test T1, $P^*(r,s^0,s^1)>0$ and using test T14, $P^*(r,s^0,s^1)$ is strictly increasing in the components of r. The identity test T3 implies that

$$P^*(1_n,s^0,s^1)=1 \qquad \text{(A16.1.3)}$$

where 1_n is a vector of ones of dimension n. Using a result attributable to Eichhorn (1978, p. 66), it can be seen that these properties of P^* are sufficient to imply that there exist positive functions $\alpha_i(s^0,s^1)$ for $i=1,\ldots,n$ such that P^* has the following representation:

$$\ln P^*(r,s^0,s^1)=\sum_{i=1}^{n}\alpha_i(s^0,s^1)\ln r_i \qquad \text{(A16.1.4)}$$

4. The continuity test T2 implies that the positive functions $\alpha_i(s^0,s^1)$ are continuous. For $\lambda>0$, the linear homogeneity test T4 implies that

$$\begin{aligned}\ln P^*(\lambda r,s^0,s^1)&=\ln\lambda+\ln P^*(r,s^0,s^1)\\&=\sum_{i=1}^{n}\alpha_i(s^0,s^1)\ln\lambda r_i \quad \text{using (A16.1.4)}\\&=\sum_{i=1}^{n}\alpha_i(s^0,s^1)\ln\lambda+\sum_{i=1}^{n}\alpha_i(s^0,s^1)\ln r_i\\&=\sum_{i=1}^{n}\alpha_i(s^0,s^1)\ln\lambda+\ln P^*(r,s^0,s^1)\\&\quad\text{using (A16.1.4)}\end{aligned} \qquad \text{(A16.1.5)}$$

Equating the right-hand sides of the first and last lines in equation (A16.1.5) shows that the functions $\alpha_i(s^0,s^1)$ must satisfy the following restriction:

$$\sum_{i=1}^{n}\alpha_i(s^0,s^1)=1 \qquad \text{(A16.1.6)}$$

for all strictly positive vectors s^0 and s^1.

5. Using the weighting test T16 and the commodity reversal test T8, equations (16.69) hold. Equation (16.69) combined with the commensurability test T9 implies that P^* satisfies the following equation:

$$P^*(1,\,\ldots,1,r_i,1,\,\ldots,1;s^0,s^1)=f(1,r_i,s^0,s^1);\quad i=1,\,\ldots,n \qquad \text{(A16.1.7)}$$

for all $r_i>0$ where f is the function defined in test T16.

6. Substitute equation (A16.1.7) into equation (A16.1.4) in order to obtain the following system of equations:

$$P^*(1,\,\ldots,1,r_i,1,\,\ldots,1;s^0,s^1)=f(1,r_i,s^0,s^1)=\alpha_i(s^0,s^1)\ln r_i \quad i=1,\,\ldots,n \qquad \text{(A16.1.8)}$$

But equation (A16.1.8) implies that the positive continuous function of $2n$ variables $\alpha_i(s^0,s^1)$ is constant with respect to all of its arguments except s_i^0 and s_i^1 and this property holds for each i. Thus each $\alpha_i(s^0,s^1)$ can be replaced by the positive continuous function of two variables $\beta_i(s_i^0,s_i^1)$ for $i=1,\ldots,n$.[77] Now replace the $\alpha_i(s^0,s^1)$ in equation (A16.1.4) by the $\beta_i(s_i^0,s_i^1)$ for $i=1,\ldots,n$ and the following representation for P^* is obtained:

$$\ln P^*(r,s^0,s^1)=\sum_{i=1}^{n}\beta_i(s_i^0,s_i^1)\ln r_i \qquad \text{(A16.1.9)}$$

7. Equation (A16.1.6) implies that the functions $\beta_i(s_i^0,s_i^1)$ also satisfy the following restrictions:

$$\sum_{i=1}^{n}s_i^0=1;\ \text{and}\sum_{i=1}^{n}s_i^1=1\ \text{implies}\sum_{i=1}^{n}\beta_i(s_i^0,s_i^1)=1 \qquad \text{(A16.1.10)}$$

8. Assume that the weighting test T17 holds and substitute equation (16.71) into equation (A16.1.9) in order to obtain the following equation:

$$\beta_i(0,0)\ln\left(\frac{p_i^1}{p_i^0}\right)=0;\quad i=1,\,\ldots,n \qquad \text{(A16.1.11)}$$

Since the p_i^1 and p_i^0 can be arbitrary positive numbers, it can be seen that equation (A16.1.11) implies

$$\beta_i(0,0)=0;\quad i=1,\,\ldots,n \qquad \text{(A16.1.12)}$$

9. Assume that the number of commodities n is equal to or greater than 3. Using equations (A16.1.10) and (A16.1.12), Theorem 2 in Aczél (1987, p. 8) can be applied and the following functional form for each of the $\beta_i(s_i^0,s_i^1)$ is obtained:

$$\beta_i(s_i^0,s_i^1)=\gamma s_i^0+(1-\gamma)s_i^1;\quad i=1,\,\ldots,n \qquad \text{(A16.1.13)}$$

where γ is a positive number satisfying $0<\gamma<1$.

10. Finally, the time reversal test T10 *or* the quantity weights symmetry test T12 can be used to show that γ must equal ½. Substituting this value for γ back into equation (A16.1.13) and then substituting that equation back into equation (A16.1.9), the functional form for P^* and hence P is determined as

$$\ln P(p^0,p^1,v^0,v^1)=\ln P^*(r,s^0,s^1)=\sum_{i=1}^{n}\frac{1}{2}(s_i^0+s_i^1)\ln\left(\frac{p_i^1}{p_i^0}\right). \qquad \text{(A16.1.14)}$$

[77] More explicitly, $\beta_1(s_1^0,s_1^1)\equiv\alpha_1(s_1^0,1,\ldots,1;s_1^1,1,\ldots,1)$ and so on. That is, in defining $\beta_1(s_1^0,s_1^1)$, the function $\alpha_1(s_1^0,1,\ldots,1;s_1^1,1,\ldots,1)$ is used where all components of the vectors s^0 and s^1 except the first are set equal to an arbitrary positive number such as 1.

THE ECONOMIC APPROACH TO INDEX NUMBER THEORY: THE SINGLE-HOUSEHOLD CASE 17

Introduction

17.1 This chapter and the next cover the economic approach to index number theory. This chapter considers the case of a *single* household, while the following chapter deals with the case of *many* households. A brief outline of the contents of the present chapter follows.

17.2 In paragraphs 17.9 to 17.17, the theory of the cost of living index for a single consumer or household is presented. This theory was originally developed by the Russian economist, A.A. Konüs (1924). The relationship between the (unobservable) true cost of living index and the observable Laspeyres and Paasche indices will be explained. It should be noted that, in the economic approach to index number theory, it is assumed that households regard the observed price data as given, while the quantity data are regarded as solutions to various economic optimization problems. Many price statisticians find the assumptions made in the economic approach to be somewhat implausible. Perhaps the best way to regard the assumptions made in the economic approach is that these assumptions simply formalize the fact that consumers tend to purchase more of a commodity if its price falls relative to other prices.

17.3 In paragraphs 17.18 to 17.26, the preferences of the consumer are restricted compared to the completely general case treated in paragraphs 17.9 to 17.17. In paragraphs 17.18 to 17.26, it is assumed that the function that represents the consumer's preferences over alternative combinations of commodities is homogeneous of degree one. This assumption means that each indifference surface (the set of commodity bundles that give the consumer the same satisfaction or utility) is a radial blow-up of a single indifference surface. With this extra assumption, the theory of the true cost of living simplifies, as will be seen.

17.4 In the sections starting with paragraphs 17.27, 17.33 and 17.44, it is shown that the Fisher, Walsh and Törnqvist price indices (which emerge as being "best" in the various non-economic approaches) are also among the "best" in the economic approach to index number theory. In these sections, the preference function of the single household will be further restricted compared to the assumptions on preferences made in the previous two sections. Specific functional forms for the consumer's utility function are assumed and it turns out that, with each of these specific assumptions, the consumer's true cost of living index can be exactly calculated using observable price and quantity data. Each of the three specific functional forms for the consumer's utility function has the property that it can approximate an arbitrary linearly homogeneous function to the second order; i.e., in economics terminology, each of these three functional forms is *flexible*. Hence, using the terminology introduced by Diewert (1976), the Fisher, Walsh and Törnqvist price indices are examples of *superlative* index number formulae.

17.5 In paragraphs 17.50 to 17.54, it is shown that the Fisher, Walsh and Törnqvist price indices approximate each other very closely using "normal" time series data. This is a very convenient result since these three index number formulae repeatedly show up as being "best" in all the approaches to index number theory. Hence this approximation result implies that it normally will not matter which of these three indices is chosen as the preferred target index for a consumer price index (CPI).

17.6 The Paasche and Laspeyres price indices have a very convenient mathematical property: they are *consistent in aggregation*. For example, if the Laspeyres formula is used to construct sub-indices for, say, food or clothing, then these sub-index values can be treated as sub-aggregate price relatives and, using the expenditure shares on these sub-aggregates, the Laspeyres formula can be applied again to form a two-stage Laspeyres price index. Consistency in aggregation means that this two-stage index is equal to the corresponding single-stage index. In paragraphs 17.55 to 17.60, it is shown that the superlative indices derived in the earlier sections are not exactly consistent in aggregation but are approximately consistent in aggregation.

17.7 In paragraphs 17.61 to 17.64, a very interesting index number formula is derived: the Lloyd (1975) and Moulton (1996a) price index. This index number formula makes use of the same information that is required in order to calculate a Laspeyres index (namely, base period expenditure shares, base period prices and current period prices), plus one other parameter (the elasticity of substitution between commodities). If information on this extra parameter can be obtained, then the resulting index can largely eliminate substitution bias and it can be calculated using basically the same information that is required to obtain the Laspeyres index.

17.8 The section starting with paragraph 17.65 considers the problem of defining a true cost of living index when the consumer has annual preferences over commodities but faces monthly (or quarterly) prices. This section attempts to provide an economic foundation for the Lowe index studied in Chapter 15. It also provides an introduction to the problems associated with the existence of seasonal commodities, which are considered at more length in Chapter 22. The final section deals with situations where there may be a zero price for a commodity in one period, but where the price is non-zero in the other period.

The Konüs cost of living index and observable bounds

17.9 This section deals with the theory of the cost of living index for a single consumer (or household) that was first developed by the Russian economist, Konüs (1924). This theory relies on the assumption of *optimizing behaviour* on the part of economic agents (consumers or producers). Thus, given a vector of commodity prices p^t that the household faces in a given time period t, it is assumed that the corresponding observed quantity vector q^t is the solution to a cost minimization problem that involves the consumer's preference or utility function f.[1] Thus in contrast to the axiomatic approach to index number theory, the economic approach does not assume that the two quantity vectors q^0 and q^1 are independent of the two price vectors p^0 and p^1. In the economic approach, the period 0 quantity vector q^0 is determined by the consumer's preference function f and the period 0 vector of prices p^0 that the consumer faces, and the period 1 quantity vector q^1 is determined by the consumer's preference function f and the period 1 vector of prices p^1.

17.10 The economic approach to index number theory assumes that "the" consumer has well-defined *preferences* over different combinations of the n consumer commodities or items.[2] Each combination of items can be represented by a positive quantity vector $q \equiv [q_1, \ldots, q_n]$. The consumer's preferences over alternative possible consumption vectors, q, are assumed to be representable by a continuous, non-decreasing and concave[3] utility function f. Thus if $f(q^1) > f(q^0)$, then the consumer prefers the consumption vector q^1 to q^0. It is further assumed that the consumer minimizes the cost of achieving the period t utility level $u^t \equiv f(q^t)$ for periods $t = 0, 1$. Thus we assume that the observed period t consumption vector q^t solves the following period t cost minimization problem:

$$C(u^t, p^t) \equiv \min_q \left\{ \sum_{i=1}^{n} p_i^t q_i : f(q) = u^t \equiv f(q^t) \right\} = \sum_{i=1}^{n} p_i^t q_i^t \quad \text{for } t = 0, 1 \qquad (17.1)$$

The period t price vector for the n commodities under consideration that the consumer faces is p^t. Note that the solution to the cost or expenditure minimization problem (17.1) for a general utility level u and general vector of commodity prices p defines the *consumer's cost function*, $C(u, p)$. The cost function will be used below in order to define the consumer's *cost of living price index*.

17.11 The Konüs (1924) family of *true cost of living indices* pertaining to two periods where the consumer faces the strictly positive price vectors $p^0 \equiv (p_1^0, \ldots, p_n^0)$ and $p^1 \equiv (p_1^1, \ldots, p_n^1)$ in periods 0 and 1, respectively, is defined as the ratio of the minimum costs of achieving the same utility level $u \equiv f(q)$, where $q \equiv (q_1, \ldots, q_n)$ is a positive reference quantity vector:

$$P_K(p^0, p^1, q) \equiv \frac{C(f(q), p^1)}{C(f(q), p^0)} \qquad (17.2)$$

Note that definition (17.2) defines a family of price indices, because there is one such index for each reference quantity vector q chosen.

17.12 It is natural to choose two specific reference quantity vectors q in definition (17.2): the observed base period quantity vector q^0 and the current period quantity vector q^1. The first of these two choices leads to the following *Laspeyres–Konüs true cost of living index*:

$$P_K(p^0, p^1, q^0) \equiv \frac{C(f(q^0), p^1)}{C(f(q^0), p^0)} = \frac{C(f(q^0), p^1)}{\sum_{i=1}^{n} p_i^0 q_i^0} \quad \text{using (17.1) for } t=0$$

$$= \frac{\min_q \left\{ \sum_{i=1}^{n} p_i^1 q_i : f(q) = f(q^0) \right\}}{\sum_{i=1}^{n} p_i^0 q_i^0} \qquad (17.3)$$

using the definition of the cost minimization problem that defines $C(f(q^0), p^1)$

$$\leq \frac{\sum_{i=1}^{n} p_i^1 q_i^0}{\sum_{i=1}^{n} p_i^0 q_i^0}$$

since $q^0 \equiv (q_1^0, \ldots, q_n^0)$ is feasible for the minimization problem

$$= P_L(p^0, p^1, q^0, q^1)$$

where P_L is the Laspeyres price index. Thus the (unobservable) Laspeyres–Konüs true cost of living index is bounded from above by the observable Laspeyres price index.[4]

17.13 The second of the two natural choices for a reference quantity vector q in definition (17.2) leads to the following *Paasche–Konüs true cost of living*

[1] For a description of the economic theory of the input and output price indices, see Balk (1998a). In the economic theory of the output price index, q^t is assumed to be the solution to a revenue maximization problem involving the output price vector p^t.

[2] In this chapter, these preferences are assumed to be invariant over time, while in the following chapter, this assumption is relaxed (one of the environmental variables could be a time variable that shifts tastes).

[3] Note that f is concave if and only if $f(\lambda q^1 + (1-\lambda)q^2) \geq \lambda f(q^1) + (1-\lambda)f(q^2)$ for all $0 \leq \lambda \leq 1$ and all $q^1 \gg 0_n$ and $q^2 \gg 0_n$. Note also that $q \geq 0_N$ means that each component of the N-dimensional vector q is non-negative, $q \gg 0_n$ means that each component of q is positive and $q > 0_n$ means that $q \geq 0_n$ but $q \neq 0_n$; i.e., q is non-negative but at least one component is positive.

[4] This inequality was first obtained by Konüs (1924; 1939, p. 17). See also Pollak (1983).

index:

$$P_K(p^0,p^1,q^1) \equiv \frac{C(f(q^1),p^1)}{C(f(q^1),p^0)} = \frac{\sum_{i=1}^n p_i^1 q_i^1}{C(f(q^1),p^0)} \quad \text{using (17.1) for } t=1$$

$$= \frac{\sum_{i=1}^n p_i^1 q_i^1}{\min_q \left\{ \sum_{i=1}^n p_i^0 q_i : f(q)=f(q^1) \right\}} \qquad (17.4)$$

using the definition of the cost minimization problem that defines

$$C(f(q^0),p^0) \geq \frac{\sum_{i=1}^n p_i^1 q_i^1}{\sum_{i=1}^n p_i^0 q_i^1} \quad \text{since } q^1 \equiv (q_1^1,\ldots,q_n^1)$$

is feasible for the minimization problem and thus

$C(f(q^1),p^0) \leq \sum_{i=1}^n p_i^0 q_i^1$ and hence

$$\frac{1}{C(f(q^1),p^0)} \geq \frac{1}{\sum_{i=1}^n p_i^0 q_i^1} = P_P(p^0,p^1,q^0,q^1)$$

where P_P is the Paasche price index. Thus the (unobservable) Paasche–Konüs true cost of living index is bounded from below by the observable Paasche price index.[5]

17.14 It is possible to illustrate the two inequalities (17.3) and (17.4) if there are only two commodities; see Figure 17.1. The solution to the period 0 cost minimization problem is the vector q^0. The straight line C represents the consumer's period 0 budget constraint, the set of quantity points q_1, q_2 such that $p_1^0 q_1 + p_2^0 q_2 = p_1^0 q_1^0 + p_2^0 q_2^0$. The curved line through q^0 is the consumer's period 0 indifference curve, the set of points q_1, q_2 such that $f(q_1,q_2) = f(q_1^0,q_2^0)$; i.e., it is the set of consumption vectors that give the same utility as the observed period 0 consumption vector q^0. The solution to the period 1 cost minimization problem is the vector q^1. The straight line D represents the consumer's period 1 budget constraint, the set of quantity points q_1, q_2 such that $p_1^1 q_1 + p_2^1 q_2 = p_1^1 q_1^1 + p_2^1 q_2^1$. The curved line through q^1 is the consumer's period 1 indifference curve, the set of points q_1, q_2 such that $f(q_1,q_2) = f(q_1^1,q_2^1)$; i.e., it is the set of consumption vectors that give the same utility as the observed period 1 consumption vector q^1. The point q^{0*} solves the hypothetical problem of minimizing the cost of achieving the base period utility level $u^0 \equiv f(q^0)$ when facing the period 1 price vector $p^1 = (p_1^1, p_2^1)$. Thus we have $C[u^0,p^1] = p_1^1 q_1^{0*} + p_2^1 q_2^{0*}$ and the dashed line A is the corresponding isocost line $p_1^1 q_1 + p_2^1 q_2 = C[u^0,p^1]$. Note that the hypothetical cost line A is parallel to the actual period 1 cost

Figure 17.1 The Laspeyres and Paasche bounds to the true cost of living index

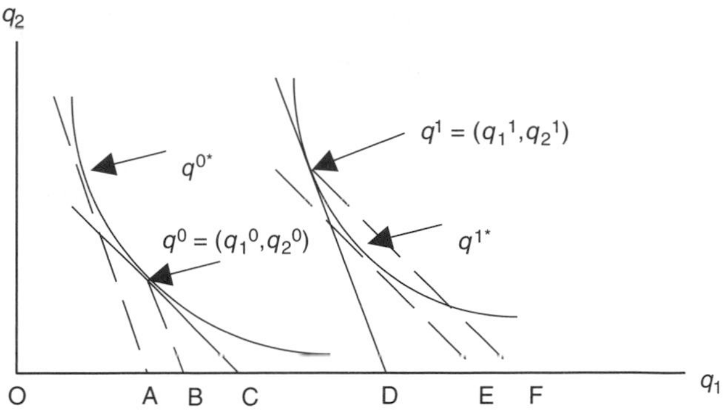

line D. From equation (17.3), the Laspeyres–Konüs true index is $C[u^0,p^1]/[p_1^0 q_1^0 + p_2^0 q_2^0]$, while the ordinary Laspeyres index is $[p_1^1 q_1^0 + p_2^1 q_2^0]/[p_1^0 q_1^0 + p_2^0 q_2^0]$. Since the denominators for these two indices are the same, the difference between the indices is attributable to the differences in their numerators. In Figure 17.1, this difference in the numerators is expressed by the fact that the cost line through A lies below the parallel cost line through B. Now if the consumer's indifference curve through the observed period 0 consumption vector q^0 were L-shaped with vertex at q^0, then the consumer would not change his or her consumption pattern in response to a change in the relative prices of the two commodities while keeping a fixed standard of living. In this case, the hypothetical vector q^{0*} would coincide with q^0, the dashed line through A would coincide with the dashed line through B and the true Laspeyres–Konüs index would coincide with the ordinary Laspeyres index. However, L-shaped indifference curves are not generally consistent with consumer behaviour; i.e., when the price of a commodity decreases, consumers generally demand more of it. Thus, in the general case, there will be a gap between the points A and B. The magnitude of this gap represents the amount of *substitution bias* between the true index and the corresponding Laspeyres index; i.e., the Laspeyres index will generally be greater than the corresponding true cost of living index, $P_K(p^0,p^1,q^0)$.

17.15 Figure 17.1 can also be used to illustrate the inequality (17.4). First note that the dashed lines E and F are parallel to the period 0 isocost line through C. The point q^{1*} solves the hypothetical problem of minimizing the cost of achieving the current period utility level $u^1 \equiv f(q^1)$ when facing the period 0 price vector $p^0 = (p_1^0, p_2^0)$. Thus we have $C[u^1,p^0] = p_1^0 q_1^{1*} + p_2^0 q_2^{1*}$ and the dashed line E is the corresponding isocost line $p_1^1 q_1 + p_2^1 q_2 = C[u^0,p^1]$. From equation (17.4), the Paasche–Konüs true index is $[p_1^1 q_1^1 + p_2^1 q_2^1]/C[u^1,p^0]$, while the ordinary Paasche index is $[p_1^1 q_1^1 + p_2^1 q_2^1]/[p_1^0 q_1^1 + p_2^0 q_2^1]$. Since the numerators for these two indices are the same, the difference between the indices is attributable to the differences in their denominators. In Figure 17.1, this difference in the denominators is expressed by the fact that the cost line through E lies below the parallel cost line through F. The magnitude of this difference

[5] This inequality is attributable to Konüs (1924; 1939, p. 19); see also Pollak (1983).

represents the amount of substitution bias between the true index and the corresponding Paasche index; i.e., the Paasche index will generally be less than the corresponding true cost of living index, $P_K(p^0, p^1, q^1)$. Note that this inequality goes in the opposite direction to the previous inequality between the two Laspeyres indices. The reason for this change in direction is attributable to the fact that one set of differences between the two indices takes place in the numerators of the indices (the Laspeyres inequalities), while the other set takes place in the denominators of the indices (the Paasche inequalities).

17.16 The bound (17.3) on the Laspeyres–Konüs true cost of living index $P_K(p^0, p^1, q^0)$ using the base period level of utility as the living standard is *one-sided*, as is the bound (17.4) on the Paasche–Konüs true cost of living index $P_K(p^0, p^1, q^1)$ using the *current period* level of utility as the living standard. In a remarkable result, Konüs (1924; 1939, p. 20) showed that there exists an intermediate consumption vector q^* that is on the straight line joining the base period consumption vector q^0 and the current period consumption vector q^1 such that the corresponding (unobservable) true cost of living index $P_K(p^0, p^1, q^*)$ is between the observable Laspeyres and Paasche indices, P_L and P_P.[6] Thus we have the existence of a number λ^* between 0 and 1 such that

$$P_L \leq P_K(p^0, p^1, \lambda^* q^0 + (1-\lambda^*)q^1) \leq P_P \text{ or}$$
$$P_P \leq P_K(p^0, p^1, \lambda^* q^0 + (1-\lambda^*)q^1) \leq P_L \qquad (17.5)$$

The inequalities (17.5) are of some practical importance. If the observable (in principle) Paasche and Laspeyres indices are not too far apart, then taking a symmetric average of these indices should provide a good approximation to a true cost of living index where the reference standard of living is somewhere between the base and current period living standards. To determine the precise symmetric average of the Paasche and Laspeyres indices, appeal can be made to the results in paragraphs 15.18 to 15.32 in Chapter 15, and the geometric mean of the Paasche and Laspeyres indices can be justified as being the "best" average, which is the Fisher price index. Thus the Fisher ideal price index receives a fairly strong justification as a good approximation to an unobservable theoretical cost of living index.

17.17 The bounds (17.3)–(17.5) are the best that can be obtained on true cost of living indices without making further assumptions. Further assumptions are made below on the class of utility functions that describe the consumer's tastes for the n commodities under consideration. With these extra assumptions, the consumer's true cost of living can be determined exactly.

The true cost of living index when preferences are homothetic

17.18 Up to now, the consumer's preference function f did not have to satisfy any particular homogeneity assumption. For the remainder of this section, it is assumed that f is (positively) *linearly homogeneous*.[7] In the economics literature, this is known as the assumption of *homothetic preferences*.[8] This assumption is not strictly justified from the viewpoint of actual economic behaviour, but it leads to economic price indices that are independent of the consumer's standard of living.[9] Under this assumption, the consumer's expenditure or cost function, $C(u,p)$ defined by equation (17.1), decomposes as follows. For positive commodity prices $p \gg 0_N$ and a positive utility level u, then, using the definition of C as the minimum cost of achieving the given utility level u, the following equalities can be derived:

$$\begin{aligned}
C(u,p) &\equiv \min_q \left\{ \sum_{i=1}^{n} p_i q_i : f(q_1, \ldots, q_n) \geq u \right\} \\
&= \min_q \left\{ \sum_{i=1}^{n} p_i q_i : \frac{1}{u} f(q_1, \ldots, q_n) \geq 1 \right\} \\
&\quad \text{dividing by } u > 0 \\
&= \min_q \left\{ \sum_{i=1}^{n} p_i q_i : f\left(\frac{q_1}{u}, \ldots, \frac{q_n}{u}\right) \geq 1 \right\} \\
&\quad \text{using the linear homogeneity of } f \\
&= u \min_q \left\{ \sum_{i=1}^{n} \frac{p_i q_i}{u} : f\left(\frac{q_1}{u}, \ldots, \frac{q_n}{u}\right) \geq 1 \right\} \\
&= u \min_z \left\{ \sum_{i=1}^{n} p_i z_i : f(z_1, \ldots, z_n) \geq 1 \right\} \quad \text{letting} \\
z_i = \frac{q_i}{u} &= uC(1,p) \quad \text{using definition (17.1)} \\
&= uc(p) \qquad (17.6)
\end{aligned}$$

[6] For more recent applications of the Konüs method of proof, see Diewert (1983a, p. 191) for an application to the consumer context and Diewert (1983b, pp. 1059–1061) for an application to the producer context.

[7] The linear homogeneity property means that f satisfies the following condition: $f(\lambda q) = \lambda f(q)$ for all $\lambda > 0$ and all $q \gg 0_n$. This assumption is fairly restrictive in the consumer context. It implies that each indifference curve is a radial projection of the unit utility indifference curve. It also implies that all income elasticities of demand are unity, which is contradicted by empirical evidence.

[8] More precisely, Shephard (1953) defined a homothetic function to be a monotonic transformation of a linearly homogeneous function. However, if a consumer's utility function is homothetic, it can always be rescaled to be linearly homogeneous without changing consumer behaviour. Hence, the homothetic preferences assumption can simply be identified with the linear homogeneity assumption.

[9] This particular branch of the economic approach to index number theory is attributable to Shephard (1953; 1970) and Samuelson and Swamy (1974). Shephard in particular realized the importance of the homotheticity assumption in conjunction with separability assumptions in justifying the existence of sub-indices of the overall cost of living index. It should be noted that, if the consumer's change in real income or utility between the two periods under consideration is not too large, then assuming that the consumer has homothetic preferences will lead to a true cost of living index which is very close to Laspeyres–Konüs and Paasche–Konüs true cost of living indices defined by equations (17.3) and (17.4). Another way of justifying the homothetic preferences assumption is to use equation (17.49), which justifies the use of the superlative Törnqvist–Theil index P_T in the context of non-homothetic preferences. Since P_T is usually numerically close to other superlative indices that are derived using the homothetic preferences assumption, it can be seen that the assumption of homotheticity will usually not be empirically misleading in the index number context.

where $c(p) = C(1, p)$ is the *unit cost function* that corresponds to f.[10] It can be shown that the unit cost function $c(p)$ satisfies the same regularity conditions that f satisfies; i.e., $c(p)$ is positive, concave and (positively) linearly homogeneous for positive price vectors.[11] Substituting equation (17.6) into equation (17.1) and using $u^t = f(q^t)$ leads to the following equation:

$$\sum_{i=1}^{n} p_i^t q_i^t = c(p^t) f(q^t) \quad \text{for } t = 0, 1 \qquad (17.7)$$

Thus, under the linear homogeneity assumption on the utility function f, observed period t expenditure on the n commodities is equal to the period t unit cost $c(p^t)$ of achieving one unit of utility times the period t utility level, $f(q^t)$. Obviously, the period t unit cost, $c(p^t)$, can be identified as the period t price level P^t and the period t level of utility, $f(q^t)$, as the period t quantity level Q^t.[12]

17.19 The linear homogeneity assumption on the consumer's preference function f leads to a simplification for the family of Konüs true cost of living indices, $P_K(p^0, p^1, q)$, defined by equation (17.2). Using this definition for an arbitrary reference quantity vector q:

$$\begin{aligned} P_K(p^0, p^1, q) &\equiv \frac{C(f(q), p^1)}{C(f(q), p^0)} \\ &= \frac{c(p^1) f(q)}{c(p^0) f(q)} \quad \text{using (17.6) twice} \\ &= \frac{c(p^1)}{c(p^0)} \qquad (17.8) \end{aligned}$$

Thus under the homothetic preferences assumption, the entire family of Konüs true cost of living indices collapses to a single index, $c(p^1)/c(p^0)$, the ratio of the minimum costs of achieving unit utility level when the consumer faces period 1 and 0 prices respectively. Put another way, under the homothetic preferences assumption, $P_K(p^0, p^1, q)$ is independent of the reference quantity vector q.

17.20 If the Konüs true cost of living index defined by the right-hand side of equation (17.8) is used as the price index concept, then the corresponding implicit quantity index defined using the product test (i.e., the product of the price index times the quantity index is equal to the value ratio) has the following form:

$$\begin{aligned} Q(p^0, p^1, q^0, q^1) &\equiv \frac{\sum_{i=1}^{n} p_i^1 q_i^1}{\sum_{i=1}^{n} p_i^t q_i^t P_K(p^0, p^1, q)} \\ &= \frac{c(p^1) f(q^1)}{c(p^0) f(q^0) P_K(p^0, p^1, q)} \quad \text{using (17.7) twice} \\ &= \frac{c(p^1) f(q^1)}{c(p^0) f(q^0) \{c(p^1)/c(p^0)\}} \quad \text{using (17.8)} \\ &= \frac{f(q^1)}{f(q^0)} \qquad (17.9) \end{aligned}$$

Thus, under the homothetic preferences assumption, the implicit quantity index that corresponds to the true cost of living price index $c(p^1)/c(p^0)$ is the utility ratio $f(q^1)/f(q^0)$. Since the utility function is assumed to be homogeneous of degree one, this is the natural definition for a quantity index.

17.21 In subsequent material, two additional results from economic theory will be needed: Wold's Identity and Shephard's Lemma. Wold's (1944, pp. 69–71; 1953, p. 145) Identity is the following result. Assuming that the consumer satisfies the cost minimization assumptions (17.1) for periods 0 and 1 and that the utility function f is differentiable at the observed quantity vectors q^0 and q^1, it can be shown[13] that the following equation holds:

$$\frac{p_i^t}{\sum_{k=1}^{n} p_k^t q_k^t} = \frac{\dfrac{\partial f(q^t)}{\partial q_i}}{\sum_{k=1}^{n} q_k^t \dfrac{\partial f(q^t)}{\partial q_k}} \quad \text{for } t = 0, 1 \text{ and } k = 1, \ldots, n \qquad (17.10)$$

where $\partial f(q^t)/\partial q_i$ denotes the partial derivative of the utility function f with respect to the ith quantity q_i, evaluated at the period t quantity vector q^t.

17.22 If the homothetic preferences assumption is made and it is assumed that the utility function is linearly homogeneous, then Wold's Identity can be simplified into an equation that will prove to be very useful:[14]

$$\frac{p_i^t}{\sum_{k=1}^{n} p_k^t q_k^t} = \frac{\partial f(q^t)/\partial q_i}{f(q^t)} \quad \text{for } t = 0, 1 \text{ and } k = 1, \ldots, n \qquad (17.11)$$

[10] Economists will recognize the producer theory counterpart to the result $C(u, p) = uc(p)$: if a producer's production function f is subject to constant returns to scale, then the corresponding total cost function $C(u, p)$ is equal to the product of the output level u times the unit cost $c(p)$.

[11] Obviously, the utility function f determines the consumer's cost function $C(u, p)$ as the solution to the cost minimization problem in the first line of equation (17.6). Then the unit cost function $c(p)$ is defined as $C(1, p)$. Thus f determines c. But we can also use c to determine f under appropriate regularity conditions. In the economics literature, this is known as *duality theory*. For additional material on duality theory and the properties of f and c, see Samuelson (1953), Shephard (1953) and Diewert (1974a; 1993b, pp.107–123).

[12] There is also a producer theory interpretation of the above theory; i.e., let f be the producer's (constant returns to scale) production function, let p be a vector of input prices that the producer faces, let q be an input vector and let $u = f(q)$ be the maximum output that can be produced using the input vector q. $C(u, p) \equiv \min_q \{\sum_{i=1}^{n} p_i q_i : f(q) \geq u\}$ is the producer's cost function in this case and $c(p^t)$ can be identified as the period t input price level, while $f(q^t)$ is the period t aggregate input level.

[13] To prove this, consider the first-order necessary conditions for the strictly positive vector q^t to solve the period t cost minimization problem. The conditions of Lagrange with respect to the vector of q variables are: $p^t = \lambda^t \nabla f(q^t)$, where λ^t is the optimal Lagrange multiplier and $\nabla f(q^t)$ is the vector of first-order partial derivatives of f evaluated at q^t. Note that this system of equations is the price equals a constant times marginal utility equations that are familiar to economists. Now take the inner product of both sides of this equation with respect to the period t quantity vector q^t and solve the resulting equation for λ^t. Substitute this solution back into the vector equation $p^t = \lambda^t \nabla f(q^t)$ and equation (17.10) is obtained.

[14] Differentiate both sides of the equation $f(\lambda q) = \lambda f(q)$ with respect to λ, and then evaluate the resulting equation at $\lambda = 1$. The equation $\sum_{i=1}^{n} f_i(q) q_i = f(q)$ is obtained where $f_i(q) \equiv \partial f(q)/\partial q_i$.

17.23 Shephard's (1953, p. 11) Lemma is the following result. Consider the period t cost minimization problem defined by equation (17.1). If the cost function $C(u,p)$ is differentiable with respect to the components of the price vector p, then the period t quantity vector q^t is equal to the vector of first-order partial derivatives of the cost function with respect to the components of p:

$$q_i^t = \frac{\partial C(u^t, p^t)}{\partial p_i} \quad \text{for } i=1,\ldots,n \text{ and } t=0,1 \qquad (17.12)$$

17.24 To explain why equation (17.12) holds, consider the following argument. Because it is assumed that the observed period t quantity vector q^t solves the cost minimization problem defined by $C(u^t, p^t)$, then q^t must be feasible for this problem so it must be the case that $f(q^t)=u^t$. Thus, q^t is a feasible solution for the following cost minimization problem where the general price vector p has replaced the specific period t price vector p^t:

$$C(u^t, p) \equiv \min_q \left\{ \sum_{i=1}^n p_i q_i : f(q_1,\ldots,q_n) \geq u^t \right\} \leq \sum_{i=1}^n p_i q_i^t \qquad (17.13)$$

where the inequality follows from the fact that $q^t \equiv (q_1^t,\ldots,q_n^t)$ is a feasible (but usually not optimal) solution for the cost minimization problem in equation (17.13). Now define for each strictly positive price vector p the function $g(p)$ as follows:

$$g(p) \equiv \sum_{i=1}^n p_i q_i^t - C(u^t, p) \qquad (17.14)$$

where, as usual, $p \equiv (p_1,\ldots,p_n)$. Using equations (17.13) and (17.1), it can be seen that $g(p)$ is minimized (over all strictly positive price vectors p) at $p=p^t$. Thus the first-order necessary conditions for minimizing a differentiable function of n variables hold, which simplify to equation (17.12).

17.25 If the homothetic preferences assumption is made and it is assumed that the utility function is linearly homogeneous, then using equation (17.6), Shephard's Lemma (17.12) becomes:

$$q_i^t = u^t \frac{\partial c(p^t)}{\partial p_i} \quad \text{for } i=1,\ldots,n \text{ and } t=0,1 \qquad (17.15)$$

Combining equations (17.15) and (17.7), the following equation is obtained:

$$\frac{q_i^t}{\sum_{k=1}^n p_k^t q_k^t} = \frac{\partial c(p^t)}{\partial p_i} \Big/ c(p^t) \quad \text{for } i=1,\ldots,n \text{ and } t=0,1 \qquad (17.16)$$

17.26 Note the symmetry of equation (17.16) with equation (17.11). It is these two equations that will be used in subsequent material in this chapter.

Superlative indices: The Fisher ideal index

17.27 Suppose the consumer has the following utility function:

$$f(q_1,\ldots,q_n) \equiv \sqrt{\sum_{i=1}^n \sum_{k=1}^n a_{ik} q_i q_k}, \quad \text{where } a_{ik} = a_{ki} \text{ for all } i \text{ and } k \qquad (17.17)$$

Differentiating $f(q)$ defined by equation (17.17) with respect to q_i yields the following equation:

$$f_i(q) = \frac{1}{2} \frac{2\sum_{k=1}^n a_{ik} q_k}{\sqrt{\sum_{j=1}^n \sum_{k=1}^n a_{jk} q_j q_k}} \quad \text{for } i=1,\ldots,n$$

$$= \frac{\sum_{k=1}^n a_{ik} q_k}{f(q)} \qquad (17.18)$$

where $f_i(q) \equiv \partial f(q^t)/\partial q_i$. In order to obtain the first equation in (17.18), it is necessary to use the symmetry conditions, $a_{ik} = a_{ki}$. Now evaluate the second equation in (17.18) at the observed period t quantity vector $q^t \equiv (q_1^t,\ldots,q_n^t)$ and divide both sides of the resulting equation by $f(q^t)$. The following equations are obtained:

$$\frac{f_i(q^t)}{f(q^t)} = \frac{\sum_{k=1}^n a_{ik} q_k^t}{\{f(q^t)\}^2} \quad \text{for } t=0,1 \text{ and } i=1,\ldots,n \qquad (17.19)$$

Assume cost minimizing behaviour for the consumer in periods 0 and 1. Since the utility function f defined by equation (17.17) is linearly homogeneous and differentiable, equation (17.11) will hold. Now recall the definition of the Fisher ideal quantity index, Q_F, defined earlier in Chapter 15:

$$Q_F(p^0, p^1, q^0, q^1) = \sqrt{\frac{\sum_{i=1}^n p_i^0 q_i^1}{\sum_{k=1}^n p_k^0 q_k^0}} \sqrt{\frac{\sum_{i=1}^n p_i^1 q_i^1}{\sum_{k=1}^n p_k^1 q_k^0}}$$

$$= \sqrt{\sum_{i=1}^n f_i(q^0) \frac{q_i^1}{f(q^0)}} \sqrt{\frac{\sum_{i=1}^n p_i^1 q_i^1}{\sum_{k=1}^n p_k^1 q_k^0}}$$

using equation (17.11) for $t=0$

$$= \sqrt{\sum_{i=1}^n f_i(q^0) \frac{q_i^1}{f(q^0)}} \Big/ \sqrt{\frac{\sum_{k=1}^n p_k^1 q_k^0}{\sum_{i=1}^n p_i^1 q_i^1}}$$

$$= \sqrt{\sum_{i=1}^{n} f_i(q^0)\frac{q_i^1}{f(q^0)}} \Big/ \sqrt{\sum_{i=1}^{n} f_i(q^1)\frac{q_i^0}{f(q^1)}}$$

using equation (17.11) for $t=1$

$$= \sqrt{\sum_{i=1}^{n}\sum_{k=1}^{n} a_{ik}q_k^0 \frac{q_i^1}{\{f(q^0)\}^2}} \Big/ \sqrt{\sum_{i=1}^{n}\sum_{k=1}^{n} a_{ik}q_k^1 \frac{q_i^0}{\{f(q^1)\}^2}}$$

using equation (17.19)

$$= \sqrt{\frac{1}{\{f(q^0)\}^2}} \Big/ \sqrt{\frac{1}{\{f(q^1)\}^2}}$$

using equation (17.17) and cancelling terms

$$= \frac{f(q^1)}{f(q^0)} \qquad (17.20)$$

Thus under the assumption that the consumer engages in cost-minimizing behaviour during periods 0 and 1 and has preferences over the n commodities that correspond to the utility function defined by equation (17.17), the Fisher ideal quantity index Q_F is exactly equal to the true quantity index, $f(q^1)/f(q^0)$.[15]

17.28 As was noted in paragraphs 15.18 to 15.23 of Chapter 15, the price index that corresponds to the Fisher quantity index Q_F using the product test (15.3) is the Fisher price index P_F, defined by equation (15.12). Let $c(p)$ be the unit cost function that corresponds to the homogeneous quadratic utility function f defined by equation (17.17). Then using equations (17.16) and (17.20), it can be seen that

$$P_F(p^0, p^1, q^0, q^1) = \frac{c(p^1)}{c(p^0)} \qquad (17.21)$$

Thus, under the assumption that the consumer engages in cost-minimizing behaviour during periods 0 and 1 and has preferences over the n commodities that correspond to the utility function defined by equation (17.17), the Fisher ideal price index P_F is exactly equal to the true price index, $c(p^1)/c(p^0)$.

17.29 A twice continuously differentiable function $f(q)$ of n variables $q \equiv (q_1, \ldots, q_n)$ can provide a *second-order approximation* to another such function $f^*(q)$ around the point q^*, if the level and all the first-order and second-order partial derivatives of the two functions coincide at q^*. It can be shown[16] that the homogeneous quadratic function f defined by equation (17.17) can provide a second-order approximation to an arbitrary f^* around any (strictly positive) point q^* in the class of linearly homogeneous functions. Thus the homogeneous quadratic functional form defined by equation (17.17) is a *flexible functional form*.[17] Diewert (1976, p. 117) termed an index number formula $Q(p^0, p^1, q^0, q^1)$ that was exactly equal to the true quantity index $f(q^1)/f(q^0)$ (where f is a flexible functional form) *a superlative index number formula*.[18] Equation (17.20) and the fact that the homogeneous quadratic function f defined by equation (17.17) is a flexible functional form show that the Fisher ideal quantity index Q_F defined by equation (15.14) is a superlative index number formula. Since the Fisher ideal price index P_F satisfies equation (17.21), where $c(p)$ is the unit cost function that is generated by the homogeneous quadratic utility function, P_F is also called a superlative index number formula.

17.30 It is possible to show that the Fisher ideal price index is a superlative index number formula by a different route. Instead of starting with the assumption that the consumer's utility function is the homogeneous quadratic function defined by equation (17.17), it is possible to start with the assumption that the consumer's unit cost function is a homogeneous quadratic.[19] Thus, suppose that the consumer has the following unit cost function:

$$c(p_1, \ldots, p_n) \equiv \sqrt{\sum_{i=1}^{n}\sum_{k=1}^{n} b_{ik}\, p_i\, p_k}$$

where $b_{ik} = b_{ki}$ for all i and k. (17.22)

Differentiating $c(p)$ defined by equation (17.22) with respect to p_i yields the following equations:

$$c_i(p) = \frac{1}{2}\frac{2\sum_{k=1}^{n} b_{ik}\, p_k}{\sqrt{\sum_{j=1}^{n}\sum_{k=1}^{n} b_{jk}\, p_j\, p_k}} \quad \text{for } i=1,\ldots,n$$

$$= \frac{\sum_{k=1}^{n} b_{ik}\, p_k}{c(q)} \qquad (17.23)$$

where $c_i(p) \equiv \partial c(p^t)/\partial p_i$. In order to obtain the first equation in (17.23), it is necessary to use the symmetry conditions. Now evaluate the second equation in (17.23) at the observed period t price vector $p^t \equiv (p_1^t, \ldots, p_n^t)$ and divide both sides of the resulting equation by $c(p^t)$. The following equation is obtained:

$$\frac{c_i(p^t)}{c(p^t)} = \frac{\sum_{k=1}^{n} b_{ik}p_k^t}{\{c(p^t)\}^2} \quad \text{for } t=0,1 \text{ and } i=1,\ldots,n \qquad (17.24)$$

As cost-minimizing behaviour for the consumer in periods 0 and 1 is being assumed and, since the unit cost function c defined by equation (17.22) is differentiable, equations (17.16) will hold. Now recall the definition of

[15] For the early history of this result, see Diewert (1976, p. 184).

[16] See Diewert (1976, p. 130) and let the parameter r equal 2.

[17] Diewert (1974a, p. 133) introduced this term into the economics literature.

[18] Fisher (1922, p. 247) used the term superlative to describe the Fisher ideal price index. Thus, Diewert adopted Fisher's terminology but attempted to give some precision to Fisher's definition of superlativeness. Fisher defined an index number formula to be superlative if it approximated the corresponding Fisher ideal results using his data set.

[19] Given the consumer's unit cost function $c(p)$, Diewert (1974a, p. 112) showed that the corresponding utility function $f(q)$ can be defined as follows: for a strictly positive quantity vector q, $f(q) \equiv 1/\max_p \{\sum_{i=1}^{n} p_i q_i : c(p) = 1\}$.

the Fisher ideal price index, P_F, given by equation (15.12) in Chapter 15:

$$P_F(p^0,p^1,q^0,q^1)=\sqrt{\frac{\sum_{i=1}^n p_i^1q_i^0}{\sum_{k=1}^n p_k^0q_k^0}}\sqrt{\frac{\sum_{i=1}^n p_i^1q_i^1}{\sum_{k=1}^n p_k^0q_k^1}}$$

$$=\sqrt{\sum_{i=1}^n p_i^1\frac{c_i(p^0)}{c(p^0)}}\sqrt{\frac{\sum_{i=1}^n p_i^1q_i^1}{\sum_{k=1}^n p_k^0q_k^1}}$$

using equation (17.16) for $t=0$

$$=\sqrt{\sum_{i=1}^n p_i^1\frac{c_i(p^0)}{c(p^0)}}\Bigg/\sqrt{\frac{\sum_{k=1}^n p_k^0q_k^1}{\sum_{i=1}^n p_i^1q_i^1}}$$

$$=\sqrt{\sum_{i=1}^n p_i^1\frac{c_i(p^0)}{c(p^0)}}\Bigg/\sqrt{\sum_{i=1}^n p_i^0\frac{c_i(p^1)}{c(p^1)}}$$

using equation (17.16) for $t=1$

$$=\sqrt{\frac{1}{\{c(p^0)\}^2}}\Bigg/\sqrt{\frac{1}{\{c(p^1)\}^2}}$$

using equation (17.22) and cancelling terms

$$=\frac{c(p^1)}{c(p^0)}. \qquad (17.25)$$

Thus, under the assumption that the consumer engages in cost-minimizing behaviour during periods 0 and 1 and has preferences over the n commodities that correspond to the unit cost function defined by equation (17.22), the Fisher ideal price index P_F is exactly equal to the true price index, $c(p^1)/c(p^0)$.[20]

17.31 Since the homogeneous quadratic unit cost function $c(p)$ defined by equation (17.22) is also a flexible functional form, the fact that the Fisher ideal price index P_F exactly equals the true price index $c(p^1)/c(p^0)$ means that P_F is a superlative index number formula.[21]

17.32 Suppose that the b_{ik} coefficients in equation (17.22) satisfy the following restrictions:

$$b_{ik}=b_ib_k \quad \text{for } i,k=1,\ldots,n \qquad (17.26)$$

where the n numbers b_i are non-negative. In this special case of equation (17.22), it can be seen that the unit cost function simplifies as follows:

$$c(p_1,\ldots,p_n)\equiv\sqrt{\sum_{i=1}^n\sum_{k=1}^n b_ib_kp_ip_k}=\sqrt{\sum_{i=1}^n b_ip_i\sum_{k=1}^n b_kp_k}=\sum_{i=1}^n b_ip_i \qquad (17.27)$$

Substituting equation (17.27) into Shephard's Lemma (17.15) yields the following expressions for the period t quantity vectors, q^t:

$$q_i^t=u^t\frac{\partial c(p^t)}{\partial p_i}=b_iu^t \quad i=1,\ldots,n;\ t=0,1 \qquad (17.28)$$

Thus if the consumer has the preferences that correspond to the unit cost function defined by equation (17.22) where the b_{ik} satisfy the restrictions (17.26), then the period 0 and 1 quantity vectors are equal to a multiple of the vector $b\equiv(b_1,\ldots,b_n)$; i.e., $q^0=b\,u^0$ and $q^1=b\,u^1$. Under these assumptions, the Fisher, Paasche and Laspeyres indices, P_F, P_P and P_L, all coincide. The preferences which correspond to the unit cost function defined by equation (17.27) are, however, not consistent with normal consumer behaviour since they imply that the consumer will not substitute away from more expensive commodities to cheaper commodities if relative prices change going from period 0 to 1.

Quadratic mean of order *r* superlative indices

17.33 It turns out that there are many other superlative index number formulae; i.e., there exist many quantity indices $Q(p^0,p^1,q^0,q^1)$ that are exactly equal to $f(q^1)/f(q^0)$ and many price indices $P(p^0,p^1,q^0,q^1)$ that are exactly equal to $c(p^1)/c(p^0)$, where the aggregator function f or the unit cost function c is a flexible functional form. Two families of superlative indices are defined below.

17.34 Suppose the consumer has the following quadratic mean of order r utility function.[22]

$$f^r(q_1,\ldots,q_n)\equiv\sqrt[r]{\sum_{i=1}^n\sum_{k=1}^n a_{ik}q_i^{r/2}q_k^{r/2}} \qquad (17.29)$$

where the parameters a_{ik} satisfy the symmetry conditions $a_{ik}=a_{ki}$ for all i and k and the parameter r satisfies the restriction $r\neq 0$. Diewert (1976, p. 130) showed that the utility function f^r defined by equation (17.29) is a flexible functional form; i.e., it can approximate an arbitrary twice continuously differentiable linearly homogeneous functional form to the second order. Note that when $r=2$, f^r equals the homogeneous quadratic function defined by equation (17.17).

[20] This result was obtained by Diewert (1976, pp. 133–134).

[21] Note that it has been shown that the Fisher index P_F is exact for the preferences defined by equation (17.17), as well as the preferences that are dual to the unit cost function defined by equation (17.22). These two classes of preferences do not coincide in general. However, if the n by n symmetric matrix A of the a_{ik} has an inverse, then it can be shown that the n by n matrix B of the b_{ik} will equal A^{-1}.

[22] The terminology is attributable to Diewert (1976, p. 129).

17.35 Define the quadratic mean of order r quantity index Q^r by:

$$Q^r(p^0,p^1,q^0,q^1) \equiv \frac{\sqrt[r]{\sum_{i=1}^{n} s_i^0 (q_i^1/q_i^0)^{r/2}}}{\sqrt[r]{\sum_{i=1}^{n} s_i^1 (q_i^1/q_i^0)^{-r/2}}} \quad (17.30)$$

where $s_i^t \equiv p_i^t q_i^t / \sum_{k=1}^{n} p_k^t q_k^t$ is the period t expenditure share for commodity i as usual.

17.36 Using exactly the same techniques as were used in paragraphs 17.27 to 17.32, it can be shown that Q^r is exact for the aggregator function f^r defined by equation (17.29); i.e., the following exact relationship between the quantity index Q^r and the utility function f^r holds:

$$Q^r(p^0,p^1,q^0,q^1) = \frac{f^r(q^1)}{f^r(q^0)} \quad (17.31)$$

Thus under the assumption that the consumer engages in cost-minimizing behaviour during periods 0 and 1 and has preferences over the n commodities that correspond to the utility function defined by equation (17.29), the quadratic mean of order r quantity index Q_F is exactly equal to the true quantity index, $f^r(q^1)/f^r(q^0)$.[23] Since Q^r is exact for f^r and f^r is a flexible functional form, it can be seen that the quadratic mean of order r quantity index Q^r is a superlative index for each $r \neq 0$. Thus there is an infinite number of superlative quantity indices.

17.37 For each quantity index Q^r, the product test (15.3) in Chapter 15 can be used in order to define the corresponding implicit quadratic mean of order r price index P^{r*}:

$$P^{r*}(p^0,p^1,q^0,q^1) \equiv \frac{\sum_{i=1}^{n} p_i^1 q_i^1}{\sum_{i=1}^{n} p_i^0 q_i^0 Q^r(p^0,p^1,q^0,q^1)} = \frac{c^{r*}(p^1)}{c^{r*}(p^0)} \quad (17.32)$$

where c^{r*} is the unit cost function that corresponds to the aggregator function f^r defined by equation (17.29). For each $r \neq 0$, the implicit quadratic mean of order r price index P^{r*} is also a superlative index.

17.38 When $r=2$, Q^r defined by equation (17.30) simplifies to Q_F, the Fisher ideal quantity index, and P^{r*} defined by equation (17.32) simplifies to P_F, the Fisher ideal price index. When $r=1$, Q^r defined by equation (17.30) simplifies to:

$$Q^1(p^0,p^1,q^0,q^1) \equiv \frac{\sum_{i=1}^{n} s_i^0 \sqrt{\frac{q_i^1}{q_i^0}}}{\sum_{i=1}^{n} s_i^1 \sqrt{\frac{q_i^0}{q_i^1}}} = \frac{\sum_{i=1}^{n} p_i^1 q_i^1}{\sum_{i=1}^{n} p_i^0 q_i^0} \frac{\sum_{i=1}^{n} p_i^0 q_i^0 \sqrt{\frac{q_i^1}{q_i^0}}}{\sum_{i=1}^{n} p_i^1 q_i^1 \sqrt{\frac{q_i^0}{q_i^1}}}$$

$$= \frac{\sum_{i=1}^{n} p_i^1 q_i^1 \sum_{i=1}^{n} p_i^0 \sqrt{q_i^0 q_i^1}}{\sum_{i=1}^{n} p_i^0 q_i^0 \sum_{i=1}^{n} p_i^1 \sqrt{q_i^0 q_i^1}}$$

$$= \frac{\sum_{i=1}^{n} p_i^1 q_i^1}{\sum_{i=1}^{n} p_i^0 q_i^0} \Bigg/ \frac{\sum_{i=1}^{n} p_i^1 \sqrt{q_i^0 q_i^1}}{\sum_{i=1}^{n} p_i^0 \sqrt{q_i^0 q_i^1}}$$

$$= \frac{\sum_{i=1}^{n} p_i^1 q_i^1}{\sum_{i=1}^{n} p_i^0 q_i^0} \Big/ P_W(p^0,p^1,q^0,q^1) \quad (17.33)$$

where P_W is the Walsh price index defined previously by equation (15.19) in Chapter 15. Thus P^{1*} is equal to P_W, the Walsh price index, and hence it is also a superlative price index.

17.39 Suppose the consumer has the following quadratic mean of order r unit cost function:[24]

$$c^r(p_1,\ldots,p_n) \equiv \sqrt[r]{\sum_{i=1}^{n}\sum_{k=1}^{n} b_{ik} p_i^{r/2} p_k^{r/2}} \quad (17.34)$$

where the parameters b_{ik} satisfy the symmetry conditions $b_{ik}=b_{ki}$ for all i and k, and the parameter r satisfies the restriction $r \neq 0$. Diewert (1976, p. 130) showed that the unit cost function c^r defined by equation (17.34) is a flexible functional form; i.e., it can approximate an arbitrary twice continuously differentiable linearly homogeneous functional form to the second order. Note that when $r=2$, c^r equals the homogeneous quadratic function defined by equation (17.22).

17.40 Define the quadratic mean of order r price index P^r by:

$$P^r(p^0,p^1,q^0,q^1) \equiv \frac{\sqrt[r]{\sum_{i=1}^{n} s_i^0 \left(\frac{p_i^1}{p_i^0}\right)^{r/2}}}{\sqrt[r]{\sum_{i=1}^{n} s_i^1 \left(\frac{p_i^1}{p_i^0}\right)^{-r/2}}} \quad (17.35)$$

where $s_i^t \equiv p_i^t q_i^t / \sum_{k=1}^{n} p_k^t q_k^t$ is the period t expenditure share for commodity i as usual.

17.41 Using exactly the same techniques as were used in paragraphs 17.27 to 17.32, it can be shown that P^r is exact for the aggregator function defined by equation (17.34); i.e., the following exact relationship between the index number formula P^r and the unit cost function c^r holds:

$$P^r(p^0,p^1,q^0,q^1) = \frac{c^r(p^1)}{c^r(p^0)} \quad (17.36)$$

Thus, under the assumption that the consumer engages in cost-minimizing behaviour during periods 0 and 1, and has preferences over the n commodities that correspond to the unit cost function defined by equation

[23] See Diewert (1976, p. 130).

[24] This terminology is attributable to Diewert (1976, p. 130), this unit cost function being first defined by Denny (1974).

(17.34), the quadratic mean of order r price index P_F is exactly equal to the true price index, $c^r(p^1)/c^r(p^0)$.[25] Since P^r is exact for c^r and c^r is a flexible functional form, it can be seen that the quadratic mean of order r price index P^r is a superlative index for each $r \neq 0$. Thus there are an infinite number of superlative price indices.

17.42 For each price index P^r, the product test (15.3) in Chapter 15 can be used in order to define the corresponding implicit quadratic mean of order r quantity index Q^{r*}:

$$Q^{r*}(p^0,p^1,q^0,q^1) \equiv \frac{\sum_{i=1}^{n} p_i^1 q_i^1}{\sum_{i=1}^{n} p_i^0 q_i^0 P^r(p^0,p^1,q^0,q^1)} = \frac{f^{r*}(p^1)}{f^{r*}(p^0)} \tag{17.37}$$

where f^{r*} is the aggregator function that corresponds to the unit cost function c^r defined by equation (17.34).[26] For each $r \neq 0$, the implicit quadratic mean of order r quantity index Q^{r*} is also a superlative index.

17.43 When $r=2$, P^r defined by equation (17.35) simplifies to P_F, the Fisher ideal price index, and Q^{r*} defined by equation (17.37) simplifies to Q_F, the Fisher ideal quantity index. When $r=1$, P^r defined by equation (17.35) simplifies to:

$$\begin{aligned} P^1(p^0,p^1,q^0,q^1) &\equiv \frac{\sum_{i=1}^{n} s_i^0 \sqrt{\frac{p_i^1}{p_i^0}}}{\sum_{i=1}^{n} s_i^1 \sqrt{\frac{p_i^0}{p_i^1}}} = \frac{\dfrac{\sum_{i=1}^{n} p_i^1 q_i^1}{\sum_{i=1}^{n} p_i^0 q_i^0} \sum_{i=1}^{n} p_i^0 q_i^0 \sqrt{\frac{p_i^1}{p_i^0}}}{\sum_{i=1}^{n} p_i^1 q_i^1 \sqrt{\frac{p_i^0}{p_i^1}}} \\ &= \frac{\sum_{i=1}^{n} p_i^1 q_i^1 \sum_{i=1}^{n} q_i^0 \sqrt{p_i^0 p_i^1}}{\sum_{i=1}^{n} p_i^0 q_i^0 \sum_{i=1}^{n} q_i^1 \sqrt{p_i^0 p_i^1}} \\ &= \frac{\sum_{i=1}^{n} p_i^1 q_i^1}{\sum_{i=1}^{n} p_i^0 q_i^0} \Bigg/ \frac{\sum_{i=1}^{n} q_i^1 \sqrt{p_i^0 p_i^1}}{\sum_{i=1}^{n} q_i^0 \sqrt{p_i^0 p_i^1}} \\ &= \frac{\sum_{i=1}^{n} p_i^1 q_i^1}{\sum_{i=1}^{n} p_i^0 q_i^0} \Big/ Q_W(p^0,p^1,q^0,q^1) \end{aligned} \tag{17.38}$$

where Q_W is the Walsh quantity index defined previously in footnote 30 of Chapter 15. Thus Q^{1*} is equal to Q_W, the Walsh quantity index, and hence it is also a superlative quantity index.

[25] See Diewert (1976, pp. 133–134).

[26] The function f^{r*} can be defined by using c^r as follows: $f^{r*}(q) \equiv 1/\max_p\{\sum_{i=1}^{n} p_i q_i : c^r(p)=1\}$.

Superlative indices: The Törnqvist index

17.44 In this section, the same assumptions that were made on the consumer in paragraphs 17.9 to 17.17 are made here. In particular, it is not assumed that the consumer's utility function f is necessarily linearly homogeneous as in paragraphs 17.18 to 17.43.

17.45 Before the main result is derived, a preliminary result is required. Suppose the function of n variables, $f(z_1,\ldots,z_n) \equiv f(z)$, is quadratic; i.e.,

$$f(z_1,\ldots,z_n) \equiv a_0 + \sum_{i=1}^{n} a_i z_i + \frac{1}{2}\sum_{i=1}^{n}\sum_{k=1}^{n} a_{ik} z_i z_k \quad \text{and } a_{ik}=a_{ki} \text{ for all } i \text{ and } k \tag{17.39}$$

where the a_i and the a_{ik} are constants. Let $f_i(z)$ denote the first-order partial derivative of f evaluated at z with respect to the ith component of z, z_i. Let $f_{ik}(z)$ denote the second-order partial derivative of f with respect to z_i and z_k. Then it is well known that the second-order Taylor series approximation to a quadratic function is exact; i.e., if f is defined by equation (17.39), then for any two points, z^0 and z^1, the following equation holds:

$$f(z^1)-f(z^0) = \sum_{i=1}^{n} f_i(z^0)\{z_i^1 - z_i^0\} + \frac{1}{2}\sum_{i=1}^{n}\sum_{k=1}^{n} f_{ik}(z^0)\{z_i^1 - z_i^0\}\{z_k^1 - z_k^0\} \tag{17.40}$$

It is less well known that an average of two first-order Taylor series approximations to a quadratic function is also exact; i.e., if f is defined by equation (17.39) above, then for any two points, z^0 and z^1, the following equation holds:[27]

$$f(z^1)-f(z^0) = \frac{1}{2}\sum_{i=1}^{n}\{f_i(z^0)+f_i(z^1)\}\{z_i^1 - z_i^0\} \tag{17.41}$$

Diewert (1976, p. 118) and Lau (1979) showed that equation (17.41) characterized a quadratic function and called the equation the *quadratic approximation lemma*. In this chapter, equation (17.41) will be called the *quadratic identity*.

17.46 Suppose that the consumer's *cost function*[28] $C(u,p)$, has the following *translog functional form*:[29]

$$\ln C(u,p) \equiv a_0 + \sum_{i=1}^{n} a_i \ln p_i + \frac{1}{2}\sum_{i=1}^{n}\sum_{k=1}^{n} a_{ik} \ln p_i \ln p_k + b_0 \ln u + \sum_{i=1}^{n} b_i \ln p_i \ln u + \frac{1}{2} b_{00}(\ln u)^2 \tag{17.42}$$

where ln is the natural logarithm function and the parameters a_i, a_{ik}, and b_i satisfy the following

[27] The proof of this and the foregoing relation is by straightforward verification.

[28] The consumer's cost function was defined by equation (17.6) above.

[29] Christensen, Jorgenson and Lau (1971) introduced this function into the economics literature.

restrictions.

$$a_{ik} = a_{ki}, \sum_{i=1}^{n} a_i = 1, \sum_{i=1}^{n} b_i = 0 \text{ and } \sum_{k=1}^{n} a_{ik} = 0$$
$$\text{for } i,k = 1,\ldots,n \quad (17.43)$$

These parameter restrictions ensure that $C(u,p)$ defined by equation (17.42) is linearly homogeneous in p, a property that a cost function must have. It can be shown that the translog cost function defined by equation (17.42) can provide a second-order Taylor series approximation to an arbitrary cost function.[30]

17.47 Assume that the consumer has preferences that correspond to the translog cost function and that the consumer engages in cost-minimizing behaviour during periods 0 and 1. Let p^0 and p^1 be the period 0 and 1 observed price vectors, and let q^0 and q^1 be the period 0 and 1 observed quantity vectors. These assumptions imply:

$$C(u^0,p^0) = \sum_{i=1}^{n} p_i^0 q_i^0 \text{ and } C(u^1,p^1) = \sum_{i=1}^{n} p_i^1 q_i^1 \quad (17.44)$$

where C is the translog cost function defined above. Now apply Shephard's Lemma, equation (17.12), and the following equation results:

$$q_i^t = \frac{\partial C(u^t,p^t)}{\partial p_i} \quad \text{for } i=1,\ldots,n \text{ and } t=0,1$$
$$= \frac{C(u^t,p^t)}{p_i^t}\frac{\partial \ln C(u^t,p^t)}{\partial \ln p_i} \quad (17.45)$$

Now use equation (17.44) to replace $C(u^t,p^t)$ in equation (17.45). After some cross multiplication, this becomes the following:

$$\frac{p_i^t q_i^t}{\sum_{k=1}^{n} p_k^t q_k^t} = s_i^t = \frac{\partial \ln C(u^t,p^t)}{\partial \ln p_i}$$
$$\text{for } i=1,\ldots,n \text{ and } t=0,1 \quad (17.46)$$

or

$$s_i^t = a_i + \sum_{k=1}^{n} a_{ik} \ln p_k^t + b_i \ln u^t \quad \text{for } i=1,\ldots,n \text{ and } t=0,1 \quad (17.47)$$

where s_i^t is the period t expenditure share on commodity i.

17.48 Define the geometric average of the period 0 and 1 utility levels as u^*; i.e., define

$$u^* \equiv \sqrt{u^0 u^1} \quad (17.48)$$

Now observe that the right-hand side of the equation that defines the natural logarithm of the translog cost function, equation (17.42), is a quadratic function of the variables $z_i \equiv \ln p_i$ if utility is held constant at the level u^*. Hence the quadratic identity (17.41) can be applied, and the following equation is obtained:

$$\begin{aligned}
&\ln C(u^*,p^1) - \ln C(u^*,p^0) \\
&= \frac{1}{2}\sum_{i=1}^{n}\left\{\frac{\partial \ln C(u^*,p^0)}{\partial \ln p_i} + \frac{\partial \ln C(u^*,p^1)}{\partial \ln p_i}\right\}\{\ln p_i^1 - \ln p_i^0\} \\
&= \frac{1}{2}\sum_{i=1}^{n}\left(a_i + \sum_{k=1}^{n} a_{ik}\ln p_k^0 + b_i \ln u^* + a_i \right. \\
&\quad \left. + \sum_{k=1}^{n} a_{ik}\ln p_k^1 + b_i \ln u^*\right)(\ln p_i^1 - \ln p_i^0) \\
&= \frac{1}{2}\sum_{i=1}^{n}\left(a_i + \sum_{k=1}^{n} a_{ik}\ln p_k^0 + b_i \ln \sqrt{u^0u^1} + a_i \right. \\
&\quad \left. + \sum_{k=1}^{n} a_{ik}\ln p_k^1 + b_i \ln \sqrt{u^0u^1}\right)(\ln p_i^1 - \ln p_i^0) \\
&= \frac{1}{2}\sum_{i=1}^{n}\left(a_i + \sum_{k=1}^{n} a_{ik}\ln p_k^0 + b_i \ln u^0 + a_i \right. \\
&\quad \left. + \sum_{k=1}^{n} a_{ik}\ln p_k^1 + b_i \ln u^1\right)(\ln p_i^1 - \ln p_i^0) \\
&= \frac{1}{2}\sum_{i=1}^{n}\left\{\frac{\partial \ln C(u^0,p^0)}{\partial \ln p_i} + \frac{\partial \ln C(u^1,p^1)}{\partial \ln p_i}\right\}(\ln p_i^1 - \ln p_i^0) \\
&= \frac{1}{2}\sum_{i=1}^{n}(s_i^0 + s_i^1)(\ln p_i^1 - \ln p_i^0) \quad \text{using equation (17.47).}
\end{aligned}$$
$$(17.49)$$

The last equation in (17.49) can be recognized as the logarithm of the Törnqvist–Theil index number formula P_T, defined earlier by equation (15.81) in Chapter 15. Hence, exponentiating both sides of equation (17.49) yields the following equality between the true cost of living between periods 0 and 1, evaluated at the intermediate utility level u^* and the observable Törnqvist–Theil index P_T:[31]

$$\frac{C(u^*,p^1)}{C(u^*,p^0)} = P_T(p^0,p^1,q^0,q^1) \quad (17.50)$$

Since the translog cost function which appears on the left-hand side of equation (17.49) is a flexible functional form, the Törnqvist–Theil price index P_T is also a superlative index.

17.49 It is somewhat mysterious how a ratio of unobservable cost functions of the form appearing on the left-hand side of the above equation can be exactly estimated by an observable index number formula. The key to this mystery is the assumption of cost-minimizing behaviour and the quadratic identity (17.41), along with the fact that derivatives of cost functions are equal to quantities, as specified by Shephard's Lemma. In fact, all the exact index number results derived in paragraphs 17.27 to 17.43 can be derived using transformations of the quadratic identity along with Shephard's Lemma (or Wold's Identity).[32] Fortunately, for most empirical applications, assuming that the

[30] It can also be shown that, if all the $b_i = 0$ and $b_{00} = 0$, then $C(u,p) = uC(1,p) \equiv uc(p)$; i.e., with these additional restrictions on the parameters of the general translog cost function, homothetic preferences are the result of these restrictions. Note that it is also assumed that utility u is scaled so that u is always positive.

[31] This result is attributable to Diewert (1976, p. 122).

[32] See Diewert (2002a).

consumer has (transformed) quadratic preferences will be an adequate assumption, so the results presented in paragraphs 17.27 to 17.49 are quite useful to index number practitioners who are willing to adopt the economic approach to index number theory.[33] Essentially, the economic approach to index number theory provides a strong justification for the use of the Fisher price index P_F defined by equation (15.12), the Törnqvist–Theil price index P_T defined by equation (15.81), the implicit quadratic mean of order r price indices P^{r*} defined by equation (17.32) (when $r=1$, this index is the Walsh price index defined by equation (15.19) in Chapter 15) and the quadratic mean of order r price indices P^r defined by equation (17.35). In the next section, we ask if it matters which one of these formulae is chosen as "best".

The approximation properties of superlative indices

17.50 The results of paragraphs 17.27 to 17.49 provide price statisticians with a large number of index number formulae which appear to be equally good from the viewpoint of the economic approach to index number theory. Two questions arise as a consequence of these results:

- Does it matter which of these formulae is chosen?
- If it does matter, which formula should be chosen?

17.51 With respect to the first question, Diewert (1978, p. 888) showed that all of the superlative index number formulae listed in paragraphs 17.27 to 17.49 approximate each other to the second order around any point where the two price vectors, p^0 and p^1, are equal and where the two quantity vectors, q^0 and q^1, are equal. In particular, this means that the following equalities are valid for all r and s not equal to 0, provided that $p^0=p^1$ and $q^0=q^1$.[34]

$$P_T(p^0,p^1,q^0,q^1)=P^r(p^0,p^1,q^0,q^1)=P^{s*}(p^0,p^1,q^0,q^1) \quad (17.51)$$

$$\frac{\partial P_T(p^0,p^1,q^0,q^1)}{\partial p_i^t}=\frac{\partial P^r(p^0,p^1,q^0,q^1)}{\partial p_i^t}=\frac{\partial P^{s*}(p^0,p^1,q^0,q^1)}{\partial p_i^t}$$

for $i=1,\ldots,n$ and $t=0,1$ (17.52)

$$\frac{\partial P_T(p^0,p^1,q^0,q^1)}{\partial q_i^t}=\frac{\partial P^r(p^0,p^1,q^0,q^1)}{\partial q_i^t}=\frac{\partial P^{s*}(p^0,p^1,q^0,q^1)}{\partial q_i^t}$$

for $i=1,\ldots,n$ and $t=0,1$ (17.53)

$$\frac{\partial^2 P_T(p^0,p^1,q^0,q^1)}{\partial p_i^t\partial p_k^t}=\frac{\partial^2 P^r(p^0,p^1,q^0,q^1)}{\partial p_i^t\partial p_k^t}=\frac{\partial^2 P^{s*}(p^0,p^1,q^0,q^1)}{\partial p_i^t\partial p_k^t}$$

for $i,k=1,\ldots,n$ and $t=0,1$ (17.54)

$$\frac{\partial^2 P_T(p^0,p^1,q^0,q^1)}{\partial p_i^t\partial q_k^t}=\frac{\partial^2 P^r(p^0,p^1,q^0,q^1)}{\partial p_i^t\partial q_k^t}=\frac{\partial^2 P^{s*}(p^0,p^1,q^0,q^1)}{\partial p_i^t\partial q_k^t}$$

for $i,k=1,\ldots,n$ and $t=0,1$ (17.55)

$$\frac{\partial^2 P_T(p^0,p^1,q^0,q^1)}{\partial q_i^t\partial q_k^t}=\frac{\partial^2 P^r(p^0,p^1,q^0,q^1)}{\partial q_i^t\partial q_k^t}=\frac{\partial^2 P^{s*}(p^0,p^1,q^0,q^1)}{\partial q_i^t\partial q_k^t}$$

for $i,k=1,\ldots,n$ for $t=0,1$ (17.56)

where the Törnqvist–Theil price index P_T is defined by equation (15.81), the implicit quadratic mean of order r price indices P^{s*} is defined by equation (17.32) and the quadratic mean of order r price indices P^r is defined by equation (17.35). Using the results in the previous paragraph, Diewert (1978, p. 884) concluded that "all superlative indices closely approximate each other".

17.52 The above conclusion is, however, not true even though the equations (17.51) to (17.56) are true. The problem is that the quadratic mean of order r price indices P^r and the implicit quadratic mean of order s price indices P^{s*} are (continuous) functions of the parameters r and s respectively. Hence, as r and s become very large in magnitude, the indices P^r and P^{s*} can differ substantially from, say, $P^2=P_F$, the Fisher ideal index. In fact, using definition (17.35) and the limiting properties of means of order r,[35] Robert Hill (2002, p. 7) showed that P^r has the following limit as r approaches plus or minus infinity:

$$\lim_{r\to+\infty} P^r(p^0,p^1,q^0,q^1)=\lim_{r\to-\infty} P^r(p^0,p^1,q^0,q^1)=\sqrt{\min_i\left(\frac{p_i^1}{p_i^0}\right)\max_i\left(\frac{p_i^1}{p_i^0}\right)} \quad (17.57)$$

[33] If, however, consumer preferences are non-homothetic and the change in utility is substantial between the two situations being compared, then it may be desirable to compute separately the Laspeyres–Konüs and Paasche–Konüs true cost of living indices defined by equations (17.3) and (17.4), $C(u^0,p^1)/C(u^0,p^0)$ and $C(u^1,p^1)/C(u^1,p^0)$, respectively. In order to do this, it would be necessary to use econometrics and estimate empirically the consumer's cost or expenditure function.

[34] To prove the equalities in equations (17.51) to (17.56), simply differentiate the various index number formulae and evaluate the derivatives at $p^0=p^1$ and $q^0=q^1$. Actually, equations (17.51) to (17.56) are still true provided that $p^1=\lambda p^0$ and $q^1=\mu q^0$ for any numbers $\lambda>0$ and $\mu>0$; i.e., provided that the period 1 price vector is proportional to the period 0 price vector and that the period 1 quantity vector is proportional to the period 0 quantity vector.

[35] See Hardy, Littlewood and Pólya (1934).

Using Hill's method of analysis, it can be shown that the implicit quadratic mean of order r price index has the following limit as r approaches plus or minus infinity:

$$\lim_{r\to+\infty} P^{r*}(p^0,p^1,q^0,q^1) = \lim_{r\to-\infty} P^{r*}(p^0,p^1,q^0,q^1,) = \frac{\sum_{i=1}^{n} p_i^1 q_i^1}{\sum_{i=1}^{n} p_i^0 q_i^0 \sqrt{\min_i\left(\frac{p_i^1}{p_i^0}\right)\max_i\left(\frac{p_i^1}{p_i^0}\right)}} \quad (17.58)$$

Thus for r large in magnitude, P^r and P^{r^*} can differ substantially from P_T, P^1, $P^{1^*}=P_W$ (the Walsh price index) and $P^2=P^{2^*}=P_F$ (the Fisher ideal index).[36]

17.53 Although Hill's theoretical and empirical results demonstrate conclusively that not all superlative indices will necessarily closely approximate each other, there is still the question of how well the more commonly used superlative indices will approximate each other. All the commonly used superlative indices, P^r and P^{r^*}, fall into the interval $0\le r\le 2$.[37] Hill (2002, p. 16) summarized how far apart the Törnqvist and Fisher indices were, making all possible bilateral comparisons between any two data points for his time series data set as follows:

> The superlative spread $S(0,2)$ is also of interest since, in practice, Törnqvist ($r=0$) and Fisher ($r=2$) are by far the two most widely used superlative indexes. In all 153 bilateral comparisons, $S(0,2)$ is less than the Paasche–Laspeyres spread and on average, the superlative spread is only 0.1 per cent. It is because attention, until now, has focussed almost exclusively on superlative indexes in the range $0\le r\le 2$ that a general misperception has persisted in the index number literature that all superlative indexes approximate each other closely.

Thus, for Hill's time series data set covering 64 components of United States gross domestic product from 1977 to 1994 and making all possible bilateral comparisons between any two years, the Fisher and Törnqvist price indices differed by only 0.1 per cent on average. This close correspondence is consistent with the results of other empirical studies using annual time series data.[38] Additional evidence on this topic may be found in Chapter 19.

17.54 In the earlier chapters of this manual, it is found that several index number formulae seem "best" when viewed from various perspectives. Thus the Fisher ideal index $P_F=P^2=P^{2^*}$ defined by equation (15.12) seemed to be best from one axiomatic viewpoint, the Törnqvist–Theil price index P_T defined by equation (15.81) seems to be best from another axiomatic perspective, as well as from the stochastic viewpoint, and the Walsh index P_W defined by equation (15.19) (which is equal to the implicit quadratic mean of order r price indices $P^{r}*$ defined by equation (17.32) when $r=1$) seems to be best from the viewpoint of the "pure" price index. The results presented in this section indicate that for "normal" time series data, these three indices will give virtually the same answer. To determine precisely which one of these three indices to use as a theoretical target or actual index, the statistical agency will have to decide which approach to bilateral index number theory is most consistent with its goals. For most practical purposes, however, it will not matter which of these three indices is chosen as a theoretical target index for making price comparisons between two periods.

Superlative indices and two-stage aggregation

17.55 Most statistical agencies use the Laspeyres formula to aggregate prices in two stages. At the first stage of aggregation, the Laspeyres formula is used to aggregate components of the overall index (e.g., food, clothing, services); then at the second stage of aggregation, these component sub-indices are further combined into the overall index. The following question then naturally arises: does the index computed in two stages coincide with the index computed in a single stage? Initially, this question is addressed in the context of the Laspeyres formula.[39]

17.56 Suppose that the price and quantity data for period t, p^t and q^t, can be written in terms of M subvectors as follows:

$$p^t=(p^{t_1},p^{t_2},\ldots,p^{t_M}) \text{ and } q^t=(q^{t_1},q^{t_2},\ldots,q^{t_M}) \quad \text{for } t=0,1 \quad (17.59)$$

where the dimensionality of the subvectors p^{tm} and q^{tm} is N_m for $m=1,2,\ldots,M$ with the sum of the dimensions N_m equal to n. These subvectors correspond to the price and quantity data for subcomponents of the consumer price index for period t. Now construct sub-indices for each of these components going from period 0 to 1. For the base period, set the price for each of these subcomponents, say P_m^0 for $m=1,2,\ldots M$, equal to 1 and set the corresponding base period subcomponent quantities, say Q_m^0 for $m=1,2,\ldots,M$, equal to the base period value of consumption for that subcomponent for $m=1,2,\ldots,M$:

$$P_m^0\equiv 1 \text{ and } Q_m^0\equiv\sum_{i=1}^{N_m} p_i^{0m}q_i^{0m} \quad \text{for } m=1,2,\ldots,M \quad (17.60)$$

Now use the Laspeyres formula in order to construct a period 1 price for each subcomponent, say P_m^1 for $m=1,2,\ldots,M$, of the CPI. Since the dimensionality of

[36] Hill (2002) documents this for two data sets. His time series data consist of annual expenditure and quantity data for 64 components of United States gross domestic product from 1977 to 1994. For this data set, Hill (2002, p. 16) found that "superlative indexes can differ by more than a factor of two (i.e., by more than 100 per cent), even though Fisher and Törnqvist never differ by more than 0.6 per cent".

[37] Diewert (1980, p. 451) showed that the Törnqvist index P_T is a limiting case of P^r, as r tends to 0.

[38] See, for example, Diewert (1978, p. 894) or Fisher (1922), which is reproduced in Diewert (1976, p. 135).

[39] Much of the material in this section is adapted from Diewert (1978) and Alterman, Diewert and Feenstra (1999). See also Balk (1996b) for a discussion of alternative definitions for the two-stage aggregation concept and references to the literature on this topic.

the subcomponent vectors, p^{tm} and q^{tm}, differs from the dimensionality of the complete period t vectors of prices and quantities, p^t and q^t, it is necessary to use different symbols for these subcomponent Laspeyres indices, say P_L^m for $m=1,2,\ldots,M$. Thus the period 1 subcomponent prices are defined as follows:

$$P_m^1 \equiv P_L^m(p^{0m}, p^{1m}, q^{0m}, q^{1m}) \equiv \frac{\sum_{i=1}^{N_m} p_i^{1m} q_i^{0m}}{\sum_{i=1}^{N_m} p_i^{0m} q_i^{0m}} \quad \text{for } m=1,2,\ldots,M \tag{17.61}$$

Once the period 1 prices for the M sub-indices have been defined by equation (17.61), then corresponding subcomponent period 1 quantities Q_m^1 for $m=1,2,\ldots,M$ can be defined by deflating the period 1 subcomponent values $\sum_{i=1}^{N_m} p_i^{1m} q_i^{1m}$ by the prices P_m^1

$$Q_m^1 \equiv \frac{\sum_{i=1}^{N_m} p_i^{1m} q_i^{1m}}{P_m^1} \quad \text{for } m=1,2,\ldots,M \tag{17.62}$$

Now define subcomponent price and quantity vectors for each period $t=0,1$ using equations (17.60) to (17.62). Thus define the period 0 and 1 subcomponent price vectors P^0 and P^1 as follows:

$$P^0 = (P_1^0, P_2^0, \ldots, P_M^0) \equiv 1_M \text{ and } P^1 = (P_1^1, P_2^1, \ldots, P_M^1) \tag{17.63}$$

where 1_M denotes a vector of ones of dimension M and the components of P^1 are defined by equation (17.61). The period 0 and 1 subcomponent quantity vectors Q^0 and Q^1 are defined as follows:

$$Q^0 = (Q_1^0, Q_2^0, \ldots, Q_M^0) \text{ and } Q^1 = (Q_1^1, Q_2^1, \ldots, Q_M^1) \tag{17.64}$$

where the components of Q^0 are defined in equation (17.60) and the components of Q^1 are defined by equation (17.62). The price and quantity vectors in equations (17.63) and (17.64) represent the results of the first-stage aggregation. Now use these vectors as inputs into the second-stage aggregation problem; i.e., apply the Laspeyres price index formula, using the information in equations (17.63) and (17.64) as inputs into the index number formula. Since the price and quantity vectors that are inputs into this second-stage aggregation problem have dimension M instead of the single-stage formula which utilized vectors of dimension n, a different symbol is required for the new Laspeyres index: this is chosen to be P_L^*. Thus the Laspeyres price index computed in two stages can be denoted as $P_L^*(P^0, P^1, Q^0, Q^1)$. Now ask whether this two-stage Laspeyres index equals the corresponding single-stage index P_L that was studied in the previous sections of this chapter; i.e., ask whether

$$P_L^*(P^0, P^1, Q^0, Q^1) = P_L(p^0, p^1, q^0, q^1). \tag{17.65}$$

If the Laspeyres formula is used at each stage of each aggregation, the answer to the above question is yes: straightforward calculations show that the Laspeyres index calculated in two stages equals the Laspeyres index calculated in one stage.

17.57 Now suppose that the Fisher or Törnqvist formula is used at each stage of the aggregation. That is, in equation (17.61), suppose that the Laspeyres formula $P_L^m(p^{0m}, p^{1m}, q^{0m}, q^{1m})$ is replaced by the Fisher formula $P_F^m(p^{0m}, p^{1m}, q^{0m}, q^{1m})$ or by the Törnqvist formula $P_T^m(p^{0m}, p^{1m}, q^{0m}, q^{1m})$; and in equation (17.65), suppose that $P_L^*(P^0, P^1, Q^0, Q^1)$ is replaced by P_F^* (or by P_T^*) and $P_L(p^0, p^1, q^0, q^1)$ is replaced by P_F (or by P_T). Then is it the case that counterparts are obtained to the two-stage aggregation result for the Laspeyres formula, equation (17.65)? The answer is no; it can be shown that, in general,

$$P_F^*(P^0, P^1, Q^0, Q^1) \neq P_F(p^0, p^1, q^0, q^1) \quad \text{and}$$
$$P_T^*(P^0, P^1, Q^0, Q^1) \neq P_T(p^0, p^1, q^0, q^1) \tag{17.66}$$

Similarly, it can be shown that the quadratic mean of order r index number formula P^r defined by equation (17.35) and the implicit quadratic mean of order r index number formula P^{r*} defined by equation (17.32) are also not consistent in aggregation.

17.58 Nevertheless, even though the Fisher and Törnqvist formulae are not exactly consistent in aggregation, it can be shown that these formulae are approximately consistent in aggregation. More specifically, it can be shown that the two-stage Fisher formula P_F^* and the single-stage Fisher formula P_F in the inequality (17.66), both regarded as functions of the $4n$ variables in the vectors p^0, p^1, q^0, q^1, approximate each other to the second order around a point where the two price vectors are equal (so that $p^0=p^1$) and where the two quantity vectors are equal (so that $q^0=q^1$), and a similar result holds for the two-stage and single-stage Törnqvist indices in equation (17.66).[40] As was seen in the previous section, the single-stage Fisher and Törnqvist indices have a similar approximation property, so all four indices in the inequality (17.66) approximate each other to the second order around an equal (or proportional) price and quantity point. Thus for normal time series data, single-stage and two-stage Fisher and Törnqvist indices will usually be numerically very close. This result is illustrated in Chapter 19 for an artificial data set.[41]

17.59 Similar approximate consistency in aggregation results (to the results for the Fisher and Törnqvist formulae explained in the previous paragraph) can be derived for the quadratic mean of order r indices, P^r, and for the implicit quadratic mean of order r indices, P^{r*}; see Diewert (1978, p. 889). Nevertheless, the results of Hill (2002) again imply that the second-order

[40] See Diewert (1978, p. 889). In other words, a string of equalities similar to equations (17.51) to (17.56) holds between the two-stage indices and their single-stage counterparts. In fact, these equalities are still true provided that $p^1=\lambda p^0$ and $q^1=\mu q^0$ for any numbers $\lambda>0$ and $\mu>0$.

[41] For an empirical comparison of the four indices, see Diewert (1978, pp. 894–895). For the Canadian consumer data considered there, the chained two-stage Fisher in 1971 was 2.3228 and the corresponding chained two-stage Törnqvist was 2.3230, the same values as for the corresponding single-stage indices.

approximation property of the single-stage quadratic mean of order r index P^r to its two-stage counterpart will break down as r approaches either plus or minus infinity. To see this, consider a simple example where there are only four commodities in total. Let the first price ratio p_1^1/p_1^0 be equal to the positive number a, let the second two price ratios p_i^1/p_i^0 equal b and let the last price ratio p_4^1/p_4^0 equal c, where we assume $a<c$ and $a \le b \le c$. Using Hill's result (17.57), the limiting value of the single-stage index is:

$$\lim_{r\to+\infty} P^r(p^0,p^1,q^0,q^1) = \lim_{r\to-\infty} P^r(p^0,p^1,q^0,q^1) = \sqrt{\min_i\left(\frac{p_i^1}{p_i^0}\right)\max_i\left(\frac{p_i^1}{p_i^0}\right)} = \sqrt{ac} \tag{17.67}$$

Now aggregate commodities 1 and 2 into a sub-aggregate and commodities 3 and 4 into another sub-aggregate. Using Hill's result (17.57) again, it is found that the limiting price index for the first sub-aggregate is $[ab]^{1/2}$ and the limiting price index for the second sub-aggregate is $[bc]^{1/2}$. Now apply the second stage of aggregation and use Hill's result once again to conclude that the limiting value of the two-stage aggregation using P^r as the index number formula is $[ab^2c]^{1/4}$. Thus the limiting value as r tends to plus or minus infinity of the single-stage aggregate over the two-stage aggregate is $[ac]^{1/2}/[ab^2c]^{1/4}=[ac/\ b^2]^{1/4}$. Now b can take on any value between a and c, and so the ratio of the single-stage limiting P^r to its two-stage counterpart can take on any value between $[c/a]^{1/4}$ and $[a/c]^{1/4}$. Since c/a is less than 1 and a/c is greater than 1, it can be seen that the ratio of the single-stage to the two-stage index can be arbitrarily far from 1 as r becomes large in magnitude with an appropriate choice of the numbers a, b and c.

17.60 The results in the previous paragraph show that some caution is required in assuming that *all* superlative indices will be approximately consistent in aggregation. However, for the three most commonly used superlative indices (the Fisher ideal P_F, the Törnqvist–Theil P_T and the Walsh P_W), the available empirical evidence indicates that these indices satisfy the consistency in aggregation property to a sufficiently high degree of approximation that users will not be unduly troubled by any inconsistencies.[42]

The Lloyd–Moulton index number formula

17.61 The index number formula that will be discussed in this section on the single-household economic approach to index number theory is a potentially very useful one for statistical agencies that are faced with the problem of producing a CPI in a timely manner. The Lloyd–Moulton formula that will be discussed in this section makes use of the same information that is required in order to implement a Laspeyres index except for one additional piece of information.

[42] See Chapter 19 for some additional evidence on this topic.

17.62 In this section, the same assumptions about the consumer are made that were made in paragraphs 17.18 to 17.26 above. In particular, it is assumed that the consumer's utility function $f(q)$ is linearly homogeneous[43] and the corresponding unit cost function is $c(p)$. It is supposed that the unit cost function has the following functional form:

$$c(p) \equiv \alpha_0\left(\sum_{i=1}^{n}\alpha_i p_i^{1-\sigma}\right)^{1/(1-\sigma)} \quad \text{if } \sigma \neq 1 \quad \text{or}$$
$$\ln c(p) \equiv \alpha_0 + \sum_{i=1}^{n}\alpha_i \ln p_i \quad \text{if } \sigma = 1 \tag{17.68}$$

where the α_i and σ are non-negative parameters with $\sum_{i=1}^{n}\alpha_i=1$. The unit cost function defined by equation (17.68) corresponds to a constant elasticity of substitution (CES) aggregator function, which was introduced into the economics literature by Arrow, Chenery, Minhas and Solow (1961).[44] The parameter σ is the elasticity of substitution; when $\sigma=0$, the unit cost function defined by equation (17.68) becomes linear in prices and hence corresponds to a fixed coefficients aggregator function which exhibits zero substitutability between all commodities. When $\sigma=1$, the corresponding aggregator or utility function is a Cobb–Douglas function. When σ approaches plus infinity, the corresponding aggregator function f approaches a linear aggregator function which exhibits infinite substitutability between each pair of inputs. The CES unit cost function defined by equation (17.68) is not a fully flexible functional form (unless the number of commodities n being aggregated is 2), but it is considerably more flexible than the zero substitutability aggregator function (this is the special case of equation (17.68) where σ is set equal to zero) that is exact for the Laspeyres and Paasche price indices.

17.63 Under the assumption of cost minimizing behaviour in period 0, Shephard's Lemma (17.12), tells us that the observed first period consumption of commodity i, q_i^0, will be equal to $u^0\ \partial c(p^0)/\partial p_i$, where $\partial c(p^0)/\partial p_i$ is the first-order partial derivative of the unit cost function with respect to the ith commodity price evaluated at the period 0 prices and $u^0=f(q^0)$ is the aggregate (unobservable) level of period 0 utility. Using the CES functional form defined by equation (17.68) and assuming that $\sigma\neq 1$, the following equations are obtained:

$$q_i^0 = u^0\alpha_0\left\{\sum_{k=1}^{n}\alpha_k(p_k^0)^r\right\}^{(1/r)-1}\alpha_i(p_i^0)^{r-1}$$
$$\text{for } r \equiv 1-\sigma \neq 0 \quad \text{and} \quad i=1,2,\ldots,n$$
$$= \frac{u^0 c(p^0)\alpha_i(p_i^0)^{r-1}}{\sum_{k=1}^{n}\alpha_k(p_k^0)^r} \tag{17.69}$$

[43] Thus homothetic preferences are assumed in this section.

[44] In the mathematics literature, this aggregator function or utility function is known as a mean of order r; see Hardy, Littlewood and Pólya (1934, pp. 12–13).

These equations can be rewritten as:

$$\frac{p_i^0 q_i^0}{u^0 c(p^0)} = \frac{\alpha_i (p_i^0)^r}{\sum_{k=1}^{n} \alpha_k (p_k^0)^r} \quad \text{for } i=1,2,\ldots,n \qquad (17.70)$$

where $r \equiv 1-\sigma$. Now consider the following Lloyd (1975) and Moulton (1996a) index number formula:

$$P_{LM}(p^0,p^1,q^0,q^1) \equiv \left\{ \sum_{i=1}^{n} s_i^0 \left(\frac{p_i^1}{p_i^0}\right)^{1-\sigma} \right\}^{1/(1-\sigma)} \quad \text{for } \sigma \neq 1 \qquad (17.71)$$

where s_i^0 is the period 0 expenditure share of commodity i, as usual:

$$s_i^0 \equiv \frac{p_i^0 q_i^0}{\sum_{k=1}^{n} p_k^0 q_k^0} \quad \text{for } i=1,2,\ldots,n$$

$$= \frac{p_i^0 q_i^0}{u^0 c(p^0)} \quad \text{using the assumption of cost minimizing behaviour}$$

$$= \frac{\alpha_i (p_i^0)^r}{\sum_{k=1}^{n} \alpha_k (p_k^0)^r} \quad \text{using equation (17.70)} \qquad (17.72)$$

If equation (17.72) is substituted into equation (17.71), it is found that:

$$P_{LM}(p^0,p^1,q^0,q^1) = \left\{ \sum_{i=1}^{n} s_i^0 \left(\frac{p_i^1}{p_i^0}\right)^r \right\}^{1/r}$$

$$= \left\{ \sum_{i=1}^{n} \frac{\alpha_i (p_i^0)^r}{\sum_{k=1}^{n} \alpha_k (p_k^0)^r} \left(\frac{p_i^1}{p_i^0}\right)^r \right\}^{1/r}$$

$$= \left\{ \frac{\sum_{i=1}^{n} \alpha_i (p_i^1)^r}{\sum_{k=1}^{n} \alpha_k (p_k^0)^r} \right\}^{1/r}$$

$$= \frac{\alpha_0 \left\{ \sum_{i=1}^{n} \alpha_i (p_i^1)^r \right\}^{1/r}}{\alpha_0 \left\{ \sum_{k=1}^{n} \alpha_k (p_k^0)^r \right\}^{1/r}}$$

$$= \frac{c(p^1)}{c(p^0)} \quad \text{using } r \equiv 1-\sigma$$

and definition (17.68). (17.73)

17.64 Equation (17.73) shows that the Lloyd–Moulton index number formula P_{LM} is exact for CES preferences. Lloyd (1975) and Moulton (1996a) independently derived this result, but it was Moulton who appreciated the significance of the formula (17.71) for statistical agency purposes. Note that in order to evaluate formula (17.71) numerically, it is necessary to have information on:

- base period expenditure shares s_i^0;
- the price relatives p_i^1/p_i^0 between the base period and the current period; and
- an estimate of the elasticity of substitution between the commodities in the aggregate, σ.

The first two pieces of information are the standard information sets that statistical agencies use to evaluate the Laspeyres price index P_L (note that P_{LM} reduces to P_L if $\sigma=0$). Hence, if the statistical agency is able to estimate the elasticity of substitution σ based on past experience,[45] then the Lloyd–Moulton price index can be evaluated using essentially the same information set that is used in order to evaluate the traditional Laspeyres index. Moreover, the resulting CPI will be free of substitution bias to a reasonable degree of approximation.[46] Of course, the practical problem with implementing this methodology is that estimates of the elasticity of substitution parameter σ are bound to be somewhat uncertain, and hence the resulting Lloyd–Moulton index may be subject to charges that it is not objective or reproducible. The statistical agency will have to balance the benefits of reducing substitution bias with these possible costs.

Annual preferences and monthly prices

17.65 Recall the definition of the Lowe index, $P_{Lo}(p^0,p^1,q)$, defined by equation (15.15) in Chapter 15. In paragraphs 15.33 to 15.64 of Chapter 15, it is noted that this formula is frequently used by statistical agencies as a target index for a CPI. It is also noted that, while the price vectors p^0 (the base period price vector) and p^1 (the current period price vector) are monthly or quarterly price vectors, the quantity vector $q \equiv (q_1, q_2, \ldots, q_n)$ which appears in this basket-type formula is usually taken to be an annual quantity vector that refers to a base year, b say, that is prior to the base period for the prices, month 0. Thus, typically, a statistical agency will produce a CPI at a monthly frequency that has the form $P_{Lo}(p^0,p^t,q^b)$, where p^0 is the price vector pertaining to the base period month for prices, month 0, p^t

[45] For the first application of this methodology (in the context of the CPI), see Shapiro and Wilcox (1997a, pp. 121–123). They calculated superlative Törnqvist indices for the United States for the years 1986–95 and then calculated the Lloyd–Moulton CES index for the same period, using various values of σ. They then chose the value of σ (which was 0.7), which caused the CES index to most closely approximate the Törnqvist index. Essentially the same methodology was used by Alterman, Diewert and Feenstra (1999) in their study of United States import and export price indices. For alternative methods for estimating σ, see Balk (2000b).

[46] What is a "reasonable" degree of approximation depends on the context. Assuming that consumers have CES preferences is not a reasonable assumption in the context of estimating elasticities of demand: at least a second-order approximation to the consumer's preferences is required in this context. In the context of approximating changes in a consumer's expenditures on the n commodities under consideration, however, it is usually adequate to assume a CES approximation.

is the price vector pertaining to the current period month for prices, month t say, and q^b is a reference basket quantity vector that refers to the base year b, which is equal to or prior to month 0.[47] The question to be addressed in the present section is: can this index be related to one based on the economic approach to index number theory?

The Lowe index as an approximation to a true cost of living index

17.66 Assume that the consumer has preferences defined over consumption vectors $q \equiv [q_1, \ldots, q_n]$ that can be represented by the continuous increasing utility function $f(q)$. Thus if $f(q^1) > f(q^0)$, then the consumer prefers the consumption vector q^1 to q^0. Let q^b be the annual consumption vector for the consumer in the base year b. Define the base year utility level u^b as the utility level that corresponds to $f(q)$ evaluated at q^b:

$$u^b \equiv f(q^b) \tag{17.74}$$

17.67 For any vector of positive commodity prices $p \equiv [p_1, \ldots, p_n]$ and for any feasible utility level u, the consumer's cost function, $C(u, p)$, can be defined in the usual way as the minimum expenditure required to achieve the utility level u when facing the prices p:

$$C(u, p) \equiv \min_q \left\{ \sum_{i=1}^{n} p_i q_i : f(q_1, \ldots, q_n) = u \right\}. \tag{17.75}$$

Let $p^b \equiv [p_1^b, \ldots, p_n^b]$ be the vector of annual prices that the consumer faced in the base year b. Assume that the observed base year consumption vector $q^b \equiv [q_1^b, \ldots, q_n^b]$ solves the following base year cost minimization problem:

$$C(u^b, p^b) \equiv \min_q \left\{ \sum_{i=1}^{n} p_i^b q_i : f(q_1, \ldots, q_n) = u^b \right\} = \sum_{i=1}^{n} p_i^b q_i^b \tag{17.76}$$

The cost function will be used below in order to define the consumer's cost of living price index.

17.68 Let p^0 and p^t be the monthly price vectors that the consumer faces in months 0 and t. Then the Konüs true cost of living index, $P_K(p^0, p^t, q^b)$, between months 0 and t, using the base year utility level $u^b = f(q^b)$ as the reference standard of living, is defined as the following ratio of minimum monthly costs of achieving the utility level u^b:

$$P_K(p^0, p^t, q^b) \equiv \frac{C(f(q^b), p^t)}{C(f(q^b), p^0)} \tag{17.77}$$

17.69 Using the definition of the monthly cost minimization problem that corresponds to the cost $C(f(q^b), p^t)$, it can be seen that the following inequality holds:

$$C(f(q^b), p^t) \equiv \min_q \left\{ \sum_{i=1}^{n} p_i^t q_i : f(q_1, \ldots, q_n) = f(q_1^b, \ldots, q_n^b) \right\} \leq \sum_{i=1}^{n} p_i^t q_i^b \tag{17.78}$$

since the base year quantity vector q^b is feasible for the cost minimization problem. Similarly, using the definition of the monthly cost minimization problem that corresponds to the month 0 cost $C(f(q^b), p^0)$, it can be seen that the following inequality holds:

$$C(f(q^b), p^0) \equiv \min_q \left\{ \sum_{i=1}^{n} p_i^0 q_i : f(q_1, \ldots, q_n) = f(q_1^b, \ldots, q_n^b) \right\} \leq \sum_{i=1}^{n} p_i^0 q_i^b \tag{17.79}$$

since the base year quantity vector q^b is feasible for the cost minimization problem.

17.70 It will prove useful to rewrite the two inequalities (17.78) and (17.79) as equalities. This can be done if non-negative substitution bias terms, e^t and e^0, are subtracted from the right-hand sides of these two inequalities. Thus the inequalities (17.78) and (17.79) can be rewritten as follows:

$$C(u^b, p^t) = \sum_{i=1}^{n} p_i^t q_i^b - e^t \tag{17.80}$$

$$C(u^b, p^0) = \sum_{i=1}^{n} p_i^0 q_i^b - e^0 \tag{17.81}$$

17.71 Using equations (17.80) and (17.81), and the definition (15.15) in Chapter 15 of the Lowe index, the following approximate equality for the Lowe index results:

$$P_{Lo}(p^0, p^t, q^b) \equiv \frac{\sum_{i=1}^{n} p_i^t q_i^b}{\sum_{i=1}^{n} p_i^0 q_i^b} = \frac{\{C(u^b, p^t) + e^t\}}{\{C(u^b, p^0) + e^0\}} \approx \frac{C(u^b, p^t)}{C(u^b, p^0)} = P_K(p^0, p^t, q^b) \tag{17.82}$$

Thus if the non-negative substitution bias terms e^0 and e^t are small, then the Lowe index between months 0 and t, $P_{Lo}(p^0, p^t, q^b)$, will be an adequate approximation to the true cost of living index between months 0 and t, $P_K(p^0, p^t, q^b)$.

17.72 A bit of algebraic manipulation shows that the Lowe index will be exactly equal to its cost of living counterpart if the substitution bias terms satisfy the following relationship:[48]

$$\frac{e^t}{e^0} = \frac{C(u^b, p^t)}{C(u^b, p^0)} = P_K(p^0, p^t, q^b) \tag{17.83}$$

[47] As noted in Chapter 15, month 0 is called the price reference period and year b is called the weight reference period.

[48] This assumes that e^0 is greater than zero. If e^0 is equal to zero, then to have equality of P_K and P_{Lo}, it must be the case that e^t is also equal to zero.

Equations (17.82) and (17.83) can be interpreted as follows: if the rate of growth in the amount of substitution bias between months 0 and t is equal to the rate of growth in the minimum cost of achieving the base year utility level u^b between months 0 and t, then the observable Lowe index, $P_{Lo}(p^0, p^t, q^b)$, will be exactly equal to its true cost of living index counterpart, $P_K(p^0, p^t, q^b)$.[49]

17.73 It is difficult to know whether condition (17.83) will hold or whether the substitution bias terms e^0 and e^t will be small. Thus, first-order and second-order Taylor series approximations to these substitution bias terms are developed in paragraphs 17.74 to 17.83.

A first-order approximation to the bias of the Lowe index

17.74 The true cost of living index between months 0 and t, using the base year utility level u^b as the reference utility level, is the ratio of two unobservable costs, $C(u^b, p^t)/C(u^b, p^0)$. However, both of these hypothetical costs can be approximated by first-order Taylor series approximations that can be evaluated using observable information on prices and base year quantities. The first-order Taylor series approximation to $C(u^b, p^t)$ around the annual base year price vector p^b is given by the following approximate equation:[50]

$$C(u^b, p^t) \approx C(u^b, p^b) + \sum_{i=1}^{n} \left[\frac{\partial C(u^b, p^b)}{\partial p_i}\right][p_i^t - p_i^b]$$

$$= C(u^b, p^b) + \sum_{i=1}^{n} q_i^b [p_i^t - p_i^b]$$

using assumption (17.76) and Shephard's Lemma (17.12)

$$= \sum_{i=1}^{n} p_i^b q_i^b + \sum_{i=1}^{n} q_i^b [p_i^t - p_i^b] \quad \text{using (17.76)}$$

$$= \sum_{i=1}^{n} p_i^t q_i^b. \qquad (17.84)$$

Similarly, the first-order Taylor series approximation to $C(u^b, p^0)$ around the annual base year price vector p^b is given by the following approximate equation:

$$C(u^b, p^0) \approx C(u^b, p^b) + \sum_{i=1}^{n} \left[\frac{\partial C(u^b, p^b)}{\partial p_i}\right][p_i^0 - p_i^b]$$

$$= C(u^b, p^b) + \sum_{i=1}^{n} q_i^b [p_i^0 - p_i^b]$$

$$= \sum_{i=1}^{n} p_i^b q_i^b + \sum_{i=1}^{n} q_i^b [p_i^0 - p_i^b]$$

$$= \sum_{i=1}^{n} p_i^0 q_i^b \qquad (17.85)$$

[49] It can be seen that, when month t is set equal to month 0, $e^t = e^0$ and $C(u^b, p^t) = C(u^b, p^0)$, and thus equation (17.83) is satisfied and $P_{Lo} = P_K$. This is not surprising since both indices are equal to unity when $t = 0$.

[50] This type of Taylor series approximation was used in Schultze and Mackie (2002, p. 91) in the cost of living index context, but it essentially dates back to Hicks (1941–42, p. 134) in the consumer surplus context. See also Diewert (1992b, p. 568) and Hausman (2002, p. 8).

17.75 Comparing approximate equation (17.84) with equation (17.80), and comparing approximate equation (17.85) with equation (17.81), it can be seen that, to the accuracy of the first-order approximations used in (17.84) and (17.85), the substitution bias terms e^t and e^0 will be zero. Using these results to reinterpret the approximate equation (17.82), it can be seen that if the month 0 and month t price vectors, p^0 and p^t, are not too different from the base year vector of prices p^b, then the Lowe index $P_{Lo}(p^0, p^t, q^b)$ will approximate the true cost of living index $P_K(p^0, p^t, q^b)$ to the accuracy of a first-order approximation. This result is quite useful, since it indicates that if the monthly price vectors p^0 and p^t are just randomly fluctuating around the base year prices p^b (with modest variances), then the Lowe index will serve as an adequate approximation to a theoretical cost of living index. However, if there are systematic long-term trends in prices and month t is fairly distant from month 0 (or the end of year b is quite distant from month 0), then the first-order approximations given by approximate equations (17.84) and (17.85) may no longer be adequate and the Lowe index may have a considerable bias relative to its cost of living counterpart. The hypothesis of long-run trends in prices will be explored in paragraphs 17.76 to 17.83.

A second-order approximation to the substitution bias of the Lowe index

17.76 A second-order Taylor series approximation to $C(u^b, p^t)$ around the base year price vector p^b is given by the following approximate equation:

$$C(u^b, p^t) \approx C(u^b, p^b) + \sum_{i=1}^{n} \left[\frac{\partial C(u^b, p^b)}{\partial p_i}\right][p_i^t - p_i^b] + \left(\frac{1}{2}\right) \sum_{i=1}^{n}\sum_{j=1}^{n} \left[\frac{\partial^2 C(u^b, p^b)}{\partial p_i \partial p_j}\right][p_i^t - p_i^b][p_j^t - p_j^b]$$

$$= \sum_{i=1}^{n} p_i^t q_i^b + \left(\frac{1}{2}\right) \sum_{i=1}^{n}\sum_{j=1}^{n} \left[\frac{\partial^2 C(u^b, p^b)}{\partial p_i \partial p_j}\right] \times [p_i^t - p_i^b][p_j^t - p_j^b] \qquad (17.86)$$

where the last equality follows using approximate equation (17.84).[51] Similarly, a second-order Taylor series approximation to $C(u^b, p^0)$ around the base year price vector p^b is given by the following approximate equation:

$$C(u^b, p^0) \approx C(u^b, p^b) + \sum_{i=1}^{n} \left[\frac{\partial C(u^b, p^b)}{\partial p_i}\right][p_i^0 - p_i^b] + \left(\frac{1}{2}\right) \sum_{i=1}^{n}\sum_{j=1}^{n} \left[\frac{\partial^2 C(u^b, p^b)}{\partial p_i \partial p_j}\right][p_i^0 - p_i^b][p_j^0 - p_j^b]$$

$$= \sum_{i=1}^{n} p_i^0 q_i^b + \left(\frac{1}{2}\right) \sum_{i=1}^{n}\sum_{j=1}^{n} \left[\frac{\partial^2 C(u^b, p^b)}{\partial p_i \partial p_j}\right] \times [p_i^0 - p_i^b][p_j^0 - p_j^b] \qquad (17.87)$$

[51] This type of second-order approximation is attributable to Hicks (1941–42, pp. 133–134; 1946, p. 331). See also Diewert (1992b, p. 568), Hausman (2002, p. 18) and Schultze and Mackie (2002, p. 91). For alternative approaches to modelling substitution bias, see Diewert (1998a; 2002c, pp. 598–603) and Hausman (2002).

where the last equality follows using the approximate equation (17.85).

17.77 Comparing approximate equation (17.86) with equation (17.80), and approximate equation (17.87) with equation (17.81), it can be seen that, to the accuracy of a second-order approximation, the month 0 and month t substitution bias terms, e^0 and e^t, will be equal to the following expressions involving the second-order partial derivatives of the consumer's cost function $\partial^2 C(u^b, p^b)/\partial p_i \partial p_j$ evaluated at the base year standard of living u^b and at the base year prices p^b:

$$e^0 \approx -\left(\frac{1}{2}\right)\sum_{i=1}^{n}\sum_{j=1}^{n}\left[\frac{\partial^2 C(u^b,p^b)}{\partial p_i \partial p_j}\right][p_i^0 - p_i^b][p_j^0 - p_j^b] \quad (17.88)$$

$$e^t \approx -\left(\frac{1}{2}\right)\sum_{i=1}^{n}\sum_{j=1}^{n}\left[\frac{\partial^2 C(u^b,p^b)}{\partial p_i \partial p_j}\right][p_i^t - p_i^b][p_j^t - p_j^b] \quad (17.89)$$

Since the consumer's cost function $C(u, p)$ is a concave function in the components of the price vector p,[52] it is known[53] that the n by n (symmetric) matrix of second-order partial derivatives $[\partial^2 C(u^b, p^b)/\partial p_i \partial p_j]$ is negative semi-definite.[54] Hence, for arbitrary price vectors p^b, p^0 and p^t, the right-hand sides of approximations (17.88) and (17.89) will be non-negative. Thus, to the accuracy of a second-order approximation, the substitution bias terms e^0 and e^t will be non-negative.

17.78 Now assume that there are long-run systematic trends in prices. Assume that the last month of the base year for quantities occurs M months prior to month 0, the base month for prices, and assume that prices trend linearly with time, starting with the last month of the base year for quantities. Thus, assume the existence of constants α_j for $j = 1, \ldots, n$ such that the price of commodity j in month t is given by:

$$p_i^t = p_i^b + \alpha_j(M + t) \quad \text{for } j = 1, \ldots, n \text{ and } t = 0, 1, \ldots, T \quad (17.90)$$

Substituting equation (17.90) into approximations (17.88) and (17.89) leads to the following second-order approximations to the two substitution bias terms, e^0 and e^t:[55]

$$e^0 \approx \gamma M^2 \quad (17.91)$$

$$e^t \approx \gamma (M + t)^2 \quad (17.92)$$

where γ is defined as follows:

$$\gamma \equiv -\left(\frac{1}{2}\right)\sum_{i=1}^{n}\sum_{j=1}^{n}\left[\frac{\partial^2 C(u^b,p^b)}{\partial p_i \partial p_j}\right]\alpha_i \alpha_j \geq 0 \quad (17.93)$$

17.79 It should be noted that the parameter γ will be zero under two sets of conditions:[56]

- All the second-order partial derivatives of the consumer's cost function $\partial^2 C(u^b, p^b)/\partial p_i \partial p_j$ are equal to zero.
- Each commodity price change parameter α_j is proportional to the corresponding commodity j base year price p_j^b.[57]

The first condition is empirically unlikely since it implies that the consumer will not substitute away from commodities of which the relative price has increased. The second condition is also empirically unlikely, since it implies that the structure of relative prices remains unchanged over time. Thus, in what follows, it will be assumed that γ is a positive number.

17.80 In order to simplify the notation in what follows, define the denominator and numerator of the month t Lowe index, $P_{Lo}(p^0, p^t, q^b)$, as a and b respectively; i.e., define:

$$a \equiv \sum_{i=1}^{n} p_i^0 q_i^b \quad (17.94)$$

$$b \equiv \sum_{i=1}^{n} p_i^t q_i^b \quad (17.95)$$

Using equation (17.90) to eliminate the month 0 prices p_i^0 from equation (17.94) and the month t prices p_i^t from equation (17.95) leads to the following expressions for a and b:

$$a = \sum_{i=1}^{n} p_i^b q_i^b + \sum_{i=1}^{n} \alpha_i q_i^b M \quad (17.96)$$

$$b = \sum_{i=1}^{n} p_i^b q_i^b + \sum_{i=1}^{n} \alpha_i q_i^b (M + t) \quad (17.97)$$

It is assumed that a and b[58] are positive and that

$$\sum_{i=1}^{n} \alpha_i q_i^b \geq 0 \quad (17.98)$$

Assumption (17.98) rules out a general deflation in prices.

17.81 Define the bias in the month t Lowe index, B^t, as the difference between the true cost of living index $P_K(p^0, p^t, q^b)$ defined by equation (17.77) and the

[52] See Diewert (1993b, pp. 109–110).

[53] See Diewert (1993b, p. 149).

[54] A symmetric n by n matrix A with ijth element equal to a_{ij} is negative semi-definite if, and only if for every vector $z \equiv [z_1, \ldots, z_n]$, it is the case that $\sum_{i=1}^{n}\sum_{j=1}^{n} a_{ij} z_i z_j \leq 0$.

[55] Note that the period 0 approximate bias defined by the right-hand side of approximation (17.91) is fixed, while the period t approximate bias defined by the right-hand side of (17.92) increases quadratically with time t. Hence, the period t approximate bias term will eventually overwhelm the period 0 approximate bias in this linear time trends case, if t is allowed to become large enough.

[56] A more general condition that ensures the positivity of γ is that the vector $[\alpha_1, \ldots, \alpha_n]$ is not an eigenvector of the matrix of second-order partial derivatives $\partial^2 C(u, p)/\partial p_i \partial p_j$ that corresponds to a zero eigenvalue.

[57] It is known that $C(u, p)$ is linearly homogeneous in the components of the price vector p; see Diewert (1993b, p. 109) for example. Hence, using Euler's Theorem on homogeneous functions, it can be shown that p^b is an eigenvector of the matrix of second-order partial derivatives $\partial^2 C(u, p)/\partial p_i \partial p_j$ that corresponds to a zero eigenvalue and thus $\sum_{i=1}^{n}\sum_{j=1}^{n}[\partial^2 C(u, p)/\partial p_i \partial p_j] p_i^b p_j^b = 0$; see Diewert (1993b, p. 149) for a detailed proof of this result.

[58] It is also assumed that $a - \gamma M^2$ is positive.

corresponding Lowe index $P_{Lo}(p^0, p^t, q^b)$:

$$B^t \equiv P_K(p^0, p^t, q^b) - P_{Lo}(p^0, p^t, q^b)$$
$$= \left\{\frac{C(u^b, p^t)}{C(u^b, p^0)}\right\} - \left(\frac{b}{a}\right)$$

using equations (17.94) and (17.95)

$$= \left\{\frac{[b-e^t]}{[a-e^0]}\right\} - \left(\frac{b}{a}\right)$$

using equations (17.80) and (17.81)

$$\approx \left\{\frac{[b-\gamma(M+t)^2]}{a-\gamma M^2}\right\} - \left(\frac{b}{a}\right)$$

using equations (17.91) and (17.92)

$$= \gamma\frac{\{(b-a)M^2 - 2aMt - at^2\}}{\{a[a-\gamma M^2]\}} \quad \text{simplifying terms}$$
$$= \gamma\frac{\left\{\left[\sum_{i=1}^n \alpha_i q_i^b t\right] M^2 - 2\left[\sum_{i=1}^n p_i^b q_i^b + \sum_{i=1}^n \alpha_i q_i^b M\right] Mt - at^2\right\}}{\{a[a-\gamma M^2]\}}$$

using equations (17.96) and (17.97)

$$= -\gamma\frac{\left\{\left[\sum_{i=1}^n \alpha_i q_i^b t\right] M^2 - 2\left[\sum_{i=1}^n p_i^b q_i^b\right] Mt + at^2\right\}}{\{a[a-\gamma M^2]\}} < 0$$

using equation (17.98). (17.99)

Thus, for $t \geq 1$, the Lowe index will have an upward bias (to the accuracy of a second-order Taylor series approximation) compared to the corresponding true cost of living index $P_K(p^0, p^t, q^b)$, since the approximate bias defined by the last expression in equation (17.99) is the sum of one non-positive and two negative terms. Moreover, this approximate bias will grow quadratically in time t.[59]

17.82 In order to give the reader some idea of the magnitude of the approximate bias B^t defined by the last line of equation (17.99), a simple special case will be considered at this point. Suppose there are only two commodities and that, at the base year, all prices and quantities are equal to 1. Thus, $p_i^b = q_i^b = 1$ for $i = 1, 2$ and $\sum_{i=1}^n p_i^b q_i^b = 2$. Assume that $M = 24$ so that the base year data on quantities take two years to process before the Lowe index can be implemented. Assume that the monthly rate of growth in price for commodity 1 is $\alpha_1 = 0.002$ so that after one year, the price of commodity 1 rises 0.024 or 2.4 per cent. Assume that commodity 2 falls in price each month with $\alpha_2 = -0.002$ so that the price of commodity 2 falls 2.4 per cent in the first year after the base year for quantities. Thus the relative price of the two commodities is steadily diverging by about 5 per cent per year. Finally, assume that $\partial^2 C(u^b, p^b)/\partial p_1 \partial p_1 = \partial^2 C(u^b, p^b)/\partial p_2 \partial p_2 = -1$ and $\partial^2 C(u^b, p^b)/\partial p_1 \partial p_2 = \partial^2 C(u^b, p^b)/\partial p_2 \partial p_1 = 1$. These assumptions imply that the own elasticity of demand for each commodity is -1 at the base year consumer equilibrium. Making all of these assumptions means that:

$$2 = \sum_{i=1}^n p_i^b q_i^b = a = b \; \sum_{i=1}^n \alpha_i q_i^b = 0 \; M = 24; \; \gamma = 0.000008 \tag{17.100}$$

Substituting the parameter values defined in equation (17.100) into equation (17.99) leads to the following formula for the approximate amount that the Lowe index will exceed the corresponding true cost of living index at month t:

$$-B^t = 0.000008\frac{(96t + 2t^2)}{2(2 - 0.004608)} \tag{17.101}$$

Evaluating equation (17.101) at $t = 12$, $t = 24$, $t = 36$, $t = 48$ and $t = 60$ leads to the following estimates for $-B^t$: 0.0029 (the approximate bias in the Lowe index at the end of the first year of operation for the index); 0.0069 (the bias after two years); 0.0121 (the bias after three years); 0.0185 (the bias after four years); 0.0260 (the bias after five years). Thus, at the end of the first year of the operation, the Lowe index will only be above the corresponding true cost of living index by approximately a third of a percentage point but, by the end of the fifth year of operation, it will exceed the corresponding cost of living index by about 2.6 percentage points, which is no longer a negligible amount.[60]

17.83 The numerical results in the previous paragraph are only indicative of the approximate magnitude of the difference between a cost of living index and the corresponding Lowe index. The important point to note is that, to the accuracy of a second-order approximation, the Lowe index will generally exceed its cost of living counterpart. The results also indicate, however, that this difference can be reduced to a negligible amount if:

- the lag in obtaining the base year quantity weights is minimized; and
- the base year is changed as frequently as possible.

It should also be noted that the numerical results depend on the assumption that long-run trends in prices exist, which may not be true,[61] and on elasticity assumptions that may not be justified.[62] Statistical agencies should prepare their own carefully constructed estimates of the differences between a Lowe index and a cost of living index in the light of their own particular circumstances.

The problem of seasonal commodities

17.84 The assumption that the consumer has annual preferences over commodities purchased in the base year

[59] If M is large relative to t, then it can be seen that the first two terms in the last equation of (17.99) can dominate the last term, which is the quadratic in t term.

[60] Note that the relatively large magnitude of M compared to t leads to a bias that grows approximately linearly with t rather than quadratically.

[61] For mathematical convenience, the trends in prices were assumed to be linear, rather than the more natural assumption of geometric trends in prices.

[62] Another key assumption that was used to derive the numerical results is the magnitude of the divergent trends in prices. If the price divergence vector is doubled to $\alpha_1 = 0.004$ and $\alpha_2 = -0.004$, then the parameter γ quadruples and the approximate bias will also quadruple.

for the quantity weights, and that these annual preferences can be used in the context of making monthly purchases of the same commodities, was a key one in relating the economic approach to index number theory to the Lowe index. This assumption that annual preferences can be used in a monthly context is, however, somewhat questionable because of the seasonal nature of some commodity purchases. The problem is that it is very likely that consumers' preference functions systematically change as the season of the year changes. National customs and weather changes cause households to purchase certain goods and services during some months and not at all for other months. For example, Christmas trees are purchased only in December and ski jackets are not usually purchased during summer months. Thus, the assumption that annual preferences are applicable during each month of the year is only acceptable as a very rough approximation to economic reality.

17.85 The economic approach to index number theory can be adapted to deal with seasonal preferences. The simplest economic approach is to assume that the consumer has annual preferences over commodities classified not only by their characteristics but also by the month of purchase.[63] Thus, instead of assuming that the consumer's annual utility function is $f(q)$ where q is an n-dimensional vector, assume that the consumer's annual utility function is $F[f^1(q^1), f^2(q^2), \ldots, f^{12}(q^{12})]$ where q^1 is an n-dimensional vector of commodity purchases made in January, q^2 is an n-dimensional vector of commodity purchases made in February, ..., and q^{12} is an n-dimensional vector of commodity purchases made in December.[64] The sub-utility functions $f^1, f^2, \ldots, f^{12}$ represent the consumer's preferences when making purchases in January, February, ..., and December, respectively. These monthly sub-utilities can then be aggregated using the macro-utility function F in order to define overall annual utility. It can be seen that these assumptions on preferences can be used to justify two types of cost of living index:

- an annual cost of living index that compares the prices in all months of a current year with the corresponding monthly prices in a base year;[65] and
- 12 monthly cost of living indices where the index for month m compares the prices of month m in the current year with the prices of month m in the base year for $m = 1, 2, \ldots, 12$.[66]

17.86 The annual Mudgett–Stone indices compare costs in a current calendar year with the corresponding costs in a base year. However, any month could be chosen as the year-ending month of the current year, and the prices and quantities of this new non-calendar year could be compared to the prices and quantities of the base year, where the January prices of the non-calendar year are matched to the January prices of the base year, the February prices of the non-calendar year are matched to the February prices of the base year, and so on. If further assumptions are made on the macro-utility function F, then this framework can be used in order to justify a third type of cost of living index: a moving year annual index.[67] This index compares the cost over the past 12 months of achieving the annual utility achieved in the base year with the base year cost, where the January costs in the current moving year are matched to January costs in the base year, the February costs in the current moving year are matched to February costs in the base year, and so on. These moving year indices can be calculated for each month of the current year and the resulting series can be interpreted as (uncentred) seasonally adjusted (annual) price indices.[68]

17.87 It should be noted that none of the three types of indices described in the previous two paragraphs is suitable for describing the movements of prices going from one month to the following month; i.e., they are not suitable for describing short-run movements in inflation. This is obvious for the first two types of index. To see the problem with the moving year indices, consider a special case where the bundle of commodities purchased in each month is entirely specific to each month. Then it is obvious that, even though all the above three types of index are well defined, none of them can describe anything useful about month-to-month changes in prices, since it is impossible to compare like with like, going from one month to the next, under the hypotheses of this special case. It is impossible to compare the incomparable.

17.88 Fortunately, it is not the case that household purchases in each month are entirely specific to the month of purchase. Thus month-to-month price comparisons can be made if the commodity space is restricted to commodities that are purchased in each month of the year. This observation leads to a fourth type of cost of living index, a month-to-month index, defined over commodities that are available in every month of the year.[69] This model can be used to justify the economic approach described in paragraphs 17.66 to 17.83. Commodities that are purchased only in certain months of the year, however, must be dropped from the scope of the index. Unfortunately, it is likely that consumers have varying monthly preferences over the commodities that are always available and, if this is the case, the month-to-month cost of living index (and the corresponding Lowe index) defined over always-available commodities will generally be subject to seasonal fluctuations. This will limit the usefulness of the

[63] This assumption and the resulting annual indices were first proposed by Mudgett (1955, p. 97) and Stone (1956, pp. 74–75).

[64] If some commodities are not available in certain months m, then those commodities can be dropped from the corresponding monthly quantity vectors q^m.

[65] For further details on how to implement this framework, see Mudgett (1955, p. 97), Stone (1956, pp. 74–75) and Diewert (1998b, pp. 459–460).

[66] For further details on how to implement this framework, see Diewert (1999a, pp. 50–51).

[67] See Diewert (1999a, pp. 56–61) for the details of this economic approach.

[68] See Diewert (1999a, pp. 67–68) for an empirical example of this approach applied to quantity indices. An empirical example of this moving year approach to price indices is presented in Chapter 22.

[69] See Diewert (1999a, pp. 51–56) for the assumptions on preferences that are required in order to justify this economic approach.

index as a short-run indicator of general inflation since it will be difficult to distinguish a seasonal movement in the index from a systematic general movement in prices.[70] Note also that if the scope of the index is restricted to always-available commodities, then the resulting month-to-month index will not be comprehensive, whereas the moving year indices will be comprehensive in the sense of using all the available price information.

17.89 The above considerations lead to the conclusion that it may be useful for statistical agencies to produce at least two consumer price indices:

- a moving year index which is comprehensive and seasonally adjusted, but which is not necessarily useful for indicating month-to-month changes in general inflation; and
- a month-to-month index which is restricted to non-seasonal commodities (and hence is not comprehensive), but which is useful for indicating short-run movements in general inflation.

The problem of a zero price increasing to a positive price

17.90 In a recent paper, Haschka (2003) raised the problem of what to do when a price which was previously zero is increased to a positive level. He gave two examples for Austria, where parking and hospital fees were raised from zero to a positive level. In this situation, it turns out that basket-type indices have an advantage over indices that are weighted geometric averages of price relatives, since basket-type indices are well defined even if some prices are zero.

17.91 The problem can be considered in the context of evaluating the Laspeyres and Paasche indices. Suppose as usual that the prices p_i^t and quantities q_i^t of the first n commodities are positive for periods 0 and 1, but that the price of commodity $n+1$ in period 0 is zero but is positive in period 1. In both periods, the consumption of commodity $n+1$ is positive. Thus the assumptions on the prices and quantities of commodity $n+1$ in the two periods under consideration can be summarized as follows:

$$p_{n+1}^0=0 \quad p_{n+1}^1>0 \quad q_{n+1}^0>0 \quad q_{n+1}^1>0 \qquad (17.102)$$

Typically, the increase in price of commodity $n+1$ from its initial non-zero level will cause consumption to fall so that $q_{n+1}^1<q_{n+1}^0$, but this inequality is not required for the analysis below.

17.92 Let the Laspeyres index between periods 0 and 1, restricted to the first n commodities, be denoted as P_L^n and let the Laspeyres index, defined over all $n+1$ commodities, be defined as P_L^{n+1}. Also let $v_i^0\equiv p_i^0q_i^0$ denote the value of expenditures on commodity i in period 0. Then by the definition of the Laspeyres index defined over all $n+1$ commodities:

$$P_L^{n+1}\equiv\frac{\sum_{i=1}^{n+1}p_i^1q_i^0}{\sum_{i=1}^{n+1}p_i^0q_i^0} = P_L^n+\frac{p_{n+1}^1q_{n+1}^0}{\sum_{i=1}^{n}v_i^0} \qquad (17.103)$$

where $p_{n+1}^0=0$ was used in order to derive the second equation above. Thus the complete Laspeyres index P_L^{n+1} defined over all $n+1$ commodities is equal to the incomplete Laspeyres index P_L^n (which can be written in traditional price relative and base period expenditure share form), plus the mixed or hybrid expenditure $p_{n+1}^1q_{n+1}^0$ divided by the base period expenditure on the first n commodities, $\sum_{i=1}^n v_i^0$. Thus the complete Laspeyres index can be calculated using the usual information available to the price statistician plus two additional pieces of information: the new non-zero price for commodity $n+1$ in period 1, p_{n+1}^1, and an estimate of consumption of commodity $n+1$ in period 0 (when it was free), q_{n+1}^0. Since it is often governments that change the previously zero price to a positive price, the decision to do this is usually announced in advance, which will give the price statistician an opportunity to form an estimate for the base period demand, q_{n+1}^0.

17.93 Let the Paasche index between periods 0 and 1, restricted to the first n commodities, be denoted as P_P^n and let the Paasche index, defined over all $n+1$ commodities, be defined as P_P^{n+1}. Also let $v_i^1\equiv p_i^1q_i^1$ denote the value of expenditures on commodity i in period 1. Then, by the definition of the Paasche index defined over all $n+1$ commodities:

$$P_P^{n+1}\equiv\frac{\sum_{i=1}^{n+1}p_i^1q_i^1}{\sum_{i=1}^{n+1}p_i^0q_i^1} = P_P^n+\frac{v_{n+1}^1}{\sum_{i=1}^{n}p_i^0q_i^1} = P_P^n+\frac{v_{n+1}^1}{\sum_{i=1}^{n}v_i^1/(p_i^1/p_i^0)} \qquad (17.104)$$

where $p_{n+1}^0=0$ was used in order to derive the second equation above. Thus the complete Paasche index P_P^{n+1} defined over all $n+1$ commodities is equal to the incomplete Paasche index P_P^n (which can be written in traditional price relative and current period expenditure share form), plus the current period expenditure on commodity $n+1$, v_{n+1}^1, divided by a sum of current period expenditures on the first n commodities, v_i^1, divided by the ith price relative for the first n commodities, p_i^1/p_i^0. Thus the complete Paasche index can be calculated using

[70] One problem with using annual weights in the context of seasonal movements in prices and quantities is that a change in price when a commodity is out of season can be greatly magnified by the use of annual weights. Baldwin (1990, p. 251) noted this problem with an annual weights price index: "But a price index is adversely affected if any seasonal good has the same basket share for all months of the year; the good will have an inappropriately small basket share in its in season months, an inappropriately large share in its off season months." Seasonality problems are considered again from a more pragmatic point of view in Chapter 22.

the usual information available to the price statistician plus information on current period expenditures.

17.94 Once the complete Laspeyres and Paasche indices have been calculated using equations (17.103) and (17.104), then the complete Fisher index can be calculated as the square root of the product of these two indices:

$$P_F^{n+1} = [P_L^{n+1} P_P^{n+1}]^{1/2} \qquad (17.105)$$

It should be noted that the complete Fisher index defined by equation (17.105) satisfies the same exact index number results as were demonstrated in paragraphs 17.27 to 17.32 above; i.e., the Fisher index remains a superlative index even if prices are zero in one period but positive in the other. Thus the Fisher price index remains a suitable target index even in the face of zero prices.

THE ECONOMIC APPROACH TO INDEX NUMBER THEORY: THE MANY-HOUSEHOLD CASE 18

Introduction

18.1 In the previous chapter on the economic approach to index numbers, it was implicitly assumed that the economy behaved as if there were a single representative consumer. In the present chapter, the economic approach is extended to an economy with many household groups or many regions. In the algebra below, an arbitrary number of households, H say, is considered. In principle, each household in the economy under consideration could have its own consumer price index. In practice, however, it will be necessary to group households into various classes. Within each class, it will be necessary to assume that the group of households in the class behaves as if it were a single household in order to apply the economic approach to index number theory. The partition of the economy into H household classes can also be given a regional interpretation: each household class could be interpreted as a group of households within a region of the country under consideration.

18.2 The concepts of a *plutocratic index* and a *conditional index* are introduced in paragraphs 18.3 to 18.13. Using the plutocratic concept, each household in the economy is given a weight in the national index that is proportional to the household's expenditures on commodities for the two periods under consideration. A conditional index is an index that depends on environmental variables that might affect household expenditures on commodities. One example of an environmental variable is the weather: if the weather is cold, then households will spend more on heating fuel. In paragraphs 18.14 to 18.22 it is shown how a national Fisher price index can approximate a plutocratic cost of living index. Finally, paragraphs 18.23 to 18.35 consider an alternative conceptual framework for a national index, the *democratic index*. Using this index concept, each household in the economy is given an equal weight in the national index (as opposed to the plutocratic concept where households that spend more get a higher weight in the national index).

Plutocratic cost of living indices and observable bounds

18.3 In this section, an economic approach to the consumer price index (CPI) is considered that is based on the *plutocratic cost of living index* that was originally defined by Prais (1959). This concept was further refined by Pollak (1980, p. 276; 1981, p. 328), who defined his *Scitovsky–Laspeyres cost of living index* as the ratio of total expenditure required to enable each household in the economy under consideration to attain its base period indifference surface at period 1 prices to the corresponding expenditure required to attain the same standard of living using period 0 prices. In the following paragraph, this concept will be explained more fully.

18.4 Suppose that there are H households (or regions) in the economy and suppose further that there are n commodities in the economy in periods 0 and 1 that households consume *and* that we wish to include in our definition of the cost of living. Denote an n-dimensional vector of commodity consumption in a given period by $q \equiv (q_1, q_2, \ldots, q_n)$ as usual. Denote the vector of period t market prices faced by household h by $p_h^t \equiv (p_{h1}^t, p_{h2}^t, \ldots, p_{hN}^t)$ for $t=0,1$. Note that it is *not* assumed that each household faces the same vector of commodity prices. In addition to the market commodities that are in the vector q, it is assumed that each household is affected by an M-dimensional vector of *environmental*[1] *or demographic*[2] *variables or public goods*, $e \equiv (e_1, e_2, \ldots, e_M)$. It is supposed that there are H households (or regions) in the economy during periods 0 and 1, and the preferences of household h over different combinations of market commodities q and environmental variables e can be represented by the continuous utility function $f^h(q, e)$ for $h = 1, 2, \ldots, H$.[3] For periods $t=0,1$ and for households $h=1,2,\ldots,H$, it is assumed that the observed household h consumption vector $q_h^t \equiv (q_{h1}^t, \ldots, q_{hN}^t)$ is a solution to the following household h expenditure minimization problem:

$$\min_q \{p_h^t q : f^h(q, e_h^t) \geq u_h^t\} \equiv C^h(u_h^t, e_h^t, p_h^t); \quad t=0,1; h=1,2,\ldots,H \tag{18.1}$$

where e_h^t is the environmental vector facing household h in period t, $u_h^t \equiv f^h(q_h^t, e_h^t)$ is the utility level achieved by household h during period t and C^h is the cost or expenditure function that is dual to the utility function f^h.[4] Basically, these assumptions mean that

[1] This is the terminology used by Pollak (1989, p. 181) in his model of the conditional cost of living concept.

[2] Caves, Christensen and Diewert (1982a, p. 1409) used the terms demographic variables or public goods to describe the vector of conditioning variables e in their generalized model of the Konüs price index or cost of living index, while Diewert (2001) used the term environmental variables.

[3] It is assumed that each $f^h(q, e)$ is continuous and increasing in the components of q and e, and is concave in the components of q.

[4] In order to simplify notation, in this section the notation $pq = \sum_{i=1}^n p_i q_i$ as the inner product between the vectors p and q is used rather than the usual summation notation.

each household has stable preferences over the same list of commodities during the two periods under consideration, the same households appear in each period and each household chooses its consumption bundle in the most cost-efficient way during each period, conditional on the environmental vector that it faces during each period. Note again that the household (or regional) prices are in general different across households (or regions).

18.5 With the above assumptions in mind, the example of Pollak (1980; 1981) and Diewert (1983a, p. 190)[5] is followed. The class of *conditional plutocratic cost of living indices*, $P^*(p^0, p^1, u, e_1, e_2, \ldots, e_H)$, pertaining to periods 0 and 1 for the arbitrary utility vector of household utilities $u \equiv (u_1, u_2, \ldots, u_H)$ and for the arbitrary vectors of household environmental variables e_h for $h = 1, 2, \ldots, H$ is defined as follows:

$$P^*(p_1^0, \ldots, p_H^0, p_1^1, \ldots, p_H^1, u, e_1, e_2, \ldots, e_H) \equiv \frac{\sum_{h=1}^{H} C^h(u_h, e_h, p_h^1)}{\sum_{h=1}^{H} C^h(u_h, e_h, p_h^0)} \quad (18.2)$$

The numerator on the right-hand side of equation (18.2) is the sum over households of the minimum cost, $C^h(u_h, e_h, p_h^1)$, for household h to achieve the arbitrary utility level u_h, given that the household h faces the arbitrary vector of household h environmental variables e_h and also faces the period 1 vector of prices p_h^1. The denominator on the right-hand side of equation (18.2) is the sum over households of the minimum cost, $C^h(u_h, e_h, p_h^0)$, for household h to achieve the *same* arbitrary utility level u_h, given that the household faces the *same* arbitrary vector of household h environmental variables e_h and also faces the period 0 vector of prices p_h^0. Thus in the numerator and denominator of equation (18.2), only the price variables are different, which is precisely what is wanted in a theoretical definition of a consumer price index.

18.6 The general definition (18.2) is now specialized by replacing the general utility vector u by either the period 0 vector of household utilities $u^0 \equiv (u_1^0, u_2^0, \ldots u_H^0)$ or the period 1 vector of household utilities $u^1 \equiv (u_1^1, u_2^1, \ldots u_H^1)$. The general definition is also specialized by replacing the general household environmental vectors $(e_1, e_2, \ldots e_H) \equiv e$ by either the period 0 vector of household environmental variables $e^0 \equiv (e_1^0, e_2^0, \ldots e_H^0)$ or the period 1 vector of household environmental variables $e^1 \equiv (e_1^1, e_2^1, \ldots, e_H^1)$. The choice of the base period vector of utility levels and base period environmental variables leads to the *Laspeyres conditional plutocratic cost of living index*, $P^*(p_1^0, \ldots, p_H^0, p_1^1, \ldots, p_H^1, u^0, e^0)$.[6] The choice of the period 1 vector of utility levels and period 1 environmental variables leads to the *Paasche conditional plutocratic cost of living index*, $P^*(p_1^0, \ldots, p_H^0, p_1^1, \ldots, p_H^1, u^1, e^1)$. It turns out that these last two indices satisfy some interesting inequalities, which are derived below.

18.7 Using definition (18.2), the Laspeyres conditional plutocratic cost of living index, $P^*(p_1^0, \ldots, p_H^0, p_1^1, \ldots, p_H^1, u^0, e^0)$, may be written as follows:

$$\begin{aligned} P^*(p_1^0, \ldots, p_H^0, p_1^1, \ldots, p_H^1, u^0, e_1^0, e_2^0, \ldots, e_H^0) &\equiv \frac{\sum_{h=1}^{H} C^h(u_h^0, e_h^0, p_h^1)}{\sum_{h=1}^{H} C^h(u_h^0, e_h^0, p_h^0)} \\ &= \frac{\sum_{h=1}^{H} C^h(u_h^0, e_h^0, p_h^1)}{\sum_{h=1}^{H} p_h^0 q_h^0} \quad \text{using equation (18.1) for } t=0 \\ &\le \frac{\sum_{h=1}^{H} p_h^1 q_h^0}{\sum_{h=1}^{H} p_h^0 q_h^0} \quad (18.3) \end{aligned}$$

since $C^h(u_h^0, e_h^0, p_h^1) \equiv \min_q \{p_h^1 q : f^h(q, e_h^0) \ge u_h^0\} \le p^1 q_h^0$ and q_h^0 is feasible for the cost minimization problem for $h = 1, 2, \ldots, H$

$$\equiv P_{PL}$$

where P_{PL} is defined to be the observable (in principle) *plutocratic Laspeyres price index*, $\sum_{h=1}^{H} p_h^1 q_h^0 / \sum_{h=1}^{H} p_h^0 q_h^0$, which uses the individual vectors of household or regional quantities for period 0, $(q_1^0, \ldots, q_H^0)$, as quantity weights.[7]

18.8 If prices are equal across households (or regions), so that

$$p_h^t = p^t \quad \text{for } t = 0, 1 \text{ and } h = 1, 2, \ldots, H, \quad (18.4)$$

then the plutocratic (or disaggregated) Laspeyres price index, P_{PL}, collapses down to the usual aggregate Laspeyres index, P_L; i.e., then P_{PL} becomes

[5] These authors provided generalizations of the plutocratic cost of living index attributable to Prais (1959). Pollak and Diewert did not include the environmental variables in their definitions of a group cost of living index.

[6] This is the concept of a cost of living index that Triplett (2001) found most useful for measuring inflation: "One might want to produce a COL *conditional* on the base period's weather experience.... In this case, the unusually cold winter does not affect the *conditional* COL subindex that holds the environment constant.... the COL subindex that holds the environment constant is probably the COL concept that is most useful for an anti-inflation policy." Hill (1999, p. 4) endorsed this point of view.

[7] Thus the plutocratic Laspeyres index can be regarded as an ordinary Laspeyres index except that each commodity consumed by each household (or in each region) is regarded as a separate commodity.

$$P_{PL} \equiv \frac{\sum_{h=1}^{H} p_h^1 q_h^0}{\sum_{h=1}^{H} p_h^0 q_h^0} = \frac{p^1 \sum_{h=1}^{H} q_h^0}{p^0 \sum_{h=1}^{H} q_h^0} = \frac{p^1 q^0}{p^0 q^0} \equiv P_L \quad (18.5)$$

where the total quantity vector in period t is defined as

$$q^t \equiv \sum_{h=1}^{H} q_h^t \quad \text{for } t=0,1 \quad (18.6)$$

18.9 The inequality (18.3) says that the theoretical Laspeyres plutocratic conditional cost of living index, $P^*(p_1^0,\ldots,p_H^0,p_1^1,\ldots,p_H^1,u^0,e^0)$, is bounded from above by the observable (in principle) plutocratic or disaggregated Laspeyres price index, P_{PL}. The special case of inequality (18.3) when the equal prices assumption (18.4) holds[8] was first obtained by Pollak (1989, p. 182) for the case of one household with environmental variables and by Pollak (1980, p. 276) for the many-household case, but where the environmental variables are absent from the household utility and cost functions.

18.10 In a similar manner, specializing definition (18.2), the Paasche conditional plutocratic cost of living index, $P^*(p_1^0,\ldots,p_H^0,p_1^1,\ldots,p_H^1,u^1,e^1)$, may be written as follows:

$$P^*(p_1^0,\ldots,p_H^0,p_1^1,\ldots,p_H^1,u^1,e_1^1,e_2^1,\ldots,e_H^1) \equiv \frac{\sum_{h=1}^{H} C^h(u_h^1,e_h^1,p_h^1)}{\sum_{h=1}^{H} C^h(u_h^1,e_h^1,p_h^0)}$$

$$= \frac{\sum_{h=1}^{H} p_h^1 q_h^1}{\sum_{h=1}^{H} C^h(u_h^1,e_h^1,p_h^0)} \quad \text{using equation (18.1) for } t=1$$

$$\geq \frac{\sum_{h=1}^{H} p_h^1 q_h^1}{\sum_{h=1}^{H} p_h^0 q_h^1} \quad \text{using a feasibility argument}$$

$$\equiv P_{PP} \quad (18.7)$$

where P_{PP} is defined to be the plutocratic or disaggregated (over households) Paasche price index, $\sum_{h=1}^{H} p_h^1 q_h^1 / \sum_{h=1}^{H} p_h^0 q_h^1$, which uses the individual vectors of household quantities for period 1, $(q_1^1,\ldots,q_H^1)$, as quantity weights.

[8] The general case was obtained by Diewert (2001, p. 222).

18.11 If prices are equal across households (or regions), so that assumptions (18.4) hold, then the disaggregated Paasche price index P_{PP} collapses down to the usual aggregate Paasche index, P_P; i.e., then P_{PP} becomes

$$P_{PP} \equiv \frac{\sum_{h=1}^{H} p_h^1 q_h^1}{\sum_{h=1}^{H} p_h^0 q_h^1} = \frac{p^1 \sum_{h=1}^{H} q_h^1}{p^0 \sum_{h=1}^{H} q_h^1} = \frac{p^1 q^1}{p^0 q^1} \equiv P_P \quad (18.8)$$

18.12 Returning to the inequality (18.7), it can be seen that the theoretical Paasche conditional plutocratic cost of living index, $P^*(p_1^0,\ldots,p_H^0,p_1^1,\ldots,p_H^1,u^1,e^1)$, is bounded from below by the observable plutocratic or disaggregated Paasche price index, P_{PP}. Diewert (1983a, p. 191) first obtained the inequality (18.7) for the case where the environmental variables are absent from the household utility and cost functions, and prices are equal across households. The general case is attributable to Diewert (2001, p. 223).

18.13 In the following section, it will be shown how to obtain a theoretical plutocratic cost of living index that is bounded from above and below rather than the theoretical indices in inequalities (18.3) and (18.7) that just have the one-sided bounds.

The Fisher plutocratic price index

18.14 Using the inequalities (18.3) and (18.7) and the continuity properties of the conditional plutocratic cost of living $P^*(p_1^0,\ldots,p_H^0,p_1^1,\ldots,p_H^1,u,e)$ defined by equation (18.2), it is possible to modify the method of proof used by Konüs (1924) and Diewert (1983a, p. 191) and establish the following result:[9]

There exists a reference utility vector $u^* \equiv (u_1^*,u_2^*,\ldots,u_H^*)$ such that the household h reference utility level u_h^* lies between the household h period 0 and 1 utility levels, u_h^0 and u_h^1 respectively for $h=1,\ldots,H$, and there exist household environmental vectors $e_h^* \equiv (e_{h1}^*,e_{h2}^*,\ldots,e_{hM}^*)$ such that the household h reference mth environmental variable e_{hm}^* lies between the household h period 0 and 1 levels for the mth environmental variable, e_{hm}^0 and e_{hm}^1 respectively for $m=1,2,\ldots,M$ and $h=1,\ldots,H$, and the conditional plutocratic cost of living index $P^*(p_1^0,\ldots,p_H^0,p_1^1,\ldots,p_H^1,u^*,e^*)$ evaluated at this intermediate reference utility vector u^* and the intermediate reference vector of household environmental variables

[9] See Diewert (2001, p. 223). Note that the household cost functions must be continuous in the environmental variables; this is a real restriction on the types of environmental variables which can be accommodated by the result.

$e^* \equiv (e_1^*, e_2^*, \ldots, e_H^*)$ lies between the observable (in principle) plutocratic Laspeyres and Paasche price indices, P_{PL} and P_{PP}, defined above by the last equalities in (18.3) and (18.7).

18.15 The above result says that the *theoretical national plutocratic conditional consumer price index* $P^*(p_1^0, \ldots, p_H^0, p_1^1, \ldots, p_H^1, u^*, e^*)$ lies between the plutocratic or disaggregated Laspeyres index P_{PL} and the plutocratic or disaggregated Paasche index P_{PP}. Hence if P_{PL} and P_{PP} are not too different, a good point approximation to the theoretical national plutocratic consumer price index will be the *plutocratic or disaggregated Fisher index* P_{PF} defined as:

$$P_{PF} \equiv \sqrt{P_{PL} P_{PP}} \tag{18.9}$$

The plutocratic Fisher price index P_{PF} is computed just like the usual Fisher price index, except that each commodity in each region (or for each household) is regarded as a separate commodity. Of course, this index will satisfy the time reversal test.

18.16 Since statistical agencies do not calculate Laspeyres, Paasche and Fisher price indices by taking inner products of price and quantity vectors, as was done in equation (18.9) and the previous definitions, it will be useful to obtain formulae for the Laspeyres and Paasche indices that depend only on price relatives and expenditure shares. In order to do this, it is necessary to introduce some notation. Define the expenditure share of household h on commodity i in period t as

$$S_{hi}^t \equiv \frac{p_{hi}^t q_{hi}^t}{\sum_{k=1}^{n} p_{hk}^t q_{hk}^t}; \quad t=0,1; \quad h=1,2,\ldots,H; \quad i=1,2,\ldots,n \tag{18.10}$$

Define the expenditure share of household h in total period t consumption as:

$$S_h^t \equiv \frac{\sum_{i=1}^{n} p_{hi}^t q_{hi}^t}{\sum_{k=1}^{H}\sum_{i=1}^{n} p_{ik}^t q_{ik}^t} = \frac{p_h^t q_h^t}{\sum_{k=1}^{H} p_k^t q_k^t} \quad t=0,1;\ h=1,2,\ldots,H \tag{18.11}$$

Finally, define the national expenditure share of commodity i in period t as:

$$\begin{aligned}
\sigma_i^t &\equiv \frac{\sum_{h=1}^{H} p_{hi}^t q_{hi}^t}{\sum_{k=1}^{H} p_k^t q_k^t} \quad t=0,1; \quad i=1,2,\ldots,n \\
&= \sum_{h=1}^{H} \left(\frac{p_{hi}^t q_{hi}^t}{p_h^t q_h^t}\right) \left(\frac{p_h^t q_h^t}{\sum_{k=1}^{H} p_k^t q_k^t}\right) \\
&= \frac{\sum_{h=1}^{H} s_{hi}^t p_h^t q_h^t}{\sum_{k=1}^{H} p_k^t q_k^t} \\
&= \sum_{h=1}^{H} s_{hi}^t S_h^t
\end{aligned} \tag{18.12}$$

The Laspeyres price index for region h (or household h) is defined as:

$$\begin{aligned}
P_{Lh} &\equiv \frac{p_h^1 q_h^0}{p_h^0 q_h^0} \quad h=1,2,\ldots,H \\
&= \frac{\sum_{i=1}^{n} \left(\frac{p_{hi}^1}{p_{hi}^0}\right) p_{hi}^0 q_{hi}^0}{p_h^0 q_h^0} \\
&= \sum_{i=1}^{n} s_{hi}^0 \left(\frac{p_{hi}^1}{p_{hi}^0}\right)
\end{aligned} \tag{18.13}$$

18.17 Referring back to equation (18.3), the plutocratic national Laspeyres price index, P_{PL}, can be rewritten as follows:

$$P_{PL} \equiv \frac{\sum_{h=1}^{H} p_h^1 q_h^0}{\sum_{h=1}^{H} p_h^0 q_h^0} \tag{18.14}$$

$$\begin{aligned}
&= \sum_{h=1}^{H} \left(\frac{p_h^1 q_h^0}{p_h^0 q_h^0}\right) \left(\frac{p_h^0 q_h^0}{\sum_{h=1}^{H} p_h^0 q_h^0}\right) = \sum_{h=1}^{H} \left(\frac{p_h^1 q_h^0}{p_h^0 q_h^0}\right) S_h^0 \\
&= \sum_{h=1}^{H} S_h^0 P_{Lh}
\end{aligned} \tag{18.15}$$

$$\begin{aligned}
&= \sum_{h=1}^{H} S_h^0 \sum_{i=1}^{n} s_{hi}^0 \left(\frac{p_{hi}^1}{p_{hi}^0}\right) \\
&= \sum_{h=1}^{H}\sum_{i=1}^{n} S_h^0 s_{hi}^0 \left(\frac{p_{hi}^1}{p_{hi}^0}\right)
\end{aligned} \tag{18.16}$$

Equation (18.15) shows that the plutocratic national Laspeyres price index is equal to a (period 0) regional expenditure share-weighted average of the regional Laspeyres price indices. Equation (18.16) shows that the national Laspeyres price index is equal to a (period 0) expenditure share-weighted average of the regional price relatives, (p_{hi}^1/p_{hi}^0), where the corresponding weight, $S_h^0 s_{hi}^0$, is the period 0 national expenditure share of commodity i in region h.

18.18 The Paasche price index for region h (or household h) is defined as:

$$\begin{aligned}
P_{Ph} &\equiv \frac{p_h^1 q_h^1}{p_h^0 q_h^1} \quad h=1,2,\ldots,H \\
&= \frac{1}{\sum_{i=1}^{n} \left(\frac{p_{hi}^0}{p_{hi}^1}\right) p_{hi}^1 q_{hi}^1 / p_h^1 q_h^1}
\end{aligned}$$

$$= \frac{1}{\sum_{i=1}^{n} s_{hi}^{1} \left(\frac{p_{hi}^{1}}{p_{hi}^{0}} \right)^{-1}}$$

$$= \left\{ \sum_{i=1}^{n} s_{hi}^{1} \left(\frac{p_{hi}^{1}}{p_{hi}^{0}} \right)^{-1} \right\}^{-1} \quad (18.17)$$

18.19 Referring back to equation (18.7), the plutocratic national Paasche price index, P_{PP}, can be rewritten as follows:

$$P_{PP} \equiv \frac{\sum_{h=1}^{H} p_h^1 q_h^1}{\sum_{h=1}^{H} p_h^0 q_h^1} \quad (18.18)$$

$$= \frac{1}{\left\{ \sum_{h=1}^{H} \left(\frac{p_h^0 q_h^1}{p_h^1 q_h^1} \right) \left(\frac{p_h^1 q_h^1}{\sum_{h=1}^{H} p_h^1 q_h^1} \right) \right\}}$$

$$= \frac{1}{\sum_{h=1}^{H} \left(\frac{p_h^1 q_h^0}{p_h^0 q_h^0} \right)^{-1} S_h^1}$$

$$= \left(\sum_{h=1}^{H} S_h^1 P_{Ph}^{-1} \right)^{-1} \quad (18.19)$$

$$= \left\{ \sum_{h=1}^{H} S_h^1 \sum_{i=1}^{n} s_{hi}^1 \left(\frac{p_{hi}^1}{p_{hi}^0} \right)^{-1} \right\}^{-1}$$

$$= \left\{ \sum_{h=1}^{H} \sum_{i=1}^{n} S_h^1 s_{hi}^1 \left(\frac{p_{hi}^1}{p_{hi}^0} \right)^{-1} \right\}^{-1} \quad (18.20)$$

Equation (18.19) shows that the national plutocratic Paasche price index is equal to a (period 1) regional expenditure share-weighted harmonic mean of the regional Paasche price indices. Equation (18.20) shows that the national Paasche price index is equal to a (period 1) expenditure share-weighted harmonic average of the regional price relatives, (p_{hi}^1/p_{hi}^0), where the weight for this price relative, $S_h^1 s_{hi}^1$, is the period 1 national expenditure share of commodity i in region h.

18.20 Of course, the share formulae for the plutocratic Paasche and Laspeyres indices, P_{PP} and P_{PL}, given by equations (18.20) and (18.16), can now be used to calculate the plutocratic Fisher index, $P_{PF} \equiv [P_{pp}\, P_{PL}]^{1/2}$.

18.21 If prices are equal across regions, the formulae (18.16) and (18.20) simplify. The formula for the plutocratic Laspeyres index becomes:

$$P_{PL} = \sum_{h=1}^{H} \sum_{i=1}^{n} S_h^0 s_{hi}^0 \left(\frac{p_{hi}^1}{p_{hi}^0} \right)$$

$$= \sum_{h=1}^{H} \sum_{i=1}^{n} S_h^0 s_{hi}^0 \left(\frac{p_i^1}{p_i^0} \right) \quad \text{using assumptions (18.4)}$$

$$= \sum_{i=1}^{n} \sigma_i^0 \left(\frac{p_i^1}{p_i^0} \right) \quad \text{using equation (18.12) for } t=0$$

$$= P_L \quad (18.21)$$

where P_L is the usual aggregate Laspeyres price index based on the assumption that each household faces the same vector of commodity prices; see equation (18.5) for the definition of P_L. Under the equal prices across households assumption, the formula for the plutocratic Paasche index becomes:

$$P_{PP} = \left\{ \sum_{h=1}^{H} \sum_{i=1}^{n} S_h^1 s_{hi}^1 \left(\frac{p_{hi}^1}{p_{hi}^0} \right)^{-1} \right\}^{-1}$$

$$= \left\{ \sum_{h=1}^{H} \sum_{i=1}^{n} S_h^1 s_{hi}^1 \left(\frac{p_i^1}{p_i^0} \right)^{-1} \right\}^{-1} \quad \text{using assumptions (18.4)}$$

$$= \left\{ \sum_{i=1}^{n} \sigma_i^1 \left(\frac{p_i^1}{p_i^0} \right)^{-1} \right\}^{-1} \quad \text{using equation (18.12) for } t=1$$

$$= P_P \quad (18.22)$$

where P_P is the usual aggregate Paasche price index based on the assumption that each household faces the same vector of commodity prices; see equation (18.8) for the definition of P_P.

18.22 Thus with the assumption that commodity prices are the same across regions, in order to calculate national Laspeyres and Paasche indices, only "national" price relatives and national commodity expenditure shares are required for the two periods under consideration. If there is regional variation in prices, however, then the simplified formulae (18.21) and (18.22) are not valid and it is necessary to use the earlier formulae (18.16) and (18.20), which require the use of regional price relatives and regional expenditure shares.

Democratic versus plutocratic cost of living indices

18.23 The plutocratic indices considered above weight each household in the economy according to the size of its expenditures in the two periods under consideration. Instead of weighting in this way, it is possible to define theoretical indices (and "practical" approximations to them) that give each household or household group in the economy an equal weight. Following Prais (1959), such an index will be called a *democratic index*. In this section, the plutocratic index number theory developed in paragraphs 18.3 to 18.22 will be reworked into the democratic framework.

18.24 Making the same assumptions as in paragraph 18.4, define the class of *conditional democratic cost of living indices*, $P_D^*(p^0, p^1, u, e_1, e_2, \ldots, e_H)$, pertaining to periods 0 and 1 for the arbitrary utility vector of household utilities $u \equiv (u_1, u_2, \ldots, u_H)$ and for the arbitrary vectors of household environmental variables e_h for $h = 1, 2, \ldots, H$ as follows:

$$P_D^*(p_1^0, \ldots, p_H^0, p_1^1, \ldots, p_H^1, u, e_1, e_2, \ldots, e_H) \equiv \sum_{h=1}^{H} \left(\frac{1}{H} \right) \frac{C^h(u_h, e_h, p_h^1)}{C^h(u_h, e_h, p_h^0)} \quad (18.23)$$

Thus P_D^* is a simple unweighted arithmetic average of the individual household conditional cost of living indices, $C^h(u_h, e_h, p_h^1)/C^h(u_h, e_h, p_h^0)$. In the numerator and denominator of these conditional indices, only the price variables are different, which is precisely what is wanted in a theoretical definition of a consumer price index. If the vector of environmental variables, e_h, is not present in the cost function of household h, then the conditional index $C^h(u_h, e_h, p_h^1)/C^h(u_h, e_h, p_h^0)$ becomes an ordinary Konüs true cost of living index of the type defined earlier in Chapter 17.

18.25 Now specialize the general definition (18.23) by replacing the general utility vector u by either the period 0 vector of household utilities $u^0 \equiv (u_1^0, u_2^0, \ldots u_H^0)$ or the period 1 vector of household utilities $u^1 \equiv (u_1^1, u_2^1, \ldots u_H^1)$. Further specialize the general definition by replacing the general household environmental vectors $(e_1, e_2, \ldots e_H) \equiv e$ by either the period 0 vector of household environmental variables $e^0 \equiv (e_1^0, e_2^0, \ldots e_H^0)$ or the period 1 vector of household environmental variables $e^1 \equiv (e_1^1, e_2^1, \ldots, e_H^1)$. The choice of the base period vector of utility levels and base period environmental variables leads to the *Laspeyres conditional democratic cost of living index*, $P_D^*(p_1^0, \ldots, p_H^0, p_1^1, \ldots, p_H^1, u^0, e^0)$, while the choice of the period 1 vector of utility levels and period 1 environmental variables leads to the *Paasche conditional democratic cost of living index*, $P_D^*(p_1^0, \ldots, p_H^0, p_1^1, \ldots, p_H^1, u^1, e^1)$. It turns out that these two democratic indices satisfy some interesting inequalities, which are derived below.

18.26 Specializing definition (18.23), the Laspeyres conditional democratic cost of living index, $P_D^*(p_1^0, \ldots, p_H^0, p_1^1, \ldots, p_H^1, u^0, e^0)$, may be written as follows:

$$P_D^*(p_1^0, \ldots, p_H^0, p_1^1, \ldots, p_H^1, u^0, e_1^0, e_2^0, \ldots, e_H^0)$$

$$\equiv \sum_{h=1}^{H} \left(\frac{1}{H}\right) \frac{C^h(u_h^0, e_h^0, p_h^1)}{C^h(u_h^0, e_h^0, p_h^0)}$$

$$= \sum_{h=1}^{H} \left(\frac{1}{H}\right) \frac{C^h(u_h^0, e_h^0, p_h^1)}{p_h^0 q_h^0}$$

using equation (18.1) for $t=0$

$$\leq \sum_{h=1}^{H} \left(\frac{1}{H}\right) \frac{p_h^1 q_h^0}{p_h^0 q_h^0} \qquad (18.24)$$

since $C^h(u_h^0, e_h^0, p_h^1) \equiv \min_q \{p_h^1 q : f^h(q, e_h^0) \geq u_h^0\} \leq p^1 q_h^0$ and q_h^0 is feasible for the cost minimization problem for $h = 1, 2, \ldots, H$

$$\equiv P_{DL}$$

where P_{DL} is defined to be the observable (in principle) democratic Laspeyres price index, $\sum_{h=1}^{H} \left(\frac{1}{H}\right) p_h^1 q_h^0 / p_h^0 q_h^0$, which uses the individual vectors of household or regional quantities for period 0, $(q_1^0, \ldots, q_H^0)$, as quantity weights.

18.27 In a similar manner, specializing definition (18.23), the Paasche conditional democratic cost of living index, $P_D^*(p_1^0, \ldots, p_H^0, p_1^1, \ldots, p_H^1, u^1, e^1)$, may be written as follows:

$$P_D^*(p_1^0, \ldots, p_H^0, p_1^1, \ldots, p_H^1, u^1, e_1^1, e_2^1, \ldots, e_H^1)$$

$$\equiv \sum_{h=1}^{H} \left(\frac{1}{H}\right) \frac{C^h(u_h^1, e_h^1, p_h^1)}{C^h(u_h^1, e_h^1, p_h^0)}$$

$$= \sum_{h=1}^{H} \left(\frac{1}{H}\right) \frac{p_h^1 q_h^1}{C^h(u_h^1, e_h^1, p_h^0)}$$

using equation (18.1) for $t=1$

$$\geq \sum_{h=1}^{H} \left(\frac{1}{H}\right) \frac{p_h^1 q_h^1}{p_h^0 q_h^1} \text{ using a feasibility argument}$$

$$\equiv P_{DP} \qquad (18.25)$$

where P_{DP} is defined to be the *democratic Paasche price index*, $\sum_{h=1}^{H} \left(\frac{1}{H}\right) p_h^1 q_h^1 / p_h^0 q_h^1$, which uses the individual vector of household h quantities for period 1, q_h^1, as quantity weights for term h in the summation of individual household Paasche indices. Thus, it can be seen that the theoretical Paasche conditional democratic cost of living index, $P_D^*(p_1^0, \ldots, p_H^0, p_1^1, \ldots, p_H^1, u^1, e^1)$, is bounded from below by the observable (in principle) democratic Paasche price index P_{DP}. Diewert (1983a, p. 191) first obtained the inequality (18.25) for the case where the environmental variables are absent from the household utility and cost functions, and prices are equal across households.

18.28 It is now shown how to obtain a theoretical democratic cost of living index that is bounded from above and below by observable indices. Using the inequalities (18.24) and (18.25) and the continuity properties of the conditional democratic cost of living $P^*(p_1^0, \ldots, p_H^0, p_1^1, \ldots, p_H^1, u, e)$ defined by equation (18.23), it is possible to modify the method of proof used by Konüs (1924) and Diewert (1983a, p. 191) and establish the following result:

> There exists a reference utility vector $u^* \equiv (u_1^*, u_2^*, \ldots, u_H^*)$ such that the household h reference utility level u_h^* lies between the household h period 0 and 1 utility levels, u_h^0 and u_h^1 respectively for $h = 1, \ldots, H$. Also, there exist household environmental vectors $e_h^* \equiv (e_{h1}^*, e_{h2}^*, \ldots, e_{hM}^*)$ such that the household h reference mth environmental variable e_{hm}^* lies between the household h period 0 and 1 levels for the mth environmental variable, e_{hm}^0 and e_{hm}^1 respectively for $m = 1, 2, \ldots, M$ and $h = 1, \ldots, H$. The conditional democratic cost of living index $P_D^*(p_1^0, \ldots, p_H^0, p_1^1, \ldots, p_H^1, u^*, e^*)$, evaluated at this intermediate reference utility vector u^* and the intermediate reference vector of household environmental variables $e^* \equiv (e_1^*, e_2^*, \ldots, e_H^*)$, lies between the observable (in principle) democratic Laspeyres and Paasche price indices, P_{DL} and P_{DP}, defined above by the last equalities in (18.24) and (18.25).

18.29 The above result says that the *theoretical national democratic conditional consumer price index* $P_D^*(p_1^0, \ldots, p_H^0, p_1^1, \ldots, p_H^1, u^*, e^*)$ lies between the democratic Laspeyres index P_{DL} and the democratic Paasche index P_{DP}. Hence if P_{DL} and P_{DP} are not too different, a good point approximation to the theoretical national democratic consumer price index will be the *democratic Fisher index* P_{DF}, defined as:

$$P_{DF} \equiv \sqrt{P_{DL} P_{DP}} \qquad (18.26)$$

The democratic Fisher price index, P_{DF}, will satisfy the time reversal test.

18.30 Again, it will be useful to obtain formulae for the democratic Laspeyres and Paasche indices that depend only on price relatives and expenditure shares. Using definition (18.10) for the household h expenditure share on commodity i during period t, s^t_{hi}, the Laspeyres and Paasche price indices for household h can be written in share form as follows:

$$P_{Lh} \equiv \frac{p^1_h q^0_h}{p^0_h q^0_h} = \sum_{i=1}^{n} s^0_{hi}\left(\frac{p^1_{hi}}{p^0_{hi}}\right); \quad h=1,\ldots,H \qquad (18.27)$$

$$P_{Ph} \equiv \frac{p^1_h q^1_h}{p^0_h q^1_h} = \left\{\sum_{i=1}^{n} s^1_{hi}\left(\frac{p^1_{hi}}{p^0_{hi}}\right)^{-1}\right\}^{-1}; \quad h=1,\ldots,H. \qquad (18.28)$$

Substituting equation (18.27) into the definition of the democratic Laspeyres index, P_{DL}, leads to the following share type formula:[10]

$$P_{DL} = \sum_{h=1}^{H}\left(\frac{1}{H}\right)\sum_{i=1}^{n} s^0_{hi}\left(\frac{p^1_{hi}}{p^0_{hi}}\right) \qquad (18.29)$$

Similarly, substituting equation (18.28) into the definition of the democratic Paasche index, P_{DP}, leads to the following share type formula:

$$P_{DL} = \sum_{h=1}^{H}\left(\frac{1}{H}\right)\left\{\sum_{i=1}^{n} s^1_{hi}\left(\frac{p^1_{hi}}{p^0_{hi}}\right)^{-1}\right\}^{-1} \qquad (18.30)$$

18.31 The formula for the democratic Laspeyres index in the previous paragraph simplifies if it can be assumed that each household faces the same vector of prices in each of the two periods under consideration. Under this condition, equation (18.28) can be rewritten as follows:

$$P_{DL} = \sum_{i-1}^{n} s^0_{di}\left(\frac{p^1_i}{p^0_i}\right) \qquad (18.31)$$

where the period 0 democratic expenditure share for commodity i, s^0_{di}, is defined as follows:

$$s^0_{di} \equiv \sum_{h=1}^{H}\left(\frac{1}{H}\right) s^0_{hi}; \quad i=1,\ldots,n \qquad (18.32)$$

Thus s^0_{di} is simply the arithmetic average (over all households) of the individual household expenditure shares on commodity i during period 0. The formula for the democratic Paasche index does not simplify in the same way, under the assumption that households face the same prices in each period, because of the harmonic form of averaging in equation (18.30).

18.32 The conclusion at this point is that democratic and plutocratic Laspeyres, Paasche and Fisher indices can be constructed by a statistical agency provided that information on household-specific price relatives, p^1_{hi}/p^0_{hi}, and expenditures is available for both periods under consideration. If expenditure information is available only for the base period, then only the Laspeyres democratic and plutocratic indices can be constructed.

18.33 It is now necessary to discuss a practical problem that statistical agencies face: namely, that existing household consumer expenditure surveys, which are used in order to form estimates of household expenditure shares, are not very accurate. Thus the detailed commodity by region expenditure shares, $S^0_h s^0_{hn}$ and $S^1_h s^1_{hn}$, which appear in the formulae for the plutocratic Laspeyres and Paasche indices, are generally measured with very large errors. Similarly, the individual household expenditure shares for the two periods under consideration, s^0_{hn} and s^1_{hn}, which are required in order to calculate the democratic Laspeyres and Paasche indices defined by equations (18.29) and (18.30) respectively, are also generally measured with substantial errors. Hence, it may lead to less overall error if the regional commodity expenditure shares s^t_{hn} are replaced by the national commodity expenditure shares σ^t_n defined by equation (18.12). Whether this approximation is justified would depend on a detailed analysis of the situation facing the statistical agency. In general, complete and accurate information on household expenditure shares will not be available to the statistical agency, and hence statistical estimation and smoothing techniques will have to be used in order to obtain expenditure weights that will be used to weight the price relatives collected by the agency.

18.34 It should be noted that the conditional index framework used above can be used to model situations where household preferences change (continuously) from the base period to the current period: simply choose the environmental variable to be time t. The theoretical results in paragraphs 18.14 and 18.28 imply the existence of cost of living indices that lie between observable Laspeyres and Paasche bounds, where the preference functions for the households are taken to be some preferences that are intermediate between the preferences pertaining to the two periods under consideration. As usual, if the observable bounds are not too far apart, taking the geometric average of the bounds leads to an adequate approximation to these theoretical cost of living indices.[11]

18.35 For criticisms and some limitations of the economic approach to index number theory, see Turvey (2000) and Diewert (2001).[12]

[10] Comparing the formula for the democratic Laspeyres index, P_{DL}, with the previous formula (18.16) for the plutocratic Laspeyres index, P_{PL}, it can be seen that the plutocratic weight for the ith price relative for household h is $S^0_h s^0_{hi}$, whereas the corresponding democratic weight is $(1/H)s^0_{hi}$. Thus households that have larger base period expenditures and hence bigger expenditure shares S^0_h get a larger weight in the plutocratic index as compared to the democratic index.

[11] For a more extensive treatment of cost of living theory in the context of taste change, see Balk (1989a).

[12] For a vigorous defence of the economic approach, see Triplett (2001).

PRICE INDICES USING AN ARTIFICIAL DATA SET 19

Introduction

19.1 In order to give the reader some idea of how much the various index numbers might differ using a "real" data set, virtually all the major indices defined in the previous chapters are computed in this chapter using an artificial data set consisting of prices and quantities for six commodities over five periods. The data are described in paragraphs 19.3 and 19.4.

19.2 The contents of the remaining sections are outlined in this paragraph. In the section starting with paragraph 19.5, two of the early unweighted indices are computed: the Carli and Jevons indices. Two of the earliest weighted indices are also computed in this section: the Laspeyres and Paasche indices. Both fixed base and chained indices are computed. In the section starting with paragraph 19.9, various asymmetrically[1] weighted indices are computed. In the section starting with paragraph 19.17, symmetrically[2] weighted indices are computed. Some of these indices are superlative, while others are not. The section starting with paragraph 19.23 computes some superlative indices using two stages of aggregation and compares the resulting two-stage indices with their single-stage counterparts. The following section computes various Lloyd–Moulton indices[3] and compares them with superlative indices. The section starting with paragraph 19.32 computes two additive percentage change decompositions for the Fisher ideal index and compares the resulting decompositions, which are found to be very similar. Up to this point, all the indices that are computed are weighted or unweighted *bilateral price indices*; i.e., the index number formula depends only on the price and quantity data pertaining to the two periods whose prices are being compared. In the final three sections of this chapter, various indices involving the data pertaining to three or more periods are computed. In the section starting with paragraph 19.37, Lowe and Young indices are computed where the data of period 1 are used as quantity or share weights in conjunction with the price data of periods 3 to 5, so that the weight reference period is 1 and the price reference period is 3. In the final two sections, various mid-year indices are computed that are based on the Lowe and Young formulae. Recall that for these two index number formulae, the price reference period does not coincide with the weight reference period. Thus these indices are not bilateral index number formulae.

The artificial data set

19.3 The period can be thought of as somewhere between a year and five years. The trends in the data are generally more pronounced than would be seen in the course of a year. The price and quantity data are listed in Tables 19.1 and 19.2. For convenience, the period t nominal expenditures, $p^t q^t \equiv \sum_{i=1}^{n} p_i^t q_i^t$, are listed along with the corresponding period t expenditure shares, $s_i^t \equiv p_i^t q_i^t / p^t q^t$, in Table 19.3.

19.4 The trends that were built into Tables 19.1 to 19.3 are now explained in this paragraph. Think of the first four commodities as the consumption of various classes of *goods* in some economy, while the last two commodities are the consumption of two classes of *services*. Think of the first good as *agricultural consumption*; its quantity fluctuates around 1 and its price also fluctuates around 1.[4] The second good is *energy consumption*; its quantity shows a gently upward trend during the five periods with some minor fluctuations. Note, however, that the price of energy fluctuates wildly from period to period.[5] The third good is *traditional manufactures*. Rather high rates of price inflation are assumed for this commodity for periods 2 and 3 which diminish to a very low inflation rate by the end of the sample period.[6] The consumption of traditional manufactured goods is more or less static in the data set. The fourth commodity is *high-technology manufactured goods*, for example computers, video cameras and compact disks. The demand for these high-technology commodities grows 12 times over the sample period, while the final period price is only one-tenth of the first period price. The fifth commodity is *traditional services*. The price trends for this commodity are similar to those of traditional manufactures, except that the period-to-period

[1] "Asymmetric weights" means that the quantity or value weights for the prices come from only one of the two periods being compared.

[2] "Symmetric weights" means that the quantity or value weights for the prices enter the index number formula in a symmetric or even-handed way.

[3] Recall from Chapter 17 that there is a separate Lloyd–Moulton index for each estimated elasticity of substitution parameter σ that is inserted into the formula.

[4] Note, however, that the expenditure share of agricultural products shows a downward trend over time as the economy develops and shifts into services.

[5] This is an example of the price bouncing phenomenon noted by Szulc (1983). Note that the fluctuations in the price of energy that are built into the data set are not that unrealistic: in the past four years, the price of a barrel of crude oil has fluctuated in the range US$12 to US$40.

[6] This corresponds roughly to the experience of most industrialized countries over the period from 1973 to the mid-1990s. Thus, roughly five years of price movement are compressed into one of our periods.

Table 19.1 Prices for six commodities

Period t	p_1^t	p_2^t	p_3^t	p_4^t	p_5^t	p_6^t
1	1.0	1.0	1.0	1.0	1.0	1.0
2	1.2	3.0	1.3	0.7	1.4	0.8
3	1.0	1.0	1.5	0.5	1.7	0.6
4	0.8	0.5	1.6	0.3	1.9	0.4
5	1.0	1.0	1.6	0.1	2.0	0.2

Table 19.2 Quantities for six commodities

Period t	q_1^t	q_2^t	q_3^t	q_4^t	q_5^t	q_6^t
1	1.0	1.0	2.0	1.0	4.5	0.5
2	0.8	0.9	1.9	1.3	4.7	0.6
3	1.0	1.1	1.8	3.0	5.0	0.8
4	1.2	1.2	1.9	6.0	5.6	1.3
5	0.9	1.2	2.0	12.0	6.5	2.5

Table 19.3 Expenditures and expenditure shares for six commodities

Period t	p^tq^t	s_1^t	s_2^t	s_3^t	s_4^t	s_5^t	s_6^t
1	10.00	0.1000	0.1000	0.2000	0.1000	0.4500	0.0500
2	14.10	0.0681	0.1915	0.1752	0.0645	0.4667	0.0340
3	15.28	0.0654	0.0720	0.1767	0.0982	0.5563	0.0314
4	17.56	0.0547	0.0342	0.1731	0.1025	0.6059	0.0296
5	20.00	0.0450	0.0600	0.1600	0.0600	0.6500	0.0250

inflation rates are a little higher. The demand for traditional services, however, grows much more strongly than for traditional manufactures. The final commodity is *high-technology services*, for example telecommunications, wireless phones, Internet services and stock market trading. For this final commodity, the price shows a very strong downward trend to end up at 20 per cent of the starting level, while demand increases fivefold. The movements of prices and quantities in this artificial data set are more pronounced than the year-to-year movements that would be encountered in a typical country, but they do illustrate the problem facing compilers of the consumer price index (CPI); namely, year-to-year price and quantity movements are far from being proportional across commodities, so the choice of index number formula will matter.

Early price indices: The Carli, Jevons, Laspeyres and Paasche indices

19.5 Every price statistician is familiar with the *Laspeyres index* P_L defined by equation (15.5) and the *Paasche index* P_P defined by equation (15.6) in Chapter 15. These indices are listed in Table 19.4 along with two unweighted indices that were considered in previous chapters: the *Carli index* defined by equation (16.45) and the *Jevons index* defined by equation (16.47) in Chapter 16. The indices in Table 19.4 compare the prices in period t with thc priccs in period 1, that is, they are *fixed base indices*. Thus the period t entry for the Carli index, P_C, is simply the arithmetic mean of the six price relatives, $\sum_{i=1}^{6}(1/6)(p_i^t/p_i^1)$, while the period t entry for the Jevons index, P_J, is the geometric mean of the six price relatives, $\prod_{i=1}^{6}(p_i^t/p_i^1)^{1/6}$.

19.6 Note that by period 5, the spread between the fixed base Laspeyres and Paasche price indices is enormous: P_L is equal to 1.4400 while P_P is 0.7968, a spread of 81 per cent. Since both these indices have exactly the same theoretical justification, it can be seen that the choice of index number formula matters a lot. The period 5 entry for the Carli index, 0.9833, falls between the corresponding Paasche and Laspeyres indices but the period 5 Jevons index, 0.6324, does not. Note that the Jevons index is always considerably below the corresponding Carli index. This will always be the case (unless prices are proportional in the two periods under consideration) because a geometric mean is always equal to or less than the corresponding arithmetic mean.[7]

19.7 It is of interest to recalculate the four indices listed in Table 19.4 using the chain principle rather than the fixed base principle. The expectation is that the spread between the Paasche and Laspeyres indices will be reduced by using the chain principle. These chain indices are listed in Table 19.5.

19.8 It can be seen comparing Tables 19.4 and 19.5 that chaining eliminated about two-thirds of the spread between the Paasche and Laspeyres indices. Nevertheless, even the chained Paasche and Laspeyres indices differ by about 18 per cent in period 5, so the choice of index number formula still matters. Note that chaining did not affect the Jevons index. This is an advantage of the index but the lack of weighting is a fatal flaw.[8] Using the economic approach to index number theory, there is an expectation that the "truth" lies between the Paasche and Laspeyres indices. From Table 19.5, it can be seen that the unweighted Jevons index is far below this acceptable range. Note that chaining did not affect the Carli index in a systematic way for the artificial data set: in periods 3 and 4, the chained Carli is above the corresponding fixed base Carli; but in period 5, the chained Carli is below the fixed base Carli.[9]

Asymmetrically weighted price indices

19.9 This section contains a systematic comparison of all of the asymmetrically weighted price indices (with

[7] According to the theorem of the arithmetic and geometric mean; see Hardy, Littlewood and Pólya (1934, p. 17).

[8] The problem with the evenly weighted geometric mean is that the price declines in high-technology goods and services are given the same weighting as the price changes in the other four commodities (which have rising or stationary price changes), but the expenditure shares of the high-technology commodities remain rather small throughout the five periods. Thus weighted price indices do not show the rate of overall price decrease that the unweighted Jevons index shows. These somewhat negative comments on the use of the unweighted geometric mean as an index number formula at higher levels of aggregation do not preclude its use at the very lowest level of aggregation, where a strong axiomatic justification for the use of this formula can be given. If probability sampling is used at the lowest level of aggregation, then the unweighted geometric mean essentially becomes the logarithmic Laspeyres index.

[9] For many data sets, the chained Carli can be expected to be above the corresponding fixed base Carli; see Szulc (1983).

Table 19.4 The fixed base Laspeyres, Paasche, Carli and Jevons indices

Period t	P_L	P_P	P_C	P_J
1	1.0000	1.0000	1.0000	1.0000
2	1.4200	1.3823	1.4000	1.2419
3	1.3450	1.2031	1.0500	0.9563
4	1.3550	1.0209	0.9167	0.7256
5	1.4400	0.7968	0.9833	0.6324

Table 19.5 Chain Laspeyres, Paasche, Carli and Jevons indices

Period t	P_L	P_P	P_C	P_J
1	1.0000	1.0000	1.0000	1.0000
2	1.4200	1.3823	1.4000	1.2419
3	1.3646	1.2740	1.1664	0.9563
4	1.3351	1.2060	0.9236	0.7256
5	1.3306	1.1234	0.9446	0.6325

Table 19.6 Asymmetrically weighted fixed base indices

Period t	P_{PAL}	P_L	P_{GP}	P_{GL}	P_P	P_{HL}
1	1.0000	1.0000	1.0000	1.0000	1.0000	1.0000
2	1.6096	1.4200	1.4846	1.3300	1.3824	1.2542
3	1.4161	1.3450	1.3268	1.2523	1.2031	1.1346
4	1.5317	1.3550	1.3282	1.1331	1.0209	0.8732
5	1.6720	1.4400	1.4153	1.0999	0.7968	0.5556

Table 19.7 Asymmetrically weighted indices using the chain principle

Period t	P_{PAL}	P_L	P_{GP}	P_{GL}	P_P	P_{HL}
1	1.0000	1.0000	1.0000	1.0000	1.0000	1.0000
2	1.6096	1.4200	1.4846	1.3300	1.3824	1.2542
3	1.6927	1.3646	1.4849	1.1578	1.2740	0.9444
4	1.6993	1.3351	1.4531	1.0968	1.2060	0.8586
5	1.7893	1.3306	1.4556	1.0266	1.1234	0.7299

the exception of the Lloyd–Moulton index, which will be considered later). The fixed base indices are listed in Table 19.6. The fixed base Laspeyres and Paasche indices, P_L and P_P, are the same as those indices listed in Table 19.4. The Palgrave index, P_{PAL}, is defined by equation (16.55). The indices denoted by P_{GL} and P_{GP} are the geometric Laspeyres and geometric Paasche indices,[10] which are special cases of the class of geometric indices defined by Konüs and Byushgens (1926); see equation (15.78). For the geometric Laspeyres index, P_{GL}, the exponent weight α_i for the ith price relative is s_i^1, where s_i^1 is the base period expenditure share for commodity i. The resulting index should be considered an alternative to the fixed base Laspeyres index, since both of these indices make use of the same information set. For the geometric Paasche index, P_{GP}, the exponent weight for the ith price relative is s_i^t, where s_i^t is the current period expenditure shares. Finally, the index P_{HL} is the harmonic Laspeyres index that was defined by equation (16.59).

19.10 By looking at the period 5 entries in Table 19.6, it can be seen that the spread between all these fixed base asymmetrically weighted indices has increased to be even larger than the earlier spread of 81 per cent between the fixed base Paasche and Laspeyres indices. In Table 19.6, the period 5 Palgrave index is about three times as big as the period 5 harmonic Laspeyres index, P_{HL}. Again, this illustrates the point that because of the non-proportional growth of prices and quantities in most economies today, the choice of index number formula is very important.

19.11 It is possible to explain why certain of the indices in Table 19.6 are bigger than others. It can be shown that a weighted arithmetic mean of n numbers is equal to or greater than the corresponding weighted geometric mean of the same n numbers, which in turn is equal to or greater than the corresponding weighted harmonic mean of the same n numbers.[11] It can be seen that the three indices P_{PAL}, P_{GP} and P_P all use the current period expenditure shares s_i^t to weight the price relatives (p_i^t/p_i^1), but P_{PAL} is a weighted arithmetic mean of these price relatives, P_{GP} is a weighted geometric mean of these price relatives and P_P is a weighted harmonic mean of these price relatives. Thus by Schlömilch's inequality, it must be the case that:[12]

$$P_{PAL} \geq P_{GP} \geq P_P \tag{19.1}$$

19.12 Table 19.6 shows that the inequalities (19.1) hold for each period. It can also be verified that the three indices P_L, P_{GL} and P_{HL} all use the base period expenditure shares s_i^1 to weight the price relatives (p_i^t/p_i^1), but P_L is a weighted arithmetic mean of these price relatives, P_{GL} is a weighted geometric mean of these price relatives, and P_{HL} is a weighted harmonic mean of these price relatives. Thus by Schlömilch's inequality, it must be the case that:[13]

$$P_L \geq P_{GL} \geq P_{HL} \tag{19.2}$$

Table 19.6 shows that the inequalities (19.2) hold for each period.

19.13 All the asymmetrically weighted price indices are compared using the chain principle and are listed in Table 19.7.

19.14 Table 19.7 shows that although the use of the chain principle dramatically reduced the spread between the Paasche and Laspeyres indices P_P and P_L compared to the corresponding fixed base entries in Table 19.6, the spread between the highest and lowest asymmetrically weighted indices in period 5 (the Palgrave index P_{PAL} and the harmonic Laspeyres index P_{HL}) does not fall as much: the fixed base spread is 1.6720/0.5556 = 3.01, while the corresponding chain spread is 1.7893/0.7299 = 2.45.

[10] Vartia (1978, p. 272) used the terms logarithmic Laspeyres and logarithmic Paasche, respectively.

[11] This follows from Schlömilch's (1858) inequality; see Hardy, Littlewood and Pólya (1934, p. 26).

[12] These inequalities were noted by Fisher (1922, p. 92) and Vartia (1978, p. 278).

[13] These inequalities were also noted by Fisher (1922, p. 92) and Vartia (1978, p. 278).

Thus, in this particular case, the use of the chain principle combined with the use of an index number formula that uses the weights of only one of the two periods being compared did not lead to a significant narrowing of the huge differences that these formulae generated using the fixed base principle. With respect to the Paasche and Laspeyres formulae, however, chaining did significantly reduce the spread between these two indices.

19.15 Is there an explanation for the results reported in the previous paragraph? It can be shown that all six of the indices that are found in the inequalities (19.1) and (19.2) approximate each other to the first order around an equal prices and quantities point. Thus with smooth trends in the data, it is expected that all the chain indices will more closely approximate each other than the fixed base indices because the changes in the individual prices and quantities are smaller using the chain principle. This expectation is realized in the case of the Paasche and Laspeyres indices, but not with the others. For some of the commodities in the data set, however, the trends in the prices and quantities are not smooth. In particular, the prices for the first two commodities (agricultural products and oil) bounce up and down. As noted by Szulc (1983), this will tend to cause the chain indices to have a wider dispersion than their fixed base counterparts. In order to determine if it is the bouncing prices problem that is causing some of the chained indices in Table 19.7 to diverge from their fixed base counterparts, all the indices in Tables 19.6 and 19.7 were computed again but excluding commodities 1 and 2 from the computations. The results of excluding these bouncing commodities may be found in Tables 19.8 and 19.9.

19.16 It can be seen that excluding the bouncing price commodities does cause the chain indices to have a much narrower spread than their fixed base counterparts. Thus, the conclusion is that if the underlying price and quantity data are subject to reasonably smooth trends over time, then the use of chain indices will narrow considerably the dispersion in the asymmetrically weighted indices. In the next section, index number formulae that use weights from both periods in a symmetric or even-handed manner are computed.

Table 19.8 Asymmetrically weighted fixed base indices for commodities 3–6

Period t	P_{PAL}	P_L	P_{GP}	P_{GL}	P_P	P_{HL}
1	1.0000	1.0000	1.0000	1.0000	1.0000	1.0000
2	1.2877	1.2500	1.2621	1.2169	1.2282	1.1754
3	1.4824	1.4313	1.3879	1.3248	1.2434	1.1741
4	1.6143	1.5312	1.4204	1.3110	1.0811	0.9754
5	1.7508	1.5500	1.4742	1.1264	0.7783	0.5000

Table 19.9 Asymmetrically weighted chained indices for commodities 3–6

Period t	P_{PAL}	P_L	P_{GP}	P_{GL}	P_P	P_{HL}
1	1.0000	1.0000	1.0000	1.0000	1.0000	1.0000
2	1.2877	1.2500	1.2621	1.2169	1.2282	1.1754
3	1.4527	1.4188	1.4029	1.3634	1.3401	1.2953
4	1.5036	1.4640	1.4249	1.3799	1.3276	1.2782
5	1.4729	1.3817	1.3477	1.2337	1.1794	1.0440

Symmetrically weighted indices: Superlative and other indices

19.17 Symmetrically weighted indices can be decomposed into two classes: *superlative indices* and *other symmetrically weighted indices*. Superlative indices have a close connection to economic theory. As was seen in paragraphs 17.27 to 17.49 of Chapter 17, a superlative index is exact for a representation of the consumer's preference function or the dual unit cost function that can provide a second-order approximation to arbitrary (homothetic) preferences. Four important superlative indices were considered in previous chapters:

- the *Fisher ideal price index* P_F, defined by equation (15.12);
- the *Walsh price index* P_W, defined by equation (15.19) (this price index also corresponds to the quantity index Q^1, defined by equation (17.33) in Chapter 17);
- the *Törnqvist–Theil price index* P_T, defined by equation (15.81);
- the *implicit Walsh price index* P_{IW} that corresponds to the Walsh quantity index Q_W defined in Chapter 15 (this is also the index P^1 defined by equation (17.38)).

19.18 These four symmetrically weighted superlative price indices are listed in Table 19.10 using the fixed base principle. Also listed in Table 19.10 are two symmetrically weighted (but not superlative) price indices:[14]

- *the Marshall–Edgeworth price index* P_{ME}, defined in paragraph 15.18;
- *the Drobisch price index* P_D, defined by equation (15.12).

19.19 Note that the Drobisch index P_D is always equal to or greater than the corresponding Fisher index P_F. This follows from the fact that the Fisher index is the geometric mean of the Paasche and Laspeyres indices, while the Drobisch index is the arithmetic mean of the Paasche and Laspeyres indices, and an arithmetic mean is always equal to or greater than the corresponding geometric mean. Comparing the fixed base asymmetrically weighted indices in Table 19.6 with the symmetrically weighted indices in Table 19.10, it can be seen that the spread between the lowest and highest index in period 5 is much less for the symmetrically weighted indices. The spread is 1.6720/0.5556 = 3.01 for the asymmetrically weighted indices, but only 1.2477/0.9801 = 1.27 for the symmetrically weighted indices. If the comparisons are restricted to the superlative indices listed for period 5 in Table 19.10, then this spread is further reduced to 1.2477/1.0712 = 1.16; i.e., the spread between the fixed base superlative indices is "only" 16 per cent compared to the fixed base spread between the Paasche and Laspeyres indices of 81 per cent (1.4400/0.7968 = 1.81). There is an expectation that the spread between the superlative indices will be further reduced by using the chain principle.

[14] Diewert (1978, p. 897) showed that the Drobisch–Sidgwick–Bowley price index approximates any superlative index to the second order around an equal price and quantity point; i.e., P_{SB} is a *pseudo-superlative index*. Straightforward computations show that the Marshall–Edgeworth index P_{ME} is also pseudo-superlative.

Table 19.10 Symmetrically weighted fixed base indices

Period t	P_T	P_{IW}	P_W	P_F	P_D	P_{ME}
1	1.0000	1.0000	1.0000	1.0000	1.0000	1.0000
2	1.4052	1.4015	1.4017	1.4011	1.4012	1.4010
3	1.2890	1.2854	1.2850	1.2721	1.2741	1.2656
4	1.2268	1.2174	1.2193	1.1762	1.1880	1.1438
5	1.2477	1.2206	1.1850	1.0712	1.1184	0.9801

Table 19.11 Symmetrically weighted indices using the chain principle

Period t	P_T	P_{IW}	P_W	P_F	P_D	P_{ME}
1	1.0000	1.0000	1.0000	1.0000	1.0000	1.0000
2	1.4052	1.4015	1.4017	1.4011	1.4012	1.4010
3	1.3112	1.3203	1.3207	1.3185	1.3193	1.3165
4	1.2624	1.2723	1.2731	1.2689	1.2706	1.2651
5	1.2224	1.2333	1.2304	1.2226	1.2270	1.2155

19.20 The symmetrically weighted indices are computed using the chain principle. The results may be found in Table 19.11.

19.21 A quick glance at Table 19.11 shows that *the combined effect of using both the chain principle as well as symmetrically weighted indices is to dramatically reduce the spread between all indices constructed using these two principles*. The spread between all the symmetrically weighted indices in period 5 is only 1.2333/1.2155 = 1.015 or 1.5 per cent and the spread between the four superlative indices in period 5 is an even smaller 1.2333/1.2224 = 1.009, or about 0.1 per cent. The spread in period 5 between the two most commonly used superlative indices, the Fisher P_F and the Törnqvist P_T, is truly tiny: 1.2226/1.2224 = 0.0002.[15]

19.22 The results listed in Table 19.11 reinforce the numerical results tabled by Hill (2002) and Diewert (1978, p. 894); *the most commonly used chained superlative indices will generally give approximately the same numerical results*.[16] In particular, the chained Fisher, Törnqvist and Walsh indices will generally approximate each other very closely.

Superlative indices constructed in two stages of aggregation

19.23 Attention is now directed to the differences between superlative indices and their counterparts that are constructed in two stages of aggregation; see paragraphs 17.55 to 17.60 of Chapter 17 for a discussion of the issues and a listing of the formulae used. Using the artificial data set, the first four commodities are combined into a *goods aggregate* and the last two commodities into a *services aggregate*. In the second stage of aggregation, the goods and services components will be aggregated into an all-items index.

19.24 The results for the two-stage aggregation procedure using period 1 as the fixed base for the Fisher index P_F, the Törnqvist index P_T and the Walsh and implicit Walsh indexes, P_W and P_{IW}, are reported in Table 19.12.

19.25 Table 19.12 shows that the fixed base single stage superlative indices generally approximate their fixed base two-stage counterparts fairly closely, with the exception of the Fisher formula. The divergence between the single-stage Fisher index P_F and its two-stage counterpart P_{F2S} in period 5 is 1.1286/1.0712 = 1.05 or 5 per cent. The other divergences are 2 per cent or less.

19.26 Using chain indices, the results of the two-stage aggregation procedure are reported in Table 19.13. Again, the single-stage and their two-stage counterparts are listed for the Fisher index P_F, the Törnqvist index P_T and the Walsh and implicit Walsh indexes, P_W and P_{IW}.

19.27 Table 19.13 shows that the chained single-stage superlative indices generally approximate their fixed base two-stage counterparts very closely indeed. The divergence between the chained single-stage Törnqvist index P_T and its two-stage counterpart P_{T2S} in period 5 is 1.2300/1.2224 = 1.006 or 0.6 per cent. The other divergences are all less than this. Given the large dispersion in period-to-period price movements, these two-stage aggregation errors are not large.

Lloyd–Moulton price indices

19.28 The next formula that will be illustrated using the artificial data set is the Lloyd (1975) and Moulton (1996) index P_{LM}, defined by equation (17.71). Recall that this formula requires an estimate for the parameter σ, *the elasticity of substitution* between all commodities being aggregated. Recall also that if σ equals 0, then the Lloyd–Moulton index collapses down to the ordinary Laspeyres index, P_L. When σ equals 1, the Lloyd–Moulton index is not defined, but it can be shown that the limit of $P_{LM\sigma}$ as σ approaches 1 is P_{GL}, the geometric Laspeyres index or the logarithmic Laspeyres index with base period shares as weights. This index uses the same basic information as the fixed base Laspeyres index P_L, and so it is a possible alternative index for CPI compilers to use. As was shown by Shapiro and Wilcox (1997a),[17] the Lloyd–Moulton index may be used to approximate a superlative index using the same information that is used in the construction of a fixed base Laspeyres index, provided that an estimate for the parameter σ is available. This methodology will be tested using the artificial data set. The superlative index that is to be approximated is the chain Fisher index[18] (which approximates the other

[15] In other periods, the differences were nevertheless larger. On average over the last four periods, the chain Fisher and the chain Törnqvist indices differed by 0.0025 percentage points.

[16] More precisely, the superlative quadratic mean of order r price indices P^r defined by equation (17.35) and the implicit quadratic mean of order r price indices P^{r*} defined by equation (17.32) will generally closely approximate each other, provided that r is in the interval $0 \leq r \leq 2$.

[17] Alterman, Diewert and Feenstra (1999) also used this methodology in the context of estimating superlative international trade price indices.

[18] Since there is still a considerable amount of dispersion among the fixed base superlative indices and practically no dispersion between the chained superlative indices, the Fisher chain index is taken as the target index rather than any of the fixed base superlative indices.

Table 19.12 Fixed base superlative single-stage and two-stage indices

Period t	P_F	P_{F2S}	P_T	P_{T2S}	P_W	P_{W2S}	P_{IW}	P_{IW2S}
1	1.0000	1.0000	1.0000	1.0000	1.0000	1.0000	1.0000	1.0000
2	1.4011	1.4004	1.4052	1.4052	1.4017	1.4015	1.4015	1.4022
3	1.2721	1.2789	1.2890	1.2872	1.2850	1.2868	1.2854	1.2862
4	1.1762	1.2019	1.2268	1.2243	1.2193	1.2253	1.2174	1.2209
5	1.0712	1.1286	1.2477	1.2441	1.1850	1.2075	1.2206	1.2240

Table 19.13 Chained superlative single-stage and two-stage indices

Period t	P_F	P_{F2S}	P_T	P_{T2S}	P_W	P_{W2S}	P_{IW}	P_{IW2S}
1	1.0000	1.0000	1.0000	1.0000	1.0000	1.0000	1.0000	1.0000
2	1.4011	1.4004	1.4052	1.4052	1.4017	1.4015	1.4015	1.4022
3	1.3185	1.3200	1.3112	1.3168	1.3207	1.3202	1.3203	1.3201
4	1.2689	1.2716	1.2624	1.2683	1.2731	1.2728	1.2723	1.2720
5	1.2226	1.2267	1.2224	1.2300	1.2304	1.2313	1.2333	1.2330

Table 19.14 Chained Fisher and fixed base Lloyd–Moulton indices

Period t	P_F	P_{LM0}	$P_{LM.2}$	$P_{LM.3}$	$P_{LM.4}$	$P_{LM.5}$	$P_{LM.6}$	$P_{LM.7}$	$P_{LM.8}$	P_{LM1}
1	1.0000	1.0000	1.0000	1.0000	1.0000	1.0000	1.0000	1.0000	1.0000	1.0000
2	1.4011	1.4200	1.4005	1.3910	1.3818	1.3727	1.3638	1.3551	1.3466	1.3300
3	1.3185	1.3450	1.3287	1.3201	1.3113	1.3021	1.2927	1.2831	1.2731	1.2523
4	1.2689	1.3550	1.3172	1.2970	1.2759	1.2540	1.2312	1.2077	1.1835	1.1331
5	1.2226	1.4400	1.3940	1.3678	1.3389	1.3073	1.2726	1.2346	1.1932	1.0999

chained superlative indices listed in Table 19.11 very closely). The chained Fisher index P_F is listed in column 2 of Table 19.14 along with the fixed base Lloyd–Moulton indices $P_{LM\sigma}$ for σ equal to 0 (this reduces to the fixed base Laspeyres index P_L), 0.2, 0.3, 0.4, 0.5, 0.6, 0.7, 0.8 and 1 (which is the fixed base geometric index P_{GL}). Note that the Lloyd–Moulton indices steadily decrease as the elasticity of substitution σ is increased.[19]

19.29 Table 19.14 shows that no single choice of the elasticity of substitution σ will lead to a Lloyd–Moulton price index $P_{LM\sigma}$ that will closely approximate the chained Fisher index P_F for periods 2, 3, 4 and 5. To approximate P_F in period 2, it is necessary to choose σ close to 0.1; to approximate P_F in period 3, choose σ close to 0.3; to approximate P_F in period 4, choose σ between 0.4 and 0.5; and to approximate P_F in period 5, choose σ between 0.7 and 0.8.[20]

19.30 The computations for the Lloyd–Moulton indices listed in Table 19.14 are now repeated except that the chain principle is used to construct the Lloyd–Moulton indices; see Table 19.15. Again, the object is to approximate the chained Fisher price index P_F which is listed as the second column in Table 19.15. In Table 19.15, P_{LM0} is the chained Laspeyres index and P_{LM1} is the chained geometric Laspeyres or geometric index using the expenditure shares of the previous period as weights.

19.31 Table 19.15 shows that again no single choice of the elasticity of substitution σ will lead to a Lloyd–Moulton price index $P_{LM\sigma}$ that will closely approximate the chained Fisher index P_F for all periods. To approximate P_F in period 2, choose σ close to 0.1; to approximate P_F in period 3, choose σ close to 0.2; to approximate P_F in period 4, choose σ between 0.2 and 0.3; and to approximate P_F in period 5, choose σ between 0.3 and 0.4. It should be noted, however, that if σ is chosen to equal to 0.3 and the resulting chained Lloyd–Moulton index $P_{LM.3}$ is used to approximate the chained Fisher index P_F, then a much better approximation to P_F results than that provided by either the chained Laspeyres index (see P_{LM0} in the third column of Table 19.15) or the fixed base Laspeyres index (see P_{LM0} in the third column of Table 19.14).[21] The tentative conclusions on the use of the Lloyd–Moulton index to approximate superlative indices that can be drawn from the above tables are:

- the elasticity of substitution parameter σ which appears in the Lloyd–Moulton formula is unlikely to remain constant over time, and hence it will be necessary for statistical agencies to update their estimates of σ at regular intervals;
- the use of the Lloyd–Moulton index as a real-time preliminary estimator for a chained superlative index

[19] This follows from Schlömilch's (1858) inequality again.

[20] Unfortunately, for this data set, neither the fixed base Laspeyres index $P_L = P_{LM0}$ nor the fixed base weighted geometric index $P_{GL} = P_{LM1}$ is very close to the chain Fisher index for all periods. For less extreme data sets, the fixed base Laspeyres and fixed base geometric indices will be closer to the chained Fisher index.

[21] For this particular data set, the fixed base or chained geometric indices using either the expenditure weights of period 1 (see the last column of Table 19.14) or using the weights of the previous period (see the last column of Table 19.15) do not approximate the chained Fisher index very closely. For less extreme data sets, however, the use of chained Laspeyres or geometric indices may approximate a chained superlative index adequately.

Table 19.15 Chained Fisher and chained Lloyd–Moulton indices

Period t	P_F	P_{LM0}	$P_{LM.2}$	$P_{LM.3}$	$P_{LM.4}$	$P_{LM.5}$	$P_{LM.6}$	$P_{LM.7}$	$P_{LM.8}$	P_{LM1}
1	1.0000	1.0000	1.0000	1.0000	1.0000	1.0000	1.0000	1.0000	1.0000	1.0000
2	1.4011	1.4200	1.4005	1.3910	1.3818	1.3727	1.3638	1.3551	1.3466	1.3300
3	1.3185	1.3646	1.3242	1.3039	1.2834	1.2628	1.2421	1.2212	1.2002	1.1578
4	1.2689	1.3351	1.2882	1.2646	1.2409	1.2171	1.1932	1.1692	1.1452	1.0968
5	1.2226	1.3306	1.2702	1.2400	1.2097	1.1793	1.1488	1.1183	1.0878	1.0266

Table 19.16 Diewert's additive percentage change decomposition of the Fisher index

Period t	$P_F - 1$	$v_{F1}\Delta p_1$	$v_{F2}\Delta p_2$	$v_{F3}\Delta p_3$	$v_{F4}\Delta p_4$	$v_{F5}\Delta p_5$	$v_{F6}\Delta p_6$
2	0.4011	0.0176	0.1877	0.0580	−0.0351	0.1840	−0.0111
3	−0.0589	−0.0118	−0.1315	0.0246	−0.0274	0.0963	−0.0092
4	−0.0376	−0.0131	−0.0345	0.0111	−0.0523	0.0635	−0.0123
5	−0.0365	0.0112	0.0316	0.0000	−0.0915	0.0316	−0.0194

seems warranted, provided that the statistical agency can provide estimates for chained superlative indices on a delayed basis. The Lloyd–Moulton index would provide a useful supplement to the traditional fixed base Laspeyres price index.

Additive percentage change decompositions for the Fisher ideal index

19.32 The next formulae to be illustrated using the artificial data set are the *additive percentage change decompositions* for the Fisher ideal index, discussed in paragraphs 16.62 to 16.73 of Chapter 16.[22] The chain links for the Fisher price index are first decomposed into additive components using the formulae (16.38) to (16.40). The results of the decomposition are listed in Table 19.16. Thus $P_F - 1$ is the percentage change in the Fisher ideal chain link going from period $t-1$ to t, and the decomposition factor $v_{Fi}\Delta P_i = v_{Fi}(P_i^t - p_i^{t-1})$ is the contribution to the total percentage change of the change in the ith price from p_i^{t-1} to p_i^t for $i=1,2,\ldots,6$.

19.33 Table 19.16 shows that the price index going from period 1 to 2 grew about 40 per cent, and the major contributors to this change were the increases in the price of commodity 2, energy (18.77 per cent), and in commodity 5, traditional services (18.4 per cent). The increase in the price of traditional manufactured goods, commodity 3, contributed 5.8 per cent to the overall increase of 40.11 per cent. The decreases in the prices of high-technology goods (commodity 4) and high-technology services (commodity 6) offset the other increases by −3.51 per cent and −1.11 per cent going from period 1 to 2. Going from period 2 to 3, the overall change in prices was negative: −5.89 per cent. The reader can read across row 3 of Table 19.16 to see what was the contribution of the six component price changes to the overall price change. It is evident that a big price change in a particular component i, combined with a big expenditure share in the two periods under consideration will lead to a big decomposition factor, v_{Fi}.

19.34 The next set of computations to be illustrated using the artificial data set is the additive percentage change decomposition for the Fisher ideal index according to Van Ijzeren (1987, p. 6), which was mentioned in footnote 43 of Chapter 16.[23] The price counterpart to the additive decomposition for a quantity index is:

$$P_F(p^0,p^1,q^0,q^1) = \frac{\sum_{i=1}^{n} q_{Fi}^* p_i^1}{\sum_{i=1}^{n} q_{Fi}^* p_i^0} \tag{19.3}$$

where the reference quantities need to be defined somehow. Van Ijzeren (1987, p. 6) showed that the following reference weights provide an exact additive representation for the Fisher ideal price index:

$$q_{Fi}^* \equiv (1/2)q_i^0 + \{(1/2)q_i^1/Q_F(p^0,p^1,q^0,q^1)\} \quad \text{for } i=1,2,\ldots,6 \tag{19.4}$$

where Q_F is the overall Fisher quantity index. Thus using the Van Ijzeren quantity weights q_{Fi}^*, the following Van Ijzeren additive percentage change decomposition for the Fisher price index is obtained:

$$P_F(p^0,p^1,q^0,q^1) - 1 = \left\{\sum_{i=1}^{6} q_{Fi}^* p_i^1 \Big/ \sum_{i=1}^{6} q_{Fi}^* p_i^0\right\} - 1 = \sum_{i=1}^{6} v_{Fi}^*\{p_i^1 - p_i^0\} \tag{19.5}$$

where the Van Ijzeren weight for commodity i, v_{Fi}^*, is defined as

$$v_{Fi}^* \equiv q_{Fi}^* \Big/ \sum_{i=1}^{6} q_{Fi}^* p_i^0 \quad \text{for } i=1,2,\ldots,6 \tag{19.6}$$

[22] See Diewert (2002a, p. 73).

[23] See Reinsdorf, Diewert and Ehemann (2002) for additional information on this decomposition.

Table 19.17 Van Ijzeren's decomposition of the Fisher price index

Period t	$P_F - 1$	$v^*_{F1}\Delta p_1$	$v^*_{F2}\Delta p_2$	$v^*_{F3}\Delta p_3$	$v^*_{F4}\Delta p_4$	$v^*_{F5}\Delta p_5$	$v^*_{F6}\Delta p_6$
2	0.4011	0.0178	0.1882	0.0579	−0.0341	0.1822	−0.0109
3	−0.0589	−0.0117	−0.1302	0.0243	−0.0274	0.0952	−0.0091
4	−0.0376	−0.0130	−0.0342	0.0110	−0.0521	0.0629	−0.0123
5	−0.0365	0.0110	0.0310	0.0000	−0.0904	0.0311	−0.0191

Table 19.18 The Lowe and Young indices, the fixed base Laspeyres, Paasche and Fisher indices, and the chained Laspeyres, Paasche and Fisher indices

Period t	P_{Lo}	P_Y	P_L	P_P	P_F	P_{LCH}	P_{PCH}	P_{FCH}
3	1.0000	1.0000	1.0000	1.0000	1.0000	1.0000	1.0000	1.0000
4	1.0074	0.9396	0.9784	0.9466	0.9624	0.9784	0.9466	0.9624
5	1.0706	0.9794	1.0105	0.8457	0.9244	0.9751	0.8818	0.9273

19.35 The chain links for the Fisher price index will be decomposed into price change components using the formulae (19.4) to (19.6), listed above. The results of the decomposition are listed in Table 19.17. Thus $P_F - 1$ is the percentage change in the Fisher ideal chain link going from period $t-1$ to t and the Van Ijzeren decomposition factor $v^*_{Fi}\Delta p_i$ is the contribution to the total percentage change of the change in the ith price from p_i^{t-1} to for $i=1,2,\ldots,6$.

19.36 Comparing the entries in Tables 19.16 and 19.17, it can be seen that the differences between the Diewert and Van Ijzeren decompositions of the Fisher price index are very small. The maximum absolute difference between the $v_{Fi}\Delta p_i$ and $v^*_{Fi}\Delta p_i$ is only 0.0018 (about 0.2 percentage points) and the average absolute difference is 0.0003. This is somewhat surprising given the very different nature of the two decompositions.[24] As was mentioned in footnote 43 of Chapter 16, the Van Ijzeren decomposition of the chain Fisher quantity index is used by the Bureau of Economic Analysis in the United States.[25]

The Lowe and Young indices

19.37 Recall that the Lowe index was defined by equation (15.15) in Chapter 15. If it is desired to compare the prices in period t with those in period 0, the formula for the Lowe index is given by equation (19.7) below:

$$P_{Lo}(p^1,p^t,q^b) \equiv \sum_{i=1}^{6} p_i^t q_i^b \Big/ \sum_{i=1}^{6} p_i^0 q_i^b \quad t=1,2,\ldots,5 \tag{19.7}$$

where $q^b \equiv [q_1^b, q_2^b, \ldots, q_6^b]$ is the quantity vector pertaining to a base period b which is prior to period 0, the base period for prices. This index will be computed for periods t equal to 3 to 5 for the artificial data set where the quantity reference period b is taken to be period 1 and the price reference period 0 is taken to be period 3; see the column with the heading P_{Lo} in Table 19.18.

19.38 For comparison purposes, the fixed base Laspeyres, Paasche and Fisher indices are also calculated for periods 3, 4 and 5, where period 3 is treated as the base period; see the columns with the headings P_L, P_P and P_F respectively. The chained Laspeyres, Paasche and Fisher indices are also calculated for periods 3, 4 and 5, and listed in Table 19.18; see the columns with the headings P_{LCH}, P_{PCH} and P_{FCH} respectively. Table 19.18 shows that the Lowe index is higher than all six of these comparison indices in periods 4 and 5. In particular, the Lowe index P_{Lo} is greater than the fixed base Laspeyres index P_L for periods 4 and 5, which is consistent with the inequality (15.37) in Chapter 15, where it was argued that the Lowe index would exceed the Laspeyres index if there were long-run trends in prices. Compared with the preferred fixed base or chained Fisher ideal target indices, P_F or P_{FCH}, the Lowe index has a considerable upward bias for this trending artificial data set.

19.39 The Young index was defined by equation (15.48) in Chapter 15 and, for convenience, this definition is repeated below:

$$P_Y(p^0,p^t,s^b) \equiv \sum_{i=1}^{n} s_i^b (p_i^t/p_i^0) \tag{19.8}$$

The base period b expenditure shares for the commodities are the s_i^b in equation (19.8) and the price reference period is period 0. This Young index will be computed for periods t equal to 3 to 5 for the artificial data set, where the quantity reference period b is taken to be period 1 and the price reference period 0 is taken to be period 3; see the column with the heading P_Y in Table 19.18.

19.40 For periods 4 and 5, the Young index is below the corresponding values for the fixed base Laspeyres index.[26] For period 4, the Young index is 0.9396, which is below the corresponding value for the Fisher index, which is 0.9624. However, for period 5, the Young index is 0.9794, which is above the corresponding values for

[24] Reinsdorf, Diewert and Ehemann (2002) nevertheless show that the terms in the two decompositions approximate each other to the second order around any point where the two price vectors are equal and where the two quantity vectors are equal.

[25] See Moulton and Seskin (1999), and Ehemann, Katz and Moulton (2002).

[26] It is noted in Chapter 15 that the Young index can be above or below the corresponding fixed base Laspeyres index, depending on the responsiveness of expenditure shares to changes in prices.

the two target Fisher indices, which are 0.9244 for the fixed base index and 0.9273 for the chained index. Thus, although the direction of the bias in the Young index is not always the same, it can be seen that it has substantial biases for the artificial data set compared to the preferred target indices.

Mid-year indices based on the Lowe formula

19.41 Recall the Lowe index formula (19.7). In most applications of the formula by statistical agencies, the quantity vector q will be taken from a period that is prior to the base period for prices, which is period 1 in the artificial data set. It is also possible, however, to use the formula as a type of mid-year index, where the reference quantity vector q could be taken to be an average of the quantity vectors pertaining to periods 1 to 5. This possible use of the formula will be explored in the present section. Thus the first Lowe index, P_{Lo1}, sets q in formula (19.7) equal to q^1, the period 1 quantity vector in the artificial data set. This index turns out to be identical to the fixed base Laspeyres index P_L, which was listed earlier in Table 19.4. The second Lowe index, P_{Lo2}, sets q in formula (19.7) equal to the average of the period 1 and 2 quantity vectors, $(1/2)(q^1+q^2)$.[27] The third Lowe index, P_{Lo3}, sets q equal to the average of the period 1 to 3 quantity vectors, $(1/3)(q^1+q^2+q^3)$. The fourth Lowe index, P_{Lo4}, sets q equal to the average of the period 1 to 4 quantity vectors, $(1/4)(q^1+q^2+q^3+q^4)$. Finally, the fifth Lowe index, P_{Lo5}, sets q equal to the average of the period 1 to 5 quantity vectors, $(1/5)(q^1+q^2+q^3+q^4+q^5)$.[28] The resulting five Lowe type indices are listed in Table 19.19.

19.42 The mid-year index $P_{MY} \equiv P_{Lo}(p^1, p^t, q^3)$ was defined in paragraphs 15.49 to 15.53 of Chapter 15; it is a Lowe type index with the "representative" quantity vector q chosen to be q^3, the quantity vector that pertains to the middle period in the span of periods under consideration (which is periods 1 to 5 in the numerical example). It is listed as the seventh column in Table 19.18.[29] The mid-year index and the five Lowe indices are compared to two of the "best" target indices, the chain Törnqvist and chain Fisher indices, P_T and P_F listed in the last two columns of Table 19.19.

19.43 From Table 19.19, it can be seen that none of the Lowe type indices (or the mid-year index) are very close to the two target indices (the chain Törnqvist and chain Fisher) for all periods.[30] With less extreme data sets, however, it is quite possible that the fifth Lowe index and the mid-year index could form adequate approximations to the target indices.

19.44 With strong trends in the price data and normal consumer substitution responses, it is unlikely that Lowe type indices, based on averages of the quantity data pertaining to the first few periods in a long time series of data, will be able to provide an adequate approximation to a chained superlative index. In general, this type of Lowe index will suffer from an upward bias compared to the target index, as can be seen from Table 19.19.

Young-type indices

19.45 Recall that the Young index was defined by equation (15.48) in Chapter 15, or equation (19.8) above. If it is desired to compare the prices in period t with those in period 1, the formula for the Young index is given by equation (19.9):

$$P_Y(p^1, p^t, s^b) \equiv \sum_{i=1}^{6} s_i^b (p_i^t/p_i^1) \quad \text{for } t=1,2,\ldots,5 \quad (19.9)$$

where the expenditure share vector $s^b \equiv [s_1^b, \ldots s_6^b]$ is "representative" for the span of periods under consideration. In most applications of the formula by statistical agencies, the base period expenditure share vector s^b will be taken from a period that is prior to the base period for prices, which is period 1 in the artificial data set. For illustrative purposes, rather than adding new data to the artificial data set, the reference share vector s^b will be taken to be an average of the expenditure share vectors pertaining to periods 1 to 5. Thus, the first Young-type index, P_{Y1}, sets s^b in formula (19.9) equal to s^1, the period 1 expenditure share vector in the artificial data set. This index turns out to be identical to the fixed base Laspeyres index P_L, shown in Table 19.4. The second Young-type index, P_{Y2}, sets s^b in formula (19.9) equal to the average of the period 1 and 2 share vectors, $(1/2)(s^1+s^2)$. The third Young-type index, P_{Y3}, sets s^b equal to the average of the period 1 to 3 share vectors, $(1/3)(s^1+s^2+s^3)$. The fourth Young-type index, P_{Y4}, sets s^b equal to the average of the period 1 to 4 share vectors, $(1/4)(s^1+s^2+s^3+s^4)$. Finally, the fifth Young-type index, P_{Y5}, sets s^b equal to the average of the period 1 to 5 share vectors, $(1/5)(s^1+s^2+s^3+s^4+s^5)$. The resulting five Young type indices are listed in Table 19.20 below. These indices are compared to two of the "best" target indices, the chained Törnqvist and chained Fisher indices, P_T and P_F listed in the last two columns of Table 19.20.

19.46 Table 19.20 shows that all the Young-type indices exhibit a substantial upward bias compared to the target chain Törnqvist and Fisher indices, P_T and P_F. Comparing Table 19.19 with Table 19.20, it can be seen that the bias in the Young-type indices becomes bigger as the expenditure shares become more representative of all five periods, whereas the upward bias in the Lowe-type indices tends to become smaller as the reference quantity vector became more representative of all periods.

[27] This is the Lowe index for the artificial data set, which will probably be the most comparable to the type of Lowe index currently computed by statistical agencies.

[28] This is Walsh's (1901, p. 431) multi-year fixed basket index, where the quantity vector is chosen to be the arithmetic average of the quantity vectors in the time period under consideration.

[29] It can be verified that if there are exact linear time trends in the quantity data, then the mid-year index P_{MY} will be exactly equal to the fifth Lowe index, P_{Lo5}.

[30] The fourth Lowe index P_{Lo4} and the mid-year index P_{MY} appear to be the closest to the target indices.

Table 19.19 The five Lowe indices, the mid-year index, and the Törnqvist and Fisher chain indices

Period t	P_{Lo1}	P_{Lo2}	P_{Lo3}	P_{Lo4}	P_{Lo5}	P_{MY}	P_T	P_F
1	1.0000	1.0000	1.0000	1.0000	1.0000	1.0000	1.0000	1.0000
2	1.4200	1.4010	1.3641	1.3068	1.2267	1.3055	1.4052	1.4011
3	1.3450	1.3366	1.2851	1.2142	1.1234	1.2031	1.3112	1.3185
4	1.3550	1.3485	1.2824	1.1926	1.0801	1.1772	1.2624	1.2689
5	1.4400	1.4252	1.3444	1.2321	1.0868	1.2157	1.2224	1.2226

Table 19.20 The five Young-type indices and the Törnqvist and Fisher chain indices

Period t	P_{Y1}	P_{Y2}	P_{Y3}	P_{Y4}	P_{Y5}	P_T	P_F
1	1.0000	1.0000	1.0000	1.0000	1.0000	1.0000	1.0000
2	1.4200	1.5148	1.4755	1.4409	1.4355	1.4052	1.4011
3	1.3450	1.3567	1.3765	1.3943	1.4144	1.3112	1.3185
4	1.3550	1.3526	1.3917	1.4267	1.4584	1.2624	1.2689
5	1.4400	1.4632	1.4918	1.5173	1.5482	1.2224	1.2226

19.47 Note that the Young type indices P_{Y2} to P_{Y5} are all bigger in magnitude than P_{Y1}, which is the ordinary fixed base Laspeyres index. It must be recognized, however, that these Young type indices are not the type of Young index that is computed by statistical agencies, in which the weight reference period precedes the price reference period. As discussed in paragraphs 19.39 to 19.42, this latter type of Young index could be above or below the corresponding fixed base Laspeyres index.

19.48 The results of this section and the previous one can be summarized as follows: it appears to be a useful exercise to attempt to find quantity weights for the Lowe formula that are representative for the entire period covered by the index, but it does not appear to be useful to do the same for the Young formula.

ELEMENTARY INDICES

20

Introduction

20.1 In all countries, the calculation of a consumer price index (CPI) proceeds in two (or more) stages. In the first stage of calculation, elementary price indices are estimated for the elementary expenditure aggregates of a CPI. In the second and higher stages of aggregation, these elementary price indices are combined to obtain higher-level indices using information on the expenditures on each of the elementary aggregates as weights. An elementary aggregate consists of the expenditures on a small and relatively homogeneous set of products defined within the consumption classification used in the CPI. Samples of prices are collected within each elementary aggregate, so that elementary aggregates serve as strata for sampling purposes.

20.2 Data on the expenditures, or quantities, of the different goods and services are typically not available within an elementary aggregate. As there are no quantity or expenditure weights, most of the index number theory outlined in Chapters 15 to 19 is not directly applicable. As was noted in Chapter 1, an elementary price index is a more primitive concept that relies on price data only.

20.3 The question of what is the most appropriate formula to use to estimate an elementary price index is considered in this chapter. The quality of a CPI depends heavily on the quality of the elementary indices, which are the basic building blocks from which CPIs are constructed.

20.4 As is explained in Chapter 6, compilers have to select representative products within an elementary aggregate and then collect a sample of prices for each of the representative products, usually from a sample of different outlets. The individual products for which prices are actually collected are described as the *sampled products*. Their prices are collected over a succession of time periods. An elementary price index is therefore typically calculated from two sets of matched price observations. In most of this chapter,[1] it is assumed that there are no missing observations and no changes in the quality of the products sampled so that the two sets of prices are perfectly matched. The treatment of new and disappearing products, and of quality change, is a separate and complex issue that is discussed in detail in Chapters 7, 8 and 21 of this manual.

20.5 Even though quantity or expenditure weights are usually not available to weight the individual elementary price quotes, it is useful to consider an *ideal framework* where expenditure information is available. This is done in the next section. The problems involved in aggregating narrowly defined price quotes over time are also discussed in that section. Thus the discussion provides a theoretical target for "practical" elementary price indices that are constructed using only information on prices.

20.6 Paragraphs 20.23 to 20.37 provide some discussion about the difficulties involved in picking a suitable level of disaggregation for the elementary aggregates. Should the elementary aggregates have a regional dimension in addition to a product dimension? Should prices be collected from retail outlets or from households? These are the types of question discussed in this section.

20.7 Paragraphs 20.38 to 20.45 introduce the main elementary index formulae that are used in practice, and paragraphs 20.46 to 20.57 develop some numerical relationships between the various indices.

20.8 Chapters 15 to 17 develop the various approaches to index number theory when information on both prices and quantities is available. It is also possible to develop axiomatic, economic or sampling (stochastic) approaches to elementary indices, and these three approaches are discussed below in paragraphs 20.58 to 20.70, 20.71 to 20.86, and 20.87, respectively.

20.9 Paragraphs 20.88 to 20.99 look at some of the recent scanner data literature that computes elementary aggregates using both price and quantity information.

20.10 Paragraphs 20.100 to 20.111 develop a simple statistical approach to elementary indices that resembles a highly simplified hedonic regression model. The concluding section presents an overview of the various results.[2]

Ideal elementary indices

20.11 The aggregates covered by a CPI or a producer price index (PPI) are usually arranged in the form of a tree-like hierarchy, such as the Classification of Individual Consumption according to Purpose (COICOP)[3] or the Nomenclature générale des Activités

[1] The problem of sample attrition and the lack of matching over time is discussed briefly in the context of classification issues in paragraphs 20.23 to 20.37.

[2] This chapter draws heavily on the recent contributions of Dalén (1992), Balk (1994; 1998b; 2002) and Diewert (1995a; 2002c).

[3] Triplett (2003, p. 160) is quite critical of the COICOP classification scheme and argues that economic theory and empirical analysis should be used to derive a more appropriate CPI classification scheme. It is nevertheless very difficult to coordinate a classification scheme that can be used by all countries.

économiques dans les Communautés Européennes [General Industrial Classification of Economic Activities within the European Communities] (NACE). Any aggregate is a set of economic transactions pertaining to a set of commodities over a specified time period. Every economic transaction relates to the change of ownership of a specific, well-defined commodity (good or service) at a particular place and date, and comes with a quantity and a price. The price index for an aggregate is calculated as a weighted average of the price indices for the sub-aggregates, the (expenditure or sales) weights and type of average being determined by the index formula. One can descend in such a hierarchy as far as available information allows the weights to be decomposed. The lowest-level aggregates are called *elementary aggregates*. They are basically of two types:

- those for which all detailed price and quantity information is available;
- those for which the statistician, considering the operational cost or the response burden of getting detailed price and quantity information about all the transactions, decides to make use of a representative sample of commodities or respondents.

20.12 The practical relevance of studying this topic is large. Since the elementary aggregates form the building blocks of a CPI or a PPI, the choice of an inappropriate formula at this level can have a tremendous impact on the overall index.

20.13 In this section, it will be assumed that detailed price and quantity information for all transactions pertaining to the elementary aggregate for the two time periods under consideration is available. This assumption allows us to define an ideal elementary aggregate. Subsequent sections will relax this strong assumption about the availability of detailed price and quantity data on transactions, but it is necessary to have a theoretically ideal target for the "practical" elementary index.

20.14 The detailed price and quantity data, although perhaps not available to the statistician, are in principle available in the outside world. It is frequently the case that at the respondent level (i.e., at the outlet or firm level) some aggregation of the individual transactions information has been executed, usually in a form that suits the respondent's financial or management information system. This level of information that is determined by the respondent could be called the *basic information level*. It is, however, not necessarily the finest level of information that could be made available to the price statistician. One could always ask the respondent to provide more disaggregated information. For instance, instead of monthly data one could ask for weekly data; or, whenever appropriate, one could ask for regional instead of global data; or one could ask for data according to a finer commodity classification. The only natural barrier to further disaggregation is the individual transaction level.[4]

20.15 It is now necessary to discuss a problem that arises when detailed data on individual transactions are available, either at the level of the individual household or at the level of an individual outlet. Recall that Chapter 15 introduces the price and quantity indices, $P(p^0, p^1, q^0, q^1)$ and $Q(p^0, p^1, q^0, q^1)$. These (bilateral) price and quantity indices decompose the value ratio V^1/V^0 into a price change part $P(p^0, p^1, q^0, q^1)$ and a quantity change part $Q(p^0, p^1, q^0, q^1)$. In this framework, it is taken for granted that the period t price and quantity for commodity i, p_i^t and q_i^t respectively, are well defined. These definitions are not, however, straightforward since individual consumers may purchase the *same* item during period *t at different prices*. Similarly, if one considers the sales of a particular shop or outlet that sells to consumers, the same item may sell at very different prices during the course of the period. Hence before a traditional bilateral price index of the form $P(p^0, p^1, q^0, q^1)$ considered in previous chapters of this manual can be applied, a non-trivial time aggregation problem must be resolved in order to obtain the basic prices p_i^t and quantities q_i^t that are the components of the price vectors p^0 and p^1 and the quantity vectors q^0 and q^1.

20.16 Walsh[5] and Davies (1924; 1932) suggested a solution to this time aggregation problem: in their view, the appropriate quantity at this very first stage of aggregation is the *total quantity purchased* of the narrowly defined item and the corresponding price is the value of purchases of this item divided by the total amount purchased, which is a *narrowly defined unit value*.

In more recent times, other researchers have adopted the Walsh and Davies solution to the time aggregation problem.[6] Note that this solution has the following advantages:

- The quantity aggregate is intuitively plausible, being the total quantity of the narrowly defined item purchased by the household (or sold by the outlet) during the time period under consideration.
- The product of the price times quantity equals the total value purchased by the household (or sold by the outlet) during the time period under consideration.

20.17 The above solution to the time aggregation problem will be adopted as the concept for the price and quantity at this very first stage of aggregation. This leaves open the question of how long the time period should be over which the unit value is calculated. This question will be considered in the following section.

20.18 Having decided on an appropriate theoretical definition of price and quantity for an item at the very

[4] See Balk (1994).

[5] Walsh explained his reasoning as follows:

> Of all the prices reported of the same kind of article, the average to be drawn is the arithmetic; and the prices should be weighted according to the relative mass quantities that were sold at them (Walsh (1901, p. 96)).
>
> Some nice questions arise as to whether only what is consumed in the country, or only what is produced in it, or both together are to be counted; and also there are difficulties as to the single price quotation that is to be given at each period to each commodity, since this, too, must be an average. Throughout the country during the period a commodity is not sold at one price, nor even at one wholesale price in its principal market. Various quantities of it are sold at different prices, and the full value is obtained by adding all the sums spent (at the same stage in its advance towards the consumer), and the average price is found by dividing the total sum (or the full value) by the total quantities (Walsh (1921a, p. 88)).

[6] See for example Szulc (1987, p. 13), Dalén (1992, p. 135), Reinsdorf (1994), Diewert (1995a, pp. 20–21), Reinsdorf and Moulton (1997), Balk (2002) and Richardson (2003).

lowest level of aggregation (i.e., a narrowly defined unit value and the total quantity sold of that item at the individual outlet, or the total quantity purchased by a single household or a group of households), it is necessary to consider how to aggregate these narrowly defined elementary prices and quantities into an overall elementary aggregate. Suppose that there are M lowest-level items or specific commodities in this chosen elementary category. Denote the period t quantity of item m by q^t_m and the corresponding time-aggregated unit value by p^t_m for $t=0,1$ and for items $m=1,2,\ldots,M$. Define the period t quantity and price vectors as $q^t \equiv [q^t_1, q^t_2, \ldots, q^t_M]$ and $p^t \equiv [p^t_1, p^t_2, \ldots, p^t_M]$ for $t=0,1$. It is now necessary to choose a theoretically ideal index number formula $P(p^0, p^1, q^0, q^1)$ that will aggregate the individual item prices into an overall aggregate price relative for the M items in the chosen elementary aggregate. This problem of choosing a functional form for $P(p^0, p^1, q^0, q^1)$ is identical to the overall index number problem that is addressed in Chapters 15–17. In these previous chapters, four different approaches to index number theory are studied, and specific index number formulae are seen as being "best" from each perspective. From the viewpoint of *fixed basket approaches*, the Fisher (1922) and Walsh (1901) price indices, P_F and P_W, appear to be "best". From the viewpoint of the *test approach*, the Fisher index appears to be "best". From the viewpoint of the *stochastic approach* to index number theory, the Törnqvist–Theil (1967) index number formula P_T emerges as being "best". Finally, from the viewpoint of the *economic approach* to index number theory, the Walsh price index P_W, the Fisher ideal index P_F and the Törnqvist–Theil index number formula P_T are all regarded as being equally desirable. It is also shown that these three index number formulae numerically approximate each other very closely, and so it does not matter very much which of these alternative indices is chosen.[7] Hence, the *theoretically ideal elementary index number formula* is taken to be one of the three formulae $P_F(p^0, p^1, q^0, q^1)$, $P_W(p^0, p^1, q^0, q^1)$ or $P_T(p^0, p^1, q^0, q^1)$ where the period t quantity of item m, q^t_m, is the total quantity of that narrowly defined item purchased by the household during period t (or sold by the outlet during period t) and the corresponding price for item m is p^t_m, the time-aggregated unit value, for $t=0,1$ and for items $m=1,2,\ldots,M$.[8]

20.19 Various "practical" elementary price indices are defined in paragraphs 20.38 to 20.45. These indices do not have quantity weights and thus are functions only of the price vectors p^0 and p^1, which contain time aggregated unit values for the M items in the elementary aggregate for periods 0 and 1. Thus when a practical elementary index number formula, say $P_E(p^0, p^1)$, is compared to an ideal elementary price index, say the Fisher price index $P_F(p^0, p^1, q^0, q^1)$, then obviously P_E will differ from P_F because the prices are not weighted according to their economic importance in the practical elementary formula.[9] Call this difference between the two index number formulae *formula approximation error*.

20.20 Practical elementary indices are subject to other types of error as well:

- The statistical agency may not be able to collect information on all M prices in the elementary aggregate; i.e., only a sample of the M prices may be collected. Call the resulting divergence between the incomplete elementary aggregate and the theoretically ideal elementary index the *sampling error*.
- Even if a price for a narrowly defined item is collected by the statistical agency, it may not be equal to the theoretically appropriate time-aggregated unit value price. This use of an inappropriate price at the very lowest level of aggregation gives rise to *time aggregation error*.[10]
- The statistical agency may classify certain distinct products as being essentially equivalent and this may result in *item aggregation error*. For example, when the same product is sold in different package sizes, only the per unit price may be collected over the different package sizes. As another example, small quality differences between products may be ignored.
- The unit value for a particular item may be constructed by aggregating over all households in a region or a certain demographic class or by aggregating over all outlets or shops that sell the item in a particular region. This may give rise to an *aggregation over agents or entities error*.

20.21 The problems of aggregation and classification are discussed in more detail in paragraphs 20.23 to 20.37.

20.22 The five main elementary index number formulae are defined in paragraphs 20.30 to 20.45, and in paragraphs 20.46 to 20.57 various numerical relationships between these five indices are developed. Paragraphs 20.58 to 20.86 develop the axiomatic and economic approaches to elementary indices, and the five main elementary formulae used in practice will be evaluated in the light of these approaches.

[7] Theorem 5 in Diewert (1978, p. 888) shows that P_F, P_T and P_W approximate each other to the second order around an equal price and quantity point; see Diewert (1978, p. 894), Hill (2002) and Chapter 19 for some empirical results.

[8] Of course, all these ideal elementary index number formulae require current period quantity (or expenditure) weights and thus are not usually "practical" formulae that can be used to produce the usual type of month-to-month CPI. Nevertheless, as statistical agencies introduce superlative indices on a retrospective basis, it may be possible to obtain more current information on weights, at least at higher levels of aggregation; see Greenlees (2003). Gudnason (2003, p. 16) also gives some examples where the Icelandic CPI obtains enough information to be able to calculate some elementary indices using a superlative formula. In any case, a target index is required at the elementary level just as one is required at higher levels of aggregation.

[9] Hausman (2002, p. 14) also noted the importance of collecting quantity data along with price data at the elementary level so that more accurate quality change adjustments can be made by statistical agencies.

[10] Many statistical agencies send price collectors to various outlets on certain days of the month to collect list prices of individual items. Usually, price collectors do not work on weekends, when many sales take place. Thus the collected prices may not be fully representative of all transactions that occur. These collected prices can be regarded as approximations to the time-aggregated unit values for those items, but they are only approximations.

Aggregation and classification problems for elementary aggregates

20.23 Hawkes and Piotrowski (2003) note that the definition of an elementary aggregate involves aggregation over *four* possible dimensions:[11]

- a *time* dimension; i.e., the item unit value could be calculated for all item transactions for a year, a month, a week, or a day;
- a *spatial* dimension; i.e., the item unit value could be calculated for all item transactions in the country, province or state, city, neighbourhood, or individual location;
- a *product* dimension; i.e., the item unit value could be calculated for all item transactions in a broad general category (e.g., food), in a more specific category (e.g., margarine), for a particular brand (ignoring package size) or for a particular narrowly defined item (e.g., a particular AC Nielsen universal product code);
- a *sectoral* (or *entity* or *economic agent*) dimension; i.e., the item unit value could be calculated for a particular class of households or a particular class of outlets.

20.24 Each of the above dimensions for choosing the domain of definition for an elementary aggregate will be discussed in turn.

20.25 As the time period is compressed, several problems emerge:

- Purchases (by households) and sales (by outlets) become erratic and sporadic. Thus the frequency of unmatched purchases or sales from one period to the next increases and in the limit (choose the time period to be one minute), nothing will be matched and bilateral index number theory fails.[12]
- As the time period becomes shorter, chained indices exhibit more "drift"; i.e., if the value at the end of a chain of periods reverts to the value in the initial period, the chained index does not revert to unity. As is discussed in paragraphs 15.76 to 15.97 of Chapter 15, it is only appropriate to use chained indices when the underlying price and quantity data exhibit relatively smooth trends. When the time period is short, seasonal fluctuations[13] and periodic sales and advertising campaigns[14] can cause prices and quantities to oscillate (or "bounce", to use Szulc's (1983, p. 548) term), and hence it is not appropriate to use chained indices under these circumstances. If fixed base indices are used in this short time period situation, then the results will usually depend very strongly on the choice of the base period. In the seasonal context, not all commodities may even be in the marketplace during the chosen base period.[15] All these problems can be mitigated by choosing a longer time period so that trends in the data will tend to dominate the short-term fluctuations.
- As the time period contracts, virtually all goods become *durable* in the sense that they yield services not only for the period of purchase but for subsequent periods. Thus the period of purchase or acquisition becomes different from the periods of use, leading to many complications.[16]
- As the time period contracts, users will not be particularly interested in the short-term fluctuations of the resulting index and there will be demands for smoothing the necessarily erratic results. Put another way, users will want the many, say, weekly or daily movements in the index to be summarized as monthly or quarterly movements in prices. Hence from the viewpoint of meeting the needs of users, there will be relatively little demand for high-frequency indices.

In view of the above considerations, it is recommended that the index number time period be at least four weeks or a month.[17]

20.26 It is also necessary to choose the spatial dimension of the elementary aggregate. Should item prices in each city or region be considered as separate aggregates or should a national item aggregate be constructed? Obviously, if it is desired to have regional CPIs which aggregate up to a national CPI, then it will be necessary to collect item prices by region. It is not clear, however, how fine the "regions" should be. They could be as fine as a grouping of households in a postal code area or as individual outlets across the country.[18] There does not seem to be a clear consensus on what the optimal degree of spatial disaggregation should be.[19]

[11] Hawkes and Piotrowski (2003, p. 31) combine the spatial and sectoral dimensions into the spatial dimension. They also acknowledge the pioneering work of Theil (1954), who identified three dimensions of aggregation: aggregation over individuals, aggregation over commodities, and aggregation over time.

[12] This point is noted in paragraphs 15.65 to 15.71 of Chapter 15 in relation to the Divisia index. David Richardson (2003, p. 51) also made the point: "Defining items with a finer granularity, as is the case if quotes in different weeks are treated as separate items, results in more missing data and more imputations."

[13] See Chapter 22 for a monthly seasonal example where chained month-to-month indices are useless.

[14] See Feenstra and Shapiro (2003) for an example of a weekly superlative index that exhibits massive chain drift. Richardson (2003, pp. 50–51) discusses the issues involved in choosing weekly unit values versus monthly unit values.

[15] See Chapter 22 for suggested solutions to these seasonality problems.

[16] See Chapter 23 for more material on the possible CPI treatment of durable goods.

[17] If there is very high inflation in the economy (or even hyperinflation), then it may be necessary to move to weekly or even daily indices. Also, it should be noted that some index number theorists feel that new theories of consumer behaviour should be developed that could use weekly or daily data: "Some studies have endorsed unit values to reduce high frequency price variation, but this implicitly assumes that the high frequency variation represents simply noise in the data and is not meaningful in the context of a COLI. That is debatable. We need to develop a theory that confronts the data, not truncate the data to fit the theory" (Triplett (2003, p. 153)). Until such new theories are adequately developed, however, a pragmatic approach is to define the item unit values over months or quarters rather than days or weeks.

[18] Iceland no longer uses regional weights but uses individual outlets as the primary geographical unit; see Gudnason (2003, p. 18).

[19] William J. Hawkes and Frank W. Piotrowski note that it is quite acceptable to use national elementary aggregates when making international comparisons between countries:

> When we try to compare egg prices across geography, however, we find that lacing across outlets won't work, because the eyelets on one side of the shoe (or outlets on one side of the river) don't match up with those on the other side. Thus, in making interspatial comparisons, we have no choice but to aggregate outlets all the way up to the regional (or, in the case of purchasing power parities, national) level. We have no hesitation about doing this for interspatial comparisons, but we are reluctant to do so for intertemporal ones. Why is this? (Hawkes and Piotrowski (2003, pp. 31–32)).

Each statistical agency will have to make its own judgements on the matter of the optimal degree of spatial disaggregation, taking into account the costs of data collection and the demands of users for a spatial dimension for the CPI.

20.27 How detailed should the product dimension be? The possibilities range from regarding all commodities in a general category as being equivalent to regarding only commodities in a particular package size made by a particular manufacturer or service provider as being equivalent. All things being equal, Triplett (2002) stresses the advantages of matching products at the most detailed level possible, since this will prevent quality differences from clouding the period-to-period price comparisons. This is sensible advice, but then what are the drawbacks to working with the finest possible commodity classification? The major drawback is that the finer the classification, the more difficult it will be to match the item purchased or sold in the base period to the same item in the current period. Hence, the finer the product classification, the smaller will be the number of matched price comparisons that are possible. This would not be a problem if the unmatched prices followed the same trend as the matched ones in a particular elementary aggregate; but in at least some circumstances, this will not be the case.[20] The finer the classification system, the more work (in principle) there will be for the statistical agency to adjust for quality or impute the prices that do not match. Choosing a relatively coarse classification system leads to a very cost-efficient system of quality adjustment (i.e., essentially no explicit quality adjustment or imputation is done for the prices that do not exactly match), but it may not be very accurate. Thus all things considered, it seems preferable to choose the finest possible classification system.

20.28 The final issue in choosing a classification scheme is the issue of choosing a sectoral dimension; i.e., should the unit value for a particular item be calculated for a particular outlet or a particular household, or for a class of outlets or households?

20.29 Before the above question can be answered, it is necessary to ask whether the individual outlet or the individual household is the appropriate finest level of entity classification. If the economic approach to the CPI is taken, then the individual household is the appropriate finest level of entity classification.[21] Obviously, a single household will not work very well as the basic unit of entity observation because of the sporadic nature of many purchases by an individual household; i.e., there will be tremendous difficulties in matching prices across periods for individual households. For a grouping of households that is sufficiently large, however, it does become feasible in theory to use the household as the entity classification, rather than the outlet as is usually done. It is not usual to use households because of the costs and difficulties involved in collecting individual household data on prices and expenditures.[22] Price information is usually collected from retail establishments or outlets that sell mainly to households. Matching problems are mitigated (but not eliminated) using this strategy because the retail outlet generally sells the same items on a continuing basis.

20.30 If expenditures by all households in a region are aggregated together, will they equal sales by the retail outlets in the region? Under certain conditions, the answer to this question is "yes". The conditions are that the outlets do not sell any items to purchasers who are not local households (no regional exports or sales to local businesses or governments) and that the regional households do not make any purchases of consumption items other than from the local outlets (no household imports or transfers of commodities to local households by governments). Obviously, these restrictive conditions will not be met in practice, but they may hold as a first approximation.

20.31 The effects of *regional aggregation* and *product aggregation* can be examined, thanks to a recent study by Koskimäki and Ylä-Jarkko (2003). This study used scanner data for the last week in September 1998 and September 2000 on butter, margarine and other vegetable fats, vegetable oils, soft drinks, fruit juices and detergents that were provided by the AC Nielsen company for Finland. At the finest level of item classification (the AC Nielsen Universal Product Code), the number of individual items in the sample was 1,028. The total number of outlets in the sample was 338. Koskimäki and Ylä-Jarkko then considered four levels of spatial disaggregation:

- the entire country (1 level);
- provinces (4 levels);
- AC Nielsen regions (15 levels);
- individual outlets (338 levels).

They also considered four levels of product disaggregation:

- the COICOP 5-digit classification (6 levels);
- the COICOP 7-digit classification (26 levels);

An answer to their question is that it is preferable to match like with like as closely as possible. This leads statisticians to prefer the finest possible level of aggregation, which, in the case of intertemporal comparisons, would be the individual household or the individual outlet. In making cross-region comparisons, however, matching is not possible unless regional item aggregates are formed, as Hawkes and Piotrowski point out above.

[20] Silver and Heravi (2001a; 2001b; 2002; 2003, p. 286) and Koskimäki and Vartia (2001) stressed this point and presented empirical evidence to back up their point. Feenstra (1994) and Balk (2000b) developed some economic theory based methods to deal with the introduction of new items.

[21] This point has been made emphatically by two authors in the recent book on scanner data and price indices:

> In any case, unit values across stores are not the prices actually faced by households and do not represent the per period price in the COLI, even if the unit values are grouped by type of retail outlet (Triplett (2003, pp. 153–154)).
>
> Furthermore, note that the relationship being estimated is not a proper consumer demand function but rather an 'establishment sales function'. Only after making further assumptions – for example, fixing the distribution of consumers across establishments – is it permissible to jump to demand functions (Ley (2003, p. 380)).

[22] However, it is not impossible to collect accurate household data in certain circumstances; see Gudnason (2003), who pioneered a receipts methodology for collecting household price and expenditure data in Iceland.

Table 20.1 Proportion of transactions in 2000 that could be matched to 1998

	COICOP 5-digit	COICOP 7-digit	AC Nielsen brand	AC Nielsen Universal Product Code
Country	1.000	1.000	0.982	0.801
Province	1.000	1.000	0.975	0.774
AC Nielsen region	1.000	1.000	0.969	0.755
Individual outlet	0.904	0.904	0.846	0.617

- the AC Nielsen brand classification (266 levels);
- the AC Nielsen individual Universal Product Code (1,028 distinct products).

20.32 In order to illustrate the ability to match products over the two-year period as a function of the degree of fineness of the classification, Koskimäki and Ylä-Jarkko (2003, p. 10) presented a table showing that the proportion of transactions that could be matched across the two years fell steadily as the fineness of the classification scheme increased. At the highest level of aggregation (the national and COICOP 5-digit), all transactions could be matched over the two-year period, but at the finest level of aggregation (338 outlets times 1,028 individual products or 347,464 classification cells in all), only 61.7 per cent of the value of transactions in 2000 could be matched back to their 1998 counterparts. Koskimäki and Ylä-Jarkko's Table 7 is reproduced as Table 20.1.

20.33 For each of the above 16 levels of product and regional disaggregation, for the products that were available in September 1998 and September 2000, Koskimäki and Ylä-Jarkko (2003, p. 9) calculated Laspeyres and Fisher price indices. Their results are reproduced below as Tables 20.2 and 20.3.

20.34 Some of the trends in Tables 20.2 and 20.3 can be explained. As the product classification is made more fine, the indices tend to fall.[23] This indicates that the new products entering the sample tend to be more expensive than the continuing products. The differences in the COICOP 5-digit results and the AC Nielsen Universal Product Code results are very big indeed and indicate that it is probably best to work at the finest level of product disaggregation, even if there is the possibility of bias because of neglecting new products. This possible bias would have to be very substantial to overturn a recommendation to work at the finest level of product disaggregation.

20.35 As the regional classification is made finer, there is a tendency for the Laspeyres indices to become larger. This can be explained by purchasers switching to the lowest-cost outlets so that the item unit values will be smaller the higher the degree of aggregation. Put another way, the Laspeyres indices calculated at the outlet level are subject to a certain amount of outlet substitution bias (if one is willing to regard this phenomenon as a bias).

[23] The results at the AC Nielsen brand level are a counter-example to this general assertion.

Table 20.2 Laspeyres price indices by type of classification, September 1998–September 2000

	COICOP 5-digit	COICOP 7-digit	AC Nielsen brand	AC Nielsen Universal Product Code
Country	1.079	1.031	1.046	1.023
Province	1.078	1.031	1.048	1.023
AC Nielsen region	1.078	1.031	1.048	1.025
Individual outlet	1.086	1.040	1.060	1.028

Table 20.3 Fisher price indices by type of classification, September 1998–September 2000

	COICOP 5-digit	COICOP 7-digit	AC Nielsen brand	AC Nielsen Universal Product Code
Country	1.080	1.032	1.048	1.015
Province	1.079	1.031	1.048	1.014
AC Nielsen region	1.079	1.030	1.047	1.014
Individual outlet	1.089	1.034	1.049	1.011

20.36 What is striking in the Tables 20.1 to 20.3 are the differences between the Laspeyres and Fisher indices at the finer levels of aggregation. For the very finest level of aggregation, the Fisher at 1.011 is 1.7 percentage points below the corresponding Laspeyres at 1.028. Thus at the finest level of aggregation, the Laspeyres for this Finnish data set has a *representativity* or *elementary substitution bias* of about 0.85 percentage points per year.

20.37 Note that the above index number comparisons are free of chain drift problems since they make direct comparisons across the two years. They should also be free of seasonal problems, since the last week in September 1998 is compared with the last week of September 2000.

Elementary indices used in practice

20.38 Suppose that there are M lowest-level items or specific commodities in a chosen elementary category. Denote the period t price of item m by p_m^t for $t=0,1$ and for items $m=1,2,\ldots,M$. Define the period t price vector as $p^t \equiv [p_1^t, p_2^t, \ldots, p_M^t]$ for $t=0,1$.

20.39 The first widely used elementary index number formula is attributable to the French economist Dutot (1738):

$$P_D(p^0,p^1) \equiv \frac{\sum_{m=1}^{M} \frac{1}{M} p_m^1}{\sum_{m=1}^{M} \frac{1}{M} p_m^0} = \frac{\sum_{m=1}^{M} p_m^1}{\sum_{m=1}^{M} p_m^0} \qquad (20.1)$$

Thus the Dutot elementary price index is equal to the arithmetic average of the M period 1 prices divided by the arithmetic average of the M period 0 prices.

20.40 The second widely used elementary index number formula is attributable to the Italian economist Carli (1764):

$$P_C(p^0, p^1) \equiv \sum_{m=1}^{M} \frac{1}{M} \frac{p_m^1}{p_m^0} \quad (20.2)$$

Thus the Carli elementary price index is equal to the arithmetic average of the M item price ratios or price relatives, p_m^1/p_m^0.

20.41 The third widely used elementary index number formula is attributable to the English economist Jevons (1863):

$$P_J(p^0, p^1) \equiv \prod_{m=1}^{M} \sqrt[M]{\frac{p_m^1}{p_m^0}} \quad (20.3)$$

Thus the Jevons elementary price index is equal to the geometric average of the M item price ratios or price relatives, p_m^1/p_m^0.

20.42 The fourth elementary index number formula P_H is the harmonic average of the M item price relatives. It was first suggested in passing as an index number formula by Jevons (1865, p. 121) and Coggeshall (1887):

$$P_H(p^0, p^1) \equiv \left[\sum_{m=1}^{M} \frac{1}{M} \left(\frac{p_m^1}{p_m^0}\right)^{-1}\right]^{-1} \quad (20.4)$$

20.43 Finally, the fifth elementary index number formula is the geometric average of the Carli and harmonic formulae; i.e., it is the geometric mean of the arithmetic and harmonic means of the M price relatives:

$$P_{CSWD}(p^0, p^1) \equiv \sqrt{P_C(p^0, p^1) P_H(p^0, p^1)} \quad (20.5)$$

This index number formula was first suggested by Fisher (1922, p. 472) as his formula 101. Fisher also observed that, empirically for his data set, P_{CSWD} was very close to the Jevons index, P_J, and these two indices were his "best" unweighted index number formulae. In more recent times, Carruthers, Sellwood and Ward (1980, p. 25) and Dalén (1992, p. 140) also proposed P_{CSWD} as an elementary index number formula.

20.44 Having defined the most commonly used elementary formulae, the question now arises: which formula is "best"? Obviously, this question cannot be answered until desirable properties for elementary indices are developed. This will be done in a systematic manner in paragraphs 20.46 to 20.57, but one desirable property for an elementary index will be noted in the present section. This is the *time reversal test*, which was noted in Chapter 15. In the present context, this test for the elementary index $P(p^0, p^1)$ becomes:

$$P(p^0, p^1)\, P(p^1, p^0) = 1 \quad (20.6)$$

This test says that if the prices in period 2 revert to the initial prices of period 0, then the product of the price change going from period 0 to 1, $P(p^0, p^1)$, times the price change going from period 1 to 2, $P(p^1, p^0)$, should equal unity; i.e., under the stated conditions, we should end up where we started. It can be verified that the Dutot, Jevons, and Carruthers–Sellwood–Ward–Dalén indices, P_D, P_J and P_{CSWD}, all satisfy the time reversal test, but that the Carli and harmonic indices, P_C and P_H, fail this test. In fact, these last two indices fail the test in the following *biased* manner:

$$P_C(p^0, p^1)\, P_C(p^1, p^0) \geq 1 \quad (20.7)$$

$$P_H(p^0, p^1)\, P_H(p^1, p^0) \leq 1 \quad (20.8)$$

with strict inequalities holding in (20.7) and (20.8) provided that the period 1 price vector p^1 is not proportional to the period 0 price vector p^0.[24] Thus the Carli index will generally have an upward bias, while the harmonic index will generally have a downward bias. Fisher (1922, pp. 66 and 383) seems to have been the first to establish the upward bias of the Carli index,[25] and he made the following observations on its use by statistical agencies: "In fields other than index numbers it is often the best form of average to use. But we shall see that the simple arithmetic average produces one of the very worst of index numbers. And if this book has no other effect than to lead to the total abandonment of the simple arithmetic type of index number, it will have served a useful purpose" (Fisher (1922, pp. 29–30).

20.45 The following section establishes some numerical relationships between the five elementary indices defined in this section. Then in the subsequent section, a more comprehensive list of desirable properties for elementary indices is developed and the five elementary formulae are evaluated in the light of these properties or tests.

Numerical relationships between the frequently used elementary indices

20.46 It can be shown[26] that the Carli, Jevons and harmonic elementary price indices satisfy the following inequalities:

$$P_H(p^0, p^1) \leq P_J(p^0, p^1) \leq P_C(p^0, p^1) \quad (20.9)$$

i.e., the harmonic index is always equal to or less than the Jevons index, which in turn is always equal to or less than the Carli index. In fact, the strict inequalities in (20.9) will hold provided that the period 0 vector of prices, p^0, is not proportional to the period 1 vector of prices, p^1.

20.47 The inequalities (20.9) do not tell us by how much the Carli index will exceed the Jevons index and by how much the Jevons index will exceed the harmonic index. Hence, in the remainder of this section, some approximate relationships between the five indices

[24] These inequalities follow from the fact that a harmonic mean of M positive numbers is always equal to or less than the corresponding arithmetic mean; see Walsh (1901, p. 517) or Fisher (1922, pp. 383–384). This inequality is a special case of Schlömilch's inequality; see Hardy, Littlewood and Pólya (1934, p. 26).

[25] See also Pigou (1920, pp. 59 and 70), Szulc (1987, p. 12) and Dalén (1992, p. 139). Dalén (1994, pp. 150–151) provides some nice intuitive explanations for the upward bias of the Carli index.

[26] Each of the three indices P_H, P_J and P_C is a mean of order r where r equals −1, 0 and 1, respectively, and so the inequalities follow from Schlömilch's inequality; see Hardy, Littlewood and Pólya (1934, p. 26).

defined in the previous section are developed that provide some practical guidance on the relative magnitudes of each of the indices.

20.48 The first approximate relationship to be derived is between the Carli index P_C and the Dutot index P_D.[27] For each period t, define the arithmetic mean of the M prices pertaining to that period as follows:

$$p^{t*} \equiv \sum_{m=1}^{M} \frac{1}{M} p_m^t; \quad t=0,1 \qquad (20.10)$$

Now define the multiplicative deviation of the mth price in period t relative to the mean price in that period, e_m^t, as follows:

$$p_m^t = p^{t*}(1+e_m^t); \quad m=1,\ldots,M; \ t=0,1 \qquad (20.11)$$

Note that equations (20.10) and (20.11) imply that the deviations e_m^t sum to zero in each period; i.e.

$$\sum_{m=1}^{M} e_m^t = 0; \quad t=0,1 \qquad (20.12)$$

20.49 Note that the Dutot index can be written as the ratio of the mean prices, p^{1*}/p^{0*}; i.e.

$$P_D(p^0,p^1) = \frac{p^{1*}}{p^{0*}} \qquad (20.13)$$

20.50 Now substitute equation (20.11) into the definition of the Jevons index (20.3):

$$\begin{aligned} P_J(p^0,p^1) &= \prod_{m=1}^{M} \sqrt[M]{\frac{p^{1*}(1+e_m^1)}{p^{0*}(1+e_m^0)}} \\ &= \frac{p^{1*}}{p^{0*}} \prod_{m=1}^{M} \sqrt[M]{\frac{(1+e_m^1)}{(1+e_m^0)}} \quad \text{using equation (20.13)} \\ &= P_D(p^0,p^1) f(e^0,e^1) \qquad (20.14) \end{aligned}$$

where $e^t \equiv [e_1^t,\ldots,e_M^t]$ for $t=0$ and 1, and where the function f is defined as follows:

$$f(e^0,e^1) \equiv \prod_{m=1}^{M} \sqrt[M]{\frac{(1+e_m^1)}{(1+e_m^0)}} \qquad (20.15)$$

20.51 Expand $f(e^0,e^1)$ by a second-order Taylor series approximation around $e^0=0_M$ and $e^1=0_M$. Using equation (20.12), it can be verified[28] that the following second-order approximate relationship between P_J and P_D is obtained:

$$\begin{aligned} P_J(p^0,p^1) &\approx P_D(p^0,p^1)[1+(1/2M)e^0e^0-(1/2M)e^1e^1] \\ &= P_D(p^0,p^1)[1+(1/2)\mathrm{var}(e^0)-(1/2)\mathrm{var}(e^1)] \qquad (20.16) \end{aligned}$$

where $\mathrm{var}(e^t)$ is the variance of the period t multiplicative deviations. Thus, for $t=0,1$:

$$\begin{aligned} \mathrm{var}(e^t) &\equiv \frac{1}{M}\sum_{m=1}^{M}(e_m^t - e_m^{t*})^2 \\ &= \frac{1}{M}\sum_{m=1}^{M}(e_m^t)^2 \quad \text{since } e_m^{t*}=0 \text{ using equation (20.12)} \\ &= \frac{1}{M} e^t e^t \qquad (20.17) \end{aligned}$$

20.52 Under normal conditions,[29] the variance of the deviations of the prices from their means in each period is likely to be approximately constant and so, under these conditions, the Jevons price index will approximate the Dutot price index to the second order.

20.53 Note that with the exception of the Dutot formula, the remaining four elementary indices defined in paragraphs 20.23 to 20.37 are functions of the relative prices of the M items being aggregated. This fact is used in order to derive some approximate relationships between these four elementary indices. Thus define the mth price relative as

$$r_m \equiv \frac{p_m^1}{p_m^0}; \quad m=1,\ldots,M \qquad (20.18)$$

20.54 Define the arithmetic mean of the m price relatives as

$$r^* \equiv \frac{1}{M}\sum_{m=1}^{M} r_m = P_C(p^0,p^1) \qquad (20.19)$$

where the last equality follows from the definition (20.2) of the Carli index. Finally, define the deviation e_m of the mth price relative r_m from the arithmetic average of the M price relatives r^* as follows:[30]

$$r_m = r^*(1+e_m); \quad m=1,\ldots,M \qquad (20.20)$$

20.55 Note that equations (20.19) and (20.20) imply that the deviations e_m sum to zero:

$$\sum_{m=1}^{M} e_m = 0 \qquad (20.21)$$

20.56 Now substitute equation (20.20) into the definitions (20.2)–(20.5) of P_C, P_J, P_H and P_{CSWD} in order to obtain the following representations for these indices in terms of the vector of deviations, $e \equiv [e_1,\ldots,e_M]$:

[27] It should be noted that the Dutot index can also be written as a weighted average of the price relatives; i.e., $P_D(p^0,p^1) \equiv \sum_{i=1}^n p_i^1 / \sum_{j=1}^n p_j^0 = \sum_{i=1}^n (p_i^1/p_i^0) p_i^0 / \sum_{j=1}^n p_j^0 = \sum_{i=1}^n (p_i^1/p_i^0) w_i^0$, where the ith weight is defined as $w_i \equiv p_i^0/\sum_{j=1}^n p_j^0$. Thus if the commodities in the elementary aggregate are heterogeneous, the commodities that are more expensive in the chosen units of measurement will get a large weight, which may not be warranted from the viewpoint of expenditures on the commodity.

[28] This approximate relationship was first obtained by Carruthers, Sellwood and Ward (1980, p. 25).

[29] If there are significant changes in the overall inflation rate, some studies indicate that the variance of deviations of prices from their means can also change. Also if M is small, then there will be sampling fluctuations in the variances of the prices from period to period.

[30] Note that the ratio-type deviations e_m, defined by equation (20.20), are different from the level-type deviations e_m^t, defined by equation (20.11).

$$P_C(p^0,p^1) = \sum_{m=1}^{M} \frac{1}{M} r_m = r^* 1 = r^* f_C(e) \quad (20.22)$$

$$P_J(p^0,p^1) = \prod_{m=1}^{M} \sqrt[M]{r_m} = r^* \prod_{m=1}^{M} \sqrt[M]{1+e_m} \equiv r^* f_J(e) \quad (20.23)$$

$$P_H(p^0,p^1) = \left[\sum_{m=1}^{M} \frac{1}{M}(r_m)^{-1}\right]^{-1} = r^* \left[\sum_{m=1}^{M} \frac{1}{M}(1+e_m)^{-1}\right]^{-1} \equiv r^* f_H(e) \quad (20.24)$$

$$P_{CSWP}(p^0,p^1) = \sqrt{P_C(p^0,p^1)P_H(p^0,p^1)} = r^* \sqrt{f_C(e) f_H(e)} \equiv r^* f_{CSWD}(e) \quad (20.25)$$

where the last identity in each of equations (20.22)–(20.25) serves to define the deviation functions, $f_C(e)$, $f_J(e)$, $f_H(e)$ and $f_{CSWD}(e)$. The second-order Taylor series approximations to each of these functions[31] around the point $e = 0_M$ are:

$$f_C(e) \approx 1 \quad (20.26)$$

$$f_J(e) \approx 1 - (1/2M)ee = 1 - (1/2)\text{var}(e) \quad (20.27)$$

$$f_H(e) \approx 1 - (1/M)ee = 1 - \text{var}(e) \quad (20.28)$$

$$f_{CSWD}(e) \approx 1 - (1/2M)ee = 1 - (1/2)\text{var}(e) \quad (20.29)$$

where repeated use of equation (20.21) is made in deriving the above approximations.[32] To the second order, the Carli index P_C will exceed the Jevons and Carruthers–Sellwood–Ward–Dalén indices, P_J and P_{CSWD}, by (1/2) r^* var(e), which is r^* times half the variance of the M price relatives p^1_m/p^0_m. Similarly, to the second order, the harmonic index P_H will lie below the Jevons and Carruthers–Sellwood–Ward–Dalén indices, P_J and P_{CSWD}, by r^* times half the variance of the M price relatives p^1_m/p^0_m.

20.57 Empirically, it is expected that the Jevons and Carruthers–Sellwood–Ward–Dalén indices will be very close to each other. Using the previous approximation result (20.16), it is expected that the Dutot index P_D will also be fairly close to P_J and P_{CSWD}, with some fluctuations over time as a result of changing variances of the period 0 and 1 deviation vectors, e^0 and e^1. Thus it is expected that these three elementary indices will give much the same numerical answers in empirical applications. In contrast, the Carli index can be expected to be substantially above these three indices, with the degree of divergence growing as the variance of the M price relatives grows. Similarly, the harmonic index can be expected to be substantially below the three middle indices, with the degree of divergence growing as the variance of the M price relatives grows.

[31] From equation (20.22), it can be seen that $f_C(e)$ is identically equal to 1 so that the expression (20.26) will be an exact equality rather than an approximation.

[32] These second-order approximations are attributable to Dalén (1992, p. 143) for the case $r^* = 1$ and to Diewert (1995a, p. 29) for the case of a general r^*.

The axiomatic approach to elementary indices

20.58 Recall the axiomatic approach to bilateral price indices $P(p^0, p^1, q^0, q^1)$ developed in Chapter 16. In the present chapter, the elementary price index $P(p^0, p^1)$ depends only on the period 0 and 1 price vectors, p^0 and p^1, respectively, so that the elementary price index does not depend on the period 0 and 1 quantity vectors, q^0 and q^1. One approach to obtaining new tests or axioms for an elementary index is to look at the 20 or so axioms listed in the Fisher axiomatic approach in Chapter 16 for bilateral price indices $P(p^0, p^1, q^0, q^1)$ and adapt those axioms to the present context; i.e., use the old bilateral tests for $P(p^0, p^1, q^0, q^1)$ that do not depend on the quantity vectors q^0 and q^1 as tests for an elementary index $P(p^0, p^1)$.[33] This is the approach taken in the present section.

20.59 The first eight tests or axioms are reasonably straightforward and uncontroversial.

T1: *Continuity*: $P(p^0, p^1)$ is a continuous function of the M positive period 0 prices $p^0 \equiv [p^0_1, \ldots, p^0_M]$ and the M positive period 1 prices $p^1 \equiv [p^1_1, \ldots, p^1_M]$.

T2: *Identity*: $P(p, p) = 1$; i.e., if the period 0 price vector equals the period 1 price vector, then the index is equal to unity.

T3: *Monotonicity in current period prices*: $P(p^0, p^1) < P(p^0, p)$ if $p^1 < p$; i.e., if any period 1 price increases, then the price index increases.

T4: *Monotonicity in base period prices*: $P(p^0, p^1) > P(p, p^1)$ if $p^0 < p$; i.e., if any period 0 price increases, then the price index decreases.

T5: *Proportionality in current period prices*: $P(p^0, \lambda p^1) = \lambda P(p^0, p^1)$ if $\lambda > 0$; i.e., if all period 1 prices are multiplied by the positive number λ, then the initial price index is also multiplied by λ.

T6: *Inverse proportionality in base period prices*: $P(\lambda p^0, p^1) = \lambda^{-1} P(p^0, p^1)$ if $\lambda > 0$; i.e., if all period 0 prices are multiplied by the positive number λ, then the initial price index is multiplied by $1/\lambda$.

T7: *Mean value test*: $\min_m \{p^1_m/p^0_m : m = 1, \ldots, M\} \leq P(p^0, p^1) \leq \max_m \{p^1_m/p^0_m : m = 1, \ldots, M\}$; i.e., the price index lies between the smallest and largest price relatives.

T8: *Symmetric treatment of outlets*: $P(p^0, p^1) = P(p^{0*}, p^{1*})$, where p^{0*} and p^{1*} denote the *same* permutation of the components of p^0 and p^1; i.e., if we change the ordering of the outlets (or households) from which we obtain the price quotations for the two periods, then the elementary index remains unchanged.

Eichhorn (1978, p. 155) showed that tests T1, T2, T3 and T5 imply test T7, so that not all of the above tests are logically independent.

20.60 The following tests are more controversial and are not necessarily accepted by all price statisticians.

T9: *The price bouncing test*: $P(p^0, p^1) = P(p^{0*}, p^{1**})$ where p^{0*} and p^{1**} denote possibly *different* permu-

[33] The approach was used by Diewert (1995a, pp. 5–17), who drew on the earlier work of Eichhorn (1978, pp. 152–160) and Dalén (1992).

tations of the components of p^0 and p^1; i.e., if the ordering of the price quotes for both periods is changed in possibly different ways, then the elementary index remains unchanged.

20.61 Obviously, test T8 is a special case of test T9 where the two permutations of the initial ordering of the prices are restricted to be the same. Thus test T9 implies test T8. Test T9 is attributable to Dalén (1992, p. 138). He justified this test by suggesting that the price index should remain unchanged if outlet prices "bounce" in such a manner that the outlets are just exchanging prices with each other over the two periods. While this test has some intuitive appeal, it is not consistent with the idea that outlet prices should be matched to each other in a one-to-one manner across the two periods. This outlet price matching is preferable to not matching prices across outlets in case there are quality differences across outlets.

20.62 The following test was also proposed by Dalén (1992) in the elementary index context:

T10: *Time reversal*: $P(p^1,p^0)=1/P(p^0,p^1)$; i.e., if the data for periods 0 and 1 are interchanged, then the resulting price index should equal the reciprocal of the original price index.

Since many price statisticians approve of the Laspeyres price index in the bilateral index context and this index does not satisfy the time reversal test, it is obvious that not all price statisticians would regard the time reversal test in the elementary index context as being a fundamental test that must be satisfied. Nevertheless, many other price statisticians do regard this test as a fundamental one since it is difficult to accept an index that gives a different answer if the ordering of time is reversed.

20.63 The following test is a strengthening of the time reversal test:

T11: *Circularity*: $P(p^0,p^1)P(p^1,p^2)=P(p^0,p^2)$; i.e., the price index going from period 0 to 1 times the price index going from period 1 to 2 equals the price index going from period 0 to 2 directly.

The circularity and identity tests imply the time reversal test (just set $p^2=p^0$). Thus the circularity test is essentially a strengthening of the time reversal test, and so price statisticians who do not accept the time reversal test are unlikely to accept the circularity test. In general, however, the circularity test seems to be a very desirable property: it is a generalization of a property that holds for a single price relative.

20.64 The following test is a very important one:

T12: *Commensurability*: $P(\lambda_1 p_1^0,\ldots,\lambda_M p_M^0;\lambda_1 p_1^1,\ldots,\lambda_M p_M^1)=P(p_1^0,\ldots,p_M^0;p_1^1,\ldots,p_M^1)=P(p^0,p^1)$ for all $\lambda_1>0,\ldots,\lambda_M>0$; i.e., if the units of measurement for each commodity are changed, then the elementary index remains unchanged.

In the bilateral index context, virtually every price statistician accepts the validity of this test. In the elementary context, however, this test is more controversial. If the M items in the elementary aggregate are all homogeneous, then it makes sense to measure all the items in the same units. Hence, if the unit of measurement of the homogeneous commodity is changed, then a modified version of test T12 should restrict all the λ_m to be the same number (say λ) and the modified test T12 becomes

$$P(\lambda p^0,\lambda p^1)=P(p^0,p^1);\quad \lambda>0 \qquad (20.30)$$

Note that this modified test T12 will be satisfied if tests T5 and T6 are satisfied. Thus if the items in the elementary aggregate are homogeneous, then there is no need for the original (unmodified) test T12.

20.65 In actual practice, there will usually be thousands of individual items in each elementary aggregate and the hypothesis of item homogeneity is not warranted. Under these circumstances, it is important that the elementary index satisfy the commensurability test, since the units of measurement of the heterogeneous items in the elementary aggregate are arbitrary, and hence the price statistician can change the index simply by changing the units of measurement for some of the items.

20.66 This completes the listing of the tests for an elementary index. There remains the task of evaluating how many tests are passed by each of the five elementary indices defined in paragraphs 20.38 to 20.45.

20.67 Straightforward computations show that the Jevons elementary index P_J satisfies all the tests, and hence emerges as being "best" from the viewpoint of this particular axiomatic approach to elementary indices.

20.68 The Dutot index P_D satisfies all the tests with the important exception of the commensurability test T12, which it fails. If there are heterogeneous items in the elementary aggregate, this is a rather serious failure and hence price statisticians should be careful in using this index under these conditions.

20.69 The geometric mean of the Carli and harmonic elementary indices, P_{CSWD}, fails only the price bouncing test T9 and the circularity test T11. The failure of these two tests is probably not a disqualifying condition, and so this index could be used by price statisticians if, for some reason, it was decided not to use the Jevons formula. As was observed in paragraphs 20.38 to 20.45, numerically, P_{CSWD} will be very close to P_J.

20.70 The Carli and harmonic elementary indices, P_C and P_H, fail the price bouncing test T9, the time reversal test T10 and the circularity test T11, and pass the other tests. The failure of tests T9 and T11 is again not a disqualifying condition, but the failure of the time reversal test T10 is a rather serious matter and so price statisticians should be cautious in using these indices.

The economic approach to elementary indices

20.71 Recall the notation and discussion in paragraphs 20.38 to 20.45. Suppose that each purchaser of the items in the elementary aggregate has preferences over a vector of purchases $q\equiv[q_1,\ldots,q_M]$ that can be represented by the linearly homogeneous aggregator (or utility) function $f(q)$. Further assume that each purchaser engages in cost-minimizing behaviour in each period. Then, as seen in Chapter 17, it can be shown that certain specific functional forms for the aggregator or utility function $f(q)$ or its dual unit cost function $c(p)$[34] lead to specific functional forms for the price index

[34] The unit cost function is defined as $c(p)\equiv\min_q\{\sum_{m=1}^M p_m q_m: f(q)=1\}$.

$P(p^0, p^1, q^0, q^1)$ with

$$P(p^0, p^1, q^0, q^1) \equiv \frac{c(p^1)}{c(p^0)} \quad (20.31)$$

20.72 Suppose that the purchasers have aggregator functions f defined as follows:[35]

$$f(q_1, \ldots, q_M) \equiv \min_m \{q_m/\alpha_m : m=1, \ldots, M\} \quad (20.32)$$

where the α_m are positive constants. Then under these assumptions, it can be shown that equation (20.31) becomes:[36]

$$\frac{c(p^1)}{c(p^0)} = \frac{p^1q^0}{p^0q^0} = \frac{p^1q^1}{p^0q^1} \quad (20.33)$$

and the quantity vectors of purchases during the two periods must be proportional; i.e.,

$$q^1 = \lambda q^0 \quad \text{for some } \lambda > 0 \quad (20.34)$$

20.73 From the first equation in (20.33), it can be seen that the true cost of living index, $c(p^1)/c(p^0)$, under assumptions (20.32) about the aggregator function f, is equal to the Laspeyres price index, $P_L(p^0, p^1, q^0, q^1) \equiv p^1q^0/p^0q^0$. It is shown below how various elementary formulae can estimate this Laspeyres formula under alternative assumptions about the sampling of prices.

20.74 In order to provide a justification for the use of the Dutot elementary formula, write the Laspeyres index number formula as follows:

$$P_L(p^0, p^1, q^0, q^1) \equiv \frac{\sum_{m=1}^{M} p_m^1 q_m^0}{\sum_{m=1}^{M} p_m^0 q_m^0} = \frac{\sum_{m=1}^{M} \rho_m^0 p_m^1}{\sum_{m=1}^{M} \rho_m^0 p_m^0} \quad (20.35)$$

where the *base period item probabilities* ρ_m^0 are defined as follows:

$$\rho_m^0 \equiv \frac{q_m^0}{\sum_{m=1}^{M} q_m^0}; \quad m=1, \ldots, M \quad (20.36)$$

Thus the base period probability for item m, ρ_m^0, is equal to the purchases of item m in the base period relative to total purchases of all items in the commodity class in the base period. Note that these definitions require that all items in the commodity class have the same units.[37]

20.75 Now it is easy to see how formula (20.35) could be turned into a rigorous sampling framework for sampling prices in the particular commodity class under consideration.[38] If item prices in the commodity class were sampled proportionally to their base period probabilities ρ_m^0, then the Laspeyres index defined by the first equality in (20.35) could be estimated by a probability-weighted Dutot index defined by the second equality in (20.35). In general, with an appropriate sampling scheme, the use of the Dutot formula at the elementary level of aggregation *for homogeneous items* can be perfectly consistent with a Laspeyres index concept.

20.76 The Dutot formula can also be consistent with a Paasche index concept. If the Paasche formula is used at the elementary level of aggregation, then the following formula is obtained:

$$P_P(p^0, p^1, q^0, q^1) \equiv \frac{\sum_{m=1}^{M} p_m^1 q_m^1}{\sum_{m=1}^{M} p_m^0 q_m^1} = \frac{\sum_{m=1}^{M} \rho_m^1 p_m^1}{\sum_{m=1}^{M} \rho_m^1 p_m^0} \quad (20.37)$$

where the period 1 item probabilities ρ_m^1 are defined as follows:

$$\rho_m^1 \equiv \frac{q_m^1}{\sum_{m=1}^{M} q_m^1}; \quad m=1, \ldots, M \quad (20.38)$$

Thus the period 1 probability for item m, ρ_m^1, is equal to the quantity purchased of item m in period 1 relative to total purchases of all items in the commodity class in that period.

20.77 Again, it is easy to see how formula (20.37) could be turned into a rigorous sampling framework for sampling prices in the particular commodity class under consideration. If item prices in the commodity class were sampled proportionally to their period 1 probabilities ρ_m^1, then the Paasche index defined by the first equality in (20.37) could be estimated by the probability-weighted Dutot index defined by the second equality in (20.37). In general, with an appropriate sampling scheme, the use of the Dutot formula at the elementary level of aggregation (for a homogeneous elementary aggregate) can be perfectly consistent with a Paasche index concept.

20.78 Rather than use the fixed basket representations for the Laspeyres and Paasche indices, it is possible to use the expenditure share representations for the Laspeyres and Paasche indices, and to use the expenditure shares s_m^0 or s_m^1 as probability weights for price relatives. Thus if the relative prices of items in the commodity class under consideration are sampled using weights that are proportional to their base period expenditure shares in the commodity class, then the following probability-weighted Carli index

$$P_C(p^0, p^1, s^0) \equiv \sum_{m=1}^{M} s_m^0 \frac{p_m^1}{p_m^0} \quad (20.39)$$

will be equal to the Laspeyres index.[39] Of course, formula (20.39) does not require the assumption of homogeneous items as did equations (20.35) and (20.37).

20.79 If the relative prices of items in the commodity class under consideration are sampled using weights that are proportional to their period 1 expenditure shares in the commodity class, then the following probability-weighted harmonic index

[35] The preferences which correspond to this f are known as Leontief (1936) or no substitution preferences.

[36] See Pollak (1983). Notation: p^1q^0 is defined as $\sum_{i=1}^{n} p_i^1 q_i^0$, etc.

[37] The probabilities defined by equation (20.36) are meaningless unless the items are homogeneous.

[38] For the details, see Balk (2002, pp. 8–10).

[39] For a rigorous derivation of a sampling framework, see Balk (2002, pp. 13–14).

$$P_H(p^0,p^1,s^1) \equiv \left(\sum_{m=1}^{M} s_m^1 \left(\frac{p_m^1}{p_m^0}\right)^{-1}\right)^{-1} \quad (20.40)$$

will be equal to the Paasche index.

20.80 The above results show that the Dutot elementary index can be justified as an approximation to an underlying Laspeyres or Paasche price index for a homogeneous elementary aggregate under appropriate price sampling schemes. The above results also show that the Carli and harmonic elementary indices can be justified as approximations to an underlying Laspeyres or Paasche price index for a heterogeneous elementary aggregate under appropriate price sampling schemes.

20.81 Recall that assumption (20.32) on f justified the Laspeyres and Paasche indices as being the "true" elementary aggregate from the viewpoint of the economic approach to elementary indices. Suppose now that assumption (20.32) is replaced by the following assumption of Cobb–Douglas (1928) preferences:[40]

$$f(q_1,\ldots,q_M) \equiv \prod_{m=1}^{M} q^{\beta_m}; \quad \beta_m > 0 \quad \text{for } m=1,\ldots,M$$
$$\text{and } \sum_{m=1}^{M} \beta_m = 1 \quad (20.41)$$

20.82 Under assumption (20.41), the true economic elementary price index is:[41]

$$\frac{c(p^1)}{c(p^0)} = \prod_{m=1}^{M} \left(\frac{p_m^1}{p_m^0}\right)^{\beta_m} \quad (20.42)$$

20.83 It turns out that if purchasers have the above Cobb–Douglas preferences, then item expenditures will be proportional over the two periods so that:

$$p_m^1 q_m^1 = \lambda p_m^0 q_m^0 \quad \text{for } m=1,\ldots,M \text{ and for some } \lambda > 0. \quad (20.43)$$

Under these conditions, the base period expenditure shares s_m^0 will equal the corresponding period 1 expenditure shares s_m^1, as well as the corresponding β_m; i.e., assumption (20.41) implies:

$$s_m^0 = s_m^1 \equiv \beta_m; \quad m=1,\ldots,M \quad (20.44)$$

Thus if the relative prices of items in the commodity class under consideration are sampled using weights that are proportional to their base period expenditure shares in the commodity class, then the following probability-weighted Jevons index

$$\ln P_J(p^0,p^1,s^0) \equiv \sum_{m=1}^{M} s_m^0 \ln \frac{p_m^1}{p_m^0} \quad (20.45)$$

will be equal to the logarithm of the true elementary price aggregate defined by equation (20.42).[42]

20.84 The above results show that the Jevons elementary index can be justified as an approximation to an underlying Cobb–Douglas price index for a heterogeneous elementary aggregate under an appropriate price sampling scheme.

20.85 The assumption of Leontief preferences implies that the quantity vectors pertaining to the two periods under consideration will be proportional; recall equation (20.34). In contrast, the assumption of Cobb–Douglas preferences implies that expenditures will be proportional over the two periods; recall equation (20.43). Index number theorists have been debating the relative merits of the proportional quantities versus proportional expenditures assumption for a long time. Authors who thought that the proportional expenditures assumption was empirically more likely include Jevons (1865, p. 295) and Ferger (1931, p. 39; 1936, p. 271). These early authors did not have the economic approach to index number theory at their disposal but they intuitively understood, along with Pierson (1895, p. 332), that substitution effects occurred and hence the proportional expenditures assumption was more plausible than the proportional quantities assumption.

20.86 The results in the previous section gave some support for the use of the unweighted Jevons elementary index over the use of the unweighted Dutot, Carli and harmonic indices, provided that the proportional expenditures assumption is more likely than the proportional quantities assumption. This support is very weak, however, since an appropriate item price sampling scheme is required in order to justify the results. Thus, using an unweighted Dutot, Carli or harmonic index (without the appropriate sampling scheme) cannot really be justified from the viewpoint of the economic approach. The results in this section nevertheless give considerable support to the use of an appropriately weighted Jevons index over the other weighted indices, since from the economic perspective, cross-item elasticities of substitution are much more likely to be close to unity (this corresponds to the case of Cobb–Douglas preferences) than to zero (this corresponds to the case of Leontief preferences). If the probability weights in the weighted Jevons index are taken to be the arithmetic average of the period 0 and 1 item expenditure shares and narrowly defined unit values are used as the price concept, then the weighted Jevons index becomes an ideal type of elementary index discussed in paragraphs 20.11 to 20.22.

The sampling approach to elementary indices

20.87 In the previous section, it is shown that appropriately weighted elementary indices are capable of approximating various economic population elementary indices, with the approximation becoming exact as the sampling approaches complete coverage. Conversely, it can be seen that, in general, it is impossible for an unweighted elementary price index of the type defined in paragraphs 20.38 to 20.45 to approach the theoretically ideal elementary price index defined in paragraphs 20.11 to 20.22, even if all item prices in the

[40] These preferences were introduced slightly earlier by Konüs and Byushgens (1926).

[41] See Pollak (1983).

[42] See Balk (2002, pp. 11–12) for a rigorous derivation.

elementary aggregate are sampled.[43] Hence, rather than just sampling prices, it will be necessary for the price statistician to collect information on the transaction values (or quantities) associated with the sampled prices in order to form sample elementary aggregates that will approach the target ideal elementary aggregate as the sample size becomes large. Thus, instead of just collecting a sample of prices, it will be necessary to collect corresponding sample quantities (or values) so that a sample Fisher, Törnqvist or Walsh price index can be constructed. This sample-based superlative elementary price index will approach the population ideal elementary index as the sample size becomes large. This approach to the construction of elementary indices in a sampling context was recommended by Pigou (1920, pp. 66–67), Fisher (1922, p. 380), Diewert (1995a, p. 25) and Balk (2002).[44] In particular, Pigou (1920, p. 67) suggested that the sample-based Fisher ideal price index be used to deflate the value ratio for the aggregate under consideration in order to obtain an estimate of the quantity ratio for the aggregate under consideration.

The use of scanner data in constructing elementary aggregates

20.88 Until fairly recently, it was not possible to determine how close an unweighted elementary index of the type defined in paragraphs 20.38 to 20.45 was to an ideal elementary aggregate. With the availability of scanner data (i.e., of detailed data on the prices and quantities of individual items that are sold in retail outlets), it has now become possible to compute ideal elementary aggregates for some item strata and compare the results with statistical agency estimates of price change for the same class of items. Of course, the statistical agency estimates of price change are usually based on the use of the Dutot, Jevons or Carli formulae. The following quotations reflect the results of many of the scanner data studies:

> A second major recent development is the willingness of statistical agencies to experiment with scanner data, which are the electronic data generated at the point of sale by the retail outlet and generally include transactions prices, quantities, location, date and time of purchase and the product described by brand, make or model. Such detailed data may prove especially useful for constructing better indices at the elementary level. Recent studies that use scanner data in this way include Silver (1995), Reinsdorf (1996), Bradley, Cook, Leaver and Moulton (1997), Dalén (1997), de Haan and Opperdoes (1997) and Hawkes (1997). Some estimates of elementary index bias (on an annual basis) that emerged from these studies were: 1.1 percentage points for television sets in the United Kingdom; 4.5 percentage points for coffee in the United States; 1.5 percentage points for ketchup, toilet tissue, milk and tuna in the United States; 1 percentage point for fats, detergents, breakfast cereals and frozen fish in Sweden; 1 percentage point for coffee in the Netherlands and 3 percentage points for coffee in the United States respectively. These bias estimates incorporate both elementary and outlet substitution biases and are significantly higher than our earlier ballpark estimates of .255 and .41 percentage points. On the other hand, it is unclear to what extent these large bias estimates can be generalized to other commodities (Diewert (1998a, pp. 54–55)).
>
> Before considering the results it is worth commenting on some general findings from scanner data. It is stressed that the results here are for an experiment in which the same data were used to compare different methods. The results for the U.K. Retail Prices Index can not be fairly compared since they are based on quite different practices and data, their data being collected by price collectors and having strengths as well as weaknesses (Fenwick, Ball, Silver and Morgan (2003)). Yet it is worth following up on Diewert's (2002c) comment on the U.K. Retail Prices Index electrical appliances section, which includes a wide variety of appliances, such as irons, toasters, refrigerators, etc. which went from 98.6 to 98.0, a drop of 0.6 percentage points from January 1998 to December 1998. He compares these results with those for washing machines and notes that "...it may be that the non washing machine components of the electrical appliances index increased in price enough over this period to cancel out the large apparent drop in the price of washing machines but I think that this is somewhat unlikely." A number of studies on similar such products have been conducted using scanner data for this period. Chained Fisher indices have been calculated from the scanner data, (the RPI (within year) indices are fixed base Laspeyres ones), and have been found to fall by about 12 per cent for televisions (Silver and Heravi, 2001a), 10 per cent for washing machines (Table 7 below), 7.5 per cent for dishwashers, 15 per cent for cameras and 5 per cent for vacuum cleaners (Silver and Heravi, 2001b). These results are quite different from those for the RPI section and suggest that the washing machine disparity, as Diewert notes, may not be an anomaly. Traditional methods and data sources seem to be giving much higher rates for the CPI than those from scanner data, though the reasons for these discrepancies were not the subject of this study (Silver and Heravi (2002, p. 25)).

20.89 The above quotations summarize the results of many elementary aggregate index number studies that are based on the use of scanner data. These studies indicate that when detailed price and quantity data are used in order to compute superlative indices or hedonic indices for an expenditure category, the resulting measures of price change are often below the corresponding official statistical agency estimates of price change for that category.[45] Sometimes the measures of price change based on the use of scanner data are considerably below the corresponding official measures.[46] These results

[43] The numerical example given in paragraphs 20.91 to 20.99 illustrates this point.

[44] Balk (2002) provides the details for this sampling framework. Hausman (2002) is another recent author who stressed the importance of collecting quantity information along with price information at the elementary level.

[45] Recall also the results obtained by Koskimäki and Ylä-Jarkko (2003) that showed the Laspeyres index considerably above the corresponding Fisher index using Finnish scanner data.

[46] Scanner data studies do not, however, always show large potential biases in official CPIs. Masato Okamoto has informed us that a large-scale comparative study in Japan is under way. Using scanner data for about 250 categories of processed food and daily necessities collected over the period 1997 to 2000, it was found that the indices based on scanner data averaged only about 0.2 percentage points below the corresponding official indices per year. Japan uses the Dutot formula at the elementary level in its official CPI.

indicate that there may be large gains in the precision of elementary indices if a weighted sampling framework is adopted.

20.90 Is there a simple intuitive explanation for the above empirical results? A partial explanation may be possible by looking at the dynamics of item demand. In any market economy, there are firms and outlets that sell items that are either declining or increasing in price. Usually, the items that decline in price experience an increase in their volume of sales. Thus the expenditure shares that are associated with items that are declining in price usually increase, and conversely for the items that increase in price. Unfortunately, elementary indices cannot pick up the effects of this negative correlation between price changes and the induced changes in expenditure shares, because elementary indices depend only on prices and not on expenditure shares.

20.91 An example can illustrate the above point. Suppose that there are only three items in the elementary aggregate and that in period 0, the price of each item is $p_m^0=1$ and the expenditure share for each item is equal so that $s_m^0=1/3$ for $m=1,2,3$. Suppose that in period 1, the price of item 1 increases to $p_1^1=1+i$, the price of item 2 remains constant at $p_2^1=1$ and the price of item 3 decreases to $p_3^1=(1+i)^{-1}$ where the item 1 rate of increase in price is $i>0$. Suppose further that the expenditure share of item 1 decreases to $s_1^1=(1/3)-\sigma$ where σ is a small number between 0 and 1/3 and the expenditure share of item 3 increases to $s_3^1=(1/3)+\sigma$.[47] The expenditure share of item 2 remains constant at $s_2^1=1/3$. The five elementary indices defined in paragraphs 20.23 to 20.37 can all be written as functions of the item 1 inflation rate i (which is also the item 3 deflation rate) as follows:

$$P_J(p^0,p^1)=[(1-i)(1+i)^{-1}]^{1/3}=1\equiv f_J(i) \qquad (20.46)$$

$$P_C(p^0,p^1)=(1/3)(1+i)+(1/3)+(1/3)(1+i)^{-1}\equiv f_C(i) \qquad (20.47)$$

$$P_H(p^0,p^1)=[(1/3)(1+i)^{-1}+(1/3)+(1/3)(1+i)]^{-1} \equiv f_H(i) \qquad (20.48)$$

$$P_{CSW}(p^0,p^1)=[P_C(p^0,p^1)P_H(p^0,p^1)]^{1/2}\equiv f_{CSW}(i) \qquad (20.49)$$

$$P_D(p^0,p^1)=(1/3)(1+i)+(1/3)+(1/3)(1+i)^{-1}\equiv f_D(i) \qquad (20.50)$$

20.92 Note that in this particular example, the Dutot index $f_D(i)$ turns out to equal the Carli index $f_C(i)$. The second-order Taylor series approximations to the five elementary indices (20.46)–(20.50) are given by the approximations (20.51)–(20.55):

$$f_J(i)\approx 1 \qquad (20.51)$$

$$f_C(i)\approx 1+(1/3)i^2 \qquad (20.52)$$

$$f_H(i)\approx 1-(1/3)i^2 \qquad (20.53)$$

$$f_{CSW}(i)\approx 1 \qquad (20.54)$$

$$f_D(i)\approx 1+(1/3)i^2 \qquad (20.55)$$

Thus for small i, the Carli and Dutot indices will be slightly greater than 1,[48] the Jevons and the Carruthers–Sellwood–Ward indices will be approximately equal to 1 and the harmonic index will be slightly less than 1. Note that the first-order Taylor series approximation to all five indices is 1. Thus, to the accuracy of a first-order approximation, all five indices equal unity.

20.93 Now calculate the Laspeyres, Paasche and Fisher indices for the elementary aggregate:

$$P_L=(1/3)(1+i)+(1/3)+(1/3)(1+i)^{-1}\equiv f_L(i) \qquad (20.56)$$

$$P_P=\{[(1/3)-\sigma](1+i)+(1/3)+[(1/3)+\sigma](1+i)^{-1}\}^{-1} \equiv f_P(i) \qquad (20.57)$$

$$P_F=(P_LP_P)^{1/2}\equiv f_F(i) \qquad (20.58)$$

20.94 First-order Taylor series approximations to the above indices (20.56)–(20.58) around $i=0$ are given by the approximations (20.59)–(20.61):

$$f_L(i)\approx 1 \qquad (20.59)$$

$$f_P(i)\approx 1-2\sigma i \qquad (20.60)$$

$$f_F(i)\approx 1-\sigma i \qquad (20.61)$$

20.95 An ideal elementary index for the three items is the Fisher ideal index $f_F(i)$. The approximations (20.51)–(20.55) and (20.61) show that the Fisher index will lie below all five elementary indices by the amount σi, taking first-order approximations to all six indices. Thus all five elementary indices will have an approximate upward bias equal to σi compared to an ideal elementary aggregate.

20.96 Suppose that the annual item inflation rate for the item rising in price is equal to 10 per cent so that $i=0.10$ (and hence the rate of price decrease for the item

[47] The parameter σ is a measure of the degree of substitutability between the various items in the elementary aggregate. It is not precisely equal to the elasticity of substitution parameter σ which appeared in the Lloyd–Moulton formula explained in paragraphs 17.61 to 17.64 of Chapter 17. However, the bigger is the elasticity of substitution, the bigger will be the σ parameter which appears in this section. David E. Lebow and Jeremy B. Rudd note that the marketing literature finds that the elasticity of substitution between brands in a narrowly defined elementary aggregate is around 2.5 (which is much higher than the Cobb–Douglas case where the elasticity of substitution is 1): "And, Gerard Tellis (1988) analyzed the results from a large number of papers in the marketing literature that estimate cross brand elasticities and found a mean elasticity (after adjusting for certain biases in the results) of 2.5" (Lebow and Rudd (2003, pp. 167–168).

[48] Recall the approximate relationship (20.16) in paragraph 20.51 between the Dutot and Jevons indices. In the present numerical example, $\text{var}(e^0)=0$ whereas $\text{var}(e^1)>0$. This explains why the Dutot index is not approximately equal to the Jevons index in this numerical example.

decreasing in price is approximately 10 per cent as well). If the expenditure share of the increasing price item declines by 5 percentage points, then $\sigma=0.05$ and the annual approximate upward bias in all five elementary indices is $\sigma i=0.05\times0.10=0.005$ or half of a percentage point. If i increases to 20 per cent and σ increases to 10 per cent, then the approximate bias increases to $\sigma i=0.10\times0.20=0.02$ or 2 per cent. Note, however, if prices in period 2 revert to the prices prevailing in period 0, then the bias will reverse itself. Hence elementary bias of the type modelled above can only cumulate over successive periods if there are long-run trends in prices and market shares.[49]

20.97 The above example is highly simplified. More sophisticated models are capable of explaining at least some of the discrepancy between official elementary indices and superlative indices calculated by using scanner data for an expenditure class. Basically, elementary indices defined without using associated quantity or value weights are incapable of picking up shifts in expenditure shares that are induced by fluctuations in item prices.[50] In order to eliminate the problem of an inability to pick up shifts in expenditure shares that are induced by fluctuations in item prices, it will be necessary to sample values along with prices in both the base and comparison periods.

20.98 A few words of caution are, however, in order at this point. The use of chained superlative indices can lead to very biased results if there are large period-to-period fluctuations in prices and quantities compared to longer-run trends in prices. In long runs, large fluctuations can be induced by seasonal factors[51] or by temporary sales.[52]

[49] White's (2000) research into Canadian outlet substitution bias indicated that not only did discount outlets have lower prices for the same items, but they also had lower inflation rates over time.

[50] Put another way, elementary indices are subject to substitution or representativity bias. In the case of Cobb–Douglas preferences, however, the parameter σ in this section would be equal to zero and the Jevons elementary aggregate would be unbiased. But the results from the marketing literature (recall Tellis (1988)) indicate that σ will be greater than zero and hence that the Jevons elementary index will have an upward bias. Thus Lebow and Rudd's (2003, p. 167) estimate that elementary substitution bias is only around 0.05 percentage points per year if the Jevons formula is used seems rather low.

[51] For an example where the use of chained superlative indices leads to a tremendous downward bias induced by seasonal fluctuations, see Chapter 22.

[52] For an example where the use of chained superlative indices leads to a tremendous upward bias induced by periodic sales, see Robert C. Feenstra and Matthew D. Shapiro (2003):

> The reason for this is that periods of *low* prices (i.e., sales) attract high purchases only when they are accompanied by advertising, and this tends to occur in the final weeks of a sale. Thus, the initial price decline, when the sale starts, does not receive as much weight in the cumulative index as the final price *increase* when the sale ends. The demand behavior that leads to this upward bias of the chained Törnqvist – with higher purchases at the end of a sale – means that consumers are very likely purchasing goods for inventory accumulation. The only theoretically correct index to use in this type of situation is a fixed base index, as demonstrated in section 5.3 (Feenstra and Shapiro (2003, p. 125)).

The use of a fixed base index in these circumstances may, however, lead to results that are highly dependent on the choice of the base period. Other solutions that could be tried in this type of circumstance are either lengthening the period of time (as discussed in paragraphs 20.23 to 20.37) or using the moving year idea explained in Chapter 22 below.

20.99 In the following section, a simple regression-based approach to the construction of elementary indices is outlined. The importance of weighting the price quotes will again emerge from the analysis.

A simple stochastic approach to elementary indices

20.100 Recall the notation used in paragraphs 20.38 to 20.45 above. Suppose the prices of the M items for period 0 and 1 are approximately equal to the right-hand sides of equations (20.62) and (20.63):

$$p_m^0 \approx \beta_m; \quad m=1,\ldots,M \tag{20.62}$$

$$p_m^1 \approx \alpha\beta_m; \quad m=1,\ldots,M \tag{20.63}$$

where α and the β_m are positive parameters. Note that there are $2M$ prices on the left-hand sides of equations (20.62) and (20.63), but only $M+1$ parameters on the right-hand sides of these equations. The basic hypothesis in the model of price behaviour defined by equations (20.62) and (20.63) is that the two price vectors p^0 and p^1 are proportional (with $p^1=\alpha p^0$ so that α is the factor of proportionality) except for random multiplicative errors. Hence α represents the value of the underlying elementary price aggregate. Taking logarithms of both sides of equations (20.62) and (20.63), and adding some random errors e_m^0 and e_m^1 to the right-hand sides of the resulting equations, the following linear regression model is obtained:

$$\ln p_m^0=\delta_m+e_m^0; \quad m=1,\ldots,M \tag{20.64}$$

$$\ln p_m^1=\gamma+\delta_m+e_m^1; \quad m=1,\ldots,M \tag{20.65}$$

where

$$\gamma\equiv\ln\alpha \text{ and } \delta_m\equiv\ln_m; \quad m=1,\ldots,M \tag{20.66}$$

20.101 Note that equations (20.64) and (20.65) can be interpreted as a highly simplified hedonic regression model.[53] The only characteristic of each commodity is the commodity itself. This model is also a special case of the country product dummy method for making international comparisons between the prices of different countries.[54] A major advantage of this regression method for constructing an elementary price index is that standard errors for the index number α can be obtained. This advantage of the stochastic approach to index number theory was stressed by Selvanathan and Rao (1994).

20.102 It can be verified that the least squares estimator for γ is:

$$\gamma^*\equiv\sum_{m=1}^{M}\frac{1}{M}\ln\frac{p_m^1}{p_m^0} \tag{20.67}$$

[53] See Chapters 7, 8 and 21 for discussion of hedonic regression models.

[54] See Summers (1973). In our special case, there are only two "countries" which are the two observations on the prices of the elementary aggregate for two periods.

20.103 If γ^* is exponentiated, then the following estimator for the elementary aggregate α is obtained:

$$\alpha^* \equiv \prod_{m=1}^{M} \sqrt[M]{\frac{p_m^1}{p_m^0}} \equiv P_J(p^0, p^1) \qquad (20.68)$$

where $P_J(p^0, p^1)$ is the Jevons elementary price index defined in paragraphs 20.38 to 20.45 above. Thus the simple regression model defined by equations (20.64) and (20.65) leads to a justification for the use of the Jevons elementary index.

20.104 Consider the following unweighted least squares model:

$$\min_{\gamma,\delta\text{'s}} \sum_{m=1}^{M} (\ln p_m^0 - \delta_m)^2 + \sum_{m=1}^{M} (\ln p_m^1 - \gamma - \delta_m)^2 \qquad (20.69)$$

It can be verified that the γ solution to the unconstrained minimization problem (20.69) is the γ^* defined by equation (20.67).

20.105 There is a problem with the unweighted least squares model defined by equation (20.69), namely, that the logarithm of each price quote is given exactly the same weight in the model no matter what the expenditure on that item was in each period. This is obviously unsatisfactory since a price that has very little economic importance (i.e., a low expenditure share in each period) is given the same weight in the regression model as a very important item. Thus it is useful to consider the following weighted least squares model:[55]

$$\min_{\gamma,\delta\text{'s}} \sum_{m=1}^{M} s_m^0 (\ln p_m^0 - \delta_m)^2 + \sum_{m=1}^{M} s_m^1 (\ln p_m^1 - \gamma - \delta_m)^2 \qquad (20.70)$$

where the period t expenditure share on commodity m is defined in the usual manner as:

$$s_m^t \equiv \frac{p_m^t q_m^t}{\sum_{m=1}^{M} p_m^t q_m^t}; \quad t=0,1; \ m=1,\ldots,M \qquad (20.71)$$

In the model (20.70), the logarithm of each item price quotation in each period is weighted by its expenditure share in that period. Note that weighting prices by their economic importance is consistent with Theil's (1967, pp. 136–138) stochastic approach to index number theory.[56]

20.106 The γ solution to the minimization problem (20.70) is

$$\gamma^{**} \equiv \frac{\sum_{m=1}^{M} h(s_m^0, s_m^1) \ln \frac{p_m^1}{p_m^0}}{\sum_{m=1}^{M} h(s_i^0, s_i^1)} \qquad (20.72)$$

where

$$h(a,b) \equiv [(1/2)a^{-1} + (1/2)b^{-1}]^{-1} = 2ab/(a+b) \qquad (20.73)$$

and $h(a,b)$ is the harmonic mean of the numbers a and b. Thus γ^{**} is a share-weighted average of the logarithms of the price ratios p_m^1/p_m^0. If γ^{**} is exponentiated, then an estimator α^{**} for the elementary aggregate α is obtained.

20.107 How does α^{**} compare to the three ideal elementary price indices defined in paragraphs 20.11 to 20.22? It can be shown[57] that α^{**} approximates those three indices to the second order around an equal price and quantity point; i.e., for most data sets, α^{**} will be very close to the Fisher, Törnqvist and Walsh elementary indices.

20.108 In fact, a slightly different weighted least squares problem that is similar to the minimization problem (20.70) will generate exactly the Törnqvist elementary index. Consider the following weighted least squares model:

$$\min_{\gamma,\delta\text{'s}} \sum_{m=1}^{M} \frac{1}{2}(s_m^0 + s_m^1)(\ln p_m^0 - \delta_m)^2 + \sum_{m=1}^{M} \frac{1}{2}(s_m^0 + s_m^1)(\ln p_m^1 - \gamma - \delta_m)^2 \qquad (20.74)$$

Thus in the model (20.74), the logarithm of each item price quotation in each period is weighted by the arithmetic average of its expenditure shares in the two periods under consideration.

20.109 The γ solution to the minimization problem (20.74) is

$$\gamma^{***} = \sum_{m=1}^{M} \frac{1}{2}(s_m^0 + s_m^1) \ln \frac{p_m^1}{p_m^0} \qquad (20.75)$$

which is the logarithm of the Törnqvist elementary index. Thus the exponential of γ^{***} is precisely the Törnqvist price index.

20.110 The results in this section provide some weak support for the use of the Jevons elementary index, but they provide much stronger support for the use of weighted elementary indices of the type defined in paragraphs 20.11 to 20.22.

20.111 The results in this section also provide support for the use of value-based weights in hedonic regressions.

Conclusion

20.112 The main results in this chapter can be summarized as follows:

- In order to define a "best" elementary index number formula, it is necessary to have a target index number concept. In paragraphs 20.11 to 20.22, it is suggested that normal bilateral index number theory applies at the elementary level as well as at higher levels and hence the target concept should be one of the Fisher, Törnqvist or Walsh formulae.
- When aggregating the prices of the same narrowly defined item within a period, the narrowly defined unit value is a reasonable target price concept.

[55] Balk (1980c) considers a similar weighted least squares model for many periods but with different weights.

[56] Theil's approach is also pursued by Rao (1995), who considered a generalization of equation (20.70) to cover the case of many time periods.

[57] Using the techniques in Diewert (1978).

- The axiomatic approach to traditional elementary indices (i.e., no quantity or value weights are available) supports the use of the Jevons formula under all circumstances.[58] If the items in the elementary aggregate are homogeneous (i.e., they have the same unit of measurement), then the Dutot formula can be used. In the case of a heterogeneous elementary aggregate (the usual case), the Carruthers–Sellwood–Ward formula can be used as an alternative to the Jevons formula, but both will give much the same numerical answers.
- The Carli index has an upward bias and the harmonic index has a downward bias.
- The economic approach to elementary indices weakly supports the use of the Jevons formula.
- None of the five unweighted elementary indices is really satisfactory. A much more satisfactory approach would be to collect quantity or value information along with price information, and form sample superlative indices as the preferred elementary indices. If a chained superlative index is calculated, however, it should be examined for chain drift; i.e., a chained index should only be used if the data are relatively smooth and subject to long-term trends rather than short-term fluctuations.
- A simple hedonic regression approach to elementary indices supports the use of the Jevons formula, but a weighted hedonic regression approach is more satisfactory. The resulting index will closely approximate the ideal indices defined in paragraphs 20.11 to 20.22.

[58] One exception to this advice is when a price can be zero in one period and positive in another comparison period. In this situation, the Jevons index will fail and the corresponding item will have to be ignored in the elementary index, or the technique outlined in paragraphs 17.90 to 17.94 of Chapter 17 could be used.

QUALITY CHANGE AND HEDONICS

21

Introduction

21.1 Chapters 15 to 20 cover theoretical issues relating to the choice of index number formula and are based on a simplifying assumption: that the aggregation is over the same $i = 1, \ldots n$ matched items in the two periods being compared. A comparison of prices between two periods requires the quality of each item to remain the same between the periods. Price collectors are asked to match items with the same quality specification in each month, so that only "pure" price changes are measured, not price changes tainted by changes in the quality of what is consumed. In practice, the quality of what is consumed does change. Furthermore, new goods and services appear on the market, and their relative price changes may differ from the price changes of existing ones. In addition, the expenditure share of these new goods and services may be substantial. Paragraphs 21.2 to 21.60 outline a theoretical framework which extends the definition of items to include their quality characteristics. It helps to provide a background for the practical implementation of quality adjustment, discussed in Chapter 7, and for ways of dealing with item substitution and new goods, covered in Chapter 8.

New and disappearing items

21.2 The assumption in the previous chapters was that the same set of items was being compared in each period. This can be considered as sampling from all the matched items available in periods 0 and t – the intersection universe[1] which includes only matched items. Yet in many product areas old items disappear and new items appear. Constraining the sample to be drawn from this intersection universe is unrealistic. Outlets may sell an item in period 0, but it may not be sold in subsequent periods t.[2] New items may be introduced after period 0 which cannot be compared with a corresponding item in period 0. These items may be variants of the old existing ones, or provide totally new services which cannot be directly compared with anything that previously existed. This universe of all items in periods 0 and t is the dynamic double universe.

21.3 There is a third universe from which prices might be sampled: a replacement universe. The prices of a sample of items in period 0 are determined and their prices are monitored in subsequent periods. If the item is discontinued and there are no longer prices to record for the particular item, prices of a comparable replacement item may be used to continue the series of prices. This universe is a replacement universe that starts with the base period universe, but also includes one-to-one replacements when an item from the sample in the base period is missing in the current period.

21.4 Ideally the replacement item is comparable in quality to the item it replaces. When a comparable replacement is unavailable, a non-comparable one may be selected. Two approaches are possible. An explicit adjustment may be made to the price of either the old or the replacement item for the quality difference, since the two items are of different quality. Alternatively, an assumption may be made that the price change of the "old" item, had it continued to exist, would have been the same as that of the overall price change of a targeted group of items from the matched universe. In this second case, an implicit adjustment is being made about the effect on price of the quality change, namely that there is no difference between the price change for the matched group and the quality-adjusted price change of the old item, had it continued to exist.[3] Here, the problem of missing items is considered from the point of view of adjusting prices for quality differences.

21.5 Three practical difficulties emerge. First, there is the problem of explicit quality adjustment between a replacement and old item. The item is no longer consumed, a replacement is found which is not strictly comparable in quality, the differences in quality are identified, and a price has to be put on these differences if the series of prices for the replacement "new" item is to be used to continue the series of prices for the "old" item.

21.6 Second, in markets where the turnover of items is high, the sample space selected from the matched universe is going to become increasingly unrepresentative of the dynamic universe, as argued in Chapter 8. Even the replacement universe may be inappropriate, as it will comprise series which only replenish themselves when an item needs replacing. Given the rapidly changing technology in many product areas, this universe may be unrepresentative. In such cases, it may be preferable to collect prices, not from matched samples, but from a sample in each period of the main (or a representative sample of) items available, even though they are of a different quality. A comparison between the average prices of such items would be biased if, say, the quality

[1] The terminology is attributable to Dalén (1998a); see also Appendix 8.1.

[2] Its absence may be temporary, being say a seasonal item; ways of treating such temporarily unavailable items are considered in Chapter 8. The concern here, however, is with items that disappear on a permanent basis.

[3] Such methods and their assumption are discussed in detail in Chapter 7.

of the items were improving. The need for, and details of, mechanisms to remove the effects of such changes from the average price comparisons are discussed in Chapter 7.

21.7 Finally, there is the problem of new and disappearing goods and services. These are ones where the new item is not a variant of the old but provides a completely new service. It is not possible to use it as a replacement for an old item by adjusting a price for the quality differential because what it provides is, by definition, something new.

21.8 There are a number of approaches to quality adjustment and these are considered in Chapter 7. One of the approaches is to make explicit adjustments to prices for the quality difference between the old and replacement items using the coefficients or predicted values from hedonic regression equations. Hedonic regressions are regressions of the prices of individual models of a product on their characteristics, for example the prices of television sets on screen size, the possession of stereo or text-retrieval features, etc. The coefficients of such variables provide estimates of the marginal values of different quantifiable characteristics of the product. They can be used to adjust the price of a non-comparable replacement item for differences in its quality as compared with the old item – for example, the replacement television set may have text-retrieval facilities when the previous version did not. It is important that a clear understanding exists of the meaning of such estimated coefficients if they are to be used for quality adjustment, especially given that their use is being promoted.[4] To understand what these estimated parameters mean, it is first necessary to conceive of items as aggregates of their characteristics. Unlike items, characteristics have no separate price attached to them. The price of the item, however, is the price of a "tied" bundle of its characteristics. Then it is necessary to consider what might determine the prices of these characteristics: economic theory points towards examining the demand and supply for characteristics (discussed in paragraphs 21.13 to 21.21) and the interaction of the two to determine an equilibrium price (see paragraphs 21.22 and 21.23). Having developed the analytical framework for such prices, it is then necessary to see what interpretation the economic theory framework allows us to put on these calculated coefficients (see paragraphs 21.24 to 21.28).

21.9 In Chapter 7, paragraphs 7.125 to 7.158, two main approaches were advised for the treatment of product areas with rapid turnover of items. If the sample in period 0 is soon outdated, the matched universe and even replacement universe will become increasingly unrepresentative of the double universe, and repeated sampling from the double universe is required. In this case, either chained indices were advised (see paragraphs 7.153 to 7.158), or one of a number of hedonic indices (see paragraphs 7.132 to 152). Such indices differ from the use of hedonic regression for adjusting prices for quality differences for a missing item. These indices use hedonic regressions, say by including a dummy variable for time on the right-hand side of the equation, to estimate the quality-adjusted price change, as outlined below and in Chapter 7, and build upon the theory in Chapter 17 and paragraphs 21.13 to 21.36. The economic theory of price indices outlined in Chapter 17 is developed to include those tied bundles of good that can be defined in terms of their characteristics as an item in the consumer's utility function. Theoretical consumer price indices are defined which include changes in the prices of characteristics. As with the price indices for goods considered in Chapter 17, there are many formulations that such indices can take, and analogous issues and formulae arise when discussing alternative approaches in paragraphs 21.40 to 21.60.

21.10 The estimation of hedonic regressions and the testing of their statistical properties are facilitated by the availability of user-friendly, yet powerful, statistical and econometric software. There are many standard problems in the estimation of regression equations, which can be resolved using the diagnostic tests available in such software, as discussed by Kennedy (1998) and Maddala (1988). There are, however, matters of functional form, the use of weighted least squares estimators and specification that are specific to the estimation of hedonic equations. Many of these are illustrated in Chapter 7, while Appendix 21.1 to this chapter considers some of the theoretical aspects; see also Gordon (1990), Griliches (1990) and Triplett (1990).

21.11 Finally, in paragraphs 21.61 to 21.68, economic theory is used to advise on the problem of new and disappearing goods and services. This problem arises where differences between existing goods and services and the new goods and services are substantive in nature and cannot be meaningfully compared, even with a quality adjustment. The economic theory of reservation prices is considered and some concern about its practical implementation is expressed.

Hedonic prices and implicit markets

Items as tied bundles of characteristics

21.12 A hedonic regression is a regression equation which relates the prices of items, p, to the quantities of characteristics, given by the vector $z = (z_1, z_2, \ldots, z_n)$, i.e.

$$p(z) = p(z_1, z_2, \ldots, z_n) \qquad (21.1)$$

where the items are defined in terms of varying amounts of their characteristics. In practice, what will be observed for each item (variant of the product) is its price, its characteristics, and possibly the quantity and thus value sold. Empirical work in this area has been concerned with two issues: estimating how the price of an item changes as a result of unit changes in each characteristic, that is, the estimated coefficients of equation (21.1); and estimating the demand and supply functions for each characteristic. The depiction of an item as a basket of characteristics, each characteristic having it own implicit (shadow) price, requires in turn the specification of a market for such characteristics, since prices result from the workings of markets. Houthakker (1952), Becker

[4] See Boskin, Dullberger, Gordon, Griliches and Jorgenson (1996 and 1998) and Schultze and Mackie (2002).

(1965), Lancaster (1966) and Muth (1966) have all identified the demand for items in terms of their characteristics. The sale of an item is the sale of a tied bundle of characteristics to a consumer whose economic behaviour in choosing between items is depicted as one of choosing between bundles of characteristics.[5] Rosen (1974) further developed the analysis by providing a structural market framework in terms of both producers and consumers. There are two sides: demand and supply. How much of each characteristic is supplied and consumed is determined by the interaction of the demand for characteristics by consumers and the supply of characteristics by producers. These are considered in turn.

The consumer or demand side

21.13 Consider Figure 21.1, from Triplett (1987, p. 634), which shows a simplified characteristics-space between only two characteristics. The hedonic surfaces p_1 and p_2 trace out all the combinations of the two characteristics z_1 and z_2 that can be purchased at prices p_1 and p_2. An indifference curve q_j^* maps the combinations of z_1 and z_2 that the consumer is indifferent about purchasing; that is, the consumer will derive the same utility from any point on the curve. The tangency of q_j^* with p_1 at A is the solution to the utility maximization problem for a given budget (price p_1) and given tastes (reflected in q_j^*).

21.14 The slope of the hedonic surface is the marginal cost to the consumer of acquiring the combination of characteristics and the slope of the utility function is the marginal utility gained from their purchase; the tangency at A is the utility-maximizing combination of characteristics to be purchased at that price. If consumers purchased any other combination of characteristics in the space of Figure 21.1, it would either cost them more to do so or lead to a lower level of utility. Position A′, for example, has more of both z_1 and z_2, and the consumer receives a higher level of utility, being on q_j, but the consumer also has to have a higher budget and pays more, p_2, for being there. Figure 17.1 in Chapter 17 illustrates in goods-space how the consumer would choose between different combinations of outputs, q_1 and q_2. The characteristics-space problem in Figure 21.1 is analogous to the goods-space one, with consumers choosing between combinations of characteristics z_1 and z_2. Note that the hedonic surface depicted in Figure 21.1 is non-linear, so relative characteristic prices are not fixed. The consumer with tastes q_k^* chooses characteristic set B at p_1. Thus the data observed in the market depend on the set of tastes. Triplett (2002) has argued that if tastes were all the same then only one model of, say, a personal computer would be purchased. But in the real world more than one model does exist, reflecting heterogeneous tastes and income levels. Rosen (1974) shows that, of all the characteristic combinations and prices at which they may be offered, the hedonic surface traces out an envelope[6] of tangencies, including q_j^* and q_k^* on p_1 in Figure 21.1. This envelope is simply a description of the locus of the points chosen. Since these points are what economic theory tells us will be observed in the market, assuming rational utility-maximizing consumers, these are the points that will be used to estimate the hedonic regression. Note further that points A and B alone will not allow the regression to determine the price of z_1 relative to z_2 since the observed data will be two combinations of outputs at the same price. The locus of points on an expansion path AA′ would, however, allow this to be determined. Of course, there may be expansion paths for consumers with different tastes, such as B, and this may give rise to conflicting valuations. The overall parameter estimates determined by the regression from transactions observed in the market are an amalgam of such data. Of course, this is just a reflection of the reality of economic life. What arises from this exposition is the fact that the form of the hedonic function is determined in part by the distribution of buyers and their tastes in the market.

Figure 21.1 Consumption and production decisions for combinations of characteristics

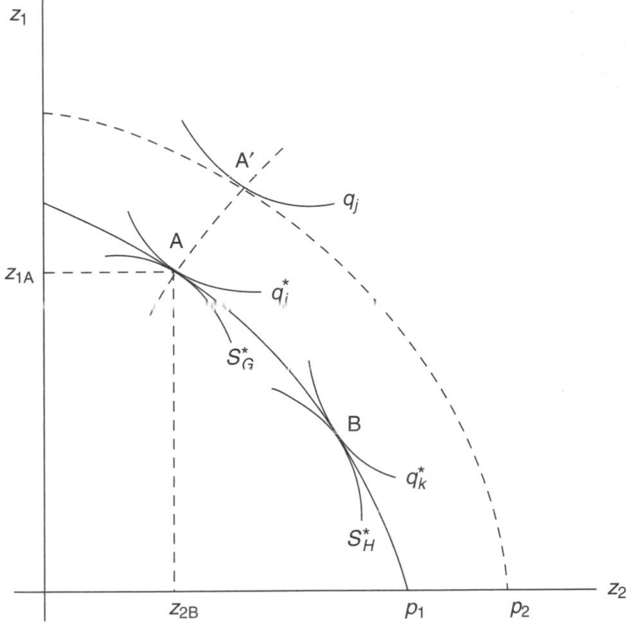

21.15 The exposition is now formalized to include parameters for tastes and a numeraire commodity[7] against which combinations of other aggregates are

[5] The range of items is assumed to be continuous in terms of the combinations of characteristics that define them. A non-continuous case can be depicted where the price functions are piece-wise linear and an optimal set of characteristics is obtained by combining the purchases of different items; see Lancaster (1971) and Gorman (1980).

[6] Note that an envelope is more formally defined by letting $f(x, y, k) = 0$ be an implicit function of x and y. The form of the function is assumed to depend on k, the tastes in this case. A different curve corresponds to each value of k in the xy plane. The envelope of this family of curves is itself a curve with the property that it is tangent to each member of the family. The equation of the envelope is obtained by taking the partial derivative of $f(x, y, k)$ with respect to k and eliminating k from the two equations $f(x, y, k) = 0$ and $\partial f(x, y, k)/\partial k = 0$; see Osgood (1925).

[7] The numeraire commodity represents all other goods and services consumed – it represents the "normal" non-hedonic commodities. The price of x is set equal to unity, and $p(z)$ and income are measured using that unit.

selected, following Rosen (1974). The hedonic function $p(z)$ describes variation in the market price of the items in terms of their characteristics. The consumer purchase decision is assumed to be based on utility maximization behaviour, the utility function being given by $U(z, x; \alpha)$ where x is a numeraire commodity, the maximization of utility being subject to a budget constraint given by income y measured as $y = x + p(z)$ (the amount spent on the numeraire commodity and the hedonic products) and α is a vector of the features of individual consumers which describe their tastes. Naturally x in the utility function can be described in terms of $y - p(z)$. Consumers maximize their utility by selecting a combination of quantities of x and characteristics z subject to a budget constraint. The market is assumed to be competitive and consumers are described as "price takers"; they only purchase the one item, so their purchase decision does not influence the market price. The price they pay for a combination of characteristics, vector z, is given by $p(z)$. Since they are optimizing consumers, the combination chosen is such that:

$$[\partial U(z, y - p(z); \alpha)/\partial z_i]/[\partial U(z, y - p(z); \alpha)/\partial x] = \partial p(z)/\partial z_i \equiv p_i(z) \qquad (21.2)$$

where $\partial p(z)/\partial z_i$ is the first derivative of the hedonic function (21.1) with respect to each z characteristic. The coefficients of the hedonic function are equal to their shadow prices, p_i, which equal the utility derived from that characteristic relative to the numeraire good for given budgets and tastes.

21.16 A *value function* θ can be defined as the value of expenditure a consumer with tastes α is willing to pay for alternative values of z at a given utility u and income y, represented by $\theta(z; u, y, \alpha)$. It defines a family of indifference curves relating the z_i to forgone x, "money". For an individual characteristic z_1, θ is the marginal rate of substitution between z_i and money, or the implicit marginal valuation that the consumer with tastes α puts on z_i at a given utility level and income. It is an indication of the reservation demand[8] price for an additional unit of z_i.[9] The price in the market is $p(z)$ and utility is maximized when $\theta(z; u, y, \alpha) = p(z)$, i.e. the purchase takes place where the surface of the indifference curve θ is tangent to the hedonic price surface. If different buyers have different value functions (tastes), some will buy more of a characteristic than others for a given price function, as illustrated in Figure 21.1.

21.17 The joint distribution function of tastes and income sets out a family of value functions each of which, when tangential to the price function, depicts a purchase and simultaneously defines the price function whose envelope is the market hedonic price function. The points of purchase traced out by the hedonic function thus depend on the budget and the tastes of the individual consumer purchasing an individual set of characteristics. If demand functions are to be traced out, the joint probability distribution of consumers with particular budgets and tastes occurring in the market needs to be specified, i.e., $F(y, \alpha)$. This function, along with equation (21.1) allows the demand equations to be represented for each characteristic.

The producer or supply side

21.18 Figure 21.1, reproduced from Triplett (1987), also shows the production side. Consider a revenue-maximizing producer whose revenue maximization problem is given by:[10]

$$R(p, v) \equiv \max_q \left\{ \sum_{n=1}^{N} p_n q_n : (q) \text{ belongs to } S(v) \right\} \qquad (21.3)$$

where $R(p, v)$ is the maximum value of output, $\sum_{n=1}^{N} p_n q_n$, that the establishment can produce, given that it faces the vector of output prices p and given that the vector of inputs v is available for use, using the period t technology. Recall that Figure 17.1 illustrates in goods-space how the producer would choose between different combinations of outputs, q_1 and q_2. In Figure 21.1 the characteristics-space problem is one of producers choosing between combinations of z_1 and z_2 to produce for a particular level of technology and inputs $S(v)$. For a particular producer with level of inputs and technology S_G^* facing a price surface p_1, the optimal production combination is at A. However, a different producer with technology and inputs S_H^* facing a price surface p_1 would produce at B. At these points, the marginal cost of z_1 with respect to z_2 is equal to its marginal price from the hedonic surface, as depicted by the tangency of the point. Production under these circumstances at any other combination would not be optimal. The envelope of tangencies such as S_G^* and S_H^* trace out the production decisions that would be observed in the market from optimizing, price-taking producers and are used as data for estimating the hedonic regressions. The hedonic function can be seen to be determined, in part, by the distribution of technologies of producers, including their output scale.

21.19 Rosen (1974) formalizes the producer side whereby price-taking producers are assumed to have cost functions described by $C(Q, z; \tau)$,[11] where $Q = Q(z)$ is the output scale – the number of units produced by an establishment offering specifications of an item with characteristics z. The producers have to decide which items to produce, i.e., which package of z. To do this, a cost minimization problem is solved which requires τ, equivalent to $S(v)$ above, a vector of the technology of each producer that describes the output combinations each producer can produce with given input costs, using that producer's factors of production and the factor prices. It is the variation in τ across producers that

[8] This is the hypothetical price which just makes the demand for the commodity equal to zero; that is, it is the price which, when inserted into the demand function, sets demand to zero. The utility function is assumed to be strictly concave, so that θ is concave in z and the value function is increasing in z_i at a decreasing rate.

[9] The utility function is assumed strictly concave so that θ is concave in z and the value function is increasing in z_i at a decreasing rate.

[10] The time superscripts are not relevant in this context.

[11] The cost function is assumed to be convex with no indivisibilities, and the marginal cost of producing one more item of a given combination of characteristics is assumed to be positive and increasing. Similarly, the marginal cost of increasing production of each component characteristic is positive and non-decreasing.

distinguishes producer A's decision as to which combination of z to produce from that of producer B in Figure 21.1. Producers are optimizers who seek to maximize profits, given by:

$$Qp(z) - C(Q, z; \tau) \qquad (21.4)$$

by selecting Q and z optimally. The supplying market is assumed to be competitive, and producers are price takers so the producer cannot influence price by a production decision. The producer's decision as to how much to produce of each z is determined by the price of z, assuming that the producer can vary Q and z in the short run.[12] Dividing the expression (21.4) by Q and setting it equal to zero, the first-order profit-maximizing conditions are given by:

$$\frac{\partial p}{\partial z_i} = p_i = \frac{C_{zi}(Q, z; \tau)}{Q} \qquad (21.5)$$

where $p = p(z_1, z_2, \ldots, z_n)$ from equation (21.1).

21.20 The marginal *unit revenue* from producing characteristic z_i is given by its shadow price in the price function and its marginal cost of production. In the producer case, the probability distribution of the technologies of firms $G(\tau)$ is necessary if the overall quantity supplied of items with given sets of characteristics is to be revealed. Since it is a profit maximization problem to select the optimal combination of characteristics to produce, marginal revenue from the additional attributes must equal their marginal cost of production per unit sold. Quantities are produced up to the point where unit revenues $p(z)$ equal their marginal production cost, evaluated at the optimum bundle of characteristics supplied.

21.21 While a value function was considered for consumers, producers require an *offer function* $\phi(z; \pi, \tau)$. The offer price is the price the seller is willing to accept for various values of z at constant profit level π, when quantities produced are optimally chosen, while $p(z)$ is the maximum price obtainable from those models in the market. Producer equilibrium is characterized by a tangency between a profit characteristics indifference surface and the market characteristics price surface where $p_i(z_i) = \varphi_{zi}(z; \pi z; \pi)$ and $p_i(z_i) = \varphi_{zi}(z; \pi z; \pi)$. Since there is a distribution of technologies $G(\tau)$, the producer equilibrium is characterized by a family of offer functions that envelop the market hedonic price function. The varying τ will depend on different factor prices for items produced in different countries, multi-product firms with economies of scale and differences in the technology, be it the quality of capital, labour or intermediate inputs and their organization. A family of production surfaces is defined for different values of τ.

[12] Rosen (1974) considered two other supply characterizations: the short run in which only M is variable and the long run in which plants can be added and retired. The determination of equilibrium supply and demand is not straightforward. A function $p(z)$ is required such that market demand for all z will equate to market supply and clear the market. But demand and supply depend on the whole $p(z)$, since any adjustment to prices to equate demand and supply for one combination of items will induce substitutions and changes for others. Rosen (1974, pp. 44–48) discusses this in some detail.

Equilibrium

21.22 The theoretical framework first defines each item as a point on a plane of several dimensions made up by the $z_1, z_2, \ldots, z_n$ quality characteristics; each item is a combination of values $z_1, z_2, \ldots, z_n$. If only two characteristics define the item, then each point in the positive space of Figure 21.1 would define an item. The characteristics are not bought individually, but as bundles of characteristics tied together to make up an item. It is assumed that the markets are differentiated so that there is a wide range of choices to be made.[13] The market is also assumed to be perfectly competitive, with consumers and producers as price takers undertaking optimizing behaviour to decide which items (tied sets of characteristics) to buy and sell. Competitive markets and optimizing behaviour are assumed so that the quantity demanded of an item equals the quantity supplied. Since the items are made up of characteristics z, the quantity demanded of all characteristics z must equal their quantity supplied. It has been shown that consumers' and producers' choices or "locations" on the plane will be dictated by consumer tastes and producer technology. Tauchen and Witte (2001, p. 4) show that the hedonic price function will differ across markets in accordance with the means and variances (and in some cases also higher moments) of the distributions of household and firm characteristics.

21.23 Rosen (1974, p. 44) notes that a buyer and seller are perfectly matched when their respective value and offer functions are tangential to each other. The common gradient at that point is given by the gradient of the market clearing implicit price function $p(z)$. The consumption and production decisions are seen in the value and offer functions to be jointly determined, for given $p(z)$, by $F(y, \alpha)$ and $G(\tau)$. In competitive markets there is a simultaneity in the determination of the hedonic equation, as the distribution of $F(y, \alpha)$ and $G(\tau)$ helps determine the quantities demanded and supplied, as well as the slope of the function. Although the decisions made by consumers and producers are as price takers, the prices taken are those from the hedonic function. There is a sense in which the hedonic function and its shadow prices emerge from the operations of the market. The product markets implicitly reveal the hedonic function. Since consumers and producers are optimizers in competitive markets, the hedonic function, in principle, gives the minimum price of any bundle of characteristics. Given all of this, Rosen (1974, p. 44) asked: What do hedonic prices mean?

What hedonic prices mean

21.24 It would be convenient if, for CPI construction, the estimated coefficients from hedonic regressions were estimates of the marginal utility based on a characteristic or user value. But theory tells us that this is not the case and that the interpretation is not clear.

21.25 There used to be an erroneous perception, in the 1960s, that the coefficients from hedonic methods

[13] So that choices among combinations of z are continuous, assume further that z possesses continuous second-order derivatives.

represented user values as opposed to resource costs. Rosen (1974), as has been shown, found that hedonic coefficients generally reflect both user values and resource costs, both supply and demand situations. The ratios of these coefficients may reflect consumers' marginal rates of substitution or producers' marginal rates of substitution (transformation) for characteristics. There is what is referred to in econometrics as an "identification" problem in which the observed prices and quantities are jointly determined by supply and demand considerations, and their underlying sources cannot be separated. The data collected on prices jointly arise from variations in demand by different consumers with different tastes and preferences, and from variations in supply by producers with different technologies.

21.26 First, it is necessary to come to terms with this simultaneity problem. Hedonic regressions are an increasingly important analytical tool, one implicitly promoted by the attention given to it in this manual, but also promoted in manuals by organizations such as the OECD (see Triplett (2002)), Eurostat (2001a) and widely used by the United States Bureau of Labor Statistics; see Kokoski, Waehrer and Rozaklis (2001) and Moulton (2001). So how do economists writing on the subject shrug their intellectual shoulders in the light of these findings?

Rosen (1974, p. 43) refers to the hedonic function as:

> ... a joint envelope of a family of value functions and another family of offer functions. An envelope function by itself reveals nothing about the underlying members that generate it; and they in turn constitute the generating structure of the observations.

Griliches (1988, p. 120) notes the following:

> My own view is that what the hedonic approach tries to do is to estimate aspects of the budget constraint facing consumers, allowing thereby the estimation of "missing" prices when quality changes. It is not in the business of estimating utility functions per se, though it can also be useful for these purposes... what is being estimated is the actual locus of intersection of the demand curves of different consumers with varying tastes and the supply curves of different producers with possible varying technologies of production. One is unlikely, therefore, to be able to recover the underlying utility and cost functions from such data alone, except in very special circumstances.

Triplett (1987) states:

> It is well-established – but still not widely understood – that the form of $h(\cdot)$ [the hedonic function] cannot be derived from the form of $Q(\cdot)$ and $t(\cdot)$ [utility and production functions], nor does $h(\cdot)$ represent a "reduced form" of supply and demand functions derived from $Q(\cdot)$ and $t(\cdot)$.

Diewert (2003a, p. 320), with his focus on the consumer side, says:

> Thus I am following Muellbauer's (1974, p. 977) example where he says that his "approach is unashamedly one-sided; only the demand side is treated ...". Its subject matter is therefore rather different from that of the recent paper by Sherwin Rosen. The supply side and simultaneity problems which may arise are ignored.

21.27 Diewert's (2003a) approach is of interest since the derivation of estimates of hedonic coefficients is one that follows the demand side only. It is a useful exercise to consider the conditions under which the hedonic coefficients are determined by only demand-side or supply-side factors – the circumstances under which clear explanations would be valid. The problem is that because the coefficients of a hedonic function are the outcome of the interaction of consumer and producer optimizing conditions, it is not possible to interpret the function only in terms of, say, producer marginal costs or consumer marginal values. Suppose, however, that the *production technology* τ is the same for each producing establishment. Buyers differ but sellers are identical. Then instead of there being a confusing family of offer functions, there is a unique offer function with the hedonic function describing the prices of characteristics the firm will supply with the given ruling technology to the current mixture of tastes. The function $p(z)$ becomes the offer function since there is no distribution of τ to confuse it. There are different tastes on the consumer side, so what appears in the market is the result of firms trying to satisfy consumer preferences, all for a constant technology and profit level; the structure of supply is revealed by the hedonic price function. In Figure 21.1 only the expansion path traced out by, say, S_H^* akin to AA′, would be revealed. Now suppose that sellers differ, but that buyers' tastes α are identical. Here the family of value functions collapses to be revealed as the hedonic function $p(z)$ which identifies the structure of demand, such as AA′ in Figure 21.1.[14] Triplett (1987, p. 632) notes that of these possibilities, uniformity of technologies is the most likely, especially when access to technology is unrestricted in the long run, while uniformity of tastes is unlikely. There may, of course, be segmented markets where tastes are more uniform, to which specific sets of items are tailored and for which hedonic equations can be estimated for individual segments.[15]

21.28 The analysis in paragraphs 21.12 to 21.27 demonstrates the ambiguity surrounding the interpretation of hedonic coefficients. This analysis is needed since issues relating to the estimation of the underlying supply and demand functions for characteristics have implications for the estimation of hedonic functions. Appendix 21.1 considers identification and estimation issues in this light. The next section provides an alternative theoretical derivation, based on Diewert (2003a), which shows the assumptions required for a demand-based (consumer-based) interpretation.

[14] Correspondingly, if the supply curves were perfectly inelastic, so that a change in price would not affect the supply of any of the differentiated products, then the variation in prices underlying the data and feeding the hedonic estimates would be determined by demand factors. The coefficients would provide estimates of user values. Similarly, if the supplying market were perfectly competitive, the estimates would be of resource costs. None of the price differences between differentiated items would be attributable to, say, novel configurations of characteristics, and no temporary monopoly profit would be achieved as a reward for this, or as a result of the exercise of market power; see Berndt (1991).

[15] Berry, Levinsohn and Pakes (1995) provide a detailed and interesting example for cars, in which makes are used as market segments. Tauchen and Witte (2001) provide a systematic theoretical study of estimation issues for supply, demand and hedonic functions, where consumers and producers and their transactions are indexed across communities.

An alternative, consumer-based hedonic theoretical formulation

21.29 This section takes a consumer-based approach to deriving theoretical hedonic functions. It assumes:

- that every consumer has the *same separable sub-utility function*, $f(z_1, \ldots, z_N)$ that gives the consumer the sub-utility $Z=f(z)$ from the purchase of one unit of the complex hedonic commodity that has the vector of characteristics $z \equiv (z_1, \ldots, z_N)$;[16]
- the sub-utility that the consumer gets from consuming Z units of the hedonic commodity is combined with the consumption of X units of a composite "other" commodity to give the consumer an overall utility of $u=U^t(X, Z)$ in period t, where U^t is the period t "macro" utility function. Rosen (1974, p. 38) normalized the price of X to be unity. This is not required in the present approach. Instead, there is an explicit period t price, p^t, for one unit of the general consumption commodity X.

21.30 The approach starts by considering the set of X and Z combinations that can yield the consumer's period t utility level, u^t. This is the set $\{(X, Z): U^t(X, Z)=u^t\}$, which is the consumer's period t indifference curve over equivalent combinations of the general consumption commodity X and the hedonic commodity Z. The equation $U^t(X, Z)=u^t$ for X is solved as a function of u^t and Z; i.e.[17]

$$X=g^t(u^t, Z) \tag{21.6}$$

It is assumed that the indifference curve slopes downward, and the stronger assumption is made that g^t is differentiable with respect to Z and

$$\partial g^t(u^t, Z)/\partial Z<0 \tag{21.7}$$

Let p^t and P^t be the prices for one unit of X and Z, respectively, in period t. The *consumer's period* t *expenditure minimization problem* may be defined as follows:

$$\begin{aligned} &\min_{X,Z}\{p^tX+P^tZ: X=g^t(u^t, Z)\} \\ &=\min_Z\{p^tg^t(u^t, Z)+P^tZ\} \end{aligned} \tag{21.8}$$

The first-order necessary condition for Z to solve equation (21.8) is:

$$p^t\partial g^t(u^t, Z)/\partial Z+P^t=0 \tag{21.9}$$

Equation (21.9) can be rearranged to give the price of the hedonic aggregate P^t as a function of the period t utility level u^t and the price of general consumption p^t:

$$P^t=-p^t\partial g^t(u^t, Z)/\partial Z>0 \tag{21.10}$$

where the inequality follows from assumption (21.7). The right-hand side of the equation (21.10) can now be interpreted as the consumer's *period* t *willingness to pay price function:*

$$w^t(Z, u^t, p^t) \equiv -p^t\partial g^t(u^t, Z)/\partial Z \tag{21.11}$$

21.31 Thus, for each point (indexed by Z) on the consumer's period t indifference curve, equation (21.11) gives the amount of money the consumer would be willing to pay per unit of Z in order to stay on the same indifference curve, which is indexed by the utility level u^t. The *period* t *willingness to pay value function* v^t can now be defined as the product of the quantity of Z consumed times the corresponding per unit willingness to pay price, $w^t(Z, u^t, p^t)$:

$$v^t(Z, u^t, p^t) \equiv Zw^t(Z, u^t, p^t)=-Zp^t\partial g^t(u^t, Z)/\partial Z \tag{21.12}$$

where the last equality follows using equation (21.11). The function v^t is the counterpart to Rosen's (1974, p. 38) value or bid function; it gives us the amount of money the consumer is willing to pay in order to consume Z units. All the above algebra has an interpretation that is independent of the hedonic model; it is simply an exposition of how to derive a willingness to pay price and value function using a consumer's preferences defined over two commodities.

21.32 It is assumed now that the consumer has a separable sub-utility function, $f(z_1, \ldots, z_N)$, which gives the consumer the sub-utility $Z=f(z)$ from the purchase of one unit of the complex hedonic commodity[18] that has the vector of characteristics $z \equiv (z_1, \ldots, z_N)$. Note that it has been assumed that the function f is time invariant. Let the consumer's period t utility function be $U^t(X, f(z))$. The above algebra on willingness to pay is still valid. In particular, the new period t willingness to pay price function, for a particular model with characteristics $z=(z_1, \ldots, z_N)$, is:

$$w^t(f(z), u^t, p^t) \equiv -p^t\partial g^t(u^t, f(z))/\partial Z \tag{21.13}$$

The new period t willingness to pay value function (which is the amount of money the consumer is willing

[16] It is not assumed that all possible models exist in the marketplace. In fact, we will assume that only a finite set of models exist in each period. It is assumed, however, that the consumer has preferences over all possible models, where each model is indexed by its vector of characteristics, $z=(z_1, \ldots, z_N)$. Thus each consumer will prefer a potential model with characteristics vector $z^1=(z_1^1, \ldots, z_N^1)$ over another potential model with the characteristics vector $z^2=(z_1^2, \ldots, z_N^2)$ if and only if $f(z^1)>f(z^2)$.

[17] If the period t indifference curve intersects both axes, then $g^t(u^t, Z)$ will only be defined for a range of non-negative Z up to an upper bound.

[18] If a consumer purchases, say, two units of a model at price P that has characteristics $z_1, \ldots, z_N$, then we can model this situation by introducing an artificial model that sells at price $2P$ and has characteristics $2z_1, \ldots, 2z_N$. Thus the hedonic surface, $Z=f(z)$, consists of only the most efficient models including the artificial models. We do not assume that $f(z)$ is a quasi-concave or concave function of z. In normal consumer demand theory, $f(z)$ can be assumed to be quasi-concave without loss of generality because linear budget constraints and the assumption of perfect divisibility will imply that "effective" indifference curves enclose convex sets. As Rosen (1974, pp. 37–38) points out, however, in the case of hedonic commodities, the various characteristics cannot be untied. Moreover, perfect divisibility cannot be assumed and not all possible combinations of characteristics will be available in the marketplace. Thus the usual assumptions made in "normal" consumer demand theory are not satisfied in the hedonic context. Note also that while we place a smoothness assumption on the macro functions $g^t(u, Z)$, namely the existence of the partial derivative $\partial g^t(u, Z)/\partial Z)$, we do not place any smoothness restrictions on the hedonic sub-utility function $f(z)$.

to pay to have the services of a model with characteristics vector z) is:

$$v^t(f(z), u^t, p^t) \equiv f(z)w^t(f(z), u^t, p^t) = -f(z)p^t \partial g^t(u^t, f(z))/\partial Z \qquad (21.14)$$

21.33 Now suppose that there are K^t models available to the consumer in period t, where model k sells at the per unit price of P_k^t and has the vector of characteristics $z_k^t \equiv (z_{1k}^t, \ldots, z_{Nk}^t)$ for $k=1,2,\ldots,K$. If the consumer purchases a unit of model k in period t, then the model price P_k^t can be equated to the appropriate willingness to pay value defined by equation (21.14), where z is replaced by z_k^t; i.e., the following equation should hold:

$$P_k^t = -f(z_k^t)p^t \partial g^t(u^t, f(z_k^t))/\partial Z \quad \text{for } t=1,\ldots,T; k=1,\ldots,K^t \qquad (21.15)$$

What is the meaning of the separability assumption? Suppose the hedonic commodity is a car and suppose that there are only three characteristics: number of seats in the vehicle, fuel economy and horsepower. The separability assumption means that the consumer can trade off these three characteristics and determine the utility of any car with any mix of these three characteristics, independently of his or her other choices of commodities. In particular, the utility ranking of car models is independent of the number of children the consumer might have or what the price of petrol might be. Obviously, the separability assumption is not likely to be exactly satisfied in the real world, but this somewhat restrictive assumption is required to make our model tractable.

21.34 Another aspect of our model needs some further explanation. It is being explicitly assumed that consumers cannot purchase fractional units of each model.; they can purchase only a non-negative integer amount of each model. That is, indivisibilities are being explicitly assumed on the supply side of our model. Thus, in each period, there is only a finite number of models of the hedonic commodity available. While the consumer is assumed to have continuous preferences over all possible combinations of characteristics $(z_1, \ldots, z_N)$ in each period, there is only a finite number of isolated models available on the market.

21.35 At this point, the model is further specialized. It is assumed that every consumer has the same hedonic sub-utility function[19] $f(z)$ and consumer i has the following *linear indifference curve macro utility function* in period t:

$$g_i^t(u_i^t, Z) \equiv -a^t Z + b_i^t u_i^t \quad \text{for } t=1,\ldots,T \text{ and } i=1,\ldots,I \qquad (21.16)$$

where a^t and b_i^t are positive constants.

For each period t and each consumer i, the period t indifference curve between combinations of X and Z is linear, with the constant slope $-a^t$ being the same for all consumers.[20] Note that this slope is allowed to change over time. Now differentiate equation (21.16) with respect to Z and substitute this partial derivative into equation (21.15). The resulting equation is:[21]

$$P_k^t = p^t a^t f(z_k^t) \quad \text{for } t=1,\ldots,T \text{ and } k=1,\ldots,K^t \qquad (21.17)$$

Define the aggregate price of one unit of Z in period t as:[22]

$$r_t \equiv p^t a^t \quad \text{for} \quad t=1,\ldots,T \qquad (21.18)$$

Now substitute equation (21.18) into equation (21.17) in order to obtain our *basic system of hedonic equations*.[23]

$$P_k^t = r_t f(z_k^t) \quad \text{for } t=1,\ldots,T \text{ and } k=1,\ldots,K^t \qquad (21.19)$$

21.36 All that is needed is to postulate a functional form for the hedonic sub-utility function f and add a stochastic specification to equation (21.19) to yield a basic hedonic regression model. The unknown parameters in f along with the period t hedonic price parameters r_t can then be estimated.[24] It is possible to generalize the above model, but get the same model

[19] The sameness assumption is very strong and needs some justification. This assumption is entirely analogous with the assumption that consumers have the same homothetic preferences over, say, food. Although this assumption is not justified for some purposes, it suffices for the purpose of constructing a price index for food, since we are mostly interested in capturing the substitution effects in the aggregate price of food as the relative prices of food components vary. In a similar fashion, we are interested in determining how the "average" consumer values a faster computer speed against more memory; i.e., we are primarily interested in hedonic substitution effects.

[20] We do not require a linear indifference curve globally, but only locally over a certain range of purchases. Alternatively, we can view the linear indifference curve as providing a first-order approximation to a non-linear indifference curve.

[21] Comparing equation (21.17) with equation (21.15), it can be seen that the simplifying assumptions (21.16) enable us to get rid of the terms $\partial g^t(u_i^t, f(z_k^t))/\partial Z$, which depend on individual consumer indifference curves between the hedonic commodity and other commodities. If we had individual household data on the consumption of hedonic and other commodities, then we could use normal consumer demand techniques in order to estimate the parameters that characterized these indifference curves.

[22] There has been a switch to subscripts from superscripts in keeping with the conventions for parameters in regression models; i.e., the constants r_t will be regression parameters in what follows. Note also that r_t is the product of the price of the "other" commodity p^t times the period t slope parameter a^t. We need to allow this slope parameter to change over time in order to be able to model the demand for high-technology hedonic commodities, which have been falling in price relative to "other" commodities; i.e., we think of a^t as decreasing over time for high-technology commodities.

[23] The basic model ends up being very similar to one of Muellbauer's (1974, pp. 988–989) hedonic models; see in particular his equation (32).

[24] It is possible to rework the above theory and give it a producer theory interpretation. The counterpart to the expenditure minimization problem (21.8) is now the following profit maximization problem: $\max_{x,z} \{P^t Z - w^t X : X = g^t(k^t, Z)\}$ where Z is hedonic output and P^t is a period t price for one unit of the hedonic output, w^t is the period t price of a variable input and X is the quantity used of it, k^t is the period t quantity of a fixed factor (capital, say) and g^t is the firm's factor requirements function. Assuming that $Z=f(z)$, we end up with the following producer theory counterpart to equation (21.15): $P_k^t = f(z_k^t)\,\partial g^t(k^t, f(z_k^t))/\partial Z$. The counterpart to assumption (21.16) is, for firm i, $g_i^t(k_i^t, Z) \equiv a^t Z - b_i^t k_i^t$ and the counterpart to equation (21.17) becomes $P_k^t = w^t a^t f(z_k^t)$. The producer theory model assumptions are, however, not as plausible as the corresponding consumer theory model assumptions. In particular, it is not very likely that each producer will have the same period t aggregate price for a unit of variable input w^t and it is not very likely that each firm producing in the hedonic market will have the same technology parameter a^t. The key assumption that will not generally be

(21.19) if the composite "other" commodity X is replaced by $h(x)$, where x is a consumption vector and h is a linearly homogeneous, increasing and concave aggregator function. Instead of equation (21.17), under these new assumptions, the following equation results:

$$P^t_k = c(p^t)a^t f(z^t_k) \quad \text{for } t = 1, \ldots, T \quad \text{and } k = 1, \ldots, K^t \tag{21.20}$$

where p^t is now the vector of prices for the x commodities in period t and c is the unit cost or expenditure function that is dual to h.[25] Now redefine r_t as $c(p^t)a^t$ and the basic system of hedonic equations (21.19) is still obtained. Equation (21.19) has one property that is likely to be present in more complex and realistic models of consumer choice. This property is that the model prices in period t are homogeneous of degree one in the general price level p^t. Thus if p^t is replaced by λp^t for any $\lambda > 0$ (think of a sudden hyperinflation where λ is large), then equations (21.17) and (21.19) imply that the model prices should become λP^t_k. Note that this homogeneity property will not hold for the following additive hedonic model:

$$P^t_k = r_t + f(z^t_k) \quad \text{for } t = 1, \ldots, T \text{ and } k = 1, \ldots, K^t \tag{21.21}$$

Thus hedonic regressions based on the linear model (21.21) may be ruled out on a priori grounds. Note that hedonic models that take the logarithm of the model price P^t_k as the dependent variable will tend to be consistent with basic hedonic equations (21.19), whereas linear models like (21.21) will not be consistent with the normal linear homogeneity properties implied by microeconomic theory.

Hedonic indices

21.37 It was noted above that hedonic functions are required for two purposes with regard to a quality adjustment. The first is when an item is no longer available and the replacement item, of which the price is used to continue the series, is of a different quality to the original price basis. The differences in quality can be established in terms of different values of a subset of the z price-determining variables. The coefficients from the hedonic regressions, as estimates of the monetary value of additional units of each quality component z, can then be used to adjust the price of, say, the old item so that it is comparable with the price of the new item[26] – so that, again, like is compared with like. This process could be described as "patching", in that an adjustment is needed to the price of the old (or new replacement) series for the quality differences, to enable the new series to be patched onto the old. A second use of hedonic functions is for estimating *hedonic indices*. These are suitable when the pace and scale of replacements of items are substantial and when an extensive use of patching might lead to extensive errors if there were some error or bias in the quality adjustment process and to sampling from a biased replacement universe (as outlined in paragraphs 21.12 to 21.36). Hedonic indices use data in each period from a refreshed sample of items, which should include those with a substantial share of sales expenditure – with sampling in each period from the double universe. There is no need to establish a preselected set of items for matching and for price collectors to keep collecting prices for that set. What is required are samples of items to be redrawn in each month along with information on their prices, characteristics and, possibly, quantities/values. The "partialling out" in the hedonic regressions controls for quality differences, as opposed to the matching of price by the price collectors. There are a number of procedures for estimating hedonic indices and these are briefly considered below.

Theoretical characteristics price indices

21.38 Theoretical cost of living indices are defined in Chapter 17 and practical index number formulae are considered as estimates of these indices. Theoretical cost of living index numbers are defined here not just on the goods produced, but also on their characteristics. The Konüs (1924) family of *true cost of living indices* pertaining to two periods, where the consumer faces the strictly positive price vectors $p^0 \equiv (p^0_1, \ldots, p^0_N)$ and $p^1 \equiv (p^1_1, \ldots, p^1_N)$ in periods 0 and 1 respectively, was defined in Chapter 17 as the ratio of the minimum costs of achieving the same utility level $u \equiv f(q)$, where $q \equiv (q_1, \ldots, q_N)$ is a positive reference quantity vector; i.e.,

$$P_K(p^0, p^1, q) \equiv C[u, p^1]/C[u, p^0] = C[f(q), p^1]/C[f(q), p^0] \tag{21.22}$$

For theoretical indices in characteristic space, the revenue functions are also defined over goods made up of bundles of characteristics represented by the hedonic function:[27]

$$\begin{aligned} P_K(p^0, p^1, q) &\equiv C[u, p^1, p(z_1)]/C[u, p^0, p(z_0)] \\ &= C[f(q), p^1, p(z_1)]/C[f(q), p^0, p(z_0)] \end{aligned} \tag{21.23}$$

21.39 The theoretical price index defined by equation (21.23) is a ratio of the period 1 to period 0 hypothetical costs to consumers of achieving a given utility. Equation

satisfied in the producer context is that each producer is able to produce the entire array of hedonic models; whereas, in the consumer context, it is quite plausible that each consumer has the possibility of purchasing and consuming each model.

[25] Define c as $c(p^t) \equiv \min_x \{p^t x : h(x) = 1\}$, where $p^t x$ denotes the inner product between the vectors p^t and x.

[26] Various mechanisms for such adjustments are outlined in paragraphs 7.103 to 7.109, and Triplett (2002). They include using the coefficients from the salient set of characteristics or using the predicted values from the regression as a whole and, in either case, making the adjustment to the old for comparison with the new, or to the new for comparison with the old, or some effective average of the two.

[27] Triplett (1987) and Diewert (2002d), following Pollak (1975), consider a two-stage budgeting process whereby that portion of utility concerned with items defined as characteristics has its theoretical index defined in terms of a cost-minimizing selection of characteristics, conditioned on an optimum output level for composite and hedonic commodities. These quantities are then fed back into the second-stage maximization of overall revenue.

(21.23) incorporates substitution effects: if the prices of some characteristics increase more than others, then utility-maximizing consumers can switch their output mix of characteristics in favour of such characteristics. The numerator in equation (21.23) is the cost of the maximum utility that the consumer could attain if faced with the commodity prices and implicit hedonic shadow prices of period 1, p^1 and $p(z^1)$, while the denominator in equation (21.23) is the maximum utility that the consumer could attain if faced with the commodity and characteristic prices of period 0, p^0 and $p(z^0)$. Note that all the variables in the numerator and denominator functions are exactly the same, except that the commodity price and characteristic price vectors differ. This is a defining characteristic of a price index. As with the economic indices in Chapter 15, there is of course an entire family of indices depending on which reference utility level is chosen. Some explicit formulations are considered in paragraphs 21.48 to 21.58, including a base period 0 reference level and a current period 1 reference level analogous to the derivation of the Laspeyres and Paasche indices in Chapter 17. Before considering such hedonic indices, two simpler formulations are first considered: hedonic regressions using dummy variables on time (paragraphs 21.40 to 21.42), and hedonic imputation indices (paragraphs 21.43 to 21.47). They are simple, and widely used because they require no information on quantities or weights. They also do not require matched data, so can be used when resampling all the data. Yet their interpretation from economic theory is therefore more limited on account of this. As will be shown in Appendix 21.1, however, weighted formulations are possible using a weighted least squares estimator.

Hedonic regressions and dummy variables of time

21.40 Let there be K characteristics of a product and let model or item i of the product in period t have the vector of characteristics $z_i^t \equiv [z_{i1}^t, \ldots, z_{iK}^t]$ for $i = 1, \ldots, I$ and $t = 1, \ldots, T$. Denote the price of model i in period t by p_i^t. A hedonic regression of the price of model i in period t on its characteristics set z_i^t is given by:

$$\ln p_i^t = \gamma_0 + \sum_{t=2}^{T} \gamma^t D^t + \sum_{k=1}^{K} \beta_k z_{ik}^t + \varepsilon_i^t \qquad (21.24)$$

where D^t are dummy variables for the time periods, D^2 being 1 in period $t = 2$, zero otherwise; D^3 being 1 in period $t = 3$, zero otherwise, etc. The coefficients γ^t are estimates of quality-adjusted price changes, having controlled for the effects of variation in quality (via $\sum_{k=1}^{K} \gamma_k z^t ki$) – but see Goldberger (1968) and Teekens and Koerts (1972) for the adjustment for estimation bias.

21.41 The above approach uses the dummy variables on time to compare prices in period 1 with prices in each subsequent period. In doing so, the β_k parameters are constrained to be constant over the period $t = 1, \ldots, T$. Such an approach is fine retrospectively, but in real time the index may be estimated as a fixed base or chained base formulation. The *fixed base* formulation would estimate the index for period 1 and 2, $I_{1,2}$, using equation (21.24) for $t = 1, 2$; the index for period 3, $I_{1,3}$, would use equation (21.24) for $t = 1, 3$; the index for period 4, $I_{1,4}$, using equation (21.24) for $t = 1, 4$ and so forth. The dummy variable in such cases would take values of 1 for the current period and 0 for the price reference period. For example, for $I_{1,4}$ it would be 1 for observations in period 4 and 0 otherwise, i.e. for observations in period 1. Only data in periods 1 and 4 are used for the estimated equation. The coefficient of the dummy variable is an estimate of quality-adjusted price change. In each case, the index constrains the estimated coefficients on the quality characteristics to be the same for the current and price reference periods, periods 1 and 4. A fixed base bilateral comparison using equation (21.24) makes use of the constrained parameter estimates over the two periods of the price comparison. *A chained* formulation would estimate $I_{1,4}$, for example, as the product of a series of links: $I_{1,4} = I_{1,2} \times I_{2,3} \times I_{3,4}$. Each successive binary comparison, or link, is combined by successive multiplication. The index for each link is estimated using equation (21.24). Because the periods of time being compared are close, it is generally more likely that the constraining of parameters required by chained time dummy hedonic indexes are considered to be less severe than that required of their fixed base counterparts.

21.42 There is no explicit weighting in these formulations, and this is a serious disadvantage. In practice, cut-off sampling might be employed to include only the most important items. If sales data are available, a weighted (by relative sales shares; see Appendix 21.1) least squares estimator, as opposed to an ordinary least squares estimator (OLS), should be used.[28] Matched data are not required for this method; items can be resampled in each period to include new technologies.

Hedonic imputation indices

21.43 An alternative approach for a comparison between period 1 and t is to estimate a hedonic regression for period t, and insert the values of the characteristics of each model existing in period 1 into the period t regression to predict, for each item, its price $\hat{p}_i^t(z_i^1)$. This would generate predictions of the price of items existing in period 1, at period t shadow prices, $\hat{p}_i^t(z_i^1), i = 1, \ldots, N$. These prices (or an average) can be compared with (the average of) the actual prices of models $i = 1, \ldots, N$ models in period 1. The averages may be arithmetic, as in a Dutot index, or geometric, as in a Jevons index. The arithmetic formulation is defined as follows:

$$\frac{\sum_{i=1}^{N} (1/N) \hat{p}_i^t(z_i^1)}{\sum_{i=1}^{N} (1/N) p_i^1(z_i^1)} \qquad (21.25a)$$

21.44 Alternatively, the characteristics of models existing in period 1 can be inserted into a regression for period t. Predicted prices of period t items generated at

[28] Ioannidis and Silver (1999) and Bode and van Dalén (2001) compared the results from these different estimators, finding notable differences, but not in all cases; see also Silver and Heravi (2003).

period 1 shadow prices (or an average) can be compared with (the average of) the actual prices in period t:

$$\frac{\sum_{i=1}^{N}(1/N)p_i^t(z_i^t)}{\sum_{i=1}^{N}(1/N)\hat{p}_i^1(z_i^t)} \qquad (21.25b)$$

21.45 For a fixed base bilateral comparison using either formula (21.25a) or (21.25b), the hedonic equation need only be estimated for one period. The denominator in formula (21.25a) is the average observed price in period 1, which should be equal to the average price that a hedonic regression based on period 1 data will predict using period 1 characteristics. The numerator, however, requires an estimated hedonic regression to predict period 1 characteristics at period t hedonic prices. Similarly, in formula (21.25b) a hedonic regression is required only for the denominator. For reasons analogous to those explained in Chapter 15, a symmetric average of these indices should have some theoretical support.

21.46 Note that all the indices described in paragraphs 21.40 to 21.45 can use matched data or all the data available in each period. If there is a new item in, say, period 4, it is included in the data set and its quality differences controlled for by the regression. Similarly, if old items drop out, they are still included in the indices in the periods in which they exist. This is part of the natural estimation procedure and differs from the use of hedonic regressions only for price adjustments to non-comparable items.

21.47 As with the dummy variable approach, there is no need for matched data. Yet there is also no explicit use of quantity weighting in these formulations, and this is a serious disadvantage. Were data on quantities or values available, it is immediately apparent that such weights could be attached to the individual $i=1,\ldots,N$ prices or their estimates. This is considered in the next section.

Superlative and exact hedonic indices

21.48 In Chapter 17, Laspeyres and Paasche bounds were defined on a theoretical basis, as were superlative indices, which treat both periods symmetrically. These superlative formulae included the Fisher index, which was seen in Chapter 16 to have desirable axiomatic properties. Furthermore, the Fisher index was supported from economic theory as a symmetric average of the Laspeyres and Paasche bounds, and was found to be the most suitable such average of the two on axiomatic grounds. The Törnqvist index also possessed desirable axiomatic properties, seemed to be best from the stochastic viewpoint, and also did not require strong assumptions for its derivation from the economic approach as a superlative index. The Laspeyres and Paasche indices were found to correspond to (be exact for) underlying (Leontief) aggregator functions with no substitution possibilities, while superlative indices were exact for flexible functional forms, including the quadratic and translog forms for the Fisher and Törnqvist indices respectively. If data on prices, characteristics and quantities are available, then analogous approaches and findings arise for hedonic indices; see Fixler and Zieschang (1992) and Feenstra (1995). Exact bounds on such an index were defined by Feenstra (1995). Consider the theoretical index in equation (21.23), but now only defined over items in terms of their characteristics. The prices are still of items, but they are wholly defined through $p(z)$. An arithmetic aggregation for a linear hedonic equation finds that a Laspeyres upper bound (as quantities supplied *decrease* with increasing relative prices) is given by:

$$\frac{\sum_{i=1}^{N} x_i^{t-1}\hat{p}_i^t}{\sum_{i=1}^{N} x_i^{t-1}p_i^{t-1}} = \sum_{i=1}^{N} s_i^{t-1}\left(\frac{\hat{p}_i^t}{p_i^{t-1}}\right) > \frac{C(u^{t-1}, p(z)^t)}{C(u^{t-1}, p(z)^{t-1})} \qquad (21.26a)$$

where the right-hand side expression is the ratio of the cost of achieving a period $t-1$ level of utility (u^{t-1}), where utility is a function of the vector of quantities; i.e., $u^{t-1}=f(x^{t-1})$; the price comparison is evaluated at a fixed level of period $t-1$ quantities and s_i^{t-1} are the shares in the total value of expenditure on product i in period $t-1$:

$$s_i^{t-1} = x_i^{t-1}p_i^{t-1} \Big/ \sum_{i=1}^{N} x_i^{t-1}p_i^{t-1}$$

21.49 The difference between a Laspeyres formula and the left-hand side of equation (21.26a) is that the price in the numerator of the left-hand side of equation (21.26a) is a predicted price:

$$\hat{p}_i^t \equiv \hat{p}_i^t(z_i^{t-1}) = \sum_{k=0}^{K} \beta_k^t z_{ik}^{t-1} \qquad (21.26b)$$

or, if a non-comparable replacement is used, then the predicted price adjusts for the difference in quality between the old and new items. That is, the predicted price

$$\hat{p}_i^t \equiv p_i^t - \sum_{i=1}^{N} \beta_k^t (z_{ik}^t - z_{ik}^{t-1}) \qquad (21.26c)$$

is the price in period t adjusted for the sum of the changes in each quality characteristic weighted by their coefficients derived from a linear hedonic regression. Note that the summation is over the same i in both periods since replacements are included when an item is missing, and (21.26c) adjusts the prices in period t for quality differences via $\sum_{i=1}^{N}\beta_k^t(z_{ik}^t - z_{ik}^{t-1})$.

21.50 A Paasche lower bound is estimated as:

$$\frac{\sum_{i=1}^{N} x_i^t p_i^t}{\sum_{i=1}^{N} x_i^t \hat{p}_i^{t-1}} = \left[\sum_{i=1}^{N} s_i^t \left(\frac{\hat{p}_i^{t-1}}{p_i^t}\right)\right]^{-1} \leq \frac{C(u^t, p(z)^t)}{C(u^t, p(z)^{t-1})} \qquad (21.27a)$$

where $s_i^t = x_i^t p_i^t / \sum_{i=1}^{N} x_i^t p_i^t$ and

$$\hat{p}_i^{t-1} \equiv \sum_{k=0}^{k} \beta_k^{t-1} z_{ik}^t \qquad (21.27b)$$

$$\hat{p}_i^{t-1} \equiv p_i^{t-1} + \sum_{k=0}^{N} \beta_k^{t-1}(z_{ik}^t - z_{ik}^{t-1}) \qquad (21.27c)$$

which are the imputation and replacement adjustment, respectively. The latter are the prices in periods $t-1$ adjusted for the sum of the changes in each quality characteristic weighted by their respective coefficients derived from a linear hedonic regression.

21.51 Following from the inequalities in (17.5), where the Laspeyres P_L and Paasche P_P indices form bounds (17.8) on their "true" P_K economic theoretic indices:

$$P_L \leq P_K \leq P_P \text{ or } P_P \leq P_K \leq P_L \qquad (21.28)$$

a suitable index is thus a Fisher geometric mean of the Laspeyres P_L and Paasche P_P indices, which incorporate hedonic adjustments for quality differences.

21.52 Thus, the approach based on using superlative and exact hedonic indices first applies the coefficients from hedonic regressions to changes in the characteristics to adjust observed prices for quality changes. Second, it incorporates a weighting system using data on the quantities sold of each model and their characteristics, rather than treating each model as equally important. Finally, it has a direct correspondence to the formulation defined using economic theory.

21.53 Semi-logarithmic hedonic regressions would supply a set of β coefficients suitable for use with the base and current period geometric bounds:

$$\prod_{i=1}^{N}\left(\frac{p_i^t}{\hat{p}_i^{t-1}}\right)^{s_i^t} \leq \frac{C(u^t, p(z)^t)}{C(u^t, p(z)^{t-1})} \leq \prod_{i=1}^{N}\left(\frac{\hat{p}_i^t}{p_i^{t-1}}\right)^{s_i^{t-1}} \qquad (21.29a)$$

$$\hat{p}_i^{t-1} \equiv \exp\left[\sum_{k=0}^{k} \beta_k^{t-1} z_k^t\right]$$

$$\hat{p}_i^t \equiv \exp\left[\sum_{k=0}^{k} \beta_k^t z_k^{t-1}\right] \qquad (21.29b)$$

$$\hat{p}_i^{t-1} \equiv p_i^{t-1} \exp\left[\sum_{i=1}^{N} \beta_k^{t-1}(z_{ik}^t - z_{ik}^{t-1})\right]$$

$$\hat{p}_i^t \equiv p_i^t \exp\left[-\sum_{i=1}^{N} \beta_k^t(z_{ik}^t - z_{ik}^{t-1})\right] \qquad (21.29c)$$

21.54 In the inequality (21.29a), the two bounds on the respective theoretical indices have been shown to be brought together. The calculation of such indices is relatively straightforward for matched data, but for unmatched data is no small task. For an example of its application for unmatched comparisons over time, see Silver and Heravi (2002; 2003) and Chapter 7, paragraphs 7.132 to 7.152, and see Kokoski, Moulton and Zieschang (1999) for matched price comparisons across regions of a country.

21.55 Exact hedonic indices can also be defined using the theoretical framework outlined by Diewert (2003a).[29] Recall the basic hedonic equation (21.19). Assume that the price P_k^t is the average price for all the models of type k sold in period t and let q_k^t be the number of units sold of model k in period t. Recall that the number of models in the marketplace during period t is K^t. Assume that there are K models in the marketplace over all T periods in our sample period. If a particular model k is not sold at all during period t, then it will be assumed that P_k^t and q_k^t are both zero. With these conventions in mind, the *total value of consumer purchases during period t* is equal to:

$$\sum_{k=1}^{K} P_k^t q_k^t = \sum_{k=1}^{K} r_t f(z_k) q_k^t \quad \text{for } t=1,\ldots,T \qquad (21.30)$$

21.56 The hedonic sub-utility function f has done all the hard work in the model by converting the utility yielded by model k in period t into a "standard" utility $f(z_k)$ that is cardinally comparable across models. For each model type k, it is only necessary to multiply by the total number of units sold in period t, q_k^t, in order to obtain the *total period* t *market quantity of the hedonic commodity*, Q_t say. This yields:[30]

$$Q_t \equiv \sum_{k=1}^{K} f(z_k) q_k^t \quad \text{for } t=1,\ldots,T \qquad (21.31)$$

21.57 The aggregate price for the hedonic commodity corresponding to Q_t is r_t. Thus in the highly simplified model outlined in paragraphs 21.29 to 21.36, the *aggregate exact period* t *price and quantity* for the hedonic commodity are r_t and Q_t defined by equation (21.31), which can readily be calculated provided that the parameters in the hedonic regression have been estimated and provided that data on quantities sold are available each period q_k^t.[31] Once r_t and Q_t have been determined for $t=1,\ldots,T$, then these aggregate price and quantity estimates for the hedonic commodity can be combined with the aggregate prices and quantities of non-hedonic commodities using normal index number theory. Any of the index number formulae considered in Chapter 17, including Laspeyres, Paasche and Fisher, can be accordingly defined based on the use of quantity information.

21.58 The above illustrates how weighted quality-adjusted price index number formulae might be constructed using data on prices, quantities and characteristics of an item. The method using dummy variables of time, described in paragraphs 21.40 to 21.42, does not require matched data. Appendix 21.1 discusses a weighting system. The use of weighted superlative indices for matched data is outlined above. Weighted superlative indices may also be applied to unmatched data, using a method

[29] The assumptions are quite different from those made by Fixler and Zieschang (1992), who took yet another approach to the construction of exact hedonic indices.

[30] This is a counterpart to the quantity index defined by Muellbauer (1974, p. 988) in one of his hedonic models; see his equation (30). Of course, treating r_t as a price for the hedonic commodity quantity aggregate defined by equation (21.31) can be justified by appealing to Hicks' (1946, pp. 312–313) aggregation theorem, since the model prices $p_k^t = r_t f(z_t)$ all have the common factor of proportionality r_t.

[31] If data are available for the q_k^t, then it is best to run sales-weighted regressions, as discussed in Appendix 21.1. If we do not have complete market data on individual model sales but we do have total sales in each period, then the hedonic regression model can be run using a sample of model prices, and period t sales can be divided by our estimated r_t parameter in order to obtain an estimator for Q_t.

outlined in Chapter 7 and in Silver and Heravi (2001a; 2001b; 2003). But what of unweighted indices, which was the concern of the initial section of this chapter? What correspondence does the unweighted hedonic time dummy index (outlined in paragraphs 21.40 to 21.42), which uses all the data, have to the matched unweighted index number formulae? This is a critical question for product areas where there is a rapid turnover of items. It was suggested above that the time dummy variable method be used instead of the matched method. So how do they differ for unweighted indices? The effect and use of weights is considered in Appendix 21.1.

Unweighted hedonic indices and unweighted matched index number formulae

21.59 Triplett (2002) and Diewert (2003a) have argued that an unweighted geometric mean Jevons index (see equation (20.3)) for matched data gives the same result as a logarithmic dummy variable hedonic index run on the same data. An index from a dummy variable hedonic regression such as equation (21.24), but in double-logarithmic (log-log) form, for matched models can be shown (see Aizcorbe, Corrado and Doms (2001)) to be equal to:

$$\ln(p^t/p^{t-1}) = \sum_{m\in Mt}(\ln p^t_m - Z^t_m)/M^t - \sum_{m\in Mt-1}(\ln p^{t-1}_m - Z^{t-1}_m)/M^{t-1} \qquad (21.32)$$

where m is the matched sample and Z^t and Z^{t-1} are the quality adjustments to the dummy variables for time in equation (21.24), that is, $\sum_{k=1}^{K}\beta_k z^t_k$. Equation (21.32) is simply the difference between two geometric means of quality-adjusted prices. The sample space $m = M_t = M_{t-1}$ is the same model in each period. Consider the introduction of a new model n introduced in period t with no counterpart in $t-1$ and the demise of an old model o so it has no counterpart in t. So in period t, the sample space M_t is composed of the period t matched items m and the new items n, and in period $t-1$ M_{t-1} is composed of the period $t-1$ matched items m and the old items. Silver and Heravi (2002) have shown the dummy variable hedonic comparison to be:

$$\begin{aligned}\ln(p^t/p^{t-1}) &= [m/(m+n)\sum_m(\ln p^t_m - Z_m)/m \\ &\quad + n/(m+n)\sum_n(\ln p^t_n - Z_n)/n] \\ &\quad - [m/(m+o)\sum_m(\ln p^{t-1}_m - Z_m)/m \\ &\quad + o/(m+o)\sum_o(\ln p^{t-1}_o - Z_o)/o] \\ &= [m/(m+n)\sum_m(\ln p^t_m - Z_m)/m \\ &\quad - m/(m+o)\sum_m(\ln p^{t-1}_m - Z_m)/m] \\ &\quad + [n/(m+n)\sum_n(\ln p^t_n - Z_n)/n \\ &\quad - o/(m+o)\sum_o(\ln p^{t-1}_o - Z_o)/o] \end{aligned} \qquad (21.33)$$

21.60 Consider the second expression in equation (21.33). First there is the price change for m matched observations. This is the change in mean prices of matched models m in period t and $t-1$ adjusted for quality. Note that the weight in period t for this matched component is the proportion of matched observations to all observations in period t, both matched and unmatched new (n). Similarly, for period $t-1$, the matched weight depends on how many matched and unmatched old observations (o) are in the sample. In the last line of equation (21.33) the change is between the unmatched new and the unmatched old mean (quality-adjusted) prices in periods t and $t-1$. Thus, the matched methods can be seen to ignore the last line in equation (21.33) and will thus differ from the hedonic dummy variable approach. It can be seen from equation (21.33) that the hedonic dummy variable approach, in its inclusion of unmatched old and new observations, may possibly differ from a geometric mean of matched prices changes, the extent of any difference depending, in this unweighted formulation, on the proportions of old and new items leaving and entering the sample and on the price changes of old and new items relative to those of matched items. If the market for products is one in which old quality-adjusted prices are unusually low while new quality-adjusted prices are unusually high, then the matched index will understate price changes; see Silver and Heravi (2002) and Berndt, Ling and Kyle (2003) for examples. Different market behaviour will lead to different forms of bias. There is a second way in which the results will differ. Index number formulae provide weights for the price changes. The Carli index, for example, weights each observation equally, while the Dutot index weights each observation according to its relative price in the base period. The Jevons index, with no assumptions as to economic behaviour, weights each observation equally. Silver (2002) has argued, however, that the weight given to each observation in an ordinary least squares regression also depends on the characteristics of the observations, some observations with unusual characteristics having more leverage. In this way, the results from the two approaches may differ even more.

New goods and services

21.61 This section briefly highlights theoretical issues relating to the incorporation of new goods into the index. Practical issues are outlined in Chapter 8, paragraphs 8.36 to 8.60. The term "new goods" will be used here to refer to those that provide a substantial and substantive change in what is provided, as opposed to more of a currently available set of service flows, such as a new model of a car that has a bigger engine. In this latter instance, there is a continuation of a service and production flow, and this may be linked to the service flow and production technology of the existing model. The practical concern with the definition of new goods as against quality changes is that the former cannot be easily linked to existing items as a continuation of an existing resource base and service flow, because of the very nature of their "newness". There are alternative definitions; Oi (1997) directs the problem of defining "new" goods to that of defining a monopoly. If there is no close substitute, the good is new. A monopoly supplier may be able to supply an item with new combinations of the hedonic z characteristics resulting from a new technology and have a monopoly power in doing so, but in practice the new good can be linked via the set of hedonic characteristics to the existing goods. In this practical sense, such goods are not considered "new" for the purposes of the manual.

21.62 The terminology adopted here is that used by Merkel (2000) for the measurement of producer price indices, but considered in the context of consumer price indices (CPIs). The aim is to distinguish between *evolutionary* and *revolutionary* goods. Evolutionary goods are replacement or supplementary models which continue to provide a similar service flow, perhaps in new ways or to different degrees. In contrast, revolutionary goods are entirely new goods not closely tied to a previously available good. Although revolutionary goods may satisfy a long-standing consumer need in a novel way, they do not fit into any established CPI item category. Thus, in principle, the underlying theory of what is meant by new goods applies as much to evolutionary as to revolutionary goods. However, the practicalities of index number construction imply a need to consider a new good in terms of something that is not an extension or a modification of an existing one. Evolutionary goods can be incorporated into an index by means of the methods discussed in Chapter 7, even though utility gains from their introduction are ignored. This procedure has further problems. Because the item is by its nature unique, it is unlikely to be incorporated into the sample as a replacement for an existing one. It would be neither comparable nor amenable to explicit adjustments to its price for quality differences with existing goods. Since it is not replacing an item, it does not have an existing weight and its introduction implies a need to reweight the index.

21.63 The main concern regarding the incorporation of new goods into the CPI is the decision on the need and timing for their inclusion. Waiting for a new good to be established or waiting for the rebasing of an index before incorporating new products may lead to errors in the measurement of price changes if the unusual price movements at critical stages in the product life cycles are ignored. There are practical approaches to the early adoption of both evolutionary and revolutionary goods, as outlined in Chapter 8. For evolutionary goods, such strategies include the rebasing of the index, resampling of items and introduction of new goods as directed sample *substitutions*; see Merkel (2000). Also of use are hedonic quality adjustments and indices outlined in Chapter 7, paragraphs 7.103 to 7.109 and 7.153 and 7.158, and paragraphs 21.37 to 21.60, which facilitate the incorporation of evolutionary goods. These goods possess a similar characteristic set to existing goods, but deliver different quantities of these characteristics. Short-run or chained frameworks outlined in paragraphs 7.153 to 7.173 may also be more appropriate for product areas with a high turnover of items. These approaches can incorporate the price change of new goods into the index as soon as prices are available for two successive periods, though issues relating to the proper weighting of such changes may remain.

21.64 For revolutionary goods, however, substitution may not be appropriate. First, revolutionary goods may not be able to be defined within the existing classification systems. Second, they may be primarily produced by a new outlet, which will require extending the sample to such outlets. Third, there will be no previous items to match them against to make a quality adjustment to prices, since by definition they are substantially different from pre-existing goods. Finally, there is no weight to attach to the new outlet or item. Sample *augmentation* is appropriate for revolutionary goods, as opposed to sample substitution for evolutionary goods. It is necessary to bring the new revolutionary goods into the sample in addition to what exists. This may involve extending the classification, the sample of outlets, and the item list within new or existing outlets (Merkel, 2000).

21.65 The second measurement issue with respect to new products is the incorporation of the welfare effect of those products at introduction. The preceding discussion has been concerned with the incorporation of price changes into the index once two successive quotations are available. Yet there is a gain to the consumer when comparing the price in the first of these periods with the price in the period that preceded its introduction *had it existed*. In the context of the CPI, the appropriate period 1 shadow price for the new good is that price that just induces the consumer of the new good to consume zero quantities in the preceding period. This is a hypothetical price. If it is relatively high in the period before the introduction of the good, but the actual price in the period of introduction is much lower, then the introduction of the new good is clearly of some benefit to the consumer. To ignore this benefit, and the change from the virtual price to the actual price in its period of introduction, is to ignore something of the price movements that give rise to expenditure changes.

21.66 The sample augmentation procedures miss the effects on price between the period preceding the introduction of a new good and its introduction. There exist in economic theory and practice the tools for estimating such effects; see Hicks (1940) and Diewert (1980, pp. 498–503). This involves setting a virtual price in the period before introduction. This price is the one at which supply is set to zero. The virtual price is compared with the actual price in the period of introduction and this is used to estimate the welfare gain from the introduction of the good. Hausman (1997) provides some estimates of consumer welfare for the introduction of a new brand of breakfast cereals, Apple-Cinnamon Cheerios. He concludes:

> The correct economic approach to the evaluation of new goods has been known for over fifty years, since Hicks' pioneering contribution. However, it has not been implemented by government statistical agencies, perhaps because of its complications and data requirements. Data are now available. The impact of new goods on consumer welfare appears to be significant according to the demand

estimates of this paper, the CPI for cereal may be too high by about 25 per cent because it does not account for new cereal brands. An estimate this large seems worth worrying about.

21.67 Shapiro and Wilcox (1997b, p. 144) share the same concerns:

> ... the rare new item that delivers services radically different from anything previously available. For example, even the earliest generation of personal computers allowed consumers to undertake tasks that previously would have been prohibitively expensive.
>
> This problem can be solved only by estimating the consumer surplus created by the introduction of each new item. Hausman (1997) argues that this must involve explicit modeling of the demand for each new item. ... Although explicit modeling of demand may be of dubious practicality for widespread implementation in the CPI, strategic application in a few selected cases might be worthwhile.

21.68 The expertise required for such estimates is considerable, and even when applied, is not beyond dispute; see Bresnahan (1997) on this last point. An alternative approach is outlined for the CPI by Balk (2000b), with empirical estimates provided by de Haan (2001), the details being provided in Chapter 8 and Appendix 8.2. While this approach is simpler than that undertaken by Hausman (1997), both require considerable statistical and econometric expertise. The inclusion of such effects on a routine basis is not something being actively considered, even by statistical offices with well-developed systems.[32]

[32] Even if virtual prices were estimated, there would still be problems with including new goods in indices such as the Laspeyres index because of the absence of weights in the base period.

Appendix 21.1 Some econometric issues

1. Hedonic regression estimates are seen in Chapter 7 to have a potential use for quality adjustment to prices. A number of issues arise from the specification and estimation of hedonic regressions, the use of diagnostic statistics, and courses of action when the standard assumptions of ordinary least squares (OLS) are seen to break down. Many of these issues are standard econometric ones and not the subject of this manual. This is not to say they are unimportant. The use of hedonic regressions requires some econometric and statistical expertise, but suitable texts are generally available; see Berndt (1991) – particularly the chapter on hedonic regressions – and Maddala (1988) and Kennedy (1998) amongst many others. Modern statistical and econometric software has adequate diagnostic tests for testing when OLS assumptions break down. There remain, however, some specific aspects which merit attention; these points are over and above the important standard econometric considerations dealt with in econometric texts.

Identification and appropriate estimators

2. Wooldridge (1996, pp. 400–401) has shown on standard econometric grounds that the estimation of supply and demand functions by OLS is biased and this bias carries over to the estimation of the hedonic function. It is first useful to consider estimation issues regarding demand and supply functions. The demand and supply functions are rarely estimated in practice. The more common approach is to estimate *offer* functions, with the marginal price offered by the firm dependent upon chosen attributes (product characteristics) and firm characteristics, and *bid* or value functions, with the marginal prices paid by a consumer dependent upon chosen attributes and consumer characteristics.[33] As noted earlier, the observed prices and quantities are the result of the interaction between structural demand and supply equations and the distributions of producer technologies and consumer tastes; they cannot reveal the parameters of the offer and value functions. Rosen (1974, pp. 50–51) suggested a procedure for determining these parameters. Since these estimates are conditioned on tastes (α) and technologies (τ), the estimation procedure needs to include empirical measures or "proxy variables" of α and τ. For the tastes α of consumers, the empirical counterparts may be socio-demographic and economic variables, which may include age, income, education and geographical region. For technologies τ, variables may include types of technologies, scale and factor prices. First, the hedonic equation is estimated in the normal manner, without these variables, using the best-fitting functional form. This is to represent the price function that consumers and producers face when making their decisions. Then, an implicit marginal price function is computed for each characteristic as $\partial p(z)/\partial zi = \hat{p}_i(z)$, where $\hat{p}(z)$ is the estimated hedonic equation. Bear in mind that in normal demand/supply studies for *products*, the prices are observed in the market. Prices for *characteristics* are unobserved; this first stage is to estimate the parameters from the hedonic regression. The actual values of each z_i bought and sold are then inserted into each implicit marginal price function to yield a numerical value for each characteristic. These marginal values are used in the second stage[34] of estimation as endogenous variables for the estimation of the demand side:

$$\hat{p}_i(z) = F(z_1, \ldots, z_K, \alpha^*) \tag{A21.1}$$

where α^* are the proxy variables for tastes; and the supply side:

$$\hat{p}_i(z) = F(z_1, \ldots, z_K, \tau^*) \tag{A21.2}$$

where τ^* are the proxy variables for technologies.

The variables τ^* drop out when there is no variation in technologies and $\hat{p}_i(z)$ is an estimate of the offer function. Similarly, the variables α^* drop out when sellers differ and buyers are identical, and cross-section estimates trace out compensated demand functions.

3. Epple (1987) has argued that Rosen's modelling strategy is likely to give rise to inappropriate estimation procedures of the demand and supply parameters. In the hedonic approach to estimating the demand for characteristics, a difficulty arises from the fact that marginal prices are likely to be endogenous – they depend on the amount of each characteristic consumed and must be estimated from the hedonic function rather than observed directly. There are two resulting problems. First, there is an identification problem (see Epple (1987)) because both the marginal price of a characteristic and the inverse bid depend on the levels of characteristics consumed. Second, if important characteristics are unmeasured and they are correlated with measured characteristics, the coefficients of measured characteristics will be biased. This applies to all econometric models, but is particularly relevant to hedonic models; on this point, see Wooldridge (1996, pp. 400–401) in particular. The equilibrium conditions for characteristic prices imply functional relationships among the characteristics of demanders, suppliers and products. This in turn reduces the likelihood that important excluded variables will be uncorrelated with the included variables of the model; see also Bartik (1988) on this point. The bias arises because buyers are differentiated by characteristics (y, α) and sellers by technologies τ. The type of item buyers will purchase is related to (y, α) and the type sellers provide to τ. On the plane of combinations of z transacted, the equilibrium ones chosen may be systematically related; the characteristics of buyers are related to those of sellers. Epple (1987) uses the example of stereo equipment: the higher income of some buyers leads to purchases of high-quality equipment, and the technical competence of sellers leads them to provide it. The consumer and producer characteristics may be correlated.

4. Wooldridge (1996, pp. 400–401) suggests that individual consumer and firm characteristics, such as income, education and input prices, should be used as instruments in estimating hedonic functions. In addition, variables other than a good's characteristics should be included as instruments if they are price-determining, such as geographical location (proximity to ports, good road systems, climate and so on). Communities of economic agents are assumed, within which consumers consume and producers produce for each other at prices that vary across communities for identical goods. Variables of the characteristics of the communities will not in themselves enter the demand and supply equation, but are price-determining for observed prices that are recorded across communities. Tauchen and Witte (2001) provide a systematic investigation of the conditions under which the characteristics of consumers, producers and communities will affect the hedonic parameter estimates for a single regression equation estimated across all communities. A key concern is whether the error term of the hedonic price function represents factors that are unobserved by both the economic agents and the researcher, or only by the researcher. In the latter case, the error term may be correlated with the product attributes; instrumental variable estimation is

[33] These are equivalent to inverse demand (or supply) functions, with the prices dependent upon the quantities demanded (or supplied) and the individual consumer (or producer) characteristics.

[34] This two-stage approach is common in the literature, though Wooldridge (1996) discusses the joint estimation of the hedonic, demand-side and supply-side functions as a system.

required. If the error term is *not* correlated with the product characteristics – preferences are quasi-linear – then a properly specified hedonic regression, including community-specific characteristics or appropriate slope dummies, can be estimated using ordinary least squares. In other cases, depending on the correlation between consumer and producer characteristics, assumptions about the error term and the method of incorporating community characteristics into the regression, instrumental variables, including consumer, producer or community dummy or characteristics, may need to be used.

Functional form

5. Triplett (1987 and 2002) argues that neither classical utility theory nor production theory can specify the functional form of the hedonic function.[35] This point dates back to Rosen (1974, p. 54), who describes the observations as being "...a joint-envelope function and cannot by themselves identify the structure of consumer preferences and producer technologies that generate them". A priori judgements as to what the form should look like may be based on ideas as to how consumers and production technologies respond to price changes. These judgements are difficult to make when the observations are jointly determined by demand and supply factors, but not impossible in rare instances. They are, however, complicated when pricing is with a mark-up, the extent of which may vary over the life cycle of a product. Some tied combinations of characteristics will have higher mark-ups than others. New item introductions are likely to be attracted to these areas of characteristic space, and this will have the effect of increasing supply and thus lowering the mark-up and price; see Cockburn and Anis (1998), Feenstra (1995, p. 647) and Triplett (1987). This again must be taken into account in any a priori reasoning – not an easy or straightforward matter.

6. It may be that in some cases the hedonic function's functional form will be straightforward. For example, prices on the web sites for options for products are often additive. The underlying cost and utility structures are unlikely jointly to generate such linear functions, but the producer or consumer is also paying for the convenience of selling in this way and is willing to bear losses or make gains if the cost or utility at higher values of z are priced lower or worth more than the price set. In general, the data should convey what the functional form should look like; imposing artificial structures simply leads to specification bias. For examples of econometric testing of hedonic functional form, see Cassel and Mendelsohn (1985), Cropper, Deck and McConnell (1988), Rasmussen and Zuehlke (1990), Bode and van Dalén (2001) and Curry, Morgan and Silver (2001).

7. The three forms prevalent in the literature are linear, semi-logarithmic and double-logarithmic (log-log). A number of studies have used econometric tests, in the absence of a clear theoretical statement, to choose between them. There have been a large number of hedonic studies and, as illustrated by Curry, Morgan and Silver (2001), in many of these the quite simple forms do well, at least in terms of the $\bar{R}^2$ presented[36] and the parameters according with a priori reasoning, usually on the consumer side. Of the three popular forms, some are favoured in testing; for example, Murray and Sarantis (1999) favoured the semi-logarithmic form, while others, for example Hoffmann (1998), found that the three functional forms scarcely differed in terms of their explanatory power. That the parameters from these simple forms accord with a priori reasoning, usually from the consumer side, is promising, but researchers should be aware that such matters are not assured. There is much that may happen on the supply side to affect parameter values. Indeed Pakes (2001) has argued that no intuitive sign can be given to the parameters of the variables, since producers may vary their price mark-ups on characteristics in ways that would result in counter-intuitive negative signs on some desirable characteristics.

8. Of the three forms, the semi-logarithmic form has much to commend it. The interpretation of its coefficients is quite straightforward, as proportionate changes in prices arise from a unit change in the value of the characteristic[37] (see Chapter 7, paragraphs 7.39 and 7.40). This is a useful formulation since quality adjustments are usually undertaken by making multiplicative as opposed to additive adjustments.

9. The semi-logarithmic form, unlike the log-log model, can incorporate dummy variables for characteristics which are either present, $z_i = 1$, or not, $z_i = 0$. Furthermore, Diewert (2002e) has argued that it is more likely that the errors from a semi-logarithmic hedonic equation are homoskedastic (have a constant variance) compared to the errors from a linear hedonic equation, since items with very large characteristic values will have high prices and are very likely to have relatively large error terms. On the other hand, models with very small amounts of characteristics will have small prices and small means, and the deviation of a model price from its mean will necessarily be small. Since an assumption of OLS is that the residuals are homoskedastic, the semi-logarithmic equation is preferred to the linear one.

10. More complicated forms are, of course, possible. Simple forms have the virtue of parsimony and allow more efficient estimates to be made for a given sample. However, parsimony is not something to be achieved at the cost of misspecification bias. First, if the hedonic function is estimated across multiple independent markets, then interaction terms are required (see Mendelsohn (1984) for fishing sites). Excluding them is tantamount to omitting variables and inappropriately constraining the estimated coefficients of the regression. Tauchen and Witte (2001) have outlined the particular biases that can arise for such omitted variables in hedonic studies. Second, it may be argued that the functional form should correspond to the aggregator for the index – linear for a Laspeyres index, logarithmic for a geometric Laspeyres index, translogarithmic for a Törnqvist index, and quadratic for a Fisher index (see Chapter 17). As Triplett (2002) notes, however, the purpose of estimating hedonic regressions is to adjust prices for quality differences; imposing a functional form on the data which is inconsistent with the data might create an error in the quality adjustment procedure. Yet, as Diewert (2003a) notes, flexible functional forms encompass these simple forms, the log-log form being a special case of the translog form given in equation (17.42) and the semi-log form being a special case of the semi-log quadratic form given in equation (17.49). If there are a priori reasons

[35] Although Arguea, Haseo and Taylor (1994) propose a linear form on the basis of arbitrage for characteristics, held to be likely in competitive markets, Triplett (2002) argues that this is unlikely to be a realistic scenario in most commodity markets.

[36] While the use of $\bar{R}^2$ as a criterion for deciding between the fit of semi-logarithmic and log-log models has some validity, its use is not advised for comparing linear models with either of these logarithmic formulations, a number of tests being appropriate for such comparisons; see Maddala (1988).

[37] There are two caveats: first, $e^{\hat{\beta}-1}$ is required for the interpretation of the coefficients, where $\hat{\beta}$ is the estimated coefficient. Second, the antilogarithms of the OLS estimated coefficients are not unbiased – the estimation of semi-logarithmic functions as transformed linear regressions requires an adjustment to provide minimum variance unbiased estimates of parameters of the conditional mean. A standard adjustment is to subtract half of the coefficient's squared standard error from the estimated coefficient; see Goldberger (1968) and Teekens and Koerts (1972).

to expect interaction terms for specific characteristics, as illustrated in the example in paragraph 7.99, then these more general forms allow this. The theory of hedonic functions neither dictates the form of the hedonic form nor restricts it.

Changing tastes and technologies

11. The estimates of the coefficients from a hedonic regression may change over time. Some of this change will be attributed to sampling error, especially if multicollinearity is present, as discussed below. But in other cases it may be a genuine reflection of changes in tastes and technologies. If a subset of the estimated coefficients from a hedonic regression is to be used to make a quality adjustment to a non-comparable replacement price, then the use of estimated out-of-date coefficients from some previous period to adjust the prices of the new replacement model may be inappropriate. There is a need to update the indices as regularly as the changes demanded.[38] Estimating hedonic imputation indices is more complicated. Silver (1999), using a simple example, showed how the estimate of quality-adjusted price changes requires a reference basket of characteristics. This is apparent for the hedonic imputation indices in paragraphs 21.37 to 21.60, where separate indices using base and current period characteristics are estimated. A symmetric average of such indices is considered appropriate. A hedonic index based on a time dummy variable implicitly constrained the estimated coefficients from the base and current periods to be the same. Diewert (2003a) formalized the problem of choosing the reference characteristics when comparing prices over time, when the parameters of the hedonic function may themselves be changing over time. He found the results of hedonic indices *not* to be invariant to the choice of reference period characteristic vector set z. He considered the use of a sales-weighted average vector of characteristics, as proposed by Silver (1999), but he notes that over long time periods this may become unrepresentative.[39] Of course, if a chained formulation is used, the weighted averages of characteristics remain reasonably up to date, although chaining has its own pros and cons (see paragraph 17.44 to 17.49 of Chapter 17). A fixed base alternative noted by Diewert (2003a) is to use a Laspeyres type comparison with the base period parameter set, and a Paasche type current period index with the current period parameter set, and take the geometric mean of the two indices for reasons similar to those given in Chapter 15, paragraphs 15.18 to 15.32. The resulting Fisher type index is akin to a geometric mean of Laspeyres and Paasche indices – given in equations (21.26) and (21.27) – based on Feenstra (1995).[40] A feature of the time dummy approach in paragraphs 21.40 to 21.42 is that it implicitly takes a symmetric average of the coefficients by constraining them to be the same. But what if, as is more likely the case, only base period hedonic regression coefficients are available? Since hedonic indices based on a symmetric average of the coefficients are desirable, the "spread" or difference between estimates based on either a current or a reference period characteristic set is an indication of potential bias and estimates of such spread may be undertaken retrospectively. If the spread is large, estimates based on the use of a single period's characteristics set, say the current period, should be treated with caution. More regular updating of the hedonic regressions is likely to reduce spread because the periods being compared will be closer and the characteristics of the items in the periods compared more similar.

Weighting

12. Ordinary least squares estimators implicitly treat each item as being of equal importance, even though some items will have quite substantial sales, while sales of others will be minimal. It is axiomatic that an item with sales of over 5,000 in a month should not be accorded the same influence in the regression estimator as one with a few transactions. Items with very low sales may be at the end of their life cycles or be custom-made. Either way, their (quality-adjusted) prices and price changes may be unusual.[41] Observations with unusual prices should not be allowed unduly to influence the index.[42]

13. The estimation of hedonic regression equations by a weighted least squares (WLS) estimator is preferable. This estimator minimizes the sum of *weighted* squared deviations between the actual prices and the predicted prices from the regression equation, as opposed to ordinary least squares (OLS), which uses an equal weight for each observation. There is a question as to whether to use quantity (volume) or expenditure weights. The use of quantity weights can be supported by considering the nature of their equivalent "price". Such prices are the average (usually the same) price over a number of transactions. The underlying sampling unit is the individual transaction, so there is a sense that the data may be replicated as being composed of, say, 12 individual observations using an OLS estimator, as opposed to a single observation with a weight of 12 using a WLS estimator. Both would yield the same result. Diewert (2002e) has argued on the grounds of representativity that sales values are the appropriate weights. Quantity weighting gives too little weight to models with high prices and too much weight to cheap models that have relatively low amounts of useful characteristics. The need to equate the weights with relative expenditure or sales value arises from a prime concern with index numbers: that they serve to decompose changes in value into their price and quantity components. Silver (2002) has shown that a WLS estimator using value weights will not necessarily give each observation a weight equal to its relative value. The estimator will give more weight to those observations with high leverage effects and residuals. Observations with values of characteristics with large deviations from their means, say very old or new models, have relatively high leverage. New and old models are likely to be priced at quite different prices than those predicted from the hedonic regression, even after taking into account their different characteristics. Such prices result, for example, from a pricing strategy designed to skim segments of the market willing to pay a premium for a new model, or from a strategy to charge relatively low prices for an old model to dump it to make way for a new one. In such cases, the influence these models have on deriving the estimated coefficients will be over and above that attributable to their value weights.

[38] Adjusting the base versus the current period price entails different data demands; see Chapter 7, paragraph 7.49.

[39] Other averages may of course be proposed; for example, the needs of an index representative of the "typical" establishment would be better met by a trimmed mean or median.

[40] Diewert (2002e) also suggests matching items where possible, and using hedonic regressions to impute the prices of the missing old and new ones. Different forms of weighting systems, including superlative ones, can be applied to this set of price data in each period for both matched and unmatched data.

[41] Such observations would have higher variances of their error terms, leading to imprecise parameter estimates. This would argue for the use of weighted least squares estimators with quantity sold as the weight. This is one of the standard treatments for heteroskedastic errors; see Berndt (1991).

[42] Silver and Heravi (2002) show that old items have above-average leverage effects and below-average residuals. Not only are they different, but they exert undue influence for their size (number of observations). See Berndt, Ling and Kyle (2003), Cockburn and Anis (1998) and Silver and Heravi (2002) for examples.

Silver (2002) suggests that leverage effects should be calculated for each observation, and those with high leverage and low weights should be deleted, and the regression rerun. Thus, while quantity or value weights are preferable to no weights (i.e., OLS), value weights are more appropriate than quantity ones and, even so, account should be taken of observations with undue influence.

14. Diewert (2002e) has also considered the issue of weighting with respect to the dummy time hedonic indices outlined in paragraphs 21.40 to 21.42. The use of WLS by value involves weights being applied to observations in both periods. However, if, for example, there is high inflation then the sales values for a model in the current period will generally be larger than those of the corresponding model in the base period and the assumption of homoskedastic residuals is unlikely to be met. Diewert (2002e) suggests the use of expenditure *shares* in each period, as opposed to values, as weights for WLS for time dummy hedonic indices. He also suggests that an average of expenditure shares in the periods being compared be used for matched models.

15. Data on sales are not always available for weights, but the major selling items can generally be identified. In such cases, it is important to restrict the number of observations of items with relatively low sales, the extent of the restriction depending on the number of observations and the skewness of the sales distribution. In some cases, items with few sales provide the variability necessary for efficient estimates of the regression equation. In other cases, their low sales may be due to factors that make them unrepresentative of the hedonic surface, their residuals being unusually high. An example is low-selling models about to be dumped to make way for new models. Unweighted regressions may thus suffer from a sampling problem – even if the prices are perfectly quality adjusted, the index can be biased because it is unduly influenced by low-selling items with unrepresentative price–characteristic relationships. In the absence of weights, regression diagnostics have a role to play in helping to determine whether the undue variance in some observations belongs to such unusual low-selling items.[43]

Multicollinearity

16. There are a priori reasons to expect, for some products, that the variation in the value of one quality characteristic is not independent of one quality characteristic or a linear combination of more than one such characteristic. As a result, parameter estimates will be unbiased yet imprecise. To illustrate this, a plot of the confidence interval for one parameter estimate against another collinear one is often described as elliptical, since the combinations of possible values they may take can easily drift from, say, high values of β_1 and low values of β_2 to high values of β_2 and low values of β_1. Since the sample size for the estimates is effectively reduced, additions to and deletions from the sample may affect the parameter estimates more than would be expected. These are standard statistical issues, dealt with by Maddala (1988) and Kennedy (1998). In a hedonic regression, multicollinearity might be expected, as some characteristics may be technologically tied to others. Producers including one characteristic may need to include others for the product to work, while consumer purchasing, say, an up-market brand may expect a certain bundle of features to come with it. Triplett (2002) argues strongly for the researcher to be aware of the features of the product and the consumer market. There are standard, though not completely reliable, indicators of multicollinearity (such as variance inflation factors), but an exploration of its nature is greatly aided by an understanding of the market along with exploration of the effects of including and excluding individual variables on the signs and coefficients and on other diagnostic test statistics; see Maddala (1988).[44]

17. If a subset of the estimated coefficients from a hedonic regression is to be used to quality-adjust a non-comparable replacement price, and if there is multicollinearity between variables in this subset and other independent variables, then the estimates of the coefficients to be used for the adjustment will be imprecise. The multicollinearity effectively reduces the sample size, and some of the effects of the variables in the subset may be wrongly ascribed to the other independent variables. The extent of this error will be determined by the strength of the multiple correlation coefficient between all such "independent" variables (the multicollinearity), the standard error or fit of the regression, the dispersion of the independent variable concerned and the sample size. These all affect the precision of the estimates since they are components in the standard error of the t-statistics. Even if multicollinearity is expected to be quite high, large sample sizes and a well-fitting model may reduce the standard errors on the t-statistics to acceptable levels. If multicollinearity is expected to be severe, the predicted value for an item's price may be computed using the whole regression and an adjustment made using this predicted value, as explained in Chapter 17, paragraphs 17.103 to 17.109. There is a sense in which it does not matter whether the variation that, for example, should have been attributed to β_1 was wrongly attributed to β_2, or vice versa if the predicted price based on both β_1 and β_2 is used.

Omitted variable bias

18. The exclusion of tastes, technology and community characteristics has already been discussed. The concern here is with product characteristics. Consider again the use of a subset of the estimated coefficients from a hedonic regression to quality-adjust a non-comparable replacement price. It is well established that multicollinearity of omitted variables with included variables leads to bias in the estimates of the coefficients of included ones. If omitted variables are independent of the included variables, then the estimates of the coefficients on the included variables are unbiased. This is acceptable in the present instance, the only caveat being that the quality adjustment for the replacement item may also require an adjustment for these omitted variables and this, as noted by Triplett (2002), has to be undertaken using a separate method and data. But what if the omitted variable is multicollinear with a subset of included variables which are to be used to quality-adjust a non-comparable item? In this case, the coefficient of the subset of the included variables may wrongly pick up some of the effects of the omitted variables. The subset of included variables will be used to quality-adjust prices for items which differ only with regard to this subset, and the price comparison will be biased if the characteristics of included and

[43] A less formal procedure is to take the standardized residuals from the regression and plot them against model characteristics that may denote low sales, such as certain brands (makes) or vintage (if not directly incorporated), or some technical feature which makes it unlikely that the item is being bought in quantity. Higher variances may be apparent from the scatter plot. If certain features are expected to have, on average, low sales, but seem to have high variances, leverages and residuals (see Silver and Heravi (2002)), a case exists for at least down-playing their influence. Bode and van Dalén (2001) use formal statistical criteria to decide between different weighting systems and compare the results of OLS and WLS, finding, as with Ioannidis and Silver (1999), that different results can arise.

[44] Triplett (2002) stresses the point that $\bar{R}_2$ alone is insufficient for this purpose.

omitted variables have different price changes. For hedonic indices using a dummy time trend, the estimates of quality-adjusted price changes will suffer from a similar bias if omitted variables that are multicollinear with the time change are excluded from the regression. What are picked up as quality-adjusted price changes over time may, in part, be changes attributable to the prices of these excluded variables. This happens when the prices of the omitted characteristics follow a different trend. Such effects are most likely when there are gradual improvements in the quality of items, such as the reliability and safety of consumer durables,[45] which are difficult to measure, at least for the sample of items in real time. The quality-adjusted price changes will thus overstate price changes in such instances.

[45] There are, of course, some commodity areas, such as airline comfort, which have been argued to have overall patterns of decreasing quality.

THE TREATMENT OF SEASONAL PRODUCTS 22

Introduction

22.1 The existence of seasonal commodities poses some significant challenges for price statisticians. *Seasonal commodities* are commodities which are either: (a) not available in the marketplace during certain seasons of the year, or (b) are available throughout the year, but there are regular fluctuations in prices or quantities that are synchronized with the season or the time of the year.[1] A commodity that satisfies (a) is termed a *strongly seasonal commodity*, whereas a commodity that satisfies (b) is called a *weakly seasonal commodity*. It is strongly seasonal commodities that create the biggest problems for price statisticians in the context of producing a monthly or quarterly consumer price index (CPI) because if a commodity price is available in only one of the two months (or quarters) being compared, then obviously it is not possible to calculate a relative price for the commodity and traditional bilateral index number theory breaks down. In other words, if a commodity is present in one month but not the next, how can the month-to-month amount of price change for that commodity be computed?[2] In this chapter, a solution to this problem is presented which "works", even if the commodities consumed are entirely different for each month of the year.[3]

22.2 There are two main sources of seasonal fluctuations in prices and quantities: (a) climate, and (b) custom.[4] In the first category, fluctuations in temperature, precipitation and hours of daylight cause fluctuations in the demand or supply for many commodities; for example, summer versus winter clothing, the demand for light and heat, holidays, etc. With respect to custom and convention as a cause of seasonal fluctuations, consider the following quotation:

> Conventional seasons have many origins – ancient religious observances, folk customs, fashions, business practices, statute law... Many of the conventional seasons have considerable effects on economic behaviour. We can count on active retail buying before Christmas, on the Thanksgiving demand for turkeys, on the first of July demand for fireworks, on the preparations for June weddings, on heavy dividend and interest payments at the beginning of each quarter, on an increase in bankruptcies in January, and so on (Mitchell (1927, p. 237)).

22.3 Examples of important seasonal commodities are: many food items; alcoholic beverages; many clothing and footwear items; water; heating oil; electricity; flowers and garden supplies; vehicle purchases; vehicle operation; many entertainment and recreation expenditures; books; insurance expenditures; wedding expenditures; recreational equipment; toys and games; software; air travel and tourism expenditures. For a "typical" country, seasonal expenditures will often amount to one-fifth to one-third of all consumer expenditures.[5]

22.4 In the context of producing a monthly or quarterly CPI, it must be recognized that there is no completely satisfactory way of dealing with strongly seasonal commodities. If a commodity is present in one month but missing from the marketplace in the next month, then none of the index number theories that were considered in Chapters 15 to 20 can be applied because all these theories assumed that the dimensionality of the commodity space was constant for the two periods being compared. However, if seasonal commodities are present in the market during each season, then, in theory, traditional index number theory can be applied in order to construct month-to-month or quarter-to-quarter price indices. This "traditional" approach to the treatment of seasonal commodities will be followed in paragraphs 22.78 to 22.90. The reason why this straightforward approach is deferred to the end of the chapter is twofold:

- The approach that restricts the index to commodities that are present in every period often does not work well in the sense that systematic biases can occur.
- The approach is not fully representative; i.e., it does not make use of information on commodities that are not present in every month or quarter.

[1] This classification of seasonal commodities corresponds to Balk's narrow and wide sense seasonal commodities; see Balk (1980a, p. 7; 1980b, p. 110; 1980c, p. 68). Diewert (1998b, p. 457) used the terms type 1 and type 2 seasonality.

[2] Victor Zarnowitz (1961, p. 238) was perhaps the first to note the importance of this problem: "But the main problem introduced by the seasonal change is precisely that the market basket is different in the consecutive months (seasons), not only in weights but presumably often also in its very composition by commodities. This is a general and complex problem which will have to be dealt with separately at later stages of our analysis."

[3] The same commodities must, however, reappear each year for each separate month.

[4] This classification dates back to Wesley C. Mitchell (1927, p. 236) at least: "Two types of seasons produce annually recurring variations in economic activity – those which are due to climates and those which are due to conventions".

[5] Alterman, Diewert and Feenstra (1999, p. 151) found that over the 40 months between September 1993 and December 1996, somewhere between 23 and 40 per cent of United States imports and exports exhibited seasonal variations in quantities, whereas only about 5 per cent of United States export and import prices exhibited seasonal fluctuations.

22.5 In the next section, a modified version of Turvey's (1979) artificial data set is introduced. This data set will be used in order to evaluate numerically all the index number formulae suggested in this chapter. It will be seen in paragraphs 22.63 to 22.77 that very large seasonal fluctuations in volumes, combined with systematic seasonal changes in price, can make month-to-month or quarter-to-quarter price indices behave rather poorly.

22.6 Even though existing index number theory cannot deal satisfactorily with seasonal commodities in the context of constructing month-to-month indices of consumer prices, it can deal satisfactorily with seasonal commodities if the focus is changed from month-to-month CPIs to CPIs that compare the prices of one month with the prices of the *same* month in a previous year. Thus, in paragraphs 22.16 to 22.34, year-over-year monthly CPIs are studied. Turvey's seasonal data set is used to evaluate the performance of these indices and they are found to perform quite well.

22.7 In paragraphs 22.35 to 22.44, the year-over-year monthly indices defined in paragraphs 23.16 to 23.34 are aggregated into an annual index that compares all the monthly prices in a given calendar year with the corresponding monthly prices in a base year. In paragraphs 22.45 to 22.54, this idea of comparing the prices of a current calendar year with the corresponding prices in a base year is extended to annual indices that compare the prices of the last 12 months with the corresponding prices in the 12 months of a base year. The resulting *rolling year indices* can be regarded as seasonally adjusted price indices. The modified Turvey data set is used to test out these year-over-year indices, and they are found to work very well on this data set.

22.8 The rolling year indices can provide an accurate gauge of the movement of prices in the current rolling year compared to the base year. This measure of price inflation can, however, be regarded as a measure of inflation for a year that is centred around a month six months prior to the last month in the current rolling year. Hence for some policy purposes, this type of index is not as useful as an index that compares the prices of the current month to the previous month, so that more up-to-date information on the movement of prices can be obtained. In paragraphs 22.55 to 22.62, it will nevertheless be shown that under certain conditions, the year-over-year monthly index for the current month, along with the year-over-year monthly index for last month, can successfully predict or forecast a rolling year index that is centred around the current month.

22.9 The year-over-year indices defined in paragraphs 22.16 to 22.34, and their annual averages studied in paragraphs 22.35 to 22.54, offer a theoretically satisfactory method for dealing with strongly seasonal commodities; i.e., commodities that are available only during certain seasons of the year. These methods rely on the year-over-year comparison of prices and hence cannot be used in the month-to-month or quarter-to-quarter type of index, which is typically the main focus of a consumer price programme. Thus there is a need for another type of index, which may not have very strong theoretical foundations, but which can deal with seasonal commodities in the context of producing a month-to-month index. In paragraphs 22.63 to 22.77, such an index is introduced and it is implemented using the artificial data set for the commodities that are available during each month of the year. Unfortunately, because of the seasonality in both prices and quantities of the always available commodities, this type of index can be systematically biased. This bias shows up for the modified Turvey data set.

22.10 Since many CPIs are month-to-month indices that use *annual basket quantity weights*, this type of index is studied in paragraphs 22.78 to 22.84. For months when the commodity is not available in the marketplace, the last available price is carried forward and used in the index. In paragraphs 22.85 and 22.86, an annual quantity basket is again used but instead of carrying forward the prices of seasonally unavailable items, an imputation method is used to fill in the missing prices. The annual basket type indices defined in paragraphs 22.78 to 22.84 are implemented using the artificial data set. Unfortunately, the empirical results are not satisfactory in that the indices show tremendous seasonal fluctuations in prices, so they would not be suitable for users who wanted up-to-date information on trends in general inflation.

22.11 In paragraphs 22.87 to 22.90, the artificial data set is used in order to evaluate another type of month-to-month index that is frequently suggested in the literature on how to deal with seasonal commodities; namely the *Bean and Stine Type C* (1924) or *Rothwell* (1958) index. Again, this index does not get rid of the tremendous seasonal fluctuations that are present in the modified Turvey data set.

22.12 Paragraphs 22.78 to 22.84 show that the annual basket type indices with carry forward of missing prices or imputation of missing prices do not get rid of seasonal fluctuations in prices. However, in paragraphs 22.91 to 22.96, it is shown how seasonally adjusted versions of these annual basket indices can be used successfully to forecast rolling year indices that are centred on the current month. In addition, the results show how these annual basket type indices can be seasonally adjusted (using information obtained from rolling year indices from prior periods or by using traditional seasonal adjustment procedures), and hence these seasonally adjusted annual basket indices could be used as successful indicators of general inflation on a timely basis.

22.13 Paragraph 23.97 outlines some conclusions.

A seasonal commodity data set

22.14 It is useful to illustrate the index number formulae defined in subsequent sections by computing them for an actual data set. Turvey (1979) constructed an artificial data set for five seasonal commodities (apples, peaches, grapes, strawberries and oranges) for four years by month so that there are $5 \times 4 \times 12 = 240$ observations in all. At certain times of the year, peaches and strawberries (commodities 2 and 4) are unavailable, so in Tables 22.1 and 22.2 the prices and quantities for these two commodities are entered as zeros.[6] The data in

[6] The corresponding prices are not zeros, but they are entered as zeros for convenience in programming the various indices.

Table 22.1 An artificial seasonal data set: Prices

Year t	Month m	$p_1^{t,m}$	$p_2^{t,m}$	$p_3^{t,m}$	$p_4^{t,m}$	$p_5^{t,m}$
1970	1	1.14	0	2.48	0	1.30
	2	1.17	0	2.75	0	1.25
	3	1.17	0	5.07	0	1.21
	4	1.40	0	5.00	0	1.22
	5	1.64	0	4.98	5.13	1.28
	6	1.75	3.15	4.78	3.48	1.33
	7	1.83	2.53	3.48	3.27	1.45
	8	1.92	1.76	2.01	0	1.54
	9	1.38	1.73	1.42	0	1.57
	10	1.10	1.94	1.39	0	1.61
	11	1.09	0	1.75	0	1.59
	12	1.10	0	2.02	0	1.41
1971	1	1.25	0	2.15	0	1.45
	2	1.36	0	2.55	0	1.36
	3	1.38	0	4.22	0	1.37
	4	1.57	0	4.36	0	1.44
	5	1.77	0	4.18	5.68	1.51
	6	1.86	3.77	4.08	3.72	1.56
	7	1.94	2.85	2.61	3.78	1.66
	8	2.02	1.98	1.79	0	1.74
	9	1.55	1.80	1.28	0	1.76
	10	1.34	1.95	1.26	0	1.77
	11	1.33	0	1.62	0	1.76
	12	1.30	0	1.81	0	1.50
1972	1	1.43	0	1.89	0	1.56
	2	1.53	0	2.38	0	1.53
	3	1.59	0	3.59	0	1.55
	4	1.73	0	3.90	0	1.62
	5	1.89	0	3.56	6.21	1.70
	6	1.98	4.69	3.51	3.98	1.78
	7	2.07	3.32	2.73	4.30	1.89
	8	2.12	2.29	1.65	0	1.91
	9	1.73	1.90	1.15	0	1.92
	10	1.56	1.97	1.15	0	1.95
	11	1.56	0	1.46	0	1.94
	12	1.49	0	1.73	0	1.64
1973	1	1.68	0	1.62	0	1.69
	2	1.82	0	2.16	0	1.69
	3	1.89	0	3.02	0	1.74
	4	2.00	0	3.45	0	1.91
	5	2.14	0	3.08	7.17	2.03
	6	2.23	6.40	3.07	4.53	2.13
	7	2.35	4.31	2.41	5.19	2.22
	8	2.40	2.98	1.49	0	2.26
	9	2.09	2.21	1.08	0	2.22
	10	2.03	2.18	1.08	0	2.31
	11	2.05	0	1.36	0	2.34
	12	1.90	0	1.57	0	1.97

Table 22.2 An artificial seasonal data set: Quantities

Year t	Month m	$q_1^{t,m}$	$q_2^{t,m}$	$q_3^{t,m}$	$q_4^{t,m}$	$q_5^{t,m}$
1970	1	3086	0	82	0	10266
	2	3765	0	35	0	9656
	3	4363	0	98	0	7940
	4	4842	0	26	0	5110
	5	4439	0	75	700	4089
	6	5323	91	82	2709	3362
	7	4165	498	96	1970	3396
	8	3224	6504	1490	0	2406
	9	4025	4923	2937	0	2486
	10	5784	865	2826	0	3222
	11	6949	0	1290	0	6958
	12	3924	0	338	0	9762
1971	1	3415	0	119	0	10888
	2	4127	0	45	0	10314
	3	4771	0	14	0	8797
	4	5290	0	11	0	5590
	5	4986	0	74	806	4377
	6	5869	98	112	3166	3681
	7	4671	548	132	2153	3748
	8	3534	6964	2216	0	2649
	9	4509	5370	4229	0	2726
	10	6299	932	4178	0	3477
	11	7753	0	1831	0	8548
	12	4285	0	496	0	10727
1972	1	3742	0	172	0	11569
	2	4518	0	67	0	10993
	3	5134	0	22	0	9621
	4	5738	0	16	0	6063
	5	5498	0	137	931	4625
	6	6420	104	171	3642	3970
	7	5157	604	202	2533	4078
	8	3881	7378	3269	0	2883
	9	4917	5839	6111	0	2957
	10	6872	1006	5964	0	3759
	11	8490	0	2824	0	8238
	12	5211	0	731	0	11827
1973	1	4051	0	250	0	12206
	2	4909	0	102	0	11698
	3	5567	0	30	0	10438
	4	6253	0	25	0	6593
	5	6101	0	220	1033	4926
	6	7023	111	252	4085	4307
	7	5671	653	266	2877	4418
	8	4187	7856	4813	0	3165
	9	5446	6291	8803	0	3211
	10	7377	1073	8778	0	4007
	11	9283	0	4517	0	8833
	12	4955	0	1073	0	12558

Tables 22.1 and 22.2 are essentially the same as the data set constructed by Turvey except that a number of adjustments have been made to it in order to illustrate various points. The two most important adjustments are:

- The data for commodity 3 (grapes) have been adjusted so that the annual Laspeyres and Paasche indices (defined in paragraphs 22.35 to 22.44) would differ more than in the original data set.[7]
- After the above adjustments were made, each price in the last year of data was escalated by the monthly inflation factor 1.008 so that month-to-month inflation for the last year of data would be at an approximate monthly rate of 1.6 per cent per month compared to about 0.8 per cent per month for the first three years of data.[8]

[7] After the first year, the price data for grapes has been adjusted downward by 30 per cent each year and the corresponding volume has been adjusted upward by 40 per cent each year. In addition, the quantity of oranges (commodity 5) for November 1971 has been changed from 3,548 to 8,548 so that the seasonal pattern of change for this commodity is similar to that of other years. For similar reasons, the price of oranges in December 1970 has been changed from 1.31 to 1.41 and in January 1971 from 1.35 to 1.45.

[8] Pierre Duguay of the Bank of Canada, while commenting on a preliminary version of this chapter, observed that rolling year indices would not be able to detect the *magnitude* of systematic changes in the month-to-month inflation rate. The original Turvey data set was roughly consistent with a month-to-month inflation rate of 0.8 per cent per month; i.e., prices grew roughly at the rate of 1.008 each month over the four years of data. This second major adjustment of the Turvey data was introduced to illustrate Duguay's observation, which is quite correct: the centred rolling year indices pick up the correct magnitude of the new inflation rate only after a lag of half a year or so. They do, however, quickly pick up the direction of change in the inflation rate.

22.15 Ralph Turvey sent his artificial data set to statistical agencies around the world, asking them to use their normal techniques to construct monthly and annual average price indices. About 20 countries replied, and Turvey (1979, p. 13) summarized the responses as follows: "It will be seen that the monthly indices display very large differences, e.g., a range of 129.12–169.50 in June, while the range of simple annual means is much smaller. It will also be seen that the indices vary as to the peak month or year."

The above (modified) data are used to test out various index number formulae in subsequent sections.

Year-over-year monthly indices

22.16 It can be seen that the existence of seasonal commodities that are present in the marketplace in one month but not the next causes the accuracy of a month-to-month index to fall.[9] A way of dealing with these strongly seasonal commodities is to change the focus from short-term month-to-month price indices and instead focus on making year-over-year price comparisons for each month of the year. In the latter type of comparison, there is a good chance that seasonal commodities that appear, say, in February will also appear in subsequent Februarys so that the overlap of commodities will be maximized in these year-over-year monthly indices.

22.17 For over a century, it has been recognized that making year-over-year comparisons[10] provides the simplest method for making comparisons that are free from the contaminating effects of seasonal fluctuations. According to W. Stanley Jevons (1884, p. 3):

> In the daily market reports, and other statistical publications, we continually find comparisons between numbers referring to the week, month, or other parts of the year, and those for the corresponding parts of a previous year. The comparison is given in this way in order to avoid any variation due to the time of the year. And it is obvious to everyone that this precaution is necessary. Every branch of industry and commerce must be affected more or less by the revolution of the seasons, and we must allow for what is due to this cause before we can learn what is due to other causes.

22.18 The economist A.W. Flux and the statistician G. Udny Yule also endorsed the idea of making year-over-year comparisons to minimize the effects of seasonal fluctuations:

> Each month the average price change compared with the corresponding month of the previous year is to be computed.... The determination of the proper seasonal variations of weights, especially in view of the liability of seasons to vary from year to year, is a task from which, I imagine, most of us would be tempted to recoil (Flux (1921, pp. 184–185)).
>
> My own inclination would be to form the index number for any month by taking ratios to the corresponding month of the year being used for reference, the year before presumably, as this would avoid any difficulties with seasonal commodities. I should then form the annual average by the geometric mean of the monthly figures (Yule (1921, p. 199)).

In more recent times, Victor Zarnowitz (1961, p. 266) also endorsed the use of year-over-year monthly indices:

> There is of course no difficulty in measuring the average price change between the same months of successive years, if a month is our unit "season", and if a constant seasonal market basket can be used, for traditional methods of price index construction can be applied in such comparisons.

22.19 In the remainder of this section, it is shown how year-over-year Fisher indices and approximations to them can be constructed.[11] For each month $m = 1, 2, \ldots, 12$, let $S(m)$ denote the set of commodities that are available in the marketplace for each year $t = 0, 1, \ldots, T$. For $t = 0, 1, \ldots, T$ and $m = 1, 2, \ldots, 12$, let $p_n^{t,m}$ and $q_n^{t,m}$ denote the price and quantity of commodity n that is in the marketplace in month m of year t, where n belongs to $S(m)$. Let $p^{t,m}$ and $q^{t,m}$ denote the month m and year t price and quantity vectors, respectively. Then *the year-over-year monthly Laspeyres, Paasche and Fisher indices* going from month m of year t to month m of year $t+1$ can be defined as follows:

$$P_L(p^{t,m}, p^{t+1,m}, q^{t,m}) = \frac{\sum_{n \in S(m)} p_n^{t+1,m} q_n^{t,m}}{\sum_{n \in S(m)} p_n^{t,m} q_n^{t,m}} \qquad m = 1, 2, \ldots, 12 \tag{22.1}$$

$$P_P(p^{t,m}, p^{t+1,m}, q^{t+1,m}) = \frac{\sum_{n \in S(m)} p_n^{t+1,m} q_n^{t+1,m}}{\sum_{n \in Sm)} p_n^{t,m} q_n^{t+1,m}} \qquad m = 1, 2, \ldots, 12 \tag{22.2}$$

$$P_F(p^{t,m}, p^{t+1,m}, q^{t,m}, q^{t+1,m}) \equiv \sqrt{P_L(p^{t,m}, p^{t+1,m}, q^{t,m}) P_P(p^{t,m}, p^{t+1,m}, q^{t+1,m})} \qquad m = 1, 2, \ldots, 12. \tag{22.3}$$

22.20 The above formulae can be rewritten in price relative and monthly expenditure share form as follows:

$$P_L(p^{t,m}, p^{t+1,m}, s^{t,m}) = \sum_{n \in S(m)} s_n^{t,m} (p_n^{t+1,m} / p_n^{t,m}) \qquad m = 1, 2, \ldots, 12 \tag{22.4}$$

[9] At the limit, if each commodity appeared in only one month of the year, then a month-to-month index would break down completely.

[10] In the seasonal price index context, this type of index corresponds to Bean and Stine's (1924, p. 31) Type D index.

[11] Diewert (1996b, p. 17–19; 1999a, p. 50) noted various separability restrictions on consumer preferences that would justify these year-over-year monthly indices from the viewpoint of the economic approach to index number theory.

$$P_P(p^{t,m},p^{t+1,m},s^{t+1,m}) = \left[\sum_{n\in S(m)} s_n^{t+1,m}(p_n^{t+1,m}/p_n^{t,m})^{-1}\right]^{-1}$$

$$m = 1,2,\ldots,12 \qquad (22.5)$$

$$P_F(p^{t,m},p^{t+1,m},s^{t,m},s^{t+1,m}) \equiv \sqrt{P_L(p^{t,m},p^{t+1,m},s^{t,m})P_P(p^{t,m},p^{t+1,m},s^{t+1,m})} = \sqrt{\sum_{n\in S(m)} s_n^{t,m}(p_n^{t+1,m}/p_n^{t,m})} \times \sqrt{\left[\sum_{n\in S(m)} s_n^{t,m}(p_n^{t+1,m}/p_n^{t,m})^{-1}\right]^{-1}}$$

$$m = 1,2,\ldots,12 \qquad (22.6)$$

where the monthly expenditure share for commodity $n \in S(m)$ for month m in year t is defined as:

$$s_n^{t,m} = \frac{p_n^{t,m}q_n^{t,m}}{\sum_{i\in S(m)} p_i^{t,m}q_i^{t,m}}$$

$$m = 1,2,\ldots,12$$

$$n \in S(m) \; t = 0,1,\ldots,T \qquad (22.7)$$

and $s^{t,m}$ denotes the vector of month m expenditure shares in year t, $[s_n^{t,m}]$ for $n \in S(m)$.

22.21 Current period expenditure shares $s_n^{t,m}$ are not likely to be available. Hence it will be necessary to approximate these shares using the corresponding expenditure shares from a base year 0.

22.22 Use the base period monthly expenditure share vectors $s^{0,m}$ in place of the vector of month m and year t expenditure shares $s^{t,m}$ in equation (22.4), and use the base period monthly expenditure share vectors $s^{0,m}$ in place of the vector of month m and year $t+1$ expenditure shares $s^{t+1,m}$ in equation (22.5). Similarly, replace the share vectors $s^{t,m}$ and $s^{t+1,m}$ in equation (22.6) by the base period expenditure share vector for month m, $s^{0,m}$. The resulting *approximate year-over-year monthly Laspeyres, Paasche and Fisher indices* are defined by equations (22.8) to (22.10):[12]

$$P_{AL}(p^{t,m},p^{t+1,m},s^{0,m}) = \sum_{n\in S(m)} s_n^{0,m}(p_n^{t+1,m}/p_n^{t,m})$$

$$m = 1,2,\ldots,12 \qquad (22.8)$$

$$P_{AP}(p^{t,m},p^{t+1,m},s^{0,m}) = \left[\sum_{n\in S(m)} s_n^{0,m}(p_n^{t+1,m}/p_n^{t,m})^{-1}\right]^{-1}$$

$$m - 1,2,\ldots,12 \qquad (22.9)$$

$$P_{AF}(p^{t,m},p^{t+1,m},s^{0,m},s^{0,m}) \equiv \sqrt{P_{AL}(p^{t,m},p^{t+1,m},s^{0,m})P_P(p^{t,m},p^{t+1,m},s^{0,m})} = \sqrt{\sum_{n\in S(m)} s_n^{t,m}(p_n^{t+1,m}/p_n^{t,m})} \times \sqrt{\left[\sum_{n\in S(m)} s_n^{t,m}(p_n^{t+1,m}/p_n^{t,m})^{-1}\right]^{-1}}$$

$$m = 1,2,\ldots,12. \qquad (22.10)$$

22.23 The approximate Fisher year-over-year monthly indices defined by equation (22.10) will provide adequate approximations to their true Fisher counterparts defined by equation (22.6) only if the monthly expenditure shares for the base year 0 are not too different from their current year t and $t+1$ counterparts. Hence, it will be useful to construct the true Fisher indices on a delayed basis in order to check the adequacy of the approximate Fisher indices defined by equation (22.10).

22.24 The year-over-year monthly approximate Fisher indices defined by equation (22.10) will normally have a certain amount of upward bias, since these indices cannot reflect long-term substitution of consumers towards commodities that are becoming relatively cheaper over time. This reinforces the case for computing true year-over-year monthly Fisher indices defined by equation (22.6) on a delayed basis so that this substitution bias can be estimated.

22.25 Note that the approximate year-over-year monthly Laspeyres and Paasche indices, P_{AL} and P_{AP} defined by equations (22.8) and (22.9) above, satisfy the following inequalities:

$$P_{AL}(p^{t,m},p^{t+1,m},s^{0,m})P_{AL}(p^{t+1,m},p^{t,m},s^{0,m}) \geq 1$$

$$m = 1,2,\ldots,12 \qquad (22.11)$$

$$P_{AP}(p^{t,m},p^{t+1,m},s^{0,m})P_{AP}(p^{t+1,m},p^{t,m},s^{0,m}) \leq 1$$

$$m = 1,2,\ldots,12 \qquad (22.12)$$

with strict inequalities if the monthly price vectors $p^{t,m}$ and $p^{t+1,m}$ are not proportional to each other.[13] The inequality (22.11) says that the approximate year-over-year monthly Laspeyres index fails the time reversal test with an upward bias, while the inequality (22.12) says that the approximate year-over-year monthly Paasche index fails the time reversal test with a downward bias. Hence the fixed weight approximate Laspeyres index P_{AL} has a built-in upward bias and the fixed weight approximate Paasche index P_{AP} has a built-in downward bias. Statistical agencies should avoid the use of these formulae. The formulae can, however, be

[12] If the monthly expenditure shares for the base year, $s_n^{0,m}$, are all equal, then the approximate Fisher index defined by equation (22.10) reduces to Fisher's (1922, p. 472) formula 101. Fisher (1922, p. 211) observed that this index was empirically very close to the unweighted geometric mean of the price relatives, while Dalén (1992, p. 143) and Diewert (1995a, p. 29) showed analytically that these two indices approximated each other to the second order. The equally weighted version of equation (22.10) was recommended as an elementary index by Carruthers, Sellwood and Ward (1980, p. 25) and Dalén (1992, p. 140).

[13] See Hardy, Littlewood and Pólya (1934, p. 26).

combined as in the approximate Fisher formula (22.10) and the resulting index should be free from any systematic formula bias (but there still could be some substitution bias).

22.26 The year-over-year monthly indices defined in this section are illustrated using the artificial data set given in Tables 22.1 and 22.2. Although fixed base indices are not formally defined in this section, these indices have similar formulae to the year-over-year indices except that the variable base year t is replaced by the fixed base year 0. The resulting 12 year-over-year monthly fixed base Laspeyres, Paasche and Fisher indices are listed in Tables 22.3 to 22.5.

22.27 Comparing the entries in Tables 22.3 and 22.4, it can be seen that the year-over-year monthly fixed base Laspeyres and Paasche price indices do not differ substantially for the early months of the year, but that there are substantial differences between the indices for the last five months of the year by the time the year 1973 is reached. The largest percentage difference between the Laspeyres and Paasche indices is 12.5 per cent for month 10 in 1973 (1.4060/1.2496 = 1.125). However, all the year-over-year monthly series show a smooth year-over-year trend.

22.28 Approximate fixed base year-over-year Laspeyres, Paasche and Fisher indices can be constructed by replacing current month expenditure shares for the five commodities by the corresponding base year monthly expenditure shares on the five commodities. The resulting approximate Laspeyres indices are equal to the original fixed base Laspeyres indices so there is no need to present the approximate Laspeyres indices in a table. The approximate year-over-year Paasche and Fisher indices do, however, differ from the fixed base Paasche and Fisher indices found in Tables 22.4 and 22.5, so these new approximate indices are listed in Tables 22.6 and 22.7.

22.29 Comparing Table 22.4 with Table 22.6, it can be seen that, with a few exceptions, the entries correspond fairly closely. One of the bigger differences is the 1973 entry for the fixed base Paasche index for month 9, which is 1.1664, while the corresponding entry for the approximate fixed base Paasche index is 1.1920, for a 2.2 per cent difference (1.1920/1.1664 = 1.022). In general, the approximate fixed base Paasche indices are somewhat bigger than the true fixed base Paasche indices, as could be expected, since the approximate indices have

Table 22.3 Year-over-year monthly fixed base Laspeyres indices

Year	Month											
	1	2	3	4	5	6	7	8	9	10	11	12
1970	1.0000	1.0000	1.0000	1.0000	1.0000	1.0000	1.0000	1.0000	1.0000	1.0000	1.0000	1.0000
1971	1.1085	1.1068	1.1476	1.1488	1.1159	1.0844	1.1103	1.0783	1.0492	1.0901	1.1284	1.0849
1972	1.2060	1.2442	1.3062	1.2783	1.2184	1.1734	1.2364	1.1827	1.1049	1.1809	1.2550	1.1960
1973	1.3281	1.4028	1.4968	1.4917	1.4105	1.3461	1.4559	1.4290	1.2636	1.4060	1.5449	1.4505

Table 22.4 Year-over-year monthly fixed base Paasche indices

Year	Month											
	1	2	3	4	5	6	7	8	9	10	11	12
1970	1.0000	1.0000	1.0000	1.0000	1.0000	1.0000	1.0000	1.0000	1.0000	1.0000	1.0000	1.0000
1971	1.1074	1.1070	1.1471	1.1486	1.1115	1.0827	1.1075	1.0699	1.0414	1.0762	1.1218	1.0824
1972	1.2023	1.2436	1.3038	1.2773	1.2024	1.1657	1.2307	1.1455	1.0695	1.1274	1.2218	1.1901
1973	1.3190	1.4009	1.4912	1.4882	1.3715	1.3266	1.4433	1.3122	1.1664	1.2496	1.4296	1.4152

Table 22.5 Year-over-year monthly fixed base Fisher indices

Year	Month											
	1	2	3	4	5	6	7	8	9	10	11	12
1970	1.0000	1.0000	1.0000	1.0000	1.0000	1.0000	1.0000	1.0000	1.0000	1.0000	1.0000	1.0000
1971	1.1080	1.1069	1.1474	1.1487	1.1137	1.0835	1.1089	1.0741	1.0453	1.0831	1.1251	1.0837
1972	1.2041	1.2439	1.3050	1.2778	1.2104	1.1695	1.2336	1.1640	1.0870	1.1538	1.2383	1.1930
1973	1.3235	1.4019	1.4940	1.4900	1.3909	1.3363	1.4496	1.3694	1.2140	1.3255	1.4861	1.4327

Table 22.6 Year-over-year approximate monthly fixed base Paasche indices

Year	Month											
	1	2	3	4	5	6	7	8	9	10	11	12
1970	1.0000	1.0000	1.0000	1.0000	1.0000	1.0000	1.0000	1.0000	1.0000	1.0000	1.0000	1.0000
1971	1.1077	1.1057	1.1468	1.1478	1.1135	1.0818	1.1062	1.0721	1.0426	1.0760	1.1209	1.0813
1972	1.2025	1.2421	1.3036	1.2757	1.2110	1.1640	1.2267	1.1567	1.0788	1.1309	1.2244	1.1862
1973	1.3165	1.3947	1.4880	1.4858	1.3926	1.3223	1.4297	1.3315	1.1920	1.2604	1.4461	1.4184

some substitution bias built into them as their expenditure shares are held fixed at the 1970 levels.

22.30 Turning now to the chained year-over-year monthly indices using the artificial data set, the resulting 12 year-over-year monthly chained Laspeyres, Paasche and Fisher indices, P_L, P_P and P_F, where the month-to-month links are defined by equations (22.4) to (22.6), are listed in Tables 22.8 to 22.10.

22.31 Comparing the entries in Tables 22.8 and 22.9, it can be seen that the year-over-year monthly chained Laspeyres and Paasche price indices have smaller differences than the corresponding fixed base Laspeyres and Paasche price indices in Tables 22.3 and 22.4. This is a typical pattern, as found in Chapter 19: the use of chained indices tends to reduce the spread between Paasche and Laspeyres indices compared to their fixed base counterparts. The largest percentage difference between corresponding entries for the chained Laspeyres and Paasche indices in Tables 22.8 and 22.9 is 4.1 per cent for month 10 in 1973 (1.3593/1.3059 = 1.041). Recall that the fixed base Laspeyres and Paasche indices differed by 12.5 per cent for the same month, so that chaining does tend to reduce the spread between these two equally plausible indices.

22.32 The chained year-over-year Fisher indices listed in Table 22.10 are regarded as the "best" estimates of year-over-year inflation using the artificial data set.

22.33 The year-over-year chained Laspeyres, Paasche and Fisher indices listed in Tables 22.8 to 22.10 can be approximated by replacing current period commodity expenditure shares for each month by the corresponding base year monthly commodity expenditure shares. The resulting 12 year-over-year monthly approximate chained Laspeyres, Paasche and Fisher indices, P_{AL}, P_{AP} and P_{AF}, where the monthly links are defined by equations (22.8) to (22.10), are listed in Tables 22.11 to 22.13.

22.34 The year-over-year chained indices listed in Tables 22.11 to 22.13 approximate their true chained counterparts listed in Tables 22.8 to 22.10 very closely. For the year 1973, the largest discrepancies are for the Paasche and Fisher indices for month 9: the chained Paasche is 1.2018, while the corresponding approximate chained Paasche is 1.2183 for a difference of 1.4 per cent, and the chained Fisher is 1.2181, while the corresponding approximate chained Fisher is 1.2305 for a difference of 1.0 per cent. It can be seen that for the modified Turvey data set, the approximate

Table 22.7 Year-over-year approximate monthly fixed base Fisher indices

Year	Month											
	1	2	3	4	5	6	7	8	9	10	11	12
1970	1.0000	1.0000	1.0000	1.0000	1.0000	1.0000	1.0000	1.0000	1.0000	1.0000	1.0000	1.0000
1971	1.1081	1.1063	1.1472	1.1483	1.1147	1.0831	1.1082	1.0752	1.0459	1.0830	1.1247	1.0831
1972	1.2043	1.2432	1.3049	1.2770	1.2147	1.1687	1.2316	1.1696	1.0918	1.1557	1.2396	1.1911
1973	1.3223	1.3987	1.4924	1.4888	1.4015	1.3341	1.4428	1.3794	1.2273	1.3312	1.4947	1.4344

Table 22.8 Year-over-year monthly chained Laspeyres indices

Year	Month											
	1	2	3	4	5	6	7	8	9	10	11	12
1970	1.0000	1.0000	1.0000	1.0000	1.0000	1.0000	1.0000	1.0000	1.0000	1.0000	1.0000	1.0000
1971	1.1085	1.1068	1.1476	1.1488	1.1159	1.0844	1.1103	1.0783	1.0492	1.0901	1.1284	1.0849
1972	1.2058	1.2440	1.3058	1.2782	1.2154	1.1720	1.2357	1.1753	1.0975	1.1690	1.2491	1.1943
1973	1.3274	1.4030	1.4951	1.4911	1.4002	1.3410	1.4522	1.3927	1.2347	1.3593	1.5177	1.4432

Table 22.9 Year-over-year monthly chained Paasche indices

Year	Month											
	1	2	3	4	5	6	7	8	9	10	11	12
1970	1.0000	1.0000	1.0000	1.0000	1.0000	1.0000	1.0000	1.0000	1.0000	1.0000	1.0000	1.0000
1971	1.1074	1.1070	1.1471	1.1486	1.1115	1.0827	1.1075	1.0699	1.0414	1.0762	1.1218	1.0824
1972	1.2039	1.2437	1.3047	1.2777	1.2074	1.1682	1.2328	1.1569	1.0798	1.1421	1.2321	1.1908
1973	1.3243	1.4024	1.4934	1.4901	1.3872	1.3346	1.4478	1.3531	1.2018	1.3059	1.4781	1.4305

Table 22.10 Year-over-year monthly chained Fisher indices

Year	Month											
	1	2	3	4	5	6	7	8	9	10	11	12
1970	1.0000	1.0000	1.0000	1.0000	1.0000	1.0000	1.0000	1.0000	1.0000	1.0000	1.0000	1.0000
1971	1.1080	1.1069	1.1474	1.1487	1.1137	1.0835	1.1089	1.0741	1.0453	1.0831	1.1251	1.0837
1972	1.2048	1.2438	1.3052	1.2780	1.2114	1.1701	1.2343	1.1660	1.0886	1.1555	1.2405	1.1926
1973	1.3258	1.4027	1.4942	1.4906	1.3937	1.3378	1.4500	1.3728	1.2181	1.3323	1.4978	1.4368

Table 22.11 Year-over-year monthly approximate chained Laspeyres indices

Year	Month 1	2	3	4	5	6	7	8	9	10	11	12
1970	1.0000	1.0000	1.0000	1.0000	1.0000	1.0000	1.0000	1.0000	1.0000	1.0000	1.0000	1.0000
1971	1.1085	1.1068	1.1476	1.1488	1.1159	1.0844	1.1103	1.0783	1.0492	1.0901	1.1284	1.0849
1972	1.2056	1.2440	1.3057	1.2778	1.2168	1.1712	1.2346	1.1770	1.0989	1.1692	1.2482	1.1939
1973	1.3255	1.4007	1.4945	1.4902	1.4054	1.3390	1.4491	1.4021	1.2429	1.3611	1.5173	1.4417

Table 22.12 Year-over-year monthly approximate chained Paasche indices

Year	Month 1	2	3	4	5	6	7	8	9	10	11	12
1970	1.0000	1.0000	1.0000	1.0000	1.0000	1.0000	1.0000	1.0000	1.0000	1.0000	1.0000	1.0000
1971	1.1077	1.1057	1.1468	1.1478	1.1135	1.0818	1.1062	1.0721	1.0426	1.0760	1.1209	1.0813
1972	1.2033	1.2424	1.3043	1.2764	1.2130	1.1664	1.2287	1.1638	1.0858	1.1438	1.2328	1.1886
1973	1.3206	1.3971	1.4914	1.4880	1.3993	1.3309	1.4386	1.3674	1.2183	1.3111	1.4839	1.4300

Table 22.13 Year-over-year monthly approximate chained Fisher indices

Year	Month 1	2	3	4	5	6	7	8	9	10	11	12
1970	1.0000	1.0000	1.0000	1.0000	1.0000	1.0000	1.0000	1.0000	1.0000	1.0000	1.0000	1.0000
1971	1.1081	1.1063	1.1472	1.1483	1.1147	1.0831	1.1082	1.0752	1.0459	1.0830	1.1247	1.0831
1972	1.2044	1.2432	1.3050	1.2771	1.2149	1.1688	1.2317	1.1704	1.0923	1.1565	1.2405	1.1912
1973	1.3231	1.3989	1.4929	1.4891	1.4024	1.3349	1.4438	1.3847	1.2305	1.3358	1.5005	1.4358

year-over-year monthly approximate Fisher indices listed in Table 22.13 approximate the theoretically preferred (but in practice unfeasible in a timely fashion) Fisher chained indices listed in Table 22.10 quite satisfactorily. Since the approximate Fisher indices are just as easy to compute as the approximate Laspeyres and Paasche indices, it may be useful to ask that statistical agencies make available to the public these approximate Fisher indices along with the approximate Laspeyres and Paasche indices.

Year-over-year annual indices

22.35 Assuming that each commodity in each season of the year is a separate "annual" commodity is the simplest and theoretically most satisfactory method for dealing with seasonal commodities when the goal is to construct annual price and quantity indices. This idea can be traced back to Bruce D. Mudgett in the consumer price context and to Richard Stone in the producer price context:

> The basic index is a yearly index and as a price or quantity index is of the same sort as those about which books and pamphlets have been written in quantity over the years (Mudgett (1955, p. 97)).

> The existence of a regular seasonal pattern in prices which more or less repeats itself year after year suggests very strongly that the varieties of a commodity available at different seasons cannot be transformed into one another without cost and that, accordingly, in all cases where seasonal variations in price are significant, the varieties available at different times of the year should be treated, in principle, as separate commodities (Stone (1956, pp. 74–75)).

22.36 Using the notation introduced in the previous section, the *Laspeyres, Paasche and Fisher annual (chain link) indices* comparing the prices of year t with those of year $t+1$ can be defined as follows:

$$P_L(p^{t,1},\ldots,p^{t,12};\,p^{t+1,1},\ldots,p^{t+1,12};\,q^{t,1},\ldots,q^{t,12}) \equiv \frac{\sum_{m=1}^{12}\sum_{n\in S(m)} p_n^{t+1,m}q_n^{t,m}}{\sum_{m=1}^{12}\sum_{n\in S(m)} p_n^{t,m}q_n^{t,m}} \tag{22.13}$$

$$P_P(p^{t,1},\ldots,p^{t,12};\,p^{t+1,1},\ldots,p^{t+1,12};\,q^{t+1,1},\ldots,q^{t+1,12}) \equiv \frac{\sum_{m=1}^{12}\sum_{n\in S(m)} p_n^{t+1,m}q_n^{t+1,m}}{\sum_{m=1}^{12}\sum_{n\in S(m)} p_n^{t,m}q_n^{t+1,m}} \tag{22.14}$$

$$\begin{aligned} &P_F(p^{t,1},\ldots,p^{t,12};\,p^{t+1,1},\ldots,p^{t+1,12};\,q^{t,1},\ldots,q^{t,12};\,q^{t+1,1},\ldots,q^{t+1,12}) \\ &\equiv \sqrt{P_L(p^{t,1},\ldots,p^{t,12};\,p^{t+1,1},\ldots,p^{t+1,12};\,q^{t,1},\ldots,q^{t,12})} \\ &\times \sqrt{P_P(p^{t,1},\ldots,p^{t,12};\,p^{t+1,1},\ldots,p^{t+1,12};\,q^{t+1,1},\ldots,q^{t+1,12})} \end{aligned} \tag{22.15}$$

22.37 The above formulae can be rewritten in price relative and monthly expenditure share form as follows:

$$P_L(p^{t,1},\ldots,p^{t,12};\ p^{t+1,1},\ldots,p^{t+1,12};\ \sigma_1^t s^{t,1},\ldots,\sigma_{12}^t s^{t,12})$$
$$\equiv \sum_{m=1}^{12}\sum_{n\in S(m)} \sigma_m^t s_n^{t,m}(p_n^{t+1,m}/p_n^{t,m})$$
$$= \sum_{m=1}^{12} \sigma_m^t P_L(p^{t,m},p^{t+1,m},s^{t,m}) \qquad (22.16)$$

$$P_P(p^{t,1},\ldots,p^{t,12};\ p^{t+1,1},\ldots,p^{t+1,12};\ \sigma_1^{t+1} s^{t+1,1},\ldots,\sigma_{12}^{t+1} s^{t+1,12})$$
$$\equiv \left[\sum_{m=1}^{12}\sum_{n\in S(m)} \sigma_m^{t+1} s_n^{t+1,m}(p_n^{t+1,m}/p_n^{t,m})^{-1}\right]^{-1}$$
$$= \left[\sum_{m=1}^{12} \sigma_m^{t+1} \sum_{n\in S(m)} s_n^{t+1,m}(p_n^{t+1,m}/p_n^{t,m})^{-1}\right]^{-1}$$
$$= \left[\sum_{m=1}^{12} \sigma_m^{t+1}[P_P(p^{t,m},p^{t+1,m},s^{t+1,m})]^{-1}\right]^{-1} \qquad (22.17)$$

where the expenditure share for month m in year t is defined as:

$$P_F(p^{t,1},\ldots,p^{t,12};\ p^{t+1,1},\ldots,p^{t+1,12};\ \sigma_1^t s^{t,1},\ldots,\sigma_{12}^t s^{t,12};\ \sigma_1^{t+1} s^{t+1,1},\ldots,\sigma_{12}^{t+1} s^{t+1,12})$$
$$\equiv \sqrt{\frac{\sum_{m=1}^{12}\sum_{n\in S(m)} \sigma_m^t s_n^{t,m}(p_n^{t+1,m}/p_n^{t,m})}{\sum_{m=1}^{12}\sum_{n\in S(m)} \sigma_m^{t+1} s_n^{t+1,m}(p_n^{t+1,m}/p_n^{t,m})^{-1}}}$$
$$= \sqrt{\frac{\sum_{m=1}^{12} \sigma_m^t[P_L(p^{t,m},p^{t+1,m},s^{t,m})]}{\sum_{m=1}^{12} \sigma_m^{t+1}[P_P(p^{t,m},p^{t+1,m},s^{t+1,m})]^{-1}}} \qquad (22.18)$$

$$\sigma_n^t \equiv \frac{\sum_{n\in S(m)} p_n^{t,m} q_n^{t,m}}{\sum_{i=1}^{12}\sum_{j\in S(i)} p_j^{t,i} q_j^{t,i}} \qquad m=1,2,\ldots,12;\ t=0,1,\ldots,T \qquad (22.19)$$

and the year-over-year monthly Laspeyres and Paasche (chain link) price indices $P_L(p^{t,m}, p^{t+1,m}, s^{t,m})$ and $P_P(p^{t,m}, p^{t+1,m}, s^{t+1,m})$ are defined by equations (22.4) and (22.5), respectively. As usual, the annual chain link Fisher index P_F defined by equation (22.18), which compares the prices in every month of year t with the corresponding prices in year $t+1$, is the geometric mean of the annual chain link Laspeyres and Paasche indices, P_L and P_P, defined by equations (22.16) and (22.17). The last equations in (22.16), (22.17) and (22.18) show that these annual indices can be defined as (monthly) share-weighted averages of the year-over-year monthly chain link Laspeyres and Paasche indices, $P_L(p^{t,m}, p^{t+1,m}, s^{t,m})$ and $P_P(p^{t,m}, p^{t+1,m}, s^{t+1,m})$, defined by equations (22.4) and (22.5). Hence once the year-over-year monthly indices defined above have been calculated numerically, it is easy to calculate the corresponding annual indices.

22.38 Fixed base counterparts to the formulae defined by equations (22.16) to (22.18) can readily be defined: simply replace the data pertaining to period t by the corresponding data pertaining to the base period 0.

22.39 The annual fixed base Laspeyres, Paasche and Fisher indices, as calculated using the data from the artificial data set tabled in paragraphs 22.14 and 22.15, are listed in Table 22.14, which shows that by 1973, the annual fixed base Laspeyres index exceeds its Paasche counterpart by 4.5 per cent. Note that each series increases steadily.

22.40 The annual fixed base Laspeyres, Paasche and Fisher indices can be approximated by replacing any current shares by the corresponding base year shares. The resulting annual approximate fixed base Laspeyres, Paasche and Fisher indices are listed in Table 22.15. Also listed in the last column of Table 22.15 is the fixed base geometric Laspeyres annual index, P_{GL}. This is the weighted geometric mean counterpart to the fixed base Laspeyres index, which is equal to a base period weighted arithmetic average of the long-term price relatives; see Chapter 19. It can be shown that P_{GL} approximates the approximate fixed base Fisher index, P_{AF}, to the second order around a point where all the long-term price relatives are equal to unity.[14] It can be seen that the entries for the Laspeyres price indices are exactly the same in Tables 22.14 and 22.15. This is as it should be, because the fixed base Laspeyres price index uses only expenditure shares from the base year 1970; hence the approximate fixed base Laspeyres index is equal to the true fixed base Laspeyres index. Comparing the columns labelled P_P and P_F in Table 22.14 with the columns P_{AP} and P_{AF} in Table 22.15 shows that the approximate Paasche and approximate Fisher indices are quite close to the corresponding annual Paasche and Fisher indices. Hence, for the artificial data set, the true annual fixed base Fisher index can be very closely approximated by the corresponding approximate Fisher index, P_{AF} (or the geometric Laspeyres index, P_{GL}), which, of course, can be computed using the same information set that is normally available to statistical agencies.

22.41 Using the artificial data set in Tables 22.1 and 22.2, the annual chained Laspeyres, Paasche and Fisher indices can readily be calculated, using the formulae (22.16) to (22.18) for the chain links. The resulting indices are listed in Table 22.16, which shows that the use of chained indices has substantially narrowed the gap between the Paasche and Laspeyres indices. The difference between the chained annual Laspeyres and Paasche indices in 1973 is only 1.5 per cent (1.3994 versus 1.3791), whereas from Table 22.14, the difference between the fixed base annual Laspeyres and Paasche indices in 1973 is 4.5 per cent (1.4144 versus 1.3536). Thus the use of chained annual indices has substantially reduced the substitution (or representativity) bias of the Laspeyres and Paasche indices. Comparing Tables 22.14 and 22.16, it can be seen that for this particular artificial data set, the annual fixed base Fisher indices are very

[14] See footnote 12.

Table 22.14 Annual fixed base Laspeyres, Paasche and Fisher price indices

Year	P_L	P_P	P_F
1970	1.0000	1.0000	1.0000
1971	1.1008	1.0961	1.0984
1972	1.2091	1.1884	1.1987
1973	1.4144	1.3536	1.3837

Table 22.15 Annual approximate fixed base Laspeyres, Paasche, Fisher and geometric Laspeyres indices

Year	P_{AL}	P_{AP}	P_{AF}	P_{GL}
1970	1.0000	1.0000	1.0000	1.0000
1971	1.1008	1.0956	1.0982 1	.0983
1972	1.2091	1.1903	1.1996	1.2003
1973	1.4144	1.3596	1.3867	1.3898

Table 22.16 Annual chained Laspeyres, Paasche and Fisher price indices

Year	P_L	P_P	P_F
1970	1.0000	1.0000	1.0000
1971	1.1008	1.0961	1.0984
1972	1.2052	1.1949	1.2001
1973	1.3994	1.3791	1.3892

Table 22.17 Annual approximate chained Laspeyres, Paasche and Fisher price indices

Year	P_{AL}	P_{AP}	P_{AF}
1970	1.0000	1.0000	1.0000
1971	1.1008	1.0956	1.0982
1972	1.2051	1.1952	1.2002
1973	1.3995	1.3794	1.3894

close to their annual chained Fisher counterparts. The annual chained Fisher indices should, however, normally be regarded as the more desirable target index to approximate, since this index will normally give better results if prices and expenditure shares are changing substantially over time.[15]

22.42 Obviously, the current year weights, $s_n^{t,m}$ and σ_m^t and $s_n^{t+1,m}$ and σ_m^{t+1}, which appear in the chain link formulae (22.16) to (22.18), can be approximated by the corresponding base year weights, $s_n^{0,m}$ and σ_m^0. This leads to the annual approximate chained Laspeyres, Paasche and Fisher indices listed in Table 22.17.

22.43 Comparing the entries in Tables 22.16 and 22.17 shows that the approximate chained annual Laspeyres, Paasche and Fisher indices are extremely close to the corresponding true chained annual Laspeyres, Paasche and Fisher indices. Hence, for the artificial data set, the true annual chained Fisher index can be very closely approximated by the corresponding approximate Fisher index, which can be computed using the same information set that is normally available to statistical agencies.

22.44 The approach to computing annual indices outlined in this section, which essentially involves taking monthly expenditure share-weighted averages of the 12 year-over-year monthly indices, should be contrasted with the approach that simply takes the arithmetic mean of the 12 monthly indices. The problem with the latter approach is that months where expenditures are below the average (e.g., February) are given the same weight in the unweighted annual average as months where expenditures are above the average (e.g., December).

Rolling year annual indices

22.45 In the previous section, the price and quantity data pertaining to the 12 months of a calendar year were compared to the 12 months of a base calendar year. There is, however, no need to restrict attention to calendar-year comparisons: any 12 consecutive months of price and quantity data could be compared to the price and quantity data of the base year, provided that the January data in the non-calendar year are compared to the January data of the base year, the February data of the non-calendar year are compared to the February data of the base year, and so on, up to the December data of the non-calendar year being compared to the December data of the base year.[16] Alterman, Diewert and Feenstra (1999, p. 70) called the resulting indices *rolling year* or *moving year* indices.[17]

22.46 In order to theoretically justify the rolling year indices from the viewpoint of the economic approach to index number theory, some restrictions on preferences are required. The details of these assumptions can be found in Diewert (1996b, pp. 32–34; 1999a, pp. 56–61).

22.47 The problems involved in constructing rolling year indices for the artificial data set are now considered. For both fixed base and chained rolling year indices, the first 13 index number calculations are the same. For the year that ends with the data for December of 1970, the index is set equal to 1 for the Laspeyres, Paasche and Fisher moving year indices. The base year data are the 44 non-zero price and quantity observations for the calendar year 1970. When the data for January 1971 become available, the three non-zero price and quantity entries for January of calendar year 1970 are dropped and replaced by the corresponding entries for January 1971. The data for the remaining months of the comparison year remain the same; i.e., for February to December of the comparison year, the data for the rolling year are set equal to the corresponding entries for February to December 1970. Thus the Laspeyres, Paasche or Fisher

[15] The gap between the Laspeyres and Paasche indices will normally be reduced using chained indices under these circumstances. Of course, if there are no substantial trends in prices, so that prices are just changing randomly, then it will generally be preferable to use the fixed base Fisher index.

[16] Diewert (1983c) suggested this type of comparison and termed the resulting index a "split year" comparison.

[17] Crump (1924, p. 185) and Mendershausen (1937, p. 245), respectively, used these terms in the context of various seasonal adjustment procedures. The term "rolling year" seems to be well established in the business literature in the United Kingdom.

rolling year index value for January 1971 compares the prices and quantities of January 1971 with the corresponding prices and quantities of January 1970. For the remaining months of this first moving year, the prices and quantities of February to December 1970 are simply compared with exactly the same prices and quantities of February to December 1970. When the data for February 1971 become available, the three non-zero price and quantity entries for February for the last rolling year (which are equal to the three non-zero price and quantity entries for February 1970) are dropped and replaced by the corresponding entries for February 1971. The resulting data become the price and quantity data for the second rolling year. The Laspeyres, Paasche or Fisher rolling year index value for February 1971 compares the prices and quantities of January and February 1971 with the corresponding prices and quantities of January and February 1970. For the remaining months of this first moving year, the prices and quantities of March to December 1970 are compared with exactly the same prices and quantities of March to December 1970. This process of exchanging the price and quantity data of the current month in 1971 with the corresponding data of the same month in the base year 1970 in order to form the price and quantity data for the latest rolling year continues until December 1971 is reached, when the current rolling year becomes the calendar year 1971. Thus the Laspeyres, Paasche and Fisher rolling year indices for December 1971 are equal to the corresponding fixed base (or chained) annual Laspeyres, Paasche and Fisher indices for 1971, listed in Tables 22.14 or 22.16.

22.48 Once the first 13 entries for the rolling year indices have been defined as indicated above, the remaining fixed base rolling year Laspeyres, Paasche and Fisher indices are constructed by taking the price and quantity data of the last 12 months and rearranging the data so that the January data in the rolling year are compared to the January data in the base year, the February data in the rolling year are compared to the February data in the base year, and so on, up to the December data in the rolling year being compared to the December data in the base year. The resulting fixed base rolling year Laspeyres, Paasche and Fisher indices for the artificial data set are listed in Table 22.18.

22.49 Once the first 13 entries for the fixed base rolling year indices have been defined as indicated above, the remaining chained rolling year Laspeyres, Paasche and Fisher indices are constructed by taking the price and quantity data of the last 12 months and comparing these data to the corresponding data of the rolling year of the 12 months preceding the current rolling year. The resulting chained rolling year Laspeyres, Paasche and Fisher indices for the artificial data set are listed in the last three columns of Table 22.18. Note that the first 13 entries of the fixed base Laspeyres, Paasche and Fisher indices are equal to the corresponding entries for the chained Laspeyres, Paasche and Fisher indices. It will also be noted that the entries for December (month 12) of 1970, 1971, 1972 and 1973 for the fixed base rolling year Laspeyres, Paasche and Fisher indices are equal to the corresponding fixed base annual Laspeyres, Paasche and Fisher indices listed in Table 22.14. Similarly, the entries in Table 22.18 for December (month 12) of 1970, 1971, 1972 and 1973 for the chained rolling year Laspeyres, Paasche and Fisher indices are equal to the corresponding chained annual Laspeyres, Paasche and Fisher indices listed in Table 22.16.

22.50 Table 22.18 shows that the rolling year indices are very smooth and free from seasonal fluctuations. For the fixed base indices, each entry can be viewed as a *seasonally adjusted annual consumer price index* that compares the data of the 12 consecutive months that end with the year and month indicated with the corresponding price and quantity data of the 12 months in the base year, 1970. Thus rolling year indices offer statistical agencies an objective and reproducible method of seasonal adjustment that can compete with existing time series methods of seasonal adjustment.[18]

22.51 Table 22.18 shows that the use of chained indices has substantially narrowed the gap between the fixed base moving year Paasche and Laspeyres indices. The difference between the rolling year chained Laspeyres and Paasche indices in December 1973 is only 1.5 per cent (1.3994 versus 1.3791), whereas the difference between the rolling year fixed base Laspeyres and Paasche indices in December 1973 is 4.5 per cent (1.4144 versus 1.3536). Thus, the use of chained indices has substantially reduced the substitution (or representativity) bias of the Laspeyres and Paasche indices. As in the previous section, the chained Fisher rolling year index is regarded as the target seasonally adjusted annual index when seasonal commodities are in the scope of the CPI. This type of index is also a suitable index for central banks to use for inflation targeting purposes.[19] The six series in Table 22.18 are charted in Figure 22.1. The fixed base Laspeyres index is the highest one, followed by the chained Laspeyres, the two Fisher indices (which are virtually indistinguishable), and the chained Paasche. Finally, the fixed base Paasche is the lowest index. An increase in the slope of each graph can clearly be seen for the last eight months, reflecting the increase in the month-to-month inflation rates that was built into the data for the last 12 months of the data set.[20]

22.52 As in the previous section, the current year weights, $s_n^{t,m}$ and σ_m^t and $s_n^{t+1,m}$ and σ_m^{t+1}, which appear

[18] For discussions on the merits of econometric or time series methods versus index number methods of seasonal adjustment, see Diewert (1999a, pp. 61–68) and Alterman, Diewert and Feenstra (1999, pp. 78–110). The basic problem with time series methods of seasonal adjustment is that the target seasonally adjusted index is very difficult to specify in an unambiguous way; i.e., there is an infinite number of possible target indices. For example, it is impossible to identify a temporary increase in inflation within a year from a changing seasonal factor. Hence different econometricians will tend to generate different seasonally adjusted series, leading to a lack of reproducibility.

[19] See Diewert (2002c) for a discussion of the measurement issues involved in choosing such an index.

[20] The arithmetic average of the 36 month-over-month inflation rates for the rolling year fixed base Fisher indices is 1.0091; the average of these rates for the first 24 months is 1.0076, for the last 12 months is 1.0120 and for the last 2 months is 1.0156. Hence, the increased month-to-month inflation rates for the last year are not fully reflected in the rolling year indices until a full 12 months have passed. However, the fact that inflation has increased for the last 12 months of data compared to the earlier months is picked up almost immediately.

Table 22.18 Rolling year Laspeyres, Paasche and Fisher price indices

Year	Month	P_L (fixed)	P_P (fixed)	P_F (fixed)	P_L (chain)	P_P (chain)	P_F (chain)
1970	12	1.0000	1.0000	1.0000	1.0000	1.0000	1.0000
1971	1	1.0082	1.0087	1.0085	1.0082	1.0087	1.0085
	2	1.0161	1.0170	1.0165	1.0161	1.0170	1.0165
	3	1.0257	1.0274	1.0265	1.0257	1.0274	1.0265
	4	1.0344	1.0364	1.0354	1.0344	1.0364	1.0354
	5	1.0427	1.0448	1.0438	1.0427	1.0448	1.0438
	6	1.0516	1.0537	1.0527	1.0516	1.0537	1.0527
	7	1.0617	1.0635	1.0626	1.0617	1.0635	1.0626
	8	1.0701	1.0706	1.0704	1.0701	1.0706	1.0704
	9	1.0750	1.0740	1.0745	1.0750	1.0740	1.0745
	10	1.0818	1.0792	1.0805	1.0818	1.0792	1.0805
	11	1.0937	1.0901	1.0919	1.0937	1.0901	1.0919
	12	1.1008	1.0961	1.0984	1.1008	1.0961	1.0984
1972	1	1.1082	1.1035	1.1058	1.1081	1.1040	1.1061
	2	1.1183	1.1137	1.1160	1.1183	1.1147	1.1165
	3	1.1287	1.1246	1.1266	1.1290	1.1260	1.1275
	4	1.1362	1.1324	1.1343	1.1366	1.1342	1.1354
	5	1.1436	1.1393	1.1414	1.1437	1.1415	1.1426
	6	1.1530	1.1481	1.1505	1.1528	1.1505	1.1517
	7	1.1645	1.1595	1.1620	1.1644	1.1622	1.1633
	8	1.1757	1.1670	1.1713	1.1747	1.1709	1.1728
	9	1.1812	1.1680	1.1746	1.1787	1.1730	1.1758
	10	1.1881	1.1712	1.1796	1.1845	1.1771	1.1808
	11	1.1999	1.1805	1.1901	1.1962	1.1869	1.1915
	12	1.2091	1.1884	1.1987	1.2052	1.1949	1.2001
1973	1	1.2184	1.1971	1.2077	1.2143	1.2047	1.2095
	2	1.2300	1.2086	1.2193	1.2263	1.2172	1.2218
	3	1.2425	1.2216	1.2320	1.2393	1.2310	1.2352
	4	1.2549	1.2341	1.2444	1.2520	1.2442	1.2481
	5	1.2687	1.2469	1.2578	1.2656	1.2579	1.2617
	6	1.2870	1.2643	1.2756	1.2835	1.2758	1.2797
	7	1.3070	1.2843	1.2956	1.3038	1.2961	1.3000
	8	1.3336	1.3020	1.3177	1.3273	1.3169	1.3221
	9	1.3492	1.3089	1.3289	1.3395	1.3268	1.3331
	10	1.3663	1.3172	1.3415	1.3537	1.3384	1.3460
	11	1.3932	1.3366	1.3646	1.3793	1.3609	1.3700
	12	1.4144	1.3536	1.3837	1.3994	1.3791	1.3892

Figure 22.1 Rolling year fixed base and chained Laspeyres, Paasche and Fisher indices

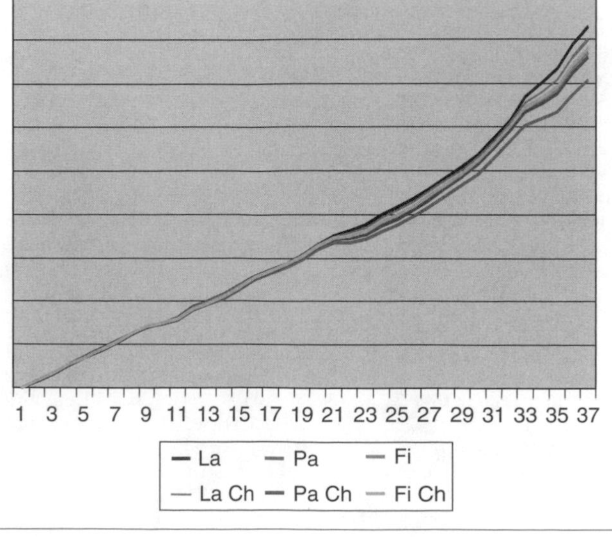

in the chain link formulae (22.16) to (22.18) or in the corresponding fixed base formulae, can be approximated by the corresponding base year weights, $s_n^{0,m}$ and σ_m^0. This leads to the annual approximate fixed base and chained rolling year Laspeyres, Paasche and Fisher indices listed in Table 22.19.

22.53 Comparing the indices in Tables 22.18 and 22.19, it can be seen that the approximate rolling year fixed base and chained Laspeyres, Paasche and Fisher indices listed in Table 22.19 are very close to their true rolling year counterparts listed in Table 22.18. In particular, the approximate chain rolling year Fisher index (which can be computed using just base year expenditure share information, along with current information on prices) is very close to the preferred target index, the rolling year chained Fisher index. In December 1973, these two indices differ by only 0.014 per cent (1.3894/1.3892 = 1.00014). The indices in Table 22.19 are charted in Figure 22.2. It can be seen that Figures 22.1 and 22.2 are very similar; in particular, the Fisher fixed base and chained indices are virtually identical in both figures.

Table 22.19 Rolling year approximate Laspeyres, Paasche and Fisher price indices

Year	Month	P_{AL} (fixed)	P_{AP} (fixed)	P_{AF} (fixed)	P_{AL} (chain)	P_{AP} (chain)	P_{AF} (chain)
1970	12	1.0000	1.0000	1.0000	1.0000	1.0000	1.0000
1971	1	1.0082	1.0074	1.0078	1.0082	1.0074	1.0078
	2	1.0161	1.0146	1.0153	1.0161	1.0146	1.0153
	3	1.0257	1.0233	1.0245	1.0257	1.0233	1.0245
	4	1.0344	1.0312	1.0328	1.0344	1.0312	1.0328
	5	1.0427	1.0390	1.0409	1.0427	1.0390	1.0409
	6	1.0516	1.0478	1.0497	1.0516	1.0478	1.0497
	7	1.0617	1.0574	1.0596	1.0617	1.0574	1.0596
	8	1.0701	1.0656	1.0679	1.0701	1.0656	1.0679
	9	1.0750	1.0702	1.0726	1.0750	1.0702	1.0726
	10	1.0818	1.0764	1.0791	1.0818	1.0764	1.0791
	11	1.0937	1.0881	1.0909	1.0937	1.0881	1.0909
	12	1.1008	1.0956	1.0982	1.1008	1.0956	1.0982
1972	1	1.1082	1.1021	1.1051	1.1083	1.1021	1.1052
	2	1.1183	1.1110	1.1147	1.1182	1.1112	1.1147
	3	1.1287	1.1196	1.1241	1.1281	1.1202	1.1241
	4	1.1362	1.1260	1.1310	1.1354	1.1268	1.1311
	5	1.1436	1.1326	1.1381	1.1427	1.1336	1.1381
	6	1.1530	1.1415	1.1472	1.1520	1.1427	1.1473
	7	1.1645	1.1522	1.1583	1.1632	1.1537	1.1584
	8	1.1757	1.1620	1.1689	1.1739	1.1642	1.1691
	9	1.1812	1.1663	1.1737	1.1791	1.1691	1.1741
	10	1.1881	1.1710	1.1795	1.1851	1.1747	1.1799
	11	1.1999	1.1807	1.1902	1.1959	1.1855	1.1907
	12	1.2091	1.1903	1.1996	1.2051	1.1952	1.2002
1973	1	1.2184	1.1980	1.2082	1.2142	1.2033	1.2087
	2	1.2300	1.2074	1.2187	1.2253	1.2133	1.2193
	3	1.2425	1.2165	1.2295	1.2367	1.2235	1.2301
	4	1.2549	1.2261	1.2404	1.2482	1.2340	1.2411
	5	1.2687	1.2379	1.2532	1.2615	1.2464	1.2540
	6	1.2870	1.2548	1.2708	1.2795	1.2640	1.2717
	7	1.3070	1.2716	1.2892	1.2985	1.2821	1.2903
	8	1.3336	1.2918	1.3125	1.3232	1.3048	1.3139
	9	1.3492	1.3063	1.3276	1.3386	1.3203	1.3294
	10	1.3663	1.3182	1.3421	1.3538	1.3345	1.3441
	11	1.3932	1.3387	1.3657	1.3782	1.3579	1.3680
	12	1.4144	1.3596	1.3867	1.3995	1.3794	1.3894

Figure 22.2 Rolling year approximate fixed base and chained Laspeyres, Paasche and Fisher indices

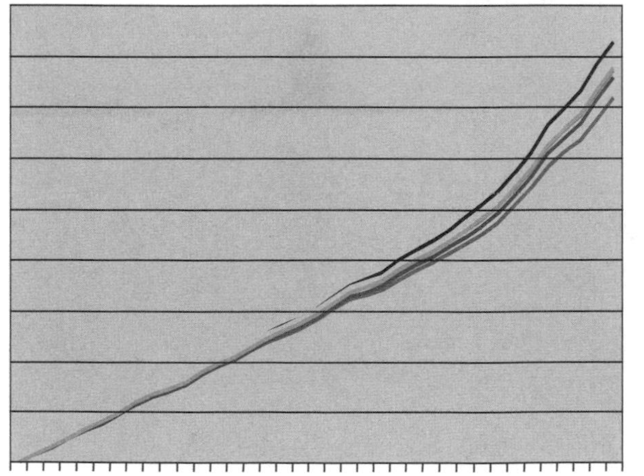

22.54 From the above tables, it can be seen that year-over-year monthly indices and their generalizations to rolling year indices perform very well using the modified Turvey data set; like is compared to like, and the existence of seasonal commodities does not lead to erratic fluctuations in the indices. The only drawback to the use of these indices is that it seems that they cannot give any information on short-term, month-to-month fluctuations in prices. This is most evident if seasonal baskets are totally different for each month since in this case, there is no possibility of comparing prices on a month-to-month basis. In the following section, it is shown how a current period year-over-year monthly index can be used to predict a rolling year index that is centred on the current month.

Predicting a rolling year index using a current period year-over-year monthly index

22.55 It might be conjectured that under a regime where the long-run trend in prices is smooth, changes in the year-over-year inflation rate for a particular month compared to the previous month could give valuable information about the long-run trend in price inflation. For the modified Turvey data set, this conjecture turns out to be true, as seen below.

22.56 The basic idea is illustrated using the fixed base Laspeyres rolling year indices listed in Table 22.18 and the year-over-year monthly fixed base Laspeyres indices listed in Table 22.3. In Table 22.18, the fixed base Laspeyres rolling year entry for December of 1971 compares the 12 months of price and quantity data pertaining to 1971 with the corresponding prices and quantities pertaining to 1970. This index number, P_L, is the first entry in Table 22.20. Thus the P_{LRY} column of Table 22.20 shows the fixed base rolling year Laspeyres index, taken from Table 22.18, starting at December 1971 and carrying through to December 1973, which is 24 observations in all. Looking at the first entry of this column, it can be seen that the index is a weighted average of year-over-year price relatives over all 12 months in 1970 and 1971. Thus this index is an average of year-over-year monthly price changes, centred between June and July of the two years for which prices are being compared. Hence, an approximation to this annual index could be obtained by taking the arithmetic average of the June and July year-over-year monthly indices pertaining to the years 1970 and 1971 (see the entries for months 6 and 7 for the year 1971 in Table 22.3, 1.0844 and 1.1103).[21] The next rolling year fixed base Laspeyres index corresponds to the January 1972 entry in Table 22.18. An approximation to this rolling year index, P_{ARY}, could be obtained by taking the arithmetic average of the July and August year-over-year monthly indices pertaining to the years 1970 and 1971 (see the entries for months 7 and 8 for the year 1971 in Table 22.3, 1.1103 and 1.0783). These arithmetic averages of the two year-over-year monthly indices that are in the middle of the corresponding rolling year are listed in the P_{ARY} column of Table 22.20. From Table 22.20, it can be seen that the P_{ARY} column does not approximate the P_{LRY} column particularly well, since the approximate indices in the P_{ARY} column are seen to have some pronounced seasonal fluctuations, whereas the rolling year indices in the P_{LRY} column are free from seasonal fluctuations.

22.57 Some seasonal adjustment factors (*SAF*) are listed in Table 22.20. For the first 12 observations, the entries in the *SAF* column are simply the ratios of the entries in the P_{LRY} column, divided by the corresponding entries in the P_{ARY} column; i.e., for the first 12 observations, the seasonal adjustment factors are simply the ratio of the rolling year indices starting at December 1971, divided by the arithmetic average of the two year-over-year monthly indices that are in the middle of the corresponding rolling year.[22] The initial 12 seasonal adjustment factors are then just repeated for the remaining entries for the *SAF* column.

Table 22.20 Rolling year fixed base Laspeyres and seasonally adjusted approximate rolling year price indices

Year	Month	P_{LRY}	P_{SAARY}	P_{ARY}	*SAF*
1971	12	1.1008	1.1008	1.0973	1.0032
1972	1	1.1082	1.1082	1.0943	1.0127
	2	1.1183	1.1183	1.0638	1.0512
	3	1.1287	1.1287	1.0696	1.0552
	4	1.1362	1.1362	1.1092	1.0243
	5	1.1436	1.1436	1.1066	1.0334
	6	1.1530	1.1530	1.1454	1.0066
	7	1.1645	1.1645	1.2251	0.9505
	8	1.1757	1.1757	1.2752	0.9220
	9	1.1812	1.1812	1.2923	0.9141
	10	1.1881	1.1881	1.2484	0.9517
	11	1.1999	1.1999	1.1959	1.0033
	12	1.2091	1.2087	1.2049	1.0032
1973	1	1.2184	1.2249	1.2096	1.0127
	2	1.2300	1.2024	1.1438	1.0512
	3	1.2425	1.2060	1.1429	1.0552
	4	1.2549	1.2475	1.2179	1.0243
	5	1.2687	1.2664	1.2255	1.0334
	6	1.2870	1.2704	1.2620	1.0066
	7	1.3070	1.2979	1.3655	0.9505
	8	1.3336	1.3367	1.4498	0.9220
	9	1.3492	1.3658	1.4943	0.9141
	10	1.3663	1.3811	1.4511	0.9517
	11	1.3932	1.3827	1.3783	1.0032
	12	1.4144	1.4188	1.4010	1.0127

22.58 Once the seasonal adjustment factors have been defined, then the approximate rolling year index P_{ARY} can be multiplied by the corresponding seasonal adjustment factor *SAF* in order to form a *seasonally adjusted approximate rolling year index*, P_{SAARY}, as listed in Table 22.20.

22.59 Comparing the P_{LRY} and P_{SAARY} columns in Table 22.20, the rolling year fixed base Laspeyres index, P_{LRY}, and the seasonally adjusted approximate rolling year index, P_{SAARY}, are identical for the first 12 observations, which follows by construction since P_{SAARY} equals the approximate rolling year index, P_{ARY}, multiplied by the seasonal adjustment factor *SAF* which in turn is equal to the rolling year Laspeyres index, P_{LRY}, divided by P_{ARY}. However, starting at December 1972, the rolling year index, P_{LRY}, differs from the corresponding seasonally adjusted approximate rolling year index, P_{SAARY}. It can be seen that for these last 13 months, P_{SAARY} is surprisingly close to P_{LRY}.[23]

Figure 22.3 shows P_{LRY}, P_{SAARY} and P_{ARY} graphically. Because of the acceleration in the monthly inflation rate for the last year of data, it can be seen that the seasonally adjusted approximate rolling year series, P_{SAARY}, does not pick up this accelerated inflation rate for the first few months of the last year (it lies well below P_{LRY} for February and March 1973) but,

[21] Obviously, if an average of the year-over-year monthly indices for May, June, July and August were taken, a better approximation to the annual index could be obtained, and if an average of the year-over-year monthly indices for April, May, June, July, August and September were taken, an even better approximation could be obtained to the annual index, and so on.

[22] Thus if *SAF* is greater than one, this means that the two months in the middle of the corresponding rolling year have year-over-year rates of price increase that average out to a number below the overall average of the year-over-year rates of price increase for the entire rolling year, and above the overall average if *SAF* is less than one.

[23] The means for the last 13 observations in columns P_{LRY} and P_{ARY} of Table 22.20 are 1.2980 and 1.2930. A regression of P_L on P_{SAARY} leads to an R^2 of 0.9662 with an estimated variance of the residual of 0.000214.

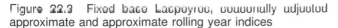

Figure 22.3 Fixed base Laspeyres, seasonally adjusted approximate and approximate rolling year indices

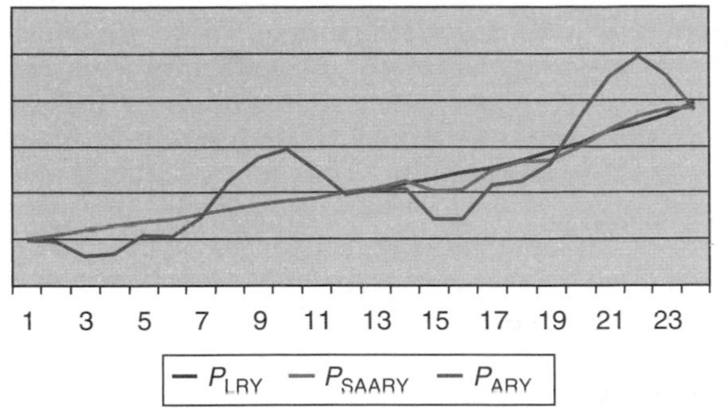

in general, it predicts the corresponding centred year quite well.

22.60 The above results for the modified Turvey data set are quite encouraging. If these results can be replicated for other data sets, then it means that statistical agencies can use the latest information on year-over-year monthly inflation to predict reasonably well the (seasonally adjusted) rolling year inflation rate for a rolling year that is centred around the last two months. Thus policy-makers and other interested users of the CPI can obtain a reasonably accurate forecast of trend inflation (centred around the current month) some six months in advance of the final estimates being calculated.

22.61 The method of seasonal adjustment used in this section is rather crude compared to some of the sophisticated econometric or statistical methods that are available. Thus, these more sophisticated methods could be used in order to improve the forecasts of trend inflation. If improved forecasting methods are used, however, it is useful to use the rolling year indices as targets for the forecasts, rather than using a statistical package that simultaneously seasonally adjusts current data and calculates a trend rate of inflation. What is being suggested here is that the rolling year concept can be used in order to eliminate the lack of reproducibility in the estimates of trend inflation that existing statistical methods of seasonal adjustment generate.[24]

22.62 In this section and the previous ones, all the suggested indices have been based on year-over-year monthly indices and their averages. In the subsequent sections of this chapter, attention will be turned to more traditional price indices that attempt to compare the prices in the current month with the prices in a previous month.

[24] The operator of a statistical seasonal adjustment package has to make somewhat arbitrary decisions on many factors. For example, are the seasonal factors additive or multiplicative? How long should the moving average be and what type of average should be calculated? Thus different operators of the seasonal adjustment package will tend to produce different estimates of the trend and the seasonal factors.

Maximum overlap month-to-month price indices

22.63 A reasonable method for dealing with seasonal commodities in the context of picking a target index for a month-to-month CPI is the following:[25]

- Determine the set of commodities that is present in the marketplace in both months of the comparison.
- For this maximum overlap set of commodities, calculate one of the three indices recommended in previous chapters; i.e., calculate the Fisher, Walsh or Törnqvist–Theil index.[26]

Thus the bilateral index number formula is applied only to the subset of commodities that is present in both periods.[27]

22.64 The question now arises: should the comparison month and the base month be adjacent months (thus leading to chained indices) or should the base month be fixed (leading to fixed base indices)? It seems reasonable to prefer chained indices over fixed base indices for two reasons:

- The set of seasonal commodities which overlaps during two consecutive months is likely to be much larger than the set obtained by comparing the prices of any given month with a fixed base month (such as January of a base year). Hence the comparisons made using chained indices will be more comprehensive and accurate than those made using a fixed base.
- In many economies, on average 2 or 3 per cent of price quotes disappear each month because of the introduction of new commodities and the disappearance of older ones. This rapid sample attrition means that fixed base indices rapidly become unrepresentative. Hence it seems preferable to use chained indices which can more closely follow marketplace developments.[28]

22.65 It will be useful to review the notation at this point and define some new notation. Let there be N commodities that are available in some month of some year and let $p_n^{t,m}$ and $q_n^{t,m}$ denote the price and quantity of commodity n that is in the marketplace[29] in month m of year t (if the commodity is unavailable, define $p_n^{t,m}$

[25] For more on the economic approach and the assumptions on consumer preferences that can justify month-to-month maximum overlap indices, see Diewert (1999a, pp. 51–56).

[26] For simplicity, only the Fisher index is considered in detail in this chapter.

[27] Keynes (1930, p. 95) called this the highest common factor method for making bilateral index number comparisons. Of course, this target index drops those strongly seasonal commodities that are not present in the marketplace during one of the two months being compared. Thus the index number comparison is not completely comprehensive. Mudgett (1955, p. 46) called the "error" in an index number comparison that is introduced by the highest common factor method (or maximum overlap method) the "homogeneity error".

[28] This rapid sample degradation essentially forces some form of chaining at the elementary level in any case.

[29] As was seen in Chapter 20, it is necessary to have a target concept for the individual prices and quantities $p_n^{t,m}$ and $q_n^{t,m}$ at the finest level of aggregation. Under most circumstances, these target concepts can be taken to be unit values (for prices) and total quantities consumed (for quantities).

and $q_n^{t,m}$ to be 0). Let $p^{t,m} \equiv [p_1^{t,m}, p_2^{t,m}, \ldots, p_N^{t,m}]$ and $q^{t,m} \equiv [q_1^{t,m}, q_2^{t,m}, \ldots, q_N^{t,m}]$ be the month m and year t price and quantity vectors, respectively. Let $S(t,m)$ be the set of commodities that is present in month m of year t and the following month. Then the maximum overlap Laspeyres, Paasche and Fisher indices going from month m of year t to the following month can be defined as follows:[30]

$$P_L(p^{t,m}, p^{t,m+1}, q^{t,m}, S(t,m)) = \frac{\sum_{n \in S(t,m)} p_n^{t,m+1} q_n^{t,m}}{\sum_{n \in S(t,m)} p_n^{t,m} q_n^{t,m}} \quad m = 1, 2, \ldots, 11 \tag{22.20}$$

$$P_P(p^{t,m}, p^{t,m+1}, q^{t,m+1}, S(t,m)) = \frac{\sum_{n \in S(t,m)} p_n^{t,m+1} q_n^{t,m+1}}{\sum_{n \in S(t,m)} p_n^{t,m} q_n^{t,m+1}} \quad m = 1, 2, \ldots, 11 \tag{22.21}$$

$$P_F(p^{t,m}, p^{t,m+1}, q^{t,m}, q^{t,m+1}, S(t,m)) \equiv \sqrt{P_L(p^{t,m}, p^{t,m+1}, q^{t,m}, S(t,m)) P_P(p^{t,m}, p^{t,m+1}, q^{t,m+1}, S(t,m))} \quad m = 1, 2, \ldots, 11. \tag{22.22}$$

Note that P_L, P_P and P_F depend on the two (complete) price and quantity vectors pertaining to months m and $m+1$ of year $t, p^{t,m}, p^{t,m+1}, q^{t,m}, q^{t,m+1}$, but they also depend on the set $S(t, m)$, which is the set of commodities that are present in both months. Thus, the commodity indices n that are in the summations on the right-hand sides of equations (22.20) to (22.22) include indices n that correspond to commodities that are present in both months, which is the meaning of $n \in S(t, m)$; i.e., n belongs to the set $S(t, m)$.

22.66 In order to rewrite the definitions (22.20) to (22.22) in expenditure share and price relative form, some additional notation is required. Define the expenditure shares of commodity n in month m and $m+1$ of year t, using the set of commodities that are present in month m of year t and the subsequent month, as follows:

$$s_n^{t,m}(t,m) = \frac{p_n^{t,m} q_n^{t,m}}{\sum_{i \in S(t,m)} p_i^{t,m} q_i^{t,m}} \quad n \in S(t,m) \quad m = 1, 2, \ldots, 11 \tag{22.23}$$

$$s_n^{t,m+1}(t,m) = \frac{p_n^{t,m+1} q_n^{t,m+1}}{\sum_{i \in S(t,m)} p_i^{t,m+1} q_i^{t,m+1}} \quad n \in S(t,m) \quad m = 1, 2, \ldots, 11 \tag{22.24}$$

The notation in equations (22.23) and (22.24) is rather messy because $s_n^{t,m+1}(t,m)$ has to be distinguished from $s_n^{t,m+1}(t,m+1)$. The expenditure share $s_n^{t,m+1}(t,m)$ is the share of commodity n in month $m+1$ of year t where n is restricted to the set of commodities that are present in month m of year t and the subsequent month, whereas $s_n^{t,m+1}(t,m+1)$ is the share of commodity n in month $m+1$ of year t but where n is restricted to the set of commodities that are present in month $m+1$ of year t and the subsequent month. Thus, the set of superscripts $t, m+1$ in $s_n^{t,m+1}(t,m)$ indicates that the expenditure share is calculated using the price and quantity data of month $m+1$ of year t and (t, m) indicates that the set of admissible commodities is restricted to the set of commodities that are present in both month m of year t and the subsequent month.

22.67 Now define vectors of expenditure shares. If commodity n is present in month m of year t and the following month, define $s_n^{t,m}(t,m)$ using equation (22.23); if this is not the case, define $s_n^{t,m}(t,m) = 0$. Similarly, if commodity n is present in month m of year t and the following month, define $s_n^{t,m+1}(t,m)$ using equation (22.24); if this is not the case, define $s_n^{t,m+1}(t,m) = 0$. Now define the N-dimensional vectors $s^{t,m}(t,m) \equiv [s_1^{t,m}(t,m), s_2^{t,m}(t,m), \ldots, s_N^{t,m}(t,m)]$ and $s^{t,m+1}(t,m) \equiv [s_1^{t,m+1}(t,m), s_2^{t,m+1}(t,m), \ldots, s_N^{t,m+1}(t,m)]$. Using these share definitions, the month-to-month Laspeyres, Paasche and Fisher formulae (22.20) to (22.22) can also be rewritten in expenditure share and price form as follows:

$$P_L(p^{t,m}, p^{t,m+1}, s^{t,m}(t,m)) \equiv \sum_{n \in S(t,m)} s_n^{t,m}(t,m)(p_n^{t,m+1}/p_n^{t,m}) \quad m = 1, 2, \ldots, 11 \tag{22.25}$$

$$P_P(p^{t,m}, p^{t,m+1}, s^{t,m+1}(t,m)) \equiv \left[\sum_{n \in S(t,m)} s_n^{t,m+1}(t,m)(p_n^{t,m+1}/p_n^{t,m})^{-1} \right]^{-1} \quad m = 1, 2, \ldots, 11 \tag{22.26}$$

$$P_F(p^{t,m}, p^{t,m+1}, s^{t,m}(t,m), s^{t,m+1}(t,m)) \equiv \sqrt{\frac{\sum_{n \in S(m)} s_n^{t,m}(t,m)(p_n^{t,m+1}/p_n^{t,m})}{\sum_{n \in S(m)} s_n^{t,m+1}(t,m)(p_n^{t,m+1}/p_n^{t,m})^{-1}}} \quad m = 1, 2, \ldots, 11. \tag{22.27}$$

22.68 It is important to recognize that the expenditure shares $s_n^{t,m}(t,m)$ that appear in the maximum overlap month-to-month Laspeyres index defined by equation (22.25) are not the expenditure shares that could be taken from a consumer expenditure survey for month m of year t: instead, they are the shares that result after expenditures on seasonal commodities that are present in month m of year t, but are not present in the following month, are dropped. Similarly, the expenditure shares $s_n^{t,m+1}(t,m)$ that appear in the maximum overlap month-to-month Paasche index defined by equation (22.26) are

[30] The formulae are slightly different for the indices that go from December to January of the following year.

Table 22.21 Month-to-month maximum overlap chained Laspeyres, Paasche and Fisher price indices

Year	Month	P_L	P_P	P_F
1970	1	1.0000	1.0000	1.0000
	2	0.9766	0.9787	0.9777
	3	0.9587	0.9594	0.9590
	4	1.0290	1.0534	1.0411
	5	1.1447	1.1752	1.1598
	6	1.1118	1.0146	1.0621
	7	1.1167	1.0102	1.0621
	8	1.1307	0.7924	0.9465
	9	1.0033	0.6717	0.8209
	10	0.9996	0.6212	0.7880
	11	1.0574	0.6289	0.8155
	12	1.0151	0.5787	0.7665
1971	1	1.0705	0.6075	0.8064
	2	1.0412	0.5938	0.7863
	3	1.0549	0.6005	0.7959
	4	1.1409	0.6564	0.8654
	5	1.2416	0.7150	0.9422
	6	1.1854	0.6006	0.8438
	7	1.2167	0.6049	0.8579
	8	1.2230	0.4838	0.7692
	9	1.0575	0.4055	0.6548
	10	1.0497	0.3837	0.6346
	11	1.1240	0.3905	0.6626
	12	1.0404	0.3471	0.6009
1972	1	1.0976	0.3655	0.6334
	2	1.1027	0.3679	0.6369
	3	1.1291	0.3765	0.6520
	4	1.1974	0.4014	0.6933
	5	1.2818	0.4290	0.7415
	6	1.2182	0.3553	0.6579
	7	1.2838	0.3637	0.6833
	8	1.2531	0.2794	0.5916
	9	1.0445	0.2283	0.4883
	10	1.0335	0.2203	0.4771
	11	1.1087	0.2256	0.5001
	12	1.0321	0.1995	0.4538
1973	1	1.0866	0.2097	0.4774
	2	1.1140	0.2152	0.4897
	3	1.1532	0.2225	0.5065
	4	1.2493	0.2398	0.5474
	5	1.3315	0.2544	0.5821
	6	1.2594	0.2085	0.5124
	7	1.3585	0.2160	0.5416
	8	1.3251	0.1656	0.4684
	9	1.0632	0.1330	0.3760
	10	1.0574	0.1326	0.3744
	11	1.1429	0.1377	0.3967
	12	1.0504	0.1204	0.3556

Table 22.22 Month-to-month chained Laspeyres, Paasche and Fisher price indices

Year	Month	$P_L(3)$	$P_P(3)$	$P_F(3)$	$P_L(2)$	$P_P(2)$	$P_F(2)$
1970	1	1.0000	1.0000	1.0000	1.0000	1.0000	1.0000
	2	0.9766	0.9787	0.9777	0.9751	0.9780	0.9765
	3	0.9587	0.9594	0.9590	0.9522	0.9574	0.9548
	4	1.0290	1.0534	1.0411	1.0223	1.0515	1.0368
	5	1.1447	1.1752	1.1598	1.1377	1.1745	1.1559
	6	1.2070	1.2399	1.2233	1.2006	1.2424	1.2214
	7	1.2694	1.3044	1.2868	1.2729	1.3204	1.2964
	8	1.3248	1.1537	1.2363	1.3419	1.3916	1.3665
	9	1.0630	0.9005	0.9784	1.1156	1.1389	1.1272
	10	0.9759	0.8173	0.8931	0.9944	1.0087	1.0015
	11	1.0324	0.8274	0.9242	0.9839	0.9975	0.9907
	12	0.9911	0.7614	0.8687	0.9214	0.9110	0.9162
1971	1	1.0452	0.7993	0.9140	0.9713	0.9562	0.9637
	2	1.0165	0.7813	0.8912	0.9420	0.9336	0.9378
	3	1.0300	0.7900	0.9020	0.9509	0.9429	0.9469
	4	1.1139	0.8636	0.9808	1.0286	1.0309	1.0298
	5	1.2122	0.9407	1.0679	1.1198	1.1260	1.1229
	6	1.2631	0.9809	1.1131	1.1682	1.1763	1.1723
	7	1.3127	1.0170	1.1554	1.2269	1.2369	1.2319
	8	1.3602	0.9380	1.1296	1.2810	1.2913	1.2861
	9	1.1232	0.7532	0.9198	1.1057	1.0988	1.1022
	10	1.0576	0.7045	0.8632	1.0194	1.0097	1.0145
	11	1.1325	0.7171	0.9012	1.0126	1.0032	1.0079
	12	1.0482	0.6373	0.8174	0.9145	0.8841	0.8992
1972	1	1.1059	0.6711	0.8615	0.9652	0.9311	0.9480
	2	1.1111	0.6755	0.8663	0.9664	0.9359	0.9510
	3	1.1377	0.6912	0.8868	0.9863	0.9567	0.9714
	4	1.2064	0.7371	0.9430	1.0459	1.0201	1.0329
	5	1.2915	0.7876	1.0086	1.1202	1.0951	1.1075
	6	1.3507	0.8235	1.0546	1.1732	1.1470	1.1600
	7	1.4091	0.8577	1.0993	1.2334	1.2069	1.2201
	8	1.4181	0.7322	1.0190	1.2562	1.2294	1.2427
	9	1.1868	0.5938	0.8395	1.1204	1.0850	1.1026
	10	1.1450	0.5696	0.8076	1.0614	1.0251	1.0431
	11	1.2283	0.5835	0.8466	1.0592	1.0222	1.0405
	12	1.1435	0.5161	0.7682	0.9480	0.8935	0.9204
1973	1	1.2038	0.5424	0.8081	1.0033	0.9408	0.9715
	2	1.2342	0.5567	0.8289	1.0240	0.9639	0.9935
	3	1.2776	0.5755	0.8574	1.0571	0.9955	1.0259
	4	1.3841	0.6203	0.9266	1.1451	1.0728	1.1084
	5	1.4752	0.6581	0.9853	1.2211	1.1446	1.1822
	6	1.5398	0.6865	1.0281	1.2763	1.1957	1.2354
	7	1.6038	0.7136	1.0698	1.3395	1.2542	1.2962
	8	1.6183	0.6110	0.9944	1.3662	1.2792	1.3220
	9	1.3927	0.5119	0.8443	1.2530	1.1649	1.2081
	10	1.3908	0.5106	0.8427	1.2505	1.1609	1.2049
	11	1.5033	0.5305	0.8930	1.2643	1.1743	1.2184
	12	1.3816	0.4637	0.8004	1.1159	1.0142	1.0638

not the expenditure shares that could be taken from a consumer expenditure survey for month $m+1$ of year t: instead, they are the shares that result after expenditures on seasonal commodities that are present in month $m+1$ of year t, but are not present in the preceding month, are dropped.[31] The maximum overlap month-to-month Fisher index defined by equation (22.27) is the geometric mean of the Laspeyres and Paasche indices defined by equations (22.25) and (22.26).

22.69 Table 22.21 lists the maximum overlap chained month-to-month Laspeyres, Paasche and Fisher price indices for the data listed in Tables 22.1 and 22.2. These indices are defined by equations (22.25), (22.26) and (22.27).

22.70 The chained maximum overlap Laspeyres, Paasche and Fisher indices for December 1973 are 1.0504, 0.1204 and 0.3556, respectively. Comparing these results to the year-over-year results listed in Tables 22.3, 22.4 and 22.5 (page 398) indicates that the results in Table 22.21 are not at all realistic. These hugely different direct indices compared with the last row of Table 22.21 indicate that the maximum overlap indices suffer from a serious downward bias for the artificial data set.

22.71 What are the factors that can explain this downward bias? It is evident that part of the problem has to do with the seasonal pattern of prices for peaches and strawberries (commodities 2 and 4). These are the commodities that are not present in the marketplace for each

[31] It is important that the expenditure shares used in an index number formula add up to unity. The use of unadjusted expenditure shares from a household expenditure survey would lead to a systematic bias in the index number formula.

month of the year. When these commodities first become available, they come into the marketplace at relatively high prices and then, in subsequent months, their prices drop substantially. The effects of these initially high prices (compared to the relatively low prices that prevailed in the last month that the commodities were available in the previous year) are not captured by the maximum overlap month-to-month indices, so the resulting indices build up a tremendous downward bias. The downward bias is most pronounced in the Paasche indices, which use the quantities or volumes of the current month. Those volumes are relatively large compared to the volumes in the initial month when the commodities become available, reflecting the effects of lower prices as the quantity dumped in the market increases.

22.72 Table 22.22 lists the results using chained Laspeyres, Paasche and Fisher indices for the artificial data set where the strongly seasonal commodities 2 and 4 are dropped from each comparison of prices. Thus, the indices in Table 22.22 are the usual chained Laspeyres, Paasche and Fisher indices restricted to commodities 1, 3 and 5, which are available in each season. The indices derived using these three commodities are labelled $P_L(3)$, $P_P(3)$ and $P_F(3)$.

22.73 The chained Laspeyres, Paasche and Fisher indices (using only the three always present commodities) for January 1973 are 1.2038, 0.5424 and 0.8081, respectively. From Tables 22.8, 22.9 and 22.10, the chained year-over-year Laspeyres, Paasche and Fisher indices for January 1973 are 1.3274, 1.3243 and 1.3258, respectively. Thus the chained indices using the always present commodities which are listed in Table 22.22 evidently suffer from substantial downward biases.

22.74 If the data in Tables 22.1 and 22.2 are examined, it can be seen that the quantities of grapes (commodity 3) on the marketplace varies tremendously over the course of a year, with substantial increases in price for the months when grapes are almost out of season. Thus the price of grapes decreases substantially as the quantity in the marketplace increases during the last half of each year, but the annual substantial increase in the price of grapes takes place in the first half of the year when quantities in the market are small. This pattern of seasonal price and quantity changes will cause the overall index to take on a downward bias.[32] To verify that this conjecture is true, see the last three columns of Table 22.22 where chained Laspeyres, Paasche and Fisher indices are calculated using only commodities 1 and 5. These indices are labelled $P_L(2)$, $P_P(2)$ and $P_F(2)$, respectively, and for January 1973 they are equal to 1.0033, 0.9408 and 0.9715, respectively. These estimates based on two always present commodities are much closer to the chained year-over-year Laspeyres, Paasche and Fisher indices for January 1973, which were 1.3274, 1.3243 and 1.3258, respectively, than the estimates based on the three always present commodities. It can be seen that the chained Laspeyres, Paasche and Fisher indices restricted to commodities 1 and 5 still have very substantial downward biases for the artificial data set. Basically, the problems are caused by the high volumes associated with low or declining prices, and the low volumes caused by high or rising prices. These weight effects make the seasonal price declines bigger than the seasonal price increases using month-to-month index number formulae with variable weights.[33]

22.75 In addition to the downward biases that show up in Tables 22.21 and 22.22, all of these month-to-month chained indices show substantial seasonal fluctuations in prices over the course of a year. Hence these month-to-month indices are of little use to policy-makers who are interested in short-term inflationary trends. Thus, if the purpose of the month-to-month CPI is to indicate changes in general inflation, then statistical agencies should be cautious about including commodities that show strong seasonal fluctuations in prices in the month-to-month index.[34] If seasonal commodities are included in a month-to-month index that is meant to indicate general inflation, then a seasonal adjustment procedure should be used to remove these strong seasonal fluctuations. Some simple types of seasonal adjustment procedures are considered in paragraphs 22.91 to 22.96.

22.76 The rather poor performance of the month-to-month indices listed in Tables 22.21 and 22.22 does not always occur in the context of seasonal commodities. In the context of calculating import and export price indices using quarterly data for the United States, Alterman, Diewert and Feenstra (1999) found that maximum overlap month-to-month indices worked reasonably well.[35] Statistical agencies should check that their month-to-month indices are at least approximately consistent with the corresponding year-over-year indices.

22.77 Obviously the various Paasche and Fisher indices computed in this section could be approximated by indices that replaced all current period expenditure shares by the corresponding expenditure shares from the base year. These approximate Paasche and Fisher

[32] Andrew Baldwin (1990, p. 264) used the Turvey data to illustrate various treatments of seasonal commodities and discusses what causes various month-to-month indices to behave badly: "It is a sad fact that for some seasonal commodity groups, monthly price changes are not meaningful, whatever the choice of formula."

[33] This remark has an application to Chapter 20 on elementary indices where irregular sales during the course of a year could induce a similar downward bias in a month-to-month index that used monthly weights. Another problem with month-to-month chained indices is that purchases and sales of individual commodities can become quite irregular as the time period becomes shorter and shorter, and the problem of zero purchases and sales becomes more pronounced. Feenstra and Shapiro (2003, p. 125) find an upward bias for their chained weekly indices for canned tuna compared to a fixed base index; their bias was caused by variable weight effects resulting from the timing of advertising expenditures. In general, these drift effects of chained indices can be reduced by lengthening the time period, so that the trends in the data become more prominent than the high-frequency fluctuations.

[34] If the purpose of the index is to compare the prices that consumers actually face in two consecutive months, ignoring the possibility that the consumer may regard a seasonal good as being qualitatively different in the two months, then the production of a month-to-month CPI that has large seasonal fluctuations can be justified.

[35] They checked the validity of their month-to-month indices by cumulating them for four quarters and comparing them to the corresponding year-over-year indices, and found only relatively small differences. However, note that irregular high-frequency fluctuations will tend to be smaller for quarters than for months, and hence chained quarterly indices can be expected to perform better than chained monthly or weekly indices.

indices will not be reproduced here since they resemble their "true" counterparts and hence are also subject to tremendous downward bias.

Annual basket indices with carry forward of unavailable prices

22.78 Recall that the Lowe (1823) index defined in earlier chapters had two reference periods:[36]

- a reference period for the vector of quantity weights;
- a reference period for the base period prices.

The Lowe index for month m is defined by the following formula:

$$P_{Lo}(p^0, p^m, q) \equiv \sum_{n=1}^{N} p_n^m q_n \Big/ \sum_{n=1}^{N} p_n^0 q_n \qquad (22.28)$$

where $p^0 \equiv [p_1^0, \ldots, p_N^0]$ is the base month price vector, $p^m \equiv [p_1^m, \ldots, p_N^m]$ is the current month m price vector, and $q \equiv [q_1, \ldots, q_N]$ is the base year reference quantity vector. For the purposes of this section, where the modified Turvey data set is used to illustrate the index numerically, the base year will be taken to be 1970. The resulting base year quantity vector turns out to be:

$$q \equiv [q_1, \ldots, q_5] = [53889,\ 12881,\ 9198,\ 5379,\ 68653]. \qquad (22.29)$$

The base period for the prices will be taken to be December 1970. For prices that are not available in the current month, the last available price is carried forward. The resulting Lowe index with carry forward of missing prices using the modified Turvey data set can be found in the P_{Lo} column of Table 22.23 on p. 412.

22.79 Andrew Baldwin's (1990, p. 258) comments on this type of annual basket (AB) index are worth quoting at length:

> For seasonal goods, the AB index is best considered an index partially adjusted for seasonal variation. It is based on annual quantities, which do not reflect the seasonal fluctuations in the volume of purchases, and on raw monthly prices, which do incorporate seasonal price fluctuations. Zarnowitz (1961, pp. 256–257) calls it an index of "a hybrid sort". Being neither of sea nor land, it does not provide an appropriate measure either of monthly or 12 month price change. The question that an AB index answers with respect to price change from January to February say, or January of one year to January of the next, is "What would the change in consumer prices have been if there were no seasonality in purchases in the months in question, but prices nonetheless retained their own seasonal behaviour?" It is hard to believe that this is a question that anyone would be interested in asking. On the other hand, the 12 month ratio of an AB index based on seasonally adjusted prices would be conceptually valid, if one were interested in eliminating seasonal influences.

Despite Baldwin's somewhat negative comments on the Lowe index, it is the index that is preferred by many statistical agencies, so it is necessary to study its properties in the context of strongly seasonal data.

22.80 Recall that the Young (1812) index was defined in earlier chapters as follows:

$$P_Y(p^0, p^m, s) \equiv \sum_{n=1}^{N} s_n (p_n^m / p_n^0) \qquad (22.30)$$

where $s \equiv [s_1, \ldots, s_N]$ is the base year reference vector of expenditure shares. For the purposes of this section, where the modified Turvey data set is used to numerically illustrate the index, the base year will be taken to be 1970. The resulting base year expenditure share vector turns out to be:

$$s \equiv [s_1, \ldots, s_5] = [0.3284,\ 0.1029,\ 0.0674,\ 0.0863,\ 0.4149]. \qquad (22.31)$$

Again, the base period for the prices will be taken to be December 1970. For prices that are not available in the current month, the last available price is carried forward. The resulting Young index with carry forward of missing prices using the modified Turvey data set can be found in the P_Y column of Table 22.23.

22.81 The geometric Laspeyres index is defined in Chapter 19 as follows:

$$P_{GL}(p^0, p^m, s) \equiv \prod_{n=1}^{N} (p_n^m / p_n^0)^{s_n}. \qquad (22.32)$$

Thus the geometric Laspeyres index makes use of the same information as the Young index except that a geometric average of the price relatives is taken instead of an arithmetic one. Again, the base year is taken to be 1970 and the base period for prices is taken to be December 1970. The index is illustrated using the modified Turvey data set with carry forward of missing prices; see the P_{GL} column of Table 22.23.

22.82 It is of interest to compare the above three indices that use annual baskets to the fixed base Laspeyres rolling year indices computed earlier. The rolling year index that ends in the current month is centred five-and-a-half months backwards. Hence the above three annual basket type indices will be compared with an arithmetic average of two rolling year indices that have their last month five and six months forward. This latter centred rolling year index is labelled P_{CRY} and is listed in the last column of Table 22.23.[37] Note the zero entries for the last six rows of this column; the data set does not extend six months into 1975, so the centred rolling year indices cannot be calculated for these last six months.

22.83 It can be seen that the Lowe, Young and geometric Laspeyres indices have a considerable amount of seasonality in them and do not at all approximate their rolling year counterparts listed in the last column of Table 22.23.[38] Hence, without seasonal adjustment,

[36] In the context of seasonal price indices, this type of index corresponds to Bean and Stine's (1924, p. 31) Type A index.

[37] This series is normalized to equal 1 in December 1970, so that it is comparable to the other month-to-month indices.

[38] The sample means of the four indices are 1.2935 (Lowe), 1.3110 (Young), 1.2877 (geometric Laspeyres) and 1.1282 (rolling year). Of course, the geometric Laspeyres indices will always be equal to or less than their Young counterparts, since a weighted geometric mean is always equal to or less than the corresponding weighted arithmetic mean.

Table 22.23 Lowe, Young, geometric Laspeyres and centred rolling year indices with carry forward prices

Year	Month	P_{LO}	P_Y	P_{GL}	P_{CRY}
1970	12	1.0000	1.0000	1.0000	1.0000
1971	1	1.0554	1.0609	1.0595	1.0091
	2	1.0711	1.0806	1.0730	1.0179
	3	1.1500	1.1452	1.1187	1.0242
	4	1.2251	1.2273	1.1942	1.0298
	5	1.3489	1.3652	1.3249	1.0388
	6	1.4428	1.4487	1.4068	1.0478
	7	1.3789	1.4058	1.3819	1.0547
	8	1.3378	1.3797	1.3409	1.0631
	9	1.1952	1.2187	1.1956	1.0729
	10	1.1543	1.1662	1.1507	1.0814
	11	1.1639	1.1723	1.1648	1.0885
	12	1.0824	1.0932	1.0900	1.0965
1972	1	1.1370	1.1523	1.1465	1.1065
	2	1.1731	1.1897	1.1810	1.1174
	3	1.2455	1.2539	1.2363	1.1254
	4	1.3155	1.3266	1.3018	1.1313
	5	1.4262	1.4508	1.4183	1.1402
	6	1.5790	1.5860	1.5446	1.1502
	7	1.5297	1.5550	1.5349	1.1591
	8	1.4416	1.4851	1.4456	1.1690
	9	1.3038	1.3342	1.2974	1.1806
	10	1.2752	1.2960	1.2668	1.1924
	11	1.2852	1.3034	1.2846	1.2049
	12	1.1844	1.2032	1.1938	1.2203
1973	1	1.2427	1.2710	1.2518	1.2386
	2	1.3003	1.3308	1.3103	1.2608
	3	1.3699	1.3951	1.3735	1.2809
	4	1.4691	1.4924	1.4675	1.2966
	5	1.5972	1.6329	1.5962	1.3176
	6	1.8480	1.8541	1.7904	1.3406
	7	1.7706	1.8010	1.7711	0.0000
	8	1.6779	1.7265	1.6745	0.0000
	9	1.5253	1.5676	1.5072	0.0000
	10	1.5371	1.5746	1.5155	0.0000
	11	1.5634	1.5987	1.5525	0.0000
	12	1.4181	1.4521	1.4236	0.0000

the Lowe, Young and geometric Laspeyres indices are not suitable predictors for their seasonally adjusted rolling year counterparts.[39] The four series, P_{LO}, P_Y, P_{GL} and P_{CRY}, listed in Table 22.23 are also plotted in Figure 22.4. It can be seen that the Young price index is generally the highest, followed by the Lowe index, while the geometric Laspeyres is the lowest of the three month-to-month indices. The centred rolling year Laspeyres counterpart index, P_{CRY}, is generally below the other three indices (and of course does not have the strong seasonal movements of the other three series), but it moves in a roughly parallel fashion to the other three indices.[40] Note that the seasonal movements of P_{LO}, P_Y, and P_{GL} are quite regular. This regularity is exploited in paragraphs 22.91 to 22.96 in order to use these month-to-month indices to predict their rolling year counterparts.

[39] In paragraphs 22.91 to 22.96, the Lowe, Young and geometric Laspeyres indices are seasonally adjusted.

[40] In Figure 22.4, P_{CRY} is artificially set equal to the June 1973 value for the index, which is the last month that the centred index can be constructed from the available data.

Figure 22.4 Lowe, Young, geometric Laspeyres and centred rolling year Laspeyres indices

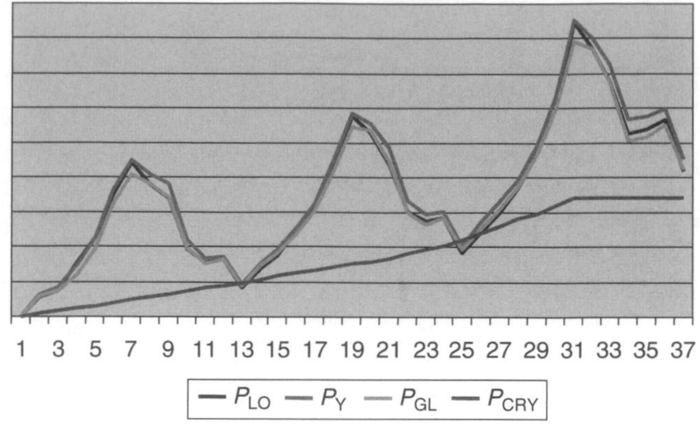

22.84 Part of the problem may be the fact that the prices of strongly seasonal goods have been carried forward for the months when the commodities are not available. This will tend to add to the amount of seasonal movements in the indices, particularly when there is high general inflation. Thus in the following section, the Lowe, Young and geometric Laspeyres indices are computed again using an imputation method for the missing prices rather than simply carrying forward the last available price.

Annual basket indices with imputation of unavailable prices

22.85 Instead of simply carrying forward the last available price of a seasonal commodity that is not sold during a particular month, it is possible to use an imputation method to fill in the missing prices. Alternative imputation methods are discussed by Armknecht and Maitland-Smith (1999) and Feenstra and Diewert (2001). The basic idea is to take the last available price and impute prices for the missing periods, using the trend of another index. This other index could be an index of available prices for the general category of commodity or higher-level components of the CPI. For the purposes of this section, the imputation index is taken to be a price index that grows at the multiplicative rate of 1.008, since the fixed base rolling year Laspeyres indices for the modified Turvey data set grow at approximately 0.8 per cent per month.[41] Using this imputation method to fill in the missing prices, the Lowe, Young and geometric Laspeyres indices defined in the previous section can be recomputed. The resulting indices are listed in Table 22.24, along with the centred rolling year index P_{CRY} for comparison purposes.

22.86 As could be expected, the Lowe, Young and geometric Laspeyres indices that use imputed prices are on average somewhat higher than their counterparts that use carry forward prices, but the variability of the

[41] For the last year of data, the imputation index is escalated by an additional monthly growth rate of 1.008.

Table 22.24 Lowe, Young, geometric Laspeyres and centred rolling year indices with imputed prices

Year	Month	P_{LOI}	P_{YI}	P_{GLI}	P_{CRY}
1970	12	1.0000	1.0000	1.0000	1.0000
1971	1	1.0568	1.0624	1.0611	1.0091
	2	1.0742	1.0836	1.0762	1.0179
	3	1.1545	1.1498	1.1238	1.0242
	4	1.2312	1.2334	1.2014	1.0298
	5	1.3524	1.3682	1.3295	1.0388
	6	1.4405	1.4464	1.4047	1.0478
	7	1.3768	1.4038	1.3798	1.0547
	8	1.3364	1.3789	1.3398	1.0631
	9	1.1949	1.2187	1.1955	1.0729
	10	1.1548	1.1670	1.1514	1.0814
	11	1.1661	1.1747	1.1672	1.0885
	12	1.0863	1.0972	1.0939	1.0965
1972	1	1.1426	1.1580	1.1523	1.1065
	2	1.1803	1.1971	1.1888	1.1174
	3	1.2544	1.2630	1.2463	1.1254
	4	1.3260	1.3374	1.3143	1.1313
	5	1.4306	1.4545	1.4244	1.1402
	6	1.5765	1.5831	1.5423	1.1502
	7	1.5273	1.5527	1.5326	1.1591
	8	1.4402	1.4841	1.4444	1.1690
	9	1.3034	1.3343	1.2972	1.1806
	10	1.2758	1.2970	1.2675	1.1924
	11	1.2875	1.3062	1.2873	1.2049
	12	1.1888	1.2078	1.1981	1.2203
1973	1	1.2506	1.2791	1.2601	1.2386
	2	1.3119	1.3426	1.3230	1.2608
	3	1.3852	1.4106	1.3909	1.2809
	4	1.4881	1.5115	1.4907	1.2966
	5	1.6064	1.6410	1.6095	1.3176
	6	1.8451	1.8505	1.7877	1.3406
	7	1.7679	1.7981	1.7684	0.0000
	8	1.6773	1.7263	1.6743	0.0000
	9	1.5271	1.5700	1.5090	0.0000
	10	1.5410	1.5792	1.5195	0.0000
	11	1.5715	1.6075	1.5613	0.0000
	12	1.4307	1.4651	1.4359	0.0000

imputed indices is generally a little lower.[42] The series listed in Table 22.24 are also plotted in Figure 22.5. It can be seen that the Lowe, Young and geometric Laspeyres indices that use imputed prices still have a huge amount of seasonality in them and do not closely approximate their rolling year counterparts listed in the last column of Table 22.24.[43] Hence, without seasonal adjustment, the Lowe, Young and geometric Laspeyres indices using imputed prices are not suitable predictors for their seasonally adjusted rolling year counterparts.[44]

[42] For the Lowe indices, the mean for the first 31 observations increases (with imputed prices) from 1.3009 to 1.3047, but the standard deviation decreases from 0.18356 to 0.18319. For the Young indices, the mean for the first 31 observations increases from 1.3186 to 1.3224, but the standard deviation decreases from 0.18781 to 0.18730. For the geometric Laspeyres indices, the mean for the first 31 observations increases from 1.2949 to 1.2994, and the standard deviation also increases slightly from 0.17582 to 0.17599. The imputed indices are preferred to the carry forward indices on general methodological grounds; in high-inflation environments, the carry forward indices will be subject to sudden jumps as the previously unavailable commodities become available.

[43] Note also that Figures 22.4 and 22.5 are very similar.

[44] In paragraphs 22.91 to 22.96, the Lowe, Young and geometric Laspeyres indices using imputed prices are seasonally adjusted.

Figure 22.5 Lowe, Young and geometric Laspeyres with imputed prices and centred rolling year indices

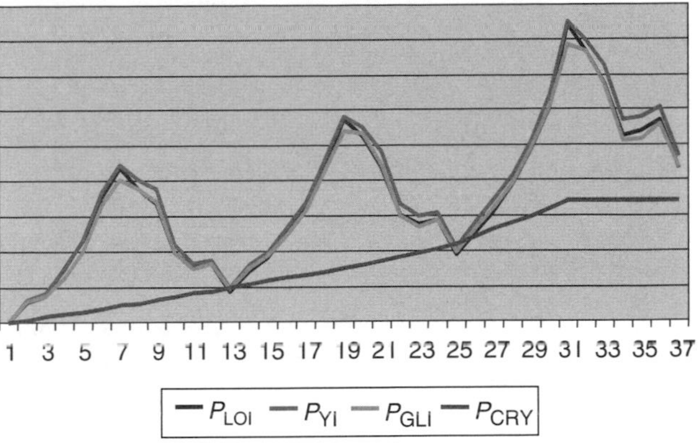

As these indices stand, they are not suitable as measures of general inflation going from month to month.

Bean and Stine Type C or Rothwell indices

22.87 The final month-to-month index[45] that is considered in this chapter is the *Bean and Stine Type C* (1924, p. 31) or *Rothwell* (1958, p. 72) index.[46] This index makes use of seasonal baskets in the base year, denoted as the vectors $q^{0,m}$ for the months $m = 1, 2, \ldots, 12$. The index also makes use of a vector of base year unit value prices, $p^0 \equiv [p_1^0, \ldots, p_5^0]$, where the nth price in this vector is defined as:

$$p_n^0 \equiv \frac{\sum_{m=1}^{12} p_n^{0,m} q_n^{0,m}}{\sum_{m=1}^{12} q_n^{0,m}} \qquad n = 1, \ldots, 5. \tag{22.33}$$

The *Rothwell price index for month m in year t* can now be defined as follows:

$$P_R(p^0, p^{t,m}, q^{0,m}) \equiv \frac{\sum_{n=1}^{5} p_n^{t,m} q_n^{0,m}}{\sum_{n=1}^{5} p_n^0 q_n^{0,m}} \qquad m = 1, \ldots, 12. \tag{22.34}$$

Thus as the month changes, the quantity weights for the index change, and hence the month-to-month movements in this index are a mixture of price and quantity changes.[47]

[45] For other suggested month-to-month indices in the seasonal context, see Balk (1980a; 1980b; 1980c; 1981).

[46] This is the index favoured by Baldwin (1990, p. 271) and many other price statisticians in the context of seasonal commodities.

[47] Rothwell (1958, p. 72) showed that the month-to-month movements in the index have the form of an expenditure ratio divided by a quantity index.

Table 22.25 The Lowe with carry forward prices, Rothwell and normalized Rothwell indices

Year	Month	P_{LO}	P_{NR}	P_R
1970	12	1.0000	1.0000	0.9750
1971	1	1.0554	1.0571	1.0306
	2	1.0711	1.0234	0.9978
	3	1.1500	1.0326	1.0068
	4	1.2251	1.1288	1.1006
	5	1.3489	1.3046	1.2720
	6	1.4428	1.2073	1.1771
	7	1.3789	1.2635	1.2319
	8	1.3378	1.2305	1.1997
	9	1.1952	1.0531	1.0268
	10	1.1543	1.0335	1.0077
	11	1.1639	1.1432	1.1146
	12	1.0824	1.0849	1.0577
1972	1	1.1370	1.1500	1.1212
	2	1.1731	1.1504	1.1216
	3	1.2455	1.1752	1.1459
	4	1.3155	1.2561	1.2247
	5	1.4262	1.4245	1.3889
	6	1.5790	1.3064	1.2737
	7	1.5297	1.4071	1.3719
	8	1.4416	1.3495	1.3158
	9	1.3038	1.1090	1.0813
	10	1.2752	1.1197	1.0917
	11	1.2852	1.2714	1.2396
	12	1.1844	1.1960	1.1661
1973	1	1.2427	1.2664	1.2348
	2	1.3003	1.2971	1.2647
	3	1.3699	1.3467	1.3130
	4	1.4691	1.4658	1.4292
	5	1.5972	1.6491	1.6078
	6	1.8480	1.4987	1.4612
	7	1.7706	1.6569	1.6155
	8	1.6779	1.6306	1.5898
	9	1.5253	1.2683	1.2366
	10	1.5371	1.3331	1.2998
	11	1.5634	1.5652	1.5261
	12	1.4181	1.4505	1.4143

22.88 Using the modified Turvey data set, the base year is chosen to be 1970 as usual and the index is started off at December 1970. The Rothwell index P_R is compared to the Lowe index with carry forward of missing prices, P_{LO}, in Table 22.25. To make the series slightly more comparable, the *normalized Rothwell index* P_{NR} is also listed in Table 22.25; this index is simply equal to the original Rothwell index divided by its first observation.

22.89 Figure 22.6, which plots the Lowe index with the carry forward of the last price and the normalized Rothwell index, shows that the Rothwell index has smaller seasonal movements than the Lowe index, and is less volatile in general.[48] It is evident that there are still large seasonal movements in the Rothwell index, and it may not be a suitable index for measuring general inflation without some sort of seasonal adjustment.

[48] For all 37 observations in Table 22.25, the Lowe index has a mean of 1.3465 and a standard deviation of 0.20313, while the normalized Rothwell index has a mean of 1.2677 and a standard deviation of 0.18271.

Figure 22.6 The Lowe and Rothwell price indices

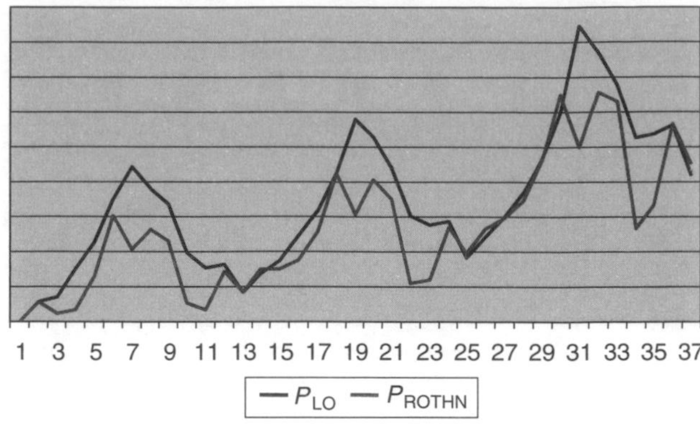

22.90 In the following section, the annual basket type indices (with and without imputation) defined in paragraphs 22.78 to 22.86 will be seasonally adjusted using essentially the same method that was used in paragraphs 22.55 to 22.62.

Forecasting rolling year indices using month-to-month annual basket indices

22.91 Recall Table 22.23 showing the Lowe, Young, geometric Laspeyres (using carry forward prices) and the centred rolling year indices for the 37 observations running from December 1970 to December 1973, P_{LO}, P_Y, P_{GL} and P_{CRY}, respectively. For each of the first three series, define a seasonal adjustment factor, SAF, as the centred rolling year index, P_{CRY}, divided by P_{LO}, P_Y and P_{GL}, respectively, for the first 12 observations. Now for each of the three series, repeat these 12 seasonal adjustment factors for observations 13 to 24, and then repeat them again for the remaining observations. These operations will create three SAF series for all 37 observations (label them SAF_{LO}, SAF_Y and SAF_{GL}, respectively). Only the first 12 observations in the P_{LO}, P_Y, P_{GL} and P_{CRY} series are used to create the three SAF series. Finally, define *seasonally adjusted Lowe, Young and geometric Laspeyres indices* by multiplying each unadjusted index by the appropriate seasonal adjustment factor:

$$P_{LOSA} \equiv P_{LO}SAF_{LO} \quad P_{YSA} \equiv P_Y SAF_Y$$
$$P_{GLSA} \equiv P_{GL}SAF_{GL}. \tag{22.35}$$

These three seasonally adjusted annual basket type indices are listed in Table 22.26 along with the target index, the centred rolling year index, P_{CRY}.

22.92 The four series in Table 22.26 coincide for their first 12 observations, which follows from the way the seasonally adjusted series were defined. Also, the last six observations are missing for the centred rolling year series, P_{CRY}, since data for the first six months of 1974 would be required in order to calculate all these index values. Note that from December 1971 to December 1973, the three seasonally adjusted annual basket type indices can be used

Table 22.26 Seasonally adjusted Lowe, Young and geometric Laspeyres indices with carry forward prices and the centred rolling year index

Year	Month	P_{LOSA}	P_{YSA}	P_{GLSA}	P_{CRY}
1970	12	1.0000	1.0000	1.0000	1.0000
1971	1	1.0091	1.0091	1.0091	1.0091
	2	1.0179	1.0179	1.0179	1.0179
	3	1.0242	1.0242	1.0242	1.0242
	4	1.0298	1.0298	1.0298	1.0298
	5	1.0388	1.0388	1.0388	1.0388
	6	1.0478	1.0478	1.0478	1.0478
	7	1.0547	1.0547	1.0547	1.0547
	8	1.0631	1.0631	1.0631	1.0631
	9	1.0729	1.0729	1.0729	1.0729
	10	1.0814	1.0814	1.0814	1.0814
	11	1.0885	1.0885	1.0885	1.0885
	12	1.0824	1.0932	1.0900	1.0965
1972	1	1.0871	1.0960	1.0919	1.1065
	2	1.1148	1.1207	1.1204	1.1174
	3	1.1093	1.1214	1.1318	1.1254
	4	1.1057	1.1132	1.1226	1.1313
	5	1.0983	1.1039	1.1120	1.1402
	6	1.1467	1.1471	1.1505	1.1502
	7	1.1701	1.1667	1.1715	1.1591
	8	1.1456	1.1443	1.1461	1.1690
	9	1.1703	1.1746	1.1642	1.1806
	10	1.1946	1.2017	1.1905	1.1924
	11	1.2019	1.2102	1.2005	1.2049
	12	1.1844	1.2032	1.1938	1.2203
1973	1	1.1882	1.2089	1.1922	1.2386
	2	1.2357	1.2536	1.2431	1.2608
	3	1.2201	1.2477	1.2575	1.2809
	4	1.2349	1.2523	1.2656	1.2966
	5	1.2299	1.2425	1.2514	1.3176
	6	1.3421	1.3410	1.3335	1.3406
	7	1.3543	1.3512	1.3518	0.0000
	8	1.3334	1.3302	1.3276	0.0000
	9	1.3692	1.3800	1.3524	0.0000
	10	1.4400	1.4601	1.4242	0.0000
	11	1.4621	1.4844	1.4508	0.0000
	12	1.4181	1.4521	1.4236	0.0000

to predict the corresponding centred rolling year entries; see Figure 22.7 for plots of these predictions. What is remarkable in Table 22.26 and Figure 22.7 is that the predicted values of these seasonally adjusted series are fairly close to the corresponding target index values.[49] This result is somewhat unexpected since the annual basket indices use price information for only two consecutive months, whereas the corresponding centred rolling year index uses price information for some 25 months.[50] It should be noted that the seasonally adjusted

Figure 22.7 Seasonally adjusted Lowe, Young and geometric Laspeyres indices with carry forward prices and the centred rolling year index

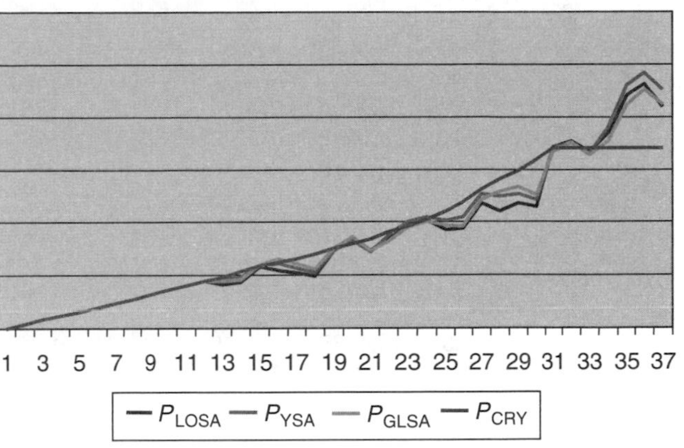

geometric Laspeyres index is generally the best predictor of the corresponding rolling year index for this data set. It can be seen from Figure 22.7 that for the first few months of 1973, the three month-to-month indices underestimate the centred rolling year inflation rate, but by the middle of 1973, the month-to-month indices are right on target.[51]

22.93 The above manipulations can be repeated, replacing the carry forward annual basket indices by their imputed counterparts; i.e., use the information in Table 22.24 (instead of Table 22.23) and in Table 22.27 (instead of Table 22.26). A seasonally adjusted version of the Rothwell index presented in the previous section may also be found in Table 22.27.[52] The five series in Table 22.27 are also represented graphically in Figure 22.8.

22.94 Again, the seasonally adjusted annual basket type indices listed in the P_{LOSA}, P_{YSA} and P_{GLSA} columns of Table 22.27 (using imputations for the missing prices) are reasonably close to the corresponding centred rolling year index listed in the last column of Table 22.27.[53] The seasonally adjusted geometric Laspeyres index is the closest to the centred rolling year index, and the seasonally adjusted Rothwell index is the furthest away. The three seasonally adjusted month-to-month indices that use annual weights, P_{LOSA}, P_{YSA} and P_{GLSA}, dip below the corresponding centred rolling year index, P_{CRY}, for the first few months of 1973 when the rate of month-to-month inflation suddenly increases, but by the middle of 1973, all four indices are fairly close to each other. The seasonally adjusted Rothwell does not do

[49] For observations 13 to 31, the seasonally adjusted series can be regressed on the centred rolling year series. For the seasonally adjusted Lowe index, an R^2 of 0.8816 is obtained; for the seasonally adjusted Young index, an R^2 of 0.9212 is obtained; and for the seasonally adjusted geometric Laspeyres index, an R^2 of 0.9423 is obtained. These fits are not as good as the fit obtained in paragraphs 22.55 to 22.62, where the seasonally adjusted approximate rolling year index is used to predict the fixed base Laspeyres rolling year index. This R^2 is 0.9662; recall the discussion of Table 22.20.

[50] For seasonal data sets that are not as regular as the modified Turvey data set, the predictive power of the seasonally adjusted annual basket type indices may be considerably less; i.e., if there are abrupt changes in the seasonal pattern of prices, these month-to-month indices cannot be expected to accurately predict a rolling year index.

[51] Recall that the last six months of P_{CRY} have been artificially held constant; six months of data for 1974 would be required to evaluate these centred rolling year index values, but these data are not available.

[52] The same seasonal adjustment technique as was defined by equations (22.35) was used.

[53] For observations 13 to 31, the seasonally adjusted series can be regressed on the centred rolling year series. For the seasonally adjusted Lowe index, an R^2 of 0.8994 is obtained; for the seasonally adjusted Young index, an R^2 of 0.9294 is obtained; and for the seasonally adjusted geometric Laspeyres index, an R^2 of 0.9495 is obtained. For the seasonally adjusted Rothwell index, an R^2 of 0.8704 is obtained, which is lower than the other three fits. For the Lowe, Young and geometric Laspeyres indices using imputed prices, these R^2 are higher than those obtained using carry forward prices.

Table 22.27 Seasonally adjusted Lowe, Young and geometric Laspeyres indices with imputed prices, seasonally adjusted Rothwell and centred rolling year indices

Year	Month	P_{LOSA}	P_{YSA}	P_{GLSA}	P_{ROTHSA}	P_{CRY}
1970	12	1.0000	1.0000	1.0000	1.0000	1.0000
1971	1	1.0091	1.0091	1.0091	1.0091	1.0091
	2	1.0179	1.0179	1.0179	1.0179	1.0179
	3	1.0242	1.0242	1.0242	1.0242	1.0242
	4	1.0298	1.0298	1.0298	1.0298	1.0298
	5	1.0388	1.0388	1.0388	1.0388	1.0388
	6	1.0478	1.0478	1.0478	1.0478	1.0478
	7	1.0547	1.0547	1.0547	1.0547	1.0547
	8	1.0631	1.0631	1.0631	1.0631	1.0631
	9	1.0729	1.0729	1.0729	1.0729	1.0729
	10	1.0814	1.0814	1.0814	1.0814	1.0814
	11	1.0885	1.0885	1.0885	1.0885	1.0885
	12	1.0863	1.0972	1.0939	1.0849	1.0965
1972	1	1.0909	1.0999	1.0958	1.0978	1.1065
	2	1.1185	1.1245	1.1244	1.1442	1.1174
	3	1.1129	1.1250	1.1359	1.1657	1.1254
	4	1.1091	1.1167	1.1266	1.1460	1.1313
	5	1.0988	1.1043	1.1129	1.1342	1.1402
	6	1.1467	1.1469	1.1505	1.1339	1.1502
	7	1.1701	1.1666	1.1715	1.1746	1.1591
	8	1.1457	1.1442	1.1461	1.1659	1.1690
	9	1.1703	1.1746	1.1642	1.1298	1.1806
	10	1.1947	1.2019	1.1905	1.1715	1.1924
	11	1.2019	1.2103	1.2005	1.2106	1.2049
	12	1.1888	1.2078	1.1981	1.1960	1.2203
1973	1	1.1941	1.2149	1.1983	1.2089	1.2386
	2	1.2431	1.2611	1.2513	1.2901	1.2608
	3	1.2289	1.2565	1.2677	1.3358	1.2809
	4	1.2447	1.2621	1.2778	1.3373	1.2966
	5	1.2338	1.2459	1.2576	1.3131	1.3176
	6	1.3421	1.3406	1.3335	1.3007	1.3406
	7	1.3543	1.3510	1.3518	1.3831	0.0000
	8	1.3343	1.3309	1.3285	1.4087	0.0000
	9	1.3712	1.3821	1.3543	1.2921	0.0000
	10	1.4430	1.4634	1.4271	1.3949	0.0000
	11	1.4669	1.4895	1.4560	1.4903	0.0000
	12	1.4307	1.4651	1.4359	1.4505	0.0000

a very good job of approximating P_{CRY} for this particular data set, although this could be a function of the rather simple method of seasonal adjustment that is used.

22.95 Comparing the results in Tables 22.26 and 22.7, it can be seen that, for the modified Turvey data set, it did not make a great deal of difference whether missing prices are carried forward or imputed; the seasonal adjustment factors picked up the lumpiness in the unadjusted indices that occurs if the carry forward method is used. Nevertheless, the three month-to-month indices that used annual weights and imputed prices did predict the corresponding centred rolling year indices somewhat better than the three indices that used carry forward prices. Hence, the use of imputed prices over carry forward prices is recommended.

22.96 The conclusions that emerge from this section are rather encouraging for statistical agencies that wish to use an annual basket type index as their flagship index.[54] It appears that for commodity groups that have strong seasonality, an annual basket type index for this group can be seasonally adjusted[55] and the resulting seasonally adjusted index value can be used as a price relative for the group at higher stages of aggregation. The preferred type of annual basket type index appears to be the geometric Laspeyres index rather than the Lowe index, but the differences between the two are not large for this data set.

[54] Taking into account the results of previous chapters, the use of the annual basket Young index is not encouraged because of its failure of the time reversal test and the resulting upward bias.

Figure 22.8 Seasonally adjusted Lowe, Young and geometric Laspeyres indices with imputed prices, seasonally adjusted Rothwell and centred rolling year indices

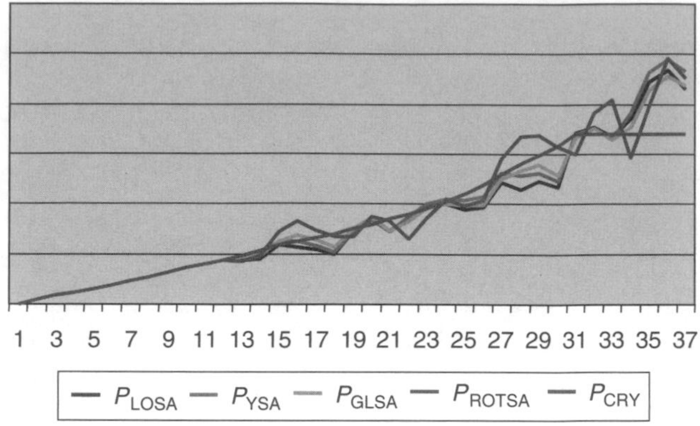

Conclusion

22.97 A number of tentative conclusions can be drawn from the results of the previous sections in this chapter:

- The inclusion of seasonal commodities in maximum overlap month-to-month indices will frequently lead to substantial biases. Hence, unless the maximum overlap month-to-month indices using seasonal commodities cumulated for a year are close to their year-over-year counterparts, the seasonal commodities should be excluded from the month-to-month index or the seasonal adjustment procedures suggested in paragraphs 22.91 to 22.96 should be used.
- Year-over-year monthly indices can always be constructed even if there are strongly seasonal commodities.[56] Many users will be interested in these indices; moreover, these indices are the building blocks for annual indices and for rolling year indices. Statistical agencies should compute these indices, which may be labelled "analytic series" in order to prevent user confusion with the primary month-to-month CPI.

[55] It is not necessary to use rolling year indices in the seasonal adjustment process, but their use is recommended because they increase the objectivity and reproducibility of the seasonally adjusted indices.

[56] There may be problems with the year-over-year indices if shifting holidays or abnormal weather changes "normal" seasonal patterns. In general, choosing a longer time period will mitigate these types of problems; i.e., quarterly seasonal patterns will be more stable than monthly patterns, which in turn will be more stable than weekly patterns.

- Rolling year indices should also be made available as analytic series. These indices will give the most reliable indicator of annual inflation at a monthly frequency. This type of index can be regarded as a seasonally adjusted CPI, and is the most natural to use as a central bank inflation target. It has the disadvantage of measuring year-over-year inflation with a lag of six months; hence it cannot be used as a short-run indicator of month-to-month inflation. Nevertheless, the techniques suggested in paragraphs 22.55 to 22.62 and 22.91 to 22.96 could be used, so that timely forecasts of these rolling year indices can be made using current price information.
- Annual basket indices can also be successfully used in the context of seasonal commodities. Most users of the CPI will, however, want to use seasonally adjusted versions of these annual basket type indices. The seasonal adjustment can be done using the index number methods explained in paragraphs 22.91 to 22.96, or traditional statistical agency seasonal adjustment procedures could be used.[57]
- From an a priori point of view, when making a price comparison between any two periods, the Paasche and Laspeyres indices are of equal importance. Under normal circumstances, the spread between the Laspeyres and Paasche indices will be reduced by using chained indices rather than fixed base indices. Hence, it is suggested that when constructing year-over-year monthly or annual indices, the chained Fisher index (or the chained Törnqvist–Theil index, which closely approximates the chained Fisher) be chosen as the target index that a statistical agency should aim to approximate. When constructing month-to-month indices, however, chained indices should always be checked against their year-over-year counterparts to check for chain drift. If substantial drift is found, the chained month-to-month indices must be replaced by fixed base indices or seasonally adjusted annual basket type indices.[58]
- If current period expenditure shares are not all that different from base year expenditure shares, approximate chained Fisher indices will normally provide a very close practical approximation to the chained Fisher target indices. Approximate Laspeyres, Paasche and Fisher indices use base period expenditure shares whenever they occur in the index number formula in place of current period (or lagged current period) expenditure shares. Approximate Laspeyres, Paasche and Fisher indices can be computed by statistical agencies using their normal information sets.
- The geometric Laspeyres index is an alternative to the approximate Fisher index; it uses the same information and will normally be close to the approximate Fisher index.

It is evident that more research needs to be carried out on the problems associated with the index number treatment of seasonal commodities. There is, as yet, no consensus on what is best practice in this area.

[57] There is, however, a problem with using traditional X-11 type seasonal adjustment procedures for seasonally adjusting the main CPI because "final" seasonal adjustment factors are generally not available until data have been collected for two or three more years. Since the main CPI cannot be revised, this may preclude using X-11 type seasonal adjustment procedures on it. Note that the index number method of seasonal adjustment explained in this chapter does not suffer from this problem.

[58] Alternatively, some sort of multilateral index number formula could be used; see, for example, Caves, Christensen and Diewert (1982a) or Feenstra and Shapiro (2003).

DURABLES AND USER COSTS

23

Introduction

23.1 When a durable good (other than housing) is purchased by a consumer, national consumer price indices (CPIs) attribute all that expenditure to the period of purchase, even though the use of the good extends beyond the period of purchase.[1] By definition, a durable good delivers services longer than the period under consideration.[2] The *System of National Accounts 1993* defines a *durable good* as follows:

> In the case of goods, the distinction between acquisition and use is analytically important. It underlies the distinction between durable and non-durable goods extensively used in economic analysis. In fact, the distinction between durable and non-durable goods is not based on physical durability as such. Instead, the distinction is based on whether the goods can be used once only for purposes of production or consumption or whether they can be used repeatedly, or continuously. For example, coal is a highly durable good in a physical sense, but it can be burnt only once. A durable good is therefore defined as one which may be used repeatedly or continuously over a period of more than a year, assuming a normal or average rate of physical usage. A consumer durable is a good that may be used for purposes of consumption repeatedly or continuously over a period of a year or more (Commission of the European Communities et al. (1993, p. 208)).

This chapter is mainly concerned with the problems involved in pricing durable goods according to the above definition.[3] Durability is more than the fact that a good can physically persist for more than a year (this is true of most goods): a durable good is distinguished from a non-durable good by its ability to deliver useful services to a consumer through repeated use over an extended period of time.

23.2 Since the benefits of using the consumer durable extend over more than one period, it may not be appropriate to charge the entire purchase cost of the durable to the initial period of purchase. If this point of view is taken, then the initial purchase cost must be distributed somehow over the useful life of the asset. This is a fundamental problem of accounting.[4]

Charles R. Hulten (1990, pp. 120–121) explains the consequences for accountants of the durability of a purchase as follows:

> Durability means that a capital good is productive for two or more time periods, and this, in turn, implies that a distinction must be made between the value of using or renting capital in any year and the value of owning the capital asset. This distinction would not necessarily lead to a measurement problem if the capital services used in any given year were paid for in that year; that is, if all capital were rented. In this case, transactions in the rental market would fix the price and quantity of capital in each time period, much as data on the price and quantity of labor services are derived from labor market transactions. But, unfortunately, much capital is utilized by its owner and the transfer of capital services between owner and user results in an implicit rent typically not observed by the statistician. Market data are thus inadequate for the task of directly estimating the price and quantity of capital services, and this has led to the development of indirect procedures for inferring the quantity of capital, like the perpetual inventory method, or to the acceptance of flawed measures, like book value.

23.3 There are three main methods for dealing with the durability problem:

- ignore the problem of distributing the initial cost of the durable over the useful life of the good and allocate the entire charge to the period of purchase. This is known as the *acquisitions approach*, and is the approach currently used by CPI statisticians for all durables, with the exception of housing;
- the *rental equivalence* or *leasing equivalence approach*. In this approach, a period price is imputed for the durable which is equal to the rental price or leasing price of an equivalent consumer durable for the same period of time;

[1] This treatment of the purchases of durable goods dates back to Alfred Marshall (1898, pp. 594–595) at least:

> We have noticed also that though the benefits which a man derives from living in his own house are commonly reckoned as part of his real income, and estimated at the net rental value of his house; the same plan is not followed with regard to the benefits which he derives from the use of his furniture and clothes. It is best here to follow the common practice, and not count as part of the national income or dividend anything that is not commonly counted as part of the income of the individual.

[2] An alternative definition of a durable good is that the good delivers services to its purchaser for a period exceeding three years: "The Bureau of Economic Analysis defines consumer durables as those durables that have an average life of at least 3 years" (Katz (1983, p. 422)).

[3] In paragraphs 23.136 to 23.145 there is a brief discussion about accounting for the purchase, consumption and inventory holdings of non-durable goods.

[4] According to Stephen Gilman (1939) and David Solomons (1961):

> The third convention is that of the annual accounting period. It is this convention which is responsible for most of the difficult accounting problems. Without this convention, accounting would be a simple matter of recording completed and fully realized transactions: an act of primitive simplicity (Gilman (1939, p. 26)).
>
> *All* the problems of income measurement are the result of our desire to attribute income to arbitrarily determined short periods of time. Everything comes right in the end; but by then it is too late to matter (Solomons (1961, p. 378)).

Note that these authors do not mention the additional complications that arise from the fact that future revenues and costs must be discounted to yield values that are equivalent to present dollars.

- the *user cost approach*. In this approach, the initial purchase cost of the durable is decomposed into two parts: one part which reflects an estimated cost of using the services of the durable for the period, and another part which is regarded as an investment that must earn some exogenous rate of return.

These three approaches will be discussed more fully in the following three sections.

23.4 The above three approaches to the treatment of durable purchases can be applied to the purchase of any durable commodity. Historically, it turns out that the rental equivalence and user cost approaches have only been applied to owner-occupied housing. In other words, the acquisitions approach to the purchase of consumer durables has been universally used by statistical agencies, with the exception of owner-occupied housing. A possible reason for this is tradition; Marshall set the standard, and statisticians have followed his example for the past century. Another possible reason is that unless the durable good has a very long useful life, it usually will not make a great deal of difference in the long run whether the acquisitions approach or one of the two alternative approaches is used. This fact is demonstrated in paragraphs 23.39 to 23.42.

23.5 **a** major component of the user cost approach to valuing the services of owner-occupied housing is the depreciation component. In paragraphs 23.43 to 23.68, a general model of depreciation for a consumer durable is presented and then specialized to the three most common models of depreciation that are in use. These models assume that homogeneous units of the durable are produced in each period so that information on the prices of the various vintages of the durable at any point in time can be used to determine the pattern of depreciation. However, many durables (like housing) are custom produced and thus the methods for determining the form of depreciation explained in paragraphs 23.43 to 23.68 are not applicable. The special problems caused by these uniquely produced consumer durables are considered in paragraphs 23.69 to 23.78.

23.6 Subsequent sections treat some of the special problems involved in implementing the user cost and rental equivalence methods for valuing the services provided by owner-occupied housing. Paragraphs 23.79 to 23.93 present a derivation for the user cost of owner-occupied housing and various approximations to it. Paragraphs 23.94 to 23.120 consider some of the costs that are tied to home-ownership, while paragraphs 23.121 to 23.133 consider how a landlord's costs might differ from a home-owner's costs. This material is relevant if the rental equivalence approach to valuing the services of owner-occupied housing is used: care must be taken to remove some costs that are embedded in market rents that home-owners do not face.

23.7 Following Marshall, statistical agencies have used alternatives to the acquisitions approach when dealing with owner-occupied housing. In addition to the rental equivalence approach (which is the usual approach by statistical agencies) and the user cost approach, a fourth approach has been used: the *payments approach*,[5] which is a type of *cash flow approach*. It is explained in paragraphs 23.134 and 23.135.

23.8 Paragraphs 23.136 to 23.145 outline some of the problems involved in implementing the three main approaches for pricing owner-occupied housing.

The acquisitions approach

23.9 The *net acquisitions approach* to the treatment of owner-occupied housing is described by Charles Goodhart (2001, p. F350) as follows:

> The first is the net acquisition approach, which is the change in the price of newly purchased owner-occupied dwellings, weighted by the net purchases of the reference population. This is an asset based measure, and therefore comes close to my preferred measure of inflation as a change in the value of money, though the change in the price of the stock of existing houses rather than just of net purchases would in some respects be even better. It is, moreover, consistent with the treatment of other durables. A few countries, e.g., Australia and New Zealand, have used it, and it is, I understand, the main contender for use in the Euro-area Harmonized Index of Consumer Prices (HICP), which currently excludes any measure of the purchase price of (new) housing, though it does include minor repairs and maintenance by home-owners, as well as all expenditures by tenants.

23.10 The weights for the net acquisitions approach are the net purchases of the household sector of houses from other institutional sectors in the base period. Note that, in principle, purchases of second-hand dwellings from other sectors are relevant here; for example, a local government may sell rental dwellings to owner-occupiers. Typically, however, newly built houses form a major part of these types of transactions. Thus the long-term price relative for this category of expenditure will be primarily the price of (new) houses (quality adjusted) in the current period relative to the price of new houses in the base period.[6] If the net acquisitions approach is applied to other consumer durables, it is extremely easy to implement: the purchase of a durable is treated in the same way as a non-durable or service purchase is treated.

23.11 One additional implication of the net acquisitions approach is that major renovations and additions to owner-occupied dwelling units could also be considered as being in scope for this approach. In practice, these costs typically are not covered in a standard CPI. The treatment of renovations and additions is considered in more detail in paragraphs 23.107 to 23.117.

23.12 Traditionally, the net acquisitions approach also includes transfer costs relating to the buying and selling of second-hand houses as expenditures that are in scope for an acquisitions type CPI. These costs are

[5] This is the term used by Goodhart (2001, pp. F350–F351).

[6] This price index may or may not include the price of the land on which the new dwelling unit is situated. Thus a new house price construction index would typically not include the land cost. The acquisitions approach concentrates on the purchases by households of goods and services that are provided by suppliers from outside the household sector. If the land on which a new house is situated was previously owned by the household sector, then presumably the cost of this land would be excluded from an acquisitions type new house price index.

mainly the costs of using a real estate agent's services and asset transfer taxes. These transfer costs are further discussed in paragraphs 23.100, 23.101 and 23.118 to 23.120.

23.13 The major advantage of the acquisitions approach is that it treats durable and non-durable purchases in a completely symmetric manner, and thus no special procedures have to be developed by a statistical agency to deal with durable goods. As will be seen later, the major disadvantage of this approach is that the expenditures associated with this approach will tend to understate the corresponding expenditures on durables that are implied by the rental equivalence and user cost approaches.

23.14 Some differences between the acquisitions approach and the other approaches are:

- If rental or leasing markets for the durable exist and the durable has a long useful life, then the expenditure weights implied by the rental equivalence or user cost approaches will typically be much larger than the corresponding expenditure weights implied by the acquisitions approach; see paragraphs 23.34 to 23.42.
- If the base year corresponds to a boom year (or a slump year) for the durable, then the base period expenditure weights may be too large or too small. Put another way, the aggregate expenditures that correspond to the acquisitions approach are likely to be more volatile than the expenditures for the aggregate that are implied by the rental equivalence or user cost approaches.
- In making comparisons of consumption across countries where the proportion of owning versus renting or leasing the durable varies greatly,[7] the use of the acquisitions approach may lead to misleading cross-country comparisons. The reason for this is that capital costs are excluded in the net acquisitions approach, whereas they are explicitly or implicitly included in the other two approaches.

23.15 More fundamentally, whether the acquisitions approach is the right one or not depends on the overall purpose of the index number. If the purpose is to measure the price of current period consumption services, then the acquisitions approach can only be regarded as an approximation to a more appropriate approach (which would be either the rental equivalence or user cost approach). If the purpose of the index is to measure monetary (or non-imputed) expenditures by households during the period, then the acquisitions approach is preferable.

The rental equivalence approach

23.16 The *rental equivalence approach* simply values the services yielded by the use of a consumer durable good for a period by the corresponding market rental value for the same durable for the same period of time (if such a rental value exists). This is the approach taken in the *System of National Accounts 1993* (*SNA 1993*) for owner-occupied housing:

> As well-organized markets for rented housing exist in most countries, the output of own-account housing services can be valued using the prices of the same kinds of services sold on the market with the general valuation rules adopted for goods and services produced on own account. In other words, the output of housing services produced by owner-occupiers is valued at the estimated rental that a tenant would pay for the same accommodation, taking into account factors such as location, neighbourhood amenities, etc. as well as the size and quality of the dwelling itself (Commission of the European Communities et al. (1993, p. 134)).

23.17 The *SNA 1993* nevertheless follows Marshall (1898, p. 595) and does not extend the rental equivalence approach to consumer durables other than housing. This seemingly inconsistent treatment of durables is explained in the *SNA 1993* as follows:

> The production of housing services for their own final consumption by owner-occupiers has always been included within the production boundary in national accounts, although it constitutes an exception to the general exclusion of own-account service production. The ratio of owner-occupied to rented dwellings can vary significantly between countries and even over short periods of time within a single country, so that both international and intertemporal comparisons of the production and consumption of housing services could be distorted if no imputation were made for the value of own-account services (Commission of the European Communities et al. (1993, p. 126)).

23.18 Eurostat's (2001) *Handbook on Price and Volume Measures in National Accounts* also recommends the rental equivalence approach for the treatment of the dwelling services for owner-occupied housing: "The output of dwelling services of owner-occupiers at current prices is in many countries estimated by linking the actual rents paid by those renting similar properties in the rented sector to those of owner-occupiers. This allows the imputation of a notional rent for the service owner-occupiers receive from their property" (Eurostat (2001, p. 99)).

23.19 The United States statistical agencies, the Bureau of Labor Statistics and the Bureau of Economic Analysis, both use the rental equivalence approach to value the services of owner-occupied housing. Arnold J. Katz (1983, p. 411) describes the Bureau of Economic Analysis (BEA) procedures as follows:

> Basically, BEA measures the gross rent (space rent) of owner-occupied housing from data on the rent paid for similar housing with the same market value. To get the service value that is added to GNP (gross housing product), the value of intermediate goods and services included in this figure (e. g., expenditures for repair and maintenance, insurance, condominium fees, and closing costs) are subtracted from the space rent. To obtain a net return (net rental income), depreciation, taxes, and net interest are subtracted from, and subsidies added to, the service value.

23.20 There are some problems with the above treatment of housing and they are discussed in later

[7] According to Hoffmann and Kurz (2002, pp. 3–4), about 60 per cent of German households live in rented dwellings, whereas only about 20 per cent of Spaniards rent their dwellings.

sections, after the user cost approach to durables has been discussed.[8]

23.21 To summarize the above material, it can be seen that the rental equivalence approach to the treatment of durables is conceptually simple: impute a current period rental or leasing price for a comparable product as the price for the purchase of a unit of a consumer durable. For existing stocks of used consumer durables, the rental equivalence approach would entail finding rental prices for comparable used units.[9] To date, as noted above, statistical agencies have not used the rental equivalence approach to the treatment of durables, with the single exception of owner-occupied housing. Note, however, that in order to implement the rental equivalence approach, it is necessary for the relevant rental or leasing markets to exist. Often this will not be the case, particularly when it is recognized that vintage specific rental prices are required for all vintages of the durable held by households.[10]

The user cost approach

23.22 The user cost approach to the treatment of durable goods is in some ways very simple: it calculates the cost of purchasing the durable at the beginning of the period, using the services of the durable during the period and then netting off from these costs the benefit that could be obtained by selling the durable at the end of the period. Several details of this procedure are, however, somewhat controversial. These involve the use of opportunity costs, which are usually imputed costs, the treatment of interest, and the treatment of capital gains or holding gains.

23.23 Another complication with the user cost approach is that it involves making distinctions between current period (flow) purchases within the period under consideration and the holdings of physical stocks of the durable at the beginning and the end of the accounting period. Up to this point in the manual, all prices and quantity purchases have been thought of as taking place at a single point in time, say the middle of the period under consideration, and consumption has been thought of as taking place within the period as well. Thus, there has been no need to consider the behaviour (and valuation) of stocks of consumer durables that households may have at their disposal. The rather complex problems involved in accounting for stocks and flows are unfamiliar to most price statisticians.

23.24 To determine the net cost of using the durable good during, say, period 0, assume that one unit of the durable good is purchased at the beginning of period 0 at the price P^0. The "used" or "second-hand" durable good can be sold at the end of period 0 at the price P_S^1. It might seem that a reasonable net cost for the use of one unit of the consumer durable during period 0 is its initial purchase price P^0 less its end of period 0 "scrap value" P_S^1. However, money received at the end of the period is not as valuable as money received at the beginning of the period. Thus, in order to convert the end of period value into its beginning of period equivalent value, it is necessary to discount the term P_S^1 by the term $1+r^0$, where r^0 is the beginning of period 0 nominal interest rate that the consumer faces. Hence the period 0 user cost u^0 for the consumer durable[11] is defined as:

$$u^0 \equiv P^0 - \frac{P_S^1}{(1+r^0)} \tag{23.1}$$

23.25 There is another way to view the user cost formula (23.1): the consumer purchases the durable at the beginning of period 0 at the price P^0 and charges himself or herself the rental price u^0. The remainder of the purchase price, I^0, defined as

$$I^0 \equiv P^0 - u^0 \tag{23.2}$$

can be regarded as an investment, which is to yield the appropriate opportunity cost of capital r^0 that the consumer faces. At the end of period 0, this rate of return could be realized provided that I^0, r^0 and the selling price of the durable at the end of the period P_S^1 satisfy the following equation:

$$I^0(1+r^0) = P_S^1 \tag{23.3}$$

Given P_S^1 and r^0, equation (23.3) determines I^0, which in turn, given P^0, determines the user cost u^0 via equation (23.2).[12]

23.26 It should be noted that some price statisticians object to the user cost concept as a valid pricing concept for a CPI:

> A suitable price concept for a CPI ought to reflect only a ratio of exchange of money for other things, not a ratio at which money in one form or time period can be traded for money in another form or time period. The ratio at which money today can be traded for money tomorrow

[8] To anticipate the later results: the main problem is that the rental equivalence approach to valuing the services of owner-occupied housing may give a higher valuation for these services than the user cost approach.

[9] Another method for determining rental price equivalents for stocks of consumer durables is to ask households what they think their durables would rent for. This approach is used by the United States Bureau of Labor Statistics in order to determine expenditure weights for owner-occupied housing; i.e., home-owners are asked to estimate what their house would rent for if it were rented to a third party; see the Bureau of Labor Statistics (1983). Lebow and Rudd (2003, p. 169) note that these estimates of imputed rents in the United States based on a consumer expenditure survey differ considerably from the corresponding Bureau of Economic Analysis estimates for imputed rents, which are derived by applying a rent-to-value ratio for rented properties to the owner-occupied stock of housing. Lebow and Rudd feel that the expenditure survey estimates may be less reliable than the ratio of rent-to-value method because of the relatively small size of the consumer expenditure survey plus the difficulties households may have in recalling or estimating expenditures.

[10] If the form of depreciation is of the "one hoss shay" or light bulb type, then the rental price for the durable will be the same for all vintages, and hence a detailed knowledge of market rentals by vintage will not be required. The light bulb model of depreciation dates back to Böhm-Bawerk (1891, p. 342). For more recent material on this model, see paragraphs 23.62 to 23.68, or Hulten (1990) or Diewert (2003b).

[11] This approach to the derivation of a user cost formula was used by Diewert (1974b), who in turn based it on an approach attributable to Hicks (1946, p. 326).

[12] This derivation for the user cost of a consumer durable was also made by Diewert (1974b, p. 504).

by paying an interest rate or by enjoying actual or expected holding gains on an appreciating asset has no part in a measure of the current purchasing power of money (Reinsdorf (2003)).

User costs are not like the prices of non-durables or services because the user cost concept involves pricing the durable at two points in time rather than at a single point in time.[13] Because the user cost concept involves prices at two points in time, money received or paid out at the first point in time is more valuable than money paid out or received at the second point in time, so interest rates creep into the user cost formula. Furthermore, because the user cost concept involves prices at two points in time, expected prices can be involved if the user cost is calculated at the beginning of the period under consideration instead of at the end. With all these complications, it is no wonder that many price statisticians would like to avoid using user costs as a pricing concept. However, even for price statisticians who would prefer to use the rental equivalence approach to the treatment of durables over the user cost approach, there is some justification for considering the user cost approach in some detail, since this approach gives insights into the economic determinants of the rental or leasing price of a durable. As is seen in paragraphs 23.121 to 23.133, the user cost for a house can differ substantially for a landlord compared to an owner. Thus adjustments should be made to market rents for dwelling units, if they are to be used as imputations for owner-occupied rents.

23.27 The user cost formula (23.1) can be put into a more familiar form if the period 0 *economic depreciation rate* δ and the period 0 *ex post asset inflation rate* i^0 are defined. Define δ by:

$$(1-\delta) \equiv P_S^1/P^1 \qquad (23.4)$$

where P_S^1 is the price of a used asset at the end of period 0 and P^1 is the price of a new asset at the end of period 0. The *period* 0 *inflation rate* for the new asset, i^0, is defined by:

$$1+i^0 \equiv P_S^1/P^1 \qquad (23.5)$$

Eliminating P^1 from equations (23.4) and (23.5) leads to the following formula for the end of period 0 used asset price:

$$P_S^1=(1-\delta)(1+i^0)P^0 \qquad (23.6)$$

Substitution of equation (23.6) into equation (23.1) yields the following expression for the *period* 0 *user cost* u^0:

$$u^0=\frac{[(1+r^0)-(1-\delta)(1+i^0)]P^0}{1+r^0} \qquad (23.7)$$

Note that r^0-i^0 can be interpreted as a period 0 *real interest rate* and $\delta(1+i^0)$ can be interpreted as an *inflation-adjusted depreciation rate*.

23.28 The user cost u^0 is expressed in terms of prices that are discounted to the beginning of period 0. It is also possible to express the user cost in terms of prices that are "discounted" to the end of period 0.[14] Define the *end of period* 0 *user cost* p^0 as:[15]

$$p^0 \equiv (1+r^0)u^0=[r^0-i^0+\delta(1+i^0)]P^0 \qquad (23.8)$$

where the last equation follows using equation (23.7). If the real interest rate r^{0*} is defined as the nominal interest rate r^0 less the asset inflation rate i^0, and the small term δi^0 is neglected, then the end of period user cost defined by equation (23.8) reduces to:

$$p^0=(r^{0*}+\delta)P^0 \qquad (23.9)$$

23.29 Abstracting from transactions costs and inflation, it can be seen that the end of period user cost defined by equation (23.9) is an *approximate rental cost*; i.e., the rental cost for the use of a consumer (or producer) durable good should equal the (real) opportunity cost of the capital tied up, $r^0{*}P^0$, plus the decline in value of the asset over the period, δP^0. Formulae (23.8) and (23.9) thus cast some light on the economic determinants of rental or leasing prices for consumer durables.

23.30 If the simplified user cost formula defined by equation (23.9) is used, then forming a price index for the user costs of a durable good is not very much more difficult than forming a price index for the purchase price of the durable good, P^0. The price statistician needs only to:

- make a reasonable assumption as to what an appropriate monthly or quarterly real interest rate r^{0*} should be;

[13] Woolford suggested that interest should be excluded from an ideal price index that measured inflation. In his view, interest is not a *contemporaneous price*; i.e., an interest rate necessarily refers to *two* points in time: a beginning point when the capital is loaned and an ending point when the capital loaned must be repaid. Thus, if attention is restricted to a domain of definition that consists of only contemporaneous prices, interest rates are excluded. Woolford (1999, p. 535) noted that his ideal inflation measure "would be contemporary in nature, capturing only the current trend in prices associated with transactions in goods and services. It would exclude interest rates on the grounds that they are intertemporal prices, representing the relative price of consuming today rather than in the future."

[14] The beginning of the period user cost u^0 discounts all monetary costs and benefits into their dollar equivalent at the beginning of period 0, whereas p^0 discounts (or appreciates) all monetary costs and benefits into their dollar equivalent at the end of period 0. This leaves open how flow transactions that take place within the period should be treated. Following the conventions used in financial accounting suggests that flow transactions taking place within the accounting period should be regarded as taking place at the end of the accounting period. Following this convention, end of period user costs should be used by the price statistician.

[15] Christensen and Jorgenson (1969) derived a user cost formula similar to equation (23.7) in a different way, using a continuous time optimization model. If the inflation rate i equals 0, then the user cost formula (23.7) reduces to that derived by Walras (1954, p. 269; first edition 1874). This zero inflation rate user cost formula was also derived by the industrial engineer A. Hamilton Church (1901, pp. 907–908), who perhaps drew on the work of Ewing Matheson (1910, p. 169, first published in 1884): "In the case of a factory where the occupancy is assured for a term of years, and the rent is a first charge on profits, the rate of interest, to be an appropriate rate, should, so far as it applies to the buildings, be equal (including the depreciation rate) to the rental which a landlord who owned but did not occupy a factory would let it for." Additional derivations of user cost formulae in discrete time have been made by Katz (1983, pp. 408–409) and Diewert (2003b).

- make an assumption as to what a reasonable monthly or quarterly depreciation rate δ should be;[16]
- collect purchase prices P^0 for the durable;
- make an estimate of the total stock of the durable which was held by the reference population during the base period for quantities. In order to construct a superlative index, estimates of the stock held will have to be made for each period.

23.31 If it is thought necessary to implement the more complicated user cost formula (23.8) in place of the simpler formula (23.9), then the situation is more complicated. As it stands, the end of period user cost formula (23.8) is an ex post user cost: the asset inflation rate i^0 cannot be calculated until the end of period 0 has been reached. Formula (23.8) can be converted into an ex ante user cost formula if i^0 is interpreted as an *anticipated asset inflation rate*. The resulting formula should approximate a market rental rate for the asset under inflationary conditions.[17]

23.32 Note that in the user cost approach to the treatment of consumer durables, the entire user cost formula (23.8) or (23.9) is the period 0 price. Thus, in the time series context, it is not necessary to deflate each component of the formula separately; the period 0 price $p^0 \equiv [r^0 - i^0 + \delta(1+i^0)]P^0$ is compared to the corresponding period 1 price, $p^1 \equiv [r^1 - i^1 + \delta(1+i^1)]P^1$ and so on.

23.33 In principle, depreciation rates can be estimated using information on the selling prices of used units of the durable good. This methodology will be explained in more detail in paragraphs 23.43 to 23.68. Before this is done, however, it will be useful to use the material in this section to explain what the relationship between the user cost and acquisition approaches to the treatment of durables is likely to be. This topic is discussed in the following section.

The relationship between user costs and acquisition costs

23.34 In this section, the user cost approach to the treatment of consumer durables is compared to the acquisitions approach. Obviously, in the short run, the value flows associated with each approach could be very different. For example, if real interest rates, $r^0 - i^0$, are very high and the economy is in a severe recession or depression, then purchases of new consumer durables, Q^0 say, could be very low and even approach zero for very long-lived assets, such as houses. In contrast, using the user cost approach zero, existing stocks of consumer durables would be carried over from previous periods and priced out at the appropriate user costs, and the resulting consumption value flow could be quite large. Thus, in the short run, the monetary values of consumption under the two approaches could be vastly different. Hence, in what follows, a (hypothetical) longer-run comparison is considered where real interest rates are held constant.[18]

23.35 Suppose that in period 0, the reference population of households purchases q^0 units of a consumer durable at the purchase price P^0. Then *the period* 0 *value of consumption from the viewpoint of the acquisitions approach* is:

$$V_A^0 \equiv P^0 q^0 \tag{23.10}$$

23.36 Recall that the end of period user cost for one new unit of the asset purchased at the beginning of period 0 is p^0 defined by equation (23.8). In order to simplify the analysis, declining balance depreciation is assumed; i.e., at the beginning of period 0, a one-period-old asset is worth $(1-\delta)P^0$; a two-period-old asset is worth $(1-\delta)^2 P^0$; a t-period-old asset is worth $(1-\delta)^t P^0$; etc. Under these hypotheses, the corresponding end of period 0 user cost for a new asset purchased at the beginning of period 0 is p^0; the end of period 0 user cost for a one-period-old asset at the beginning of period 0 is $(1-\delta)p^0$; the corresponding user cost for a two-period-old asset at the beginning of period 0 is $(1-\delta)^2 p^0$; the corresponding user cost for a t-period-old asset at the beginning of period 0 is $(1-\delta)^t p^0$; etc.[19] The final simplifying assumption is that household purchases of the consumer durable have been growing at the geometric rate g into the indefinite past. This means that if household purchases of the durable were q^0 in period 0, then in the previous period the households purchased $q^0/(1+g)$ new units; two periods ago, they purchased $q^0/(1+g)^2$ new units; t periods ago, they purchased $q^0/(1+g)^t$ new units; etc. Putting all of these assumptions together, it can be seen that *the period* 0 *value of consumption from the viewpoint of the user cost approach* is:

$$V_U^0 \equiv p^0 q^0 + \frac{(1-\delta)p^0 q^0}{1+g} + \frac{(1-\delta)^2 p^0 q^0}{(1+g)^2} + \ldots \tag{23.11}$$

$$= \frac{(1+g)p^0 q^0}{g+\delta} \quad \text{summing the infinite series}$$

$$= \frac{(1+g)[r^0 - i^0 + \delta(1+i^0)]P^0 q^0}{g+\delta} \quad \text{using equation (23.8)} \tag{23.12}$$

23.37 Equation (23.12) can be simplified by letting the asset inflation rate i^0 be 0 (or by replacing $r^0 - i^0$ by the real interest rate r^{0*} and by ignoring the small term δi^0). Under these conditions, the ratio of the user cost

[16] The geometric model for depreciation, explained in more detail in paragraphs 23.43 to 23.68, requires only a single monthly or quarterly depreciation rate. Other models of depreciation may require the estimation of a sequence of vintage depreciation rates. If the estimated annual geometric depreciation rate is δ_a, then the corresponding monthly geometric depreciation rate δ can be obtained by solving the equation $(1-\delta)^{12} = 1-\delta_a$. Similarly, if the estimated annual real interest rate is r_a^*, then the corresponding monthly real interest rate r^* can be obtained by solving the equation $(1+r^*)^{12} = 1+r_a^*$.

[17] Since landlords must set their rent at the beginning of the period (and in fact, they usually set their rent for an extended period of time), if the user cost approach is used to model the economic determinants of market rental rates, then the asset inflation rate i^0 should be interpreted as an expected inflation rate rather than an ex post actual inflation rate.

[18] The following material is based on Diewert (2002c).

[19] For many consumer durables, the "one hoss shay" assumption for depreciation may be more realistic than the declining balance model; see paragraphs 23.43 to 23.68, or Hulten (1990) or Diewert and Lawrence (2000).

flow of consumption (23.12) to the acquisitions measure of consumption in period 0, (23.10), is:

$$\frac{V_U^0}{V_A^0} = \frac{(1+g)(r^{0*}+\delta)}{g+\delta} \qquad (23.13)$$

23.38 Using formula (23.13), it can be seen that if $1+g>0$ and $\delta+g>0$, then V_U^0/V_A^0 will be greater than unity if

$$r^{0*} > \frac{g(1-\delta)}{1+g} \qquad (23.14)$$

a condition that will usually be satisfied.[20] Thus under normal conditions and over a longer time horizon, household expenditures on consumer durables using the user cost approach will tend to exceed the corresponding money outlays on new purchases of the consumer durable. The difference between the two approaches will tend to grow as the life of the asset increases (i.e., as the depreciation rate δ decreases).

23.39 To get a rough idea of the possible magnitude of the value ratio for the two approaches, V_U^0/V_A^0, equation (23.13) is evaluated for a "housing" example using annual data where the depreciation rate is 2 per cent (i.e., $\delta=0.02$), the real interest rate is 4 per cent (i.e., $r^{0*}=0.04$) and the growth rate for the production of new houses is 1 per cent (i.e., $g=0.01$). In this base case, the ratio of user cost expenditures on housing to the purchases of new housing in the same period, V_U^0/V_A^0, is 2.02. If the depreciation rate is increased to 3 per cent, then V_U^0/V_A^0 decreases to 1.77; if the depreciation rate is reduced to 1 per cent, then V_U^0/V_A^0 increases to 2.53. Again looking at the base case, if the real interest rate is increased to 5 per cent, then V_U^0/V_A^0 increases to 2.36, while if the real interest rate is reduced to 3 per cent, then V_U^0/V_A^0 decreases to 1.68. Finally, if the growth rate for new houses is increased to 2 per cent, then V_U^0/V_A^0 decreases to 1.53, while if the growth rate is reduced to 0, then V_U^0/V_A^0 increases to 3.00. Thus an acquisitions approach to housing in the CPI is likely to give about half the expenditure weight that a user cost approach would give.

23.40 For shorter-lived assets, the difference between the acquisitions approach and the user cost approach will not be so large, indicating that the acquisitions approach is approximately "correct" as a measure of consumption services.[21]

[20] Note that if the real interest rate r^0 equals g, the real rate of growth in purchases of the durable, then from the ratio (23.13), $V_U^0/V_A^0=(1+g)$ and the acquisitions approach will be more or less equivalent to the user cost approach over the long run.

[21] The simplified user cost approach can be used for other consumer durables as well. In formula (23.13), let $r^{0*}=0.04$, $g=0.01$ and $\delta=0.15$. Under these conditions, $V_U^0/V_A^0=1.20$; i.e., for a declining balance depreciation rate of 15 per cent, the user cost approach leads to an estimated value of consumption that is 20 per cent higher than the acquisitions approach under the conditions specified. Thus for consumer durable depreciation rates that are lower than 15 per cent, it could be useful for the statistical agency to produce user costs for these goods and for the national accounts division to produce the corresponding consumption flows as "analytic series". It should be noted that this extends the present national accounts treatment of housing to other long-lived consumer durables. Note also that this revised treatment of consumption in the national accounts would tend to make rich countries richer, since poorer countries hold fewer long-lived consumer durables on a per capita basis.

23.41 The following is a list of some of the problems and difficulties that might arise in implementing a user cost approach to purchases of a consumer durable:[22]

- It is difficult to determine what the relevant nominal interest rate r^0 is for each household. If a consumer has to borrow to finance the cost of a durable good purchase, then this interest rate will typically be much higher than the safe rate of return that would be the appropriate opportunity cost rate of return for a consumer who had no need to borrow funds to finance the purchase.[23] It may be necessary to simply use a benchmark interest rate that would be determined by either the government, a national statistical agency or an accounting standards board.
- It will generally be difficult to determine what the relevant depreciation rate is for the consumer durable.[24]
- Ex post user costs based on formula (23.8) will be too volatile to be acceptable to users[25] (owing to the volatility of the asset inflation rate i^0), and hence an ex ante user cost concept will have to be used. This creates difficulties in that different national statistical agencies will generally make different assumptions and use different methods to construct forecasted structures and land inflation rates. Hence, the resulting ex ante user costs of the durable may not be comparable across countries.[26]
- The user cost formula (23.8) must be generalized to accommodate various taxes that may be associated

[22] For additional material on difficulties with the user cost approach, see Diewert (1980, pp. 475–479) and Katz (1983, pp. 415–422).

[23] Katz (1983, pp. 415–416) comments on the difficulties involved in determining the appropriate rate of interest to use:

> There are numerous alternatives: a rate on financial borrowings, on savings, and a weighted average of the two; a rate on nonfinancial investments. e.g. residential housing, perhaps adjusted for capital gains, and the consumer's subjective rate of time preference. Furthermore, there is some controversy about whether it should be the maximum observed rate, the average observed rate, or the rate of return earned on investments that have the same degree of risk and liquidity as the durables whose services are being valued.

[24] It is not necessary to assume declining balance depreciation in the user cost approach: any pattern of depreciation can be accommodated, including "one hoss shay" depreciation, where the durable yields a constant stream of services over time until it is scrapped. See Diewert and Lawrence (2000) for some empirical examples for Canada, using different assumptions about the form of depreciation. For references to the depreciation literature and for empirical methods for estimating depreciation rates, see Hulten and Wykoff (1981a; 1981b; 1996) and Jorgenson (1996).

[25] Goodhart (2001, p. F351) comments on the practical difficulties of using ex post user costs for housing, as follows:

> An even more theoretical user cost approach is to measure the cost foregone by living in an owner-occupied property as compared with selling it at the beginning of the period and repurchasing it at the end . . . But this gives the absurd result that as house prices rise, so the opportunity cost falls; indeed the more virulent the inflation of housing asset prices, the more negative would this measure become. Although it has some academic aficionados, this flies in the face of common sense; I am glad to say that no country has adopted this method.

As will be seen later, Iceland has in fact adopted a simplified user cost framework.

[26] For additional material on the difficulties involved in constructing ex ante user costs, see Diewert (1980, pp. 475–486) and Katz (1983, pp. 419–420). For empirical comparisons of different user cost formulae, see Harper, Berndt and Wood (1989) and Diewert and Lawrence (2000).

with the purchase of a durable or with the continuing use of the durable.[27]

23.42 Some of the problems associated with estimating depreciation rates will be discussed in the next section.

Alternative models of depreciation

A general model of depreciation for (unchanging) consumer durables

23.43 In this subsection, a "general" model of depreciation for durable goods that appear on the market each period without undergoing quality change will be presented. In three subsequent subsections, this general model will be specialized to the three most common models of depreciation that appear in the literature. In paragraphs 23.69 to 23.78 below, the additional problems that occur when the durable is built as a unique good will be discussed.

23.44 The main tool that can be used to identify depreciation rates for a durable good is the (cross-sectional) sequence of vintage asset prices that units of the good sell for on the second-hand market at any point of time.[28]

23.45 Some notation is required. Let P^0 be the price of a newly produced unit of the durable good at the beginning of period 0 (this is the same notation as was used earlier). Let P_v^t be the second-hand market price at the beginning of period t of a unit of the durable good that is v periods old.[29] Let δ_v^0 be the period 0 depreciation rate for a unit of the durable good that is v periods old at the beginning of period 0. These depreciation rates can be defined recursively, starting with the period 0 depreciation rate for a brand new unit, δ_0^0, using the period 0 vintage asset prices P_v^0 as follows:

$$1-\delta_0^0=P_1^0/P^0 \tag{23.15}$$

Once δ_0^0 has been defined by equation (23.15), the period 0 cross-sectional depreciation rate for a unit of the durable good that is one period old at the beginning of period 0, δ_1^0, can be defined using the following equation:

$$(1-\delta_1^0)(1-\delta_0^0)=P_2^0/P^0 \tag{23.16}$$

Note that P_2^0 is the beginning of period 0 asset price of a unit of the durable good that is two periods old, and it is compared to the price of a brand new unit of the durable, P^0 (which is equal to P_0^0 using the vintage good notation).

23.46 Given that the period 0 cross-sectional depreciation rates for units of the durable that are 0, 1, 2, . . . , $v-1$ periods old at the beginning of period 0 are defined (these are the depreciation rates $\delta_0^0, \delta_1^0, \delta_2^0, \ldots, \delta_{v-1}^0$), then the period 0 cross-sectional depreciation rate for units of the durable that are v periods old at the beginning of period 0 can be defined using the following equation:

$$(1-\delta_v^0)\ldots(1-\delta_1^0)(1-\delta_0^0)=P_{v+1}^0/P^0 \tag{23.17}$$

23.47 It should be clear how the sequence of period 0 vintage asset prices P_v^0 can be converted into a sequence of period 0 vintage depreciation rates. It should also be clear that the sequence of equations (23.15)–(23.17) can be repeated using the vintage asset price data pertaining to the beginning of period t, P_v^t, in order to obtain a sequence of period t vintage depreciation rates, δ_v^t. In the literature, it is usually assumed that the sequence of vintage depreciation rates, δ_v^t, is independent of the period t so that:

$$\delta_v^t=\delta_v \quad \text{for all periods } t \text{ and all vintages } v \tag{23.18}$$

23.48 The above material shows how the sequence of vintage or used durable goods prices at a point in time can be used in order to estimate depreciation rates. This type of methodology, with a few extra modifications to account for differing ages of retirement, was pioneered by Beidelman (1973; 1976) and Hulten and Wykoff (1981a; 1981b; 1996).[30]

23.49 Recall the user cost formula for a new unit of the durable good under consideration defined by equation (23.1). The same approach can be used in order to define a sequence of period 0 user costs for all vintages v of the durable. Thus suppose that P_{v+1}^{1a} is the *anticipated end of period* 0 *price* of a unit of the durable good that is v periods old at the beginning of period 0, and let r^0 be the consumer's opportunity cost of capital. Then the discounted to the beginning of period 0 *user cost* of a unit of the durable good that is v periods old at the beginning of period 0, u_v^0, is defined as follows:

$$u_v^0 \equiv P_v^0-P_{v+1}^{1a}/(1+r^0) \quad v=0,1,2,\ldots \tag{23.19}$$

23.50 It is now necessary to specify how the end of period 0 anticipated vintage asset prices P_v^{1a} are related to their counterpart beginning of period 0 vintage asset

[27] For example, property taxes are associated with the use of housing services and hence should be included in the user cost formula; see paragraphs 23.100 and 23.101. As Katz (1983, p. 418) noted, taxation issues also have an impact on the choice of the interest rate: "Should the rate of return be a before or after tax rate?" From the viewpoint of a household that is not borrowing to finance the purchase of the durable, an after tax rate of return seems appropriate; but from the point of view of a leasing firm, a before tax rate of return seems appropriate. This difference helps to explain why rental equivalence prices for the durable might be higher than user cost prices.

[28] Another information source that could be used to identify depreciation rates for the durable good is the sequence of vintage rental or leasing prices that might exist for some consumer durables. In the closely related capital measurement literature, the general framework for an internally consistent treatment of capital services and capital stocks in a set of vintage accounts was set out by Jorgenson (1989) and Hulten (1990, pp. 127–129; 1996, pp. 152–160).

[29] Using this notation for vintages, it can be seen that the vintage $v=0$ price at the beginning of period $t=0$, P_0^0, is equal to the price of a new unit of the good, P^0. If these second-hand vintage prices depend on how intensively the durable good has been used in previous periods, then it will be necessary to further classify the durable good not only by its vintage v, but also according to the intensity of its use. In this case, think of the sequence of vintage asset prices, P_v^0, as corresponding to the prevailing market prices of the various vintages of the good at the beginning of period 0 for assets that have been used at "average" intensities.

[30] See also Jorgenson (1996) for a review of the empirical literature on the estimation of depreciation rates.

prices P_v^0. The assumption that is made now is that the entire sequence of vintage asset prices at the end of period 0 is equal to the corresponding sequence of asset prices at the beginning of period 0 times a general anticipated period 0 inflation rate factor $(1+i^0)$, where i^0 is the anticipated period 0 (general) asset inflation rate. Thus it is assumed that

$$P_v^{1a}=(1+i^0)P_v^0 \quad v=0,1,2,\ldots \tag{23.20}$$

Substituting equations (23.20) and (23.15)–(23.18) into equation (23.19) leads to the following beginning of *period* 0 *sequence of vintage user costs*:[31]

$$\begin{aligned} u_v^0 &= (1-\delta_{v-1})(1-\delta_{v-2})\ldots(1-\delta_0) \\ &\quad\times[(1+r^0)-(1+i^0)(1-\delta_v)]P^0/(1+r^0) \\ &= (1-\delta_{v-1})(1-\delta_{v-2})\ldots(1-\delta_0) \\ &\quad\times[r^0-i^0+\delta_v(1+i^0)]P^0/(1+r^0) \quad v=0,1,2,\ldots \end{aligned} \tag{23.21}$$

23.51 Note that if $v=0$, then the u_0^0 defined by equation (23.21) agrees with the user cost formula for a new purchase of the durable u^0 that was derived earlier in equation (23.7).

23.52 The sequence of vintage user costs u_v^0 defined by equation (23.21) are expressed in terms of prices that are discounted to the beginning of period 0. However, as was done in paragraphs 23.22 to 23.33, it is also possible to express the user costs in terms of prices that are "discounted" to the end of period 0. Thus, define the sequence of vintage *end of period* 0 *user cost*, p_v^0, as follows:

$$\begin{aligned} p_v^0 \equiv (1+r^0)u_v^0 &= (1-\delta_{v-1})(1-\delta_{v-2})\ldots(1-\delta_0) \\ &\quad\times[r^0-i^0+\delta_v(1+i^0)]P^0 \quad v=0,1,2,\ldots \end{aligned} \tag{23.22}$$

23.53 If the real interest rate r^{0*} is defined as the nominal interest rate r^0 less the asset inflation rate i^0, and the small terms $\delta_v i^0$ are neglected in equation (23.22), then the sequence of end of period user costs defined by equation (23.22) reduces to:

$$p_v^0=(1-\delta_{v-1})(1-\delta_{v-2})\ldots(1-\delta_0)[r^{0*}+\delta_v]P^0 \quad v=0,1,2,\ldots \tag{23.23}$$

Thus, if the price statistician has estimates for the vintage depreciation rates δ_v and the real interest rate $r^{0}*$, and is able to collect a sample of prices for new units of the durable good P^0, then the sequence of vintage user costs defined by equation (23.23) can be calculated. To complete the model, the price statistician should gather information on the stocks held by the household sector of each vintage of the durable good. Then normal index number theory can be applied to these p and Q values, with the set of p being vintage user costs and the set of Q being the vintage stocks pertaining to each period. For some worked examples of this methodology under various assumptions about depreciation rates and the calculation of expected asset inflation rates, see Diewert and Lawrence (2000) and Diewert (2003c).[32]

23.54 In the following three subsections, the general methodology described above is specialized by making additional assumptions about the form of the vintage depreciation rates δ_v.

Geometric or declining balance depreciation

23.55 The *declining balance method of depreciation* dates back to Matheson (1910, p. 55) at least.[33] In terms of the algebra presented in the previous subsection, the method is very simple: all the cross-sectional vintage depreciation rates δ_v^0 defined by equations (23.15)–(23.17) are assumed to be equal to the same rate δ, where δ is a positive number less than one; i.e., for all time periods t and all vintages v, it is assumed that

$$\delta_v^t=\delta \quad v=0,1,2,\ldots \tag{23.24}$$

Substitution of equation (23.24) into equation (23.22) leads to the following formula for the sequence of *period* 0 *vintage user costs*:

$$\begin{aligned} p_v^0 &= (1-\delta)^v[(1+r^0)-(1+i^0)(1-\delta)]P^0 \quad v=0,1,2,\ldots \\ &= (1-\delta)^v p_0^0 \end{aligned} \tag{23.25}$$

23.56 The second set of equations in (23.25) says that *all the vintage user costs are proportional to the user cost for a new asset*. This proportionality means that it is not necessary to use an index number formula to aggregate over vintages to form a durable services aggregate. To see this, it is useful to calculate the aggregate value of services yielded by all vintages of the consumer durable at the beginning of period 0. Let q^{-v} be the quantity of the durable purchased by the household sector v periods ago for $v=1,2,\ldots$ and let q^0 be the new purchases of the durable during period 0. The beginning of period 0 price for these vintages of age v will be p_v^0, defined by equation (23.25) above. Thus the aggregate services of all vintages of the good, including those purchased in period 0, will have the following value, S^0:

$$\begin{aligned} S^0 &= p_0^0q^0+p_1^0q^{-1}+p_2^0q^{-2}+\ldots \\ &= p_0^0q^0+(1-\delta)p_0^0q^{-1}+(1-\delta)^2p_0^0q^{-2}+\ldots \end{aligned}$$

using equation (23.25)

$$\begin{aligned} &= p_0^0[q^0+(1-\delta)q^{-1}+(1-\delta)^2q^{-2}+\ldots] \\ &= p_0^0Q^0 \end{aligned} \tag{23.26}$$

[31] When $v=0$, define $\delta_{-1}\equiv 1$; i.e., the terms in front of the square brackets on the right-hand side of equation (23.21) are set equal to 1.

[32] Additional examples and discussion can be found in two recent OECD manuals on productivity measurement and the measurement of capital; see OECD (2001a; 2001b).

[33] A case for attributing the method to Walras (1954, pp. 268–269) could be made, but he did not lay out all of the details. Matheson (1910, p. 91) used the term "diminishing value" to describe the method. Hotelling (1925, p. 350) used the term "the reducing balance method", while Canning (1929, p. 276) used the term "the declining balance formula".

where the period 0 aggregate (quality-adjusted) quantity of durable services consumed in period 0, Q^0, is defined as

$$Q^0 \equiv q^0 + (1-\delta)q^{-1} + (1-\delta)^2 q^{-2} + \ldots \qquad (23.27)$$

23.57 Thus the *period* 0 *services quantity aggregate* Q^0 is equal to new purchases of the durable in period 0, q^0, plus one minus the depreciation rate δ times the purchases of the durable in the previous period, q^{-1}, plus the square of one minus the depreciation rate times the purchases of the durable two periods ago, q^{-2}, and so on. The service price that can be applied to this quantity aggregate is p_0^0, and the imputed rental price or user cost for a new unit of the durable purchased in period 0.

23.58 If the depreciation rate δ and the purchases of the durable in prior periods are known, then the aggregate service quantity Q^0 can readily be calculated using equation (23.27). Then, using equation (23.26), it can be seen that the value of the services of the durable (over all vintages), S^t, decomposes into the price term p_0^0 times the quantity term Q^0. Hence, it is not necessary to use an index number formula to aggregate over vintages using this depreciation model.

Straight line depreciation

23.59 Another very common model of depreciation is the *straight line model.*[34] In this model, a most probable length of life for the durable is somehow determined, say L periods, so that after being used for L periods, the durable is scrapped. In the straight line depreciation model, it is assumed that the period 0 cross-sectional vintage asset prices P_v^0 follow the following pattern of linear decline relative to the period 0 price of a new asset P^0:

$$\frac{P_v^0}{P^0} = \frac{L-v}{L} \quad \text{for } v=0,1,2,\ldots,L-1 \qquad (23.28)$$

For $v=L, L+1, \ldots$, it is assumed that $P_v^0=0$. Now substitute equations (23.20) and (23.28) into the beginning of the period user cost formula (23.19) in order to obtain the following sequence of *period* 0 *vintage user costs* for the durable:

$$\begin{aligned} u_v^0 &= P_v^0-(1+i^0)P_{v+1}^0/(1+r^0) \quad \text{for } v=0,1,2,\ldots,L-1 \\ &= \frac{(L-v)P^0}{L} - \frac{(1+i^0)(L-v-1)P^0}{(1+r^0)L} \\ &= \frac{P^0}{1+r^{0*}}\left[\frac{(L-v)r^{0*}}{L} + \frac{1}{L}\right] \end{aligned} \qquad (23.29)$$

where the *asset-specific real interest rate for period* 0, r^{0*}, is defined by

$$1+r^{0*} \equiv \frac{1+r^0}{1+i^0} \qquad (23.30)$$

23.60 The user costs for units of the durable good that are older than L periods are zero; i.e., $u_v^0 \equiv 0$ for $v \geq L$. Looking at the terms in square brackets on the right-hand side of equation (23.29), it can be seen that the first term is a real interest opportunity cost for holding and using the unit of the durable that is v periods old (and this imputed interest cost declines as the durable good ages), and the second term is a depreciation term that is equal to the constant rate $1/L$.

23.61 In this model of depreciation, it is necessary to keep track of household purchases of the durable for L periods and weight up each vintage quantity q^{-v} of these purchases by the corresponding vintage user cost u_v^0, defined by equation (23.29), or the end of period vintage user costs p_v^0, defined as $(1+r^0)u_v^0$, could be used.[35]

"One hoss shay" or light bulb depreciation

23.62 The final model of depreciation that is in common use is the "light bulb" or "*one hoss shay*" *model of depreciation.*[36] In this model, the durable delivers the same services for each vintage: a chair is a chair, no matter what its age (until it falls to pieces and is scrapped). Thus this model also requires an estimate of the most probable life L of the consumer durable.[37]

In the "one hoss shay" model, it is assumed that the sequence of vintage beginning of the period user costs u_v^0, defined by the first line of equation (23.29), is *constant* for all vintages younger than the asset lifetime L; i.e., it is assumed that

$$\begin{aligned} u^0 = u_v^0 &= P_v^0-(1+i^0)P_{v+1}^0/(1+r^0) \quad \text{for } v=0,1,2,\ldots,L-1 \\ &= P_v^0-\gamma P_{v+1}^0 \end{aligned} \qquad (23.31)$$

where the *discount factor* γ is defined as

$$\gamma \equiv \frac{1+i^0}{1+r^0} = \frac{1}{1+r^{0*}} \qquad (23.32)$$

and the asset-specific real interest rate r^{0*} was defined by equation (23.30). Now the second equation in (23.31) can be used to express the *vintage v asset price* P_v^0 in terms of the common user cost u^0 and the vintage $v+1$ asset price, P_{v+1}^0, so that

$$P_v^0 = u^0 + \gamma P_{v+1}^0 \qquad (23.33)$$

23.63 Now start out using equation (23.33) with $v=0$, then substitute out P_1^0 using equation (23.33) with $v=1$, then substitute out P_2^0 using equation (23.33) with $v=2$, etc. The process finally ends after L such

[34] This model of depreciation dates back to the late 1800s; see Matheson (1910, p. 55), Garcke and Fells (1893, p. 98) or Canning (1929, pp. 265–266).

[35] A worked example using this model of depreciation can be found in Diewert (2003b).

[36] This model can be traced back to Böhm-Bawerk (1891, p. 342). For a more comprehensive exposition, see Hulten (1990, p. 124) or Diewert (2003b).

[37] The assumption of a single life L for a durable can be relaxed using a methodology attributable to Charles R. Hulten:

> We have thus far taken the date of retirement T to be the same for all assets in a given cohort (all assets put in place in a given year). However, there is no reason for this to be true, and the theory is readily extended to allow for different retirement dates. A given cohort can be broken into components, or subcohorts, according to date of retirement and a separate T assigned to each. Each subcohort can then be characterized by its own efficiency sequence, which depends among other things on the subcohort's useful life T_i (Hulten (1990, p. 125)).

substitutions, when P^0_L is reached and, of course, P^0_l equals zero. The following equation is obtained:

$$\begin{aligned} P^0 &= u^0 + \gamma u^0 + \gamma^2 u^0 + \ldots + \gamma^{L-1} u^0 \\ &= u^0[1+\gamma+\gamma^2+\ldots+\gamma^{L-1}] \\ &= u^0\left[\frac{1}{1-\gamma} - \frac{\gamma^L}{1-\gamma}\right] \quad \text{provided that } \gamma < 1 \\ &= u^0\left[\frac{1-\gamma^L}{1-\gamma}\right]. \end{aligned} \tag{23.34}$$

23.64 Now use the last equation in (23.34) in order to solve for the constant over vintages (beginning of the period) user cost for this model, u^0, in terms of the period 0 price for a new unit of the durable, P^0, and the discount factor γ defined by equation (23.32):

$$u^0 = \left[\frac{1-\gamma}{1-\gamma^L}\right] P^0. \tag{23.35}$$

23.65 The *end of period* 0 *user cost*, p^0, is, as usual, equal to the beginning of period 0 user cost, u^0, times the nominal interest rate factor, $1+r^0$:

$$p^0 \equiv (1+r^0)u^0 \tag{23.36}$$

23.66 The *aggregate services of all vintages* of the good, including those purchased in period 0, will have the following value, S^0:

$$\begin{aligned} S^0 &= p^0_0 q^0 + p^0_1 q^{-1} + p^0_2 q^{-2} + \ldots \\ &= p^0[q^0 + q^{-1} + q^{-2} + \ldots + q^{-(L-1)}] \\ &= p^0 Q^0 \end{aligned} \tag{23.37}$$

where the *period* 0 *aggregate (quality-adjusted) quantity of durable services* consumed in period 0, Q^0, is defined as follows for this "one hoss shay" depreciation model:

$$Q^0 \equiv q^0 + q^{-1} + q^{-2} + \ldots + q^{-(L-1)} \tag{23.38}$$

23.67 Thus in this model of depreciation, the vintage quantity aggregate is the simple sum of household purchases over the last L periods. As was the case with the geometric depreciation model, the "one hoss shay" model does not require index number aggregation over vintages: there is a constant service price p^0, and the associated period 0 quantity Q^0 is a weighted sum of past purchases for the geometric model and a simple sum over the purchases of the last L periods for the light bulb model.[38]

23.68 How can the different models of depreciation be distinguished empirically? In principle, information on the prices of second-hand durable goods may be used in order to decide which model of depreciation best fits the empirical facts. In practice, this is difficult to do, and hence different statistical agencies may make different assumptions about the "correct" pattern of depreciation (which generates the "correct" pattern of vintage user costs), based on whatever information they have at their disposal.

[38] Thus equation (23.38) is the quantity aggregate counterpart to equation (23.27).

Unique durable goods and the user cost approach

23.69 In the previous sections, it was assumed that a newly produced unit of the durable good remained the same from period to period. This means that the various vintages of the durable good repeat themselves going from period to period. Hence, a particular vintage of the good in the current period can be compared with the same vintage in the next period. In particular, consider the period 0 user cost of a new unit of a durable good, p^0_0, defined by equation (23.8). For convenience, the formula is repeated here:

$$p^0_0 = [(1+r^0)-(1+i^0)(1-\delta_0)]P^0 = [r^0 - i^0 + \delta_0(1+i^0)]P^0 \tag{23.39}$$

23.70 Recall that P^0 is the beginning of period 0 purchase price for the durable, r^0 is the nominal opportunity cost of capital that the household faces in period 0, i^0 is the anticipated period 0 inflation rate for the durable good, and δ_0 is the one-period depreciation rate for a new unit of the durable good. In previous sections, it was assumed that the period 0 user cost p^0_0 for a new unit of the durable could be compared with the corresponding period 1 user cost p^1_0 for a new unit of the durable purchased in period 1. This period 1 user cost can be defined as follows:

$$p^1_0 = [(1+r^1)-(1+i^1)(1-\delta_0)]P^1 = [r^1 - i^1 + \delta_0(1+i^1)]P^1 \tag{23.40}$$

23.71 However, many durable goods are produced as *one of a kind* models. For example, a new house may have many features that are specific to that particular house. An exact duplicate of it is unlikely to be built in the following period. Thus, if the user cost for the house is constructed for period 0 using formula (23.39), where the new house price P^0 plays a key role, then since there will not necessarily be a comparable new house price for the same type of unit in period 1, it will not be possible to construct the period 1 user cost for a house of the same type, p^1_0 defined by equation (23.40), because the comparable new house price P^1 will not be available.

23.72 Recall the notation that was introduced in paragraphs 23.43 to 23.54 above, where P^t_v was the second-hand market price at the beginning of period t of a unit of a durable good that is v periods old. Define δ_v to be the depreciation rate for a unit of the durable good that is v periods old at the beginning of the period under consideration. Using this notation, the user cost of the house (which is now one period old) for period 1, p^1_1, can be defined as follows:

$$p^1_1 \equiv (1+r^1)P^1_1 - (1+i^1)(1-\delta_1)P^1_1 \tag{23.41}$$

where P^1_1 is the beginning of period 1 price for the house that is now one period old, r^1 is the nominal opportunity cost of capital that the household faces in period 1, i^1 is the anticipated period 1 inflation rate for the durable good and δ_1 is the one-period depreciation rate for a house that is one period old. For a unique durable good, there is no beginning of period 1 price for a new unit of the durable, P^1, but it is natural to impute this price as the potentially observable market price for the used durable, P_1^1, divided by one minus the period 0 depreciation rate, δ_0; i.e., define an imputed period 1 price for a new unit of the unique durable as follows:

$$P^1 \equiv \frac{P_1^1}{(1-\delta_0)} \qquad (23.42)$$

23.73 If equation (23.42) is solved for P_1^1 and the solution is substituted into the user cost defined by equation (23.41), then the following expression is obtained for p_1^1, *the period* 1 *user cost of a one-period-old unique consumer durable*:

$$p_1^1 \equiv (1-\delta_0)[(1+r^1)-(1+i^1)(1-\delta_1)]P^1 \qquad (23.43)$$

23.74 If it is further assumed that the unique consumer durable follows the geometric model of depreciation, then

$$\delta = \delta_0 = \delta_1 \qquad (23.44)$$

Substituting equation (23.44) into equations (23.43) and (23.40) leads to the following relationship between *the imputed rental cost in period* 1 *of a new unit of the consumer durable*, p_0^1, and *the period* 1 *user cost of the one-period-old consumer durable*, p_1^1:

$$p_1^0 = \frac{p_1^1}{(1-\delta)} \qquad (23.45)$$

23.75 Thus, in order to obtain an imputed rental price for the unique consumer durable for period 1, p_0^1, that is comparable to the period 0 rental price for a new unit of the consumer durable, p_0^0, it is necessary to make a quality adjustment to the period 1 rental price for the one-period-old durable, p_1^1, by dividing this latter price by one minus the one-period geometric depreciation rate, δ. This observation has implications for the quality adjustment of observed market rents of houses. Without this type of quality adjustment, observed dwelling unit rents will have a downward bias, since the observed rents do not adjust for the gradual lowering of the quality of the unit as a result of depreciation of the unit.[39]

23.76 Note that in order to obtain an imputed purchase price for the unique consumer durable for period 1, P^1, that is comparable to the period 0 purchase price for a new unit of the consumer durable, P^0, it is necessary to make a quality adjustment to the period 1 used asset price for the one-period-old durable, P_1^1, by dividing this latter price by one minus the period 0 depreciation rate, δ_0; recall equation (23.42) above.[40]

23.77 This section concludes with some observations on the difficulties for economic measurement that occur when attempting to determine depreciation rates empirically for unique assets. Consider again equation (23.42), which allows the potentially observable market price of the unique asset at the beginning of period 1, P_1^1, to be expressed as being equal to $(1-\delta_0)P^1$, where P^1 is a hypothetical period 1 price for a new unit of the unique asset. If it is assumed that this hypothetical period 1 new asset price is equal to the period 0 to 1 inflation rate factor $(1+i^0)$ times the observable period 0 asset price P^0, then the following relationship between the two observable asset prices is obtained:

$$P_1^1 = (1-\delta_0)(1+i^0)P^0 \qquad (23.46)$$

Thus the potentially observable period 1 used asset price P_1^1 is equal to the period 0 new asset price P^0 times the product of two factors: $(1-\delta_0)$, a quality adjustment factor that takes into account the effects of ageing on the unique asset; and $(1+i^0)$, a period-to-period pure price change factor holding quality constant. The problem with unique assets is that cross-sectional information on used asset prices at any point in time is no longer available to make it possible to sort out the separate effects of these two factors. Thus there is a fundamental identification problem with unique assets; without extra information or assumptions, it will be impossible to distinguish the separate effects of asset deterioration and asset inflation.[41] In practice, this identification problem is solved by making somewhat arbitrary assumptions about the form of depreciation that the asset is expected to experience.[42]

23.78 Housing is the primary example of a unique asset. However, in addition to the problems outlined in this section, there are other major problems associated with this particular form of unique asset. These problems are discussed in the following sections.

The user cost of owner-occupied housing

23.79 Owner-occupied housing is typically an example of a unique consumer durable, so the material on the quality adjustment of both stock and rental prices developed in the previous section applies to this commodity. Owner-occupied housing is, however, also an

[39] There is an exception to this general observation: if housing depreciation is of the "one hoss shay" type, then there is no need to quality-adjust observed rents for the same unit over time. However, "one hoss shay" depreciation is empirically unlikely in the housing market since renters are generally willing to pay a rent premium for a new unit over an older unit of the same type. For empirical evidence of this age premium, see Malpezzi, Ozanne and Thibodeau (1987), and Hoffmann and Kurz (2002, p. 19).

[40] This type of quality adjustment to the asset prices for unique consumer durables will always be necessary; i.e., there is no exception to this rule, as was the case for "one hoss shay" depreciation in the context of quality-adjusting rental prices.

[41] Special cases of this fundamental identification problem have been noted in the context of various econometric housing models, by Martin J. Bailey, Richard F. Muth and Hugh O. Nourse (1963, p. 936): "For some purposes one might want to adjust the price index for depreciation. Unfortunately, a depreciation adjustment cannot be readily estimated along with the price index using our regression method.... In applying our method, therefore, additional information would be needed in order to adjust the price index for depreciation."

[42] For example, if the unique asset is a painting by a master, then the depreciation rate can be assumed to be very close to zero. As another example, a reasonable guess at the likely length of life L of the unique asset could be made, and then the "one hoss shay" or straight line depreciation models could be implemented. Alternatively, the length of life L could be converted into an equivalent geometric depreciation rate δ using the conversion rule $\delta = n/L$, where n is a number between 1 and 2.

example of a composite good; i.e., two distinct commodities are bundled together and sold (or rented) at a single price. The two distinct commodities are:

- the structure;
- the land on which the structure is situated.

23.80 To model this situation, consider a particular newly constructed dwelling unit that is purchased at the beginning of period 0. Suppose that the purchase price is V^0. This value can be regarded as the sum of a cost of producing the structure, say $P_S^0 Q_S^0$, where Q_S^0 is the number of square metres of floor space in the structure and P_S^0 is the beginning of period 0 price of construction per square metre, and the cost of the land, say $P_L^0 Q_L^0$, where Q_L^0 is the number of square metres of the ground on which the structure is situated and the associated land, and P_L^0 is the beginning of period 0 price of the land per square metre.[43] Thus at the beginning of period 0, *the value of the dwelling unit*, V^0, is defined as follows:

$$V^0 = P_S^0 Q_S^0 + P_L^0 Q_L^0 \quad (23.47)$$

23.81 Suppose that the anticipated price of a unit of a new structure at the beginning of period 1 is P_S^{1a} and that the anticipated price of a unit of land at the beginning of period 1 is P_L^{1a}. Define the *period* 0 *anticipated inflation rates for new structures and land*, i_S^0 and i_L^0, respectively, as follows:

$$1 + i_S^0 \equiv \frac{P_S^{1a}}{P_S^0} \quad (23.48)$$

$$1 + i_L^0 \equiv \frac{P_L^{1a}}{P_L^0} \quad (23.49)$$

23.82 Let δ_0 be the period 0 depreciation rate for the structure. Then the anticipated beginning of period 1 value for the structure and the associated land is equal to

$$V^{1a} = P_S^{1a}(1-\delta_0)Q_S^0 + P_L^{1a}Q_L^0 \quad (23.50)$$

Note the presence of the depreciation term $(1-\delta_0)$ on the right-hand side of equation (23.50). Should this term be associated with the expected beginning of period 1 price for a new unit of structure P_S^{1a} or with the structure quantity term Q_S^0? On the principle that like should be compared with like for prices, it seems preferable to associate $(1-\delta_0)$ with the quantity term Q_S^0. This is consistent with the treatment of unique assets that was suggested in the previous section; i.e., the initial quantity of structure Q_S^0 should be quality adjusted downwards to the amount $(1-\delta_0)\ Q_S^0$ at the beginning of period 1.

23.83 Now calculate the cost (including the imputed opportunity cost of capital r^0) of buying the dwelling unit at the beginning of period 0 and (hypothetically) selling it at the end of period 0. The following end of period 0 *user cost or imputed rental cost* R^0 for the dwelling unit is obtained using equations (23.47)–(23.50):

$$\begin{aligned} R^0 &= V^0(1+r^0) - V^{1a} \\ &= [P_S^0 Q_S^0 + P_L^0 Q_L^0](1+r^0) - [P_S^{1a}(1-\delta_0)Q_S^0 + P_L^{1a}Q_L^0] \\ &= [P_S^0 Q_S^0 + P_L^0 Q_L^0](1+r^0) \\ &\quad - [P_S^0(1+i_S^0)(1-\delta_0)Q_S^0 + P_L^0(1+i_L^0)Q_L^0] \\ &= p_S^0 Q_S^0 + p_L^0 Q_L^0 \end{aligned} \quad (23.51)$$

where separate period 0 *user costs of structure and land*, p_S^0 and p_L^0, are defined as follows:

$$\begin{aligned} p_S^0 &\equiv [(1+r^0)-(1+i_S^0)(1-\delta_0)]P_S^0 \\ &= [r^0 - i_S^0 + \delta_0(1+i_S^0)]P_S^0 \end{aligned} \quad (23.52)$$

$$\begin{aligned} p_L^0 &\equiv [(1+r^0)-(1+i_L^0)]P_L^0 \\ &= [r^0 - i_L^0]P_L^0 \end{aligned} \quad (23.53)$$

23.84 Note that the above algebra indicates some of the major determinants of market rents for rented properties. The user cost formulae defined by equations (23.52) and (23.53) can be further simplified if the same approximations that were made in paragraphs 23.22 to 23.33 are made here (recall equation (23.9); i.e., assume that the terms $r^0 - i_S^0$ and $r^0 - i_L^0$ can be approximated by a real interest rate r^{0*} and neglect the small term δ_0 times i_S^0 in equation (23.52). Then the user costs defined by equations (23.52) and (23.53) reduce to:

$$p_S^0 \approx [r^{0*} + \delta_0]P_S^0 \quad (23.54)$$

$$p_L^0 \approx r^{0*} P_L^0 \quad (23.55)$$

23.85 Thus the imputed rent for an owner-occupied dwelling unit is made up of three main costs:

- the real opportunity cost of the financial capital tied up in the structure;
- the real opportunity cost of the financial capital tied up in the land;
- the depreciation cost of the structure.

23.86 The above simplified approach to the user cost of housing can be even further simplified by assuming that the ratio of the quantity of land to structure is fixed, and so the aggregate user cost of housing is equal to $[r^{0*} + \delta]P_H^0$, where P_H is a quality-adjusted housing price index that is based on all properties sold in the country to households during the period under consideration and δ is a geometric depreciation rate that applies to the composite of household structure and land. This extremely simplified approach is used in Iceland; see Gudnason (2003, pp. 28–29).[44] A variant of this

[43] If the dwelling unit is part of a multiple unit structure, then the land associated with it will be the appropriate share of the total land space.

[44] The real interest rate that is used is approximately 4 per cent per year and the combined depreciation rate for land and structures is assumed to equal 1.25 per cent per year. The depreciation rate for structures alone is estimated to be 1.5 per cent per year. Property taxes are accounted for separately in the Icelandic CPI. Housing price information is provided by the State Evaluation Board, based on property sales data of both new and old housing. The State Evaluation Board also estimates the value of the housing stock and land in Iceland, using a hedonic regression model based on property sales data. The value of each household's dwelling is collected in the household budget survey.

approach is used by the United States Bureau of Economic Analysis: Lebow and Rudd (2003, p. 168) note that the United States national accounts imputation for the services of owner-occupied housing is obtained by applying rent-to-value ratios for tenant-occupied housing to the stock of owner-occupied housing. The rent-to-value ratio can be regarded as an estimate of the applicable real interest rate plus the depreciation rate.

23.87 Returning to the period 0 imputed rental cost model for a new structure defined by equations (23.47)–(23.53), now calculate the cost (including the imputed opportunity cost of capital r^1) of buying the used dwelling unit at the beginning of period 1 and (hypothetically) selling it at the end of period 1. Thus at the beginning of period 1, the value of the depreciated dwelling unit is V^1 defined as follows:

$$V^1 = P_S^1(1-\delta_0)Q_S^0 + P_L^1 Q_L^0 \qquad (23.56)$$

where P_S^1 is the beginning of period 1 construction price for building a new dwelling unit of the same type and P_L^1 is the beginning of period 1 price of land for the dwelling unit. Note that equation (23.56) is an *end of period* 0 *ex post or actual value* of the dwelling unit, whereas the similar expression (23.50) defined a *beginning of period* 0 *ex ante or anticipated value* of the dwelling unit.

23.88 Suppose that the anticipated price of a unit of a new structure at the beginning of period 2 is P_S^{2a} and that the anticipated price of a unit of land at the beginning of period 2 is P_L^{2a}. Define *the period* 1 *anticipated inflation rates for new structures and land*, i_S^1 and i_L^1, respectively, as follows:

$$1 + i_S^1 \equiv P_S^{2a}/P_S^1 \qquad (23.57)$$

$$1 + i_L^1 \equiv P_L^{2a}/P_L^1 \qquad (23.58)$$

23.89 Let δ_1 be the period 1 depreciation rate for the structure. Then *the anticipated beginning of period* 2 *value for the structure and the associated land* is equal to

$$V^{2a} = P_S^{2a}(1-\delta_0)(1-\delta_1)Q_S^0 + P_L^{2a}Q_L^0 \qquad (23.59)$$

23.90 The following end of period 1 *user cost or imputed rental cost*, R_1^1, for a one-period-old dwelling unit is obtained using equations (23.56)–(23.59):

$$\begin{aligned} R_1^1 &\equiv V^1(1+r^1) - V^{2a} \\ &= [P_S^1(1-\delta_0)Q_S^0 + P_L^1Q_L^0](1+r^1) \\ &\quad -[P_S^{2a}(1-\delta_0)(1-\delta_1)Q_S^0 + P_L^{2a}Q_L^0] \\ &= [P_S^1(1-\delta_0)Q_S^0 + P_L^1Q_L^0](1+r^1) \\ &\quad -[P_S^1(1+i_S^1)(1-\delta_0)(1-\delta_1)Q_S^0 + P_L^1(1+i_L^1)Q_L^0] \\ &= p_{S1}^1(1-\delta_0)Q_S^0 + p_L^1Q_L^0 \end{aligned} \qquad (23.60)$$

where the period 1 *user costs of one-period-old structures and land*, p_{S1}^1 and p_L^1, are defined as follows:

$$\begin{aligned} p_{S1}^1 &\equiv [(1+r^1)-(1+i_S^1)(1-\delta_1)]P_S^1 \\ &= [r^1 - i_S^1 + \delta_1(1+i_S^1)]P_S^1 \end{aligned} \qquad (23.61)$$

$$p_L^1 \equiv [(1+r^1)-(1+i_L^1)]P_L^1 = [r^1 - i_L^1]P_L^1 \qquad (23.62)$$

23.91 Comparing the period 0 user cost of land, p_L^0, defined by equation (23.53) with the period 1 user cost of land, p_L^1, defined by equation (23.62), it can be seen that these user costs have exactly the same form and hence are comparable. However, comparing the period 0 user cost for a new structure, p_S^0, defined by equation (23.52) with the period 1 user cost for a one-period-old structure, p_S^1, defined by equation (23.61), it can be seen that these user costs are not quite comparable unless the period 0 depreciation rate δ_0 is equal to the period 1 depreciation rate δ_1. If declining balance depreciation for structures is assumed, then $\delta_0 = \delta_1 = \delta$, where δ is the common depreciation rate across all periods. Under this assumption, p_S^1 is comparable to the period 0 user cost for a new unit of structures p_S^0. Even under the assumption of geometric depreciation, it can be seen that the period 1 imputed rent for a one-period-old dwelling unit, R_1^1, defined by equation (23.60) is not comparable to the corresponding period 0 imputed rent for a new dwelling unit, R^0, defined by equation (23.51). The imputed rent R^1 that would be comparable to R^0 can be defined as follows:

$$R^1 \equiv p_S^1Q_S^0 + p_L^1Q_L^0 = R_1^1 + p_S^1\delta Q_S^0 \qquad (23.63)$$

where the period 1 user cost of structures, p_S^1, is defined by the right-hand side of equation (23.61), with δ_1 equal to the common depreciation rate δ and the period 1 user cost of land, p_L^1, defined by equation (23.62). Equation (23.63) has the following implication for the quality adjustment of the price of a rented property: if R^0 is the observed rent of the unit in period 0 and R_1^1 is the observed rent for the same dwelling unit in period 1, then the observed rent R_1^1 is *too low* compared to R^0 and so the period 1 observed rent should be quality adjusted upwards by the period 1 rental price for structures, p_S^1, times the amount of physical depreciation, δQ_S^0, in the structure that occurred in the previous period. This is the same point that was made in paragraphs 23.69 to 23.78, but in this section the complications arising from the fact that housing services are a mixture of structure and land services are taken into account.

23.92 It is evident that the main drivers for the user costs of structures and land are a price index for new dwelling construction, P_S^t, and a price index for residential land, P_L^t. Most statistical agencies have a constant quality price index for new residential structures, since this index is required in the national accounts in order to deflate investment expenditures on residential structures. This index could be used as an approximation to P_S^t.[45] The national accounts also require an

[45] This index may only be an approximation since it covers the construction of rented properties, as well as owner-occupied dwellings.

imputation for the services of owner-occupied housing and thus the constant quality price component of this imputation may be suitable for CPI purposes.[46] If the national accounts division also computes quarterly real balance sheets for the economy, then a price index for residential land may be available to the prices division. Even if this is the case, there will be problems in producing this price index for land on a timely basis and at a monthly frequency.[47] A further possible source of information on land prices may be found in land title registry offices and in the records of real estate firms. The associated information on transactions involving the same property can be used in a hedonic regression framework; see for example, Malpezzi, Ozanne and Thibodeau (1987).[48]

23.93 There are many other difficulties associated with measuring the price and quantity of owner-occupied housing services. The following section discusses some of the problems involved in modelling the costs of certain expenditures that are tied to the ownership of a home.

The treatment of costs that are tied to owner-occupied housing

23.94 There are many costs that are quite directly tied to home-ownership. It is not always clear, however, how these costs can be decomposed into price and quantity components. Several of these cost components are listed below, and some ways of forming their associated prices are suggested.

The treatment of mortgage interest costs

23.95 The derivation of the user cost or expected rental price that an owner of a home should charge for the use of the dwelling unit for one period implicitly assumes that the owner has no mortgage interest costs, so the interest rate r^0 refers to the owner's opportunity cost of equity capital. In this section, the case where the owner has a mortgage on the property is considered.

23.96 Recall the notation in the previous section where the user cost or imputed rental cost, R^0, for an equity-financed dwelling unit is obtained; see equation (23.51). Suppose now that the property purchase is partly financed by a mortgage of M^0 dollars at the beginning of period 0. Let f^0 be the fraction of the beginning of period 0 market value of the property that is financed by the mortgage so that

$$M^0 = f^0 V^0 = f^0[P_S^0 Q_S^0 + P_L^0 Q_L^0] \qquad (23.64)$$

23.97 Let the one-period nominal mortgage interest rate be r_M^0. The owner's period 0 benefits of owning the dwelling unit remain the same as in the previous section and are equal to V^{1a}, defined by equation (23.50). However, the period 0 costs are now made up of an explicit mortgage interest cost equal to $M^0(1+r_M^0)$ plus an imputed equity cost equal to $(1-f^0)V^0(1+r^0)$. Thus the new imputed rent for using the property during period 0 is now

$$\begin{aligned} R^0 &\equiv (1-f^0)V^0(1+r^0) + M^0(1+r_M^0) - V^{1a} \\ &= (1-f^0)[P_S^0 Q_S^0 + P_L^0 Q_L^0](1+r^0) \\ &\quad + f^0[P_S^0 Q_S^0 + P_L^0 Q_L^0](1+r_M^0) - [P_S^{1a}(1-\delta_0)Q_S^0 + P_L^{1a} Q_L^0] \\ &= p_S^{0*} Q_S^0 + p_L^{0*} Q_L^0 \end{aligned} \qquad (23.65)$$

where the new mortgage interest adjusted period 0 *user costs of structures and land*, p_S^{0*} and p_L^{0*}, are defined as follows:

$$\begin{aligned} p_S^{0*} &\equiv [(1+r^0)(1-f^0) + (1+r_M^0)f^0 - (1+i_S^0)(1-\delta_0)]P_S^0 \\ &= [r^0(1-f^0) + r_M^0 f^0 - i_S^0 + \delta_0(1+i_S^0)]P_S^0 \\ &= [(r^0 - i_S^0)(1-f^0) + (r_M^0 - i_S^0)f^0 + \delta_0(1+i_S^0)]P_S^0 \end{aligned} \qquad (23.66)$$

$$\begin{aligned} p_L^{0*} &\equiv [(1+r^0)(1-f^0) + (1+r_M^0)f^0 - (1+i_L^0)]P_L^0 \\ &= [r^0(1-f^0) + r_M^0 f^0 - i_L^0]P_L^0 \\ &= [(r^0 - i_L^0)(1-f^0) + (r_M^0 - i_L^0)f^0]P_L^0 \end{aligned} \qquad (23.67)$$

23.98 Comparing the new user costs for structures and land defined by equations (23.66) and (23.67) with the corresponding equity-financed user costs defined by equations (23.52) and (23.53), it can be seen that the old equity opportunity cost of capital r^0 is now replaced by a weighted average of this equity opportunity cost and the mortgage interest rate, $r^0(1-f^0) + r_M^0 f^0$, where f^0 is the fraction of the beginning of period 0 value of the dwelling unit that is financed by the mortgage.

23.99 Central bankers often object to the inclusion of mortgage interest in a CPI. Examination of the last equation in (23.66) and in (23.67) nevertheless shows that the *nominal* mortgage interest rate r_M^0 has an offsetting benefit resulting from *anticipated price inflation* in the price of structures, i_S^0 in equation (23.66), and in the price of land, i_L^0 in equation (23.67), so, as usual, what counts in these user cost formulae are real interest costs rather than nominal ones.

[46] However, the national accounts imputation for the services of owner-occupied housing will only be produced on a quarterly basis, and so some additional work will be required to produce a price deflator on a monthly basis. Also, even though the *SNA 1993* recommends that the imputation for the services of owner-occupied housing be based on the rental equivalent method, it may be the case that the imputation covers only the imputed depreciation on the structure part of owner-occupied housing. As was pointed out above, there are two other important additional components that should also be included in owner-occupied housing services; namely, the imputed real interest on the structures and the land on which the structure is situated. These latter two components of imputed expenditures are likely to be considerably larger than the depreciation component.

[47] Another source of information on the value of residential land may be available from the local property tax authorities, particularly if properties are assessed at market values.

[48] Many hedonic regression studies use the logarithm of a transaction price as the dependent variable. This specification of the hedonic model is usually not consistent with the additive nature of the structure and land components of a property, and the multiplicative nature of the depreciation adjustment, as appearing in equations (23.47) and (23.56) which defined the value of a specific property in successive periods.

The treatment of property taxes

23.100 Recall the user costs of structures and land defined by equations (23.52) and (23.53). It is now supposed that the owner of the housing unit must pay the property taxes T_S^0 and T_L^0 for the use of the structure and land, respectively, during period 0.[49] Define *the period* 0 *structures tax rate* τ_S^0 and *land tax rate* τ_L^0, as follows:

$$\tau_S^0 \equiv \frac{T_S^0}{P_S^0 Q_S^0} \tag{23.68}$$

$$\tau_L^0 \equiv \frac{T_L^0}{P_L^0 Q_L^0} \tag{23.69}$$

23.101 The *new imputed rent for using the property during period* 0, R^0, including the property tax costs, is defined as follows:

$$\begin{aligned} R^0 &\equiv V^0(1+r^0)+T_S^0+T_S^0-V^{1a} \\ &=[P_S^0 Q_S^0+P_L^0 Q_L^0](1+r^0)+\tau_S^0 P_S^0 Q_S^0+\tau_L^0 P_L^0 Q_L^0 \\ &\quad -[P_S^0(1+i_S^0)(1-\delta_0)Q_S^0+P_L^0(1+i_L^0)Q_L^0] \\ &=p_S^0 Q_S^0+p_L^0 Q_L^0 \end{aligned} \tag{23.70}$$

where separate period 0 tax-adjusted *user costs of structures and land*, p_S^0 and p_L^0, are defined as follows:

$$\begin{aligned} p_S^0 &\equiv [(1+r^0)-(1+i_S^0)(1-\delta_0)+\tau_S^0]P_S^0 \\ &=[r^0-i_S^0+\delta_0(1+i_S^0)+\tau_S^0]P_S^0 \end{aligned} \tag{23.71}$$

$$\begin{aligned} p_L^0 &\equiv [(1+r^0)-(1+i_L^0)+\tau_L^0]P_L^0 \\ &=[r^0-i_L^0+\tau_L^0]P_L^0 \end{aligned} \tag{23.72}$$

Thus the property tax rates, τ_S^0 and τ_L^0, defined by equations (23.68) and (23.69), enter the user costs of structures and land, p_S^0 and p_L^0, defined by equations (23.71) and (23.72), in a simple additive manner; i.e., these terms are additive to the previous depreciation and real interest rate terms.[50]

The treatment of property insurance

23.102 At first glance, it would seem that *property insurance* could be treated in the same manner as the treatment of property taxes in the previous subsection. Thus, let C_S^0 be the cost of insuring the structure at the beginning of period 0 and define *the period* 0 *structures premium rate* γ_S^0 as follows:

$$\gamma_S^0 \equiv \frac{C_S^0}{P_S^0 Q_S^0} \tag{23.73}$$

23.103 The new *imputed rent* for using the property during period 0, R^0, including property tax and insurance costs, is defined as follows:

$$R^0 \equiv V^0(1+r^0)+T_S^0+T_S^0+C_S^0-V^{1a}=p_S^0 Q_S^0+p_L^0 Q_L^0 \tag{23.74}$$

where separate period 0 tax and insurance adjusted *user costs of structures and land*, p_S^0 and p_L^0, are defined as follows:

$$\begin{aligned} p_S^0 &\equiv [(1+r^0)-(1+i_S^0)(1-\delta_0)+\tau_S^0+\gamma_S^0] \\ P_S^0 &=[r^0-i_S^0+\delta_0(1+i_S^0)+\tau_S^0+\gamma_S^0]P_S^0 \end{aligned} \tag{23.75}$$

$$p_L^0 \equiv [(1+r^0)-(1+i_L^0)+\tau_L^0]P_L^0=[r^0-i_L^0+\tau_L^0]P_L^0 \tag{23.76}$$

23.104 Thus the insurance premium rate γ_S^0 appears in the user cost of structures, p_S^0, defined by equation (23.75), in an additive manner, analogous to the additive property tax rate term.[51] If it is desired to have a separate CPI price component for insurance, then the corresponding period 0 and 1 prices can be defined as $\gamma_S^0 P_S^0$ and $\gamma_S^1 P_S^1$, respectively, while the corresponding period 0 and 1 expenditures can be defined as $\gamma_S^0 P_S^0 Q_S^0$ and $\gamma_S^1 P_S^1(1-\delta)Q_S^0$, respectively.[52] Of course, if this separate treatment is implemented, then these terms have to be dropped from the corresponding user costs of structures.

23.105 The above treatment of property taxation and insurance assumes that the property taxes and the premium payments are made at the end of the period under consideration; see equation (23.74) above. While this may be an acceptable approximation for the payment of property taxes, it is not acceptable for the payment of insurance premiums: the premium must be paid at the beginning of the period of protection rather than at the end. When this complication is taken into account, the user cost of structures becomes

$$\begin{aligned} p_S^0 &\equiv [(1+r^0)-(1+i_S^0)(1-\delta_0)+\tau_S^0+\gamma_S^0(1+r^0)]P_S^0 \\ &=[r^0-i_S^0+\delta_0(1+i_S^0)+\tau_S^0+\gamma_S^0(1+r^0)]P_S^0 \end{aligned} \tag{23.77}$$

23.106 There are some additional problems associated with the modelling of property insurance:

- The above user cost derivations assume that the risk of property damage remains constant from period to period. If the risk of damage changes, then an argument can be made for quality adjustment of the premium to hold constant the risk so that like can be compared with like.
- The gross premium approach to insurance is taken in the above treatment; i.e., it is assumed that dwelling owners pay premiums for property protection

[49] If there is no breakdown of the property taxes into structure and land components, then just impute the overall tax into structure and land components based on the beginning of the period values of both components.

[50] If the price statistician uses the national accounts imputation for the value of owner-occupied housing services, care should be taken to ensure that the value of property taxes is included in this imputation.

[51] This treatment of property insurance dates back to Walras (1954, pp. 268–269).

[52] Similarly, if it is desired to have a separate CPI price component for property taxes on structures, then the corresponding period 0 and 1 prices can be defined as $\tau_S^0 P_S^0$ and $\tau_S^1 P_S^1$, respectively, while the corresponding period 0 and 1 expenditures can be defined as $\tau_S^0 P_S^0 Q_S^0$ and $\tau_S^1 P_S^1(1-\delta)Q_S^0$, respectively.

services, no matter whether they have a claim or not. In the net premium approach, payments to settle claims are subtracted from the gross premium payments.

- The property protection may not be complete; i.e., the insurance policy may have various limitations on the type of claim that is allowed and there may be a deductible or damage threshold, below which no claim is allowed. If the deductible changes from period to period, then the price statistician is faced with a rather complex quality adjustment problem.

Thus it can be seen that there are many difficult problems that remain to be resolved in this area.

The treatment of maintenance and renovation expenditures

23.107 Another problem associated with home-ownership is the treatment of maintenance expenditures, major repair expenditures and expenditures associated with renovations or additions.

23.108 Empirical evidence suggests that the normal decline in a structure resulting from the effects of ageing and use can be offset by maintenance and renovation expenditures. How exactly should these expenditures be treated in the context of modelling the costs and benefits of home-ownership?

23.109 A common approach in the national accounts literature is to treat major renovation and repair expenditures as capital formation, and smaller routine maintenance and repair expenditures as current expenditures. If this approach is followed in the CPI context, then these smaller routine maintenance expenditures can be treated in the same manner as other non-durable goods and services. The major renovation and repair expenditures do not enter the CPI in the period that they are made, but are capitalized and added to expenditures on new structures for the period under consideration, so that period 0 investment in structures in constant dollars, I_S^0 say,[53] would include both types of expenditures. Let Q_S^0 and Q_S^1 be the stocks (in constant quality units) of owner-occupied structures in the reference population at the beginning of period 0 and 1, respectively. Then if the geometric model of depreciation is used, so that the constant period-to-period depreciation rate δ is applicable, then the beginning of period 1 stock of owner-occupied structures Q_S^1 is related to the beginning of period 0 stock of structures Q_S^0 and the period 0 investment in structures I_S^0, according to the following equation:

$$Q_S^1 = (1-\delta)Q_S^0 + I_S^0 \tag{23.78}$$

23.110 Thus, if declining balance depreciation is assumed for structures, then the treatment of major repair and renovation expenditures does not pose major conceptual problems using a conventional capital accumulation model: it is only necessary to have an estimate for the monthly or quarterly depreciation rate δ, a starting value for the stock of owner-occupied structures for some period, information on new purchases of residential housing structures by the household sector, information on expenditures by owners on major repairs and renovations, and a construction price index for new residential structures. With this information on a timely basis, up-to-date CPI weights for the stock of owner-occupied structures could be constructed.[54]

23.111 This section concludes by looking at how major repair and renovation expenditures could be treated in a repeat sales regression model that uses transactions data on the sale of the same housing unit in two or more periods. In order to minimize notational complexities, consider a highly simplified situation where data on the sale of N houses of a relatively homogeneous type for two consecutive periods are available. Suppose that these sale prices are V_n^0 for period 0 and V_n^1 for period 1, for $n=1, 2, \ldots, N$. Suppose that a price index for structures of this type of property in period 0, P_S^0, and a corresponding price index for land in period 0, P_L^0, have been constructed.[55] The price statistician's problem is to use the data on the matched sales for the two periods in order to construct estimates of these two indices for period 1; i.e., the problem is to construct P_S^1 and P_L^1.

23.112 The period 0 *dwelling unit values* for the N properties can be decomposed into the structure and land components as follows:

$$V_n^0 = V_{Sn}^0 + V_{Ln}^0 = \alpha_n P_S^0 Q_{Sn}^0 + \beta_n P_L^0 Q_{Ln}^0; \quad n=1,2,\ldots,N \tag{23.79}$$

where V_{Sn}^0 and V_{Ln}^0 are the estimated period 0 values of the structure and land of property n in period 0, P_S^0 and P_L^0 are the (known) price index values for structures and land for all properties of this type in period 0, and Q_{Sn}^0 and Q_{Ln}^0 are (known) estimates of the quantity of structures and land for property n. The numbers α_n and β_n are property n quality adjustment factors that convert the property standardized values of structures and land, $P_S^0 Q_{Sn}^0$ and $P_L^0 Q_{Sn}^0$, respectively, into the period 0 actual market values, V_{Sn}^0 and V_{Ln}^0, respectively; i.e., if estimates of the period 0 market values of the structures and land for property n are available, then α_n and β_n can be defined as follows:

$$\alpha_n \equiv \frac{V_{Sn}^0}{P_S^0 Q_{Sn}^0}; \quad \beta_n \equiv \frac{V_{Ln}^0}{P_L^0 Q_{Ln}^0}; \quad n=1,\ldots,N \tag{23.80}$$

23.113 Suppose that information on the dollar amount of major repairs and renovations made to property n during period 0, VR_n^0, are also available for each property n in the sample of properties. Then the period 1 value for property n, V_n^1, should be approximately equal to

[53] Let VI_S^0 be the nominal value of investment in new owner-occupied structures in period 0, plus the value of major renovation expenditures made during period 0. Then the constant dollar quantity of investment could be defined as $I_S^0 \equiv VI_S^0/P_S^0$, where P_S^0 is the period 0 construction price index for new structures.

[54] The practical problems involved in obtaining all this information on a timely basis are, however, not trivial.

[55] If these period 0 indices are not available, then set P_S^0 and P_L^0 equal to 1.

$$V_n^1 = \alpha_n P_S^1 (1-\delta) Q_{Sn}^0 + VR_n^0 + \beta_n P_L^1 Q_{Ln}^0; \quad n = 1, \ldots, N \tag{23.81}$$

where δ is the geometric depreciation rate for structures. All the variables on the right-hand side of equation (23.81) are assumed to be known, with the exception of the period 1 price index values for structures and land, P_S^1 and P_L^1, respectively, and the one-period geometric depreciation rate, δ. If the number of observations N is greater than three, then it would appear that these three parameters, P_S^1, P_L^1 and δ, could be estimated by a linear regression using the N equations in (23.81) as estimating equations. It turns out, however, that this is not quite correct. The problem is that the parameters P_S^1 and $(1-\delta)$ appear in equation (23.81) in a multiplicative fashion so that while the product of these two terms will be identified by the regression, the individual terms cannot be uniquely identified. This is just a reappearance of the same problem that was discussed in paragraphs 23.69 to 23.78 in relation to unique consumer durables: the separate effects of ageing of the asset (depreciation or capital consumption) and price appreciation over time cannot be separately identified using just market data.[56]

23.114 There are three possible solutions to this identification problem:

- use an external estimate of the depreciation rate δ;
- use an external construction price index P_S^1 instead of estimating it as a parameter in equations (23.81);
- abandon the repeat sales approach and use a hedonic regression approach instead.

23.115 What would a hedonic regression model look like, taking into account the approximate additivity of the value of the housing structure and the value of the land on which the structure is situated? If the renovations problem is ignored and geometric depreciation of the structure is assumed, then the value of a housing unit n in period t that is v periods old, V_n^t, should be approximately equal to the depreciated value of the structure plus the value of the land plus an error term; i.e., the following relationship should hold approximately:

$$V_n^t = P_S^t (1-\delta)^v Q_{Sn} + P_L^t Q_L + u_n^t \tag{23.82}$$

where δ is the one-period geometric depreciation rate, Q_{Sn} is the number of square metres of floor space of the original structure for housing unit n, Q_L is the number of square metres of land on which the housing structure is situated, and u_n^t is an error term. P_S^t is the beginning of *period t price level for structures* of this type and P_L^t is the corresponding *price of land* for this class of housing units. As long as there is more than one vintage of structure in the sample (i.e., more than one v), then the parameters P_S^t, P_L^t and δ can be identified by running a non-linear regression model using equation (23.82). Why can the price levels be identified in the present hedonic regression model, whereas they could not be identified in the repeat sales model? The answer is that the hedonic model (23.82) does not assume property-specific quality adjustment factors for each housing unit; instead, all the housing units in the sample are assumed to be of comparable quality once prices are adjusted for the age of the unit and the quantity (in square metres) of original structure and the quantity of land.

23.116 Unfortunately, many housing structures that may have started off as identical structures do not remain the same over time, because of differing standards of maintenance, as well as major renovations and additions to some of the structures. To model this phenomenon, let R_n^t be real maintenance, repair and renovation expenditures on housing unit n during period t, and suppose that these real expenditures depreciate at the geometric rate δ_R. It is reasonable to assume that these expenditures add to the value of the housing unit, and so equation (23.82) should be replaced by the following equation:

$$V_n^t = P_S^t (1-\delta)^v Q_{Sn} + P_R^t [R_n^t + (1-\delta_R) R_n^{t-1} + (1-\delta_R)^2 R_n^{t-2} + \cdots + (1-\delta_R)^v R_n^{t-v}] + P_L^t Q_L + u_n^t \tag{23.83}$$

where P_R^t is the period t price level for real maintenance, repair and renovation expenditures on this class of housing units. If information on these real renovation and repair expenditures, $R_n^t, R_n^{t-1}, R_n^{t-2}, \ldots, R_n^{t-v}$, is available for each housing unit in the sample of housing units that sold in period t, then the parameters P_S^t, P_L^t, P_R^t, δ and δ_R can be identified by running a non-linear regression model using equation (23.83).[57] A major practical problem with implementing a hedonic regression model along the above lines is that, usually, accurate data on renovation and repair expenditures on a particular dwelling unit between the construction of the initial housing unit and the present period are not available. Without accurate data on repairs and renovations, it will be impossible to obtain accurate estimates of the unknown parameters in the hedonic regression model.

23.117 A final practical problem with the above hedonic regression model will be mentioned. Theoretically, "normal" maintenance expenditures could be included in the renovation expenditure terms, R_n^t, in equation (23.83). If this is done, then including normal maintenance expenditures in R_n^t will have the effect of increasing the estimated depreciation rates δ and δ_R. Thus different statistical agencies, with different criteria

[56] Recall equation (23.46). This fundamental identification problem was recognized by Bailey, Muth and Nourse (1963, p. 936) in the original repeat sales housing article, but it was ignored by them and subsequent users of the repeat sales methodology. Another problem with the housing hedonic regression literature is that, usually, the logarithm of the purchase price is taken as the dependent variable in the regression. While this specification has some advantages, it does not recognize properly the additive nature of the structure and land components of the housing property. A final problem with the traditional hedonic housing literature is that, usually, separate price indices for land and structures are not estimated. It is important to allow for separate price indices for these two components since, usually, the price of land is more volatile and tends to increase faster than the price of structures over long periods of time.

[57] Alternatively, if price levels are available for P_S^t and P_R^t from construction price indices, then these parameters do not have to be estimated.

for deciding where to draw the line between "normal" maintenance and "major" repair and renovations, will produce different estimated depreciation rates.

The treatment of the transactions costs of home purchase

23.118 Another cost of home-ownership needs to be discussed. Normally, when a family purchases a dwelling unit, they have to pay certain fees and costs, which can include:

- the commissions of real estate agents who help the family find the "right" property;
- various transactions taxes that governments can impose on the sale of the property;
- various legal fees that might be associated with the transfer of title for the property.

23.119 Should the above fees be considered as expenditure in the period of purchase, or should they simply be regarded as part of the purchase price of the property and hence be depreciated over time in a manner analogous to the treatment of structures in the national accounts?

23.120 An argument can be made for either treatment. From the viewpoint of the opportunity cost treatment of purchases of durable goods, the relevant price of the dwelling unit in the periods following the purchase of the property is the after tax and transactions fees value of the property. This viewpoint suggests that the transactions costs of the purchaser should be counted as expenses in the period of purchase. From the viewpoint of a landlord who has just purchased a dwelling unit for rental purposes, however, it would not be sensible to charge the tenant the full cost of these transactions fees in the first month of rent. The landlord would tend to capitalize these costs and recover them gradually over the time period that the landlord expects to own the property. Thus, either treatment could be justified and the statistical agency will have to decide which treatment is most convenient from its particular perspective.

User costs for landlords versus owners

23.121 In the previous section, the various costs associated with home-ownership were discussed. Both home-owners and landlords face these costs. Thus, they will be reflected in market rents, and this must be kept in mind if the imputed rent approach is used to value the services of owner-occupied housing. If some or all of these associated costs of owner-occupied housing are covered elsewhere in the CPI (e.g., home insurance could be separately covered), then the value of imputed rents for owner-occupied housing must be reduced by the amount of these expenditures covered elsewhere.

23.122 In addition to the costs of home-ownership covered in the previous section, landlords face a number of additional costs compared to the home-owner. These additional costs will be reflected in market rents. Thus, if market rents are used to impute the services provided by the ownership of a dwelling unit, then these extra costs should also be removed from the market rents that are used for imputation purposes, since they will not be relevant for owner-occupiers. These additional landlord-specific costs are discussed in paragraphs 23.123 to 23.133.

Damage costs

23.123 Tenants do not have the same incentive to take care of a rented property compared to an owned property, so depreciation costs for a rented property are likely to exceed depreciation rates for comparable owned properties. Usually, landlords demand damage deposits, but often these deposits are not sufficient to cover the costs of the actual damages that some tenants inflict.

Non-payment of rent and vacancy costs

23.124 At times, tenants run into financial difficulties and are unable to pay landlords the rent that is owned. Usually, eviction is a long-drawn-out process, and so landlords can lose several months of rent before a non-paying tenant finally leaves. The landlord also incurs extra costs compared to a home-owner when a rented property remains vacant because of lack of demand.[58] These extra costs will be reflected in market rents but should not be reflected in the user costs of owner-occupied housing.

Billing and maintenance costs

23.125 A landlord may have to rent office space and employ staff to send out monthly bills to tenants, and employ staff to respond to requests for maintenance. A home-owner who gives his or her time in order to provide maintenance services[59] offers this time at his or her *after income tax wage rate*, which may be lower than the *before income tax wage rate* that a landlord must pay his or her employees. The net effect of these factors leads to higher market rents compared to the corresponding owner-occupied user cost.

The opportunity cost of capital

23.126 The home-owner's *after tax* opportunity cost of capital that appeared in the various user cost formulae considered earlier in this chapter will typically be *lower* than the landlord's *before tax* opportunity cost of capital. Put another way, the landlord has an extra income tax cost compared to the home-owner. In addition, the landlord may face a higher risk premium for the use of capital because of the risks of damage and non-payment of rent. Care must be taken that these additional landlord costs are not counted twice.

[58] The demand for rented properties can vary substantially over the business cycle, and this can lead to depressed rents or very high rents compared to the user costs of home-ownership. Thus imputed rents based on market rents of similar properties can differ substantially from the corresponding user costs of owner-occupied housing over the business cycle.

[59] Typically, these imputed maintenance costs will not appear in the CPI, but if the user cost of an owned dwelling unit is to be comparable with the market rent of a similar property, these imputed labour costs should be included.

The supply of additional services for rented properties

23.127 Often, properties that are to let will contain some major consumer durables that home-owners have to provide themselves, such as refrigerators, stoves, washing-machines, driers and air conditioning units. In addition, landlords may pay for electricity or fuel in some rented apartments. Thus, to make the market rental comparable to an owner-occupied imputed rent, the market rental should be adjusted downwards to account for the above factors (which will appear elsewhere in the expenditures of owner-occupiers).

23.128 The factors listed above will tend to make observed market rental prices higher than the corresponding user cost for an owner-occupier of a property of the same quality. Thus, if the imputed rental approach is used to value the services of owner-occupied housing, then these market-based rents should be adjusted downward to account for the above factors.

23.129 Although all the above factors will tend to lead to an upward bias if unadjusted market rental rates are used to impute the services of owner-occupied housing, there is another factor not discussed thus far that could lead to a large downward bias. That factor is rent controls.

23.130 Under normal conditions, the acquisitions approach to the treatment of owner-occupied housing will give rise to the smallest expenditures, the user cost approach will give rise to the next highest level of expenditures, and the use of imputed market rentals will give the largest level of expenditures for owner-occupied housing. For the first two approaches, a main driver of the price of owner-occupied housing is the price of new housing construction. For the user cost approach, another main driver is the price of land. For the imputed rent approach, the main driver of the price of owner-occupied housing is the rental price index.

23.131 The above discussion is far from being complete and definitive, but it does illustrate that it is not completely straightforward to impute market rental rates to owner-occupied dwelling units. Care must be taken to ensure that the "correct" expenditure weights are constructed.

23.132 As can be seen from the material above, the treatment of owner-occupied housing presents special difficulties. Astin (1999, p. 5) discussed some of the difficulties that the European Union encountered in trying to find the "best" approach to use in its Harmonized Index of Consumer Prices (HICP), as follows:

> A special coverage problem concerns owner-occupied housing. This has always been one of the most difficult sectors to deal with in CPIs.
>
> Strictly, the price of housing should not be included in a CPI because it is classified as capital. On the other hand, the national accounts classifies imputed rents of owner-occupiers as part of consumers' expenditure. This is a reasonable thing to do if the aim is to measure the volume of consumption of the capital resource of housing. But that is not what a CPI is measuring.
>
> Some countries, following the compensation index concept, would prefer to have mortgage interest included in the HICP. This approach could indeed be defended for a compensation index, because there is no doubt that the monthly mortgage payment is an important element in the budget of many households: a rise in the interest rate acts in exactly the same way as a price increase from the point of view of the individual household. But this is not acceptable for a wider inflation index.
>
> So, after many hours of debate, the Working Party came to the conclusion that there were just two options. The first was to simply exclude owner-occupied housing from the HICP. One could at least argue that this was a form of harmonization, although it is worrying that there are such large differences between Member States in the percentages of the population which own or rent their dwellings. Exclusion also falls in line with the international guideline issued 10 years ago by the ILO. Furthermore, it would be possible to supplement the HICP with a separate house price index, which could be used by analysts as part of a battery of inflation indicators.
>
> The second option was to include owner-occupied housing on the basis of acquisition costs, essentially treating them like any other durable. Most secondhand housing would be excluded: in practice the index would include new houses plus a small volume of housing new to the household sector (sales from the company or government sectors to the household sector).
>
> The main problem here is practical: several countries do not have new house price indices and their construction could be difficult and costly. A Task Force is at present examining these matters. Final recommendations are due at the end of 1999.

Because of the complexities involved in modelling the treatment of owner-occupied housing, final recommendations have still not emerged for the HICP.

23.133 A fourth approach to the treatment of housing will be studied in the following section. Since this approach has only been applied to owner-occupied dwellings, it is not as "universal" as the other three approaches.[60]

The payments approach

23.134 A fourth possible approach to the treatment of owner-occupied housing, the *payments approach*, is described by Charles Goodhart (2001, pp. F350–F351) as follows:

> The second main approach is the payments approach, measuring actual cash outflows, on down payments, mortgage repayments and mortgage interest, or some subset of the above. This approach always, however, includes mortgage interest payments. This, though common, is analytically unsound. First, the procedure is not carried out consistently across purchases. Other goods bought on the basis of credit, e.g., credit card credit, are usually not treated as more expensive on that account (though they have been in New Zealand). Second, the treatment of interest flows is not consistent across persons. If a borrower is worse off in some sense when interest rates rise, then equivalently a lender owning an interest bearing asset is better off; why measure one and not the other? If I sell an interest earning asset, say a

[60] The acquisitions, user cost and rental equivalence approaches can be applied to any consumer durable, but to apply the rental equivalence approach, appropriate rental or leasing markets for the durable must exist.

money market mutual fund holding, to buy a house, why am I treated differently to someone who borrows on a (variable rate) mortgage? Third, should not the question of the price of any purchase be assessed separately from the issue of how that might be financed? Imports, inventories and all business purchases tend to be purchased in part on credit. Should we regard imports as more expensive, when the cost of trade credit rises? Money, moreover, is fungible. As we know from calculations of mortgage equity withdrawal, the loan may be secured on the house but used to pay for furniture. When interest rates rise, is the furniture thereby more expensive? Moreover, the actual cash out-payments totally ignore changes in the ongoing value of the house whether by depreciation, or capital loss/gain, which will often dwarf the cash flow. Despite its problems, such a cash payment approach was used in the United Kingdom until 1994 and still is in Ireland.

23.135 Thus, the *payments approach* to owner-occupied housing is a kind of *cash flow approach* to the costs of operating an owner-occupied dwelling. Possible objections to this approach are that it ignores the opportunity costs of holding the equity in the owner-occupied dwelling, it ignores depreciation, and it uses nominal interest rates without any offset for inflation. If the payments approach is adjusted for these imputed costs, however, then the result is a rather complicated user cost approach to the treatment of housing. Nevertheless, as was mentioned in Chapter 10, under some conditions, the payments approach to the treatment of owner-occupied housing may be a reasonable compromise. In general, the payments approach will tend to lead to much smaller monthly expenditures on owner-occupied housing than the other three main approaches, except during periods of high inflation, when the nominal mortgage rate term becomes very large without any offsetting item for inflation.[61]

Alternative approaches for pricing owner-occupied housing

23.136 For consumer durables that have long useful lives, the usual acquisitions approach will not be adequate for CPI users who desire prices that measure the service flows that consumer durables generate. This is particularly true for owner-occupied housing. Hence it will be useful to many users if, in addition to the acquisitions approach, the statistical agency implements a variant of either the rental equivalence approach or the user cost approach for long-lived consumer durables and for owner-occupied housing in particular. Users can then decide which approach best suits their purposes. Any one of the three main approaches could be chosen as the approach that would be used in the "headline" CPI. The other two approaches could be made available to users as analytic tables.

[61] If there is high inflation, then the statistical agency using the payments approach may want to consider adjusting nominal mortgage interest rates for the inflation component, as is done in paragraphs 23.95 to 23.99. For additional material on the payments approach, see Chapter 10.

23.137 We conclude this chapter by outlining some of the problems involved in implementing the three main approaches to the measurement of price change for owner-occupied housing.

The acquisitions approach

23.138 In order to implement the acquisitions approach, a constant quality price index for the sales of new residential housing units will be required.

The rental equivalence approach

Option 1: Using home-owners' estimates of rents

23.139 In this option, home-owners would be surveyed and asked to estimate a rental price for their housing unit. Problems with this approach are:

- Home-owners may not be able to provide very accurate estimates for the rental value of their dwelling unit.
- The statistical agency should make an adjustment to these estimated rents over time in order to take into account the effects of depreciation, which causes the quality of the unit to decline slowly over time (unless this effect is offset by renovation and repair expenditures).[62]
- Care must be taken to determine exactly what extra services are included in the home-owner's estimated rent; i.e., does the rent include insurance, electricity and fuel or the use of various consumer durables in addition to the structure? If so, these extra services should be stripped out of the rent, since they are covered elsewhere in the CPI.[63]

Option 2: Using a hedonic regression model of the rental market to impute rents

23.140 In this option, the statistical agency would collect data on rented properties and their characteristics, and then use this information to construct a hedonic regression model for the housing rental market.[64] This model would then be used to impute prices for owner-occupied properties. Problems with this approach are:

- It is information intensive; in addition to requiring information on the rents and characteristics of rented properties, information on the characteristics of owner-occupied properties would also be required.
- The characteristics of the owner-occupied population could be quite different from the characteristics of the rental population. In particular, if the rental market for housing is subject to rent controls, this approach is not recommended.

[62] Recall paragraphs 23.79 to 23.93.

[63] It could be argued that these extra services that might be included in the rent are mainly a weighting issue; i.e., that the trend in the home-owner's estimated rent would be a reasonably accurate estimate of the trend in the rents after adjusting for the extra services included in the rent.

[64] See Hoffmann and Kurz (2002) for an example of such a model.

- Hedonic regression models suffer from a lack of reproducibility in that different researchers will have different characteristics in the model and use different functional forms.
- From the previous discussions, it is seen that market rents can be considerably higher than the opportunity costs of home-owners. Hence, using market rents to impute rents for owner-occupiers may lead to rents that are too high.[65] On the other hand, if there are rent controls or a temporary glut of rented properties, then market rents could be too low compared to the opportunity costs of home-owners.
- There is some evidence that depreciation is somewhat different for rental units compared to owner-occupied housing units.[66] If this is so, then the imputation procedure will be somewhat incorrect. However, all studies that estimate depreciation for owner-occupied housing suffer from biases resulting from the inadequate treatment of land and the lack of information on repair, renovation and maintenance expenditures over the life of the dwelling unit. It is not certain that depreciation for rental units is significantly different from that for owner-occupied units.

The user cost approach

23.141 It is first necessary to decide whether an ex ante or ex post user cost of housing is to be calculated. It seems that the ex ante approach is the more useful for CPI purposes; these are the prices that should appear in economic models of consumer choice. Moreover, the ex post approach will lead to user costs that fluctuate too much to suit the needs of most users. Of course, the problem with the ex ante approach is that it will be difficult to estimate anticipated inflation rates for house prices.

Option 3: The rent-to-value approach

23.142 In this option, the statistical agency collects information on market rents paid for a sample of rented properties, but it also collects information on the sales price of these rented properties when they are sold. Using these two pieces of information, the statistical agency can form an estimated *rent-to-value ratio* for rented properties of various types. It can be seen that this rent-to-value ratio represents an estimate of all the terms that go into an ex ante user cost formula, except the asset price of the property; i.e., the rent-to-value ratio for a particular property can be regarded as an estimate of the interest rate less anticipated housing inflation plus the depreciation rate plus the other miscellaneous rates discussed in paragraphs 23.94 to 23.120, such as insurance and property tax rates. Under the assumption that these rates remain reasonably constant over the short run, changes in user costs are equal to changes in the price of owner-occupied housing. Thus, this approach can be implemented if a constant quality price index for the stock value of owner-occupied housing can be developed. It may be decided to approximate the comprehensive price index for owner-occupied housing by a new housing price index. If this is done, the approach essentially reduces to the acquisitions approach, except that the weights will generally be larger using this user cost approach than those obtained using the acquisitions approach.[67] Problems with this approach include:

- It will require a considerable amount of resources to construct a constant quality price index for the stock of owner-occupied housing units. If a hedonic regression model is used, there are problems associated with the reproducibility of the results.
- Rent-to-value ratios can change considerably over time. Hence it will be necessary to keep collecting information on rents and selling prices of rented properties.
- As was noted in paragraphs 23.121 and 23.122, the user cost structure of rented properties can be quite different from the corresponding user cost structure of owner-occupied properties. Hence, the use of rent-to-value ratios can give misleading results.[68]

Option 4: The simplified user cost approach

23.143 This approach is similar to that of Option 3 above, but instead of using the rent-to-value ratio to estimate the sum of the various rates in the user cost formula, direct estimates are made of these rates. If the simplified Icelandic user cost approach discussed in paragraphs 23.79 to 23.93 is used, all that is required is a constant quality owner-occupied housing price index, an estimated real interest rate, and an estimated composite depreciation rate on the structure and land together. Problems with this approach are:

- As was the case with Option 3 above, it will require a considerable amount of resources to construct a constant quality price index for the stock of owner-occupied housing units. If a hedonic regression model is used, there are problems associated with the reproducibility of the results.
- It is not known with any degree of certainty what the appropriate real interest rate should be.
- Similarly, it is difficult to determine what the "correct" depreciation rate should be.[69]

---

[65] Again, it could argued that this is a mainly a weighting issue; i.e., that the trend in market rents would be a reasonably accurate estimate for the trend in home-owners' opportunity costs.

[66] According to Stephen Malpezzi, Larry Ozanne and Thomas G. Thibodeau (1987, p. 382): "The average depreciation rate for rental property is remarkably constant, ranging from 0.58 per cent to 0.60 per cent over the 25 year period. Depreciation rates for owner-occupied units show more variation than the estimated rates for renter occupied units. The average depreciation rate for owner-occupied housing ranges from 0.9 per cent in year 1 to 0.28 per cent in year 20."

[67] Recall the discussion in paragraphs 23.34 to 23.42.

[68] This is primarily a weighting issue, however, so the trend in the constant quality stock of owner-occupied housing price index should be an adequate approximation to the trend in owner-occupied user costs.

[69] Because of the lack of information on repairs and renovations, estimated housing depreciation rates vary widely:

> One striking feature with the results of all three approaches used in these and related studies is their variability: estimates range from about a half per cent per year to two and a half per cent (Malpezzi, Ozanne and Thibodeau (1987, pp. 373–375).

This problem is complicated by the fact that, over time, the price of land tends to increase faster than the price of building a residential structure, so the land price component of an owner-occupied housing unit will tend to increase in importance, which in turn will tend to decrease the composite depreciation rate.

Option 5: A national accounting approach

23.144 This approach makes use of the fact that the national accounts division of the statistical agency will usually collect data on investment in residential housing, as well as on repair and renovation expenditures on housing. In addition, many statistical agencies will also construct estimates for the stock of residential dwelling units, so that estimates for the structures' depreciation rates are available. Finally, if the statistical agency also constructs a national balance sheet, then estimates for the value of residential land will also be available. Thus, all the basic ingredients that are necessary to construct stocks for residential structures and the associated land stocks are available. If, in addition, assumptions about the appropriate nominal interest rate and about expected prices for structures and land are made,[70] then aggregate user costs of residential structures and residential land can be constructed. The proportion of these stocks that is rented can be deducted, and estimates for the user costs and corresponding values for owner-occupied residential land and structures can be made. Of course, it would be almost impossible to do all this on a current basis, but all the above computations can be done for a base period in order to obtain appropriate weights for owner-occupied structures and land. Then, it can be seen that the main drivers for the monthly user costs are the price of a new structure and the price of residential land. Hence, if timely monthly indicators for these two prices can be developed, the entire procedure is feasible. Problems with this approach include:

- As was the case with Option 4 above, it will be difficult to determine what the "correct" depreciation rates and real interest rates are.[71]
- It will be difficult to construct a monthly price of residential land index.
- It may be difficult to convert the residential housing investment price deflator from a quarterly to a monthly basis.

23.145 All the above five options have their advantages and disadvantages; there does not appear to be a clear "winning" option. Thus, each statistical agency will have to decide whether they have the resources to implement any of these five options in addition to the usual acquisitions approach to the treatment of owner-occupied housing. From the viewpoint of the cost of living approach to the CPI, any one of the five options would be an adequate approximation to the ideal treatment from the perspective of measuring the flow of consumption services in each period.[72]

[70] Alternatively, an appropriate real interest rate can be assumed.

[71] As usual, however, it can be argued that errors in estimating these parameters will mainly affect the weights used in the price index.

[72] For consumer durables that do not change in quality over time, Option 5 will probably suffice.

A GLOSSARY OF MAIN TERMS

The appendix to this glossary gives the main aggregate index number formulae used for consumer price index (CPI) purposes and also explains the interrelationships between them.

Acquisitions approach	An approach to CPIs in which consumption is identified with the consumption goods and services acquired by a household in some period (as distinct from those wholly or partially used up for purposes of consumption). Depending on the intended scope of the CPI, acquisitions may include not only goods and services purchased, but also those acquired by own-account production or as social transfers in kind from government or non-profit institutions.
Additivity	At current prices, the value of an aggregate is identical to the sum of the values of its components. Additivity requires this identity to be preserved for the extrapolated values of the aggregate and its components when their current values in some period are extrapolated using a set of interrelated quantity indices; or, alternatively, when the current values of an aggregate and its components in some period are deflated using a set of interrelated price indices.
Aggregate	A set of transactions relating to a specified flow of goods and services, such as the total purchases made by resident households on consumer goods and services in some period. The term "aggregate" is also used to mean the value of the designated set of transactions.
Aggregation	The process of combining, or adding, different sets of transactions to obtain larger sets of transactions. The larger set is described as having a higher *level* of aggregation than the sets of which it is composed. The term "aggregation" is also used to mean the process of adding the values of the lower-level aggregates to obtain higher-level aggregates. In the case of price indices, it means the process by which price indices for lower-level aggregates are averaged, or otherwise combined, to obtain price indices for higher level aggregates.
Axiomatic, or test approach	The approach to index number theory that determines the choice of index number formula on the basis of its mathematical properties. A list of tests is drawn up, each test requiring an index to possess a certain property or satisfy a certain axiom. An index number may then be chosen on the basis of the number of tests satisfied. Not all tests may be considered to be equally important and the failure to satisfy one or two key tests may be considered sufficient grounds for rejecting an index.
Base period	The base period is usually understood to mean the period with which all the other periods are compared. The term may, however, have different meanings in different contexts. Three types of base period may be distinguished: • the *price reference period* – the period that provides the prices to which the prices in other periods are compared. The prices of the price reference period appear in the denominators of the price relatives, or price ratios, used to calculate the index. The price reference period is typically designated as period 0; • the *weight reference period* – the period, usually one or more years, of which the expenditures serve as weights for the index. When the expenditures are *hybrid* (i.e., the quantities of one period are valued at the prices of some other period), the weight reference period is the period to which the quantities refer. The weight reference period is typically designated as period b in this manual; • the *index reference period* – the period for which the value of the index is set equal to 100. It should be noted that, in practice, the duration of the weight reference period for a CPI is typically a year, or even two or more years, whereas the CPI is calculated monthly or quarterly, the duration of the price reference period being a month or quarter. Thus, the weight and price reference periods seldom coincide in practice, at least when a CPI is first calculated, although the price and index reference periods frequently coincide.
Basket	A specified set of quantities of goods and services. In a CPI context, the set may comprise the actual quantities of consumption goods or services acquired or used by households in some period, or may be made up of hypothetical quantities.
Basket price index	A price index that measures the proportionate change between periods 0 and t in the total value of a specified basket of goods and services: that is, $\sum p^t q / \sum p^0 q$, where the terms q are the specified quantities. See *Lowe index*.
Bias	A systematic tendency for the calculated CPI to diverge from some ideal or preferred index, resulting from the method of data collection or processing, or the index formula used. See *Cost of living bias* and *Representativity bias*.
Bouncing	A situation in which the set of prices for the second period is simply a reordering of the set of prices for the first period, the price relatives thus being obtained by matching each price in the first period with another price from the same set of prices.

Carli price index	An elementary price index defined as a simple, or unweighted, arithmetic average of the sample price relatives.
Carry forward	A situation in which a missing price in some period is imputed as being equal to the last price observed for that item.
Central product classification (CPC)	An internationally agreed classification of goods and services based on the physical characteristics of goods or on the nature of the services rendered.
Chain index	An index number series for a long sequence of periods obtained by linking together index numbers spanning shorter sequences of periods. See *Linking*; see also *equation (6) of the Appendix.*
Characteristics	The physical and economic attributes of a good or service that serve to identify it and enable it to be classified.
Circularity (transitivity)	An index number property such that, if ${}_jI_k$ denotes a particular kind of price index that measures the change between periods j and k, then ${}_jI_l \equiv {}_jI_k \cdot {}_kI_l$ where the indices ${}_jI_l$ and ${}_kI_l$ are of the same type. When an index is transitive, the index that compares periods j and l indirectly through period k is identical with the index that compares j and l directly. One test that might be required under the axiomatic approach is that the index number should be transitive.
Collective consumption	Goods and services that are consumed simultaneously by a group of consumers or by the community as a whole; for example, defence services provided by the State.
Commensurability	See *Invariance to changes in the units of measurement test.*
Commodity reversal test	A test that might be used under the axiomatic approach, which requires that, for a given set of products, the price index should remain unchanged when the ordering of the products is changed.
Component	A subset of the goods and services that make up some defined aggregate.
Conditional cost of living index	A conditional cost of living index measures the change in the cost of maintaining a given utility level, or standard of living, on the assumption that all the factors, *except the prices covered by the index*, that influence the consumer's utility or welfare (e.g., the state of the physical environment) remain constant. See *Cost of living index.*
Consistency in aggregation	An index is said to be consistent in aggregation when the index for some aggregate has the same value whether it is calculated directly in a single operation, without distinguishing its components, or whether it is calculated in two or more steps by first calculating separate indices, or sub-indices, for its components, or sub-components, and then aggregating them, the same formula being used at each step.
Consumer price index (CPI)	A monthly or quarterly price index compiled and published by an official statistical agency that measures changes in the prices of consumption goods and services acquired or used by households. Its exact definition may vary from country to country.
Consumers	Individual persons or groups of persons living together as households.
Consumption	There are several types of consumption: • *intermediate consumption* consists of the goods and services used by enterprises as inputs into their processes of production; it is excluded from CPIs; • *collective consumption* consists mainly of the collective services provided by governments to the community as a whole; it is excluded from CPIs; • *final individual consumption* consists of goods and services that individual households may acquire in order to satisfy their own needs and wants. See also *Households' consumption expenditures.*
Consumption of own production	Goods or services that are consumed by the same household that produces them. The housing services consumed by owner-occupiers fall within this category. If goods and services produced and consumed within the same household are to be included in CPIs, prices must be imputed for them. Their inclusion or exclusion depends on the intended scope of the CPI.
Continuity	The property whereby the price index is a continuous function of its price and quantity vectors.
Cost of living bias	An alternative term used to describe *Substitution bias.*
Cost of living index (COLI)	An index that measures the change between two periods in the minimum expenditures that *would* be incurred by a utility-maximizing consumer, whose preferences or tastes remain unchanged, in order to maintain a given level of utility (or standard of living or welfare). As consumers may be expected to change the quantities they consume in response to changes in relative prices (see *Substitution effect*), the COLI is not a basket index. The expenditures in one or other, or possibly both, periods cannot usually be observed. COLIs cannot be directly calculated but may be approximated by superlative indices. See *Conditional cost of living index.*
Coverage	The set of goods and services of which the prices are actually included in the index. For practical reasons, coverage may have to be less than the ideal scope of the index, that is, the set of goods and services that the compilers of the index would prefer to include if it were feasible.

Current period, or comparison period In principle, the current period should refer to the most recent period for which the index has been compiled or is being compiled. The term is widely used, however, to mean the comparison period; that is, the period that is compared with the base period, usually the price reference or index reference period. It is also widely used simply to mean the later of the two periods being compared. The exact meaning is usually clear in the context.

Current prices The actual prices prevailing in the period in question.

Current value The actual value of some aggregate in the period in question: the quantities in the period multiplied by the prices of the same period.

Cut-off sampling A sampling procedure in which a predetermined threshold is established with all units in the universe at or above the threshold being included in the sample, and all units below the threshold being excluded. The threshold is usually specified in terms of the size of some relevant variable, the largest sampling units being included and the rest given a zero chance of inclusion. In the case of retail outlets, size may be defined in terms of sales.

Deflation The division of the current value of some aggregate by a price index (described as a *deflator*) in order to revalue its quantities at the prices of the price reference period.

Democratic index A form of CPI in which each household is given equal weight in the calculation of the index, irrespectively of the size of its expenditures.

Discount A deduction from the list or advertised price of a good or a service that is available to specific customers under specific conditions. Examples include cash discounts, prompt payment discounts, volume discounts, trade discounts and advertising discounts.

Divisia index A price or quantity index that treats both prices and quantities as continuous functions of time. By differentiating with respect to time, the rate of change in the value of the aggregate in question is partitioned into two components, one of which is the price index and the other the quantity index. In practice, the indices cannot be calculated directly, but it may be possible to approximate them by chain indices in which indices measuring the changes between consecutive periods are linked together.

Domain An alternative term for the scope of an index.

Drift A chain index is said to drift if it does not return to unity when prices in the current period return to their levels in the base period. Chain indices are liable to drift when prices fluctuate over the periods they cover.

Drobisch price index The arithmetic average of the Laspeyres price index and the Paasche price index.

Durable consumption good A consumption good that can be used repeatedly or continuously for purposes of consumption over a long period of time, typically several years.

Dutot index An elementary price index defined as the ratio of the unweighted arithmetic averages of the prices in the two periods compared.

Economic approach The economic approach to index number theory assumes that the quantities are functions of the prices, the observed data being generated as solutions to various economic optimization problems. In the CPI context, the economic approach usually requires the CPI to be some kind of cost of living index.

Edgeworth price index A basket price index in which the quantities in the basket are simple arithmetic averages of the quantities consumed in the two periods.

Editing The process of scrutinizing and checking the prices reported by price collectors. Some checks may be carried out by computers using statistical programs written for the purpose.

Elementary aggregate The smallest aggregate for which expenditure data are available and used for CPI purposes. The values of the elementary aggregates are used to weight the price indices for elementary aggregates to obtain higher-level indices. The range of goods and services covered by an elementary aggregate should be relatively narrow, and may be further narrowed by confining the goods and services to those sold in particular types of outlet or in particular locations. Elementary aggregates also serve as strata for the sampling of prices.

Elementary price index An elementary index is a price index for an elementary aggregate. Expenditure weights cannot usually be assigned to the price relatives for the sampled products within an elementary aggregate, although other kinds of weighting may be explicitly or implicitly introduced into the calculation of elementary indices. Three examples of elementary index number formulae are the Carli, the Dutot and the Jevons.

Expenditure weights See *Weights*.

Explicit quality adjustment A direct estimate of how much of the change in the price of a product is attributable to changes in its physical or economic characteristics. It requires an evaluation of the contributions of the differences in particular characteristics to the differences in the observed prices of two products. It includes quality adjustments based on hedonic methods. See also *Implicit quality adjustment*.

Factor reversal test	Suppose the prices and quantities in a price index are interchanged to yield a quantity index of exactly the same functional form as the price index. Under the axiomatic approach, the factor reversal test requires that the product of this quantity index and the original price index should be identical to the proportionate change in the value of the aggregate in question.
Fisher price index	The geometric average of the Laspeyres price index and the Paasche price index. It is a symmetric index and a superlative index.
Fixed basket indices	A time series of basket indices that all use the same basket; see *equation (4) of the Appendix*. In a CPI context, the fixed basket usually consists of the total quantities consumed by the designated set of households over a period of a year or more.
Fixed weight indices	An abbreviated description for a series of weighted arithmetic averages of price relatives that all use the same weights; see *equation (13) of the Appendix*. The weights are usually either actual or hybrid expenditure shares.
Geometric Laspeyres index	A weighted geometric average of the price relatives using the expenditure shares of the price reference period as weights. Also called Logarithmic Laspeyres index.
Goods	Physical objects for which a demand exists, over which ownership rights can be established and for which ownership can be transferred between units by engaging in transactions on the market.
Hedonic method	A regression model in which the market prices of different products are expressed as a function of their characteristics. Non-numerical characteristics are represented by dummy variables. Each regression coefficient is treated as an estimate of the marginal contribution of that characteristic to the total price. The estimates may be used to predict the price of a new product for which the mix of characteristics is different from that of any product already on the market. The hedonic method can therefore be used to estimate the effects of quality changes on prices.
Higher-level index	An aggregate index as distinct from an elementary index.
Household budget surveys (HBSs)	Sample surveys of households in which the households are asked to provide data on, or estimates of, the amounts they spend on consumption goods and services, and for other purposes over a given period of time.
Households	Households may be either individual persons living alone or groups of persons living together who make common provision for food or other essentials for living. Most countries choose to exclude groups of persons living in large institutional households (barracks, retirement homes, etc.) from the scope of their CPIs.
Households' consumption expenditures	Expenditures on final consumption goods and services incurred by individual households on their own behalf. They exclude expenditures incurred by governments or non-profit institutions on goods or services provided to households as free social transfers in kind.
Hybrid values or expenditures	Hypothetical values, or expenditures, in which the quantities are valued at a different set of prices from those at which they were actually bought or sold: for example, when the quantities purchased in an earlier period, such as b, are valued at the prices prevailing in a later period, such as 0.
Hybrid weights	Weights defined as hybrid value, or hybrid expenditure, shares.
Identity test	A test under the axiomatic approach that requires that, if each and every price remains unchanged between the two periods, the price index must equal unity.
Implicit quality adjustment	Inferring indirectly the change in the quality of a product of which the characteristics change over time by estimating, or assuming, the pure price change that has occurred. For example, if the pure price change is assumed to be equal to the average for some other group of products, the implied change in quality is equal to the actual observed price change divided by the assumed pure price change. If the whole of the observed price change is assumed to be pure price change, there is assumed to be no change in quality. See also *Explicit quality adjustment*.
Imputed price	The price assigned to an item for which the price is missing in a particular period. The term "imputed price" may also refer to the price assigned to an item that is not sold on the market, such as a good or service produced for own consumption, including housing services produced by owner-occupiers, or one received as payment in kind or as a free transfer from a government or non-profit institution.
Indexation	The periodic adjustment of the money values of some regular scheduled payments based on the movement of the CPI or some other price index. The payments may be wages or salaries, social security or other pensions, other social security benefits, rents, interest payments, etc.
Index reference period	The period for which the value of the index is set at 100.
Institutional unit	A national accounts concept defined as an economic entity that is capable, in its own right, of owning assets, incurring liabilities and engaging in economic activities and transactions with other entities. Households are institutional units. Other kinds of units include enterprises and governments.
Invariance to changes in the units of measurement test	A test under the axiomatic approach that requires that the price index does not change when the units of quantity to which the prices refer are changed: for example, when the price of some drink is quoted per litre rather than per pint. This test is also described as the commensurability test.

Invariance to proportional change in current or base quantities test	A test under the axiomatic approach that requires that the price index remains unchanged when all the base period quantities, or all the current period quantities, are multiplied by a positive scalar
Inverse proportionality in base year prices test	A test which may be invoked under the axiomatic approach that requires that, if all the base period prices are multiplied by the positive scalar λ, the new price index is $1/\lambda$ times the old price index.
Item	An individual good or service in the sample of products selected for pricing.
Item or product rotation	The deliberate replacement of a sampled item, or product, for which prices are being collected, by another product before the replaced product has disappeared from the market or individual outlet. It is designed to keep the sample of products up to date and reduce the need for forced replacements caused by the disappearance of products.
Jevons price index	An elementary price index defined as the unweighted geometric average of the sample price relatives.
Laspeyres price index	A basket index in which the basket is composed of the actual quantities of goods and services in the earlier of the two periods compared, the price reference period; see *equation (3) of the Appendix*. It can also be expressed as a weighted arithmetic average of the price relatives that uses the expenditure shares in the earlier period as weights; see *equations (7) to (10) of the Appendix*. The earlier period serves as both the weight reference period and the price reference period.
Linking	Splicing together two consecutive sequences of price observations, or price indices, that overlap in one or more periods. When the two sequences overlap by a single period, the usual procedure is simply to rescale one or other sequence so that the value in the overlap period is the same in both sequences and the spliced sequences form one continuous series. See *equation (6) of the Appendix*.
Lowe index	A price index that measures the proportionate change between periods 0 and t in the total value of a specified basket of goods and services; that is, $\sum p^t q / \sum p^0 q$, where the terms q are the specified quantities. The basket does not necessarily have to consist of the actual quantities in some period. See *Appendix*. This type of index is described in the manual as a Lowe index after the index number pioneer who first proposed this general type of index. The class of indices covered by this definition is very broad and includes, by appropriate specification of the terms q, the Laspeyres, Paasche, Edgeworth and Walsh indices, for example. Lowe indices are widely used for CPI purposes, the quantities in the basket typically being those of some weight reference period b, which precedes the price reference period 0.
Lower-level index	An elementary index as distinct from an aggregate index.
Matched products or models	The practice of pricing exactly the same product in two or more consecutive periods. It is designed to ensure that the observed price changes are not affected by quality change. The change in price between two perfectly matched products is described as a pure price change.
Mean value test for prices	A test under the axiomatic approach, which requires that the price index should lie between the smallest price relative and the largest price relative.
Non-probability sampling	The deliberate, i.e. non-random, selection of a sample of outlets and products on the basis of the knowledge or judgement of the person responsible. Also known as purposive sampling and judgemental sampling.
"One hoss shay"	A model of depreciation, in which the durable delivers the same services for each vintage: a chair is a chair, no matter what its age (until it falls to pieces and is scrapped). Also known as the light bulb model of depreciation.
Outlier	A term that is generally used to describe any extreme value in a set of survey data. In a CPI context, it is used for an extreme value of price or price relative that requires further investigation or that has been verified as being correct.
Owner-occupied housing	Dwellings owned by the households that live in them. The dwellings are fixed assets that their owners use to produce housing services for their own consumption, these services being usually included within the scope of the CPI. The rents may be imputed by the rents payable on the market for equivalent accommodation or by user costs. See *Rental equivalence* and *User cost*.
Paasche price index	A basket index in which the basket is composed of the actual quantities of goods and services in the later of the two periods compared. The later period serves as the weight reference period and the earlier period as the price reference period. The Paasche index can also be expressed as a weighted harmonic average of the price relatives that uses the actual expenditure shares in the later period as weights. See *equations (7) to (11) of the Appendix*.
Price reference period	The period of which the prices appear in the denominators of the price relatives. See also *Base period*.
Price relative	The ratio of the price of an individual product in one period to the price of that same product in some other period.

Price updating	A procedure whereby the quantities in an earlier period are revalued at the prices of a later period. The resulting expenditures are hybrid. In practice, the price-updated expenditures may be obtained by multiplying the original expenditures by price relatives or price indices.
Probability proportional to size sampling (PPS)	A sampling procedure whereby each unit in the universe has a probability of selection proportional to the size of some known variable, such as the value of the sales of an outlet.
Probability sampling	The random selection of a sample of units, such as outlets or products, in such a way that each unit in the universe has a known non-zero probability of selection.
Products	A generic term used to mean a good or a service. Individual sampled products selected for pricing are often described as items.
Proportionality in current prices test	A test under the axiomatic approach that requires that, if all current period prices are multiplied by the positive scalar λ, the new price index is λ times the old price index.
Purchaser's price	The amount payable by the purchaser to acquire a good or service. The purchaser's price includes any charges incurred in order to take delivery at the time and place required by the purchaser.
Pure price change	The change in the price of a good or service of which the characteristics are unchanged; or the change in the price after adjusting for any change in quality.
Quality adjustment	An adjustment to the change in the price of a product of which the characteristics change over time that is designed to remove the contribution of the change in the characteristics to the observed price change. In a CPI context, the adjustment is needed when the price of a replacement product has to be compared with the price of the product it replaces. In practice, the required adjustment can only be estimated. Different methods of estimation, including hedonic methods, may be used in different circumstances. See *Explicit quality adjustment* and *Implicit quality adjustment*.
Quantity relative	The ratio of the quantity of a product in one period to the quantity of that same product in some other period.
Quantity weights	A term sometimes used to describe the quantities in the basket. However, expenditures rather than quantities act as weights for price relatives. See *Weights*.
Rebasing	Rebasing may have different meanings in different contexts. It may mean: • changing the weights used for a series of indices; or • changing the price reference period used for a series of indices; or • changing the index reference period for a series of indices. The weights, price reference period and index reference period may be changed separately or at the same time.
Reference population	The set of households included within the scope of the index.
Rental equivalence	The estimation of the imputed rents payable by owner-occupiers on the basis of the rents payable on the market for accommodation of the same type.
Replacement product	A product chosen to replace a product for which prices have been collected previously, either because the previous product has disappeared altogether or because it accounts for a diminishing share of the sales of the outlet, or the expenditures within the elementary aggregate.
Representative product	A product, or category of products, that accounts for a significant proportion of the total expenditures within an elementary aggregate, and/or for which the average price change is expected to be close to the average for all products within the aggregate.
Representativity bias	Bias in a basket index that results from the use of quantities that are not representative of the two periods compared; that is, that systematically diverge from the average quantities consumed in the two periods. For example, representativity bias may result from the use of an old, out-of-date basket which deviates systematically from the baskets in both the periods compared. In practice, representativity bias tends to be similar to substitution bias, as it is attributable to the same economic factors.
Reweighting	Replacing the weights used in an index by a new set of weights.
Sample augmentation	Maintaining and adding to the sample of outlets in the survey panel to ensure that they continue to be representative of the population of outlets. A fixed sample of outlets tends to be depleted over time, as outlets cease trading or stop responding. Including new outlets also tends to facilitate the inclusion of new products in the CPI.
Sampled price	The price collected for a sampled product, sometimes described as a price quote.
Sampled product	An individual product that is included in the sample selected for pricing within an elementary aggregate.
Sample rotation	Limiting the length of time that outlets and/or products are included in the price surveys by dropping a proportion of them, or possibly all of them, after a certain period of time and selecting a new sample of outlets and/or products. Rotation is designed to keep the sample up to date.

Sampling frame	A list of the units in the universe from which a sample of units can be selected. The list may contain information about the units, which may be used for PPS sampling. Examples of lists that may be used for retail outlets are business registers, telephone directories ("yellow pages"), local authority records, trade directories, etc. Such lists may not cover all the units in the designated universe and may also include units that do not form part of that universe.
Scanner data	Detailed data on sales of consumer goods obtained by scanning the bar codes for individual products at electronic points of sale in retail outlets. The data can provide detailed information about quantities, characteristics and values of goods sold, as well as their prices. Scanner data constitute a rapidly expanding source of data with considerable potential for CPI purposes. They are increasingly used for purposes of hedonic analysis.
Scope	The set of products for which the index is intended to measure the price changes. The scope of a CPI will generally be defined in terms of a designated set of consumption goods and services purchased by a designated set of households. In practice, certain goods and services or households may have to be excluded because it is too difficult, time-consuming or costly to collect the relevant data on expenditures or prices: for example, illegal expenditures. The coverage of an index denotes the actual set of products included, as distinct from the intended scope of the index.
Seasonal products	Seasonal products are products that either are not available on the market during certain seasons or periods of the year, or are available throughout the year but with regular fluctuations in their quantities and prices that are linked to the season or time of the year.
Specification	A description or list of the characteristics that can be used to identify an individual sampled product to be priced. A tight specification is a fairly precise description of an item intended to narrow the range of items from which a price collector might choose, possibly reducing it to a unique item, such as a particular brand of television set identified by a specific code number. A loose specification is a generic description of a range of items that allows the price collector some discretion as to which particular item or model to select for pricing, such as colour television sets of a particular size.
Stochastic approach	The approach to index number theory that treats the observed price relatives as if they were a random sample drawn from a defined universe for which the mean can be interpreted as the general rate of inflation. The sample mean provides an estimate of the rate of inflation.
Substitute	A product of which the characteristics are similar to those of another product and that can be used to meet the same kinds of consumer needs or wants.
Substitution	The replacement of products by substitutes, typically in response to changes in relative prices. Rational utility-maximizing consumers, as price takers, typically react to changes in relative prices by reducing, at least marginally, their consumption of goods and services that have become relatively dearer and increasing their consumption of substitutes that have become relatively cheaper. Substitution results in a negative correlation between the quantity and price relatives.
Substitution bias	This is generally understood to be the bias that results when a basket index is used to estimate a cost of living index, because a basket index cannot take account of the effects on the cost of living of the substitutions made by consumers in response to changes in relative prices. In general, the earlier the period of which the basket is used, the greater the upward bias in the index; see also *Representativity bias*.
Substitution effect	The effect of substitution on the value of an index.
Superlative index	A type of index formula that can be expected to approximate to the cost of living index. An index is said to be exact when it equals the true cost of living index for consumers whose preferences can be represented by a particular functional form. A superlative index is then defined as an index that is exact for a flexible functional form that can provide a second-order approximation to other twice-differentiable functions around the same point. The Fisher, the Törnqvist and the Walsh price indices are examples of superlative indices. Superlative indices are generally symmetric indices.
Symmetric index	An index that treats both periods symmetrically by attaching equal importance to the price and expenditure data in both periods. The price and expenditure data for both periods enter into the index formula in a symmetric way.
System of National Accounts (SNA)	A coherent, consistent and integrated set of macroeconomic accounts, balance sheets and tables based on a set of internationally agreed concepts, definitions, classifications and accounting rules. Household income and consumption expenditure accounts form part of the SNA. The expenditure data are one of the sources that are used to estimate expenditure weights for CPI purposes.
Time reversal	An index number property such that, if ${}_jI_k$ denotes a particular kind of price index formula that measures the change from period j to period k, then ${}_jI_k \equiv 1/{}_kI_j$ where ${}_kI_j$ measures the change from period k to period j. When an index has this property, the change is the same whether it is measured forwards from the first to the second period or backwards from the second to the first period. An index may be required to satisfy the time reversal test under the axiomatic approach.
Törnqvist price index	A symmetric index defined as the weighted geometric average of the price relatives in which the weights are simple arithmetic averages of the expenditure shares in the two periods. It is a superlative index. Also known as the Törnqvist–Theil price index.

Transitivity	See *Circularity*.
Unit value or average value	The unit value of a set of homogeneous products is the total value of the purchases/sales divided by the sum of the quantities. It is therefore a quantity-weighted average of the different prices at which the product is purchased/sold. Unit values may change over time as a result of a change in the mix of the products sold at different prices, even if the prices do not change.
User cost	The cost incurred over a period of time by the owner of a fixed asset or consumer durable as a consequence of using it to provide a flow of capital or consumption services. User cost consists mainly of the depreciation of the asset or durable (measured at current prices and not at historic cost) plus the capital, or interest, cost.
Uses approach	An approach to CPIs in which the consumption in some period is identified with the consumption goods and services actually used up by a household to satisfy their needs and wants (as distinct from the consumption goods and services acquired). In this approach, the consumption of consumer durables in a given period is measured by the values of the flows of services provided by the stocks of durables owned by households. These values may be estimated by the user costs.
Value	Price times quantity. The value of the expenditures on a set of homogeneous products can be factored uniquely into its price and quantity components. Similarly, the change over time in the value of a set of homogeneous products can be factored uniquely into the change in the unit value and the change in the total quantities. There are, however, many different ways of factoring the change over time in the value of a set of heterogeneous products into its price and quantity components, a phenomenon that gives rise to the index number problem.
Walsh price index	A basket index in which the quantities are geometric averages of the quantities in the two periods; see the *Appendix*. It is a symmetric index and a superlative index.
Weight reference period	The period of which the expenditure shares serve as the weights for a Young index, or of which the quantities make up the basket for a Lowe index. There may be no weight reference period when the expenditure shares for the two periods are averaged, as in the Törnqvist index, or when the quantities are averaged, as in the Walsh index. See also *Base period*.
Weighted arithmetic average index	An index defined as a weighted arithmetic average of the price relatives: namely, $\sum w(p^t/p^0)$, where the weights w sum to unity.
Weights	A set of numbers summing to unity that are used to calculate averages. In a CPI context, the weights are generally actual or hybrid expenditure shares that sum to unity by definition. They are used to average price relatives, or elementary price indices; see the *Appendix*. Quantities of different kinds of products are not commensurate and not additive. They cannot serve as weights. The quantities that make up a basket should therefore not be described as quantity weights.
Young index	A Young index is a weighted arithmetic average of the price relatives, $\sum w(p^t/p^0)$, in which the terms w refer to the actual expenditure shares of period b, the weight reference period; that is, $w = s^b = p^b q^b / \sum p^b q^b$. It is a weighted version of the Carli index.

Appendix to the glossary. Some basic index number formulae and terminology

1. Throughout this Appendix, the sums are understood to be running over all items n.

A *basket* price index is an index of the form

$$\frac{\sum p_n^t q_n}{\sum p_n^0 q_n} \qquad (A.1)$$

which compares the prices of period t with those of (an earlier) price reference period 0, using a certain specified quantity basket. The basket does not have to consist of the actual quantities in any particular period. This general type of index is called a Lowe price index after the index number pioneer who first proposed this general type of index. The family of Lowe indices includes some well-known indices as special cases:

- when $q_n = q_n^0$, we get the Laspeyres index;
- when $q_n = q_n^t$, we get the Paasche index;
- when $q_n = (q_n^0 + q_n^1)/2$, we get the Marshall–Edgeworth index;
- and when $q_n = (q_n^0 q_n^t)^{1/2}$, we get the Walsh index.

In practice, statistical offices frequently work with a Lowe index in which $q_n = q_n^b$, where b denotes some weight reference period that is typically prior to 0.

2. A useful feature of a Lowe index for period t relative to period 0 is that it can be decomposed, or factored, into the product of two or more indices of the same type: for instance, as the product of an index for period $t-1$ relative to period 0 and an index for period t relative to period $t-1$. Formally,

$$\frac{\sum p_n^t q_n}{\sum p_n^0 q_n} = \frac{\sum p_n^{t-1} q_n}{\sum p_n^0 q_n} \frac{\sum p_n^t q_n}{\sum p_n^{t-1} q_n} \qquad (A.2)$$

In particular, when $q_n = q_n^0$, expression (2) turns into

$$\frac{\sum p_n^t q_n^0}{\sum p_n^0 q_n^0} = \frac{\sum p_n^{t-1} q_n^0}{\sum p_n^0 q_n^0} \frac{\sum p_n^t q_n^0}{\sum p_n^{t-1} q_n^0} \qquad (A.3)$$

The left-hand side of expression (3) is a direct Laspeyres index. Note that only the first of the indices that make up the right-hand side is itself a Laspeyres index, the second being a Lowe index for period t relative to period $t-1$ that uses the quantity basket of period 0 (not $t-1$). Some statistical offices describe the index on the right-hand side of expression (3) as a modified Laspeyres index.

3. In a time series context, say when t runs from 1 to T, the series

$$\frac{\sum p_n^1 q_n}{\sum p_n^0 q_n}, \frac{\sum p_n^2 q_n}{\sum p_n^0 q_n}, \ldots, \frac{\sum p_n^T q_n}{\sum p_n^0 q_n} \qquad (A.4)$$

is termed a series of *fixed basket* price indices. In particular, when $q_n = q_n^0$, we get a series of Laspeyres indices.

4. At period T one could change to a new quantity basket q', and calculate from this period onwards

$$\frac{\sum p_n^{T+1} q_n'}{\sum p_n^T q_n'}, \frac{\sum p_n^{T+2} q_n'}{\sum p_n^T q_n'}, \frac{\sum p_n^{T+3} q_n'}{\sum p_n^T q_n'}, \ldots \qquad (A.5)$$

To relate the prices of periods $T+1$, $T+2$, $T+3, \ldots$ to those of period 0, chain linking can be used to transform the series (5) into a series of the form

$$\frac{\sum p_n^T q_n}{\sum p_n^0 q_n} \frac{\sum p_n^{T+1} q_n'}{\sum p_n^T q_n'}, \frac{\sum p_n^T q_n}{\sum p_n^0 q_n} \frac{\sum p_n^{T+2} q_n'}{\sum p_n^T q_n'}, \frac{\sum p_n^T q_n}{\sum p_n^0 q_n} \frac{\sum p_n^{T+3} q_n'}{\sum p_n^T q_n'}, \ldots \qquad (A.6)$$

This could be termed a series of *chain-linked fixed basket* price indices. In particular, when $q_n = q_n^0$ and $q_n' = q_n^T$, we get a series of chain-linked Laspeyres indices. Since the basket is changed at period T, the adjective fixed applies literally only over a certain number of time intervals. The basket is fixed from period 1 to period T, and is again fixed from period $T+1$ onwards. When the time intervals during which the basket is kept fixed are of the same length, such as one, two or five years, this feature can be made explicit by describing the index as an annual, bi-annual or five-yearly chain-linked fixed basket price index.

5. A *weighted arithmetic-average* price index (so-called to distinguish it from a geometric or other kind of average) is an index of the form

$$\sum w_n (p_n^t / p_n^0) \qquad (A.7)$$

which compares the prices of period t with those of period 0, using a certain set of weights adding up to 1. In particular, when the weights are the period b value shares

$$w_n = s_n^b \equiv p_n^b q_n^b / \sum p_n^b q_n^b \qquad (A.8)$$

we obtain the Young index.

Note that any basket price index (1) can be expressed in the form (7), since

$$\frac{\sum p_n^t q_n}{\sum p_n^0 q_n} = \sum \frac{p_n^0 q_n}{\sum p_n^0 q_n} \frac{p_n^t}{p_n^0}. \qquad (A.9)$$

When the weights are the period 0 value shares,

$$w_n = s_n^0 \equiv p_n^0 q_n^0 / \sum p_n^0 q_n^0 \qquad (A.10)$$

expression (7) turns into the Laspeyres index. When

$$w_n = p_n^0 q_n^t / \sum p_n^0 q_n^t \qquad (A.11)$$

that is, hybrid period (0, t) value shares, we get the Paasche index.

One could also think of setting

$$w_n = s_n^b (p_n^0 / p_n^b) / \sum s_n^b (p_n^0 / p_n^b) = p_n^0 q_n^b / \sum p_n^0 q_n^b \qquad (A.12)$$

that is, price-updated period b value shares.

Note that hybrid value shares, such as given by expressions (11) or (12), are not observable but must be constructed.

6. In a time series context, when t runs from 1 to T, the series

$$\sum w_n (p_n^1 / p_n^0), \sum w_n (p_n^2 / p_n^0), \ldots, \sum w_n (p_n^T / p_n^0) \qquad (A.13)$$

is termed a series of *fixed weighted arithmetic-average* price indices. In particular, when the weights are equal to the period 0 expenditure shares, we get a series of Laspeyres indices, and when the weights are equal to the price-updated period b expenditure shares, we get a series of Lowe indices in which the quantities in the basket are those of period b.

7. In period T one could change to a new set of weights w', and calculate from this period onwards

$$\sum w_n' (p_n^{T+1} / p_n^T), \sum w_n' (p_n^{T+2} / p_n^T), \sum w_n' (p_n^{T+3} / p_n^T), \ldots \qquad (A.14)$$

or, using chain-linking to relate the prices of periods $T+1$, $T+2$, $T+3$, ... to those of period 0,

$$\sum w_n(p_n^T/p_n^0)\sum w_n'(p_n^{T+1}/p_n^T),$$
$$\sum w_n(p_n^T/p_n^0)\sum w_n'(p_n^{T+2}/p_n^T),\ldots. \quad \text{(A.15)}$$

This could be termed a series of *chain-linked fixed weighted arithmetic-average* price indices. In particular, when $w_n = s_n^0$ and $w_n' = s_n^T$, we get a series of chain-linked Laspeyres indices. When $w_n = s_n^b(p_n^0/p_n^b)/\sum s_n^b(p_n^0/p_n^b)$ and $w_n' = s_n^{b'}(p_n^T/p_n^{b'})/\sum s_n^{b'}(p_n^T/p_n^{b'})$ for some later period b', we get a series of chain-linked Lowe indices.

8. Again, since the weights are changed at period T, the adjective fixed applies literally only over a certain number of time intervals. The weights are fixed from period 1 to period T, and are again fixed from period $T+1$ onwards. When the time intervals during which the weights are kept fixed are of the same length, this feature can be made explicit by adding a temporal adjective, such as annual, bi-annual or five-yearly.

Annex 1

Harmonized Indices of Consumer Prices (European Union)

1 Introduction

The Harmonized Indices of Consumer Prices (HICPs) are a set of European Union consumer price indices (CPIs) calculated according to a harmonized approach and a single set of definitions. This annex outlines the aims and history of the HICPs, summarizes the most important harmonized standards and notes some key items on the agenda for further harmonization. The HICP development project is ongoing. This annex describes the state of development of the HICPs at mid-2003. The HICPs have a legal basis in that their production, and many elements of the specific methodology to be used, are stated in and required by a series of legally binding European Union Regulations. References for the full set of HICP legal standards are given at the end of this annex.

1.1 The main HICPs

The HICPs on which most attention is focused are:

- the Monetary Union Index of Consumer Prices (MUICP) – an aggregate index covering the countries within the euro-zone;
- the European Index of Consumer Prices (EICP) – for the euro-zone plus the other European Union countries;
- the national HICPs – for each of the Member States of the European Union (EU).

Beyond these are also the European Economic Area Index of Consumer Prices (EEAICP) and HICPs for the individual EEA countries.

There are also interim HICPs for Candidate and, in particular, Acceding Countries.[1] It is expected that once those countries accede to the EU their HICPs will be fully comparable to those of the existing Member States. The national HICPs are produced by the national statistical institutes, while the country-group aggregates are produced by Eurostat.

1.2 Uses of the HICPs

As explained elsewhere in this manual, CPIs have a variety of potential uses, for example for indexing social benefits or contracts, or as inputs to various types of economic analyses. The drive for the harmonization project has been the use of the HICPs as convergence criteria and the main measure for monitoring price stability in the euro-zone. The HICPs have been set up to provide the best measure for international comparisons of consumer price inflation within the EU and the euro-zone, for assessing price convergence and stability in the context of monetary policy analysis.

In the early stages of the project, the most important use of the HICPs was in the assessment of the price stability and price convergence required for entry into the European Economic and Monetary Union. More recently, the focus of interest has shifted towards country-group aggregates – and in particular the MUICP. This change of emphasis reflects the European Central Bank's objective of price stability and the view that the HICPs are the most appropriate price measure for assessing price stability.

The focus of the HICPs on measuring price stability and convergence, and on international comparisons, does not mean that a wider range of users should not or cannot use HICPs for other purposes. Depending on the precise purpose the user has in mind, the HICPs may be the best available price statistics. All users of the HICPs should note, however, that the HICPs are revisable; the indices may change after the first results are published.

1.3 Brief history of the HICPs

On 23 October 1995, the European Union's Council of Ministers adopted a Regulation providing the legal basis for the establishment of a harmonized methodology for compiling consumer price indices in the Member States and European Economic Area Countries.

This Regulation[2] (hereinafter referred to as the HICP Framework Regulation) required HICPs to be produced and published, that they use a common reference base, employ a common coverage of consumer goods and services, and share a common classification. In the context of the HICP Framework Regulation, a series of specific implementing measures has been adopted.

As mentioned above, early in the harmonization project the most important use of the HICPs was for the application of the criterion of price stability in preparation for Economic and Monetary Union in Europe.

On 1 January 1999, Economic and Monetary Union began, with 11 countries participating in the single currency – the euro. From that date, there has been a common monetary policy, with common interest rates, operating within the euro-zone under the control of the European Central Bank (ECB).

The maintenance of price stability is the primary objective of the European System of Central Banks. The President of the ECB announced in October 1998[3] that it would be operating a flexible monetary policy

[1] The composition of the country groups at the end of 2003 is as follows:
Euro-zone countries: Austria, Belgium, Finland, France, Germany, Greece, Ireland, Italy, Luxembourg, Netherlands, Portugal, Spain.
EU countries: Euro-zone countries plus Denmark, Sweden, United Kingdom.
European Economic Area countries: EU countries plus Iceland, Norway.
Acceding countries: Cyprus, Czech Republic, Estonia, Hungary, Latvia, Lithuania, Malta, Poland, Slovakia, Slovenia.
Candidate countries: Acceding countries plus Bulgaria, Romania, Turkey.
When countries accede to the EU or the euro-zone, the composition of those aggregates is revised accordingly.

[2] Council Regulation (EC) No. 2494/95.

[3] ECB press release of 13 Oct. 1998.

strategy, ensuring price stability in the euro-zone based on a monetary reference value and a mix of other indicators. In this context, the Governing Council of the ECB stated: "Price stability shall be defined as a year-on-year increase in the Harmonized Index of Consumer Prices (HICP) for the euro area of below 2%. Price stability is to be maintained over the medium term."

In 2003 the ECB reaffirmed its inflation target of October 1998, founded on the HICP for the euro-zone, and added that: "At the same time, the Governing Council agreed that in the pursuit of price stability it will aim to maintain inflation rates close to 2% over the medium term."[4]

1.4 Stepwise harmonization

The HICP Framework Regulation laid down a stepwise approach to harmonization, whereby each step requiring specific implementing measures would be legislated in the form of further legally binding standards.

The HICP Framework Regulation established that the EU's Statistical Programme Committee would act as the so-called Regulatory Committee, and would therefore be responsible for adopting the further harmonization standards to be given legal force. The Statistical Programme Committee is the most senior statistical committee of the EU, comprising the directors of the national statistical institutes.

1.5 Minimum standards

The approach taken to harmonization has been to build, as far as possible, on the EU Member States' existing data sources and methodologies for their national CPIs. The legal standards typically take the form of minimum standards, whereby more than one solution to a harmonization issue may usually be allowed so long as comparability is not threatened.

Within this framework, by mid-2003, a series of 13 legally binding standards and some additional guidelines had been drawn up and implemented in collaboration with the EU Member States.

1.6 Compliance monitoring

Given the importance accorded to the accuracy, reliability and comparability of the HICPs in the EU, Eurostat operates a system of compliance monitoring to ensure that the legal framework is adhered to. This includes, in particular, compliance assessments on the basis of questionnaires and visits by Eurostat officials to the EU national statistical institutes to study in more detail their work on their HICPs.

2 Basic concepts and definitions

2.1 Aim and scope of the HICPs

The aim of the HICPs was stated to be to measure inflation on a comparable basis, taking into account differences in national definitions. This, however, requires an operational definition of the term "inflation".

Given the opinion and the needs of the HICPs' main users, it was decided to compute the HICPs as Laspeyres-type price indices, based on the prices of goods and services available for purchase in the economic territory of each EU Member State for the purpose of directly satisfying consumer needs.

Based on this concept and by reference to national accounts, specifically the European System of Accounts (ESA 95), the coverage in practice of the HICPs was taken to be household final monetary consumption expenditure[5] (HFMCE). This definition effectively prescribes the goods and services, the population and the geographic territory to be covered, as well as the prices and the weights to be used.

The HICP may thus be described as a Laspeyres-type "consumer inflation" or "pure price" index, which measures average price changes on the basis of the changed expenditure of maintaining the consumption pattern of households and the composition of the consumer population in the base or reference period.

The term "pure price index" indicates that it is only changes in prices that should be reflected in the HICP measure between the current and the base or reference period. The HICP is therefore not a cost of living index. That is, it is not intended to be a measure of the change in the minimum cost for achieving the same standard of living (i.e. constant utility) from two different consumption patterns realized in the two periods compared, and where factors other than pure price changes may enter the index.

2.2 Household final monetary consumption expenditure

The coverage of the HICPs is delimited by HFMCE, and so concerns that part of final consumption expenditure which is:

- by households irrespective of their nationality or residence status;
- in monetary transactions;
- on the economic territory of the EU Member State;
- on goods and services that are used for the direct satisfaction of individual needs or wants;
- in one or both of the time periods being compared.

The prices used in the HICP should be the prices paid by households to purchase individual goods and services in monetary transactions. The purchaser's price is the price for the products that the purchaser actually pays at the time of purchase.

The weights of the HICP are the aggregate expenditures by households on any set of goods and services covered by the HICP, expressed as a proportion of the total expenditure on all goods and services within the coverage of the HICP.

The HICPs are classified according to the four-digit categories and sub-categories of the COICOP/HICP (Classification of Individual Consumption according to Purpose, adapted to the needs of HICPs).

[4] ECB press release of 8 May 2003.

[5] Council Regulation (EC) No. 1688/98.

2.3 Links to national accounts concepts

The concept of HFMCE not only specified the coverage, the prices and the weights for the HICP, but also established a link between HICPs and ESA 95 that has proved useful to analysts and policy-makers. HICP definitions follow ESA 95 wherever possible and when to do so is consistent with the aims and uses of the HICP.

That said, there are some differences between the coverage of the HICPs and that of household final consumption expenditure (HFCE) as defined by national accounts, in particular the treatment of owner-occupied housing. A full list of these differences is given below.

2.4 Some basic requirements for HICPs

The relative distribution of consumers' expenditure on individual products varies from country to country. Hence, there is no uniform basket applying to all EU Member States. The weights used in the compilation of HICPs may relate to a reference period up to seven years prior to the current year. In practice, this results in a complete weight and sample revision of national HICPs in at least five-yearly intervals, taking into account that a period of about two years may be needed to integrate results of a full consumer expenditure survey. Adjustments must nevertheless be made each year for any especially large changes in expenditure patterns, to minimize any disparities that could arise from different update frequencies.

To keep the HICPs broadly in step with each other and up to date, new products must be included when they achieve a significant relative importance. HICPs must also be shown to be based on appropriate sampling procedures, taking into account the national diversity of products and prices.

The samples must be kept up to date, in particular by banning the practice whereby missing prices are simply assumed to be equal to the last observed prices. In order to measure pure price changes, the prices included in HICPs need to be adjusted for changes in the quality of goods and services. Certain inappropriate quality adjustment practices, such as so-called automatic linking, may not be used.

HICP aggregates for country groups are calculated as the weighted averages of the national HICPs, using the weights of the countries and sub-indices concerned. The weight of a country is its share of HFMCE in the total. For the MUICP the weights are all naturally expressed in euros, whereas for the EICP and the EEAICP the aggregations use purchasing power standards. The MUICP is treated as a single entity within the EICP and EEAICP aggregates.[6]

[6] For technical notes see:
Eurostat News Release 21/97 of 5 March 1997, *Harmonizing the way EU measures inflation.*
Eurostat Memo 8/98 of 4 May 1998, *New monetary union index of consumer prices (MUICP).*
Eurostat Memo 02/00 of 18 February 2000, *Improved EU Harmonized Index of Consumer Prices: Extended coverage and earlier release dates for the HICP.*
Further details can be found in the Compendium of HICP reference documents : http://europa.eu.int/comm/eurostat/Public/datashop/print-catalogue/EN?catalogue=Eurostat&product=KS-AO-01-005-_-I-EN

3 Coverage

3.1 Goods and services

The coverage of goods and services in the HICPs has been expanded over time. The HICPs now cover virtually all of HMFCE. The main difference to the ESA 95 concept of HFCE is the exclusion of imputed expenditures of owner-occupied housing.

The initial coverage of goods and services in the HICPs, although fairly comprehensive, reflected for the most part what was common to the national consumer price indices. Since then, with considerable effort and cooperation by EU Member States, coverage has been extended to virtually all consumers' expenditure, in the sense of HFMCE. In particular, the difficult areas of health, education and social protection services are now covered, as are insurance and financial services. These are included in the HICPs according to agreed definitions, thus ensuring comparability despite major institutional differences.

In the initial coverage of the HICPs,[7] some difficult categories such as health and educational services, where there are major institutional differences between EU Member States, were not fully covered. In 1998 a further legal standard[8] amended the initial coverage of goods and services and laid down a staged procedure to extend the coverage of the HICP. Another legal standard extending the coverage entered into effect with the index for January 2000.[9] The next step took place with the publication of the January 2001 index.[10]

3.2 Geographic and population coverage

The HICP Framework Regulation required the HICPs to be based on the prices of goods and services available for purchase on the economic territory of the EU Member State for the purposes of directly satisfying consumer needs. As regards the economic territory and the consumers concerned, a harmonized definition of the geographic and population coverage of the HICP was necessary, both to achieve comparability and to avoid gaps or double counting when aggregating national HICPs.

In 1998 a legal standard[11] specified that the HICP should cover all HFMCE which takes place on the economic territory of an EU Member State. In particular, HICP coverage should include expenditure by foreign visitors and expenditure by individuals living in institutions, but should exclude the expenditure by residents whilst in a foreign country (the so-called domestic concept). All private households should be included, irrespective of the area in which they live or their position in the income distribution. Expenditure incurred for business purposes should be excluded.

The choice of the domestic concept reflected the role of the MUICP in measuring price stability in the euro-zone.

[7] Commission Regulation (EC) No. 1749/96.
[8] Council Regulation (EC) No. 1687/98.
[9] Commission Regulation (EC) No. 1749/1999.
[10] Commission Regulation (EC) No. 2166/1999.
[11] Council Regulation (EC) No. 1688/98.

Price changes in the euro-zone are measured by aggregating price changes taking place within the individual EU Member States. Expenditure and price changes to be measured within the economic territory should include those affecting foreign visitors and exclude those affecting residents whilst in a foreign country.

It is an HICP requirement that HICPs should be compiled using weights which reflect the HFMCE of all households. HICPs which cover only a subset of households should nevertheless be regarded as comparable if this difference in practice accounts for less than one part per thousand of the total expenditure to be covered by the HICP.

4 Weights, index formulae and price sampling

4.1 Weights

The HICP Framework Regulation requires HICP weights to be sufficiently up to date to ensure comparability, whilst at the same time avoiding the cost of conducting household budget surveys more than every five years.

An HICP legal standard[12] gives minimum standards for the quality of HICP weights. It aims to guarantee the quality of weights used to construct the HICP and minimize the disparities between HICPs which might arise from different update frequencies.

Concerning the quality of HICP weights, the weights should be sufficiently up to date to ensure comparability whilst avoiding unnecessary costs. Differences in the frequency of updating of the weights could, but not necessarily would, lead to differences in measured inflation and non-comparability. Imposing the cost of high precision for all weights or frequent updating of weights was not considered justified. On the other hand, it is difficult to be sure that an HICP using weights up to seven years old will provide a reliable and relevant measure of current inflation.

The legal standard on the quality of HICP weights requires a minimum action of review and adjustment to ensure that the quality of weights used to construct HICPs is sufficient. It establishes a comparability threshold in relation to the proposed reference practice.

The review requirement involves checking each year those weights which are judged to be most critical for reliability and relevance and, hence, for the comparability of the overall HICP. These are primarily the weights for index components where significant market changes have accompanied atypical price movements. Where a weight is identified as deficient, EU Member States should make an improved estimate and introduce an appropriate adjustment, from the following January index, where this would exceed the threshold effect of 0.1 percentage points (on average for one year compared with the previous year). The aim is to ensure that the adjusted weights are the best estimates that can be made on the information available.

[12] Commission Regulation (EC) No. 2454/97.

4.2 Index formulae

The choice of the index formula to be used for the HICP is made at two levels:

- the level of the macro-formula; that is, the choice between a chained index with annual links and a fixed base index with links up to five years.
- the level of the micro-formula; within each level there is the issue of reference period, both for prices and for weights.

4.2.1 Macro index formula

The HICP is required to be a Laspeyres-type index.[13] Although the HICPs produced by the EU Member States differ in detail, they can all be broadly described as Laspeyres-type indices. They are all price indices in which the month-to-month movements in prices are measured as an average of price indices using expenditure weights which are an appropriate reflection of the consumption pattern of the consumer population in the weight reference period.

In practice, there are three types of base period used in the construction of HICPs:

- the base period to which the volumes of the current expenditure weights refer ("weight reference period");
- the base period from which the current price change is measured, i.e. the time reference of the prices used for the valuation of the volumes in the current weights ("index reference period");
- the period in which the index base is set to 100 ("index base period").

The HICP is, depending on to the macro-formula applied in practice for its computation, potentially a chained index. It should be stressed that this is the equivalent chain form of the fixed base index which simply allows chained and fixed indices to be expressed by a common formula. The chaining becomes effective if and only if there are changes to the weights currently used, for instance on the grounds of the review as required by the HICP standard on the quality of HICP weightings.[14]

In practice, some EU Member States compile fixed base HICPs, while others compute chain HICPs with annual weight updating. In order to obtain a set of HICPs with sub-indices allowing for consistent aggregations, it is necessary to present the HICPs as if they were all computed with the same formula. Hence, it was necessary to apply a common index base period and reference period.

By mid-2003, the HICP Framework Regulation defined the common index base period with 1996 = 100. In order to obtain also a common index reference period, the weights are "price updated" to each December.

4.2.2 Elementary aggregates

An HICP legal standard[15] defines elementary aggregates by reference to the expenditure or consumption

[13] Council Regulation (EC) No. 2494/95, Article 9.

[14] Commission Regulation (EC) No. 2454/97.

[15] Commission Regulation (EC) No. 1749/96.

covered by the most detailed level of stratification of the HICP, and within which reliable expenditure information is not available for weighting purposes. An elementary aggregate index is a price index for an elementary aggregate comprising only price data.

For the HICPs the ratio of geometric mean prices or the ratio of arithmetic mean prices are the two formulae which should be used within elementary aggregates. The arithmetic mean of price relatives may only be applied in exceptional cases and where it can be shown that it is comparable.

4.2.3 The level at which macro-aggregation changes into elementary aggregation

The level of elementary aggregation interacts with other design features such as sampling procedures and the availability of weighting information. Depending on the sources of the weights used, elementary aggregation may start at different levels in different countries in the product, geographic and outlet hierarchies.

Differences in national practices can affect the resulting HICPs but this issue was, in the first instance, not considered to be a priority for harmonization and no action has been undertaken up until now. This issue is likely to be taken up again as the harmonization process develops.

4.3 Sampling of prices

There are three important sampling dimensions to take into account:

- the item dimension;
- the outlet dimension;
- the regional dimension.

Each of these dimensions may in turn be divided into sampling stages.

In the product dimension, a selection or sample of representative items is sometimes first made within the national statistical office, and then a further selection is made by price collectors in the field. In the outlet dimension, there is often first a selection of geographical areas, followed by a sample of outlets being taken within each of them.

Random sampling is not easily achieved when it comes to the collection of prices for a CPI and in practice most EU Member States follow purposive sampling procedures for their HICPs. Irrespective of the sampling method used, small effective sampling sizes may lead to random errors of a size that in itself may constitute a comparability problem.

For Member States using purposive sampling, the numbers of elementary aggregates and of prices within the elementary aggregates give an indication of the degree of coverage of the universe of outlets and items.

HICPs should be constructed from target samples which take into account the weight of each Classification of Individual Consumption according to Purpose (COICOP)/HICP category. HICPs which have sufficient elementary aggregates to represent the diversity of items within the category and sufficient prices within each elementary aggregate to take account of the variation of price movements in the population are regarded as reliable and comparable.

Concerning the replacement of products and outlets, a replacement may take place because an item or an outlet has disappeared from the market or because an item or an outlet is no longer considered to be representative. Market developments with regard to products and outlets are likely to constitute an important source of non-comparability. However, there is an important interaction with the choice of the index formula and sampling practices here. For example, the use of tight as opposed to loose product specifications may lead to quite different issues in respect to quality adjustment.

5 Specific HICP standards

5.1 Timing of entering purchaser prices into the HICP

Differences between Member States in the time of entering purchaser prices into the HICP may be particularly important for products where there is a significant time difference between the time of purchase, payment, or delivery and the time of consumption.

An HICP legal standard[16] harmonized practices and made the compilation of the HICP more transparent by setting down detailed rules for the timing of entering purchaser prices into the HICP. It uses ESA 95 as the source of its definitions and it is consistent with the ESA 95 definitions in as far as they are consistent with the purposes of the HICP.

In particular, ESA 95 states that goods and services should in general be recorded when the payables are created, that is, when the purchaser incurs a liability to the seller. However, expenditure on services in ESA 95 is recorded when the delivery of the service is completed. In the HICP, volumes are generally valued at purchaser prices following the acquisition principle. This implies for the purposes of the HICP that prices for goods shall be entered into the HICP for the month in which they are observed, and that prices for services shall be entered into the HICP for the month in which the consumption of the service at the observed prices can commence.

5.2 The treatment of price reductions

An HICP legal standard[17] lays down detailed rules for the treatment of price reductions. The standard reflects what was common practice in many EU Member States. The standard defines the general principles under which transient reductions in prices should be taken into account. It requires that price reductions must be: (i) attributable to the purchase of an individual good or service; (ii) available to all potential consumers with no special conditions attached; (iii) known to the buyer at the time when he or she entered into the agreement to buy the product concerned; and (iv) claimable at the time of purchase or within such a time period from the actual purchase that they might be expected to have a

[16] Commission Regulation (EC) No. 2601/2000.

[17] Commission Regulation (EC) No. 2602/2000.

significant influence on the quantities buyers are willing to buy.

Further guidelines supplement the legal standard, giving advice on how various price reduction schemes should be treated, such as:

- sales prices (e.g. stock-clearing sales and closing-down sales, seasonal sales, end of range or line sales, and damaged, shop-soiled or defective goods);
- credit and payment arrangements: a zero-interest loan when buying a new durable;
- inducements in the form of extra quantities or gifts;
- discounts available only to a restricted group of households;
- regular rebates or refunds (e.g. bottle deposits);
- irregular rebates or refunds (e.g. loyalty rebates schemes and cards).

5.3 Missing observations

In order to ban practices which can lead to serious biases, EU Member States are asked to maintain and provide a statement of their target sample from month to month. Where prices are not observed, they must be estimated by an appropriate procedure.

A legal standard[18] deals with minimum standards for price observation. Where the target sample requires monthly price observation, but observation fails because of the non-availability of the item or for any other reason, estimated prices may be used for the first or second month but replacement prices shall be used from the third month.

5.4 Quality adjustment

For the HICPs, quality change is said to occur whenever the Member State judges that a change in specification has resulted in a significant difference in utility (or functionality) to the consumer between a new variety or model of a good or service and the good or service previously selected for pricing. A quality change does not arise when there is a comprehensive revision of the HICP sample.

Quality adjustment is defined as the procedure of making an allowance for a quality change by increasing or reducing the observed current or reference prices by a factor or an amount equivalent to the value of that quality change.

Under the HICP legal standard[19] EU Member States are required to examine their quality adjustment procedures and to avoid the so-called automatic linking method, which is equivalent to the assumption that the difference in price between two successive models is wholly attributable to a difference in quality.

Where quality changes occur, EU Member States should make appropriate quality adjustments based on explicit estimates of the value of the quality change. In the absence of national estimates, EU Member States should use Eurostat estimates where these are available and relevant. Eurostat should assist in this process by setting up a database of quality change estimates provided both by Member States themselves and from other sources. Where no estimates are available, price changes should be estimated as the whole difference between the price of the substitute and that of the item it has replaced. Furthermore, Member Sates are required to monitor the incidence of quality changes and the adjustments made in order to demonstrate their compliance.

Despite the existing legal standards, differences between HICPs may arise because the same changes in the physical characteristics of an item are still perceived and treated in different ways in different countries. This is not to say that the same quality characteristic must be valued to the same extent in different EU Member States, only that the principles and procedures for valuation should be harmonized. In practice, differences in quality adjustment procedures between countries may not average out across the goods and services covered by the indices. On the contrary, they are likely to cumulate to differences well in excess of 0.1 percentage points.

Quality adjustment is one of the most, if not the most, intractable harmonization issues for the HICP. Eurostat and the EU Member States are currently involved in both general and conceptual discussions of methods and in the examination of the results of empirical studies of quality change and quality adjustment.

5.5 Rejected price observations

HICP guidelines concerning the rejection of price observations specify the procedures to be followed for the validation and adjustment of price observations. The guidelines require that, in general, the prices reported by the price collectors should be accepted. Rejection or adjustment of reported prices, for example the correction of an unusually high or low price change, should not be carried out by automatic procedures, but only by reference to specific information on the individual price observation, such as a repeated observation. If, following a validation procedure, the reported price has nevertheless still to be rejected, the rejected price should be treated according to the rules for missing observations.

The guidelines leave it to the EU Member States to apply methods other than the specified methods. Where an EU Member State does not use the described methods, Eurostat may request it to show that the resulting HICP does not differ systematically from an HICP constructed in line with the described methods by more than 0.1 percentage points on average, taking one year against the previous year.

5.6 Newly significant goods and services

What is meant by the term "new goods" is not always precise. In particular, there is no sharp dividing-line between new models and varieties of previously existing products and genuinely new innovative products which fulfil needs that could not be fulfilled before.

Neither the formulae used to calculate the index, nor the frequency of renewing the basket of goods and services, can fully address the basic problem: the risk of bias if the introduction of new models and varieties is

[18] Commission Regulation (EC) No. 1749/96, Article 6.

[19] Commission Regulation (EC) No. 1749/96.

used as an occasion to implement price increases or decreases.

The HICP Framework Regulation[20] contains a requirement to maintain the relevance of HICPs, meaning that steps must be taken to ensure that HICPs keep broadly in step with each other and are up to date in terms of market developments. The HICP legal standard concerning newly significant goods and services (NSGS) aims to ensure that new products are incorporated in the HICP as soon as they achieve a sales volume of one part per thousand of total consumers' expenditure in the EU Member State.[21]

The term "newly significant" can be interpreted in a wide sense, that is in the sense of being new to the index.

There are two ways whereby new products are introduced into the HICP if they have gained a significant part of consumption:

- replacement: the new product replaces an already existing product that has lost importance, so a more up-to-date representative is brought into the sample;
- addition: the new product is brought into the index in addition to the products which are already covered, as representative for a purpose not yet represented in the index.

The HICP standard on NSGS relates to additions, not to replacements.

Additions are brought into the index for two main reasons:

- a new product (e.g. mobile phones), which had not been represented in the index, and would not normally be considered as a replacement because it was radically different from the existing products. It would be added as a new category within an existing category;
- a product had been previously available, but not explicitly represented in the index because the consumption of the product was too low. Inclusion is not undertaken as a replacement within a category, but by adding a new category within an existing category.

In the case of additions, the price of the new product is collected in addition to the already observed products; and the minimum standard on NSGS offers the following treatments:

- either adjust the weights of the relevant category of COICOP/HICP; or
- adjust the weights within the relevant category of COICOP/HICP; or
- assign part of the weight specifically to the new product (i.e. below the 4-digit level of COICOP/HICP).

5.7 Tariff prices

Many tariff prices faced by consumers relate to products which are or have been regulated by government, or are or have been provided in a monopoly or a monopoly-like situation. Changes are, however, taking place in many EU countries in such markets, as the markets are opened up, and it is important that the impact on consumer inflation is appropriately captured in the HICPs since such products account for a large proportion of the total expenditure.

HICP sub-indices involving tariff prices are, in practice, often obtained centrally or directly from suppliers such as major retail chains, or computed by the Member States based on data on tariff prices and their underlying consumption patterns provided by suppliers.

The requirement for the HICP was not only to determine what statistical standards are required to ensure that EU Member States measure the same price change in a comparable and reliable way, but also to give such legal powers as are necessary to ensure that Member States are in position to have access to the data they need.

An HICP legal standard[22] lays down minimum standards for the treatment of tariffs:

- It clarifies the obligation of suppliers to provide Member States with the necessary data.[23]
- It defines the procedure to follow in the case of changes in the tariff structure. The HICP approach is based on the Laspeyres fixed basket concept, with consumption patterns as up to date as necessary to determine the immediate impact of the tariff change on the index population. The HICP should reflect the price change on the basis of the changed expenditure of maintaining the consumption pattern chosen by households prior to the given change in the tariff. The aim of this principle is to avoid showing the changes in the consumption pattern because of a change in a tariff.

5.8 Insurance

The initial coverage of the HICP included home-contents insurance and motor insurance. Since January 2000, the HICPs have also covered all insurance connected with the dwelling which is typically paid by the tenant, not only contents insurance, and private health, civil liability and travel insurance.[24] Life insurance is excluded from the coverage of the HICP, as it is considered as a household saving.

In 1997, an HICP legal standard[25] stated that the weights and prices for insurance should be measured net of claims. However, a price index for gross premiums may be used as a proxy or estimate for changes in the "prices" of net premiums.

As the initial legal standard still left scope for some procedural differences, a further standard[26] was adopted in 1999. Following the HFMCE concept, the standard retained the net concept for insurance, reflecting the use of the HICP as a measure of consumer price inflation in terms of prices actually charged.

EU household budget surveys cover all expenditure, including expenditure financed out of claims. Hence, the use of the net concept avoids the possibility of double

[20] Council Regulation (EC) No. 2494/95.

[21] Commission Regulation (EC) No. 1749/96, Article 2(b).

[22] Commission Regulation (EC) No. 2464/98.

[23] The legal basis is provided by Council Regulation (EC) No. 2494/95.

[24] Council Regulation (EC) No. 1687/98.

[25] Commission Regulation (EC) No. 2214/97.

[26] Commission Regulation (EC) No. 1617/1999.

counting or gaps. It also ensures that the overall HICP measures the change in the price for the insurance service, and that the other sub-indices, in particular those for the purchase and the repair of vehicles, major household appliances and other durables, measure the change in price for the repair and replacement of such products.

5.8.1 Weights for insurance

According to the HICP legal standard,[27] weights should reflect the so-called service charge. This is defined as follows:

Gross insurance premiums (net of insurance tax)
+/– Changes in the actuarial provisions other than for life-insurance risks
= Actual premiums earned
\+ Premium supplements
– Claims due
+/– Changes in technical provisions against outstanding life insurance risks
= Implicit service charge (net of insurance tax)
(+ Insurance tax)
= Implicit service charge

The actuarial provisions in the above definition are the technical provisions for outstanding risks which exist for almost any insurance type. The HICP legal standard also states that the weights should be based on average expenditure over three years. This is aimed at using more stable estimates of the service charge and minimizing the risk of negative weights.

According to ESA 95, payments as a result of claims are treated as current transfers from the insurance companies to policy-holders and other parties to the claim and, therefore, enter into households' disposable income. The HICP standard[28] on the treatment of insurance requires explicitly that the weights of other sub-indices (e.g. those for the purchase or repair of vehicles, for major household appliances and other durables) should include all expenditure financed out of claims where it is incurred by or on behalf of the household sector. If, for example, a damaged car is repaired then the expenditure should be reflected in the weight for car maintenance and repairs. The same holds true if the repair is paid directly by the insurance company, since the latter is considered to be acting on the policy-holder's behalf.

5.8.2 Prices for insurance

As the net concept of insurance is not applicable at the individual consumer level for pricing in practice, and because the information is not available each month, gross premiums are followed. In practice, gross premiums (or the value of the insured good) are often indexed by the CPI or by other price or cost indices. This effect should be reflected in the HICP; the gross insurance premiums should not be adjusted to exclude this indexation.

Supplementary guidelines on insurance are in the process of being elaborated. They will aim at providing practical guidance on some further technically difficult areas.

5.9 Health, education and social protection services

Several HICP legal standards concern health, education and social protection services.[29] The standards state that the purchaser prices of goods and services in the health, education and social protection sectors to be used in the HICP should, in accordance with the usual approach and with ESA 95, concern the amounts to be paid by consumers net of reimbursements. Reimbursements are defined as payments to households by government units, social security administrations or non-profit institutions serving households, that are made as direct consequences of purchases of individually specified goods and services, initially paid for by households. Payments of claims to households by insurance companies do not constitute reimbursements.

The HICP sub-indices concerned should be calculated using a formula consistent with the Laspeyres type formula used for other sub-indices, i.e., they should reflect the price change on the basis of the changed expenditure of maintaining the consumption pattern of households and the composition of the consumer population in the base or reference period. In accordance with the Laspeyres principle and the HICP standards on tariff prices, changes in purchaser prices, which reflect changes in the rules determining them, should be shown as price changes in the HICP, as should changes in the purchaser prices resulting from changes in purchasers' incomes.

If EU Member States choose to use a procedure which differs from that described above, they are required to describe the procedure before it is used so that it may be assessed against the legal standard.

5.10 Financial services

EU Member States had traditionally followed different practices in the measurement of prices for financial services in their national CPIs and applied different methods for defining the weights. There was scope for non-comparability by excluding service charges expressed as a proportion of transaction values. A harmonized methodology for the treatment of such charges was thus considered necessary.

The HICP legal standard concerning prices expressed as a proportion of transaction values[30] provides some clarifications, in particular with respect to the coverage of administrative charges of "private pension funds and the like" and "estate agent fees".

The standard says that where service charges are defined as a proportion of the transaction value, the purchaser prices should be defined as the proportion itself, multiplied by the value of a representative

[27] Commission Regulation (EC) No. 1617/1999.

[28] Commission Regulation (EC) No. 1617/1999.

[29] Commission Regulation (EC) No. 1749/96, as amended by Council Regulation (EC) No. 1687/98, requires extended coverage in the health, education and social protection sectors. Council Regulation (EC) No. 2166/1999 defines the methodological details.

[30] Commission Regulation (EC) No. 1920/2001.

unit transaction in the base or reference period. The HICP should include charges expressed as a flat fee or flat rate but exclude interest payments and interest-like charges. Changes in purchaser prices which reflect changes in the rules determining them, as well as changes in the purchaser prices resulting from changes in the values of the representative unit transactions, should be shown as price changes in the HICP. The change in the values of the representative unit transactions may be estimated by the change in a price index which represents appropriately the unit transactions concerned.

Supplementary guidelines on financial services are in the process of being elaborated. These guidelines aim at providing practical guidance on some technically difficult issues in this area.

5.11 Data processing equipment

Prices for data processing equipment tend to differ very much from the development of the all-items HICP. At the same time, there has been a considerable increase in the relative importance of such equipment in HFMCE. In view of these circumstances and the significant differences in national practices in the treatment of data processing equipment, there was a need to establish some minimum common guidelines for the HICPs.

The HICP guidelines on data processing equipment specify that Member States should cover personal computers and associated items in their HICPs. Where direct sellers are a significant source of supply, they should be covered in addition to other outlets. Prices may be obtained from magazines instead of, or as well as, direct observation in retail outlets.

The HICP standards concerning the annual review of the weights[31] are extended to verifying the weights to the level of the major components of the sub-index for data processing equipment. Those major components should comprise a component index for personal computers.

5.12 Owner-occupied housing

Measurement of the services provided by owner-occupied housing is a notoriously difficult issue for CPIs. It is sometimes stated that these services are not an issue that should concern consumer price indices, and sometimes that they are an issue and so should be covered, but that practical solutions concerning how they should be measured are elusive.

In the HICPs, the imputed prices for the services provided by owner-occupied housing are currently excluded. The exclusion of imputed services relating to owner-occupied housing has removed a potentially very important source of non-comparability between HICPs. It should be noted that, for their national CPIs, EU Member States use a variety of methods–for example, some use an approach involving imputed rents, some include mortgage interest in their CPI, while others entirely exclude the shelter costs of owner-occupiers. Other monetary consumption expenditures related to owner occupied housing, for example, expenditure on minor property maintenance and repairs, are included in the HICP.

Currently a price index based on the net acquisitions of housing by the consumers is being piloted for possible inclusion in the HICP in future. It will be compiled separately from the HICPs on an experimental basis before any decision is made to incorporate it within the HICPs.

5.13 Revisions

Since the main purpose of the HICP is to inform the monetary policy for the euro-zone by the ECB, and the HICP is a revisable index, a clear and transparent policy with respect to revisions is of paramount importance. Also, for the HICP harmonization process, a decision was necessary on how to implement improvements whilst at the same time minimizing the difficulties caused to users by introducing discontinuities into the published HICP series.

A legal standard[32] states that the published HICP series may be revised for mistakes, new or improved information, and changes in the system of harmonized rules. In particular:

- Mistakes should be corrected and any revisions that may result from such corrections should be implemented without unnecessary delay.
- New or improved information, for example a more up-to-date weighting structure, may result in revisions which should be implemented, provided that Eurostat does not oppose the timing of the revisions to be made.
- Changes in the system of harmonized rules should not require revisions of published HICPs unless otherwise stated in the particular implementing measure. The impact of such changes should be assessed. Only if it is likely that the impact is significant should the impact then be estimated for each of the 12 following months, starting with the index for January in which the change takes place.

6 Links between the HICP and National Accounts deflator of HFCE

6.1 Monetary expenditures

There are some differences between the concept of household final consumption expenditure (HFCE) used in national accounts and that of household final monetary consumption expenditure (HFMCE) used for the HICP. The HICP covers only the part of HFCE that is considered relevant to inflation measurement for monetary policy purposes, that is, only the part which involves actual monetary transactions. Imputed expenditures, in particular imputed services provided by owner-occupied shelter, are thus excluded from the HICP.

[31] Commission Regulation (EC) No. 2454/97.

[32] Commission Regulation (EC) No. 1921/2001.

6.2 Domestic concept

For the HICP, HFMCE is defined on the domestic concept, while HFCE in national accounts is defined on the national concept. Thus HFMCE in the HICPs excludes household final monetary consumption expenditure by residents abroad, outside the economic territory of the EU Member State, but includes household final monetary consumption expenditure by non-residents on the economic territory of the EU Member State. HFMCE includes extraterritorial enclaves such as embassies and foreign military bases situated within the EU Member State but excludes territorial enclaves situated in the rest of the world.

6.3 Imputed expenditures and owner-occupied housing

As noted above, HFMCE excludes imputed services from owner-occupied housing. Also excluded are incomes in kind and own final consumption, to the extent that they are covered within HFCE, because they also do not involve monetary transactions.

6.4 Life insurance and pension funds

HFMCE excludes the service charge of life insurance and the administrative charges of private pension funds.

6.5 Commissions

HFMCE excludes commissions to estate agents in connection with the sale or purchase of non-financial assets. It includes payments for services of housing agents in connection with rental transactions.

6.6 Games of chance, prostitution and narcotics

On price measurement grounds, HFMCE is defined to exclude games of chance, prostitution and narcotics.

6.7 Time of recording

Both in HICPs and ESA 95, volumes are generally valued at purchaser prices, following the acquisition principle. However, expenditure on services in ESA 95 is recorded when the delivery of the service is completed, whilst service prices are recorded in the HICP in the month for which consumption at the observed prices can commence.

6.8 Household consumption deflator

The points listed above can result in differences between the national accounts deflator of HFCE and the HICP. Furthermore, there are differences between these two price measures regarding the index formulae and the weighting schemes applied. While the HICP is defined as a Laspeyres type price index, national accounts deflators are Paasche type indices. Deflators are used to derive volume indices that are of the Laspeyres type.

7 Release and timeliness of the HICPs

7.1 Full HICPs

The full set of HICPs is published each month according to a pre-announced schedule – in general between 17 and 19 days after the end of the month in question. This schedule has advanced significantly since the HICP was first published, as a result of a series of improvements to timeliness made in both the EU Member States and at Eurostat.

7.2 Flash estimate of the MUICP

Eurostat also publishes each month a flash estimate for the MUICP – the HICP for the euro-zone as a whole. This flash estimate is based on the results from the first countries to publish their national estimates and on energy price data. It gives an early indication of what the MUICP is likely to show when the full data set is available. The estimation procedure combines historical information with partial information on price developments in the most recent months to give a total index for the euro-zone. No detailed breakdown is available. Over the two years up to June 2003, the flash estimate exactly anticipated the full estimate 14 times, eight times differed by 0.1, and twice differed by 0.2 – the last time in April 2002. The MUICP flash estimate is generally released on the last working day of the month in question.

7.3 Data

The HICP data which are released each month cover the price indices themselves, annual average price indices and rates of change, and monthly and annual rates of change. None of these are seasonally adjusted.

As well as the all-items HICPs, the full range of around 100 COICOP/HICP indices for different goods and services are made available. The main headings are as follows:

- food;
- alcohol and tobacco;
- clothing;
- housing;
- household equipment;
- health;
- transport;
- communications;
- recreation and culture;
- education;
- hotels and restaurants;
- miscellaneous.

In addition, a series of special aggregates is released, including, for example:

- the MUICP, excluding energy;
- the MUICP, excluding energy, food, alcohol and tobacco;
- the MUICP, excluding unprocessed food;
- the MUICP, excluding energy and seasonal goods;
- the MUICP, excluding tobacco.

The weights for the component goods and services and the individual countries are also made available.

All of the HICPs, including the complete list of component indices and special aggregates, are accessible via the Eurostat web site[33] and Euro-indicators web site.[34]

The Euro-indicators web site gives quick access to the latest headline figures and most important sub-indices. The Eurostat web site also gives access to the monthly news releases, more detailed data, and contact points in many countries through which comprehensive data can be obtained.

7.4 Metadata

The Eurostat web site also gives access to the compendium of HICP reference documents,[35] which contains detailed reports on the functioning of the HICP, in addition to the HICP legal standards and guidelines, and some technical notes.

8 Agenda for further harmonization

The progress made on the harmonization of CPIs does not mean that development is at an end. There are several major issues where further harmonization will still be necessary. Currently, work is in progress on:

- Quality adjustment and sampling: Eurostat and the EU Member States are following up an action plan concerning this subject. The aim is to agree on some more concrete best practices for a range of specific goods and services, in particular for cars, consumer durables, books and CDs, clothing, computers and telecommunications services. The existing HICP standard which addressed this issue in 1996 was only a first step – it is not in itself a sufficient guarantee of full comparability.
- Owner-occupied housing: the imputed expenditures for the consumption of the service provided by owner-occupied housing are currently excluded from the HICPs. Pilot calculations are being carried out using an approach based on the acquisition prices of housing that is new to the household sector – mainly newly constructed dwellings. Indices will be compiled separately from the HICPs on an experimental basis before any decision is made to incorporate them within the HICPs.

Other issues currently on the agenda include:

- minimum sampling standards in the field of price collection;
- more comprehensive systems to assess EU Member States' compliance with the existing Regulations and other guidance. More comprehensive quality assurance of the HICP compilation process in the widest sense is needed;
- support for those countries seeking to join the EU, the Acceding and Candidate Countries, to ensure that their HICPs are fully comparable;
- the consolidation of the legal framework for HICPs, and the production in due course of a methodological manual to assist both compilers and users.

[33] http://europa.eu.int/comm/eurostat/

[34] http://europa.eu.int/comm/euroindicators/

[35] http://europa.eu.int/comm/eurostat/Public/datashop/print-catalogue/EN?catalogue=Eurostat&product=KS-AO-01-005-_-I-EN

9 Regulations concerning HICPs (as at June 2003)

Council Regulation (EC) No 2494/95 of 23 October 1995 concerning Harmonized Indices of Consumer Prices (OJ L 257, 27.10.1995, p. 1).

Commission Regulation (EC) No. 1749/96 of 9 September 1996 on initial implementing measures for Council Regulation (EC) No. 2494/95 concerning Harmonized Indices of Consumer Prices (OJ L 229, 10.9.1996, p. 3).

Commission Regulation (EC) No. 2214/96 of 20 November 1996 concerning Harmonized Indices of Consumer Prices: transmission and dissemination of sub-indices of the HICP (OJ L 296, 21.11.1996, p. 8).

Commission Regulation (EC) No. 2454/97 of 10 December 1997 laying down detailed rules for the implementation of Council Regulation (EC) No. 2494/95 as regards minimum standards for the quality of HICP weightings (OJ L 340, 11.12.1997, p. 24).

Council Regulation (EC) No. 1687/98 of 20 July 1998 amending Commission Regulation (EC) No. 1749/96 concerning the coverage of goods and services of the Harmonized Index of Consumer Prices (OJ L 214, 31.7.1998, p. 12).

Council Regulation (EC) No. 1688/98 of 20 July 1998 amending Commission Regulation (EC) No. 1749/96 concerning the geographic and population coverage of the Harmonized Index of Consumer Prices (OJ L 214, 31.7.1998, p. 23).

Commission Regulation (EC) No. 2646/98 of 9 December 1998 laying down detailed rules for the implementation of Council Regulation (EC) No. 2494/95 as regards minimum standards for the treatment of tariffs in the Harmonized Index of Consumer Prices (OJ L 335, 10.12.1998, p. 30).

Commission Regulation (EC) No. 1617/1999 of 23 July 1999 laying down detailed rules for the implementation of Council Regulation (EC) No. 2494/95 as regards minimum standards for the treatment of insurance in the Harmonized Index of Consumer Prices and modifying Commission Regulation (EC) No. 2214/96 (OJ L 192, 24.7.1999, p. 9).

Commission Regulation (EC) No. 1749/1999 of 23 July 1999 amending Regulation (EC) No. 2214/96, concerning the sub-indices of the Harmonized Indices of Consumer Prices (OJ L 214, 13.8.1999, p. 1 – corrigenda published in OJ L 214, 13.8.1999, p. 1).

Council Regulation (EC) No. 2166/1999 of 8 October 1999 laying down detailed rules for the implementation of Regulation (EC) No. 2494/95 as regards minimum standards for the treatment of products in the health, education and social protection sectors in the Harmonized Index of Consumer Prices (OJ L 266, 14.10.1999, p. 1).

Commission Regulation (EC) No. 2601/2000 of 17 November 2000 laying down detailed rules for the implementation of Council Regulation (EC) No. 2494/95 as regards the timing of entering purchaser prices into the Harmonized Index of Consumer Prices (OJ L 300, 29.11.2000, p. 14).

Commission Regulation (EC) No. 2602/2000 of 17 November 2000 laying down detailed rules for the implementation of Council Regulation (EC) No. 2494/95 as regards minimum standards for the treatment of price reductions in the Harmonized Index of Consumer Prices (OJ L 300, 29.11.2000, p. 16).

Commission Regulation (EC) No. 1920/2001 of 28 September 2001 laying down detailed rules for the implementation of Council Regulation (EC) No. 2494/95 as regards minimum standards for the treatment of service charges proportional to transaction values in the Harmonized Index of Consumer Prices and amending Commission (EC) No. 2214/96. (OJ L 261, 29.9.2001, p. 46 – corrigenda published in OJ L 295, 13.11.2001, p. 34).

Commission Regulation (EC) No. 1921/2001 of 28 September 2001 laying down detailed rules for the implementation of Council Regulation (EC) No. 2494/95 as regards minimum standards for revisions of the Harmonized Index of Consumer Prices and amending Regulation (EC) No. 2602/2000 (OJ L 261, 29.9.2001, p. 49 – corrigenda published in OJ L 295, 13.11.2001, p. 34).

All these legal acts can be found on the following web site: http://europa.eu.int/celex/

Annex 2

Classification of Individual Consumption according to Purpose (COICOP)-Extract

COICOP: BREAKDOWN OF INDIVIDUAL CONSUMPTION EXPENDITURE OF HOUSEHOLDS BY DIVISION AND GROUP

01	***FOOD AND NON-ALCOHOLIC BEVERAGES***
01.1	FOOD
01.2	NON-ALCOHOLIC BEVERAGES
02	***ALCOHOLIC BEVERAGES, TOBACCO AND NARCOTICS***
02.1	ALCOHOLIC BEVERAGES
02.2	TOBACCO
02.3	NARCOTICS
03	***CLOTHING AND FOOTWEAR***
03.1	CLOTHING
03.2	FOOTWEAR
04	***HOUSING, WATER, ELECTRICITY, GAS AND OTHER FUELS***
04.1	ACTUAL RENTALS FOR HOUSING
04.2	IMPUTED RENTALS FOR HOUSING
04.3	MAINTENANCE AND REPAIR OF THE DWELLING
04.4	WATER SUPPLY AND MISCELLANEOUS SERVICES RELATING TO THE DWELLING
04.5	ELECTRICITY, GAS AND OTHER FUELS
05	***FURNISHINGS, HOUSEHOLD EQUIPMENT AND ROUTINE HOUSEHOLD MAINTENANCE***
05.1	FURNITURE AND FURNISHINGS, CARPETS AND OTHER FLOOR COVERINGS
05.2	HOUSEHOLD TEXTILES
05.3	HOUSEHOLD APPLIANCES
05.4	GLASSWARE, TABLEWARE AND HOUSEHOLD UTENSILS
05.5	TOOLS AND EQUIPMENT FOR HOUSE AND GARDEN
05.6	GOODS AND SERVICES FOR ROUTINE HOUSEHOLD MAINTENANCE
06	***HEALTH***
06.1	MEDICAL PRODUCTS, APPLIANCES AND EQUIPMENT
06.2	OUTPATIENT SERVICES
06.3	HOSPITAL SERVICES
07	***TRANSPORT***
07.1	PURCHASE OF VEHICLES
07.2	OPERATION OF PERSONAL TRANSPORT EQUIPMENT
07.3	TRANSPORT SERVICES
08	***COMMUNICATION***
08.1	POSTAL SERVICES
08.2	TELEPHONE AND TELEFAX EQUIPMENT
08.3	TELEPHONE AND TELEFAX SERVICES
09	***RECREATION AND CULTURE***
09.1	AUDIO-VISUAL, PHOTOGRAPHIC AND INFORMATION PROCESSING EQUIPMENT
09.2	OTHER MAJOR DURABLES FOR RECREATION AND CULTURE
09.3	OTHER RECREATIONAL ITEMS AND EQUIPMENT, GARDENS AND PETS
09.4	RECREATIONAL AND CULTURAL SERVICES
09.5	NEWSPAPERS, BOOKS AND STATIONERY
09.6	PACKAGE HOLIDAYS
10	***EDUCATION***
10.1	PRE-PRIMARY AND PRIMARY EDUCATION
10.2	SECONDARY EDUCATION
10.3	POST-SECONDARY NON-TERTIARY EDUCATION
10.4	TERTIARY EDUCATION
10.5	EDUCATION NOT DEFINABLE BY LEVEL
11	***RESTAURANTS AND HOTELS***
11.1	CATERING SERVICES
11.2	ACCOMMODATION SERVICES
12	***MISCELLANEOUS GOODS AND SERVICES***
12.1	PERSONAL CARE
12.2	PROSTITUTION
12.3	PERSONAL EFFECTS N.E.C.
12.4	SOCIAL PROTECTION
12.5	INSURANCE
12.6	FINANCIAL SERVICES N.E.C.
12.7	OTHER SERVICES N.E.C.

COICOP: DEFINITION BY CLASS

01–12 INDIVIDUAL CONSUMPTION EXPENDITURE OF HOUSEHOLDS

01 FOOD AND NON-ALCOHOLIC BEVERAGES

01.1 FOOD

The food products classified here are those purchased for consumption at home. The group excludes: food products sold for immediate consumption away from the home by hotels, restaurants, cafés, bars, kiosks, street vendors, automatic vending machines, etc. (11.1.1); cooked dishes prepared by restaurants for consumption off their premises (11.1.1); cooked dishes prepared by catering contractors whether collected by the customer or delivered to the customer's home (11.1.1); and products sold specifically as pet foods (09.3.4).

01.1.1 Bread and cereals (ND)

- Rice in all forms;
- maize, wheat, barley, oats, rye and other cereals in the form of grain, flour or meal;

- bread and other bakery products (crispbread, rusks, toasted bread, biscuits, gingerbread, wafers, waffles, crumpets, muffins, croissants, cakes, tarts, pies, quiches, pizzas, etc.);
- mixes and doughs for the preparation of bakery products;
- pasta products in all forms; couscous;
- cereal preparations (cornflakes, oatflakes, etc.) and other cereal products (malt, malt flour, malt extract, potato starch, tapioca, sago and other starches).

Includes: farinaceous-based products prepared with meat, fish, seafood, cheese, vegetables or fruit.

Excludes: meat pies (01.1.2); fish pies (01.1.3); sweetcorn (01.1.7).

01.1.2 Meat (ND)

- Fresh, chilled or frozen meat of:
  - bovine animals, swine, sheep and goat;
  - horse, mule, donkey, camel and the like;
  - poultry (chicken, duck, goose, turkey, guinea fowl);
  - hare, rabbit and game (antelope, deer, boar, pheasant, grouse, pigeon, quail, etc.);
- fresh, chilled or frozen edible offal;
- dried, salted or smoked meat and edible offal (sausages, salami, bacon, ham, pâté, etc.);
- other preserved or processed meat and meat-based preparations (canned meat, meat extracts, meat juices, meat pies, etc.).

Includes: meat and edible offal of marine mammals (seals, walruses, whales, etc.) and exotic animals (kangaroo, ostrich, alligator, etc.); animals and poultry purchased live for consumption as food.

Excludes: land and sea snails (01.1.3); lard and other edible animal fats (01.1.5); soups, broths and stocks containing meat (01.1.9).

01.1.3 Fish and seafood (ND)

- Fresh, chilled or frozen fish;
- fresh, chilled or frozen seafood (crustaceans, molluscs and other shellfish, sea snails);
- dried, smoked or salted fish and seafood;
- other preserved or processed fish and seafood and fish and seafood-based preparations (canned fish and seafood, caviar and other hard roes, fish pies, etc.).

Includes: land crabs, land snails and frogs; fish and seafood purchased live for consumption as food.

Excludes: soups, broths and stocks containing fish and seafood (01.1.9).

01.1.4 Milk, cheese and eggs (ND)

- Raw milk; pasteurized or sterilized milk;
- condensed, evaporated or powdered milk;
- yoghurt, cream, milk-based desserts, milk-based beverages and other similar milk-based products;
- cheese and curd;
- eggs and egg products made wholly from eggs.

Includes: milk, cream and yoghurt containing sugar, cocoa, fruit or flavourings; dairy products not based on milk such as soya milk.

Excludes: butter and butter products (01.1.5).

01.1.5 Oils and fats (ND)

- Butter and butter products (butter oil, ghee, etc.);
- margarine (including "diet" margarine) and other vegetable fats (including peanut butter);
- edible oils (olive oil, corn oil, sunflower-seed oil, cottonseed oil, soybean oil, groundnut oil, walnut oil, etc.);
- edible animal fats (lard, etc.).

Excludes: cod or halibut liver oil (06.1.1).

01.1.6 Fruit (ND)

- Fresh, chilled or frozen fruit;
- dried fruit, fruit peel, fruit kernels, nuts and edible seeds;
- preserved fruit and fruit-based products.

Includes: melons and water melons.

Excludes: vegetables cultivated for their fruit such as aubergines, cucumbers and tomatoes (01.1.7); jams, marmalades, compotes, jellies, fruit purées and pastes (01.1.8); parts of plants preserved in sugar (01.1.8); fruit juices and syrups (01.2.2).

01.1.7 Vegetables (ND)

- Fresh, chilled, frozen or dried vegetables cultivated for their leaves or stalks (asparagus, broccoli, cauliflower, endives, fennel, spinach, etc.), for their fruit (aubergines, cucumbers, courgettes, green peppers, pumpkins, tomatoes, etc.), and for their roots (beetroots, carrots, onions, parsnips, radishes, turnips, etc.);
- fresh or chilled potatoes and other tuber vegetables (manioc, arrowroot, cassava, sweet potatoes, etc.);
- preserved or processed vegetables and vegetable-based products;

Note: ND, SD, D and S denote non-durable goods, semi-durable goods, durable goods and services, respectively.

- products of tuber vegetables (flours, meals, flakes, purées, chips and crisps) including frozen preparations such as chipped potatoes.

Includes: olives; garlic; pulses; sweetcorn; sea fennel and other edible seaweed; mushrooms and other edible fungi.

Excludes: potato starch, tapioca, sago and other starches (01.1.1); soups, broths and stocks containing vegetables (01.1.9); culinary herbs (parsley, rosemary, thyme, etc.) and spices (pepper, pimento, ginger, etc.) (01.1.9); vegetable juices (01.2.2).

01.1.8 Sugar, jam, honey, chocolate and confectionery (ND)

- Cane or beet sugar, unrefined or refined, powdered, crystallized or in lumps;
- jams, marmalades, compotes, jellies, fruit purées and pastes, natural and artificial honey, maple syrup, molasses and parts of plants preserved in sugar;
- chocolate in bars or slabs, chewing gum, sweets, toffees, pastilles and other confectionery products;
- cocoa-based foods and cocoa-based dessert preparations;
- edible ice, ice cream and sorbet.

Includes: artificial sugar substitutes.

Excludes: cocoa and chocolate-based powder (01.2.1).

01.1.9 Food products n.e.c. (ND)

- Salt, spices (pepper, pimento, ginger, etc.), culinary herbs (parsley, rosemary, thyme, etc.), sauces, condiments, seasonings (mustard, mayonnaise, ketchup, soy sauce, etc.), vinegar;
- prepared baking powders, baker's yeast, dessert preparations, soups, broths, stocks, culinary ingredients, etc.;
- homogenized baby food and dietary preparations irrespective of the composition.

Excludes: milk-based desserts (01.1.4); soya milk (01.1.4); artificial sugar substitutes (01.1.8); cocoa-based dessert preparations (01.1.8).

01.2 NON-ALCOHOLIC BEVERAGES

The non-alcoholic beverages classified here are those purchased for consumption at home. The group excludes non-alcoholic beverages sold for immediate consumption away from the home by hotels, restaurants, cafés, bars, kiosks, street vendors, automatic vending machines, etc. (11.1.1).

01.2.1 Coffee, tea and cocoa (ND)

- Coffee, whether or not decaffeinated, roasted or ground, including instant coffee;
- tea, maté and other plant products for infusions;
- cocoa, whether or not sweetened, and chocolate-based powder.

Includes: cocoa-based beverage preparations; coffee and tea substitutes; extracts and essences of coffee and tea.

Excludes: chocolate in bars or slabs (01.1.8); cocoa-based food and cocoa-based dessert preparations (01.1.8).

01.2.2 Mineral waters, soft drinks, fruit and vegetable juices (ND)

- Mineral or spring waters; all drinking water sold in containers;
- soft drinks such as sodas, lemonades and colas;
- fruit and vegetable juices;
- syrups and concentrates for the preparation of beverages.

Excludes: non-alcoholic beverages which are generally alcoholic such as non-alcoholic beer (02.1).

02 ALCOHOLIC BEVERAGES, TOBACCO AND NARCOTICS

02.1 ALCOHOLIC BEVERAGES

The alcoholic beverages classified here are those purchased for consumption at home. The group excludes alcoholic beverages sold for immediate consumption away from the home by hotels, restaurants, cafés, bars, kiosks, street vendors, automatic vending machines, etc. (11.1.1).

The beverages classified here include low- or non-alcoholic beverages which are generally alcoholic such as non-alcoholic beer.

02.1.1 Spirits (ND)

- Eaux-de-vie, liqueurs and other spirits.

Includes: mead; aperitifs other than wine-based aperitifs (02.1.2).

02.1.2 Wine (ND)

- Wine, cider and perry, including sake;
- wine-based aperitifs, fortified wines, champagne and other sparkling wines.

02.1.3 Beer (ND)

- All kinds of beer such as ale, lager and porter.

Includes: low-alcoholic beer and non-alcoholic beer; shandy.

02.2 TOBACCO

This group covers all purchases of tobacco by households, including purchases of tobacco in restaurants, cafés, bars, service stations, etc.

02.2.0 Tobacco (ND)

- Cigarettes; cigarette tobacco and cigarette papers;
- cigars, pipe tobacco, chewing tobacco or snuff.

Excludes: other smokers' articles (12.3.2).

02.3 NARCOTICS

02.3.0 Narcotics (ND)

- Marijuana, opium, cocaine and their derivatives;
- other vegetable-based narcotics such as cola nuts, betel leaves and betel nuts;
- other narcotics including chemicals and man-made drugs.

03 CLOTHING AND FOOTWEAR

03.1 CLOTHING

03.1.1 Clothing materials (SD)

- Clothing materials of natural fibres, of man-made fibres and of their mixtures.

Excludes: furnishing fabrics (05.2.0).

03.1.2 Garments (SD)

- Garments for men, women, children (3 to 13 years) and infants (0 to 2 years), either ready-to-wear or made-to-measure, in all materials (including leather, furs, plastics and rubber), for everyday wear, for sport or for work:
  - capes, overcoats, raincoats, anoraks, parkas, blousons, jackets, trousers, waistcoats, suits, costumes, dresses, skirts, etc.;
  - shirts, blouses, pullovers, sweaters, cardigans, shorts, swimsuits, tracksuits, jogging suits, sweatshirts, T-shirts, leotards, etc.;
  - vests, underpants, socks, stockings, tights, petticoats, brassières, knickers, slips, girdles, corsets, body stockings, etc.;
  - pyjamas, nightshirts, nightdresses, housecoats, dressing gowns, bathrobes, etc.;
  - baby clothes and babies' booties made of fabric.

Excludes: articles of medical hosiery such as elasticated stockings (06.1.2); babies' napkins (12.1.3).

03.1.3 Other articles of clothing and clothing accessories (SD)

- Ties, handkerchiefs, scarves, squares, gloves, mittens, muffs, belts, braces, aprons, smocks, bibs, sleeve protectors, hats, caps, berets, bonnets, etc.;
- sewing threads, knitting yarns and accessories for making clothing such as buckles, buttons, press studs, zip fasteners, ribbons, laces, trimmings, etc.

Includes: gardening gloves and working gloves; crash helmets for motorcycles and bicycles.

Excludes: gloves and other articles made of rubber (05.6.1); pins, safety pins, sewing needles, knitting needles, thimbles (05.6.1); protective headgear for sports (09.3.2); other protective gear for sports such as life jackets, boxing gloves, body padding, belts, supports, etc. (09.3.2); paper handkerchiefs (12.1.3); watches, jewellery, cuff links, tiepins (12.3.1); walking sticks and canes, umbrellas and parasols, fans, keyrings (12.3.2).

03.1.4 Cleaning, repair and hire of clothing (S)

- Dry-cleaning, laundering and dyeing of garments;
- darning, mending, repair and altering of garments;
- hire of garments.

Includes: total value of the repair service (that is, both the cost of labour and the cost of materials are covered).

Excludes: materials, threads, accessories, etc. purchased by households with the intention of undertaking the repairs themselves (03.1.1) or (03.1.3); repair of household linen and other household textiles (05.2.0); dry-cleaning, laundering, dyeing and hiring of household linen and other household textiles (05.6.2).

03.2 FOOTWEAR

03.2.1 Shoes and other footwear (SD)

- All footwear for men, women, children (3 to 13 years) and infants (0 to 2 years) including sports footwear suitable for everyday or leisure wear (shoes for jogging, cross-training, tennis, basket ball, boating, etc.).

Includes: gaiters, leggings and similar articles; shoelaces; parts of footwear, such as heels, soles, etc., purchased by households with the intention of repairing footwear themselves.

Excludes: babies' booties made of fabric (03.1.2); shoe-trees, shoehorns and polishes, creams and other shoe-cleaning articles (05.6.1); orthopaedic footwear (06.1.3); game-specific footwear (ski boots, football boots, golfing shoes and other such footwear fitted with ice-skates, rollers, spikes, studs, etc.) (09.3.2); shin-guards, cricket pads and other such protective apparel for sport (09.3.2).

03.2.2 **Repair and hire of footwear (S)**

- Repair of footwear; shoe-cleaning services;
- hire of footwear.

Includes: total value of the repair service (that is, both the cost of labour and the cost of materials are covered).

Excludes: parts of footwear, such as heels, soles, etc., purchased by households with the intention of undertaking the repair themselves (03.2.1); polishes, creams and other shoe-cleaning articles (05.6.1); repair (09.3.2) or hire (09.4.1) of game-specific footwear (ski boots, football boots, golfing shoes and other such footwear fitted with ice-skates, rollers, spikes, studs, etc.).

04 HOUSING, WATER, ELECTRICITY, GAS AND OTHER FUELS

04.1 ACTUAL RENTALS FOR HOUSING

Rentals normally include payment for the use of the land on which the property stands, the dwelling occupied, the fixtures and fittings for heating, plumbing, lighting, etc., and, in the case of a dwelling let furnished, the furniture.

Rentals also include payment for the use of a garage to provide parking in connection with the dwelling. The garage does not have to be physically contiguous to the dwelling; nor does it have to be leased from the same landlord.

Rentals do not include payment for the use of garages or parking spaces not providing parking in connection with the dwelling (07.2.4). Nor do they include charges for water supply (04.4.1), refuse collection (04.4.2) and sewage collection (04.4.3); co-proprietor charges for caretaking, gardening, stairwell cleaning, heating and lighting, maintenance of lifts and refuse disposal chutes, etc. in multi-occupied buildings (04.4.4); charges for electricity (04.5.1) and gas (04.5.2); charges for heating and hot water supplied by district heating plants (04.5.5).

04.1.1 **Actual rentals paid by tenants (S)**

- Rentals actually paid by tenants or sub-tenants occupying unfurnished or furnished premises as their main residence.

Includes: payments by households occupying a room in a hotel or boarding house as their main residence.

Excludes: accommodation services of educational establishments and hostels (11.2.0) and of retirement homes for elderly persons (12.4.0).

04.1.2 **Other actual rentals (S)**

- Rentals actually paid for secondary residences.

Excludes: accommodation services of holiday villages and holiday centres (11.2.0).

04.2 IMPUTED RENTALS FOR HOUSING

For coverage see note to (04.1) above.

04.2.1 **Imputed rentals of owner-occupiers (S)**

- Imputed rentals of owners occupying their main residence.

04.2.2 **Other imputed rentals (S)**

- Imputed rentals for secondary residences;
- imputed rentals of households paying a reduced rental or housed free.

04.3 MAINTENANCE AND REPAIR OF THE DWELLING

Maintenance and repair of dwellings are distinguished by two features: first, they are activities that have to be undertaken regularly in order to maintain the dwelling in good working order; second, they do not change the dwelling's performance, capacity or expected service life.

There are two types of maintenance and repair of dwellings: those which are minor, such as interior decoration and repairs to fittings, and which are commonly carried out by both tenants and owners; and those which are major, such as replastering walls or repairing roofs, and which are carried out by owners only.

Only expenditures which tenants and owner-occupiers incur on materials and services for minor maintenance and repair are part of individual consumption expenditure of households. Expenditures which owner-occupiers incur on materials and services for major maintenance and repair are not part of individual consumption expenditure of households.

Purchases of materials made by tenants or owner-occupiers with the intention of undertaking the maintenance or repair themselves should be shown under (04.3.1). If tenants or owner-occupiers pay an enterprise to carry out the maintenance or repair, the total value of the service, including the costs of the materials used, should be shown under (04.3.2).

04.3.1 **Materials for the maintenance and repair of the dwelling (ND)**

- Products and materials, such as paints and varnishes, renderings, wallpapers, fabric wall coverings, window panes, plaster, cement, putty, wallpaper pastes, etc., purchased for minor maintenance and repair of the dwelling.

Includes: small plumbing items (pipes, taps, joints, etc.), surfacing materials (floorboards, ceramic tiles, etc.) and brushes and scrapers for paint, varnish and wallpaper.

Excludes: fitted carpets and linoleum (05.1.2); hand tools, door fittings, power sockets, wiring flex and lamp bulbs (05.5.2); brooms, scrubbing brushes, dusting brushes and cleaning products (05.6.1); products, materials and fixtures used for major maintenance and repair (intermediate consumption) or for extension and conversion of the dwelling (capital formation).

04.3.2 Services for the maintenance and repair of the dwelling (S)

- Services of plumbers, electricians, carpenters, glaziers, painters, decorators, floor polishers, etc. engaged for minor maintenance and repair of the dwelling.

Includes: total value of the service (that is, both the cost of labour and the cost of materials are covered).

Excludes: separate purchases of materials made by households with the intention of undertaking the maintenance or repair themselves (04.3.1); services engaged for major maintenance and repair (intermediate consumption) or for extension and conversion of the dwelling (capital formation).

04.4 WATER SUPPLY AND MISCELLANEOUS SERVICES RELATING TO THE DWELLING

04.4.1 Water supply (ND)

- Water supply.

Includes: associated expenditure such as hire of meters, reading of meters, standing charges, etc.

Excludes: drinking water sold in bottles or containers (01.2.2); hot water or steam purchased from district heating plants (04.5.5).

04.4.2 Refuse collection (S)

- Refuse collection and disposal.

04.4.3 Sewage collection (S)

- Sewage collection and disposal.

04.4.4 Other services relating to the dwelling n.e.c. (S)

- Co-proprietor charges for caretaking, gardening, stairwell cleaning, heating and lighting, maintenance of lifts and refuse disposal chutes, etc. in multi-occupied buildings;
- security services;
- snow removal and chimney sweeping.

Excludes: household services such as window cleaning, disinfecting, fumigation and pest extermination (05.6.2); bodyguards (12.7.0).

04.5 ELECTRICITY, GAS AND OTHER FUELS

04.5.1 Electricity (ND)

- Electricity.

Includes: associated expenditure such as hire of meters, reading of meters, standing charges, etc.

04.5.2 Gas (ND)

- Town gas and natural gas;
- liquefied hydrocarbons (butane, propane, etc.).

Includes: associated expenditure such as hire of meters, reading of meters, storage containers, standing charges, etc.

04.5.3 Liquid fuels (ND)

- Domestic heating and lighting oils.

04.5.4 Solid fuels (ND)

- Coal, coke, briquettes, firewood, charcoal, peat and the like.

04.5.5 Heat energy (ND)

- Hot water and steam purchased from district heating plants.

Includes: associated expenditure such as hire of meters, reading of meters, standing charges, etc.; ice used for cooling and refrigeration purposes.

05 FURNISHINGS, HOUSEHOLD EQUIPMENT AND ROUTINE HOUSEHOLD MAINTENANCE

05.1 FURNITURE AND FURNISHINGS, CARPETS AND OTHER FLOOR COVERINGS

05.1.1 Furniture and furnishings (D)

- Beds, sofas, couches, tables, chairs, cupboards, chests of drawers and bookshelves;
- lighting equipment such as ceiling lights, standard lamps, globe lights and bedside lamps;

- pictures, sculptures, engravings, tapestries and other art objects including reproductions of works of art and other ornaments;
- screens, folding partitions and other furniture and fixtures.

Includes: delivery and installation when applicable; base mattresses, mattresses, tatamis; bathroom cabinets; baby furniture such as cradles, high chairs and playpens; blinds; camping and garden furniture; mirrors, candleholders and candlesticks.

Excludes: bedding and sunshades (05.2.0); safes (05.3.1); ornamental glass and ceramic articles (05.4.0); clocks (12.3.1); wall thermometers and barometers (12.3.2); carrycots and pushchairs (12.3.2); works of art and antique furniture acquired primarily as stores of value (capital formation).

05.1.2 Carpets and other floor coverings (D)

- Loose carpets, fitted carpets, linoleum and other such floor coverings.

Includes: laying of floor coverings.

Excludes: bathroom mats, rush mats and doormats (05.2.0); antique floor coverings acquired primarily as stores of value (capital formation).

05.1.3 Repair of furniture, furnishings and floor coverings (S)

- Repair of furniture, furnishings and floor coverings.

Includes: total value of the service (that is, both the cost of labour and the cost of materials are covered); restoration of works of art, antique furniture and antique floor coverings other than those acquired primarily as stores of value (capital formation).

Excludes: separate purchases of materials made by households with the intention of undertaking the repair themselves (05.1.1) or (05.1.2); dry-cleaning of carpets (05.6.2).

05.2 HOUSEHOLD TEXTILES

05.2.0 Household textiles (SD)

- Furnishing fabrics, curtain material, curtains, double curtains, awnings, door curtains and fabric blinds;
- bedding such as futons, pillows, bolsters and hammocks;
- bedlinen such as sheets, pillowcases, blankets, travelling rugs, plaids, eiderdowns, counterpanes and mosquito nets;
- table linen and bathroom linen such as tablecloths, table napkins, towels and face cloths;
- other household textiles such as shopping bags, laundry bags, shoe bags, covers for clothes and furniture, flags, sunshades, etc.;
- repair of such articles.

Includes: cloth bought by the piece; oilcloth; bathroom mats, rush mats and doormats.

Excludes: fabric wall coverings (04.3.1); tapestries (05.1.1); floor coverings such as carpets and fitted carpets (05.1.2); electric blankets (05.3.2); covers for motor cars, motorcycles, etc. (07.2.1); air mattresses and sleeping bags (09.3.2).

05.3 HOUSEHOLD APPLIANCES

05.3.1 Major household appliances whether electric or not (D)

- Refrigerators, freezers and fridge-freezers;
- washing machines, dryers, drying cabinets, dishwashers, ironing and pressing machines;
- cookers, spit roasters, hobs, ranges, ovens and microwave ovens;
- air-conditioners, humidifiers, space heaters, water heaters, ventilators and extractor hoods;
- vacuum cleaners, steam-cleaning machines, carpet shampooing machines and machines for scrubbing, waxing and polishing floors;
- other major household appliances such as safes, sewing machines, knitting machines, water softeners, etc.

Includes: delivery and installation of the appliances when applicable.

Excludes: such appliances that are built into the structure of the building (capital formation).

05.3.2 Small electric household appliances (SD)

- Coffee mills, coffee-makers, juice extractors, can-openers, food mixers, deep fryers, meat grills, knives, toasters, ice cream makers, sorbet makers, yoghurt makers, hotplates, irons, kettles, fans, electric blankets, etc.

Excludes: small non-electric household articles and kitchen utensils (05.4.0); household scales (05.4.0); personal weighing machines and baby scales (12.1.3).

05.3.3 Repair of household appliances (S)

- Repair of household appliances.

Includes: total value of the service (that is, both the cost of labour and the cost of materials are covered); charges for the leasing or rental of major household appliances.

Excludes: separate purchases of materials made by households with the intention of undertaking the repair themselves (05.3.1) or (05.3.2).

05.4 GLASSWARE, TABLEWARE AND HOUSEHOLD UTENSILS

05.4.0 Glassware, tableware and household utensils (SD)

- Glassware, crystal ware, ceramic ware and china ware of the kind used for table, kitchen, bathroom, toilet, office and indoor decoration;
- cutlery, flatware and silverware;
- non-electric kitchen utensils of all materials such as saucepans, stewpots, pressure cookers, frying pans, coffee mills, purée makers, mincers, hotplates, household scales and other such mechanical devices;
- non-electric household articles of all materials such as containers for bread, coffee, spices, etc., waste bins, waste-paper baskets, laundry baskets, portable money boxes and strongboxes, towel rails, bottle racks, irons and ironing boards, letter boxes, feeding bottles, thermos flasks and iceboxes;
- repair of such articles.

Excludes: lighting equipment (05.1.1); electric household appliances (05.3.1) or (05.3.2); cardboard tableware (05.6.1); personal weighing machines and baby scales (12.1.3); ashtrays (12.3.2).

05.5 TOOLS AND EQUIPMENT FOR HOUSE AND GARDEN

05.5.1 Major tools and equipment (D)

- Motorized tools and equipment such as electric drills, saws, sanders and hedge cutters, garden tractors, lawnmowers, cultivators, chainsaws and water pumps;
- repair of such articles.

Includes: charges for the leasing or rental of do-it-yourself machinery and equipment.

05.5.2 Small tools and miscellaneous accessories (SD)

- Hand tools such as saws, hammers, screwdrivers, wrenches, spanners, pliers, trimming knives, rasps and files;
- garden tools such as wheelbarrows, watering cans, hoses, spades, shovels, rakes, forks, scythes, sickles and secateurs;
- ladders and steps;
- door fittings (hinges, handles and locks), fittings for radiators and fireplaces, other metal articles for the house (curtain rails, carpet rods, hooks, etc.) or for the garden (chains, grids, stakes and hoop segments for fencing and bordering);
- small electric accessories such as power sockets, switches, wiring flex, electric bulbs, fluorescent lighting tubes, torches, flashlights, hand lamps, electric batteries for general use, bells and alarms;
- repair of such articles.

05.6 GOODS AND SERVICES FOR ROUTINE HOUSEHOLD MAINTENANCE

05.6.1 Non-durable household goods (ND)

- Cleaning and maintenance products such as soaps, washing powders, washing liquids, scouring powders, detergents, disinfectant bleaches, softeners, conditioners, window-cleaning products, waxes, polishes, dyes, unblocking agents, disinfectants, insecticides, pesticides, fungicides and distilled water;
- articles for cleaning such as brooms, scrubbing brushes, dustpans and dust brushes, dusters, tea towels, floorcloths, household sponges, scourers, steel wool and chamois leathers;
- paper products such as filters, tablecloths and table napkins, kitchen paper, vacuum cleaner bags and cardboard tableware, including aluminium foil and plastic bin liners;
- other non-durable household articles such as matches, candles, lamp wicks, methylated spirits, clothes-pegs, clothes hangers, pins, safety pins, sewing needles, knitting needles, thimbles, nails, screws, nuts and bolts, tacks, washers, glues and adhesive tapes for household use, string, twine and rubber gloves.

Includes: polishes, creams and other shoe-cleaning articles; fire extinguishers for households.

Excludes: brushes and scrapers for paint, varnish and wallpaper (04.3.1); fire extinguishers for transport equipment (07.2.1); products specifically for the cleaning and maintenance of transport equipment such as paints, chrome cleaners, sealing compounds and bodywork polishes (07.2.1); horticultural products for the upkeep of ornamental gardens (09.3.3); paper handkerchiefs, toilet paper, toilet soaps, toilet sponges and other products for personal hygiene (12.1.3); cigarette, cigar and pipe lighters and lighter fuel (12.3.2).

05.6.2 Domestic services and household services (S)

- Domestic services supplied by paid staff employed in private service such as butlers,

cooks, maids, drivers, gardeners, governesses, secretaries, tutors and au pairs,
- similar services, including babysitting and housework, supplied by enterprises or self-employed persons;
- household services such as window cleaning, disinfecting, fumigation and pest extermination;
- dry-cleaning, laundering and dyeing of household linen, household textiles and carpets;
- hire of furniture, furnishings, carpets, household equipment and household linen.

Excludes: dry-cleaning, laundering and dyeing of garments (03.1.4); refuse collection (04.4.2); sewerage collection (04.4.3); co-proprietor charges for caretaking, gardening, stairwell cleaning, heating and lighting, maintenance of lifts and refuse disposal chutes, etc. in multi-occupied buildings (04.4.4); security services (04.4.4); snow removal and chimney sweeping (04.4.4); removal and storage services (07.3.6); services of wet-nurses, crèches, day-care centres and other child-minding facilities (12.4.0); bodyguards (12.7.0).

06 HEALTH

This division also includes health services purchased from school and university health centres.

06.1 MEDICAL PRODUCTS, APPLIANCES AND EQUIPMENT

This group covers medicaments, prostheses, medical appliances and equipment and other health-related products purchased by individuals or households, either with or without a prescription, usually from dispensing chemists, pharmacists or medical equipment suppliers. They are intended for consumption or use outside a health facility or institution. Such products supplied directly to outpatients by medical, dental and paramedical practitioners or to in-patients by hospitals and the like are included in outpatient services (06.2) or hospital services (06.3).

06.1.1 Pharmaceutical products (ND)

- Medicinal preparations, medicinal drugs, patent medicines, serums and vaccines, vitamins and minerals, cod liver oil and halibut liver oil, oral contraceptives.

Excludes: veterinary products (09.3.4); articles for personal hygiene such as medicinal soaps (12.1.3).

06.1.2 Other medical products (ND)

- Clinical thermometers, adhesive and non-adhesive bandages, hypodermic syringes, first-aid kits, hot-water bottles and ice bags, medical hosiery items such as elasticated stockings and knee supports, pregnancy tests, condoms and other mechanical contraceptive devices.

06.1.3 Therapeutic appliances and equipment (D)

- Corrective eyeglasses and contact lenses, hearing aids, glass eyes, artificial limbs and other prosthetic devices, orthopaedic braces and supports, orthopaedic footwear, surgical belts, trusses and supports, neck braces, medical massage equipment and health lamps, powered and unpowered wheelchairs and invalid carriages, "special" beds, crutches, electronic and other devices for monitoring blood pressure, etc.;
- repair of such articles.

Includes: dentures but not fitting costs.

Excludes: hire of therapeutic equipment (06.2.3); protective goggles, belts and supports for sport (09.3.2); sunglasses not fitted with corrective lenses (12.3.2).

06.2 OUTPATIENT SERVICES

This group covers medical, dental and paramedical services delivered to outpatients by medical, dental and paramedical practitioners and auxiliaries. The services may be delivered at home, in individual or group consulting facilities, dispensaries or the outpatient clinics of hospitals and the like.

Outpatient services include the medicaments, prostheses, medical appliances and equipment and other health-related products supplied directly to outpatients by medical, dental and paramedical practitioners and auxiliaries.

Medical, dental and paramedical services provided to in-patients by hospitals and the like are included in hospital services (06.3).

06.2.1 Medical services (S)

- Consultations of physicians in general or specialist practice.

Includes: services of orthodontic specialists.

Excludes: services of medical analysis laboratories and x-ray centres (06.2.3); services of practitioners of traditional medicine (06.2.3).

06.2.2 Dental services (S)

- Services of dentists, oral hygienists and other dental auxiliaries.

Includes: fitting costs of dentures.

Excludes: dentures (06.1.3); services of orthodontic specialists (06.2.1); services of medical analysis laboratories and x-ray centres (06.2.3).

06.2.3 Paramedical services (S)

- Services of medical analysis laboratories and x-ray centres;
- services of freelance nurses and midwives;
- services of freelance acupuncturists, chiropractors, optometrists, physiotherapists, speech therapists, etc.;
- medically prescribed corrective-gymnastic therapy;
- outpatient thermal bath or sea-water treatments;
- ambulance services;
- hire of therapeutic equipment.

Includes: services of practitioners of traditional medicine.

06.3 HOSPITAL SERVICES

Hospitalization is defined as occurring when a patient is accommodated in a hospital for the duration of the treatment. Hospital day-care and home-based hospital treatment are included, as are hospices for terminally ill persons.

This group covers the services of general and specialist hospitals, the services of medical centres, maternity centres, nursing homes and convalescent homes which chiefly provide in-patient health care, the services of institutions serving old people in which medical monitoring is an essential component and the services of rehabilitation centres providing in-patient health care and rehabilitative therapy where the objective is to treat the patient rather than to provide long-term support.

Hospitals are defined as institutions which offer in-patient care under direct supervision of qualified medical doctors. Medical centres, maternity centres, nursing homes and convalescent homes also provide in-patient care but their services are supervised and frequently delivered by staff of lower qualification than medical doctors.

This group does not cover the services of facilities, such as surgeries, clinics and dispensaries, devoted exclusively to outpatient care (06.2). Nor does it include the services of retirement homes for elderly persons, institutions for disabled persons and rehabilitation centres providing primarily long-term support (12.4).

06.3.0 Hospital services (S)

- Hospital services comprise the provision of the following services to hospital in-patients:
  - basic services: administration; accommodation; food and drink; supervision and care by non-specialist staff (nursing auxiliaries); first aid and resuscitation; ambulance transport; provision of medicines and other pharmaceutical products; provision of therapeutic appliances and equipment;
  - medical services: services of physicians in general or specialist practice, of surgeons and of dentists; medical analyses and x-rays; paramedical services such as those of nurses, midwives, chiropractors, optometrists, physiotherapists, speech therapists, etc.

07 TRANSPORT

07.1 PURCHASE OF VEHICLES

Purchases of recreational vehicles such as camper vans, caravans, trailers, aeroplanes and boats are covered by (09.2.1).

07.1.1 Motor cars (D)

- Motor cars, passenger vans, station wagons, estate cars and the like with either two-wheel drive or four-wheel drive.

Excludes: invalid carriages (06.1.3); camper vans (09.2.1); golf carts (09.2.1).

07.1.2 Motor cycles (D)

- Motor cycles of all types, scooters and powered bicycles.

Includes: sidecars; snowmobiles.

Excludes: invalid carriages (06.1.3); golf carts (09.2.1).

07.1.3 Bicycles (D)

- Bicycles and tricycles of all types.

Includes: rickshaws.

Excludes: toy bicycles and tricycles (09.3.1).

07.1.4 Animal-drawn vehicles (D)

- Animal-drawn vehicles.

Includes: animals required to draw the vehicles and related equipment (yokes, collars, harnesses, bridles, reins, etc.).

Excludes: horses and ponies, horse- or pony-drawn vehicles and related equipment purchased for recreational purposes (09.2.1).

07.2 OPERATION OF PERSONAL TRANSPORT EQUIPMENT

Purchases of spare parts, accessories or lubricants made by households with the intention of undertaking the maintenance, repair or intervention themselves should be shown under (07.2.1) or (07.2.2). If households pay an enterprise to carry out the maintenance, repair or fitting, the total value of the service, including the costs of the materials used, should be shown under (07.2.3).

07.2.1 Spare parts and accessories for personal transport equipment (SD)

- Tyres (new, used or retreaded), inner tubes, spark plugs, batteries, shock absorbers, filters, pumps and other spare parts or accessories for personal transport equipment.

Includes: fire extinguishers for transport equipment; products specifically for the cleaning and maintenance of transport equipment such as paints, chrome cleaners, sealing compounds and bodywork polishes; covers for motor cars, motorcycles, etc.

Excludes: crash helmets for motorcycles and bicycles (03.1.3); non-specific products for cleaning and maintenance such as distilled water, household sponges, chamois leathers, detergents, etc. (05.6.1); charges for the fitting of spare parts and accessories and for the painting, washing and polishing of bodywork (07.2.3); radio-telephones (08.2.0); car radios (09.1.1); baby seats for cars (12.3.2).

07.2.2 Fuels and lubricants for personal transport equipment (ND)

- Petrol and other fuels such as diesel, liquid petroleum gas, alcohol and two-stroke mixtures;
- lubricants, brake and transmission fluids, coolants and additives.

Includes: fuel for major tools and equipment covered under (05.5.1) and recreational vehicles covered under (09.2.1).

Excludes: charges for oil changes and greasing (07.2.3).

07.2.3 Maintenance and repair of personal transport equipment (S)

- Services purchased for the maintenance and repair of personal transport equipment such as fitting of parts and accessories, wheel balancing, technical inspection, breakdown services, oil changes, greasing and washing.

Includes: total value of the service (that is, both the cost of labour and the cost of materials are covered).

Excludes: separate purchases of spare parts, accessories or lubricants made by households with the intention of undertaking the maintenance or repair themselves (07.2.1) or (07.2.2); roadworthiness tests (07.2.4).

07.2.4 Other services in respect of personal transport equipment (S)

- Hire of garages or parking spaces not providing parking in connection with the dwelling;
- toll facilities (bridges, tunnels, shuttle ferries, motorways) and parking meters;
- driving lessons, driving tests and driving licences;
- roadworthiness tests;
- hire of personal transport equipment without drivers.

Excludes: hire of a car with driver (07.3.2); service charges for insurance in respect of personal transport equipment (12.5.4).

07.3 TRANSPORT SERVICES

Purchases of transport services are generally classified by mode of transport. When a ticket covers two or more modes of transport – for example, intra-urban bus and underground or inter-urban train and ferry – and the expenditure cannot be apportioned between them, then such purchases should be classified in (07.3.5).

Costs of meals, snacks, drinks, refreshments or accommodation services have to be included if covered by the fare and not separately priced. If separately priced, these costs have to be classified in Division 11.

School transport services are included, but ambulance services are excluded (06.2.3).

07.3.1 Passenger transport by railway (S)

- Transport of individuals and groups of persons and luggage by train, tram and underground.

Includes: transport of private vehicles.

Excludes: funicular transport (07.3.6).

07.3.2 Passenger transport by road (S)

- Transport of individuals and groups of persons and luggage by bus, coach, taxi and hired car with driver.

07.3.3 Passenger transport by air (S)

- Transport of individuals and groups of persons and luggage by aeroplane and helicopter.

07.3.4 Passenger transport by sea and inland waterway (S)

- Transport of individuals and groups of persons and luggage by ship, boat, ferry, hovercraft and hydrofoil.

Includes: transport of private vehicles.

07.3.5 Combined passenger transport (S)

- Transport of individuals and groups of persons and luggage by two or more modes of transport when the expenditure cannot be apportioned between them.

Includes: transport of private vehicles.

Excludes: package holidays (09.6.0).

07.3.6 Other purchased transport services (S)

- Funicular, cable-car and chairlift transport;
- removal and storage services;
- services of porters and left-luggage and luggage-forwarding offices;
- travel agents' commissions, if separately priced.

Excludes: cable-car and chairlift transport at ski resorts and holiday centres (09.4.1).

08 COMMUNICATION

08.1 POSTAL SERVICES

08.1.0 Postal services (S)

- Payments for the delivery of letters, postcards and parcels;
- private mail and parcel delivery.

Includes: all purchases of new postage stamps, pre-franked postcards and aerogrammes.

Excludes: purchase of used or cancelled postage stamps (09.3.1); financial services of post offices (12.6.2).

08.2 TELEPHONE AND TELEFAX EQUIPMENT

08.2.0 Telephone and telefax equipment (D)

- Purchases of telephones, radio-telephones, telefax machines, telephone-answering machines and telephone loudspeakers;
- repair of such equipment.

Excludes: telefax and telephone-answering facilities provided by personal computers (09.1.3).

08.3 TELEPHONE AND TELEFAX SERVICES

08.3.0 Telephone and telefax services (S)

- Installation and subscription costs of personal telephone equipment;
- telephone calls from a private line or from a public line (public telephone box, post office cabin, etc.); telephone calls from hotels, cafés, restaurants and the like;
- telegraphy, telex and telefax services;
- information transmission services; Internet connection services;
- hire of telephones, telefax machines, telephone-answering machines and telephone loudspeakers.

Includes: radio-telephony, radio-telegraphy and radiotelex services.

09 RECREATION AND CULTURE

09.1 AUDIO-VISUAL, PHOTOGRAPHIC AND INFORMATION PROCESSING EQUIPMENT

09.1.1 Equipment for the reception, recording and reproduction of sound and pictures (D)

- Television sets, video cassette players and recorders, television aerials of all types;
- radio sets, car radios, radio clocks, two-way radios, amateur radio receivers and transmitters;
- gramophones, tape players and recorders, cassette players and recorders, CD-players, personal stereos, stereo systems and their constituent units (turntables, tuners, amplifiers, speakers, etc.), microphones and earphones.

Excludes: video cameras, camcorders and sound-recording cameras (09.1.2).

09.1.2 Photographic and cinematographic equipment and optical instruments (D)

- Still cameras, movie cameras and sound-recording cameras, video cameras and camcorders, film and slide projectors, enlargers and film processing equipment, accessories (screens, viewers, lenses, flash attachments, filters, exposure meters, etc.);
- binoculars, microscopes, telescopes and compasses.

09.1.3 Information processing equipment (D)

- Personal computers, visual display units, printers and miscellaneous accessories accompanying them; computer software packages such as operating systems, applications, languages, etc.;
- calculators, including pocket calculators;
- typewriters and word processors.

Includes: telefax and telephone-answering facilities provided by personal computers.

Excludes: pre-recorded diskettes and CD-ROMs containing books, dictionaries, encyclopaedias, foreign language trainers, multimedia presentations, etc. in the form of software (09.1.4); video game software (09.3.1); video game computers that plug into a television set (09.3.1); typewriter ribbons (09.5.4); toner and ink cartridges (09.5.4); slide rules (09.5.4).

09.1.4 Recording media (SD)

- Records and compact discs;
- pre-recorded tapes, cassettes, video cassettes, diskettes and CD-ROMs for tape recorders,

cassette recorders, video recorders and personal computers;
- unrecorded tapes, cassettes, video cassettes, diskettes and CD-ROMs for tape recorders, cassette recorders, video recorders and personal computers;
- unexposed films, cartridges and disks for photographic and cinematographic use.

Includes: pre-recorded tapes and compact discs of novels, plays, poetry, etc.; pre-recorded diskettes and CD-ROMs containing books, dictionaries, encyclopaedias, foreign language trainers, multimedia presentations, etc. in the form of software; photographic supplies such as paper and flashbulbs; unexposed film the price of which includes the cost of processing without separately identifying it.

Excludes: batteries (05.5.2); computer software packages such as operating systems, applications, languages, etc. (09.1.3); video game software, video game cassettes and video game CD-ROMs (09.3.1); development of films and printing of photographs (09.4.2).

09.1.5 Repair of audio-visual, photographic and information processing equipment (S)

- Repair of audio-visual, photographic and information processing equipment.

Includes: total value of the service (that is, both the cost of labour and the cost of materials are covered).

Excludes: separate purchases of materials made by households with the intention of undertaking the repair themselves (09.1.1), (09.1.2) or (09.1.3).

09.2 OTHER MAJOR DURABLES FOR RECREATION AND CULTURE

09.2.1 Major durables for outdoor recreation (D)

- Camper vans, caravans and trailers;
- aeroplanes, microlight aircraft, gliders, hang-gliders and hot-air balloons;
- boats, outboard motors, sails, rigging and superstructures;
- horses and ponies, horse- or pony-drawn vehicles and related equipment (harnesses, bridles, reins, saddles, etc.);
- major items for games and sport such as canoes, kayaks, windsurfing boards, sea-diving equipment and golf carts.

Includes: fitting out of boats, camper vans, caravans, etc.

Excludes: horses and ponies, horse- or pony-drawn vehicles and related equipment purchased for personal transport (07.1.4); inflatable boats, rafts and swimming pools for children and the beach (09.3.2).

09.2.2 Musical instruments and major durables for indoor recreation (D)

- Musical instruments of all sizes, including electronic musical instruments, such as pianos, organs, violins, guitars, drums, trumpets, clarinets, flutes, recorders, harmonicas, etc.;
- billiard tables, ping-pong tables, pinball machines, gaming machines, etc.

Excludes: toys (09.3.1).

09.2.3 Maintenance and repair of other major durables for recreation and culture (S)

- Maintenance and repair of other major durables for recreation and culture.

Includes: total value of the service (that is, both the cost of labour and the cost of materials are covered); laying up for winter of boats, camper vans, caravans, etc.; hangar services for private planes; marina services for boats; veterinary and other services (stabling, feeding, farriery, etc.) for horses and ponies purchased for recreational purposes.

Excludes: fuel for recreational vehicles (07.2.2); separate purchases of materials made by households with the intention of undertaking the maintenance or repair themselves (09.2.1) or (09.2.2); veterinary and other services for pets (09.3.5).

09.3 OTHER RECREATIONAL ITEMS AND EQUIPMENT, GARDENS AND PETS

09.3.1 Games, toys and hobbies (SD)

- Card games, parlour games, chess sets and the like;
- toys of all kinds including dolls, soft toys, toy cars and trains, toy bicycles and tricycles, toy construction sets, puzzles, plasticine, electronic games, masks, disguises, jokes, novelties, fireworks and rockets, festoons and Christmas tree decorations;
- stamp-collecting requisites (used or cancelled postage stamps, stamp albums, etc.), other items for collections (coins, medals, minerals, zoological and botanical specimens, etc.) and other tools and articles n.e.c. for hobbies.

Includes: video-game software; video-game computers that plug into a television set; video-game cassettes and video-game CD-ROMs.

Excludes: collectors' items falling into the category of works of art or antiques (05.1.1); unused postage stamps (08.1.0); Christmas trees (09.3.3); children's scrapbooks (09.5.1).

09.3.2 Equipment for sport, camping and open-air recreation (SD)

- Gymnastic, physical education and sport equipment such as balls, shuttlecocks, nets, rackets, bats, skis, golf clubs, foils, sabres, poles, weights, discuses, javelins, dumb-bells, chest expanders and other body-building equipment;
- parachutes and other sky-diving equipment;
- firearms and ammunition for hunting, sport and personal protection;
- fishing rods and other equipment for fishing;
- equipment for beach and open-air games, such as bowls, croquet, frisbee, volleyball, and inflatable boats, rafts and swimming pools;
- camping equipment such as tents and accessories, sleeping bags, backpacks, air mattresses and inflating pumps, camping stoves and barbecues;
- repair of such articles.

Includes: game-specific footwear (ski boots, football boots, golfing shoes and other such footwear fitted with ice-skates, rollers, spikes, studs, etc.); protective headgear for sports; other protective gear for sports such as life jackets, boxing gloves, body padding, shin-guards, goggles, belts, supports, etc.

Excludes: crash helmets for motor cycles and bicycles (03.1.3); camping and garden furniture (05.1.1).

09.3.3 Gardens, plants and flowers (ND)

- Natural or artificial flowers and foliage, plants, shrubs, bulbs, tubers, seeds, fertilizers, composts, garden peat, turf for lawns, specially treated soils for ornamental gardens, horticultural preparations, pots and pot holders.

Includes: natural and artificial Christmas trees; delivery charges for flowers and plants.

Excludes: gardening gloves (03.1.3); gardening services (04.4.4) or (05.6.2); gardening equipment (05.5.1); gardening tools (05.5.2); insecticides and pesticides for household use (05.6.1).

09.3.4 Pets and related products (ND)

- Pets, pet foods, veterinary and grooming products for pets, collars, leashes, kennels, birdcages, fish tanks, cat litter, etc.

Excludes: horses and ponies (07.1.4) or (09.2.1); veterinary services (09.3.5).

09.3.5 Veterinary and other services for pets (S)

- Veterinary and other services for pets such as grooming, boarding, tattooing and training.

Excludes: veterinary and other services (stabling, farriery, etc.) for horses and ponies purchased for recreational purposes (09.2.3).

09.4 RECREATIONAL AND CULTURAL SERVICES

09.4.1 Recreational and sporting services (S)

- Services provided by:
  - sports stadiums, horse-racing courses, motor-racing circuits, velodromes, etc.;
  - skating rinks, swimming pools, golf courses, gymnasia, fitness centres, tennis courts, squash courts and bowling alleys;
  - fairgrounds and amusement parks;
  - roundabouts, see-saws and other playground facilities for children;
  - pin-ball machines and other games for adults other than games of chance;
  - ski slopes, ski lifts and the like;
- hire of equipment and accessories for sport and recreation, such as aeroplanes, boats, horses, skiing and camping equipment;
- out-of-school individual or group lessons in bridge, chess, aerobics, dancing, music, skating, skiing, swimming or other pastimes;
- services of mountain guides, tour guides, etc.;
- navigational aid services for boating.

Includes: hire of game-specific footwear (ski boots, football boots, golfing shoes and other such footwear fitted with ice-skates, rollers, spikes, studs, etc.).

Excludes: cable-car and chairlift transport not at ski resorts or holiday centres (07.3.6).

09.4.2 Cultural services (S)

- Services provided by:
  - cinemas, theatres, opera houses, concert halls, music halls, circuses, sound and light shows;
  - museums, libraries, art galleries, exhibitions;
  - historic monuments, national parks, zoological and botanical gardens, aquaria;
- hire of equipment and accessories for culture, such as television sets, video cassettes, etc.;
- television and radio broadcasting, in particular licence fees for television equipment and subscriptions to television networks;
- services of photographers such as film developing, print processing, enlarging, portrait photography, wedding photography, etc.

Includes: services of musicians, clowns, performers for private entertainments.

09.4.3 Games of chance (S)

- Service charges for lotteries, bookmakers, totalizators, casinos and other gambling establishments, gaming machines, bingo halls, scratch cards, sweepstakes, etc. (Service charge is defined as the difference between the amounts paid for lottery tickets or placed in bets and the amounts paid out to winners.)

09.5 NEWSPAPERS, BOOKS AND STATIONERY

09.5.1 Books (SD)

- Books, including atlases, dictionaries, encyclopaedias, textbooks, guidebooks and musical scores.

Includes: scrapbooks and albums for children; bookbinding.

Excludes: pre-recorded tapes and compact discs of novels, plays, poetry, etc. (09.1.4); pre-recorded diskettes and CD-ROMs containing books, dictionaries, encyclopaedias, foreign language trainers, etc. in the form of software (09.1.4); stamp albums (09.3.1).

09.5.2 Newspapers and periodicals (ND)

- Newspapers, magazines and other periodicals.

09.5.3 Miscellaneous printed matter (ND)

- Catalogues and advertising material;
- posters, plain or picture postcards, calendars;
- greeting cards and visiting cards, announcement and message cards;
- maps and globes.

Excludes: pre-franked postcards and aerogrammes (08.1.0); stamp albums (09.3.1).

09.5.4 Stationery and drawing materials (ND)

- Writing pads, envelopes, account books, notebooks, diaries, etc.;
- pens, pencils, fountain pens, ballpoint pens, felt-tip pens, inks, erasers, pencil sharpeners, etc.;
- stencils, carbon paper, typewriter ribbons, inking pads, correcting fluids, etc.;
- paper punches, paper cutters, paper scissors, office glues and adhesives, staplers and staples, paper clips, drawing pins, etc.;
- drawing and painting materials such as canvas, paper, card, paints, crayons, pastels and brushes.

Includes: toner and ink cartridges; educational materials such as exercise books, slide rules, geometry instruments, slates, chalks and pencil boxes.

Excludes: pocket calculators (09.1.3).

09.6 PACKAGE HOLIDAYS

09.6.0 Package holidays (S)

- All-inclusive holidays or tours which provide for travel, food, accommodation, guides, etc.

Includes: half-day and one-day excursion tours; pilgrimages.

10 EDUCATION

This division covers educational services only. It does not include expenditures on educational materials, such as books (09.5.1) and stationery (09.5.4), or education support services, such as health-care services (06), transport services (07.3), catering services (11.1.2) and accommodation services (11.2.0).

It includes education by radio or television broadcasting.

The breakdown of educational services is based upon the level categories of the 1997 International Standard Classification of Education (ISCED-97) of the United Nations Educational, Scientific and Cultural Organization (UNESCO).

10.1 PRE-PRIMARY AND PRIMARY EDUCATION

10.1.0 Pre-primary and primary education (S)

- Levels 0 and 1 of ISCED-97: pre-primary and primary education.

Includes: literacy programmes for students too old for primary school.

10.2 SECONDARY EDUCATION

10.2.0 Secondary education (S)

- Levels 2 and 3 of ISCED-97: lower-secondary and upper-secondary education.

Includes: out-of-school secondary education for adults and young people.

10.3 POST-SECONDARY NON-TERTIARY EDUCATION

10.3.0 Post-secondary non-tertiary education (S)

- Level 4 of ISCED-97: post-secondary non-tertiary education.

Includes: out-of-school post-secondary non-tertiary education for adults and young people.

10.4 TERTIARY EDUCATION

10.4.0 Tertiary education (S)

– Levels 5 and 6 of ISCED-97: first stage and second stage of tertiary education.

10.5 EDUCATION NOT DEFINABLE BY LEVEL

10.5.0 Education not definable by level (S)

– Educational programmes, generally for adults, which do not require any special prior instruction, in particular vocational training and cultural development.

Excludes: driving lessons (07.2.4); recreational training courses such as sport or bridge lessons given by independent teachers (09.4.1).

11 RESTAURANTS AND HOTELS

11.1 CATERING SERVICES

11.1.1 Restaurants, cafés and the like (S)

– Catering services (meals, snacks, drinks and refreshments) provided by restaurants, cafés, buffets, bars, tearooms, etc., including those provided:
  - in places providing recreational, cultural, sporting or entertainment services: theatres, cinemas, sports stadiums, swimming pools, sports complexes, museums, art galleries, nightclubs, dancing establishments, etc.;
  - on public transport (coaches, trains, boats, aeroplanes, etc.) when priced separately;

– also included are:
  - the sale of food products and beverages for immediate consumption by kiosks, street vendors and the like, including food products and beverages dispensed ready for consumption by automatic vending machines;
  - the sale of cooked dishes by restaurants for consumption off their premises;
  - the sale of cooked dishes by catering contractors whether collected by the customer or delivered to the customer's home.

Includes: tips.

Excludes: tobacco purchases (02.2.0); telephone calls (08.3.0).

11.1.2 Canteens (S)

– Catering services of works canteens, office canteens and canteens in schools, universities and other educational establishments.

Includes: university refectories, military messes and wardrooms.

Excludes: food and drink provided to hospital in-patients (06.3.0).

11.2 ACCOMMODATION SERVICES

11.2.0 Accommodation services (S)

– Accommodation services of:
  - hotels, boarding houses, motels, inns and establishments offering "bed and breakfast";
  - holiday villages and holiday centres, camping and caravan sites, youth hostels and mountain chalets;
  - boarding schools, universities and other educational establishments;
  - public transport (trains, boats, etc.) when priced separately;
  - hostels for young workers or immigrants.

Includes: tips, porters.

Excludes: payments of households occupying a room in a hotel or boarding house as their main residence (04.1.1); rentals paid by households for a secondary residence for the duration of a holiday (04.1.2); telephone calls (08.3.0); catering services in such establishments except for breakfast or other meals included in the price of the accommodation (11.1.1); housing in orphanages, homes for disabled or maladjusted persons (12.4.0).

12 MISCELLANEOUS GOODS AND SERVICES

12.1 PERSONAL CARE

12.1.1 Hairdressing salons and personal grooming establishments (S)

– Services of hairdressing salons, barbers, beauty shops, manicures, pedicures, Turkish baths, saunas, solariums, non-medical massages, etc.

Includes: bodycare, depilation and the like.

Excludes: spas (06.2.3) or (06.3.0); fitness centres (09.4.1).

12.1.2 Electric appliances for personal care (SD)

– Electric razors and hair trimmers, hand-held and hood hairdryers, curling tongs and styling combs, sunlamps, vibrators, electric toothbrushes and other electric appliances for dental hygiene, etc.;

– repair of such appliances.

12.1.3 Other appliances, articles and products for personal care (ND)

- Non-electric appliances: razors and hair trimmers and blades therefor, scissors, nail files, combs, shaving brushes, hairbrushes, toothbrushes, nail brushes, hairpins, curlers, personal weighing machines, baby scales, etc.;
- articles for personal hygiene: toilet soap, medicinal soap, cleansing oil and milk, shaving soap, shaving cream and foam, toothpaste, etc.;
- beauty products: lipstick, nail varnish, make-up and make-up removal products (including powder compacts, brushes and powder puffs), hair lacquers and lotions, pre-shave and after-shave products, sunbathing products, hair removers, perfumes and toilet waters, personal deodorants, bath products, etc.;
- other products: toilet paper, paper handkerchiefs, paper towels, sanitary towels, cotton wool, cotton tops, babies' napkins, toilet sponges, etc.

Excludes: handkerchiefs made of fabric (03.1.3).

12.2 PROSTITUTION

12.2.0 Prostitution (S)

- Services provided by prostitutes and the like.

12.3 PERSONAL EFFECTS N.E.C.

12.3.1 Jewellery, clocks and watches (D)

- Precious stones and metals and jewellery fashioned out of such stones and metals;
- costume jewellery, cuff links and tiepins;
- clocks, watches, stopwatches, alarm clocks, travel clocks;
- repair of such articles.

Excludes: ornaments (05.1.1) or (05.4.0); radio clocks (09.1.1); precious stones and metals and jewellery fashioned out of such stones and metals acquired primarily as stores of value (capital formation).

12.3.2 Other personal effects (SD)

- Travel goods and other carriers of personal effects: suitcases, trunks, travel bags, attaché cases, satchels, hand-bags, wallets, purses, etc.;
- articles for babies: baby carriages, push-chairs, carrycots, recliners, car beds and seats, back-carriers, front carriers, reins and harnesses, etc.;
- articles for smokers: pipes, lighters, cigarette cases, cigar cutters, ashtrays, etc.;
- miscellaneous personal articles: sunglasses, walking sticks and canes, umbrellas and parasols, fans, keyrings, etc.;
- funerary articles: coffins, gravestones, urns, etc.;
- repair of such articles.

Includes: lighter fuel; wall thermometers and barometers.

Excludes: baby furniture (05.1.1); shopping bags (05.2.0); feeding bottles (05.4.0).

12.4 SOCIAL PROTECTION

Social protection as defined here covers assistance and support services provided to persons who are: elderly, disabled, having occupational injuries and diseases, survivors, unemployed, destitute, homeless, low-income earners, indigenous people, immigrants, refugees, alcohol and substance abusers, etc. It also covers assistance and support services provided to families and children.

12.4.0 Social protection (S)

Such services include residential care, home help, day care and rehabilitation. More specifically, this class covers payments by households for:

- Retirement homes for elderly persons, residences for disabled persons, rehabilitation centres providing long-term support for patients rather than health care and rehabilitative therapy, schools for disabled persons where the main aim is to help students overcome their disability;
- help to maintain elderly and disabled persons at home (home-cleaning services, meal programmes, day-care centres, day-care services and holiday-care services);
- wet-nurses, crèches, play schools and other child-minding facilities;
- counselling, guidance, arbitration, fostering and adoption services for families.

12.5 INSURANCE

Service charges for insurance are classified by type of insurance, namely: life insurance and non-life insurance (that is, insurance in connection with the dwelling, health, transport, etc.). Service charges for multi-risk insurance covering several risks should be classified on the basis of the cost of the principal risk if it is not possible to allocate the service charges to the various risks covered.

Service charge is defined as the difference between claims due and premiums earned and premium supplement.

12.5.1 Life insurance (S)

- Service charges for life assurance, death benefit assurance, education assurance, etc.

12.5.2 Insurance connected with the dwelling (S)

- Service charges paid by owner-occupiers and by tenants for the kinds of insurance typically taken out by tenants against fire, theft, water damage, etc.

Excludes: service charges paid by owner-occupiers for the kinds of insurance typically taken out by landlords (intermediate consumption).

12.5.3 Insurance connected with health (S)

- Service charges for private sickness and accident insurance.

12.5.4 Insurance connected with transport (S)

- Service charges for insurance in respect of personal transport equipment;
- service charges for travel insurance and luggage insurance.

12.5.5 Other insurance (S)

- Service charges for other insurance such as civil liability for injury or damage to third parties or their property.

Excludes: civil liability or damage to third parties or their property arising from the operation of personal transport equipment (12.5.4).

12.6 FINANCIAL SERVICES N.E.C.

12.6.1 FISIM (S)

- Financial intermediation services indirectly measured.

12.6.2 Other financial services n.e.c. (S)

- Actual charges for the financial services of banks, post offices, saving banks, money changers and similar financial institutions;
- fees and service charges of brokers, investment counsellors, tax consultants and the like;
- administrative charges of private pension funds and the like.

12.7 OTHER SERVICES N.E.C.

12.7.0 Other services n.e.c. (S)

- Fees for legal services, employment agencies, etc.;
- charges for undertaking and other funeral services;
- payment for the services of estate agents, housing agents, auctioneers, salesroom operators and other intermediaries;
- payment for photocopies and other reproductions of documents;
- fees for the issue of birth, marriage and death certificates and other administrative documents;
- payment for newspaper notices and advertisements;
- payment for the services of graphologists, astrologers, private detectives, bodyguards, matrimonial agencies and marriage guidance counsellors, public writers, miscellaneous concessions (seats, toilets, cloakrooms), etc.

Annex 3

Resolution concerning consumer price indices adopted by the Seventeenth International Conference of Labour Statisticians, 2003

Preamble*

The Seventeenth International Conference of Labour Statisticians,

Having been convened at Geneva by the Governing Body of the ILO and having met from 24 November to 3 December 2003,

Recalling the resolution adopted by the Fourteenth International Conference of Labour Statisticians concerning consumer price indices and recognizing the continuing validity of the basic principles recommended therein and, in particular, the fact that the consumer price index (CPI) is designed primarily to measure the changes over time in the general level of prices of goods and services that a reference population acquires, uses or pays for,

Recognizing the need to modify and broaden the existing standards in the light of recent methodological and computational developments to enhance the usefulness of the international standards in the provision of technical guidelines to all countries,

Recognizing the usefulness of such standards in enhancing the international comparability of the statistics,

Recognizing that the CPI is used for a wide variety of purposes and that governments should be encouraged to identify the (priority) purposes a CPI is to serve, to provide adequate resources for its compilation, and to guarantee the professional independence of its compilers,

Recognizing that the (priority) objectives and uses of a CPI differ among countries and that, therefore, a single standard could not be applied universally,

Recognizing that the CPI needs to be credible to observers and users, both national and international, and that better understanding of the principles and procedures used to compile the index will enhance the users' confidence in the index,

Agrees that the principles and methods used in constructing a CPI should be based on the guidelines and methods that are generally accepted as constituting good statistical practices;

Adopts, this third day of December 2003, the following resolution which replaces the previous one adopted in 1987:

The nature and meaning of a consumer price index

1. The CPI is a current social and economic indicator that is constructed to measure changes over time in the general level of prices of consumer goods and services that households acquire, use or pay for consumption.

2. The index aims to measure the change in consumer prices over time. This may be done by measuring the cost of purchasing a fixed basket of consumer goods and services of constant quality and similar characteristics, with the products in the basket being selected to be representative of households' expenditure during a year or other specified period. Such an index is called a fixed basket price index.

3. The index may also aim to measure the effects of price changes on the cost of achieving a constant standard of living (i.e. level of utility or welfare). This concept is called a cost-of-living index (COLI). A fixed basket price index, or another appropriate design, may be employed as an approximation to a COLI.

The uses of a consumer price index

4. The CPI is used for a wide variety of purposes, the two most common ones being: (i) to adjust wages as well as social security and other benefits to compensate, partly or completely, for changes in the cost of living or in consumer prices; and (ii) to provide an average measure of price inflation for the household sector as a whole, for use as a macroeconomic indicator. CPI sub-indices are also used to deflate components of household final consumption expenditure in the national accounts and the value of retail sales to obtain estimates of changes in their volume.

5. CPIs are also used for other purposes, such as monitoring the overall rate of price inflation for all sectors of the economy, the adjustment of government fees and charges, the adjustment of payments in commercial contracts, and for formulating and assessing fiscal and monetary policies and trade and exchange rate policies. In these types of cases, the CPI is used as more appropriate measures do not exist at present, or because other characteristics of the CPI (e.g. high profile, wide acceptance, predictable publication schedule, etc.) are seen to outweigh any conceptual or technical deficiencies.

6. Given that the CPI may be used for many purposes, it is unlikely that one index can perform equally satisfactorily in all applications. It may therefore be appropriate to construct a number of alternative price indices for specific purposes, if the requirements of the users justify the extra expense. Each index should be properly defined and named to avoid confusion and a "headline" CPI measure should be explicitly identified.

7. Where only one index is compiled, it is the main use that should determine the type of index compiled, the range of goods and services covered, its geographic coverage, the households it relates to, as well as to the concept of price and the formula used. If there are several major uses, it is likely that compromises may have to be made with regard to how the CPI is constructed. Users should be informed of the compromises made and of the limitations of such an index.

Scope of the index

8. The scope of the index depends on the main use for which it is intended, and should be defined in terms of

*All annexes referred to in the footnotes are the annexes to the resolution.

the type of households, geographic areas, and the categories of consumer goods and services acquired, used or paid for by the reference population.

9. If the primary use of the CPI is for adjusting money incomes, a relevant group of households, such as wage and salary earners, may be the appropriate target population. For this use, all consumption expenditures by these households, at home and abroad, may be covered. If the primary use of the CPI is to measure inflation in the domestic economy, it may be appropriate to cover consumption expenditures made within the country, rather than the expenditures of households resident within the country.

10. In general, the reference population for a national index should be defined very widely. If any income groups, types of households or particular geographic areas are excluded, for example, for cost or practical considerations, then this should be explicitly stated.

11. The geographic scope refers to the geographic coverage of price collection and of consumption expenditures of the reference population and both should be defined as widely as possible, and preferably consistently. If price collection is restricted to particular areas due to resource constraints, then this should be specified. The geographic coverage of the consumption expenditure may be defined either as covering consumption expenditure of the resident population (resident consumption) or consumption expenditure within the country (domestic consumption).

12. Significant differences in the expenditure patterns and/or price movements between specific population groups or regions may exist, and care should be taken to ensure that they are represented in the index. Separate indices for these population groups or regions may be computed if there is sufficient demand to justify the additional cost.

13. In accordance with its main purpose, the CPI should conceptually cover all types of consumer goods and services of significance to the reference population, without any omission of those that may not be legally available or may be considered socially undesirable. Where appropriate, special aggregates may be constructed to assist those users who may wish to exclude certain categories of goods or services for particular applications or for analysis. Whenever certain goods or services have been excluded from the index, this should be clearly documented.

14. Goods and services purchased for business purposes, expenditures on assets such as works of art, financial investment (as distinct from financial services), and payments of income taxes, social security contributions and fines are not considered to be consumer goods or services and should be excluded from the coverage of the index. Some countries regard expenditures on the purchase of houses entirely as a capital investment and, as such, exclude them from the index.

Acquisition, use or payment

15. In determining the scope of the index, the time of recording and valuation of consumption, it is important to consider whether the purposes for which the index is used are best satisfied by defining consumption in terms of "acquisition", "use", or "payment".[1] The "acquisition" approach is often used when the primary purpose of the index is to serve as a macroeconomic indicator. The "payment" approach is often used when the primary purpose of the index is for the adjustment of compensation or income. Where the aim of the index is to measure changes in the cost of living, the "use" approach may be most suitable. The decision regarding the approach to follow for a particular group of products should in principle be based on the purpose of the index, as well as on the costs and the acceptability of the decision to the users who should be informed of the approach followed for different products. Because of the practical difficulties in uniformly defining consumption and estimating the flow of services provided by other durable goods in terms of "use", it may be necessary to adopt a mixed approach, e.g. "use" for owner-occupied housing and "acquisition" or "payment" basis for other consumer durables.

16. The differences between the three approaches are most pronounced in dealing with products for which the times of acquisition, use and payment do not coincide, such as owner-occupied housing, durable goods and products acquired on credit.

17. The most complex and important of the products mentioned above is owner-occupied housing. In most countries, a significant proportion of households are owner-occupiers of their housing, with the housing being characterized by a long useful life and a high purchase outlay (price). Under the "acquisition" approach, the value of the new dwellings acquired in the weight reference period may be used for deriving the weight (and the full price of the dwelling is included in the CPI at the time of acquisition, regardless of when the consumption is taking place). Under the "payment" approach, the weights reflect the amounts actually paid out for housing (and the prices enter the CPI in the period(s) when the prices are paid). Under the "use" approach the weights are based on the value of the flow of housing services consumed during the weight reference period estimated using an implicit or notional cost (and prices or estimated opportunity costs enter the CPI when the consumption is taking place).

18. Own-account consumption, remuneration in kind and/or goods and services provided without charge or subsidized by governments and non-profit institutions serving households may be important in some countries where the purpose of the index is best satisfied by defining consumption in terms of "use" or "acquisition" (under the payment approach these are out of scope). The inclusion of these products will require special valuation and pricing techniques.

Basket and weights

19. Decisions on the composition of the basket and the weights follow directly from the scope, as well as from the choice between the "acquisition", "use" or "payment" approaches.

[1]See Annex 1.

20. Once defined, the expenditures that fall within the scope of the index should be grouped into similar categories in a hierarchical classification system, e.g. divisions/groups/classes, for compilation as well as analytical purposes. There should be consistency between the classification used for index compilation and the one used for household expenditure statistics. The CPI classification should meet the needs of users for special sub-indices. For the purposes of international comparisons, the classification should also be reconcilable with the most recent version of the UN *Classification of Individual Consumption according to Purpose* (COICOP), at least at its division level.[2]

21. In order to facilitate the analysis and interpretation of the results of the index, it may be desirable to classify goods and services according to various supplementary classifications, e.g. source of origin, durability and seasonality. Calculation of the CPI by using various classifications should generate the same overall results as the original index.

22. The classification should also provide a framework for the allocation of expenditure weights. Expenditures at the lowest level of the classification system, expressed as a proportion of the total expenditure, determine the weights to be used at this level. When the weights are to remain fixed for several years, the objective should be to adopt weights that are representative of the contemporary household behaviour.

23. The two main sources for deriving the weights are the results from household expenditure surveys (HESs) and national accounts estimates on household consumption expenditure. The results from an HES are appropriate for an index defined to cover the consumption expenditures of reference population groups resident within the country, while national account estimates are suitable for an index defined to cover consumption expenditures within the country. The decision about what source or sources to use and how they should be used depends on the main purpose of the index and on the availability and quality of appropriate data.

24. The information from the main source (HESs or national accounts) should be supplemented with all other available information on the expenditure pattern. Sources of such information that can be used for disaggregating the expenditures are surveys of sales in retail outlets, point-of-purchase surveys, surveys of production, export and import data and administrative sources. Based on these data the weights for certain products may be further disaggregated by region and type of outlet. Where the data obtained from different sources relate to different periods, it is important to ensure, before weights are allocated, that expenditures are adjusted so that they have the same reference period.

25. Where the weight reference period differs significantly from the price reference period, the weights should be price updated to take account of price changes between the weight reference period and price reference period. Where it is likely that price-updated weights are less representative of the consumption pattern in the price reference period this procedure may be omitted.

26. Weights should be reviewed and if appropriate revised as often as accurate and reliable data are available for this to be done, but at least once every five years. Revisions are important to reduce the impact on the index of product substitutions and to ensure the basket of goods and services and their weights remain representative.[3] For some categories, it may be necessary to update the weights more frequently as such weights are likely to become out of date more quickly than higher-level weights. In periods of high inflation, the weights should be updated frequently.

27. When a new basket (structure or weights) replaces the old, a continuous CPI series should be created by linking[4] together the index numbers based on the new basket of goods and services to those based on the earlier basket. The particular procedure used to link index number series will depend on the particular index compilation technique used. The objective is to ensure that the technique used to introduce a new basket does not, of itself, alter the level of the index.

28. Completely new types of goods and services (i.e. goods and services that cannot be classified to any of the existing elementary aggregates) should normally be considered for inclusion only during one of the periodic review and reweighting exercises. A new model or variety of an existing product that can be fitted within an existing elementary aggregate should be included at the time it is assessed as having a significant and sustainable market share. If a quality change is detected an appropriate quality adjustment should be made.[5]

29. Some products such as seasonal products, insurance, second-hand goods, expenditure abroad, interest, own production, expenditures on purchase and construction of dwellings, etc., may need special treatment when constructing their weights. The way these products are dealt with should be determined by the main purpose of the index, national circumstances and the practicalities of compilation.

30. Seasonal products should be included in the basket. It is possible to use: (i) a fixed weight approach which uses the same weight for the seasonal product in all months using an imputed price in the out-of-season months; or (ii) a variable weights approach where a changing weight is attached to the product in various months. The decision on the approach should be based on national circumstances.

31. The expenditure weights for second-hand goods should be based either on the net expenditure of the reference population on such goods, or the gross expenditure, depending on the purpose of the index.

32. When consumption from own production is within the scope of the index, the weights should be based on the value of quantities consumed from own production. Valuation of consumption from own production should be made on the basis of prices prevailing

[2] See Annex 4.

[3] See Annex 1.

[4] See Annex 2.

[5] See Annex 2.

on the market, unless there is some reason to conclude that market prices are not relevant or cannot be reliably observed, or there is no interest in using hypothetically imputed prices. In this case the expenditures and prices for the inputs into the production of these goods and services could be used instead. The third option is to valuate it by using quality-adjusted market prices.

Sampling for price collection

33. A CPI is an estimate based on a sample of households to estimate weights, and a sample of zones within regions, a sample of outlets, a sample of goods and services and a sample of time periods for price observation.

34. The sample size and sample selection methods for both outlets and the goods and services for which price movements over time are to be observed should ensure that the prices collected are representative and sufficient to meet the requirements for the accuracy of the index, but also that the collection process is cost-effective. The sample of prices should reflect the importance, in terms of relative expenditures, of the goods and services available for purchase by consumers in the reference period, the number, types and geographic spread of outlets that are relevant for each good and service, and the dispersion of prices and price changes across outlets.

35. Probability sampling techniques are the preferred methods, in principle, as they permit sound statistical inference and control over the representativity of the sample. In addition, they permit estimation of sampling variation (errors). However, they may be costly to implement and can result in the selection of products that are very difficult to price to constant quality.

36. In cases where appropriate sampling frames are lacking and it is too costly to obtain them, samples of outlets and products have to be obtained by non-probability methods. Statisticians should use available information and apply their best judgement to ensure that representative samples are selected. The possibility of applying cut-off or detailed quota sampling[6] strategy may be considered, especially where the sample size is small. A mixture of probability and non-probability sampling techniques may be used.

37. Efficient and representative sampling, whether random or purposive, requires comprehensive and up-to-date sampling frames for outlets and products. Sample selection can be done either by head office from centrally held sampling frames, or in the field by price collectors, or by a mixture of the two. In the first case, price collectors should be given precise instructions on which outlets to visit and which products to price. In the second case, price collectors should be given detailed and unambiguous guidelines on the local sampling procedures to be adopted. Statistical business registers, business telephone directories, results from the point-of-purchase surveys or from surveys of sales in different types of outlets, and lists of Internet sellers may be used as sampling frames for the central selection of outlets. Catalogues or other product lists drawn up by major manufacturers, wholesalers or trade associations, or lists of products that are specific to individual outlets such as large supermarkets might be used as the sampling frame for selection of products. Data scanned by bar-code readers at the cashier's desk (electronic databases) can be particularly helpful in the selection of goods and services.

38. The sample of outlets and of goods and services should be reviewed periodically and updated where necessary to maintain its representativeness.

Index calculation

39. The compilation of a CPI consists of collecting and processing price and expenditure data according to specified concepts, definitions, methods and practices. The detailed procedures that are applied will depend on particular circumstances.

40. CPIs are calculated in steps. In the first step, the elementary aggregate indices are calculated. In the subsequent steps, higher-level indices are calculated by aggregating the elementary aggregate indices.

Elementary aggregate indices

41. The elementary aggregate is the smallest and relatively homogeneous set of goods or services for which expenditure data are defined (used) for CPI purposes. It is the only aggregate for which an index number is constructed without any explicit expenditure weights, although other kinds of weights might be explicitly or implicitly introduced into the calculation. The set of goods or services covered by an elementary aggregate should be similar in their end-uses and are expected to have similar price movements. They may be defined not only in terms of their characteristics but also in terms of the type of location and outlet in which they are sold. The degree of homogeneity achieved in practice will depend on the availability of corresponding expenditure data.

42. An elementary index is a price index for an elementary aggregate. As expenditure weights usually cannot be attached to the prices or price relatives for the sampled products within the elementary aggregate, an elementary index is usually calculated as an unweighted average of the prices or price relatives. When some information on weights is available, this should be taken into account when compiling the elementary indices.

43. There are several ways in which the prices, or the price relatives, might be averaged. The three most commonly used formulae are the ratio of arithmetic mean prices (RAP), the geometric mean (GM) and the arithmetic mean of price relatives (APR). The choice of formula depends on the purpose of the index, the sample design and the mathematical properties of the formula. It is possible to use different formulae for different elementary aggregates within the same CPI. It is recommended that the GM formula be used, particularly where there is a need to reflect substitution within the elementary aggregate or where the dispersion in prices or price changes within the elementary aggregate is large. The GM has many advantages because of its mathematical properties. The RAP may be used for

[6]See Annex 1.

elementary aggregates that are homogeneous and where consumers have only limited opportunity to substitute or where substitution is not to be reflected in the index. The APR formula should be avoided in its chained form, as it is known to result in biased estimates of the elementary indices.

44. The elementary index may be computed by using either a chained or direct form of the formula chosen. The use of a chained form may make the estimation of missing prices and the introduction of replacement products easier.

Upper-level indices

45. These price indices are constructed as weighted averages of elementary aggregate indices. Several types of formulae can be used to average the elementary aggregate indices. In order to compile a timely index, the practical option is to use a formula that relies on the weights relating to some past period. One such formula is the Laspeyres-type index, the formula used by most national statistical agencies.

46. For some purposes it may be appropriate to calculate the index retrospectively by using an index number formula that employs both base period weights and current period weights, such as the Fisher, Törnqvist or Walsh index. Comparing the difference between the index of this type and the Laspeyres-type index can give some indication of the combined impact of income changes, preference changes and substitution effects over the period in question, providing important information for producers and users of the CPI.

47. Where the change in an upper-level index between two consecutive periods such as $t-1$ and t is calculated as the weighted average of the individual indices between $t-1$ and t, care should be taken to ensure that the weights are updated to take account of the price changes between the price reference period 0 and the preceding period $t-1$. Failure to do so may result in a biased index.

Price observations

48. The number and quality of the prices collected are critical determinants of the reliability of the index, along with the specifications of the products priced. Standard methods for collecting and processing price information should be developed and procedures put in place for collecting them systematically and accurately at regular intervals. Price collectors should be well trained and well supervised, and should be provided with a comprehensive manual explaining the procedures they have to follow.

Collection

49. An important consideration is whether the index or parts of the index should relate to monthly (or quarterly) average prices or to prices for a specific period of time (e.g. a single day or week in a month). This decision is related to a number of issues, which include the use of an index, the practicalities of carrying out price collection and the pattern of price movements. When point-in-time pricing is adopted, prices should be collected over a very small number of days each month (or quarter). The interval between price observations should be uniform for each product. Since the length of the month (or quarter) varies, this uniformity needs to be defined carefully. When the aim is monthly (or quarterly) average prices, the prices collected should be representative of the period to which they refer.

50. Attention should also be paid to the time of day selected for price observation. For example, in the case of perishable goods, price observations may need to be collected at the same time on the same day of the week and not just before closing time, when stocks may be low, or sold cheaply to minimize wastage.

51. Price collection should be carried out in such a way as to be representative of all geographical areas within the scope of the index. Special care should be taken where significant differences in price movements between areas may be expected.

52. Prices should be collected in all types of outlets that are important, including Internet sellers, open-air markets and informal markets, and in free markets as well as price-controlled markets. Where more than one type of outlet is important for a particular type of product, this should be reflected in the initial sample design and an appropriately weighted average should be used in the calculation of the index.

53. Specifications should be provided detailing the variety and size of the products for which price information is to be collected. These should be precise enough to identify all the price-determining characteristics that are necessary to ensure that, as far as possible, the same goods and services are priced in successive periods in the same outlet. The specifications should include, for example, make, model, size, terms of payment, conditions of delivery, type of guarantees and type of outlet. This information could be used in the procedures used for replacement and for quality adjustment.

54. Prices to be collected are actual transaction prices, including indirect taxes and non-conditional discounts, that would be paid, agreed or costed (accepted) by the reference population. Where prices are not displayed or have to be negotiated, where quantity units are poorly defined or where actual purchase prices may deviate from listed or fixed prices, it may be necessary for the price collectors to purchase products in order to determine the transaction prices. A budget may be provided for any such purchases. When this is not possible, consideration may be given to interviewing customers about the prices actually paid. Tips for services, where compulsory, should be treated as part of the price paid.

55. Exceptional prices charged for stale, shop-soiled, damaged or otherwise imperfect goods sold at clearance prices should be excluded, unless the sale of such products is a permanent and widespread phenomenon. Sale prices, discounts, cut prices and special offers should be included when applicable to all customers without there being significant limits to the quantities that can be purchased by each customer.

56. In periods of price control or rationing, where limited supplies are available at prices which are held at a low level by measures such as subsidies to the sellers, government procurement, price control, etc., such prices as well as those charged on any significant unrestricted markets should be collected. The different price observations should be combined in a way that uses the best information available with respect to the actual prices paid and the relative importance of the different types of sales.

57. For each type of product, different alternatives for collecting prices should be carefully investigated, to ensure that the price observations could be made reliably and effectively. Means of collection could include visits to outlets with paper forms or hand-held devices, interviews with customers, computer-assisted telephone interviews, mail-out questionnaires, brochures, price lists provided by large or monopoly suppliers of services, scanner data and prices posted on the Internet. For each alternative, the possible cost advantages need to be balanced against an assessment of the reliability and timeliness of each of the alternatives.

58. Where centrally regulated or centrally fixed prices are collected from the regulatory authorities, checks should be made to ascertain whether the goods and services in question are actually sold and whether these prices are in fact paid. For goods and services where the prices paid are determined by combinations of subscription fees and piece rates (e.g. for newspapers, journals, public transport, electricity and telecommunications) care must be taken to ensure that a representative range of price offers is observed. Care must also be taken to ensure that prices charged to different types of consumers are observed, e.g. those linked to the age of the purchaser or to memberships of particular associations.

59. The collected price information should be reviewed for comparability and consistency with previous observations, the presence of replacements, unusual or large price changes and to ensure that price conversions of goods priced in multiple units or varying quantities are properly calculated. Extremely large or unusual price changes should be examined to determine whether they are genuine price changes or are due to changes in quality. Procedures should be put in place for checking the reliability of all price observations. This could include a programme of direct pricing and/or selective repricing of some products shortly after the initial observation was made.

60. Consistent procedures should be established for dealing with missing price observations because of, e.g. inability to contact the seller, non-response, observation rejected as unreliable or products temporarily unavailable. Prices of non-seasonal products that are temporarily unavailable should be estimated until they reappear or are replaced, by using appropriate estimation procedures, e.g. imputation on the basis of price changes of similar non-missing products. Carrying forward the last observed price should be avoided, especially in periods of high inflation.

Replacements

61. Replacement of a product will be necessary when it disappears permanently. Replacement should be made within the first three months (quarter) of the product becoming unavailable. It may also be necessary when the product is no longer available or sold in significant quantities or under normal sale conditions. Clear and precise rules should be developed for selecting the replacement product. Depending on the frequency of sampling and the potential for accurate quality adjustment, the most commonly used alternatives are to select: (i) the most similar to the replaced variety; (ii) the most popular variety among those that belong to the same elementary aggregate; and (iii) the variety most likely to be available in the future. Precise procedures should be laid down for price adjustments with respect to the difference in characteristics when replacements are necessary, so that the impact of changes in quality is excluded from the observed price.

62. Replacement of an outlet may be motivated if prices cannot be obtained, e.g. because it has closed permanently, because of a decline in representativeness or because the outlet no longer cooperates. Clear rules should be established on when to discontinue price observations from a selected outlet, on the criteria for selecting a replacement, as well as on the adjustments that may be required to price observations or weights. Such rules should be consistent with the objectives of the index and with the way in which the outlet sample has been determined.

63. Deletion of an entire elementary aggregate will be necessary if all products in that elementary aggregate disappear from most or all outlets and it is not possible to locate a sufficient number of price observations to continue to compile a reliable index for this elementary aggregate. In such situations, it is necessary to redistribute the weight assigned to the elementary aggregate among the other elementary aggregates included in the next level of aggregation.

Quality changes

64. The same product should be priced in each period as long as it is representative. However, in practice, products that can be observed at different time periods may differ with respect to package sizes, weights, volumes, features and terms of sale, as well as other characteristics. Thus it is necessary to monitor the characteristics of the products being priced to ensure that the impact of any differences in price-relevant or utility-relevant characteristics can be excluded from the estimated price change.

65. Identifying changes in quality or utility is relatively more difficult for complex durable goods and services. It is necessary, therefore, to collect a considerable amount of information on the relevant characteristics of the products for which prices are collected. The most important information can be obtained in the course of collecting prices. Other sources of information on price-relevant or utility-relevant characteristics can be producers, importers or wholesalers of the goods included and the study of articles and advertisements in trade publications.

66. When a quality change is detected, an adjustment must be made to the price, so that the index reflects as nearly as possible the pure price change. If this is not done, the index will either record a price change that has not taken place or fail to record a price change that did happen. The choice of method for such adjustments will depend on the particular goods and services involved. Great care needs to be exercised because the accuracy of the resulting index depends on the quality of this process. To assume automatically that all price change is a reflection of the change in quality should be avoided, as should the automatic assumption that products with different qualities are essentially equivalent.

67. The methods for estimating quality-adjusted prices[7] may be:

(a) *Explicit (or direct) quality adjustment methods* that directly estimate the value of the quality difference between the old and new product and adjust one of the prices accordingly. Pure price change is then implicitly estimated as the difference in the adjusted prices.

(b) *Implicit (or indirect) quality adjustment methods* which estimate the pure price change component of the price difference between the old and new products based on the price changes observed for similar products. The difference between the estimate of pure price change and the observed price change is considered as change due to quality difference.

Some of these methods are complex, costly and difficult to apply. The methods used should as far as possible be based on objective criteria.

Accuracy

68. As with all statistics, CPI estimates are subject to errors that may arise from a variety of sources.[8] Compilers of CPIs need to be aware of the possible sources of error, and to take steps during the design of the index, its construction and compilation processes to minimize their impact, for which adequate resources should be allocated.

69. The following are some well-known sources of potential error, either in pricing or in index construction, that over time can lead to errors in the overall CPI: incorrect selection of products and incorrect observation and recording of their prices; incorrect selection of outlets and timing of price collection; failure to observe and adjust correctly for quality changes; appearance of new goods and outlets; failure to adjust for product and outlet substitution or loss of representativity; the use of inappropriate formulae for computing elementary aggregate and upper level indices.

70. To reduce the index's potential for giving a misleading picture, it is in general essential to update weights and baskets regularly, to employ unbiased elementary aggregate formulae, to make appropriate adjustments for quality change, to allow adequately and correctly for new products, and to take proper account of substitution issues as well as quality control of the entire compilation process.

Dissemination

71. The CPI estimate should be computed and publicly released as quickly as possible after the end of the period to which it refers, and according to a pre-announced timetable. It should be made available to all users at the same time, in a convenient form, and should be accompanied by a short methodological explanation. Rules relating to its release should be made publicly available and strictly observed. In particular, they should include details of who has pre-release access to the results, why, under what conditions, and how long before the official release time.

72. The general CPI should be compiled and released monthly. Where there is no strong user demand for a monthly series or countries do not have the necessary resources, the CPI may be prepared and released quarterly. Depending on national circumstances, sub-indices may be released with a frequency that corresponds to users' needs.

73. When it is found that published index estimates have been seriously distorted because of errors or mistakes made in their compilation, corrections should be made and published. Such corrections should be made as soon as possible after detection according to publicly available policy for correction. Where the CPI is widely used for adjustment purposes for wages and contracts, retrospective revisions should be avoided to the extent possible.

74. The publication of the CPI results should show the index level from the index reference period. It is also useful to present derived indices, such as the one that shows changes in the major aggregates between: (i) the current month and the previous month; (ii) the current month and the same month of the previous year; and (iii) the average of the latest 12 months and the average of the previous 12 months. The indices should be presented in both seasonally adjusted and unadjusted terms, if seasonally adjusted data are available.

75. Comments and interpretation of the index should accompany its publication to assist users. An analysis of the contributions of various products or group of products to the overall change and an explanation of any unusual factors affecting the price changes of the major contributors to the overall change should be included.

76. Indices for the major expenditure groups should also be compiled and released. Consideration should be given to compiling indices for the divisions and groups of the COICOP.[9] Sub-indices for different regions or population groups, and alternative indices designed for analytical purposes, may be compiled and publicly released if there is a demand from users, they are judged to be reliable and their preparation is cost effective.

77. The index reference period may be chosen to coincide with the latest weight reference period or it could be established to coincide with the base period of other statistical series. It should be changed as frequently as necessary to ensure that the index numbers remain easy to present and understand.

[7] See Annex 2.

[8] See Annex 3.

[9] See Annex 4.

78. Average prices and price ranges for important and reasonably homogeneous products may be estimated and published in order to support the research and analytical needs of users.

79. Countries should report national CPI results and methodological information to the International Labour Office as soon as possible after their national release.

80. Comparing national CPI movements across countries is difficult because of the different measurement approaches used by countries for certain products, particularly housing and financial services. The exclusion of housing (actual rents and either imputed rents or acquisition of new houses, and maintenance and repair of dwelling) and financial services from the all-items index will make the resulting estimates of price change for the remaining products more comparable across countries. Therefore, in addition to the all-items index, countries should, if possible, compile and provide for dissemination to the international community an index that excludes housing and financial services. It should be emphasized, though, that even for the remaining products in scope, there can still be difficulties when making international comparisons of changes in consumer prices.

Consultations and integrity

81. The compiling agency should have the professional independence, competence and resources necessary to support a high quality CPI programme. The UN *Fundamental Principles of Official Statistics*[10] and the ILO *Guidelines concerning dissemination practices for labour statistics*[11] should be respected.

82. The agency responsible for the index should consult representatives of users on issues of importance for the CPI, particularly during preparations for any changes to the methodology used in compiling the CPI. One way of organizing such consultations is through the establishment of advisory committee(s) on which social partners, as well as other users and independent experts, might be represented.

83. In order to ensure public confidence in the index, a full description of the data collection procedures and the index methodology should be prepared and made widely available. Reference to this description should be made when the CPI is published. The documentation should include an explanation of the main objectives of the index, details of the weights, the index number formulae used, and a discussion of the accuracy of the index estimates. The precise identities of the outlets and goods and services used for price collection should not be revealed.

84. Users should be informed in advance of any changes that are going to be made to the scope, weights or methodology used to estimate the CPI.

85. Technical guidance on the compilation of consumer price indices is provided in the *Consumer price index manual: Theory and practice*.[12] This manual should be updated periodically in order to reflect current best practice.

Annex 1

Terminology and definitions

(a) "Consumer goods" are goods or services that are used by households for the satisfaction of individual needs or wants.

(b) "Consumption expenditures" are expenditure on consumer goods and services and can be defined in terms of "acquisition",[13] "use", or "payment":
- "acquisition" indicates that it is the total value of the goods and services acquired during a given period that should be taken into account, irrespective of whether they were wholly paid for or used during the period. This approach could be extended to include the estimated values of own-account production and social transfers in kind received from government or non-profit institutions. The prices enter the CPI in the period when consumers accept or agree prices, as distinct from the time payment is made;
- "use" indicates that it is the total value of all goods and services actually consumed during a given period that should be taken into account; for durable goods this approach requires valuing the services provided by these goods during the period. The prices (opportunity costs) enter the CPI in the period of consumption;
- "payment" indicates that it is the total payment made for goods and services during a given period that should be taken into account, without regard to whether they were delivered or used during the period. The prices enter the CPI in the period or periods when the payment is made.

(c) "Scope of the index" refers to the population groups, geographic areas, products and outlets for which the index is constructed.

(d) "Coverage" of the index is the set of goods and services represented in the index. For practical reasons, coverage may have to be less than what corresponds to the defined scope of the index.

(e) "Reference population" refers to that specific population group for which the index has been constructed.

(f) "Weights" are the aggregate consumption expenditures on any set of goods and services expressed as a proportion of the total consumption expenditures on all goods and services within the scope of the index in the weight reference period. They are a set of numbers summing up to unity.

(g) "Price updating of weights" is a procedure that is used to bring the expenditure weights in line with the index or price reference period. The price-updated weights are calculated by multiplying the

[10] UN Economic and Social Council, 1994.

[11] Sixteenth International Conference of Labour Statisticians, 1998.

[12] ILO/IMF/OECD/Eurostat/UNECE/World Bank, Geneva, 2004.

[13] This definition differs from the one adopted by the Fourteenth ICLS (1987).

weights from the weight reference period by elementary indices measuring the price changes between weight reference and price reference period and rescaling to sum to unity.

(h) "Index reference period" is the period for which the value of the index is set at 100.0.

(i) "Price reference period" is the period whose prices are compared with the prices in the current period. The period whose prices appear in the denominators of the price relatives.

(j) The "weight reference period" is the period, usually a year, whose estimates of the volume of consumption and its components are used to calculate the weights.

(k) "Probability sampling" is the selection of a sample of units, such as outlets or products, in such a way that each unit in the universe has a known non-zero probability of selection.

(l) "Cut-off sampling" is a sampling procedure in which a predetermined threshold is established with all units in the relevant population at or above the threshold being eligible for inclusion in the sample and all units below the threshold being excluded. The threshold is usually specified in terms of the size of some relevant variable (such as some percentage of total sales), the largest sampling units being included and the rest excluded.

(m) "Quota sampling" is a non-probability method where the population is divided into certain strata. For each stratum, the number ("quota") of elements to be included in the sample is specified. The price collector simply "fills the quotas", which means, in the case of outlet sampling, that the selection of the outlets is based on the judgement of the price collectors and the specified criteria.

(n) "Imputed expenditures" are the expenditures assigned to a product that has not been purchased, such as a product that has been produced by the household for its own consumption (including housing services produced by owner-occupiers), a product received as payment in kind or as a free transfer from government or non-profit institutions.

(o) "Imputed price" refers to the estimated price of a product whose price during a particular period has not been observed and is therefore missing. It is also the price assigned to a product for which the expenditures have been imputed, see (n).

(p) "Outlet" indicates a shop, market stall, service establishment, Internet seller or other place where goods and/or services are sold or provided to consumers for non-business use.

(q) "Linking" means joining together two consecutive sequences of price observations, or price indices, that overlap in one or more periods, by rescaling one of them so that the value in the overlap period is the same in both sequences, thus combining them into a single continuous series.

(r) "Price" is defined as the value of one unit of a product, for which the quantities are perfectly homogeneous not only in a physical sense but also in respect of a number of other characteristics.

(s) "Pure price change" is that change in the price of a good or service which is not due to any change in its quality. When the quality does change, the pure price change is the price change remaining after eliminating the estimated contribution of the change in quality to the observed price change.

(t) "Quality adjustment" refers to the process of adjusting the observed prices of a product to remove the effect of any changes in the quality of that product over time so that pure price change may be identified.

(u) "Consumer substitution" occurs when, faced with changes in relative price, consumers buy more of the good that has become relatively cheaper and less of the good that has become relatively more expensive. It may occur between varieties of the same product or between different expenditure categories.

Annex 2

Quality adjustment methods

Implicit quality adjustment methods

1. The "overlap" method assumes that the entire price difference at a common point in time between the disappearing product and its replacement is due to a difference in quality.
2. The "overall mean imputation" method first calculates the average price change for an aggregate without the disappearing product and its replacement, and then uses that rate of price change to impute a price change for the disappearing product. It assumes that the pure price difference between the disappearing product and its replacement is equal to the average price changes for continuing (non-missing) products.
3. The "class mean imputation" method is a variant of the overall mean imputation method. The only difference is in the source of the imputed rate of price change to period $t+1$ for the disappearing product. Rather than using the average index change for all the non-missing products in the aggregate, the imputed rate of price change is estimated using only those price changes of the products that were judged essentially equivalent or were directly quality-adjusted.

Explicit quality adjustment methods

4. The "expert's adjustment" method relies on the judgement of one or more industry experts, commodity specialists, price statisticians or price collectors on the value of any quality difference between the old and replacement product. None, some, or all of the price difference may be attributed to the improved quality.
5. The "differences in production costs" approach relies on the information provided by the manufacturers on the production costs of new features of the replacements (new models), to which retail mark-ups and associated indirect taxes are then added. This approach is most practicable in markets with a

relatively small number of producers, with infrequent and predictable model updates. However, it should be used with caution as it is possible for new production techniques to reduce costs while simultaneously improving quality.

6. The "quantity adjustment" method is applicable to products for which the replacement product is of a different size to the previously available one. It should only be used if the differences in quantities do not have an impact on the quality of the good.
7. The "option cost" method adjusts the price of the replacements for the value of the new observable characteristics. An example of this is the addition of a feature that earlier has been a priced option as standard to a new automobile model.
8. A "hedonic" regression method estimates the price of a product as a function of the characteristics it possesses. The relationship between the prices and all relevant and observable price-determining characteristics is first estimated and then results are used in the estimation of the index.

Annex 3

Types of errors

- "Quality change error" is the error that can occur as a result of the index's failure to make proper allowance for changes in the quality of goods and services.
- "New goods error" is the failure to reflect either price changes in new products not yet sampled, or given a COLI objective, the welfare gain to consumers when those products appear.
- "Outlet substitution error" can occur when consumers shift their purchases among outlets for the same product without proper reflection of this shift in the data collection for the index.
- "New outlets error" is conceptually identical to new goods error. It arises because of the failure to reflect either price changes in new outlets not yet sampled, or the welfare gain to consumers when the new outlets appear.
- "Upper-level substitution error" arises when the index does not reflect consumer substitution among the basic categories of consumption owing to the use of an inappropriate method for aggregating elementary aggregates in the construction of the overall index value. Only relevant to a COLI, although an equivalent (representativity error) may be defined from the perspective of the pure price index.
- "Elementary index error" arises from the use of an inappropriate method for aggregating price quotations at the very lowest level of aggregation. The elementary index error can take two forms: formula error and lower-level substitution error. The index suffers from formula error if, as a result of the properties of the formula, the result produced is biased relative to what would have been the result if a pure price change could have been estimated. The index suffers from lower-level substitution error if it does not reflect consumer substitution among the products contained in the elementary aggregate.
- "Selection error" arises when the sample of price observations is not fully representative of the intended population of outlets or products. The first four types of errors listed above can be seen as special cases of this type of error.

Annex 4

Classification of Individual Consumption according to Purpose (COICOP)[14]

(breakdown of individual consumption expenditure of households by division and group)

01 Food and non-alcoholic beverages
01.1 Food
01.2 Non-alcoholic beverages

02 Alcoholic beverages, tobacco and narcotics
02.1 Alcoholic beverages
02.2 Tobacco
02.3 Narcotics

03 Clothing and footwear
03.1 Clothing
03.2 Footwear

04 Housing, water, electricity, gas and other fuels
04.1 Actual rentals for housing
04.2 Imputed rentals for housing
04.3 Maintenance and repair of the dwelling
04.4 Water supply and miscellaneous services related to the dwelling
04.5 Electricity, gas and other fuels

05 Furnishings, household equipment and routine household maintenance
05.1 Furniture and furnishings, carpets and other floor coverings
05.2 Household textiles
05.3 Household appliances
05.4 Glassware, tableware and household utensils
05.5 Tools and equipment for house and garden
05.6 Goods and services for routine household maintenance

06 Health
06.1 Medical products, appliances and equipment
06.2 Outpatient services
06.3 Hospital services

07 Transport
07.1 Purchase of vehicles
07.2 Operation of personal transport equipment
07.3 Transport services

08 Communication
08.1 Postal services
08.2 Telephone and telefax equipment
08.3 Telephone and telefax services

[14] See Annex 2 on p. 465 for explanatory notes.

09 Recreation and culture
- 09.1 Audio-visual, photographic and information processing equipment
- 09.2 Other major durables for recreation and culture
- 09.3 Other recreational products and equipment, gardens and pets
- 09.4 Recreational and cultural services
- 09.5 Newspapers, books and stationery
- 09.6 Package holidays

10 Education
- 10.1 Pre-primary and primary education
- 10.2 Secondary education
- 10.3 Post-secondary non-tertiary education
- 10.4 Tertiary education
- 10.5 Education not definable by level

11 Restaurants and hotels
- 11.1 Catering services
- 11.2 Accommodation services

12 Miscellaneous goods and services
- 12.1 Personal care
- 12.2 Prostitution
- 12.3 Personal effects n.e.c.
- 12.4 Social protection
- 12.5 Insurance
- 12.6 Financial services n.e.c.
- 12.7 Other services n.e.c.

Annex 4

Spatial comparisons of consumer prices, purchasing power parities and the International Comparison Program

1 Introduction

This annex deals with the problem of comparing price levels across different areas or regions within a country, as well as across countries. Even though international price comparisons are required to handle differences in currencies in different countries, the index number problems involved in price comparisons across countries mirror those encountered in comparisons over time. There is a large body of literature on cross-country comparisons of prices and real income undertaken under the auspices of the International Comparison Program (ICP). While not providing an exhaustive account of the related problems and relevant aggregation methods, this annex aims to achieve a degree of completeness in the coverage of the problem of consumer price comparisons in the manual by adding the spatial and international dimensions to the temporal comparisons dealt with in various chapters of the manual. The annex also attempts to identify possible avenues for a closer integration between spatial and temporal comparisons of consumer prices.

The main objectives of the annex are: (i) to provide a brief summary of the index number problems encountered in the process of international and inter-area price comparisons and to highlight the need for the development and use of specialized aggregation methods; (ii) to describe a few aggregation methods used in deriving purchasing power parities (PPPs) and spatial measures of price levels; (iii) to examine the relationship between the ICP and PPPs for cross-country comparisons with the CPI; and (iv) to explore the feasibility of integrating the ICP activities with the streamlined activities of national statistical offices for the compilation of the CPI.

The annex is also designed to provide an introduction for the statisticians in various national statistical offices who may currently be involved in consumer price index (CPI) compilation to the issues and methods involved in spatial comparisons of consumer prices. The annex outlines some of the principal differences in the approaches to spatial comparisons. Countries embarking on inter-area or regional consumer price comparisons, as well as those countries that may participate in the ICP in the near future, may find the contents of the annex useful.

2 Differences between temporal and spatial comparisons

There are several major qualitative differences in the nature of price comparisons involved in the standard CPI comparisons over time and price comparisons over space involving regions or countries. These differences highlight the need for specialized methods for aggregating price data in deriving summary measures of price levels, as well as specific types of data requirements associated with cross-country and inter-area comparisons.

The foremost difference is the absence of a natural ordering of price and quantity observations in the context of cross-country or inter-area comparisons. The CPI framework and methods are devised to measure changes over time. Therefore, the price observations appear in a chronological order. The presence of a natural ordering of price observations makes it possible to examine the feasibility and relative merits of the fixed and chain index numbers. For example, in the context of constructing price comparisons across countries within the OECD, or across states within the United States, it is impossible to arrive at an ordering which facilitates chained comparisons.

The multilateral nature of spatial comparisons is a distinguishing feature of price comparisons across regions and countries. When price levels of goods and services across different countries are compared, it is essential that such comparisons are undertaken for every pair of regions being considered. If the World Bank is interested in comparisons of real income in different countries, it is necessary for the Bank to be able to make comparisons between all pairs of countries involved. This multilateral nature of comparisons creates several problems. First, the number of comparisons (one for each pair) can be quite large, and presentation and use of such results may be quite unwieldy. For example, if a particular comparison exercise involves 20 countries, then it requires 190 ($20 \times 19/2$) separate binary comparisons involving distinct pairs of countries. Second, results from such a large tableau of binary comparisons require a degree of consistency. This requirement translates into the "transitivity" condition described below.

The uses and applications of inter-area price comparisons may differ significantly from general consumer price indices. The CPI is probably the most significant economic statistic produced in any country. It is not only used as a general measure of price changes over time, but often in assessing and calibrating monetary policy. Despite the conceptual similarities in price comparisons over time and across space, spatial price comparisons are useful in comparisons of standards of living and well-being in different regions of a country or across countries. Such comparisons are essential in assessing development and in ensuring more balanced growth in different regions. There is considerable demand for measures of CPI across different cities and different states and regions (rural versus urban) within countries. However, there are very few countries where inter-area price level comparisons are readily available. Kokoski et al. (1999) demonstrate the feasibility of deriving meaningful inter-area price comparisons within the United States using the price data collected across different states.

International comparisons of prices, in the form of PPPs from the ICP, are used by international organizations and individual researchers in assessing growth and productivity performance of countries, and also in making meaningful comparisons of various national income aggregates (including government expenditure) across different countries. Currently, consensus is emerging among researchers and practitioners that price comparisons and PPPs are necessary in assessing the nature and extent of global poverty and its distribution across countries and regions of the world. Several recent research papers by Ward (2001), Prennushi (2001), Astin (2001) and Dwyer et al. (2001), presented at the joint World Bank–OECD Seminar on Purchasing Power Parities, 30 January to 2 February 2001, highlight a number of important applications of PPPs derived from international comparisons of prices under the ICP. Eurostat has recently embarked on a programme to extend the current ICP for its EU Member States to cover regional comparisons within different countries.

In recognition of the major analytical differences between the standard CPI comparisons over time and spatial and cross-country comparisons of consumer prices and PPPs, considerable research efforts have focused on the development of the data and methods necessary for spatial comparisons of prices. A brief summary of the results of this research is given below.

3 Data requirements for spatial comparisons

The basic data requirements for spatial comparisons are very similar to the data required for standard CPI calculation. The main components are the data on prices of a large range of products representative of the consumption baskets of households and information on weights associated with various product categories reflecting the importance attached to different products. Within the CPI, it is common practice to collect price quotations from different outlets scattered throughout the country. The selection of the outlets and areas from which prices are collected is based on complex multistage sampling designs. The expenditure weights are based on a classification of goods and services using a standard system such as the Classification of Individual Consumption according to Purpose (COICOP) or a similar national classification. The lowest level of product classification at which expenditure weights are available is used in identifying the elementary indices and higher-level indices at progressively higher levels of aggregation, leading ultimately to the total household expenditure level.

Spatial comparisons pose several problems in terms of identifying products that are to be priced from different areas, regions or countries involved in a comparison exercise. This problem is less severe when fairly similar or homogeneous areas are being compared. In cases where comparisons involve areas that are fairly heterogeneous, two problems arise. The first arises from major differences in the consumption baskets. For example, when comparisons are made between two states, say Minnesota and Florida, there may be major differences in the consumption baskets at the detailed level, even though the major expenditure categories may be identical. This problem is somewhat similar to the treatment of disappearing and new goods in the context of the CPI, but is more serious when cross-country comparisons are being attempted. The second problem arises from major differences in the quality of items. The quality differences may be measured through several product characteristics, with allowances and adjustments being made at the appropriate stage of index number calculation. Kokoski et al. (1999) demonstrate the feasibility of making inter-area price comparisons for heterogeneous goods.

Changes in quality are likely to be more gradual in the case of temporal comparisons, but can be a serious problem when comparisons across countries are attempted. The ICP follows the principle of identity in dealing with the problem of quality differences across countries. A comprehensive list of products with detailed product specifications is developed at the planning stages of any cross-country comparison exercise. These items are priced in different countries from various outlets distributed across the country, a procedure very similar to that used in the CPI. Development of the product listing is, however, a difficult step, with the degree of difficulty depending upon the size and heterogeneity of the group of countries involved. The use of a product listing, based on the identity principle, can have serious implications for the representativeness of the product list of the consumption baskets in different countries. There are several operational procedures used by international organizations in handling these problems relating to the compilation of price data. A more detailed account of the problems and recommended solutions can be found in *ICP Handbook* (United Nations, 1992) and the recent publication by OECD (1999) on its international comparison work.

Once the price data are compiled, the next stage in the CPI compilation is the aggregation of item-specific price changes to measure price movements for various categories of consumption expenditure. At this stage, it is necessary to have information on consumption patterns. This information is usually drawn from household expenditure surveys. These surveys are regularly conducted in most countries by the respective national statistical organizations. For purposes of making inter-area comparisons of consumer prices, the corresponding requirement is the availability of household expenditure survey data specific to each area included in the comparisons. In many cases, for reasons relating to sampling and statistical reliability, detailed expenditure pattern data may not be available for all the regions.

Spatial comparisons of consumer prices pose specific problems because of the non-overlapping nature of the consumption baskets, major differences in the quality of items priced in different regions and countries, and the non-availability of crucial data on region-specific expenditure patterns. These problems require the development of new analytical techniques that can handle major differences in quality. National statistical offices may need additional financial resources in order to provide reliable and meaningful price comparisons between different cities, areas and regions within countries, and to compile reliable data for the more difficult task of inter-country comparisons of prices and real consumption.

4 Aggregation methods for spatial comparisons

This section briefly describes the types of aggregation methods that are commonly used in cross-country comparisons of prices. Since most of these methods have been developed in the context of the ICP, and are equally valid for inter-area or regional comparisons, the discussion below uses countries as spatial entities. This section is further divided into three parts. The first deals with the notation and conceptual framework necessary to deal with multilateral spatial comparisons. The second describes the construction of elementary indices for aggregation of prices when no quantity or expenditure information is available. Finally, a small selection of index number methods used in spatial price comparisons are presented.

4.1 Notation and conceptual framework

Consider the case involving comparisons across M countries, and price and quantity data on N commodities. These commodities refer to goods and services that are priced in all the countries. If the commodities refer to items below the elementary level at which no quantity or expenditure share data are available, we make use of only the price data. At this stage, all the problems relating to non-overlapping commodity lists and existence of quality differences are set aside so that the main focus is just on the aggregation issues. Let $p^j = [p_1^j, \ldots p_N^j]$ and $q^j = [q_1^j, \ldots q_N^j]$ represent the price and quantity vectors from country j ($j = 1, 2, \ldots, M$). In the case of international comparisons, all the prices are expressed in the respective national currency units. As in the case of the CPI computation, the problem is one of decomposing the differences in the value aggregates

$$V^j = \sum_{i=1}^{N} p_i^j q_i^j \tag{A4.1}$$

into measures of price and real expenditure components.

Since there are M sets of price and quantity vectors and, therefore, $M(M-1)/2$ binary comparisons between all distinct pairs of countries, a simpler notation is used in this annex in the place of the notation generally used in the manual. Let I_{jk} denote the (consumer) price index number for country k with country j as the base. If j and k are, respectively, the United States and India, and if $I_{jk} = 22.50$, then the index is interpreted to mean that 22.50 Indian rupees have the same purchasing power as one US dollar for the goods and services covered in computing the index. Thus the index can also be interpreted as the PPP between the currencies of j and k. This interpretation is consistent with the meaning accorded to the CPI. Since currency denominations are involved here, a proper measure of relative price level differences can be obtained if the PPP is compared to the exchange rate prevailing at the time when comparisons are made.

Because of the multilateral nature of spatial comparisons, when M countries are involved, it is necessary to provide comparisons between all pairs of countries. Thus, it becomes necessary to compute each and every entry in the following matrix of binary comparisons:

$$I = \begin{bmatrix} I_{11} & I_{12} & I_{1k} & I_{1M} \\ I_{21} & I_{22} & I_{2k} & I_{2M} \\ I_{j1} & I_{j2} & I_{jk} & I_{jM} \\ I_{M1} & I_{M2} & I_{Mk} & I_{MM} \end{bmatrix} \tag{A4.2}$$

Several points concerning the matrix, I, are worth noting. First, the matrix can be large if the number of countries (or regions) involved is large. Second, the results recorded in the matrix need to be internally consistent. All the index number issues and various approaches discussed in the manual apply directly to each binary comparison involving two countries. Diewert (1986, 1999b) provides a summary of the microeconomic theoretical and test approaches to cross-country comparisons. Thus, it is possible to apply Fisher, Törnqvist, Walsh or other index number formulae described in the manual.

In order to ensure meaningful interpretation of the results from multilateral cross-country comparisons, the index number methods applied need to satisfy a number of basic requirements, only the most important of which are discussed below. Kravis et al. (1982), OECD (1999) and United Nations (1992) provide a complete list of these requirements.

Transitivity. An index number formula I_{jk} is said to satisfy the transitivity property if and only if for all choices of j, k and ℓ (j, k, $\ell = 1, 2, \ldots, M$), the index satisfies

$$I_{jk} = I_{j\ell} \times I_{\ell k} \tag{A4.3}$$

Equation (A4.3) requires that the application of a formula to make a direct comparison, I_{jk}, should result in the same numerical measure as an indirect comparison between j and k through a link country ℓ. Note that the transitivity property ensures internal consistency of index numbers in the matrix given in equation (A4.2). It guarantees that the PPP for two currencies, say A and B, is the same whether it is derived through a direct comparison of A and B or through an indirect comparison that compares A with C and C with B, which are then combined to provide an indirect PPP for A and B. This requirement arises mainly from the spatial nature of the comparisons where no natural ordering of the countries involved could be imposed without a value judgement. Most of the commonly used index number procedures do not satisfy this requirement. The following result is useful in constructing transitive index numbers.

An index number formula I_{jk} satisfies the transitivity property in (A4.3) if and only if there exist M positive real numbers $\lambda_1, \lambda_2, \ldots, \lambda_M$, such that

$$I_{jk} = \frac{\lambda_k}{\lambda_j} \tag{A4.4}$$

for all j and k.

The proof of this result is straightforward (Rao and Banerjee, 1984). The result is important since it shows that, when the transitivity property is satisfied, all that is necessary is to measure M real numbers $\lambda_1, \lambda_2, \ldots, \lambda_M$, and then all the necessary indices in (A4.2) can be calculated using these M numbers, thus reducing the dimension of the problem involved. Two important points may be noted. First, the numbers λ_j in equation (A4.4) are not unique, since any scalar multiplication of a vector of λ_j can also lead to the same matrix of index numbers as that derived from the original λ_j. Therefore, these λ_j need to be determined (in any empirical exercise) up to a factor of proportionality. Second, these λ_j can be interpreted as the PPP of currencies involved. This particular result formed the basis of the work of statisticians such as Geary (1958) and Khamis (1970), who proposed aggregation methods designed to compute PPPs directly from the price and quantity data without invoking the index number literature.

Base invariance. An index number formula is said to be base invariant if a comparison between a given pair of countries (j, k) is invariant to the order in which the countries are listed. This implies that multilateral comparisons should be invariant to all possible permutations of the data set. For example, consider a set of transitive comparisons derived using a particular country (say the United States) as a star country. Under this scheme, price comparison between any pair of countries, say A and B, is effected through the United States which serves as a link country. Therefore,

$$PPP_{A,B} = PPP_{A,USA} \times PPP_{USA,B}$$

This scheme is inadmissible under the base invariance criterion since the choice of the star country clearly affects the PPP of currencies of countries A and B. Further, the United States is accorded a special status, in the form of a link country, in deriving transitive multilateral comparisons.

Characteristicity. This is a requirement outlined in Drechsler (1973). This property requires that any set of multilateral comparisons satisfying the transitivity property should retain the essential features of the binary comparisons constructed without the transitivity requirement. Since condition (A4.3) implies that a transitive comparison between a pair of countries j and k is necessarily influenced by the price and quantity data for all the other countries, the characteristicity property requires that distortions resulting from adherence to the transitivity property should be kept at a minimum. Balk (2001) shows that a complete adherence to the characteristicity principle in its extreme (complete preservation of all binary comparisons) would imply that price indices, and hence PPPs, cannot depend upon any quantity or expenditure share weights. This is an extreme result, which is to be avoided in all index number comparisons. The Elteto–Koves–Szulc (EKS) method for multilateral comparisons, discussed below, has its origins in the characteristicity property.

4.2 Index number methods for spatial comparisons

Spatial price comparisons in general, and international comparisons in particular, use index number methods for aggregating price and quantity data at two different levels. The first is the basic heading level. This is normally the lowest level of aggregation at which expenditure data and weights are available. These basic headings usually consist of a fairly homogeneous group of items that are priced in different outlets in the countries. The subsequent levels of aggregation lead to indices for broad expenditure categories, and finally to the whole consumption basket.

4.2.1 Aggregation below the basic heading level

Two commonly used index number methods are described below. These procedures explicitly allow for the possibility that price data may not be available for all items in the product list constructed for a given international comparison exercise. Such a situation is possible in the case of temporal comparisons, but is usually limited to a small number of commodities that are either disappearing or new goods.

The Elteto–Koves–Szulc (EKS) Method. A variant of the original method proposed in Elteto and Koves (1964) and Szulc (1964) is generally used in aggregating price data below the basic heading level. The EKS method involves two stages. In the first stage, binary comparisons are constructed using price relatives of those commodities for which prices are available in both countries. If n_{jk} is the number of commodities that are priced in both countries, then the current practice within ICP constructs a binary elementary index using the following formula:

$$I_{jk} = \prod_{i=1}^{n_{jk}} \left[\frac{p_i^k}{p_i^j} \right]^{1/n_{jk}} \qquad \text{(A4.5)}$$

Obviously, these indices are not transitive, since each index is based on prices of a different set of commodities. The EKS procedure is then used in deriving a transitive set of indices. The resulting formula for the construction of elementary indices for spatial comparisons is given by

$$I_{jk}^{EKS} = \prod_{\ell=1}^{M} \left[I_{j\ell} I_{\ell k} \right]^{1/M} \qquad \text{(A4.6)}$$

The elementary index number formula in (A4.5) is similar to the formula used in the construction of the CPI. The principal difference results from the fact that not all commodities are priced in all countries and that there is a need for transitivity at all stages of aggregation. The properties of these indices are discussed in Chapter 20 of the manual.

The OECD (1999) uses a slightly modified variant of the binary indices shown in equation (A4.5). A formula that mimics the standard Fisher index is used, but without the use of any expenditure shares since the aggregation is below the basic heading level. This procedure tries to account for the fact that not all commodities for which prices are collected are really characteristic or important in one or both of the countries. The procedure takes explicit account of those commodities which are starred, indicating that the item is important in a given country. The modified EKS method uses the same formula as above, but the binary index on the right-hand side is replaced by:

$$I_{js} = \left\{ \prod_{i \in M(s)} \left[\frac{p_i^s}{p_i^j} \right]^{\frac{1}{n(s)}} \prod_{i \in M(j)} \left[\frac{p_i^s}{p_i^j} \right]^{\frac{1}{n(j)}} \right\}^{\frac{1}{2}} \qquad \text{(A4.7)}$$

where $n(s)$ and $n(j)$ are, respectively, the number of starred items in countries s and j; $M(s)$ and $M(j)$ are, respectively, the sets of commodities that are starred (considered representative) in different countries.

Use of equations (A4.5) and (A4.6) for the construction of spatial CPI numbers at the basic heading level has its problems. The most important problem is that these formulae do not take into consideration whether or not the commodities priced in different countries are "representative" of the consumption in different countries within the basic heading. A related problem is whether or not the coverage of the commodities, priced with respect to the basic heading to which they belong, is adequate. These issues are currently being researched, and Rao (2001b) offers a modified approach that attaches weights proportional to coverage and representativeness.

While there has been much research on the properties of index number formulae for the construction of elementary indices within the CPI framework (Diewert (1995a), Dalén (1992) and Turvey (1996)), there has been very little research on the properties of elementary indices within the context of international comparisons.

The Country–Product–Dummy (CPD) Method. The CPD method was originally proposed by Summers (1973) as a tool to deal with missing price observations. The method is a simple statistical device that can be used in deriving the PPPs for a particular basic heading by simply regressing the logarithm of observed prices against a set of dummy variables, defined with respect to commodities and countries. Thus the procedure involves the model:

$$\ln p_i^j = \eta_1 D_1 + \eta_2 D_2 + \ldots + \eta_n D_n + \pi_1 D_1^* + \pi_2 D_2^* + \ldots + \pi_M D_M + u_i^j \qquad \text{(A4.8)}$$

where D_i $(I=1,2,\ldots,n)$ and $D_j^*(j=1,2,\ldots,M)$ are, respectively, dummy variables for the N commodities in the basic heading and M countries involved in the comparisons.

Once this regression equation is estimated, the PPP for currency of country k with country j as base can be obtained by

$$\text{PPP}^j = \exp(\hat{\pi}_j) \qquad \text{(A4.9)}$$

where $\hat{\pi}_j$ is the estimator of π_j in equation (A4.8). Then the desired index at the basic heading level is given by

$$I_{jk} = \frac{\text{PPP}_k}{\text{PPP}_j}. \qquad \text{(A4.10)}$$

The exponential of the difference in the estimates of π_j and π_k obtained from the regression equation provides the necessary index number.

The CPD model offers a number of generalizations that can explicitly account for a number of data-related problems. The model can be easily generalized to account for differences in quality measured through a set of product characteristics. The feasibility of this approach to inter-area comparisons of consumer prices within the United States was demonstrated in Kokoski et al. (1999). Rao and Timmer (2000) examined the feasibility of using a generalized CPD model to incorporate various measures of reliability in the context of aggregating unit value ratios to provide comparisons at the manufacturing branch level. Rao (2001b) discusses a few model specifications that are appropriate for aggregation below the basic heading level within the context of the ICP.

The EKS method, described in equations (A4.6)–(A4.8), is the procedure that is currently used by all the international organizations for purposes of aggregation below the basic heading level. The CPD and EKS methods yield identical basic heading parities when all the commodities are priced in all the countries. Ferrari and Riani (1998) and Ferrari et al. (1996) present a number of analytical results relating to these methods.

While the sampling issues relating to the selection and distribution of outlets and the frequency of price quotations are considered important for the construction of the elementary indices within the CPI, issues that are crucial for the construction of PPPs below the basic heading for inter-country comparisons are quite different. Issues of quality differences and non-availability of goods and services in all the comparison countries are far more important in spatial comparisons of consumer prices.

4.2.2 Aggregation above the basic heading level

This section presents a small selection of the range of aggregation methods used in the context of spatial comparisons. A more comprehensive analysis of the spatial aggregation methods developed over the past three decades is presented by Balk (2001).

This level of aggregation is similar to the stage where elementary indices are aggregated to derive the overall CPI. In the case of temporal comparisons involving two time periods, all the methods and approaches described in the manual are appropriate, and in most cases the national statistical offices use the Laspeyres, Fisher or some variants of these formulae for CPI construction. However, the multilateral nature of spatial comparisons necessitates slightly different approaches to their construction.

A number of index number methods for aggregation above the basic heading level have been developed over the past three decades but, in the interest of brevity, only the principal methods are discussed below. These are the Geary–Khamis and EKS methods for international comparisons, the principal aggregation methods used in various international comparison exercises by the ICP, the OECD, Eurostat and FAO.

Several approaches to the construction of multilateral index numbers that satisfy transitivity and base invariance properties are discussed below. Four distinct approaches emerged during ICP work carried out between 1970 and the early 2000s. The first and most straightforward is the EKS approach, which uses binary results as building-blocks for multilateral comparisons. The second is the Geary–Khamis approach, which provides a methodology for computing PPPs of currencies and international average prices of commodities, using the price–quantity data at the basic heading level. The third is the stochastic approach based on the CPD method and its generalizations that can be used in econometrically estimating the PPPs using a regression framework. The fourth and the last approach discussed here is the linking approach to the construction of chained comparisons based on the concept of the minimum spanning tree. This is generating considerable interest and is explored further in the last section of this annex. These four approaches are by no means exhaustive, but they represent major strands of research and development in this area.

The EKS Method. The EKS system is a simple method of generating transitive multilateral index numbers from a system of binary index numbers, with the property that the resulting multilateral indices deviate the least (according to a specific criterion) from the binary indices. Since the seminal paper by Drechsler (1973), it has been well recognized that (transitive) multilateral systems necessarily deviate from their binary counterparts and therefore result in a loss of "characteristicity". The EKS system is designed to minimize such loss of characteristicity. The original EKS system uses the Fisher binary indices, but the work of Caves, Christensen and Diewert (1982b) and Rao and Banerjee (1984) recognizes that other binary indices could be used in conjunction with the EKS technique. For any pair of countries j and k, if F_{jk} represents the Fisher binary index, then

$$EKS_{jk} = \prod_{\ell=1}^{M} \left[F_{j\ell}.F_{\ell k}\right]^{1/M} \qquad \text{(A4.11)}$$

provides the EKS index.

There are several notable features of the EKS technique. First, it is based on the premise that direct binary comparisons, derived using any chosen formula, provide the best comparison between pairs of countries. Second, even though the EKS index in equation (A4.11) is defined using the Fisher index, this approach can be applied in conjunction with any other index number formula. For example, the Fisher index in equation (A4.11) may be replaced by another superlative index, such as the Törnqvist index. Caves, Christensen and Diewert (1982b) suggest the use of a Törnqvist-based EKS formula for spatial comparisons. Third, the EKS index in equation (A4.11) is the multilateral index that deviates the least from the matrix of non-transitive binary indices, when the deviations are measured using a logarithmic distance function. Finally, the EKS index can be interpreted as a simple geometric mean of all indirect comparisons between j and k through all possible link countries.

The simple unweighted nature of the EKS index has attracted attention in recent years. Since different binary comparisons have different levels of reliability, measured using various criteria, it is necessary to reflect these differences in defining weighted EKS index numbers. Rao and Timmer (2000), Rao et al. (2000) and Rao (2001b) provide illustrations of how weighted EKS indices can be generated in order to account for various data-related problems.

The Geary–Khamis (GK) Method. The GK method was originally proposed by Geary (1958) and subsequently developed by Khamis (1970, 1972 and 1984). The GK method has been the principal aggregation method in most of the ICP phases to date. Since 1996, the OECD has produced and published international comparisons based on both the EKS and GK methods.

The GK method provides a way of calculating PPPs of currencies of different countries from the observed price and quantity data (applied at the basic heading level). The concept of PPP is applicable even when the currency unit is the same in several areas of a country. The GK method simultaneously determines international average prices of different countries. Let P_i denote the international average price of ith commodity. The GK method is defined through the following system of interrelated equations, defined for each country j and each commodity i,

$$P_i = \frac{\sum_{j=1}^{M} p_i^j q_i^j / PPP_j}{\sum_{j=1}^{M} q_i^j} \quad \text{and} \quad PPP_j = \frac{\sum_{i=1}^{N} p_i^j q_i^j}{\sum_{i=1}^{N} P_i q_i^j} \qquad \text{(A4.12)}$$

These simultaneous equations are then solved to yield numerical values of PPPs and Ps, after selecting one of the currencies as a numeraire. Once the PPPs are solved, the spatial price index numbers are simply defined as

$$I_{jk} = \frac{PPP_k}{PPP_j} \qquad \text{(A4.13)}$$

One of the main reasons for the continued use of the GK method is "additivity". Additivity requires that aggregates, such as real domestic product, derived by converting national aggregates using PPPs, should be equal to aggregates derived through valuation of quantities at international prices. Thus additivity requires

$$\sum_{i=1}^{n} p_i^j q_i^j / PPP_j = \sum_{i=1}^{n} P_i q_i^j \qquad \text{(A4.14)}$$

This requirement is satisfied automatically by the PPPs and Ps derived from the GK system defined in equation (A4.12). The GK system is also useful in analysing the structure of real GDP and shares of different components across different countries. This system provides a framework within which internationally comparable national accounts could be constructed. However, the GK system is not rooted in standard economic theory and fails several test properties (Diewert, 1986). There has been considerable debate among practitioners concerning the average prices resulting from the GK system. The system has the potential to reflect the price structure of the richer countries, and therefore has the tendency to overstate the real income of the poorer countries.

Weighted Country–Product–Dummy (CPD) Method. It is possible to generalize the CPD method discussed in the context of aggregation below the basic heading level. Rao (1995) has generalized the CPD method by incorporating quantity and value data directly into the CPD method described in equation (A4.8). The basic idea behind this generalization comes from the fact that the standard CPD regression model attempts to track the logarithm of the observed prices using an unweighted residual sum of squares. In the spirit of the standard index number approach, where price index numbers are required to track price changes of more important commodities more closely, a more appropriate procedure would be to find estimates of the parameters that are likely to track important commodities more closely. This is achieved by minimizing a weighted residual sum of squares, with each observation weighted according to the expenditure share of the commodity in a given country. Thus the generalized CPD method suggests that estimation of the equation

$$\ln p_{ij} = \pi_1 D_1 + \pi_2 D_2 + \ldots + \pi_M D_M + \eta_1 D_1^* + \eta_2 D_2^* + \ldots + \eta_n D_n^* + u_{ij} \quad \text{(A4.15)}$$

be conducted after weighting each observation according to its value share. This is equivalent to the application of ordinary least squares to the following transformed equation obtained by premultiplying equation (A4.15) by $\sqrt{w_{ij}}$. The resulting equation is:

$$\sqrt{w_{ij}} \ln p_{ij} = \pi_1 \sqrt{w_{ij}} D_1 + \pi_2 \sqrt{w_{ij}} D_2 + \ldots + \pi_M \sqrt{w_{ij}} D_M + \eta_1 \sqrt{w_{ij}} D_1^* + \ldots + \eta_n \sqrt{w_{ij}} D_n^* + v_{ij} \quad \text{(A4.16)}$$

where $w_{ij} = p_{ij} q_{ij} / \sum_{i=1}^{N} p_{ij} q_{ij}$ is the value share of the ith basic heading in the jth country.

Rao (1995) has shown that the international prices and PPPs resulting from the estimates of parameters in equation (A4.13) are identical to those derived using the Rao method for international comparisons, described in Rao (1990). Thus the weighted CPD method may be considered as a bridge between the GK approach to international comparisons and the standard stochastic approach to index numbers.

Kokoski et al. (1999) outline a procedure which makes use of the CPD method to adjust for differences in quality characteristics of various consumer items for the construction of inter-area CPIs using United States data. Estimates derived from the CPD method are subsequently used in the application of the multilateral Törnqvist index derived after imposing the transitivity condition. Hence the approach used in Kokoski et al. (1999) may be described as a mixed stochastic and index number approach to multilateral spatial comparisons of CPI numbers.

Spatial linking and chaining approach. In recent years, a new approach to inter-area and inter-country comparisons of prices has been given serious consideration. This approach advocates spatial chaining of binary comparisons where links are identified using a procedure based on a measure of distance or reliability of binary comparisons involved. This approach is in sharp contrast to the general approach to multilateral comparisons, where either all the binary comparisons are used, as in the case of the EKS method, or all the price and quantity data are simultaneously used, as in the case of the GK and CPD approaches.

Using the graphical theoretical concept of minimum spanning trees, Hill (1999c, 1999d) proposed a method of deriving a system of transitive multilateral comparisons from a matrix of binary comparisons. The Hill approach is based on the fact that direct binary comparisons may not always be the best.

For any pair of countries j and k, Hill suggests a measure of distance (indicating the reliability of the binary comparison) using the Laspeyres–Paasche spread defined as

$$D(j,k) = \left| \ln\left(\frac{L(j,k}{P(j,k)} \right) \right| \quad \text{(A4.17)}$$

where $L(j, k)$ and $P(j, k)$ are, respectively, binary Laspeyres and Paasche price index numbers. Note that the same distance function emerges if price index numbers are replaced by quantity index numbers. $D(j, k)$ is equal to zero if the price structures or quantity structures are identical in countries, j and k. Thus, this distance function serves as an indicator of similarity of price and quantity structures in these countries.

Using a matrix of distances calculated for all pairs of countries, Hill (1999c, 1999d) suggests that a minimum spanning tree (MST) be extracted and used in constructing chained links between all pairs of countries. The MST has the property that a chained comparison between any pair of countries has the least distance, and therefore can be considered as the most reliable. It also has the property that the sum of the distances between all the links, in the MST, is the least when compared to all possible tree-configurations. For purposes of illustrating the concepts involved, Figure A4.1.1 shows the MST for Europe constructed using ICP data for Europe for the 1985 benchmark year.

It is evident from the MST presented here that a comparison between Germany and Portugal is through a chain involving Ireland, Luxembourg and Spain. This chained comparison is deemed to be better than a direct comparison between these two countries. There are a number of issues yet to be resolved regarding the use of the MST. Nonetheless, an MST provides a formalization of a somewhat intuitive notion of linking dissimilar countries using a chain of similar countries.

Once the MST is identified, a transitive comparison between a given pair of countries in a particular exercise is constructed using binary indices calculated using a chosen formula, such as the Fisher or Törnqvist index, and the links indicated in the MST. Thus, if a comparison between Sweden and Denmark is needed, then the MST approach suggests the following index for this comparison:

$$I^{MST}_{\text{Sweden, Denmark}} = F_{\text{Sweden, Finland}} \times F_{\text{Finland, Denmark}}$$

where F denotes the Fisher index.

Figure A4.1 A minimum spanning tree: Europe

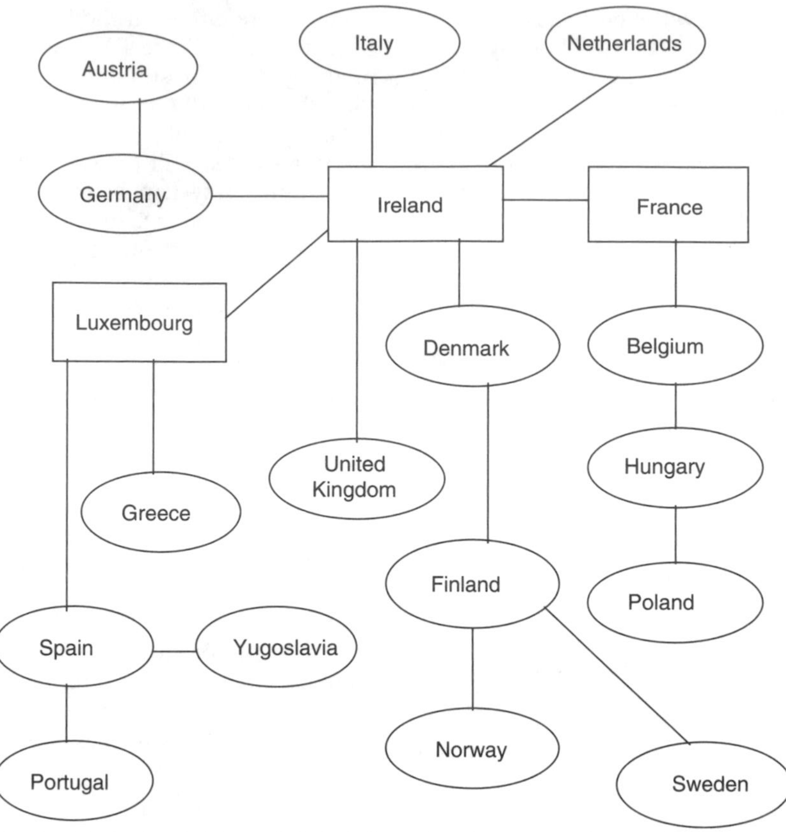

Since the MST provides a unique chain of links between any two countries, comparisons are uniquely defined. The spanning trees are, however, sensitive to the countries included, and the types of measures used in assessing the degree of reliability or comparability of any two countries. Aten et al. (2001) examine the sensitivity of the spanning trees and the resulting comparisons based on a range of measures including some similarity indices. Rao et al. (2000) applied the spanning tree approach to the construction of multilateral, agricultural input, output and productivity indices, using United States state-level agricultural production data.

5 Integration of the CPI and inter-area and international comparisons

The best available inter-area and international price comparisons for consumer goods and services use data from the national statistical offices compiling CPIs. In recent critical reviews of the ICP by Ryten (1998), and of the OECD–Eurostat PPPs by Castles (1997), the accuracy and reliability of international comparisons have been assessed as being less than adequate. Castles notes the difficulties encountered in comparing like goods from country to country, and Ryten argues for the need to secure greater support from national statistical offices in compiling price data for the ICP. Both reviews recommended examination of the feasibility of integrating ICP work with that of the normal CPI work undertaken by the national statistical offices. Since this annex deals with spatial and international comparisons, it is appropriate now to examine and identify possible steps involved in a more integrated approach to the CPI and ICP activities.

This section first provides an assessment of potential benefits that could flow from the integration of CPI and ICP activities with statistical systems in general, and price statistics in particular, at both global and national levels. It is useful to note here that the ICP provides cross-country comparisons of prices of goods and services that enter private consumption, government consumption and investment. Thus ICP encompasses all components of gross domestic product (GDP). In contrast, the CPI focuses mainly on movements in prices of consumer goods and services. The nature and scope of the CPI and ICP activities and the limits on the extent of an integrated approach are discussed briefly. The final subsection identifies a number of useful initiatives that could provide a framework for a practical, more integrated approach to these important activities involving inter-temporal, inter-area and international comparisons of consumer prices and the ICP.

5.1 Benefits from CPI and ICP integration

Globalization and the resulting expansion in international trade and financial flows have led to an ever-increasing demand for internationally comparable statistics that can be used in assessing the economic performance of nations. The ICP plays a major role in meeting this demand by providing internationally comparable national income aggregates, such as private and government consumption and capital formation. The ICP has also provided valuable information on relative international prices of goods and services, at a reasonably disaggregated level, which is used by researchers around the world. The most popular by-products of the international comparisons are the Penn World Tables and the World Development Indicators, which are considered invaluable sources of data for research on global inequality, poverty and econometric analysis of productivity growth, and the study of catch-up and convergence among nations.

The potential benefits of the ICP are somewhat diminished by the long lags in making international comparisons available to potential users. The coverage of the ICP is not extensive and the number of countries covered varies across regions. The limited coverage of ICP in some regions reflects the resource needs associated with the compilation of price data specifically for the purpose of the ICP. It is in this area where significant benefits can be derived if the ICP activities can be integrated with the CPI work of the national statistical offices.

At the global level, the potential benefits are many and varied. A few are listed below:

- increased country coverage, leading to a better framework for extrapolations;
- improved quality of the estimates resulting from the use of extensive price data collected for CPI purposes, rather than basing comparisons on products with specifications that may not be representative of the consumption baskets of the countries involved;
- benefits from research on methods for quality adjustment. Such methods are necessary to make adjustments for differences in product quality across countries;
- the development of regional PPPs, which are likely to make ICP results more consistent with domestic price movements and more acceptable to national governments;
- construction of internationally comparable national accounts, in a common currency unit, complementing the existing national accounts in national currency units. Such accounts will be a useful addition to the international statistical data bases that will enable global-level research on country and regional economic performance, and long-term catch-up, and convergence among countries;
- reliable estimates of PPPs along with domestic rates of inflation, providing a complete matrix of temporal–spatial price differences that can be used to better understand the factors influencing national price levels and exchange rate movements.

Several benefits may also be derived by the national statistical offices from an integrated approach to the compilation of CPI and PPPs. The nature of benefits derived will, however, vary depending on the stage of development of the countries involved. For more developed countries with well-established statistical agencies and programmes, the benefits derived are through the synergies arising out of a joint approach to spatial and temporal comparisons. These are as follows:

- Recent work on CPI and ICP manuals addresses the important issue of quality change over time and quality differences across countries. Efforts are being channelled into finding suitable statistical methods that can be used in the measurement of price-level changes leading to reductions in potential biases.
- The treatment of new and disappearing products within the CPI is also an important problem associated with increased globalization, the expansion of free trade and the removal of tariff barriers. Thus national statistical offices, especially in developed countries, are often confronted with the problem of accounting for new goods, and goods subject to rapid quality changes.
- The regular compilation of the national accounts statistics and the measurement of price change through the CPI, and extending to inter-area and international comparisons, can provide information needed to assess the levels of, and movements in, real income.

In the case of developing countries with inadequate statistical infrastructure, benefits from an integrated approach could be significant and aid statistical capacity building in such countries. These benefits include:

- strengthening statistical infrastructure and institution building. Efforts to implement the CPI manual and its recommendations, along with participation in the ICP activity, are likely to identify deficiencies in a country's infrastructure and the lack of institutional capacity. In some countries, it may be necessary to strengthen management and planning functions, recruit new staff, and provide training to conduct household expenditure and other general price surveys;
- strengthening of data collection, processing systems and dissemination. Designing and conducting sample surveys to international standards is a lengthy and demanding exercise. It may be necessary to develop a systematic plan to improve survey designs to coordinate surveys of economic and business entities, and to conduct periodic censuses of economic activity. Computerization of data-processing activities may also be required;
- improvement in the measurement of income inequality and poverty. Improved price and expenditure data can be used to improve national and international estimates of poverty;
- improved regional comparisons. PPPs compiled for regions and for neighbouring countries can provide useful insights into the dynamics of regional development, and help identify the regions with special needs and required assistance. Comparisons with neighbouring countries, in terms of relative price differences and real income changes, can provide powerful incentives to pursue policies for growth and low inflation.

There are many potential applications of the PPPs from the ICP. Several papers (by Astin (2001), Ward (2001) and Prennushi (2001), in particular) at the recent OECD–World Bank (2001) seminar dealt with some important applications of PPPs at Eurostat and the OECD, and at the global level in the assessment of poverty and inequality.

5.2 Salient features of CPI and ICP integration

In order to identify strategies for closer integration of temporal CPI compilation with wider inter-area and cross-country comparisons of consumer prices and PPPs at the level of GDP, it is necessary to examine the main features and the context in which such an integration will occur. The important issues are the scope and coverage of these two endeavours from the perspective of national statistical offices, and a general framework of price comparisons within which both these activities are placed. This section deals with these two aspects.

The scope and coverage of the CPI and ICP are vastly different. The CPI is a measure of changes, over time, in prices of goods and services that belong to the consumption baskets of households in a given country. In contrast, the ICP provides a measure of price-level differences across countries, covering all components of the expenditure side of the national accounts. The main components of GDP used in ICP comparisons are household consumption, government consumption, capital formation and net exports. In line with the *SNA 1993*, the ICP merges the portion of government expenditure that provides goods and services to households with private consumption to form household consumption. Thus, the scope and coverage of goods and services in the ICP is much wider than that of the CPI. The household consumption concept used is, however, almost identical to that used in constructing the CPI. Any integration of CPI and ICP work will necessarily be confined to the household consumption aggregate of the national accounts.

Within the ICP, price quotations from different countries are obtained for a large number of goods and services with very well-defined product specifications. This approach, described as the "tight specification" approach, is used in the ICP. The tight specification approach requires a sufficient description of the product so that it is uniquely defined in the "law of one price" sense, and so that it can be recognized in a range of localities and time periods wherever and whenever it is available. The product listing is determined on the basis of the group of countries included in an international comparison exercise. While this approach provides a solution to the problem of quality variations across countries, the commodities priced for ICP purposes may not be representative of the consumption baskets in respective countries. Thus, commodities priced may not be representative of the items consumed in the countries, which usually make up the bundle of goods and services for the construction of the CPI.

The degree of success of integrating ICP activity with the CPI compilation depends upon the extent to which these two activities can draw on a common pool of data and information available at the national level. The intersection of data sets for the CPI and the ICP is represented in figure A4.2.

The following marked areas are of particular significance:

(1) Common set of goods and services between the CPI and ICP lists. These price data can be used directly in an integrated approach to these two activities.

(2) and (3) Subset of ICP goods and services for which prices can be derived after making quality adjustments to products listed in the CPI basket. These are the goods and services that are not identical, but close enough for quality adjustments to be made based on the characteristics of the goods and services.

(4) Set of goods and services in the CPI basket that has no direct component in the ICP basket.

(5) ICP basket of goods and services under headings of the expenditure side of the national accounts that has no direct relevance or correspondence with CPI.

Figure A4.2 shows that if the integration between the ICP and the CPI is to be successful, the ICP comparisons should necessarily be restricted to country groupings where the basket of goods and services representing household consumption within the ICP has a significant overlap with the country-specific CPI baskets. Such an overlap can be achieved only when country groupings within the ICP comparisons exhibit similarities in their CPI consumption baskets. This has implications for the ICP and its regionalization programme.

In examining the CPI and ICP activities, it is also necessary to consider a range of temporal and spatial price comparisons of interest to national statistical offices in the course of providing a comprehensive set of economic statistics for policy-makers and other analysts. It is possible to consider these activities in a sequence indicating the progression involved in these price comparison activities (figure A4.3).

The schematic diagram uses the standard CPI activity of estimating annual or quarterly price changes for the nation as a whole. In most countries, national CPI figures are supplemented by area-specific CPI estimates for either capital cities or regions within the country. A natural progression, where data permit, is to undertake spatial comparisons of prices. At present, very few

Figure A4.2 Price data for CPI and ICP activities

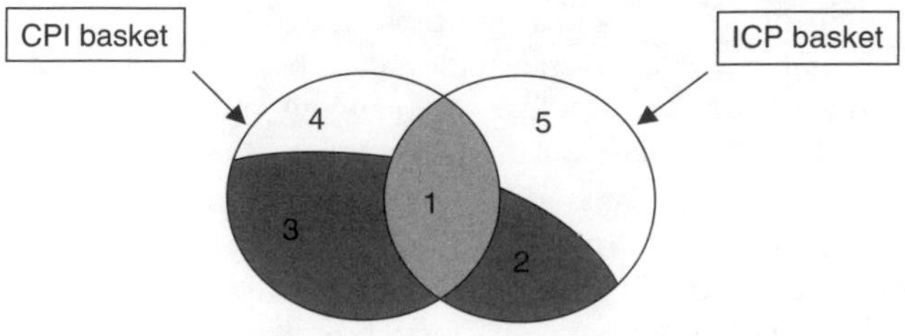

Figure A4.3 A sequence of price comparisons

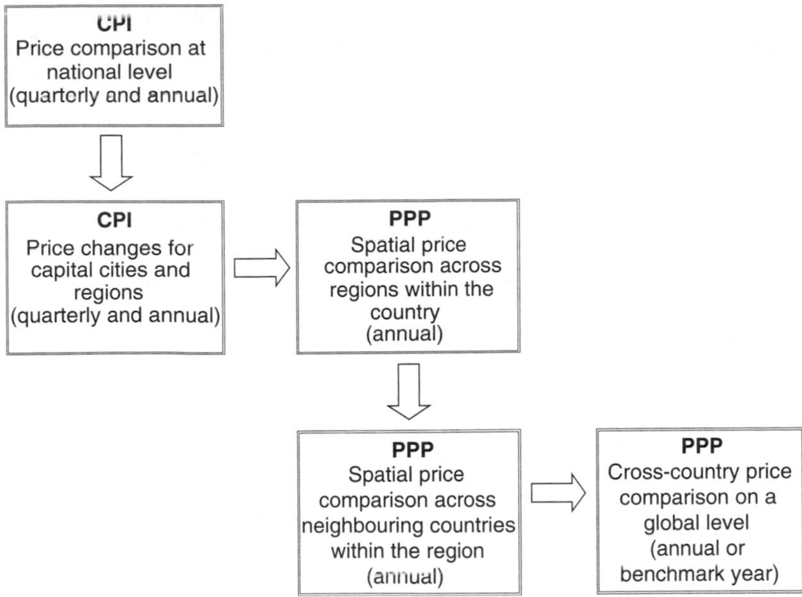

countries appear to produce such indices on a regular basis. A fairly significant jump from this level is to undertake price comparisons, on a bilateral or multilateral basis, with geographically contiguous countries or countries within a political or economic grouping. The last element in this chain is the participation of the national statistical offices in a global price comparison exercise such as the ICP. At present, national statistical offices are mostly involved at the two extreme ends of this spectrum. The general level of involvement of national statistical offices in the ICP is likely to be more enthusiastic, however, when they gain experience from their participation in inter-area comparisons within the country and intra-regional comparisons involving countries in geographical proximity.

5.3 Two core strategies for CPI and ICP integration

Based on the brief discussion of the CPI and ICP activities undertaken by participating national statistical offices, it is possible to identify two major strategies that will result in a level of integration between these two activities that can benefit both programmes and the systems of economic statistics in the participating countries. Both of these strategies emerge from the need to maximize the flow of data from the CPI and ICP, and at the same time provide a framework for improving temporal and inter-area consumer price comparisons within a country.

Use of characteristics approach. This approach was proposed in Zieschang et al. (2001) and alluded to in Rao (2001a). The characteristics approach begins with a market study by a national statistical office analyst to determine a set of price-determining characteristics. These product characteristics, such as size, features, nature of the sale transaction, type of outlet, and so on, are determined according to the available information about the impact of the detailed characteristic on price at a point in time or over a specified reference period, such as a year. Under this approach, product prices are collected and at the same time the product characteristics are also recorded.

In the standard CPI context, the product listing remains fairly constant, except in cases where an old variety or product is replaced by a new one. When spatial comparisons are undertaken, however, the overlap in products may be limited. In such cases, the characteristics approach becomes useful. This approach is in direct contrast with pricing very specific products in all the countries, or in areas within a country, thus limiting the overlap and the usefulness of the resulting CPIs.

The characteristics approach requires price and characteristics data for a sufficiently wide variety of detailed commodities or specifications in the item group to estimate a regression model of price on characteristics. Such models are known as hedonic regression models, where the logarithm of price is regressed on various characteristics. For spatial comparisons, this approach is very similar to the country–product–dummy (CPD) method discussed above in this annex. Kokoski et al. (1999) describe a method of producing "exact", characteristics-adjusted, economic index number comparisons between areas that allow for hedonic equation parameters to differ from one area to another. This method can be classified as a variant of the weighted CPD method along with a multilateral Törnqvist index number.

The main advantages of the characteristics approach is that it is not critically based on the overlap in commodity bundles for different areas or countries, but on the sample size and number of commodities for which prices and quality characteristics are collected. The sample size needs to be large enough to enable efficient estimation of the parameters involved.

In order to facilitate cooperation with the ICP, in addition to having a well-structured database for the CPI that is extended to cover characteristics, the interests of national statistical offices are ultimately best served by implementing product and characteristic classification schemes consistent with internationally agreed standards. In order to make this approach operational, it is necessary that such classification schemes are established by making use of some of the existing classifications, for example the Central Product Classification (CPC) or the Classification of Individual Consumption according to Purpose (COICOP). These product classifications need to be extended to include a core set of standard characteristics for each category within the classification.

Notwithstanding the benefits of the characteristics approach, implementing a scheme of product characteristics classification requires all the countries or parties involved to agree to a specific standard and to allocate the necessary resources for such an endeavour. Until comprehensive data sets with price and characteristics of products become available, it may be necessary to explore other possible approaches that can be used in conjunction with the present "tight specification" approach used in ICP exercises.

Linking approach to international comparisons. If maximizing the overlap with the CPI is one of the principal objectives of the ICP, then multilateral cross-country comparisons need to be built up from bilateral comparisons, where pairs of countries are identified on the basis of the maximum overlap in their national CPI baskets. Once such pairs of countries are identified, then multilateral comparisons can be built using chains constructed on the basis of links. This approach is somewhat similar to the MST approach proposed by Hill. While the basic criterion in Hill's approach uses variability in price relatives, measured using the Laspeyres–Paasche spread, the approach suggested here requires measures of overlap of price data as the principal criterion.

The linking approach needs a multi-stage framework. In the first stage, it is necessary to identify groups of countries to form regions or clusters. The principal criteria that should be used are, first, the extent of overlap that can be achieved between pairs of countries within the group and some measures of similarity in the expenditure patterns. In the second stage, an MST approach should be used to identify the exact links within a regional cluster of countries. Once multilateral regional PPPs are constructed, and PPPs for the GDP and its major components are derived, then the next stage will involve linking various regional comparisons to derive a set of global comparisons and PPPs.

Application of the chaining procedure represents a major shift from the present approach to ICP work. Currently, comparisons within the ICP are based essentially on a top-down approach, where a commodity listing based on the "tight specification" approach is determined in the first instance, and then price data from different countries are collected. Where the ICP work is regionalized, regions are essentially determined on geographical considerations and not on any data-based considerations. If cross-country comparisons are to be based on nationally available CPI data, it is necessary to use a bottom-up approach, where all the operational procedures, including the determination of clusters and links, need to be built with the data available from the national sources provided by the national statistical offices. The application of spatial linking procedures will minimize the need for quality adjustments of the type described under the characteristics approach to price data collection.

The integration of spatial and temporal comparisons has the potential to provide a consistent set of temporal, inter-area and inter-country comparisons, and at the same time improve the quality of the underlying comparisons. It is an exciting prospect, but several challenges need to be met before a truly integrated approach to spatial and temporal consumer price comparisons can be achieved.

BIBLIOGRAPHY

Abraham, K.G., J.S. Greenlees and B.R. Moulton. 1998. "Working to Improve the Consumer Price Index", in *Journal of Economic Perspectives*, Vol. 12, No. 1, pp. 27–36.

Aczél, J. 1987. *A Short Course on Functional Equations* (Dordrecht: Reidel Publishing Co.).

Advisory Commission to Study the Consumer Price Index. 1995. *Toward a More Accurate Measure of the Cost of Living*, Interim Report to the Senate Finance Committee, Sep. 15 (Washington, D.C.).

Aizcorbe, A.M., and P.C. Jackman. 1993. "The commodity substitution effect in CPI data, 1982–91", in *Monthly Labor Review*, Vol. 116, No. 12, pp. 25–33.

Aizcorbe, A., C. Corrado and M. Doms. 2001. *Constructing Price and Quantity Indexes for High Technology Goods*, Industrial Output Section, Division of Research and Statistics (Washington, D.C.: Board of Governors of the Federal Reserve System).

Alterman, W.F., W.E. Diewert and R.C. Feenstra. 1999. *International Trade Price Indexes and Seasonal Commodities* (Washington, D.C.: Bureau of Labor Statistics).

Anderson, R.G., B.E. Jones and T. Nesmith. 1997. "Building New Monetary Services Indexes: Concepts, Data and Methods", in *Federal Reserve Bank of St. Louis Review*, Vol. 79, No. 1, pp. 53–83.

Ardilly, P. and F. Guglielmetti. 1993. "La précision de l'indice des prix: mesure et optimisation", in *Economie et Statistique*, No. 267, juillet.

Arguea, N.M., C. Haseo and G.A. Taylor. 1994. "Estimating Consumer Preferences using Market Data: An Application to U.S. Automobile Demand", in *Journal of Applied Econometrics*, Vol. 9, pp. 1–18.

Armknecht, P.A. 1996. *Improving the Efficiency of the U.S. CPI*, Working Paper No. 96/103 (Washington, D.C.: IMF).

—— and D. Weyback. 1989. "Adjustments for Quality Change in the U.S. Consumer Price Index", in *Journal of Official Statistics*, Vol. 5, No. 2, pp. 107–123.

—— and F. Maitland-Smith. 1999. *Price Imputation and Other Techniques for Dealing with Missing Observations, Seasonality and Quality Change in Price Indices*, Working Paper No. 99/78 (Washington, D.C.: IMF), June. Available at: http://www.imf.org/external/pubs/ft/wp/1999/wp9978.pdf

——, W.F. Lane and K.J. Stewart. 1997. "New Products and the U.S. Consumer Price Index", in R.C. Feenstra and M.D. Shapiro (eds.): *Scanner Data and Price Indexes*, NBER Studies in Income and Wealth (Chicago, IL: University of Chicago Press, 2003), pp. 375–391.

Arrow, K.J., H.B. Chenery, B.S. Minhas and R.M. Solow. 1961. "Capital–Labor Substitution and Economic Efficiency", in *Review of Economics and Statistics*, Vol. 63, pp. 225–250.

Astin, J. 1999. "The European Union Harmonized Indices of Consumer Prices. HICP)", in R. Gudnason and T. Gylfadottir (eds.): *Proceedings of the Ottawa Group Fifth Meeting*, Reykjavik, Iceland, 25–27 Aug.; also published in *Statistical Journal of the United Nations ECE*, Vol. 16, pp. 123–135. Available at: http://www.statcan.ca/secure/english/ottawa group/

——. 2001. *New Uses of PPPs within the European Union*, Paper presented at the Joint World Bank–OECD Seminar on Purchasing Power Parities: Recent Advances in Methods and Applications, Washington, D.C., Jan. 30–Feb. 2.

Aten, B., R. Summers and A. Heston. 2001. *An Explanation of Stability in Country Price Structures: Implications for Spatial–temporal Comparisons*, Paper presented at the Joint World Bank–OECD Seminar on Purchasing Power Parities: Recent Advances in Methods and Applications, Washington, D.C., Jan. 30–Feb. 2.

Australian Bureau of Statistics. 1997. *An Analytical Framework for Price Indexes in Australia*, Information Paper, Catalogue No. 6421.0. Available at: http://www.abs.gov.au

——. 2000. *Price Index and The New Tax System*, Information Paper, Catalogue No. 6425.0. Available at: http://www.abs.gov.au

——. 2003. *Australian Consumer Price Index: Concepts, Sources and Methods*, Catalogue No. 6461.0. Available at: http://www.abs.gov.au/

Bailey, M.J., Muth, R.F. and Nourse, H.O. 1963. "A Regression Method for Real Estate Price Construction", in *Journal of the American Statistical Association*, Vol. 58, pp. 933–942.

Baker, D. 1998. "Does the CPI Overstate Inflation? An Analysis of the Boskin Commission Report", in D. Baker (ed.): *Getting Prices Right* (Washington, D.C.: Economic Policy Institute), pp. 79–155.

Baldwin, A. 1990. "Seasonal Baskets in Consumer Price Indexes", in *Journal of Official Statistics*, Vol. 6, No. 3, pp. 251–273.

Balk, B.M. 1980a. "Seasonal Products in Agriculture and Horticulture and Methods for Computing Price Indices", in *Statistical Studies No. 24* (The Hague: Netherlands Central Bureau of Statistics).

——. 1980b. "Seasonal Commodities and the Construction of Annual and Monthly Price Indexes", in *Statistische Hefte*, Vol. 21, pp. 110–116.

——. 1980c. "A Method for Constructing Price Indices for Seasonal Commodities", in *The Journal of the Royal Statistical Society Series A*, Vol. 143, pp. 68–75.

——. 1981. "A Simple Method for Constructing Price Indices for Seasonal Commodities", in *Statistische Hefte*, Vol. 22, pp. 72–78.

——. 1983. "Does There Exist a Relation between Inflation and Relative Price Change Variability? The Effect of the Aggregation Level", in *Economic Letters*, Vol. 13, pp. 173–180.

——. 1985. "A Simple Characterization of Fisher's Price Index", in *Statistische Hefte*, Vol. 26, pp. 59–63.

——. 1989a. "Changing Consumer Preferences and the Cost of Living Index: Theory and Nonparametric Expressions", in *Zeitschrift für Nationalökonomie*, Vol. 50, No. 2, pp. 157–169.

——. 1989b. "On Calculating the Precision of Consumer Price Indices", in *Contributed Papers 47th Session of the ISI* (Paris).

——. 1990. "On Calculating Cost-of-Living Index Numbers for Arbitrary Income Levels", in *Econometrica*, Vol. 58, No. 1, pp. 75–92.

——. 1994. *On the First Step in the Calculation of a Consumer Price Index*, Paper presented at First Meeting of the International Working Group on Price Indices, Ottawa, Oct. 31–Nov. 4. Available at: http://www.ottawagroup.org

——. 1995. "Axiomatic Price Index Theory: A Survey", in *International Statistical Review*, Vol. 63, pp. 69–93.

——. 1996a. "A Comparison of Ten Methods for Multilateral International Price and Volume Comparisons", in *Journal of Official Statistics*, Vol. 12, pp. 199–222.

——. 1996b. "Consistency in Aggregation and Stuvel Indices", in *The Review of Income and Wealth*, Vol. 42, pp. 353–363.

——. 1998a. *Industrial Price, Quantity and Productivity Indices* (Boston, MA: Kluwer Academic Publishers).

——. 1998b. *On the Use of Unit Value Indices as Consumer Price Subindices*, Paper presented at the Fourth Meeting of the International Working Group on Price Indices, Washington, D.C., Apr. 22–24. Available at: http://www.ottawagroup.org

——. 2000a. *Divisia Price and Quantity Indexes 75 Years After*, Draft Paper, Department of Statistical Methods (Voorburg: Statistics Netherlands).

——. 2000b. *On Curing the CPI's Substitution and New Goods Bias*, Research Paper 0005, Department of Statistical Methods (Voorburg: Statistics Netherlands).

——. 2001. *Aggregation Methods in International Comparisons: What have we Learned?*, Report Series Research in Management ERS-2001-41-MKT, Erasmus Research Institute of Management (Rotterdam: Erasmus University).

——. 2002. *Price Indexes for Elementary Aggregates: The Sampling Approach*, Research Report, Methods and Informatics Department (Voorburg: Statistics Netherlands).

—— and W.E. Diewert. 2001. "A Characterization of the Törnqvist Price Index", in *Economics Letters*, Vol. 73, pp. 279–281.

—— and H.M.P. Kersten. 1986. "On the Precision of Consumer Price Indices Caused by the Sampling Variability of Budget Surveys", in *Journal of Economic and Social Measurement*, Vol. 14, pp. 19–35.

Bartik, T.J. 1988. "Measuring the Benefits of Land Improvements in Hedonic Models", in *Land Economics*, Vol. 64, No. 2, pp. 172–183.

Bascher, J. and T. Lacroix. 1999. *Dishwashers and PCs in the French CPI: Hedonic Modeling, from Design to Practice*, Paper presented at the Fifth Meeting of the International Working Group on Price Indices, Reykjavik, Aug. 25–27. Available at: http://www.ottawagroup.org

Baxter, M. (ed.). 1998. *The Retail Prices Index. Technical Manual* (London: Office for National Statistics, UK).

Bean, L.H. and O.C. Stine. 1924. "Four Types of Index Numbers of Farm Prices", in *Journal of the American Statistical Association*, Vol. 19, pp. 30–35.

Becker, G.S. 1965. "A Theory of the Allocation of Time", in *Economic Journal*, Vol. 75, pp. 493–517.

Beidelman, C. 1973. *Valuation of Used Capital Assets* (Sarasota, FL: American Accounting Association).

——. 1976. "Economic Depreciation in a Capital Goods Industry", in *National Tax Journal*, Vol. 29, pp. 379–390.

Berndt, E.R. 1991. *The Practice of Econometrics: Classic and Contemporary* (Reading, MA: Addison-Wesley).

——, D. Ling and M.K. Kyle. 2003. "The Long Shadow of Patent Expiration: Generic Entry and Rx to OTC Switches", in M. Shapiro and R.C. Feenstra (eds.): *Scanner Data and Price Indexes*, NBER Studies in Income and Wealth (Chicago, IL: University of Chicago Press), pp. 229–273.

——, L.T. Bui, D.H. Lucking-Reiley and G.L. Urban. 1997. "The Roles of Marketing, Product Quality and Price Competition in the Growth and Composition of the U.S. Anti-Ulcer Drug Industry", in T. Bresnahan and R.J. Gordon: *The Economics of New Goods*, NBER Studies in Income and Wealth (Chicago and London: University of Chicago Press), pp. 277–232.

——, Z. Griliches and N.J. Rappaport. 1995. "Econometric Estimates of Price Indexes for Personal Computers in the 1990s", in *Journal of Econometrics*, Vol. 68, pp. 243–68.

Berry S., J. Levinsohn and A. Pakes. 1995. "Automobile Prices in Market Equilibrium", in *Econometrica*, Vol. 63, No. 4, pp. 841–890; also published as NBER Working Paper No. W4264, July 1996, available at: http://www.nber.org.

Beuerlein, I. 2001. *The German consumer price index for telecommunication services: a user profile approach for mobile technology and Internet access*, Paper presented at the Sixth Meeting of the International Working Group on Price Indices, Canberra, Apr. 2–6. Available at: http://www.ottawagroup.org/

Bode, B. and van J. Dalén. 2001. *Quality-Corrected Price Indexes of New Passenger Cars in the Netherlands, 1990–1999*, Paper presented at the Sixth Meeting of the International Working Group on Price Indices, Canberra, Apr. 2–6. Available at: http://www.ottawagroup.org

Böhm-Bawerk, E.V. 1891. *The Positive Theory of Capital*, translated from the original German edition of 1888 by W. Smart (New York: G.E. Stechert).

Boon, M. 1998. "Sampling designs in compiling consumer price indices: current practices at EU statistical institutes", in *Research in Official Statistics*, Vol. 1, No. 2, pp. 39–52.

Bortkiewicz, L.V. 1923. "Zweck und Struktur einer Preisindexzahl", in *Nordisk Statistisk Tidsskrift* 2, pp. 369–408.

Boskin, M.J. (Chair), E.R. Dullberger, R.J. Gordon, Z. Griliches and D.W. Jorgenson. 1996. *Final Report of the Commission to Study the Consumer Price Index*, U.S. Senate, Committee on Finance (Washington, D.C.: U.S. Government Printing Office).

——. 1998. "Consumer Prices in the Consumer Price Index and the Cost of Living", in *Journal of Economic Perspectives*, Vol. 12, No. 1, pp. 3–26.

Bowley, A.L. 1899. "Wages, Nominal and Real", in R.H.I. Palgrave. (ed.): *Dictionary of Political Economy*, Volume 3 (London: Macmillan), pp. 640–651.

——. 1901. *Elements of Statistics* (Westminster: Orchard House).

——. 1919. "The Measurement of Changes in the Cost of Living", in *Journal of the Royal Statistical Society*, Vol. 82, pp. 343–361.

Bradley, R., B. Cook, S.E. Leaver and B. R. Moulton. 1997. *An Overview of Research on Potential Uses of Scanner Data in the U.S. CPI*, Paper presented at the Third Meeting of the International Working Group on Price Indices, Voorburg, Apr. 16–18. Available at: http://www.ottawagroup.org

Braithwait, S.D. 1980. "The Substitution Bias of the Laspeyres Price Index: An Analysis Using Estimated Cost-of-Living Indexes", in *American Economic Review*, Vol. 70, No. 1, pp. 64–77.

Bresnahan, T.F. 1997. "Comment", in T.F. Bresnahan and R.J. Gordon (eds.): *The Economics of New Goods*, NBER Studies in Income and Wealth (Chicago, IL: University of Chicago Press), pp. 237–247.

Canning, J.B. 1929. *The Economics of Accountancy* (New York: The Ronald Press Co.).

Carli, G.-R. 1804. "Del valore e della proporzione dei metalli monetati", in *Scrittori classici italiani di economia politica*, Vol. 13 (Milano: G.G. Destefanis), pp. 297–366; originally published in 1764.

Carruthers, A.G., D.J. Sellwood and P.W. Ward. 1980. "Recent Developments in the Retail Prices Index", in *The Statistician*, Vol. 29, pp. 1–32.

Cassel, E. and R. Mendelsohn. 1985. "On the Choice of Functional Forms for Hedonic Price Equations: Comment", in *Journal of Urban Economics*, Vol. 18, Sep., pp. 135–142.

Castles, I. 1997. *The OECD–EUROSTAT PPP Program: Review of Practice and Procedures* (Paris: OECD).

Caves, D.W., L.R. Christensen and W.E. Diewert. 1982a. "The Economic Theory of Index Numbers and the Measurement of Input, Output and Productivity", in *Econometrica*, Vol. 50, 1393–1414.

——, L.R. Christensen and W.E. Diewert. 1982b. "Multilateral Comparisons of Output, Input and Productivity using Superlative Index Numbers", in *Economic Journal*, Vol. 92, pp. 73–86.

Cecchetti, S.G. 1997. "Measuring Inflation for Central Bankers", in *Federal Reserve Bank of St. Louis Review*, Vol. 79, pp. 143–155.

Christensen, L.R. and D.W. Jorgenson. 1969. "The Measurement of U.S. Real Capital Input, 1929–1967", in *Review of Income and Wealth*, Vol. 15, No. 4, pp. 293–320.

——, —— and L.J. Lau. 1971. "Conjugate Duality and the Transcendental Logarithmic Production Function", in *Econometrica*, Vol. 39, pp. 255–256.

Church, A.H. 1901. "The Proper Distribution of Establishment Charges, Part III", in *The Engineering Magazine*, Vol. 21, pp. 904–912.

Clements, K.W. and H.Y. Izan. 1981. "A Note on Estimating Divisia Index Numbers", in *International Economic Review*, Vol. 22, pp. 745–747.

—— and H.Y. Izan. 1987. "The Measurement of Inflation: A Stochastic Approach", in *Journal of Business and Economic Statistics*, Vol. 5, pp. 339–350.

Cobb, C. and P.H. Douglas. 1928. "A Theory of Production", in *American Economic Review*, Vol. 18, pp. 39–165.

Cochran, W.G. 1977. *Sampling Techniques*, 3rd edition (New York: Wiley).

Cockburn, I.M. and A.H. Anis. 1998. *Hedonic Analysis and Arthritic Drugs*, Working Paper 6574 (Cambridge, MA: National Bureau of Economic Research).

Coggeshall, F. 1887. "The Arithmetic, Geometric and Harmonic Means", in *Quarterly Journal of Economics*, Vol. 1, pp. 83–86.

Combris, P., S. Lecocqs and M. Visser. 1997. "Estimation of a Hedonic Price Equation for Bordeaux Wine: Does Quality Matter?", in *Economic Journal*, Vol. 107, No. 441, pp. 390–402.

Commission of the European Communities (Eurostat), IMF, OECD, United Nations and World Bank. 1993. *System of National Accounts 1993* (Brussels/Luxembourg, New York, Paris, Washington, D.C.).

Congressional Budget Office (CBO). 1994. *Is the Growth of the CPI a Biased Measure of Changes in the Cost of Living?*, CBO Paper, Oct. (Washington, D.C.).

Crawford, A. 1998. "Measurement Biases in the Canadian CPI: An Update", in *Bank of Canada Review*, Spring, pp. 39–56.

Cropper, M.L., L.L. Deck and K.E. McConnell. 1988. "On the Choice of Functional Form for Hedonic Price Functions", in *Review of Economics and Statistics*, Vol. 70, No. 4, pp. 668–675.

Crump, N. 1924. "The Interrelation and Distribution of Prices and their Incidence Upon Price Stabilization", in *Journal of the Royal Statistical Society*, Vol. 87, pp. 167–206.

Cunningham, A.W.F. 1996. *Measurement Bias in Price Indices: An Application to the UK's RPI*, Bank of England Working Paper 47 (London: Bank of England).

Curry, B., P. Morgan and M. Silver. 2001. "Hedonic Regressions: Misspecification and Neural Networks", in *Applied Economics*, Vol. 33, pp. 659–671.

Czinkota, M.R. and I. Ronkainen. 1997. "International Business and Trade in the Next Decade: Report from a Delphi Study", in *Journal of International Business Studies*, Vol. 28, No. 4, pp. 827–844.

Dalén, J. 1992. "Computing Elementary Aggregates in the Swedish Consumer Price Index", in *Journal of Official Statistics*, Vol. 8, pp. 129–147.

——. 1994. *Sensitivity Analyses for Harmonizing European Consumer Price Indices*, Paper presented at the First Meeting of the International Working Group on Price Indices, Ottawa, Oct. 31–Nov. 4. Available at: http://www.ottawagroup.org

——. 1995. "Quantifying errors in the Swedish consumer price index", in *Journal of Official Statistics*, Vol. 13, No. 3, pp. 347–356.

——. 1997. *Experiments with Swedish Scanner Data*, Paper presented at the Third Meeting of the International Working Group on Price Indices, Voorburg, Apr. 16–18. Available at: http://www.ottawagroup.org.

——. 1998a. *On the Statistical Objective of a Laspeyres Price Index*, Paper presented at the Fourth Meeting of the International Working Group on Price Indices, Washington, D.C., Apr. 22–24. Available at: http://www.ottawagroup.org.

——. 1998b. "Studies on the Comparability of Consumer Price Indices", in *International Statistical Review*, Vol. 66, No. 1, pp. 83–113.

——. 1999a. "On Reliability, Uncertainty and Bias in Consumer Price Indexes", in M. Silver and D. Fenwick (eds.): *Proceedings of the Measurement of Inflation Conference* (Cardiff: Cardiff University), pp. 184–190.

——. 1999b. *A note on the Variance of the Sample Geometric Mean*, Research Report 1991: 1, Department of Statistics (Stockholm: Stockholm University).

—— and O. Muelteel. 1998. *Variance estimation in the Luxembourg CPI*, Cellule "Statistique et décision" (Luxembourg: Centre de Recherche Public–Centre Universitaire).

—— and E. Ohlsson. 1995. "Variance Estimation in the Swedish Consumer Price Index", in *Journal of Business and Economic Statistics*, Vol. 13, No. 3, pp. 347–356.

Dalton, K.V., J.S. Greenlees, and K.J. Stewart. 1998. "Incorporating a Geometric Mean Formula into the CPI", in *Monthly Labor Review*, Vol. 121, No. 10, pp. 3–7.

Davies, G.R. 1924. "The Problem of a Standard Index Number Formula", in *Journal of the American Statistical Association*, Vol. 19, pp. 180–188.

——. 1932. "Index Numbers in Mathematical Economics", in *Journal of the American Statistical Association*, Vol. 27, pp. 58–64.

de Haan, J. 2001. *Generalised Fisher Price Indexes and the Use of Scanner Data in the CPI*, Unpublished Paper (Voorburg: Statistics Netherlands).

——. 2003. *Time Dummy Approaches to Hedonic Price Measurement*, Paper presented at the Seventh Meeting of the International Working Group on Price Indices, Paris, May 27–29. Available at: http://www.insee.fr/

—— and E. Opperdoes. 1997. *Estimation of the Coffee Price Index Using Scanner Data: Simulation of Official Practices*, Paper presented at the Third Meeting of the International Working Group on Price Indices, Voorburg, Apr. 16–18. Available at: http://www.ottawagroup.org

——, E. Opperdoes, and C. Schut. 1997. *Item Sampling in the Consumer Price Index: A Case Study using Scanner Data*, Research Report (Voorburg: Statistics Netherlands).

——, E. Opperdoes, and C. Schut. 1999. "Item Selection in the Consumer Price Index: Cut-off Versus Probability Sampling", in *Survey Methodology*, Vol. 25, No. 1, pp. 31–41.

Deaton, A. 1998. "Getting prices right: What should be done?", in *Journal of Economic Perspectives*, Vol. 12, No. 1, pp. 37–46.

Denny, M. 1974. "The Relationship Between Functional Forms for the Production System", in *Canadian Journal of Economics*, Vol. 7, pp. 21–31.

Diewert, W.E. 1974a. "Applications of Duality Theory", in M.D. Intriligator and D.A. Kendrick (eds.): *Frontiers of Quantitative Economics*, Vol. II (Amsterdam: North-Holland) pp. 106–171.

——. 1974b. "Intertemporal Consumer Theory and the Demand for Durables", in *Econometrica*, Vol. 42, pp. 497–516.

——. 1976. "Exact and Superlative Index Numbers", in *Journal of Econometrics*, Vol. 4, pp. 114–145.

——. 1978. "Superlative Index Numbers and Consistency in Aggregation", in *Econometrica*, Vol. 46, pp. 883–900.

——. 1980. "Aggregation Problems in the Measurement of Capital", in D. Usher (ed.): *The Measurement of Capital*, NBER Studies in Income and Wealth (Chicago, IL: University of Chicago Press), pp. 433–528.

——. 1983a. "The Theory of the Cost of Living Index and the Measurement of Welfare Change", in W.E. Diewert and C. Montmarquette (eds.): *Price Level Measurement* (Ottawa: Statistics Canada), pp. 163–233; reprinted in W.E. Diewert (ed.): *Price Level Measurement* (Amsterdam: North-Holland, 1990), pp. 79–147.

——. 1983b. "The Theory of the Output Price Index and the Measurement of Real Output Change", in W.E. Diewert and C. Montmarquette (eds.): *Price Level Measurement* (Ottawa: Statistics Canada), pp. 1049–1113.

——. 1983c. "The Treatment of Seasonality in a Cost of Living Index", in W.E. Diewert and C. Montmarquette (eds.): *Price Level Measurement* (Ottawa: Statistics Canada), pp. 1019–1045.

——. 1986. *Microeconomic Approaches to the Theory of International Comparisons*, Technical Working Paper No. 53 (Cambridge, MA: National Bureau of Economic Research).

——. 1992a. "Fisher Ideal Output, Input and Productivity Indexes Revisited", in *Journal of Productivity Analysis*, Vol. 3, pp. 211–248.

——. 1992b. "Exact and Superlative Welfare Change Indicators", in *Economic Inquiry*, Vol. 30, pp. 565–582.

——. 1993a. "The Early History of Price Index Research", in W.E. Diewert and A.O. Nakamura (eds.): *Essays in Index Number Theory*, Vol. 1, Contributions to Economic Analysis 217 (Amsterdam: North-Holland), pp. 33–65.

——. 1993b. "Duality Approaches to Microeconomic Theory", in W.E. Diewert and A.O. Nakamura (eds.): *Essays in Index Number Theory*, Vol. 1, Contributions to Economic Analysis 217 (Amsterdam: North-Holland), pp. 105–175.

——. 1993c. "Symmetric Means and Choice under Uncertainty", in W.E. Diewert and A.O. Nakamura (eds.): *Essays in Index Number Theory*, Vol. 1, Contributions to Economic Analysis 217 (Amsterdam: North-Holland), pp. 355–433.

——. 1993d. "Overview of Volume 1", in W.E. Diewert and A.O. Nakamura (eds.): *Essays in Index Number Theory*, Vol. 1, Contributions to Economic Analysis 217 (Amsterdam: North-Holland) pp. 1–31.

——. 1995a. *Axiomatic and Economic Approaches to Elementary Price Indexes*, Discussion Paper No. 95–01, Department of Economics (Vancouver: University of British Columbia). Available at: http://www.econ.ubc.ca

——. 1995b. *On the Stochastic Approach to Index Numbers*, Discussion Paper No. 95–31, Department of Economics (Vancouver: University of British Columbia). Available at: http://www.econ.ubc.ca

——. 1996a. "Price and Volume Measures in the National Accounts", in J. Kendrick (ed.): *The New System of National Economic Accounts* (Norwell, MA: Kluwer Academic Publishers), pp. 237–285.

——. 1996b. *Seasonal Commodities, High Inflation and Index Number Theory*, Discussion Paper 96–06, Department of Economics (Vancouver: University of British Columbia).

——. 1996c. *Sources of Bias in Consumer Price Indexes*, Discussion Paper, School of Economics (Sydney: University of New South Wales).

——. 1997. "Commentary on Mathew D. Shapiro and David W. Wilcox: Alternative Strategies for Aggregating Price in the CPI", in *The Federal Reserve Bank of St. Louis Review*, Vol. 79, No. 3, pp. 127–137.

——. 1998a. "Index Number Issues in the Consumer Price Index", in *The Journal of Economic Perspectives*, Vol. 12, No. 1, pp. 47–58.

——. 1998b. "High Inflation, Seasonal Commodities and Annual Index Numbers", in *Macroeconomic Dynamics*, Vol. 2, pp. 456–471.

——. 1999a. "Index Number Approaches to Seasonal Adjustment", in *Macroeconomic Dynamics*, Vol. 3, pp. 48–68.

——. 1999b. "Axiomatic and Economic Approaches to Multilateral Comparisons", in A. Heston and R.E. Lipsey (eds.): *International and Interarea Comparisons of Income, Output and Prices* (Chicago, IL: University of Chicago Press), pp. 13–87.

——. 2000. *Notes on Producing an Annual Superlative Index Using Monthly Price Data*, Discussion Paper No. 00-08, Department of Economics (Vancouver: University of British Columbia). Available at: http://www.econ.ubc.ca

——. 2001. "The Consumer Price Index and Index Number Purpose", in *Journal of Economic and Social Measurement*, Vol. 27, pp. 167–240.

——. 2002a. "The Quadratic Approximation Lemma and Decompositions of Superlative Indexes", in *Journal of Economic and Social Measurement*, Vol. 28, pp. 63–88.

——. 2002b. *Similarity and Dissimilarity Indexes: An Axiomatic Approach*, Discussion Paper No. 02-10, Department of Economics (Vancouver: University of British Columbia). Available at: http://www.econ.ubc.ca

——. 2002c. "Harmonized Indexes of Consumer Prices: Their Conceptual Foundations", in *Swiss Journal of Economics and Statistics*, Vol. 138, No. 4, pp. 547–637.

——. 2002d. *Notes on Hedonic Producer Price Indexes*, Unpublished Paper, Department of Economics (Vancouver: University of British Columbia), Jan.

——. 2002e. *Hedonic Regressions: A Review of Some Unresolved Issues*, Unpublished Paper, Department of Economics (Vancouver: University of British Columbia).

——. 2003a. "Hedonic Regressions: A Consumer Theory Approach", in R.C. Feenstra and M.D. Shapiro (eds.): *Scanner Data and Price Indexes*, NBER Studies in Income and Wealth (Chicago, IL: The University of Chicago Press), pp. 317–348.

——. 2003b. *Measuring Capital*, NBER Working Paper W9526 (Cambridge, MA: National Bureau of Economic Research).

—— and D.A. Lawrence. 2000. "Progress in Measuring the Price and Quantity of Capital", in L.J. Lau (ed.): *Econometrics Volume 2: Econometrics and the cost of Capital: Essays in Honor of Dale W. Jorgenson* (Cambridge, MA: The MIT Press), pp. 273–326.

Dikhanov, Y. 1997. *The Sensitivity of PPP-Based Income Estimates to Choice of Aggregation Procedures*, Unpublished Paper, International Economics Department (Washington, D.C.: World Bank), Jan.

Dippo, C.S. and C.A. Jacobs. 1983. "Area Sampling Redesign for the Consumer Price Index", in *Proceedings of the Survey Research Methods Section, American Statistical Association*, pp. 118–123.

Divisia, F. 1926. *L'indice monétaire et la théorie de la monnaie* (Paris: Société anonyme du Recueil Sirey).

Drechsler, L. 1973. "Weighting of Index Numbers in Multilateral International Comparisons", in *Review of Income and Wealth*, Vol. 19, pp. 17–34.

Drobisch, M. W. 1871a. "Ueber die Berechnung der Veränderungen der Waarenpreise und des Geldwerths", in *Jahrbücher für Nationalökonomie und Statistik*, Vol. 16, pp. 143–156.

—— 1871b. "Ueber einige Einwürfe gegen die in diesen Jahrbüchern veröffentlichte neue Methode, die Veränderungen der Waarenpreise und des Geldwerths zu berechten", in *Jahrbücher für Nationalökonomie und Statistik*, Vol. 16, pp. 416–427.

Ducharme, L.M. 1997. "The Canadian Consumer Price Index and the Bias Issue: Present and Future Outlooks" in L.M. Ducharme (ed.): *Bias in the CPI: Experiences from Five OECD Countries*, Prices Division Analytical Series, No. 10 (Ottawa: Statistics Canada), pp. 13–24.

Duggan, J. E. and R. Gillingham. 1999. "The Effect of Errors in the CPI on Social Security Finances", in *Journal of Business and Economic Statistics*, Vol. 17, No. 2, pp. 161–169.

Dulberger, E.R. 1989. "The Application of an Hedonic Model to a Quality-Adjusted Price Index For Computer Processors", in D. Jorgenson and R. Landau (eds.): *Technology and Capital Formation* (Cambridge, MA: MIT Press).

——. 1993. "Sources of Price Decline in Computer Processors: Selected Electronic Components", in M. Foss, M.E. Manser and A.H. Young (eds.): *Price Measurement and their Uses*, NBER Studies in Income and Wealth (Chicago, IL: University of Chicago Press), pp. 103–124.

Dutot, C. 1738. *Réflections politiques sur les finances et le commerce*, Vol. 1 (La Haye: Les frères Vaillant et N. Prevost).

Dwyer, L., P. Forsyth and D.S. Prasada Rao. 2001. *PPPs and the Price Competitiveness of International Tourism Destinations*, Paper presented at the Joint World Bank–OECD Seminar on Purchasing Power Parities: Recent Advances in Methods and Applications, Washington, D.C., Jan. 30–Feb. 2.

Edgeworth, F.Y. 1888. "Some New Methods of Measuring Variation in General Prices", in *Journal of the Royal Statistical Society*, Vol. 51, pp. 346–368.

——. 1923. "The Doctrine of Index Numbers According to Mr. Correa Walsh", in *The Economic Journal*, Vol. 11, pp. 343–351.

——. 1925. *Papers Relating to Political Economy*, Vol. 1 (New York: Burt Franklin).

Edwards, R. 1997. "Measuring Inflation in Australia", in L.M. Ducharme (ed.): *Bias in the CPI: Experiences from Five OECD Countries*, Prices Division Analytical Series, No. 10 (Ottawa: Statistics Canada), pp. 5–12.

Ehemann, C., A.J. Katz and B.R. Moulton. 2002. "The Chain-Additivity Issue and the U.S. National Accounts", in *Journal of Economic and Social Measurement*, Vol. 28, pp. 37–49.

Eichhorn, W. 1978. *Functional Equations in Economics* (Reading, MA: Addison-Wesley Publishing Company).

—— and J. Voeller. 1976. *Theory of the Price Index*, Lecture Notes in Economics and Mathematical Systems, Vol. 140 (Berlin: Springer-Verlag).

Eldridge, L.P. 1999. "How price indexes affect BLS productivity measures", in *Monthly Labor Review*, Vol. 122, No. 2, pp. 35–46.

Elteto, O. and P. Koves. 1964. "On an Index Number Computation Problem in International Comparison", in *Statisztikai Szemle*, Vol. 42, pp. 507–518 (in Czech).

Epple, D. 1987. "Hedonic Prices and Implicit Markets: Estimating Demand and Supply Functions for Differentiated Products", in *Journal of Political Economy*, Vol. 95, pp. 59–80.

European Foundation for Quality Management Excellence Model (Brussels: European Foundation for Quality Management). Available at: http://www.efqm.org

Eurostat. 1993. *Classification of Products by Activity in the European Economic Community* (CPA) (Luxembourg).

——. 2001a. *Compendium of HICP Reference Documents* (Luxembourg: Unit B3, Harmonisation of Price Indices), Mar.

——. 2001b. *Handbook on Price and Volume Measures in National Accounts* (Luxembourg: European Commission).

Feenstra, R.C. 1994. "New Product Varieties and the Measurement of International Prices", in *American Economic Review*, Vol. 34, pp. 157–177.

——. 1995. "Exact Hedonic Price Indices", in *Review of Economics and Statistics*, Vol. 77, pp. 634–654.

—— and C.R. Shiells. 1997. "Bias in U.S. Import Prices and Demand", in T.F. Bresnahan and R.J. Gordon (eds.): *The Economics of New Goods*, NBER Studies in Income and Wealth (Chicago, IL: University of Chicago), pp. 249–276.

—— and M.D. Shapiro. 2003. "High Frequency Substitution and the Measurement of Price Indexes", in R.C. Feenstra and M.D. Shapiro (eds.): *Scanner Data and Price Indexes*, NBER Studies in Income and Wealth (Chicago, IL: The University of Chicago Press), pp. 123–146.

—— and W.E. Diewert. 2001. *Imputation and Price Indexes: Theory and Evidence from the International Price Program*, Working Paper No. 335 (Washington, D.C.: Bureau of Labor Statistics). Available at: http://www.bls.gov

Fenwick, D. 1997. "The Boskin Report from a United Kingdom Perspective", in L.M. Ducharme (ed.): *Bias in the CPI: Experiences from Five OECD Countries*, Prices Division Analytical Series, No. 10 (Ottawa: Statistics Canada), pp. 45–52.

——, A. Ball, M. Silver and P.H. Morgan. 2003. "Price Collection and Quality Assurance of Item Sampling in the Retail Price Index: How Can Scanner Data Help?", in M. Shapiro and R. Feenstra (eds.): *Scanner Data and Price Indexes*, NBER Studies in Income and Wealth (Chicago, IL: University of Chicago Press, 2003), pp. 67–87.

Ferger, W.F. 1931. "The Nature and Use of the Harmonic Mean", in *Journal of the American Statistical Association*, Vol. 26, pp. 36–40.

——. 1936. "Distinctive Concepts of Price and Purchasing Power Index Numbers", in *Journal of the American Statistical Association*, Vol. 31, pp. 258–272.

Ferrari, G. and M. Riani. 1998. "On Purchasing Power Parities Calculation at the Basic Heading Level", in *Statistica*, Vol. LVIII, pp. 91–108.

——, G. Gozzi and M. Riani. 1996. "Comparing GEKS and EPD Approaches for Calculating PPPs at the Basic Heading level", in Eurostat: *Improving the Quality of Price Indices: CPI and PPP* (Luxembourg).

Fisher, F.M. and K. Shell. 1972. "The Pure Theory of the National Output Deflator", in *The Economic Theory of Price Indexes* (New York: Academic Press), pp. 49–113.

Fisher, I. 1897. "The Role of Capital in Economic Theory", in *Economic Journal*, Vol. 7, pp. 511–537.

——. 1911. *The Purchasing Power of Money* (London: Macmillan).

——. 1921. "The Best Form of Index Number", in *Journal of the American Statistical Association*, Vol. 17, pp. 533–537.

——. 1922. *The Making of Index Numbers* (Boston, MA: Houghton-Mifflin).

Fisher, W.C. 1913. "The Tabular Standard in Massachusetts History", in *Quarterly Journal of Economics*, Vol. 27, pp. 417–451.

Fixler, D. and K.D. Zieschang. 1992. "Incorporating Ancillary Measures of Processes and Quality Change into a Superlative Productivity Index", in *Journal of Productivity Analysis*, Vol. 2, pp. 245–267.

—— and K.D. Zieshang. 2001. *Price Indices for Financial Services*, Paper presented at the Sixth Meeting of the International Working Group on Price Indices, Canberra, Apr. 2–6. Available at: http://www.ottawagroup.org

Flux, A.W. 1921. "The Measurement of Price Change", in *Journal of the Royal Statistical Society*, Vol. 84, pp. 167–199.

Forsyth, F.G., and R.F. Fowler. 1981. "The Theory and Practice of Chain Price Index Numbers", in *Journal of the Royal Statistical Society A*, Vol. 144, No. 2, pp. 224–247.

Frisch, R. 1930. "Necessary and Sufficient Conditions Regarding the Form of an Index Number Which Shall Meet Certain of Fisher's Tests", in *Journal of the American Statistical Association*, Vol. 25, pp. 397–406.

——. 1936. "Annual Survey of General Economic Theory: The Problem of Index Numbers", in *Econometrica*, Vol. 4, pp. 1–38.

Frost, S. 2001. *The Construction of Price Indices for Deposit and Loan Facilities*, Paper presented at the Sixth Meeting of the International Working Group on Price Indices, Canberra, Apr. 2–6. Available at: www.ottawagroup.org/

Funke, H. and J. Voeller. 1978. "A Note on the Characterization of Fisher's Ideal Index", in W. Eichhorn, R. Henn, O. Opitz and R.W. Shephard (eds.): *Theory and Applications of Economic Indices* (Würzburg: Physica-Verlag), pp. 177–181.

——, G. Hacker and J. Voeller. 1979. "Fisher's Circular Test Reconsidered", in *Schweizerische Zeitschrift für Volkswirtshaft und Statistik*, Vol. 115, pp. 677–687.

Garcke, E. and J.M. Fells. 1893. *Factory Accounts: Their Principles and Practice*, Fourth Edition (First Edition 1887) (London: Crosby, Lockwood and Son).

Geary, R.C. 1958. "A note on the comparison of exchange rates and purchasing power between countries", in *Journal of the Royal Statistical Society* (Series A), Vol. 121, pp. 97–99.

Genereux, P.A. 1983. "Impact of the Choice of Formulae on the Canadian Consumer Price Index" in W.E. Diewert and C. Montmarquette (eds.): *Price Level Measurement* (Ottawa: Statistics Canada), pp. 489–535.

Gilman, S. 1939. *Accounting Concepts of Profit* (New York: The Rolland Press Co.).

Goldberger, A.A. 1968. "The Interpretation and Estimation of Cobb–Douglas Functions", in *Econometrica*, Vol. 35, pp. 464–472.

Goodhart, C. 2001. "What Weights should be Given to Asset Prices in the Measurement of Inflation?", in *Economic Journal*, Vol. 111, June, F335–F356.

Gordon, R.J. 1990. *The Measurement of Durable Goods Prices* (Chicago, IL: University of Chicago Press).

—— and Z. Griliches. 1997. "Quality Change and New Products", in *American Economic Review: Papers and Proceedings of the Hundred and Fourth Annual Meeting of the American Economic Association*, Vol. 87, No. 2, pp. 84–88.

Gorman, W.M. 1980. "A Possible Procedure for Analyzing Quality Differentials in the Egg Market", in *Review of Economic Studies*, Vol. 47, pp. 843–856.

Greenlees, J. 1997. "Expenditure Weight Updates and Measured Inflation", Paper presented at the Third Meeting of the International Working Group on Price Indices, Voorburg, Apr. 16–18.

——. 1999. *Random Errors and Superlative Indexes*, Paper presented at the Annual Conference of the Western Economic Association, 8 July, San Diego, CA.

——. 2000. "Consumer Price Indexes: Methods for Quality and Variety Change", in *Statistical Journal of the United Nations Economic Commission for Europe*, Vol. 17, No. 1, pp. 37–58.

——. 2003. *Introducing the Chained Consumer Price Index*, Paper presented at the Seventh Meeting of the International

Working Group on Price Indices, Paris, May 27–29. Available at: http://www.insee.fr

Griliches, Z. 1988. *Technology, Education and Productivity: Early Papers with Notes to Subsequent Literature* (New York: Basil Blackwell).

——. 1990. "Hedonic Price Indices and the Measurement of Capital and Productivity: Some Historical Reflections", in E.R. Berndt and J.E. Triplett (eds.): *Fifty Years of Economic Measurement: The Jubilee of the Conference on Research in Income and Wealth*, NBER Studies in Income and Wealth (Chicago, IL: University of Chicago Press), pp. 185–206.

Guðnason. 1999. *Use of Cash Register Data*, Paper presented at the Fifth Meeting of the International Working Group on Price Indices, Reykjavik, Aug. 25–27. Available at: http://www.ottawagroup.org

Gudnason, R. 2003. *How do we Measure Inflation? Some Measurement Problems*, Paper presented at the Seventh Meeting of the International Working Group on Price Indices, May 27–29, Paris. Available at: http://www.insee.fr

Hardy, G.H., J.E. Littlewood and G. Pólya. 1934. *Inequalities* (Cambridge: Cambridge University Press).

Harper, M.J., E.R. Berndt and D.O. Wood. 1989. "Rates of Return and Capital Aggregation Using Alternative Rental Prices", in D.W. Jorgenson and R. Landau (eds.): *Technology and Capital Formation* (Cambridge, MA: The MIT Press), pp. 331–372.

Haschka, P. 2003. *Simple Methods of Explicit QA for Services in Complex Pricing Schemes*, Paper presented at the Seventh Meeting of the International Working Group on Price Indices, May 27–29, Paris. Available at: http://www.insee.fr

Hausman, J.A. 1997. "Valuation of New Goods Under Perfect and Imperfect Conditions", in T.F. Bresnahan and R.J. Gordon (eds.): *The Economics of New Goods*, NBER Studies in Income and Wealth (Chicago, IL: University of Chicago Press), pp. 209–237.

——. 1999. "Cellular Telephone, New Products, and the CPI", in *Journal of Business and Economic Statistics*, Vol. 17, No. 2, pp. 188–194.

——. 2002. *Sources of Bias and Solutions to Bias in the CPI*, NBER Working Paper 9298 (Cambridge, MA: National Bureau of Economic Research).

Hawkes, W.J. 1997. *Reconciliation of Consumer Price Index Trends in Average Prices for Quasi-Homogeneous Goods Using Scanning Data*, Paper presented at the Third Meeting of the International Working Group on Price Indices, Voorburg, Apr. 16–18. Available at: http://www.ottawagroup.org

—— and F.W. Piotrowski. 2003. "Using Scanner Data to Improve the Quality of Measurement in the Consumer Price Index", in R.C. Feenstra and M.D. Shapiro (eds.): *Scanner Data and Price Indexes*, NBER Studies in Income and Wealth (Chicago, IL: University of Chicago Press), pp. 17–38.

Haworth, M.F., D. Fenwick and R. Beaven. 1997. *Recent Developments in the UK Retail Prices Index: Quality Management*, Paper presented at the Third Meeting of the International Working Group on Price Indices, Voorburg, Apr. 16–18. Available at: http://www.ottawagroup.org.

Hicks, J.R. 1940. "The Valuation of the Social Income", in *Economica*, Vol. 7, pp. 105–124.

——. 1941–42. "Consumers' Surplus and Index Numbers", in *The Review of Economic Studies*, Vol. 9, pp. 126–137.

——. 1946. *Value and Capital*, Second Edition (Oxford: Clarendon Press).

Hıdıroglou M.A. and J.-M. Berthelot. 1986. "Statistical editing and imputation for periodic business surveys", in *Survey Methodology*, Vol. 12, No. 1, pp. 73–83.

Hill, R.J. 1995. *Purchasing Power Methods of Making International Comparisons*, Ph.D. Dissertation (Vancouver: University of British Columbia).

——. 1999a. "Comparing Price Levels across Countries Using Minimum Spanning Trees", in *The Review of Economics and Statistics*, Vol. 81, pp. 135–142.

——. 1999b. "International Comparisons using Spanning Trees", in A. Heston and R.E. Lipsey (eds.): *International and Interarea Comparisons of Income, Output and Prices*, NBER Studies in Income and Wealth (Chicago, IL: University of Chicago Press), pp. 109–120.

——. 1999c. "Chained PPPs and Minimum Spanning Trees", in A. Heston and R.E. Lipsey (eds.): *International and Interarea Comparisons of Income, Output and Prices*, NBER Studies in Income and Wealth (Chicago, IL: Chicago University Press), pp. 327–364.

——. 1999d. "Comparing Price Levels Across Countries Using Minimum Spanning Trees", in *The Review of Economics and Statistics*, Vol. 81, pp. 135–142.

——. 2001. "Measuring Inflation and Growth Using Spanning Trees", in *International Economic Review*, Vol. 42, pp. 167–185.

——. 2002. *Superlative Index Numbers: Not All of them Are Super*, Discussion Paper No. 2002/04, School of Economics (Sydney: University of New South Wales).

Hill, T.P. 1988. "Recent Developments in Index Number Theory and Practice", in *OECD Economic Studies*, Vol. 10, pp. 123–148.

——. 1993. "Price and Volume Measures", in *System of National Accounts 1993* (Brussels/Luxembourg, New York, Paris, New York, and Washington, D.C.: Commission of the European Communities, IMF, OECD, World Bank and United Nations), pp. 379–406.

——. 1996. *Inflation Accounting: A Manual on National Accounting under Conditions of High Inflation* (OECD: Paris).

——. 1998. "The Measurement of Inflation and Changes in the Cost of Living", in *Statistical Journal of the United Nations ECE*, Vol. 15, pp. 37–51.

——. 1999. *COL Indexes and Inflation Indexes*, Paper tabled at the Fifth Meeting of the International Working Group on Price Indices, Reykjavik, Aug. 25–27. Available at: http://www.ottawagroup.org

Hillinger, C. 2002. *A General Theory of Price and Quantity Aggregation and Welfare Measurement*, CISifo Working Paper No. 818 (Munich: University of Munich).

Hoffmann, J. 1998. *Problems of Inflation Measurement in Germany*, Discussion Paper 1/98, Economic Research Group of the Deutsche Bundesbank (Frankfurt: Deutsche Bundesbank).

——. 1999. *The Treatment of Quality Changes in the German Consumer Price Index*, Paper presented at the Fifth Meeting of the International Working Group on Price Indices, Reykjavik, Aug. 25–27. Available at: http://www.ottawagroup.org

—— and C. Kurz. 2002. *Rent Indices for Housing in West Germany: 1985 to 1998*, Discussion Paper 01/02, Economic Research Centre of the Deutsche Bundesbank (Frankfurt: Deutsche Bundesbank).

Holdway, M. 1999. *An Alternative Methodology: Valuing Quality Changes for Microprocessors in the PPI*, Unpublished Paper (Washington, D.C.: Bureau of Labor Statistics).

Hotelling, H. 1925. "A General Mathematical Theory of Depreciation", in *Journal of the American Statistical Association*, Vol. 20, pp. 340–353.

Houthakker, H.S. 1952. "Compensated Changes in Quantities and Qualities Consumed", in *Review of Economic Studies*, Vol. 19, pp. 155–164.

Hoven, L. 1999. *Some Observations on Quality Adjustment in the Netherlands*, Unpublished Paper, Department of Consumer Prices (Voorburg: Statistics Netherland).

Hulten, C.R. 1973. "Divisia Index Numbers", in *Econometrica*, Vol. 41, pp. 1017–1026.

——. 1990. "The Measurement of Capital", in E.R. Berndt and J.E. Triplett (eds.): *Fifty Years of Economic Measurement: The Jubilee of the Conference on Research in Income and Wealth*, NBER Studies in Income and Wealth (Chicago, IL: University of Chicago Press), pp. 119–158.

——. 1996. "Capital and Wealth in the Revised SNA", in J.W. Kendrick (ed.): *The New System of National Accounts* (New York: Kluwer Academic Publishers), pp. 149–181.

—— and F.C. Wykoff. 1981a. "The Estimation of Economic Depreciation using Vintage Asset Prices", in *Journal of Econometrics*, Vol. 15, pp. 367–396.

——. 1981b. "The Measurement of Economic Depreciation", in C.R. Hulten (ed.): *Depreciation, Inflation and the Taxation of Income from Capital* (Washington, D.C.: The Urban Institute Press), pp. 81–125.

——. 1996. "Issues in the Measurement of Economic Depreciation: Introductory Remarks", in *Economic Inquiry*, Vol. 34, pp. 10–23.

International Labour Organization (ILO). 1987. *Report of the Fourteenth International Conference of Labour Statisticians* (Geneva).

——. 1990. *ISCO-88: International Standard Classification of Occupations* (Geneva).

——. 1998. "Guidelines concerning dissemination practices for labour statistics", in *Report of the Sixteenth International Conference of Labour Statisticians* (Geneva). Web address: http://www.ilo.org/public/english/bureau/stat/standards/guidelines/index.htm)

——. 2003. *Report III to the Seventeenth International Conference of Labour Statisticians* (Geneva).

ILO, IMF, OECD, Eurostat, UNECE and the World Bank. 2004. *Producer Price Index Manual* (Brussels/Luxembourg, Geneva, Washington, D.C., Geneva, Washington, D.C.).

International Monetary Fund (IMF). *General Data Dissemination System (GDDS)*. Web address: http://dsbb.imf.org/Applications/web/gdds/gddshome/

——. *Special Data Dissemination Standard (SDDS)*. Web address: http://dsbb.imf.org/Applications/web/sddshome

——. 1993. *Balance of Payments Manual, Fifth Edition* (Washington, D.C.).

——. 2001. *Government Financial Statistics Manual* (Washington, D.C.).

Ioannidis, C. and M. Silver. 1999. "Estimating Hedonic Indices: An Application to UK Television Sets", in *Journal of Economics. Zeitschrift für Nationalökonomie*, Vol. 69, No. 1, pp. 71–94.

ISO 9000. Geneva, International Standards Organization, 1994. Web address: http://iso.ch

ISO 9001. Geneva, International Standards Organization, 2000. Web address: http://iso.ch

Jacobsen, J. 1997. *Variance Estimation and Sample Allocation in the Finnish CPI*, Memo written for Statistics Finland, Mar. 11.

Jensen, J.L.W.V. 1906. "Sur les fonctions convexes et les inégalités entre les valeurs moyennes", in *Acta Math.*, Vol. 8, pp. 94–96.

Jevons, W.S. 1863. "A Serious Fall in the Price of Gold Ascertained and its Social Effects Set Forth", reprinted in *Investigations in Currency and Finance* (London: Macmillan and Co., 1884), pp. 13–118.

——. 1865. "The Variation of Prices and the Value of the Currency since 1782", in *Journal of the Statistical Society of London*, Vol. 28, pp. 294–320; reprinted in *Investigations in Currency and Finance* (London: Macmillan and Co., 1884), pp. 119–150.

——. 1884. "A Serious Fall in the Value of Gold Ascertained and its Social Effects Set Forth. 1863", in *Investigations in Currency and Finance* (London: Macmillan and Co.), pp. 13–118.

Jorgenson, D.W. 1989. "Capital as a Factor of Production", in D.W. Jorgenson and R. Landau (eds.): *Technology and Capital Formation* (Cambridge, MA: The MIT Press), pp. 1–35.

——. 1996. "Empirical Studies of Depreciation", in *Economic Inquiry*, Vol. 34, pp. 24–42.

—— and Z. Griliches. 1967. "The Explanation of Productivity Change", in *Review of Economic Studies*, Vol. 34, pp. 249–283.

Katz, A.J. 1983. "Valuing the Services of Consumer Durables", in *The Review of Income and Wealth*, Vol. 29, pp. 405–427.

Kennedy, P. 1998. *A Guide to Econometrics* (Oxford: Blackwell Publishers).

Kenny, P.B. 1995. *Errors in the Retail Prices Index*, Memo written for the UK Central Statistical Office/Office for National Statistics, 8 Mar.

Keynes, J.M. 1930. *A Treatise on Money in Two Volumes: 1: The Pure Theory of Money* (London: Macmillan).

Khamis, S.H. 1970. "Properties and Conditions for the Existence of a New Type if Index Numbers", in *Sankhya*, Series B, Vol. 32, pp. 81–98.

——. 1972. "A New System of index Numbers for National and International Purposes", in *Journal of the Royal Statistical Society*, Series A, Vol. 135, pp. 96–121.

——. 1984. "On Aggregation methods for International Comparisons", in *Review of Income and Wealth*, Vol. 30, No. 2, pp. 185–205.

Knibbs, Sir G.H. 1924. "The Nature of an Unequivocal Price Index and Quantity Index", in *Journal of the American Statistical Association*, Vol. 19, pp. 42–60 and 196–205.

Kokoski, M.F., K. Waehrer and P. Rozaklis. 2001. *Using Hedonic Methods for Quality Adjustment in the CPI: The Consumer Audio Products Component*, Working Paper No. 344 (Washington, D.C.: Bureau of Labor Statistics).

——, B.R. Moulton and K.D. Zieschang. 1999. "Interarea Price Comparisons for Heterogeneous Goods and Several Levels of Commodity Aggregation", in A. Heston and R.E. Lipsey (eds.): *International and Interarea Comparisons of Income, Output and Prices*, NBER Studies in Income and Wealth (Chicago, IL: University of Chicago Press), pp. 123–166.

Konüs, A.A. 1924. "The Problem of the True Index of the Cost of Living", in *The Economic Bulletin of the Institute of*

Economic Conjuncture (in Russian), No. 9–10, pp. 64–71; published in English in 1939 in *Econometrica*, Vol. 7, pp. 10–29

—— and S.S. Byushgens. 1926. "K probleme pokupatelnoi cili deneg", in *Voprosi Konyunkturi*, Vol. 2, pp. 151–172.

Koskimäki, T. and M. Ylä-Jarkko. 2003. *Segmented Markets and CPI Elementary Classifications*, Paper presented at the Seventh Meeting of the International Working Group on Price Indices, Paris, May 27–29. Available at: http://www.insee.fr/

—— and Y. Vartia. 2001. *Beyond Matched Pairs and Griliches Type Hedonic Methods for Controlling Quality Changes in CPI Subindices*, Paper presented at the Sixth Meeting of the International Working Group on Price Indices, Canberra, Apr. 2–6. Available at: http://www.ottawagroup.org

Kotler, P. 1991. *Marketing Management*, Seventh Edition (Englewood Cliffs, NJ: Prentice Hall).

Kravis, I.B., A.W. Heston and R. Summers. 1982. *World Product and Income: International Comparisons of Real Gross Domestic Product* (Baltimore, MD: Johns Hopkins University Press).

Krueger, A.B. and A. Siskind. 1998. "Using Survey Data to Assess Bias in the Consumer Price Index", in *Monthly Labor Review*, Vol. 121, No. 4, pp. 24–33.

Lancaster, K.J. 1966. "A New Approach to Consumer Theory", in *Journal of Political Economy*, Vol. 74, No. 2, pp. 132–156.

——. 1971. *Consumer Demand: A New Approach* (New York: Columbia University Press).

Lane, W. 2001. *Addressing the New Goods Problem in the Consumer Price Index*, Paper presented at the Sixth Meeting of the International Working Group on Price Indices, Canberra, Apr. 2–6. Available at http://www.ottawa.org

Laspeyres, E. 1871. "Die Berechnung einer mittleren Waarenpreissteigerung", in *Jahrbücher für Nationalökonomie und Statistik*, Vol. 16, pp. 296–314.

Lau, L.J. 1979. "On Exact Index Numbers", in *Review of Economics and Statistics*, Vol. 61, pp. 73–82.

Leaver, S.G. and D. Swanson. 1992. "Estimating Variances for the U.S. Consumer Price Index for 1987–1991", in American Statistical Association: *Proceedings of the Survey Research Methods Section* (Alexandria, VS), pp. 740–745.

—— and R. Valliant. 1995. "Statistical Problems in Estimating the U.S. Consumer Price Index", in Cox et al. (eds.): *Business Survey Methods* (New York: Wiley).

Lebow, D.E. and J.B. Rudd. 2003. "Measurement Error in the Consumer Price Index: Where Do We Stand?", in *Journal of Economic Literature*, Vol. 41, pp. 159–201.

——, J.M. Roberts and D.J. Stockton. 1994. *Monetary Policy and the 'Price Level'*, Unpublished Paper (Washington, D.C.: Board of Governors of the Federal Reserve System), July.

Lehr, J. 1885. *Beiträge zur Statistik der Preise* (Frankfurt: J.D. Sauerlander).

Leontief, W. 1936. "Composite Commodities and the Problem of Index Numbers", in *Econometrica*, Vol. 4, pp. 39–59.

Lequiller, F. 1997. "Does the French Consumer Price Index Overstate Inflation?", in L.M. Ducharme (ed.): *Bias in the CPI: Experiences from Five OECD Countries*, Prices Division Analytical Series, No. 10 (Ottawa: Statistics Canada), pp. 25–43.

Levy, F., H. Beamish, R.J. Murnane and D. Aurtor. 1999. *Computerization and Skills: Example from a Car Dealership*, Brookings Program on Output and Productivity Measurement in the Services Sector, Workshop on Measuring the Output of Business Services, May 14, (Washington, D.C.: Brookings Institution).

Ley, E. 2003. "Comment", in R.C. Feenstra and M.D. Shapiro (eds.): *Scanner Data and Price Indexes*, NBER Studies in Income and Wealth (Chicago, IL: University of Chicago Press), pp. 379–382.

Liegey Jr., P.R. 1992. "Adjusting apparel indices in the CPI for quality differences", in M.F. Foss, M. Manser and A. Young (eds.): *Price Measurements and their Uses*, NBER Studies in Income and Wealth (Chicago, IL: University of Chicago Press).

——. 1994. "Apparel Price Indexes: Effects of Hedonic Adjustments", in *Monthly Labor Review*, Vol. 117, pp. 38–45.

—— 2000. *Hedonic Quality Adjustment Methods for Microwave Ovens in the U.S. CPI*, Methodology Paper (Washington, D.C.: Bureau of Labor Statistics).

Linder, F. 1996. *Reducing bias in the estimation of consumer price indices by using integrated data*, Research Report (Voorburg: Statistics Netherlands).

Lloyd, P.J. 1975. "Substitution Effects and Biases in Nontrue Price Indices", in *American Economic Review*, Vol. 65, pp. 301–313.

Lowe, J. 1823. *The Present State of England in Regard to Agriculture, Trade and Finance*, Second Edition (London: Longman, Hurst, Rees, Orme and Brown).

Lowe, R. 1996. "The Type and Extent of Quality Changes in the Canadian CPI", in J. Dalén (ed.): *Proceedings of the Second Meeting of the International Working Group on Price Indices* (Stockholm: Statistics Sweden), pp. 231–249. Available at: http://www.ottawagroup.org

——. 1999. *The Use of the Regression Approach to Quality Change for Durables in Canada*, Paper presented at the Fifth Meeting of the International Working Group on Price Indices, Reykjavik, Aug. 25–27. Available at: http://www.ottawagroup.org

Maddala, G.S. 1988. *Introduction to Econometrics* (New York: Macmillan).

Malmquist, S. 1953. "Index Numbers and Indifference Surfaces", in *Trabajos de Estadística*, Vol. 4, pp. 209–242.

Malpezzi, S., L. Ozanne and T. Thibodeau. 1987. "Microeconomic Estimates of Housing Depreciation", in *Land Economics*, Vol. 63, pp. 372–385.

Manser, M.E. and R.J. McDonald. 1988. "An Analysis of Substitution Bias in Measuring Inflation, 1959–85", in *Econometrica*, Vol. 56, No. 4, pp. 909–930.

Marshall, A. 1887. "Remedies for Fluctuations of General Prices", in *Contemporary Review*, Vol. 51, pp. 355–375.

——. 1898. *Principles of Economics*, Fourth Edition (London: The Macmillan Co.).

Matheson, E. 1910. *The Depreciation of Factories and their Valuation*, Fourth Edition (London: E. & F.N. Spon).

McClelland, R. and M. Reinsdorf. 1999. *Small Sample Bias in Geometric Mean and Seasoned CPI Component Indexes*, Economic Working Paper (Washington, D.C.: Bureau of Labor Statistics).

McCracken, P.M., J. Tobin et al. 1999. *Measuring Prices in A Dynamic Economy: Re-Examining the CPI* (New York: The Conference Board).

Mendelsohn, R. 1984. "Estimating the Structural Equations of Implicit Market and Household Production Functions", in *Review of Economics and Statistics*, Vol. 66, No. 4, pp. 673–677.

Mendershausen, H. 1937. "Annual Survey of Statistical Technique: Methods of Computing and Eliminating Changing Seasonal Fluctuations", in *Econometrica*, Vol. 5, pp. 234–262.

Merkel, F.K. 2000. *Addressing New Item Bias in the Producer Price Indexes: A PPI Quality Improvement Initiative*, Unpublished Paper (Washington, D.C.: Bureau of Labor Statistics).

Mitchell, W.C. 1927. *Business Cycles* (New York: National Bureau of Economic Research).

Moulton, B.R. 1996a. *Constant Elasticity Cost-of-Living Index in Share Relative Form* (Washington, D.C.: Bureau of Labor Statistics), Dec.

——. 1996b. "Bias in the Consumer Price Index: What is the Evidence?", in *Journal of Economic Perspectives*, Vol. 10, No. 4, pp. 159–177.

——. 2001. "The Expanding Role of Hedonic Methods in the Official Statistics of the United States", in *Proceedings of a Symposium on Hedonic Methods* (Wiesbaden: Deutches Bundesbank and German Federal Statistical Office), June.

—— and K.E. Moses. 1997. "Addressing the Quality Change Issue in the Consumer Price Index", in *Brooking Papers on Economic Activity*, Vol. 1, pp. 305–366.

—— and E.P. Seskin. 1999. "A Preview of the 1999 Comprehensive Revision of the National Income and Product Accounts", in *Survey of Current Business*, Vol. 79, pp. 6–17.

——, T. LaFleur and K.E. Moses. 1999. "Research on Improved Quality Adjustment in the CPI: The Case of Televisions", in W. Lane (ed.): *Proceedings of the Fourth Meeting of the International Working Group on Price Indices* (Washington, D.C.: Bureau of Labor Statistics), pp. 77–99. Available at: http://www.ottawagroup.org

Mudgett, B.D. 1955. "The Measurement of Seasonal Movements in Price and Quantity Indexes", in *Journal of the American Statistical Association*, Vol. 50, pp. 93–98.

Muellbauer, J. 1974. "Household Production Theory, Quality, and the 'Hedonic Technique'", in *The American Economic Review*, Vol. 64, No. 6, pp. 977–994.

Murray, J. and N. Sarantis. 1999. "Price–Quality Relationships and Hedonic Price Indexes for Cars in the United Kingdom", in *International Journal of the Economics of Business*, Vol. 6, No. 1, pp. 1–23.

Muth, R.F. 1966. "Household Production and Consumer Demand Functions", in *Econometrica*, Vol. 34, pp. 699–708.

Nevo, A. 2001. *New Products, Quality Changes, and Welfare Measures Computed from Estimated Demand Systems*, NBER Working Paper #W8425 (Cambridge, MA: National Bureau of Economic Research).

Norberg, A. 1999. "Quality Adjustment: The Case of Clothing", in M. Silver and D. Fenwick (eds.): *Proceedings of the Measurement of Inflation Conference* (Cardiff: Cardiff University). Available at: http://www.cardiff.ac.uk

Nordhaus, W.D. 1998. "Quality Change in Price Indexes", in *Journal of Economic Perspectives*, Vol. 12, No. 1, pp. 59–68.

Obst, Carl. 2000. "A Review of Bias in the CPI", in *Statistical Journal of the United Nations ECE*, Vol. 17, pp. 37–58.

Office for National Statistics (UK). 1998. *The Retail Prices Index: A Technical Manual.* Available at: http://www.statistics.gov.uk

Oi, W.Y. 1997. "The Welfare Implications of Invention", in T.F. Bresnahan and R.J. Gordon (eds.): *The Economics of New Goods*, NBER Studies in Income and Wealth (Chicago, IL: University of Chicago Press), pp. 109–141.

Okamoto, M. 1999. *Empirical Study of Outlet Sampling Using Scanner Data*, Paper presented at the ILO/ECE Joint Meeting on CPI, Geneva, Nov. 3–5. Available at: http://www.unece.org

——. 2001. *Mid-Year Basket Index as a Practical Approximation to a Superlative Index*, Paper presented at the Sixth Meeting of the International Working Group on Price Indices, Canberra, Apr. 2–6. Available at: http://www.ottawagroup.org

Opperdoes, E. 2001. *Some Empirical Experiments with CES Functions*, Unpublished Paper (Voorburg: Statistics Netherlands).

Organisation for Economic Co-operation and Development (OECD). 1997. *Synthesis Paper on Shortcomings of the Consumer Price Index Measure of Inflation for Economic Policy Purposes*, Paper prepared for Working Party No. 1 on Macroeconomic and Structural Policy Analysis, ECO/CPE/WP1(97)12, Sep. (Paris).

——. 1998. *FISM, A Note by the OECD Secretariat*, Prepared for the Joint OECD/ESCAP Meeting on National Accounts – 1993 System of National Accounts: Five Years On, Bangkok, May 4–8.

——. 1999. *Purchasing Power Parities and Real Expenditures* (Paris).

——. 2001a. *Measuring Productivity: Measurement of Aggregate and Industry-Level Productivity Growth* (Paris).

——. 2001b. *Measuring Capital: Measurement of Capital Stocks, Consumption of Fixed Capital and Capital Services* (Paris).

Osgood, W.F. 1925. *Advanced Calculus* (New York: Macmillan).

Paasche, H. 1874. "Über die Preisentwicklung der letzten Jahre nach den Hamburger Borsennotirungen", in *Jahrbücher für Nationalökonomie und Statistik*, Vol. 12, pp. 168–178.

Pakes, A. 2001. *A Reconsideration of Hedonic Price Indices with an Application to PC's*, Working Paper No. 8715 (Cambridge, MA: National Bureau of Economic Research), revised November 2001.

Palgrave, R.H.I. 1886. "Currency and Standard of Value in England, France and India and the Rates of Exchange Between these Countries", in *Memorandum submitted to the Royal Commission on Depression of Trade and Industry*, Third Report, Appendix B, pp. 312–390.

Parker, P. 1992. "Price Elasticity Dynamics Over the Adoption Life Cycle", in *Journal of Marketing Research*, Vol. XXIX, pp. 358–367.

Pierson, N.G. 1895. "Index Numbers and Appreciation of Gold", in *Economic Journal*, Vol. 5, pp. 329–335.

——. 1896. "Further Considerations on Index-Numbers", in *Economic Journal*, Vol. 6, pp. 127–131.

Pigou, A.C. 1920. *The Economics of Welfare* (London: Macmillan).

Pollak, R.A. 1975. "Subindexes of the Cost of Living", in *International Economic Review*, Vol. 16, pp. 135–160.

——. 1980. "Group Cost-of-Living Indexes", in *American Economic Review*, Vol. 70, pp. 273–278.

——. 1981. "The Social Cost-of-Living Index", in *Journal of Public Economics*, Vol. 15, pp. 311–336.

——. 1983. "The Theory of the Cost-of-Living Index", in W.E. Diewert and C. Montmarquette (eds.): *Price Level Measurement* (Ottawa: Statistics Canada), pp. 87–161; reprinted in R.A. Pollak: *The Theory of the Cost-of-Living Index* (Oxford: Oxford University Press, 1989), pp. 3–52;

also reprinted in W.E. Diewert (ed.): *Price Level Measurement* (Amsterdam: North-Holland, 1990), pp. 5–77.

——. 1989. "The Treatment of the Environment in the Cost-of-Living Index", in R.A. Pollak: *The Theory of the Cost-of-Living Index* (Oxford: Oxford University Press), pp. 181–185.

——. 1998. "The Consumer Price Index: A Research Agenda and Three Proposals", in *Journal of Economic Perspectives*, Vol. 12, No. 1, pp. 69–78.

Popkin, J. 1997. "Improving the CPI: The Record and Suggested Next Steps", in *Business Economics*, July, pp. 42–47.

Prais, S.J. 1959. "Whose Cost of Living?", in *The Review of Economic Studies*, Vol. 26, pp. 126–134.

Prennushi, G. 2001. *PPPs and Global Poverty: Strengths and Weaknesses*, Paper presented at the Joint World Bank–OECD Seminar on Purchasing Power Parities: Recent Advances in Methods and Applications, Washington, D.C., Jan. 30–Feb. 2.

Price Statistics Review Committee. 1961. *The Price Statistics of the Federal Government* (New York: National Bureau of Economic Research).

Rameshwar, S. 1998. "A Note on Weights for Consumer Price Indices", in *Inter-Stat No. 18* (Luxembourg, London, Paris: Eurostat, DfID, INSEE), pp. 89–96.

Rao, D.S. Prasada. 1990. "A System of Log-Change Index Numbers for Multilateral Comparisons", in J. Salazar-Carrillo and D.S. Prasada Rao (eds.): *Comparisons of Prices and Real Products in Latin America* (Amsterdam: North-Holland).

——. 1995. *On the Equivalence of the Generalized Country-Product-Dummy (CPD) Method and the Rao-System for Multilateral Comparisons*, Working Paper No. 5, Centre for International Comparisons (Philadelphia, PA: University of Pennsylvania).

——. 1997. "Aggregation Methods for International Comparison of Purchasing Power Parities and Real Income: Analytical Issues and Some Recent Developments", in *Proceedings of the International Statistical Institute, 51st Session*, pp. 197–200.

——. 2001a. *Integration of CPI and ICP: Methodological Issues, Feasibility and Recommendations*, Paper presented at the Joint World Bank–OECD Seminar on Purchasing Power Parities: Recent Advances in Methods and Applications, Washington, D.C., Jan. 30–Feb. 2.

——. 2001b. *Weighted EKS and Generalized Country Product Dummy Methods for Aggregation at Basic Heading Level and above Basic Heading Level*, Paper presented at the Joint World Bank–OECD Seminar on Purchasing Power Parities: Recent Advances in Methods and Applications, Washington, D.C., Jan. 30–Feb. 2.

—— and K.S. Banerjee. 1984. " A Multilateral Index Number System Based on the Factorial Approach", in *Statistische Hefte*, Vol. 27, pp. 297–313.

—— and M. Timmer. 2000. *Multilateralisation of Manufacturing Sector comparisons: Issues, Methods and Empirical Results*, Research Memorandum No. GD 47 (Groningen: Groningen Growth and Development Centre).

——, C.J. O'Donnell and E. Ball. 2000. *Transitive Multilateral Comparisons of Agricultural Output and Productivity Using Minimum Spanning Trees and Generalized EKS Methods*, Paper presented at the Workshop on Agricultural Productivity: Data, Methods, and Measures, March 9–10, Washington, D.C.

Rasmussen, D.W. and T.W. Zuehlke. 1990. "On the Choice of Functional Form for Hedonic Price Functions", in *The Review of Economics and Statistics*, Vol. 72, pp. 668–675.

Reese, M. 2000. *Hedonic Quality Adjustment Methods for College Textbooks for the U.S. CPI*, Methodology paper (Cambridge, MA: Bureau of Labor Statistics). Available at: http://www.bls.gov.

Reinsdorf, M.B. 1993. "The Effect of Outlet Price Differentials on the U.S. Consumer Price Index", in M.F. Foss, M.E. Manser and A.H. Young (eds.): *Price Measurement and their Uses*, NBER Studies in Income and Wealth (Chicago, IL: University of Chicago Press), pp. 227–254.

——. 1994. *Price Dispersion, Seller Substitution and the U.S. CPI*, Working Paper 252 (Washington, D.C.: Bureau of Labor Statistics).

—— 1996. *Constructing Basic Component Indexes for the U.S. CPI from Scanner Data: A Test Using Data on Coffee*, Working Paper 277 (Washington, D.C.: Bureau of Labor Statistics.).

——. 1998. *Divisia Indices and the Representative Consumer Problem*, Paper presented at the Fourth Meeting of the International Working Group on Price Indices, Washington, D.C., Apr. 22–24. Available at: http://www.ottawa-group.org

——. 2003. Personal Communication, Sep. 9.

—— and B.R. Moulton. 1997. "The Construction of Basic Components of Cost-of-Living Indexes", in T.F. Bresnahan and R.J. Gordon (eds.): *The Economics of New Goods*, NBER Studies in Income and Wealth (Chicago, IL: University of Chicago Press).

——, P. Liegey, and K. Stewart. 1996. *New Ways of Handling Quality Change in the U.S. Consumer Price Index*, Working Paper 276 (Washington, D.C.: Bureau of Labor Statistics).

——, W.E. Diewert and C. Ehemann. 2002. "Additive Decompositions for the Fisher, Törnqvist and Geometric Mean Indexes", in *Journal of Economic and Social Measurement*, Vol. 28, pp. 51–61.

Richardson, D.H. 2003. "Scanner Indexes for the Consumer Price Index", in R.C. Feenstra and M.D. Shapiro (eds.): *Scanner Data and Price Indexes*, NBER Studies in Income and Wealth (Chicago, IL: The University of Chicago Press), pp. 39–65.

Rosén, B. 1997a. "Asymptotic Theory for Order Sampling", in *Journal of Statistical Planning and Inference*, Vol. 62, pp. 135–158.

——. 1997b. "On Sampling with Probability Proportional to Size", in *Journal of Statistical Planning and Inference*, Vol. 62, pp. 159–191.

Rosen, S. 1974. "Hedonic Prices and Implicit Markets: Product Differentiation and Pure Competition", in *Journal of Political Economy*, Vol. 82, pp. 34–49.

Rothwell, D.P. 1958. "Use of Varying Seasonal Weights in Price Index Construction", in *Journal of the American Statistical Association*, Vol. 53, pp. 66–77.

Ryten, J. 1998. *The Evaluation of the International Comparison Project (ICP)*, (Washington, D.C.: IMF).

Samuelson, P.A. 1953. "Prices of Factors and Goods in General Equilibrium", *Review of Economic Studies*, Vol. 21, pp. 1–20.

—— and S. Swamy. 1974. "Invariant Economic Index Numbers and Canonical Duality: Survey and Synthesis", in *American Economic Review*, Vol. 64, pp. 566–593.

Särndal, C.-E., B. Swensson and J. Wretman. 1992. *Model Assisted Survey Sampling* (New York: Springer-Verlag).

Schlömilch, O. 1858. "Über Mittelgrössen verschiedener Ordnungen", in *Zeitschrift für Mathematik und Physik*, Vol. 3, pp. 308–310.

Schultz, B.J. (Szulc). 1996. "Treatment of Changes in Product Quality in Consumer Price Indices", in J. Dalén (ed.): *Proceedings of the Second Meeting of the International Working Group on Price Indices* (Stockholm: Statistics Sweden), pp. 209–229. Available at: http://www.ottawa-group.org

——. 1999. "Effects of Using Various Macro-Index Formulae in Longitudinal Price and Comparisons: Empirical Studies", in W. Lane (ed.): *Proceedings of the Fourth Meeting of the International Working Group on Price Indices* (Washington, D.C.: Bureau of Labor Statistics), pp. 236–249. Available at: http://www.ottawagroup.org

Schultze, C.L. and C. Mackie (eds.). 2002. *At What Price? Conceptualizing and Measuring Cost-of-Living and Price Indices* (Washington, D.C.: National Academy Press).

Scrope, G.P. 1833. *Principles of Political Economy* (London: Longman, Rees, Orme, Brown, Green and Longman).

Sellwood, D. 2001. *Improving Quality Adjustment in Practice*, Paper presented at the Sixth Meeting of the International Working Group on Price Indices, Canberra, Apr. 2–6. Available at: http://www.ottawagroup.org

Selvanathan, E.A. and D.S. Prasada Rao. 1994. *Index Numbers: A Stochastic Approach* (Ann Arbor, MI: University of Michigan Press).

Shapiro, M.D. and D.W. Wilcox. 1997a. "Alternative Strategies for Aggregating Prices in the CPI", in *Federal Reserve Bank of St. Louis Review*, Vol. 79, No. 3, pp. 113–125.

—— and D.W. Wilcox. 1997b. *Mismeasurement in the Consumer Price Index: An Evaluation*, Working Paper No. W5590 (Cambridge, MA: National Bureau of Economic Research). Available at: http:// www.nber.org

Shephard, R.W. 1953. *Cost and Production Functions* (Princeton, NJ: Princeton University Press).

——. 1970. *Theory of Cost and Production Functions* (Princeton, NJ: Princeton University Press).

Shepler, N. 2000. *Developing a Hedonic Regression Model for Refrigerators in the U.S. CPI*, Methodology paper (Washington, D.C.: Bureau of Labor Statistics). Web site: http://www.bls.gov/cpi/cpirfr.htm.

Shiratsuka, S. 1999. "Measurement Errors in the Japanese Consumer Price Index", in *Monetary and Economic Studies*, Vol. 17, No. 3, pp. 69–102.

Sidgwick, H. 1883. *The Principles of Political Economy* (London: Macmillan).

Silver, M. 1995. "Elementary Aggregates, Micro-Indices and Scanner Data: Some Issues in the Compilation of Consumer Price Indices", in *Review of Income and Wealth*, Vol. 41, pp. 427–438.

——. 1999. "An Evaluation of the Use of Hedonic Regressions for Basic Components of Consumer Price Indices", in *Review of Income and Wealth*, Vol. 45, No. 1, pp. 41–56.

——. 2002. *The Use of Weights in Hedonic Regressions: The Measurement of Quality Adjusted Price Changes*, Unpublished Paper, Cardiff Business School (Cardiff: Cardiff University).

—— and S. Heravi. 2001a. "Scanner Data and the Measurement of Inflation", in *The Economic Journal*, 111 June, F384–F405

—— and S. Heravi. 2001b. *Hedonic Price Indices and the Matched Models Approach*, Unpublished Paper, Cardiff Business School (Cardiff: Cardiff University).

—— and S. Heravi. 2002. *Why the CPI Matched Models Method May Fail Us*, Working Paper 144 (Frankfurt: European Central Bank).

—— and S. Heravi. 2003. "The Measurement of Quality Adjusted Price Changes", in R.C. Feenstra and M.D. Shapiro (eds.): *Scanner Data and Price Indexes*, NBER Studies in Income and Wealth (Chicago, IL: University of Chicago Press), pp. 277–316.

Sitter, R.R. and R. Balshaw. 1998. *Evaluation of Bias and Variance Estimation of the RPI*, Confidential Report to the Office for National Statistics (UK) (British Columbia: Simon Fraser University).

Solomons, D. 1961. "Economic and Accounting Concepts of Income", in *The Accounting Review*, Vol. 36, pp. 374–383.

Solow, R.M. 1957. "Technical Change and the Aggregate Production Function", in *Review of Economics and Statistics*, Vol. 39, pp. 312–320.

Statistics Sweden. 2001. *Swedish Consumer Price Index: A Handbook of Methods* (Stockholm).

Stone, R. 1956. *Quantity and Price Indexes in the National Accounts* (Paris: OECD).

Summers, R. 1973. "International Price Comparisons Based Upon Incomplete Data", in *Review of Income and Wealth*, Vol. 19, No. 1, pp. 1–16.

Sundgren, B. 1993. "Statistical Metainformation Systems Pragmatics, Semantics", Syntatctics, in *Statistical Journal of the United Nations Economic Commission for Europe*, Vol. 10, No. 2, pp. 121–142.

Szulc, B.J. (Schultz) 1964. "Index Numbers of Multilateral Regional Comparisons" (in Polish), in *Przeglad Statysticzny*, Vol. 3, pp. 239–254.

——. 1983. "Linking Price Index Numbers," in W.E. Diewert and C. Montmarquette (eds.): *Price Level Measurement* (Ottawa: Statistics Canada), pp. 537–566.

——. 1987. "Price Indices below the Basic Aggregation Level", in *Bulletin of Labour Statistics*, Vol. 2, pp. 9–16.

Tauchen, H. and A.D. Witte. 2001. *Estimating Hedonic Models; Implications of the Theory*, Technical Working Paper No. 271 (Cambridge, MA: National Bureau of Economic Research). Available at: http://www.nber.org

Teekens, R. and J. Koerts. 1972. "Some Statistical Implications of the Log Transformations of Multiplicative Models", in *Econometrica*, Vol. 40, No. 5, pp. 793–819.

Tellis, G.J. 1988. "The Price Elasticity of Selective Demand: A Meta-Analysis of Econometric Models of Sales", in *Journal of Marketing Research*, Vol. 25, pp. 167–177.

Theil, H. 1954. *Linear Aggregation of Economic Relations* (Amsterdam: North-Holland).

——. 1967. *Economics and Information Theory* (Amsterdam: North-Holland).

Törnqvist, L. 1936. "The Bank of Finland's Consumption Price Index", in *Bank of Finland Monthly Bulletin*, Vol. 10, pp. 1–8.

—— and E. Törnqvist. 1937. "Vilket är förhållandet mellan finska markens och svenska kronans köpkraft?", in *Ekonomiska Samfundets Tidskrift*, Vol. 39, pp. 1–39; reprinted in *Collected Scientific Papers of Leo Törnqvist* (Helsinki: The Research Institute of the Finnish Economy, 1981), pp. 121–160.

Trajtenberg, M. 1989. *Economic Analysis of Product Innovation: The Case of CT Scanners*, (Cambridge, MA: Harvard University Press).

Triplett, J.E. 1981. "Reconciling the CPI and the PCE Deflator", in *Monthly Labor Review*, Sep., pp. 3–15.

——. 1983. "Concepts of Quality in Input and Output Price Measures: A Resolution of the User-Value Resource-Cost Debate", in M.F. Foss (ed.): *The U.S. National Income and Product Accounts: Selected Topics*, NBER Studies in Income and Wealth (Chicago, IL: University of Chicago Press), pp. 269–311.

——. 1987. "Hedonic Functions and Hedonic Indices", in J. Eatwell, M. Milgate and P. Newman (eds.): *The New Palgrave: A Dictionary of Economics*, Vol. 2 (London: Macmillan), pp. 630–634.

——. 1990. "Hedonic Methods in Statistical Agency Environments: An Intellectual Biopsy", in E.R. Berndt and J.E. Triplett (eds.): *Fifty Years of Economic Measurement: The Jubilee of the Conference on Research in Income and Wealth*, NBER Studies in Income and Wealth (Chicago, IL: University of Chicago Press), pp. 207–238.

——. 1997. "Current Status of the Debate on the Consumer Price Index in the U.S.", in L.M. Ducharme (ed.): *Bias in the CPI: Experiences from Five OECD Countries*, Prices Division Analytical Series, No. 10 (Ottawa: Statistics Canada), pp. 53–60.

——. 1999. "The Solow Productivity Paradox: What do Computers do to Productivity?", in *Canadian Journal of Economics*, Vol. 32, No. 2, Apr., pp. 309–334.

——. 2001. "Should the Cost-of-Living Index Provide the Conceptual Framework for a Consumer Price Index?", in *The Economic Journal*, Vol. 111, June, F311–F334.

——. 2002. *Handbook on Quality Adjustment of Price Indexes for Information and Communication Technology Products*, Draft, OECD Directorate for Science, Technology and Industry (Paris: OECD).

——. 2003. "Using Scanner Data in Consumer Price Indexes: Some Neglected Conceptual Considerations", in R.C. Feenstra and M.D. Shapiro (eds.): *Scanner Data and Price Indexes*, NBER Studies in Income and Wealth (Chicago, IL: University of Chicago Press), pp. 151–162.

Trivedi, P.K. 1981. "Some Discrete Approximations to Divisia Integral Indices", in *International Economic Review*, Vol. 22, pp. 71–77.

Turvey, R. 1979. "The Treatment of Seasonal Items in Consumer Price Indices", in *Bulletin of Labour Statistics*, Fourth Quarter (Geneva: ILO), pp. 13–33.

——. 1996. *Elementary Aggregate (micro) Indexes*, Paper presented at the Eurostat Seminar on Improving the Quality of Price Indices: CPI and PPP, Florence, Dec. 18–20, 1995.

——. 1998. "New Outlets and New Products", in B. Balk (ed.): *Proceedings of the Third Meeting of the International Working Group on Price Indices* (Voorburg: Statistics Netherlands), pp. 97–110.

——. 1999. "Incorporating New Models into a CPI: PCs as an Example", in M. Silver and D. Fenwick (eds.): *Proceedings of the Measurement of Inflation Conference* (Luxembourg, London, Cardiff: Eurostat, Office for National Statistics, Cardiff University). Available at: http://www.cardiff.ac.uk

——. 2000. "True Cost of Living Indexes", in R. Gudnason and D. Gylfadóttir (eds.): *Proceedings of the Fifth Meeting of the International Working Group on Price Indices* (Reykjavik: Statistics Iceland). Available at: http://www.ottawagroup.org

—— et al. 1989. *Consumer Price Indices: An ILO Manual* (Geneva: ILO).

U.S. Bureau of Labor Statistics. 1983. "Changing the Home Ownership Component Of the Consumer Price Index to Rental Equivalence", in *CPI Detailed Report* (Washington, D.C.).

——. 1997. *BLS Handbook of Methods*, Bulletin 2490 (Washington, D.C.).

——. 1998. "Measurement Issues in the Consumer Price Index", in *Statistical Journal of the United Nations ECE*, Vol. 15, pp. 1–36.

U.S. General Accounting Office. 2000. *Consumer Price Index: Update of Boskin Commission's Estimate of Bias*, Report GAO/GGD-00–50 (Washington, D.C.), Feb.

U.S. Senate, Committee on Finance. 1996. *Final Report of the Advisory Commission to Study the Consumer Price Index*, Print 104–72, 104 Cong., 2nd Session (Washington, D.C.: Government Printing Office).

United Nations. 1990. *International Standard Industrial Classification of All Economic Activities*, Statistical Papers Series M, No. 4, Rev. 3 (New York)

——. 1992. *Handbook of the International Comparison Program*, Series F, No. 62 (New York).

——. 1994. *Fundamental Principles of Official Statistics*, Adopted by the UN Statistical Commission. UN Economic and Social Council, 1994, Report of the Special Session of the Statistical Commission, New York, 11–15 Apr., 1994, E/1994/29 (New York).

——. 1998a. *Principles and Recommendations for Population and Housing Censuses. Revision 1*, Statistical Papers Series M, No. 67/Rev. 1, Sales No. E.98.XVII.8 (New York).

——. 1998b. *Central Product Classification. CPC. Version 1.0*, Statistical Papers Series M, No. 77, Ver. 1.0 (New York).

——. 1999. *Classifications of Expenditure According to Purpose*, Statistical Papers Series M, No. 84 (New York).

——. 2002. *International Standard Industrial Classification of All Economic Activities*, ISIC, Revision 3.1 (New York: United Nations Statistical Division).

Van Ijzeren, J. 1987. *Bias in International Index Numbers: A Mathematical Elucidation*, Dissertation for the Hungarian Academy of Sciences (The Hague: Koninklijke Bibliotheek).

van Mulligen, P.H. 2003. *Quality aspects in price indices and international comparisons: Applications of the hedonic method*, Ph.D. thesis (Groningen: University of Groningen). Web site: http://www.cbs.nl/en/publications/articles/general/theses/theses.htm.

Vartia, Y.O. 1976. *Relative Changes and Index Numbers* (Helsinki: The Research Institute of the Finnish Economy).

——. 1978. "Fisher's Five-Tined Fork and Other Quantum Theories of Index Numbers", in W. Eichhorn, R. Henn, O. Opitz and R.W. Shephard (eds.): *Theory and Applications of Economic Indices* (Würzburg: Physica-Verlag), pp. 271–295.

Ville, J. 1946. "The Existence-Conditions of a Total Utility Function" (in French); translated in 1951 in *The Review of Economic Studies*, Vol. 19, pp. 123–128.

Vogt, A. 1977. "Zum Indexproblem: Geometrische Darstellung sowie eine neue Formel", in *Schweizerische Zeitschrift für Volkswirtschaft und Statistik*, Vol. 113, pp. 73–88.

——. 1978. "Divisia Indices on Different Paths", in W. Eichhorn, R. Henn, O. Opitz and R.W. Shephard (eds.): *Theory and Applications of Economic Indices* (Würzburg: Physica-Verlag), pp. 297–305.

——. 1980. "Der Zeit und der Faktorumkehrtest als 'Finders of Tests'", in *Statistische Hefte*, Vol. 21, pp. 66–71.

—— and J. Barta. 1997. *The Making of Tests for Index Numbers* (Heidelberg: Physica-Verlag).

von Auer, L. 2001. *An Axiomatic Checkup for Price Indices*, Working Paper No. 1/2001, Faculty of Economics and Management (Magdeburg: Otto von Guericke University).

——. 2002. "Spurious Inflation: The Legacy of Laspeyres and Others", in *The Quarterly Review of Economics and Finance*, Vol. 42, pp. 529–542.

von der Lippe, P. 2001. *Chain Indices: A Study in Price Index Theory*, Publication Series Spectrum of Federal Statistics, Vol. 16 (Wiesbaden: Statistisches Bundesamt).

Walras, L. 1954. *Elements of Pure Economics*, translated from French by W. Jaffe (London: George Allen and Unwin); first published in 1874.

Walsh, C.M. 1901. *The Measurement of General Exchange Value* (New York: Macmillan and Co.).

——. 1921a. *The Problem of Estimation* (London: P.S. King & Son).

——. 1921b. "Discussion", in *Journal of the American Statistical Association*, Vol. 17, pp. 537–544.

——. 1932. "Index Numbers", in E.R.A. Seligman (ed.): *Encyclopedia of the Social Sciences*, Vol. 7 (New York: The Macmillan Co.), pp. 652–658.

Ward, M. 2001. *True Comparisons in Real and Money Terms*, Paper presented at the Joint World Bank–OECD Seminar on Purchasing Power Parities: Recent Advances in Methods and Applications, Washington, D.C., Jan. 30–Feb. 2.

Westergaard, H. 1890. *Die Grundzüge der Theorie der Statistik* (Jena: Fischer).

White, A.G. 1999. "Measurement Biases in Consumer Price Indexes", in *International Statistical Review*, Vol. 67, No. 3, pp. 301–325.

——. 2000. "Outlet Types and the Canadian Consumer Price Index", in *Canadian Journal of Economics*, Vol. 33, pp. 488–505.

Wold, H. 1944. "A Synthesis of Pure Demand Analysis, Part 3", in *Skandinavisk Aktuarietidskrift*, Vol. 27, pp. 69–120.

——. 1953. *Demand Analysis* (New York: John Wiley).

Wooldridge, J.M. 1996. "Estimating Systems of Equations with Different Instruments for Different Equations", in *Journal of Econometrics*, Vol. 74, pp. 387–405.

Woolford, K. 1999. "Measuring Inflation: A Framework Based on Domestic Final Purchases", in M. Silver and D. Fenwick: *Proceedings of the Measurement of Inflation Conference* (Cardiff: Cardiff University), pp. 534–543.

——. 2001. *Financial Services in the Consumer Price Index*, Paper presented at the Sixth Meeting of the International Working Group on Price Indices, Canberra, Apr. 2–6. Available at: http://www.ottawagroup.org

Wynne, M.A. 1997. "Commentary", in *Federal Reserve Bank of St. Louis Review*, Vol. 79, No. 3, pp. 161–167.

——. 1999. *Core Inflation: A Review of Some Conceptual Issues*, Research Department Working Paper 99–03 (Dallas, TX: Federal Reserve Bank of Dallas).

—— and F.D. Sigalla. 1994. "The Consumer Price Index", in *Federal Reserve Bank of Dallas Economic Review*, Second Quarter, pp. 1–22.

Young, A. 1812. *An Inquiry into the Progressive Value of Money in England as Marked by the Price of Agricultural Products* (Piccadilly: Hatchard).

Yule, G.U. 1921. "Discussion of Mr. Flux's Paper", in *Journal of the Royal Statistical* Society, Vol. 84, pp. 199–202.

Zarnowitz, V. 1961. "Index Numbers and the Seasonality of Quantities and Prices", in G.J. Stigler (Chair): *The Price Statistics of the Federal Government* (New York: National Bureau of Economic Research), pp. 233–304.

Zieschang, K.D. 1988. *The Characteristics Approach to the Problem of New and Disappearing Goods in Price Indexes*, Working Paper No. 183 (Washington, D.C.: Bureau of Labor Statistics).

——, P.A. Armnecht and D. Smith. 2001. *Integrated Inter-Area and International Price Comparisons with Consumer Price Index Compilation*, Paper presented at the Joint World Bank–OECD Seminar on Purchasing Power Parities: Recent Advances in Methods and Applications, Washington, D.C., Jan. 30–Feb. 2.

INDEX

Note: References are to chapter and paragraph, or annex or appendix numbers (not to pages). *(g)* indicates an entry in the glossary and (where applicable) the glossary appendix. *(t)*, *(f)* or *(b)* appended to paragraph numbers indicate tables, figures or boxes adjoining relevant text; the addition of "*" (e.g. *(t*)*) indicates that the table, etc. is located immediately after - but not relevant to - that paragraph (the paragraph number is merely a locator).